Mangan Communications, Inc.

Federal Motor Carrier Safety Regulations
Administrator Edition

Including:

49 CFR Parts 40, 325-399, Appendixes A-G to Subchapter B
DOT Interpretations
Medical Advisory Criteria for Evaluation Under 49 CFR Part 391.41
Overview of Federal and State Regulations Concerning Interstate Motor Operations
Motor Carrier Safety Progress Report
Bridge Formula Weights
Federal Motor Carrier Safety Administration Field Offices
Costs of Highway Crashes Worksheet
Revenue Necessary to Pay for Accident Losses

As Prescribed by the Department of Transportation (DOT)

Updated through February 1, 2007

This publication is also available on CD-ROM

Changing the Complex Into Compliance®
Mangan Communications, Inc.
http://www.mancomm.com

Copyright © MMVII

by

Patent Pending

315 West Fourth Street
Davenport, Iowa 52801
(563) 323-6245
1-800-MANCOMM
(6 2 6 - 2 6 6 6)
Fax: (563) 323-0804

Website: http://www.mancomm.com
E-mail: safetyinfo@mancomm.com

All rights reserved. Printed in the U.S.A. Except as permitted under the United States Copyright Act of 1976, no part of this publication may be reproduced or distributed in any form or by any means, or stored in a database or any other retrieval system, without the prior written permission of the publisher. Although the Federal Regulations published as promulgated are in public domain, the formatting and sequence of the regulations and other materials contained herein are subject to the copyright laws.

While every effort has been made to ensure that the information contained herein is accurate and complete at the time of printing, the frequency of changes in the regulations makes it impossible to guarantee the complete accuracy of the information that follows. Therefore, neither Mangan Communications, Inc., nor its subsidiaries shall be liable for any damages resulting from the use of or reliance upon this publication. Furthermore, the appearance of products, services, companies, organizations or causes in the 49 CFR does not in any way imply endorsement by Mangan Communications, Inc., or its subsidiaries.

This publication is constructed to provide accurate information in regard to the material included. It is sold with the understanding that the publisher is not involved in providing accounting, legal, or other professional service. If legal consultation or other expert advice is required, the services of a professional person should be engaged.

Library of Congress Control Number: 2007921011
ISBN: 1-59959-049-2

RegLogic®... a better way

RegLogic® is a revolutionary, patent-pending technology for formatting information to give you the most comprehensive books of government regulations you've ever seen.

▶ Quick Reference

Cut the time it takes to find regulation information in half with **RegLogic®**. Each regulation is organized in outline format with indenting to make accessing information quicker. Color-coding, bold text, and italics further organize government regulations for fast reference, while the index sorts information by section *AND* page number.

- **Color-coding for fast reference**
- **Bold text and italics for further organization**
- **Outline format with indenting to ease locating regulations**
- **Bracket revisions enhance outline organization**
- **Easy-to-use index, including section numbers *and* page numbers in color for easy access**

▶ Easy Understanding

Stop squinting at graphics and tables for regulatory compliance by switching to **RegLogic®**. Each graphic is redrawn and enhanced with coloring and shading, colored arrows point out information more clearly, and legible text takes guesswork out of the picture. Tables have color-coded headings and clearly defined lines, making information quickly accessible.

- **Clear, legible text**
- **Coloring and shading make graphics more realistic**
- **Color-coded headings**
- **Clearly defined lines**

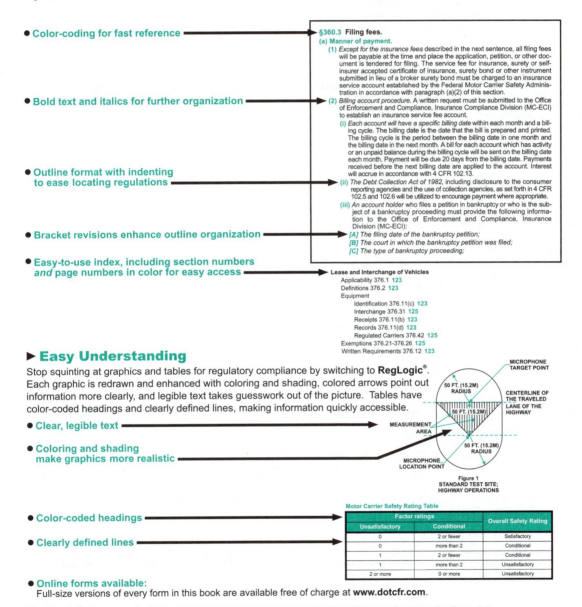

- **Online forms available:**
  Full-size versions of every form in this book are available free of charge at **www.dotcfr.com**.

RegLogic® is a one-of-a-kind approach that you will find only from Mangan Communications, Inc.

Recent changes in regulations:

August 10, 2006 (Federal Register Volume 71, No. 154)
In the August 10, 2006, Federal Register, the Department of Transportation's Federal Motor Carrier Safety Administration (FMCSA) amended 49 CFR to redesignate Part 1420 as Part 369 due to the transfer of responsibility for the Motor Carrier Financial and Operating Statistics Program from the Research and Innovative Technology Administration (RITA) to the FMCSA. In addition, minor technical amendments are made to the redesignated sections. This edition of the Federal Register included amendments to the following sections appearing herein.

§§369.1-369.11	§§1420.1-1420.11 are redesignated as §§369.1-369.11.
Part 369	An authority citation for redesignated Part 369 is added and all references to the 'Bureau of Transportation Statistics' are revised.
§369.1	Redesignated §369.1 is revised.
§369.5	Redesignated §369.5 is revised.
§369.6	Redesignated §369.6 is revised.
§369.8	Paragraphs (c) and (d) in redesignated §369.8 are revised.
§369.10	Paragraphs (b)(1) and (2) in redesignated §369.10 are revised.
§369.11	Redesignated §369.11 is revised.

August 23, 2006 (Federal Register Volume 71, No. 163)
In the August 23, 2006, Federal Register, the Department of Transportation (DOT) amended 49 CFR Part 40 to add state-licensed or certified marriage and family therapists to the list of professionals eligible to be substance abuse professionals appearing in Subpart O and to make technical amendments to its drug and alcohol testing procedural rule. The technical amendments clarify certain provisions of the rule and address omissions and typographical errors. This edition of the Federal Register included amendments to the following sections appearing herein.

Part 40	All references to 'RSPA' are revised to 'PHMSA'.
§40.3	The address for the Division of Workplace Programs is updated and a reference to the 'Research and Special Programs Administration (RSPA)' is replaced with a reference to the 'Pipeline and Hazardous Material Safety Administration'.
§40.23	Paragraph (c) is revised to correct the alcohol test result range that requires temporary removal of an employee from performing safety-sensitive functions.
§40.73	Paragraph (a)(2) is revised.
§40.83	Paragraphs (c)(2) and (4) are revised.
§40.191	Paragraph (a)(7) is revised.
§40.267	Paragraph (c)(5) is revised.
§40.269	Paragraph (b) is revised.
§40.281	Paragraph (a)(4) is revised, paragraph (a)(5) is redesignated as paragraph (a)(6), and new paragraph (a)(5) is added.
§40.283	Paragraph (a) is revised.

August 28, 2006 (Federal Register Volume 71, No. 166)
In the August 28, 2006, Federal Register, the Federal Motor Carrier Safety Administration (FMCSA) amended 49 CFR Parts 350, 390, and 392 to adopt the interim regulations published in the Federal Register in August 2002, with minor changes intended to clarify the definition of operating authority in order to assist enforcement officers in identifying the correct violations and avoid confusing operating authority with other registration requirements. This edition of the Federal Register included amendments to the following sections appearing herein.

Part 350	The authority citation for Part 350 is revised.
§350.105	A definition for the term 'operating authority' is added.
§350.201	Paragraph (t) is revised.
Part 390	The authority citation for Part 390 is revised.
§390.5	A definition for the term 'operating authority' is added and the definition of the term 'out-of-service' is revised.
§392.9a	Paragraphs (a) through (c) are revised.

September 22, 2006 (Federal Register Volume 71, No. 184)
In the September 22, 2006, Federal Register, the DOT amended 49 CFR Part 40 to correct a typographical error and to add text to its drug and alcohol testing procedural rule that was omitted from the Federal Register issued on August 23, 2006. This edition of the Federal Register included amendments to the following sections appearing herein.

§40.3	A reference to the 'Pipeline and Hazardous Material Safety Administration' is revised.
§40.281	The introductory text is revised.

January 11, 2007 (Federal Register Volume 72, No. 7)
In the January 11, 2007, Federal Register, the DOT amended 49 CFR Part 40 to provide procedures for use of a new breath tube alcohol screening device (ASD) recently approved by the National Highway Transportation Safety Administration (NHTSA) and to remove procedures for a previously approved breath tube ASD no longer being manufactured. This edition of the Federal Register included amendments to the following sections appearing herein.

Part 40	The authority citation for Part 40 is revised.
§40.245	Paragraphs (b)(1), (2), (3), (6), (8), (9), and (10) are revised.
§40.267	Paragraph (a)(4) is added.

Disclaimer

Although the author and publisher of this book have made every effort to ensure the accuracy and timeliness of the information contained herein, the author and publisher assume no liability with respect to loss or damage caused by or alleged to be caused by reliance on any information contained herein and disclaim any and all warranties, expressed or implied.

Table of Contents

Part 40 - Procedures for Transportation Workplace Drug and Alcohol Testing Programs

Subpart A - Administrative Provisions 1
§§40.1-40.7

Subpart B - Employer Responsibilities 3
§§40.11-40.29

Subpart C - Urine Collection Personnel 6
§§40.31-40.37

Subpart D - Collection Sites, Forms, Equipment and Supplies Used in DOT Urine Collections 8
§§40.41-40.51

Subpart E - Urine Specimen Collections 10
§§40.61-40.73

Subpart F - Drug Testing Laboratories 13
§§40.81 40.113

Subpart G - Medical Review Officers and the Verification Process 17
§§40.121-40.169

Subpart H - Split Specimen Tests 24
§§40.171-40.189

Subpart I - Problems in Drug Tests 26
§§40.191-40.209

Subpart J - Alcohol Testing Personnel 30
§§40.211-40.217

Subpart K - Testing Sites, Forms, Equipment and Supplies Used in Alcohol Testing 32
§§40.221-40.235

Subpart L - Alcohol Screening Tests 33
§§40.241-40.247

Subpart M - Alcohol Confirmation Tests 35
§§40.251-40.255

Subpart N - Problems in Alcohol Testing 36
§§40.261-40.277

Subpart O - Substance Abuse Professionals and the Return-to-Duty Process 38
§§40.281-40.313

Subpart P - Confidentiality and Release of Information 42
§§40.321-40.333

Subpart Q - Roles and Responsibilities of Service Agents 44
§§40.341 40.355

Subpart R - Public Interest Exclusions 45
§§40.361-40.413

Appendix A to Part 40 - Appendix H to Part 40 49

Part 325 - Compliance with Interstate Motor Carrier Noise Emission Standards

Subpart A - General Provisions 57
§§325.1-325.9

Subpart B - Administrative Provisions 58
§§325.11 -325.13

Subpart C - Instrumentation 58
§§325.21 -325.27

Subpart D - Measurement of Noise Emissions; Highway Operations 58
§§325.31 -325.39

Subpart E - Measurement of Noise Emissions; Stationary Test 59
§§325.51 -325.59

Subpart F - Correction Factors 61
§§325.71 -325.79

Subpart G - Exhaust Systems and Tires 62
§§325.91 -325.93

Part 350 - Commercial Motor Carrier Safety Assistance Program

Subpart A - General 63
§§350.101 -350.111

Subpart B - Requirements for Participation 63
§§350.201 -350.217

Subpart C - Funding 66
§§350.301 -350.345

Part 355 - Compatibility of State Laws and Regulations Affecting Interstate Motor Carrier Operations

Subpart A - General Applicability and Definitions 71
§§355.1 -355.5

Subpart B - Requirements 71
§§355.21 -355.25

Appendix A to Part 355 71

Part 356 - Motor Carrier Routing Regulations

§§356.1 -356.13 73

Part 360 - Fees for Motor Carrier Registration and Insurance

§§360.1 -360.5 76

Part 365 - Rules Governing Applications for Operating Authority

Subpart A - How to Apply for Operating Authority 77
§§365.101 -365.123

Subpart B - How to Oppose Requests for Authority 78
§§365.201 -365.207

Subpart C - General Rules Governing the Application Process 78
§§365.301 -365.309

Subpart D - Transfer of Operating Rights Under 49 U.S.C. 10926 78
§§365.401 -365.413

Subpart E - Special Rules for Certain Mexico-domiciled Carriers 79
§§365.501 -Appendix A to Subpart E

Part 366 - Designation of Process Agent

§§366.1 -366.6 83

Part 367 - Standards for Registration with States

§§367.1 -Appendix A to Part 367 86

Part 368 - Application for a Certificate of Registration to Operate in Municipalities in the United States on the United States-Mexico International Border or Within the Commercial Zones of Such Municipalities

§§368.1 -368.8 87

Part 369 - Reports of Motor Carriers

§§369.1 -369.11 89

Part 370 - Principles and Practices for the Investigation and Voluntary Disposition of Loss and Damage Claims and Processing Salvage

§§370.1 -370.11 93

Part 371 - Brokers of Property
§§371.1 -371.13   95

Part 372 - Exemptions, Commercial Zones, and Terminal Areas

Subpart A - Exemptions   97
§§372.101 -372.117

Subpart B - Commercial Zones   99
§§372.201 -372.243

Subpart C - Terminal Areas   102
§§372.300 -372.303

Part 373 - Receipts and Bills

Subpart A - Motor Carrier Receipts and Bills   103
§§373.101 -373.105

Subpart B - Freight Forwarders; Bills of Lading   103
§373.201

Part 374 - Passenger Carrier Regulations

Subpart A - Discrimination in Operations of Interstate Motor Common Carriers of Passengers   105
§§374.101 -374.113

Subpart B - Limitation of Smoking on Interstate Passenger Carrier Vehicles   105
§374.201

Subpart C - Adequacy of Intercity Motor Common Carrier Passenger Service   105
§§374.301 -374.319

Subpart D - Notice of and Procedures for Baggage Excess Value Declaration   107
§§374.401 -374.405

Subpart E - Incidental Charter Rights   107
§§374.503 -374.505

Part 375 - Transportation of Household Goods in Interstate Commerce; Consumer Protection Regulations

Subpart A - General Requirements   109
§§375.101 -375.105

Subpart B - Before Offering Services to My Customers   109
§§375.201 -375.221

Subpart C - Service Options Provided   111
§§375.301 -375.303

Subpart D - Estimating Charges   111
§§375.401 -375.409

Subpart E - Pick Up of Shipments of Household Goods   113
§§375.501 -375.521

Subpart F - Transportation of Shipments   115
§§375.601 -375.609

Subpart G - Delivery of Shipments   116
§§375.701 -375.709

Subpart H - Collection of Charges   116
§§375.801 -375.807

Subpart I - Penalties   116
§375.901

Appendix A to Part 375   117

Part 376 - Lease and Interchange of Vehicles

Subpart A - General Applicability and Definitions   131
§§376.1 -376.2

Subpart B - Leasing Regulations   131
§§376.11 -376.12

Subpart C - Exemptions for the Leasing Regulations   133
§§376.21 -376.26

Subpart D - Interchange Regulations   133
§376.31

Subpart E - Private Carriers and Shippers   133
§376.42

Part 377 - Payment of Transportation Charges

Subpart A - Handling of C.O.D. Shipments   135
§§377.101 -377.105

Subpart B - Extension of Credit to Shippers by Motor Common Carriers, Water Common Carriers, and Household Goods Freight Forwarders   135
§§377.201 -377.217

Part 378 - Procedures Governing the Processing, Investigation, and Disposition of Overcharge, Duplicate Payment, or Overcollection Claims

§§378.1 -378.9   137

Part 379 - Preservation of Records

§§379.1 -Appendix A to Part 379   139

Part 380 - Special Training Requirements

Subpart A - Longer Combination Vehicle (LCV) Driver-Training and Driver-Instructor Requirements — General   143
§§380.101 -380.113

Subpart B - LCV Driver-Training Program   144
§§380.201 -380.205

Subpart C - LCV Driver-Instructor Requirements   145
§§380.301 -380.305

Subpart D - Driver-Training Certification   145
§380.401

Subpart E - Entry-Level Driver Training Requirements   145
§§380.501 -380.513

Appendix to Part 380   146

Part 381 - Waivers, Exemptions, and Pilot Programs

Subpart A - General   149
§§381.100-381.110

Subpart B - Procedures for Requesting Waivers   149
§§381.200 -381.225

Subpart C - Procedures for Applying for Exemptions   149
§§381.300 -381.330

Subpart D - Initiation of Pilot Programs   150
§§381.400 -381.420

Subpart E - Administrative Procedures for Pilot Programs   151
§§381.500-381.520

Subpart F - Preemption of State Rules   151
§381.600

Part 382 - Controlled Substances and Alcohol Use and Testing

Subpart A - General   153
§§382.101 -382.121

Subpart B - Prohibitions   156
§§382.201 -382.215

Subpart C - Tests Required   157
§§382.301 -382.311

Subpart D - Handling of Test Results, Records Retention, and Confidentiality   163
§§382.401 -382.413

Subpart E - Consequences for Drivers Engaging in Substance Use-Related Conduct   166
§§382.501 -382.507

Subpart F - Alcohol Misuse & Controlled Substances Use Information, Training, & Referral   166
§§382.601 -382.605

Part 383 - Commercial Driver's License Standards; Requirements and Penalties

Subpart A - General   171
§§383.1 -383.7

Subpart B - Single License Requirement   176
§§383.21 -383.23

Subpart C - Notification Requirements and Employer Responsibilities   177
§§383.31-383.37

Subpart D - Driver Disqualifications and Penalties   178
§§383.51 -383.53

Subpart E - Testing and Licensing Procedures   183
§§383.71 -383.77

Subpart F - Vehicle Groups and Endorsements   186
§§383.91 -383.95

Subpart G - Required Knowledge and Skills   188
§§383.110 -Appendix to Subpart G

Subpart H - Tests   191
§§383.131-383.135

Subpart I - Requirement for Transportation Security Administration Approval of Hazardous Materials Endorsement Issuances   192
§383.141

Subpart J - Commercial Driver's License Document   192
§§383.151 -383.155

Part 384 - State Compliance with Commercial Driver's License Program

Subpart A - General 195
§§384.101 -384.107

Subpart B - Minimum Standards for Substantial Compliance by States 195
§§384.201 -384.233

Subpart C - Procedures for Determining State Compliance 197
§§384.301 -384.309

Subpart D - Consequences of State Noncompliance 198
§§384.401 -384.407

Part 385 - Safety Fitness Procedures

Subpart A - General 201
§§385.1 -385.19

Subpart B - Safety Monitoring System for Mexico-Domiciled Carriers 203
§§385.101-385.119

Subpart C - Certification of Safety Auditors, Safety Investigators, and Safety Inspectors 205
§§385.201 -385.205

Subpart D - New Entrant Safety Assurance Program 205
§§385.301 -385.337

Subpart E - Hazardous Materials Safety Permits 207
§§385.401 -385.423

Appendix A to Part 385 - Appendix B to Part 385 210

Part 386 - Rules of Practice for Motor Carrier, Broker, Freight Forwarder, and Hazardous Materials Proceedings

Subpart A - Scope of Rules; Definitions and General Provisions 217
§§386.1 -386.8

Subpart B - Commencement of Proceedings, Pleadings 219
§§386.11 -386.18

Subpart C - Settlement Agreements 221
§386.22

Subpart D - General Rules and Hearings 221
§§386.31-386.58

Subpart E - Decision 225
§§386.61 -386.67

Subpart F - Injunctions and Imminent Hazards 226
§§386.71 -386.72

Subpart G - Penalties 226
§§386.81 -386.84

Appendix A to Part 386 - Appendix B to Part 386 228

Part 387 - Minimum Levels of Financial Responsibility for Motor Carriers

Subpart A - Motor Carriers of Property 231
§§387.1 -387.17

Subpart B - Motor Carriers of Passengers 234
§§387.25 -387.41

Subpart C - Surety Bonds and Policies of Insurance for Motor Carriers and Property Brokers 237
§§387.301 -387.323

Subpart D - Surety Bonds and Policies of Insurance for Freight Forwarders 242
§§387.401 -387.419

Part 388 - Cooperative Agreements with States
§§388.1 -388.8 243

Part 389 - Rulemaking Procedures — Federal Motor Carrier Safety Regulations

Subpart A - General 245
§§389.1 -389.7

Subpart B - Procedures for Adoption of Rules 245
§§389.11 -389.37

Part 390 - Federal Motor Carrier Safety Regulations; General

Subpart A - General Applicability and Definitions 247
§§390.1 -390.7

Subpart B - General Requirements and Information 255
§§390.9 -390.37

Subpart C - [Reserved] 259

Part 391 - Qualifications of Drivers and Longer Combination Vehicle (LCV) Driver Instructors

Subpart A - General 261
§§391.1 -391.2

Subpart B - Qualification and Disqualification of Drivers 261
§§391.11 -391.15

Subpart C - Background and Character 263
§§391.21 -391.27

Subpart D - Tests 266
§§391.31 -391.33

Subpart E - Physical Qualifications and Examinations 267
§§391.41 -391.49

Subpart F - Files and Records 275
§§391.51 -391.55

Subpart G - Limited Exemptions 275
§§391.61 -391.71

Part 392 - Driving of Commercial Motor Vehicles

Subpart A - General 279
§§392.1 -392.9a

Subpart B - Driving of Commercial Motor Vehicles 281
§§392.10-392.18

Subpart C - Stopped Commercial Motor Vehicles 282
§§392.20-392.25

Subpart D - Use of Lighted Lamps and Reflectors 282
§§392.30-392.33

Subpart E - License Revocation; Duties of Driver 282
§§392.40-392.42

Subpart F - Fueling Precautions 282
§§392.50 -392.52

Subpart G - Prohibited Practices 283
§§392.60 -392.71

Part 393 - Parts and Accessories Necessary for Safe Operation

Subpart A - General 285
§§393.1 -393.7

Subpart B - Lamps, Reflective Devices, and Electrical Wiring 288
§§393.9 -393.33

Subpart C - Brakes 297
§§393.40 -393.55

Subpart D - Glazing and Window Construction 303
§§393.60 -393.63

Subpart E - Fuel Systems 305
§§393.65 -393.69

Subpart F - Coupling Devices and Towing Methods 307
§§393.70 -393.71

Subpart G - Miscellaneous Parts and Accessories 312
§§393.75-393.94

Subpart H - Emergency Equipment 317
§393.95

Subpart I - Protection Against Shifting and Falling Cargo 318
§§393.100 -393.136

Subpart J - Frames, Cab and Body Components, Wheels, Steering, and Suspension Systems 327
§§393.201 -393.209

Part 394 - [Reserved] 327

Part 395 - Hours of Service of Drivers
§§395.0 -395.15 329

Part 396 - Inspection, Repair, and Maintenance
§§396.1 -396.25 349

Part 397 - Transportation of Hazardous Materials; Driving and Parking Rules

Subpart A - General 355
§§397.1 -397.19

Subpart B - [Reserved] 357

Subpart C - Routing of Non-Radioactive Hazardous Materials 357
§§397.61 -397.77

Subpart D - Routing of Class 7 (Radioactive) Materials 360
§§397.101 -397.103

Subpart E - Preemption Procedures 361
§§397.201 -397.225

Part 398 - Transportation of Migrant Workers
§§398.1 -398.8   365

Part 399 - Employee Safety and Health Standards

Subparts A-K - [Reserved]   369

Subpart L - Step, Handhold, and Deck Requirements for Commercial Motor Vehicles   369
§§399.201 -399.211

Appendixes to Subchapter B (Parts 350-399)

Appendix A - [Reserved]   371
Appendix B - Special Agents   371
Appendix C - [Reserved]   371
Appendix D - [Reserved]   371
Appendix E - [Reserved]   371
Appendix F - Commercial Zones   371
Appendix G - Minimum Periodic Inspection Standards   381

Addendum

Medical Advisory Criteria for Evaluation Under 49 Part CFR 391.41   385
Interstate Motor Operations   388
Useful Addresses and Telephone Numbers for State Agencies   389
Motor Carrier Safety Progress Report   391
Bridge Formula Weights   392
FMCSA Offices   396
Costs of Highway Crashes Worksheet   398
Revenue Necessary to Pay for Accident Losses   399

Notes

Part 40 - Procedures for Transportation Workplace Drug and Alcohol Testing Programs (Page 1 in the Driver Edition)

> **Pre-Employment Alcohol Testing**
> *Question 1:* Can an employer wishing to conduct pre-employment alcohol testing, do so?
> *Guidance:* A DOT-regulated employer (except under USCG and PHMSA rules) wishing to conduct pre-employment alcohol testing under DOT authority may do so if certain conditions are met.
> The testing must be accomplished for all applicants (i.e., the employer cannot select for testing some applicants and not others) and the testing must be conducted as a post-offer requirement (i.e., the employer needs to inform the applicant that he or she has the job if he or she passes a DOT alcohol test).
> In addition, the testing and its consequences must comply with requirements of Part 40.

Subpart A - Administrative Provisions

§40.1 Who does this regulation cover?
(a) **This part tells all parties** who conduct drug and alcohol tests required by Department of Transportation (DOT) agency regulations how to conduct these tests and what procedures to use.
(b) **This part concerns the activities** of transportation employers, safety-sensitive transportation employees (including self-employed individuals, contractors and volunteers as covered by DOT agency regulations), and service agents.
(c) **Nothing in this part is intended** to supersede or conflict with the implementation of the Federal Railroad Administration's post-accident testing program (see 49 CFR 219.200).

§40.3 What do the terms used in this regulation mean?
In this part, the terms listed in this section have the following meanings:

Adulterated specimen. A specimen that contains a substance that is not expected to be present in human urine, or contains a substance expected to be present but is at a concentration so high that it is not consistent with human urine.

Affiliate. Persons are affiliates of one another if, directly or indirectly, one controls or has the power to control the other, or a third party controls or has the power to control both. Indicators of control include, but are not limited to: interlocking management or ownership; shared interest among family members; shared facilities or equipment; or common use of employees. Following the issuance of a public interest exclusion, an organization having the same or similar management, ownership, or principal employees as the service agent concerning whom a public interest exclusion is in effect is regarded as an affiliate. This definition is used in connection with the public interest exclusion procedures of Subpart R of this part.

Air blank. In evidential breath testing devices (EBTs) using gas chromatography technology, a reading of the device's internal standard. In all other EBTs, a reading of ambient air containing no alcohol.

Alcohol. The intoxicating agent in beverage alcohol, ethyl alcohol or other low molecular weight alcohols, including methyl or isopropyl alcohol.

Alcohol concentration. The alcohol in a volume of breath expressed in terms of grams of alcohol per 210 liters of breath as indicated by a breath test under this part.

Alcohol confirmation test. A subsequent test using an EBT, following a screening test with a result of 0.02 or greater, that provides quantitative data about the alcohol concentration.

Alcohol screening device (ASD). A breath or saliva device, other than an EBT, that is approved by the National Highway Traffic Safety Administration (NHTSA) and placed on a conforming products list (CPL) for such devices.

Alcohol screening test. An analytic procedure to determine whether an employee may have a prohibited concentration of alcohol in a breath or saliva specimen.

Alcohol testing site. A place selected by the employer where employees present themselves for the purpose of providing breath or saliva for an alcohol test.

Alcohol use. The drinking or swallowing of any beverage, liquid mixture or preparation (including any medication), containing alcohol.

Blind specimen or blind performance test specimen. A specimen submitted to a laboratory for quality control testing purposes, with a fictitious identifier, so that the laboratory cannot distinguish it from an employee specimen.

Breath Alcohol Technician (BAT). A person who instructs and assists employees in the alcohol testing process and operates an evidential breath testing device.

Cancelled test. A drug or alcohol test that has a problem identified that cannot be or has not been corrected, or which this part otherwise requires to be cancelled. A cancelled test is neither a positive nor a negative test.

Chain of custody. The procedure used to document the handling of the urine specimen from the time the employee gives the specimen to the collector until the specimen is destroyed. This procedure uses the Federal Drug Testing Custody and Control Form (CCF).

Collection container. A container into which the employee urinates to provide the specimen for a drug test.

Collection site. A place selected by the employer where employees present themselves for the purpose of providing a urine specimen for a drug test.

Collector. A person who instructs and assists employees at a collection site, who receives and makes an initial inspection of the specimen provided by those employees, and who initiates and completes the CCF.

Confirmation (or confirmatory) drug test. A second analytical procedure performed on a urine specimen to identify and quantify the presence of a specific drug or drug metabolite.

Confirmation (or confirmatory) validity test. A second test performed on a urine specimen to further support a validity test result.

Confirmed drug test. A confirmation test result received by an MRO from a laboratory.

Consortium/Third-party administrator (C/TPA). A service agent that provides or coordinates the provision of a variety of drug and alcohol testing services to employers. C/TPAs typically perform administrative tasks concerning the operation of the employers' drug and alcohol testing programs. This term includes, but is not limited to, groups of employers who join together to administer, as a single entity, the DOT drug and alcohol testing programs of its members. C/TPAs are not "employers" for purposes of this part.

Continuing education. Training for medical review officers (MROs) and substance abuse professionals (SAPs) who have completed qualification training and are performing MRO or SAP functions, designed to keep MROs and SAPs current on changes and developments in the DOT drug and alcohol testing program.

Designated employer representative (DER). An employee authorized by the employer to take immediate action(s) to remove employees from safety-sensitive duties, or cause employees to be removed from these covered duties, and to make required decisions in the testing and evaluation processes. The DER also receives test results and other communications for the employer, consistent with the requirements of this part. Service agents cannot act as DERs.

Dilute specimen. A specimen with creatinine and specific gravity values that are lower than expected for human urine.

DOT, The Department, DOT agency. These terms encompass all DOT agencies, including, but not limited to, the United States Coast Guard (USCG), the Federal Aviation Administration (FAA), the Federal Railroad Administration (FRA), the Federal Motor Carrier Safety Administration (FMCSA), the Federal Transit Administration (FTA), the National Highway Traffic Safety Administration (NHTSA), the Pipeline and Hazardous Materials Safety Administration (PHMSA), and the Office of the Secretary (OST). These terms include any designee of a DOT agency.

Drugs. The drugs for which tests are required under this part and DOT agency regulations are marijuana, cocaine, amphetamines, phencyclidine (PCP), and opiates.

Employee. Any person who is designated in a DOT agency regulation as subject to drug testing and/or alcohol testing. The term includes individuals currently performing safety-sensitive functions designated in DOT agency regulations and applicants for employment subject to pre-employment testing. For purposes of drug testing under this part, the term employee has the same meaning as the term "donor" as found on CCF and related guidance materials produced by the Department of Health and Human Services.

Employer. A person or entity employing one or more employees (including an individual who is self-employed) subject to DOT agency regulations requiring compliance with this part. The term includes an employer's officers, representatives, and management personnel. Service agents are not employers for the purposes of this part.

Error Correction Training. Training provided to BATs, collectors, and screening test technicians (STTs) following an error that resulted in the cancellation of a drug or alcohol test. Error correction training must be provided in person or by a means that provides real-time observation and interaction between the instructor and trainee.

Evidential Breath Testing Device (EBT). A device approved by NHTSA for the evidential testing of breath at the .02 and .04 alcohol concentrations, placed on NHTSA's Conforming Products List (CPL) for "Evidential Breath Measurement Devices" and identified on the CPL as conforming with the model specifications available from NHTSA's Traffic Safety Program.

HHS. The Department of Health and Human Services or any designee of the Secretary, Department of Health and Human Services.

Initial drug test. The test used to differentiate a negative specimen from one that requires further testing for drugs or drug metabolites.

Initial validity test. The first test used to determine if a specimen is adulterated, diluted, or substituted.

Invalid drug test. The result of a drug test for a urine specimen that contains an unidentified adulterant or an unidentified interfering substance, has abnormal physical characteristics, or has an endogenous substance at an abnormal concentration that prevents the laboratory from completing or obtaining a valid drug test result.

Laboratory. Any U.S. laboratory certified by HHS under the National Laboratory Certification Program as meeting the minimum standards of Subpart C of the HHS Mandatory Guidelines for Federal Workplace Drug Testing Programs; or, in the case of foreign laboratories, a laboratory approved for participation by DOT under this part. (The HHS Mandatory Guidelines for Federal Workplace Drug Testing Programs are available on the internet at http://www.health.org/workpl.htm or from the Division of Workplace Programs, 1 Choke Cherry Road, Room 2-1035, Rockville MD 20587.)

Medical Review Officer (MRO). A person who is a licensed physician and who is responsible for receiving and reviewing laboratory results generated by an employer's drug testing program and evaluating medical explanations for certain drug test results.

Office of Drug and Alcohol Policy and Compliance (ODAPC). The office in the Office of the Secretary, DOT, that is responsible for coordinating drug and alcohol testing program matters within the Department and providing information concerning the implementation of this part.

Primary specimen. In drug testing, the urine specimen bottle that is opened and tested by a first laboratory to determine whether the employee has a drug or drug metabolite in his or her system; and for the purpose of validity testing. The primary specimen is distinguished from the split specimen, defined in this section.

Qualification Training. The training required in order for a collector, BAT, MRO, SAP, or STT to be qualified to perform their functions in the DOT drug and alcohol testing program. Qualification training may be provided by any appropriate means (e.g., classroom instruction, internet application, CD-ROM, video).

Refresher Training. The training required periodically for qualified collectors, BATs, and STTs to review basic requirements and provide instruction concerning changes in technology (e.g., new testing methods that may be authorized) and amendments, interpretations, guidance, and issues concerning this part and DOT agency drug and alcohol testing regulations. Refresher training can be provided by any appropriate means (e.g., classroom instruction, internet application, CD-ROM, video).

Screening Test Technician (STT). A person who instructs and assists employees in the alcohol testing process and operates an ASD.

Secretary. The Secretary of Transportation or the Secretary's designee.

Service agent. Any person or entity, other than an employee of the employer, who provides services specified under this part to employers and/or employees in connection with DOT drug and alcohol testing requirements. This includes, but is not limited to, collectors, BATs and STTs, laboratories, MROs, substance abuse professionals, and C/TPAs. To act as service agents, persons and organizations must meet the qualifications set forth in applicable sections of this part. Service agents are not employers for purposes of this part.

Shipping container. A container that is used for transporting and protecting urine specimen bottles and associated documents from the collection site to the laboratory.

Specimen bottle. The bottle that, after being sealed and labeled according to the procedures in this part, is used to hold the urine specimen during transportation to the laboratory.

Split specimen. In drug testing, a part of the urine specimen that is sent to a first laboratory and retained unopened, and which is transported to a second laboratory in the event that the employee requests that it be tested following a verified positive test of the primary specimen or a verified adulterated or substituted test result.

Stand-down. The practice of temporarily removing an employee from the performance of safety-sensitive functions based only on a report from a laboratory to the MRO of a confirmed positive test for a drug or drug metabolite, an adulterated test, or a substituted test, before the MRO has completed verification of the test result.

Substance Abuse Professional (SAP). A person who evaluates employees who have violated a DOT drug and alcohol regulation and makes recommendations concerning education, treatment, follow-up testing, and aftercare.

Substituted specimen. A specimen with creatinine and specific gravity values that are so diminished that they are not consistent with human urine.

Verified test. A drug test result or validity testing result from an HHS-certified laboratory that has undergone review and final determination by the MRO.

§40.3 DOT Interpretations

Question 1: Can the employer himself or herself act as a Designated Employer Representative (DER), as opposed to appointing another employee to play this role?

Guidance: The employer (e.g., the owner of a small business) may act personally as the DER.

The employer may also appoint an employee or employees to play this role.

The DER must exercise his or her authority to remove an employee from safety sensitive functions either directly or by causing the employee to be removed from performing these functions (e.g., by having the employee's supervisor effect the actual removal).

The employer may not delegate the DER role to a service agent. Only the employer or an actual employee of the employer may perform this function.

The Department will not authorize a "DER-for-hire" concept (e.g., a person under contract by several companies to serve as their DER), either.

§§40.3 and 40.15(d) DOT Interpretations

Question 1: If a C/TPA is hired as an "independent safety consultant" that executes all aspects of the employer's safety and drug and alcohol testing programs, can the C/TPA act as a DER?

Guidance: Service agents are prohibited from acting as DERs under any circumstances.

The fact that an organization that is called an "independent safety consultant" acts as a consultant to an employer for purposes of executing a drug and alcohol testing or safety program does not make it any less a service agent. It is still prohibited from acting as a DER.

§40.5 Who issues authoritative interpretations of this regulation?

ODAPC and the DOT Office of General Counsel (OGC) provide written interpretations of the provisions of this part. These written DOT interpretations are the only official and authoritative interpretations concerning the provisions of this part. DOT agencies may incorporate ODAPC/OGC interpretations in written guidance they issue concerning drug and alcohol testing matters. Only Part 40 interpretations issued after August 1, 2001, are considered valid.

§40.7 How can you get an exemption from a requirement in this regulation?

(a) **If you want an exemption** from any provision of this part, you must request it in writing from the Office of the Secretary of Transportation, under the provisions and standards of 49 CFR Part 5. You must send requests for an exemption to the following address:

Department of Transportation
Deputy Assistant General Counsel for Regulation and Enforcement
400 7th Street, SW., Room 10424
Washington, DC 20590

Subpart B - Employer Responsibilities

(b) Under the standards of 49 CFR Part 5, we will grant the request only if the request documents special or exceptional circumstances, not likely to be generally applicable and not contemplated in connection with the rulemaking that established this part, that make your compliance with a specific provision of this part impracticable.

(c) If we grant you an exemption, you must agree to take steps we specify to comply with the intent of the provision from which an exemption is granted.

(d) We will issue written responses to all exemption requests.

Subpart B - Employer Responsibilities

§40.11 What are the general responsibilities of employers under this regulation?

(a) As an employer, you are responsible for meeting all applicable requirements and procedures of this part.

(b) You are responsible for all actions of your officials, representatives, and agents (including service agents) in carrying out the requirements of the DOT agency regulations.

(c) All agreements and arrangements, written or unwritten, between and among employers and service agents concerning the implementation of DOT drug and alcohol testing requirements are deemed, as a matter of law, to require compliance with all applicable provisions of this part and DOT agency drug and alcohol testing regulations. Compliance with these provisions is a material term of all such agreements and arrangements.

§40.13 How do DOT drug and alcohol tests relate to non-DOT tests?

(a) DOT tests must be completely separate from non-DOT tests in all respects.

(b) DOT tests must take priority and must be conducted and completed before a non-DOT test is begun. For example, you must discard any excess urine left over from a DOT test and collect a separate void for the subsequent non-DOT test.

(c) Except as provided in paragraph (d) of this section, you must not perform any tests on DOT urine or breath specimens other than those specifically authorized by this part or DOT agency regulations. For example, you may not test a DOT urine specimen for additional drugs, and a laboratory is prohibited from making a DOT urine specimen available for a DNA test or other types of specimen identity testing.

(d) The single exception to paragraph (c) of this section is when a DOT drug test collection is conducted as part of a physical examination required by DOT agency regulations. It is permissible to conduct required medical tests related to this physical examination (e.g., for glucose) on any urine remaining in the collection container after the drug test urine specimens have been sealed into the specimen bottles.

(e) No one is permitted to change or disregard the results of DOT tests based on the results of non-DOT tests. For example, as an employer you must not disregard a verified positive DOT drug test result because the employee presents a negative test result from a blood or urine specimen collected by the employee's physician or a DNA test result purporting to question the identity of the DOT specimen.

(f) As an employer, you must not use the CCF or the ATF in your non-DOT drug and alcohol testing programs. This prohibition includes the use of the DOT forms with references to DOT programs and agencies crossed out. You also must always use the CCF and ATF for all your DOT-mandated drug and alcohol tests.

§40.15 May an employer use a service agent to meet DOT drug and alcohol testing requirements?

(a) As an employer, you may use a service agent to perform the tasks needed to comply with this part and DOT agency drug and alcohol testing regulations, consistent with the requirements of Subpart Q and other applicable provisions of this part.

(b) As an employer, you are responsible for ensuring that the service agents you use meet the qualifications set forth in this part (e.g., §40.121 for MROs). You may require service agents to show you documentation that they meet the requirements of this part (e.g., documentation of MRO qualifications required by §40.121(e)).

(c) You remain responsible for compliance with all applicable requirements of this part and other DOT drug and alcohol testing regulations, even when you use a service agent. If you violate this part or other DOT drug and alcohol testing regulations because a service agent has not provided services as our rules require, a DOT agency can subject you to sanctions. Your good faith use of a service agent is not a defense in an enforcement action initiated by a DOT agency in which your alleged noncompliance with this part or a DOT agency drug and alcohol regulation may have resulted from the service agent's conduct.

(d) As an employer, you must not permit a service agent to act as your DER.

> **§§40.3 and 40.15(d) DOT Interpretations**
>
> *Question 1:* If a C/TPA is hired as an "independent safety consultant" that executes all aspects of the employer's safety and drug and alcohol testing programs, can the C/TPA act as a DER?
>
> *Guidance:* Service agents are prohibited from acting as DERs under any circumstances.
>
> The fact that an organization that is called an "independent safety consultant" acts as a consultant to an employer for purposes of executing a drug and alcohol testing or safety program does not make it any less a service agent. It is still prohibited from acting as a DER.

§40.17 Is an employer responsible for obtaining information from its service agents?

Yes, as an employer, you are responsible for obtaining information required by this part from your service agents. This is true whether or not you choose to use a C/TPA as an intermediary in transmitting information to you. For example, suppose an applicant for a safety-sensitive job takes a pre-employment drug test, but there is a significant delay in your receipt of the test result from an MRO or C/TPA. You must not assume that "no news is good news" and permit the applicant to perform safety-sensitive duties before receiving the result. This is a violation of the Department's regulations.

§40.19 [Reserved]

§40.21 May an employer stand down an employee before the MRO has completed the verification process?

(a) As an employer, you are prohibited from standing employees down, except consistent with a waiver a DOT agency grants under this section.

(b) You may make a request to the concerned DOT agency for a waiver from the prohibition of paragraph (a) of this section. Such a waiver, if granted, permits you to stand an employee down following the MRO's receipt of a laboratory report of a confirmed positive test for a drug or drug metabolite, an adulterated test, or a substituted test pertaining to the employee.

(1) *For this purpose,* the concerned DOT agency is the one whose drug and alcohol testing rules apply to the majority of the covered employees in your organization. The concerned DOT agency uses its applicable procedures for considering requests for waivers.

(2) *Before taking action on a waiver request,* the concerned DOT agency coordinates with other DOT agencies that regulate the employer's other covered employees.

(3) *The concerned DOT agency* provides a written response to each employer that petitions for a waiver, setting forth the reasons for the agency's decision on the waiver request.

(c) Your request for a waiver must include, as a minimum, the following elements:

(1) *Information about your organization:*

(i) *Your determination that standing employees down* is necessary for safety in your organization and a statement of your basis for it, including any data on safety problems or incidents that could have been prevented if a stand-down procedure had been in place;

(ii) *Data showing* the number of confirmed laboratory positive, adulterated, and substituted test results for your employees over the two calendar years preceding your waiver request, and the number and percentage of those test results that were verified positive, adulterated, or substituted by the MRO;

(iii) *Information about the work situation* of the employees subject to stand-down, including a description of the size and organization of the unit(s) in which the employees work, the process through which employees will be informed of the stand-down, whether there is an in-house MRO, and whether your organization has a medical disqualification or stand-down policy for employees in situations other than drug and alcohol testing; and

(iv) *A statement of which DOT agencies regulate your employees.*

(2) *Your proposed written company policy* concerning stand-down, which must include the following elements:
  (i) *Your assurance* that you will distribute copies of your written policy to all employees that it covers;
  (ii) *Your means of ensuring* that no information about the confirmed positive, adulterated, or substituted test result or the reason for the employee's temporary removal from performance of safety-sensitive functions becomes available, directly or indirectly, to anyone in your organization (or subsequently to another employer) other than the employee, the MRO and the DER;
  (iii) *Your means of ensuring* that all covered employees in a particular job category in your organization are treated the same way with respect to stand-down;
  (iv) *Your means of ensuring* that a covered employee will be subject to stand-down only with respect to the actual performance of safety-sensitive duties;
  (v) *Your means of ensuring* that you will not take any action adversely affecting the employee's pay and benefits pending the completion of the MRO's verification process. This includes continuing to pay the employee during the period of the stand-down in the same way you would have paid him or her had he or she not been stood down;
  (vi) *Your means of ensuring* that the verification process will commence no later than the time an employee is temporarily removed from the performance of safety-sensitive functions and that the period of stand-down for any employee will not exceed five days, unless you are informed in writing by the MRO that a longer period is needed to complete the verification process; and
  (vii) *Your means of ensuring* that, in the event that the MRO verifies the test negative or cancels it —
    [A] *You return the employee immediately* to the performance of safety-sensitive duties;
    [B] *The employee suffers* no adverse personnel or financial consequences as a result; and
    [C] *You maintain no individually identifiable record* that the employee had a confirmed laboratory positive, adulterated, or substituted test result (i.e., you maintain a record of the test only as a negative or cancelled test).
(d) **The Administrator of the concerned DOT agency,** or his or her designee, may grant a waiver request only if he or she determines that, in the context of your organization, there is a high probability that the procedures you propose will effectively enhance safety and protect the interests of employees in fairness and confidentiality.
  (1) *The Administrator, or his or her designee,* may impose any conditions he or she deems appropriate on the grant of a waiver.
  (2) *The Administrator, or his or her designee,* may immediately suspend or revoke the waiver if he or she determines that you have failed to protect effectively the interests of employees in fairness and confidentiality, that you have failed to comply with the requirements of this section, or that you have failed to comply with any other conditions the DOT agency has attached to the waiver.
(e) **You must not stand employees down** in the absence of a waiver, or inconsistent with the terms of your waiver. If you do, you are in violation of this part and DOT agency drug testing regulations, and you are subject to enforcement action by the DOT agency just as you are for other violations of this part and DOT agency rules.

§40.21 DOT Interpretations

Question 1: Can union hiring halls, driver-leasing companies, and other entities have a stand-down policy, or is the ability to obtain a waiver for this purpose limited to actual employers?
Guidance: The rule permits "employers" to apply for a stand-down waiver. It does not permit any other entity to do so.

Only entities that are viewed as "employers" for purposes of DOT agency drug and alcohol testing regulations can apply for stand-down waivers. If a DOT agency rule provides that hiring halls, leasing agencies, etc. are treated as employers, such organizations could apply for a stand-down waiver.

Question 2: Does an employer need a stand-down waiver in order to implement a policy that requires employees to cease performing safety-sensitive functions following a reasonable suspicion or post-accident test?

Guidance: §40.21 requires an employer to obtain a waiver to do one very specific thing: remove employees from performance of safety-sensitive functions on the basis of the report of confirmed laboratory test results that have not yet been verified by the MRO. An employer does not need a §40.21 waiver to take other actions involving the performance of safety-sensitive functions.

For example, an employer could (if it is not prohibited by DOT agency regulations and it is consistent with applicable labor-management agreements) have a company policy saying that, on the basis of an event (e.g., the occurrence of an accident that requires a DOT post-accident test, the finding of reasonable suspicion that leads to a DOT reasonable suspicion test), the employee would immediately stop performing safety-sensitive functions. Such a policy, which is not triggered by the MRO's receipt of a confirmed laboratory test result, would not require a §40.21 waiver.

It would not be appropriate for an employer to remove employees from performance of safety-sensitive functions pending the result of a random or follow-up test, since there is no triggering event to which the action could rationally be tied.

§40.23 What actions do employers take after receiving verified test results?

(a) **As an employer who receives** a verified positive drug test result, you must immediately remove the employee involved from performing safety-sensitive functions. You must take this action upon receiving the initial report of the verified positive test result. Do not wait to receive the written report or the result of a split specimen test.
(b) **As an employer who receives** a verified adulterated or substituted drug test result, you must consider this a refusal to test and immediately remove the employee involved from performing safety-sensitive functions. You must take this action on receiving the initial report of the verified adulterated or substituted test result. Do not wait to receive the written report or the result of a split specimen test.
(c) **As an employer who receives** an alcohol test result of 0.04 or higher, you must immediately remove the employee involved from performing safety-sensitive functions. If you receive an alcohol test result of 0.02 - 0.039, you must temporarily remove the employee involved from performing safety-sensitive functions, as provided in applicable DOT agency regulations. Do not wait to receive the written report of the result of the test.
(d) **As an employer, when an employee** has a verified positive, adulterated, or substituted test result, or has otherwise violated a DOT agency drug and alcohol regulation, you must not return the employee to the performance of safety-sensitive functions until or unless the employee successfully completes the return-to-duty process of Subpart O of this part.
(e) **As an employer who receives a drug test result** indicating that the employee's specimen was dilute, take action as provided in §40.197.
(f) **As an employer who receives a drug test result** indicating that the employee's specimen was invalid and that a second collection must take place under direct observation —
  (1) *You must immediately direct the employee* to provide a new specimen under direct observation.
  (2) *You must not attach consequences* to the finding that the test was invalid other than collecting a new specimen under direct observation.
  (3) *You must not give any advance notice* of this test requirement to the employee.
  (4) *You must instruct the collector* to note on the CCF the same reason (e.g. random test, post-accident test) as for the original collection.
(g) **As an employer who receives** a cancelled test result when a negative result is required (e.g., pre-employment, return-to-duty, or follow-up test), you must direct the employee to provide another specimen immediately.
(h) **As an employer, you may also be required** to take additional actions required by DOT agency regulations (e.g., FAA rules require some positive drug tests to be reported to the Federal Air Surgeon).
(i) **As an employer, you must not alter** a drug or alcohol test result transmitted to you by an MRO, BAT, or C/TPA.

Subpart B - Employer Responsibilities §40.25 (j)

§40.25 Must an employer check on the drug and alcohol testing record of employees it is intending to use to perform safety-sensitive duties?

(a) **Yes, as an employer, you must,** after obtaining an employee's written consent, request the information about the employee listed in paragraph (b) of this section. This requirement applies only to employees seeking to begin performing safety-sensitive duties for you for the first time (i.e., a new hire, an employee transfers into a safety-sensitive position). If the employee refuses to provide this written consent, you must not permit the employee to perform safety-sensitive functions.

(b) **You must request the information** listed in this paragraph (b) from DOT-regulated employers who have employed the employee during any period during the two years before the date of the employee's application or transfer:

(1) *Alcohol tests with a result of 0.04 or higher alcohol concentration;*
(2) *Verified positive drug tests;*
(3) *Refusals to be tested* (including verified adulterated or substituted drug test results);
(4) *Other violations of DOT agency* drug and alcohol testing regulations; and
(5) *With respect to any employee* who violated a DOT drug and alcohol regulation, documentation of the employee's successful completion of DOT return-to-duty requirements (including follow-up tests). If the previous employer does not have information about the return-do-duty process (e.g., an employer who did not hire an employee who tested positive on a pre-employment test), you must seek to obtain this information from the employee.

(c) **The information obtained** from a previous employer includes any drug or alcohol test information obtained from previous employers under this section or other applicable DOT agency regulations.

(d) **If feasible, you must obtain and review** this information before the employee first performs safety-sensitive functions. If this is not feasible, you must obtain and review the information as soon as possible. However, you must not permit the employee to perform safety-sensitive functions after 30 days from the date on which the employee first performed safety-sensitive functions, unless you have obtained or made and documented a good faith effort to obtain this information.

(e) **If you obtain information that the employee** has violated a DOT agency drug and alcohol regulation, you must not use the employee to perform safety-sensitive functions unless you also obtain information that the employee has subsequently complied with the return-to-duty requirements of Subpart O of this part and DOT agency drug and alcohol regulations.

(f) **You must provide to each of the employers** from whom you request information under paragraph (b) of this section written consent for the release of the information cited in paragraph (a) of this section.

(g) **The release of information under this section** must be in any written form (e.g., fax, e-mail, letter) that ensures confidentiality. As the previous employer, you must maintain a written record of the information released, including the date, the party to whom it was released, and a summary of the information provided.

(h) **If you are an employer from whom information** is requested under paragraph (b) of this section, you must, after reviewing the employee's specific, written consent, immediately release the requested information to the employer making the inquiry.

(i) **As the employer requesting the information** required under this section, you must maintain a written, confidential record of the information you obtain or of the good faith efforts you made to obtain the information. You must retain this information for three years from the date of the employee's first performance of safety-sensitive duties for you.

(j) **As the employer, you must also ask the employee** whether he or she has tested positive, or refused to test, on any pre-employment drug or alcohol test administered by an employer to which the employee applied for, but did not obtain, safety-sensitive transportation work covered by DOT agency drug and alcohol testing rules during the past two years. If the employee admits that he or she had a positive test or a refusal to test, you must not use the employee to perform safety-sensitive functions for you, until and unless the employee documents successful completion of the return-to-duty process (see paragraphs (b)(5) and (e) of this section).

§40.25 DOT Interpretations

Question 1: When an employer is inquiring about an applicant's previous DOT drug and alcohol test results, is the employer required to send the inquiry via certified mail?

Guidance: No. Certified mail is not required.

The employer can make this inquiry through a variety of means, including mail (certified or not), fax, telephone, or email.

However, the employer must provide the former employer the signed release or a faxed or scanned copy of the employee's signed release.

The former employer must respond via a written response (e.g., fax, letter, email) that ensures confidentiality.

The employer should document an attempt or attempts to contact and contacts with previous employers, no matter how they were made, so that it can show a good faith effort to obtain the required information.

Question 2: When a previous employer receives an inquiry from a new employer for drug and alcohol testing information, does the previous employer provide information it may have received from other employers in the past?

Guidance: As an employer, when you receive an inquiry about a former employee, you must provide all the information in your possession concerning the employee's DOT drug and alcohol tests that occurred in the two years preceding the inquiry.

This includes information you received about an employee from a former employer (e.g., in response to the Federal Motor Carrier Safety Administration's pre-employment inquiry requirement).

It is not a violation of Part 40 or DOT agency rules if you provide, in addition, information about the employee's DOT drug and alcohol tests obtained from former employers that dates back more than two years ago.

If you are an employer regulated by the FAA, this does not impact your requirements under the Pilot Record Act.

Question 3: If an applicant admits to testing positive on or refusing to take a pre-employment test within the past two years, must the applicant be held out of safety-sensitive duties if he or she did not complete the return-to-duty process (i.e., the SAP process)?

Guidance: If the applicant admits that he or she had a positive or a refusal to test result on a pre-employment test, the employer is not permitted to use the applicant to perform safety-sensitive duties until and unless the applicant documents successful completion of the return-to-duty process.

This Part 40 requirement applies whether or not the pre-employment positive or refusal occurred before, on, or after August 1, 2001.

Should no proof exist that the return-no-duty process was successfully complied with by the applicant, a current return-to-duty process must occur before the individual can again perform safety-sensitive functions.

Question 4: When an employee leaves an employer for a period of time (but not exceeding two years) and returns to that same employer, must the employer once again seek to obtain information it may have received previously from other employers?

Guidance: No. If the information received previously is still on file with the employer, the employer need not seek to obtain the testing data again.

However, the employer must seek information from all other employers for whom the employee performed safety-sensitive duties since the employee last worked for the employer.

Question 5: May the previous employer delay sending an employee's drug and alcohol testing information to the gaining employer pending payment for the cost of the information?

Guidance: No. Part 40 specifically requires that previous employers immediately provide the gaining employer with the appropriate drug and alcohol testing information.

No one (i.e., previous employer, service agent [to include C/TPA], employer information/data broker) may withhold this information from the requesting employer pending payment for it.

Question 6: Will FMCSA- and FAA-regulated employers complying with the drug and alcohol information records check requirements contained in the Federal Motor Carrier Safety Administration (FMCSA) regulation 49 CFR Part 391 and the Federal Aviation Administration (FAA) Pilot Record Improvement Act be considered compliant with §40.25?

Guidance: Yes. Employers who are required by and who comply with the FMCSA's three-year requirement for obtaining and providing employee drug and alcohol testing information are considered to have satisfied the two-year requirement contained in §40.25.

Likewise, employers who are required by and who comply with the FAA's five-year requirement for obtaining and providing employee drug and alcohol testing information are considered to have satisfied the two-year requirement contained in §40.25.

These employers do not need to seek separately the §40.25 information if the employer adheres to the FMCSA and FAA regulations, as appropriate, for obtaining an employee's prior drug and alcohol testing information.

§40.26 What form must an employer use to report Management Information System (MIS) data to a DOT agency?

As an employer, when you are required to report MIS data to a DOT agency, you must use the form and instructions at Appendix H to Part 40. You must submit the MIS report in accordance with rule requirements (e.g., dates for submission; selection of companies required to submit, and method of reporting) established by the DOT agency regulating your operation.

§40.27 May an employer require an employee to sign a consent or release in connection with the DOT drug and alcohol testing program?

No, as an employer, you must not require an employee to sign a consent, release, waiver of liability, or indemnification agreement with respect to any part of the drug or alcohol testing process covered by this part (including, but not limited to, collections, laboratory testing, MRO and SAP services).

§40.29 Where is other information on employer responsibilities found in this regulation?

You can find other information on the responsibilities of employers in the following sections of this part:

§40.3 - Definition.
§40.35 - Information about DERs that employers must provide collectors.
§40.45 - Modifying CCFs, Use of foreign-language CCFs.
§40.47 - Use of non-Federal forms for DOT tests or Federal CCFs for non-DOT tests.
§40.67 - Requirements for direct observation.
§§40.103-40.105 - Blind specimen requirements.
§40.173 - Responsibility to ensure test of split specimen.
§40.193 - Action in "shy bladder" situations.
§40.197 - Actions following report of a dilute specimen.
§40.207 - Actions following a report of a cancelled drug test.
§40.209 - Actions following and consequences of non-fatal flaws in drug tests.
§40.215 - Information about DERs that employers must provide BATs and STTs.
§40.225 - Modifying ATFs; use of foreign-language ATFs.
§40.227 - Use of non-DOT forms for DOT tests or DOT ATFs for non-DOT tests.
§40.235 (c) and (d) - Responsibility to follow instructions for ASDs.
§40.255 (b) - Receipt and storage of alcohol test information.
§40.265 (c)-(e) - Actions in "shy lung" situations.
§40.267 - Cancellation of alcohol tests.
§40.271 - Actions in "correctable flaw" situations in alcohol tests.
§40.273 - Actions following cancelled tests in alcohol tests.
§40.275 - Actions in "non-fatal flaw" situations in alcohol tests.
§§40.287-40.289 - Responsibilities concerning SAP services.
§§40.295-40.297 - Prohibition on seeking second SAP evaluation or changing SAP recommendation.
§40.303 - Responsibilities concerning aftercare recommendations.
§40.305 - Responsibilities concerning return-to-duty decision.
§40.309 - Responsibilities concerning follow-up tests.
§40.321 - General confidentiality requirement.
§40.323 - Release of confidential information in litigation.
§40.331 - Other circumstances for the release of confidential information.
§40.333 - Record retention requirements.
§40.345 - Choice of who reports drug testing information to employers.

Subpart C - Urine Collection Personnel

§40.31 Who may collect urine specimens for DOT drug testing?

(a) Collectors meeting the requirements of this subpart are the only persons authorized to collect urine specimens for DOT drug testing.
(b) A collector must meet training requirements of §40.33.
(c) As the immediate supervisor of an employee being tested, you may not act as the collector when that employee is tested, unless no other collector is available and you are permitted to do so under DOT agency drug and alcohol regulations.
(d) You must not act as the collector for the employee being tested if you work for a HHS-certified laboratory (e.g., as a technician or accessioner) and could link the employee with a urine specimen, drug testing result, or laboratory report.

§40.33 What training requirements must a collector meet?

To be permitted to act as a collector in the DOT drug testing program, you must meet each of the requirements of this section:

(a) *Basic information.* You must be knowledgeable about this part, the current "DOT Urine Specimen Collection Procedures Guidelines," and DOT agency regulations applicable to the employers for whom you perform collections, and you must keep current on any changes to these materials. The DOT Urine Specimen Collection Procedures Guidelines document is available from ODAPC (Department of Transportation, 400 7th Street, SW., Room 10403, Washington DC, 20590, 202-366-3784, or on the ODAPC web site (http://www.dot.gov/ost/dapc)).

(b) *Qualification training.* You must receive qualification training meeting the requirements of this paragraph. Qualification training must provide instruction on the following subjects:
   (1) *All steps necessary to complete a collection correctly* and the proper completion and transmission of the CCF;
   (2) *"Problem" collections* (e.g., situations like "shy bladder" and attempts to tamper with a specimen);
   (3) *Fatal flaws, correctable flaws,* and how to correct problems in collections; and
   (4) *The collector's responsibility* for maintaining the integrity of the collection process, ensuring the privacy of employees being tested, ensuring the security of the specimen, and avoiding conduct or statements that could be viewed as offensive or inappropriate;

(c) *Initial Proficiency Demonstration.* Following your completion of qualification training under paragraph (b) of this section, you must demonstrate proficiency in collections under this part by completing five consecutive error-free mock collections.
   (1) *The five mock collections* must include two uneventful collection scenarios, one insufficient quantity of urine scenario, one temperature out of range scenario, and one scenario in which the employee refuses to sign the CCF and initial the specimen bottle tamper-evident seal.
   (2) *Another person* must monitor and evaluate your performance, in person or by a means that provides real-time observation and interaction between the instructor and trainee, and attest in writing that the mock collections are "error-free." This person must be a qualified collector who has demonstrated necessary knowledge, skills, and abilities by —
      (i) *Regularly conducting DOT drug test collections* for a period of at least a year;
      (ii) *Conducting collector training* under this part for a year; or
      (iii) *Successfully completing a "train the trainer" course.*

(d) **Schedule for qualification training** and initial proficiency demonstration. The following is the schedule for qualification training and the initial proficiency demonstration you must meet:
   (1) *If you became a collector before August 1, 2001,* and you have already met the requirements of paragraphs (b) and (c) of this section, you do not have to meet them again.
   (2) *If you became a collector before August 1, 2001,* and have yet to meet the requirements of paragraphs (b) and (c) of this section, you must do so no later than January 31, 2003.
   (3) *If you become a collector on or after August 1, 2001,* you must meet the requirements of paragraphs (b) and (c) of this section before you begin to perform collector functions.

(e) *Refresher training.* No less frequently than every five years from the date on which you satisfactorily complete the requirements of paragraphs (b) and (c) of this section, you must complete refresher training that meets all the requirements of paragraphs (b) and (c) of this section.

(f) Error Correction Training. If you make a mistake in the collection process that causes a test to be cancelled (i.e., a fatal or uncorrected flaw), you must undergo error correction training. This training must occur within 30 days of the date you are notified of the error that led to the need for retraining.

   (1) *Error correction training must be provided* and your proficiency documented in writing by a person who meets the requirements of paragraph (c)(2) of this section.
   (2) *Error correction training is required* to cover only the subject matter area(s) in which the error that caused the test to be cancelled occurred.
   (3) *As part of the error correction training,* you must demonstrate your proficiency in the collection procedures of this part by completing three consecutive error-free mock collections. The mock collections must include one uneventful scenario and two scenarios related to the area(s) in which your error(s) occurred. The person providing the training must monitor and evaluate your performance and attest in writing that the mock collections were "error-free."

(g) Documentation. You must maintain documentation showing that you currently meet all requirements of this section. You must provide this documentation on request to DOT agency representatives and to employers and C/TPAs who are using or negotiating to use your services.

§40.33 DOT Interpretations

Question 1: If a collector makes a mistake resulting in a cancellation of a test before he or she has obtained qualification training (e.g., in the period before January 31, 2003), does he or she have to obtain error correction training under §40.33(f)?

Guidance: Yes. If a collector makes a mistake that causes a test to be cancelled, the collector must undergo error correction training (even if the collector has yet to undergo qualification training). There are no exceptions to this requirement.

Question 2: A collector who is notified that he or she made a mistake has 30 days in which to obtain error correction training. Can the collector continue to perform DOT collections during this 30-day period?

Guidance: Yes. A collector may continue to perform DOT collections during this period.

After 30 days have elapsed following the notification to the collector of the need to obtain error correction training, the collector is no longer qualified to conduct DOT collections until and unless he or she has successfully completed error correction training.

As provided in §40.209(b)(3), collection of a specimen by a collector who has not met training requirements does not result in the cancellation of the test, assuming the collection is otherwise proper. However, use of an unqualified collector can result in enforcement action.

Question 3: Who is responsible for notifying a collector that error correction training is needed?

Guidance: The MRO, in canceling a drug test, will determine if the collector is at fault.

When the MRO reports the cancelled test to the employer, the MRO will note the reason for the cancellation and that, if appropriate, it was the result of collector error.

The employer or service agent (e.g., MRO, C/TPA) designated by the employer is responsible for notifying the collection site of the error and the retraining requirement; and for ensuring that the training takes place.

Question 4: Must collectors, BATs, STTs, MROs, and SAPs maintain documentation of meeting training requirements on their persons?

Guidance: These individuals are responsible for maintaining documentation that they currently meet all training requirements (see, for example, §40.33(g)).

However, they are not required to keep this documentation on their person.

They must be able to produce this documentation within a short, reasonable time of a request by a DOT representative or an employer.

Nothing precludes an organization (e.g., a collection site) from also maintaining a file of the training records of its personnel, if it wishes to do so.

Question 5: What does the rule require with respect to the qualifications of persons who train collectors?

Guidance: Part 40 does not specify any set of specific qualifications for persons who train collectors.

The training must cover the items required by Part 40.

Question 6: Does a person who monitors proficiency demonstrations as a part of collector qualification training have to be a qualified collector?

Guidance: Yes. It is very important for persons who monitor mock collections to have a thorough "book" and practical knowledge of relevant DOT rules and procedures. It is also very important that, before determining whether trainees have successfully completed a proficiency demonstration, the monitor have experienced and successfully completed the same training that collectors have to undergo.

Consequently, mock collection monitors have to meet collector qualification training requirements. In addition, the monitor must meet any one of three other requirements:

- The monitor can be a qualified collector who has regularly conducted DOT drug testing collections for a least a year before serving as a monitor; or
- The monitor can be a qualified collector who has had a "train-the-trainer" course. Such a course could include the mandatory elements of collector qualification training as well as instruction on how to conduct training effectively; or
- The monitor can be a qualified collector who has conducted collector training under Part 40 for at least a year before serving as a monitor.

Monitors in the second and third categories do not need to practice actively as collectors, so long as they have met collector qualification requirements.

Individuals acting as collectors prior to August 1, 2001, have until January 31, 2003, to meet qualification training requirements. In the meantime, such collectors can serve as monitors even though they may not have met the qualification and mock collection requirements (so long as they meet any one of the three other requirements).

Question 7: Is error correction training required if a drug test is cancelled due to a specimen having an insufficient amount of urine?

Guidance: If the laboratory finds there is an insufficient amount of urine in the primary bottle for analysis, the laboratory will report to the MRO that the specimen is "rejected for testing" (unless the laboratory can redesignate the specimens). Subsequently, the MRO must cancel the test.

The MRO should seek to determine (with the assistance of the laboratory) if the specimen leaked in transit or if not enough urine was collected.

Specimen leakage while in transit to a laboratory will not cause a cancellation requiring the collector to have error correction training.

If the laboratory finds no evidence of leakage, indications would be strong that the collector failed to collect the appropriate amount of urine. If this were the case, the collector would need error correction training.

If specimen leakage is a recurrent problem for a collection site, the MRO may be wise to inquire whether or not the shipping containers used are sufficient to adequately protect the specimens or whether or not collectors are securing the bottle lids properly.

§§40.33, 40.121, 40.213, 40.281 DOT Interpretations

Question 1: Because Part 40 requires collectors, MROs, BATs and STTs, and SAPs to maintain their own training records, can employers or training entities refuse to provide these service agents their training records?

Guidance: No. Employers and trainers who provide training for these service agents must not withhold training documentation from them when they have successfully completed the training requirements.

If a collector, BAT, STT, MRO, or SAP is not in possession of training documentation, he or she is in violation of Part 40.

Therefore, Part 40 does not permit the withholding of such documentation from these service agents.

§40.35 What information about the DER must employers provide to collectors?

As an employer, you must provide to collectors the name and telephone number of the appropriate DER (and C/TPA, where applicable) to contact about any problems or issues that may arise during the testing process.

> **§§40.35, 40.45, 40.345 DOT Interpretations**
>
> *Question 1:* How should the employer's decision to have a C/TPA act as intermediary in the handling of drug test results be documented?
>
> *Guidance:* When an employer chooses to use the C/TPA as the intermediary in the transmission of the MRO's verified drug test results, this decision should be communicated from the employer to the MRO and the C/TPA.
>
> We advise the MRO to obtain some documentation of the employer's decision prior to sending results through the C/TPA. Documentation could be in the form of a letter, an email, or record of a telephone conversation with the employer.
>
> DOT also recommends that MROs maintain listings of the names, addresses, and phone numbers of C/TPA points of contact.

§40.37 Where is other information on the role of collectors found in this regulation?

You can find other information on the role and functions of collectors in the following sections of this part:

§40.3 - Definition.
§40.43 - Steps to prepare and secure collection sites.
§§40.45-40.47 - Use of CCF.
§§40.49-40.51 - Use of collection kit and shipping materials.
§§40.61-40.63 - Preliminary steps in collections.
§40.65 - Role in checking specimens.
§40.67 - Role in directly observed collections.
§40.69 - Role in monitored collections.
§40.71 - Role in split specimen collections.
§40.73 - Chain of custody completion and finishing the collection process.
§40.103 - Processing blind specimens.
§40.191 - Action in case of refusals to take test.
§40.193 - Action in "shy bladder" situations.
§§40.199-40.205 - Collector errors in tests, effects, and means of correction.

Subpart D - Collection Sites, Forms, Equipment and Supplies Used in DOT Urine Collections

§40.41 Where does a urine collection for a DOT drug test take place?

(a) *A urine collection for a DOT drug test* must take place in a collection site meeting the requirements of this section.

(b) *If you are operating a collection site,* you must ensure that it meets the security requirements of §40.43.

(c) *If you are operating a collection site,* you must have all necessary personnel, materials, equipment, facilities and supervision to provide for the collection, temporary storage, and shipping of urine specimens to a laboratory, and a suitable clean surface for writing.

(d) *Your collection site must include* a facility for urination described in either paragraph (e) or paragraph (f) of this section.

(e) *The first, and preferred, type of facility for urination* that a collection site may include is a single-toilet room, having a full-length privacy door, within which urination can occur.

(1) *No one but the employee* may be present in the room during the collection, except for the observer in the event of a directly observed collection.

(2) *You must have a source of water* for washing hands, that, if practicable, should be external to the closed room where urination occurs. If an external source is not available, you may meet this requirement by securing all sources of water and other substances that could be used for adulteration and substitution (e.g., water faucets, soap dispensers) and providing moist towelettes outside the closed room.

(f) *The second type of facility for urination* that a collection site may include is a multistall restroom.

(1) *Such a site must provide substantial visual privacy* (e.g., a toilet stall with a partial-length door) and meet all other applicable requirements of this section.

(2) *If you use a multi-stall restroom, you must either —*

(i) *Secure all sources of water* and other substances that could be used for adulteration and substitution (e.g., water faucets, soap dispensers) and place bluing agent in all toilets or secure the toilets to prevent access; or

(ii) *Conduct all collections in the facility* as monitored collections (see §40.69 for procedures). This is the only circumstance in which you may conduct a monitored collection.

(3) *No one but the employee may be present* in the multistall restroom during the collection, except for the monitor in the event of a monitored collection or the observer in the event of a directly observed collection.

(g) *A collection site may be in a medical facility,* a mobile facility (e.g., a van), a dedicated collection facility, or any other location meeting the requirements of this section.

§40.43 What steps must operators of collection sites take to protect the security and integrity of urine collections?

(a) *Collectors and operators of collection sites* must take the steps listed in this section to prevent unauthorized access that could compromise the integrity of collections.

(b) *As a collector,* you must do the following before each collection to deter tampering with specimens:

(1) *Secure any water sources* or otherwise make them unavailable to employees (e.g., turn off water inlet, tape handles to prevent opening faucets);

(2) *Ensure that the water in the toilet is blue;*

(3) *Ensure that* no soap, disinfectants, cleaning agents, or other possible adulterants are present;

(4) *Inspect the site to ensure* that no foreign or unauthorized substances are present;

(5) *Tape or otherwise secure shut* any movable toilet tank top, or put bluing in the tank;

(6) *Ensure that undetected access* (e.g., through a door not in your view) is not possible;

(7) *Secure areas and items* (e.g., ledges, trash receptacles, paper towel holders, under-sink areas) that appear suitable for concealing contaminants; and

(8) *Recheck items* in paragraphs (b)(1) through (7) of this section following each collection to ensure the site's continued integrity.

(c) *If the collection site uses a facility* normally used for other purposes, like a public rest room or hospital examining room, you must, as a collector, also ensure before the collection that:

(1) *Access to collection materials and specimens* is effectively restricted; and

(2) *The facility* is secured against access during the procedure to ensure privacy to the employee and prevent distraction of the collector. Limited-access signs must be posted.

(d) *As a collector,* you must take the following additional steps to ensure security during the collection process:

(1) *To avoid distraction* that could compromise security, you are limited to conducting a collection for only one employee at a time. However, during the time one employee is in the period for drinking fluids in a "shy bladder" situation (see §40.193(b)), you may conduct a collection for another employee.

(2) *To the greatest extent you can,* keep an employee's collection container within view of both you and the employee between the time the employee has urinated and the specimen is sealed.

(3) *Ensure you are the only person* in addition to the employee who handles the specimen before it is poured into the bottles and sealed with tamper-evident seals.

(4) *In the time* between when the employee gives you the specimen and when you seal the specimen, remain within the collection site.

(5) *Maintain personal control* over each specimen and CCF throughout the collection process.

(e) *If you are operating a collection site,* you must implement a policy and procedures to prevent unauthorized personnel from entering any part of the site in which urine specimens are collected or stored.

(1) *Only employees being tested,* collectors and other collection site workers, DERs, employee and employer representatives authorized by the employer (e.g., employer policy, collective bargaining agreement), and DOT agency representatives are authorized persons for purposes of this paragraph (e).

Subpart D - Collection Sites, Forms, Equipment and Supplies Used in DOT Urine Collections §40.45 (e)

(2) *Except for the observer* in a directly observed collection or the monitor in the case of a monitored collection, you must not permit anyone to enter the urination facility in which employees provide specimens.

(3) *You must ensure that all authorized persons* are under the supervision of a collector at all times when permitted into the site.

(4) *You or the collector may remove any person* who obstructs, interferes with, or causes a delay in the collection process.

(f) **If you are operating a collection site,** you must minimize the number of persons handling specimens.

§§40.193 and 40.43 DOT Interpretations

Question 1: Generally, only one collector is supposed to supervise a collection for an employee. However, given the time span involved, it is possible that two collectors could be involved in a shy bladder collection (e.g., because of a shift change during the three-hour period between the first and second collection attempts). How should this be handled?

Guidance: In this situation, it is permissible for one collector to turn the process over to another collector to complete the collection.

The first collector would document the start time for the 3-hour period. The second would provide his or her name and signature after the second collection, as the collector of record. The Remarks line (Step 2 of the CCF) would be used to document the transition (including the first collector's name and the start time for the shy bladder procedure).

§40.45 What form is used to document a DOT urine collection?

(a) **The Federal Drug Testing** Custody and Control Form (CCF) must be used to document every urine collection required by the DOT drug testing program. The CCF must be a five-part carbonless manifold form. You may view this form on the Department's web site (*http://www.dot.gov/ost/dapc*) or the HHS web site (*http://www.workplace.samhsa.gov*).

(b) **You must not use a non-Federal form** or an expired Federal form to conduct a DOT urine collection. As a laboratory, C/TPA or other party that provides CCFs to employers, collection sites, or other customers, you must not provide copies of an expired Federal form to these participants. You must also affirmatively notify these participants that they must not use an expired Federal form (e.g., that beginning August 1, 2001, they may not use the old 7-part Federal CCF for DOT urine collections).

(c) **As a participant in the DOT drug testing program,** you are not permitted to modify or revise the CCF except as follows:

(1) *You may include,* in the area outside the border of the form, other information needed for billing or other purposes necessary to the collection process.

(2) *The CCF must include* the names, addresses, telephone numbers and fax numbers of the employer and the MRO, which may be preprinted, typed, or handwritten. The MRO information must include the specific physician's name and address, as opposed to only a generic clinic, health care organization, or company name. This information is required, and it is prohibited for an employer, collector, service agent or any other party to omit it. In addition, a C/TPA's name, address, fax number, and telephone number may be included, but is not required. The employer may use a C/TPA's address in place of its own, but must continue to include its name, telephone number, and fax number.

(3) *As an employer,* you may add the name of the DOT agency under whose authority the test occurred as part of the employer information.

(4) *As a collector,* you may use a CCF with your name, address, telephone number, and fax number preprinted, but under no circumstances may you sign the form before the collection event.

(d) **Under no circumstances** may the CCF transmit personal identifying information about an employee (other than a social security number (SSN) or other employee identification (ID) number) to a laboratory.

(e) **As an employer, you may use** an equivalent foreign-language version of the CCF approved by ODAPC. You may use such a non-English language form only in a situation where both the employee and collector understand and can use the form in that language.

§40.45 DOT Interpretations

Question 1: Where can billing information be entered onto the Federal Drug Testing Custody and Control Form (CCF)?

Guidance: §40.45(c)(1) states that the CCF may include billing information if the information is in the area outside the border of the form.

Therefore, if account codes or collection site codes are entered, they must be placed outside the border, only.

CCFs with this information pre-printed inside the border (i.e., in the Step 1 box) may be used until the supply of these forms is exhausted. CCFs produced or re-ordered after February 15, 2002, must not have this information inside the border.

No corrective action is needed nor will a result be impacted if the CCF contains this information inside the border. However, employers and service providers may be subject to enforcement action if this requirement is not met.

Question 2: What actual address is required for "Collection Site Address" in Step 1 of the CCF, and what telephone number should the collector provide?

Guidance: The collection site address should reflect the location where the collection takes place. If the collection takes place at a clinic, the actual address of that clinic should be used: not a corporate or a "main office" address of the clinic/collection company.

If the collection takes place on-site at the employer's place of business (e.g., a bus terminal, a rail yard), the actual address of the employer site should be used.

If the collection takes place in a "mobile unit" or takes place at an accident site, the collector should enter the actual location address of the collection (or as near an approximation as possible, under the circumstances).

The required collector telephone number should be the number at which it is most likely that the laboratory, MRO, or employer, if necessary, may contact the collector and the collector's supervisor.

Pre-printing certain information onto the CCF is problematic if the information is subject to change.

Question 3: Can a collector mark through pre-printed employer, MRO, collection site, and/or laboratory information on the CCF if that information is not accurate for a particular collection?

Guidance: Yes. When the collector has no "blank" CCFs and the CCFs on-hand contain inaccurate pre-printed employer, MRO, collection site, and/or laboratory information, the collector is permitted to "line through" the inaccurate information and insert legibly the proper information.

The likelihood of a collection site having CCFs with inaccurate information increases with unexpected collection events (e.g., employee arrives unannounced for post-accident testing).

If the specimen will be sent to a laboratory different than the one pre-printed on the available CCF, it becomes important for the collector to modify the CCF so that it reflects the name and address of the laboratory to which the specimen will actually be sent. It is also important for the collector to line through any pre-printed billing code and insert the appropriate one, if it is available.

Finally, laboratories should honor collection site requests to provide an adequate number of "blank" CCFs for use during unexpected collection events. It is important to note that the DOT permits overprinting or pre-printing of CCFs in an effort to streamline the entire testing process, not to limit the distribution of the forms to collection sites.

Question 4: May the MRO's address entered on the CCF be a post-office box number only?

Guidance: No. The address must contain at least a number and street address.

The reason for this requirement is that CCFs are often delivered by courier or messenger services who do not deliver items to post office box addresses.

The post-office box can be included, but not in lieu of the number and street address.

> **§§40.35, 40.45, 40.345 DOT Interpretations**
>
> *Question 1:* How should the employer's decision to have a C/TPA act as intermediary in the handling of drug test results be documented?
>
> *Guidance:* When an employer chooses to use the C/TPA as the intermediary in the transmission of the MRO's verified drug test results, this decision should be communicated from the employer to the MRO and the C/TPA.
>
> We advise the MRO to obtain some documentation of the employer's decision prior to sending results through the C/TPA. Documentation could be in the form of a letter, an email, or record of a telephone conversation with the employer.
>
> DOT also recommends that MROs maintain listings of the names, addresses, and phone numbers of C/TPA points of contact.

§40.47 May employers use the CCF for non-Federal collections or non-Federal forms for DOT collections?

(a) **No, as an employer,** you are prohibited from using the CCF for non-Federal urine collections. You are also prohibited from using non-Federal forms for DOT urine collections. Doing either subjects you to enforcement action under DOT agency regulations.

(b) (1) *In the rare case where the collector,* either by mistake or as the only means to conduct a test under difficult circumstances (e.g., post-accident or reasonable suspicion test with insufficient time to obtain the CCF), uses a non-Federal form for a DOT collection, the use of a non-Federal form does not present a reason for the laboratory to reject the specimen for testing or for an MRO to cancel the result.

(2) *The use of the non-Federal form is a "correctable flaw."* As an MRO, to correct the problem you must follow the procedures of §40.205(b)(2).

§40.49 What materials are used to collect urine specimens?

For each DOT drug test, you must use a collection kit meeting the requirements of Appendix A of this part.

§40.51 What materials are used to send urine specimens to the laboratory?

(a) **Except as provided in paragraph (b) of this section,** you must use a shipping container that adequately protects the specimen bottles from shipment damage in the transport of specimens from the collection site to the laboratory.

(b) **You are not required to use a shipping container** if a laboratory courier hand-delivers the specimens from the collection site to the laboratory.

Subpart E - Urine Specimen Collections

§40.61 What are the preliminary steps in the collection process?

As the collector, you must take the following steps before actually beginning a collection:

(a) **When a specific time for an employee's test** has been scheduled, or the collection site is at the employee's work site, and the employee does not appear at the collection site at the scheduled time, contact the DER to determine the appropriate interval within which the DER has determined the employee is authorized to arrive. If the employee's arrival is delayed beyond that time, you must notify the DER that the employee has not reported for testing. In a situation where a C/TPA has notified an owner/operator or other individual employee to report for testing and the employee does not appear, the C/TPA must notify the employee that he or she has refused to test (see §40.191(a)(1)).

(b) **Ensure that, when the employee enters** the collection site, you begin the testing process without undue delay. For example, you must not wait because the employee says he or she is not ready or is unable to urinate or because an authorized employer or employee representative is delayed in arriving.

(1) *If the employee is also going to take* a DOT alcohol test, you must, to the greatest extent practicable, ensure that the alcohol test is completed before the urine collection process begins.

Example to Paragraph (b)(1): An employee enters the test site for both a drug and an alcohol test. Normally, the collector would wait until the BAT had completed the alcohol test process before beginning the drug test process. However, there are some situations in which an exception to this normal practice would be reasonable. One such situation might be if several people were waiting for the BAT to conduct alcohol tests, but a drug testing collector in the same facility were free. Someone waiting might be able to complete a drug test without unduly delaying his or her alcohol test. Collectors and BATs should work together, however, to ensure that post-accident and reasonable suspicion alcohol tests happen as soon as possible (e.g., by moving the employee to the head of the line for alcohol tests).

(2) *If the employee needs medical attention* (e.g., an injured employee in an emergency medical facility who is required to have a post-accident test), do not delay this treatment to collect a specimen.

(3) *You must not collect,* by catheterization or other means, urine from an unconscious employee to conduct a drug test under this part. Nor may you catheterize a conscious employee. However, you must inform an employee who normally voids through self-catheterization that the employee is required to provide a specimen in that manner.

(4) *If, as an employee,* you normally void through self-catheterization, and decline to do so, this constitutes a refusal to test.

(c) **Require the employee to provide positive identification.** You must see a photo ID issued by the employer (other than in the case of an owner-operator or other self-employed individual) or a Federal, state, or local government (e.g., a driver's license). You may not accept faxes or photocopies of identification. Positive identification by an employer representative (not a co-worker or another employee being tested) is also acceptable. If the employee cannot produce positive identification, you must contact a DER to verify the identity of the employee.

(d) **If the employee asks, provide your identification** to the employee. Your identification must include your name and your employer's name, but does not have to include your picture, address, or telephone number.

(e) **Explain the basic collection procedure** to the employee, including showing the employee the instructions on the back of the CCF.

(f) **Direct the employee to remove outer clothing** (e.g., coveralls, jacket, coat, hat) that could be used to conceal items or substances that could be used to tamper with a specimen. You must also direct the employee to leave these garments and any briefcase, purse, or other personal belongings with you or in a mutually agreeable location. You must advise the employee that failure to comply with your directions constitutes a refusal to test.

(1) *If the employee asks for a receipt* for any belongings left with you, you must provide one.

(2) *You must allow the employee to keep his or her wallet.*

(3) *You must not ask the employee* to remove other clothing (e.g., shirts, pants, dresses, underwear), to remove all clothing, or to change into a hospital or examination gown (unless the urine collection is being accomplished simultaneously with a DOT agency-authorized medical examination).

(4) *You must direct the employee* to empty his or her pockets and display the items in them to ensure that no items are present which could be used to adulterate the specimen. If nothing is there that can be used to adulterate a specimen, the employee can place the items back into his or her pockets. As the employee, you must allow the collector to make this observation.

(5) *If, in your duties under paragraph (f)(4) of this section,* you find any material that could be used to tamper with a specimen, you must:

(i) *Determine if the material* appears to be brought to the collection site with the intent to alter the specimen, and, if it is, conduct a directly observed collection using direct observation procedures (see §40.67); or

(ii) *Determine if the material* appears to be inadvertently brought to the collection site (e.g., eye drops), secure and maintain it until the collection process is completed and conduct a normal (i.e., unobserved) collection.

(g) **You must instruct the employee** not to list medications that he or she is currently taking on the CCF. (The employee may make notes of medications on the back of the employee copy of the form for his or her own convenience, but these notes must not be transmitted to anyone else.)

> **§40.61 DOT Interpretations**
>
> *Question 1:* May a DOT urine specimen be obtained via catheterization from a patient who is catheterized as part of a medical procedure or who is unconscious?
>
> *Guidance:* No one is ever permitted to obtain a urine specimen for DOT testing purposes from an unconscious individual, whether by catheterization or any other means.
>
> No one is permitted to catheterize a conscious employee for the purpose of collecting urine for a DOT drug test.

Subpart E - Urine Specimen Collections §40.67 (c)

However, if a person has been catheterized for medical purposes (e.g., a conscious, hospitalized patient in a post-accident test situation), it is permissible to use urine collected by this means for DOT testing purposes. All necessary documentation for a DOT collection must be provided (e.g., the CCF).

In addition, an employee who normally voids through self-catheterization is required to provide a specimen in that manner.

§40.63 What steps does the collector take in the collection process before the employee provides a urine specimen?

As the collector, you must take the following steps before the employee provides the urine specimen:

(a) Complete Step 1 of the CCF.

(b) Instruct the employee to wash and dry his or her hands at this time. You must tell the employee not to wash his or her hands again until after delivering the specimen to you. You must not give the employee any further access to water or other materials that could be used to adulterate or dilute a specimen.

(c) Select, or allow the employee to select, an individually wrapped or sealed collection container from collection kit materials. Either you or the employee, with both of you present, must unwrap or break the seal of the collection container. You must not unwrap or break the seal on any specimen bottle at this time. You must not allow the employee to take anything from the collection kit into the room used for urination except the collection container.

(d) Direct the employee to go into the room used for urination, provide a specimen of at least 45 mL, not flush the toilet, and return to you with the specimen as soon as the employee has completed the void.

   (1) *Except in the case* of an observed or a monitored collection (see §§40.67 and 40.69), neither you nor anyone else may go into the room with the employee.

   (2) *As the collector, you may set a reasonable time limit for voiding.*

(e) You must pay careful attention to the employee during the entire collection process to note any conduct that clearly indicates an attempt to tamper with a specimen (e.g., substitute urine in plain view or an attempt to bring into the collection site an adulterant or urine substitute). If you detect such conduct, you must require that a collection take place immediately under direct observation (see §40.67) and note the conduct and the fact that the collection was observed in the "Remarks" line of the CCF (Step 2). You must also, as soon as possible, inform the DER and collection site supervisor that a collection took place under direct observation and the reason for doing so.

§40.65 What does the collector check for when the employee presents a specimen?

As a collector, you must check the following when the employee gives the collection container to you:

(a) Sufficiency of specimen. You must check to ensure that the specimen contains at least 45 mL of urine.

   (1) *If it does not,* you must follow "shy bladder" procedures (see §40.193(b)).

   (2) *When you follow "shy bladder" procedures,* you must discard the original specimen, unless another problem (i.e., temperature out of range, signs of tampering) also exists.

   (3) *You are never permitted* to combine urine collected from separate voids to create a specimen.

   (4) *You must discard any excess urine.*

(b) Temperature. You must check the temperature of the specimen no later than four minutes after the employee has given you the specimen.

   (1) *The acceptable temperature range is 32-38 °C / 90-100 °F.*

   (2) *You must determine* the temperature of the specimen by reading the temperature strip attached to the collection container.

   (3) *If the specimen temperature* is within the acceptable range, you must mark the "Yes" box on the CCF (Step 2).

   (4) *If the specimen temperature* is outside the acceptable range, you must mark the "No" box and enter in the "Remarks" line (Step 2) your findings about the temperature.

   (5) *If the specimen temperature* is outside the acceptable range, you must immediately conduct a new collection using direct observation procedures (see §40.67).

   (6) *In a case where a specimen is collected* under direct observation because of the temperature being out of range, you must process both the original specimen and the specimen collected using direct observation and send the two sets of specimens to the laboratory. This is true even in a case in which the original specimen has insufficient volume but the temperature is out of range. You must also, as soon as possible, inform the DER and collection site supervisor that a collection took place under direct observation and the reason for doing so.

   (7) *In a case where the employee* refuses to provide another specimen (see §40.191(a)(3)) or refuses to provide another specimen under direct observation (see §40.191(a)(4)), you must notify the DER. As soon as you have notified the DER, you must discard any specimen the employee has provided previously during the collection procedure.

(c) Signs of tampering. You must inspect the specimen for unusual color, presence of foreign objects or material, or other signs of tampering (e.g., if you notice any unusual odor).

   (1) *If it is apparent from this inspection* that the employee has tampered with the specimen (e.g., blue dye in the specimen, excessive foaming when shaken, smell of bleach), you must immediately conduct a new collection using direct observation procedures (see §40.67).

   (2) *In a case where a specimen* is collected under direct observation because of showing signs of tampering, you must process both the original specimen and the specimen collected using direct observation and send the two sets of specimens to the laboratory. This is true even in a case in which the original specimen has insufficient volume but it shows signs of tampering. You must also, as soon as possible, inform the DER and collection site supervisor that a collection took place under direct observation and the reason for doing so.

   (3) *In a case where the employee* refuses to provide a specimen under direct observation (see §40.191(a)(4)), you must discard any specimen the employee provided previously during the collection procedure. Then you must notify the DER as soon as practicable.

§40.65 DOT Interpretations

Question 1: Part 40 directs the collector to discard the first specimen if the temperature was out of range or the specimen showed signs of tampering <u>and</u> the employee refused to provide a second specimen under direct observation. The Urine Specimen Collection Guidelines [at Section 8, Directly Observed Collection, Number 7] indicate that, in such a situation, the first specimen should be retained and sent to the laboratory. Which requirement is correct?

Guidance: When a specimen is out of temperature range or shows signs of tampering <u>and</u> the employee refuses to provide a second specimen under direct observation, it is considered a refusal to test. The collector does <u>not</u> retain the first specimen, but discards it.

The requirement in the Urine Specimen Collection Guidelines, Version 1.0, to retain the specimen and send it to the laboratory, was inserted inadvertently.

Urine Specimen Collection Guidelines, Version 1.01, contain the proper procedures as directed by §40.65.

§40.67 When and how is a directly observed collection conducted?

(a) As an employer, you must direct an immediate collection under direct observation with no advance notice to the employee, if:

   (1) *The laboratory reported to the MRO* that a specimen is invalid, and the MRO reported to you that there was not an adequate medical explanation for the result;

   (2) *The MRO reported to you* that the original positive, adulterated, or substituted test result had to be cancelled because the test of the split specimen could not be pezrformed; or

   (3) *The laboratory reported to the MRO* that the specimen was negative-dilute with a creatinine concentration greater than or equal to 2 mg/dL but less than or equal to 5 mg/dL, and the MRO reported the specimen to you as negative-dilute and that a second collection must take place under direct observation (see §40.197(b)(1)).

(b) As an employer, you may direct a collection under direct observation of an employee if the drug test is a return-to-duty test or a follow-up test.

(c) As a collector, you must immediately conduct a collection under direct observation if:

   (1) *You are directed by the DER to do so* (see paragraphs (a) and (b) of this section); or

   (2) *You observed materials* brought to the collection site or the employee's conduct clearly indicates an attempt to tamper with a specimen (see §§40.61(f)(5)(i) and 40.63(e)); or

11

(3) *The temperature on the original specimen* was out of range (see §40.65(b)(5)); or
(4) *The original specimen* appeared to have been tampered with (see §40.65(c)(1)).
(d) (1) *As the employer,* you must explain to the employee the reason for a directly observed collection under paragraph (a) or (b) of this section.
(2) *As the collector,* you must explain to the employee the reason, if known, under this part for a directly observed collection under paragraphs (c)(1) through (3) of this section.
(e) As the collector, you must complete a new CCF for the directly observed collection.
(1) *You must mark* the "reason for test" block (Step 1) the same as for the first collection.
(2) *You must check* the "Observed, (Enter Remark)" box and enter the reason (see §40.67(b)) in the "Remarks" line (Step 2).
(f) In a case where two sets of specimens are being sent to the laboratory because of suspected tampering with the specimen at the collection site, enter on the "Remarks" line of the CCF (Step 2) for each specimen a notation to this effect (e.g., collection 1 of 2, or 2 of 2) and the specimen ID number of the other specimen.
(g) As the collector, you must ensure that the observer is the same gender as the employee. You must never permit an opposite gender person to act as the observer. The observer can be a different person from the collector and need not be a qualified collector.
(h) As the collector, if someone else is to observe the collection (e.g., in order to ensure a same gender observer), you must verbally instruct that person to follow procedures at paragraphs (i) and (j) of this section. If you, the collector, are the observer, you too must follow these procedures.
(i) As the observer, you must watch the employee urinate into the collection container. Specifically, you are to watch the urine go from the employee's body into the collection container.
(j) As the observer but not the collector, you must not take the collection container from the employee, but you must observe the specimen as the employee takes it to the collector.
(k) As the collector, when someone else has acted as the observer, you must include the observer's name in the "Remarks" line of the CCF (Step 2).
(l) As the employee, if you decline to allow a directly observed collection required or permitted under this section to occur, this is a refusal to test.
(m) As the collector, when you learn that a directly observed collection should have been collected but was not, you must inform the employer that it must direct the employee to have an immediate recollection under direct observation.

§§40.67 and 40.69 DOT Interpretations
Question 1: Can the monitor (or direct observer) of a collection be a co-worker or immediate supervisor of the employee?
Guidance: The immediate supervisor of a particular employee may not act as the collector when that employee is tested, unless no other collector is available and the supervisor is permitted to do so under a DOT operating administration's drug and alcohol regulation.

The immediate supervisor may act as a monitor or observer (if same gender) if there is no alternate method at the collection site to conduct a monitored or observed collection.

An employee who is in a safety-sensitive position and subject to the DOT drug testing rules should not be a collector, an observer, or a monitor for co-workers who are in the same testing pool or who work together with that employee on a daily basis.

§40.69 How is a monitored collection conducted?
(a) As the collector, you must secure the room being used for the monitored collection so that no one except the employee and the monitor can enter it until after the collection has been completed.
(b) As the collector, you must ensure that the monitor is the same gender as the employee, unless the monitor is a medical professional (e.g., nurse, doctor, physician's assistant, technologist, or technician licensed or certified to practice in the jurisdiction in which the collection takes place). The monitor can be a different person from the collector and need not be a qualified collector.
(c) As the collector, if someone else is to monitor the collection (e.g., in order to ensure a same-gender monitor), you must verbally instruct that person to follow the procedures of paragraphs (d) and (e) of this section. If you, the collector, are the monitor, you must follow these procedures.
(d) As the monitor, you must not watch the employee urinate into the collection container. If you hear sounds or make other observations indicating an attempt to tamper with a specimen, there must be an additional collection under direct observation (see §§40.63(e), 40.65(c), and 40.67(b)).
(e) As the monitor, you must ensure that the employee takes the collection container directly to the collector as soon as the employee has exited the enclosure.
(f) As the collector, when someone else has acted as the monitor, you must note that person's name in the "Remarks" line of the CCF (Step 2).
(g) As the employee being tested, if you decline to permit a collection authorized under this section to be monitored, it is a refusal to test.

§§40.67 and 40.69 DOT Interpretations
Question 1: Can the monitor (or direct observer) of a collection be a co-worker or immediate supervisor of the employee?
Guidance: The immediate supervisor of a particular employee may not act as the collector when that employee is tested, unless no other collector is available and the supervisor is permitted to do so under a DOT operating administration's drug and alcohol regulation.

The immediate supervisor may act as a monitor or observer (if same gender) if there is no alternate method at the collection site to conduct a monitored or observed collection.

An employee who is in a safety-sensitive position and subject to the DOT drug testing rules should not be a collector, an observer, or a monitor for co-workers who are in the same testing pool or who work together with that employee on a daily basis.

§40.71 How does the collector prepare the specimens?
(a) All collections under DOT agency drug testing regulations must be split specimen collections.
(b) As the collector, you must take the following steps, in order, after the employee brings the urine specimen to you. You must take these steps in the presence of the employee.
(1) *Check the box on the CCF* (Step 2) indicating that this was a split specimen collection.
(2) *You, not the employee,* must first pour at least 30 mL of urine from the collection container into one specimen bottle, to be used for the primary specimen.
(3) *You, not the employee,* must then pour at least 15 mL of urine from the collection container into the second specimen bottle to be used for the split specimen.
(4) *You, not the employee,* must place and secure (i.e., tighten or snap) the lids/caps on the bottles.
(5) *You, not the employee,* must seal the bottles by placing the tamper-evident bottle seals over the bottle caps/lids and down the sides of the bottles.
(6) *You, not the employee,* must then write the date on the tamper-evident bottle seals.
(7) *You must then ensure that the employee* initials the tamper-evident bottle seals for the purpose of certifying that the bottles contain the specimens he or she provided. If the employee fails or refuses to do so, you must note this in the "Remarks" line of the CCF (Step 2) and complete the collection process.
(8) *You must discard any urine left over* in the collection container after both specimen bottles have been appropriately filled and sealed. There is one exception to this requirement: you may use excess urine to conduct clinical tests (e.g., protein, glucose) if the collection was conducted in conjunction with a physical examination required by a DOT agency regulation. Neither you nor anyone else may conduct further testing (such as adulteration testing) on this excess urine and the employee has no legal right to demand that the excess urine be turned over to the employee.

§40.73 How is the collection process completed?
(a) As the collector, you must do the following things to complete the collection process. You must complete the steps called for in paragraphs (a)(1) through (a)(7) of this section in the employee's presence.
(1) *Direct the employee* to read and sign the certification statement on Copy 2 (Step 5) of the CCF and provide date of birth, printed name, and day and evening contact telephone numbers. If the employee refuses to sign the CCF or to provide date of birth, printed name, or telephone numbers, you must note this in the "Remarks" line (Step 2) of the CCF, and complete the collection. If the employee refuses to fill out any information, you must, as a minimum, print the employee's name in the appropriate place.

Subpart F - Drug Testing Laboratories §40.83 (h)

(2) *Complete the chain of custody on the CCF* (Step 4) by printing your name (NOTE: you may pre-print your name), recording the time and date of the collection, signing the statement, and entering the name of the delivery service transferring the specimen to the laboratory.
(3) *Ensure that all copies of the CCF are legible and complete.*
(4) *Remove Copy 5 of the CCF and give it to the employee.*
(5) *Place the specimen bottles* and Copy 1 of the CCF in the appropriate pouches of the plastic bag.
(6) *Secure both pouches of the plastic bag.*
(7) *Advise the employee that he or she may leave the collection site.*
(8) *To prepare the sealed plastic bag* containing the specimens and CCF for shipment you must:
   (i) *Place the sealed plastic bag* in a shipping container (e.g., standard courier box) designed to minimize the possibility of damage during shipment. (More than one sealed plastic bag can be placed into a single shipping container if you are doing multiple collections.)
   (ii) *Seal the container as appropriate.*
   (iii) *If a laboratory courier* hand-delivers the specimens from the collection site to the laboratory, prepare the sealed plastic bag for shipment as directed by the courier service.
(9) *Send Copy 2 of the CCF to the MRO* and Copy 4 to the DER. You must fax or otherwise transmit these copies to the MRO and DER within 24 hours or during the next business day. Keep Copy 3 for at least 30 days, unless otherwise specified by applicable DOT agency regulations.

(b) **As a collector or collection site,** you must ensure that each specimen you collect is shipped to a laboratory as quickly as possible, but in any case within 24 hours or during the next business day.

§§40.73 and 40.193 DOT Interpretations

Question 1: What is the preferred method for the collector to get the MRO copy of the CCF to the MRO?

Guidance: The promptness of reporting suffers when the mail is used to convey the MRO copy from the collection site.

Even though we permit other means (e.g., overnight courier service) of transmitting MRO copies from the collection site to the MRO, collectors should fax the MRO copies when possible.

If the faxed copy is not legible, the MRO must request another faxed copy or a hard copy.

Subpart F - Drug Testing Laboratories

§40.81 What laboratories may be used for DOT drug testing?

(a) **As a drug testing laboratory located in the U.S.,** you are permitted to participate in DOT drug testing only if you are certified by HHS under the National Laboratory Certification Program (NLCP) for all testing required under this part.
(b) **As a drug testing laboratory located** in Canada or Mexico which is not certified by HHS under the NLCP, you are permitted to participate in DOT drug testing only if:
   (1) *The DOT,* based on a written recommendation from HHS, has approved your laboratory as meeting HHS laboratory certification standards or deemed your laboratory fully equivalent to a laboratory meeting HHS laboratory certification standards for all testing required under this part; or
   (2) *The DOT,* based on a written recommendation from HHS, has recognized a Canadian or Mexican certifying organization as having equivalent laboratory certification standards and procedures to those of HHS, and the Canadian or Mexican certifying organization has certified your laboratory under those equivalent standards and procedures.
(c) **As a laboratory participating** in the DOT drug testing program, you must comply with the requirements of this part. You must also comply with all applicable requirements of HHS in testing DOT specimens, whether or not the HHS requirements are explicitly stated in this part.
(d) **If DOT determines** that you are in noncompliance with this part, you could be subject to PIE proceedings under Subpart R of this part. If the Department issues a PIE with respect to you, you are ineligible to participate in the DOT drug testing program even if you continue to meet the requirements of paragraph (a) or (b) of this section.

§40.83 How do laboratories process incoming specimens?

As the laboratory, you must do the following when you receive a DOT specimen:

(a) **You are authorized to receive** only the laboratory copy of the CCF. You are not authorized to receive other copies of the CCF nor any copies of the alcohol testing form.
(b) **You must comply with applicable provisions** of the HHS Guidelines concerning accessioning and processing urine drug specimens.
(c) **You must inspect each specimen and CCF** for the following "fatal flaws":
   (1) *The specimen ID numbers* on the specimen bottle and the CCF do not match;
   (2) *The specimen bottle seal is broken* or shows evidence of tampering, unless a split specimen can be redesignated (see paragraph (h) of this section);
   (3) *The collector's printed name and signature* are omitted from the CCF; and
   (4) *There is an insufficient amount of urine* in the primary bottle for analysis, unless the specimens can be redesignated (see paragraph (h) of this section).
(d) **When you find a specimen** meeting the criteria of paragraph (c) of this section, you must document your findings and stop the testing process. Report the result in accordance with §40.97(a)(3).
(e) **You must inspect each CCF for the presence** of the collector's signature on the certification statement in Step 4 of the CCF. Upon finding that the signature is omitted, document the flaw and continue the testing process.
   (1) *In such a case,* you must retain the specimen for a minimum of 5 business days from the date on which you initiated action to correct the flaw.
   (2) *You must then attempt to correct the flaw* by following the procedures of §40.205(b)(1).
   (3) *If the flaw is not corrected,* report the result as rejected for testing in accordance with §40.97(a)(3).
(f) **If you determine that the specimen temperature** was not checked and the "Remarks" line did not contain an entry regarding the temperature being outside of range, you must then attempt to correct the problem by following the procedures of §40.208.
   (1) *In such a case,* you must continue your efforts to correct the problem for five business days, before you report the result.
   (2) *When you have obtained the correction,* or five business days have elapsed, report the result in accordance with §40.97(a).
(g) **If you determine that a CCF** that fails to meet the requirements of §40.45(a) (e.g., a non-Federal form or an expired Federal form was used for the collection), you must attempt to correct the use of the improper form by following the procedures of §40.205(b)(2).
   (1) *In such a case,* you must retain the specimen for a minimum of 5 business days from the date on which you initiated action to correct the problem.
   (2) *During the period August 1 - October 31, 2001,* you are not required to reject a test conducted on an expired Federal CCF because this problem is not corrected. Beginning November 1, 2001, if the problem(s) is not corrected, you must reject the test and report the result in accordance with §40.97(a)(3).
(h) **If the CCF is marked** indicating that a split specimen collection was collected and if the split specimen does not accompany the primary, has leaked, or is otherwise unavailable for testing, you must still test the primary specimen and follow appropriate procedures outlined in §40.175(b) regarding the unavailability of the split specimen for testing.
   (1) *The primary specimen and the split specimen* can be redesignated (i.e., Bottle B is redesignated as Bottle A, and vice-versa) if:
      (i) *The primary specimen* appears to have leaked out of its sealed bottle and the laboratory believes a sufficient amount of urine exists in the split specimen to conduct all appropriate primary laboratory testing; or
      (ii) *The primary specimen is labeled as Bottle B,* and the split specimen as Bottle A; or
      (iii) *The laboratory opens the split specimen* instead of the primary specimen, the primary specimen remains sealed, and the laboratory believes a sufficient amount of urine exists in the split specimen to conduct all appropriate primary laboratory testing; or

(iv) *The primary specimen seal is broken* but the split specimen remains sealed and the laboratory believes a sufficient amount of urine exists in the split specimen to conduct all appropriate primary laboratory testing.

(2) *In situations outlined* in paragraph (g)(1) of this section, the laboratory shall mark through the "A" and write "B," then initial and date the change. A corresponding change shall be made to the other bottle by marking through the "B" and writing "A," and initialing and dating the change.

(i) A notation shall be made on Copy 1 of the CCF (Step 5a) and on any laboratory internal chain of custody documents, as appropriate, for any fatal or correctable flaw.

§40.83 DOT Interpretations

Question 1: If the primary laboratory must redesignate bottle B for bottle A, can the laboratory test the specimen if only 15 mL of urine is present in the redesignated bottle A?

Guidance: The Department permits specimen redesignation only in limited circumstances – one such occurrence would be if the A specimen has leaked in transit, leaving only the B specimen to be tested. In such a case, the laboratory should test the redesignated specimen despite the fact that, under normal circumstances, a sufficient amount of specimen would not have been available for testing.

§40.85 What drugs do laboratories test for?

As a laboratory, you must test for the following five drugs or classes of drugs in a DOT drug test. You must not test "DOT specimens" for any other drugs.

(a) Marijuana metabolites.
(b) Cocaine metabolites.
(c) Amphetamines.
(d) Opiate metabolites.
(e) Phencyclidine (PCP).

§40.87 What are the cutoff concentrations for initial and confirmation tests?

(a) As a laboratory, you must use the cutoff concentrations displayed in the following table for initial and confirmation drug tests. All cutoff concentrations are expressed in nanograms per milliliter (ng/mL). The table follows:

Type of Drug or Metabolite	Initial Test	Confirmation Test
(1) Marijuana metabolites	50	
(i) Delta-9-tetrahydrocannabinol-9-carboxylic acid (THC)		15
(2) Cocaine metabolites (Benzoylecgonine)	300	150
(3) Phencyclidine (PCP)	25	25
(4) Amphetamines	1000	
(i) Amphetamine		500
(ii) Methamphetamine		500 (Specimen must also contain amphetamine at a concentration of greater than or equal to 200 ng/mL.)
(5) Opiate metabolites	2000	
(i) Codeine		2000
(ii) Morphine		2000
(iii) 6-acetylmorphine (6-AM)		10 (Test for 6-AM in the specimen. Conduct this test only when specimen contains morphine at a concentration greater than or equal to 2000 ng/mL.)

(b) On an initial drug test, you must report a result below the cutoff concentration as negative. If the result is at or above the cutoff concentration, you must conduct a confirmation test.

(c) On a confirmation drug test, you must report a result below the cutoff concentration as negative and a result at or above the cutoff concentration as confirmed positive.

(d) You must report quantitative values for morphine or codeine at 15,000 ng/mL or above.

§40.89 What is validity testing, and are laboratories required to conduct it?

(a) Specimen validity testing is the evaluation of the specimen to determine if it is consistent with normal human urine. The purpose of validity testing is to determine whether certain adulterants or foreign substances were added to the urine, if the urine was diluted, or if the specimen was substituted.

(b) As a laboratory, you are authorized to conduct validity testing.

§40.91 What validity tests must laboratories conduct on primary specimens?

As a laboratory, when you conduct validity testing under §40.89, you must conduct it in accordance with the requirements of this section.

(a) You must determine the creatinine concentration on each primary specimen. You must also determine its specific gravity if you find the creatinine concentration to be less than 20 mg/dL.

(b) You must determine the pH of each primary specimen.

(c) You must perform one or more validity tests for oxidizing adulterants on each primary specimen.

(d) You must perform additional validity tests on the primary specimen when the following conditions are observed:

(1) *Abnormal physical characteristics;*
(2) *Reactions or responses* characteristic of an adulterant obtained during initial or confirmatory drug tests (e.g., non-recovery of internal standards, unusual response); or
(3) *Possible unidentified interfering substance or adulterant.*

(e) If you determine that the specimen is invalid and HHS guidelines direct you to contact the MRO, you must contact the MRO and together decide if testing the primary specimen by another HHS certified laboratory would be useful in being able to report a positive or adulterated test result.

§40.93 What criteria do laboratories use to establish that a specimen is dilute or substituted?

(a) As a laboratory, you must consider the primary specimen to be dilute when:

(1) *The creatinine concentration* is greater than or equal to 2 mg/dL but less than 20 mg/dL, and
(2) *The specific gravity* is greater than 1.0010 but less than 1.0030 on a single aliquot.

(b) As a laboratory, you must consider the primary specimen to be substituted when the creatinine concentration is less than 2 mg/dL and the specific gravity is less than or equal to 1.0010 or greater than or equal to 1.0200 on both the initial and confirmatory creatinine tests and on both the initial and confirmatory specific gravity tests on two separate aliquots.

§40.95 What criteria do laboratories use to establish that a specimen is adulterated?

(a) As a laboratory, you must consider the primary specimen to be adulterated if you determine that —

(1) *A substance* that is not expected to be present in human urine is identified in the specimen;
(2) *A substance* that is expected to be present in human urine is identified at a concentration so high that it is not consistent with human urine; or
(3) *The physical characteristics of the specimen* are outside the normal expected range for human urine.

(b) In making your determination under paragraph (a) of this section, you must apply the criteria in current HHS requirements or specimen validity guidance.

§40.97 What do laboratories report and how do they report it?

(a) As a laboratory, you must report the results for each primary specimen tested as one or more of the following:

(1) *Negative;*
(2) *Negative-dilute,* with numerical values for creatinine and specific gravity;
(3) *Rejected for testing,* with remark(s);
(4) *Positive,* with drug(s)/metabolite(s) noted;
(5) *Positive,* with drug(s)/metabolite(s) noted — dilute;
(6) *Adulterated,* with numerical values (when applicable), with remark(s);
(7) *Substituted,* with numerical values for creatinine and specific gravity; or
(8) *Invalid result,* with remark(s).

Subpart F - Drug Testing Laboratories §40.101 (b)

(b) As a laboratory, you must report laboratory results directly, and only, to the MRO at his or her place of business. You must not report results to or through the DER or a service agent (e.g., C/TPA).
  (1) *Negative results:* You must fax, courier, mail, or electronically transmit a legible image or copy of the fully-completed Copy 1 of the CCF which has been signed by the certifying scientist, or you may provide the laboratory results report electronically (i.e., computer data file).
    (i) *If you elect to provide the laboratory results report,* you must include the following elements, as a minimum, in the report format:
      [A] *Laboratory name and address;*
      [B] *Employer's name* (you may include I.D. or account number);
      [C] *Medical review officer's name;*
      [D] *Specimen I.D. number;*
      [E] *Donor's SSN or employee I.D. number, if provided;*
      [F] *Reason for test, if provided;*
      [G] *Collector's name and telephone number;*
      [H] *Date of the collection;*
      [I] *Date received at the laboratory;*
      [J] *Date certifying scientist released the results;*
      [K] *Certifying scientist's name;*
      [L] *Results (e.g., positive, adulterated)* as listed in paragraph (a) of this section; and
      [M] *Remarks section,* with an explanation of any situation in which a correctable flaw has been corrected.
    (ii) *You may release the laboratory results report* only after review and approval by the certifying scientist. It must reflect the same test result information as contained on the CCF signed by the certifying scientist. The information contained in the laboratory results report may not contain information that does not appear on the CCF.
    (iii) *The results report may be transmitted* through any means that ensures accuracy and confidentiality. You, as the laboratory, together with the MRO, must ensure that the information is adequately protected from unauthorized access or release, both during transmission and in storage.
  (2) *Non-negative results:* You must fax, courier, mail, or electronically transmit a legible image or copy of the fully-completed Copy 1 of the CCF that has been signed by the certifying scientist. In addition, you may provide the electronic laboratory results report following the format and procedures set forth in paragraphs (b)(1)(i) and (ii) of this section.
(c) In transmitting laboratory results to the MRO, you, as the laboratory, together with the MRO, must ensure that the information is adequately protected from unauthorized access or release, both during transmission and in storage. If the results are provided by fax, the fax connection must have a fixed telephone number accessible only to authorized individuals.
(d) You must transmit test results to the MRO in a timely manner, preferably the same day that review by the certifying scientist is completed.
(e) (1) *You must provide quantitative values* for confirmed positive drug test results to the MRO when the MRO requests you to do so in writing. The MRO's request may be either a general request covering all such results you send to the MRO or a specific case-by-case request.
  (2) *You must provide the numerical values* that support the adulterated (when applicable) or substituted result, without a request from the MRO.
  (3) *You must also provide to the MRO* numerical values for creatinine and specific gravity for the negative-dilute test result, without a request from the MRO.
(f) You must provide quantitative values for confirmed opiate results for morphine or codeine at 15,000 ng/mL or above, even if the MRO has not requested quantitative values for the test result.

§40.97 DOT Interpretations
Question 1: Must a certifying scientist's signature be on Copy 1 of the CCF if the drug test result is negative?
Guidance: The certifying scientist's signature must be on Copy 1 of the CCF for non-negative results only.
Therefore, the certifying scientist may simply initial (and date) the CCF when the test result is negative.

§§40.97 and 40.209 DOT Interpretations
Question 1: After the laboratory reports a test result, someone (e.g., the employer, a service agent) discovers that the CCF listed the wrong reason for the test (e.g., the CCF says the test was a pre-employment test when it was actually a random test). How is this corrected and by whom?
Guidance: This is another example of an error that does not have a significant adverse effect on the right of an employee to have a fair and accurate test (see §40.209).
The test is not cancelled as the result of such a mistake.
While concerned parties may wish to correct the faulty description of the reason for the test, Part 40 does not require a correction to be made.
Employers or their designated service agents should ensure that appropriate changes are documented (e.g., for MIS reporting purposes).

§40.99 How long does the laboratory retain specimens after testing?
(a) As a laboratory testing the primary specimen, you must retain a specimen that was reported with positive, adulterated, substituted, or invalid results for a minimum of one year.
(b) You must keep such a specimen in secure, long-term, frozen storage in accordance with HHS requirements.
(c) Within the one-year period, the MRO, the employee, the employer, or a DOT agency may request in writing that you retain a specimen for an additional period of time (e.g., for the purpose of preserving evidence for litigation or a safety investigation). If you receive such a request, you must comply with it. If you do not receive such a request, you may discard the specimen at the end of the year.
(d) If you have not sent the split specimen to another laboratory for testing, you must retain the split specimen for an employee's test for the same period of time that you retain the primary specimen and under the same storage conditions.
(e) As the laboratory testing the split specimen, you must meet the requirements of paragraphs (a) through (d) of this section with respect to the split specimen.

§§40.103, 40.99, 40.333 DOT Interpretations
Question 1: What are the retention requirements for blind specimens and records of blind specimen tests?
Guidance: Laboratories, employers and other parties required to retain specimens and records of tests should retain blind specimens and records of blind specimen tests in exactly the same way and for the same periods of time as they do actual employee specimens and test records.
For example, an employer would keep a record of a blind positive test for five years and a blind negative test for two years.
Laboratories would keep blind specimens for negatives in accordance with their SOPs and non-negatives for one year.

§40.101 What relationship may a laboratory have with an MRO?
(a) As a laboratory, you may not enter into any relationship with an MRO that creates a conflict of interest or the appearance of a conflict of interest with the MRO's responsibilities for the employer. You may not derive any financial benefit by having an employer use a specific MRO.
(b) The following are examples of relationships between laboratories and MROs that the Department regards as creating conflicts of interest, or the appearance of such conflicts. This following list of examples is not intended to be exclusive or exhaustive:
  (1) *The laboratory employs an MRO* who reviews test results produced by the laboratory;
  (2) *The laboratory has a contract or retainer* with the MRO for the review of test results produced by the laboratory;
  (3) *The laboratory designates* which MRO the employer is to use, gives the employer a slate of MROs from which to choose, or recommends certain MROs;
  (4) *The laboratory gives the employer* a discount or other incentive to use a particular MRO;
  (5) *The laboratory has its place of business* co-located with that of an MRO or MRO staff who review test results produced by the laboratory; or
  (6) *The laboratory permits an MRO,* or an MRO's organization, to have a financial interest in the laboratory.

§40.103 What are the requirements for submitting blind specimens to a laboratory?

(a) **As an employer or C/TPA with an aggregate** of 2000 or more DOT-covered employees, you must send blind specimens to laboratories you use. If you have an aggregate of fewer than 2000 DOT-covered employees, you are not required to provide blind specimens.

(b) **To each laboratory to which you send** at least 100 specimens in a year, you must transmit a number of blind specimens equivalent to one percent of the specimens you send to that laboratory, up to a maximum of 50 blind specimens in each quarter (i.e., January-March, April-June, July-September, October-December). As a C/TPA, you must apply this percentage to the total number of DOT-covered employees' specimens you send to the laboratory. Your blind specimen submissions must be evenly spread throughout the year. The following examples illustrate how this requirement works:

Example 1 to Paragraph (b). You send 2500 specimens to Lab X in Year 1. In this case, you would send 25 blind specimens to Lab X in Year 1. To meet the even distribution requirement, you would send 6 in each of three quarters and 7 in the other.

Example 2 to Paragraph (b). You send 2000 specimens to Lab X and 1000 specimens to Lab Y in Year 1. In this case, you would send 20 blind specimens to Lab X and 10 to Lab Y in Year 1. The even distribution requirement would apply in a similar way to that described in Example 1.

Example 3 to Paragraph (b). Same as Example 2, except that you also send 20 specimens to Lab Z. In this case, you would send blind specimens to Labs X and Y as in Example 2. You would not have to send any blind specimens to Lab Z, because you sent fewer than 100 specimens to Lab Z.

Example 4 to Paragraph (b). You are a C/TPA sending 2000 specimens to Lab X in Year 1. These 2000 specimens represent 200 small employers who have an average of 10 covered employees each. In this case you — not the individual employers — send 20 blind specimens to Lab X in Year 1, again ensuring even distribution. The individual employers you represent are not required to provide any blind specimens on their own.

Example 5 to Paragraph (b). You are a large C/TPA that sends 40,000 specimens to Lab Y in Year 1. One percent of that figure is 400. However, the 50 blind specimen per quarter "cap" means that you need send only 50 blind specimens per quarter, rather than the 100 per quarter you would have to send to meet the one percent rate. Your annual total would be 200, rather than 400, blind specimens.

(c) **Approximately 75 percent** of the specimens you submit must be blank (i.e., containing no drugs, nor adulterated or substituted). Approximately 15 percent must be positive for one or more of the five drugs involved in DOT tests, and approximately 10 percent must either be adulterated with a substance cited in HHS guidance or substituted (i.e., having specific gravity and creatinine meeting the criteria of §40.93(b)).

(1) *The blind specimens* that you submit that contain drugs, that are adulterated with a substance cited in HHS guidance, or that are substituted must be validated as to their contents by the supplier using initial and confirmatory tests.

(2) *The supplier must provide information* regarding the shelf life of the blind specimens.

(3) *If the blind specimen is drug positive,* the concentration of drug it contains must be between 1.5 and 2 times the initial drug test cutoff concentration.

(4) *If the blind specimen is adulterated with nitrite,* the concentration of nitrite it contains must be between 1.5 and 2 times the initial validity test cutoff concentration.

(5) *If the blind specimen is adulterated by altering pH,* the pH must be less than or equal to 2, or greater than or equal to 12.

(6) *If the blind specimen is substituted,* the creatinine must be less than or equal to 2, and the specific gravity must be 1.000.

(d) **You must ensure that each blind specimen** is indistinguishable to the laboratory from a normal specimen.

(1) *You must submit* blind specimens to the laboratory using the same channels (e.g., via a regular collection site) through which employees' specimens are sent to the laboratory.

(2) *You must ensure* that the collector uses a CCF, places fictional initials on the specimen bottle label/seal, indicates for the MRO on Copy 2 that the specimen is a blind specimen, and discards Copies 4 and 5 (employer and employee copies).

(3) *You must ensure that all blind specimens include split specimens.*

§40.103 DOT Interpretations

Question 1: Must an employer or C/TPA who is required to submit blind specimens to laboratories send adulterated or substituted blinds if the employer or C/TPA is not yet having specimens undergo validity testing?

Guidance: At the present time, validity testing remains an employer option.

Therefore, if an employer or C/TPA required to submit blind specimens is not conducting validity testing during the course of its normal testing, the employer or C/TPA needs not send adulterated or substituted blind specimens to the laboratories used.

However, if an employer or C/TPA conducts validity testing, adulterated or substituted blind specimens must be sent to the laboratories used.

Part 40 requires that approximately 75 percent of the blinds must be blank (i.e., containing no drugs, nor adulterated or substituted); 15 percent must be positive for one or more drugs; and 10 percent must be adulterated or substituted.

If the employer or C/TPA is not exercising the option to conduct validity testing, approximately 75 percent of blinds must be blank and 25 percent must be positive for one or more drugs.

Question 2: Requirements for submitting quarterly blind specimens to the laboratory went into effect mid-quarter, August 1, 2001. How are the new requirements for blind sample submission to be calculated? Are the blinds for July, 2001 to be calculated on the old Part 40 regulations and August and September, 2001 blind calculations based on new Part 40 regulations?

Guidance: It is acceptable to send in blind specimens for July 2001, based on the requirements of the old Part 40 and for August-September based on the new Part 40 that went into effect August 1, 2001.

§§40.103, 40.99, 40.333 DOT Interpretations

Question 1: What are the retention requirements for blind specimens and records of blind specimen tests?

Guidance: Laboratories, employers and other parties required to retain specimens and records of tests should retain blind specimens and records of blind specimen tests in exactly the same way and for the same periods of time as they do actual employee specimens and test records.

For example, an employer would keep a record of a blind positive test for five years and a blind negative test for two years.

Laboratories would keep blind specimens for negatives in accordance with their SOPs and non-negatives for one year.

§40.105 What happens if the laboratory reports a result different from that expected for a blind specimen?

(a) **If you are an employer, MRO, or C/TPA** who submits a blind specimen, and if the result reported to the MRO is different from the result expected, you must investigate the discrepancy.

(b) **If the unexpected result is a false negative,** you must provide the laboratory with the expected results (obtained from the supplier of the blind specimen), and direct the laboratory to determine the reason for the discrepancy.

(c) **If the unexpected result is a false positive,** you must provide the laboratory with the expected results (obtained from the supplier of the blind specimen), and direct the laboratory to determine the reason for the discrepancy. You must also notify ODAPC of the discrepancy by telephone (202-366-3784) or e-mail (addresses are listed on the ODAPC web site, http://www.dot.gov/ost/dapc). ODAPC will notify HHS who will take appropriate action.

§40.107 Who may inspect laboratories?

As a laboratory, you must permit an inspection, with or without prior notice, by ODAPC, a DOT agency, or a DOT-regulated employer that contracts with the laboratory for drug testing under the DOT drug testing program, or the designee of such an employer.

§40.109 What documentation must the laboratory keep, and for how long?

(a) **As a laboratory, you must retain all records** pertaining to each employee urine specimen for a minimum of two years.

(b) **As a laboratory,** you must also keep for two years employer-specific data required in §40.111.

(c) **Within the two-year period,** the MRO, the employee, the employer, or a DOT agency may request in writing that you retain the records for an additional period of time (e.g., for the purpose of preserving evidence for litigation or a safety investigation). If you receive such a request, you must comply with it. If you do not receive such a request, you may discard the records at the end of the two-year period.

§40.111 When and how must a laboratory disclose statistical summaries and other information it maintains?

(a) **As a laboratory,** you must transmit an aggregate statistical summary, by employer, of the data listed in Appendix B to this part to the employer on a semi-annual basis.

(1) *The summary must not reveal the identity of any employee.*

Subpart G - Medical Review Officers and the Verification Process §40.123 (b)

(2) *In order to avoid sending data* from which it is likely that information about an employee's test result can be readily inferred, you must not send a summary if the employer has fewer than five aggregate tests results.

(3) *The summary must be sent by January 20* of each year for July 1 through December 31 of the prior year.

(4) *The summary must also be sent by July 20* of each year for January 1 through June 30 of the current year.

(b) **When the employer requests a summary** in response to an inspection, audit, or review by a DOT agency, you must provide it unless the employer had fewer than five aggregate test results. In that case, you must send the employer a report indicating that not enough testing was conducted to warrant a summary. You may transmit the summary or report by hard copy, fax, or other electronic means.

(c) **You must also release information** to appropriate parties as provided in §§40.329 and 40.331.

§40.113 Where is other information concerning laboratories found in this regulation?

You can find more information concerning laboratories in several sections of this part:

§40.3 - Definition.
§40.13 - Prohibition on making specimens available for other purposes.
§40.31 - Conflicts of interest concerning collectors.
§40.47 - Laboratory rejections of test for improper form.
§40.125 - Conflicts of interest concerning MROs.
§40.175 - Role of first laboratory in split specimen tests.
§40.177 - Role of second laboratory in split specimen tests (drugs).
§40.179 - Role of second laboratory in split specimen tests (adulterants).
§40.181 - Role of second laboratory in split specimen tests (substitution).
§§40.183-40.185 - Transmission of split specimen test results to MRO.
§§40.201-40.205 - Role in correcting errors.
§40.329 - Release of information to employees.
§40.331 - Limits on release of information.
§40.355 - Role with respect to other service agents.

Subpart G - Medical Review Officers and the Verification Process

§40.121 Who is qualified to act as an MRO?

To be qualified to act as an MRO in the DOT drug testing program, you must meet each of the requirements of this section:

(a) **Credentials.** You must be a licensed physician (Doctor of Medicine or Osteopathy). If you are a licensed physician in any U.S., Canadian, or Mexican jurisdiction and meet the other requirements of this section, you are authorized to perform MRO services with respect to all covered employees, wherever they are located. For example, if you are licensed as an M.D. in one state or province in the U.S., Canada, or Mexico, you are not limited to performing MRO functions in that state or province, and you may perform MRO functions for employees in other states or provinces without becoming licensed to practice medicine in the other jurisdictions.

(b) **Basic knowledge.** You must be knowledgeable in the following areas:

(1) *You must be knowledgeable about* and have clinical experience in controlled substances abuse disorders, including detailed knowledge of alternative medical explanations for laboratory confirmed drug test results.

(2) *You must be knowledgeable about issues* relating to adulterated and substituted specimens as well as the possible medical causes of specimens having an invalid result.

(3) *You must be knowledgeable about this part,* the DOT MRO Guidelines, and the DOT agency regulations applicable to the employers for whom you evaluate drug test results, and you must keep current on any changes to these materials. The DOT MRO Guidelines document is available from ODAPC (Department of Transportation, 400 7th Street, SW., Room 10403, Washington, DC 20590, 202-366-3784, or on the ODAPC web site (http://www.dot.gov/ost/dapc).

(c) **Qualification training.** You must receive qualification training meeting the requirements of this paragraph (c).

(1) *Qualification training must provide instruction* on the following subjects:

(i) Collection procedures for urine specimens;
(ii) Chain of custody, reporting, and recordkeeping;
(iii) Interpretation of drug and validity tests results;
(iv) The role and responsibilities of the MRO in the DOT drug testing program;
(v) The interaction with other participants in the program (e.g., DERs, SAPs); and
(vi) Provisions of this part and DOT agency rules applying to employers for whom you review test results, including changes and updates to this part and DOT agency rules, guidance, interpretations, and policies affecting the performance of MRO functions, as well as issues that MROs confront in carrying out their duties under this part and DOT agency rules.

(2) *Following your completion* of qualification training under paragraph (c)(1) of this section, you must satisfactorily complete an examination administered by a nationally-recognized MRO certification board or subspecialty board for medical practitioners in the field of medical review of DOT-mandated drug tests. The examination must comprehensively cover all the elements of qualification training listed in paragraph (c)(1) of this section.

(3) *The following is the schedule* for qualification training you must meet:

(i) *If you became an MRO* before August 1, 2001, and have already met the qualification training requirement, you do not have to meet it again.

(ii) *If you became an MRO* before August 1, 2001, but have not yet met the qualification training requirement, you must do so no later than January 31, 2003.

(iii) *If you become an MRO* on or after August 1, 2001, you must meet the qualification training requirement before you begin to perform MRO functions.

(d) **Continuing education.** During each three-year period from the date on which you satisfactorily complete the examination under paragraph (c)(2) of this section, you must complete continuing education consisting of at least 12 professional development hours (e.g., Continuing Education Medical Units) relevant to performing MRO functions.

(1) *This continuing education* must include material concerning new technologies, interpretations, recent guidance, rule changes, and other information about developments in MRO practice, pertaining to the DOT program, since the time you met the qualification training requirements of this section.

(2) *Your continuing education activities* must include assessment tools to assist you in determining whether you have adequately learned the material.

(3) *If you are an MRO* who completed the qualification training and examination requirements prior to August 1, 2001, you must complete your first increment of 12 CEU hours before August 1, 2004.

(e) **Documentation.** You must maintain documentation showing that you currently meet all requirements of this section. You must provide this documentation on request to DOT agency representatives and to employers and C/TPAs who are using or negotiating to use your services.

> **§§40.33, 40.121, 40.213, 40.281 DOT Interpretations**
>
> *Question 1:* Because Part 40 requires collectors, MROs, BATs and STTs, and SAPs to maintain their own training records, can employers or training entities refuse to provide these service agents their training records?
>
> *Guidance:* No. Employers and trainers who provide training for these service agents must not withhold training documentation from them when they have successfully completed the training requirements.
>
> If a collector, BAT, STT, MRO, or SAP is not in possession of training documentation, he or she is in violation of Part 40.
>
> Therefore, Part 40 does not permit the withholding of such documentation from these service agents.

§40.123 What are the MRO's responsibilities in the DOT drug testing program?

As an MRO, you have the following basic responsibilities:

(a) **Acting as an independent** and impartial "gatekeeper" and advocate for the accuracy and integrity of the drug testing process.

(b) **Providing a quality assurance review** of the drug testing process for the specimens under your purview. This includes, but is not limited to:

(1) *Ensuring the review of the CCF* on all specimen collections for the purposes of determining whether there is a problem that

may cause a test to be cancelled (see §§40.199-40.203). As an MRO, you are not required to review laboratory internal chain of custody documentation. No one is permitted to cancel a test because you have not reviewed this documentation;

(2) *Providing feedback to employers,* collection sites and laboratories regarding performance issues where necessary; and

(3) *Reporting to and consulting* with the ODAPC or a relevant DOT agency when you wish DOT assistance in resolving any program issue. As an employer or service agent, you are prohibited from limiting or attempting to limit the MRO's access to DOT for this purpose and from retaliating in any way against an MRO for discussing drug testing issues with DOT.

(c) You must determine whether there is a legitimate medical explanation for confirmed positive, adulterated, substituted, and invalid drug tests results from the laboratory.

(d) While you provide medical review of employees' test results, this part does not deem that you have established a doctor-patient relationship with the employees whose tests you review.

(e) You must act to investigate and correct problems where possible and notify appropriate parties (e.g., HHS, DOT, employers, service agents) where assistance is needed, (e.g., cancelled or problematic tests, incorrect results, problems with blind specimens).

(f) You must ensure the timely flow of test results and other information to employers.

(g) You must protect the confidentiality of the drug testing information.

(h) You must perform all your functions in compliance with this part and other DOT agency regulations.

§40.125 What relationship may an MRO have with a laboratory?

As an MRO, you may not enter into any relationship with an employer's laboratory that creates a conflict of interest or the appearance of a conflict of interest with your responsibilities to that employer. You may not derive any financial benefit by having an employer use a specific laboratory. For examples of relationships between laboratories and MROs that the Department views as creating a conflict of interest or the appearance of such a conflict, see §40.101(b).

§40.127 What are the MRO's functions in reviewing negative test results?

As the MRO, you must do the following with respect to negative drug test results you receive from a laboratory, prior to verifying the result and releasing it to the DER:

(a) Review Copy 2 of the CCF to determine if there are any fatal or correctable errors that may require you to initiate corrective action or to cancel the test (see §§40.199 and 40.203).

(b) Review the negative laboratory test result and ensure that it is consistent with the information contained on the CCF.

(c) Before you report a negative test result, you must have in your possession the following documents:

(1) *Copy 2 of the CCF,* a legible copy of it, or any other CCF copy containing the employee's signature; and

(2) *A legible copy* (fax, photocopy, image) of Copy 1 of the CCF or the electronic laboratory results report that conveys the negative laboratory test result.

(d) If the copy of the documentation provided to you by the collector or laboratory appears unclear, you must request that the collector or laboratory send you a legible copy.

(e) On Copy 2 of the CCF, place a check mark in the "Negative" box (Step 6), provide your name, and sign, initial, or stamp and date the verification statement.

(f) Report the result in a confidential manner (see §§40.163-40.167).

(g) Staff under your direct, personal supervision may perform the administrative functions of this section for you, but only you can cancel a test. If you cancel a laboratory-confirmed negative result, check the "Test Cancelled" box (Step 6) on Copy 2 of the CCF, make appropriate annotation in the "Remarks" line, provide your name, and sign, initial or stamp and date the verification statement.

(1) *On specimen results* that are reviewed by your staff, you are responsible for assuring the quality of their work.

(2) *You are required to personally review* at least 5 percent of all CCFs reviewed by your staff on a quarterly basis, including all results that required a corrective action. However, you need not review more than 500 negative results in any quarter.

(3) *Your review must, as a minimum,* include the CCF, negative laboratory test result, any accompanying corrective documents, and the report sent to the employer. You must correct any errors that you discover. You must take action as necessary to ensure compliance by your staff with this part and document your corrective action. You must attest to the quality assurance review by initialing the CCFs that you review.

(4) *You must make these CCFs* easily identifiable and retrievable by you for review by DOT agencies.

§40.127 DOT Interpretations

Question 1: How should the MRO's review of negative results processed by the MRO's staff take place?

Guidance: The MRO's personal review of the MRO's staff work (to include the CCFs, lab results documentation, corrective documents, and results reports to employers) should be spread throughout the quarter.

Even if the MRO has reviewed the required 500 per quarter, the MRO must still review all those that needed corrective actions.

The MRO need not review a sampling from all employers or transportation industries he or she serves.

The MRO must provide documentation of the CCF quality assurance review to DOT agency representatives regardless of their DOT agency affiliation (e.g., an FRA inspector can obtain and review documents generated from an FAA-sanctioned test). Part 40 is a One-DOT effort.

§40.129 What are the MRO's functions in reviewing laboratory confirmed positive, adulterated, substituted, or invalid drug test results?

(a) As the MRO, you must do the following with respect to confirmed positive, adulterated, substituted, or invalid drug tests you receive from a laboratory, before you verify the result and release it to the DER:

(1) *Review Copy 2 of the CCF* to determine if there are any fatal or correctable errors that may require you to cancel the test (see §§40.199 and 40.203). Staff under your direct, personal supervision may conduct this administrative review for you, but only you may verify or cancel a test.

(2) *Review Copy 1 of the CCF* and ensure that it is consistent with the information contained on Copy 2, that the test result is legible, and that the certifying scientist signed the form. You are not required to review any other documentation generated by the laboratory during their analysis or handling of the specimen (e.g., the laboratory internal chain of custody).

(3) *If the copy of the documentation* provided to you by the collector or laboratory appears unclear, you must request that the collector or laboratory send you a legible copy.

(4) *Except in the circumstances* spelled out in §40.133, conduct a verification interview. This interview must include direct contact in person or by telephone between you and the employee. You may initiate the verification process based on the laboratory results report.

(5) *Verify the test result* as either negative, positive, test cancelled, or refusal to test because of adulteration or substitution, consistent with the requirements of §§40.135-40.145 and 40.159.

(b) Before you report a verified negative, positive, test cancelled, refusal to test because of adulteration or substitution, you must have in your possession the following documents:

(1) *Copy 2 of the CCF,* a legible copy of it, or any other CCF copy containing the employee's signature; and

(2) *A legible copy* (fax, photocopy, image) of Copy 1 of the CCF, containing the certifying scientist's signature.

(c) With respect to verified positive test results, place a check mark in the "Positive" box (Step 6) on Copy 2 of the CCF, indicate the drug(s)/metabolite(s) detected on the "Remarks" line, sign and date the verification statement.

(d) If you cancel a laboratory confirmed positive, adulterated, substituted, or invalid drug test report, check the "test cancelled" box (Step 6) on Copy 2 of the CCF, make appropriate annotation in the "Remarks" line, sign, provide your name, and date the verification statement.

(e) Report the result in a confidential manner (see §§40.163-40.167).

(f) With respect to adulteration or substitution test results, check the "refusal to test because:" box (Step 6) on Copy 2 of the CCF, check the "Adulterated" or "Substituted" box, as appropriate, make appropriate annotation in the "Remarks" line, sign and date the verification statement.

(g) As the MRO, your actions concerning reporting confirmed positive, adulterated, or substituted results to the employer before you have completed the verification process are also governed by the stand-down provisions of §40.21.

Subpart G - Medical Review Officers and the Verification Process §40.133 (c)

(1) *If an employer has a stand-down policy* that meets the requirements of §40.21, you may report to the DER that you have received an employee's laboratory confirmed positive, adulterated, or substituted test result, consistent with the terms of the waiver the employer received. You must not provide any further details about the test result (e.g., the name of the drug involved).

(2) *If the employer does not have a stand-down policy* that meets the requirements of §40.21, you must not inform the employer that you have received an employee's laboratory confirmed positive, adulterated, or substituted test result until you verify the test result. For example, as an MRO employed directly by a company, you must not tell anyone on the company's staff or management that you have received an employee's laboratory confirmed test result.

§40.131 How does the MRO or DER notify an employee of the verification process after a confirmed positive, adulterated, substituted, or invalid test result?

(a) **When, as the MRO,** you receive a confirmed positive, adulterated, substituted, or invalid test result from the laboratory, you must contact the employee directly (i.e., actually talk to the employee), on a confidential basis, to determine whether the employee wants to discuss the test result. In making this contact, you must explain to the employee that, if he or she declines to discuss the result, you will verify the test as positive or as a refusal to test because of adulteration or substitution, as applicable.

(b) **As the MRO,** staff under your personal supervision may conduct this initial contact for you.

  (1) *This staff contact must be limited* to scheduling the discussion between you and the employee and explaining the consequences of the employee's declining to speak with you (i.e., that the MRO will verify the test without input from the employee). If the employee declines to speak with you, the staff person must document the employee's decision, including the date and time.

  (2) *A staff person must not gather* any medical information or information concerning possible explanations for the test result.

  (3) *A staff person may advise an employee* to have medical information (e.g., prescriptions, information forming the basis of a legitimate medical explanation for a confirmed positive test result) ready to present at the interview with the MRO.

  (4) *Since you are required to speak personally* with the employee, face-to-face or on the phone, your staff must not inquire if the employee wishes to speak with you.

(c) **As the MRO,** you or your staff must make reasonable efforts to reach the employee at the day and evening telephone numbers listed on the CCF. Reasonable efforts include, as a minimum, three attempts, spaced reasonably over a 24-hour period, to reach the employee at the day and evening telephone numbers listed on the CCF. If you or your staff cannot reach the employee directly after making these efforts, you or your staff must take the following steps:

  (1) *Document the efforts you made* to contact the employee, including dates and times. If both phone numbers are incorrect (e.g., disconnected, wrong number), you may take the actions listed in paragraph (c)(2) of this section without waiting the full 24-hour period.

  (2) *Contact the DER, instructing the DER to contact the employee.*

    (i) *You must simply direct the DER* to inform the employee to contact you.

    (ii) *You must not inform the DER* that the employee has a confirmed positive, adulterated, substituted, or invalid test result.

    (iii) *You must document the dates and times* of your attempts to contact the DER, and you must document the name of the DER you contacted and the date and time of the contact.

(d) **As the DER,** you must attempt to contact the employee immediately, using procedures that protect, as much as possible, the confidentiality of the MRO's request that the employee contact the MRO. If you successfully contact the employee (i.e., actually talk to the employee), you must document the date and time of the contact, and inform the MRO. You must inform the employee that he or she should contact the MRO immediately. You must also inform the employee of the consequences of failing to contact the MRO within the next 72 hours (see §40.133(a)(2)).

  (1) *As the DER,* you must not inform anyone else working for the employer that you are seeking to contact the employee on behalf of the MRO.

  (2) *If, as the DER,* you have made all reasonable efforts to contact the employee but failed to do so, you may place the employee on temporary medically unqualified status or medical leave. Reasonable efforts include, as a minimum, three attempts, spaced reasonably over a 24-hour period, to reach the employee at the day and evening telephone numbers listed on the CCF.

    (i) *As the DER,* you must document the dates and times of these efforts.

    (ii) *If, as the DER,* you are unable to contact the employee within this 24-hour period, you must leave a message for the employee by any practicable means (e.g., voice mail, e-mail, letter) to contact the MRO and inform the MRO of the date and time of this attempted contact.

§40.131 DOT Interpretations

Question 1: Must an MRO use the full 24-hour period to contact the donor if the MRO is sure that the donor is not and will not be available at the phone numbers provided by the donor?

Guidance: §40.131(a)(1) states that if the phone numbers provided by the donor are wrong, an MRO may contact the DER to inform the donor to contact the MRO without waiting the full 24 hours.

If the MRO discovers that phone numbers provided by the donor will not permit the MRO to contact the donor within the 24-hour period, the MRO may contact the DER immediately. For example, the MRO may discover that the employee is not expected to be available for another five days at the number provided.

Question 2: Is it appropriate for the MRO to attempt to contact the employee after normal office hours?

Guidance: Yes. Copy 2 of the CCF contains spaces for the employee's daytime and evening telephone numbers. We expect MROs or their staffs to attempt to contact the employee at the evening phone number if the employee is not available at the daytime number.

§40.133 Under what circumstances may the MRO verify a test as positive, or as a refusal to test because of adulteration or substitution, without interviewing the employee?

(a) **As the MRO,** you normally may verify a confirmed positive test (for any drug or drug metabolite, including opiates), or as a refusal to test because of adulteration or substitution, only after interviewing the employee as provided in §§40.135-40.145. However, there are three circumstances in which you may verify such a result without an interview:

  (1) *You may verify a test result* as a positive or refusal to test, as applicable, if the employee expressly declines the opportunity to discuss the test with you. You must maintain complete documentation of this occurrence, including notation of informing, or attempting to inform, the employee of the consequences of not exercising the option to speak with you.

  (2) *You may verify a test result* as a positive or refusal to test, as applicable, if the DER has successfully made and documented a contact with the employee and instructed the employee to contact you and more than 72 hours have passed since the time the DER contacted the employee.

  (3) *You may verify a test result* as a positive or refusal to test, as applicable, if neither you nor the DER, after making and documenting all reasonable efforts, has been able to contact the employee within ten days of the date on which the MRO receives the confirmed test result from the laboratory.

(b) **As the MRO,** when you verify a test result as a positive or refusal to test under this section, you must document the date, time and reason, following the instructions in §40.163.

(c) **As the MRO,** after you have verified a test result as a positive or refusal to test under this section and reported the result to the DER, you must allow the employee to present information to you within 60 days of the verification documenting that serious illness, injury, or other circumstances unavoidably precluded contact with the MRO and/or DER in the times provided. On the basis of such information, you may reopen the verification, allowing the employee to present information concerning whether there is a legitimate medical explanation for the confirmed test result.

§40.135 What does the MRO tell the employee at the beginning of the verification interview?

(a) *As the MRO,* you must tell the employee that the laboratory has determined that the employee's test result was positive, adulterated, substituted, or invalid, as applicable. You must also tell the employee of the drugs for which his or her specimen tested positive, or the basis for the finding of adulteration or substitution.

(b) *You must explain the verification interview process* to the employee and inform the employee that your decision will be based on information the employee provides in the interview.

(c) *You must explain that,* if further medical evaluation is needed for the verification process, the employee must comply with your request for this evaluation and that failure to do so is equivalent of expressly declining to discuss the test result.

(d) *As the MRO,* you must warn an employee who has a confirmed positive, adulterated, substituted or invalid test that you are required to provide to third parties drug test result information and medical information affecting the performance of safety-sensitive duties that the employee gives you in the verification process without the employee's consent (see §40.327).

  (1) *You must give this warning to the employee* before obtaining any medical information as part of the verification process.

  (2) *For purposes of this paragraph (d),* medical information includes information on medications or other substances affecting the performance of safety-sensitive duties that the employee reports using or medical conditions the employee reports having.

  (3) *For purposes of this paragraph (d),* the persons to whom this information may be provided include the employer, a SAP evaluating the employee as part of the return to duty process (see §40.293(g)), DOT, another Federal safety agency (e.g., the NTSB), or any state safety agency as required by state law.

(e) *You must also advise the employee that,* after informing any third party about any medication the employee is using pursuant to a legally valid prescription under the Controlled Substances Act, you will allow 5 days for the employee to have the prescribing physician contact you to determine if the medication can be changed to one that does not make the employee medically unqualified or does not pose a significant safety risk. If, as an MRO, you receive such information from the prescribing physician, you must transmit this information to any third party to whom you previously provided information about the safety risks of the employee's other medication.

§40.137 On what basis does the MRO verify test results involving marijuana, cocaine, amphetamines, or PCP?

(a) *As the MRO,* you must verify a confirmed positive test result for marijuana, cocaine, amphetamines, and/or PCP unless the employee presents a legitimate medical explanation for the presence of the drug(s)/metabolite(s) in his or her system.

(b) *You must offer the employee an opportunity* to present a legitimate medical explanation in all cases.

(c) *The employee has the burden of proof* that a legitimate medical explanation exists. The employee must present information meeting this burden at the time of the verification interview. As the MRO, you have discretion to extend the time available to the employee for this purpose for up to five days before verifying the test result, if you determine that there is a reasonable basis to believe that the employee will be able to produce relevant evidence concerning a legitimate medical explanation within that time.

(d) *If you determine* that there is a legitimate medical explanation, you must verify the test result as negative. Otherwise, you must verify the test result as positive.

(e) *In determining* whether a legitimate medical explanation exists, you may consider the employee's use of a medication from a foreign country. You must exercise your professional judgment consistently with the following principles:

  (1) *There can be a legitimate medical explanation* only with respect to a substance that is obtained legally in a foreign country.

  (2) *There can be a legitimate medical explanation* only with respect to a substance that has a legitimate medical use. Use of a drug of abuse (e.g., heroin, PCP, marijuana) or any other substance (see §40.151(f) and (g)) that cannot be viewed as having a legitimate medical use can never be the basis for a legitimate medical explanation, even if the substance is obtained legally in a foreign country.

  (3) *Use of the substance* can form the basis of a legitimate medical explanation only if it is used consistently with its proper and intended medical purpose.

  (4) *Even if you find* that there is a legitimate medical explanation under this paragraph (e) and verify a test negative, you may have a responsibility to raise fitness-for-duty considerations with the employer (see §40.327).

§40.139 On what basis does the MRO verify test results involving opiates?

As the MRO, you must proceed as follows when you receive a laboratory confirmed positive opiate result:

(a) *If the laboratory detects* the presence of 6-acetylmorphine (6-AM) in the specimen, you must verify the test result positive.

(b) *In the absence of 6-AM,* if the laboratory detects the presence of either morphine or codeine at 15,000 ng/mL or above, you must verify the test result positive unless the employee presents a legitimate medical explanation for the presence of the drug or drug metabolite in his or her system, as in the case of other drugs (see §40.137). Consumption of food products (e.g., poppy seeds) must not be considered a legitimate medical explanation for the employee having morphine or codeine at these concentrations.

(c) *For all other opiate positive results,* you must verify a confirmed positive test result for opiates only if you determine that there is clinical evidence, in addition to the urine test, of unauthorized use of any opium, opiate, or opium derivative (i.e., morphine, heroin, or codeine).

  (1) *As an MRO,* it is your responsibility to use your best professional and ethical judgement and discretion to determine whether there is clinical evidence of unauthorized use of opiates. Examples of information that you may consider in making this judgement include, but are not limited to, the following:

    (i) *Recent needle tracks;*

    (ii) *Behavioral and psychological signs* of acute opiate intoxication or withdrawal;

    (iii) *Clinical history of unauthorized use* recent enough to have produced the laboratory test result;

    (iv) *Use of a medication from a foreign country.* See §40.137(e) for guidance on how to make this determination.

  (2) *In order to establish the clinical evidence* referenced in paragraphs (c)(1)(i) and (ii) of this section, personal observation of the employee is essential.

    (i) *Therefore, you, as the MRO,* must conduct, or cause another physician to conduct, a face-to-face examination of the employee.

    (ii) *No face-to-face examination is needed* in establishing the clinical evidence referenced in paragraph (c)(1)(iii) or (iv) of this section.

  (3) *To be the basis* of a verified positive result for opiates, the clinical evidence you find must concern a drug that the laboratory found in the specimen. (For example, if the test confirmed the presence of codeine, and the employee admits to unauthorized use of hydrocodone, you do not have grounds for verifying the test positive. The admission must be for the substance that was found).

  (4) *As the MRO,* you have the burden of establishing that there is clinical evidence of unauthorized use of opiates referenced in this paragraph (c). If you cannot make this determination (e.g., there is not sufficient clinical evidence or history), you must verify the test as negative. The employee does not need to show you that a legitimate medical explanation exists if no clinical evidence is established.

§40.141 How does the MRO obtain information for the verification decision?

As the MRO, you must do the following as you make the determinations needed for a verification decision:

(a) *You must conduct a medical interview.* You must review the employee's medical history and any other relevant biomedical factors presented to you by the employee. You may direct the employee to undergo further medical evaluation by you or another physician.

(b) *If the employee asserts that the presence* of a drug or drug metabolite in his or her specimen results from taking prescription medication, you must review and take all reasonable and necessary steps to verify the authenticity of all medical records the employee provides. You may contact the employee's physician or other relevant medical personnel for further information.

§40.143 [Reserved]

Subpart G - Medical Review Officers and the Verification Process

§40.145 On what basis does the MRO verify test results involving adulteration or substitution?

(a) **As an MRO,** when you receive a laboratory report that a specimen is adulterated or substituted, you must treat that report in the same way you treat the laboratory's report of a confirmed positive for a drug or drug metabolite.

(b) **You must follow the same procedures** used for verification of a confirmed positive test for a drug or drug metabolite (see §§40.129-40.135, 40.141, 40.151), except as otherwise provided in this section.

(c) **In the verification interview,** you must explain the laboratory findings to the employee and address technical questions or issues the employee may raise.

(d) **You must offer the employee the opportunity** to present a legitimate medical explanation for the laboratory findings with respect to presence of the adulterant in, or the creatinine and specific gravity findings for, the specimen.

(e) **The employee has the burden of proof** that there is a legitimate medical explanation.

(1) *To meet this burden* in the case of an adulterated specimen, the employee must demonstrate that the adulterant found by the laboratory entered the specimen through physiological means.

(2) *To meet this burden* in the case of a substituted specimen, the employee must demonstrate that he or she did produce or could have produced urine through physiological means, meeting the creatinine concentration criterion of less than 2 mg/dL and the specific gravity criteria of less than or equal to 1.0010 or greater than or equal to 1.0200 (see §40.93(b)).

(3) *The employee must present information* meeting this burden at the time of the verification interview. As the MRO, you have discretion to extend the time available to the employee for this purpose for up to five days before verifying the specimen, if you determine that there is a reasonable basis to believe that the employee will be able to produce relevant evidence supporting a legitimate medical explanation within that time.

(f) *As the MRO or the employer,* you are not responsible for arranging, conducting, or paying for any studies, examinations or analyses to determine whether a legitimate medical explanation exists.

(g) *As the MRO,* you must exercise your best professional judgment in deciding whether the employee has established a legitimate medical explanation.

(1) *If you determine that the employee's explanation* does not present a reasonable basis for concluding that there may be a legitimate medical explanation, you must report the test to the DER as a verified refusal to test because of adulteration or substitution, as applicable.

(2) *If you believe that the employee's explanation* may present a reasonable basis for concluding that there is a legitimate medical explanation, you must direct the employee to obtain, within the five-day period set forth in paragraph (e)(3) of this section, a further medical evaluation. This evaluation must be performed by a licensed physician (the "referral physician"), acceptable to you, with expertise in the medical issues raised by the employee's explanation. (The MRO may perform this evaluation if the MRO has appropriate expertise.)

(i) *As the MRO or employer,* you are not responsible for finding or paying a referral physician. However, on request of the employee, you must provide reasonable assistance to the employee's efforts to find such a physician. The final choice of the referral physician is the employee's, as long as the physician is acceptable to you.

(ii) *As the MRO,* you must consult with the referral physician, providing guidance to him or her concerning his or her responsibilities under this section. As part of this consultation, you must provide the following information to the referral physician:

[A] That the employee was required to take a DOT drug test, but the laboratory reported that the specimen was adulterated or substituted, which is treated as a refusal to test;

[B] The consequences of the appropriate DOT agency regulation for refusing to take the required drug test;

[C] That the referral physician must agree to follow the requirements of paragraphs (g)(3) through (g)(4) of this section; and

[D] That the referral physician must provide you with a signed statement of his or her recommendations.

(3) *As the referral physician,* you must evaluate the employee and consider any evidence the employee presents concerning the employee's medical explanation. You may conduct additional tests to determine whether there is a legitimate medical explanation. Any additional urine tests must be performed in an HHS-certified laboratory.

(4) *As the referral physician,* you must then make a written recommendation to the MRO about whether the MRO should determine that there is a legitimate medical explanation. As the MRO, you must seriously consider and assess the referral physician's recommendation in deciding whether there is a legitimate medical explanation.

(5) *As the MRO,* if you determine that there is a legitimate medical explanation, you must cancel the test and inform ODAPC in writing of the determination and the basis for it (e.g., referral physician's findings, evidence produced by the employee).

(6) *As the MRO,* if you determine that there is not a legitimate medical explanation, you must report the test to the DER as a verified refusal to test because of adulteration or substitution.

(h) **The following are examples of types of evidence** an employee could present to support an assertion of a legitimate medical explanation for a substituted result.

(1) *Medically valid evidence* demonstrating that the employee is capable of physiologically producing urine meeting the creatinine and specific gravity criteria of §40.93(b).

(i) *To be regarded as medically valid,* the evidence must have been gathered using appropriate methodology and controls to ensure its accuracy and reliability.

(ii) *Assertion by the employee* that his or her personal characteristics (e.g., with respect to race, gender, weight, diet, working conditions) are responsible for the substituted result does not, in itself, constitute a legitimate medical explanation. To make a case that there is a legitimate medical explanation, the employee must present evidence showing that the cited personal characteristics actually result in the physiological production of urine meeting the creatinine and specific gravity criteria of §40.93(b).

(2) *Information from a medical evaluation* under paragraph (g) of this section that the individual has a medical condition that has been demonstrated to cause the employee to physiologically produce urine meeting the creatinine and specific gravity criteria of §40.93(b).

(i) *A finding or diagnosis by the physician* that an employee has a medical condition, in itself, does not constitute a legitimate medical explanation.

(ii) *To establish* there is a legitimate medical explanation, the employee must demonstrate that the cited medical condition actually results in the physiological production of urine meeting the creatinine and specific gravity criteria of §40.93(b).

§40.147 [Reserved]

§40.149 May the MRO change a verified positive drug test result or refusal to test?

(a) **As the MRO,** you may change a verified positive or refusal to test drug test result only in the following situations:

(1) *When you have reopened a verification* that was done without an interview with an employee (see §40.133(c)).

(2) *If you receive information,* not available to you at the time of the original verification, demonstrating that the laboratory made an error in identifying (e.g., a paperwork mistake) or testing (e.g., a false positive or negative) the employee's primary or split specimen. For example, suppose the laboratory originally reported a positive test result for Employee X and a negative result for Employee Y. You verified the test results as reported to you. Then the laboratory notifies you that it mixed up the two test results, and X was really negative and Y was really positive. You would change X's test result from positive to negative and contact Y to conduct a verification interview.

(3) If, within 60 days of the original verification decision —

(i) *You receive information* that could not reasonably have been provided to you at the time of the decision demonstrating that there is a legitimate medical explanation for the presence of drug(s)/metabolite(s) in the employee's specimen; or

(ii) *You receive credible* new or additional evidence that a legitimate medical explanation for an adulterated or substituted result exists.

Example to Paragraph (a)(3): If the employee's physician provides you a valid prescription that he or she failed to find at the time of the original verification, you may change the test result from positive to negative if you conclude that the prescription provides a legitimate medical explanation for the drug(s)/metabolite(s) in the employee's specimen.

(4) *If you receive the information* in paragraph (a)(3) of this section after the 60-day period, you must consult with ODAPC prior to changing the result.

(5) *When you have made* an administrative error and reported an incorrect result.

(b) *If you change the result,* you must immediately notify the DER in writing, as provided in §§40.163-40.165.

(c) *You are the only person* permitted to change a verified test result, such as a verified positive test result or a determination that an individual has refused to test because of adulteration or substitution. This is because, as the MRO, you have the sole authority under this part to make medical determinations leading to a verified test (e.g., a determination that there was or was not a legitimate medical explanation for a laboratory test result). For example, an arbitrator is not permitted to overturn the medical judgment of the MRO that the employee failed to present a legitimate medical explanation for a positive, adulterated, or substituted test result of his or her specimen.

§40.149 DOT Interpretations

Question 1: Can arbitrators change or overturn the MRO's determination about the verification of a test result?

Guidance: No. The MRO is the only person authorized to change a verified test result (see §40.149(c)). The MRO can do so with respect to a verification decision he or she has made, in the circumstances described in §40.149.

An arbitrator is someone who derives his authority from the employer, or from a labor-management agreement. The arbitrator cannot exercise authority that the employer could not exercise on its own. The arbitrator could not overturn a decision of the MRO concerning a test verification any more than the employer could on its own.

This prohibition applies to substantive decisions the MRO makes about the merits of a test (e.g., with respect to whether there is a legitimate medical explanation for a positive, adulterated, or substituted test result or whether a medical condition precluded an individual from providing a sufficient specimen).

An arbitrator could determine that a test result should be cancelled because of a defect in the drug testing process involving the MRO (e.g., that the MRO failed to afford the employee the opportunity for a verification interview). But an arbitrator could not overturn the substantive judgment of the MRO about whether, for example, the information submitted by the employee constituted a legitimate medical explanation.

§§40.149 and 40.209 DOT Interpretations

Question 1: What is an employer to do if an arbitrator's decision claims to overturn the result of a DOT drug or alcohol test on grounds contrary to DOT regulations?

Guidance: There could be instances in which an arbitrator makes a decision that purports to cancel a DOT test for reasons that the DOT regulation does not recognize as valid.

For example, the arbitrator might make a decision based on disagreement with an MRO's judgment about a legitimate medical explanation (see §40.149) or on the basis of a procedural error that is not sufficient to cancel a test (see §40.209).

Such a test result remains valid under DOT regulations, notwithstanding the arbitrator's decision. Consequently, as a matter of Federal safety regulation, the employer must not return the employee to the performance of safety-sensitive functions until the employee has completed the return to duty process.

The employer may still be bound to implement the personnel policy outcome of the arbitrator's decision in such a case. This can result in hardship for the employer (e.g., being required to pay an individual at the same time as the Department's rules prevent the individual from performing the duties of his job).

§40.151 What are MROs prohibited from doing as part of the verification process?

As an MRO, you are prohibited from doing the following as part of the verification process:

(a) *You must not consider* any evidence from tests of urine samples or other body fluids or tissues (e.g., blood or hair samples) that are not collected or tested in accordance with this part. For example, if an employee tells you he went to his own physician, provided a urine specimen, sent it to a laboratory, and received a negative test result or a DNA test result questioning the identity of his DOT specimen, you are required to ignore this test result.

(b) *It is not your function to make decisions* about factual disputes between the employee and the collector concerning matters occurring at the collection site that are not reflected on the CCF (e.g., concerning allegations that the collector left the area or left open urine containers where other people could access them).

(c) *It is not your function to determine* whether the employer should have directed that a test occur. For example, if an employee tells you that the employer misidentified her as the subject of a random test, or directed her to take a reasonable suspicion or post-accident test without proper grounds under a DOT agency drug or alcohol regulation, you must inform the employee that you cannot play a role in deciding these issues.

(d) *It is not your function to consider explanations* of confirmed positive, adulterated, or substituted test results that would not, even if true, constitute a legitimate medical explanation. For example, an employee may tell you that someone slipped amphetamines into her drink at a party, that she unknowingly ingested a marijuana brownie, or that she traveled in a closed car with several people smoking crack. MROs are unlikely to be able to verify the facts of such passive or unknowing ingestion stories. Even if true, such stories do not present a legitimate medical explanation. Consequently, you must not declare a test as negative based on an explanation of this kind.

(e) *You must not verify a test negative* based on information that a physician recommended that the employee use a drug listed in Schedule I of the Controlled Substances Act. (e.g., under a state law that purports to authorize such recommendations, such as the "medical marijuana" laws that some states have adopted).

(f) *You must not accept an assertion of consumption* or other use of a hemp or other non-prescription marijuana-related product as a basis for verifying a marijuana test negative. You also must not accept such an explanation related to consumption of coca teas as a basis for verifying a cocaine test result as negative. Consuming or using such a product is not a legitimate medical explanation.

(g) *You must not accept an assertion* that there is a legitimate medical explanation for the presence of PCP or 6-AM in a specimen. There are no legitimate medical explanations for the presence of these substances.

(h) *You must not accept,* as a legitimate medical explanation for an adulterated specimen, an assertion that soap, bleach, or glutaraldehyde entered a specimen through physiological means. There are no physiological means through which these substances can enter a specimen.

(i) *You must not accept,* as a legitimate medical explanation for a substituted specimen, an assertion that an employee can produce urine with no detectable creatinine. There are no physiological means through which a person can produce a urine specimen having this characteristic.

§40.153 How does the MRO notify employees of their right to a test of the split specimen?

(a) *As the MRO,* when you have verified a drug test as positive for a drug or drug metabolite, or as a refusal to test because of adulteration or substitution, you must notify the employee of his or her right to have the split specimen tested. You must also notify the employee of the procedures for requesting a test of the split specimen.

(b) *You must inform the employee* that he or she has 72 hours from the time you provide this notification to him or her to request a test of the split specimen.

(c) *You must tell the employee how to contact you* to make this request. You must provide telephone numbers or other information that will allow the employee to make this request. As the MRO, you must have the ability to receive the employee's calls at all times during the 72 hour period (e.g., by use of an answering machine with a "time stamp" feature when there is no one in your office to answer the phone).

(d) *You must tell the employee* that if he or she makes this request within 72 hours, the employer must ensure that the test takes place, and that the employee is not required to pay for the test from his or her own funds before the test takes place. You must also tell the employee that the employer may seek reimbursement for the cost of the test (see §40.173).

(e) *You must tell the employee* that additional tests of the specimen (e.g., DNA tests) are not authorized.

Subpart G - Medical Review Officers and the Verification Process

§40.155 What does the MRO do when a negative or positive test result is also dilute?

(a) **When the laboratory reports** that a specimen is dilute, you must, as the MRO, report to the DER that the specimen, in addition to being negative or positive, is dilute.

(b) **You must check the "dilute" box (Step 6) on Copy 2 of the CCF.**

(c) **When you report a dilute specimen** to the DER, you must explain to the DER the employer's obligations and choices under §40.197, to include the requirement for an immediate recollection under direct observation if the creatinine concentration of a negative-dilute specimen was greater than or equal to 2 mg/dL but less than or equal to 5 mg/dL.

§40.157 [Reserved]

§40.159 What does the MRO do when a drug test result is invalid?

(a) **As the MRO, when the laboratory reports** that the test result is an invalid result, you must do the following:

 (1) *Discuss the laboratory results* with a certifying scientist to obtain more specific information.

 (2) *Contact the employee* and inform the employee that the specimen was invalid or contained an unexplained interfering substance. In contacting the employee, use the procedures set forth in §40.131.

 (3) *After explaining the limits of disclosure* (see §§40.135(d) and 40.327), you should inquire as to medications the employee may have taken that may interfere with some immunoassay tests.

 (4) *If the employee gives an explanation that is acceptable, you must:*

  (i) *Place a check mark* in the "Test Cancelled" box (Step 6) on Copy 2 of the CCF and enter "Invalid Result" and "direct observation collection not required" on the "Remarks" line.

  (ii) *Report to the DER that the test is cancelled,* the reason for cancellation, and that no further action is required unless a negative test result is required (i.e., pre-employment, return-to-duty, or follow-up tests).

 (5) *If the employee* is unable to provide an explanation and/or a valid prescription for a medication that interfered with the immunoassay test but denies having adulterated the specimen, you must:

  (i) *Place a check mark* in the "Test Cancelled" box (Step 6) on Copy 2 of the CCF and enter "Invalid Result" and "direct observation collection required" on the "Remarks" line.

  (ii) *Report to the DER that the test is cancelled,* the reason for cancellation, and that a second collection must take place immediately under direct observation.

  (iii) *Instruct the employer* to ensure that the employee has the minimum possible advance notice that he or she must go to the collection site.

(b) **You may only report an invalid test result** when you are in possession of a legible copy of Copy 1 of the CCF. In addition, you must have Copy 2 of the CCF, a legible copy of it, or any other copy of the CCF containing the employee's signature.

(c) **If the employee admits** to having adulterated or substituted the specimen, you must, on the same day, write and sign your own statement of what the employee told you. You must then report a refusal to test in accordance with §40.163.

§40.159 DOT Interpretations

Question 1: What does an MRO do when a drug test result is invalid due to "color discrepancy?"

Guidance: If "Invalid — Color difference" is the only result reported to you, you must follow the guidance of §40.159 by contacting the laboratory to obtain more specific information about the color difference between the specimens, and contacting the donor to obtain a legitimate explanation for the color difference. While there is no legitimate medical reason for anyone being able to provide a specimen that separates into two different colors when placed in two different bottles, the interview is necessary to determine appropriate follow-on action.

You must determine whether the donor has provided you with a legitimate explanation for the color difference (e.g., the collector used two separate voids for the collection), or not (e.g., no clue as to how the colors changed by the time the specimens reached the laboratory).

You must follow §40.159 for canceling the result, reporting the result to the employer, determining whether a recollection is necessary, and, if so, should it be under direct observation. If the laboratory has also reported to you that the specimen is positive, adulterated, or substituted, or substituted, then you must process the results in accordance with §40.129-131. If you determine (i.e., verify) the final result to be positive, adulterated, or substituted, then no additional action is required by you due to the color difference. You must not direct the employee to take another test.

Notify the employer that the collector must receive "error correction training" as required by §40.33(f). The area of Part 40 in which the collector needs to be retrained is §40.65(a).

§40.161 What does the MRO do when a drug test specimen is rejected for testing?

As the MRO, when the laboratory reports that the specimen is rejected for testing (e.g., because of a fatal or uncorrected flaw), you must do the following:

(a) **Place a check mark in the "Test Cancelled" box** (Step 6) on Copy 2 of the CCF and enter the reason on the "Remarks" line.

(b) **Report to the DER that the test is cancelled** and the reason for cancellation, and that no further action is required unless a negative test is required (e.g., in the case of a pre-employment, return-to-duty, or follow-up test).

(c) **You may only report a test cancelled** because of a rejected for testing test result when you are in possession of a legible copy of Copy 1 of the CCF. In addition, you must have Copy 2 of the CCF, a legible copy of it, or any other copy of the CCF containing the employee's signature.

§40.163 How does the MRO report drug test results?

(a) **As the MRO,** it is your responsibility to report all drug test results to the employer.

(b) **You may use a signed or stamped and dated** legible photocopy of Copy 2 of the CCF to report test results.

(c) **If you do not report test results using Copy 2** of the CCF for this purpose, you must provide a written report (e.g., a letter) for each test result. This report must, as a minimum, include the following information:

 (1) *Full name, as indicated on the CCF, of the employee tested;*

 (2) *Specimen ID number from the CCF* and the donor SSN or employee ID number;

 (3) *Reason for the test, if indicated on the CCF* (e.g., random, post-accident);

 (4) *Date of the collection;*

 (5) *Date you received Copy 2 of the CCF;*

 (6) *Result of the test* (i.e., positive, negative, dilute, refusal to test, test cancelled) and the date the result was verified by the MRO;

 (7) *For verified positive tests,* the drug(s)/metabolite(s) for which the test was positive;

 (8) *For cancelled tests, the reason for cancellation; and*

 (9) *For refusals to test,* the reason for the refusal determination (e.g., in the case of an adulterated test result, the name of the adulterant).

(d) **As an exception to the reporting requirements** of paragraph (b) and (c) of this section, the MRO may report negative results using an electronic data file.

 (1) *If you report negatives* using an electronic data file, the report must contain, as a minimum, the information specified in paragraph (c) of this section, as applicable for negative test results.

 (2) *In addition,* the report must contain your name, address, and phone number, the name of any person other than you reporting the results, and the date the electronic results report is released.

(e) **You must retain a signed or stamped and dated copy** of Copy 2 of the CCF in your records. If you do not use Copy 2 for reporting results, you must maintain a copy of the signed or stamped and dated letter in addition to the signed or stamped and dated Copy 2. If you use the electronic data file to report negatives, you must maintain a retrievable copy of that report in a format suitable for inspection and auditing by a DOT representative.

(f) **You must not use Copy 1 of the CCF to report drug test results.**

(g) You must not provide quantitative values to the DER or C/TPA for drug or validity test results. However, you must provide the test information in your possession to a SAP who consults with you (see §40.293(g)).

§40.163 DOT Interpretations

Question 1: Is it acceptable for an MRO to transmit a number of reports of drug test results per page to the employer, rather than one per page?

Guidance: The Department recommends that MROs use Copy 2 of the CCF as the means of reporting all drug test results to employers. However, if you use a written report (all results) or an electronic report (negative results) meeting all the requirements of §40.163, rather than using Copy 2 of the CCF for this purpose, you must put only one such report on each page. This will help to prevent inadvertent breaches of confidentiality by the employer resulting from photocopying a multiple-result report and putting a copy in the file of each employee involved.

Question 2: If the MRO uses a written report instead of a copy of the CCF to report results to employers, how should those reports be signed?

Guidance: The MRO must sign all reports of non-negative results (i.e., positives, refusals, tests canceled, and invalids).

The MRO or an MRO's staff member may rubber stamp and initial negative results. The rubber stamp should identify the MRO.

Each written report should be dated and indicate the address of the MRO.

Question 3: May the MRO report an "interim" or "preliminary" test result to the employer (or C/TPA) while awaiting receipt of the MRO copy and/or the laboratory result?

Guidance: No. An MRO must not report tests results until and unless he or she has received all required information from the collection site and laboratory.

This means the MRO must have Copy 2 or a legible copy of Copy 2 (or any legible copy of a CCF page signed by the employee) and must have the drug test result (sent in the appropriate manners for negatives and non-negatives) from the laboratory.

An MRO sending "in-progress" negative or non-negative results will be considered to be in violation of Part 40.

§40.165 To whom does the MRO transmit reports of drug test results?

(a) As the MRO, you must report all drug test results to the DER, except in the circumstances provided for in §40.345.

(b) If the employer elects to receive reports of results through a C/TPA, acting as an intermediary as provided in §40.345, you must report the results through the designated C/TPA.

§40.167 How are MRO reports of drug results transmitted to the employer?

As the MRO or C/TPA who transmits drug test results to the employer, you must comply with the following requirements:

(a) You must report the results in a confidential manner.

(b) You must transmit to the DER on the same day the MRO verifies the result or the next business day all verified positive test results, results requiring an immediate collection under direct observation, adulterated or substituted specimen results, and other refusals to test.

  (1) *Direct telephone contact with the DER* is the preferred method of immediate reporting. Follow up your phone call with appropriate documentation (see §40.163).

  (2) *You are responsible* for identifying yourself to the DER, and the DER must have a means to confirm your identification.

  (3) *The MRO's report* that you transmit to the employer must contain all of the information required by §40.163.

(c) You must transmit the MRO's report(s) of verified tests to the DER so that the DER receives it within two days of verification by the MRO.

  (1) *You must fax, courier, mail, or electronically transmit* a legible image or copy of either the signed or stamped and dated Copy 2 or the written report (see §40.163(b) and (c)).

  (2) *Negative results reported electronically* (i.e., computer data file) do not require an image of Copy 2 or the written report.

(d) In transmitting test results, you or the C/TPA and the employer must ensure the security of the transmission and limit access to any transmission, storage, or retrieval systems.

(e) MRO reports are not subject to modification or change by anyone other than the MRO, as provided in §40.149(c).

§40.169 Where is other information concerning the role of MROs and the verification process found in this regulation?

You can find more information concerning the role of MROs in several sections of this part:

§40.3 - Definition.
§§40.47-40.49 - Correction of form and kit errors.
§40.67 - Role in direct observation and other atypical test situations.
§40.83 - Laboratory handling of fatal and correctable flaws.
§40.97 - Laboratory handling of test results and quantitative values.
§40.99 - Authorization of longer laboratory retention of specimens.
§40.101 - Relationship with laboratories; avoidance of conflicts of interest.
§40.105 - Notification of discrepancies in blind specimen results.
§40.171 - Request for test of split specimen.
§40.187 - Action concerning split specimen test results.
§40.193 - Role in "shy bladder" situations.
§40.195 - Role in cancelling tests.
§§40.199-40.203 - Documenting errors in tests.
§40.327 - Confidentiality and release of information.
§40.347 - Transfer of records.
§40.353 - Relationships with service agents.

Subpart H - Split Specimen Tests

§40.171 How does an employee request a test of a split specimen?

(a) As an employee, when the MRO has notified you that you have a verified positive drug test or refusal to test because of adulteration or substitution, you have 72 hours from the time of notification to request a test of the split specimen. The request may be verbal or in writing. If you make this request to the MRO within 72 hours, you trigger the requirements of this section for a test of the split specimen.

(b) (1) *If, as an employee,* you have not requested a test of the split specimen within 72 hours, you may present to the MRO information documenting that serious injury, illness, lack of actual notice of the verified test result, inability to contact the MRO (e.g., there was no one in the MRO's office and the answering machine was not working), or other circumstances unavoidably prevented you from making a timely request.

  (2) *As the MRO,* if you conclude from the employee's information that there was a legitimate reason for the employee's failure to contact you within 72 hours, you must direct that the test of the split specimen take place, just as you would when there is a timely request.

(c) When the employee makes a timely request for a test of the split specimen under paragraphs (a) and (b) of this section, you must, as the MRO, immediately provide written notice to the laboratory that tested the primary specimen, directing the laboratory to forward the split specimen to a second HHS-certified laboratory. You must also document the date and time of the employee's request.

§40.171 DOT Interpretations

Question 1: Can someone other than the employee direct that an MRO have the employee's split specimen tested?

Guidance: No. Because the split specimen exists to provide the employee with "due process" in the event that he or she desires to challenge the primary specimen's results, only the employee can request that the split specimen be tested.

In addition, an employer or a union (or other labor representative) may not act on the behalf of the employee in requesting that the split specimen be tested.

The employee must make the request directly to the MRO.

Question 2: Can a split specimen be sent to a second laboratory that is under the same corporate title as the primary laboratory?

Guidance: Yes. The rule requires the split to be tested at a different or second HHS-certified laboratory. For example, if the primary specimen was tested at XYZ Laboratory in Dallas, TX, the split specimen may be sent to XYZ Laboratory in Chicago, IL.

HHS certifies each laboratory separately and on its own merits. Laboratories on the HHS listing of certified laboratories, even those under the same corporate title, are individually certified and are considered separate and unique from one another.

Question 3: Can the MRO require an employee's split specimen test request to be in writing rather than verbal?

Guidance: 40.171(a) states that the employee's request may be verbal or in writing. Therefore, the MRO <u>must</u> accept a verbal request.

The MRO may ask the employee for written documentation, but must immediately honor the verbal request.

An MRO should always document whether or not an employee requested to have the split tested.

The MRO must document the date and time of the employee's request.

§40.173 Who is responsible for paying for the test of a split specimen?

(a) **As the employer,** you are responsible for making sure (e.g., by establishing appropriate accounts with laboratories for testing split specimens) that the MRO, first laboratory, and second laboratory perform the functions noted in §§40.175-40.185 in a timely manner, once the employee has made a timely request for a test of the split specimen.

(b) **As the employer,** you must not condition your compliance with these requirements on the employee's direct payment to the MRO or laboratory or the employee's agreement to reimburse you for the costs of testing. For example, if you ask the employee to pay for some or all of the cost of testing the split specimen, and the employee is unwilling or unable to do so, you must ensure that the test takes place in a timely manner, even though this means that you pay for it.

(c) **As the employer,** you may seek payment or reimbursement of all or part of the cost of the split specimen from the employee (e.g., through your written company policy or a collective bargaining agreement). This part takes no position on who ultimately pays the cost of the test, so long as the employer ensures that the testing is conducted as required and the results released appropriately.

§40.175 What steps does the first laboratory take with a split specimen?

(a) **As the laboratory** at which the primary and split specimen first arrive, you must check to see whether the split specimen is available for testing.

(b) **If the split specimen is unavailable** or appears insufficient, you must then do the following:
  (1) *Continue the testing process* for the primary specimen as you would normally. Report the results for the primary specimen without providing the MRO information regarding the unavailable split specimen.
  (2) *Upon receiving a letter from the MRO* instructing you to forward the split specimen to another laboratory for testing, report to the MRO that the split specimen is unavailable for testing. Provide as much information as you can about the cause of the unavailability.

(c) **As the laboratory that tested the primary specimen,** you are not authorized to open the split specimen under any circumstances (except when the split specimen is redesignated as provided in §40.83).

(d) **When you receive written notice from the MRO** instructing you to send the split specimen to another HHS-certified laboratory, you must forward the following items to the second laboratory:
  (1) *The split specimen in its original specimen bottle,* with the seal intact;
  (2) *A copy of the MRO's written request;* and
  (3) *A copy of Copy 1 of the CCF,* which identifies the drug(s)/metabolite(s) or the validity criteria to be tested for.

(e) **You must not send to the second laboratory** any information about the identity of the employee. Inadvertent disclosure does not, however, cause a fatal flaw.

(f) **This subpart does not prescribe** who gets to decide which HHS-certified laboratory is used to test the split specimen. That decision is left to the parties involved.

§40.177 What does the second laboratory do with the split specimen when it is tested to reconfirm the presence of a drug or drug metabolite?

(a) **As the laboratory testing the split specimen,** you must test the split specimen for the drug(s)/drug metabolite(s) detected in the primary specimen.

(b) **You must conduct this test without regard** to the cutoff concentrations of §40.87.

(c) **If the test fails to reconfirm the presence** of the drug(s)/drug metabolite(s) that were reported positive in the primary specimen, you must conduct validity tests in an attempt to determine the reason for being unable to reconfirm the presence of the drug(s)/metabolite(s). You should conduct the same validity tests as you would conduct on a primary specimen set forth in §40.91.

(d) **In addition, if the test fails to reconfirm the presence** of the drugs/drugs metabolites or validity criteria that were reported in the primary specimen, you may transmit the specimen or an aliquot of it to another HHS-certified laboratory that will conduct another reconfirmation test.

§40.179 What does the second laboratory do with the split specimen when it is tested to reconfirm an adulterated test result?

As the laboratory testing the split specimen, you must test the split specimen for the adulterant detected in the primary specimen, using the criteria of §40.95 just as you would do for a primary specimen. The result of the primary specimen is reconfirmed if the split specimen meets these criteria.

§40.181 What does the second laboratory do with the split specimen when it is tested to reconfirm a substituted test result?

As the laboratory testing the split specimen, you must test the split specimen using the criteria of §40.93(b), just as you would do for a primary specimen. The result of the primary specimen is reconfirmed if the split specimen meets these criteria.

§40.183 What information do laboratories report to MROs regarding split specimen results?

(a) **As the laboratory responsible** for testing the split specimen, you must report split specimen test results by checking the "Reconfirmed" box or the "Failed to Reconfirm" box (Step 5(b)) on Copy 1 of the CCF.

(b) **If you check the "Failed to Reconfirm" box,** one of the following statements must be included (as appropriate) on the "Reason" line (Step 5(b)):
  (1) "Drug(s)/Drug Metabolite(s) Not Detected."
  (2) "Adulterant not found within criteria."
  (3) "Specimen not consistent with substitution criteria [specify creatinine, specific gravity, or both]."
  (4) "Specimen not available for testing."

(c) **As the laboratory certifying scientist,** enter your name, sign, and date the CCF.

§40.185 Through what methods and to whom must a laboratory report split specimen results?

(a) **As the laboratory testing the split specimen,** you must report laboratory results directly, and only, to the MRO at his or her place of business. You must not report results to or through the DER or another service agent (e.g., a C/TPA).

(b) **You must fax, courier, mail, or electronically transmit** a legible image or copy of the fully-completed Copy 1 of the CCF, which has been signed by the certifying scientist.

(c) **You must transmit the laboratory result** to the MRO immediately, preferably on the same day or next business day as the result is signed and released.

§40.187 What does the MRO do with split specimen laboratory results?

As an MRO, you must take the following actions when a laboratory reports the following results of split specimen tests:

(a) **Reconfirmed.**
  (1) *In the case of a reconfirmed* positive test for a drug or drug metabolite, report the reconfirmation to the DER and the employee.

(2) *In the case of a reconfirmed* adulterated or substituted result, report to the DER and the employee that the specimen was adulterated or substituted, either of which constitutes a refusal to test. Therefore, "refusal to test" is the final result.

(3) *In the case of a reconfirmed* substituted result, in which the creatinine concentration for the primary specimen was less than 2 mg/dL and the creatinine concentration of the split specimen is between 2 and 5 mg/DL, inclusive, report the result to the employer as "dilute" and instruct the employer to conduct an immediate recollection under direct observation.

(b) **Failed to Reconfirm: Drug(s)/Drug Metabolite(s) Not Detected.**
  (1) *Report to the DER and the employee* that both tests must be cancelled.
  (2) *Using the format in Appendix D to this part,* inform ODAPC of the failure to reconfirm.

(c) **Failed to Reconfirm:** Adulteration or Substitution (as appropriate) Criteria Not Met.
  (1) *Report to the DER and the employee* that both tests must be cancelled.
  (2) *Using the format in Appendix D to this part,* inform ODAPC of the failure to reconfirm.

(d) **Failed to Reconfirm: Specimen not Available for Testing.**
  (1) *Report to the DER and the employee* that both tests must be cancelled and the reason for cancellation.
  (2) *Direct the DER* to ensure the immediate collection of another specimen from the employee under direct observation, with no notice given to the employee of this collection requirement until immediately before the collection.
  (3) *Using the format in Appendix D to this part,* notify ODAPC of the failure to reconfirm.

(e) **Failed to Reconfirm: Specimen Results Invalid.**
  (1) *Report to the DER and the employee* that both tests must be cancelled and the reason for cancellation.
  (2) *Direct the DER* to ensure the immediate collection of another specimen from the employee under direct observation, with no notice given to the employee of this collection requirement until immediately before the collection.
  (3) *Using the format in Appendix D to this part,* notify ODAPC of the failure to reconfirm.

(f) **Failed to Reconfirm: Split Specimen Adulterated.**
  (1) *Contact the employee and inform the employee* that the laboratory has determined that his or her split specimen is adulterated.
  (2) *Follow the procedures of §40.145* to determine if there is a legitimate medical explanation for the laboratory finding of adulteration.
  (3) *If you determine* that there is a legitimate medical explanation for the adulterated test result, report to the DER and the employee that the test is cancelled. Using the format in Appendix D to this part, notify ODAPC of the result.
  (4) *If you determine* that there is not a legitimate medical explanation for the adulterated test result, take the following steps:
    (i) *Report the test to the DER* and the employee as a verified refusal to test. Inform the employee that he or she has 72 hours to request a test of the primary specimen to determine if the adulterant found in the split specimen also is present in the primary specimen.
    (ii) *Except that the request* is for a test of the primary specimen and is being made to the laboratory that tested the primary specimen, follow the procedures of §§40.153, 40.171, 40.173, 40.179, and 40.185.
    (iii) *As the laboratory that tests* the primary specimen to reconfirm the presence of the adulterant found in the split specimen, report your result to the MRO on a photocopy (faxed, mailed, scanned, couriered) of Copy 1 of the CCF.
    (iv) *If the test of the primary specimen* reconfirms the adulteration finding of the split specimen, as the MRO you must report the test result as a refusal as provided in §40.187(a)(2).
    (v) *If the test of the primary specimen* fails to reconfirm the adulteration finding of the split specimen, as the MRO you cancel the test. Follow the procedures of paragraph (e) of this section in this situation.

(g) **Enter your name, sign and date (Step 7) of Copy 2 of the CCF.**

(h) **Send a legible copy of Copy 2 of the CCF** (or a signed and dated letter, see §40.163) to the employer and keep a copy for your records. Transmit the document as provided in §40.167.

§40.187 DOT Interpretations

Question 1: What must an MRO do when he or she determines that there is no split laboratory capable of testing the adulterant identified by the primary laboratory after the employee has asked for the split to be tested?

Guidance:

The department views this situation as closely paralleling the MRO reporting requirement, at §40.187(d), when the split specimen is not available for testing after the request to test the split is made by the employee. Therefore, the MRO needs to follow similar steps.

- The MRO must report to the employer that the specimen, "Failed to Reconfirm: Split Laboratory not Available for Testing."
- The MRO must also report to the DER and the employee that the test result must be cancelled and the reason for the cancellation.
- The MRO must direct the DER to ensure the immediate collection of another specimen from the employee under direct observation, with no notice give to the employee of this collection requirement until immediately before the collection.
- Finally, the MRO must notify ODAPC of the failure to reconfirm.

The result of the collection under direct observation will be the result of record for this testing event.

§40.189 Where is other information concerning split specimens found in this regulation?

You can find more information concerning split specimens in several sections of this part:

§40.3 - Definition.
§40.65 - Quantity of split specimen.
§40.67 - Directly observed test when split specimen is unavailable.
§§40.71-40.73 - Collection process for split specimens.
§40.83 - Laboratory accessioning of split specimens.
§40.99 - Laboratory retention of split specimens
§40.103 - Blind split specimens.
§40.153 - MRO notice to employees on tests of split specimen.
§§40.193 and 40.201 - MRO actions on insufficient or unavailable split specimens.
Appendix D to Part 40 - Report format for split specimen failure to reconfirm.

Subpart I - Problems in Drug Tests

§40.191 What is a refusal to take a DOT drug test, and what are the consequences?

(a) **As an employee, you have refused to take a drug test if you:**
  (1) *Fail to appear for any test* (except a pre-employment test) within a reasonable time, as determined by the employer, consistent with applicable DOT agency regulations, after being directed to do so by the employer. This includes the failure of an employee (including an owner-operator) to appear for a test when called by a C/TPA (see §40.61(a));
  (2) *Fail to remain at the testing site* until the testing process is complete; provided, that an employee who leaves the testing site before the testing process commences (see §40.63(c)) for a pre-employment test is not deemed to have refused to test;
  (3) *Fail to provide a urine specimen* for any drug test required by this part or DOT agency regulations; provided, that an employee who does not provide a urine specimen because he or she has left the testing site before the testing process commences (see §40.63(c)) for a pre-employment test is not deemed to have refused to test;
  (4) *In the case* of a directly observed or monitored collection in a drug test, fail to permit the observation or monitoring of your provision of a specimen (see §§40.67(l) and 40.69(g));
  (5) *Fail to provide* a sufficient amount of urine when directed, and it has been determined, through a required medical evaluation, that there was no adequate medical explanation for the failure (see §40.193(d)(2));
  (6) *Fail or decline to take an additional drug test* the employer or collector has directed you to take (see, for instance, §40.197(b));

Subpart I - Problems in Drug Tests §40.193 (i)

(7) *Fail to undergo* a medical examination or evaluation, as directed by the MRO as part of the verification process, or as directed by the DER under § 40.193(d). In the case of a pre-employment drug test, the employee is deemed to have refused to test on this basis only if the pre-employment test is conducted following a contingent offer of employment. If there was no contingent offer of employment, the MRO will cancel the test; or

(8) *Fail to cooperate* with any part of the testing process (e.g., refuse to empty pockets when so directed by the collector, behave in a confrontational way that disrupts the collection process).

(b) **As an employee,** if the MRO reports that you have a verified adulterated or substituted test result, you have refused to take a drug test.

(c) **As an employee,** if you refuse to take a drug test, you incur the consequences specified under DOT agency regulations for a violation of those DOT agency regulations.

(d) **As a collector or an MRO,** when an employee refuses to participate in the part of the testing process in which you are involved, you must terminate the portion of the testing process in which you are involved, document the refusal on the CCF (including, in the case of the collector, printing the employee's name on Copy 2 of the CCF), immediately notify the DER by any means (e.g., telephone or secure fax machine) that ensures that the refusal notification is immediately received. As a referral physician (e.g., physician evaluating a "shy bladder" condition or a claim of a legitimate medical explanation in a validity testing situation), you must notify the MRO, who in turn will notify the DER.

(1) *As the collector,* you must note the refusal in the "Remarks" line (Step 2), and sign and date the CCF.

(2) *As the MRO,* you must note the refusal by checking the "refused to test because" box (Step 6) on Copy 2 of the CCF, and add the reason on the "Remarks" line. You must then sign and date the CCF.

(e) **As an employee,** when you refuse to take a non-DOT test or to sign a non-DOT form, you have not refused to take a DOT test. There are no consequences under DOT agency regulations for refusing to take a non-DOT test.

§§40.191 and 40.193 DOT Interpretations

Question 1: Do collectors sign the CCF in situations in which a urine specimen is not provided during a collection (i.e., a refusal to provide a specimen; a shy bladder situation)?

Guidance: In any such case, the collector would check the box in Step 2 of the CCF indicating that no specimen was provided and enter an explanatory remark.

The collector would then provide his or her name and signature in Step 4 of the CCF.

The employee's name and phone number should be included on the MRO copy.

The collector would then transmit the CCF copies to the appropriate parties (e.g., employer, MRO).

§40.193 What happens when an employee does not provide a sufficient amount of urine for a drug test?

(a) **This section prescribes procedures for situations** in which an employee does not provide a sufficient amount of urine to permit a drug test (i.e., 45 mL of urine).

(b) **As the collector, you must do the following:**

(1) *Discard the insufficient specimen,* except where the insufficient specimen was out of temperature range or showed evidence of adulteration or tampering (see §40.65(b) and (c)).

(2) *Urge the employee to drink* up to 40 ounces of fluid, distributed reasonably through a period of up to three hours, or until the individual has provided a sufficient urine specimen, whichever occurs first. It is not a refusal to test if the employee declines to drink. Document on the Remarks line of the CCF (Step 2), and inform the employee of, the time at which the three-hour period begins and ends.

(3) *If the employee refuses to make the attempt* to provide a new urine specimen or leaves the collection site before the collection process is complete, you must discontinue the collection, note the fact on the "Remarks" line of the CCF (Step 2), and immediately notify the DER. This is a refusal to test.

(4) *If the employee has not provided* a sufficient specimen within three hours of the first unsuccessful attempt to provide the specimen, you must discontinue the collection, note the fact on the "Remarks" line of the CCF (Step 2), and immediately notify the DER.

(5) *Send Copy 2 of the CCF to the MRO* and Copy 4 to the DER. You must send or fax these copies to the MRO and DER within 24 hours or the next business day.

(c) **As the DER, when the collector informs you** that the employee has not provided a sufficient amount of urine (see paragraph (b)(4) of this section), you must, after consulting with the MRO, direct the employee to obtain, within five days, an evaluation from a licensed physician, acceptable to the MRO, who has expertise in the medical issues raised by the employee's failure to provide a sufficient specimen. (The MRO may perform this evaluation if the MRO has appropriate expertise.)

(1) *As the MRO,* if another physician will perform the evaluation, you must provide the other physician with the following information and instructions:

(i) *That the employee* was required to take a DOT drug test, but was unable to provide a sufficient amount of urine to complete the test;

(ii) *The consequences* of the appropriate DOT agency regulation for refusing to take the required drug test;

(iii) *That the referral physician* must agree to follow the requirements of paragraphs (d) through (g) of this section.

(2) [Reserved]

(d) **As the referral physician conducting this evaluation,** you must recommend that the MRO make one of the following determinations:

(1) *A medical condition has,* or with a high degree of probability could have, precluded the employee from providing a sufficient amount of urine. As the MRO, if you accept this recommendation, you must:

(i) Check "Test Cancelled" (Step 6) on the CCF; and

(ii) Sign and date the CCF.

(2) *There is not an adequate basis* for determining that a medical condition has, or with a high degree of probability could have, precluded the employee from providing a sufficient amount of urine. As the MRO, if you accept this recommendation, you must:

(i) Check "Refusal to test because" (Step 6) on the CCF and enter reason in the remarks line; and

(ii) Sign and date the CCF.

(e) **For purposes of this paragraph,** a medical condition includes an ascertainable physiological condition (e.g., a urinary system dysfunction) or a medically documented pre-existing psychological disorder, but does not include unsupported assertions of "situational anxiety" or dehydration.

(f) **As the referral physician making the evaluation,** after completing your evaluation, you must provide a written statement of your recommendations and the basis for them to the MRO. You must not include in this statement detailed information on the employee's medical condition beyond what is necessary to explain your conclusion.

(g) **If, as the referral physician making this evaluation** in the case of a pre-employment test, you determine that the employee's medical condition is a serious and permanent or long-term disability that is highly likely to prevent the employee from providing a sufficient amount of urine for a very long or indefinite period of time, you must set forth your determination and the reasons for it in your written statement to the MRO. As the MRO, upon receiving such a report, you must follow the requirements of §40.195, where applicable.

(h) **As the MRO,** you must seriously consider and assess the referral physician's recommendations in making your determination about whether the employee has a medical condition that has, or with a high degree of probability could have, precluded the employee from providing a sufficient amount of urine. You must report your determination to the DER in writing as soon as you make it.

(i) **As the employer,** when you receive a report from the MRO indicating that a test is cancelled as provided in paragraph (d)(1) of this section, you take no further action with respect to the employee. The employee remains in the random testing pool.

§§40.73 and 40.193 DOT Interpretations
Question 1: What is the preferred method for the collector to get the MRO copy of the CCF to the MRO?
Guidance: The promptness of reporting suffers when the mail is used to convey the MRO copy from the collection site.

Even though we permit other means (e.g., overnight courier service) of transmitting MRO copies from the collection site to the MRO, collectors should fax the MRO copies when possible.

If the faxed copy is not legible, the MRO must request another faxed copy or a hard copy.

§§40.191 and 40.193 DOT Interpretations
Question 1: Do collectors sign the CCF in situations in which a urine specimen is not provided during a collection (i.e., a refusal to provide a specimen; a shy bladder situation)?
Guidance: In any such case, the collector would check the box in Step 2 of the CCF indicating that no specimen was provided and enter an explanatory remark.

The collector would then provide his or her name and signature in Step 4 of the CCF.

The employee's name and phone number should be included on the MRO copy.

The collector would then transmit the CCF copies to the appropriate parties (e.g., employer, MRO).

§§40.193 and 40.43 DOT Interpretations
Question 1: Generally, only one collector is supposed to supervise a collection for an employee. However, given the time span involved, it is possible that two collectors could be involved in a shy bladder collection (e.g., because of a shift change during the three-hour period between the first and second collection attempts). How should this be handled?
Guidance: In this situation, it is permissible for one collector to turn the process over to another collector to complete the collection.

The first collector would document the start time for the 3-hour period. The second would provide his or her name and signature after the second collection, as the collector of record. The Remarks line (Step 2 of the CCF) would be used to document the transition (including the first collector's name and the start time for the shy bladder procedure).

§§40.193 and 40.265 DOT Interpretations
Question 1: Do the five days within which an employee is given to obtain a medical evaluation after providing an insufficient amount of urine or breath include holidays and weekends, or does this refer to five business days?
Guidance: The five-day limit for obtaining an examination by a licensed physician refers to business days.

Therefore, holidays and weekend days should not be included in the 5-day time frame.

§40.195 What happens when an individual is unable to provide a sufficient amount of urine for a pre-employment, follow-up or return-to-duty test because of a permanent or long-term medical condition?

(a) **This section concerns a situation** in which an employee has a medical condition that precludes him or her from providing a sufficient specimen for a pre-employment follow-up or return-to-duty test and the condition involves a permanent or long-term disability. As the MRO in this situation, you must do the following:
  (1) *You must determine* if there is clinical evidence that the individual is an illicit drug user. You must make this determination by personally conducting, or causing to be conducted, a medical evaluation and through consultation with the employee's physician and/or the physician who conducted the evaluation under §40.193(d).
  (2) *If you do not personally conduct* the medical evaluation, you must ensure that one is conducted by a licensed physician acceptable to you.
  (3) *For purposes of this section,* the MRO or the physician conducting the evaluation may conduct an alternative test (e.g., blood) as part of the medically appropriate procedures in determining clinical evidence of drug use.
(b) **If the medical evaluation reveals** no clinical evidence of drug use, as the MRO, you must report the result to the employer as a negative test with written notations regarding results of both the evaluation conducted under §40.193(d) and any further medical examination. This report must state the basis for the determination that a permanent or long-term medical condition exists, making provision of a sufficient urine specimen impossible, and for the determination that no signs and symptoms of drug use exist.
  (1) *Check "Negative" (Step 6) on the CCF.*
  (2) *Sign and date the CCF.*
(c) **If the medical evaluation reveals** clinical evidence of drug use, as the MRO, you must report the result to the employer as a cancelled test with written notations regarding results of both the evaluation conducted under §40.193(d) and any further medical examination. This report must state that a permanent or long-term medical condition exists, making provision of a sufficient urine specimen impossible, and state the reason for the determination that signs and symptoms of drug use exist. Because this is a cancelled test, it does not serve the purposes of a negative test (i.e., the employer is not authorized to allow the employee to begin or resume performing safety-sensitive functions, because a negative test is needed for that purpose).
(d) **For purposes of this section,** permanent or long-term medical conditions are those physiological, anatomic, or psychological abnormalities documented as being present prior to the attempted collection, and considered not amenable to correction or cure for an extended period of time, if ever.
  (1) *Examples would include destruction* (any cause) of the glomerular filtration system leading to renal failure; unrepaired traumatic disruption of the urinary tract; or a severe psychiatric disorder focused on genito-urinary matters.
  (2) *Acute or temporary medical conditions,* such as cystitis, urethritis or prostatitis, though they might interfere with collection for a limited period of time, cannot receive the same exceptional consideration as the permanent or long-term conditions discussed in paragraph (d)(1) of this section.

§40.197 What happens when an employer receives a report of a dilute specimen?
(a) **As the employer,** if the MRO informs you that a positive drug test was dilute, you simply treat the test as a verified positive test. You must not direct the employee to take another test based on the fact that the specimen was dilute.
(b) **As an employer,** if the MRO informs you that a negative test was dilute, take the following action:
  (1) *If the MRO directs you* to conduct a recollection under direct observation (i.e., because the creatinine concentration of the specimen was equal to or greater than 2 mg/dL, but less than or equal to 5 mg/dL (see §40.155(c)), you must do so immediately.
  (2) *Otherwise* (i.e., if the creatinine concentration of the dilute specimen is greater than 5 mg/dL), you may, but are not required to, direct the employee to take another test immediately.
    (i) *Such recollections must not be collected* under direct observation, unless there is another basis for use of direct observation (see §40.67(b) and (c)).
    (ii) *You must treat all employees the same* for this purpose. For example, you must not retest some employees and not others. You may, however, establish different policies for different types of tests (e.g., conduct retests in pre-employment situations, but not in random test situations). You must inform your employees in advance of your decisions on these matters.
(c) **The following provisions** apply to all tests you direct an employee to take under paragraph (b) of this section:
  (1) *You must ensure* that the employee is given the minimum possible advance notice that he or she must go to the collection site;
  (2) *You must treat the result* of the test you directed the employee to take under paragraph (b) of this section — and not a prior test — as the test result of record, on which you rely for purposes of this part;
  (3) *If the result of the test* you directed the employee to take under paragraph (b) of this section is also negative and dilute, you are not permitted to make the employee take an additional test because the result was dilute. Provided, however, that if the MRO directs you to conduct a recollection

under direct observation under paragraph (b)(1) of this section, you must immediately do so.

(4) *If the employee declines to take a test* you directed him or her to take under paragraph (b) of this section, the employee has refused the test for purposes of this part and DOT agency regulations.

§40.197 DOT Interpretations

Question 1: May an employer have a policy of declining to hire applicants who have a negative dilute test result on a pre-employment drug test?

Guidance: The Department's rules do not require an employer to hire anyone. That decision is an employer's.

While §40.197(b) authorizes an employer to obtain one additional test following a negative dilute result (in pre-employment or other testing situations), a negative dilute test result is a valid negative test for DOT's purposes.

Because a negative dilute test result is a negative test for DOT program purposes, the employer is authorized to have the applicant begin performing safety-sensitive functions.

If the employer declines to hire the applicant in this situation, the employer's decision is based solely on its own policy. The employer cannot claim that its action is required or authorized by DOT rules.

§40.199 What problems always cause a drug test to be cancelled?

(a) **As the MRO,** when the laboratory discovers a "fatal flaw" during its processing of incoming specimens (see §40.83), the laboratory will report to you that the specimen has been "Rejected for Testing" (with the reason stated). You must always cancel such a test.

(b) **The following are "fatal flaws":**
   (1) *There is no printed collector's name and no collector's signature;*
   (2) *The specimen ID numbers* on the specimen bottle and the CCF do not match;
   (3) *The specimen bottle seal is broken* or shows evidence of tampering (and a split specimen cannot be redesignated, see §40.83(g)); and
   (4) *Because of leakage or other causes,* there is an insufficient amount of urine in the primary specimen bottle for analysis and the specimens cannot be redesignated (see §40.83(g)).

(c) **You must report the result as provided in §40.161.**

§40.201 What problems always cause a drug test to be cancelled and may result in a requirement for another collection?

As the MRO, you must cancel a drug test when a laboratory reports that any of the following problems have occurred. You must inform the DER that the test was cancelled. You must also direct the DER to ensure that an additional collection occurs immediately, if required by the applicable procedures specified in paragraphs (a) through (e) of this section.

(a) **The laboratory reports an "Invalid Result."** You must follow applicable procedures in §40.159 (recollection under direct observation may be required).

(b) **The laboratory reports the result** as "Rejected for Testing." You must follow applicable procedures in §40.161 (a recollection may be required).

(c) **The laboratory's test of the primary specimen** is positive and the split specimen is reported by the laboratory as "Failure to Reconfirm: Drug(s)/Drug Metabolite(s) Not Detected." You must follow applicable procedures in §40.187(b) (no recollection is required in this case).

(d) **The laboratory's test result** for the primary specimen is adulterated or substituted and the split specimen is reported by the laboratory as "Adulterant not found within criteria," or "specimen not consistent with substitution criteria," as applicable. You must follow applicable procedures in §40.187(c) (no recollection is required in this case).

(e) **The laboratory's test of the primary specimen** is positive, adulterated, or substituted and the split specimen is unavailable for testing. You must follow applicable procedures in §40.187(d) (recollection under direct observation is required in this case).

(f) **The examining physician has determined** that there is an acceptable medical explanation of the employee's failure to provide a sufficient amount of urine. You must follow applicable procedures in §40.193(d)(1) (no recollection is required in this case).

§40.203 What problems cause a drug test to be cancelled unless they are corrected?

(a) **As the MRO,** when a laboratory discovers a "correctable flaw" during its processing of incoming specimens (see §40.83), the laboratory will attempt to correct it. If the laboratory is unsuccessful in this attempt, it will report to you that the specimen has been "Rejected for Testing" (with the reason stated).

(b) **The following is a "correctable flaw"** that laboratories must attempt to correct: The collector's signature is omitted on the certification statement on the CCF.

(c) **As the MRO,** when you discover a "correctable flaw" during your review of the CCF, you must cancel the test unless the flaw is corrected.

(d) **The following are correctable flaws** that you must attempt to correct:
   (1) *The employee's signature* is omitted from the certification statement, unless the employee's failure or refusal to sign is noted on the "Remarks" line of the CCF.
   (2) *The certifying scientist's signature* is omitted on the laboratory copy of the CCF for a positive, adulterated, substituted, or invalid test result.
   (3) *The collector uses a non-Federal form* or an expired Federal form for the test. This flaw may be corrected through the procedure set forth in §40.205(b)(2), provided that the collection testing process has been conducted in accordance with the procedures of this part in an HHS-certified laboratory. During the period August 1 - October 31, 2001, you are not required to cancel a test because of the use of an expired Federal form. Beginning November 1, 2001, if the problem is not corrected, you must cancel the test.

§40.203 DOT Interpretations

Question 1: If a collector makes an error on a CCF and the collector is not available to sign a corrective statement (e.g., collector on vacation, no longer with the company), can the collector's supervisor sign the corrective statement for the collector?

Guidance: If the error was the use of a non-DOT form (to include use of the old Federal CCF), the collector or the collector's supervisor may sign the corrective statement explaining the circumstances of why a non-DOT form was used.

If the missing information is the printed name and signature of the collector, neither the collector nor the supervisor may supply the missing information. This is a fatal, uncorrectable flaw.

If the CCF contains the printed name of the collector, but the signature is missing, the collector or the collector's supervisor may attest that collector performed the collection, but did not sign his or her name.

If the employee's signature is omitted and there is no notation in the "Remarks" line, only the collector can provide the corrective statement. The collector's supervisor cannot sign the corrective statement.

§40.205 How are drug test problems corrected?

(a) **As a collector, you have the responsibility** of trying to successfully complete a collection procedure for each employee.
   (1) *If, during or shortly after the collection process,* you become aware of any event that prevents the completion of a valid test or collection (e.g., a procedural or paperwork error), you must try to correct the problem promptly, if doing so is practicable. You may conduct another collection as part of this effort.
   (2) *If another collection is necessary,* you must begin the new collection procedure as soon as possible, using a new CCF and a new collection kit.

(b) **If, as a collector, laboratory, MRO, employer,** or other person implementing these drug testing regulations, you become aware of a problem that can be corrected (see §40.203), but which has not already been corrected under paragraph (a) of this section, you must take all practicable action to correct the problem so that the test is not cancelled.
   (1) *If the problem resulted* from the omission of required information, you must, as the person responsible for providing that information, supply in writing the missing information and a statement that it is true and accurate. For example, suppose you are a collector, and you forgot to make a notation on the "Remarks" line of the CCF that the employee did not sign the certification. You would, when the problem is called to your attention, supply a signed statement that the employee failed or refused to sign the certification and that your statement is

true and accurate. You must supply this information on the same business day on which you are notified of the problem, transmitting it by fax or courier.

(2) *If the problem* is the use of a non-Federal form or an expired Federal form, you must provide a signed statement (i.e., a memorandum for the record). It must state that the incorrect form contains all the information needed for a valid DOT drug test, and that the incorrect form was used inadvertently or as the only means of conducting a test, in circumstances beyond your control. The statement must also list the steps you have taken to prevent future use of non-Federal forms or expired Federal forms for DOT tests. For this flaw to be corrected, the test of the specimen must have occurred at a HHS-certified laboratory where it was tested consistent with the requirements of this part. You must supply this information on the same business day on which you are notified of the problem, transmitting it by fax or courier.

(3) *You must maintain the written documentation* of a correction with the CCF.

(4) *You must mark the CCF in such a way* (e.g., stamp noting correction) as to make it obvious on the face of the CCF that you corrected the flaw.

(c) **If the correction does not take place,** as the MRO you must cancel the test.

§40.207 What is the effect of a cancelled drug test?
(a) **A cancelled drug test is neither positive nor negative.**

(1) *As an employer,* you must not attach to a cancelled test the consequences of a positive test or other violation of a DOT drug testing regulation (e.g., removal from a safety-sensitive position).

(2) *As an employer,* you must not use a cancelled test for the purposes of a negative test to authorize the employee to perform safety-sensitive functions (i.e., in the case of a pre-employment, return-to-duty, or follow-up test).

(3) *However, as an employer,* you must not direct a recollection for an employee because a test has been cancelled, except in the situations cited in paragraph (a)(2) of this section or other provisions of this part that require another test to be conducted (e.g., §§40.159(a)(5) and 40.187(b)).

(b) **A cancelled test does not count toward compliance** with DOT requirements (e.g., being applied toward the number of tests needed to meet the employer's minimum random testing rate).

(c) **A cancelled DOT test does not provide a valid basis** for an employer to conduct a non-DOT test (i.e., a test under company authority).

§40.208 What problem requires corrective action but does not result in the cancellation of a test?
(a) **If, as a laboratory, collector, employer,** or other person implementing the DOT drug testing program, you become aware that the specimen temperature on the CCF was not checked and the "Remarks" line did not contain an entry regarding the temperature being out of range, you must take corrective action, including securing a memorandum for the record explaining the problem and taking appropriate action to ensure that the problem does not recur.

(b) **This error does not result in the cancellation of the test.**

(c) **As an employer or service agent, this error,** even though not sufficient to cancel a drug test result, may subject you to enforcement action under DOT agency regulations or Subpart R of this part.

§40.209 What procedural problems do not result in the cancellation of a test and do not require collection?
(a) **As a collector, laboratory, MRO, employer,** or other person administering the drug testing process, you must document any errors in the testing process of which you become aware, even if they are not considered problems that will cause a test to be cancelled as listed in this subpart. Decisions about the ultimate impact of these errors will be determined by other administrative or legal proceedings, subject to the limitations of paragraph (b) of this section.

(b) **No person concerned with the testing process** may declare a test cancelled based on an error that does not have a significant adverse effect on the right of the employee to have a fair and accurate test. Matters that do not result in the cancellation of a test include, but are not limited to, the following:

(1) *A minor administrative mistake* (e.g., the omission of the employee's middle initial, a transposition of numbers in the employee's social security number);

(2) *An error* that does not affect employee protections under this part (e.g., the collector's failure to add bluing agent to the toilet bowl, which adversely affects only the ability of the collector to detect tampering with the specimen by the employee);

(3) *The collection of a specimen* by a collector who is required to have been trained (see §40.33), but who has not met this requirement;

(4) *A delay in the collection process* (see §40.61(a));

(5) *Verification of a test result* by an MRO who has the basic credentials to be qualified as an MRO (see §40.121(a) through (b)) but who has not met training and/or documentation requirements (see §40.121(c) through (e));

(6) *The failure to directly observe or monitor* a collection that the rule requires or permits to be directly observed or monitored, or the unauthorized use of direct observation or monitoring for a collection;

(7) *The fact that a test was conducted in a facility* that does not meet the requirements of §40.41;

(8) *If the specific name of the courier on the CCF* is omitted or erroneous;

(9) *Personal identifying information* is inadvertently contained on the CCF (e.g., the employee signs his or her name on the laboratory copy); or

(10) *Claims that the employee was improperly selected for testing.*

(c) **As an employer or service agent,** these types of errors, even though not sufficient to cancel a drug test result, may subject you to enforcement action under DOT agency regulations or action under Subpart R of this part.

§§40.97 and 40.209 DOT Interpretations
Question 1: After the laboratory reports a test result, someone (e.g., the employer, a service agent) discovers that the CCF listed the wrong reason for the test (e.g., the CCF says the test was a pre-employment test when it was actually a random test). How is this corrected and by whom?

Guidance: This is another example of an error that does not have a significant adverse effect on the right of an employee to have a fair and accurate test (see §40.209).

The test is not cancelled as the result of such a mistake.

While concerned parties may wish to correct the faulty description of the reason for the test, Part 40 does not require a correction to be made.

Employers or their designated service agents should ensure that appropriate changes are documented (e.g., for MIS reporting purposes).

§§40.149 and 40.209 DOT Interpretations
Question 1: What is an employer to do if an arbitrator's decision claims to overturn the result of a DOT drug or alcohol test on grounds contrary to DOT regulations?

Guidance: There could be instances in which an arbitrator makes a decision that purports to cancel a DOT test for reasons that the DOT regulation does not recognize as valid.

For example, the arbitrator might make a decision based on disagreement with an MRO's judgment about a legitimate medical explanation (see §40.149) or on the basis of a procedural error that is not sufficient to cancel a test (see §40.209).

Such a test result remains valid under DOT regulations, notwithstanding the arbitrator's decision. Consequently, as a matter of Federal safety regulation, the employer must not return the employee to the performance of safety-sensitive functions until the employee has completed the return to duty process.

The employer may still be bound to implement the personnel policy outcome of the arbitrator's decision in such a case. This can result in hardship for the employer (e.g., being required to pay an individual at the same time as the Department's rules prevent the individual from performing the duties of his job).

Subpart J - Alcohol Testing Personnel

§40.211 Who conducts DOT alcohol tests?
(a) **Screening test technicians (STTs)** and breath alcohol technicians (BATs) meeting their respective requirements of this subpart are the only people authorized to conduct DOT alcohol tests.

(b) **An STT can conduct only alcohol screening tests,** but a BAT can conduct alcohol screening and confirmation tests.

Subpart J - Alcohol Testing Personnel §40.217

(c) As a BAT- or STT-qualified immediate supervisor of a particular employee, you may not act as the STT or BAT when that employee is tested, unless no other STT or BAT is available and DOT agency regulations do not prohibit you from doing so.

§40.213 What training requirements must STTs and BATs meet?

To be permitted to act as a BAT or STT in the DOT alcohol testing program, you must meet each of the requirements of this section:

(a) *Basic information.* You must be knowledgeable about the alcohol testing procedures in this part and the current DOT guidance. These documents and information are available from ODAPC (Department of Transportation, 400 7th Street, SW., Room 10403, Washington DC, 20590, 202-366-3784, or on the ODAPC web site, *http://www.dot.gov/ost/dapc*).

(b) *Qualification training.* You must receive qualification training meeting the requirements of this paragraph (b).

   (1) *Qualification training must be in accordance* with the DOT Model BAT or STT Course, as applicable. The DOT Model Courses are available from ODAPC (Department of Transportation, 400 7th Street, SW., Room 10403, Washington DC, 20590, 202-366-3784, or on the ODAPC web site, *http://www.dot.gov/ost/dapc*). The training can also be provided using a course of instruction equivalent to the DOT Model Courses. On request, ODAPC will review BAT and STT instruction courses for equivalency.

   (2) *Qualification training must include* training to proficiency in using the alcohol testing procedures of this part and in the operation of the particular alcohol testing device(s) (i.e., the ASD(s) or EBT(s)) you will be using.

   (3) *The training must emphasize* that you are responsible for maintaining the integrity of the testing process, ensuring the privacy of employees being tested, and avoiding conduct or statements that could be viewed as offensive or inappropriate.

   (4) *The instructor must be an individual* who has demonstrated necessary knowledge, skills, and abilities by regularly conducting DOT alcohol tests as an STT or BAT, as applicable, for a period of at least a year, who has conducted STT or BAT training, as applicable, under this part for a year, or who has successfully completed a "train the trainer" course.

(c) *Initial Proficiency Demonstration.* Following your completion of qualification training under paragraph (b) of this section, you must demonstrate proficiency in alcohol testing under this part by completing seven consecutive error-free mock tests (BATs) or five consecutive error-free tests (STTs).

   (1) *Another person* must monitor and evaluate your performance, in person or by a means that provides real-time observation and interaction between the instructor and trainee, and attest in writing that the mock collections are "error-free." This person must be an individual who meets the requirements of paragraph (b)(4) of this section.

   (2) *These tests must use* the alcohol testing devices (e.g., EBT(s) or ASD(s)) that you will use as a BAT or STT.

   (3) *If you are an STT who will be using an ASD* that indicates readings by changes, contrasts, or other readings in color, you must demonstrate as part of the mock test that you are able to discern changes, contrasts, or readings correctly.

(d) *Schedule for qualification training* and initial proficiency demonstration. The following is the schedule for qualification training and the initial proficiency demonstration you must meet:

   (1) *If you became a BAT or STT* before August 1, 2001, you were required to have met the requirements set forth in paragraphs (b) and (c) of this section, and you do not have to meet them again.

   (2) *If you become a BAT or STT* on or after August 1, 2001, you must meet the requirements of paragraphs (b) and (c) of this section before you begin to perform BAT or STT functions.

(e) *Refresher training.* No less frequently than every five years from the date on which you satisfactorily complete the requirements of paragraphs (b) and (c) of this section, you must complete refresher training that meets all the requirements of paragraphs (b) and (c) of this section. If you are a BAT or STT who completed qualification training before January 1, 1998, you are not required to complete refresher training until January 1, 2003.

(f) *Error Correction Training.* If you make a mistake in the alcohol testing process that causes a test to be cancelled (i.e., a fatal or uncorrected flaw), you must undergo error correction training. This training must occur within 30 days of the date you are notified of the error that led to the need for retraining.

   (1) *Error correction training must be provided* and your proficiency documented in writing by a person who meets the requirements of paragraph (b)(4) of this section.

   (2) *Error correction training is required* to cover only the subject matter area(s) in which the error that caused the test to be cancelled occurred.

   (3) *As part of the error correction training,* you must demonstrate your proficiency in the alcohol testing procedures of this part by completing three consecutive error-free mock tests. The mock tests must include one uneventful scenario and two scenarios related to the area(s) in which your error(s) occurred. The person providing the training must monitor and evaluate your performance and attest in writing that the mock tests were error-free.

(g) *Documentation.* You must maintain documentation showing that you currently meet all requirements of this section. You must provide this documentation on request to DOT agency representatives and to employers and C/TPAs who are negotiating to use your services.

(h) *Other persons who may serve as BATs or STTs.*

   (1) *Anyone meeting the requirements* of this section to be a BAT may act as an STT, provided that the individual has demonstrated initial proficiency in the operation of the ASD that he or she is using, as provided in paragraph (c) of this section.

   (2) *Law enforcement officers* who have been certified by state or local governments to conduct breath alcohol testing are deemed to be qualified as BATs. They are not required to also complete the training requirements of this section in order to act as BATs. In order for a test conducted by such an officer to be accepted under DOT alcohol testing regulations, the officer must have been certified by a state or local government to use the EBT or ASD that was used for the test.

§40.213 DOT Interpretations

Question 1: Is error correction training required if an alcohol test is cancelled due to equipment failure?
Guidance: Normally, equipment failure will not require the BAT to have error correction training.
However, if it is determined that the equipment failure was related to the BAT's failure to properly maintain equipment (e.g., the EBT), error correction training would be in order.
In addition, error correction would be required if the BAT does not attempt to accomplish the test following equipment failure using another device – provided that another device was reasonably available.

§§40.33, 40.121, 40.213, 40.281 DOT Interpretations

Question 1: Because Part 40 requires collectors, MROs, BATs and STTs, and SAPs to maintain their own training records, can employers or training entities refuse to provide these service agents their training records?
Guidance: No. Employers and trainers who provide training for these service agents must not withhold training documentation from them when they have successfully completed the training requirements.
If a collector, BAT, STT, MRO, or SAP is not in possession of training documentation, he or she is in violation of Part 40.
Therefore, Part 40 does not permit the withholding of such documentation from these service agents.

§40.215 What information about the DER do employers have to provide to BATs and STTs?

As an employer, you must provide to the STTs and BATs the name and telephone number of the appropriate DER (and C/TPA, where applicable) to contact about any problems or issues that may arise during the testing process.

§40.217 Where is other information on the role of STTs and BATs found in this regulation?

You can find other information on the role and functions of STTs and BATs in the following sections of this part:

§40.3 - Definitions.
§40.223 - Responsibility for supervising employees being tested.
§§40.225-40.227 - Use of the alcohol testing form.
§§40.241-40.245 - Screening test procedures with ASDs and EBTs.
§§40.251-40.255 - Confirmation test procedures.

§40.261 - Refusals to test.
§§40.263-40.265 - Insufficient saliva or breath.
§40.267 - Problems requiring cancellation of tests.
§§40.269-40.271 - Correcting problems in tests.

Subpart K - Testing Sites, Forms, Equipment and Supplies Used in Alcohol Testing

§40.221 Where does an alcohol test take place?

(a) **A DOT alcohol test must take place** at an alcohol testing site meeting the requirements of this section.

(b) **If you are operating an alcohol testing site,** you must ensure that it meets the security requirements of §40.223.

(c) **If you are operating an alcohol testing site,** you must ensure that it provides visual and aural privacy to the employee being tested, sufficient to prevent unauthorized persons from seeing or hearing test results.

(d) **If you are operating an alcohol testing site,** you must ensure that it has all needed personnel, materials, equipment, and facilities to provide for the collection and analysis of breath and/or saliva samples, and a suitable clean surface for writing.

(e) **If an alcohol testing site fully meeting** all the visual and aural privacy requirements of paragraph (c) is not readily available, this part allows a reasonable suspicion or post-accident test to be conducted at a site that partially meets these requirements. In this case, the site must afford visual and aural privacy to the employee to the greatest extent practicable.

(f) **An alcohol testing site can be in a medical facility,** a mobile facility (e.g., a van), a dedicated collection facility, or any other location meeting the requirements of this section.

§40.223 What steps must be taken to protect the security of alcohol testing sites?

(a) **If you are a BAT, STT, or other person** operating an alcohol testing site, you must prevent unauthorized personnel from entering the testing site.
  (1) *The only people* you are to treat as authorized persons are employees being tested, BATs, STTs, and other alcohol testing site workers, DERs, employee representatives authorized by the employer (e.g., on the basis of employer policy or labor-management agreement), and DOT agency representatives.
  (2) *You must ensure* that all persons are under the supervision of a BAT or STT at all times when permitted into the site.
  (3) *You may remove any person* who obstructs, interferes with, or causes unnecessary delay in the testing process.

(b) **As the BAT or STT,** you must not allow any person other than you, the employee, or a DOT agency representative to actually witness the testing process (see §§40.241-40.255).

(c) **If you are operating an alcohol testing site,** you must ensure that when an EBT or ASD is not being used for testing, you store it in a secure place.

(d) **If you are operating an alcohol testing site,** you must ensure that no one other than BATs or other employees of the site have access to the site when an EBT is unsecured.

(e) **As a BAT or STT,** to avoid distraction that could compromise security, you are limited to conducting an alcohol test for only one employee at a time.
  (1) *When an EBT screening test on an employee* indicates an alcohol concentration of 0.02 or higher, and the same EBT will be used for the confirmation test, you are not allowed to use the EBT for a test on another employee before completing the confirmation test on the first employee.
  (2) *As a BAT who will conduct* both the screening and the confirmation test, you are to complete the entire screening and confirmation process on one employee before starting the screening process on another employee.
  (3) *You are not allowed* to leave the alcohol testing site while the testing process for a given employee is in progress, except to notify a supervisor or contact a DER for assistance in the case an employee or other person who obstructs, interferes with, or unnecessarily delays the testing process.

§40.225 What form is used for an alcohol test?

(a) **The DOT Alcohol Testing Form (ATF)** must be used for every DOT alcohol test beginning February 1, 2002. The ATF must be a three-part carbonless manifold form. The ATF is found in Appendix G to this part. You may view this form on the ODAPC web site (http://www.dot.gov/ost/dapc).

(b) **As an employer in the DOT alcohol testing program,** you are not permitted to modify or revise the ATF except as follows:
  (1) *You may include* other information needed for billing purposes, outside the boundaries of the form.
  (2) *You may use an ATF* directly generated by an EBT which omits the space for affixing a separate printed result to the ATF, provided the EBT prints the result directly on the ATF.
  (3) *You may use an ATF* that has the employer's name, address, and telephone number preprinted. In addition, a C/TPA's name, address, and telephone number may be included, to assist with negative results.
  (4) *You may use an ATF* in which all pages are printed on white paper. You may modify the ATF by using colored paper, or have clearly discernable borders or designation statements on Copy 2 and Copy 3. When colors are used, they must be green for Copy 2 and blue for Copy 3.
  (5) *As a BAT or STT,* you may add, on the "Remarks" line of the ATF, the name of the DOT agency under whose authority the test occurred.
  (6) *As a BAT or STT,* you may use a ATF that has your name, address, and telephone number preprinted, but under no circumstances can your signature be preprinted.

(c) **As an employer,** you may use an equivalent foreign-language version of the ATF approved by ODAPC. You may use such a non-English language form only in a situation where both the employee and BAT/STT understand and can use the form in that language.

§40.227 May employers use the ATF for non-DOT tests, or non-DOT forms for DOT tests?

(a) **No, as an employer, BAT, or STT,** you are prohibited from using the ATF for non-DOT alcohol tests. You are also prohibited from using non-DOT forms for DOT alcohol tests. Doing either subjects you to enforcement action under DOT agency regulations.

(b) **If the STT or BAT, either by mistake,** or as the only means to conduct a test under difficult circumstances (e.g., post-accident test with insufficient time to obtain the ATF), uses a non-DOT form for a DOT test, the use of a non-DOT form does not, in and of itself, require the employer or service agent to cancel the test. However, in order for the test to be considered valid, a signed statement must be obtained from the STT or BAT in accordance with §40.271(b).

§40.229 What devices are used to conduct alcohol screening tests?

EBTs and ASDs on the NHTSA conforming products lists (CPL) for evidential and non-evidential devices are the only devices you are allowed to use to conduct alcohol screening tests under this part. You may use an ASD that is on the NHTSA CPL for DOT alcohol tests only if there are instructions for its use in this part. An ASD can be used only for screening tests for alcohol, and may not be used for confirmation tests.

> **§§40.229 and 40.231 DOT Interpretations**
>
> *Question 1:* Is an employer considered to be in compliance with Part 40 if EBTs are not available within 30 minutes of an alcohol screening test location?
>
> *Guidance:* An employer is not considered to be in compliance if an EBT is not available for use within 30 minutes to confirm the screening test.
>
> However, there may exist unusual circumstances (e.g., post-accident testing) in which an EBT is not available within the appropriate time frame. In such a case, the employer would not be considered out of compliance with the regulation if documentation exists showing a "good faith" effort to get an EBT. [It is important to note that most operating administrations give employers up to 8 hours to administer the appropriate alcohol test following a qualifying accident.]

§40.231 What devices are used to conduct alcohol confirmation tests?

(a) **EBTs on the NHTSA CPL for evidential devices** that meet the requirements of paragraph (b) of this section are the only devices you may use to conduct alcohol confirmation tests under this part. Note that, among devices on the CPL for EBTs, only those devices listed without an asterisk (*) are authorized for use in confirmation testing in the DOT alcohol testing program.

Subpart L - Alcohol Screening Tests

§40.243 (e)

(b) To conduct a confirmation test, you must use an EBT that has the following capabilities:
  (1) *Provides a printed triplicate result* (or three consecutive identical copies of a result) of each breath test;
  (2) *Assigns a unique number* to each completed test, which the BAT and employee can read before each test and which is printed on each copy of the result;
  (3) *Prints, on each copy of the result,* the manufacturer's name for the device, its serial number, and the time of the test;
  (4) *Distinguishes alcohol from acetone* at the 0.02 alcohol concentration level;
  (5) *Tests an air blank;* and
  (6) *Performs an external calibration check*

§§40.229 and 40.231 DOT Interpretations

Question 1: Is an employer considered to be in compliance with Part 40 if EBTs are not available within 30 minutes of an alcohol screening test location?

Guidance: An employer is not considered to be in compliance if an EBT is not available for use within 30 minutes to confirm the screening test.

However, there may exist unusual circumstances (e.g., post-accident testing) in which an EBT is not available within the appropriate time frame. In such a case, the employer would not be considered out of compliance with the regulation if documentation exists showing a "good faith" effort to get an EBT. (It is important to note that most operating administrations give employers up to 8 hours to administer the appropriate alcohol test following a qualifying accident.)

§40.233 What are the requirements for proper use and care of EBTs?

(a) As an EBT manufacturer, you must submit, for NHTSA approval, a quality assurance plan (QAP) for your EBT before NHTSA places the EBT on the CPL.
  (1) *Your QAP must specify the methods used* to perform external calibration checks on the EBT, the tolerances within which the EBT is regarded as being in proper calibration, and the intervals at which these checks must be performed. In designating these intervals, your QAP must take into account factors like frequency of use, environmental conditions (e.g., temperature, humidity, altitude) and type of operation (e.g., stationary or mobile).
  (2) *Your QAP must also specify* the inspection, maintenance, and calibration requirements and intervals for the EBT.
(b) As the manufacturer, you must include, with each EBT, instructions for its use and care consistent with the QAP.
(c) As the user of the EBT (e.g., employer, service agent), you must do the following:
  (1) *You must follow the manufacturer's instructions* (see paragraph (b) of this section), including performance of external calibration checks at the intervals the instructions specify.
  (2) *In conducting external calibration checks,* you must use only calibration devices appearing on NHTSA's CPL for "Calibrating Units for Breath Alcohol Tests."
  (3) *If an EBT fails an external check of calibration,* you must take the EBT out of service. You may not use the EBT again for DOT alcohol testing until it is repaired and passes an external calibration check.
  (4) *You must maintain* records of the inspection, maintenance, and calibration of EBTs as provided in §40.333(a)(2).
  (5) *You must ensure* that inspection, maintenance, and calibration of the EBT are performed by its manufacturer or a maintenance representative certified either by the manufacturer or by a state health agency or other appropriate state agency.

§40.235 What are the requirements for proper use and care of ASDs?

(a) As an ASD manufacturer, you must submit, for NHTSA approval, a QAP for your ASD before NHTSA places the ASD on the CPL. Your QAP must specify the methods used for quality control checks, temperatures at which the ASD must be stored and used, the shelf life of the device, and environmental conditions (e.g., temperature, altitude, humidity) that may affect the ASD's performance.
(b) As a manufacturer, you must include with each ASD instructions for its use and care consistent with the QAP. The instructions must include directions on the proper use of the ASD, and, where applicable the time within which the device must be read, and the manner in which the reading is made.
(c) As the user of the ASD (e.g., employer, STT), you must follow the QAP instructions.
(d) You are not permitted to use an ASD that does not pass the specified quality control checks or that has passed its expiration date.
(e) As an employer, with respect to breath ASDs, you must also follow the device use and care requirements of §40.233.

Subpart L - Alcohol Screening Tests

§40.241 What are the first steps in any alcohol screening test?

As the BAT or STT you will take the following steps to begin all alcohol screening tests, regardless of the type of testing device you are using:

(a) When a specific time for an employee's test has been scheduled, or the collection site is at the employee's worksite, and the employee does not appear at the collection site at the scheduled time, contact the DER to determine the appropriate interval within which the DER has determined the employee is authorized to arrive. If the employee's arrival is delayed beyond that time, you must notify the DER that the employee has not reported for testing. In a situation where a C/TPA has notified an owner/operator or other individual employee to report for testing and the employee does not appear, the C/TPA must notify the employee that he or she has refused to test.

(b) Ensure that, when the employee enters the alcohol testing site, you begin the alcohol testing process without undue delay. For example, you must not wait because the employee says he or she is not ready or because an authorized employer or employee representative is delayed in arriving.
  (1) *If the employee* is also going to take a DOT drug test, you must, to the greatest extent practicable, ensure that the alcohol test is completed before the urine collection process begins.
  (2) *If the employee* needs medical attention (e.g., an injured employee in an emergency medical facility who is required to have a post-accident test), do not delay this treatment to conduct a test.

(c) Require the employee to provide positive identification. You must see a photo ID issued by the employer (other than in the case of an owner-operator or other self-employer individual) or a Federal, State, or local government (e.g., a driver's license). You may not accept faxes or photocopies of identification. Positive identification by an employer representative (not a co-worker or another employee being tested) is also acceptable. If the employee cannot produce positive identification, you must contact a DER to verify the identity of the employee.

(d) If the employee asks, provide your identification to the employee. Your identification must include your name and your employer's name but is not required to include your picture, address, or telephone number.

(e) Explain the testing procedure to the employee, including showing the employee the instructions on the back of the ATF.

(f) Complete Step 1 of the ATF.

(g) Direct the employee to complete Step 2 on the ATF and sign the certification. If the employee refuses to sign this certification, you must document this refusal on the "Remarks" line of the ATF and immediately notify the DER. This is a refusal to test.

§40.243 What is the procedure for an alcohol screening test using an EBT or non-evidential breath ASD?

As the BAT or STT, you must take the following steps:

(a) Select, or allow the employee to select, an individually wrapped or sealed mouthpiece from the testing materials.

(b) Open the individually wrapped or sealed mouthpiece in view of the employee and insert it into the device in accordance with the manufacturer's instructions.

(c) Instruct the employee to blow steadily and forcefully into the mouthpiece for at least six seconds or until the device indicates that an adequate amount of breath has been obtained.

(d) Show the employee the displayed test result.

(e) If the device is one that prints the test number, testing device name and serial number, time, and result directly onto the ATF, you must check to ensure that the information has been printed correctly onto the ATF.

(f) *If the device is one* that prints the test number, testing device name and serial number, time and result, but on a separate printout rather than directly onto the ATF, you must affix the printout of the information to the designated space on the ATF with tamper-evident tape or use a self-adhesive label that is tamper-evident.

(g) *If the device is one* that does not print the test number, testing device name and serial number, time, and result, or it is a device not being used with a printer, you must record this information in Step 3 of the ATF.

---

§§40.243, 40.253, 40.275, Appendix G to Part 40 DOT Interpretations

Question 1: Is it acceptable to affix printed alcohol test results on the back of the Alcohol Testing Form (ATF) rather than on the front?

Guidance: §§40.243(f) and 40.253(g) instruct the BAT to affix the printout of the information from the alcohol testing device to the designated space on the ATF.

The designated space on the ATF is on the front of the form. That is where BATs and STTs should affix the printouts.

However, because the instructions on the ATF also permit the printout to be affixed to the back of the ATF, the Department has no objections to having the printouts on the back of the ATF.

---

§40.245 What is the procedure for an alcohol screening test using a saliva ASD or a breath tube ASD?

(a) As the STT or BAT, you must take the following steps when using the saliva ASD:

(1) *Check the expiration date* on the device or on the package containing the device and show it to the employee. You may not use the device after its expiration date.

(2) *Open an individually wrapped* or sealed package containing the device in the presence of the employee.

(3) *Offer the employee the opportunity* to use the device. If the employee uses it, you must instruct the employee to insert it into his or her mouth and use it in a manner described by the device's manufacturer.

(4) *If the employee chooses not to use the device,* or in all cases in which a new test is necessary because the device did not activate (see paragraph (a)(7) of this section), you must insert the device into the employee's mouth and gather saliva in the manner described by the device's manufacturer. You must wear single-use examination or similar gloves while doing so and change them following each test.

(5) *When the device is removed* from the employee's mouth, you must follow the manufacturer's instructions regarding necessary next steps in ensuring that the device has activated.

(6) (i) *If you were unable* to successfully follow the procedures of paragraphs (a)(3) through (a)(5) of this section (e.g., the device breaks, you drop the device on the floor), you must discard the device and conduct a new test using a new device.

(ii) *The new device you use* must be one that has been under your control or that of the employee before the test.

(iii) *You must note on the "Remarks" line* of the ATF the reason for the new test. (Note: You may continue using the same ATF with which you began the test.)

(iv) *You must offer the employee* the choice of using the device or having you use it unless the employee, in the opinion of the STT or BAT, was responsible (e.g., the employee dropped the device) for the new test needing to be conducted.

(v) *If you are unable to successfully follow* the procedures of paragraphs (a)(3) through (a)(5) of this section on the new test, you must end the collection and put an explanation on the "Remarks" line of the ATF.

(vi) *You must then direct the employee* to take a new test immediately, using an EBT for the screening test.

(7) *If you are able to successfully follow* the procedures of paragraphs (a)(3) through (a)(5) of this section, but the device does not activate, you must discard the device and conduct a new test, in the same manner as provided in paragraph (a)(6) of this section. In this case, you must place the device into the employee's mouth to collect saliva for the new test.

(8) *You must read the result* displayed on the device no sooner than the device's manufacturer instructs. In all cases the result displayed must be read within 15 minutes of the test. You must then show the device and it's reading to the employee and enter the result on the ATF.

(9) *You must never re-use* devices, swabs, gloves or other materials used in saliva testing.

(10) *You must note the fact* that you used a saliva ASD in Step 3 of the ATF.

(b) As the STT or BAT, you must take the following steps when using the breath tube ASD:

(1) *Check the expiration date* on the detector device and the electronic analyzer or on the package containing the device and the analyzer and show it to the employee. You must not use the device or the analyzer after their expiration date. You must not use an analyzer which is not specifically precalibrated for the device being used in the collection.

(2) *Remove the device from the package* and secure an inflation bag onto the appropriate end of the device, as directed by the manufacturer on the device's instructions.

(3) *Break the tube's ampoule* in the presence of the employee.

(4) *Offer the employee the opportunity to use the device.* If the employee chooses to use (e.g. hold) the device, instruct the employee to blow forcefully and steadily into the blowing end of device until the inflation bag fills with air (approximately 12 seconds).

(5) *If the employee chooses not to hold the device,* you must hold it and provide the use instructions in paragraph (b)(4) of this section.

(6) *When the employee completes the breath process,* take the device from the employee (or if you were holding it, remove it from the employee's mouth), remove the inflation bag, and prepare the device to be read by the analyzer in accordance with the manufacturer's directions.

(7) (i) *If you were unable* to successfully follow the procedures of paragraphs (b)(4) through (b)(6) of this section (e.g., the device breaks apart, the employee did not fill the inflation bag), you must discard the device and conduct a new test using a new one.

(ii) *The new device you use* must be one that has been under your control or that of the employer before the test.

(iii) *You must note* on the "Remarks" line of the ATF the reason for the new test. (Note: You may continue using the same ATF with which you began the test.)

(iv) *You must offer the employee* the choice of holding the device or having you hold it unless the employee, in your opinion, was responsible (e.g., the employee failed to fill the inflation bag) for the new test needing to be conducted.

(v) *If you are unable to successfully follow* the procedures of paragraphs (b)(4) through (b)(6) of this section on the new test, you must end the collection and put an explanation on the "Remarks" line of the ATF.

(vi) *You must then direct the employee* to take a new test immediately, using another type of ASD (e.g., saliva device) or an EBT.

(8) *If you were able to successfully follow the procedures* of paragraphs (b)(4) through (b)(6) of this section and after having waited the required amount of time directed by the manufacturer for the detector device to incubate, you must place the device in the analyzer in accordance with the manufacturer's directions. The result must be read from the analyzer no earlier then the required incubation time of the device. In all cases, the result must be read within 15 minutes of the test.

(9) *You must follow the manufacturer's instructions* for determining the result of the test. You must show the analyzer result to the employee and record the result on Step 3 of the ATF.

(10) *You must never re-use detector devices* or any gloves used in breath tube testing. The inflation bag must be voided of air following removal from a device. Inflation bags and electronic analyzers may be re-used but only in accordance with the manufacturer's directions.

(11) *You must note the fact* that you used a breath tube device in Step 3 of the ATF.

§40.247 What procedures does the BAT or STT follow after a screening test result?

(a) If the test result is an alcohol concentration of less than 0.02, as the BAT or STT, you must do the following:

(1) *Sign and date Step 3 of the ATF;* and

(2) *Transmit the result to the DER* in a confidential manner, as provided in §40.255.

(b) If the test result is an alcohol concentration of 0.02 or higher, as the BAT or STT, you must direct the employee to take a confirmation test.

Subpart M - Alcohol Confirmation Tests

(1) *If you are the BAT* who will conduct the confirmation test, you must then conduct the test using the procedures beginning at §40.251.

(2) *If you are not the BAT* who will conduct the confirmation test, direct the employee to take a confirmation test, sign and date Step 3 of the ATF, and give the employee Copy 2 of the ATF.

(3) *If the confirmation test* will be performed at a different site from the screening test, you must take the following additional steps:

  (i) *Advise the employee* not to eat, drink, put anything (e.g., cigarette, chewing gum) into his or her mouth, or belch;

  (ii) *Tell the employee* the reason for the waiting period required by §40.251(a) (i.e., to prevent an accumulation of mouth alcohol from leading to an artificially high reading);

  (iii) *Explain that following your instructions* concerning the waiting period is to the employee's benefit;

  (iv) *Explain that the confirmation test* will be conducted at the end of the waiting period, even if the instructions have not been followed;

  (v) *Note on the "Remarks" line of the ATF* that the waiting period instructions were provided;

  (vi) *Instruct the person accompanying the employee* to carry a copy of the ATF to the BAT who will perform the confirmation test; and

  (vii) *Ensure that* you or another BAT, STT, or employer representative observe the employee as he or she is transported to the confirmation testing site. You must direct the employee not to attempt to drive a motor vehicle to the confirmation testing site.

(c) If the screening test is invalid, you must, as the BAT or STT, tell the employee the test is cancelled and note the problem on the "Remarks" line of the ATF. If practicable, repeat the testing process (see §40.271).

Subpart M - Alcohol Confirmation Tests

§40.251 What are the first steps in an alcohol confirmation test?

As the BAT for an alcohol confirmation test, you must follow these steps to begin the confirmation test process:

(a) You must carry out a requirement for a waiting period before the confirmation test, by taking the following steps:

(1) *You must ensure that the waiting period* lasts at least 15 minutes, starting with the completion of the screening test. After the waiting period has elapsed, you should begin the confirmation test as soon as possible, but not more than 30 minutes after the completion of the screening test.

  (i) *If the confirmation test* is taking place at a different location from the screening test (see §40.247(b)(3)) the time of transit between sites counts toward the waiting period if the STT or BAT who conducted the screening test provided the waiting period instructions.

  (ii) *If you cannot verify,* through review of the ATF, that waiting period instructions were provided, then you must carry out the waiting period requirement.

  (iii) *You or another BAT or STT,* or an employer representative, must observe the employee during the waiting period.

(2) *Concerning the waiting period, you must tell the employee:*

  (i) *Not to eat, drink, put anything* (e.g., cigarette, chewing gum) into his or her mouth, or belch;

  (ii) *The reason for the waiting period* (i.e., to prevent an accumulation of mouth alcohol from leading to an artificially high reading);

  (iii) *That following your instructions* concerning the waiting period is to the employee's benefit; and

  (iv) *That the confirmation test* will be conducted at the end of the waiting period, even if the instructions have not been followed.

(3) *If you become aware* that the employee has not followed the instructions, you must note this on the "Remarks" line of the ATF.

(b) If you did not conduct the screening test for the employee, you must require positive identification of the employee, explain the confirmation procedures, and use a new ATF. You must note on the "Remarks" line of the ATF that a different BAT or STT conducted the screening test.

(c) Complete Step 1 of the ATF.

(d) Direct the employee to complete Step 2 on the ATF and sign the certification. If the employee refuses to sign this certification, you must document this refusal on the "Remarks" line of the ATF and immediately notify the DER. This is a refusal to test.

(e) Even if more than 30 minutes have passed since the screening test result was obtained, you must begin the confirmation test procedures in §40.253, not another screening test.

(f) You must note on the "Remarks" line of the ATF the time that elapsed between the two events, and if the confirmation test could not begin within 30 minutes of the screening test, the reason why.

(g) Beginning the confirmation test procedures after the 30 minutes have elapsed does not invalidate the screening or confirmation tests, but it may constitute a regulatory violation subject to DOT agency sanction.

§40.253 What are the procedures for conducting an alcohol confirmation test?

As the BAT conducting an alcohol confirmation test, you must follow these steps in order to complete the confirmation test process:

(a) In the presence of the employee, you must conduct an air blank on the EBT you are using before beginning the confirmation test and show the reading to the employee.

(1) *If the reading is 0.00, the test may proceed.* If the reading is greater than 0.00, you must conduct another air blank.

(2) *If the reading on the second air blank is 0.00,* the test may proceed. If the reading is greater than 0.00, you must take the EBT out of service.

(3) *If you take an EBT out of service for this reason,* no one may use it for testing until the EBT is found to be within tolerance limits on an external check of calibration.

(4) *You must proceed* with the test of the employee using another EBT, if one is available.

(b) You must open a new individually wrapped or sealed mouthpiece in view of the employee and insert it into the device in accordance with the manufacturer's instructions.

(c) You must ensure that you and the employee read the unique test number displayed on the EBT.

(d) You must instruct the employee to blow steadily and forcefully into the mouthpiece for at least six seconds or until the device indicates that an adequate amount of breath has been obtained.

(e) You must show the employee the result displayed on the EBT.

(f) You must show the employee the result and unique test number that the EBT prints out either directly onto the ATF or onto a separate printout.

(g) If the EBT provides a separate printout of the result, you must attach the printout to the designated space on the ATF with tamper-evident tape, or use a self-adhesive label that is tamper-evident.

---

§§40.243, 40.253, 40.275, Appendix G to Part 40 DOT Interpretations

Question 1: Is it acceptable to affix printed alcohol test results on the back of the Alcohol Testing Form (ATF) rather than on the front?

Guidance: §§40.243(f) and 40.253(g) instruct the BAT to affix the printout of the information from the alcohol testing device to the designated space on the ATF.

The designated space on the ATF is on the front of the form. That is where BATs and STTs should affix the printouts.

However, because the instructions on the ATF also permit the printout to be affixed to the back of the ATF, the Department has no objections to having the printouts on the back of the ATF.

---

§40.255 What happens next after the alcohol confirmation test result?

(a) After the EBT has printed the result of an alcohol confirmation test, you must, as the BAT, take the following additional steps:

(1) *Sign and date Step 3 of the ATF.*

(2) *If the alcohol confirmation test result* is lower than 0.02, nothing further is required of the employee. As the BAT, you must sign and date Step 3 of the ATF.

(3) *If the alcohol confirmation test result* is 0.02 or higher, direct the employee to sign and date Step 4 of the ATF. If the employee does not do so, you must note this on the "Remarks" line of the ATF. However, this is not considered a refusal to test.

(4) *If the test is invalid,* tell the employee the test is cancelled and note the problem on the "Remarks" line of the ATF. If practicable, conduct a re-test. (see §40.271).

(5) *Immediately transmit the result* directly to the DER in a confidential manner.
  (i) *You may transmit the results* using Copy 1 of the ATF, in person, by telephone, or by electronic means. In any case, you must immediately notify the DER of any result of 0.02 or greater by any means (e.g., telephone or secure fax machine) that ensures the result is immediately received by the DER. You must not transmit these results through C/TPAs or other service agents.
  (ii) *If you do not make* the initial transmission in writing, you must follow up the initial transmission with Copy 1 of the ATF.
(b) **As an employer,** you must take the following steps with respect to the receipt and storage of alcohol test result information:
  (1) *If you receive any test results* that are not in writing (e.g., by telephone or electronic means), you must establish a mechanism to establish the identity of the BAT sending you the results.
  (2) *You must store all test result information* in a way that protects confidentiality.

Subpart N - Problems in Alcohol Testing

§40.261 What is a refusal to take an alcohol test, and what are the consequences?

(a) **As an employee,** you are considered to have refused to take an alcohol test if you:
  (1) *Fail to appear for any test* (except a pre-employment test) within a reasonable time, as determined by the employer, consistent with applicable DOT agency regulations, after being directed to do so by the employer. This includes the failure of an employee (including an owner-operator) to appear for a test when called by a C/TPA (see §40.241(a));
  (2) *Fail to remain at the testing site* until the testing process is complete; *Provided,* That an employee who leaves the testing site before the testing process commences (see §40.243(a)) for a pre-employment test is not deemed to have refused to test;
  (3) *Fail to provide* an adequate amount of saliva or breath for any alcohol test required by this part or DOT agency regulations; *Provided,* That an employee who does not provide an adequate amount of breath or saliva because he or she has left the testing site before the testing process commences (see §40.243(a)) for a pre-employment test is not deemed to have refused to test;
  (4) *Fail to provide a sufficient breath specimen,* and the physician has determined, through a required medical evaluation, that there was no adequate medical explanation for the failure (see §40.265(c));
  (5) *Fail to undergo* a medical examination or evaluation, as directed by the employer as part of the insufficient breath procedures outlined at §40.265(c);
  (6) *Fail to sign the certification* at Step 2 of the ATF (see §§40.241(g) and 40.251(d)); or
  (7) *Fail to cooperate with any part of the testing process.*
(b) **As an employee,** if you refuse to take an alcohol test, you incur the same consequences specified under DOT agency regulations for a violation of those DOT agency regulations.
(c) **As a BAT or an STT, or as the physician** evaluating a "shy lung" situation, when an employee refuses to test as provided in paragraph (a) of this section, you must terminate the portion of the testing process in which you are involved, document the refusal on the ATF (or in a separate document which you cause to be attached to the form), immediately notify the DER by any means (e.g., telephone or secure fax machine) that ensures the refusal notification is immediately received. You must make this notification directly to the DER (not using a C/TPA as an intermediary).
(d) **As an employee,** when you refuse to take a non-DOT test or to sign a non-DOT form, you have not refused to take a DOT test. There are no consequences under DOT agency regulations for such a refusal.

§40.263 What happens when an employee is unable to provide a sufficient amount of saliva for an alcohol screening test?

(a) **As the STT,** you must take the following steps if an employee is unable to provide sufficient saliva to complete a test on a saliva screening device (e.g., the employee does not provide sufficient saliva to activate the device).
  (1) *You must conduct* a new screening test using a new screening device.
  (2) *If the employee* refuses to make the attempt to complete the new test, you must discontinue testing, note the fact on the "Remarks" line of the ATF, and immediately notify the DER. This is a refusal to test.
  (3) *If the employee* has not provided a sufficient amount of saliva to complete the new test, you must note the fact on the "Remarks" line of the ATF and immediately notify the DER.
(b) **As the DER,** when the STT informs you that the employee has not provided a sufficient amount of saliva (see paragraph (a)(3) of this section), you must immediately arrange to administer an alcohol test to the employee using an EBT or other breath testing device.

§40.265 What happens when an employee is unable to provide a sufficient amount of breath for an alcohol test?

(a) *If an employee does not provide* a sufficient amount of breath to permit a valid breath test, you must take the steps listed in this section.
(b) **As the BAT or STT,** you must instruct the employee to attempt again to provide a sufficient amount of breath and about the proper way to do so.
  (1) *If the employee refuses to make the attempt,* you must discontinue the test, note the fact on the "Remarks" line of the ATF, and immediately notify the DER. This is a refusal to test.
  (2) *If the employee again attempts* and fails to provide a sufficient amount of breath, you may provide another opportunity to the employee to do so if you believe that there is a strong likelihood that it could result in providing a sufficient amount of breath.
  (3) *When the employee's attempts* under paragraph (b)(2) of this section have failed to produce a sufficient amount of breath, you must note the fact on the "Remarks" line of the ATF and immediately notify the DER.
  (4) *If you are using an EBT* that has the capability of operating manually, you may attempt to conduct the test in manual mode.
  (5) *If you are qualified to use a saliva ASD* and you are in the screening test stage, you may change to a saliva ASD only to complete the screening test.
(c) **As the employer,** when the BAT or STT informs you that the employee has not provided a sufficient amount of breath, you must direct the employee to obtain, within five days, an evaluation from a licensed physician who is acceptable to you and who has expertise in the medical issues raised by the employee's failure to provide a sufficient specimen.
  (1) *You are required to provide the physician* who will conduct the evaluation with the following information and instructions:
    (i) *That the employee* was required to take a DOT breath alcohol test, but was unable to provide a sufficient amount of breath to complete the test;
    (ii) *The consequences* of the appropriate DOT agency regulation for refusing to take the required alcohol test;
    (iii) *That the physician must provide you* with a signed statement of his or her conclusions; and
    (iv) *That the physician,* in his or her reasonable medical judgment, must base those conclusions on one of the following determinations:
      [A] *A medical condition* has, or with a high degree of probability could have, precluded the employee from providing a sufficient amount of breath. The physician must not include in the signed statement detailed information on the employee's medical condition. In this case, the test is cancelled.
      [B] *There is not an adequate basis* for determining that a medical condition has, or with a high degree of probability could have, precluded the employee from providing a sufficient amount of breath. This constitutes a refusal to test.
      [C] *For purposes* of paragraphs (c)(1)(iv)[A] and [B] of this section, a medical condition includes an ascertainable physiological condition (e.g., a respiratory system dysfunction) or a medically documented pre-existing psychological disorder, but does not include unsupported assertions of "situational anxiety" or hyperventilation.
  (2) *As the physician making the evaluation,* after making your determination, you must provide a written statement of your conclusions and the basis for them to the DER directly (and

not through a C/TPA acting as an intermediary). You must not include in this statement detailed information on the employee's medical condition beyond what is necessary to explain your conclusion.

(3) *Upon receipt of the report* from the examining physician, as the DER you must immediately inform the employee and take appropriate action based upon your DOT agency regulations.

§§40.193 and 40.265 DOT Interpretations

Question 1: Do the five days within which an employee is given to obtain a medical evaluation after providing an insufficient amount of urine or breath include holidays and weekends, or does this refer to five business days?

Guidance: The five-day limit for obtaining an examination by a licensed physician refers to business days.

Therefore, holidays and weekend days should not be included in the 5-day time frame.

§40.267 What problems always cause an alcohol test to be cancelled?

As an employer, a BAT, or an STT, you must cancel an alcohol test if any of the following problems occur. These are "fatal flaws." You must inform the DER that the test was cancelled and must be treated as if the test never occurred. These problems are:

(a) **In the case of a screening test conducted** on a saliva ASD or a breath tube ASD:
  (1) *The STT or BAT reads the result* either sooner than or later than the time allotted by the manufacturer and this Part (see §40.245(a)(8) for the saliva ASD and §40.245(b)(8) for the breath tube ASD).
  (2) *The saliva ASD does not activate* (see §40.245(a)(7)); or
  (3) *The device is used for a test* after the expiration date printed on the device or on its package (see §40.245(a)(1) for the saliva ASD and §40.245(b)(1) for the breath tube ASD).
  (4) *The breath tube ASD is tested with an analyzer* which has not been pre-calibrated for that device's specific lot (see § 40.245(b)(1)).

(b) **In the case of a screening or confirmation test** conducted on an EBT, the sequential test number or alcohol concentration displayed on the EBT is not the same as the sequential test number or alcohol concentration on the printed result (see §40.253(c), (e) and (f)).

(c) **In the case of a confirmation test:**
  (1) *The BAT conducts the confirmation test* before the end of the minimum 15-minute waiting period (see §40.251(a)(1));
  (2) *The BAT does not conduct an air blank* before the confirmation test (see §40.253(a));
  (3) *There is not a 0.00 result on the air blank* conducted before the confirmation test (see §40.253(a)(1) and (2));
  (4) *The EBT does not print the result* (see §40.253(f)); or
  (5) *The next external calibration check of the EBT* produces a result that differs by more than the tolerance stated in the QAP from the known value of the test standard. In this case, every result of 0.02 or above obtained on the EBT since the last valid external calibration check is cancelled (see §40.233(a)(1) and (c)(3)).

§40.269 What problems cause an alcohol test to be cancelled unless they are corrected?

As a BAT or STT, or employer, you must cancel an alcohol test if any of the following problems occur, unless they are corrected. These are "correctable flaws." These problems are:

(a) **The BAT or STT does not sign the ATF** (see §§40.247(a)(1) and 40.255(a)(1)).
(b) **The BAT or STT fails to note** on the "Remarks" line of the ATF that the employee has not signed the ATF after the result is obtained (see §40.255(a)(3)).
(c) **The BAT or STT uses a non-DOT form for the test (see §40.225(a)).**

§40.271 How are alcohol testing problems corrected?

(a) **As a BAT or STT,** you have the responsibility of trying to complete successfully an alcohol test for each employee.
  (1) *If, during or shortly after the testing process,* you become aware of any event that will cause the test to be cancelled (see §40.267), you must try to correct the problem promptly, if practicable. You may repeat the testing process as part of this effort.
  (2) *If repeating the testing process is necessary,* you must begin a new test as soon as possible. You must use a new ATF, a new sequential test number, and, if needed, a new ASD and/or a new EBT. It is permissible to use additional technical capabilities of the EBT (e.g., manual operation) if you have been trained to do so in accordance with §40.213(c).
  (3) *If repeating the testing process is necessary,* you are not limited in the number of attempts to complete the test, provided that the employee is making a good faith effort to comply with the testing process.
  (4) *If another testing device is not available* for the new test at the testing site, you must immediately notify the DER and advise the DER that the test could not be completed. As the DER who receives this information, you must make all reasonable efforts to ensure that the test is conducted at another testing site as soon as possible.

(b) **If, as an STT, BAT, employer or other service agent** administering the testing process, you become aware of a "correctable flaw" (see §40.269) that has not already been corrected, you must take all practicable action to correct the problem so that the test is not cancelled.
  (1) *If the problem resulted* from the omission of required information, you must, as the person responsible for providing that information, supply in writing the missing information and a signed statement that it is true and accurate. For example, suppose you are a BAT and you forgot to make a notation on the "Remarks" line of the ATF that the employee did not sign the certification. You would, when the problem is called to your attention, supply a signed statement that the employee failed or refused to sign the certification after the result was obtained, and that your signed statement is true and accurate.
  (2) *If the problem is the use of a non-DOT form,* you must, as the person responsible for the use of the incorrect form, certify in writing that the incorrect form contains all the information needed for a valid DOT alcohol test. You must also provide a signed statement that the incorrect form was used inadvertently or as the only means of conducting a test, in circumstances beyond your control, and the steps you have taken to prevent future use of non-DOT forms for DOT tests. You must supply this information on the same business day on which you are notified of the problem, transmitting it by fax or courier.

(c) **If you cannot correct the problem, you must cancel the test.**

§40.273 What is the effect of a cancelled alcohol test?

(a) **A cancelled alcohol test is neither positive nor negative.**
  (1) *As an employer,* you must not attach to a cancelled test the consequences of a test result that is 0.02 or greater (e.g., removal from a safety-sensitive position).
  (2) *As an employer,* you must not use a cancelled test in a situation where an employee needs a test result that is below 0.02 (e.g., in the case of a return-to-duty or follow-up test to authorize the employee to perform safety-sensitive functions).
  (3) *As an employer,* you must not direct a recollection for an employee because a test has been cancelled, except in the situations cited in paragraph (a)(2) of this section or other provisions of this part.

(b) **A cancelled test** does not count toward compliance with DOT requirements, such as a minimum random testing rate.

(c) **When a test must be cancelled,** if you are the BAT, STT, or other person who determines that the cancellation is necessary, you must inform the affected DER within 48 hours of the cancellation.

(d) **A cancelled DOT test** does not provide a valid basis for an employer to conduct a non-DOT test (i.e., a test under company authority).

§40.275 What is the effect of procedural problems that are not sufficient to cancel an alcohol test?

(a) **As an STT, BAT, employer, or a service agent** administering the testing process, you must document any errors in the testing process of which you become aware, even if they are not "fatal flaws" or "correctable flaws" listed in this subpart. Decisions about the ultimate impact of these errors will be determined by administrative or legal proceedings, subject to the limitation of paragraph (b) of this section.

(b) **No person concerned with the testing process** may declare a test cancelled based on a mistake in the process that does not have a significant adverse effect on the right of the employee to a fair and accurate test. For example, it is inconsistent with this part to cancel a test based on a minor administrative mistake (e.g., the omission of the employee's middle initial) or an error that does not affect employee protections under this part. Nor does the failure of an employee to sign in Step 4 of the ATF result in the cancellation of the test. Nor is a test to be cancelled on the basis of a claim by an employee that he or she was improperly selected for testing.

(c) **As an employer,** these errors, even though not sufficient to cancel an alcohol test result, may subject you to enforcement action under DOT agency regulations.

> **§§40.243, 40.253, 40.275, Appendix G to Part 40 DOT Interpretations**
>
> *Question 1:* Is it acceptable to affix printed alcohol test results on the back of the Alcohol Testing Form (ATF) rather than on the front?
>
> *Guidance:* §§40.243(f) and 40.253(g) instruct the BAT to affix the printout of the information from the alcohol testing device to the designated space on the ATF.
>
> The designated space on the ATF is on the front of the form. That is where BATs and STTs should affix the printouts.
>
> However, because the instructions on the ATF also permit the printout to be affixed to the back of the ATF, the Department has no objections to having the printouts on the back of the ATF.

§40.277 Are alcohol tests other than saliva or breath permitted under these regulations?

No, other types of alcohol tests (e.g., blood and urine) are not authorized for testing done under this part. Only saliva or breath for screening tests and breath for confirmation tests using approved devices are permitted.

Subpart O - Substance Abuse Professionals and the Return-to-Duty Process

§40.281 Who is qualified to act as a SAP?

To be permitted to act as a SAP in the DOT drug and alcohol testing program, you must meet each of the requirements of this section:

(a) **Credentials.** You must have one of the following credentials:
   (1) *You are a licensed physician (Doctor of Medicine or Osteopathy);*
   (2) *You are a licensed or certified social worker;*
   (3) *You are a licensed or certified psychologist;*
   (4) *You are a licensed or certified* employee assistance professional;
   (5) *You are a state licensed or certified* marriage and family therpist; or
   (6) *You are a drug and alcohol counselor* certified by the National Association of Alcoholism and Drug Abuse Counselors Certification Commission (NAADAC); or by the International Certification Reciprocity Consortium/Alcohol and Other Drug Abuse (ICRC); or by the National Board for Certified Counselors, Inc. and Affiliates/Master Addictions Counselor (NBCC).

(b) **Basic knowledge.** You must be knowledgeable in the following areas:
   (1) *You must be knowledgeable about* and have clinical experience in the diagnosis and treatment of alcohol and controlled substances-related disorders.
   (2) *You must be knowledgeable about the SAP function* as it relates to employer interests in safety-sensitive duties.
   (3) *You must be knowledgeable about this part,* the DOT agency regulations applicable to the employers for whom you evaluate employees, and the DOT SAP Guidelines, and you keep current on any changes to these materials. These documents are available from ODAPC (Department of Transportation, 400 7th Street, SW., Room 10403, Washington DC, 20590 (202-366-3784), or on the ODAPC web site (*http://www.dot.gov/ost/dapc*)).

(c) **Qualification training.** You must receive qualification training meeting the requirements of this paragraph (c).
   (1) *Qualification training* must provide instruction on the following subjects:
      (i) *Background, rationale, and coverage* of the Department's drug and alcohol testing program;
      (ii) *49 CFR Part 40* and DOT agency drug and alcohol testing rules;
      (iii) *Key DOT drug testing requirements,* including collections, laboratory testing, MRO review, and problems in drug testing;
      (iv) *Key DOT alcohol testing requirements,* including the testing process, the role of BATs and STTs, and problems in alcohol tests;
      (v) *SAP qualifications and prohibitions;*
      (vi) *The role of the SAP* in the return-to-duty process, including the initial employee evaluation, referrals for education and/or treatment, the follow-up evaluation, continuing treatment recommendations, and the follow-up testing plan;
      (vii) *SAP consultation and communication* with employers, MROs, and treatment providers;
      (viii) *Reporting and recordkeeping requirements;*
      (ix) *Issues that SAPs confront* in carrying out their duties under the program.
   (2) *Following your completion* of qualification training under paragraph (c)(1) of this section, you must satisfactorily complete an examination administered by a nationally-recognized professional or training organization. The examination must comprehensively cover all the elements of qualification training listed in paragraph (c)(1) of this section.
   (3) *The following is the schedule* for qualification training you must meet:
      (i) *If you became an SAP* before August 1, 2001, you must meet the qualification training requirement no later than December 31, 2003.
      (ii) *If you become an SAP* between August 1, 2001, and December 31, 2003, you must meet the qualification training requirement no later than December 31, 2003.
      (iii) *If you become an SAP* on or after January 1, 2004, you must meet the qualification training requirement before you begin to perform SAP functions.

(d) **Continuing education.** During each three-year period from the date on which you satisfactorily complete the examination under paragraph (c)(2) of this section, you must complete continuing education consisting of at least 12 professional development hours (e.g., CEUs) relevant to performing SAP functions.
   (1) *This continuing education* must include material concerning new technologies, interpretations, recent guidance, rule changes, and other information about developments in SAP practice, pertaining to the DOT program, since the time you met the qualification training requirements of this section.
   (2) *Your continuing education activities* must include documentable assessment tools to assist you in determining whether you have adequately learned the material.

(e) **Documentation.** You must maintain documentation showing that you currently meet all requirements of this section. You must provide this documentation on request to DOT agency representatives and to employers and C/TPAs who are using or contemplating using your services.

> **§§40.33, 40.121, 40.213, 40.281 DOT Interpretations**
>
> *Question 1:* Because Part 40 requires collectors, MROs, BATs and STTs, and SAPs to maintain their own training records, can employers or training entities refuse to provide these service agents their training records?
>
> *Guidance:* No. Employers and trainers who provide training for these service agents must not withhold training documentation from them when they have successfully completed the training requirements.
>
> If a collector, BAT, STT, MRO, or SAP is not in possession of training documentation, he or she is in violation of Part 40.
>
> Therefore, Part 40 does not permit the withholding of such documentation from these service agents.

§40.283 How does a certification organization obtain recognition for its members as SAPs?

(a) **If you represent a certification organization** that wants DOT to authorize its certified drug and alcohol counselors to be added to §40.281(a)(6), you may submit a written petition to DOT requesting a review of your petition for inclusion.

(b) **You must obtain** the National Commission for Certifying Agencies (NCCA) accreditation before DOT will act on your petition.

(c) **You must also meet the minimum requirements** of Appendix E to this part before DOT will act on your petition.

§40.285 When is a SAP evaluation required?

(a) **As an employee, when you have violated** DOT drug and alcohol regulations, you cannot again perform any DOT safety-sensitive duties for any employer until and unless you complete the SAP evaluation, referral, and education/treatment process set forth in this subpart and in applicable DOT agency regulations. The first step in this process is an SAP evaluation.

(b) **For purposes of this subpart,** a verified positive DOT drug test result, a DOT alcohol test with a result indicating an alcohol concentration of 0.04 or greater, a refusal to test (including by adulterating or substituting a urine specimen) or any other violation of the

Subpart O - Substance Abuse Professionals and the Return-to-Duty Process

prohibition on the use of alcohol or drugs under a DOT agency regulation constitutes a DOT drug and alcohol regulation violation.

§40.287 What information is an employer required to provide concerning SAP services to an employee who has a DOT drug and alcohol regulation violation?

As an employer, you must provide to each employee (including an applicant or new employee) who violates a DOT drug and alcohol regulation a listing of SAPs readily available to the employee and acceptable to you, with names, addresses, and telephone numbers. You cannot charge the employee any fee for compiling or providing this list. You may provide this list yourself or through a C/TPA or other service agent.

§40.289 Are employers required to provide SAP and treatment services to employees?

(a) **As an employer,** you are not required to provide an SAP evaluation or any subsequent recommended education or treatment for an employee who has violated a DOT drug and alcohol regulation.

(b) **However, if you offer that employee** an opportunity to return to a DOT safety-sensitive duty following a violation, you must, before the employee again performs that duty, ensure that the employee receives an evaluation by an SAP meeting the requirements of §40.281 and that the employee successfully complies with the SAP's evaluation recommendations.

(c) **Payment for SAP evaluations and services** is left for employers and employees to decide and may be governed by existing management-labor agreements and health care benefits.

§40.291 What is the role of the SAP in the evaluation, referral, and treatment process of an employee who has violated DOT agency drug and alcohol testing regulations?

(a) **As an SAP, you are charged with:**
  (1) *Making a face-to-face clinical assessment* and evaluation to determine what assistance is needed by the employee to resolve problems associated with alcohol and/or drug use;
  (2) *Referring the employee* to an appropriate education and/or treatment program;
  (3) *Conducting a face-to-face follow-up evaluation* to determine if the employee has actively participated in the education and/or treatment program and has demonstrated successful compliance with the initial assessment and evaluation recommendations;
  (4) *Providing the DER* with a follow-up drug and/or alcohol testing plan for the employee; and
  (5) *Providing the employee and employer* with recommendations for continuing education and/or treatment.

(b) **As a SAP,** you are not an advocate for the employer or employee. Your function is to protect the public interest in safety by professionally evaluating the employee and recommending appropriate education/treatment, follow-up tests, and aftercare.

§§40.291 and 40.293 DOT Interpretations

Question 1: Suppose the SAP fails to make the required recommendation for education and/or treatment of an employee who has violated a DOT agency drug or alcohol testing rule, and simply sends the employee back to the employer for a return-to-duty (RTD) test. What is the employer to do?

Guidance: The employer should not administer an RTD test under these circumstances.

The employer should refer the employee back to the SAP with direction to prescribe education and/or treatment and conduct a re-evaluation of the employee to determine whether the employee has successfully complied with the SAP's instructions.

If the employer has compounded the problem by having conducted the RTD test and returned the employee to safety-sensitive duties (i.e., only realizes that a mistake has been made some time after the fact), the employer should work with the SAP to "go back and do it right."

This means that the employee should be removed from performance of safety-sensitive functions, referred back to the SAP for an education and/or treatment prescription, and re-evaluated by the SAP for successful compliance. Following the receipt of a successful compliance report from the SAP, the employer would conduct another RTD test before returning the employee to performance of safety-sensitive functions.

§40.293 What is the SAP's function in conducting the initial evaluation of an employee?

As an SAP, for every employee who comes to you following a DOT drug and alcohol regulation violation, you must accomplish the following:

(a) **Provide a comprehensive face-to-face assessment** and clinical evaluation.

(b) **Recommend a course of education** and/or treatment with which the employee must demonstrate successful compliance prior to returning to DOT safety-sensitive duty.
  (1) *You must make such a recommendation* for every individual who has violated a DOT drug and alcohol regulation.
  (2) *You must make a recommendation* for education and/or treatment that will, to the greatest extent possible, protect public safety in the event that the employee returns to the performance of safety-sensitive functions.

(c) **Appropriate education may include,** but is not limited to, self-help groups (e.g., Alcoholics Anonymous) and community lectures, where attendance can be independently verified, and bona fide drug and alcohol education courses.

(d) **Appropriate treatment may include,** but is not limited to, in-patient hospitalization, partial in-patient treatment, out-patient counseling programs, and aftercare.

(e) **You must provide a written report** directly to the DER highlighting your specific recommendations for assistance (see §40.311(c)).

(f) **For purposes of your role** in the evaluation process, you must assume that a verified positive test result has conclusively established that the employee committed a DOT drug and alcohol regulation violation. You must not take into consideration in any way, as a factor in determining what your recommendation will be, any of the following:
  (1) *A claim by the employee* that the test was unjustified or inaccurate;
  (2) *Statements by the employee* that attempt to mitigate the seriousness of a violation of a DOT drug or alcohol regulation (e.g., related to assertions of use of hemp oil, "medical marijuana" use, "contact positives," poppy seed ingestion, job stress); or
  (3) *Personal opinions you may have* about the justification or rationale for drug and alcohol testing.

(g) **In the course of gathering information** for purposes of your evaluation in the case of a drug-related violation, you may consult with the MRO. As the MRO, you are required to cooperate with the SAP and provide available information the SAP requests. It is not necessary to obtain the consent of the employee to provide this information.

§§40.291 and 40.293 DOT Interpretations

Question 1: Suppose the SAP fails to make the required recommendation for education and/or treatment of an employee who has violated a DOT agency drug or alcohol testing rule, and simply sends the employee back to the employer for a return-do-duty (RTD) test. What is the employer to do?

Guidance: The employer should not administer an RTD test under these circumstances.

The employer should refer the employee back to the SAP with direction to prescribe education and/or treatment and conduct a re-evaluation of the employee to determine whether the employee has successfully complied with the SAP's instructions.

If the employer has compounded the problem by having conducted the RTD test and returned the employee to safety-sensitive duties (i.e., only realizes that a mistake has been made some time after the fact), the employer should work with the SAP to "go back and do it right."

This means that the employee should be removed from performance of safety-sensitive functions, referred back to the SAP for an education and/or treatment prescription, and re-evaluated by the SAP for successful compliance. Following the receipt of a successful compliance report from the SAP, the employer would conduct another RTD test before returning the employee to performance of safety-sensitive functions.

§40.295 May employees or employers seek a second SAP evaluation if they disagree with the first SAP's recommendations?

(a) **As an employee with a DOT** drug and alcohol regulation violation, when you have been evaluated by a SAP, you must not seek a second SAP's evaluation in order to obtain another recommendation.

(b) **As an employer,** you must not seek a second SAP's evaluation if the employee has already been evaluated by a qualified SAP. If the employee, contrary to paragraph (a) of this section, has obtained a second SAP evaluation, as an employer you may not rely on it for any purpose under this part.

§40.297 Does anyone have the authority to change a SAP's initial evaluation?

(a) **Except as provided** in paragraph (b) of this section, no one (e.g., an employer, employee, a managed-care provider, any service agent) may change in any way the SAP's evaluation or recommendations for assistance. For example, a third party is not permitted to make more or less stringent a SAP's recommendation by changing the SAP's evaluation or seeking another SAP's evaluation.

(b) **The SAP who made the initial evaluation** may modify his or her initial evaluation and recommendations based on new or additional information (e.g., from an education or treatment program).

§40.299 What is the SAP's role and what are the limits on a SAP's discretion in referring employees for education and treatment?

(a) **As a SAP,** upon your determination of the best recommendation for assistance, you will serve as a referral source to assist the employee's entry into an education and/or treatment program.

(b) **To prevent the appearance** of a conflict of interest, you must not refer an employee requiring assistance to your private practice or to a person or organization from which you receive payment or to a person or organization in which you have a financial interest. You are precluded from making referrals to entities with which you are financially associated.

(c) **There are four exceptions** to the prohibitions contained in paragraph (b) of this section. You may refer an employee to any of the following providers of assistance, regardless of your relationship with them:

  (1) *A public agency* (e.g., treatment facility) operated by a state, county, or municipality;

  (2) *The employer or a person or organization* under contract to the employer to provide alcohol or drug treatment and/or education services (e.g., the employer's contracted treatment provider);

  (3) *The sole source* of therapeutically appropriate treatment under the employee's health insurance program (e.g., the single substance abuse in-patient treatment program made available by the employee's insurance coverage plan); or

  (4) *The sole source* of therapeutically appropriate treatment reasonably available to the employee (e.g., the only treatment facility or education program reasonably located within the general commuting area).

§40.301 What is the SAP's function in the follow-up evaluation of an employee?

(a) **As a SAP,** after you have prescribed assistance under §40.293, you must re-evaluate the employee to determine if the employee has successfully carried out your education and/or treatment recommendations.

  (1) *This is your way to gauge for the employer* the employee's ability to demonstrate successful compliance with the education and/or treatment plan.

  (2) *Your evaluation may serve* as one of the reasons the employer decides to return the employee to safety-sensitive duty.

(b) **As the SAP** making the follow-up evaluation determination, you must:

  (1) *Confer with or obtain appropriate documentation* from the appropriate education and/or treatment program professionals where the employee was referred; and

  (2) *Conduct a face-to-face clinical interview* with the employee to determine if the employee demonstrates successful compliance with your initial evaluation recommendations.

(c) (1) *If the employee has demonstrated* successful compliance, you must provide a written report directly to the DER highlighting your clinical determination that the employee has done so with your initial evaluation recommendation (see §40.311(d)).

  (2) *You may determine* that an employee has successfully demonstrated compliance even though the employee has not yet completed the full regimen of education and/or treatment you recommended or needs additional assistance. For example, if the employee has successfully completed the 30-day in-patient program you prescribed, you may make a "successful compliance" determination even though you conclude that the employee has not yet completed the out-patient counseling you recommended or should continue in an aftercare program.

(d) (1) *As the SAP,* if you believe, as a result of the follow-up evaluation, that the employee has not demonstrated successful compliance with your recommendations, you must provide written notice directly to the DER (see §40.311(e)).

  (2) *As an employer* who receives the SAP's written notice that the employee has not successfully complied with the SAP's recommendations, you must not return the employee to the performance of safety-sensitive duties.

  (3) *As the SAP,* you may conduct additional follow-up evaluation(s) if the employer determines that doing so is consistent with the employee's progress as you have reported it and with the employer's policy and/or labor-management agreements.

  (4) *As the employer,* following a SAP report that the employee has not demonstrated successful compliance, you may take personnel action consistent with your policy and/or labor-management agreements.

§40.303 What happens if the SAP believes the employee needs additional treatment, aftercare, or support group services even after the employee returns to safety-sensitive duties?

(a) **As a SAP,** if you believe that ongoing services (in addition to follow-up tests) are needed to assist an employee to maintain sobriety or abstinence from drug use after the employee resumes the performance of safety-sensitive duties, you must provide recommendations for these services in your follow-up evaluation report (see §40.311(d)(10)).

(b) **As an employer receiving a recommendation** for these services from a SAP, you may, as part of a return-to-duty agreement with the employee, require the employee to participate in the recommended services. You may monitor and document the employee's participation in the recommended services. You may also make use of SAP and employee assistance program (EAP) services in assisting and monitoring employees' compliance with SAP recommendations. Nothing in this section permits an employer to fail to carry out its obligations with respect to follow-up testing (see §40.309).

(c) **As an employee,** you are obligated to comply with the SAP's recommendations for these services. If you fail or refuse to do so, you may be subject to disciplinary action by your employer.

§40.305 How does the return-to-duty process conclude?

(a) **As the employer,** if you decide that you want to permit the employee to return to the performance of safety-sensitive functions, you must ensure that the employee takes a return-to-duty test. This test cannot occur until after the SAP has determined that the employee has successfully complied with prescribed education and/or treatment. The employee must have a negative drug test result and/or an alcohol test with an alcohol concentration of less than 0.02 before resuming performance of safety-sensitive duties.

(b) **As an employer,** you must not return an employee to safety-sensitive duties until the employee meets the conditions of paragraph (a) of this section. However, you are not required to return an employee to safety-sensitive duties because the employee has met these conditions. That is a personnel decision that you have the discretion to make, subject to collective bargaining agreements or other legal requirements.

(c) **As a SAP or MRO,** you must not make a "fitness for duty" determination as part of this re-evaluation unless required to do so under an applicable DOT agency regulation. It is the employer, rather than you, who must decide whether to put the employee back to work in a safety-sensitive position.

§40.307 What is the SAP's function in prescribing the employee's follow-up tests?

(a) **As a SAP,** for each employee who has committed a DOT drug or alcohol regulation violation, and who seeks to resume the performance of safety-sensitive functions, you must establish a written follow-up testing plan. You do not establish this plan until after you determine that the employee has successfully complied with your recommendations for education and/or treatment.

Subpart O - Substance Abuse Professionals and the Return-to-Duty Process §40.311 (g)

(b) You must present a copy of this plan directly to the DER (see §40.311(d)(9)).

(c) You are the sole determiner of the number and frequency of follow-up tests and whether these tests will be for drugs, alcohol, or both, unless otherwise directed by the appropriate DOT agency regulation. For example, if the employee had a positive drug test, but your evaluation or the treatment program professionals determined that the employee had an alcohol problem as well, you should require that the employee have follow-up tests for both drugs and alcohol.

(d) However, you must, at a minimum, direct that the employee be subject to six unannounced follow-up tests in the first 12 months of safety-sensitive duty following the employee's return to safety-sensitive functions.

(1) *You may require* a greater number of follow-up tests during the first 12-month period of safety-sensitive duty (e.g., you may require one test a month during the 12-month period; you may require two tests per month during the first 6-month period and one test per month during the final 6-month period).

(2) *You may also require* follow-up tests during the 48 months of safety-sensitive duty following this first 12-month period.

(3) *You are not to establish the actual dates* for the follow-up tests you prescribe. The decision on specific dates to test is the employer's.

(4) *As the employer,* you must not impose additional testing requirements (e.g., under company authority) on the employee that go beyond the SAP's follow-up testing plan.

(e) The requirements of the SAP's follow-up testing plan "follow the employee" to subsequent employers or through breaks in service.

Example 1 to Paragraph (e): The employee returns to duty with Employer A. Two months afterward, after completing the first two of six follow-up tests required by the SAP's plan, the employee quits his job with Employer A and begins to work in a similar position for Employer B. The employee remains obligated to complete the four additional tests during the next 10 months of safety-sensitive duty, and Employer B is responsible for ensuring that the employee does so. Employer B learns of this obligation through the inquiry it makes under §40.25.

Example 2 to Paragraph (e): The employee returns to duty with Employer A. Three months later, after the employee completes the first two of six follow-up tests required by the SAP's plan, Employer A lays the employee off for economic or seasonal employment reasons. Four months later, Employer A recalls the employee. Employer A must ensure that the employee completes the remaining four follow-up tests during the next nine months.

(f) As the SAP, you may modify the determinations you have made concerning follow-up tests. For example, even if you recommended follow-up testing beyond the first 12-months, you can terminate the testing requirement at any time after the first year of testing. You must not, however, modify the requirement that the employee take at least six follow-up tests within the first 12 months after returning to the performance of safety-sensitive functions.

§40.307 DOT Interpretations

Question 1: May an employer conduct follow-up testing under company authority that goes beyond the follow-up testing which the SAP determines necessary?

Guidance: No. The regulation (at §40.307(d)(4)) and SAP guidelines state that employers must not impose additional testing requirements that go beyond the SAP's follow-up testing plan. This includes additional testing requirements under company authority.

In addition to follow-up testing and random testing, an employer has other means available to ascertain an employee's alcohol- and drug-free performance and functions.

- The employer can choose to monitor the employee's compliance with the SAP's recommendations for continuing treatment and/or education as part of a return-to-duty agreement with the employee.
- The employer can conduct reasonable suspicion testing if the employee exhibits signs and symptoms of drug or alcohol use.
- The employer can meet regularly with the employee to discuss the employee's continuing sobriety and drug-free status.

The Department is not opposed to an employer discussing his or her desires for having more than the minimum rule requirement (i.e., 6 tests in the first year) for follow-up testing with SAPs they intend to utilize.

§40.309 What are the employer's responsibilities with respect to the SAP's directions for follow-up tests?

(a) As the employer, you must carry out the SAP's follow-up testing requirements. You may not allow the employee to continue to perform safety-sensitive functions unless follow-up testing is conducted as directed by the SAP.

(b) You should schedule follow-up tests on dates of your own choosing, but you must ensure that the tests are unannounced with no discernable pattern as to their timing, and that the employee is given no advance notice.

(c) You cannot substitute any other tests (e.g., those carried out under the random testing program) conducted on the employee for this follow-up testing requirement.

(d) You cannot count a follow-up test that has been cancelled as a completed test. A cancelled follow-up test must be recollected.

§40.311 What are the requirements concerning SAP reports?

(a) As the SAP conducting the required evaluations, you must send the written reports required by this section in writing directly to the DER and not to a third party or entity for forwarding to the DER (except as provided in §40.355(e)). You may, however, forward the document simultaneously to the DER and to a C/TPA.

(b) As an employer, you must ensure that you receive SAP written reports directly from the SAP performing the evaluation and that no third party or entity changed the SAP's report in any way.

(c) The SAP's written report, following an initial evaluation that determines what level of assistance is needed to address the employee's drug and/or alcohol problems, must be on the SAP's own letterhead (and not the letterhead of another service agent) signed and dated by the SAP, and must contain the following delineated items:

(1) *Employee's name and SSN;*
(2) *Employer's name and address;*
(3) *Reason for the assessment* (specific violation of DOT regulations and violation date);
(4) *Date(s) of the assessment;*
(5) *SAP's education and/or treatment recommendation; and*
(6) *SAP's telephone number.*

(d) The SAP's written report concerning a follow-up evaluation that determines the employee has demonstrated successful compliance must be on the SAP's own letterhead (and not the letterhead of another service agent), signed by the SAP and dated, and must contain the following items:

(1) *Employee's name and SSN;*
(2) *Employer's name and address;*
(3) *Reason for the initial assessment* (specific violation of DOT regulations and violation date);
(4) *Date(s) of the initial assessment* and synopsis of the treatment plan;
(5) *Name of practice(s) or service(s)* providing the recommended education and/or treatment;
(6) *Inclusive dates of employee's program participation;*
(7) *Clinical characterization of employee's program participation;*
(8) *SAP's clinical determination* as to whether the employee has demonstrated successful compliance;
(9) *Follow-up testing plan;*
(10) *Employee's continuing care needs* with specific treatment, aftercare, and/or support group services recommendations; and
(11) *SAP's telephone number.*

(e) The SAP's written report concerning a follow-up evaluation that determines the employee has not demonstrated successful compliance must be on the SAP's own letterhead (and not the letterhead of another service agent), signed by the SAP and dated, and must contain the following items:

(1) *Employee's name and SSN;*
(2) *Employer's name and address;*
(3) *Reason for the initial assessment (specific DOT violation and date);*
(4) *Date(s) of initial assessment and synopsis of treatment plan;*
(5) *Name of practice(s) or service(s)* providing the recommended education and/or treatment;
(6) *Inclusive dates of employee's program participation;*
(7) *Clinical characterization of employee's program participation;*
(8) *Date(s) of the first follow-up evaluation;*
(9) *Date(s) of any further follow-up evaluation the SAP has scheduled;*
(10) *SAP's clinical reasons* for determining that the employee has not demonstrated successful compliance; and
(11) *SAP's telephone number.*

(f) As a SAP, you must also provide these written reports directly to the employee if the employee has no current employer and to the gaining DOT regulated employer in the event the employee obtains another transportation industry safety-sensitive position.

(g) As a SAP, you are to maintain copies of your reports to employers for 5 years, and your employee clinical records in accordance with Federal, state, and local laws regarding record maintenance, confidentiality, and release of information. You must make these records available, on request, to DOT agency representatives (e.g., inspectors conducting an audit or safety investigation) and representatives of the NTSB in an accident investigation.

(h) **As an employer,** you must maintain your reports from SAPs for 5 years from the date you received them.

§40.311 DOT Interpretations

Question 1: What is meant by "SAP's own letterhead?

Guidance: By "SAP's own letterhead" we mean the letterhead the SAP uses in his or her daily counseling practice.

If the SAP is in private practice, the SAP should use the letterhead of his or her practice.

If the SAP works as an employee assistance professional for an organization, the SAP should use the employee assistance program's letterhead.

If the SAP works for a community mental health service, the SAP should use the community mental health service's letterhead.

The Department wants to avoid a SAP network provider requiring the SAP to use the provider's letterhead rather than that of the SAP.

The Department wants to avoid another service agent contracting the SAP's services to require the contracted SAP to use the service agent's letterhead.

The Department wants to avoid any appearance that anyone changed the SAP's recommendations or that the SAP's report failed to go directly from the SAP to the employer.

The Department does not want the SAP to use a "fill-in-the-blanks"/ "check-the-appropriate-boxes" type of pre-printed form, including any that are issued to the SAP by a SAP network provider, to which the network or SAP would affix the SAP's letterhead information.

The SAP must generate and complete all information on the SAP report.

§40.313 Where is other information on SAP functions and the return-to-duty process found in this regulation?

You can find other information on the role and functions of SAPs in the following sections of this part:

§40.3 - Definition.

§40.347 - Service agent assistance with SAP-required follow-up testing.

§40.355 - Transmission of SAP reports.

§40.329(c) - Making SAP reports available to employees on request.

Appendix E to Part 40 - SAP Equivalency Requirements for Certification Organizations.

Subpart P - Confidentiality and Release of Information

§40.321 What is the general confidentiality rule for drug and alcohol test information?

Except as otherwise provided in this subpart, as a service agent or employer participating in the DOT drug or alcohol testing process, you are prohibited from releasing individual test results or medical information about an employee to third parties without the employee's specific written consent.

(a) A **third party** is any person or organization to whom other subparts of this regulation do not explicitly authorize or require the transmission of information in the course of the drug or alcohol testing process.

(b) **Specific written consent** means a statement signed by the employee that he or she agrees to the release of a particular piece of information to a particular, explicitly identified, person or organization at a particular time. "Blanket releases," in which an employee agrees to a release of a category of information (e.g., all test results) or to release information to a category of parties (e.g., other employers who are members of a C/TPA, companies to which the employee may apply for employment), are prohibited under this part.

§40.323 May program participants release drug or alcohol test information in connection with legal proceedings?

(a) **As an employer,** you may release information pertaining to an employee's drug or alcohol test without the employee's consent in certain legal proceedings.

(1) *These proceedings include a lawsuit* (e.g., a wrongful discharge action), grievance (e.g., an arbitration concerning disciplinary action taken by the employer), or administrative proceeding (e.g., an unemployment compensation hearing) brought by, or on behalf of, an employee and resulting from a positive DOT drug or alcohol test or a refusal to test (including, but not limited to, adulterated or substituted test results).

(2) *These proceedings also include* a criminal or civil action resulting from an employee's performance of safety-sensitive duties, in which a court of competent jurisdiction determines that the drug or alcohol test information sought is relevant to the case and issues an order directing the employer to produce the information. For example, in personal injury litigation following a truck or bus collision, the court could determine that a post-accident drug test result of an employee is relevant to determining whether the driver or the driver's employer was negligent. The employer is authorized to respond to the court's order to produce the records.

(b) **In such a proceeding,** you may release the information to the decisionmaker in the proceeding (e.g., the court in a lawsuit). You may release the information only with a binding stipulation that the decisionmaker to whom it is released will make it available only to parties to the proceeding.

(c) **If you are a service agent,** and the employer requests its employee's drug or alcohol testing information from you to use in a legal proceeding as authorized in paragraph (a) of this section (e.g., the laboratory's data package), you must provide the requested information to the employer.

(d) **As an employer or service agent,** you must immediately notify the employee in writing of any information you release under this section.

§40.325 [Reserved]

§40.327 When must the MRO report medical information gathered in the verification process?

(a) **As the MRO, you must,** except as provided in paragraph (c) of this section, report drug test results and medical information you learned as part of the verification process to third parties without the employee's consent if you determine, in your reasonable medical judgment, that:

(1) *The information is likely to result* in the employee being determined to be medically unqualified under an applicable DOT agency regulation; or

(2) *The information indicates* that continued performance by the employee of his or her safety-sensitive function is likely to pose a significant safety risk.

(b) **The third parties to whom you are authorized** to provide information by this section include the employer, a physician or other health care provider responsible for determining the medical qualifications of the employee under an applicable DOT agency safety regulation, an SAP evaluating the employee as part of the return to duty process (see §40.293(g)), a DOT agency, or the National Transportation Safety Board in the course of an accident investigation.

(c) **If the law of a foreign country** (e.g., Canada) prohibits you from providing medical information to the employer, you may comply with that prohibition.

§40.327 DOT Interpretations

Question 1: If an MRO knows the identity of a physician responsible for determining whether a DOT-regulated employee is physically qualified to perform safety-sensitive duties (e.g., under Federal Motor Carrier Safety Administration regulations for physical qualifications of motor carrier drivers) for another company, can the MRO report drug test result as well as medical information to that physician?

Guidance: Under §40.327(a), an MRO must report drug test results and medical information to third parties without the employee's consent, under certain circumstances spelled out in the rule.

Under §40.327(b), a physician responsible for determining the medical qualifications of an employee under an applicable DOT agency safety regulation is a party to whom the MRO is instructed to provide this information.

Consequently, if an MRO knows the identity of such a physician — even if the physician performs this function for a different employer — the MRO would provide the information. The MRO is not required to affirmatively seek out such physicians, however.

Subpart P - Confidentiality and Release of Information §40.333 (e)

§40.329 What information must laboratories, MROs, and other service agents release to employees?

(a) **As an MRO or service agent you must provide,** within 10 business days of receiving a written request from an employee, copies of any records pertaining to the employee's use of alcohol and/or drugs, including records of the employee's DOT-mandated drug and/or alcohol tests. You may charge no more than the cost of preparation and reproduction for copies of these records.

(b) **As a laboratory, you must provide,** within 10 business days of receiving a written request from an employee, and made through the MRO, the records relating to the results of the employee's drug test (i.e., laboratory report and data package). You may charge no more than the cost of preparation and reproduction for copies of these records.

(c) **As an SAP, you must make available to an employee,** on request, a copy of all SAP reports (see §40.311). However, you must redact follow-up testing information from the report before providing it to the employee.

§40.329 DOT Interpretations

Question 1: If an employee requests his/her records from the MRO, do these records include the MRO's notes and comments or only copies of the CCF and laboratory result?

Guidance: In general, the MRO should provide all records that are available related to that employee, to include written notes, checklists, or comments. All of this information was obtained from the employee or from appropriate individuals or organizations (with the employee's authorization) or from documentation provided by the employee.

Consistent with appropriate medical record constraints, the MRO may need to withhold or interpret sensitive medical, psychiatric, and mental health record information.

§40.331 To what additional parties must employers and service agents release information?

As an employer or service agent you must release information under the following circumstances:

(a) **If you receive a specific, written consent** from an employee authorizing the release of information about that employee's drug or alcohol tests to an identified person, you must provide the information to the identified person. For example, as an employer, when you receive a written request from a former employee to provide information to a subsequent employer, you must do so. In providing the information, you must comply with the terms of the employee's consent.

(b) **If you are an employer, you must,** upon request of DOT agency representatives, provide the following:
   (1) *Access to your facilities used for this part* and DOT agency drug and alcohol program functions.
   (2) *All written, printed, and computer-based* drug and alcohol program records and reports (including copies of name-specific records or reports), files, materials, data, documents/documentation, agreements, contracts, policies, and statements that are required by this part and DOT agency regulations. You must provide this information at your principal place of business in the time required by the DOT agency.
   (3) *All items in paragraph (b)(2) of this section* must be easily accessible, legible, and provided in an organized manner. If electronic records do not meet these standards, they must be converted to printed documentation that meets these standards.

(c) **If you are a service agent, you must,** upon request of DOT agency representatives, provide the following:
   (1) *Access to your facilities used for this part* and DOT agency drug and alcohol program functions.
   (2) *All written, printed, and computer-based* drug and alcohol program records and reports (including copies of name-specific records or reports), files, materials, data, documents/documentation, agreements, contracts, policies, and statements that are required by this part and DOT agency regulations. You must provide this information at your principal place of business in the time required by the DOT agency.
   (3) *All items in paragraph (c)(2) of this section* must be easily accessible, legible, and provided in an organized manner. If electronic records do not meet these standards, they must be converted to printed documentation that meets these standards.

(d) **If requested by the National Transportation Safety Board** as part of an accident investigation, you must provide information concerning post-accident tests administered after the accident.

(e) **If requested by a Federal, state, or local safety agency** with regulatory authority over you or the employee, you must provide drug and alcohol test records concerning the employee.

(f) **Except as otherwise provided in this part,** as a laboratory you must not release or provide a specimen or a part of a specimen to a requesting party, without first obtaining written consent from ODAPC. If a party seeks a court order directing you to release a specimen or part of a specimen contrary to any provision of this part, you must take necessary legal steps to contest the issuance of the order (e.g., seek to quash a subpoena, citing the requirements of §40.13). This part does not require you to disobey a court order, however.

§40.333 What records must employers keep?

(a) **As an employer, you must keep the following records** for the following periods of time:
   (1) *You must keep the following records for five years:*
      (i) *Records of alcohol test results* indicating an alcohol concentration of 0.02 or greater;
      (ii) *Records of verified positive drug test results;*
      (iii) *Documentation of refusals* to take required alcohol and/or drug tests (including substituted or adulterated drug test results);
      (iv) *SAP reports; and*
      (v) *All follow-up tests and schedules for follow-up tests.*
   (2) *You must keep records for three years* of information obtained from previous employers under §40.25 concerning drug and alcohol test results of employees.
   (3) *You must keep records* of the inspection, maintenance, and calibration of EBTs, for two years.
   (4) *You must keep records* of negative and cancelled drug test results and alcohol test results with a concentration of less than 0.02 for one year.

(b) **You do not have to keep records** related to a program requirement that does not apply to you (e.g., a maritime employer who does not have a DOT-mandated random alcohol testing program need not maintain random alcohol testing records).

(c) **You must maintain the records** in a location with controlled access.

(d) **A service agent may maintain these records for you.** However, you must ensure that you can produce these records at your principal place of business in the time required by the DOT agency. For example, as a motor carrier, when an FMCSA inspector requests your records, you must ensure that you can provide them within two business days.

(e) **If you store records electronically,** where permitted by this part, you must ensure that the records are easily accessible, legible, and formatted and stored in an organized manner. If electronic records do not meet these criteria, you must convert them to printed documentation in a rapid and readily auditable manner, at the request of DOT agency personnel.

§40.333 DOT Interpretations

Question 1: When records are stored and transferred electronically, how should they be made available to DOT representatives?

Guidance: The obligations of employers and service agents to make records available expeditiously to DOT representatives apply regardless of how the records are maintained.

All records must be easily and quickly accessible, legible, and formatted and stored in a well-organized and orderly way.

If electronic records do not meet these criteria, then the employer or service agent must convert them to printed documentation in a rapid and readily auditable way.

§§40.103, 40.99, 40.333 DOT Interpretations

Question 1: What are the retention requirements for blind specimens and records of blind specimen tests?

Guidance: Laboratories, employers and other parties required to retain specimens and records of tests should retain blind specimens and records of blind specimen tests in exactly the same way and for the same periods of time as they do actual employee specimens and test records.

For example, an employer would keep a record of a blind positive test for five years and a blind negative test for two years.

Laboratories would keep blind specimens for negatives in accordance with their SOPs and non-negatives for one year.

Subpart Q - Roles and Responsibilities of Service Agents

§40.341 Must service agents comply with DOT drug and alcohol testing requirements?

(a) **As a service agent,** the services you provide to transportation employers must meet the requirements of this part and the DOT agency drug and alcohol testing regulations.

(b) **If you do not comply,** DOT may take action under the Public Interest Exclusions procedures of this part (see Subpart R of this part) or applicable provisions of other DOT agency regulations.

§40.343 What tasks may a service agent perform for an employer?

As a service agent, you may perform for employers the tasks needed to comply with DOT agency drug and alcohol testing regulations, subject to the requirements and limitations of this part.

§40.345 In what circumstances may a C/TPA act as an intermediary in the transmission of drug and alcohol testing information to employers?

(a) **As a C/TPA or other service agent,** you may act as an intermediary in the transmission of drug and alcohol testing information in the circumstances specified in this section only if the employer chooses to have you do so. Each employer makes the decision about whether to receive some or all of this information from you, acting as an intermediary, rather than directly from the service agent who originates the information (e.g., an MRO or BAT).

(b) **The specific provisions of this part** concerning which you may act as an intermediary are listed in Appendix F to this part. These are the only situations in which you may act as an intermediary. You are prohibited from doing so in all other situations.

(c) **In every case, you must ensure that,** in transmitting information to employers, you meet all requirements (e.g., concerning confidentiality and timing) that would apply if the service agent originating the information (e.g., an MRO or collector) sent the information directly to the employer. For example, if you transmit drug testing results from MROs to DERs, you must transmit each drug test result to the DER in compliance with the MRO requirements set forth in §40.167.

> **§§40.35, 40.45, 40.345 DOT Interpretations**
>
> *Question 1:* How should the employer's decision to have a C/TPA act as intermediary in the handling of drug test results be documented?
>
> *Guidance:* When an employer chooses to use the C/TPA as the intermediary in the transmission of the MRO's verified drug test results, this decision should be communicated from the employer to the MRO and the C/TPA.
>
> We advise the MRO to obtain some documentation of the employer's decision prior to sending results through the C/TPA.
>
> Documentation could be in the form of a letter, an email, or record of a telephone conversation with the employer.
>
> DOT also recommends that MROs maintain listings of the names, addresses, and phone numbers of C/TPA points of contact.

§40.347 What functions may C/TPAs perform with respect to administering testing?

As a C/TPA, except as otherwise specified in this part, you may perform the following functions for employers concerning random selection and other selections for testing.

(a) **You may operate random testing programs for employers** and may assist (i.e., through contracting with laboratories or collection sites, conducting collections) employers with other types of testing (e.g., pre-employment, post-accident, reasonable suspicion, return-to-duty, and follow-up).

(b) **You may combine employees** from more than one employer or one transportation industry in a random pool if permitted by all the DOT agency drug and alcohol testing regulations involved.

   (1) *If you combine employees* from more than one transportation industry, you must ensure that the random testing rate is at least equal to the highest rate required by each DOT agency.

   (2) *Employees not covered* by DOT agency regulations may not be part of the same random pool with DOT covered employees.

(c) **You may assist employers** in ensuring that follow-up testing is conducted in accordance with the plan established by the SAP. However, neither you nor the employer are permitted to randomly select employees from a "follow-up pool" for follow-up testing.

§40.349 What records may a service agent receive and maintain?

(a) **Except where otherwise specified in this part,** as a service agent you may receive and maintain all records concerning DOT drug and alcohol testing programs, including positive, negative, and refusal to test individual test results. You do not need the employee's consent to receive and maintain these records.

(b) **You may maintain all information needed** for operating a drug/alcohol program (e.g., CCFs, ATFs, names of employees in random pools, random selection lists, copies of notices to employers of selected employees) on behalf of an employer.

(c) **If a service agent** originating drug or alcohol testing information, such as an MRO or BAT, sends the information directly to the DER, he or she may also provide the information simultaneously to you, as a C/TPA or other service agent who maintains this information for the employer.

(d) **If you are serving as an intermediary** in transmitting information that is required to be provided to the employer, you must ensure that it reaches the employer in the same time periods required elsewhere in this part.

(e) **You must ensure that you can make available** to the employer within two business days any information the employer is asked to produce by a DOT agency representative.

(f) **On request of an employer, you must,** at any time on the request of an employer, transfer immediately all records pertaining to the employer and its employees to the employer or to any other service agent the employer designates. You must carry out this transfer as soon as the employer requests it. You are not required to obtain employee consent for this transfer. You must not charge more than your reasonable administrative costs for conducting this transfer. You may not charge a fee for the release of these records.

(g) **If you are planning to go out of business** or your organization will be bought by or merged with another organization, you must immediately notify all employers and offer to transfer all records pertaining to the employer and its employees to the employer or to any other service agent the employer designates. You must carry out this transfer as soon as the employer requests it. You are not required to obtain employee consent for this transfer. You must not charge more than your reasonable administrative costs for conducting this transfer. You may not charge a fee for the release of these records.

§40.351 What confidentiality requirements apply to service agents?

Except where otherwise specified in this part, as a service agent the following confidentiality requirements apply to you:

(a) **When you receive or maintain** confidential information about employees (e.g., individual test results), you must follow the same confidentiality regulations as the employer with respect to the use and release of this information.

(b) **You must follow all confidentiality** and records retention requirements applicable to employers.

(c) **You may not provide individual test results** or other confidential information to another employer without a specific, written consent from the employee. For example, suppose you are a C/TPA that has employers X and Y as clients. Employee Jones works for X, and you maintain Jones' drug and alcohol test for X. Jones wants to change jobs and work for Y. You may not inform Y of the result of a test conducted for X without having a specific, written consent from Jones. Likewise, you may not provide this information to employer Z, who is not a C/TPA member, without this consent.

(d) **You must not use blanket consent forms** authorizing the release of employee testing information.

(e) **You must establish** adequate confidentiality and security measures to ensure that confidential employee records are not available to unauthorized persons. This includes protecting the physical security of records, access controls, and computer security measures to safeguard confidential data in electronic data bases.

§40.353 What principles govern the interaction between MROs and other service agents?

As a service agent other than an MRO (e.g., a C/TPA), the following principles govern your interaction with MROs:

(a) **You may provide MRO services to employers,** directly or through contract, if you meet all applicable provisions of this part.

(b) **If you employ or contract for an MRO,** the MRO must perform duties independently and confidentially. When you have a relationship with an MRO, you must structure the relationship to ensure that this independence and confidentiality are not compromised. Specific means (including both physical and operational measures, as appropriate) to separate MRO functions and other service agent functions are essential.

(c) **Only your staff** who are actually under the day-to-day supervision and control of an MRO with respect to MRO functions may perform these functions. This does not mean that those staff may not perform other functions at other times. However, the designation of your staff to perform MRO functions under MRO supervision must be limited and not used as a subterfuge to circumvent confidentiality and other requirements of this part and DOT agency regulations. You must ensure that MRO staff operate under controls sufficient to ensure that the independence and confidentiality of the MRO process are not compromised.

(d) **Like other MROs,** an MRO you employ or contract with must personally conduct verification interviews with employees and must personally make all verification decisions. Consequently, your staff cannot perform these functions.

§40.355 What limitations apply to the activities of service agents?

As a service agent, you are subject to the following limitations concerning your activities in the DOT drug and alcohol testing program.

(a) **You must not require an employee** to sign a consent, release, waiver of liability, or indemnification agreement with respect to any part of the drug or alcohol testing process covered by this part (including, but not limited to, collections, laboratory testing, MRO, and SAP services). No one may do so on behalf of a service agent.

(b) **You must not act as an intermediary** in the transmission of drug test results from the laboratory to the MRO. That is, the laboratory may not send results to you, with you in turn sending them to the MRO for verification. For example, a practice in which the laboratory transmits results to your computer system, and you then assign the results to a particular MRO, is not permitted.

(c) **You must not transmit drug test results** directly from the laboratory to the employer (by electronic or other means) or to a service agent who forwards them to the employer. All confirmed laboratory results must be processed by the MRO before they are released to any other party.

(d) **You must not act as an intermediary** in the transmission of alcohol test results of 0.02 or higher from the STT or BAT to the DER.

(e) **Except as provided in paragraph (f) of this section,** you must not act as an intermediary in the transmission of individual SAP reports to the actual employer. That is, the SAP may not send such reports to you, with you in turn sending them to the actual employer. However, you may maintain individual SAP summary reports and follow-up testing plans after they are sent to the DER, and the SAP may transmit such reports to you simultaneously with sending them to the DER.

(f) **As an exception to paragraph (e) of this section,** you may act as an intermediary in the transmission of SAP report from the SAP to an owner-operator or other self-employed individual.

(g) **Except as provided in paragraph (h) of this section,** you must not make decisions to test an employee based upon reasonable suspicion, post-accident, return-to-duty, and follow-up determination criteria. These are duties the actual employer cannot delegate to a C/TPA. You may, however, provide advice and information to employers regarding these testing issues and how the employer should schedule required testing.

(h) **As an exception to paragraph (g) of this section,** you may make decisions to test an employee based upon reasonable suspicion, post-accident, return-to-duty, and follow-up determination criteria with respect to an owner-operator or other self-employed individual.

(i) **Except as provided in paragraph (j) of this section,** you must not make a determination that an employee has refused a drug or alcohol test. This is a non-delegable duty of the actual employer. You may, however, provide advice and information to employers regarding refusal-to-test issues.

(j) **As an exception to paragraph (i) of this section,** you may make a determination that an employee has refused a drug or alcohol test, if:
  (1) *You schedule a required test* for an owner-operator or other self-employed individual, and the individual fails to appear for the test without a legitimate reason; or
  (2) *As an MRO,* you determine that an individual has refused to test on the basis of adulteration or substitution.

(k) **You must not act as a DER.** For example, while you may be responsible for transmitting information to the employer about test results, you must not act on behalf of the employer in actions to remove employees from safety-sensitive duties.

(l) **In transmitting documents to laboratories,** you must ensure that you send to the laboratory that conducts testing only the laboratory copy of the CCF. You must not transmit other copies of the CCF or any ATFs to the laboratory.

(m) **You must not impose conditions or requirements** on employers that DOT regulations do not authorize. For example, as a C/TPA serving employers in the pipeline or motor carrier industry, you must not require employers to have provisions in their DOT plans that PHMSA or FMCSA regulations do not require.

(n) **You must not intentionally delay the transmission** of drug or alcohol testing-related documents concerning actions you have performed, because of a payment dispute or other reasons.

Example 1 to Paragraph (n): A laboratory that has tested a specimen must not delay transmitting the documentation of the test result to an MRO because of a billing or payment dispute with the MRO or a C/TPA.
Example 2 to Paragraph (n): An MRO or SAP who has interviewed an employee must not delay sending a verified test result or SAP report to the employer because of such a dispute with the employer or employee.
Example 3 to Paragraph (n): A collector who has performed a urine specimen collection must not delay sending the drug specimen and CCF to the laboratory because of a payment or other dispute with the laboratory or a C/TPA.
Example 4 to Paragraph (n): A BAT who has conducted an alcohol test must not delay sending test result information to an employer or C/TPA because of a payment or other dispute with the employer or C/TPA.

(o) **While you must follow the DOT agency regulations,** the actual employer remains accountable to DOT for compliance, and your failure to implement any aspect of the program as required in this part and other applicable DOT agency regulations makes the employer subject to enforcement action by the Department.

Subpart R - Public Interest Exclusions

§40.361 What is the purpose of a public interest exclusion (PIE)?

(a) **To protect the public interest,** including protecting transportation employers and employees from serious noncompliance with DOT drug and alcohol testing rules, the Department's policy is to ensure that employers conduct business only with responsible service agents.

(b) **The Department therefore uses PIEs** to exclude from participation in DOT's drug and alcohol testing program any service agent who, by serious noncompliance with this part or other DOT agency drug and alcohol testing regulations, has shown that it is not currently acting in a responsible manner.

(c) **A PIE is a serious action that the Department takes** only to protect the public interest. We intend to use PIEs only to remedy situations of serious noncompliance. PIEs are not used for the purpose of punishment.

(d) **Nothing in this subpart precludes** a DOT agency or the Inspector General from taking other action authorized by its regulations with respect to service agents or employers that violate its regulations.

§40.363 On what basis may the Department issue a PIE?

(a) **If you are a service agent,** the Department may issue a PIE concerning you if we determine that you have failed or refused to provide drug or alcohol testing services consistent with the requirements of this part or a DOT agency drug and alcohol regulation.

(b) **The Department also may issue a PIE** if you have failed to cooperate with DOT agency representatives concerning inspections, complaint investigations, compliance and enforcement reviews, or requests for documents and other information about compliance with this part or DOT agency drug and alcohol regulations.

§40.365 What is the Department's policy concerning starting a PIE proceeding?

(a) **It is the Department's policy** to start a PIE proceeding only in cases of serious, uncorrected noncompliance with the provisions of this part, affecting such matters as safety, the outcomes of test results, privacy and confidentiality, due process and fairness for employees, the honesty and integrity of the testing program, and cooperation with or provision of information to DOT agency representatives.

(b) **The following are examples** of the kinds of serious noncompliance that, as a matter of policy, the Department views as appropriate grounds for starting a PIE proceeding. These examples are not intended to be an exhaustive or exclusive list of the grounds for starting a PIE proceeding. We intend them to illustrate the level of seriousness that the Department believes supports starting a PIE proceeding. The examples follow:

(1) *For an MRO,* verifying tests positive without interviewing the employees as required by this part or providing MRO services without meeting the qualifications for an MRO required by this part;
(2) *For a laboratory,* refusing to provide information to the Department, an employer, or an employee as required by this part; failing or refusing to conduct a validity testing program when required by this part; or a pattern or practice of testing errors that result in the cancellation of tests. (As a general matter of policy, the Department does not intend to initiate a PIE proceeding concerning a laboratory with respect to matters on which HHS initiates certification actions under its laboratory guidelines.);
(3) *For a collector,* a pattern or practice of directly observing collections when doing so is unauthorized, or failing or refusing to directly observe collections when doing so is mandatory;
(4) *For collectors, BATs, or STTs,* a pattern or practice of using forms, testing equipment, or collection kits that do not meet the standards in this part;
(5) *For a collector, BAT, or STT,* a pattern or practice of "fatal flaws" or other significant uncorrected errors in the collection process;
(6) *For a laboratory, MRO or C/TPA,* failing or refusing to report tests results as required by this part or DOT agency regulations;
(7) *For a laboratory,* falsifying, concealing, or destroying documentation concerning any part of the drug testing process, including, but not limited to, documents in a "litigation package";
(8) *For SAPs,* providing SAP services while not meeting SAP qualifications required by this part or performing evaluations without face-to-face interviews;
(9) *For any service agent,* maintaining a relationship with another party that constitutes a conflict of interest under this part (e.g., a laboratory that derives a financial benefit from having an employer use a specific MRO);
(10) *For any service agent,* representing falsely that the service agent or its activities is approved or certified by the Department or a DOT agency;
(11) *For any service agent,* disclosing an employee's test result information to any party this part or a DOT agency regulation does not authorize, including by obtaining a "blanket" consent from employees or by creating a data base from which employers or others can retrieve an employee's DOT test results without the specific consent of the employee;
(12) *For any service agent,* interfering or attempting to interfere with the ability of an MRO to communicate with the Department, or retaliating against an MRO for communicating with the Department;
(13) *For any service agent,* directing or recommending that an employer fail or refuse to implement any provision of this part; or
(14) *With respect to noncompliance* with a DOT agency regulation, conduct that affects important provisions of Department-wide concern (e.g., failure to properly conduct the selection process for random testing).

§40.367 Who initiates a PIE proceeding?
The following DOT officials may initiate a PIE proceeding:
(a) The drug and alcohol program manager of a DOT agency;
(b) An official of ODAPC, other than the Director; or
(c) The designee of any of these officials.

§40.369 What is the discretion of an initiating official in starting a PIE proceeding?
(a) Initiating officials have broad discretion in deciding whether to start a PIE proceeding.
(b) In exercising this discretion, the initiating official must consider the Department's policy regarding the seriousness of the service agent's conduct (see §40.365) and all information he or she has obtained to this point concerning the facts of the case. The initiating official may also consider the availability of the resources needed to pursue a PIE proceeding.
(c) A decision not to initiate a PIE proceeding does not necessarily mean that the Department regards a service agent as being in compliance or that the Department may not use other applicable remedies in a situation of noncompliance.

§40.371 On what information does an initiating official rely in deciding whether to start a PIE proceeding?
(a) An initiating official may rely on credible information from any source as the basis for starting a PIE proceeding.

(b) Before sending a correction notice (see §40.373), the initiating official informally contacts the service agent to determine if there is any information that may affect the initiating official's determination about whether it is necessary to send a correction notice. The initiating official may take any information resulting from this contact into account in determining whether to proceed under this subpart.

§40.373 Before starting a PIE proceeding, does the initiating official give the service agent an opportunity to correct problems?
(a) If you are a service agent, the initiating official must send you a correction notice before starting a PIE proceeding.
(b) The correction notice identifies the specific areas in which you must come into compliance in order to avoid being subject to a PIE proceeding.
(c) If you make and document changes needed to come into compliance in the areas listed in the correction notice to the satisfaction of the initiating official within 60 days of the date you receive the notice, the initiating official does not start a PIE proceeding. The initiating official may conduct appropriate fact finding to verify that you have made and maintained satisfactory corrections. When he or she is satisfied that you are in compliance, the initiating official sends you a notice that the matter is concluded.

§40.375 How does the initiating official start a PIE proceeding?
(a) As a service agent, if your compliance matter is not correctable (see §40.373(a)), or if have not resolved compliance matters as provided in §40.373(c), the initiating official starts a PIE proceeding by sending you a notice of proposed exclusion (NOPE). The NOPE contains the initiating official's recommendations concerning the issuance of a PIE, but it is not a decision by the Department to issue a PIE.
(b) The NOPE includes the following information:
(1) *A statement that the initiating official* is recommending that the Department issue a PIE concerning you;
(2) *The factual basis for the initiating official's belief* that you are not providing drug and/or alcohol testing services to DOT-regulated employers consistent with the requirements of this part or are in serious noncompliance with a DOT agency drug and alcohol regulation;
(3) *The factual basis for the initiating official's belief* that your noncompliance has not been or cannot be corrected;
(4) *The initiating official's recommendation for the scope of the PIE;*
(5) *The initiating official's recommendation* for the duration of the PIE; and
(6) *A statement that you may contest the issuance* of the proposed PIE, as provided in §40.379.
(c) The initiating official sends a copy of the NOPE to the ODAPC Director at the same time he or she sends the NOPE to you.

§40.377 Who decides whether to issue a PIE?
(a) The ODAPC Director, or his or her designee, decides whether to issue a PIE. If a designee is acting as the decisionmaker, all references in this subpart to the Director refer to the designee.
(b) To ensure his or her impartiality, the Director plays no role in the initiating official's determination about whether to start a PIE proceeding.
(c) There is a "firewall" between the initiating official and the Director. This means that the initiating official and the Director are prohibited from having any discussion, contact, or exchange of information with one another about the matter, except for documents and discussions that are part of the record of the proceeding.

§40.379 How do you contest the issuance of a PIE?
(a) If you receive a NOPE, you may contest the issuance of the PIE.
(b) If you want to contest the proposed PIE, you must provide the Director information and argument in opposition to the proposed PIE in writing, in person, and/or through a representative. To contest the proposed PIE, you must take one or more of the steps listed in this paragraph (b) within 30 days after you receive the NOPE.
(1) *You may request that the Director* dismiss the proposed PIE without further proceedings, on the basis that it does not concern serious noncompliance with this part or DOT agency regulations, consistent with the Department's policy as stated in §40.365.
(2) *You may present written information and arguments,* consistent with the provisions of §40.381, contesting the proposed PIE.

Subpart R - Public Interest Exclusions §40.391 (g)

(3) *You may arrange with the Director* for an informal meeting to present your information and arguments.

(c) **If you do not take any of the actions** listed in paragraph (b) of this section within 30 days after you receive the NOPE, the matter proceeds as an uncontested case. In this event, the Director makes his or her decision based on the record provided by the initiating official (i.e., the NOPE and any supporting information or testimony) and any additional information the Director obtains.

§40.381 What information do you present to contest the proposed issuance of a PIE?

(a) **As a service agent** who wants to contest a proposed PIE, you must present at least the following information to the Director:
(1) *Specific facts* that contradict the statements contained in the NOPE (see §40.375(b)(2) and (3)). A general denial is insufficient to raise a genuine dispute over facts material to the issuance of a PIE;
(2) *Identification of any existing, proposed or prior PIE; and*
(3) *Identification of your affiliates, if any.*

(b) **You may provide** any information and arguments you wish concerning the proposed issuance, scope and duration of the PIE (see §40.375 (b)(4) and (5)).

(c) **You may provide** any additional relevant information or arguments concerning any of the issues in the matter.

§40.383 What procedures apply if you contest the issuance of a PIE?

(a) **DOT conducts PIE proceedings** in a fair and informal manner. The Director may use flexible procedures to allow you to present matters in opposition. The Director is not required to follow formal rules of evidence or procedure in creating the record of the proceeding.

(b) **The Director will consider any information or argument** he or she determines to be relevant to the decision on the matter.

(c) **You may submit any documentary evidence** you want the Director to consider. In addition, if you have arranged an informal meeting with the Director, you may present witnesses and confront any person the initiating official presents as a witness against you.

(d) **In cases** where there are material factual issues in dispute, the Director or his or her designee may conduct additional fact-finding.

(e) **If you have arranged a meeting with the Director,** the Director will make a transcribed record of the meeting available to you on your request. You must pay the cost of transcribing and copying the meeting record.

§40.385 Who bears the burden of proof in a PIE proceeding?

(a) **As the proponent of issuing a PIE,** the initiating official bears the burden of proof.

(b) **This burden is to demonstrate,** by a preponderance of the evidence, that the service agent was in serious noncompliance with the requirements of this part for drug and/or alcohol testing-related services or with the requirements of another DOT agency drug and alcohol testing regulation.

§40.387 What matters does the Director decide concerning a proposed PIE?

(a) **Following the service agent's response** (see §40.379(b)) or, if no response is received, after 30 days have passed from the date on which the service agent received the NOPE, the Director may take one of the following steps:
(1) *In response to a request from the service agent* (see §40.379 (b)(1)) or on his or her own motion, the Director may dismiss a PIE proceeding if he or she determines that it does not concern serious noncompliance with this part or DOT agency regulations, consistent with the Department's policy as stated in §40.365.
  (i) *If the Director dismisses a proposed PIE* under this paragraph (a), the action is closed with respect to the noncompliance alleged in the NOPE.
  (ii) *The Department may initiate* a new PIE proceeding against you on the basis of different or subsequent conduct that is in noncompliance with this part or other DOT drug and alcohol testing rules.
(2) *If the Director determines* that the initiating official's submission does not have complete information needed for a decision, the Director may remand the matter to the initiating official. The initiating official may resubmit the matter to the Director when the needed information is complete. If the basis for the proposed PIE has changed, the initiating official must send an amended NOPE to the service agent.

(b) **The Director makes determinations** concerning the following matters in any PIE proceeding that he or she decides on the merits:
(1) *Any material facts that are in dispute;*
(2) *Whether the facts support issuing a PIE;*
(3) *The scope of any PIE that is issued; and*
(4) *The duration of any PIE that is issued.*

§40.389 What factors may the Director consider?

This section lists examples of the kind of mitigating and aggravating factors that the Director may consider in determining whether to issue a PIE concerning you, as well as the scope and duration of a PIE. This list is not exhaustive or exclusive. The Director may consider other factors if appropriate in the circumstances of a particular case. The list of examples follows:

(a) **The actual or potential harm that results** or may result from your noncompliance;

(b) **The frequency of incidents** and/or duration of the noncompliance;

(c) **Whether there is a pattern or prior history of noncompliance;**

(d) **Whether the noncompliance was pervasive** within your organization, including such factors as the following:
(1) *Whether and to what extent* your organization planned, initiated, or carried out the noncompliance;
(2) *The positions held by individuals* involved in the noncompliance, and whether your principals tolerated their noncompliance; and
(3) *Whether you had effective standards* of conduct and control systems (both with respect to your own organization and any contractors or affiliates) at the time the noncompliance occurred;

(e) **Whether you have demonstrated** an appropriate compliance disposition, including such factors as the following:
(1) *Whether you have accepted responsibility* for the noncompliance and recognize the seriousness of the conduct that led to the cause for issuance of the PIE;
(2) *Whether you have cooperated fully* with the Department during the investigation. The Director may consider when the cooperation began and whether you disclosed all pertinent information known to you;
(3) *Whether you have fully investigated* the circumstances of the noncompliance forming the basis for the PIE and, if so, have made the result of the investigation available to the Director;
(4) *Whether you have taken* appropriate disciplinary action against the individuals responsible for the activity that constitutes the grounds for issuance of the PIE; and
(5) *Whether your organization* has taken appropriate corrective actions or remedial measures, including implementing actions to prevent recurrence;

(f) **With respect to noncompliance** with a DOT agency regulation, the degree to which the noncompliance affects matters common to the DOT drug and alcohol testing program;

(g) **Other factors appropriate to the circumstances of the case.**

§40.391 What is the scope of a PIE?

(a) **The scope of a PIE is the Department's determination** about the divisions, organizational elements, types of services, affiliates, and/or individuals (including direct employees of a service agent and its contractors) to which a PIE applies.

(b) **If, as a service agent, the Department issues** a PIE concerning you, the PIE applies to all your divisions, organizational elements, and types of services that are involved with or affected by the noncompliance that forms the factual basis for issuing the PIE.

(c) **In the NOPE (see §40.375(b)(4)),** the initiating official sets forth his or her recommendation for the scope of the PIE. The proposed scope of the PIE is one of the elements of the proceeding that the service agent may contest (see §40.381(b)) and about which the Director makes a decision (see §40.387(b)(3)).

(d) **In recommending and deciding the scope of the PIE,** the initiating official and Director, respectively, must take into account the provisions of paragraphs (e) through (j) of this section.

(e) **The pervasiveness of the noncompliance** within a service agent's organization (see §40.389(d)) is an important consideration in determining the scope of a PIE. The appropriate scope of a PIE grows broader as the pervasiveness of the noncompliance increases.

(f) **The application of a PIE is not limited** to the specific location or employer at which the conduct that forms the factual basis for issuing the PIE was discovered.

(g) **A PIE applies to your affiliates,** if the affiliate is involved with or affected by the conduct that forms the factual basis for issuing the PIE.

47

(h) **A PIE applies to individuals** who are officers, employees, directors, shareholders, partners, or other individuals associated with your organization in the following circumstances:
  (1) *Conduct forming any part of the factual basis* of the PIE occurred in connection with the individual's performance of duties by or on behalf of your organization; or
  (2) *The individual knew of,* had reason to know of, approved, or acquiesced in such conduct. The individual's acceptance of benefits derived from such conduct is evidence of such knowledge, acquiescence, or approval.
(i) **If a contractor to your organization** is solely responsible for the conduct that forms the factual basis for a PIE, the PIE does not apply to the service agent itself unless the service agent knew or should have known about the conduct and did not take action to correct it.
(j) **PIEs do not apply to drug and alcohol testing** that DOT does not regulate.
(k) **The following examples illustrate** how the Department intends the provisions of this section to work:
Example 1 to §40.391. Service Agent P provides a variety of drug testing services. P's SAP services are involved in a serious violation of this Part 40. However, P's other services fully comply with this part, and P's overall management did not plan or concur in the noncompliance, which in fact was contrary to P's articulated standards. Because the noncompliance was isolated in one area of the organization's activities, and did not pervade the entire organization, the scope of the PIE could be limited to SAP services.
Example 2 to §40.391. Service Agent Q provides a similar variety of services. The conduct forming the factual basis for a PIE concerns collections for a transit authority. As in Example 1, the noncompliance is not pervasive throughout Q's organization. The PIE would apply to collections at all locations served by Q, not just the particular transit authority or not just in the State in which the transit authority is located.
Example 3 to §40.391. Service Agent R provides a similar array of services. One or more of the following problems exists: R's activities in several areas — collections, MROs, SAPs, protecting the confidentiality of information — are involved in serious noncompliance; DOT determines that R's management knew or should have known about serious noncompliance in one or more areas, but management did not take timely corrective action; or, in response to an inquiry from DOT personnel, R's management refuses to provide information about its operations. In each of these three cases, the scope of the PIE would include all aspects of R's services.
Example 4 to §40.391. Service Agent W provides only one kind of service (e.g., laboratory or MRO services). The Department issues a PIE concerning these services. Because W only provides this one kind of service, the PIE necessarily applies to all its operations.
Example 5 to §40.391. Service Agent X, by exercising reasonably prudent oversight of its collection contractor, should have known that the contractor was making numerous "fatal flaws" in tests. Alternatively, X received a correction notice pointing out these problems in its contractor's collections. In neither case did X take action to correct the problem. X, as well as the contractor, would be subject to a PIE with respect to collections.
Example 6 to §40.391. Service Agent Y could not reasonably have known that one of its MROs was regularly failing to interview employees before verifying tests positive. When it received a correction notice, Y immediately dismissed the erring MRO. In this case, the MRO would be subject to a PIE but Y would not.
Example 7 to §40.391. The Department issues a PIE with respect to Service Agent Z. Z provides services for DOT-regulated transportation employers, a Federal agency under the HHS-regulated Federal employee testing program, and various private businesses and public agencies that DOT does not regulate. The PIE applies only to the DOT-regulated transportation employers with respect to their DOT-mandated testing, not to the Federal agency or the other public agencies and private businesses. The PIE does not prevent the non-DOT regulated entities from continuing to use Z's services.

§40.393 How long does a PIE stay in effect?

(a) **In the NOPE (see §40.375(b)(5)),** the initiating official proposes the duration of the PIE. The duration of the PIE is one of the elements of the proceeding that the service agent may contest (see §40.381(b)) and about which the Director makes a decision (see §40.387(b)(4)).
(b) **In deciding upon the duration of the PIE,** the Director considers the seriousness of the conduct on which the PIE is based and the continued need to protect employers and employees from the service agent's noncompliance. The Director considers factors such as those listed in §40.389 in making this decision.
(c) **The duration of a PIE** will be between one and five years, unless the Director reduces its duration under §40.407.

§40.395 Can you settle a PIE proceeding?

At any time before the Director's decision, you and the initiating official can, with the Director's concurrence, settle a PIE proceeding.

§40.397 When does the Director make a PIE decision?

The Director makes his or her decision within 60 days of the date when the record of a PIE proceeding is complete (including any meeting with the Director and any additional fact-finding that is necessary). The Director may extend this period for good cause for additional periods of up to 30 days.

§40.399 How does the Department notify service agents of its decision?

If you are a service agent involved in a PIE proceeding, the Director provides you written notice as soon as he or she makes a PIE decision. The notice includes the following elements:

(a) **If the decision is not to issue a PIE,** a statement of the reasons for the decision, including findings of fact with respect to any material factual issues that were in dispute.
(b) **If the decision is to issue a PIE —**
  (1) *A reference to the NOPE;*
  (2) *A statement of the reasons for the decision,* including findings of fact with respect to any material factual issues that were in dispute;
  (3) *A statement of the scope of the PIE;* and
  (4) *A statement of the duration of the PIE.*

§40.401 How does the Department notify employers and the public about a PIE?

(a) **The Department maintains a document** called the "List of Excluded Drug and Alcohol Service Agents." This document may be found on the Department's web site (*http://www.dot.gov/ost/dapc*). You may also request a copy of the document from ODAPC.
(b) **When the Director issues a PIE,** he or she adds to the List the name and address of the service agent, and any other persons or organizations, to whom the PIE applies and information about the scope and duration of the PIE.
(c) **When a service agent ceases to be subject to a PIE,** the Director removes this information from the List.
(d) **The Department also publishes** a Federal Register notice to inform the public on any occasion on which a service agent is added to or taken off the List.

§40.403 Must a service agent notify its clients when the Department issues a PIE?

(a) **As a service agent,** if the Department issues a PIE concerning you, you must notify each of your DOT-regulated employer clients, in writing, about the issuance, scope, duration, and effect of the PIE. You may meet this requirement by sending a copy of the Director's PIE decision or by a separate notice. You must send this notice to each client within three business days of receiving from the Department the notice provided for in §40.399(b).
(b) **As part of the notice you send** under paragraph (a) of this section, you must offer to transfer immediately all records pertaining to the employer and its employees to the employer or to any other service agent the employer designates. You must carry out this transfer as soon as the employer requests it.

§40.405 May the Federal courts review PIE decisions?

The Director's decision is a final administrative action of the Department. Like all final administrative actions of Federal agencies, the Director's decision is subject to judicial review under the Administrative Procedure Act (5 U.S.C. 551 et. seq).

§40.407 May a service agent ask to have a PIE reduced or terminated?

(a) **Yes, as a service agent concerning whom** the Department has issued a PIE, you may request that the Director terminate a PIE or reduce its duration and/or scope. This process is limited to the issues of duration and scope. It is not an appeal or reconsideration of the decision to issue the PIE.
(b) **Your request must be in writing** and supported with documentation.
(c) **You must wait at least nine months** from the date on which the Director issued the PIE to make this request.
(d) **The initiating official who was the proponent** of the PIE may provide information and arguments concerning your request to the Director.
(e) **If the Director verifies that the sources** of your noncompliance have been eliminated and that all drug or alcohol testing-related services you would provide to DOT-regulated employers will be consistent with the requirements of this part, the Director may issue a notice terminating or reducing the PIE.

§40.409 What does the issuance of a PIE mean to transportation employers?

(a) **As an employer,** you are deemed to have notice of the issuance of a PIE when it appears on the List mentioned in §40.401(a) or the notice of the PIE appears in the Federal Register as provided in §40.401(d). You should check this List to ensure that any service agents you are using or planning to use are not subject to a PIE.
(b) **As an employer who is using a service agent** concerning whom a PIE is issued, you must stop using the services of the service agent no later than 90 days after the Department has published the decision in the Federal Register or posted it on its web site. You may apply to the ODAPC Director for an extension of 30 days if you demonstrate that you cannot find a substitute service agent within 90 days.
(c) **Except during the period provided in paragraph (b)** of this section, you must not, as an employer, use the services of a service

agent that are covered by a PIE that the Director has issued under this subpart. If you do so, you are in violation of the Department's regulations and subject to applicable DOT agency sanctions (e.g., civil penalties, withholding of Federal financial assistance).

(d) You also must not obtain drug or alcohol testing services through a contractor or affiliate of the service agent to whom the PIE applies.

Example to Paragraph (d): Service Agent R was subject to a PIE with respect to SAP services. As an employer, not only must you not use R's own SAP services, but you also must not use SAP services you arrange through R, such as services provided by a subcontractor or affiliate of R or a person or organization that receives financial gain from its relationship with R.

(e) This section's prohibition on using the services of a service agent concerning which the Director has issued a PIE applies to employers in all industries subject to DOT drug and alcohol testing regulations.

Example to Paragraph (e): The initiating official for a PIE was the FAA drug and alcohol program manager, and the conduct forming the basis of the PIE pertained to the aviation industry. As a motor carrier, transit authority, pipeline, railroad, or maritime employer, you are also prohibited from using the services of the service agent involved in connection with the DOT drug and alcohol testing program.

(f) The issuance of a PIE does not result in the cancellation of drug or alcohol tests conducted using the service agent involved before the issuance of the Director's decision or up to 90 days following its publication in the Federal Register or posting on the Department's web site, unless otherwise specified in the Director's PIE decision or the Director grants an extension as provided in paragraph (b) of this section.

Example to Paragraph (f): The Department issues a PIE concerning Service Agent N on September 1. All tests conducted using N's services before September 1, and through November 30, are valid for all purposes under DOT drug and alcohol testing regulations, assuming they meet all other regulatory requirements.

§40.411 What is the role of the DOT Inspector General's office?

(a) Any person may bring concerns about waste, fraud, or abuse on the part of a service agent to the attention of the DOT Office of Inspector General.

(b) In appropriate cases, the Office of Inspector General may pursue criminal or civil remedies against a service agent.

(c) The Office of Inspector General may provide factual information to other DOT officials for use in a PIE proceeding.

§40.413 How are notices sent to service agents?

(a) If you are a service agent, DOT sends notices to you, including correction notices, notices of proposed exclusion, decision notices, and other notices, in any of the ways mentioned in paragraph (b) or (c) of this section.

(b) DOT may send a notice to you, your identified counsel, your agent for service of process, or any of your partners, officers, directors, owners, or joint venturers to the last known street address, fax number, or e-mail address. DOT deems the notice to have been received by you if sent to any of these persons.

(c) DOT considers notices to be received by you —
  (1) *When delivered,* if DOT mails the notice to the last known street address, or five days after we send it if the letter is undeliverable;
  (2) *When sent,* if DOT sends the notice by fax or five days after we send it if the fax is undeliverable; or
  (3) *When delivered,* if DOT sends the notice by e-mail or five days after DOT sends it if the e-mail is undeliverable.

Appendix A to Part 40 — DOT Standards for Urine Collection Kits

The Collection Kit Contents:

1. Collection Container
  a. *Single-use container,* made of plastic, large enough to easily catch and hold at least 55 mL of urine voided from the body.
  b. *Must have graduated volume markings* clearly noting levels of 45 mL and above.
  c. *Must have a temperature strip* providing graduated temperature readings 32-38° C / 90-100° F, that is affixed or can be affixed at a proper level on the outside of the collection container. Other methodologies (e.g., temperature device built into the wall of the container) are acceptable provided the temperature measurement is accurate and such that there is no potential for contamination of the specimen.
  d. *Must be individually wrapped* in a sealed plastic bag or shrink wrapping; or must have a peelable, sealed lid or other easily visible tamper-evident system.
  e. *May be made available separately* at collection sites to address shy bladder situations when several voids may be required to complete the testing process.

2. Plastic Specimen Bottles
  a. *Each bottle must be large enough* to hold at least 35 mL; or alternatively, they may be two distinct sizes of specimen bottles provided that the bottle designed to hold the primary specimen holds at least 35 mL of urine and the bottle designed to hold the split specimen holds at least 20 mL.
  b. *Must have screw-on or snap-on caps* that prevent seepage of the urine from the bottles during shipment.
  c. *Must have markings* clearly indicating the appropriate levels (30 mL for the primary specimen and 15 mL for the split) of urine that must be poured into the bottles.
  d. *Must be designed* so that the required tamper-evident bottle seals made available on the CCF fit with no damage to the seal when the employee initials it nor with the chance that the seal overlap would conceal printed information.
  e. *Must be wrapped* (with caps) together in a sealed plastic bag or shrink wrapping separate from the collection container; or must be wrapped (with cap) individually in sealed plastic bags or shrink wrapping; or must have peelable, sealed lid or other easily visible tamper-evident system.
  f. *Plastic material must be leak resistant.*

3. Leak-resistant Plastic Bag
  a. *Must have two sealable compartments or pouches* which are leak-resistant; one large enough to hold two specimen bottles and the other large enough to hold the CCF paperwork.
  b. *The sealing methodology* must be such that once the compartments are sealed, any tampering or attempts to open either compartment will be evident.

4. Absorbent material
Each kit must contain enough absorbent material to absorb the entire contents of both specimen bottles. Absorbent material must be designed to fit inside the leak-resistant plastic bag pouch into which the specimen bottles are placed.

5. Shipping Container
  a. *Must be designed* to adequately protect the specimen bottles from shipment damage in the transport of specimens from the collection site to the laboratory (e.g., standard courier box, small cardboard box, plastic container).
  b. *May be made available separately at collection sites* rather than being part of an actual kit sent to collection sites.
  c. *A shipping container is not necessary* if a laboratory courier hand-delivers the specimen bottles in the plastic leak-proof bags from the collection site to the laboratory.

Appendix B to Part 40 — DOT Drug Testing Semi-Annual Laboratory Report

The following items are required on each report:
Reporting Period: (inclusive dates)
Laboratory Identification: (name and address)
Employer Identification: (name; may include billing code or ID code)
C/C/TPA Identification: (where applicable; name and address)

1. Number of specimen results reported: (total number)
  By test type:
  a. *Pre-employment testing:* (number)
  b. *Post-accident testing:* (number)
  c. *Random testing:* (number)
  d. *Reasonable suspicion/cause testing:* (number)
  e. *Return-to-duty testing:* (number)
  f. *Follow-up testing:* (number)
  g. *Type not noted on CCF:* (number)

2. Number of specimens reported as:
  a. *Negative:* (total number)
  b. *Negative-dilute:* (number)

3. Number of specimens reported as Rejected for Testing: (total number)
  By reason:
  a. *Fatal flaw:* (number)
  b. *Uncorrected flaw:* (number)

4. Number of specimens reported as Positive: (total number)
  By drug:
  a. *Marijuana Metabolite:* (number)
  b. *Cocaine Metabolite:* (number)
  c. *Opiates:*
    (1) *Codeine:* (number)
    (2) *Morphine:* (number)

Appendix C Part 40 - Procedures for Transportation Workplace Drug and Alcohol Testing Programs

   (3) *6-AM:* (number)
  d. *Phencyclidine:* (number)
  e. *Amphetamines:* (number)
   (1) *Amphetamine:* (number)
   (2) *Methamphetamine:* (number):
5. **Adulterated:** (number)
6. **Substituted:** (number)
7. **Invalid results:** (number)

Appendix C to Part 40 [Reserved]

Appendix D to Part 40 Report Format: Split Specimen Failure To Reconfirm

Fax or mail to:
Department of Transportation
Office of Drug and Alcohol Policy and Compliance
400 7th Street, SW., Room 10403
Washington, DC 20590
(fax) 202-366-3897.

1. *MRO name, address, phone number, and fax number.*
2. *Collection site name, address, and phone number.*
3. *Date of collection.*
4. *Specimen I.D. number.*
5. *Laboratory accession number.*
6. *Primary specimen laboratory name, address, and phone number.*
7. *Date result reported or certified by primary laboratory.*
8. *Split specimen laboratory name, address, and phone number.*
9. *Date split specimen result* reported or certified by split specimen laboratory.
10. *Primary specimen results* (e.g., name of drug, adulterant) in the primary specimen.
11. *Reason for split specimen failure-to-reconfirm result* (e.g., drug or adulterant not present, specimen invalid, split not collected, insufficient volume).
12. *Actions taken by the MRO* (e.g., notified employer of failure to reconfirm and requirement for recollection).
13. *Additional information explaining the reason for cancellation.*
14. *Name of individual submitting the report (if not the MRO).*

Appendix E to Part 40 SAP Equivalency Requirements for Certification Organizations

1. **Experience:** Minimum requirements are for three years of full-time supervised experience or 6,000 hours of supervised experience as an alcoholism and/or drug abuse counselor. The supervision must be provided by a licensed or certified practitioner. Supervised experience is important if the individual is to be considered a professional in the field of alcohol and drug abuse evaluation and counseling.
2. **Education:** There exists a requirement of 270 contact hours of education and training in alcoholism and/or drug abuse or related training. These hours can take the form of formal education, in-service training, and professional development courses. Part of any professional counselor's development is participation in formal and non-formal education opportunities within the field.
3. **Continuing Education:** The certified counselor must receive at least 40-60 hours of continuing education units (CEU) during each two year period. These CEUs are important to the counselor's keeping abreast of changes and improvements in the field.
4. **Testing:** A passing score on a national test is a requirement. The test must accurately measure the application of the knowledge, skills, and abilities possessed by the counselor. The test establishes a national standard that must be met to practice.
5. **Testing Validity:** The certification examination must be reviewed by an independent authority for validity (examination reliability and relationship to the knowledge, skills, and abilities required by the counseling field). The reliability of the exam is paramount if counselor attributes are to be accurately measured. The examination passing score point must be placed at an appropriate minimal level score as gauged by statistically reliable methodology.
6. **Measurable Knowledge Base:** The certification process must be based upon measurable knowledge possessed by the applicant and verified through collateral data and testing. That level of knowledge must be of sufficient quantity to ensure a high quality of SAP evaluation and referral services.
7. **Measurable Skills Base:** The certification process must be based upon measurable skills possessed by the applicant and verified through collateral data and testing. That level of skills must be of sufficient quality to ensure a high quality of SAP evaluation and referral services.
8. **Quality Assurance Plan:** The certification agency must ensure that a means exists to determine that applicant records are verified as being true by the certification staff. This is an important check to ensure that true information is being accepted by the certifying agency.
9. **Code of Ethics:** Certified counselors must pledge to adhere to an ethical standard for practice. It must be understood that code violations could result in de-certification. These standards are vital in maintaining the integrity of practitioners. High ethical standards are required to ensure quality of client care and confidentiality of client information as well as to guard against inappropriate referral practices.
10. **Re-certification Program:** Certification is not just a one-time event. It is a continuing privilege with continuing requirements. Among these are continuing education, continuing state certification, and concomitant adherence to the code of ethics. Re-certification serves as a protector of client interests by removing poor performers from the certified practice.
11. **Fifty State Coverage:** Certification must be available to qualified counselors in all 50 States and, therefore, the test must be available to qualified applicants in all 50 States. Because many companies are multi-State operators, consistency in SAP evaluation quality and opportunities is paramount. The test need not be given in all 50 States but should be accessible to candidates from all States.
12. **National Commission for Certifying Agencies** (NCCA) Accreditation: Having NCCA accreditation is a means of demonstrating to the Department of Transportation that your certification has been reviewed by a panel of impartial experts that have determined that your examination(s) has met stringent and appropriate testing standards.

Appendix F to Part 40 Drug and Alcohol Testing Information that C/TPAs May Transmit to Employers

1. **If you are a C/TPA,** you may, acting as an intermediary, transmit the information in the following sections of this part to the DER for an employer, if the employer chooses to have you do so. These are the only items that you are permitted to transmit to the employer as an intermediary. The use of C/TPA intermediaries is prohibited in all other cases, such as transmission of laboratory drug test results to MROs, the transmission of medical information from MROs to employers, the transmission of SAP reports to employers, the transmission of positive alcohol test results, and the transmission of medical information from MROs to employers.
2. **In every case, you must ensure that,** in transmitting the information, you meet all requirements (e.g., concerning confidentiality and timing) that would apply if the party originating the information (e.g., an MRO or collector) sent the information directly to the employer. For example, if you transmit MROs' drug testing results to DERs, you must transmit each drug test result to the DER in compliance with the requirements for MROs set forth in §40.167.

Drug testing information

§40.25: Previous two years' test results

§40.35: Notice to collectors of contact information for DER

§40.61(a): Notification to DER that an employee is a "no show" for a drug test

§40.63(e): Notification to DER of a collection under direct observation

§40.65(b)(6) and (7) and (c)(2) and (3): Notification to DER of a refusal to provide a specimen or an insufficient specimen

§40.73(a)(9): Transmission of CCF copies to DER (However, MRO copy of CCF must be sent by collector directly to the MRO, not through the C/TPA.)

§40.111(a): Transmission of laboratory statistical report to employer

§40.127(f): Report of test results to DER

§§40.127(g), 40.129(d), 40.159(a)(4)(ii), 40.161(b): Reports to DER that test is cancelled

§40.129(d): Report of test results to DER

§40.129(g)(1): Report to DER of confirmed positive test in stand-down situation

§40.149(b): Report to DER of changed test result

§40.155(a): Report to DER of dilute specimen

§40.167(b) and (c): Reports of test results to DER

§40.187(a)-(f): Reports to DER concerning the reconfirmation of tests

Part 40 - Procedures for Transportation Workplace Drug and Alcohol Testing Programs   Appendix G

§40.191(d): Notice to DER concerning refusals to test

§40.193(b)(3): Notification to DER of refusal in shy bladder situation

§40.193(b)(4): Notification to DER of insufficient specimen

§40.193(b)(5): Transmission of CCF copies to DER (not to MRO)

§40.199: Report to DER of cancelled test and direction to DER for additional collection

§40.201: Report to DER of cancelled test

Alcohol testing information

§40.215: Notice to BATs and STTs of contact information for DER

§40.241(b)(1): Notification to DER that an employee is a "no show" for an alcohol test

§40.247(a)(2): Transmission of alcohol screening test results only when the test result is less than 0.02

§40.255(a)(4): Transmission of alcohol confirmation test results only when the test result is less than 0.02

§40.263(a)(3) and (b)(3): Notification of insufficient saliva and failure to provide sufficient amount of breath

Appendix G to Part 40 Alcohol Testing Form

The following form is the alcohol testing form required for use in the DOT alcohol testing program beginning August 1, 2001. Use of the form is authorized beginning January 18, 2001.

§§40.243, 40.253, 40.275, Appendix G to Part 40 DOT Interpretations

Question 1: Is it acceptable to affix printed alcohol test results on the back of the Alcohol Testing Form (ATF) rather than on the front?

Guidance: §§40.243(f) and 40.253(g) instruct the BAT to affix the printout of the information from the alcohol testing device to the designated space on the ATF.

The designated space on the ATF is on the front of the form. That is where BATs and STTs should affix the printouts.

However, because the instructions on the ATF also permit the printout to be affixed to the back of the ATF, the Department has no objections to having the printouts on the back of the ATF.

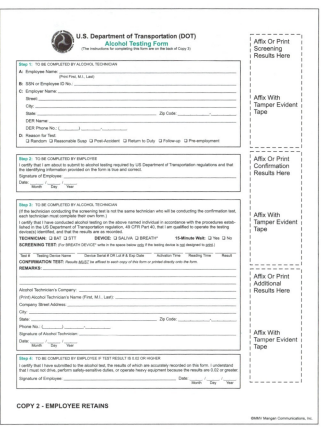

* Full-size forms available free of charge at www.dotcfr.com.

* Full-size forms available free of charge at www.dotcfr.com.

* Full-size forms available free of charge at www.dotcfr.com.

Appendix H   **Part 40 - Procedures for Transportation Workplace Drug and Alcohol Testing Programs**

* Full-size forms available free of charge at www.dotcfr.com.

* Full-size forms available free of charge at www.dotcfr.com.

Appendix H to Part 40   DOT Drug and Alcohol Testing Management Information System (MIS) Data Collection Form

The following form and instructions must be used when an employer is required to report MIS data to a DOT agency.

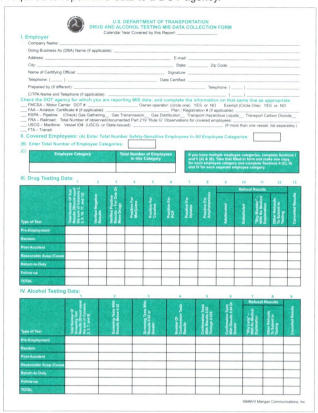

* Full-size forms available free of charge at www.dotcfr.com.

* Full-size forms available free of charge at www.dotcfr.com.

Part 40 - Procedures for Transportation Workplace Drug and Alcohol Testing Programs Appendix H

U.S. Department of Transportation Drug and Alcohol Testing MIS Data Collection Form Instruction Sheet

This Management Information System (MIS) form is made-up of four sections: employer information; covered employees (i.e., employees performing DOT regulated safety-sensitive duties) information; drug testing data; and alcohol testing data. The employer information needs only to be provided once per submission. However, you must submit a separate page of data for each employee category for which you report testing data. If you are preparing reports for more than one DOT agency then you must submit DOT agency-specific forms.

Please print entries legibly in black ink.

TIP — Read the entire instructions before starting. Please note that USCG-regulated employers do not report alcohol test results on the MIS form.

Calendar Year Covered by this Report: Enter the appropriate year.

Section I. Employer

1. **Enter your company's name,** to include when applicable, your "doing business as" name; current address, city, state, and zip code; and an e-mail address, if available.
2. **Enter the printed name, signature,** and complete telephone number of the company official certifying the accuracy of the report and the date that person certified the report as complete.
3. **If someone other than the certifying official** completed the MIS form, enter that person's name and phone number on the appropriate lines provided.
4. **If a Consortium/Third Party Administrator (C/TPA)** performs administrative services for your drug and alcohol program operation, enter its name and phone number on the appropriate lines provided.
5. **DOT Agency Information:** Check the box next to the DOT agency for which you are completing this MIS form. Again, if you are submitting to multiple DOT agencies, you must use separate forms for each DOT agency.
    a. *If you are completing the form for FMCSA,* enter your FMCSA DOT Number, as appropriate. In addition, you must indicate whether you are an owner-operator (i.e., an employer who employs only himself or herself as a driver) and whether you are exempt from providing MIS data. Exemptions are noted in the FMCSA regulation at 382.103(d).
    b. *If you are completing the form for FAA,* enter your FAA Certificate Number and FAA Antidrug Plan/Registration Number, when applicable.
    c. *If you are completing the form for PHMSA,* check the additional box(s) indicating your type of operation.
    d. *If you are completing the form for FRA,* enter the number of observed/documented Part 219 "Rule G" Observations for covered employees.
    e. *If you are submitting the form for USCG,* enter the vessel ID number. If there is more than one number, enter the numbers separately.

Section II. Covered Employees

1. **In Box II-A,** enter the total number of covered employees (i.e., employees performing DOT regulated safety-sensitive duties) who work for your company. Then enter, in Box II-B, the total number of employee categories that number represents. If you have employees, some of whom perform duties under one DOT agency and others of whom perform duties under another DOT agency, enter only the number of those employees performing duties under the DOT agency for whom you are submitting the form. If you have covered employees who perform multi-DOT agency functions (e.g., an employee drives a commercial motor vehicle and performs pipeline maintenance duties for you), count the employee only on the MIS report for the DOT agency regulating more than 50 percent of the employee's safety-sensitive function.

[Example: If you are submitting the information for the FRA and you have 2000 covered employees performing duties in all FRA-covered service categories — you would enter "2000" in the first box (II-A) and "5" in the second box (II-B), because FRA has five safety-sensitive employee categories and you have employees in all of these groups. If you have 1000 employees performing safety-sensitive duties in three FRA-covered service categories (e.g., engine service, train service, and dispatcher/operation), you would enter "1000" in the first box (II-A) and "3" in the second box (II-B).]

TIP — To calculate the total number of covered employees, add the total number of covered employees eligible for testing during each random testing selection period for the year and divide that total by the number of random testing periods. (However, no company will need to factor the average number of employees more often than once per month.) For instance, a company conducting random testing quarterly needs to add the total of covered employees they had in the random pool when each selection was made; then divide this number by 4 to obtain the yearly average number of covered employees. It is extremely important that you place all eligible employees into these random pools. [As an example, if Company A had 1500 employees in the first quarter random pool, 2250 in the second quarter, 2750 in the third quarter, and 1500 in the fourth quarter; 1500 + 2250 + 2750 + 1500 = 8000; 8000 / 4 = 2000; the total number of covered employees for the year would be reported as, "2000."

If you conduct random selections more often than once per month (e.g., you select daily, weekly, bi-weekly), you do not need to compute this total number of covered employees rate more than on a once per month basis. Therefore, employers need not compute the covered employees rate more than 12 times per year.]

2. **If you are reporting multiple employee categories,** enter the specific employee category in box II-C; and provide the number of employees performing safety-sensitive duties in that specific category.

[Example: You are submitting data to the FTA and you have 2000 covered employees. You have 1750 personnel performing revenue vehicle operation and the remaining 250 are performing revenue vehicle and equipment maintenance. When you provide vehicle operation information, you would enter "Revenue Vehicle Operation" in the first II-C box and "1750" in the second II-C box. When you provide data on the maintenance personnel, you would enter "Revenue Vehicle and Equipment Maintenance" in the first II-C box and "250" in the second II-C box.]

TIP — A separate form for each employee category must be submitted. You may do this by filling out a single MIS form through Section II-B and then make one copy for each additional employee category you are reporting. [For instance, if you are submitting the MIS form for the FMCSA, you need only submit one form for all FMCSA covered employees working for you — your only category of employees is "driver." If you are reporting testing data to the FAA and you employ only flight crewmembers, flight attendants, and aircraft maintenance workers, you need to complete one form for each category — three forms in all. If you are reporting to FAA and have all FAA categories of covered employees, you must submit eight forms.]

Here is a full listing of covered-employee categories:

FMCSA *(one category):* Driver

FAA *(eight categories):* Flight Crewmember; Flight Attendant; Flight Instructor; Aircraft Dispatcher; Aircraft Maintenance; Ground Security Coordinator; Aviation Screener; Air Traffic Controller

PHMSA *(one category):* Operation/Maintenance/Emergency Response

FRA *(five categories):* Engine Service; Train Service; Dispatcher/Operation; Signal Service; Other [Includes yardmasters, hostlers (non-engineer craft), bridge tenders, switch tenders, and other miscellaneous employees performing 49 CFR 228.5(c) defined covered service.]

USCG *(one category):* Crewmember

FTA *(five categories):* Revenue Vehicle Operation; Revenue Vehicle and Equipment Maintenance; Revenue Vehicle Control/Dispatch; CDL/Non-Revenue Vehicle; Armed Security Personnel

Section III. Drug Testing Data

This section summarizes the drug testing results for all covered employees (to include applicants). The table in this section requires drug test data by test type and by result. The categories of test types are: Pre-Employment; Random; Post-Accident; Reasonable Suspicion/Reasonable Cause; Return-to Duty; and Follow-Up.

The categories of type of results are: Total Number of Test Results [excluding cancelled tests and blind specimens]; Verified Negative; Verified Positive; Positive for Marijuana; Positive for Cocaine; Positive for PCP; Positive for Opiates; Positive for Amphetamines; Refusals due to Adulterated, Substituted, "Shy Bladder" with No Medical Explanation, and Other Refusals to Submit to Testing; and Cancelled Results.

TIP — Do not enter data on blind specimens submitted to laboratories. Be sure to enter all pre-employment testing data regardless of whether an applicant was hired or not. You do not need to separate reasonable suspicion and reasonable cause drug testing data on the MIS form. [Therefore, if you conducted only reasonable suspicion drug testing (i.e. FMCSA and FTA), enter that data; if you conducted only reasonable cause drug testing (i.e., FAA, PHMSA, and USCG); or if you conducted both under FRA drug testing rules, simply enter the data with no differentiation.] For USCG, enter any "Serious Marine Incident" testing in the Post-Accident row. For FRA, do not enter post accident data (the FRA does not collect this data on the MIS form). Finally, you may leave blank any row or column in which there were no results, or you may enter "0" (zero) instead. Please note that cancelled tests are not included in the "total number of test results" column.

Section III, Column 1. Total Number of Test Results — This column requires a count of the total number of test results in each testing category during the entire reporting year. Count the number of test results

Appendix H   Part 40 - Procedures for Transportation Workplace Drug and Alcohol Testing Programs

as the number of testing events resulting in negative, positive, and refusal results. Do not count cancelled tests and blind specimens in this total.

[Example: A company that conducted fifty pre-employment tests would enter "50" on the Pre-Employment row. If it conducted one hundred random tests, "100" would be entered on the Random row. If that company did no post-accident, reasonable suspicion, reasonable cause, return-to-duty, or follow-up tests, those categories will be left blank or zeros entered.]

Section III, Column 2. Verified Negative Results — This column requires a count of the number of tests in each testing category that the Medical Review Officer (MRO) reported as negative. Do not count a negative-dilute result if, subsequently, the employee underwent a second collection; the second test is the test of record.

[Example: If forty-seven of the company's fifty pre-employment tests were reported negative, "47" would be entered in Column 2 on the Pre-Employment row. If ninety of the company's one hundred random test results were reported negative, "90" would be entered in Column 2 on the Random row. Because the company did no other testing, those other categories would be left blank or zeros entered.]

Section III, Column 3. Verified Positive Results — For One or More Drugs — This column requires a count of the number of tests in each testing category that the MRO reported as positive for one or more drugs. When the MRO reports a test positive for two drugs, it would count as one positive test.

[Example: If one of the fifty pre-employment tests was positive for two drugs, "1" would be entered in Column 3 on the Pre-Employment row. If four of the company's one hundred random test results were reported positive (three for one drug and one for two drugs), "4" would be entered in Column 3 on the Random row.]

Section III, Columns 4 through 8. Positive (for specific drugs) — These columns require entry of the by-drug data for which specimens were reported positive by the MRO.

[Example: The pre-employment positive test reported by the MRO was positive for marijuana, "1" would be entered in Column 4 on the Pre-Employment row. If three of the four positive results for random testing were reported by the MRO to be positive for marijuana, "3" would be entered in Column 4 on the Random row. If one of the four positive results for random testing was reported positive for both PCP and opiates, "1" would be entered in Column 6 on the Random row and "1" would be entered in Column 7 of the Random row.]

TIP — *Column 1 should equal the sum of Columns 2, 3, 9, 10, 11, and 12. Remember you have not counted specimen results that were ultimately cancelled or were from blind specimens. So, Column 1 = Column 2 + Column 3 + Column 9 + Column 10 + Column 11 + Column 12. Certainly, double check your records to determine if your actual results count is reflective of all negative, positive, and refusal counts.*

An MRO may report that a specimen is positive for more than one drug. When that happens, to use the company example above (i.e., one random test was positive for both PCP and opiates), the positive results should be recorded in the appropriate columns — PCP and opiates in this case. There is no expectation for Columns 4 through 8 numbers to add up to the numbers in Column 3 when you report multiple positives.

Section III, Columns 9 through 12. Refusal Results — The refusal section is divided into four refusal groups — they are: Adulterated; Substituted; "Shy Bladder" — With No Medical Explanation; and Other Refusals to Submit to Testing. The MRO reports two of these refusal types — adulterated and substituted specimen results — because of laboratory test findings.

When an individual does not provide enough urine at the collection site, the MRO conducts or causes to have conducted a medical evaluation to determine if there exists a medical reason for the person's inability to provide the appropriate amount of urine. If there is no medical reason to support the inability, the MRO reports the result to the employer as a refusal to test: Refusals of this type are reported in the "Shy Bladder" — With No Medical Explanation category.

Finally, additional reasons exist for a test to be considered a refusal. Some examples are: the employee fails to report to the collection site as directed by the employer; the employee leaves the collection site without permission; the employee fails to empty his or her pockets at the collection site; the employee refuses to have a required shy bladder evaluation. Again, these are only four examples: there are more.

Section III, Column 9. Adulterated — This column requires the count of the number of tests reported by the MRO as refusals because the specimens were adulterated.

[Example: If one of the fifty pre-employment tests was adulterated, "1" would be entered in Column 9 of the Pre-Employment row.]

Section III, Column 10. Substituted — This column requires the count of the number of tests reported by the MRO as refusals because the specimens were substituted.

[Example: If one of the 100 random tests was substituted, "1" would be entered in Column 10 of the Random row.]

Section III, Column 11. "Shy Bladder" — With No Medical Explanation — This column requires the count of the number of tests reported by the MRO as being a refusal because there was no legitimate medical reason for an insufficient amount of urine.

[Example: If one of the 100 random tests was a refusal because of shy bladder, "1" would be entered in Column 11 of the Random row.]

Section III, Column 12. Other Refusals to Submit to Testing — This column requires the count of refusals other than those already entered in Columns 9 through 11.

[Example: If the company entered "100" as the number of random specimens collected, however it had five employees who refused to be tested without submitting specimens: two did not show up at the collection site as directed; one refused to empty his pockets at the collection site; and two left the collection site rather than submit to a required directly observed collection. Because of these five refusal events, "5" would be entered in Column 11 of the Random row.]

TIP — *Even though some testing events result in a refusal in which no urine was collected and sent to the laboratory, a "refusal" is still a final test result. Therefore, your overall numbers for test results (in Column 1) will equal the total number of negative tests (Column 2); positives (Column 3); and refusals (Columns 9, 10, 11, and 12). Do not worry that no urine was processed at the laboratory for some refusals; all refusals are counted as a testing event for MIS purposes and for establishing random rates.*

Section III, Column 13. Cancelled Tests — This column requires the count of the number of tests in each testing category that the MRO reported as cancelled. You must not count any cancelled tests in Column 1 or in any other column. For instance, you must not count a positive result (in Column 3) if it had ultimately been cancelled for any reason (e.g., specimen was initially reported positive, but the split failed to reconfirm.)

[Example: If a pre-employment test was reported cancelled, "1" would be entered in Column 13 on the Pre-Employment row. If three of the company's random test results were reported cancelled, "3" would be entered in Column 13 on the Random row.]

Total Line. Columns 1 through 13 — This line requires you to add the numbers in each column and provide the totals.

Section IV. Alcohol Testing Data

This section summarizes the alcohol testing conducted for all covered employees (to include applicants). The table in this section requires alcohol test data by test type and by result. The categories of test types are: Pre-Employment; Random; Post-Accident; Reasonable Suspicion/Reasonable Cause; Return-to Duty; and Follow-Up.

The categories of results are: Number of Screening Test Results; Screening Tests with Results Below 0.02; Screening Tests with Results 0.02 Or Greater; Number of Confirmation Tests Results; Confirmation Tests with Results 0.02 through 0.039; Confirmation Tests with Results 0.04 Or Greater; Refusals due to "Shy Lung" with No Medical Explanation, and Other Refusals to Submit to Testing; and Cancelled Results.

TIP — *Be sure to enter all pre-employment testing data regardless of whether an applicant was hired or not. Of course, for most employers pre-employment alcohol testing is optional, so you may not have conducted this type of testing. You do not need to separate "reasonable suspicion" and "reasonable cause" alcohol testing data on the MIS form. [Therefore, if you conducted only reasonable suspicion alcohol testing (i.e., FMCSA, FAA, FTA, and PHMSA), enter that data; if you conducted both reasonable suspicion and reasonable cause alcohol testing (i.e., FRA), simply enter the data with no differentiation.] PHMSA does not authorize "random" testing for alcohol. Finally, you may leave blank any row or column in which there were no results, or you may enter "0" (zero) instead. Please note that USCG-regulated employers do not report alcohol test results on the MIS form: Do not fill-out Section IV if you are a USCG-regulated employer.*

Section IV, Column 1. Total Number of Screening Test Results — This column requires a count of the total number of screening test results in each testing category during the entire reporting year. Count the number of screening tests as the number of screening test events with final screening results of below 0.02, of 0.02 through 0.039, of 0.04 or greater, and all refusals. Do not count cancelled tests in this total.

[Example: A company that conducted twenty pre-employment tests would enter "20" on the Pre-Employment row. If it conducted fifty random tests, "50" would be entered. If that company did no post-accident, reasonable suspicion, reasonable cause, return-to-duty, or follow-up tests, those categories will be left blank or zeros entered.]

Section IV, Column 2. Screening Tests With Results Below 0.02 — This column requires a count of the number of tests in each testing category that the BAT or STT reported as being below 0.02 on the screening test.

[Example: If seventeen of the company's twenty pre-employment screening tests were reported as being below 0.02, "17" would be entered in Column 2 on the Pre-Employment row. If forty-four of the company's fifty random screening test results were reported as being below 0.02, "44" would be entered in Column 2 on the Random row. Because the company did no other testing, those other categories would be left blank or zeros entered.]

Section IV, Column 3. Screening Tests With Results 0.02 Or Greater — This column requires a count of the number of screening tests in each testing category that the BAT or STT reported as being 0.02 or greater on the screening test.

Part 40 - Procedures for Transportation Workplace Drug and Alcohol Testing Programs — Appendix H

[Example: If one of the twenty pre-employment tests was reported as being 0.02 or greater, "1" would be entered in Column 3 on the Pre-Employment row. If four of the company's fifty random test results were reported as being 0.02 or greater, "4" would be entered in Column 3 on the Random row.]

Section IV, Column 4. Number of Confirmation Test Results — This column requires entry of the number of confirmation tests that were conducted by a BAT as a result of the screening tests that were found to be 0.02 or greater. In effect, all screening tests of 0.02 or greater should have resulted in confirmation tests. Ideally the number of tests in Column 3 and Column 4 should be the same. However, we know that this required confirmation test sometimes does not occur. In any case, the number of confirmation tests that were actually performed should be entered in Column 4.

[Example: If the one pre-employment screening test reported as 0.02 or greater had a subsequent confirmation test performed by a BAT, "1" would be entered in Column 4 on the Pre-Employment row. If three of the four random screening tests that were found to be 0.02 or greater had a subsequent confirmation test performed by a BAT, "3" would be entered in Column 4 on the Random row.]

Section IV, Column 5. Confirmation Tests With Results 0.02 Through 0.039 — This column requires entry of the number of confirmation tests that were conducted by a BAT that led to results that were 0.02 through 0.039.

[Example: If one of pre-employment confirmation test yielded a result of 0.042, Column 5 of the Pre-Employment row would be left blank or zeros entered. If two of the random confirmation tests yielded results of 0.03 and 0.032, "2" would be entered in Column 5 of the Random row.]

Section IV, Column 6. Confirmation Tests With Results 0.04 Or Greater — This column requires entry of the number of confirmation tests that were conducted by a BAT that led to results that were 0.04 or greater.

[Example: Because the one pre-employment confirmation test yielded a result of 0.042, "1" would be entered in Column 6 of the Pre-Employment row. If one of the random confirmation tests yielded a result of 0.04, "1" would be entered in Column 6 of the Random row.]

TIP — *Column 1 should equal the sum of Columns 2, 3, 7, and 8. The number of screening tests results should reflect the number of screening tests you have no matter the result (below 0.02 or at or above 0.02, plus refusals to test), unless of course, the tests were ultimately cancelled. So, Column 1 = Column 2 + Column 3 + Column 7 + Column 8. Certainly, double check your records to determine if your actual screening results count is reflective of all these counts.*

There is no need to record MIS confirmation tests results below 0.02: That is why we have no column for it on the form. [If the random test that screened 0.02 went to a confirmation test, and that confirmation test yielded a result below 0.02, there is no place for that confirmed result to be entered.] We assume that if a confirmation test was completed but not listed in either Column 5 or Column 6, the result was below 0.02. In addition, if the confirmation test ended up being cancelled, it should not have been included in Columns 1, 3, or 4 in the first place.

Section IV, Columns 7 and 8. Refusal Results — The refusal section is divided into two refusal groups — they are: Shy Lung — With No Medical Explanation; and Other Refusals To Submit to Testing.

When an individual does not provide enough breath at the test site, the company requires the employee to have a medical evaluation to determine if there exists a medical reason for the person's inability to provide the appropriate amount of breath. If there is no medical reason to support the inability as reported by the examining physician, the employer calls the result a refusal to test: Refusals of this type are reported in the "Shy Lung — With No Medical Explanation" category. Finally, additional reasons exist for a test to be considered a refusal. Some examples are: the employee fails to report to the test site as directed by the employer; the employee leaves the test site without permission; the employee fails to sign the certification at Step 2 of the ATF; the employee refuses to have a required shy lung evaluation. Again, these are only four examples; there are more.

Section IV, Column 7. "Shy Lung" — With No Medical Explanation — This column requires the count of the number of tests in which there is no medical reason to support the employee's inability to provide an adequate breath as reported by the examining physician; subsequently, the employer called the result a refusal to test.

[Example: If one of the 50 random tests was a refusal because of shy lung, "1" would be entered in Column 7 of the Random row.]

Section IV, Column 8. Other Refusals to Submit to Testing — This column requires the count of refusals other than those already entered in Column 7.

[Example: The company entered "50" as the number of random specimens collected, however it had one employee who did not show up at the testing site as directed. Because of this one refusal event, "1" would be entered in Column 8 of the Random row.]

TIP — *Even though some testing events result in a refusal in which no breath (or saliva) was tested, there is an expectation that your overall numbers for screening tests (in Column 1) will equal the total number of screening tests with results below 0.02 (Column 2); screening tests with results 0.02 or greater (Column 3); and refusals (Columns 7 and 8). Do not worry that no breath (or saliva) was tested for some refusals; all refusals are counted as a screening test event for MIS purposes and for establishing random rates.*

Section IV, Column 9. Cancelled Tests — This column requires the count of the number of tests in each testing category that the BAT or STT reported as cancelled. Do not count any cancelled tests in Column 1 or in any other column other than Column 9. For instance, you must not count a 0.04 screening result or confirmation result in any column, other than Column 9, if the test was ultimately cancelled for some reason (e.g., a required air blank was not performed.)

[Example: If a pre-employment test was reported cancelled, "1" would be entered in Column 9 on the Pre-Employment row. If three of the company's random test results were reported cancelled, "3" would be entered in Column 13 on the Random row.]

Total Line. Columns 1 through 9 — This line requires you to add the numbers in each column and provide the totals.

Notes

Part 325 - Compliance with Interstate Motor Carrier Noise Emission Standards

Subpart A - General Provisions

§325.1 Scope of the rules in this part.

(a) **The rules in this part prescribe procedures** for inspection, surveillance, and measurement of motor vehicles and motor vehicle equipment operated by motor carriers to determine whether those vehicles and that equipment conform to the Interstate Motor Carrier Noise Emission Standards of the Environmental Protection Agency, 40 CFR Part 202.

(b) **Except as provided in paragraph (c) of this section,** the rules in this part apply to motor carriers engaged in interstate commerce. The rules apply at any time or under any condition of highway grade, load, acceleration or deceleration.

(c) **The rules in this part do not apply to —**
  (1) *A motor vehicle* that has a Gross Vehicle Weight Rating (GVWR) of 10,000 pounds (4,536 kg.) or less;
  (2) *A combination of motor vehicles* that has a Gross Combination Weight Rating (GCWR) of 10,000 pounds (4,536 kg.) or less;
  (3) *The sound generated by a warning device,* such as a horn or siren, installed in a motor vehicle, unless such device is intentionally sounded in order to preclude an otherwise valid noise emission measurement;
  (4) *An emergency motor vehicle,* such as a fire engine, an ambulance, a police van, or a rescue van, when it is responding to an emergency call;
  (5) *A snow plow in operation;* or
  (6) *The sound generated by auxiliary equipment* which is normally operated only when the motor vehicle on which it is installed is stopped or is operating at a speed of 5 miles per hour (8 kph) or less, unless such device is intentionally operated at speeds greater than 5 mph (8 kph) in order to preclude an otherwise valid noise measurement. Examples of that type of auxiliary equipment include, but are not limited to, cranes, asphalt, spreaders, ditch diggers, liquid or slurry pumps, auxiliary air compressors, welders, and trash compactors.

§325.1 DOT Interpretations

Question 1: What noise emission requirements are applicable to auxiliary generators?
Guidance: Auxiliary generators which normally operate only when a CMV is stopped or moving at 5 mph or less are "auxiliary equipment" of the kind contemplated by EPA and are, therefore, exempt from the noise limits in Part 325. However, noise from generators that run while the CMV is moving at higher speeds would be measured as part of total vehicle noise.

Question 2: Do refrigeration units on tractor-trailer combinations fall within the exemption listed in Part 325, Subpart A of the FMCSRs?
Guidance: No.

§325.3 Effective date.

The rules in this part are effective on October 15, 1975.

§325.5 Definitions.

(a) **Statutory definitions.** All terms defined in the Noise Control Act of 1972 (Pub. L. 92-574, 86 Stat. 1234) are used as they are defined in that Act.

(b) **Definitions in standards.** All terms defined in §202.10 of the Interstate Motor Carrier Noise Emission Standards, 40 CFR 202.10, are used as they are defined in that section.

(c) **Additional definitions.**
  (1) **Hard test site** means any test site having the ground surface covered with concrete, asphalt, packed dirt, gravel, or similar reflective material for more than 1/2 the distance between the microphone target point and the microphone location point.
  (2) **Soft test site** means any test site having the ground surface covered with grass, other ground cover, or similar absorptive material for 1/2 or more of the distance between the microphone target point and the microphone location point.
  (3) **Ground cover** means any of various low, dense-growing plants, such as ivy, myrtle, low weeds, or brush.
  (4) **Traffic railing** means any longitudinal highway traffic barrier system installed along the side or median of a highway. For the purpose of this part, a traffic railing must have at least 35 percent of its vertical height, from the ground surface to the top of the railing, open to free space in order to qualify as an acceptable object within a noise measurement test site. Further, for the purposes of this part, posts or other discrete supports shall be ignored when ascertaining open free space.
  (5) **Relatively flat** when used to describe a noise measurement site means a site which does not contain significant concave curvatures or slope reversals that may result in the focusing of sound waves toward the microphone location point.

§325.7 Allowable noise levels.

Motor vehicle noise emissions, when measured according to the rules of this part, shall not exceed the values specified in Table 1.

Table 1 - Maximum Permissible Sound Level Readings (Decibel (A))[1,2]

If the distance between the microphone location point and the microphone target point is —	Highway operation test				Stationary tests	
	Soft site		Hard Site		Soft site	Hard site
	35 mi/h or less	Above 35 mi/h	35 mi/h or less	Above 35 mi/h		
31 ft (9.5 m) or more but less than 35 ft (10.7 m)	87	91	89	93	89	91
35 ft (10.7 m) or more but less than 39 ft (11.9 m)	86	90	88	92	88	90
39 ft (11.9 m) or more but less than 43 ft (13.1 m)	85	89	87	91	87	89
43 ft (13.1 m) or more but less than 48 ft (14.6 m)	84	88	86	90	86	88
48 ft (14.6 m) or more but less than 58 ft (17.1 m)	83	87	85	89	85	87
58 ft (17.1 m) or more but less than 70 ft (21.3 m)	82	86	84	88	84	86
70 ft (21.3 m) or more but less than 83 ft (25.3 m)	81	85	83	87	83	85

1. The speeds shown refer to measurements taken at sites having speed limits as indicated. These speed limits do not necessarily have to be posted.
2. This table is based on motor carrier noise emission requirements specified in 40 CFR 202.20 and 40 CFR 202.21.

§325.9 Measurement tolerances.

(a) **Measurement tolerances will be allowed** to take into account the effects of the following factors:
  (1) *The consensus standard practice* of reporting filed sound level measurements to the nearest whole decibel.
  (2) *Variations resulting from commercial instrument tolerances.*
  (3) *Variations resulting from the topography* of the noise measurement site.
  (4) *Variations resulting from atmospheric conditions* such as wind, ambient temperature, and atmospheric pressure.
  (5) *Variations resulting from reflected sound* from small objects allowed within the test site.
  (6) *The interpretation of the effects* of the above cited factors by enforcement personnel.

(b) **Measurement tolerances shall not exceed 2 decibels** for a given measurement.

Subpart B - Administrative Provisions

§325.11 Issuance, amendment, and revocation of the rules in this part.

The procedures specified in Part 389 of this chapter for the issuance, amendment, or revocation of the Federal Motor Carrier Safety Regulations apply to rulemaking proceedings for the issuance, amendment, or revocation of the rules in this part.

§325.13 Inspection and examination of motor vehicles.

(a) **Any special agent** of the Federal Motor Carrier Safety Administration (designated in Appendix B to Subchapter B of this chapter) is authorized to inspect, examine, and test a motor vehicle operated by a motor carrier in accordance with the procedures specified in this part for the purpose of ascertaining whether the motor vehicle and equipment installed on the motor vehicle conforms to the Interstate Motor Carrier Noise Emission Standards of the Environmental Protection Agency, 40 CFR Part 202.

(b) **A motor carrier, its officers, drivers,** agents, and employees must, at any time, submit a motor vehicle used in its operations for inspection, examination, and testing for the purpose of ascertaining whether the motor vehicle and equipment installed on it conforms to the Interstate Motor Carrier Noise Emission Standards of the Environmental Protection Agency, 40 CFR Part 202.

(c) **Prescribed inspection report.** Form MCS-141, Noise Level Compliance Check shall be used to record findings from motor vehicles selected for noise emission inspection by authorized employees.

(d) **Motor carrier's disposition of form MCS-141.**
  (1) *The driver of any motor vehicle* receiving a Form MCS-141 shall deliver such MCS-141 to the motor carrier operating the vehicle upon his/her arrival at the next terminal or facility of the motor carrier, if such arrival occurs within twenty-four (24) hours. If the driver does not arrive at a terminal or facility of the motor carrier operating the vehicle within twenty-four (24) hours he/she shall immediately mail the Form MCS-141 to the motor carrier. For operating convenience, motor carriers may designate any shop, terminal, facility, or person to which it may instruct its drivers to deliver or forward Form MCS-141. It shall be the sole responsibility of the motor carrier that Form MCS-141 is returned to the Federal Motor Carrier Safety Administration[1], in accordance with the terms prescribed thereon and in paragraphs (d)(2) and (3) of this section. A driver, if himself/herself a motor carrier, shall return Form MCS-141 to the Federal Motor Carrier Safety Administration, in accordance with the terms prescribed thereon and in paragraphs (d)(2) and (3) of this section.
  (2) *Motor carriers shall carefully examine* Forms MCS-141. Appropriate corrective action shall be taken on vehicles found to be not in compliance with the requirements of this part.
  (3) *Motor carriers must complete* the "Motor Carrier Certification of Action Taken" on Form MCS-141 in accordance with the terms prescribed thereon. Motor carriers must return Forms MCS-141 to the Division Office at the address indicated on Form MCS-141 within fifteen (15) days following the date of the vehicle inspection.

Subpart C - Instrumentation

§325.21 Scope of the rules in this subpart.

The rules in this subpart specify criteria for sound level measurement systems which are used to make the sound level measurements specified in Subpart D and Subpart E of this part.

§325.23 Type of measurement systems which may be used.

The sound level measurement system must meet or exceed the requirements of American National Standard Specification for Sound Level Meters (ANSI S1.4-1971), approved April 27, 1971, issued by the American National Standards Institute,[2] throughout the applicable frequency range for either:

(a) **A Type 1 sound level meter;**
(b) **A Type 2 sound level meter; or**
(c) **A Type S sound level meter which has —**
  (1) *A weighing frequency response;*
  (2) *Fast dynamic characteristics of its indicating instrument; and*
  (3) *A relative response level tolerance* consistent with those of either a Type 1 or Type 2 sound level meter, as specified in section 3.2 of ANSI S1.4-1971.

§325.25 Calibration of measurement systems.

(a) (1) *The sound level measurement system* must be calibrated and appropriately adjusted at one or more frequencies in the range from 250 to 1,000 Hz at the beginning of each series of measurements and at intervals of 5-15 minutes thereafter, until it has been determined that the sound level measurement system has not significantly drifted from its calibrated level. Once this fact has been established, calibrations may be made at intervals of once every hour. A significant drift shall be considered to have occurred if a 0.3 dB or more excursion is noted from the system's predetermined reference calibration level. In the case of systems using displays with whole decibel increments, the operator may visually judge when the 0.3 dB drift has been met or exceeded.

(2) *The sound level measurement system* must be checked periodically by its manufacturer, a representative of its manufacturer, or a person of equivalent special competence to verify that its accuracy meets the manufacturer's design criteria.

(b) **An acoustical calibrator** of the microphone coupler type designed for the sound level measurement system in use shall be used to calibrate the sound level measurement system in accordance with paragraph (a) of this section. The calibration must meet or exceed the accuracy requirements specified in section 5.4.1 of the American National Standard Institute Standard Methods for Measurements of Sound Pressure Levels (ANSI S1.13-1971) for field method measurements.

§325.27 Use of a windscreen.

A properly installed windscreen, of the type recommended by the manufacturer of the Sound Level Measurement System, shall be used during the time that noise emission measurements are being taken.

Subpart D - Measurement of Noise Emissions; Highway Operations

§325.31 Scope of the rules in this subpart.

The rules in this subpart specify conditions and procedures for measurement of the sound level generated by a motor vehicle engaged in a highway operation for the purpose of ascertaining whether the motor vehicle conforms to the Standards for Highway Operations set forth in 40 CFR 202.20.

§325.33 Site characteristics; highway operations.

(a) **Measurement shall be made at a test site** which is adjacent to, and includes a portion of, a traveled lane of a public highway. A microphone target point shall be established on the centerline of the traveled lane of the highway, and a microphone location point shall be established on the ground surface not less than 31 feet (9.5 m) or more than 83 feet (25.3 m) from the microphone target point and on a line that is perpendicular to the centerline of the traveled lane of the highway and that passes through the microphone target point. In the case of a standard test site, the microphone location point is 50 feet (15.2 m) from the microphone target point. Within the test site is a triangular measurement area.

---

1. Editor's Note: The phrase 'Federal Motor Carrier Safety Administration' replaces the phrase 'Federal Highway Administration' in the CFR in accordance with an amendment appearing in the October 1, 2001, Federal Register.

2. Copies of the specification may be secured from the American National Standards Institute, 1430 Broadway, New York, New York, 10018.

A plan view diagram of a standard test site, having an open site within a 50-foot (15.2 m) radius of both the microphone target point and the microphone location point, is shown in Figure 1. Measurements may be made at a test site having smaller or greater dimensions in accordance with the rules in Subpart F of this part.

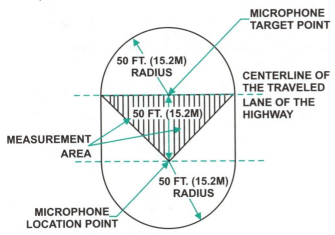

**Figure 1
STANDARD TEST SITE;
HIGHWAY OPERATIONS**

(b) **The test site must be an open site,** essentially free of large sound-reflecting objects. However, the following objects may be within the test site, including the triangular measurement area:
  (1) *Small cylindrical objects* such as fire hydrants or telephone or utility poles.
  (2) *Rural mailboxes.*
  (3) *Traffic railings of any type of construction* except solid concrete barriers (see §325.5(c)(4)).
  (4) *One or more curbs* having a vertical height of 1 foot (.3 m) or less.

(c) **The following objects may be within the test site** if they are outside of the triangular measurement area of the site:
  (1) *Any vertical surface* (such as billboard), regardless of size, having a lower edge more than 15 feet (4.6 m) higher than the surface of the traveled lane of the highway.
  (2) *Any uniformly smooth sloping surface* slanting away from the highway (such as a rise in grade alongside the highway) with a slope that is less than 45 degrees above the horizontal.
  (3) *Any surface slanting away from the highway* that is 45 degrees or more and not more than 90 degrees above the horizontal, if all points on the surface are more than 15 feet (4.6 m) above the surface of the traveled lane of the highway.

(d) **The surface of the ground within the measurement area** must be relatively flat (see §325.5(c)(5)). The site shall be a "soft" test site. However, if the site is determined to be "hard," the correction factor specified in §325.75(a) of this part shall be applied to the measurement.

(e) **The traveled lane of the highway within the test site** must be dry, paved with relatively smooth concrete or asphalt, and substantially free of —
  (1) *Holes or other defects* which would cause a motor vehicle to emit irregular tire, body, or chassis impact noise; and
  (2) *Loose material,* such as gravel or sand.

(f) **The traveled lane of the highway** on which the microphone target point is situated must not pass through a tunnel or underpass located within 200 feet (61 m) of that point.

§325.35 Ambient conditions; highway operations.

(a) (1) *Sound.* The ambient A-weighted sound level at the microphone location point shall be measured, in the absence of motor vehicle noise emanating from within the clear zone, with fast meter response using a sound level measurement system that conforms to the rules of §325.23.
  (2) *The measured ambient level* must be 10 dB(A) or more below that level specified in §325.7, Table 1, which corresponds to the maximum permissible sound level reading which is applicable at the test site at the time of testing.

(b) **Wind.** The wind velocity at the test shall be measured at the beginning of each series of noise measurements and at intervals of 5-15 minutes thereafter until it has been established that the wind velocity is essentially constant. Once this fact has been established, wind velocity measurements may be made at intervals of once every hour. Noise measurements may only be made if the measured wind velocity is 12 mph (19.3 kph) or less. Gust wind measurements of up to 20 mph (33.2 kph) are allowed.

(c) **Precipitation.** Measurements are prohibited under any condition of precipitation, however, measurements may be made with snow on the ground. The ground surface within the measurement area must be free of standing water.

§325.37 Location and operation of sound level measurement system; highway operations.

(a) **The microphone of a sound level measurement system** that conforms to the rules in §325.23 of this part shall be located at a height of not less than 2 feet (.6 m) nor more than 6 feet (1.8 M) above the plane of the roadway surface and not less than 3 1/2 feet (1.1 m) above the surface on which the microphone stands. The preferred microphone height on flat terrain is 4 feet (1.2 m).

(b) (1) *When the sound level measurement system* is hand-held or is otherwise monitored by a person located near its microphone, the holder must orient himself/herself relative to the highway in a manner consistent with the recommendation of the manufacturer of the sound level measurement system.
  (2) *In no case shall the holder or observer* be closer than 2 feet (.6 m) from the system's microphone, nor shall he/she locate himself/herself between the microphone and the vehicle being measured.

(c) **The microphone of the sound level measurement system** shall be oriented toward the traveled lane of the highway at the microphone target point at an angle that is consistent with the recommendation of the system's manufacturer. If the manufacturer of the system does not recommend an angle of orientation for its microphone, the microphone shall be oriented toward the highway at an angle of not less than 70 degrees and not more than perpendicular to the horizontal plane of the traveled lane of the highway at the microphone target point.

(d) **The sound level measurement system shall be set** to the A-weighting network and "fast" meter response mode.

§325.39 Measurement procedure; highway operations.

(a) **In accordance with the rules in this subpart,** a measurement shall be made of the sound level generated by a motor vehicle operating through the measurement area on the traveled lane of the highway within the test site, regardless of the highway grade, load, acceleration or deceleration.

(b) **The sound level generated by the motor vehicle** is the highest reading observed on the sound level measurement system as the vehicle passes through the measurement area, corrected, when appropriate, in accordance with the rules in Subpart F of this part. (Table 1 in §325.7 lists the range of maximum permissible sound level readings for various test conditions.) The sound level of the vehicle being measured must be observed to rise at least 6 dB(A) before the maximum sound level occurs and to fall at least 6 dB(A) after the maximum sound level occurs in order to be considered a valid sound level reading.

Subpart E - Measurement of Noise Emissions; Stationary Test

§325.51 Scope of the rules in this subpart.

(a) **The rules in this subpart** specify conditions and procedures for measuring the sound level generated by a vehicle when the vehicle's engine is rapidly accelerated from idle to governed speed at wide open throttle with the vehicle stationary, its transmission in neutral, and its clutch engaged, for the purpose of ascertaining whether the motor vehicle conforms to the Standard for Operation Under Stationary Test, 40 CFR 202.21.

(b) **The rules in this subpart** apply only to a motor vehicle that is equipped with an engine speed governor.

(c) **Tests conducted in accordance with the rules** of this subpart may be made on either side of the vehicle.

§325.53 Site characteristics; stationary test.

(a) (1) *The motor vehicle to be tested* shall be parked on the test site. A microphone target point shall be established on the ground surface of the site on the centerline of the lane in which the motor vehicle is parked at a point that is within 3 feet (.9 m) of the longitudinal position of the vehicle's exhaust system outlet(s). A microphone location point shall be established on the ground surface not less than 31 feet (9.5 m) and not more than 83 feet (25.3 m) from the microphone target point. Within the test site is a triangular measurement area. A plan view diagram of a standard test site, having an open site within a 50-foot (15.2 m) radius of both the microphone target point and the microphone location point, is shown in Figure 2.

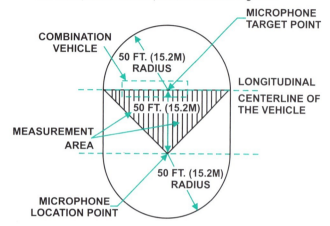

Figure 2
STANDARD TEST SITE; STATIONARY TEST

(2) *Measurements may be made at a test site* having smaller or greater dimensions in accordance with the rules in Subpart F of this part.

(b) *The test site must be an open site,* essentially free of large sound-reflecting objects. However, the following objects may be within the test site, including the triangular measurement area:
  (1) *Small cylindrical objects* such as fire hydrants or telephone or utility poles.
  (2) *Rural mailboxes.*
  (3) *Traffic railings of any type of construction* except solid concrete barriers (see §325.5(c)(4)).
  (4) *One or more curbs having a height of 1 foot (.3 m) or less.*

(c) *The following objects may be within the test site* if they are outside of the triangular measurement area of the site:
  (1) *Any vertical surface, regardless of size* (such as a billboard), having a lower edge more than 15 feet (4.6 m) above the ground.
  (2) *Any uniformly smooth surface* slanting away from the vehicle with a slope that is less than 45 degrees above the horizontal.
  (3) *Any surface slanting away from the vehicle* that is 45 degrees or more and not more than 90 degrees above the horizontal, if all points on the surface are more than 15 feet (4.6 m) above the surface of the ground in the test site.

(d) *The surface of the ground within the measurement area* must be relatively flat. (See §325.5(c)(5)). The site shall be a "hard" site. However, if the site is determined to be "soft," the correction factor specified in §325.75(b) of this part shall be applied to the measurement.

§325.55 Ambient conditions; stationary test.

(a) (1) *Sound.* The ambient A-weighted sound level at the microphone location point shall be measured, in the absence of motor vehicle noise emanating from within the clear zone, with fast meter response using a sound level measurement system that conforms to the rules of §325.23.
  (2) *The measured ambient level* must be 10 dB(A) or more below that level specified in §325.7, Table 1, which corresponds to the maximum permissible sound level reading which is applicable at the test site at the time of testing.

(b) *Wind.* The wind velocity at the test site shall be measured at the beginning of each series of noise measurements and at intervals of 5-15 minutes thereafter until it has been established that the wind velocity is essentially constant. Once this fact has been established, wind velocity measurements may be made at intervals of once every hour. Noise measurements may only be made if the measured wind velocity is 12 mph (19.3 kph) or less. Gust wind measurements of up to 20 mph (33.2 kph) are allowed.

(c) *Precipitation.* Measurements are prohibited under any conditions of precipitation, however, measurements may be made with snow on the ground. The ground within the measurement area must be free of standing water.

§325.57 Location and operation of sound level measurement systems; stationary test.

(a) *The microphone of a sound level measurement system* that conforms to the rules in §325.23 shall be located at a height of not less than 2 feet (.6 m) nor more than 6 feet (1.8 m) above the plane of the roadway surface and not less than 3 1/2 feet (1.1 m) above the surface on which the microphone stands. The preferred microphone height on flat terrain is 4 feet (1.2 m).

(b) *When the sound level measurement system* is hand-held or otherwise monitored by a person located near its microphone, the holder must orient himself/herself relative to the highway in a manner consistent with the recommendation of the manufacturer of the sound level measurement system. In no case shall the holder or observer be closer than 2 feet (.6 m) from the system's microphone, nor shall he/she locate himself/herself between the microphone and the vehicle being measured.

(c) *The microphone of the sound level measurement system* shall be oriented toward the vehicle at an angle that is consistent with the recommendation of the system's manufacturer. If the manufacturer of the system does not recommend an angle of orientation for its microphone, the microphone shall be oriented at an angle of not less than 70 degrees and not more than perpendicular to the horizontal plane of the test site at the microphone target point.

(d) *The sound level measurement system shall be set* to the A-weighting network and "fast" meter response mode.

§325.59 Measurement procedure; stationary test.

In accordance with the rules in this subpart, a measurement shall be made of the sound level generated by a stationary motor vehicle as follows:

(a) *Park the motor vehicle on the test site* as specified in §325.53 of this subpart. If the motor vehicle is a combination (articulated) vehicle, park the combination so that the longitudinal centerlines of the towing vehicle and the towed vehicle or vehicles are in substantial alignment.

(b) *Turn off all auxiliary equipment which is installed* on the motor vehicle and which is designed to operate under normal conditions only when the vehicle is operating at a speed of 5 mph (8 kph) or less. Examples of such equipment include cranes, asphalt spreaders, liquid or slurry pumps, auxiliary air compressors, welders, and trash compactors.

(c) *If the motor vehicle's engine radiator fan drive* is equipped with a clutch or similar device that automatically either reduces the rotational speed of the fan or completely disengages the fan from its power source in response to reduced engine cooling loads, park the vehicle before testing with its engine running at high idle or any other speed the operator may choose, for sufficient time but not more than 10 minutes, to permit the engine radiator fan to automatically disengage when the vehicle's noise emissions are measured under stationary test.

(d) *With the motor vehicle's transmission in neutral* and its clutch engaged, rapidly accelerate the vehicle's engine from idle to its maximum governed speed with wide open throttle. Return the engine's speed to idle.

(e) *Observe the maximum reading* on the sound level measurement system during the time the procedures specified in paragraph (d) of this section are followed. Record that reading, if the reading has not been influenced by extraneous noise sources such as motor vehicles operating on adjacent roadways.

(f) *Repeat the procedures specified in paragraphs (d) and (e)* of this section until the first two maximum sound level readings that are within 2 dB(A) of each other are recorded. Numerically average those two maximum sound level readings. When appropriate, correct the average figure in accordance with the rules in Subpart F of this part.

(g) *The average figure, corrected as appropriate,* contained in accordance with paragraph (f) of this section, is the sound level generated by the motor vehicle for the purpose of determining whether it conforms to the Standard for Operation Under Stationary Test, 40 CFR 202.21. (Table 1 in §325.7 lists the range of maximum permissible sound level readings for various test conditions.)

Subpart F - Correction Factors

§325.71 Scope of the rules in this subpart.
(a) **The rules in this subpart specify correction factors** which are added to, or subtracted from, the reading of the sound level generated by a motor vehicle, as displayed on a sound level measurement system, during the measurement of the motor vehicle's sound level emissions at a test site which is not a standard site.

(b) **The purpose of adding or subtracting a correction factor** is to equate the sound level reading actually generated by the motor vehicle to the sound level reading it would have generated if the measurement had been made at a standard test site.

§325.73 Microphone distance correction factors.[1]
If the distance between the microphone location point and the microphone target point is other than 50 feet (15.2 m), the maximum observed sound level reading generated by the motor vehicle in accordance with §325.39 of this part or the numerical average of the recorded maximum observed sound level readings generated by the motor vehicle in accordance with §325.59 of this part shall be corrected as specified in the following table:

Table 2 - Distance Correction Factors

If the distance between the microphone location point and the microphone target point is	The value dB(A) to be applied to the observed sound level reading is —
31 feet (9.5 m) or more but less than 35 feet (10.7 m)	-4
35 feet (10.7 m) or more but less than 39 feet (11.9 m)	-3
39 feet (11.9 m) or more but less than 43 feet (13.1 m)	-2
43 feet (13.1 m) or more but less than 48 feet (14.6 m)	-1
48 feet (14.6 m) or more but less than 58 feet (17.7 m)	0
58 feet (17.7 m) or more but less than 70 feet (21.3 m)	+1
70 feet (21.3 m) or more but less than 83 feet (25.3 m)	+2

§325.75 Ground surface correction factors.[1]
(a) **Highway operations.** When measurements are made in accordance with the rules in Subpart D of this part upon a test site which is "hard," a correction factor of 2 dB(A) shall be subtracted from the maximum observed sound level reading generated by the motor vehicle to determine whether the motor vehicle conforms to the Standards for Highway Operations, 40 CFR 202.20.

(b) **Stationary Test.** When measurements are made in accordance with the rules in Subpart E of this part upon a test site which is "soft," a correction factor of 2 dB(A) shall be added to the numerical average of the recorded maximum observed sound level readings generated by the motor vehicle to determine whether the motor vehicle conforms to the Standard for Operation Under Stationary Test, 40 CFR 202.21.

---

1. Table 1, in §325.7 is a tabulation of the maximum allowable sound level readings taking into account both the distance correction factors contained in §325.73 and the ground surface correction factors contained in §325.75.

§325.77 Computation of open site requirements — nonstandard sites.
(a) **If the distance between the microphone location point** and the microphone target point is other than 50 feet (15.2 m), the test site must be an open site within a radius from both points which is equal to the distance between the microphone location point and the microphone target point.

(b) **Plan view diagrams of nonstandard test sites** are shown in Figures 3 and 4. Figure 3 illustrates a test site which is larger than a standard test site and is based upon a 60-foot (18.3 m) distance between the microphone location point and the microphone target point. (See §325.79(b)(1) for an example of the application of the correction factor to a sound level reading obtained at such a site.) Figure 4 illustrates a test site which is smaller than a standard test site and is based upon a 35-foot (10.7 m) distance between the microphone location point and the microphone target point. (See §325.79(b)(2) for an example of the application of the correction factor to a sound level reading obtained at such a site.)

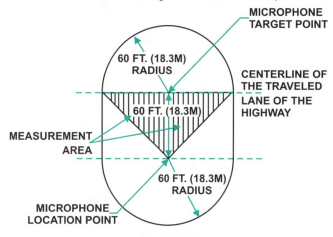

Figure 3
NON-STANDARD TEST SITE;
(60 FT. [18.3M] DISTANCE BETWEEN
MICROPHONE LOCATION AND TARGET POINTS)

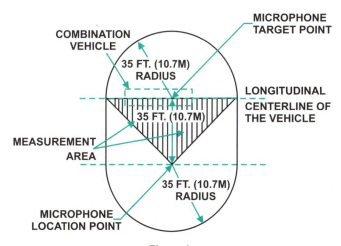

Figure 4
NON-STANDARD TEST SITE;
(35 FT. [10.7M] DISTANCE BETWEEN
MICROPHONE LOCATION AND TARGET POINTS)

§325.79 Application of correction factors.

(a) If two correction factors apply to a measurement they are applied cumulatively.

(b) The following examples illustrate the application of correction factors to sound level measurement readings:

(1) *Example 1 — Highway operations.* Assume that a motor vehicle generates a maximum observed sound level reading of 86 dB(A) during a measurement in accordance with the rules in Subpart D of this part. Assume also that the distance between the microphone location point and the microphone target point is 60 feet (18.3 m) and that the measurement area of the test site is acoustically "hard." The corrected sound level generated by the motor vehicle would be 85 dB(A), calculated as follows:

```
  86 dB(A) Uncorrected reading
  +1 dB(A) Distance correction factor
  -2 dB(A) Ground surface correction factor
  ─────────
  85 dB(A) Corrected reading
```

(2) *Example 2 — Stationary test.* Assume that a motor vehicle generates maximum sound level readings which average 88 dB(A) during a measurement in accordance with the rules in Subpart E of this part. Assume also that the distance between the microphone location point and the microphone target point is 35 feet (10.7 m), and that the measurement area of the test site is acoustically "soft." The corrected sound level generated by the motor vehicle would be 87 dB(A), calculated as follows:

```
  88 dB(A) Uncorrected average of readings
  -3 dB(A) Distance correction factor
  +2 dB(A) Ground surface correction factor
  ─────────
  87 dB(A) Corrected reading
```

Subpart G - Exhaust Systems and Tires

§325.91 Exhaust systems.

A motor vehicle does not conform to the visual exhaust system inspection requirements, 40 CFR 202.22, of the Interstate Motor Carrier Noise Emission Standards, if inspection of the exhaust system of the motor vehicle discloses that the system —

(a) Has a defect which adversely affects sound reduction, such as exhaust gas leaks or alteration or deterioration of muffler elements, (small traces of soot on flexible exhaust pipe sections shall not constitute a violation of this subpart);

(b) Is not equipped with either a muffler or other noise dissipative device, such as a turbocharger (supercharger driven by exhaust gases); or

(c) Is equipped with a cut-out, by-pass, or similar device, unless such device is designed as an exhaust gas driven cargo unloading system.

§325.93 Tires.

(a) Except as provided in paragraph (b) of this section, a motor vehicle does not conform to the visual tire inspection requirements, 40 CFR 202.23, of the Interstate Motor Carrier Noise Emissions Standards, if inspection of any tire on which the vehicle is operating discloses that the tire has a tread pattern composed primarily of cavities in the tread (excluding sipes and local chunking) which are not vented by grooves to the tire shoulder or circumferentially to each other around the tire.

(b) Paragraph (a) of this section does not apply to a motor vehicle operated on a tire having a tread pattern of the type specified in that paragraph, if the motor carrier who operates the motor vehicle demonstrates to the satisfaction of the Administrator or his/her designee that either —

(1) *The tire did not have that type of tread pattern* when it was originally manufactured or newly remanufactured; or

(2) *The motor vehicle generates* a maximum sound level reading of 90 dB(A) or less when measured at a standard test site for highway operations at a distance of 15.3 meters (50 feet) and under the following conditions:

(i) *The measurement must be made* at a time and place and under conditions specified by the Administrator or his/her designee.

(ii) *The motor vehicle must be operated* on the same tires that were installed on it when the inspection specified in paragraph (a) of this section occurred.

(iii) *The motor vehicle must be operated* on a highway having a posted speed limit of more than 56.3 kph (35 mph).

(iv) *The sound level measurement must be made* while the motor vehicle is operating at the posted speed limit.

Part 350 - Commercial Motor Carrier Safety Assistance Program

Subpart A - General

§350.101 What is the Motor Carrier Safety Assistance Program (MCSAP)?

The MCSAP is a Federal grant program that provides financial assistance to States to reduce the number and severity of accidents and hazardous materials incidents involving commercial motor vehicles (CMV). The goal of the MCSAP is to reduce CMV-involved accidents, fatalities, and injuries through consistent, uniform, and effective CMV safety programs. Investing grant monies in appropriate safety programs will increase the likelihood that safety defects, driver deficiencies, and unsafe motor carrier practices will be detected and corrected before they become contributing factors to accidents. The MCSAP also sets forth the conditions for participation by States and local jurisdictions and promotes the adoption and uniform enforcement of safety rules, regulations, and standards compatible with the Federal Motor Carrier Safety Regulations (FMCSRs) and Federal Hazardous Material Regulations (HMRs) for both interstate and intrastate motor carriers and drivers.

§350.103 What is the purpose of this part?

The purpose of this part is to ensure the Federal Motor Carrier Safety Administration (FMCSA), States, and other political jurisdictions work in partnership to establish programs to improve motor carrier, CMV, and driver safety to support a safe and efficient transportation system.

§350.105 What definitions are used in this part?

10-year average accident rate means for each State, the aggregate number of large truck-involved fatal crashes (as reported in the Fatality Analysis Reporting System (FARS)) for a 10-year period divided by the aggregate vehicle miles traveled (VMT) (as defined by the Federal Motor Carrier Safety Administration (FMCSA)) for the same 10-year period.

Accident rate means for each State, the total number of fatal crashes involving large trucks (as measured by the FARS for each State) divided by the total VMT as defined by the FMCSA for each State for all vehicles.

Agency means Federal Motor Carrier Safety Administration.

Administrative Takedown Funds means funds deducted by the FMCSA each fiscal year from the amount made available for the MCSAP for expenses incurred in the administration of the MCSAP, including expenses to train State and local government employees.

Administrator means Federal Motor Carrier Safety Administrator.

Basic Program Funds means the total MCSAP funds less the High Priority Activity, Border Activity, Administrative Takedown, and Incentive Funds.

Border Activity Funds means funds provided to States, local governments, and other persons carrying out programs, activities, and projects relating to CMV safety and regulatory enforcement supporting the North American Free Trade Agreement (NAFTA) at the U.S. border. Up to 5 percent of total MCSAP funds are available for these activities.

Commercial motor vehicle (CMV) means a motor vehicle that has any of the following characteristics:

(1) *A gross vehicle weight (GVW),* gross vehicle weight rating (GVWR), gross combination weight (GCW), or gross combination weight rating (GCWR) of 4,537 kilograms (10,001 pounds) or more.

(2) *Regardless of weight,* is designed or used to transport 16 or more passengers, including driver.

(3) *Regardless of weight,* is used in the transportation of hazardous materials and is required to be placarded pursuant to 49 CFR Part 172, Subpart F.

Commercial vehicle safety plan (CVSP) means the document outlining the State's CMV safety objectives, strategies, activities and performance measures.

Compatible or **Compatibility** means State laws and regulations applicable to interstate commerce and to intrastate movement of hazardous materials are identical to the FMCSRs and the HMRs or have the same effect as the FMCSRs. State laws applicable to intrastate commerce are either identical to, or have the same effect as, the FMCSRs or fall within the established limited variances under §350.341.

High Priority Activity Funds means funds provided to States, local governments, and other persons carrying out activities and projects that directly support the MCSAP, are national in scope in that the successful activity or project could potentially be applied in other States on a national scale, and improve CMV safety and compliance with CMV safety regulations. Up to 5 percent of total MCSAP funds are available for these activities.

Incentive Funds means funds awarded to States achieving reductions in CMV involved fatal accidents, CMV fatal accident rate, or meeting specified CMV safety program performance criteria.

Large truck means a truck over 10,000 pounds gross vehicle weight rating including single unit trucks and truck tractors (FARS definition).

Motor carrier means a for-hire motor carrier or private motor carrier. The term includes a motor carrier's agents, officers, or representatives responsible for hiring, supervising, training, assigning, or dispatching a driver or concerned with the installation, inspection, and maintenance of motor vehicle equipment or accessories or both.

North American Standard Inspection means the methodology used by State CMV safety inspectors to conduct safety inspections of CMVs. This consists of various levels of inspection of the vehicle or driver or both. The inspection criteria are developed by the FMCSA in conjunction with the Commercial Vehicle Safety Alliance (CVSA), an association of States, Canadian Provinces, and Mexico whose members agree to adopt these standards for inspecting CMVs in their jurisdiction.

Operating Authority means the registration required by 49 U.S.C. 13902, 49 CFR Part 365, 49 CFR Part 368, and 49 CFR Part 392.9a.

§350.107 What jurisdictions are eligible for MCSAP funding?

All of the States, the District of Columbia, the Commonwealth of Puerto Rico, the Commonwealth of the Northern Mariana Islands, American Samoa, Guam, and the Virgin Islands are eligible to receive MCSAP grants directly from the FMCSA. For purposes of this subpart, all references to "State" or "States" include these jurisdictions.

§350.109 What are the national program elements?

The national program elements include the following five activities:

(a) **Driver/vehicle inspections.**
(b) **Traffic enforcement.**
(c) **Compliance reviews.**
(d) **Public education and awareness.**
(e) **Data collection.**

§350.111 What constitutes "traffic enforcement" for the purpose of the MCSAP?

Traffic enforcement means enforcement activities of State or local officials, including stopping CMVs operating on highways, streets, or roads for violations of State or local motor vehicle or traffic laws (e.g., speeding, following too closely, reckless driving, improper lane change). To be eligible for funding through the grant, traffic enforcement must include an appropriate North American Standard Inspection of the CMV or driver or both prior to releasing the driver or CMV for resumption of operations.

Subpart B - Requirements for Participation

§350.201 What conditions must a State meet to qualify for Basic Program Funds?

Each State must meet the following twenty-two conditions:

(a) **Assume responsibility for improving motor carrier safety** and adopting and enforcing State safety laws and regulations that are compatible with the FMCSRs (49 CFR Parts 390-397) and the HMRs (49 CFR parts 107 (Subparts F and G only), 171-173, 177, 178 and 180), except as may be determined by the Administrator to be inapplicable to a State enforcement program.

(b) **Implement a performance-based program** by the beginning of Fiscal Year 2000 and submit a CVSP which will serve as the basis for monitoring and evaluating the State's performance.

(c) **Designate, in its State Certification,** the lead State agency responsible for implementing the CVSP.

(d) **Ensure that only agencies** having the legal authority, resources, and qualified personnel necessary to enforce the FMCSRs and HMRs or compatible State laws or regulations are assigned to perform functions in accordance with the approved CVSP.

§350.203 Part 350 - Commercial Motor Carrier Safety Assistance Program

(e) **Allocate adequate funds** for the administration of the CVSP, including the enforcement of the FMCSRs, HMRs, or compatible State laws or regulations.
(f) **Maintain the aggregate expenditure of funds** by the State and its political subdivisions, exclusive of Federal funds, for motor carrier and highway hazardous materials safety enforcement, eligible for funding under this part, at a level at least equal to the average expenditure for Federal or State fiscal years 1997, 1998, and 1999.
(g) **Provide legal authority** for a right of entry and inspection adequate to carry out the CVSP.
(h) **Prepare and submit to the FMCSA,** upon request, all reports required in connection with the CVSP or other conditions of the grant.
(i) **Adopt and use the reporting standards and forms** required by the FMCSA to record work activities performed under the CVSP.
(j) **Require registrants of CMVs to declare,** at the time of registration, their knowledge of applicable FMCSRs, HMRs, or compatible State laws or regulations.
(k) **Grant maximum reciprocity for inspections conducted** under the North American Standard Inspection through the use of a nationally accepted system that allows ready identification of previously inspected CMVs.
(l) **Conduct CMV size and weight enforcement activities** funded under this program only to the extent those activities do not diminish the effectiveness of other CMV safety enforcement programs.
(m) **Coordinate the CVSP,** data collection and information systems, with State highway safety programs under Title 23 United States Code (U.S.C.).
(n) **Ensure participation in SAFETYNET** and other information systems by all appropriate jurisdictions receiving funding under this section.
(o) **Ensure information is exchanged** with other States in a timely manner.
(p) **Emphasize and improve enforcement** of State and local traffic laws and regulations related to CMV safety.
(q) **Promote activities in support** of the national program elements listed in §350.109, including the following three activities:
  (1) *Activities aimed at removing* impaired CMV drivers from the highways through adequate enforcement of restrictions on the use of alcohol and controlled substances and by ensuring ready roadside access to alcohol detection and measuring equipment.
  (2) *Activities aimed at providing* an appropriate level of training to MCSAP personnel to recognize drivers impaired by alcohol or controlled substances.
  (3) *Interdiction activities affecting the transportation* of controlled substances by CMV drivers and training on appropriate strategies for carrying out those interdiction activities.
(r) **Enforce requirements relating** to the licensing of CMV drivers, including checking the status of commercial drivers' licenses (CDL).
(s) **Require the proper and timely correction** of all CMV safety violations noted during inspections carried out with MCSAP funds.
(t) (1) *Enforce operating authority requirements* under 49 U.S.C. 13902, 49 CFR Part 365, 49 CFR Part 368, and 49 CFR Part 392.9a by placing out of service a vehicle operated by a motor carrier without operating authority or beyond the scope of its operating authority.
  (2) *Enforce financial responsibility requirements* under 49 U.S.C. 13906, 31138, 31139, and 49 CFR Part 387.
(u) **Adopt and maintain** consistent, effective, and reasonable sanctions for violations of CMV, driver, and hazardous materials regulations.
(v) **Ensure that MCSAP agencies have policies** that stipulate roadside inspections will be conducted at locations that are adequate to protect the safety of drivers and enforcement personnel.

§350.203 [Reserved]

§350.205 How and when does a State apply for MCSAP funding?

(a) **The lead agency, designated by the Governor,** must submit the State's CVSP to the Motor Carrier State Director, FMCSA, on or before August 1 of each year.
(b) **This deadline may, for good cause,** be extended by the State Director for a period not to exceed 30 calendar days.
(c) **For a State to receive funding,** the CVSP must be complete and include all required documents.

§350.207 What response does a State receive to its CVSP submission?

(a) **The FMCSA will notify the State, in writing,** within 30 days of receipt of the CVSP whether:
  (1) *The plan is approved.*
  (2) *Approval of the plan is withheld* because the CVSP does not meet the requirements of this part, or is not adequate to ensure effective enforcement of the FMCSRs and HMRs or compatible State laws and regulations.
(b) **If approval is withheld,** the State will have 30 days from the date of the notice to modify and resubmit the plan.
(c) **Disapproval of a resubmitted plan is final.**
(d) **Any State aggrieved by an adverse decision** under this section may seek judicial review under 5 U.S.C. Chapter 7.

§350.209 How does a State demonstrate that it satisfies the conditions for Basic Program funding?

(a) **The Governor, the State's Attorney General,** or other State official specifically designated by the Governor, must execute a State Certification as described in §350.211.
(b) **The State must submit the State Certification** along with its CVSP, and supplement it with a copy of any State law, regulation, or form pertaining to CMV safety adopted since the State's last certification that bears on the items contained in §350.201 of this subpart.

§350.211 What is the format of the certification required by §350.209?

The State's certification must be consistent with the following content:
I (name), (title), on behalf of the State (or Commonwealth) of (State), as requested by the Administrator as a condition of approval of a grant under the authority of 49 U.S.C. 31102, as amended, do hereby certify as follows:

1. **The State has adopted commercial motor carrier** and highway hazardous materials safety rules and regulations that are compatible with the FMCSRs and the HMRs.
2. **The State has designated** (name of State CMV safety agency) as the lead agency to administer the CVSP for the grant sought and (names of agencies) to perform defined functions under the plan. These agencies have the legal authority, resources, and qualified personnel necessary to enforce the State's commercial motor carrier, driver, and highway hazardous materials safety laws or regulations.
3. **The State will obligate the funds or resources necessary** to provide a matching share to the Federal assistance provided in the grant to administer the plan submitted and to enforce the State's commercial motor carrier safety, driver, and hazardous materials laws or regulations in a manner consistent with the approved plan.
4. **The laws of the State** provide the State's enforcement officials right of entry and inspection sufficient to carry out the purposes of the CVSP, as approved, and provide that the State will grant maximum reciprocity for inspections conducted pursuant to the North American Standard Inspection procedure, through the use of a nationally accepted system allowing ready identification of previously inspected CMVs.
5. **The State requires that all reports relating to the program** be submitted to the appropriate State agency or agencies, and the State will make these reports available, in a timely manner, to the FMCSA on request.
6. **The State has uniform reporting requirements** and uses FMCSA designated forms for record keeping, inspection, and other enforcement activities.
7. **The State has in effect a requirement** that registrants of CMVs declare their knowledge of the applicable Federal or State CMV safety laws or regulations.
8. **The State will maintain** the level of its expenditures, exclusive of Federal assistance, at least at the level of the average of the aggregate expenditures of the State and its political subdivisions during State or Federal fiscal years 1997, 1998, and 1999. These expenditures must cover at least the following four program areas, if applicable:
  (a) *Motor carrier safety programs in accordance with 49 CFR 350.301.*
  (b) *Size and weight enforcement programs.*
  (c) *Traffic safety.*
  (d) *Drug interdiction enforcement programs.*

Subpart B - Requirements for Participation §350.215 (f)

9. **The State will ensure** that CMV size and weight enforcement activities funded with MCSAP funds will not diminish the effectiveness of other CMV safety enforcement programs.
10. **The State will ensure** that violation fines imposed and collected by the State are consistent, effective, and equitable.
11. **The State will ensure it has a program** for timely and appropriate correction of all violations discovered during inspections conducted using MCSAP funds.
12. **The State will ensure** that the CVSP, data collection, and information systems are coordinated with the State highway safety program under Title 23, U.S. Code. The name of the Governor's highway safety representative (or other authorized State official through whom coordination was accomplished) is _____. (Name)
13. **The State participates in SAFETYNET** and ensures information is exchanged with other States in a timely manner.
14. **The State has undertaken efforts** to emphasize and improve enforcement of State and local traffic laws as they pertain to CMV safety.
15. **The State will ensure that MCSAP agencies** have departmental policies stipulating that roadside inspections will be conducted at locations that are adequate to protect the safety of drivers and enforcement personnel.
16. **The State will ensure** that requirements relating to the licensing of CMV drivers are enforced, including checking the status of CDLs.
17. **The State or a local recipient of MCSAP funds** will certify that it meets the minimum Federal standards set forth in 49 CFR Part 385, Subpart C, for training and experience of employees performing safety audits, compliance reviews, or driver/vehicle roadside inspections.

Date_____
Signature_____

§350.213 What must a State CVSP include?

The State's CVSP must reflect a performance-based program, and contain the following eighteen items:

(a) **A general overview section** that must include the following two items:
  (1) *A statement of the State agency goal or mission.*
  (2) *A program summary of the effectiveness* of the prior years' activities in reducing CMV accidents, injuries and fatalities, and improving driver and motor carrier safety performance. Data periods used must be consistent from year to year. This may be calendar year or fiscal year or any 12-month period of time for which the State's data is current. The summary must show trends supported by safety and program performance data collected over several years. It must identify safety or performance problems in the State and those problems must be addressed in the new or modified CVSP.
(b) **A brief narrative describing how the State program** addresses the national program elements listed in §350.109. The plan must address these elements even if there are no planned activities in a program area. The rationale for the resource allocation decision must be explained. The narrative section must include a description of how the State supports the activities identified in §350.201(q) and (t).
  (1) *Activities aimed at removing* impaired CMV drivers from the highways through adequate enforcement of restrictions on the use of alcohol and controlled substances and by ensuring ready roadside access to alcohol detection and measuring equipment.
  (2) *Activities aimed at providing* an appropriate level of training to MCSAP personnel to recognize drivers impaired by alcohol or controlled substances.
  (3) *Interdiction activities affecting the transportation* of controlled substances by CMV drivers and training on appropriate strategies for carrying out those interdiction activities.
  (4) *Activities to enforce registration requirements* under 49 U.S.C. 13902 and 49 CFR Part 365 and financial responsibility requirements under 49 U.S.C. 13906, 31138 and 31139 and 49 CFR Part 387.

(c) **A definitive problem statement for each objective,** supported by data or other information. The CVSP must identify the source of the data, and who is responsible for its collection, maintenance, and analysis.
(d) **Performance objectives, stated in quantifiable terms,** to be achieved through the State plan. Objectives must include a measurable reduction in highway accidents or hazardous materials incidents involving CMVs. The objective may also include documented improvements in other program areas (e.g., legislative or regulatory authority, enforcement results, or resource allocations).
(e) **Strategies to be employed to achieve** performance objectives. Strategies may include education, enforcement, legislation, use of technology and improvements to safety infrastructure.
(f) **Specific activities intended to achieve** the stated strategies and objectives. Planned activities must be eligible under this program as defined in §§350.309 and 350.311.
(g) **Specific quantifiable performance measures,** as appropriate. These performance measures will be used to assist the State in monitoring the progress of its program and preparing an annual evaluation.
(h) **A description of the State's method** for ongoing monitoring of the progress of its plan. This should include who will conduct the monitoring, the frequency with which it will be carried out, and how and to whom reports will be made.
(i) **An objective evaluation that discusses** the progress towards individual objectives listed under the "Performance Objectives" section of the previous year's CVSP and identifies any safety or performance problems discovered. States will identify those problems as new objectives or make modifications to the existing objectives in the next CVSP.
(j) **A budget which supports the CVSP,** describing the expenditures for allocable costs such as personnel and related costs, equipment purchases, printing, information systems costs, and other eligible costs consistent with §§350.311 and 350.309.
(k) **A budget summary form** including planned expenditures for that fiscal year and projected number of activities in each national program element, except data collection.
(l) **The results of the annual review** to determine the compatibility of State laws and regulations with the FMCSRs and HMRs.
(m) **A copy of any new law or regulation** affecting CMV safety enforcement that was enacted by the State since the last CVSP was submitted.
(n) **Executed State Certification as outlined in §350.211.**
(o) **Executed MCSAP-1 form.**
(p) **List of MCSAP contacts.**
(q) **Annual Certification of Compatibility, §350.331.**
(r) **State Training Plan.**

§350.215 What are the consequences for a State that fails to perform according to an approved CVSP or otherwise fails to meet the conditions of this part?

(a) **If a State is not performing according to an approved plan** or not adequately meeting conditions set forth in §350.201, the Administrator may issue a written notice of proposed determination of nonconformity to the Governor of the State or the official designated in the plan. The notice will set forth the reasons for the proposed determination.
(b) **The State will have 30 days** from the date of the notice to reply. The reply must address the deficiencies or incompatibility cited in the notice and provide documentation as necessary.
(c) **After considering the State's reply,** the Administrator will make a final decision.
(d) **In the event the State fails timely to reply** to a notice of proposed determination of nonconformity, the notice becomes the Administrator's final determination of nonconformity.
(e) **Any adverse decision will result in immediate cessation** of Federal funding under this part.
(f) **Any State aggrieved by an adverse decision** under this section may seek judicial review under 5 U.S.C. Chapter 7.

§350.217 What are the consequences for a State with a CDL program not in substantial compliance with 49 CFR Part 384, Subpart B?

(a) **A State with a CDL program** not in substantial compliance with 49 CFR Part 384, Subpart B, as required by 49 CFR Part 384, Subpart C, is subject to the loss of all Motor Carrier Safety Assistance Program (MCSAP) grant funds authorized under §103(b)(1) of the Motor Carrier Safety Improvement Act of 1999 [Pub. L. 106-159, 113 Stat. 1748] and loss of certain Federal-aid highway funds, as specified in 49 CFR Part 384, Subpart D.

(b) **Withheld MCSAP grant funds** will be restored to the State if the State meets the conditions of §384.403(b) of this subchapter.

Subpart C - Funding

§350.301 What level of effort must a State maintain to qualify for MCSAP funding?

(a) **The State must maintain** the average aggregate expenditure (monies spent during the base period of Federal or State fiscal years 1997, 1998, and 1999) of State funds for motor carrier and highway hazardous materials safety enforcement purposes, in the year in which the grant is sought.

(b) **Determination of a State's level of effort** must not include the following three things:
  (1) *Federal funds received for support* of motor carrier and hazardous materials safety enforcement.
  (2) *State matching funds.*
  (3) *State funds used* for federally sponsored demonstration or pilot CMV safety programs.

(c) **The State must include costs** associated with activities performed during the base period by State or local agencies currently receiving or projected to receive funds under this part. It must include only those activities which meet the current requirements for funding eligibility under the grant program.

§350.303 What are the State and Federal shares of expenses incurred under an approved CVSP?

(a) **The FMCSA will reimburse up to 80 percent** of the eligible costs incurred in the administration of an approved CVSP.

(b) **In-kind contributions are acceptable** in meeting the State's matching share if they represent eligible costs as established by 49 CFR Part 18 or agency policy.

§350.305 Are U.S. Territories subject to the matching funds requirement?

The Administrator waives the requirement for matching funds for the Virgin Islands, American Samoa, Guam, and the Commonwealth of the Northern Mariana Islands.

§350.307 How long are MCSAP funds available to a State?

The funds obligated to a State will remain available for the rest of the fiscal year in which they were obligated and the next full fiscal year. The State must account for any prior year's unexpended funds in the annual CVSP. Funds must be expended in the order in which they are obligated.

§350.309 What activities are eligible for reimbursement under the MCSAP?

The primary activities eligible for reimbursement are:

(a) **The five national program elements listed in §350.109 of this part.**

(b) **Sanitary food transportation inspections** performed under 49 U.S.C. 5708.

(c) **The following three activities,** when accompanied by an appropriate North American Standard Inspection and inspection report:
  (1) *Enforcement of size and weight regulations* conducted at locations other than fixed weight facilities, at specific geographical locations where the weight of the vehicle can significantly affect the safe operation of the vehicle, or at seaports where intermodal shipping containers enter and exit the United States.
  (2) *Detection of the unlawful presence* of controlled substances in a CMV or on the driver or any occupant of a CMV.
  (3) *Enforcement of State traffic laws and regulations* designed to promote the safe operation of CMVs.

§350.311 What specific items are eligible for reimbursement under the MCSAP?

All reimbursable items must be necessary, reasonable, allocable to the approved CVSP, and allowable under this part and 49 CFR Part 18. The eligibility of specific items is subject to review by the FMCSA. The following six types of expenses are eligible for reimbursement:

(a) **Personnel expenses,** including recruitment and screening, training, salaries and fringe benefits, and supervision.

(b) **Equipment and travel expenses,** including per diem, directly related to the enforcement of safety regulations, including vehicles, uniforms, communications equipment, special inspection equipment, vehicle maintenance, fuel, and oil.

(c) **Indirect expenses for facilities,** except fixed scales, used to conduct inspections or house enforcement personnel, support staff, and equipment to the extent they are measurable and recurring (e.g., rent and overhead).

(d) **Expenses related to data acquisition,** storage, and analysis that are specifically identifiable as program-related to develop a data base to coordinate resources and improve efficiency.

(e) **Clerical and administrative expenses,** to the extent necessary and directly attributable to the MCSAP.

(f) **Expenses related to the improvement of real property** (e.g., installation of lights for the inspection of vehicles at night). Acquisition of real property, land, or buildings are not eligible costs.

§350.313 How are MCSAP funds allocated?

(a) **After deducting administrative expenses authorized** in 49 U.S.C. 31104(e), the MCSAP funds are allocated as follows:
  (1) *Up to 5 percent of the MCSAP funds* appropriated for each fiscal year may be distributed for High Priority Activities and Projects at the discretion of the Administrator.
  (2) *Up to 5 percent of the MCSAP funds* appropriated for each fiscal year may be distributed for Border CMV Safety and Enforcement Programs at the discretion of the Administrator.
  (3) *The remaining funds will be allocated* among qualifying States in two ways:
    (i) As Basic Program Funds in accordance with §350.323 of this part,
    (ii) As Incentive Funds in accordance with §350.327 of this part.

(b) **The funding provided in paragraphs (a)(1) and (a)(2) of** this section may be awarded through contract, cooperative agreement, or grant. The FMCSA will notify States if it intends to solicit State grant proposals for any portion of this funding.

(c) **The funding provided under paragraphs (a)(1) and (a)(2)** of this section may be made available to State MCSAP lead agencies, local governments, and other persons that use and train qualified officers and employees in coordination with State motor vehicle safety agencies.

§350.315 How may Basic Program Funds be used?

Basic Program Funds may be used for any eligible activity or item consistent with §§350.309 and 350.311.

§350.317 What are Incentive Funds and how may they be used?

Incentive Funds are monies, in addition to Basic Program Funds, provided to States that achieve reduction in CMV-involved fatal accidents, CMV fatal accident rate, or that meet specified CMV safety performance criteria. Incentive Funds may be used for any eligible activity or item consistent with §§350.309 and 350.311.

§350.319 What are permissible uses of High Priority Activity Funds?

(a) **The FMCSA may generally use these funds** to support, enrich, or evaluate State CMV safety programs and to accomplish the five objectives listed below:
  (1) *Implement, promote, and maintain* national programs to improve CMV safety.
  (2) *Increase compliance with CMV safety regulations.*
  (3) *Increase public awareness about CMV safety.*
  (4) *Provide education on CMV safety and related issues.*
  (5) *Demonstrate new safety related technologies.*

(b) **These funds will be allocated,** at the discretion of the FMCSA, to States, local governments, and other organizations that use and train qualified officers and employees in coordination with State safety agencies.

Subpart C - Funding §350.333 (a)

(c) **The FMCSA will notify the States when such funds are available.**
(d) **The Administrator may designate up to 5 percent** of the annual MCSAP funding for these projects and activities.

§350.321 What are permissible uses of Border Activity Funds?

(a) **The FMCSA may generally use such funds** to develop and implement a national program addressing CMV safety and enforcement activities along the United States' borders.
(b) **These funds will be allocated,** at the discretion of the FMCSA, to States, local governments, and other organizations that use and train qualified officials and employees in coordination with State safety agencies. The FMCSA will notify the States when such funds are available. The Administrator may designate up to 5 percent of the annual MCSAP funding for these projects and activities.

§350.323 What criteria are used in the Basic Program Funds allocation?

(a) **The funds are distributed proportionally to the States** using the following four, equally weighted (25 percent), factors.
   (1) *1997 Road miles* (all highways) as defined by the FMCSA.
   (2) *All vehicle miles traveled (VMT)* as defined by the FMCSA.
   (3) *Population* — annual census estimates as issued by the U.S. Census Bureau.
   (4) *Special fuel consumption* (net after reciprocity adjustment) as defined by the FMCSA.
(b) **Distribution of Basic Program Funds is subject** to a maximum and minimum allocation as illustrated in the Table to this section, as follows:

Table to §350.323(b) - Basic Program Fund Allocation Limitations

Recipient	Maximum allocation	Minimum allocation
States and Puerto Rico	4.944% of the Basic Program Funds	$350,000 or 0.44% of Basic Program Funds, whichever is greater
U.S. Territories		$350,000 (fixed amount)

§350.325 [Reserved]

§350.327 How may States qualify for Incentive Funds?

(a) **A State may qualify for Incentive Funds** if it can demonstrate that its CMV safety program has shown improvement in any or all of the following five categories:
   (1) *Reduction of large truck-involved fatal accidents.*
   (2) *Reduction of large truck-involved fatal accident rate* or maintenance of a large truck-involved fatal accident rate that is among the lowest 10 percent of such rates of MCSAP recipients.
   (3) *Upload of CMV accident reports* in accordance with current FMCSA policy guidelines.
   (4) *Verification of CDLs during all roadside inspections.*
   (5) *Upload of CMV inspection data* in accordance with current FMCSA policy guidelines.
(b) **Incentive Funds will be distributed based upon** the five following safety and program performance factors:
   (1) *Five shares will be awarded to States* that reduce the number of large truck-involved fatal accidents for the most recent calendar year for which data are available when compared to the 10-year average number of large truck-involved fatal accidents ending with the preceding year. The 10-year average will be computed from the number of large truck-involved fatal crashes, as reported by the FARS, administered by the National Highway Traffic Safety Administration (NHTSA).
   (2) *Four shares will be awarded to States* that reduce the fatal-accident rate for the most recent calendar year for which data are available when compared to each State's average fatal accident rate for the preceding 10-year period. States with the lowest 10 percent of accident rates in the most recent calendar year for which data are available will be awarded three shares if the rate for the State is the same as its average accident rate for the preceding 10-year period.
   (3) *Two shares will be awarded to States* that upload CMV accident data within FMCSA policy guidelines.
   (4) *Two shares will be awarded to States* that certify their MCSAP inspection agencies have departmental policies that stipulate CDLs are verified, as part of the inspection process, through Commercial Driver's License Information System (CDLIS), National Law Enforcement Tracking System (NLETS), or the State licensing authority.
   (5) *Two shares will be awarded to States* that upload CMV inspection reports within current FMCSA policy guidelines.
(c) **The total of all States' shares awarded will be divided** into the dollar amount of Incentive Funds available, thereby establishing the value of one share. Each State's incentive allocation will then be determined by multiplying the State's percentage participation in the formula allocation of Basic Program Funds, by the number of shares it received that year, multiplied by the dollar value of one share.
(d) **States may use Incentive Funds** for any eligible CMV safety purpose.
(e) **Incentive Funds are subject** to the same State matching requirements as Basic Program Funds.
(f) **A State must annually certify compliance** with the applicable incentive criteria to receive Incentive Funds. A State must submit the required certification as part of its CVSP or as a separate document.

§350.329 How may a State or a local agency qualify for High Priority or Border Activity Funds?

(a) **States must meet the requirements of §350.201, as applicable.**
(b) **Local agencies must meet the following nine conditions:**
   (1) *Prepare a proposal in accordance with §350.213, as applicable.*
   (2) *Coordinate the proposal* with the State lead MCSAP agency to ensure the proposal is consistent with State and national CMV safety program priorities.
   (3) *Certify that your local jurisdiction* has the legal authority, resources, and trained and qualified personnel necessary to perform the functions specified in the proposal.
   (4) *Designate a person who will be responsible* for implementation, reporting, and administering the approved proposal and will be the primary contact for the project.
   (5) *Agree to fund up to 20 percent of the proposed request.*
   (6) *Agree to prepare and submit all reports* required in connection with the proposal or other conditions of the grant.
   (7) *Agree to use the forms and reporting criteria* required by the State lead MCSAP agency and/or the FMCSA to record work activities to be performed under the proposal.
   (8) *Certify that the local agency will impose sanctions* for violations of CMV and driver laws and regulations that are consistent with those of the State.
   (9) *Certify participation in national data bases* appropriate to the project.

§350.331 How does a State ensure its laws and regulations are compatible with the FMCSRs and HMRs?

(a) **A State must review any new law or regulation** affecting CMV safety as soon as possible, but in any event immediately after enactment or issuance, for compatibility with the FMCSRs and HMRs.
(b) **If the review determines that the new law or regulation** is incompatible with the FMCSRs and/or HMRs, the State must immediately notify the Motor Carrier State Director.
(c) **A State must conduct an annual review** of its laws and regulations for compatibility and report the results of that review in the annual CVSP in accordance with §350.213(l) along with a certification of compliance, no later than August 1 of each year. The report must include the following two items:
   (1) *A copy of the State law, regulation, or policy* relating to CMV safety that was adopted since the State's last report.
   (2) *A certification,* executed by the State's Governor, Attorney General, or other State official specifically designated by the Governor, stating that the annual review was performed and that State CMV safety laws remain compatible with the FMCSRs and HMRs. If State CMV laws are no longer compatible, the certifying official shall explain.
(d) **As soon as practical after the effective date** of any newly enacted regulation or amendment to the FMCSRs or HMRs, but no later than three years after that date, the State must amend its laws or regulations to make them compatible with the FMCSRs and/or HMRs, as amended.

§350.333 What are the guidelines for the compatibility review?

(a) **The State law or regulation must apply to all segments** of the motor carrier industry (i.e., for-hire and private motor carriers of property and passengers).

(b) **Laws and regulations reviewed** for the CDL compliance report are excluded from the compatibility review.

(c) **Definitions of words or terms must be consistent** with those in the FMCSRs and HMRs.

(d) **A State must identify any law or regulation** that is not the same as the corresponding Federal regulation and evaluate it in accordance with the table to this section as follows:

Table to §350.333 - Guidelines for the State Law and Regulation Compatibility Review

Law or regulation has same effect as corresponding Federal regulation	Applies to interstate or intrastate commerce	Less stringent or more stringent	Action authorized
(1) Yes	....	....	Compatible — Interstate and intrastate commerce enforcement authorized
(2) No	Intrastate	....	Refer to §350.341
(3) No	Interstate	Less stringent	Enforcement prohibited
(4) No	Interstate	More stringent	Enforcement authorized if the State can demonstrate the law or regulation has a safety benefit or does not create an undue burden upon interstate commerce (See 49 CFR Part 355)

§350.335 What are the consequences if my State has laws or regulations incompatible with the Federal regulations?

(a) **A State that currently has compatible** CMV safety laws and regulations pertaining to interstate commerce (i.e., rules identical to the FMCSRs and HMRs) and intrastate commerce (i.e., rules identical to or within the tolerance guidelines for the FMCSRs and identical to the HMRs) but enacts a law or regulation which results in an incompatible rule will not be eligible for Basic Program Funds nor Incentive Funds.

(b) **A State that fails to adopt any new regulation** or amendment to the FMCSRs or HMRs within three years of its effective date will be deemed to have incompatible regulations and will not be eligible for Basic Program nor Incentive Funds.

(c) **Those States with incompatible laws or regulations** pertaining to intrastate commerce and receiving 50 percent of their basic formula allocation on April 20, 2000 will continue at that level of funding until those incompatibilities are removed, provided no further incompatibilities are created.

(d) **Upon a finding by the FMCSA,** based upon its own initiative or upon a petition of any person, including any State, that your State law, regulation or enforcement practice pertaining to CMV safety, in either interstate or intrastate commerce, is incompatible with the FMCSRs or HMRs, the FMCSA may initiate a proceeding under §350.215 for withdrawal of eligibility for all Basic Program and Incentive Funds.

(e) **Any decision regarding the compatibility** of your State law or regulation with the HMRs that requires an interpretation will be referred to the Research and Special Programs Administration of the DOT for such interpretation before proceeding under §350.215.

§350.337 How may State laws and regulations governing motor carriers, CMV drivers, and CMVs in interstate commerce differ from the FMCSRs and still be considered compatible?

States are not required to adopt 49 CFR Parts 398 and 399, Subparts A through E and H of Part 107, and §§171.15 and 171.16, as applicable to either interstate or intrastate commerce.

§350.339 What are tolerance guidelines?

Tolerance guidelines set forth the limited deviations from the FMCSRs allowed in your State's laws and regulations. These variances apply only to motor carriers, CMV drivers and CMVs engaged in intrastate commerce and not subject to Federal jurisdiction.

§350.341 What specific variances from the FMCSRs are allowed for State laws and regulations governing motor carriers, CMV drivers, and CMVs engaged in intrastate commerce and not subject to Federal jurisdiction?

(a) **A State may exempt a CMV** from all or part of its laws or regulations applicable to intrastate commerce, provided that neither the GVW, GVWR, GCW, nor GCWR of the vehicle equals or exceeds 11,801 kg (26,001 lbs.). However, a State may not exempt a CMV from such laws or regulations if the vehicle:

(1) *Transports hazardous materials requiring a placard.*

(2) *Is designed or used to transport* 16 or more people, including the driver.

(b) **State laws and regulations applicable** to intrastate commerce may not grant exemptions based upon the type of transportation being performed (e.g., for-hire, private, etc.).

(c) **A State may retain those exemptions** from its motor carrier safety laws and regulations that were in effect before April, 1988, are still in effect, and apply to specific industries operating in intrastate commerce.

(d) **State laws and regulations** applicable to intrastate commerce must not include exemptions based upon the distance a motor carrier or driver operates from the work reporting location. This prohibition does not apply to those exemptions already contained in the FMCSRs nor to the extension of the mileage radius exemption contained in 49 CFR 395.1(e) from 100 to 150 miles.

(e) **Hours of service** — State hours-of-service limitations applied to intrastate transportation may vary to the extent of allowing the following:

(1) *A 12-hour driving limit,* provided driving a CMV after having been on duty more than 16 hours is prohibited.

(2) *Driving prohibitions for drivers* who have been on duty 70 hours in 7 consecutive days or 80 hours in 8 consecutive days.

(f) **Age of CMV driver** — All CMV drivers must be at least 18 years of age.

(g) **Grandfather clauses** — States may provide grandfather clauses in their rules and regulations if such exemptions are uniform or in substantial harmony with the FMCSRs and provide an orderly transition to full regulatory adoption at a later date.

(h) **Driver qualifications:**

(1) *Intrastate drivers who do not meet* the physical qualification standards in 49 CFR 391.41 may continue to be qualified to operate a CMV in intrastate commerce if the following three conditions are met:

(i) *The driver was qualified* under existing State law or regulation at the time the State adopted physical qualification standards compatible with the Federal standards in 49 CFR 391.41.

(ii) *The otherwise non-qualifying* medical or physical condition has not substantially worsened.

(iii) *No other non-qualifying* medical or physical condition has developed.

(2) *The State may adopt or continue programs* granting variances to intrastate drivers with medical or physical conditions that would otherwise be non-qualifying under the State's equivalent of 49 CFR 391.41 if the variances are based upon sound medical judgment combined with appropriate performance standards ensuring no adverse affect on safety.

§350.343 How may a State obtain a new exemption for State laws and regulations for a specific industry involved in intrastate commerce?

The FMCSA strongly discourages exemptions for specific industries, but will consider such requests if the State submits documentation containing information supporting evaluation of the following 10 factors:

(a) **Type and scope of the industry exemption requested,** including percentage of industry affected, number of vehicles, mileage traveled, number of companies involved.

(b) **Type and scope of the requirement** to which the exemption would apply.

(c) **Safety performance of that specific industry** (e.g., accident frequency, rates and comparative figures).

(d) **Inspection information** (e.g., number of violations per inspection, driver and vehicle out-of-service information).

(e) **Other CMV safety regulations** enforced by other State agencies not participating in the MCSAP.

(f) **Commodity transported (e.g., livestock, grain).**

(g) **Similar variations granted** and the circumstances under which they were granted.

(h) **Justification for the exemption.**

(i) **Identifiable effects on safety.**

(j) **State's economic environment** and its ability to compete in foreign and domestic markets.

§350.345 How does a State apply for additional variances from the FMCSRs?

Any State may apply to the Administrator for a variance from the FMCSRs for intrastate commerce. The variance will be granted only if the State satisfactorily demonstrates that the State law, regulation or enforcement practice:

(a) **Achieves substantially the same purpose** as the similar Federal regulation.

(b) **Does not apply to interstate commerce.**

(c) **Is not likely to have an adverse impact on safety.**

Part 350 - Commercial Motor Carrier Safety Assistance Program

Notes

Part 355 - Compatibility of State Laws and Regulations Affecting Interstate Motor Carrier Operations

Subpart A - General Applicability and Definitions

§355.1 Purpose.
(a) **To promote adoption and enforcement** of State laws and regulations pertaining to commercial motor vehicle safety that are compatible with appropriate parts of the Federal Motor Carrier Safety Regulations.
(b) **To provide guidelines for a continuous regulatory review** of State laws and regulations.
(c) **To establish deadlines for States to achieve compatibility** with appropriate parts of the Federal Motor Carrier Safety Regulations with respect to interstate commerce.

§355.3 Applicability.
These provisions apply to any State that adopts or enforces laws or regulations pertaining to commercial motor vehicle safety in interstate commerce.

§355.5 Definitions.
Unless specifically defined in this section, terms used in this part are subject to the definitions in 49 CFR 390.5.

Compatible or **Compatibility** means that State laws and regulations applicable to interstate commerce and to intrastate movement of hazardous materials are identical to the FMCSRs and the HMRs or have the same effect as the FMCSRs; and that State laws applicable to intrastate commerce are either identical to, or have the same effect as, the FMCSRs or fall within the established limited variances under §§350.341, 350.343, and 350.345 of this subchapter.

Federal Hazardous Materials Regulations (FHMRs) means those safety regulations which are contained in Parts 107, 171-173, 177, 178 and 180, except Part 107 and §§171.15 and 171.16.

Federal Motor Carrier Safety Regulations (FMCSRs) means those safety regulations which are contained in Parts 390, 391, 392, 393, 395, 396, and 397 of this subchapter.

State means a State of the United States, the District of Columbia, the Commonwealth of Puerto Rico, the Commonwealth of the Northern Mariana Islands, American Samoa, Guam and the Virgin Islands.

Subpart B - Requirements

§355.21 Regulatory review.
(a) **General.** Each State shall annually analyze its laws and regulations, including those of its political subdivisions, which pertain to commercial motor vehicle safety to determine whether its laws and regulations are compatible with the Federal Motor Carrier Safety Regulations. Guidelines for the regulatory review are provided in the appendix to this part.
(b) **Responsibility.** The State agency designated as lead agency for the administration of grants made pursuant to Part 350 of this subchapter is responsible for reviewing and analyzing State laws and regulations for compliance with this part. In the absence of an officially designated Motor Carrier Safety Assistance Program (MCSAP) lead agency or in its discretion, the State shall designate another agency responsible to review and determine compliance with these regulations.
(c) **State review.**
  (1) *The State shall determine* which of its laws and regulations pertaining to commercial motor vehicle safety are the same as the Federal Motor Carrier Safety or Federal Hazardous Materials Regulations. With respect to any State law or regulation which is not the same as the FMCSRs (FHMRs must be identical), the State shall identify such law or regulation and determine whether:
    (i) *It has the same effect* as a corresponding section of the Federal Motor Carrier Safety Regulations;
    (ii) *It applies to interstate commerce;*
    (iii) *It is more stringent than the FMCSRs* in that it is more restrictive or places a greater burden on any entity subject to its provisions.
  (2) *If the inconsistent State law or regulation* applies to interstate commerce and is more stringent than the FMCSRs, the State shall determine:
    (i) *The safety benefits* associated with such State law or regulation; and
    (ii) *The effect of the enforcement* of such State law or regulation on interstate commerce.
  (3) *If the inconsistent State law or regulation* does not apply to interstate commerce or is less stringent than the FMCSRs, the guidelines for participation in the Motor Carrier Safety Assistance Program in §§350.341, 350.343, and 350.345 of this subchapter shall apply.

§355.23 Submission of results.
Each State shall submit the results of its regulatory review annually with its certification of compliance under §350.209 of this subchapter. It shall submit the results of the regulatory review with the certification no later than August 1 of each year with the Commercial Vehicle Safety Plan (CVSP). The State shall include copies of pertinent laws and regulations.

§355.25 Adopting and enforcing compatible laws and regulations.
(a) **General.** No State shall have in effect or enforce any State law or regulation pertaining to commercial motor vehicle safety in interstate commerce which the Administrator finds to be incompatible with the provisions of the Federal Motor Carrier Safety Regulations.
(b) **New state requirements.** No State shall implement any changes to a law or regulation which makes that or any other law or regulation incompatible with a provision of the Federal Motor Carrier Safety Regulations.
(c) **Enforcement.** To enforce compliance with this section, the Administrator will initiate a rulemaking proceeding under Part 389 of this subchapter to declare the incompatible State law or regulation pertaining to commercial motor vehicle safety unenforceable in interstate commerce.
(d) **Waiver of determination.** Any person (including any State) may petition for a waiver of a determination made under paragraph (c) of this section. Such petition will also be considered in a rulemaking proceeding under Part 389. Waivers shall be granted only upon a satisfactory showing that continued enforcement of the incompatible State law or regulation is not contrary to the public interest and is consistent with the safe operation of commercial motor vehicles.
(e) **Consolidation of proceedings.** The Administrator may consolidate any action to enforce this section with other proceedings required under this section if the Administrator determines that such consolidation will not adversely affect any party to any such proceeding.

Appendix A to Part 355 Guidelines for the Regulatory Review.
Each State shall review its laws and regulations to achieve compatibility with the Federal Motor Carrier Safety Regulations (FMCSRs). Each State shall coznsider all related requirements on enforcement of the State's motor carrier safety regulations. The documentation shall be simple and brief.

Scope
The State review required by §355.21 may be limited to those laws and regulations previously determined to be incompatible in the report of the Commercial Motor Vehicle Safety Regulatory Review Panel issued in August 1990, or by subsequent determination by the Administrator under this part, and any State laws or regulations enacted or issued after August 1990.

Applicability
The requirements must apply to all segments of the motor carrier industry common, contract, and private carriers of property and for-hire carriers of passengers.

Definitions
Definitions of terms must be consistent with those in the FMCSRs.

Driver Qualifications
Require a driver to be properly licensed to drive a commercial motor vehicle; require a driver to be in good physical health, at least 21 years of age, able to operate a vehicle safely, and maintain a good driving record; prohibit drug and alcohol abuse; require a motor carrier to maintain a driver qualification file for each driver; and require a motor carrier to ensure that a driver is medically qualified.

NOTE: The requirements for testing apply only to drivers of commercial motor vehicles as defined in 49 CFR Part 383.

Appendix A Part 355 - Compatibility of State Laws & Regs. Affecting Interstate Motor Carrier Operations

Driving of Motor Vehicles

Prohibit possession, use, or driving under the influence of alcohol or other controlled substances (while on duty); and establish 0.04 percent as the level of alcohol in the blood at which a driver is considered under the influence of alcohol.

Parts and Accessories Necessary for Safe Operation

Require operational lights and reflectors; require systematically arranged and installed wiring; and require brakes working at the required performance level, and other key components included in 49 CFR Part 393.

Hours of Service of Drivers

Prohibit a motor carrier from allowing or requiring any driver to drive: More than 10 hours following 8 consecutive hours off duty; after being on duty 15 hours, after being on duty more than 60 hours in any 7 consecutive days; or after being on duty more than 70 hours in any 8 consecutive days.

Require a driver to prepare a record-of-duty status for each 24-hour period. The driver and motor carrier must retain the records.

Inspection and Maintenance

Prohibit a commercial motor vehicle from being operated when it is likely to cause an accident or a breakdown; require the driver to conduct a walk-around inspection of the vehicle before driving it to ensure that it can be safely operated; require the driver to prepare a driver vehicle inspection report; and require commercial motor vehicles to be inspected at least annually.

Hazardous Materials

Require a motor carrier or a person operating a commercial motor vehicle transporting hazardous materials to follow the safety and hazardous materials requirements.

State Determinations

1. **Each State must determine** whether its requirements affecting interstate motor carriers are "less stringent" than the Federal requirements. "Less stringent" requirements represent either gaps in the State requirements in relation to the Federal requirements as summarized under item number one in this appendix or State requirements which are less restrictive than the Federal requirements.

   a. *An example of a gap* is when a State does not have the authority to regulate the safety of for-hire carriers of passengers or has the authority but chooses to exempt the carrier.

   b. *An example of a less restrictive State requirement* is when a State allows a person under 21 years of age to operate a commercial motor vehicle in interstate commerce.

2. **Each State must determine** whether its requirements affecting interstate motor carriers are "more stringent" than the Federal requirements: "More stringent" requirements are more restrictive or inclusive in relation to the Federal requirements as summarized under item number one in this appendix. For example, a requirement that a driver must have 2 days off after working 5 consecutive days. The State would demonstrate that its more stringent requirements:

   a. *Have a "safety benefit;"* for example, result in fewer accidents or reduce the risk of accidents;

   b. *Do not create* "an undue burden on interstate commerce," e.g., do not delay, interfere with, or increase that cost or the administrative burden for a motor carrier transporting property or passengers in interstate commerce; and

   c. *Are otherwise compatible with Federal safety requirements.*

3. **A State must adopt and enforce** in a consistent manner the requirements referenced in the above guidelines in order for the FMCSA to accept the State's determination that it has compatible safety requirements affecting interstate motor carrier operations.

   Generally, the States would have up to 3 years from the effective date of the new Federal requirement to adopt and enforce compatible requirements. The FMCSA would specify the deadline when promulgating future Federal safety requirements. The requirements are considered of equal importance.

Part 356 - Motor Carrier Routing Regulations

§356.1 Authority to serve a particular area — construction.

(a) Service at municipality. A motor carrier of property, motor passenger carrier of express, and freight forwarder authorized to serve a municipality may serve all points within that municipality's commercial zone not beyond the territorial limits, if any, fixed in such authority.

(b) Service at unincorporated community. A motor carrier of property, motor passenger carrier of express, and freight forwarder, authorized to serve an unincorporated community having a post office of the same name, may serve all points in the United States not beyond the territorial limits, if any, fixed in such authority, as follows:

   (1) *All points within 3 miles of the post office* in such unincorporated community if it has a population of less than 2,500; within 4 miles if it has a population of 2,500 but less than 25,000; and within 6 miles if it has a population of 25,000 or more;

   (2) *At all points in any municipality* any part of which is within the limits described in paragraph (b)(1) of this section; and

   (3) *At all points in any municipality* wholly surrounded, or so surrounded except for a water boundary, by any municipality included under the terms of paragraph (b)(2) of this section.

§356.3 Regular route motor passenger service.

(a) A motor common carrier authorized to transport passengers over regular routes may serve:

   (1) *All points on its authorized route;*

   (2) *All municipalities* wholly within one airline mile of its authorized route;

   (3) *All unincorporated areas* within one airline mile of its authorized route; and

   (4) *All military posts, airports, schools,* and similar establishments that may be entered within one airline mile of its authorized route, but operations within any part of such establishment more than one airline mile from such authorized route may not be over a public road.

(b) This section does not apply to those motor passenger common carriers authorized to operate within:

   (1) *New York, NY;*

   (2) *Rockland, Westchester, Orange, or Nassau Counties, NY;*

   (3) *Fairfield County, CT;* and

   (4) *Passaic, Bergen,* Essex, Hudson, Union, Morris, Somerset, Middlesex, or Monmouth Counties, NJ.

§356.5 Traversal authority.

(a) Scope. An irregular route motor carrier may operate between authorized service points over any reasonably direct or logical route unless expressly prohibited.

(b) Requirements. Before commencing operations, the carrier must, regarding each State traversed:

   (1) *Notify the State regulatory body in writing,* attaching a copy of its operating rights;

   (2) *Designate a process agent;* and

   (3) *Comply with 49 CFR 387.315.*

§356.7 Tacking.

Unless expressly prohibited, a motor common carrier of property holding separate authorities which have common service points may join, or *tack*, those authorities at the common point, or *gateway*, for the purpose of performing through service as follows:

(a) Regular route authorities may be tacked with one another;

(b) Regular route authority may be tacked with irregular route authority;

(c) Irregular route authorities may be tacked with one another if the authorities were granted pursuant to application filed on or before November 23, 1973, and the distance between the points at which service is provided, when measured through the gateway point, is 300 miles or less; and

(d) Irregular route authorities may be tacked with one another if the authorities involved contain a specific provision granting the right to tack.

§356.9 Elimination of routing restrictions — regular route carriers.

(a) Regular route authorities — construction. All certificates that, either singly or in combination, authorize the transportation by a motor common carrier of property over:

   (1) *A single regular route;* or

   (2) *Over two or more regular routes* that can lawfully be tacked at a common service point, shall be construed as authorizing transportation between authorized service points over any available route.

(b) Service at authorized points. A common carrier departing from its authorized service routes under paragraph (a) of this section shall continue to serve points authorized to be served on or in connection with its authorized service routes.

(c) Intermediate point service. A common carrier conducting operations under paragraph (a) of this section may serve points on, and within one airline mile of, an alternative route it elects to use if all the following conditions are met:

   (1) *The carrier is authorized* to serve all intermediate points (without regard to nominal restrictions) on the underlying service route;

   (2) *The alternative route* involves the use of a superhighway (i.e., a limited access highway with split-level crossings);

   (3) *The alternative superhighway route,* including highways connecting the superhighway portion of the route with the carrier's authorized service route,

      (i) *Extends in the same general direction* as the carrier's authorized service route and

      (ii) *Is wholly within 25 airline miles* of the carrier's authorized service route; and

   (4) *Service is provided in the same manner as,* and subject to any restrictions that apply to, service over the authorized service route.

§356.11 Elimination of gateways — regular and irregular route carriers.

A motor common carrier of property holding separate grants of authority (including regular route authority), one or more of which authorizes transportation over irregular routes, where the authorities have a common service point at which they can lawfully be tacked to perform through service, may perform such through service over any available route.

§356.13 Redesignated highways.

Where a highway over which a regular route motor common carrier of property is authorized to operate is assigned a new designation, such as a new number, letter, or name, the carrier shall advise the FMCSA by letter, and shall provide information concerning the new and the old designation, the points between which the highway is redesignated, and each place where the highway is referred to in the carrier's authority. The new designation of the highway will be shown in the carrier's certificate when the FMCSA has occasion to reissue it.

Part 356 - Motor Carrier Routing Regulations

Notes

Part 360 - Fees for Motor Carrier Registration and Insurance

§360.1 Fees for records search, review, copying, certification, and related services.

Certifications and copies of public records and documents on file with the Federal Motor Carrier Safety Administration will be furnished on the following basis, pursuant to the Freedom of Information Act regulations at 49 CFR Part 7:

(a) Certificate of the Director, Office of Data Analysis and Information Systems, as to the authenticity of documents, $9.00;

(b) Service involved in checking records to be certified to determine authenticity, including clerical work, etc., incidental thereto, at the rate of $16.00 per hour;

(c) Copies of the public documents, at the rate of $.80 per letter size or legal size exposure. A minimum charge of $5.00 will be made for this service; and

(d) Search and copying services requiring ADP processing, as follows:

(1) *A fee of $42.00 per hour* for professional staff time will be charged when it is required to fulfill a request for ADP data.

(2) *The fee for computer searches* will be set at the current rate for computer service. Information on those charges can be obtained from the Office of Data Analysis and Information Systems (MC-PSDRIS).

(3) *Printing shall be charged* at the rate of $.10 per page of computer generated output with a minimum charge of $.25. A charge of $30 per reel of magnetic tape will be made if the tape is to be permanently retained by the requestor.

§360.3 Filing fees.

(a) Manner of payment.

(1) *Except for the insurance fees* described in the next sentence, all filing fees will be payable at the time and place the application, petition, or other document is tendered for filing. The service fee for insurance, surety or self-insurer accepted certificate of insurance, surety bond or other instrument submitted in lieu of a broker surety bond must be charged to an insurance service account established by the Federal Motor Carrier Safety Administration in accordance with paragraph (a)(2) of this section.

(2) *Billing account procedure.* A written request must be submitted to the Office of Enforcement and Compliance, Insurance Compliance Division (MC-PSDECI) to establish an insurance service fee account.

(i) *Each account will have a specific billing date* within each month and a billing cycle. The billing date is the date that the bill is prepared and printed. The billing cycle is the period between the billing date in one month and the billing date in the next month. A bill for each account which has activity or an unpaid balance during the billing cycle will be sent on the billing date each month. Payment will be due 20 days from the billing date. Payments received before the next billing date are applied to the account. Interest will accrue in accordance with 4 CFR 102.13.

(ii) *The Debt Collection Act of 1982,* including disclosure to the consumer reporting agencies and the use of collection agencies, as set forth in 4 CFR 102.5 and 102.6 will be utilized to encourage payment where appropriate.

(iii) *An account holder* who files a petition in bankruptcy or who is the subject of a bankruptcy proceeding must provide the following information to the Office of Enforcement and Compliance, Insurance Division (MC-PSDECI):

[A] *The filing date of the bankruptcy petition;*

[B] *The court in which the bankruptcy petition was filed;*

[C] *The type of bankruptcy proceeding;*

[D] *The name, address, and telephone number* of its representative in the bankruptcy proceeding; and

[E] *The name, address, and telephone number* of the bankruptcy trustee, if one has been appointed.

(3) *Fees will be payable* to the Federal Motor Carrier Safety Administration by a check payable in United States currency drawn upon funds deposited in a United States or foreign bank or other financial institution, money order payable in United States' currency, or credit card (VISA or MASTERCARD).

(b) Any filing that is not accompanied by the appropriate filing fee is deficient except for filings that satisfy the deferred payment procedures in paragraph (a) of this section.

(c) Fees not refundable. Fees will be assessed for every filing in the type of proceeding listed in the schedule of fees contained in paragraph (f) of this section, subject to the exceptions contained in paragraphs (d) and (e) of this section. After the application, petition, or other document has been accepted for filing by the Federal Motor Carrier Safety Administration, the filing fee will not be refunded, regardless of whether the application, petition, or other document is granted or approved, denied, rejected before docketing, dismissed, or withdrawn.

(d) Related or consolidated proceedings.

(1) *Separate fees need not be paid* for related applications filed by the same applicant which would be the subject of one proceeding. (This does not mean requests for multiple types of operating authority filed on forms in the OP-1 series under the regulations at 49 CFR Part 365. A separate filing fee is required for each type of authority sought in each transportation mode, e.g., common, contract, and broker authority for motor property carriers.)

(2) *Separate fees will be assessed* for the filing of temporary operating authority applications as provided in paragraph (f)(6) of this section, regardless of whether such applications are related to an application for corresponding permanent operating authority.

(3) *The Federal Motor Carrier Safety Administration* may reject concurrently filed applications, petitions, or other documents asserted to be related and refund the filing fee if, in its judgment, they embrace two or more severable matters which should be the subject of separate proceedings.

(e) Waiver or reduction of filing fees. It is the general policy of the Federal Motor Carrier Safety Administration not to waive or reduce filing fees except as described as follows:

(1) *Filing fees are waived* for an application or other proceeding which is filed by a Federal government agency, or a State or local government entity. For purposes of this section the phrases "Federal government agency" or "government entity" do not include a quasi-governmental corporation or government subsidized transportation company.

(2) *In extraordinary situations* the Federal Motor Carrier Safety Administration will accept requests for waivers or fee reductions in accordance with the following procedure:

(i) *When to request.* At the time that a filing is submitted to the Federal Motor Carrier Safety Administration the applicant may request a waiver or reduction of the fee prescribed in this part. Such request should be addressed to the Director, Office of Data Analysis and Information Systems.

(ii) *Basis.* The applicant must show the waiver or reduction of the fee is in the best interest of the public, or that payment of the fee would impose an undue hardship upon the requestor.

(iii) *Federal Motor Carrier Safety Administration action.* The Director, Office of Data Analysis and Information Systems, will notify the applicant of the decision to grant or deny the request for waiver or reduction.

(f) Schedule of filing fees.

Type of Proceeding		Fee
Part I: Licensing:		
(1)	An application for motor carrier operating authority, a certificate of registration for certain foreign carriers, property broker authority, or freight forwarder authority.	$300
(2)	A petition to interpret or clarify an operating authority.	3,000
(3)	A request seeking the modification of operating authority only to the extent of making a ministerial correction, when the original error was caused by applicant, a change in the name of the shipper or owner of a plant site, or the change of a highway name or number.	50

§360.5 Part 360 - Fees for Motor Carrier Registration and Insurance

(continued)

Type of Proceeding		Fee
(4)	A petition to renew authority to transport explosives.	250
(5)	An application for authority to deviate from authorized regular-route authority.	150
(6)	An application for motor carrier temporary authority issued in an emergency situation.	100
(7)	Request for name change of a motor carrier, property broker, or freight forwarder.	14
(8)	An application involving the merger, transfer, or lease of the operating rights of motor passenger and property carriers, property brokers, and household goods freight forwarders under 49 U.S.C. 10321 and 10926.	300
(9)-(49)	[Reserved]	
Part II: Insurance:		
(50)	(i) An application for original qualification as self-insurer for bodily injury and property damage insurance (BI&PD).	4,200
	(ii) An application for original qualification as self-insurer for cargo insurance.	420
(51)	A service fee for insurer, surety, or self-insurer accepted certificate of insurance, surety bond, and other instrument submitted in lieu of a broker surety bond.	$10 per accepted certificate, surety bond or other instrument submitted in lieu of a broker surety bond.
(52)	A petition for reinstatement of revoked operating authority.	80
(53)-(79)	[Reserved]	
Part III: Services:		
(80)	Request for service or pleading list for proceedings.	13 per list
(81)	Faxed copies of operating authority to applicants or their representatives who did not receive a served copy.	5

(g) Returned check policy.
(1) *If a check submitted to the FMCSA* for a filing or service fee is dishonored by a bank or financial institution on which it is drawn, the FMCSA will notify the person who submitted the check that:
  (i) *All work will be suspended* on the filing or proceeding, until the check is made good;
  (ii) *A returned check charge of $6.00* and any bank charges incurred by the FMCSA as a result of the dishonored check must be submitted with the filing fee which is outstanding; and
  (iii) *If payment is not made* within the time specified by the FMCSA, the proceeding will be dismissed or the filing may be rejected.
(2) *If a person repeatedly submits dishonored checks* to the FMCSA for filing fees, the FMCSA may notify the person that all future filing fees must be submitted in the form of a certified or cashier's check, money order, or credit card.

§360.5 Updating user fees.

(a) **Update.** Each fee established in this part may be updated in accordance with this section as deemed necessary by the FMCSA.
(b) **Publication and effective dates.** Updated fees shall be published in the Federal Register and shall become effective 30 days after publication.
(c) **Payment of fees.** Any person submitting a filing for which a fee is established shall pay the fee in effect at the time of the filing.
(d) **Method of updating fees.** Each fee shall be updated by updating the cost components comprising the fee. Cost components shall be updated as follows:
  (1) *Direct labor costs* shall be updated by multiplying base level direct labor costs by percentage changes in average wages and salaries of FMCSA employees. Base level direct labor costs are direct labor costs determined by the cost study in Regulations Governing Fees For Service, 1 I.C.C. 2d 60 (1984), or subsequent cost studies. The base period for measuring changes shall be April 1984 or the year of the last cost study.
  (2) *Operations overhead shall be developed each year* on the basis of current relationships existing on a weighted basis, for indirect labor applicable to the first supervisory work centers directly associated with user fee activity. Actual updating of operations overhead will be accomplished by applying the current percentage factor to updated direct labor, including current governmental overhead costs.
  (3) (i) *Office general and administrative costs* shall be developed each year on the basis of current levels costs, i.e., dividing actual office general and administrative costs for the current fiscal year by total office costs for the office directly associated with user fee activity. Actual updating of office general and administrative costs will be accomplished by applying the current percentage factor to updated direct labor, including current governmental overhead and current operations overhead costs.
    (ii) *FMCSA general and administrative costs* shall be developed each year on the basis of current level costs; i.e., dividing actual FMCSA general and administrative costs for the current fiscal year by total agency expenses for the current fiscal year. Actual updating of FMCSA general and administrative costs will be accomplished by applying the current percentage factor to updated direct labor, including current governmental overhead, operations overhead and office general and administrative costs.
  (4) *Publication costs* shall be adjusted on the basis of known changes in the costs applicable to publication of material in the Federal Register or FMCSA Register. (This rounding procedure excludes copying, printing and search fees.)
(e) **Rounding of updated fees.** Updated fees shall be rounded in the following manner:
  (1) *Fees between $1 and $30* will be rounded to the nearest $1;
  (2) *Fees between $30 and $100* will be rounded to the nearest $10;
  (3) *Fees between $100 and $999* will be rounded to the nearest $50; and
  (4) *Fees above $1,000* will be rounded to the nearest $100.

Part 365 - Rules Governing Applications for Operating Authority

Subpart A - How to Apply for Operating Authority

§365.101 Applications governed by these rules.
These rules govern the handling of applications for operating authority of the following type:
- **(a) Applications for certificates and permits** to operate as a motor common or contract carrier of property or passengers.
- **(b) Applications for permits to operate as a freight forwarder.**
- **(c)** [Reserved]
- **(d) Applications for licenses to operate as a broker** of motor vehicle transportation.
- **(e) Applications for certificates under 49 U.S.C. 13902(b)(3)** to operate as a motor common carrier of passengers in intrastate commerce on a route over which applicant holds interstate authority as of November 19, 1982.
- **(f) Applications for certificates under 49 U.S.C. 13902(b)(3)** to operate as a motor common carrier of passengers in intrastate commerce on a route over which applicant has been granted or will be granted interstate authority after November 19, 1982.
- **(g) Applications for temporary motor carrier authority.**
- **(h) Applications for Mexico-domiciled motor carriers** to operate in foreign commerce as common, contract or private motor carriers of property (including exempt items) between Mexico and all points in the United States. Under NAFTA Annex I, page I-U-20, a Mexico-domiciled motor carrier may not provide point-to-point transportation services, including express delivery services, within the United States for goods other than international cargo.

§365.103 Modified procedure.
The FMCSA will handle licensing application proceedings using the modified procedure, if possible. The applicant and protestants send statements made under oath (verified statements) to each other and to the FMCSA. There are no personal appearances or formal hearings.

§365.105 Starting the application process: Form OP-1.
- **(a) All applicants must file the appropriate form** in the OP-1 series, effective January 1, 1995. Form OP-1 for motor property carriers and brokers of general freight and household goods; Form OP-1(P) for motor passenger carriers; Form OP-1(FF) for freight forwarders; and Form OP-1(MX) for Mexico-domiciled motor property carriers, including household goods and motor passenger carriers. A separate filing fee in the amount set forth at 49 CFR 360.3(f)(1) is required for each type of authority sought in each transportation mode.
- **(b) Obtain forms at a FMCSA Division Office in each State** or at one of the FMCSA Service Centers. Addresses and phone numbers for the Division Offices and Service Centers can be found at: http://www.fmcsa.dot.gov/aboutus/fieldoffices. The forms and information about filing procedures can be downloaded at: http://www.fmcsa.dot.gov/factsfigs/formspubs; and from the do-it-yourself website at: http://www.diy.dot.gov.

§365.107 Types of applications.
- **(a) Fitness applications.** Motor property applications and certain types of motor passenger applications require only the finding that the applicant is fit, willing and able to perform the involved operations and to comply with all applicable statutory and regulatory provisions. These applications can be opposed only on the grounds that applicant is not fit [e.g., is not in compliance with applicable financial responsibility and safety fitness requirements]. These applications are:
  - (1) *Motor common and contract carrier of property* (except household goods), Mexican motor property carriers that perform private carriage and transport exempt items, and motor contract carrier of passengers transportation.
  - (2) *Motor carrier brokerage of general commodities* (except household goods).
  - (3) *Certain types of motor passenger applications* as described in Form OP-1 (P).
- **(b) Motor passenger "public interest" applications** as described in Form OP-1 (P).
- **(c) Intrastate motor passenger applications** under 49 U.S.C. 13902 (b)(3) as described in Form OP-1, Schedule B.
- **(d) Motor common carrier** of household goods applications, including Mexican carrier applicants. These applications require a finding that:
  - (1) *The applicant is fit, willing, and able* to provide the involved transportation and to comply with all applicable statutory and regulatory provisions; and
  - (2) *The service proposed* will serve a useful public purpose, responsive to a public demand or need.
- **(e) Motor contract carrier** of household goods, household goods property broker, and freight forwarder applications. These applications require a finding that:
  - (1) *The applicant is fit, willing, and able* to provide the involved transportation and to comply with all applicable statutory and regulatory provisions; and
  - (2) *The transportation to be provided* will be consistent with the public interest and the national transportation policy of 49 U.S.C. 13101.
- **(f) Temporary authority (TA) for motor and water carriers.** These applications require a finding that there is or soon will be an immediate transportation need that cannot be met by existing carrier service.
- **(g) In view of the expedited time frames** established in this part for processing requests for permanent authority, applications for TA will be entertained only in exceptional circumstances (i.e., natural disasters or national emergencies) when evidence of immediate service need can be specifically documented in a narrative supplement appended to Form OP-1 for motor property carriers, Form OP-1MX for Mexican property carriers and, Form OP-1(P) for motor passenger carriers.

§365.109 FMCSA review of the application.
- **(a) FMCSA staff will review the application** for correctness, completeness, and adequacy of the evidence (the prima facie case).
  - (1) *Minor errors will be corrected without notification to the applicant.*
  - (2) *Materially incomplete applications* will be rejected. Applications that are in substantial compliance with these rules may be accepted.
  - (3) *All motor carrier applications* will be reviewed for consistency with the FMCSA's operational safety fitness policy. Applicants with "Unsatisfactory" safety fitness ratings from DOT will have their applications rejected.
  - (4) *FMCSA staff will review completed applications* that conform with the FMCSA's safety fitness policy and that are accompanied by evidence of adequate financial responsibility.
  - (5) *Financial responsibility is indicated* by filing within 20 days from the date an application notice is published in the FMCSA Register:
    - (i) *Form BMC-91 or 91X or BMC 82 surety bond* — Bodily injury and property damage (motor property and passenger carriers; household goods freight forwarders that provide pickup or delivery service directly or by using a local delivery service under their control).
    - (ii) *Form BMC-84* — Surety bond or Form BMC-85 — trust fund agreement (property brokers of general commodities and household goods).
    - (iii) *Form BMC-34 or BMC 83 surety bond* — Cargo liability (motor property common carriers and household goods freight forwarders).
  - (6) *Applicants also must submit Form BOC-3* — designation of legal process agents — within 20 days from the date an application notice is published in the FMCSA Register.
  - (7) *Applicants seeking to conduct operations* for which tariffs are required may not commence such operations until tariffs are in effect.
  - (8) *All applications must be completed in English.*
- **(b) A summary of the application will be published** as a preliminary grant of authority in the FMCSA Register to give notice to the public in case anyone wishes to oppose the application.

§365.111 Appeals to rejections of the application.
- **(a) An applicant has the right** to appeal rejection of the application. The appeal must be filed at the FMCSA within 10 days of the date of the letter of rejection.
- **(b) If the appeal is successful** and the filing is found to be proper, the application shall be deemed to have been properly filed as of the decision date of the appeal.

§365.113 Changing the request for authority or filing supplementary evidence after the application is filed.

(a) Once the application is filed, the applicant may supplement evidence only with approval of the FMCSA.

(b) Amendments to the application generally are not permitted, but in appropriate instances may be entertained at the discretion of the FMCSA.

§365.115 After publication in the FMCSA Register.

(a) Interested persons have 10 days from the date of FMCSA Register publication to file protests. See Subpart B of this part.

(b) If no one opposes the application, the grant published in the FMCSA Register will become effective by issuance of a certificate, permit, or license.

§365.117 Obtaining a copy of the application.

After publication, interested persons may request a copy of the application by contacting the FMCSA-designated contract agent (as identified in the FMCSA Register).

§365.119 Opposed applications.

If the application is opposed, opposing parties are required to send a copy of their protest to the applicant.

§365.121 Filing a reply statement.

(a) If the application is opposed, applicant may file a reply statement. This statement is due within 20 days after FMCSA Register publication.

(b) The reply statement may not contain new evidence. It shall only rebut or further explain matters previously raised.

(c) The reply statement need not be notarized or verified. Applicant understands that the oath in the application form applies to all evidence submitted in the application. Separate legal arguments by counsel need not be notarized or verified.

§365.123 Applicant withdrawal.

If the applicant wishes to withdraw an application, it shall request dismissal in writing.

Subpart B - How to Oppose Requests for Authority

§365.201 Definitions.

A person wishing to oppose a request for permanent authority files a **protest**. A person filing a valid protest becomes a **protestant**.

§365.203 Time for filing.

A protest shall be filed (received at the FMCSA) within 10 days after notice of the application appears in the FMCSA Register. A copy of the protest shall be sent to applicant's representative at the same time. Failure timely to file a protest waives further participation in the proceeding.

§365.205 Contents of the protest.

(a) All information upon which the protestant plans to rely is put into the protest.

(b) A protest must be verified, as follows:

I, _____, verify under penalty of perjury under laws of the United States of America, that the information above is true and correct. Further, I certify that I am qualified and authorized to file this protest. (See 18 U.S.C. 1001 and 18 U.S.C. 1621 for penalties.)

_____
(Signature and Date)

(c) A protest not in substantial compliance with applicable statutory standards or these rules may be rejected.

(d) Protests must respond directly to the statutory standards for FMCSA review of the application. As these standards vary for particular types of applications, potential protestants should refer to the general criteria addressed at §365.107 and may consult the FMCSA at (202) 366-9805 for further assistance in developing their evidence.

§365.207 Withdrawal.

A protestant wishing to withdraw from a proceeding shall inform the FMCSA and applicant in writing.

Subpart C - General Rules Governing the Application Process

§365.301 Applicable rules.

Generally, all application proceedings are governed by the FMCSA's Rules of Practice at Part 386 of this chapter except as designated below.

§365.303 Contacting another party.

When a person wishes to contact a party or serve a pleading or letter on that party, it shall do so through its representative. The phone and FAX numbers and address of applicant's representative shall be listed in the FMCSA Register.

§365.305 Serving copies of pleadings.

(a) An applicant must serve all pleadings and letters on the FMCSA and all known participants in the proceeding, except that a reply to a motion need only be served on the moving party.

(b) A protestant need serve only the FMCSA and applicant with pleadings or letters.

§365.307 Replies to motions.

Replies to motions filed under this part are due within 5 days of the date the motion is filed at the FMCSA.

§365.309 FAX filings.

FAX filings of applications and supporting evidence are not permitted. To assist parties in meeting the expedited time frames established for protesting an application, however, the FMCSA will accept FAX filings of protests and any reply or rebuttal evidence. FAX filings of these pleadings must be followed by the original document, plus one copy for FMCSA recordkeeping purposes.

Subpart D - Transfer of Operating Rights Under 49 U.S.C. 10926

§365.401 Scope of rules.

These rules define the procedures that enable motor passenger and property carriers, property brokers, and household goods freight forwarders to obtain approval from the FMCSA to merge, transfer, or lease their operating rights in financial transactions not subject to 49 U.S.C. 11343. Transactions covered by these rules are governed by 49 U.S.C. 10321 and 10926. The filing fee is set forth at 49 CFR 360.3(f)(8).

§365.403 Definitions.

For the purposes of this part, the following definitions apply:

(a) **Transfer.** Transfers include all transactions (i.e., the sale or lease of interstate operating rights,[1] or the merger of two or more carriers or a carrier into a noncarrier) subject to 49 U.S.C. 10926, as well as the sale of property brokers' licenses under 49 U.S.C. 10321.

(b) **Operating rights.** Operating rights include:
   (1) Certificates and permits issued to motor carriers;
   (2) Permits issued to freight forwarders;
   (3) Licenses issued to property brokers; and
   (4) Certificates of Registration issued to motor carriers. The term also includes authority held by virtue of the gateway elimination regulations published in the Federal Register as letter-notices.

(c) **Certificate of registration.** The evidence of a motor carrier's right to engage in interstate or foreign commerce within a single State is established by a corresponding State certificate.

(d) **Person.** An individual, partnership, corporation, company, association, or other form of business, or a trustee, receiver, assignee, or personal representative of any of these.

(e) **Record holder.** The person shown on the records of the FMCSA as the legal owner of the operating rights.

(f) **Control.** A relationship between persons that includes actual control, legal control, and the power to exercise control, through or by common directors, officers, stockholders, a voting trust, a holding or investment company, or any other means.

(g) **Category 1 transfers.** Transactions in which the person to whom the operating rights would be transferred is not an FMCSA carrier and is not affiliated with any FMCSA carrier.

---

1. The execution of a chattel mortgage, deed of trust, or other similar document does not constitute a transfer or require the FMCSA's approval. However, a foreclosure for the purpose of transferring an operating right to satisfy a judgment or claim against the record holder may not be effected without approval of the FMCSA.

Subpart E - Special Rules for Certain Mexico-domiciled Carriers §365.503 (a)

(h) Category 2 transfers. Transactions in which the person to whom the operating rights would be transferred is an FMCSA carrier and/or is affiliated with an FMCSA carrier.

§365.405 Applications.

(a) Procedural requirements.

(1) *At least 10 days before consummation,* an original and two copies of a properly completed Form OP-FC-1 and any attachments (see paragraph (b)(1)(viii) of this section) must be filed with the FMCSA, Licensing Team (MC-PSDRIS), 400 Seventh Street, SW., Room 8214, Washington, DC 20590.

(2) *At any time* after the expiration of the 10-day waiting period, applicants may consummate the transaction, subject to the subsequent approval of the application by the FMCSA, as described below. The transferee may commence operations under the rights acquired from the transferor upon its compliance with the FMCSA's regulations governing insurance, and process agents. See 49 CFR Parts 387, Subpart C, and 366, respectively. In the alternative, applicants may wait until the FMCSA has issued a decision on their application before transferring the operating rights. If the transferee wants the transferor's operating authority to be reissued in its name, it should furnish the FMCSA with a statement executed by both transferor and transferee indicating that the transaction has been consummated. Authority will not be reissued until after the FMCSA has approved the transaction.

(b) Information required.

(1) *In category 1 and category 2 transfers,* applicants must furnish the following information:

(i) *Full name, address, and signatures* of the transferee and transferor.

(ii) *A copy of the transferor's operating authority* involved in the transfer proceeding.

(iii) *A short summary of the essential terms of the transaction.*

(iv) *If relevant,* the status of proceedings for the transfer of State certificate(s) corresponding to the Certificates of Registration being transferred.

(v) *A statement as to whether the transfer* will or will not significantly affect the quality of the human environment.

(vi) *Certification by transferor and transferee* of their current respective safety ratings by the United States Department of Transportation (i.e., satisfactory, conditional, unsatisfactory, or unrated).

(vii) *Certification by the transferee* that it has sufficient insurance coverage under 49 U.S.C. 13906 for the service it intends to provide.

(viii) *Information to demonstrate* that the proposed transaction is consistent with the national transportation policy and satisfies the criteria for approval set forth at §365.409 of this part. (Such information may be appended to the application form and, if provided, would be embraced by the oath and verification contained on that form.)

(ix) *If motor carrier operating rights* are being transferred, certification by the transferee that it is not domiciled in Mexico nor owned or controlled by persons of that country.

(2) *Category 2 applicants* must also submit the following additional information:

(i) *Name(s) of the carrier(s),* if any, with which the transferee is affiliated.

(ii) *Aggregate revenues* of the transferor, transferee, and their carrier affiliates from interstate transportation sources for a 1-year period ending not earlier than 6 months before the date of the agreement of the parties concerning the transaction. If revenues exceed $2 million, the transfer may be subject to 49 U.S.C. 14303 rather than these rules.

§365.407 Notice.

The FMCSA will give notice of approved transfer applications through publication in the FMCSA Register.

§365.409 FMCSA action and criteria for approval.

A transfer will be approved under this section if:

(a) The transaction is not subject to 49 U.S.C. 14303; and

(b) The transaction is consistent with the public interest; however,

(c) If the transferor or transferee has an "Unsatisfactory" safety fitness rating from DOT, the transfer may be denied. If an application is denied, the FMCSA will set forth the basis for its action in a decision or letter notice. If parties with "Unsatisfactory" safety fitness ratings consummate a transaction pursuant to the 10-day rule at §365.405 of this part prior to the notification of FMCSA action, they do so at their own risk and subject to any conditions we may impose subsequently. Transactions that have been consummated but later are denied by the FMCSA are null and void and must be rescinded. Similarly, if applications contain false or misleading information, they are void *ab initio*.

§365.411 Responsive pleadings.

(a) Protests must be filed within 20 days after the date of publication of an approved transfer application in the FMCSA Register. Protests received prior to the notice will be rejected. Applicants may respond within 20 days after the due date of protests. Petitions for reconsideration of decisions denying applications must be filed within 20 days after the date of service of such decisions.

(b) Protests and petitions for reconsideration must be filed with the FMCSA Licensing Team (MC-PSDRIS), 400 Seventh Street, SW., Room 8214, Washington, DC 20590, and be served on appropriate parties.

§365.413 Procedures for changing the name or business form of a motor carrier, freight forwarder, or property broker.

(a) Scope. These procedures apply in the following circumstances:

(1) *A change in the form of a business,* such as the incorporation of a partnership or sole proprietorship;

(2) *A change in the legal name* of a corporation or partnership or change in the trade name or assumed name of any entity;

(3) *A transfer of operating rights* from a deceased or incapacitated spouse to the other spouse;

(4) *A reincorporation and merger* for the purpose of effecting a name change;

(5) *An amalgamation or consolidation* of a carrier and a noncarrier into a new carrier having a different name from either of the predecessor entities; and

(6) *A change in the State of incorporation* accomplished by dissolving the corporation in one State and reincorporating in another State.

(b) Procedures. To accomplish these changes, a letter must be sent to the FMCSA, Licensing Team (MC-PSDRIS), Washington, DC 20590. The envelope should be marked "NAME CHANGE". The applicant must provide:

(1) *The docket number(s)* and name of the carrier requesting the change;

(2) *A copy of the articles of incorporation* and the State certificate reflecting the incorporation;

(3) *The name(s) of the owner(s)* of the stock and the distribution of the shares;

(4) *The names of the officers and directors of the corporation; and*

(5) *A statement that there is no change* in the ownership, management, or control of the business. When this procedure is being used to transfer operating rights from a deceased or incapacitated spouse to the other spouse, documentation that the other spouse has the legal right to effect such change must be included with the request. The fee for filing a name change request is in §360.3(f) of this chapter.

Subpart E - Special Rules for Certain Mexico-domiciled Carriers

§365.501 Scope of rules.

(a) The rules in this subpart govern the application by a Mexico-domiciled motor carrier to provide transportation of property or passengers in interstate commerce between Mexico and points in the United States beyond the municipalities and commercial zones along the United States-Mexico international border.

(b) A Mexico-domiciled carrier may not provide point-to-point transportation services, including express delivery services, within the United States for goods other than international cargo.

§365.503 Application.

(a) Each applicant applying under this subpart must submit an application that consists of:

(1) *Form OP-1 (MX)* — Application to Register Mexican Carriers for Motor Carrier Authority To Operate Beyond U.S. Municipalities and Commercial Zones on the U.S.-Mexico Border;

(2) *Form MCS-150* — Motor Carrier Identification Report; and

(3) *A notification of the means used* to designate process agents, either by submission in the application package of Form BOC-3 — Designation of Agents-Motor Carriers, Brokers and Freight Forwarders or a letter stating that the applicant will use a process agent service that will submit the Form BOC-3 electronically.

(b) **The Federal Motor Carrier Safety Administration (FMCSA) will** only process your application if it meets the following conditions:
   (1) *The application must be completed in English;*
   (2) *The information supplied* must be accurate, complete, and include all required supporting documents and applicable certifications in accordance with the instructions to Form OP-1 (MX), Form MCS-150, and Form BOC-3;
   (3) *The application must include* the filing fee payable to the FMCSA in the amount set forth at 49 CFR 360.3(f)(1); and
   (4) *The application must be signed by the applicant.*

(c) **You must submit the application** to the address provided in Form OP-1(MX).

(d) **You may obtain the application forms** from any FMCSA Division Office or download it from the FMCSA website at: http://www.fmcsa.dot.gov/factsfigs/formspubs.htm.

§365.505 Re-registration and fee waiver for certain applicants.

(a) **If you filed an application using Form OP-1(MX)** before May 3, 2002, you are required to file a new Form OP-1(MX). You do not need to submit a new fee when you file a new application under this subpart.

(b) **If you hold a Certificate of Registration issued** before April 18, 2002, authorizing operations beyond the municipalities along the United States-Mexico border and beyond the commercial zones of such municipalities, you are required to file an OP-1(MX) if you want to continue those operations. You do not need to submit a fee when you file an application under this subpart.
   (1) *You must file the application by November 4, 2003.*
   (2) *The FMCSA may suspend or revoke* the Certificate of Registration of any applicable holder that fails to comply with the procedures set forth in this section.
   (3) *Certificates of Registration issued* before April 18, 2002, will remain valid until the FMCSA acts on the OP-1(MX) application.

§365.507 FMCSA action on the application.

(a) **The FMCSA will review and act** on each application submitted under this subpart in accordance with the procedures set out in this part.

(b) **The FMCSA will validate the accuracy of information** and certifications provided in the application by checking data maintained in databases of the governments of Mexico and the United States.

(c) **Pre-authorization safety audit.** Every Mexico-domiciled carrier that applies under this part must satisfactorily complete an FMCSA-administered safety audit before FMCSA will grant provisional operating authority to operate in the United States. The safety audit is a review by the FMCSA of the carrier's written procedures and records to validate the accuracy of information and certifications provided in the application and determine whether the carrier has established or exercises the basic safety management controls necessary to ensure safe operations. The FMCSA will evaluate the results of the safety audit using the criteria in Appendix A to this subpart.

(d) **If a carrier successfully completes** the pre-authorization safety audit and the FMCSA approves its application submitted under this subpart, FMCSA will publish a summary of the application as a preliminary grant of authority in the FMCSA Register to give notice to the public in case anyone wishes to oppose the application, as required in §365.109(b) of this part.

(e) **If the FMCSA grants provisional operating authority** to the applicant, it will assign a distinctive USDOT Number that identifies the motor carrier as authorized to operate beyond the municipalities in the United States on the U.S.-Mexico international border and beyond the commercial zones of such municipalities. In order to operate in the United States, a Mexico-domiciled motor carrier with provisional operating authority must:
   (1) *Have its surety or insurance provider* file proof of financial responsibility in the form of certificates of insurance, surety bonds, and endorsements, as required by §387.301 of this subchapter;
   (2) *File a hard copy of,* or have its process agent(s) electronically submit, Form BOC-3 — Designation of Agents — Motor Carriers, Brokers and Freight Forwarders, as required by Part 366 of this subchapter; and
   (3) *Comply with all provisions* of the safety monitoring system in Subpart B of Part 385 of this subchapter, including successfully passing CVSA Level I inspections at least every 90 days and having decals affixed to each commercial motor vehicle operated in the United States as required by §385.103(c) of this subchapter.

(f) **The FMCSA may grant permanent operating authority** to a Mexico-domiciled carrier no earlier than 18 months after the date that provisional operating authority is granted and only after successful completion to the satisfaction of the FMCSA of the safety monitoring system for Mexico-domiciled carriers set out in Subpart B of Part 385 of this subchapter. Successful completion includes obtaining a satisfactory safety rating as the result of a compliance review.

§365.509 Requirement to notify FMCSA of change in applicant information.

(a) **A motor carrier subject to this subpart** must notify the FMCSA of any changes or corrections to the information in parts I, IA or II submitted on the Form OP-1(MX) or the Form BOC-3 — Designation of Agents — Motor Carriers, Brokers and Freight Forwarders during the application process or after having been granted provisional operating authority. The carrier must notify the FMCSA in writing within 45 days of the change or correction.

(b) **If a carrier fails to comply** with paragraph (a) of this section, the FMCSA may suspend or revoke its operating authority until it meets those requirements.

§365.511 Requirement for CVSA inspection of vehicles during first three consecutive years of permanent operating authority.

A Mexico-domiciled motor carrier granted permanent operating authority must have its vehicles inspected by Commercial Vehicle Safety Alliance (CVSA)-certified inspectors every three months and display a current inspection decal attesting to the successful completion of such an inspection for at least three consecutive years after receiving permanent operating authority from the FMCSA.

Appendix A to Subpart E — Explanation of Pre-Authorization Safety Audit Evaluation Criteria for Mexico-Domiciled Motor Carriers.

I. General

(a) **Section 350 of the Fiscal Year 2002** DOT Appropriations Act (Pub. L. 107-87) directed the FMCSA to perform a safety audit of each Mexico-domiciled motor carrier before the FMCSA grants the carrier provisional operating authority to operate beyond United States municipalities and commercial zones on the United States-Mexico international border.

(b) **The FMCSA will decide whether it will conduct** the safety audit at the Mexico-domiciled motor carrier's principal place of business in Mexico or at a location specified by the FMCSA in the United States, in accordance with the statutory requirements that 50 percent of all safety audits must be conducted on-site and onsite inspections cover at least 50 percent of estimated truck traffic in any year. All records and documents must be made available for examination within 48 hours after a request is made. Saturdays, Sundays, and Federal holidays are excluded from the computation of the 48-hour period.

(c) **The safety audit will include:**
   (1) *Verification of available performance data* and safety management programs;
   (2) *Verification of a controlled substances* and alcohol testing program consistent with Part 40 of this title;
   (3) *Verification of the carrier's system of compliance* with hours-of-service rules in Part 395 of this subchapter, including recordkeeping and retention;
   (4) *Verification of proof of financial responsibility;*
   (5) *Review of available data* concerning the carrier's safety history, and other information necessary to determine the carrier's preparedness to comply with the Federal Motor Carrier Safety Regulations, Parts 382 through 399 of this subchapter, and the Federal Hazardous Material Regulations, Parts 171 through 180 of this title;
   (6) *Inspection of available commercial motor vehicles* to be used under provisional operating authority, if any of these vehicles have not received a decal required by §385.103(d) of this subchapter;

Subpart E - Special Rules for Certain Mexico-domiciled Carriers   Appendix A to Subpart E

(7) *Evaluation of the carrier's* safety inspection, maintenance, and repair facilities or management systems, including verification of records of periodic vehicle inspections;

(8) *Verification of drivers' qualifications,* including confirmation of the validity of the Licencia de Federal de Conductor of each driver the carrier intends to assign to operate under its provisional operating authority; and

(9) *An interview of carrier officials* to review safety management controls and evaluate any written safety oversight policies and practices.

(d) **To successfully complete the safety audit,** a Mexico-domiciled motor carrier must demonstrate to the FMCSA that it has the required elements in paragraphs (c)(2), (3), (4), (7), and (8) above and other basic safety management controls in place which function adequately to ensure minimum acceptable compliance with the applicable safety requirements. The FMCSA developed a "safety audit evaluation criteria," which uses data from the safety audit and roadside inspections to determine that each applicant for provisional operating authority has basic safety management controls in place.

(e) **The safety audit evaluation process** developed by the FMCSA is used to:

(1) *Evaluate basic safety management controls* and determine if each Mexico-domiciled carrier and each driver is able to operate safely in the United States beyond municipalities and commercial zones on the United States-Mexico international border; and

(2) *Identify motor carriers and drivers* who are having safety problems and need improvement in their compliance with the FMCSRs and the HMRs, before FMCSA grants the carriers provisional operating authority to operate beyond United States municipalities and commercial zones on the United States-Mexico international border.

II. Source of the Data for the Safety Audit Evaluation Criteria

(a) **The FMCSA's evaluation criteria** are built upon the operational tool known as the safety audit. The FMCSA developed this tool to assist auditors and investigators in assessing the adequacy of a Mexico-domiciled carrier's basic safety management controls.

(b) **The safety audit is a review** of a Mexico-domiciled motor carrier's operation and is used to:

(1) *Determine if a carrier* has the basic safety management controls required by 49 U.S.C. 31144;

(2) *Meet the requirements of Section 350* of the DOT Appropriations Act; and

(3) *In the event* that a carrier is found not to be in compliance with applicable FMCSRs and HMRs, the safety audit can be used to educate the carrier on how to comply with U.S. safety rules.

(c) **Documents such as those contained** in driver qualification files, records of duty status, vehicle maintenance records, and other records are reviewed for compliance with the FMCSRs and HMRs. Violations are cited on the safety audit. Performance-based information, when available, is utilized to evaluate the carrier's compliance with the vehicle regulations. Recordable accident information is also collected.

III. Overall Determination of the Carrier's Basic Safety Management Controls

(a) **The carrier will not be granted** provisional operating authority if the FMCSA fails to:

(1) *Verify a controlled substances* and alcohol testing program consistent with Part 40 of this title;

(2) *Verify a system of compliance* with hours-of-service rules of this subchapter, including recordkeeping and retention;

(3) *Verify proof of financial responsibility;*

(4) *Verify records of periodic vehicle inspections;* and

(5) *Verify drivers' qualifications of each driver* the carrier intends to assign to operate under such authority, as required by Parts 383 and 391 of this subchapter, including confirming the validity of each driver's Licencia de Federal de Conductor.

(b) **If the FMCSA confirms each item** under II (a)(1) through (5) above, the carrier will be granted provisional operating authority, except if FMCSA finds the carrier has inadequate basic safety management controls in at least three separate factors described in part III below. If FMCSA makes such a determination, the carrier's application for provisional operating authority will be denied.

IV. Evaluation of Regulatory Compliance

(a) **During the safety audit,** the FMCSA gathers information by reviewing a motor carrier's compliance with "acute" and "critical" regulations of the FMCSRs and HMRs.

(b) **Acute regulations are those** where noncompliance is so severe as to require immediate corrective actions by a motor carrier regardless of the overall basic safety management controls of the motor carrier.

(c) **Critical regulations are those** where noncompliance relates to management and/or operational controls. These are indicative of breakdowns in a carrier's management controls.

(d) **The list of the acute and critical regulations,** which are used in determining if a carrier has basic safety management controls in place, is included in Appendix B, VII. List of Acute and Critical Regulations to Part 385 of this subchapter.

(e) **Noncompliance with acute and critical regulations** are indicators of inadequate safety management controls and usually higher than average accident rates.

(f) **Parts of the FMCSRs and the HMRs** having similar characteristics are combined together into six regulatory areas called "factors." The regulatory factors, evaluated on the adequacy of the carrier's safety management controls, are:

(1) *Factor 1 — General: Parts 387 and 390;*

(2) *Factor 2 — Driver: Parts 382, 383 and 391;*

(3) *Factor 3 — Operational: Parts 392 and 395;*

(4) *Factor 4 — Vehicle: Parts 393, 396* and inspection data for the last 12 months;

(5) *Factor 5 — Hazardous Materials: Parts 171, 177, 180 and 397;* and

(6) *Factor 6 — Accident: Recordable Accident Rate per Million Miles.*

(g) **For each instance of noncompliance** with an acute regulation, 1.5 points will be assessed.

(h) **For each instance of noncompliance** with a critical regulation, 1 point will be assessed.

(i) **Vehicle Factor.**

(1) *When at least three vehicle inspections* are recorded in the Motor Carrier Management Information System (MCMIS) during the twelve months before the safety audit or performed at the time of the review, the Vehicle Factor (Part 396) will be evaluated on the basis of the Out-of-Service (OOS) rates and noncompliance with acute and critical regulations. The results of the review of the OOS rate will affect the Vehicle Factor as follows:

(i) *If the motor carrier* has had at least three roadside inspections in the twelve months before the safety audit, and the vehicle OOS rate is 34 percent or higher, one point will be assessed against the carrier. That point will be added to any other points assessed for discovered noncompliance with acute and critical regulations of Part 396 to determine the carrier's level of safety management control for that factor.

(ii) *If the motor carrier's vehicle OOS rate* is less than 34 percent, or if there are less than three inspections, the determination of the carrier's level of safety management controls will only be based on discovered noncompliance with the acute and critical regulations of Part 396.

(2) *Over two million inspections* occur on the roadside each year in the United States. This vehicle inspection information is retained in the MCMIS and is integral to evaluating motor carriers' ability to successfully maintain their vehicles, thus preventing them from being placed OOS during roadside inspections. Each safety audit will continue to have the requirements of Part 396, Inspection, Repair, and Maintenance, reviewed as indicated by the above explanation.

(j) **Accident Factor.**

(1) *In addition to the five regulatory factors,* a sixth factor is included in the process to address the accident history of the motor carrier. This factor is the recordable accident rate, which the carrier has experienced during the past 12 months. Recordable accident, as defined in 49 CFR 390.5, means an accident involving a commercial motor vehicle operating on a public road in interstate or intrastate commerce which results in a fatality; a bodily injury to a person who, as a result of the injury, immediately receives medical treatment away from the scene of the accident; or one or more motor vehicles incurring disabling damage as a result of the accident requiring the motor vehicle to be transported away from the scene by a tow truck or other motor vehicle.

(2) *Experience has shown that urban carriers,* those motor carriers operating entirely within a radius of less than 100 air miles (normally urban areas), have a higher exposure to accident situations because of their environment and normally have higher accident rates.

Appendix A to Subpart E — Part 365 - Rules Governing Applications for Operating Authority

(3) *The recordable accident rate* will be used in determining the carrier's basic safety management controls in Factor 6, Accident. It will be used only when a carrier incurs two or more recordable accidents within the 12 months before the safety audit. An urban carrier (a carrier operating entirely within a radius of 100 air miles) with a recordable rate per million miles greater than 1.7 will be deemed to have inadequate basic safety management controls for the accident factor. All other carriers with a recordable accident rate per million miles greater than 1.5 will be deemed to have inadequate basic safety management controls for the accident factor. The rates are the result of roughly doubling the United States national average accident rate in Fiscal Years 1994, 1995, and 1996.

(4) *The FMCSA will continue to consider preventability* when a new entrant contests the evaluation of the accident factor by presenting compelling evidence that the recordable rate is not a fair means of evaluating its accident factor. Preventability will be determined according to the following standard: "If a driver, who exercises normal judgment and foresight, could have foreseen the possibility of the accident that in fact occurred, and avoided it by taking steps within his/her control which would not have risked causing another kind of mishap, the accident was preventable."

(k) **Factor Ratings.**

(1) *The following table* shows the five regulatory factors, parts of the FMCSRs and HMRs associated with each factor, and the accident factor. Each carrier's level of basic safety management controls with each factor is determined as follows:

(i) *Factor 1 — General: Parts 390 and 387;*

(ii) *Factor 2 — Driver: Parts 382, 383, and 391;*

(iii) *Factor 3 — Operational: Parts 392 and 395;*

(iv) *Factor 4 — Vehicle: Parts 393, 396* and the Out of Service Rate;

(v) *Factor 5 — Hazardous Materials: Parts 171, 177, 180* and 397; and

(vi) *Factor 6 — Accident: Recordable Accident Rate* per Million Miles;

(2) *For paragraphs III (k)(1)(i) through (v) (Factors 1 through 5),* if the combined violations of acute and or critical regulations for each factor is equal to three or more points, the carrier is determined not to have basic safety management controls for that individual factor.

(3) *For paragraphs III (k)(1)(vi),* if the recordable accident rate is greater than 1.7 recordable accidents per million miles for an urban carrier (1.5 for all other carriers), the carrier is determined to have inadequate basic safety management controls.

(l) **Notwithstanding FMCSA verification of the items** listed in part II (a)(1) through (5) above, if the safety audit determines the carrier has inadequate basic safety management controls in at least three separate factors described in part III, the carrier's application for provisional operating authority will be denied. For example, FMCSA evaluates a carrier finding:

(1) *One instance of noncompliance with a critical regulation* in Part 387 scoring one point for Factor 1;

(2) *Two instances of noncompliance with acute regulations* in Part 382 scoring three points for Factor 2;

(3) *Three instances of noncompliance with critical regulations* in Part 396 scoring three points for Factor 4; and

(4) *Three instances of noncompliance with acute regulations* in Parts 171 and 397 scoring four and one-half (4.5) points for Factor 5.

Under this example, the carrier will not receive provisional operating authority because it scored three or more points for Factors 2, 4, and 5 and FMCSA determined the carrier had inadequate basic safety management controls in at least three separate factors.

Part 366 - Designation of Process Agent

§366.1 Applicability.
These rules, relating to the filing of designations of persons upon whom court process may be served, govern motor carriers and brokers and, as of the moment of succession, their fiduciaries (as defined at 49 CFR 387.319(a)).

§366.2 Form of designation.
Designations shall be made on Form BOC-3, Designation of Agent for Service of Process. Only one completed current form may be on file. It must include all States for which agent designations are required. One copy must be retained by the carrier or broker at its principal place of business.

§366.3 Eligible persons.
All persons (as defined at 49 U.S.C. 13102(16)) designated must reside or maintain an office in the State for which they are designated. If a State official is designated, evidence of his willingness to accept service of process must be furnished.

§366.4 Required States.
(a) **Motor carriers.** Every motor carrier (of property or passengers) shall make a designation for each State in which it is authorized to operate and for each State traversed during such operations. Every motor carrier (including private carriers) operating in the United States in the course of transportation between points in a foreign country shall file a designation for each State traversed.

(b) **Brokers.** Every broker shall make a designation for each State in which its offices are located or in which contracts will be written.

§366.5 Blanket designations.
Where an association or corporation has filed with the FMCSA a list of process agents for each State, motor carriers may make the required designations by using the following statement:

Those persons named in the list of process agents on file with the Federal Motor Carrier Safety Administration by _____ (Name of association or corporation) and any subsequently filed revisions thereof, for the States in which this carrier is or may be authorized to operate, including States traversed during such operations, except those States for which individual designations are named.

§366.6 Cancellation or change.
A designation may be canceled or changed only by a new designation except that, where a carrier or broker ceases to be subject to §366.4 in whole or in part for 1 year, designation is no longer required and may be canceled without making another designation.

Part 366 - Designation of Process Agent

Notes

Part 367 - Standards for Registration with States

§367.1 Definitions.
(a) **The Secretary.** The Secretary of Transportation.
(b) **Motor carrier and carrier.** A person authorized to engage in the transportation of passengers or property, as a common or contract carrier, in interstate or foreign commerce, under the provisions of 49 U.S.C. 13902.
(c) **Motor vehicle.** A self-propelled or motor driven vehicle operated by a motor carrier in interstate or foreign commerce under authority issued by the Secretary.
(d) **Principal place of business.** A single location that serves as a motor carrier's headquarters and where it maintains or can make available its operational records.
(e) **State.** A State of the United States or the District of Columbia.

§367.2 Participation by States.
(a) A State is eligible to participate as a registration State and to receive fee revenue only if, as of January 1, 1991, it charged or collected a fee for a vehicle identification stamp or a number pursuant to the provisions of the predecessor to this part.
(b) An eligible State that intends either to commence or to cease participating in the registration program must publish notice of its intention by the 1st day of July of the year preceding the registration year in which it will commence or cease participating.

§367.3 Selection of registration State.
(a) Each motor carrier required to register and pay filing fees must select a single participating State as its registration State. The carrier must select the State in which it maintains its principal place of business, if such State is a participating State. A carrier that maintains its principal place of business outside of a participating State must select the State in which it will operate the largest number of motor vehicles during the next registration year. In the event a carrier will operate the same largest number of vehicles in more than one State, it must select one of those States.
(b) A carrier may not change its registration State unless it changes its principal place of business or its registration State ceases participating in the program, in which case the carrier must select a registration State for the next registration year under the standards of paragraph (a) of this section.
(c) A carrier must give notice of its selection to the State commission of its selected registration State, and, the State commission of its prior registration State, within 30 days after it has made its selection. If a carrier changes its principal place of business during the annual registration period specified in §367.4(b)(2), the carrier may continue to use its prior registration State, if any, for the next registration year.
(d) A carrier must give notice of its selection to its insurer or insurers as soon as practicable after it has made its selection.

§367.4 Requirements for registration.
(a) Except as provided in paragraph (c)(1) of this section with regard to a carrier operating under temporary authority, only a motor carrier holding a certificate or permit issued by the Secretary under 49 U.S.C. 13902 shall be required to register under these standards.
(b) A motor carrier operating in interstate or foreign commerce in one or more participating States under a certificate or permit issued by the Secretary shall be required to register annually with a single registration State, and such registration shall be deemed to satisfy the registration requirements of all participating States.
  (1) The registration year will be the calendar year.
  (2) A carrier must file its annual registration application between the 1st day of August and the 30th day of November of the year preceding the registration year. A carrier that intends to commence operating during the current registration year may register at any time, but it must do so before it commences operating.
  (3) The registration application must be in the form appended to this part and must contain the information and be accompanied by the fees specified in paragraph (c) of this section. There will be no prorating of fees to account for partial year operations.
  (4) A carrier that has changed its registration State since its last filing must identify the registration State with which it previously filed.
(c) A motor carrier must file, or cause to be filed, the following with its registration State:
  (1) *Copies of its certificates and/or permits.* A carrier must supplement its filing by submitting copies of any new operating authorities as they are issued. Once a carrier has submitted copies of its authorities, it may thereafter satisfy the filing requirement by certifying that the copies are on file. A carrier may, with the permission of its registration State, submit a summary of its operating authorities in lieu of copies. A carrier granted emergency temporary authority or temporary authority having a duration of 120 days or less is not required to file evidence of such authority, but it must otherwise comply with the requirements of this section;
  (2) *A copy of its proof of public liability security* submitted to and accepted by the Secretary under 49 CFR Part 387, Subpart C or a copy of an order of the Secretary approving a public liability self-insurance application or other public liability security or agreement under the provisions of that part. A carrier must supplement its filings as necessary to ensure that current information is on file. Once a carrier has submitted, or caused to be submitted, a copy of its proof or order of the Secretary, it may thereafter satisfy the filing requirement by certifying that it has done so and that its security, self-insurance, or agreement remains in effect;
  (3) *A copy of its designation of an agent or agents* for service of process submitted to and accepted by the Secretary under 49 CFR Part 366. A carrier must supplement its filings as necessary to ensure that current information is on file. Once a carrier has submitted a copy of its designation, it may thereafter satisfy the filing requirement by certifying that its designation is on file; and
  (4) *A fee for the filing of proof of insurance.* In support of such fee, the carrier must submit the following information:
    (i) *The number of motor vehicles* it intends to operate in each participating State during the next registration year;
    (ii) *The per vehicle fee* each pertinent participating State charges, which fee must equal the fee, not to exceed $10, that such State collected or charged as of November 15, 1991;
    (iii) *The total fee due each participating State;* and
    (iv) *The total of all fees* specified in paragraph (c)(4)(iii) of this section.
(d) Consistent with its obligations under paragraph (c)(2) of this section, a carrier must cause to be timely filed with its registration State copies of any notices of cancellation or of any replacement certificates of insurance, surety bonds, or other security filed with the Secretary under 49 CFR Part 387, Subpart C.
(e) A carrier must make such supplemental filings at any time during the registration year as may be necessary to specify additional vehicles and/or States of operation and to pay additional fees.
(f) A motor carrier must submit to its insurer or insurers a copy of the supporting information, including any supplemental information, filed with its registration State under paragraphs (c)(4) and (e) of this section.
(g) The charging or collection of any fee that is not in accordance with the fee system established above is deemed a burden on interstate commerce. This includes fees for the registration or filing of evidence of insurance whether assessed directly upon the carrier or indirectly upon the insurance provider or other party who seeks reimbursement from the carrier.
(h) To the extent any State registration requirement imposes obligations in excess of those specified in this part, the requirement is an unreasonable burden on transportation within the Secretary's jurisdiction under 49 U.S.C. 13501.

§367.5 Registration receipts.
(a) On compliance by a motor carrier with the annual or supplemental registration requirements of §367.4, the registration State must issue the carrier a receipt reflecting that the carrier has filed the required proof of insurance and paid fees in accordance with the requirements of that section. The registration State also must issue a number of official copies of the receipt equal to the number of motor vehicles for which fees have been paid.
  (1) *The receipt and official copies* must contain only information identifying the carrier and specifying the States for which fees were paid. Supplemental receipts and official copies need contain only information relating to their underlying supplemental registrations.

(b) **Receipts and official copies issued** pursuant to a filing made during the annual registration period specified in §367.4(b)(2) must be issued within 30 days of filing of a fully acceptable registration application. All other receipts and official copies must be issued by the 30th day following the date of filing of a fully acceptable supplemental registration application. All receipts and official copies shall expire at midnight on the 31st day of December of the registration year for which they were issued.

(c) **A carrier is permitted to operate its motor vehicles** only in those participating States with respect to which it has paid appropriate fees, as indicated on the receipts and official copies. It may not operate more motor vehicles in a participating State than the number for which it has paid fees.

(d) **A motor carrier may not copy or alter** a receipt or an official copy of a receipt.

(e) **A motor carrier must maintain** in each of its motor vehicles an official copy of its receipt indicating that it has filed the required proof of insurance and paid appropriate fees for each State in which it operates.

(f) **A motor carrier may transfer** its official copies of its receipts from vehicles taken out of service to their replacement vehicles.

(g) **The driver of a motor vehicle must present** an official copy of a receipt for inspection by any authorized government personnel on reasonable demand.

(h) **No registration State shall require decals,** stamps, cab cards, or any other means of registering or identifying specific vehicles operated by a motor carrier.

§367.6 Registration State accounting.

(a) **A participating State must, on or before** the last day of each month, allocate and remit to each other participating State the appropriate portion of the fee revenue registrants submitted during the preceding month. Each remittance must be accompanied by a supporting statement identifying registrants and specifying the number of motor vehicles for which each registrant submitted fees. A participating State must submit a report of "no activity" to any other participating State for which it collected no fees during any month.

(b) **A participating State must maintain records** of fee revenue received from and remitted to each other participating State. Such records must specify the fees received from and remitted to each participating State with respect to each motor carrier registrant. A participating State must retain such records for a minimum of 3 years.

(c) **A participating State must keep records** pertaining to each of the motor carriers for which it acts as a registration State. The records must, at a minimum, include copies of annual and supplemental registration applications containing the information required by §367.4(c). A registration State must retain all such records for a minimum of 3 years.

§367.7 Violations unlawful; criminal penalties and civil sanctions.

Any violation of the provisions of these standards is unlawful. Nothing in these standards shall be construed to prevent a State from imposing criminal penalties or civil sanctions upon any person or organization violating any provision of them.

Appendix A to Part 367 Uniform Application for Single State Registration for Motor Carriers Registered with the Secretary of Transportation.

* Full-size forms available free of charge at www.dotcfr.com.

Part 368 - Application for a Certificate of Registration to Operate in Municipalities in the United States on the United States-Mexico International Border or Within the Commercial Zones of Such Municipalities

§368.1 Certificate of registration.
(a) **A Mexico-domiciled motor carrier** must apply to the FMCSA and receive a Certificate of Registration to provide interstate transportation in municipalities in the United States on the United States-Mexico international border or within the commercial zones of such municipalities as defined in 49 U.S.C. 13902(c)(4)(A).

(b) **A certificate of registration** permits only interstate transportation of property in municipalities in the United States on the United States-Mexico international border or within the commercial zones of such municipalities. A holder of a Certificate of Registration who operates a vehicle beyond this area is subject to applicable penalties and out-of-service orders.

§368.2 Definitions.
Interstate transportation means transportation described at 49 U.S.C. 13501, and transportation in the United States otherwise exempt from the Secretary's jurisdiction under 49 U.S.C. 13506(b)(1).

Mexico-domiciled motor carrier means a motor carrier of property whose principal place of business is located in Mexico.

§368.3 Applying for a certificate of registration.
(a) **If you wish to obtain a certificate of registration** under this part, you must submit an application that includes the following:
  (1) *Form OP-2* — Application for Mexican Certificate of Registration for Foreign Motor Carriers and Foreign Motor Private Carriers Under 49 U.S.C. 13902;
  (2) *Form MCS-150* — Motor Carrier Identification Report; and
  (3) *A notification of the means used* to designate process agents, either by submission in the application package of Form BOC-3 — Designation of Agents — Motor Carriers, Brokers and Freight Forwarders or a letter stating that the applicant will use a process agent service that will submit the Form BOC-3 electronically.

(b) **The FMCSA will only process your application** for a Certificate of Registration if it meets the following conditions:
  (1) *The application must be completed in English;*
  (2) *The information supplied* must be accurate and complete in accordance with the instructions to the Form OP-2, Form MCS-150 and Form BOC-3;
  (3) *The application must include* all the required supporting documents and applicable certifications set forth in the instructions to the Form OP-2, Form MCS-150 and Form BOC-3;
  (4) *The application must include* the filing fee payable to the FMCSA in the amount set forth in 49 CFR 360.3(f)(1); and
  (5) *The application must be signed by the applicant.*

(c) **If you fail to furnish the complete application** as described under paragraph (b) of this section your application may be rejected.

(d) **If you submit false information under this section,** you will be subject to applicable Federal penalties.

(e) **You must submit the application to the address** provided in the instructions to the Form OP-2.

(f) **You may obtain the application described** in paragraph (a) of this section from any FMCSA Division Office or download it from the FMCSA web site at: *http://www.fmcsa.dot.gov/factsfigs/formspubs.htm.*

§368.4 Requirement to notify FMCSA of change in applicant information.
(a) **You must notify the FMCSA** of any changes or corrections to the information in Parts I, IA or II submitted on the Form OP-2 or the Form BOC-3 — Designation of Agents — Motor Carriers, Brokers and Freight Forwarders during the application process or while you have a Certificate of Registration. You must notify the FMCSA in writing within 45 days of the change or correction.

(b) **If you fail to comply** with paragraph (a) of this section, the FMCSA may suspend or revoke the Certificate of Registration until you meet those requirements.

§368.5 Re-registration of certain carriers holding certificates of registration.
(a) **Each holder of a certificate of registration** that permits operations only in municipalities in the United States along the United States-Mexico international border or in commercial zones of such municipalities issued before April 18, 2002, who wishes to continue solely in those operations must submit an application according to procedures established under §368.3 of this part, except the filing fee in paragraph (b)(4) of that section is waived. You must file your application by October 20, 2003.

(b) **The FMCSA may suspend or revoke** the certificate of registration of any registrant that fails to comply with the procedures set forth in this section.

(c) **Certificates of registration** issued before April 18, 2002, remain valid until the FMCSA acts on the OP-2 application filed according to paragraph (a) of this section.

§368.6 FMCSA action on the application.
(a) **The Federal Motor Carrier Safety Administration** will review the application for correctness, completeness, and adequacy of information. Non-material errors will be corrected without notice to the applicant. Incomplete applications may be rejected.

(b) **If the applicant does not require or is not eligible** for a Certificate of Registration, the FMCSA will deny the application and notify the applicant.

(c) **The FMCSA will validate the accuracy of information** and certifications provided in the application against data maintained in databases of the governments of Mexico and the United States.

(d) **If the FMCSA determines that the application** and certifications demonstrate that the application is consistent with the FMCSA's safety fitness policy, it will issue a provisional Certificate of Registration, including a distinctive USDOT Number that identifies the motor carrier as permitted to provide interstate transportation of property solely in municipalities in the United States on the U.S.-Mexico international border or within the commercial zones of such municipalities.

(e) **The FMCSA may issue** a permanent Certificate of Registration to the holder of a provisional Certificate of Registration no earlier than 18 months after the date of issuance of the Certificate and only after completion to the satisfaction of the FMCSA of the safety monitoring system for Mexico-domiciled carriers set out in Subpart B of Part 385 of this subchapter.

(f) **Notice of the authority sought will not be published** in either the Federal Register or the FMCSA Register. Protests or comments will not be allowed. There will be no oral hearings.

§368.7 Requirement to carry certificate of registration in the vehicle.
A holder of a Certificate of Registration must maintain a copy of the Certificate of Registration in any vehicle providing transportation service within the scope of the Certificate, and make it available upon request to any State or Federal authorized inspector or enforcement officer.

§368.8 Appeals.
An applicant has the right to appeal denial of the application. The appeal must be in writing and specify in detail why the agency's decision to deny the application was wrong. The appeal must be filed with the Director, Office of Data Analysis and Information Systems within 20 days of the date of the letter denying the application. The decision of the Director will be the final agency order.

Part 368 - Application for a Certificate of Registration to Operate in Municipalities

Notes

Part 369 - Reports of Motor Carriers

§369.1 Annual reports of motor carriers of property, motor carriers of household goods, and dual property carriers.

(a) Annual Report Form M. All class I and class II common and contract carriers of property, including household goods and dual property motor carriers, must file Motor Carrier Annual Report Form M (Form M). Carriers must file the annual report on or before March 31 of the year following the year to which it relates. For classification criteria, see §369.2.

(b) Quarterly Report Form QFR. All class I common motor carriers of property and class I household goods motor carriers must file Motor Carrier Quarterly Report Form QFR (Form QFR). The quarterly accounting periods end on March 31, June 30, September 30, and December 31. The quarterly reports must be filed within 30 calendar days after the end of the reporting quarter.

(c) Where to file reports. Carriers must file the quarterly and annual reports with the Federal Motor Carrier Safety Administration at the address in §369.6. You can obtain blank copies of the report forms from the Federal Motor Carrier Safety Administration.

§369.2 Classification of carriers--motor carriers of property, household goods carriers, and dual property carriers.

(a) Common and contract motor carriers of property are grouped into the following three classes:

Class I. Carriers having annual carrier operating revenues (including interstate and intrastate) of $10 million or more after applying the revenue deflator formula in Note A.

Class II. Carriers having annual carrier operating revenues (including interstate and intrastate) of at least $3 million but less than $10 million after applying the revenue deflator formula in Note A.

Class III. Carriers having annual carrier operating revenues (including interstate and intrastate) of less than $3 million after applying the revenue deflator formula in Note A.

(b)(1) The class to which any carrier belongs shall be determined by annual carrier operating revenues (excluding revenues from private carriage, compensated intercorporate hauling, and leasing vehicles with drivers to private carriers) after applying the revenue deflator formula in Note A. Upward and downward classification will be effective as of January 1 of the year immediately following the third consecutive year of revenue qualification.

(2) *Any carrier which begins new operations* by obtaining operating authority not previously held or extends its existing authority by obtaining additional operating rights shall be classified in accordance with a reasonable estimate of its annual carrier operating revenues after applying the revenue deflator formula shown in Note A.

(3) *When a business combination* occurs such as a merger, reorganization, or consolidation, the surviving carrier shall be reclassified effective as of January 1 of the next calendar year on the basis of the combined revenues for the year when the combination occurred after applying the revenue deflator formula shown in Note A.

(4) *Carriers must notify* the Federal Motor Carrier Safety Administration (FMCSA) of any change in classification or any change in annual operating revenues that would cause a change in classification. The carrier may request a waiver or an exception from these regulations in unusual or extenuating circumstances, where the classification process will unduly burden the carrier, such as partial liquidation or curtailment or elimination of contracted services. The request must be in writing, specifying the conditions justifying the waiver or exception. FMCSA will notify the carriers of any change in classification.

(5) *Carriers not required to file an Annual Report* Form M may be required to file the Worksheet for Calculating Carrier Classification. All carriers will be notified of any classification changes.

Note A: Each carrier's operating revenues will be deflated annually using the Producers Price Index (PPI) of Finished Goods before comparing those revenues with the dollar revenue limits prescribed in paragraph (a) of this section. The PPI is published monthly by the Bureau of Labor Statistics. The formula to be applied is as follows:

$$\text{Current year's annual operating revenues} \times \frac{\text{1994 average PPI}}{\text{Current year's average PPI}} = \text{Adjusted annual operating revenues}$$

§369.3 Classification of carriers--motor carriers of passengers.

(a) Common and contract carriers of passengers are grouped into the following two classes:

Class I Carriers having average annual gross transportation operating revenues (including interstate and intrastate) of $5 million or more from passenger motor carrier operations after applying the revenue deflator formula as shown in the Note.

Class II Carriers having average annual gross transportation operating revenues (including interstate or intrastate) of less than $5 million from passenger motor carrier operations after applying the revenue deflator formula as shown in the Note.

(b)(1) The class to which any carrier belongs shall be determined by annual carrier operating revenues after applying the revenue deflator formula as shown in the Note. Upward and downward reclassification will be effective as of January 1 of the year immediately following the third consecutive year of revenue qualification.

(2) *Any carrier which begins new operations* (obtains operating authority not previously held) or extends its existing authority (obtains additional operating rights) shall be classified in accordance with a reasonable estimate of its annual carrier operating revenues after applying the revenue deflator formula shown in the Note.

(3) *When a business combination occurs,* such as a merger, reorganization, or consolidation, the surviving carrier shall be reclassified effective as of January 1 of the next calendar year on the basis of the combined revenues for the year when the combination occurred after applying the revenue deflator formula shown in the Note.

(4) *Carriers shall notify the FMCSA* of any change in classification or when their annual operating revenues exceed the Class II limit by writing to the Federal Motor Carrier Safety Administration at the address in §369.6. In unusual circumstances where the classification regulations and reporting requirements will unduly burden the carrier, the carrier may request from the FMCSA a waiver from these regulations. This request shall be in writing specifying the conditions justifying the waiver. The FMCSA then shall notify carriers of any change in classification or reporting requirements.

(c) For classification purposes, the FMCSA shall publish in the Federal Register annually an index number which shall be used for adjusting gross annual operating revenues. The index number (deflator) is based on the Producer Price Index of Finished Goods and is used to eliminate the effects of inflation from the classification process.

Note: Each carrier's operating revenues will be deflated annually using the Producers Price Index (PPI) of Finished Goods before comparing them with the dollar revenue limits prescribed in paragraph (a) of this section. The PPI is published monthly by the Bureau of Labor Statistics. The formula to be applied is as follows:

$$\text{Current year's annual operating revenues} \times \frac{\text{1986 average PPI}}{\text{Current year's average PPI}} = \text{Adjusted annual operating revenues}$$

§369.4 Annual and quarterly reports of Class I carriers of passengers.

(a) All Class I motor carriers of passengers shall complete and file Motor Carrier Quarterly and Annual Report Form MP-1 for Motor Carriers of Passengers (Form MP-1). Other than Class I carriers are not required to file Form MP-1.

(b) Motor Carrier Quarterly and Annual Report Form MP-1 shall be used to file both quarterly and annual selected motor carrier data. The annual accounting period shall be based either (1) on the 31st day of December in each year, or (2) an accounting year of thirteen 4-week periods ending at the close of the last 7 days of each calendar year. A carrier electing to adopt an accounting year of thirteen 4-week periods shall file with the FMCSA a statement showing the day on which its accounting year will close. A subsequent change in the accounting period may not be made except by authority of the FMCSA. The quarterly accounting period shall end on March 31, June 30, September 30, and December 31. The quarterly report shall be filed within 30 days after the end of the reporting quarter. The annual report shall be filed on or before March 31 of the year following the year to which it relates.

(c) The quarterly and annual report shall be filed in duplicate to the Federal Motor Carrier Safety Administration at the address in §369.6. Copies of Form MP-1 may be obtained from the FMCSA.

§369.5 Records.
Books, records and carrier operating documents shall be retained as prescribed in 49 CFR part 379, Preservation of Records.

§369.6 Address.
The following address must be used by motor carriers when submitting a report, requesting an exemption from filing a report, or requesting an exemption from public release of a report: Federal Motor Carrier Safety Administration, Office of Information Management, 400 Seventh St., SW., Washington, DC 20590. This address may also be used for general correspondence regarding the data collection program described in this section.

§369.7 [Reserved]

§369.8 Requests for exemptions from filing.
(a) *In General.* This section governs requests for exemptions from filing of reports required under §369.1.

(b) *Criteria.* The Federal Motor Carrier Safety Administration (FMCSA) may grant a request upon a proper showing that the exemption is necessary to preserve confidential business information that is not otherwise publicly available. Information is considered to be confidential when:
  (1) *Disclosure of the information* in the carrier's report would be likely to cause substantial harm to the carrier's competitive position; or
  (2) *Disclosure of information* in the report would be likely to impair protectable government interests.

(c) *Contents of a request.* The contents of a request for an exemption from filing must contain, at a minimum, the contents that are required for a request for an exemption from public release contained in §369.9(c). A carrier's request may include any other grounds as to why the request should be granted.

(d) *When requests are due.* The timing of a request for an exemption from filing is the same as the timing for a request for an exemption from public release contained in §369.9(d). The table below summarizes report and request due dates.

Report	Request due	
	Report due by	by
Annual Form M	March 31	March 31
First Quarter Form QFR	April 30	March 31
Second Quarter Form QFR	July 31	March 31
Third Quarter Form QFR	October 31	March 31
Fourth Quarter Form QFR	January 31	March 31

(e) *Decision to grant or deny a request.*
  (1) *A request will be denied* if it fails to provide all of the supporting information required in paragraph (c) of this section or if the supporting information is insufficient to establish that information in the carrier's report meets the criteria in paragraph (b) of this section.
  (2) *FMCSA will grant or deny each request* within a reasonable period of time. FMCSA will notify the carrier of its decision. The decision by FMCSA shall be administratively final.

(f) *Pendency. While a request is pending,* the carrier is required to submit any reports required under §369.1.

(g) *Period of exemptions.* If a request for an exemption under this section is granted, the carrier will be exempt from the reporting requirements of §369.1 for a period of three reporting years.

(h) *Modification of a decision to grant a request.* If a request is granted it remains in effect in accordance with its terms, unless modified by a later finding that the decision was clearly erroneous. If FMCSA believes such a finding should be made, FMCSA will notify the requesting carrier in writing of the reasons for the modification. The carrier may seek reconsideration of the modification.

§369.9 Requests for exemptions from public release.
(a) *In General.* This section governs requests for exemptions from public release of reports filed under §369.1.

(b) *Criteria.* The Federal Motor Carrier Safety Administration (FMCSA) will grant a request upon a proper showing that the carrier is not a publicly held corporation or that the carrier is not subject to financial reporting requirements of the Securities and Exchange Commission, and that the exemption is necessary to avoid competitive harm and to avoid the disclosure of information that qualifies as trade secret or privileged or confidential information under 5 U.S.C. 552(b)(4). Information is considered to be confidential when:
  (1) *Disclosure of the information* in the carrier's report would be likely to cause substantial harm to the carrier's competitive position; or
  (2) *Disclosure of information in the report* would be likely to impair protectable government interests.

(c) *Contents of a request.* A request for an exemption from public release must contain information supporting the claim. While the supporting information may contain opinions, the request must consist of objective data to the extent possible. General or non-specific assertions or analysis will be insufficient to support a request if FMCSA is unable to find that the criteria are met. The supporting information must show:
  (1) *That the information claimed to be confidential* is a trade secret, or commercial or financial information that is privileged or confidential.
  (2) *Measures taken by the carrier* to ensure that the information has not been disclosed or otherwise made available to any person, company, or organization other then the carrier.
  (3) *Insofar as is known by the carrier,* the extent to which the information has been disclosed, or otherwise become available, to persons other than the carrier, and why such disclosure or availability does not compromise the confidential nature of the information.
  (4) *If the carrier asserts that disclosure* would be likely to result in substantial competitive harm, what the harmful effects of disclosure would be, why the effects should be viewed as substantial, and the causal relationship between the effects and disclosure.
  (5) *If the carrier asserts that disclosure* would be likely to impair protectable government interests, what the effects of disclosure are likely to be and why disclosure is likely to impair such interests.

(d) *When requests are due.*
  (1) *Requests for an exemption under this section* may be made at any time during the year. However, a request will be deemed applicable to only those reports due on or after the date the request is received. Requests received after a report's due date will only be considered for the following year's report.
  (2) *A request will be deemed received* on the date the request is physically received or, if it is sent by mail, on the date it is postmarked.
  (3) *FMCSA will only allow a late request* if there are extenuating circumstances and the carrier gives adequate notice within a reasonable time of the extenuating circumstances.
  (4) *A carrier submitting a request* relating to the annual report can also request that it cover the quarterly reports for the upcoming year. In this case FMCSA will decide both requests at the same time. Requests covering the quarterly reports must be received by the due date of the annual report which relates to the prior year. The table in paragraph (e) of this section summarizes report, request, and decision due dates.

(e) *Decision to grant or deny a request.*
  (1) *After each due date of each annual report* specified in §369.1, FMCSA will publish a notice in the Federal Register requesting comments on any requests received under this section that are valid and pending.
  (2) *A request will be granted only if it provides* all of the supporting information required in paragraph (c) of this section and if the supporting information is sufficient to establish that information in the carrier's report meets the criteria in paragraph (b) of this section.
  (3) *If the carrier fails to comply with the timing requirements* of paragraph (d) of this section, the claim for confidentiality will be waived unless FMCSA is notified of extenuating circumstances before the information is disclosed to the public and FMCSA finds that the extenuating circumstances warrant consideration of the claim.
  (4) *FMCSA will grant or deny each request* no later than 90 days after the request's due date as defined in paragraph (d) of this section. The decision by FMCSA shall be administratively final. The table below summarizes report, request, and decision due dates.

Part 369 - Reports of Motor Carriers §369.11

Report	Report due	Request due	Decision due
Annual Form M	March 31	March 31	June 30
First Quarter Form QFR	April 30	March 31	June 30
Second Quarter Form QFR	July 31	March 31	June 30
Third Quarter Form QFR	October 31	March 31	June 30
Fourth Quarter Form QFR	January 31	March 31	June 30

(5) *If a request is granted,* FMCSA will notify carrier of that decision and of any appropriate limitations.

(6) *If a request for confidentiality is denied,* FMCSA will notify the carrier of that decision and that the information will be made available to the public not less than ten working days after the carrier has received notice of the denial. The notice will specify the reasons for denying the request.

(f) *Pendency.* A request is deemed pending from the date it is received by FMCSA until it is granted or denied by FMCSA. FMCSA will not release publicly, unless otherwise required by law, any report for which a valid request for an exemption from public release is pending.

(g) *Period of exemptions.* If a request for an exemption under this section is granted, FMCSA will not publicly release the reports covered by the granted exemption, unless otherwise required by law, for a period of three years from the report's due date.

(h) *Modification of a decision to grant a request.* If a request is granted it remains in effect in accordance with its terms, unless modified by a later finding that the decision was clearly erroneous. If FMCSA believes such a finding should be made, FMCSA will notify the requesting carrier in writing of the reasons for the modification and that the carrier's report will be made available to the public in not less than ten working days from the date of receipt of notice under this paragraph. The carrier may seek reconsideration of the modification.

§369.10 Public release of motor carrier of property data.

(a) *In general.* Unless otherwise provided in this section, the data contained in a report filed under §369.1 shall be made publicly available, but no sooner than the due date for the report.

(b) *Exceptions relating to exemptions from public release.*

(1) *If a request for an exemption* from public release is pending under §369.9, FMCSA will not publicly release the reports covered by the request until at least the time that a decision to grant or deny the request is made.

(2) *If a carrier is granted an exemption* from public release under §369.9, FMCSA will not publicly release the reports covered by the granted exemption for a period of three years from the report's due date.

(c) *Other exceptions.* Notwithstanding any other provision of this part, information may be released:

(1) *If the data are included in aggregate* industry statistics that do not identify the individual carrier;

(2) To other components of the Department of Transportation for their internal use only;

(3) *If required by law;*

(4) *With the consent of the carrier filing the report;* or

(5) *To contractors,* if necessary for the performance of a contract with FMCSA.

§369.11 Quarterly reports of passenger revenues, expenses, and statistics.

Commencing with reports for the quarter ended March 31, 1968, and for subsequent quarters thereafter, until further order, all class I common and contract motor carriers of passengers, as defined in §369.3(a), shall compile and file quarterly reports in accordance with Motor Carrier Quarterly and Annual Report, Form MP-1. Such quarterly reports shall be filed in duplicate in the FMCSA Office of Information Management at the address in §369.6, within 30 days after the close of the period to which it relates.

Part 369 - Reports of Motor Carriers

NOTES

Part 370 - Principles and Practices for the Investigation and Voluntary Disposition of Loss and Damage Claims and Processing Salvage

§370.1 Applicability of regulations.

The regulations set forth in this part shall govern the processing of claims for loss, damage, injury, or delay to property transported or accepted for transportation, in interstate or foreign commerce, by each motor carrier, water carrier, and freight forwarder (hereinafter called carrier), subject to 49 U.S.C. Subtitle IV, Part B.

§370.3 Filing of claims.

(a) Compliance with regulations. A claim for loss or damage to baggage or for loss, damage, injury, or delay to cargo, shall not be voluntarily paid by a carrier unless filed, as provided in paragraph (b) of this section, with the receiving or delivering carrier, or carrier issuing the bill of lading, receipt, ticket, or baggage check, or carrier on whose line the alleged loss, damage, injury, or delay occurred, within the specified time limits applicable thereto and as otherwise may be required by law, the terms of the bill of lading or other contract of carriage, and all tariff provisions applicable thereto.

(b) Minimum filing requirements. A written or electronic communication (when agreed to by the carrier and shipper or receiver involved) from a claimant, filed with a proper carrier within the time limits specified in the bill of lading or contract of carriage or transportation and:

(1) *Containing facts* sufficient to identify the baggage or shipment (or shipments) of property,
(2) *Asserting liability* for alleged loss, damage, injury, or delay, and
(3) *Making claim* for the payment of a specified or determinable amount of money, shall be considered as sufficient compliance with the provisions for filing claims embraced in the bill of lading or other contract of carriage; Provided, however, That where claims are electronically handled, procedures are established to ensure reasonable carrier access to supporting documents.

(c) Documents not constituting claims. Bad order reports, appraisal reports of damage, notations of shortage or damage, or both, on freight bills, delivery receipts, or other documents, or inspection reports issued by carriers or their inspection agencies, whether the extent of loss or damage is indicated in dollars and cents or otherwise, shall, standing alone, not be considered by carriers as sufficient to comply with the minimum claim filing requirements specified in paragraph (b) of this section.

(d) Claims filed for uncertain amounts. Whenever a claim is presented against a proper carrier for an uncertain amount, such as "$100 more or less," the carrier against whom such claim is filed shall determine the condition of the baggage or shipment involved at the time of delivery by it, if it was delivered, and shall ascertain as nearly as possible the extent, if any, of the loss or damage for which it may be responsible. It shall not, however, voluntarily pay a claim under such circumstances unless and until a formal claim in writing for a specified or determinable amount of money shall have been filed in accordance with the provisions of paragraph (b) of this section.

(e) Other claims. If investigation of a claim develops that one or more other carriers has been presented with a similar claim on the same shipment, the carrier investigating such claim shall communicate with each such other carrier and, prior to any agreement entered into between or among them as to the proper disposition of such claim or claims, shall notify all claimants of the receipt of conflicting or overlapping claims and shall require further substantiation, on the part of each claimant of his/her title to the property involved or his/her right with respect to such claim.

§370.5 Acknowledgment of claims.

(a) Each carrier shall, upon receipt in writing or by electronic transmission of a proper claim in the manner and form described in the regulations in the past, acknowledge the receipt of such claim in writing or electronically to the claimant within 30 days after the date of its receipt by the carrier unless the carrier shall have paid or declined such claim in writing or electronically within 30 days of the receipt thereof. The carrier shall indicate in its acknowledgment to the claimant what, if any, additional documentary evidence or other pertinent information may be required by it further to process the claim as its preliminary examination of the claim, as filed, may have revealed.

(b) The carrier shall at the time each claim is received create a separate file and assign thereto a successive claim file number and note that number on all documents filed in support of the claim and all records and correspondence with respect to the claim, including the acknowledgment of receipt. At the time such claim is received the carrier shall cause the date of receipt to be recorded on the face of the claim document, and the date of receipt shall also appear in the carrier's acknowledgment of receipt to the claimant. The carrier shall also cause the claim file number to be noted on the shipping order, if in its possession, and the delivery receipt, if any, covering such shipment, unless the carrier has established an orderly and consistent internal procedure for assuring:

(1) *That all information* contained in shipping orders, delivery receipts, tally sheets, and all other pertinent records made with respect to the transportation of the shipment on which claim is made, is available for examination upon receipt of a claim;
(2) *That all such records and documents* (or true and complete reproductions thereof) are in fact examined in the course of the investigation of the claim (and an appropriate record is made that such examination has in fact taken place); and
(3) *That such procedures* prevent the duplicate or otherwise unlawful payment of claims.

§370.7 Investigation of claims.

(a) Prompt investigation required. Each claim filed against a carrier in the manner prescribed in this part shall be promptly and thoroughly investigated if investigation has not already been made prior to receipt of the claim.

(b) Supporting documents. When a necessary part of an investigation, each claim shall be supported by the original bill of lading, evidence of the freight charges, if any, and either the original invoice, a photographic copy of the original invoice, or an exact copy thereof or any extract made therefrom, certified by the claimant to be true and correct with respect to the property and value involved in the claim; or certification of prices or values, with trade or other discounts, allowance, or deductions, of any nature whatsoever and the terms thereof, or depreciation reflected thereon; Provided, however, That where property involved in a claim has not been invoiced to the consignee shown on the bill of lading or where an invoice does not show price or value, or where the property involved has been sold, or where the property has been transferred at bookkeeping values only, the carrier shall, before voluntarily paying a claim, require the claimant to establish the destination value in the quantity, shipped, transported, or involved; Provided, further, That when supporting documents are determined to be a necessary part of an investigation, the supporting documents are retained by the carriers for possible FMCSA inspection.

(c) Verification of loss. When an asserted claim for loss of an entire package or an entire shipment cannot be otherwise authenticated upon investigation, the carrier shall obtain from the consignee of the shipment involved a certified statement in writing that the property for which the claim is filed has not been received from any other source.

§370.9 Disposition of claims.

(a) Each carrier subject to 49 U.S.C. Subtitle IV, Part B which receives a written or electronically transmitted claim for loss or damage to baggage or for loss, damage, injury, or delay to property transported shall pay, decline, or make a firm compromise settlement offer in writing or electronically to the claimant within 120 days after receipt of the claim by the carrier; Provided, however, That, if the claim cannot be processed and disposed of within 120 days after the receipt thereof, the carrier shall at that time and at the expiration of each succeeding 60-day period while the claim remains pending, advise the claimant in writing or electronically of the status of the claim and the reason for the delay in making final disposition thereof and it shall retain a copy of such advice to the claimant in its claim file thereon.

(b) When settling a claim for loss or damage, a common carrier by motor vehicle of household goods as defined in §375.1(b)(1) of this chapter shall use the replacement costs of the lost or damaged item as a base to apply a depreciation factor to arrive at the current actual value of the lost or damaged item: Provided, That where an item cannot be replaced or no suitable replacement is obtainable, the proper measure of damages shall be the original costs, augmented by a factor derived from a consumer price index, and adjusted downward by a factor depreciation over average useful life.

§370.11 Processing of salvage.

(a) **Whenever baggage or material, goods,** or other property transported by a carrier subject to the provisions in this part is damaged or alleged to be damaged and is, as a consequence thereof, not delivered or is rejected or refused upon tender thereof to the owner, consignee, or person entitled to receive such property, the carrier, after giving due notice, whenever practicable to do so, to the owner and other parties that may have an interest therein, and unless advised to the contrary after giving such notice, shall undertake to sell or dispose of such property directly or by the employment of a competent salvage agent. The carrier shall only dispose of the property in a manner that will fairly and equally protect the best interests of all persons having an interest therein. The carrier shall make an itemized record sufficient to identify the property involved so as to be able to correlate it to the shipment or transportation involved, and claim, if any, filed thereon. The carrier also shall assign to each lot of such property a successive lot number and note that lot number on its record of shipment and claim, if any claim is filed thereon.

(b) **Whenever disposition of salvage material or goods** shall be made directly to an agent or employee of a carrier or through a salvage agent or company in which the carrier or one or more of its directors, officers, or managers has any interest, financial or otherwise, that carrier's salvage records shall fully reflect the particulars of each such transaction or relationship, or both, as the case may be.

(c) **Upon receipt of a claim on a shipment** on which salvage has been processed in the manner prescribed in this section, the carrier shall record in its claim file thereon the lot number assigned, the amount of money recovered, if any, from the disposition of such property, and the date of transmittal of such money to the person or persons lawfully entitled to receive the same.

Part 371 - Brokers of Property

§371.1 Applicability.
This part applies, to the extent provided therein, to all brokers of transportation by motor vehicle as defined in §371.2.

§371.2 Definitions.
(a) **Broker** means a person who, for compensation, arranges, or offers to arrange, the transportation of property by an authorized motor carrier. Motor carriers, or persons who are employees or bona fide agents of carriers, are not brokers within the meaning of this section when they arrange or offer to arrange the transportation of shipments which they are authorized to transport and which they have accepted and legally bound themselves to transport.

(b) **Bona fide agents** are persons who are part of the normal organization of a motor carrier and perform duties under the carrier's directions pursuant to a preexisting agreement which provides for a continuing relationship, precluding the exercise of discretion on the part of the agent in allocating traffic between the carrier and others.

(c) **Brokerage** or **brokerage service** is the arranging of transportation or the physical movement of a motor vehicle or of property. It can be performed on behalf of a motor carrier, consignor, or consignee.

(d) **Non-brokerage service** is all other service performed by a broker on behalf of a motor carrier, consignor, or consignee.

§371.3 Records to be kept by brokers.
(a) *A broker shall keep a record of each transaction.* For purposes of this section, brokers may keep master lists of consignors and the address and registration number of the carrier, rather than repeating this information for each transaction. The record shall show:
  (1) The name and address of the consignor;
  (2) The name, address, and registration number of the originating motor carrier;
  (3) The bill of lading or freight bill number;
  (4) *The amount of compensation* received by the broker for the brokerage service performed and the name of the payer;
  (5) *A description of any non-brokerage service* performed in connection with each shipment or other activity, the amount of compensation received for the service, and the name of the payer; and
  (6) *The amount of any freight charges* collected by the broker and the date of payment to the carrier.

(b) *Brokers shall keep the records required by this section* for a period of three years.

(c) *Each party to a brokered transaction* has the right to review the record of the transaction required to be kept by these rules.

§371.7 Misrepresentation.
(a) *A broker shall not perform or offer to perform* any brokerage service (including advertising), in any name other than that in which its registration is issued.

(b) *A broker shall not, directly or indirectly,* represent its operations to be that of a carrier. Any advertising shall show the broker status of the operation.

§371.9 Rebating and compensation.
(a) *A broker shall not charge or receive compensation* from a motor carrier for brokerage service where:
  (1) *The broker owns* or has a material beneficial interest in the shipment or
  (2) *The broker is able to exercise control* over the shipment because the broker owns the shipper, the shipper owns the broker, or there is common ownership of the two.

(b) *A broker shall not give or offer to give* anything of value to any shipper, consignor or consignee (or their officers or employees) except inexpensive advertising items given for promotional purposes.

§371.10 Duties and obligations of brokers.
Where the broker acts on behalf of a person bound by law or the FMCSA regulation as to the transmittal of bills or payments, the broker must also abide by the law or regulations which apply to that person.

§371.13 Accounting.
Each broker who engages in any other business shall maintain accounts so that the revenues and expenses relating to the brokerage portion of its business are segregated from its other activities. Expenses that are common shall be allocated on an equitable basis; however, the broker must be prepared to explain the basis for the allocation.

Part 371 - Brokers of Property

Notes

Part 372 - Exemptions, Commercial Zones, and Terminal Areas

Subpart A - Exemptions

§372.101 Casual, occasional, or reciprocal transportation of passengers for compensation when such transportation is sold or arranged by anyone for compensation.

The partial exemption from regulation under the provisions of 49 U.S.C. Subtitle IV, Part B of the casual, occasional, and reciprocal transportation of passengers by motor vehicle in interstate or foreign commerce for compensation as provided in 49 U.S.C. 13506(b) be, and it is hereby, removed to the extent necessary to make applicable all provisions of 49 U.S.C. Subtitle IV, Part B to such transportation when sold or offered for sale, or provided or procured or furnished or arranged for, by any person who sells, offers for sale, provides, furnishes, contracts, or arranges for such transportation for compensation or as a regular occupation or business.

§372.103 Motor vehicles employed solely in transporting school children and teachers to or from school.

The exemption set forth in 49 U.S.C. 13506(a)(1) shall not be construed as being inapplicable to motor vehicles being used at the time of operation in the transportation of schoolchildren and teachers to or from school, even though such motor vehicles are employed at other times in transportation beyond the scope of the exemption.

§372.107 Definitions.

As used in the regulations in this part, the following terms shall have the meaning shown:

(a) Cooperative association. The term "cooperative association" means an association which conforms to the following definition in the Agricultural Marketing Act, approved June 15, 1929, as amended (12 U.S.C. 1141j):

As used in this Act, the term *cooperative association* means any association in which farmers act together in processing, preparing for market, handling, and/or marketing the farm products of persons so engaged, and also means any association in which farmers act together in purchasing, testing, grading, processing, distributing, and/or furnishing farm supplies and/or farm business services. Provided, however, That such associations are operated for the mutual benefit of the members thereof as such producers or purchasers and conform to one or both of the following requirements:

First. That no member of the association is allowed more than one vote because of the amount of stock or membership capital he may own therein; and

Second. That the association does not pay dividends on stock or membership capital in excess of 8 per centum per annum.

And in any case to the following:

Third. That the association shall not deal in farm products, farm supplies and farm business services with or for nonmembers in an amount greater in value than the total amount of such business transacted by it with or for members. All business transacted by any cooperative association for or on behalf of the United States or any agency or instrumentality thereof shall be disregarded in determining the volume of member and nonmember business transacted by such association.

Associations which do not conform to such definition are not eligible to operate under the partial exemption of 49 U.S.C. 13506(a)(5).

(b) Federation of cooperative associations. The term "federation of cooperative associations" means a federation composed of either two or more cooperative associations, or one or more farmers, which federation possesses no greater powers or purposes than a cooperative association as defined in paragraph (a) of this section. Federations of cooperative associations which do not conform to such definition are not eligible to operate under the partial exemption of 49 U.S.C. 13506(a)(5).

(c) Member. The term "member" means any farmer or cooperative association which has consented to be, has been accepted as, and is a member in good standing in accordance with the constitution, bylaws, or rules of the cooperative association or federation of cooperative associations.

(d) Farmer. The term "farmer" means any individual, partnership, corporation, or other business entity to the extent engaged in farming operations either as a producer of agricultural commodities or as a farm owner.

(e) Interstate transportation. The term "interstate transportation" means transportation by motor vehicle in interstate or foreign commerce subject to the FMCSA's jurisdiction as set forth in 49 U.S.C. 13501.

(f) Member transportation. The term "member transportation" means transportation performed by a cooperative association or federation of cooperative associations for itself or for its members, but does not include transportation performed in furtherance of the nonfarm business of such members.

(g) Nonmember transportation. The term "nonmember transportation" means transportation performed by a cooperative association or federation of cooperative associations other than member transportation as defined in paragraph (f) of this section.

(h) Fiscal year. The term "fiscal year" means the annual accounting period adopted by the cooperative association or federation of cooperative associations for Federal income tax reporting purposes.

§372.109 Computation of tonnage allowable in nonfarm-non-member transportation.

Interstate transportation performed by a cooperative association or federation of cooperative associations for nonmembers who are not farmers, cooperative associations, or federations of associations or the United States Government for compensation, (except transportation otherwise exempt under Subtitle IV, Part B, Chapter 135 of Title 49 of the United States Code) shall be limited to that which is incidental to its primary transportation operation and necessary for its effective performance. It shall in no event exceed 25 percent of its total interstate transportation services in any fiscal year, measured in terms of tonnage. A cooperative association or federation of cooperative associations may transport its own property, its members' property, property of other farmers and the property of other cooperatives or federations in accordance with existing law, except where the provisions of §372.111 may be applicable to the limit on member/nonmember transportation.

(a) The phrase "incidental to its primary transportation operation and necessary for its effective performance" means that the interstate transportation of the cooperative association or federation of cooperation association for nonmembers as described above is performed with the same trucks or tractors employed in a prior or subsequent trip in the primary transportation operation of the cooperative association or federation, that it is not economically feasible to operate the trucks or tractors empty on return trips (outbound trips in cases where the primary transportation operation is inbound to the association or federation), and that the additional income obtained from such transportation is necessary to make the primary transportation operation financially practicable. Transportation for nonmembers as described above performed by a cooperative or federation through the use of trucks or tractors trip-leased for one-way movements with the cooperative association or federation acting as leasee, is not incidental and necessary;

(b) The base tonnage to which the 25-percent limitation is applied is all tonnage of all kinds transported by the cooperative association or federation of cooperative associations in interstate or foreign commerce, whether for itself, its members or nonmembers, for or on behalf of the United States or any agency or instrumentality thereof, and that performed within the exemption provided by 49 U.S.C. 13506(a)(5).

§372.111 Nonmember transportation limitation and record keeping.

(a) Overall limitation of nonmember transportation. No cooperative association or federation of cooperative associations may engage in nonmember interstate transportation for compensation in any fiscal year which, measured in terms of tonnage, exceeds its total interstate member transportation in such fiscal year.

(b) Records of interstate transportation when nonmember transportation is performed. Any cooperative association or federation of cooperative associations performing interstate transportation for nonmembers shall prepare and retain for a period of at least two years written records of all interstate transportation performed for members and nonmembers. These records shall contain:

(1) The date of the shipment,
(2) The names and addresses of the consignor and consignee,
(3) The origin and destination of the shipment,
(4) A description of the articles in the shipment,
(5) The weight or volume of the shipment,
(6) A description of the equipment used either by unit number or license number and, in the event this equipment is nonowned, the name and address of its owners and drivers,

§372.113

(7) *The total charges collected,*
(8) *A copy of all leases executed* by the cooperative association or federation of cooperative associations to obtain equipment to perform transportation under 49 U.S.C. 13506(a)(5),
(9) *Whether the transportation performed is:*
   (i) *Member transportation,*
   (ii) *Nonmember transportation* for nonmembers who are farmers, cooperative associations, or federations thereof,
   (iii) *Other nonmember transportation,* and if of class (iii), how the transportation was incidental and necessary as defined in §372.109(a).

§372.113   [Reserved]

§372.115   Commodities that are not exempt under 49 U.S.C. 13506(a)(6).

49 U.S.C. 13506(a)(6) provides an exemption from regulation for motor vehicles used in carrying ordinary livestock, fish, and unmanufactured agricultural commodities. Certain specific commodities have been statutorily determined to be non-exempt. Administrative Ruling No. 133, which is reproduced below, is a list of those commodities that are non-exempt by statute.

Administrative Ruling No. 133
List of Commodities That Are Not Exempt by Statute Under 49 U.S.C. 13506(a)(6)

Animal fats
Butter
Canned fruits and vegetables
Carnauba wax as imported in slabs or chunks
Cattle, slaughtered
Charcoal
Cheese
Coal
Cocoa beans
Coffee, beans, roasted, or instant
Copra meal
Cotton yarn
Cottonseed cake or meal
Diatomaceous earth
Dinners, frozen
Feeds:
   Alfalfa meal
   Alfalfa pellets
   Beet pulp
   Bran shorts
   Copra meal
   Corn gluten
   Distilled corn grain residues, with or without solubles added
   Fish meal
   Hominy feed
   Middlings
   Pelletized ground refuse screenings
   Wheat bran
   Wheat shorts
Fertilizer, commercial
Fish:
   Canned or salted as a treatment for preserving
   Cooked or partially cooked fish or shrimp, frozen or unfrozen
   Hermetically sealed in containers as a treatment for preserving
   Oil from fishes
   Preserved, or treated for preserving, such as smoked, salted, pickled, spiced, corned or kippered
Flagstone
Flaxseed meal
Flour
Forest products:
   Resin products, such as turpentine
Fruits and Berries:
   Bananas, fresh, dried, dehydrated, or frozen
   Canned
   Frozen
   Hulls of oranges after juice extractions
   Juice, fruit, plain or concentrated
   Pies, frozen
   Preserved, such as jam
   Purees, strawberry and other, frozen
Grains:
   Oils extracted from grain
   Popcorn, popped
   Rice, precooked
   Wheat germ
Gravel
Hair, hog or other animal, product of slaughter of animal
Hay, sweetened with 3 percent molasses by weight
Hemp fiber
Hides, green and salted
Insecticides
Limestone, agricultural
Livestock:
   Monkeys
   Race horses
   Show horses
   Zoo animals
Lumber, rough sawed or planed
Maple syrup
Meal:
   Alfalfa
   Copra
   Cottonseed
   Fish
   Flaxseed
   Linseed
   Peanut
   Soybean
Meat and meat products, fresh, frozen or canned
Milk and Cream:
   Chocolate
   Condensed
   Sterilized in hermetically sealed cans
Molasses
Nuts (including peanuts):
   Peanut meal
   Roasted or boiled
Oil, mint
Oil, extracted from vegetables, grain, seed, fish or other commodity
Pelts
Pies, frozen
Pigeons, racing
Pulp, beet
Pulp, sugar cane
Rock (except natural crushed, vesicular rock to be used for decorative purposes)
Rubber, crude, in bales
Rubber, latex, natural, liquid, from which water has been extracted and to which ammonia has been added
Sand
Seeds:
   Oil extracted from seeds
Skins, animal
Soil, potting
Soil, top
Soup, frozen
Sugar
Sugar cane pulp
Sugar raw
Syrup, cane
Syrup, maple
Tea
Tobacco:
   Cigars and cigarettes
   Homogenized

Smoking
Top Soil
Trees:
    Sawed into lumber
Vegetables:
    Candied sweet potatoes, frozen
    Canned
    Cooked
    French fried potatoes
    Oil, extracted from vegetables
    Soup, frozen
    Soybean meal
Wool imported from a foreign country
Wool tops and noils
Wool waste (carded, spun, woven, or knitted)
Wool yarn

NOTE 1: Under 49 U.S.C. 13506(a)(6)(D), any listed fish or shellfish product that is not intended for human consumption is exempt.

NOTE 2: Under 49 U.S.C. 13506(a)(6)(E), any listed livestock feed, poultry feed, agricultural seeds, or plants that are transported to a site of agricultural production or to a business enterprise engaged in the sale to agricultural producers of goods used in agricultural production is exempt.

§372.117 Motor transportation of passengers incidental to transportation by aircraft.

(a) Passengers having an immediately prior or subsequent movement by air. The transportation of passengers by motor vehicle is transportation incidental to transportation by aircraft provided (1) that it is confined to the transportation of passengers who have had or will have an immediately prior or immediately subsequent movement by air and (2) that the zone within which motor transportation is incidental to transportation by aircraft, except as it may be individually determined as provided in section (c) herein, shall not exceed in size the area encompassed by a 25-mile radius of the boundary of the airport at which the passengers arrive or depart and by the boundaries of the commercial zones (as defined by the Secretary) of any municipalities any part of whose commercial zones falls within the 25-mile radius of the pertinent airport.

(b) Substituted motor-for-air transportation due to emergency conditions. Transportation of passengers by motor vehicle is transportation incidental to transportation by aircraft if it constitutes substituted motor-for-air service performed at the expense of the air carrier in emergency situations arising from the inability of the air carrier to perform air transportation due to adverse weather conditions, equipment failure, or other causes beyond the control of the air carrier.

(c) Individual determination of exempt zones. Upon its own motion or upon petition filed by any interested person, the Secretary may in an appropriate proceeding, determine whether the area within which the transportation by motor vehicle of passengers having an immediately prior or subsequent movement by air must be performed, in order to come within the provisions of paragraph (a) of this section, should be individually determined with respect to any particular airport or city served by an airport, and whether there should be established therefor appropriate boundaries differing in extent from this defined in paragraph (a)(2) of this section.

(d) Exempt zones and operations —
  (1) *Dulles and Baltimore-Washington International Airports.* The transportation by motor vehicle, in interstate or foreign commerce, of passengers, having an immediately prior or subsequent movement by air, between Dulles International Airport, near Chantilly, Va., and Baltimore-Washington International Airport, near Baltimore, Md., is partially exempt from regulation under 49 U.S.C. 13506(a)(8)(A).

  (2) *Savannah, Ga., Airport.* The transportation by motor vehicle, in interstate or foreign commerce, of passengers, having an immediately prior or subsequent movement by air, between Savannah, Ga., Airport and all points on Hilton Head Island, SC, is partially exempt from regulation under 49 U.S.C. 13506(a)(8)(A).

  (3) *Chicago O'Hare International Airport (Chicago, Ill.).* The transportation by motor vehicle, in interstate or foreign commerce, of passengers, having an immediately prior or subsequent movement by air, between O'Hare International Airport, at Chicago, Ill., on the one hand, and, on the other, points in Indiana on and north of U.S. Highway 30 and on and west of Indiana Highway 49, is partially exempt from regulation under 49 U.S.C. 13506(a)(8)(A).

Subpart B - Commercial Zones

§372.201 Albany, NY.

The zone adjacent to, and commercially a part of Albany, N.Y., within which transportation by motor vehicle, in interstate or foreign commerce, not under common control, management, or arrangement for a continuous carriage or shipment to or from a point beyond such zone, is partially exempt from regulations under 49 U.S.C. 13506(b)(1) includes and is comprised of all points as follows:

(a) The municipality of Albany, N.Y., itself.

(b) All points within a line drawn eight miles beyond the municipal limits of Albany.

(c) All points in that area more than eight miles beyond the municipal limits of Albany bounded by a line as follows: Beginning at that point on the western boundary of Cohoes, N.Y., where it crosses the line described in paragraph (b) of this section, thence along the western and northern boundary of Cohoes to the Mohawk River thence along such river to the northern boundary of the Town of Waterford thence along the northern and eastern boundaries of the Town of Waterford to the northern boundary of the City of Troy (all of which city is included under the next provision).

(d) All of any municipality any part of which is within the limits of the combined areas defined in paragraphs (b) and (c) of this section, and

(e) All of any municipality wholly surrounded, or so surrounded except for a water boundary, by the municipality of Albany or any other municipality included under the terms of paragraph (d) of this section.

§372.203 Beaumont, TX.

The zone adjacent to, and commercially a part of Beaumont, Tex., within which transportation by motor vehicle in interstate or foreign commerce, not under common control, management, or arrangement for a continuous carriage or shipment to or from a point beyond such zone, is partially exempt from regulation under 49 U.S.C. 13506(b)(1) includes and is comprised of all points as follows:

(a) The municipality of Beaumont, Tex., itself;

(b) All points within a line drawn 8 miles beyond the municipal limits of Beaumont;

(c) All points in Jefferson County and Orange County, Tex.;

(d) All of any municipality any part of which is within the limits of the combined areas defined in paragraphs (b) and (c) of this section, and

(e) All of any municipality wholly surrounded, or so surrounded except for a water boundary, by the municipality of Beaumont or by any other municipality included under the terms of paragraph (d) of this section.

§372.205 Charleston, S.C.

The zone adjacent to, and commercially a part of Charleston, S.C., within which transportation by motor vehicle in interstate or foreign commerce, not under common control, management, or arrangement for a continuous carriage or shipment to or from a point beyond such zone, is partially exempt from regulation under 49 U.S.C. 13506(b)(1) includes and is comprised of all points as follows:

(a) The municipality of Charleston, S.C., itself;

(b) All points within a line drawn 6 miles beyond the municipal limits of Charleston;

(c) Those points in Charleston County, S.C., which are not within the areas described in paragraph (b) of this section; and those points in Berkley County, S.C., which are not within the areas described in paragraph (b) of this section, and which are west of South Carolina Highway 41; and all points in Dorchester County, SC.

(d) All of any municipality any part of which is within the limits of the combined areas defined in paragraphs (b) and (c) of this section, and

(e) All of any municipality wholly surrounded, or so surrounded except for a water boundary, by the municipality of Charleston or by any other municipality included under the terms of paragraph (d) of this section.

§372.207 Charleston, WV.

The zone adjacent to, and commercially a part of Charleston, W. Va., within which transportation by motor vehicle in interstate or foreign commerce, not under common control, management, or arrangement for a continuous carriage or shipment to or from a point beyond such zone, is partially exempt from regulation under 49 U.S.C. 13506(b)(1) includes and is comprised of all points as follows:

(a) The municipality of Charleston, W. Va., itself;

(b) **All points within a line drawn 6 miles** beyond the municipal limits of Charleston;
(c) **Those points in Kanawha County, W. Va.,** which are not within the area described in paragraph (b) of this section; and those points in Putnam County, W. Va., south of West Virginia Highway 34;
(d) **All of any municipality any part of which** is within the limits of the combined areas defined in paragraphs (b) and (c) of this section, and
(e) **All of any municipality wholly surrounded,** or so surrounded except for a water boundary, by the municipality of Charleston or by any other municipality included under the terms of paragraph (d) of this section.

§372.209 Lake Charles, LA.

The zone adjacent to, and commercially a part of Lake Charles, La., within which transportation by motor vehicle in interstate or foreign commerce, not under common control, management, or arrangement for a continuous carriage or shipment to or from a point beyond such zone, is partially exempt from regulation under 49 U.S.C. 13506(b)(1) includes and is comprised of all points as follows:

(a) **The municipality of Lake Charles, La., itself;**
(b) **All points within a line drawn 6 miles** beyond the municipal limits of Lake Charles;
(c) **Those points in Calcasieu Parish, La.,** which are not within the area described in paragraph (b) of this section; and which are east of Louisiana Highway 27 (western section);
(d) **All of any municipality any part of which** is within the limits of the combined areas defined in paragraphs (b) and (c) of this section, and
(e) **All of any municipality wholly surrounded,** or so surrounded except for a water boundary, by the municipality of Lake Charles or by any other municipality included under the terms of paragraph (d) of this section.

§372.211 Pittsburgh, PA.

The zone adjacent to, and commercially a part of Pittsburgh within which transportation by motor vehicle in interstate or foreign commerce, not under common control, management, or arrangement for a continuous carriage or shipment to or from a point beyond such zone, is partially exempt from regulation under 49 U.S.C. 13506(b)(1) includes and is comprised of all points as follows:

(a) **The municipality of Pittsburgh, Pa., itself;**
(b) **All points within a line drawn 15 miles** beyond the municipal limits of Pittsburgh;
(c) **Those points in Allegheny County, Pa.,** which are not within the area described in paragraph (b) of this section;
(d) **All of any municipality any part of which** is within the limits of the combined areas defined in paragraphs (b) and (c) of this section, and
(e) **All of any municipality wholly surrounded,** or so surrounded except for a water boundary, by the municipality of Pittsburgh by any other municipality included under the terms of paragraph (d) of this section.

§372.213 Pueblo, CO.

The zone adjacent to, and commercially a part of Pueblo, Colo., within which transportation by motor vehicle in interstate or foreign commerce, not under common control, management, or arrangement for a continuous carriage or shipment to or from a point beyond such zone, is partially exempt from regulations under 49 U.S.C. 13506(b)(1) includes and is comprised of all points as follows:

(a) **The municipality of Pueblo, Colo., itself;**
(b) **All points within a line drawn 6 miles** beyond the municipal limits of Pueblo;
(c) **Those points in Pueblo County, Colo.,** which are not within the area described in paragraph (b) of this section;
(d) **All of any municipality any part of which** is within the limits of the combined areas defined in paragraphs (b) and (c) of this section, and
(e) **All of any municipality wholly surrounded,** or so surrounded except for a water boundary, by the municipality included under the terms of paragraph (d) of this section.

§372.215 Ravenswood, WV.

The zone adjacent to, and commercially a part of Ravenswood, W. Va., within which transportation by motor vehicle in interstate or foreign commerce, not under common control, management, or arrangement for a continuous carriage or shipment to or from a point beyond such zone, is partially exempt from regulation under 49 U.S.C. 13506(b)(1) includes and is comprised of all points as follows:

(a) **The municipality of Ravenswood, W. Va., itself;**
(b) **All points within a line drawn 4 miles** beyond the municipal limits of Ravenswood;
(c) **Those points in Jackson County, W. Va.,** which are not within the area described in paragraph (b) of this section, and which are north of U.S. Highway 33;
(d) **All of any municipality any part of which** is within the limits of the combined areas defined in paragraphs (b) and (c) of this section, and
(e) **All of any municipality wholly surrounded,** or so surrounded except for a water boundary, by the municipality of Ravenswood or by any other municipality included under the terms of paragraph (d) of this section.

§372.217 Seattle, WA.

The zone adjacent to, and commercially a part of Seattle, Wash., within which transportation by motor vehicle in interstate or foreign commerce, not under common control, management, or arrangement for a continuous carriage or shipment to or from a point beyond such zone, is partially exempt from regulation under 49 U.S.C. 13506(b)(1) includes and is comprised of all points as follows:

(a) **The municipality of Seattle, Wash., itself;**
(b) **All points within a line drawn 15 miles** beyond the municipal limits of Seattle;
(c) **Those points in King County, Wash.,** which are not within the area described in paragraph (b) of this section, and which are west of a line beginning at the intersection of the line described in paragraph (b) of this section and Washington Highway 18, thence northerly along Washington Highway 18 to junction of Interstate Highway 90, thence westerly along Interstate Highway 90 to junction Washington Highway 203, thence northerly along Washington Highway 203 to the King County line; and those points in Snohomish County, Wash., which are not within the area described in paragraph (b) of this section and which are west of Washington Highway 9; and those points in Kitsap County, Wash., which are not within the area described in paragraph (b) of this section lying within the area bounded by a line beginning at the intersection of the line described in paragraph (b) of this section and Washington Highway 3 to the boundary of Olympic View Industrial Park/Bremerton-Kitsap County Airport, thence westerly, southerly, easterly, and northerly along the boundary of Olympic View Industrial Park/Bremerton-Kitsap County Airport to its juncture with Washington Highway 3 to its intersection with the line described in paragraph (b) of this section.
(d) **All of any municipality any part of which** is within the limits of the combined areas defined in paragraphs (b) and (c) of this section, and
(e) **All of any municipality wholly surrounded,** or so surrounded except for a water boundary, by the municipality of Seattle or by any other municipality included under the terms of paragraph (d) of this section.

§372.219 Washington, DC.

The zone adjacent to, and commercially a part of Washington, D.C., within which transportation by motor vehicle in interstate or foreign commerce, not under common control, management, or arrangement for a continuous carriage or shipment to or from a point beyond such zone, is partially exempt from regulation under 49 U.S.C. 13506(b)(1) includes and is comprised of all points as follows:

(a) **The municipality of Washington, D.C., itself;**
(b) **All points within a line drawn 15 miles** beyond the municipal limits of Washington, DC
(c) **All points in Fairfax and Loudoun Counties, VA,** and all points in Prince William County, VA, including the City of Manassas, VA, and the City of Manassas Park, VA.
(d) **All of any municipality any part of which** is within the limits of the combined areas defined in paragraphs (b) and (c) of this section, and
(e) **All of any municipality wholly surrounded,** or so surrounded except for a water boundary, by the municipality of Washington, D.C., or by any other municipality included under the terms of paragraph (d) of this section.

§372.221 Twin Cities.

For the purpose of determining commercial zones, utilizing the general population-mileage formula as set forth in §372.241, each of the following combinations of cities shall be considered as a single municipality:

(a) **Having a population equal to the sum** of their combined populations, and
(b) **Having boundaries comprised** of their combined corporate limits, with the common portion thereof disregarded:
  (1) Bluefield, Va.-W. Va.
  (2) Bristol, Va.-Tenn.
  (3) Davenport, Iowa, and Rock Island and Moline, Ill.
  (4) Delmar, Del-Md.
  (5) Harrison, Ohio-West Harrison, Ind.
  (6) Junction City, Ark.-La.
  (7) Kansas City, Mo.-Kansas City, Kans.
  (8) Minneapolis-St. Paul, Minn.
  (9) St. Louis, Mo.-East St. Louis, Ill.
  (10) Texarkana, Ark.-Tex.
  (11) Texhoma, Tex.-Okla.
  (12) Union City, Ind.-Ohio.

§372.223 Consolidated governments.

The zone adjacent to, and commercially a part of a consolidated government within which transportation by motor vehicle, in interstate or foreign commerce, not under common control, management, or arrangement for a continuous carriage or shipment to or from a point beyond the zone, is partially exempt from regulation under 49 U.S.C. 13506(b)(1) includes and is comprised of all points as follows:

(a) **All points within the boundaries of the consolidated government.**
(b) **All points beyond the boundaries** of the consolidated government which were at any time within the commercial zone of the formerly independent core municipality.
(c) **When the present population** of the formerly independent core municipality is identifiable, all points beyond the boundaries of the consolidated government which are within the territory determined by the most recent population-mileage formula measured from the limits of the formerly independent core municipality.
(d) **All of any municipality wholly surrounded,** or so surrounded except for a water boundary, by the consolidated government or by any other municipality included under the terms of paragraphs (a), (b), or (c) of this section.

§372.225 Lexington-Fayette Urban County, KY.

The zone adjacent to and commercially a part of Lexington-Fayette Urban County, Ky., within which transportation by motor vehicle, in interstate or foreign commerce, not under a common control, management, or arrangement for a continuous carriage or shipment to or from a point beyond the zone, is partially exempt from regulation under 49 U.S.C. 13506(b)(1) includes and is comprised of all points as follows:

(a) **Lexington-Fayette Urban County, Ky., itself.**
(b) **All other municipalities and unincorporated areas** within 5 miles of the intersection of U.S. Highway 27 (Nicholasville Road) with the corporate boundary line between Jessamine County, Ky., and Lexington-Fayette Urban County, Ky.

§372.227 Syracuse, NY.

The zone adjacent to, and commercially a part of Syracuse, N.Y., within which transportation by motor vehicle, in interstate or foreign commerce, not under common control, management, or arrangement for shipment to or from points beyond such zone, is partially exempt from regulation under 49 U.S.C. 13506(b)(1) includes and is comprised of all points as follows:

(a) **The municipality of Syracuse, N.Y., itself;**
(b) **All points within a line drawn 10 miles** beyond the municipal limits of Syracuse;
(c) **Those points in the towns** of Van Buren and Lysander, Onondaga County, N.Y., which are not within the area described in paragraph (b) of this section, but which are within an area bounded by a line beginning at the intersection of new New York Highway 48 with the line described in (b) of this section, thence northwesterly along new New York Highway 48 to junction New York Highway 370, thence westerly along New York Highway 370 to junction Emerick Road, thence northerly along Emerick Road to junction Dunham Road, thence northerly along Dunham road to junction New York Highway 192, thence easterly along New York Highway 192 to junction new New York Highway 48, thence northerly along new New York Highway 48 to junction New York Highway 213, thence easterly along New York Highway 213 to junction New York Highway 213A, thence easterly along New York Highway 213A to junction New York Highway 37, thence southerly along New York Highway 37 to its intersection with the line in (b) above;
(d) **All of any municipality any part of which** is within the limits of the combined area defined in (b) and (c) of this section, and
(e) **All of any municipality wholly surrounded,** or so surrounded except for a water boundary, by the municipality of Syracuse or any other municipality included under the terms of (d) of this section.

§372.229 Spokane, WA.

The zone adjacent to, and commercially a part of Spokane, WA, within which transportation by motor vehicle, in interstate or foreign commerce, not under control, management, or arrangement for shipment to or from points beyond such zone, is partially exempt from regulation under 49 U.S.C. 13506(b)(1) includes and is comprised of all points as follows:

(a) **The municipality of Spokane, WA, itself,**
(b) **All points within a line drawn 8 miles** beyond the municipal limits of Spokane;
(c) **All points within that area more than 8 miles** beyond the municipal limits of Spokane bounded by a line as follows: From the intersection of the line described in (b) of this section and U.S. Highway 2, thence westerly along U.S. Highway 2 to junction Brooks Road, thence southerly along Brooks Road to junction Hallett Road, thence easterly along Hallett Road to its intersection with the line described in (b) of this section;
(d) **All of any municipality any part of which** is within the limits of the combined areas in (b) and (c) of this section; and
(e) **All of any municipality wholly surrounded,** or so surrounded except for a water boundary, by the municipality of Spokane or any other municipality included under the terms of (d) of this section.

§372.231 Tacoma, WA.

The zone adjacent to, and commercially a part of Tacoma, WA, within which transportation by motor vehicle, in interstate or foreign commerce, not under common control, management, or arrangement for shipment to or from points beyond such zone, is partially exempt from regulation under 49 U.S.C. 13506(b)(1), includes and is comprised of all points as follows:

(a) **The municipality of Tacoma, WA, itself;**
(b) **All points within a line drawn 8 miles** beyond the municipal limits of Tacoma;
(c) **Those points in Pierce County, WA,** which are not within the area described in paragraph (b) of this section, but which are on Washington Highway 162 beginning at its intersection with the line described in paragraph (b) of this section, extending to and including Orting, WA, and all points within the Orting commercial zone.
(d) **All of any municipality any part of which** is within the limits of the combined area defined in (b) and (c) of this section, and
(e) **All of any municipality wholly surrounded,** or so surrounded except for a water boundary, by the municipality of Tacoma or any other municipality included under the terms of (d) of this section.

§372.233 Chicago, IL.

The zone adjacent to, and commercially a part of Chicago, IL, within which transportation by motor vehicle, in interstate or foreign commerce, not under common control, management, or arrangement for a shipment to or from such zone, is partially exempt from regulation under 49 U.S.C. 13506(b)(1), includes and is comprised of all points as follows:

(a) **The municipality of Chicago, IL, itself;**
(b) **All points within a line drawn 20 miles** beyond the municipal limits of Chicago;
(c) **All points in Lake County, IL.**
(d) **All of any municipality any part of which** is within the limits of the combined area defined in paragraphs (b) and (c) of this section, and
(e) **All of any municipality wholly surrounded,** or so surrounded except for a water boundary, by the municipality included under the terms of paragraph (d) of this section.

§372.235 New York, NY.

The zone adjacent to, and commercially a part of, New York, NY, within which transportation by motor vehicle, in interstate or foreign commerce, not under common control, management, or arrangement for shipment to or from points beyond such zone is partially exempt from regulation under 49 U.S.C. 13506(b)(1), includes and is comprised of all points as follows:

(a) The municipality of New York, NY, itself;
(b) All points within a line drawn 20 miles beyond the municipal limits of New York, NY;
(c) All points in Morris County, NJ;
(d) All of any municipality any part of which is within the limits of the combined areas defined in paragraphs (b) and (c); and
(e) All of any municipality wholly surrounded, or so surrounded except by a water boundary, by the municipality of New York or by any other municipality included under the terms of paragraph (d) of this section.

§372.237 Cameron, Hidalgo, Starr, and Willacy Counties, TX.

(a) Transportation within a zone comprised of Cameron, Hidalgo, Starr, and Willacy Counties, TX, by motor carriers of property, in interstate or foreign commerce, not under common control, management, or arrangement for shipment to or from points beyond such zone, is partially exempt from regulation under 49 U.S.C. 13506(b)(1).
(b) To the extent that commercial zones of municipalities within the four counties (as determined under §372.241) extend beyond the boundaries of this four-county zone, the areas of such commercial zones shall be considered to be part of the zone and partially exempt from regulation under 49 U.S.C. 13506(b)(1).

§372.239 Definitions.

For the purposes of this part, the following terms are defined:

(a) **Municipality** means any city, town, village, or borough which has been created by special legislative act or which has been, otherwise, individually incorporated or chartered pursuant to general State laws, or which is recognized as such, under the Constitution or by the laws of the State in which located, and which has a local government. It does not include a town of the township or New England type.
(b) **Contiguous municipalities** means municipalities, as defined in paragraph (a) of this section, which have at some point a common municipal or corporate boundary.
(c) **Unincorporated area** means any area not within the corporate or municipal boundaries of any municipality as defined in paragraph (a) of this section.

§372.241 Commercial zones determined generally, with exceptions.

The commercial zone of each municipality in the United States, with the exceptions indicated in the note at the end of this section, within which the transportation of passengers or property, in interstate or foreign commerce, when not under a common control, management, or arrangement for a continuous carriage or shipment to or from a point without such zone, is exempt from all provisions of 49 U.S.C. Subtitle IV, Part B shall be deemed to consist of:

(a) The municipality itself, hereinafter called the base municipality;
(b) All municipalities which are contiguous to the base municipality;
(c) All other municipalities and all unincorporated areas within the United States which are adjacent to the base municipality as follows:
  (1) When the base municipality has a population less than 2,500 all unincorporated areas within 3 miles of its corporate limits and all of any other municipality any part of which is within 3 miles of the corporate limits of the base municipality,
  (2) When the base municipality has a population of 2,500 but less than 25,000 all unincorporated areas within 4 miles of its corporate limits and all of any other municipality any part of which is within 4 miles of the corporate limits of the base municipality.
  (3) When the base municipality has a population of 25,000 but less than 100,000 all unincorporated areas within 6 miles of its corporate limits and all of any other municipality any part of which is within 6 miles of the corporate limits of the base municipality, and
  (4) When the base municipality has a population of 100,000 but less than 200,000 all unincorporated areas within 8 miles of its corporate limits and all of any other municipality any part of which is within 8 miles of the corporate limits of the base municipality.
  (5) When the base municipality has a population of 200,000 but less than 500,000 all unincorporated areas within 10 miles of its corporate limits and all of any other municipality any part of which is within 10 miles of the corporate limits of the base municipality.
  (6) When the base municipality has a population of 500,000 but less than 1 million, all unincorporated areas within 15 miles of its corporate limits and all of any other municipality any part of which is within 15 miles of the corporate limits of the base municipality.
  (7) When the base municipality has a population of 1 million or more, all unincorporated areas within 20 miles of its corporate limits and all of any other municipality any part of which is within 20 miles of the corporate limits of the base municipality, and
(d) All municipalities wholly surrounded, or so surrounded except for a water boundary, by the base municipality, by any municipality contiguous thereto, or by any municipality adjacent thereto which is included in the commercial zone of such base municipality under the provisions of paragraph (c) of this section.

NOTE: Except: Municipalities the commercial zones of which have been or are hereafter individually or specially determined.

§372.243 Controlling distances and population data.

In the application of §372.241:

(a) Air-line distances or mileages about corporate limits of municipalities shall be used.
(b) The population of any municipality shall be deemed to be the highest figure shown for that municipality in any decennial census since (and including) the 1940 decennial census.
(c) Contraction of municipal boundaries will not alter the size of commercial zones.

Subpart C - Terminal Areas

§372.300 Distances and population data.

In the application of this subpart, distances and population data shall be determined in the same manner as provided in 49 CFR 372.243. See also definitions in 49 CFR 372.239.

§372.301 Terminal areas of motor carriers and freight forwarders at municipalities served.

The terminal area within the meaning of 49 U.S.C. 13503 of any motor carrier of property or freight forwarder subject to 49 U.S.C. Subtitle IV, Part B at any municipality authorized to be served by such motor carrier of property or motor carrier of passengers in the transportation of express or freight forwarder, within which transportation by motor carrier in the performance of transfer, collection, or delivery services may be performed by, or for, such motor carrier of property or freight forwarder without compliance with the provisions of 49 U.S.C. Subtitle IV, Part B consists of and includes all points or places which are:

(a) Within the commercial zone, as defined by the Secretary, of that municipality, and
(b) Not beyond the limits of the operating authority of such motor carrier of property or freight forwarder.

§372.303 Terminal areas of motor carriers and freight forwarders at unincorporated communities served.

The terminal areas within the meaning of 49 U.S.C. 13503 of any motor carrier of property or freight forwarder subject to 49 U.S.C. Subtitle IV, Part B, at any unincorporated community having a post office of the same name which is authorized to be served by such motor carrier of property or motor carrier of passengers in the transportation of express or freight forwarder, within which transportation by motor vehicle in the performance of transfer, collection, or delivery services may be performed by, or for, such motor carrier of property or freight forwarder without compliance with the provisions of 49 U.S.C. Subtitle IV, Part B, consists of:

(a) All points in the United States which are located within the limits of the operating authority of the motor carrier of property or freight forwarder involved, and within 3 miles of the post office at such authorized unincorporated point if it has a population less than 2,500, within 4 miles if it has a population of 2,500 but less than 25,000, or within 6 miles if it has a population of 25,000 or more;
(b) All of any municipality any part of which is included under paragraph (a) of this section; and
(c) Any municipality wholly surrounded by any municipality included under paragraph (b) of this section, or so wholly surrounded except for a water boundary.

Part 373 - Receipts and Bills

Subpart A - Motor Carrier Receipts and Bills

§373.101 Motor Carrier bills of lading.

Every motor common carrier shall issue a receipt or bill of lading for property tendered for transportation in interstate or foreign commerce containing the following information:
(a) *Names of consignor and consignee.*
(b) *Origin and destination points.*
(c) *Number of packages.*
(d) *Description of freight.*
(e) *Weight, volume, or measurement of freight* (if applicable to the rating of the freight).

The carrier shall keep a record of this information as prescribed in 49 CFR Part 379.

§373.103 Expense bills.

(a) *Property.* Every motor common carrier shall issue a freight or expense bill for each shipment transported containing the following information:
(1) *Names of consignor and consignee* (except on a reconsigned shipment, not the name of the original consignor).
(2) *Date of shipment.*
(3) *Origin and destination points* (except on a reconsigned shipment, not the original shipping point unless the final consignee pays the charges from that point).
(4) *Number of packages.*
(5) *Description of freight.*
(6) *Weight, volume, or measurement of freight* (if applicable to the rating of the freight).
(7) *Exact rate(s) assessed.*
(8) *Total charges due,* including the nature and amount of any charges for special service and the points at which such service was rendered.
(9) *Route of movement* and name of each carrier participating in the transportation.
(10) *Transfer point(s) through which shipment moved.*
(11) *Address where remittance must be made* or address of bill issuer's principal place of business.

The shipper or receiver owing the charges shall be given the original freight or expense bill and the carrier shall keep a copy as prescribed at 49 CFR Part 379. If the bill is electronically transmitted (when agreed to by the carrier and payor), a receipted copy shall be given to the payor upon payment.

(b) *Charter service.* Every motor passenger common carrier providing charter service shall issue an expense bill containing the following information:
(1) *Serial number,* consisting of one of a series of consecutive numbers assigned in advance and imprinted on the bill.
(2) *Name of carrier.*
(3) *Names of payor and organization,* if any, for which transportation is performed.
(4) *Date(s) transportation was performed.*
(5) *Origin, destination, and general routing of trip.*
(6) *Identification and seating capacity of each vehicle used.*
(7) *Number of persons transported.*
(8) *Mileage upon which charges are based,* including any deadhead mileage, separately noted.
(9) *Applicable rates per mile, hour, day, or other unit.*
(10) *Itemized charges for transportation,* including special services and fees.
(11) *Total charges assessed and collected.*

The carrier shall keep a copy of all expense bills issued for the period prescribed at 49 CFR Part 379. If any expense bill is spoiled, voided, or unused for any reason, a copy or written record of its disposition shall be retained for a like period.

§373.105 Low value packages.

The carrier and shipper may elect to waive the above provisions and use a more streamlined recordkeeping or documentation system for distribution of "low value" packages. This includes the option of shipping such packages under the provisions of 49 U.S.C. 14706(c). The shipper is responsible ultimately for determining which packages should be designated as low value. A useful guideline for this determination is an invoice value less than or equal to the costs of preparing a loss or damage claim.

Subpart B - Freight Forwarders; Bills of Lading

§373.201 Bills of lading for freight forwarders.

Every household goods freight forwarder (HHGFF) shall issue the shipper through bills of lading, covering transportation from origin to ultimate destination, on each shipment for which it arranges transportation in interstate commerce. Where a motor common carrier receives freight at the origin and issues a receipt therefor on its form with a notation showing the HHGFF's name, the HHGFF, upon receiving the shipment at the "on line" or consolidating station, shall issue a through bill of lading on its form as of the date the carrier receives the shipment.

Part 373 - Receipts and Bills

Notes

Part 374 - Passenger Carrier Regulations

Subpart A - Discrimination in Operations of Interstate Motor Common Carriers of Passengers

§374.101 Discrimination prohibited.

No motor common carrier of passengers subject to 49 U.S.C. Subtitle IV, Part B shall operate a motor vehicle in interstate or foreign commerce on which the seating of passengers is based upon race, color, creed, or national origin.

§374.103 Notice to be printed on tickets.

Every motor common carrier of passengers subject to 49 U.S.C. Subtitle IV, Part B shall cause to be printed on every ticket sold by it for transportation on any vehicle operated in interstate or foreign commerce a plainly legible notice as follows: "Seating aboard vehicles operated in interstate or foreign commerce is without regard to race, color, creed, or national origin."

NOTE: The following interpretation of the provisions of §374.103 (formerly §1055.2) appears at 27 FR 230, Jan. 9, 1962:
The words, "Seating aboard vehicles operated in interstate or foreign commerce is without regard to race, color, creed, or national origin", should appear on the face of every ticket coming within the purview of the section. If the ticket is in parts or consists of additional elements, such as coupons, identification stubs, or checks, it shall be sufficient for the purposes of §374.103 that the notice appear only once on the ticket and be placed on the face of that portion of the ticket which is held by the passenger.

§374.105 Discrimination in terminal facilities.

No motor common carrier of passengers subject to 49 U.S.C. Subtitle IV, Part B shall in the operation of vehicles in interstate or foreign commerce provide, maintain arrangements for, utilize, make available, adhere to any understanding for the availability of, or follow any practice which includes the availability of, any terminal facilities which are so operated, arranged, or maintained as to involve any separation of any portion thereof, or in the use thereof on the basis of race, color, creed, or national origin.

§374.107 Notice to be posted at terminal facilities.

No motor common carrier of passengers subject to 49 U.S.C. Subtitle IV, Part B shall in the operation of vehicles in interstate or foreign commerce utilize any terminal facility in which there is not conspicuously displayed and maintained so as to be readily visible to the public a plainly legible sign or placard containing the full text of these regulations. Such sign or placard shall be captioned: "Public Notice: Regulations Applicable to Vehicles and Terminal Facilities of Interstate Motor Common Carriers of Passengers, by order of the Secretary, U.S. Department of Transportation."

§374.109 Carriers not relieved of existing obligations.

Nothing in this regulation shall be construed to relieve any interstate motor common carrier of passengers subject to 49 U.S.C. Subtitle IV, Part B of any of its obligations under 49 U.S.C. Subtitle IV, Part B or its certificate(s) of public convenience and necessity.

§374.111 Reports of interference with regulations.

Every motor common carrier of passengers subject to 49 U.S.C. Subtitle IV, Part B operating vehicles in interstate or foreign commerce shall report to the Secretary, within fifteen (15) days of its occurrence, any interference by any person, municipality, county, parish, State, or body politic with its observance of the requirements of these regulations in this part. Such report shall include a statement of the action that such carrier may have taken to eliminate any such interference.

§374.113 Definitions.

For the purpose of these regulations the following terms and phrases are defined:

(a) **Terminal facilities.** As used in these regulations the term "terminal facilities" means all facilities, including waiting room, rest room, eating, drinking, and ticket sales facilities which a motor common carrier makes available to passengers of a motor vehicle operated in interstate or foreign commerce as a regular part of their transportation.

(b) **Separation.** As used in §374.105, the term "separation" includes, among other things, the display of any sign indicating that any portion of the terminal facilities are separated, allocated, restricted, provided, available, used, or otherwise distinguished on the basis of race, color, creed, or national origin.

Subpart B - Limitation of Smoking on Interstate Passenger Carrier Vehicles

§374.201 Prohibition against smoking on interstate passenger-carrying motor vehicles.

(a) All motor common carriers of passengers subject to 49 U.S.C. Subtitle IV, Part B, shall prohibit smoking (including the carrying of lit cigars, cigarettes, and pipes) on vehicles transporting passengers in scheduled or special service in interstate commerce.

(b) Each carrier shall take such action as is necessary to ensure that smoking by passengers, drivers, and other employees is not permitted in violation of this section. This shall include making appropriate announcements to passengers, the posting of the international no-smoking symbol, and the posting of signs in all vehicles transporting passengers in letters in sharp color contrast to the background, and of such size, shape, and color as to be readily legible. Such signs and symbols shall be kept and maintained in such a manner as to remain legible and shall indicate that smoking is prohibited by Federal regulation.

(c) The provisions of paragraph (a) of this section shall not apply to charter operations as defined in §374.503 of this part.

Subpart C - Adequacy of Intercity Motor Common Carrier Passenger Service

§374.301 Applicability.

These rules govern only motor passenger common carriers conducting regular-route operations.

§374.303 Definitions.

(a) **Carrier** means a motor passenger common carrier.
(b) **Bus** means a passenger-carrying vehicle, regardless of design or seating capacity, used in a carrier's authorized operations.
(c) **Facility** means any structure provided by or for a carrier at or near which buses pick up or discharge passengers.
(d) **Terminal** means a facility operated or used by a carrier chiefly to furnish passengers transportation services and accommodations.
(e) **Station** means a facility, other than a terminal, operated by or for a carrier to accommodate passengers.
(f) **Service** means passenger transportation by bus between authorized points or over authorized routes.
(g) **Commuter service** means passenger transportation wholly between points not more than 100 airline miles apart and not involving through-bus, connecting, or interline services to or from points beyond 100 airline miles. The usual characteristics of commuter service include reduced fare, multiple-ride, and commutation tickets, and peak morning and evening operations.
(h) **Baggage** means property a passenger takes with him for his personal use or convenience.
(i) **Restroom** means a room in a bus or terminal equipped with a toilet, washbowl, soap or a reasonable alternative, mirror, wastebasket, and toilet paper.

§374.305 Ticketing and information.

(a) Information service.
  (1) *During business hours* at each terminal or station, information shall be provided as to schedules, tickets, fares, baggage, and other carrier services.
  (2) *Carrier agents and personnel* who sell or offer to sell tickets, or who provide information concerning tickets and carrier services, shall be competent and adequately informed.

(b) Telephone information service. Every facility where tickets are sold shall provide telephonic information to the traveling public, including current bus schedules and fare information, when open for ticket sales.

(c) Schedules. Printed, regular-route schedules shall be provided to the traveling public at all facilities where tickets for such services are sold. Each schedule shall show the points along the carrier's route(s) where facilities are located or where the bus trips originate or terminate, and each schedule shall indicate the arrival or departure time for each such point.

(d) Ticket refunds. Each carrier shall refund unused tickets upon request, consistent with its governing tariff, at each place where tickets are sold, within 30 days after the request.

(e) Announcements. No scheduled bus (except in commuter service) shall depart from a terminal or station until a public announcement of the departure and boarding point has been given. The announcement shall be given at least 5 minutes before the initial departure and before departures from points where the bus is scheduled to stop for more than 5 minutes.

§374.307 Baggage service.

(a) Checking procedures.
(1) *Carriers shall issue receipts,* which may be in the form of preprinted tickets, for all checked services baggage.
(2) (i) *If baggage checking service* is not provided at the side of the bus, all baggage checked at a baggage checking counter at least 30 minutes but not more than 1 hour before departure shall be transported on the same schedule as the ticketed passenger.
(ii) *If baggage checking service* is provided at the side of the bus, passengers checking baggage at the baggage checking counter less than 30 minutes before the scheduled departure shall be notified that their baggage may not travel on the same schedule. Such baggage must then be placed on the next available bus to its destination. All baggage checked at the side of the bus during boarding, or at alternative locations provided for such purpose, shall be transported on the same schedule as the ticketed passenger.

(b) Baggage security. All checked baggage shall be placed in a secure or attended area prohibited to the public. Baggage being readied for loading shall not be left unattended.

(c) Baggage liability.
(1) *No carrier may totally exempt its liability* for articles offered as checked baggage, unless those articles have been exempted by the Secretary. (Other liability is subject to Subpart D of this part). A notice listing exempted articles shall be prominently posted at every location where baggage is accepted for checking.
(2) *Carriers may refuse to accept as checked baggage* and, if unknowingly accepted, may disclaim liability for loss or damage to the following articles:
(i) *Articles whose transportation as checked baggage* is prohibited by law or regulation;
(ii) *Fragile or perishable articles,* articles whose dimensions exceed the size limitations in the carrier's tariff, receptacles with articles attached or protruding, guns, and materials that have a disagreeable odor;
(iii) *Money;* and
(iv) *Those other articles that the Secretary exempts* upon petition by the carrier.
(3) *Carriers need not offer excess value coverage* on articles of extraordinary value (including, but not limited to, negotiable instruments, papers, manuscripts, irreplaceable publications, documents, jewelry, and watches).

(d) Express shipments. Passengers and their baggage always take precedence over express shipments.

(e) Baggage at destination. All checked baggage shall be made available to the passenger within a reasonable time, not to exceed 30 minutes, after arrival at the passenger's destination. If not, the carrier shall deliver the baggage to the passenger's local address at the carrier's expense.

(f) Lost or delayed baggage.
(1) *Checked baggage that cannot be located* within 1 hour after the arrival of the bus upon which it was supposed to be transported shall be designated as lost. The carrier shall notify the passenger at that time and furnish him with an appropriate tracing form.
(2) *Every carrier shall make available* at each ticket window and baggage counter a single form suitable both for tracing and for filing claims for lost or misplaced baggage. The form shall be prepared in duplicate and signed by the passenger and carrier representative. The carrier or its agent shall receive the signed original, with any necessary documentation and additional information, and the claim check, for which a receipt shall be given. The passenger shall retain the duplicate copy.
(3) *The carrier shall make* immediate and diligent efforts to recover lost baggage.
(4) *A passenger may fill out a tracing form* for lost unchecked baggage. The carrier shall forward recovered unchecked baggage to the terminal or station nearest the address shown on the tracing form and shall notify the passenger that the baggage will be held on a will-call basis.

(g) Settlement of claims. Notwithstanding 49 CFR 370.9, if lost checked baggage cannot be located within 15 days, the carrier shall immediately process the matter as a claim. The date on which the carrier or its agent received the tracing form shall be considered the first day of a 60-day period in which a claim must be resolved by a firm offer of settlement or by a written explanation of denial of the claim.

§374.309 Terminal facilities.

(a) Passenger security. All terminals and stations must provide adequate security for passengers and their attendants and be regularly patrolled.

(b) Outside facilities. At terminals and stations that are closed when buses are scheduled to arrive or depart, there shall be available, to the extent possible, a public telephone, outside lighting, posted schedule information, overhead shelter, information on local accommodations, and telephone numbers for local taxi service and police.

(c) Maintenance. Terminals shall be clean.

§374.311 Service responsibility.

(a) Schedules. Carriers shall establish schedules that can be reasonably met, including connections at junction points, to serve adequately all authorized points.

(b) Continuity of service. No carrier shall change an existing regular-route schedule without first filing a written notice with the FMCSA's Division Office(s). The carrier shall display conspicuously a copy of such notice in each facility and on each bus affected. Such notice shall be displayed for a reasonable time before it becomes effective and shall contain the carrier's name, a description of the proposed schedule change, the effective date thereof, the reasons for the change, the availability of alternate service, and the name and address of the carrier representative passengers may contact.

(c) Trip interruptions. A carrier shall mitigate, to the extent possible, any passenger inconvenience it causes by disrupting travel plans.

(d) Seating and reservations. A carrier shall provide sufficient buses to meet passengers' normal travel demands, including ordinary weekend and usual seasonal or holiday demand. Passengers (except commuters) shall be guaranteed, to the extent possible, passage and seating.

(e) Inspection of rest stops. Each carrier shall inspect periodically all rest stops it uses to ensure that they are clean.

§374.313 Equipment.

(a) Temperature control. A carrier shall maintain a reasonable temperature on each bus (except in commuter service).

(b) Restrooms. Each bus (except in commuter service) seating more than 14 passengers (not including the driver) shall have a clean, regularly maintained restroom, free of offensive odor. A bus may be operated without a restroom if it makes reasonable rest stops.

(c) Bus servicing. Each bus shall be kept clean, with all required items in good working order.

§374.315 Transportation of passengers with disabilities.

Service provided by a carrier to passengers with disabilities is governed by the provisions of 42 U.S.C. 12101 et seq., and regulations promulgated thereunder by the Secretary of Transportation (49 CFR Parts 27, 37, and 38) and the Attorney General (28 CFR Part 36), incorporating the guidelines established by the Architectural and Transportation Barriers Compliance Board (36 CFR Part 1191).

§374.317 Identification — bus and driver.

Each bus and driver providing service shall be identified in a manner visible to passengers. The driver may be identified by name or company number.

§374.319 Relief from provisions.

(a) Petitions. Where compliance with any rule would impose an undue burden on a carrier, it may petition the Federal Motor Carrier Safety Administration either to treat it as though it were conducting a commuter service or to waive the rule. The request for relief must be justified by appropriate verified statements.

(b) Notice to the public. The carrier shall display conspicuously, for at least 30 days, in each facility and on each bus affected, a notice of the filing of any petition. The notice shall contain the carrier's name and address, a concise description of and reasons for the relief sought, and a statement that any interested person may file written comments with the Federal Motor Carrier Safety Administration (with one copy mailed to the carrier) on or before a specific date that is at least 30 days later than the date the notice is posted.

Subpart D - Notice of and Procedures for Baggage Excess Value Declaration

§374.401 Minimum permissible limitations for baggage liability.

(a) **Motor common carriers of passengers and baggage** subject to 49 U.S.C. 13501 may not publish tariff provisions limiting their liability for loss or damage to baggage checked by a passenger transported in regular route or special operations unless:

(1) *The amount for which liability is limited* is $250 or greater per adult fare, and

(2) *The provisions permit the passenger,* for an additional charge, to declare a value in excess of the limited amount, and allow the passenger to recover the increased amount (but not higher than the actual value) in event of loss or damage. The carriers may publish a maximum value for which they will be liable, but that maximum value may not be less than $1,000. Appropriate identification must be attached securely by the passenger to each item of baggage checked, indicating in a clear and legible manner the name and address to which the baggage should be forwarded if lost and subsequently recovered. Identification tags shall be made immediately available by the carriers to passengers upon request.

(3) *Carriers need not offer excess value coverage* on articles listed in §374.307(c)(3).

§374.403 Notice of passenger's ability to declare excess value on baggage.

(a) **All motor common carriers** of passengers and baggage subject to 49 U.S.C. Subtitle IV, Part B, which provide in their tariffs for the declaration of baggage in excess of a free baggage allowance limitation, shall provide clear and adequate notice to the public of the opportunity to declare such excess value on baggage.

(b) **The notice referred to in paragraph (a)** of this section shall be in large and clear print, and shall state as follows:

Notice — Baggage Liability

This motor carrier is not liable for loss or damage to properly identified baggage in an amount exceeding $____. If a passenger desires additional coverage for the value of his baggage he may, upon checking his baggage, declare that his baggage has a value in excess of the above limitation and pay a charge as follows:

Identify Your Baggage

Under FMCSA regulations, all baggage must be properly identified. Luggage tags should indicate clearly the name and address to which lost baggage should be forwarded. Free luggage tags are available at all ticket windows and baggage counters.

The statement of charges for excess value declaration shall be clear, and any other pertinent provisions may be added at the bottom in clear and readable print.

(c) **The notice referred to in paragraphs (a) and (b)** of this section shall be (1) placed in a position near the ticket seller, sufficiently conspicuous to apprise the public of its provisions, (2) placed on a form to be attached to each ticket issued (and the ticket seller shall, where possible, provide oral notice to each ticket purchaser to read the form attached to the ticket), (3) placed in a position at or near any location where baggage may be checked, sufficiently conspicuous to apprise each passenger checking baggage of its provisions, and (4) placed in a position at each boarding point or waiting area used by the carrier at facilities maintained by the carrier or its agents, sufficiently conspicuous to apprise each boarding passenger of the provisions of the said notice.

§374.405 Baggage excess value declaration procedures.

All motor common carriers of passengers and baggage subject to 49 U.S.C. Subtitle IV, Part B, which provide in their tariffs for the declaration of baggage value in excess of a free baggage allowance limitation, shall provide for the declaration of excess value on baggage at any time or place where provision is made for baggage checking, including (a) at a baggage checking counter until 15 minutes before scheduled boarding time, and (b) at the side of the bus or at a baggage checking counter in reasonable proximity to the boarding area during boarding at a terminal or any authorized service point.

Subpart E - Incidental Charter Rights

§374.501 Applicability.

The regulations in this part apply to incidental charter rights authorized under 49 U.S.C. 13506 [49 U.S.C. 10932(c)]. These regulations do not apply to interpreting authority contained in a certificate to transport passengers in special and/or charter operations.

§374.503 Authority.

Motor carriers transporting passengers, in interstate or foreign commerce, over regular routes authorized in a certificate issued as a result of an application filed before January 2, 1967, may transport special or chartered parties, in interstate or foreign commerce, between any points and places in the United States (including Alaska and Hawaii). The term "special or chartered party" means a group of passengers who, with a common purpose and under a single contract, and at a fixed charge for the vehicle in accordance with the carrier's tariff, have acquired the exclusive use of a passenger-carrying motor vehicle to travel together as a group to a specified destination or for a particular itinerary.

§374.505 Exceptions.

(a) **Incidental charter rights do not authorize** the transportation of passengers to whom the carrier has sold individual tickets or with whom the carrier has made separate and individual transportation arrangements.

(b) **Service provided under incidental charter rights** may not be operated between the same points or over the same route so frequently as to constitute a regular-route service.

(c) **Passenger transportation within** the Washington Metropolitan Area Transit District (as defined in the Washington Metropolitan Area Transportation Regulation Compact, Pub. L. No. 86-794, 74 Stat. 1031 (1960), as amended by Pub. L. No. 87-767, 76 Stat. (1962) is not authorized by these regulations, but is subject to the jurisdiction and regulations of the Washington Metropolitan Area Transportation Commission.

(d) **A private or public recipient** of governmental assistance (within the meaning of 49 U.S.C. 13902(b)(8)) may provide service under incidental charter rights only for special or chartered parties originating in the area in which the private or public recipient provides regularly scheduled mass transportation services under the specific qualifying certificate that confers its incidental charter rights.

Part 374 - Passenger Carrier Regulations

Notes

Part 375 - Transportation of Household Goods in Interstate Commerce; Consumer Protection Regulations

Subpart A - General Requirements

§375.101 Who must follow these regulations?

You, a for-hire motor carrier engaged in the interstate transportation of household goods, must follow these regulations when offering your services to individual shippers. You are subject to this part only when you transport household goods for individual shippers by motor vehicle in interstate commerce as defined in §390.5 of this subchapter.

§375.103 What are the definitions of terms used in this part?

Terms used in this part are defined as follows. You may find other terms used in these regulations defined in 49 U.S.C. 13102. The definitions contained in this part control. If terms are used in this part and the terms are neither defined here nor in 49 U.S.C. 13102, the terms will have the ordinary practical meaning of such terms.

Advertisement means any communication to the public in connection with an offer or sale of any interstate household goods transportation service. This includes written or electronic database listings of your name, address, and telephone number in an on-line database. This excludes listings of your name, address, and telephone number in a telephone directory or similar publication. However, Yellow Pages advertising is included in the definition.

Cashier's check means a check that has all four of the following characteristics:
(1) *Drawn on a bank as defined in 12 CFR 229.2.*
(2) *Signed by an officer or employee of the bank* on behalf of the bank as drawer.
(3) *A direct obligation of the bank.*
(4) *Provided to a customer of the bank* or acquired from the bank for remittance purposes.

Certified scale means any scale inspected and certified by an authorized scale inspection and licensing authority, and designed for weighing motor vehicles, including trailers or semi-trailers not attached to a tractor, or designed as a platform or warehouse type scale.

Commercial shipper means any person who is named as the consignor or consignee in a bill of lading contract who is not the owner of the goods being transported but who assumes the responsibility for payment of the transportation and other tariff charges for the account of the beneficial owner of the goods. The beneficial owner of the goods is normally an employee of the consignor and/or consignee. A freight forwarder tendering a shipment to a carrier in furtherance of freight forwarder operations is also a commercial shipper. The Federal government is a government bill of lading shipper, not a commercial shipper.

Force majeure means a defense protecting the parties in the event that a part of the contract cannot be performed due to causes which are outside the control of the parties and could not be avoided by exercise of due care.

Government bill of lading shipper means any person whose property is transported under the terms and conditions of a government bill of lading issued by any department or agency of the Federal government to the carrier responsible for the transportation of the shipment.

Household goods, as used in connection with transportation, means the personal effects or property used, or to be used, in a dwelling, when part of the equipment or supplies of the dwelling. Transportation of the household goods must be arranged and paid for by the individual shipper or by another individual on behalf of the shipper. Household goods includes property moving from a factory or store if purchased with the intent to use in a dwelling and transported at the request of the householder, who also pays the transportation charges.

Individual shipper means any person who is the consignor or consignee of a household goods shipment identified as such in the bill of lading contract. The individual shipper owns the goods being transported and pays the transportation charges.

May means an option. You may do something, but it is not a requirement.

Must means a legal obligation. You must do something.

Order for service means a document authorizing you to transport an individual shipper's household goods.

Reasonable dispatch means the performance of transportation on the dates, or during the period, agreed upon by you and the individual shipper and shown on the Order For Service/Bill of Lading. For example, if you deliberately withhold any shipment from delivery after an individual shipper offers to pay the binding estimate or 110 percent of a non-binding estimate, you have not transported the goods with reasonable dispatch. The term "reasonable dispatch" excludes transportation provided under your tariff provisions requiring guaranteed service dates. You will have the defenses of force majeure, i.e., superior or irresistible force, as construed by the courts.

Should means a recommendation. We recommend you do something, but it is not a requirement.

Surface Transportation Board means an agency within the Department of Transportation. The Surface Transportation Board regulates household goods carrier tariffs among other responsibilities.

Tariff means an issuance (in whole or in part) containing rates, rules, regulations, classifications or other provisions related to a motor carrier's transportation services. The Surface Transportation Board requires a tariff contain specific items under §1312.3(a) of this title. These specific items include an accurate description of the services offered to the public and the specific applicable rates (or the basis for calculating the specific applicable rates) and service terms. A tariff must be arranged in a way that allows for the determination of the exact rate(s) and service terms applicable to any given shipment.

We, us, and **our** means the Federal Motor Carrier Safety Administration (FMCSA).

You and **your** means a motor carrier engaged in the interstate transportation of household goods and its household goods agents.

§375.105 What are the information collection requirements of this part?

(a) The information collection requirements of this part have been reviewed by the Office of Management and Budget pursuant to the Paperwork Reduction Act of 1995 (44 U.S.C. 3501 et seq.) and have been assigned OMB control number 2126-0025.

(b) The information collection requirements are found in the following sections: §§375.205, 375.207, 375.209, 375.211, 375.213, 375.215, 375.217, 375.303, 375.401, 375.403, 375.405, 375.409, 375.501, 375.503, 375.505, 375.507, 375.515, 375.519, 375.521, 375.605, 375.607, 375.609, 375.803, 375.805, and 375.807.

Subpart B - Before Offering Services to My Customers

Liability Considerations

§375.201 What is my normal liability for loss and damage when I accept goods from an individual shipper?

(a) In general, you are legally liable for loss or damage if it happens during performance of any transportation of household goods and all related services identified on your lawful bill of lading.

(b) You are liable for loss of, or damage to, any household goods to the extent provided in the current Surface Transportation Board's released rates order. Contact the Surface Transportation Board for a current copy of the Released Rates of Motor Carrier Shipments of Household Goods. The rate may be increased annually by the carrier based on the Department of Commerce's Cost of Living Adjustment.

(c) As required by §375.303(g), you may have additional liability if you sell liability insurance and you fail to issue a copy of the insurance policy or other appropriate evidence of insurance.

(d) You must, in a clear and concise manner, disclose to the individual shipper the limits of your liability.

§375.203 What actions of an individual shipper may limit or reduce my normal liability?

(a) If an individual shipper includes perishable, dangerous, or hazardous articles in the shipment without your knowledge, you need not assume liability for those articles or for the loss or damage caused by their inclusion in the shipment. If the shipper requests that you accept such articles for transportation, you may elect to limit your liability for any loss or damage by appropriately published tariff provisions.

(b) If an individual shipper agrees to ship household goods released at a value greater than 60 cents per pound ($1.32 per kilogram) per article, your liability for loss and damage may be limited to $100 per pound ($220 per kilogram) per article if the individual shipper fails to notify you in writing of articles valued at more than $100 per pound ($220 per kilogram).

(c) *If an individual shipper notifies you in writing* that an article valued at greater than $100 per pound ($220 per kilogram) will be included in the shipment, the shipper will be entitled to full recovery up to the declared value of the article or articles, not to exceed the declared value of the entire shipment.

General Responsibilities

§375.205 May I have agents?

(a) **You may have agents provided you comply** with paragraphs (b) and (c) of this section. A household goods agent is defined as either one of the following two types of agents:

(1) *A prime agent* provides a transportation service for you or on your behalf, including the selling of, or arranging for, a transportation service. You permit or require the agent to provide services under the terms of an agreement or arrangement with you. A prime agent does not provide services on an emergency or temporary basis. A prime agent does not include a household goods broker or freight forwarder.

(2) *An emergency or temporary agent* provides origin or destination services on your behalf, excluding the selling of, or arranging for, a transportation service. You permit or require the agent to provide such services under the terms of an agreement or arrangement with you. The agent performs such services only on an emergency or temporary basis.

(b) **If you have agents,** you must have written agreements between you and your prime agents. You and your retained prime agent must sign the agreements.

(c) **Copies of all your prime agent agreements** must be in your files for a period of at least 24 months following the date of termination of each agreement.

§375.207 What items must be in my advertisements?

(a) **You and your agents must publish and use** only truthful, straightforward, and honest advertisements.

(b) **You must include,** and you must require each of your agents to include, in all advertisements for all services (including any accessorial services incidental to or part of interstate household goods transportation), the following two elements:

(1) *Your name or trade name,* as it appears on our document assigning you a U.S. DOT number, or the name or trade name of the motor carrier under whose operating authority the advertised service will originate.

(2) *Your U.S. DOT number,* assigned by us authorizing you to operate as a for-hire motor carrier transporting household goods.

(c) **Your FMCSA-assigned U.S. DOT number** must be displayed only in the following form in every advertisement: U.S. DOT No. (assigned number).

§375.209 How must I handle complaints and inquiries?

(a) **You must establish and maintain a procedure** for responding to complaints and inquiries from your individual shippers.

(b) **Your procedure must include all four of the following items:**

(1) *A communications system* allowing individual shippers to communicate with your principal place of business by telephone.

(2) *A telephone number.*

(3) *A clear and concise statement* about who must pay for complaint and inquiry telephone calls.

(4) *A written or electronic record system* for recording all inquiries and complaints received from an individual shipper by any means of communication.

(c) **You must produce a clear and concise written description** of your procedure for distribution to individual shippers.

§375.211 Must I have an arbitration program?

(a) **You must have an arbitration program** to resolve property loss and damage disputes for individual shippers. You must establish and maintain an arbitration program with the following 11 minimum elements:

(1) *You must design your arbitration program* to prevent you from having any special advantage in any case where the claimant resides or does business at a place distant from your principal or other place of business.

(2) *Before execution of the order for service,* you must provide notice to the individual shipper of the availability of neutral arbitration, including all three of the following items:

(i) *A summary of the arbitration procedure.*

(ii) *Any applicable costs.*

(iii) *A disclosure of the legal effects of election to use arbitration.*

(3) *Upon the individual shipper's request,* you must provide information and forms you consider necessary for initiating an action to resolve a dispute under arbitration.

(4) *You must require each person you authorize* to arbitrate to be independent of the parties to the dispute and capable of resolving such disputes, and you must ensure the arbitrator is authorized and able to obtain from you or the individual shipper any material or relevant information to carry out a fair and expeditious decisionmaking process.

(5) *You must not charge the individual shipper* more than one-half of the total cost for instituting the arbitration proceeding against you. In the arbitrator's decision, the arbitrator may determine which party must pay the cost or a portion of the cost of the arbitration proceeding, including the cost of instituting the proceeding.

(6) *You must refrain from requiring the individual shipper* to agree to use arbitration before a dispute arises.

(7) *Arbitration must be binding for claims of $5,000 or less,* if the individual shipper requests arbitration.

(8) *Arbitration must be binding for claims of more than $5,000,* if the individual shipper requests arbitration and the carrier agrees to it.

(9) *If all parties agree,* the arbitrator may provide for an oral presentation of a dispute by a party or representative of a party.

(10) *The arbitrator must render a decision* within 60 days of receipt of written notification of the dispute, and a decision by an arbitrator may include any remedies appropriate under the circumstances.

(11) *The arbitrator may extend the 60-day period* for a reasonable period if you or the individual shipper fail to provide, in a timely manner, any information the arbitrator reasonably requires to resolve the dispute.

(b) **You must produce and distribute** a concise, easy-to-read, accurate summary of your arbitration program, including the items in this section.

§375.213 What information must I provide to a prospective individual shipper?

(a) **Before you execute an order for service** for a shipment of household goods, you must furnish to your prospective individual shipper, all five of the following documents:

(1) *The contents of Appendix A of this part,* "Your Rights and Responsibilities When You Move."

(2) *A concise, easy-to-read, accurate estimate of your charges.*

(3) *A notice of the availability of the applicable sections* of your tariff for the estimate of charges, including an explanation that individual shippers may examine these tariff sections or have copies sent to them upon request.

(4) *A concise, easy-to-read, accurate summary* of the your arbitration program.

(5) *A concise, easy to read, accurate summary* of your customer complaint and inquiry handling procedures. Included in this description must be both of the following two items:

(i) *The main telephone number* the individual shipper may use to communicate with you.

(ii) *A clear and concise statement* concerning who must pay for telephone calls.

(b) **To comply with paragraph (a)(1) of this section,** you must produce and distribute a document with the text and general order of Appendix A to this part as it appears. The following three items also apply:

(1) *If we, the Federal Motor Carrier Safety Administration,* choose to modify the text or general order of Appendix A, we will provide the public appropriate notice in the Federal Register and an opportunity for comment as required by Part 389 of this chapter before making you change anything.

(2) *If you publish the document,* you may choose the dimensions of the publication as long as the type font size is at least 10 point or greater and the size of the booklet is at least as large as 36 square inches (232 square centimeters).

(3) *If you publish the document,* you may choose the color and design of the front and back covers of the publication. The following words must appear prominently on the front cover in at least 12 point or greater bold or full-faced type: "Your Rights And Responsibilities When You Move. Furnished By Your Mover, As Required By Federal Law." You may substitute your name or trade name in place of "Your Mover" if you wish (for example, Furnished by XYZ Van Lines, As Required By Federal Law).

Subpart D - Estimating Charges §375.401 (e)

(c) *Paragraphs (b)(2) and (b)(3) of this section* do not apply to exact copies of Appendix A published in the Federal Register or the Code of Federal Regulations.

Collecting Transportation Charges

§375.215 How must I collect charges?

You must issue an honest, truthful freight or expense bill in accordance with Subpart A of Part 373 of this chapter. All rates and charges for the transportation and related services must be in accordance with your appropriately published tariff provisions in effect, including the method of payment.

§375.217 How must I collect charges upon delivery?

(a) **You must specify the form of payment** when you prepare the estimate. You and your agents must honor the form of payment at delivery, except when a shipper agrees to a change in writing.

(b) **You must specify the same form of payment** provided in paragraph (a) of this section when you prepare the order for service and the bill of lading.

(c) **Charge or credit card payments:**
   (1) *If you agree to accept payment* by charge or credit card, you must arrange with the individual shipper for the delivery only at a time when you can obtain authorization for the shipper's credit card transaction.
   (2) *Paragraph (c)(1) of this section* does not apply to you when you have equipped your motor vehicle(s) to process card transactions.

(d) **You may maintain a tariff** setting forth nondiscriminatory rules governing collect-on-delivery service and the collection of collect-on-delivery funds.

(e) **If an individual shipper pays you** at least 110 percent of the approximate costs of a non-binding estimate on a collect-on-delivery shipment, you must relinquish possession of the shipment at the time of delivery.

§375.219 May I extend credit to shippers?

You may extend credit to shippers, but, if you do, it must be in accordance with §375.807.

§375.221 May I use a charge or credit card plan for payments?

(a) **You may provide in your tariff** for the acceptance of charge or credit cards for the payment of freight charges. Accepting charge or credit card payments is different than extending credit to shippers in §§375.219 and 375.807. Once you provide an estimate you are bound by the provisions in your tariff regarding payment as of the estimate date, until completion of any transaction that results from that estimate, unless otherwise agreed with a shipper under §375.217(a).

(b) **You may accept charge or credit cards** whenever shipments are transported under agreements and tariffs requiring payment by cash, certified check, money order, or a cashier's check.

(c) **If you allow an individual shipper** to pay for a freight or expense bill by charge or credit card, you are deeming such payment to be the same as payment by cash, certified check, money order, or a cashier's check.

(d) **The charge or credit card plans you participate in** must be identified in your tariff rules as items permitting the acceptance of the charge or credit cards.

(e) **If an individual shipper** causes a charge or credit card issuer to reverse a charge transaction, you may consider the individual shipper's action tantamount to forcing you to provide an involuntary extension of your credit. In such instances, the rules in §375.807 apply.

Subpart C - Service Options Provided

§375.301 What service options may I provide?

(a) **You may design your household goods service** to provide individual shippers with a wide range of specialized service and pricing features. Many carriers provide at least the following five service options:
   (1) *Space reservation.*
   (2) *Expedited service.*
   (3) *Exclusive use of a vehicle.*
   (4) *Guaranteed service on or between agreed dates.*
   (5) *Liability insurance.*

(b) **If you sell liability insurance,** you must follow the requirements in §375.303.

§375.303 If I sell liability insurance coverage, what must I do?

(a) **You, your employee, or an agent** may sell, offer to sell, or procure liability insurance coverage for loss or damage to shipments of any individual shipper only when the individual shipper releases the shipment for transportation at a value not exceeding 60 cents per pound ($1.32 per kilogram) per article.

(b) **You may offer, sell, or procure** any type of insurance policy on behalf of the individual shipper covering loss or damage in excess of the specified carrier liability.

(c) **If you sell, offer to sell,** or procure liability insurance coverage for loss or damage to shipments:
   (1) *You must issue to the individual shipper* a policy or other appropriate evidence of the insurance that the individual shipper purchased.
   (2) *You must provide a copy of the policy* or other appropriate evidence to the individual shipper at the time you sell or procure the insurance.
   (3) *You must issue policies written in plain English.*
   (4) *You must clearly specify* the nature and extent of coverage under the policy.
   (5) *Your failure to issue a policy,* or other appropriate evidence of insurance purchased, to an individual shipper will subject you to full liability for any claims to recover loss or damage attributed to you.
   (6) *You must provide in your tariff* for the provision of selling, offering to sell, or procuring liability insurance coverage. The tariff must also provide for the base transportation charge, including your assumption of full liability for the value of the shipment. This would be in the event you fail to issue a policy or other appropriate evidence of insurance to the individual shipper at the time of purchase.

Subpart D - Estimating Charges

§375.401 Must I estimate charges?

(a) **Before you execute an order for service** for a shipment of household goods for an individual shipper, you must estimate the total charges in writing. The written estimate must be one of the following two types:
   (1) *A binding estimate,* an agreement made in advance with your individual shipper. It guarantees the total cost of the move based upon the quantities and services shown on your estimate.
   (2) *A non-binding estimate,* what you believe the total cost will be for the move, based upon the estimated weight or volume of the shipment and the accessorial services requested. A non-binding estimate is not binding on you. You will base the final charges upon the actual weight of the individual shipper's shipment and the tariff provisions in effect.

(b) **You must specify the form of payment** you and your agent will honor at delivery. Payment forms may include, but are not limited to, cash, a certified check, a money order, a cashier's check, a specific charge card such as American Express™, a specific credit card such as Visa™, or your credit as allowed by §375.807.

(c) **For non-binding estimates,** you must provide your reasonably accurate estimate of the approximate costs the individual shipper should expect to pay for the transportation and services of such shipments. If you provide an inaccurately low estimate, you may be limiting the amount you will collect at the time of delivery as provided in §375.407.

(d) **If you provide a shipper with an estimate** based on volume that will later be converted to a weight-based rate, you must provide the shipper an explanation in writing of the formula used to calculate the conversion to weight. You must specify the final charges will be based on actual weight and services subject to the 110 percent rule at delivery.

(e) **You must determine charges** for any accessorial services such as elevators, long carries, etc., before preparing the order for service and the bill of lading for binding or non-binding estimates. If you fail to ask the shipper about such charges and fail to determine such charges before preparing the order for service and the bill of lading, you must deliver the goods and bill the shipper after 30 days for the additional charges.

(f) **You and the individual shipper** must sign the estimate of charges. You must provide a dated copy of the estimate of charges to the individual shipper at the time you sign the estimate.

(g) **Before loading a household goods shipment,** and upon mutual agreement of both you and the individual shipper, you may amend an estimate of charges. You may not amend the estimate after loading the shipment.

§375.403 How must I provide a binding estimate?

(a) **You may provide a guaranteed binding estimate** of the total shipment charges to the individual shipper, so long as it is provided for in your tariff. The individual shipper must pay the amount for the services included in your estimate. You must comply with the following nine requirements:

(1) *You must provide a binding estimate in writing* to the individual shipper or other person responsible for payment of the freight charges.

(2) *You must retain a copy of each binding estimate* as an attachment to be made an integral part of the bill of lading contract.

(3) *You must clearly indicate* upon each binding estimate's face the estimate is binding upon you and the individual shipper. Each binding estimate must also clearly indicate on its face the charges shown are the charges being assessed for only those services specifically identified in the estimate.

(4) *You must clearly describe* binding estimate shipments and all services you are providing.

(5) *If it appears* an individual shipper has tendered additional household goods or requires additional services not identified in the binding estimate, you are not required to honor the estimate. If an agreement cannot be reached as to the price or service requirements for the additional goods or services, you are not required to service the shipment. However, if you do service the shipment, before loading the shipment, you must do one of the following three things:
  (i) *Reaffirm your binding estimate.*
  (ii) *Negotiate a revised written binding estimate* listing the additional household goods or services.
  (iii) *Agree with the individual shipper,* in writing, that both of you will consider the original binding estimate as a non-binding estimate subject to §375.405.

(6) *Once you load a shipment,* failure to execute a new binding estimate or a non-binding estimate signifies you have reaffirmed the original binding estimate. You may not collect more than the amount of the original binding estimate.

(7) *If you believe additional services are necessary* to properly service a shipment after the household goods are in transit, you must inform the individual shipper what the additional services are before performing those services. You must allow the shipper at least one hour to determine whether he or she wants the additional services performed. If the individual shipper agrees to pay for the additional services, you must execute a written attachment to be made an integral part of the bill of lading contract and have the individual shipper sign the written attachment. This may be done through fax transmissions; e-mail; overnight courier; or certified mail, return receipt requested. You must bill the individual shipper for the additional services after 30 days from delivery. If the individual shipper does not agree to pay the additional services, the carrier should perform only those additional services as are required to complete the delivery, and bill the individual shipper for the additional services after 30 days from delivery.

(8) *If the individual shipper requests additional services* after the household goods are in transit, you must inform the individual shipper of the additional charges that will be billed. You must require full payment at destination of the original binding estimate only. You must bill for the payment of the balance of any remaining charges for additional services no sooner than 30 days after the date of delivery. For example, if your binding estimate to an individual shipper estimated total charges at delivery as $1,000, but your actual charges at destination are $1,500, you must deliver the shipment upon payment of $1,000. You must then issue freight or expense bills no sooner than 30 days after the date of delivery for the remaining $500.

(9) *Failure to relinquish possession of a shipment* upon an individual shipper's offer to pay the binding estimate amount constitutes a failure to transport a shipment with "reasonable dispatch" and subjects you to cargo delay claims pursuant to Part 370 of this chapter.

(b) **If you do not provide a binding estimate** to an individual shipper, you must provide a non-binding estimate to the individual shipper in accordance with §375.405.

(c) **You must retain a copy of the binding estimate** for each move you perform for at least one year from the date you made the estimate and keep it as an attachment to be made an integral part of the bill of lading contract.

§375.405 How must I provide a non-binding estimate?

(a) **If you do not provide a binding estimate** to an individual shipper in accordance with §375.403, you must provide a non-binding written estimate to the individual shipper.

(b) **If you provide a non-binding estimate** to an individual shipper, you must provide your reasonably accurate estimate of the approximate costs the individual shipper should expect to pay for the transportation and services of the shipment. You must comply with the following ten requirements:

(1) *You must provide* reasonably accurate non-binding estimates based upon the estimated weight or volume of the shipment and services required. If you provide a shipper with an estimate based on volume that will later be converted to a weight-based rate, you must provide the shipper an explanation in writing of the formula used to calculate the conversion to weight.

(2) *You must explain to the individual shipper* final charges calculated for shipments moved on non-binding estimates will be those appearing in your tariffs applicable to the transportation. You must explain to the individual shipper these final charges may exceed the approximate costs appearing in your estimate.

(3) *You must furnish non-binding estimates* without charge and in writing to the individual shipper or other person responsible for payment of the freight charges.

(4) *You must retain a copy of each non-binding estimate* as an attachment to be made an integral part of the bill of lading contract.

(5) *You must clearly indicate* on the face of a non-binding estimate, the estimate is not binding upon you and the charges shown are the approximate charges to be assessed for the services identified in the estimate. The estimate must clearly state that the shipper may not be required to pay more than 110 percent of the non-binding estimate at the time of delivery.

(6) *You must clearly describe* on the face of a non-binding estimate the entire shipment and all services you are providing.

(7) *If it appears an individual shipper* has tendered additional household goods or requires additional services not identified in the non-binding estimate, you are not required to honor the estimate. If an agreement cannot be reached as to the price or service requirements for the additional goods or services, you are not required to service the shipment. However, if you do service the shipment, before loading the shipment, you must do one of the following two things:
  (i) *Reaffirm your non-binding estimate.*
  (ii) *Negotiate a revised written non-binding estimate* listing the additional household goods or services.

(8) *Once you load a shipment,* failure to execute a new non-binding estimate signifies you have reaffirmed the original non-binding estimate. You may not collect more than 110 percent of the amount of the original non-binding estimate at destination.

(9) *If you believe additional services are necessary* to properly service a shipment after the household goods are in transit, you must inform the individual shipper what the additional services are before performing those services. You must allow the shipper at least one hour to determine whether he or she wants the additional services performed. If the individual shipper agrees to pay for the additional services, you must execute a written attachment to be made an integral part of the bill of lading contract and have the individual shipper sign the written attachment. This may be done through fax transmissions; e-mail; overnight courier; or certified mail, return receipt requested. You must bill the individual shipper for the additional services after 30 days from delivery. If the individual shipper does not agree to pay the additional services, the carrier should perform only those additional services as are required to complete the delivery, and bill the individual shipper for the additional services after 30 days from delivery.

Subpart E - Pick Up of Shipments of Household Goods §375.501 (h)

(10) *If the individual shipper requests additional services* after the household goods are in-transit, you must inform the individual shipper additional charges will be billed. You may require full payment at destination of no more than 110 percent of the original non-binding estimate. You must bill for the payment of the balance of any remaining charges after 30 days after delivery. For example, if your non-binding estimate to an individual shipper estimated total charges at delivery as $1,000, but your actual charges at destination are $1,500, you must deliver the shipment upon payment of $1,100 (110 percent of the estimated charges) and forego demanding immediate payment of the balance. You then must issue a freight or expense bill for the remaining $400 after the 30-day period expires.

(c) **If you furnish a non-binding estimate,** you must enter the estimated charges upon the order for service and upon the bill of lading.

(d) **You must retain a copy of the non-binding estimate** for each move you perform for at least one year from the date you made the estimate and keep it as an attachment to be made an integral part of the bill of lading contract.

§375.407 Under what circumstances must I relinquish possession of a collect-on-delivery shipment transported under a non-binding estimate?

(a) **If an individual shipper pays you** at least 110 percent of the approximate costs of a non-binding estimate on a collect-on-delivery shipment, you must relinquish possession of the shipment at the time of delivery. You must accept the form of payment agreed to at the time of estimate, unless the shipper agrees in writing to a change in the form of payment.

(b) **Failure to relinquish possession of a shipment** upon an individual shipper's offer to pay 110 percent of the estimated charges constitutes a failure to transport the shipment with "reasonable dispatch" and subjects you to cargo delay claims pursuant to Part 370 of this chapter.

(c) **You must defer billing for the payment of the balance** of any remaining charges for a period of 30 days following the date of delivery. After this 30-day period, you may demand payment of the balance of any remaining charges, as explained in §375.405.

§375.409 May household goods brokers provide estimates?

A household goods broker must not provide an individual shipper with an estimate of charges for the transportation of household goods unless there is a written agreement between the broker and you, the carrier, adopting the broker's estimate as your own estimate. If you make such an agreement with a broker, you must ensure compliance with all requirements of this part pertaining to estimates, including the requirement that you must relinquish possession of the shipment if the shipper pays you 110 percent of a non-binding estimate at the time of delivery.

Subpart E - Pick Up of Shipments of Household Goods

Before Loading

§375.501 Must I write up an order for service?

(a) **Before you receive a shipment of household goods** you will move for an individual shipper, you must prepare an order for service. The order for service must contain the information described in the following 15 items:

(1) *Your name and address* and the FMCSA U.S. DOT number assigned to the mover who is responsible for performing the service.
(2) *The individual shipper's name, address,* and, if available, telephone number(s).
(3) *The name, address, and telephone number* of the delivering mover's office or agent located at or nearest to the destination of the shipment.
(4) *A telephone number* where the individual shipper/consignee may contact you or your designated agent.
(5) *One of the following three entries must be on the order for service:*
  (i) *The agreed pickup date and agreed delivery date of the move.*
  (ii) *The agreed period(s) of the entire move.*
  (iii) *If you are transporting the shipment* on a guaranteed service basis, the guaranteed dates or periods for pickup, transportation, and delivery. You must enter any penalty or per diem requirements upon the agreement under this item.

(6) *The names and addresses* of any other motor carriers, when known, who will participate in interline transportation of the shipment.
(7) *The form of payment* you and your agents will honor at delivery. The payment information must be the same that was entered on the estimate.
(8) *The terms and conditions* for payment of the total charges, including notice of any minimum charges.
(9) *The maximum amount* you will demand at the time of delivery to obtain possession of the shipment, when you transport on a collect-on-delivery basis.
(10) *The Surface Transportation Board's* required released rates valuation statement, and the charges, if any, for optional valuation coverage. The released rates may be increased annually by the carrier based on the Department of Commerce's Cost of Living Adjustment.
(11) *A complete description* of any special or accessorial services ordered and minimum weight or volume charges applicable to the shipment, subject to the following two conditions:
  (i) *If you provide service for individual shippers* on rates based upon the transportation of a minimum weight or volume, you must indicate on the order for service the minimum weight- or volume-based rates, and the minimum charges applicable to the shipment.
  (ii) *If you do not indicate* the minimum rates and charges, your tariff must provide you will compute the final charges relating to such a shipment based upon the actual weight or volume of the shipment.
(12) *Any identification or registration number* you assign to the shipment.
(13) *For non-binding estimates,* your reasonably accurate estimate of the amount of the charges, the method of payment of total charges, and the maximum amount (no more than 110 percent of the non-binding estimate) you will demand at the time of delivery to relinquish possession of the shipment.
(14) *For binding estimates,* the amount of charges you will demand based upon the binding estimate and the terms of payment under this estimate.
(15) *Whether the individual shipper* requests notification of the charges before delivery. The individual shipper must provide you with the fax number(s) or address(es) where you will transmit the notifications by fax transmission; e-mail; overnight courier; or certified mail, return receipt requested.

(b) **You, your agent, or your driver** must inform the individual shipper if you reasonably expect a special or accessorial service is necessary to safely transport a shipment. You must refuse to accept the shipment when you reasonably expect a special or accessorial service is necessary to safely transport a shipment and the individual shipper refuses to purchase the special or accessorial service. You must make a written note if the shipper refuses any special or accessorial services that you reasonably expect to be necessary.

(c) **You and the individual shipper** must sign the order for service. You must provide a dated copy of the order for service to the individual shipper at the time you sign the order.

(d) (1) *You may provide the individual shipper* with blank or incomplete estimates, orders for service, bills of lading, or any other blank or incomplete documents pertaining to the move.
(2) *You may require the individual shipper* to sign an incomplete document at origin provided it contains all relevant shipping information except the actual shipment weight and any other information necessary to determine the final charges for all services performed.

(e) **You must provide the individual shipper** the opportunity to rescind the order for service without any penalty for a three-day period after the shipper signs the order for service, if the shipper scheduled the shipment to be loaded more than three days after signing the order.

(f) **Before loading the shipment,** and upon mutual agreement of both you and the individual shipper, you may amend an order for service.

(g) **You must retain a copy of the order for service** for each move you perform for at least one year from the date you made the order for service and keep it as an attachment to be made an integral part of the bill of lading contract.

(h) **You have the option** of placing the valuation statement on either the order for service or the bill of lading, provided the order for service or bill of lading states the appropriate valuation selected by the shipper.

§375.503 Must I write up an inventory?

(a) **You must prepare a written, itemized inventory** for each shipment of household goods you transport for an individual shipper. The inventory must identify every carton and every uncartoned item that is included in the shipment. When you prepare the inventory, an identification number that corresponds to the inventory must be placed on each article that is included in the shipment.

(b) **You must prepare the inventory** before or at the time of loading in the vehicle for transportation in a manner that provides the individual shipper with the opportunity to observe and verify the accuracy of the inventory if he or she so requests.

(c) **You must furnish a complete copy of the inventory** to the individual shipper before or at the time of loading the shipment. A copy of the inventory, signed by both you and the individual shipper, must be provided to the shipper, together with a copy of the bill of lading, before or at the time you load the shipment.

(d) **Upon delivery,** you must provide the individual shipper with the opportunity to observe and verify that the same articles are being delivered and the condition of those articles. You must also provide the individual shipper the opportunity to note in writing any missing articles and the condition of any damaged or destroyed articles. In addition, you must also provide the shipper with a copy of all such notations.

(e) **You must retain inventories for each move you perform** for at least one year from the date you made the inventory and keep it as an attachment to be made an integral part of the bill of lading contract.

§375.505 Must I write up a bill of lading?

(a) **You must issue a bill of lading.** The bill of lading must contain the terms and conditions of the contract. A bill of lading may be combined with an order for service to include all the items required by §375.501 of this subpart. You must furnish a partially complete copy of the bill of lading to the individual shipper before the vehicle leaves the residence at origin. The partially complete bill of lading must contain all relevant shipment information, except the actual shipment weight and any other information necessary to determine the final charges for all services performed.

(b) **On a bill of lading, you must include the following 14 items:**
   (1) *Your name and address,* or the name and address of the motor carrier issuing the bill of lading.
   (2) *The names and addresses* of any other motor carriers, when known, who will participate in transportation of the shipment.
   (3) *The name, address, and telephone number* of your office (or the office of your agent) where the individual shipper can contact you in relation to the transportation of the shipment.
   (4) *The form of payment* you and your agents will honor at delivery. The payment information must be the same that was entered on the estimate and order for service.
   (5) *When you transport* on a collect-on-delivery basis, the name, address, and if furnished, the telephone number, facsimile number, or e-mail address of a person to notify about the charges. The notification may also be made by overnight courier or certified mail, return receipt requested.
   (6) *For non-guaranteed service,* the agreed date or period of time for pickup of the shipment and the agreed date or period of time for the delivery of the shipment. The agreed dates or periods for pickup and delivery entered upon the bill of lading must conform to the agreed dates or periods of time for pickup and delivery entered upon the order for service or a proper amendment to the order for service.
   (7) *For guaranteed service,* subject to tariff provisions, the dates for pickup and delivery, and any penalty or per diem entitlements due the individual shipper under the agreement.
   (8) *The actual date of pickup.*
   (9) *The company or carrier identification number* of the vehicle(s) upon which you load the individual shipper's shipment.
   (10) *The terms and conditions* for payment of the total charges, including notice of any minimum charges.
   (11) *The maximum amount you will demand* at the time of delivery to obtain possession of the shipment, when you transport under a collect-on-delivery basis.
   (12) *The Surface Transportation Board's* required released rates valuation statement, and the charges, if any, for optional valuation coverage. The released rates may be increased annually by the carrier based on the Department of Commerce's Cost of Living Adjustment.
   (13) *Evidence of any insurance coverage* sold to or procured for the individual shipper from an independent insurer, including the amount of the premium for such insurance.
   (14) *Each attachment to the bill of lading.* Each attachment is an integral part of the bill of lading contract. If not provided elsewhere to the shipper, the following three items must be added as an attachment to the bill of lading.
      (i) *The binding or non-binding estimate.*
      (ii) *The order for service.*
      (iii) *The inventory.*

(c) **A copy of the bill of lading** must accompany a shipment at all times while in your (or your agent's) possession. Before the vehicle leaves the residence of origin, the bill of lading must be in the possession of the driver responsible for the shipment.

(d) **You must retain bills of lading** for each move you perform for at least one year from the date you created the bill of lading.

(e) **You have the option of placing** the valuation statement on either the order for service or the bill of lading, provided the order for service or bill of lading states the appropriate valuation selected by the shipper.

Weighing the Shipment

§375.507 Must I determine the weight of a shipment?

(a) **When you transport household goods** on a non-binding estimate dependent upon the shipment weight, you must determine the weight of each shipment transported before the assessment of any charges.

(b) **You must weigh the shipment upon a certified scale.**

(c) **You must provide a written explanation** of volume to weight conversions, when you provide an estimate by volume and convert the volume to weight.

§375.509 How must I determine the weight of a shipment?

(a) **You must weigh the shipment** by using one of the following two methods:
   (1) *First method — origin weigh.* You determine the difference between the tare weight of the vehicle before loading at the origin of the shipment and the gross weight of the same vehicle after loading the shipment.
   (2) *Second method — back weigh.* You determine the difference between the gross weight of the vehicle with the shipment loaded and the tare weight of the same vehicle after you unload the shipment.

(b) **The following three conditions must exist** for both the tare and gross weighings:
   (1) *The vehicle must have installed or loaded* all pads, dollies, hand trucks, ramps, and other equipment required in the transportation of the shipment.
   (2) *The driver and other persons must be off the vehicle* at the time of either weighing.
   (3) *The fuel tanks on the vehicle* must be full at the time of each weighing, or, in the alternative, when you use the first method — origin weigh, in paragraph (a)(1) of this section, where the tare weighing is the first weighing performed, you must refrain from adding fuel between the two weighings.

(c) **You may detach the trailer** of a tractor-trailer vehicle combination from the tractor and have the trailer weighed separately at each weighing provided the length of the scale platform is adequate to accommodate and support the entire trailer at one time.

(d) **You must use the net weight** of shipments transported in containers. You must calculate the difference between the tare weight of the container (including all pads, blocking and bracing used in the transportation of the shipment) and the gross weight of the container with the shipment loaded in the container.

§375.511 May I use an alternative method for shipments weighing 3,000 pounds or less?

For shipments weighing 3,000 pounds or less (1,362 kilograms or less), you may weigh the shipment upon a platform or warehouse certified scale before loading for transportation or after unloading.

§375.513 Must I give the individual shipper an opportunity to observe the weighing?

You must give the individual shipper or any other person responsible for the payment of the freight charges the right to observe all weighings of the shipment. You must advise the individual shipper, or any other person entitled to observe the weighings, where and when each weighing will occur. You must give the person who will observe the weighings a reasonable opportunity to be present to observe the weighings.

Subpart F - Transportation of Shipments §375.609 (e)

§375.515 May an individual shipper waive his/her right to observe each weighing?

(a) *If an individual shipper* elects not to observe a weighing, the shipper is presumed to have waived that right.

(b) *If an individual shipper* elects not to observe a reweighing, the shipper must waive that right in writing. The individual shipper may send the waiver notification via fax transmission; e-mail; overnight courier; or certified mail, return receipt requested.

(c) *Waiver of the right to observe* a weighing or re-weighing does not affect any other rights of the individual shipper under this part or otherwise.

§375.517 May an individual shipper demand re-weighing?
After you inform the individual shipper of the billing weight and total charges and before actually beginning to unload a shipment weighed at origin (first method under §375.509(a)(1)), the individual shipper may demand a re-weigh. You must base your freight bill charges upon the re-weigh weight.

§375.519 Must I obtain weight tickets?

(a) *You must obtain weight tickets* whenever we require you to weigh the shipment in accordance with this subpart. You must obtain a separate weight ticket for each weighing. The weigh master must sign each weight ticket. Each weight ticket must contain the following six items:
(1) *The complete name and location of the scale.*
(2) *The date of each weighing.*
(3) *The identification of the weight entries* as being the tare, gross, or net weights.
(4) *The company or carrier identification of the vehicle.*
(5) *The last name of the individual shipper* as it appears on the bill of lading.
(6) *The carrier's shipment registration or bill of lading number.*

(b) *When both weighings* are performed on the same scale, one weight ticket may be used to record both weighings.

(c) *As part of the file on the shipment,* you must retain the original weight ticket or tickets relating to the determination of the weight of a shipment.

(d) *All freight bills you present to an individual shipper* must include true copies of all weight tickets obtained in the determination of the shipment weight in order to collect any shipment charges dependent upon the weight transported.

§375.521 What must I do if an individual shipper wants to know the actual weight or charges for a shipment before I tender delivery?

(a) *If an individual shipper of a shipment being transported* on a collect-on-delivery basis specifically requests notification of the actual weight or volume and charges on the shipment, you must comply with this request. This requirement is conditioned upon the individual shipper's supplying you with an address or telephone number where the individual shipper will receive the communication. You must make your notification by telephone; in person; fax transmissions; e-mail; overnight courier; or certified mail, return receipt requested.

(b) *The individual shipper must receive your notification* at least one full 24-hour day before any tender of the shipment for delivery, excluding Saturdays, Sundays and Federal holidays.

(c) *You may disregard the 24-hour notification requirement* on shipments in any one of the following three circumstances:
(1) *The shipment will be back weighed* (i.e., weighed at destination).
(2) *Pickup and delivery* encompass two consecutive weekdays, if the individual shipper agrees.
(3) *The shipment is moving* under a non-binding estimate and the maximum payment required at time of delivery is 110 percent of the estimated charges, but only if the individual shipper agrees to waive the 24-hour notification requirement.

Subpart F - Transportation of Shipments

§375.601 Must I transport the shipment in a timely manner?
Yes. Transportation in a timely manner is also known as "reasonable dispatch service." You must provide reasonable dispatch service to all individual shippers, except for transportation on the basis of guaranteed pickup and delivery dates.

§375.603 When must I tender a shipment for delivery?
You must tender a shipment for delivery for an individual shipper on the agreed delivery date or within the period specified on the bill of lading. Upon the request or concurrence of the individual shipper, you may waive this requirement.

§375.605 How must I notify an individual shipper of any service delays?

(a) *When you are unable to perform* either the pickup or delivery of a shipment on the dates or during the periods specified in the order for service and as soon as the delay becomes apparent to you, you must notify the individual shipper of the delay, at your expense, in one of the following six ways:
(1) *By telephone.*
(2) *In person.*
(3) *Fax transmissions.*
(4) *E-mail.*
(5) *Overnight courier.*
(6) *Certified mail, return receipt requested.*

(b) *You must advise the individual shipper* of the dates or periods you expect to be able to pick up and/or deliver the shipment. You must consider the needs of the individual shipper in your advisement. You also must do the following four things:
(1) *You must prepare a written record* of the date, time, and manner of notification.
(2) *You must prepare a written record* of your amended date or period for pick-up or delivery.
(3) *You must retain these records* as a part of your file on the shipment. The retention period is one year from the date of notification.
(4) *You must furnish a copy of the notice* to the individual shipper by first class mail or in person if the individual shipper requests a copy of the notice.

§375.607 What must I do if I am able to tender a shipment for final delivery more than 24 hours before a specified date?

(a) *You may ask the individual shipper* to accept an early delivery date. If the individual shipper does not concur with your request or the individual shipper does not request an early delivery date, you may, at your discretion, place a shipment in storage under your own account and at your own expense in a warehouse located near the destination of the shipment. If you place the shipment in storage, you must comply with paragraph (b) of this section. You may comply with paragraph (c) of this section, at your discretion.

(b) *You must immediately notify the individual shipper* of the name and address of the warehouse where you place the shipment. You must make and keep a record of your notification as a part of your shipment records. You have responsibility for the shipment under the terms and conditions of the bill of lading. You are responsible for the charges for redelivery, handling, and storage until you make final delivery.

(c) *You may limit your responsibility* under paragraph (b) of this section up to the agreed delivery date or the first day of the period of time of delivery as specified in the bill of lading.

§375.609 What must I do for shippers who store household goods in transit?

(a) *If you are holding goods for storage-in-transit (SIT)* and the period of time is about to expire, you must comply with this section.

(b) *You must notify the individual shipper,* in writing of the following four items:
(1) *The date of conversion to permanent storage.*
(2) *The existence of a nine-month period* after the date of conversion to permanent storage when the individual shipper may file claims against you for loss or damage occurring to the goods in transit or during the storage-in-transit period.
(3) *The fact your liability is ending.*
(4) *The fact the individual shipper's property* will be subject to the rules, regulations, and charges of the warehouseman.

(c) *You must make this notification at least 10 days* before the expiration date of either one of the following two periods:
(1) *The specified period of time* when the goods are to be held in storage.
(2) *The maximum period of time* provided in your tariff for storage-in-transit.

(d) *You must notify the individual shipper* by facsimile transmission; e-mail; overnight courier; or certified mail, return receipt requested.

(e) *If you are holding household goods in storage-in-transit* for a period of time less than 10 days, you must give notification to the individual shipper of the information specified in paragraph (b) of this section one day before the expiration date of the specified time when the goods are to be held in such storage.

(f) **You must maintain a record of notifications** as part of the records of the shipment.

(g) **Your failure or refusal to notify the individual shipper** will automatically effect a continuance of your carrier liability according to the applicable tariff provisions with respect to storage-in-transit, until the end of the day following the date when you actually gave notice.

Subpart G - Delivery of Shipments

§375.701 May I provide for a release of liability on my delivery receipt?

(a) **Your delivery receipt or shipping document** must not contain any language purporting to release or discharge you or your agents from liability.

(b) **The delivery receipt may include a statement** the property was received in apparent good condition except as noted on the shipping documents.

§375.703 What is the maximum collect-on-delivery amount I may demand at the time of delivery?

(a) **On a binding estimate,** the maximum amount is the exact estimate of the charges.

(b) **On a non-binding estimate,** the maximum amount is 110 percent of the non-binding estimate of the charges.

§375.705 If a shipment is transported on more than one vehicle, what charges may I collect at delivery?

(a) **At your discretion, you may do one of the following three things:**
  (1) *You may defer the collection of all charges* until you deliver the entire shipment.
  (2) *If you have determined* the charges for the entire shipment, you may collect charges for the portion of the shipment tendered for delivery. You must determine the percentage of the charges for the entire shipment represented by the portion of the shipment tendered for delivery.
  (3) *If you cannot reasonably calculate* the charges for the entire shipment, you must determine the charges for the portion of the shipment being delivered. You must collect this amount. The total charges you assess for the transportation of the separate portions of the shipment must not be more than the charges due for the entire shipment.

(b) **In the event of the loss or destruction** of any part of a shipment transported on more than one vehicle, you must collect the charges as provided in §375.707.

§375.707 If a shipment is partially lost or destroyed, what charges may I collect at delivery?

(a) **If a shipment is partially lost or destroyed,** you may first collect your freight charges for the entire shipment, if you choose. If you do this, you must refund the portion of your published freight charges corresponding to the portion of the lost or destroyed shipment (including any charges for accessorial or terminal services), at the time you dispose of claims for loss, damage, or injury to the articles in the shipment under Part 370 of this chapter.

(b) **To calculate the amount of charges** applicable to the shipment as delivered, you must multiply the percentage corresponding to the delivered shipment by the total charges applicable to the shipment tendered by the individual shipper. The following four conditions also apply:
  (1) *If the charges computed* exceed the charges otherwise applicable to the shipment as delivered, the lesser of those charges must apply. This will apply only to the transportation of household goods and not to charges for other services the individual shipper ordered.
  (2) *You must collect any specific valuation charge due.*
  (3) *You may disregard paragraph (a) of this section* if loss or destruction was due to an act or omission of the individual shipper.
  (4) *You must determine, at your own expense,* the proportion of the shipment, based on actual or constructive weight, not lost or destroyed in transit.

(c) **The individual shipper's rights are in addition to,** and not in lieu of, any other rights the individual shipper may have with respect to a shipment of household goods you or your agent(s) partially lost or destroyed in transit. This applies whether or not the individual shipper exercises its rights provided in paragraph (a) of this section.

§375.709 If a shipment is totally lost or destroyed, what charges may I collect at delivery?

(a) **You are forbidden from collecting, or requiring** an individual shipper to pay, any freight charges (including any charges for accessorial or terminal services) when a household goods shipment is totally lost or destroyed in transit. The following two conditions also apply:
  (1) *You must collect any specific valuation charge due.*
  (2) *You may disregard paragraph (a) of this section* if loss or destruction was due to an act or omission of the individual shipper.

(b) **The individual shipper's rights are in addition to,** and not in lieu of, any other rights the individual shipper may have with respect to a shipment of household goods you or your agent(s) totally lost or destroyed in transit. This applies whether or not the individual shipper exercises its rights provided in paragraph (a) of this section.

Subpart H - Collection of Charges

§375.801 What types of charges apply to Subpart H?

This subpart applies to all shipments of household goods that:
(a) **Entail a balance due freight or expense bill, or**
(b) **Are transported on an extension of credit basis.**

§375.803 How must I present my freight or expense bill?

You must present your freight or expense bill in accordance with §375.807 of this subpart.

§375.805 If I am forced to relinquish a collect-on-delivery shipment before the payment of ALL charges, how do I collect the balance?

On "collect-on-delivery" shipments, you must present your freight bill for all transportation charges within 15 days as required by §375.807.

§375.807 What actions may I take to collect the charges upon my freight bill?

(a) **You must present a freight bill within 15 days** (excluding Saturdays, Sundays, and Federal holidays) of the date of delivery of a shipment at its destination.

(b) **The credit period must be seven days** (including Saturdays, Sundays, and Federal holidays).

(c) **You must provide in your tariffs the following four things:**
  (1) *You must automatically extend* the credit period to a total of 30 calendar days for any shipper who has not paid your freight bill within the 7-day period.
  (2) *You will assess a service charge* to each individual shipper equal to one percent of the amount of the freight bill, subject to a $20 minimum charge, for the extension of the credit period. You will assess the service charge for each 30-day extension the charges go unpaid.
  (3) *You must deny credit to any shipper* who fails to pay a duly-presented freight bill within the 30-day period. You may grant credit to the individual shipper when the individual shipper satisfies he/she will promptly pay all future freight bills duly presented.
  (4) *You must ensure all payments of freight bills* are strictly in accordance with the rules and regulations of this part for the settlement of your rates and charges.

Subpart I - Penalties

§375.901 What penalties do we impose for violations of this part?

The penalty provisions of 49 U.S.C. Chapter 149, Civil and Criminal Penalties apply to this part. These penalties do not overlap. Notwithstanding these civil penalties, nothing in this section shall deprive any holder of a receipt or a bill of lading any remedy or right of action under existing law.

Part 375 - Transportation of Household Goods in Interstate Commerce — Appendix A

Appendix A to Part 375 Your Rights and Responsibilities When You Move

You must furnish this document to prospective individual shippers as required by 49 CFR 375.213. The text as it appears in this appendix may be reprinted in a form and manner chosen by you, provided it complies with §375.213(b)(2) and (b)(3). You are not required to italicize titles of sections.

YOUR RIGHTS AND RESPONSIBILITIES WHEN YOU MOVE
OMB No. 2126-0025

Furnished by Your Mover, as Required by Federal Law
Authority: 49 U.S.C. 13301, 13704, 13707, and 14104; 49 CFR 1.73.

What Is Included in This Pamphlet?
In this pamphlet, you will find a discussion of each of these topics:
Why Was I Given This Pamphlet?
What Are the Most Important Points I Should Remember From This Pamphlet?
What If I Have More Questions?

Subpart A - General Requirements
Who must follow the regulations?
What definitions are used in this pamphlet?

Subpart B - Before Requesting Services From Any Mover
What is my mover's normal liability for loss or damage when my mover accepts goods from me?
What actions by me limit or reduce my mover's normal liability?
What are dangerous or hazardous materials that may limit or reduce my mover's normal liability?
May my mover have agents?
What items must be in my mover's advertisements?
How must my mover handle complaints and inquiries?
Do I have the right to inspect my mover's tariffs (schedules of charges) applicable to my move?
Must my mover have an arbitration program?
Must my mover inform me about my rights and responsibilities under Federal law?
What other information must my mover provide to me?
How must my mover collect charges?
May my mover collect charges upon delivery?
May my mover extend credit to me?
May my mover accept charge or credit cards for my payments?

Subpart C - Service Options Provided
What service options may my mover provide?
If my mover sells liability insurance coverage, what must my mover do?

Subpart D - Estimating Charges
Must my mover estimate the transportation and accessorial charges for my move?
How must my mover estimate charges under the regulations?
What payment arrangements must my mover have in place to secure delivery of my household goods shipment?

Subpart E - Pickup of My Shipment of Household Goods
Must my mover write up an order for service?
Must my mover write up an inventory of the shipment?
Must my mover write up a bill of lading?
Should I reach an agreement with my mover about pickup and delivery times?
Must my mover determine the weight of my shipment?
How must my mover determine the weight of my shipment?
What must my mover do if I want to know the actual weight or charges for my shipment before delivery?

Subpart F - Transportation of My Shipment
Must my mover transport the shipment in a timely manner?
What must my mover do if it is able to deliver my shipment more than 24 hours before I am able to accept delivery?
What must my mover do for me when I store household goods in transit?

Subpart G - Delivery of My shipment
May my mover ask me to sign a delivery receipt releasing it from liability?
What is the maximum collect-on-delivery amount my mover may demand I pay at the time of delivery?
If my shipment is transported on more than one vehicle, what charges may my mover collect at delivery?
If my shipment is partially or totally lost or destroyed, what charges may my mover collect at delivery?
How must my mover calculate the charges applicable to the shipment as delivered?

Subpart H - Collection of Charges
Does this subpart apply to most shipments?
How must my mover present its freight or expense bill to me?
If I forced my mover to relinquish a collect-on-delivery shipment before the payment of ALL charges, how must my mover collect the balance?
What actions may my mover take to collect from me the charges in its freight bill?
Do I have a right to file a claim to recover money for property my mover lost or damaged?

Subpart I - Resolving Disputes With My Mover
What may I do to resolve disputes with my mover?

Why Was I Given This Pamphlet?
The Federal Motor Carrier Safety Administration's (FMCSA) regulations protect consumers on interstate moves and define the rights and responsibilities of consumers and household goods carriers.

The household goods carrier (mover) gave you this booklet to provide information about your rights and responsibilities as an individual shipper of household goods. Your primary responsibility is to select a reputable household goods carrier, ensure that you understand the terms and conditions of the contract, and understand and pursue the remedies that are available to you in case problems arise. You should talk to your mover if you have further questions. The mover will also furnish you with additional written information describing its procedure for handling your questions and complaints. The additional written information will include a telephone number you can call to obtain additional information about your move.

What Are the Most Important Points I Should Remember From This Pamphlet?

1. *Movers must give written estimates.*
2. *Movers may give binding estimates.*
3. *Non-binding estimates are not always accurate;* actual charges may exceed the estimate.
4. *If your mover provides you* (or someone representing you) with any partially complete document for your signature, you should verify the document is as complete as possible before signing it. Make sure the document contains all relevant shipping information, except the actual shipment weight and any other information necessary to determine the final charges for all services performed.
5. *You may request from your mover* the availability of guaranteed pickup and delivery dates.
6. *Be sure you understand the mover's responsibility* for loss or damage, and request an explanation of the difference between valuation and actual insurance.
7. *You have the right to be present* each time your shipment is weighed.
8. *You may request a reweigh of your shipment.*
9. *If you agree to move under a non-binding estimate,* you should confirm with your mover — in writing — the method of payment at delivery as cash, certified check, cashier's check, money order, or credit card.
10. *Movers must offer a dispute settlement program* as an alternative means of settling loss or damage claims. Ask your mover for details.
11. *You should ask the person you speak to* whether he or she works for the actual mover or a household goods broker. A household goods broker only arranges for the transportation. A household goods broker must not represent itself as a mover. A household goods broker does not own trucks of its own. The broker is required to find an authorized mover to provide the transportation. You should know that a household goods broker generally has no authority to provide you an estimate on behalf of a specific mover. If a household goods broker provides you an estimate, it may not be binding on the actual mover and you may have to pay the actual charges the mover incurs. A household goods broker is not responsible for loss or damage.

117

12. *You may request complaint information* about movers from the Federal Motor Carrier Safety Administration under the Freedom of Information Act. You may be assessed a fee to obtain this information. See 49 CFR Part 7 for the schedule of fees.
13. *You should seek estimates* from at least three different movers. You should not disclose any information to the different movers about their competitors, as it may affect the accuracy of their estimates.

What If I Have More Questions?

If this pamphlet does not answer all of your questions about your move, do not hesitate to ask your mover's representative who handled the arrangements for your move, the driver who transports your shipment, or the mover's main office for additional information.

Subpart A - General Requirements

The primary responsibility for your protection lies with you in selecting a reputable household goods carrier, ensuring you understand the terms and conditions of your contract with your mover, and understanding and pursuing the remedies that are available to you in case problems arise.

Who Must Follow the Regulations?

The regulations inform motor carriers engaged in the interstate transportation of household goods (movers) what standards they must follow when offering services to you. You, an individual shipper, are not directly subject to the regulations. However, your mover may be required by the regulations to force you to pay on time. The regulations only apply to your mover when the mover transports your household goods by motor vehicle in interstate commerce — that is, when you are moving from one State to another. The regulations do not apply when your interstate move takes place within a single commercial zone. A commercial zone is roughly equivalent to the local metropolitan area of a city or town. For example, a move between Brooklyn, NY, and Hackensack, NJ, would be considered to be within the New York City commercial zone and would not be subject to these regulations. Commercial zones are defined in 49 CFR Part 372.

What Definitions Are Used in This Pamphlet?

Accessorial (Additional) Services — These are services such as packing, appliance servicing, unpacking, or piano stair carries that you request to be performed (or that are necessary because of landlord requirements or other special circumstances). Charges for these services may be in addition to the line haul charges.

Advanced Charges — These are charges for services performed by someone other than the mover. A professional, craftsman, or other third party may perform these services at your request. The mover pays for these services and adds the charges to your bill of lading charges.

Advertisement — This is any communication to the public in connection with an offer or sale of any interstate household goods transportation service. This will include written or electronic database listings of your mover's name, address, and telephone number in an on-line database. This excludes listings of your mover's name, address, and telephone number in a telephone directory or similar publication. However, Yellow Pages advertising is included within the definition.

Agent — A local moving company authorized to act on behalf of a larger, national company.

Appliance Service by Third Party — The preparation of major electrical appliances to make them safe for shipment. Charges for these services may be in addition to the line haul charges.

Bill of Lading — The receipt for your goods and the contract for their transportation.

Carrier — The mover transporting your household goods.

Cash on Delivery (COD) — This means payment is required at the time of delivery at the destination residence (or warehouse).

Certified Scale — Any scale designed for weighing motor vehicles, including trailers or semitrailers not attached to a tractor, and certified by an authorized scale inspection and licensing authority. A certified scale may also be a platform or warehouse type scale that is properly inspected and certified.

Estimate, Binding — This is an agreement made in advance with your mover. It guarantees the total cost of the move based upon the quantities and services shown on the estimate.

Estimate, Non-Binding — This is what your mover believes the cost will be, based upon the estimated weight of the shipment and the accessorial services requested. A non-binding estimate is not binding on the mover. The final charges will be based upon the actual weight of your shipment, the services provided, and the tariff provisions in effect.

Expedited Service — This is an agreement with the mover to perform transportation by a set date in exchange for charges based upon a higher minimum weight.

Flight Charge — A charge for carrying items up or down flights of stairs. Charges for these services may be in addition to the line haul charges.

Guaranteed Pickup and Delivery Service — An additional level of service featuring guaranteed dates of service. Your mover will provide reimbursement to you for delays. This premium service is often subject to minimum weight requirements.

High Value Article — These are items included in a shipment valued at more than $100 per pound ($220 per kilogram).

Household Goods, as used in connection with transportation, means the personal effects or property used, or to be used, in a dwelling, when part of the equipment or supplies of the dwelling. Transportation of the household goods must be arranged and paid for by you or by another individual on your behalf. This may include items moving from a factory or store when you purchase them to use in your dwelling. You must request that these items be transported, and you (or another individual on your behalf) must pay the transportation charges to the mover.

Inventory — The detailed descriptive list of your household goods showing the number and condition of each item.

Line Haul Charges — The charges for the vehicle transportation portion of your move. These charges, if separately stated, apply in addition to the accessorial service charges.

Long Carry — A charge for carrying articles excessive distances between the mover's vehicle and your residence. Charges for these services may be in addition to the line haul charges.

May — An option. You or your mover may do something, but it is not a requirement.

Mover — A motor carrier engaged in the transportation of household goods and its household goods agents.

Must — A legal obligation. You or your mover must do something.

Order for Service — The document authorizing the mover to transport your household goods.

Order (Bill of Lading) Number — The number used to identify and track your shipment.

Peak Season Rates — Higher line haul charges applicable during the summer months.

Pickup and Delivery Charges — Separate transportation charges applicable for transporting your shipment between the storage-in-transit warehouse and your residence.

Reasonable Dispatch — The performance of transportation on the dates, or during the period of time, agreed upon by you and your mover and shown on the Order for Service/Bill of Lading. For example, if your mover deliberately withholds any shipment from delivery after you offer to pay the binding estimate or 110 percent of a non-binding estimate, your mover has not transported the goods with reasonable dispatch. The term "reasonable dispatch" excludes transportation provided under your mover's tariff provisions requiring guaranteed service dates. Your mover will have the defense of force majeure, i.e., that the contract cannot be performed owing to causes that are outside the control of the parties and that could not be avoided by exercise of due care.

Should — A recommendation. We recommend you or your mover do something, but it is not a requirement.

Shuttle Service — The use of a smaller vehicle to provide service to residences not accessible to the mover's normal line haul vehicles.

Storage-In-Transit (SIT) — The temporary warehouse storage of your shipment pending further transportation, with or without notification to you. If you (or someone representing you) cannot accept delivery on the agreed-upon date or within the agreed-upon time period (for example, because your home is not quite ready to occupy), your mover may place your shipment into SIT without notifying you. In those circumstances, you will be responsible for the added charges for SIT service, as well as the warehouse handling and final delivery charges.

However, your mover also may place your shipment into SIT if your mover was able to make delivery before the agreed-upon date (or before the first day of the agreed-upon delivery period), but you did not concur with early delivery. In those circumstances, your mover must notify you immediately of the SIT, and your mover is fully responsible for redelivery charges, handling charges, and storage charges.

Part 375 - Transportation of Household Goods in Interstate Commerce — Appendix A

Surface Transportation Board — An agency within the U.S. Department of Transportation that regulates household goods carrier tariffs, among other responsibilities. The Surface Transportation Board's address is 1925 K Street, NW., Washington, DC 20423-0001 Tele. 202-565-1674.

Tariff — An issuance (in whole or in part) containing rates, rules, regulations, classifications, or other provisions. The Surface Transportation Board requires that a tariff contain three specific items. First, an accurate description of the services the mover offers to the public. Second, the specific applicable rates (or the basis for calculating the specific applicable rates) and service terms for services offered to the public. Third, the mover's tariff must be arranged in a way that allows you to determine the exact rate(s) and service terms applicable to your shipment.

Valuation — The degree of worth of the shipment. The valuation charge compensates the mover for assuming a greater degree of liability than is provided for in its base transportation charges.

Warehouse Handling — A charge may be applicable each time SIT service is provided. Charges for these services may be in addition to the line haul charges. This charge compensates the mover for the physical placement and removal of items within the warehouse.

We, Us, and **Our** — The Federal Motor Carrier Safety Administration (FMCSA).

You and **Your** — You are an individual shipper of household goods. You are a consignor or consignee of a household goods shipment and your mover identifies you as such in the bill of lading contract. You own the goods being transported and pay the transportation charges to the mover.

Where may other terms used in this pamphlet be defined?

You may find other terms used in this pamphlet defined in 49 U.S.C. 13102. The statute controls the definitions in this pamphlet. If terms are used in this pamphlet and the terms are defined neither here nor in 49 U.S.C. 13102, the terms will have the ordinary practical meaning of such terms.

Subpart B - Before Requesting Services From Any Mover

What Is My Mover's Normal Liability for Loss or Damage When My Mover Accepts Goods From Me?

In general, your mover is legally liable for loss or damage that occurs during performance of any transportation of household goods and of all related services identified on your mover's lawful bill of lading.

Your mover is liable for loss of, or damage to, any household goods to the extent provided in the current Surface Transportation Board's Released Rates Order. You may obtain a copy of the current Released Rates Order by contacting the Surface Transportation Board at the address provided under the definition of the Surface Transportation Board. The rate may be increased annually by your mover based on the U.S. Department of Commerce's Cost of Living Adjustment. Your mover may have additional liability if your mover sells liability insurance to you.

All moving companies are required to assume liability for the value of the goods transported. However, there are different levels of liability, and you should be aware of the amount of protection provided and the charges for each option.

Basically, most movers offer two different levels of liability (options 1 and 2 below) under the terms of their tariffs and the Surface Transportation Board's Released Rates Orders. These orders govern the moving industry.

Option 1: Released Value

This is the most economical protection option available. This no-additional-cost option provides minimal protection. Under this option, the mover assumes liability for no more than 60 cents per pound ($1.32 cents per kilogram), per article. Loss or damage claims are settled based upon the pound (kilogram) weight of the article multiplied by 60 cents per pound ($1.32 cents per kilogram). For example, if your mover lost or destroyed a 10-pound (4.54-kilogram) stereo component valued at $1,000, your mover would be liable for no more than $6.00. Obviously, you should think carefully before agreeing to such an arrangement. There is no extra charge for this minimal protection, but you must sign a specific statement on the bill of lading agreeing to it.

Option 2: Full Value Protection (FVP)

Under this option, the mover is liable for the replacement value of lost or damaged goods (as long as it doesn't exceed the total declared value of the shipment). If you elect to purchase full value protection, and your mover loses, damages or destroys your articles, your mover must repair, replace with like items, or settle in cash at the current market replacement value, regardless of the age of the lost or damaged item. The minimum declared value of a shipment under this option is $5,000 or $4.00 times the actual total weight (in pounds) of the shipment, whichever is greater. For example, the minimum declared value for a 4,000-pound (1,814.4-kilogram) shipment would be $16,000. Your mover may offer you FVP with a $250 or $500 deductible, or with no deductible at all. The amount of the deductible will affect the cost of your FVP coverage. The $4.00 per pound minimum valuation rate may be increased annually by your mover based on changes in the household furnishings element of the Consumer Price Index established by the U.S. Department of Labor's Bureau of Labor Statistics.

Unless you specifically agree to other arrangements, the mover must assume liability for the entire shipment based upon this option. The approximate cost for FVP is $8.50 for each $1,000 of declared value; however, it may vary by mover. In the example above, the valuation charge for a shipment valued at $16,000 would be $136.00. As noted above, this fee may be adjusted annually by your mover based on changes in the household furnishings element of the Consumer Price Index.

Under both of these liability options, movers are permitted to limit their liability for loss or damage to articles of extraordinary value, unless you specifically list these articles on the shipping documents. An article of extraordinary value is any item whose value exceeds $100 per pound ($220 per kilogram). Ask your mover for a complete explanation of this limitation before your move. It is your responsibility to study this provision carefully and make the necessary declaration.

These optional levels of liability are not insurance agreements governed by State insurance laws, but instead are authorized under Released Rates Orders of the Surface Transportation Board of the U.S. Department of Transportation.

In addition to these options, some movers may also offer to sell, or procure for you, separate liability insurance from a third-party insurance company when you release your shipment for transportation at the minimum released value of 60 cents per pound ($1.32 per kilogram) per article (option 1). This is not valuation coverage governed by Federal law, but optional insurance regulated under State law. If you purchase this separate coverage and your mover is responsible for loss or damage, the mover is liable only for an amount not exceeding 60 cents per pound ($1.32 per kilogram) per article, and the balance of the loss is recoverable from the insurance company up to the amount of insurance purchased. The mover's representative can advise you of the availability of such liability insurance, and the cost.

If you purchase liability insurance from or through your mover, the mover is required to issue a policy or other written record of the purchase and to provide you with a copy of the policy or other document at the time of purchase. If the mover fails to comply with this requirement, the mover becomes fully liable for any claim for loss or damage attributed to its negligence.

What Actions by Me Limit or Reduce My Mover's Normal Liability?

Your actions may limit or reduce your mover's normal liability under the following three circumstances:

(1) *You include* perishable, dangerous, or hazardous materials in your household goods without your mover's knowledge.

(2) *You choose liability option 1* but ship household goods valued at more than 60 cents per pound ($1.32 per kilogram) per article.

(3) *You fail to notify your mover in writing* of articles valued at more than $100 per pound ($220 per kilogram). (If you do notify your mover, you will be entitled to full recovery up to the declared value of the article or articles, not to exceed the declared value of the entire shipment.)

What Are Dangerous or Hazardous Materials That May Limit or Reduce My Mover's Normal Liability?

Federal law forbids you to ship hazardous materials in your household goods boxes or luggage without informing your mover. A violation can result in five years' imprisonment and penalties of $250,000 or more (49 U.S.C. 5124). You could also lose or damage your household goods by fire, explosion, or contamination.

If you offer hazardous materials to your mover, you are considered a hazardous materials shipper and must comply with the hazardous materials requirements in 49 CFR Parts 171, 172, and 173, including but not limited to package labeling and marking, shipping papers, and emergency response information. Your mover must comply with 49 CFR Parts 171, 172, 173, and 177 as a hazardous materials carrier.

Hazardous materials include explosives, compressed gases, flammable liquids and solids, oxidizers, poisons, corrosives, and radioactive materials. Examples: Nail polish remover, paints, paint thinners, lighter fluid, gasoline, fireworks, oxygen bottles, propane cylinders, automotive repair and maintenance chemicals, and radiopharmaceuticals.

There are special exceptions for small quantities (up to 70 ounces total) of medicinal and toilet articles carried in your household goods and certain smoking materials carried on your person. For further information, contact your mover.

May My Mover Have Agents?

Yes, your mover may have agents. If your mover has agents, your mover must have written agreements with its prime agents. Your mover and its retained prime agent must sign their agreements. Copies of your mover's prime agent agreements must be in your mover's files for a period of at least 24 months following the date of termination of each agreement.

What Items Must Be in My Mover's Advertisements?

Your mover must publish and use only truthful, straightforward, and honest advertisements. Your mover must include certain information in all advertisements for all services (including any accessorial services incidental to or part of interstate transportation). Your mover must require each of its agents to include the same information in its advertisements. The information must include the following two pieces of information about your mover:

(1) *Name or trade name of the mover* under whose USDOT number the advertised service will originate.

(2) *USDOT number, assigned by FMCSA,* authorizing your mover to operate.

Your mover must display the information as: USDOT No. (assigned number). You should compare the name or trade name of the mover and its USDOT number to the name and USDOT number on the sides of the truck(s) that arrive at your residence. The names and numbers should be identical. If the names and numbers are not identical, you should ask your mover immediately why they are not. You should not allow the mover to load your household goods on its truck(s) until you obtain a satisfactory response from the mover's local agent. The discrepancies may warn of problems you will have later in your business dealings with this mover.

How Must My Mover Handle Complaints and Inquiries?

All movers are expected to respond promptly to complaints or inquiries from you, the customer. Should you have a complaint or question about your move, you should first attempt to obtain a satisfactory response from the mover's local agent, the sales representative who handled the arrangements for your move, or the driver assigned to your shipment.

If for any reason you are unable to obtain a satisfactory response from one of these persons, you should then contact the mover's principal office. When you make such a call, be sure to have available your copies of all documents relating to your move. Particularly important is the number assigned to your shipment by your mover.

Interstate movers are also required to offer neutral arbitration as a means of resolving consumer loss or damage disputes involving loss of or damage to household goods. Your mover is required to provide you with information regarding its arbitration program. You have the right to pursue court action under 49 U.S.C. 14706 to seek judicial redress directly rather than participate in your mover's arbitration program.

All interstate moving companies are required to maintain a complaint and inquiry procedure to assist their customers. At the time you make the arrangements for your move, you should ask the mover's representative for a description of the mover's procedure, the telephone number to be used to contact the mover, and whether the mover will pay for such telephone calls. Your mover's procedure must include the following four things:

(1) *A communications system* allowing you to communicate with your mover's principal place of business by telephone.

(2) *A telephone number.*

(3) *A clear and concise statement* about who must pay for complaint and inquiry telephone calls.

(4) *A written or electronic record system* for recording all inquiries and complaints received from you by any means of communication.

Your mover must give you a clear and concise written description of its procedure. You may want to be certain that the system is in place.

Do I Have the Right to Inspect My Mover's Tariffs (Schedules of Charges) Applicable to My Move?

Federal law requires your mover to advise you of your right to inspect your mover's tariffs (its schedules of rates or charges) governing your shipment. Movers' tariffs are made a part of the contract of carriage (bill of lading) between you and the mover. You may inspect the tariff at the mover's facility, or, upon request, the mover will furnish you a free copy of any tariff provision containing the mover's rates, rules, or charges governing your shipment.

Tariffs may include provisions limiting the mover's liability. This would generally be described in a section on declaring value on the bill of lading. A second tariff provision may set the periods for filing claims. This would generally be described in Section 6 on the reverse side of a bill of lading. A third tariff provision may reserve your mover's right to assess additional charges for additional services performed. For non-binding estimates, another tariff provision may base charges upon the exact weight of the goods transported. Your mover's tariff may contain other provisions that apply to your move. Ask your mover what they might be, and request a copy.

Must My Mover Have an Arbitration Program?

Your mover must have an arbitration program for your use in resolving disputes concerning loss or damage to your household goods. You have the right not to participate in the arbitration program. You may pursue court action under 49 U.S.C. 14706 to seek judicial remedies directly. Your mover must establish and maintain an arbitration program with the following 11 minimum elements:

(1) *The arbitration program offered to you* must prevent your mover from having any special advantage because you live or work in a place distant from the mover's principal or other place of business.

(2) *Before your household goods* are tendered for transport, your mover must provide notice to you of the availability of neutral arbitration, including the following three things:
   (a) *A summary of the arbitration procedure.*
   (b) *Any applicable costs.*
   (c) *A disclosure of the legal effects of electing to use arbitration.*

(3) *Upon your request,* your mover must provide information and forms it considers necessary for initiating an action to resolve a dispute under arbitration.

(4) *Each person authorized to arbitrate* must be independent of the parties to the dispute and capable of resolving such disputes fairly and expeditiously. Your mover must ensure the arbitrator is authorized and able to obtain from you or your mover any material or relevant information to carry out a fair and expeditious decision-making process.

(5) *You must not be required to pay* more than one-half of the arbitration's cost. The arbitrator may determine the percentage of payment of the costs for each party in the arbitration decision, but must not make you pay more than half.

(6) *Your mover must not require you* to agree to use arbitration before a dispute arises.

(7) *You will be bound by arbitration* for claims of $5,000 or less if you request arbitration.

(8) *You will be bound by arbitration* for claims of more than $5,000 only if you request arbitration and your mover agrees to it.

(9) *If you and your mover both agree,* the arbitrator may provide for an oral presentation of a dispute by a party or representative of a party.

(10) *The arbitrator must render a decision* within 60 days of receipt of written notification of the dispute, and a decision by an arbitrator may include any remedies appropriate under the circumstances.

(11) *The 60-day period may be extended* for a reasonable period if you fail, or your mover fails, to provide information in a timely manner.

Your mover must produce and distribute a concise, easy-to-read, accurate summary of its arbitration program.

Must My Mover Inform Me About My Rights and Responsibilities Under Federal Law?

Yes, your mover must inform you about your rights and responsibilities under Federal law. Your mover must produce and distribute this document. It should be in the general order and contain the text of Appendix A to 49 CFR Part 375.

What Other Information Must My Mover Provide Me?

Before your mover executes an order for service for a shipment of household goods, your mover must furnish you with the following four documents:

(1) *The contents of Appendix A,* "Your Rights and Responsibilities When You Move" — this pamphlet.

(2) *A concise, easy-to-read, accurate summary* of your mover's arbitration program.

Part 375 - Transportation of Household Goods in Interstate Commerce — Appendix A

(3) *A notice of availability of the applicable sections* of your mover's tariff for the estimate of charges, including an explanation that you may examine the tariff sections or have copies sent to you upon request.

(4) *A concise, easy-to-read, accurate summary* of your mover's customer complaint and inquiry handling procedures. Included in this summary must be the following two items:

(a) *The main telephone number you may use* to communicate with your mover.

(b) *A clear and concise statement* concerning who must pay for telephone calls.

Your mover may, at its discretion, provide additional information to you.

How Must My Mover Collect Charges?

Your mover must issue you an honest, truthful freight or expense bill for each shipment transported. Your mover's freight or expense bill must contain the following 19 items:

(1) *Name of the consignor.*
(2) *Name of the consignees.*
(3) *Date of the shipment.*
(4) *Origin point.*
(5) *Destination points.*
(6) *Number of packages.*
(7) *Description of the freight.*
(8) *Weight of the freight* (if applicable to the rating of the freight).
(9) *The volume of the freight* (if applicable to the rating of the freight).
(10) *The measurement of the freight* (if applicable to the rating of the freight).
(11) *Exact rate(s) assessed.*
(12) *Disclosure of the actual rates,* charges, and allowances for the transportation service, when your mover electronically presents or transmits freight or expense bills to you. These rates must be in accordance with the mover's applicable tariff.
(13) *An indication of whether adjustments may apply to the bill.*
(14) *Total charges due and acceptable methods of payment.*
(15) *The nature and amount of any special service charges.*
(16) *The points where special services were rendered.*
(17) *Route of movement and name of each mover* participating in the transportation.
(18) *Transfer points where shipments moved.*
(19) *Address where you must pay* or address of bill issuer's principal place of business.

Your mover must present its freight or expense bill to you within 15 days of the date of delivery of a shipment at its destination. The computation of time excludes Saturdays, Sundays, and Federal holidays. (Bills for charges exceeding 110 percent of a non-binding estimate, and for additional services requested or found necessary after the shipment is in transit, will be presented no sooner than 30 days after the date of delivery.)

If your mover lacks sufficient information to compute its charges, your mover must present its freight bill for payment within 15 days of the date when sufficient information does become available.

May My Mover Collect Charges Upon Delivery?

Yes. Your mover must specify the form of payment acceptable at delivery when the mover prepares an estimate and order for service. The mover and its agents must honor the form of payment at delivery, except when you mutually agree to a change in writing. The mover must also specify the same form of payment when it prepares your bill of lading, unless you agree to a change. See also "May my mover accept charge or credit cards for my payments?"

You must be prepared to pay 10 percent more than the estimated amount, if your goods are moving under a non-binding estimate. Every collect-on-delivery shipper must have available 110 percent of the estimate at the time of delivery.

May My Mover Extend Credit to Me?

Extending credit to you is not the same as accepting your charge or credit card(s) as payment. Your mover may extend credit to you in the amount of the tariff charges. If your mover extends credit to you, your mover becomes like a bank offering you a line of credit, whose size and interest rate are determined by your ability to pay its tariff charges within the credit period. Your mover must ensure you will pay its tariff charges within the credit period. Your mover may relinquish possession of freight before you pay its tariff charges, at its discretion.

The credit period must begin on the day following presentation of your mover's freight bill to you. Under Federal regulation, the standard credit period is 7 days, excluding Saturdays, Sundays, and Federal holidays. Your mover must also extend the credit period to a total of 30 calendar days if the freight bill is not paid within the 7-day period. A service charge equal to one percent of the amount of the freight bill, subject to a $20 minimum, will be assessed for this extension and for each additional 30-day period the charges go unpaid.

Your failure to pay within the credit period will require your mover to determine whether you will comply with the Federal household goods transportation credit regulations in good faith in the future before extending credit again.

May My Mover Accept Charge or Credit Cards for My Payments?

Your mover may allow you to use a charge or credit card for payment of the freight charges. Your mover may accept charge or credit cards whenever you ship with it under an agreement and tariff requiring payment by cash or cash equivalents. Cash equivalents are a certified check, money order, or cashier's check (a check that a financial institution — bank, credit union, savings and loan — draws upon itself and that is signed by an officer of the financial institution).

If your mover allows you to pay for a freight or expense bill by charge or credit card, your mover deems such a payment to be equivalent to payment by cash, certified check, or cashier's check. It must note in writing on the order for service and the bill of lading whether you may pay for the transportation and related services using a charge or credit card. You should ask your mover at the time the estimate is written whether it will accept charge or credit cards at delivery.

The mover must specify what charge or credit cards it will accept, such as American Express™, Discover™, MasterCard™, or Visa™. If your mover agrees to accept payment by charge or credit card, you must arrange with your mover for the delivery only at a time when your mover can obtain authorization for your credit card transaction.

If you cause a charge or credit card issuer to reverse a transaction, your mover may consider your action tantamount to forcing your mover to provide an involuntary extension of its credit.

Subpart C - Service Options Provided

What Service Options May My Mover Provide?

Your mover may provide any service options it chooses. It is customary for movers to offer several price and service options.

The total cost of your move may increase if you want additional or special services. Before you agree to have your shipment moved under a bill of lading providing special service, you should have a clear understanding with your mover of what the additional cost will be. You should always consider whether other movers may provide the services you require without requiring you to pay the additional charges.

One service option is a space reservation. If you agree to have your shipment transported under a space reservation agreement, you will pay for a minimum number of cubic feet of space in the moving van regardless of how much space in the van your shipment actually occupies.

A second option is expedited service. This aids you if you must have your shipments transported on or between specific dates when the mover could not ordinarily agree to do so in its normal operations.

A third customary service option is exclusive use of a vehicle. If for any reason you desire or require that your shipment be moved by itself on the mover's truck or trailer, most movers will provide such service.

Another service option is guaranteed service on or between agreed dates. You enter into an agreement with the mover where the mover provides for your shipment to be picked up, transported to destination, and delivered on specific guaranteed dates. If the mover fails to provide the service as agreed, you are entitled to be compensated at a predetermined amount or a daily rate (per diem) regardless of the expense you might actually have incurred as a result of the mover's failure to perform.

Before requesting or agreeing to any of these price and service options, be sure to ask the mover's representatives about the final costs you will pay.

Transport of Shipments on Two or More Vehicles

Although all movers try to move each shipment on one truck, it becomes necessary, at times, to divide a shipment among two or more trucks. This may occur if your mover has underestimated the cubic feet (meters) of space required for your shipment and it will not all fit on the first truck. Your mover will pick up the remainder, or "leave behind," on a second truck at a later time, and this part of your shipment may arrive at the destination later than the first truck. When this occurs, your transportation charges will be determined as if the entire shipment had moved on one truck.

If it is important for you to avoid this inconvenience of a "leave behind," be sure your estimate includes an accurate calculation of the cubic feet (meters) required for your shipment. Ask your estimator to use a "Table of Measurements" form in making this calculation. Consider asking for a binding estimate. A binding estimate is more likely to be conservative with regard to cubic feet (meters) than a non-binding estimate. If the mover offers space reservation service, consider purchasing this service for the necessary amount of space plus some margin for error. In any case, you would be prudent to "prioritize" your goods in advance of the move so the driver will load the more essential items on the first truck if some are left behind.

If My Mover Sells Liability Insurance Coverage, What Must My Mover Do?

If your mover provides the service of selling additional liability insurance, your mover must follow certain regulations.

Your mover, its employees, or its agents, may sell, offer to sell, or procure additional liability insurance coverage for you for loss or damage to your shipment if you release the shipment for transportation at a value not exceeding 60 cents per pound ($1.32 per kilogram) per article.

Your mover may offer, sell, or procure any type of insurance policy covering loss or damage in excess of its specified liability.

Your mover must issue you a policy or other appropriate evidence of the insurance you purchased. Your mover must provide a copy of the policy or other appropriate evidence to you at the time your mover sells or procures the insurance. Your mover must issue policies written in plain English.

Your mover must clearly specify the nature and extent of coverage under the policy. Your mover's failure to issue you a policy, or other appropriate evidence of insurance you purchased, will subject your mover to full liability for any claims to recover loss or damage attributed to it.

Your mover's tariff must provide for liability insurance coverage. The tariff must also provide for the base transportation charge, including its assumption of full liability for the value of the shipment. This would offer you a degree of protection in the event your mover fails to issue you a policy or other appropriate evidence of insurance at the time of purchase.

Subpart D - Estimating Charges

Must My Mover Estimate the Transportation and Accessorial Charges for My Move?

We require your mover to prepare a written estimate on every shipment transported for you. You are entitled to a copy of the written estimate when your mover prepares it. Your mover must provide you a written estimate of all charges, including transportation, accessorial, and advance charges. Your mover's "rate quote" is not an estimate. You and your mover must sign the estimate of charges. Your mover must provide you with a dated copy of the estimate of charges at the time you sign the estimate.

You should be aware that if you receive an estimate from a household goods broker, the mover is not required to accept the estimate. Be sure to obtain a written estimate from the mover if a mover tells you orally that it will accept the broker's estimate.

Your mover must specify the form of payment the mover and its delivering agent will honor at delivery. Payment forms may include but are not limited to cash, certified check, money order, cashier's check, a specific charge card such as American Express ^{TM}, a specific credit card such as Visa ^{TM}, and your mover's own credit.

If your mover provides you with an estimate based on volume that will later be converted to a weight-based rate, the mover must provide you an explanation in writing of the formula used to calculate the conversion to weight. Your mover must specify that the final charges will be based on actual weight and services. Before loading your household goods, and upon mutual agreement between you and your mover, your mover may amend an estimate of charges. Your mover may not amend the estimate after loading the shipment.

A binding estimate is an agreement made in advance with your mover. It guarantees the total cost of the move based upon the quantities and services shown on your mover's estimate.

A non-binding estimate is what your mover believes the total cost will be for the move, based upon the estimated weight of the shipment and the accessorial services requested. A non-binding estimate is not binding on your mover. Your mover will base the final charges upon the actual weight of your shipment, the services provided, and its tariff provisions in effect. You must be prepared to pay 10 percent more than the estimated amount at delivery.

How Must My Mover Estimate Charges Under the Regulations?
Binding Estimates

Your mover may charge you for providing a binding estimate. The binding estimate must clearly describe the shipment and all services provided.

When you receive a binding estimate, you cannot be required to pay any more than the estimated amount at delivery. If you have requested the mover provide more services than those included in the estimate, the mover must not demand full payment for those added services at time of delivery. Instead, the mover must bill for those services later, as explained below. Such services might include destination charges that often are not known at origin (such as long carry charges, shuttle charges, or extra stair carry charges).

A binding estimate must be in writing, and a copy must be made available to you before you move.

If you agree to a binding estimate, you are responsible for paying the charges due by cash, certified check, money order, or cashier's check. The charges are due your mover at the time of delivery unless your mover agrees, before you move, to extend credit or to accept payment by a specific charge card such as American Express ^{TM} or a specific credit card such as Visa ^{TM}. If you are unable to pay at the time the shipment is delivered, the mover may place your shipment in storage at your expense until you pay the charges.

Other requirements of binding estimates include the following eight elements:

(1) *Your mover must retain a copy* of each binding estimate as an attachment to the bill of lading.

(2) *Your mover must clearly indicate* upon each binding estimate's face that the estimate is binding upon you and your mover. Each binding estimate must also clearly indicate on its face that the charges shown are the charges to be assessed for only those services specifically identified in the estimate.

(3) *Your mover must clearly describe* binding estimate shipments and all services to be provided.

(4) *If, before loading your shipment,* your mover believes you are tendering additional household goods or are requiring additional services not identified in the binding estimate, and you and your mover cannot reach an agreement, your mover may refuse to service the shipment. If your mover agrees to service the shipment, your mover must do one of the following three things:

  (a) *Reaffirm the binding estimate.*
  (b) *Negotiate a revised written binding estimate* listing the additional household goods or services.
  (c) *Add an attachment to the contract, in writing,* stating you both will consider the original binding estimate as a non-binding estimate. You should read more below. This may seriously affect how much you may pay for the entire move.

(5) *Once your mover loads your shipment,* your mover's failure to execute a new binding estimate or to agree with you to treat the original estimate as a non-binding estimate signifies it has reaffirmed the original binding estimate. Your mover may not collect more than the amount of the original binding estimate, except as provided in the next two paragraphs.

(6) *Your mover may believe* additional services are necessary to properly service your shipment after your household goods are in transit. Your mover must inform you what the additional services are before performing them. Your mover must allow you at least one hour to determine whether you want the additional services performed. Such additional services include carrying your furniture up additional stairs or using an elevator. If these services do not appear on your mover's estimate, your mover must deliver your shipment and bill you later for the additional services.

If you agree to pay for the additional services, your mover must execute a written attachment to be made an integral part of the bill of lading and have you sign the written attachment. This may be done through fax transmissions. You will be billed for the additional services 30 days following the date of delivery.

(7) *If you add additional services* after your household goods are in transit, you will be billed for the additional services but only be expected to pay the full amount of the binding estimate to receive delivery. Your mover must bill you for the balance of any remaining charges for these additional services no sooner than 30 days after delivery. For example, if your binding estimate shows total charges at delivery should be $1,000 but

Part 375 - Transportation of Household Goods in Interstate Commerce — Appendix A

your actual charges at destination are $1,500, your mover must deliver the shipment upon payment of $1,000. The mover must bill you for the remaining $500 no sooner than 30 days after the date of delivery.

(8) *Failure of your mover* to relinquish possession of a shipment upon your offer to pay the binding estimate amount constitutes your mover's failure to transport a shipment with "reasonable dispatch" and subjects your mover to cargo delay claims pursuant to 49 CFR Part 370.

Non-Binding Estimates

Your mover is not permitted to charge you for giving a non-binding estimate.

A non-binding estimate is not a bid or contract. Your mover provides it to you to give you a general idea of the cost of the move, but it does not bind your mover to the estimated cost. You should expect the final cost to be more than the estimate. The actual cost will be in accordance with your mover's tariffs. Federal law requires your mover to collect the charges shown in its tariffs, regardless of what your mover writes in its non-binding estimates. That is why it is important to ask for copies of the applicable portions of the mover's tariffs before deciding on a mover. The charges contained in movers' tariffs are essentially the same for the same weight shipment moving the same distance. If you obtain different non-binding estimates from different movers, you must pay only the amount specified in your mover's tariff. Therefore, a non-binding estimate may have no effect on the amount that you will ultimately have to pay.

You must be prepared to pay 10 percent more than the estimated amount at the time of delivery. Every collect-on-delivery shipper must have available 110 percent of the estimate at the time of delivery. If you order additional services from your mover after your goods are in transit, the mover will then bill you 30 days after delivery for any remaining charges.

Non-binding estimates must be in writing and clearly describe the shipment and all services provided. Any time a mover provides such an estimate, the amount of the charges estimated must be on the order for service and bill of lading related to your shipment. When you are given a non-binding estimate, do not sign or accept the order for service or bill of lading unless the mover enters the amount estimated on each form it prepares.

Other requirements of non-binding estimates include the following 10 elements:

(1) *Your mover must provide* reasonably accurate non-binding estimates based upon the estimated weight of the shipment and services required.

(2) *Your mover must explain to you* that all charges on shipments moved under non-binding estimates will be those appearing in your mover's tariffs applicable to the transportation. If your mover provides a non-binding estimate of approximate costs, your mover is not bound by such an estimate.

(3) *Your mover must furnish non-binding estimates* without charge and in writing to you.

(4) *Your mover must retain a copy* of each non-binding estimate as an attachment to the bill of lading.

(5) *Your mover must clearly indicate* on the face of a non-binding estimate that the estimate is not binding upon your mover and the charges shown are the approximate charges to be assessed for the services identified in the estimate.

(6) *Your mover must clearly describe* on the face of a non-binding estimate the entire shipment and all services to be provided.

(7) *If, before loading your shipment,* your mover believes you are tendering additional household goods or requiring additional services not identified in the non-binding estimate, and you and your mover cannot reach an agreement, your mover may refuse to service the shipment. If your mover agrees to service the shipment, your mover must do one of the following two things:
  (a) Reaffirm the non-binding estimate.
  (b) Negotiate a revised written non-binding estimate listing the additional household goods or services.

(8) *Once your mover loads your shipment,* your mover's failure to execute a new estimate signifies it has reaffirmed the original non-binding estimate. Your mover may not collect more than 110 percent of the amount of this estimate at destination.

(9) *Your mover may believe* additional services are necessary to properly service your shipment after your household goods are in transit. Your mover must inform you what the additional services are before performing them. Your mover must allow you at least one hour to determine whether you want the additional services performed. Such additional services include carrying your furniture up additional stairs or using an elevator. If these services do not appear on your mover's estimate, your mover must deliver your shipment and bill you later for the additional services.

If you agree to pay for the additional services, your mover must execute a written attachment to be made an integral part of the bill of lading and have you sign the written attachment. This may be done through fax transmissions. You will be billed for the additional services after 30 days from delivery.

(10) *If you add additional services* after your household goods are in transit, you will be billed for the additional services. To receive delivery, however, you are required to pay no more than 110 percent of the non-binding estimate. At least 30 days after delivery, your mover must bill you for any remaining balance, including the additional services you requested. For example, if your non-binding estimate shows total charges at delivery should be $1,000 but your actual charges at destination are $1,500, your mover must deliver the shipment upon payment of $1,100. The mover must bill you for the remaining $400 no sooner than 30 days after the date of delivery.

If your mover furnishes a non-binding estimate, your mover must enter the estimated charges upon the order for service and upon the bill of lading.

Your mover must retain a record of all estimates of charges for each move performed for at least one year from the date your mover made the estimate.

What Payment Arrangements Must My Mover Have in Place To Secure Delivery of My Household Goods Shipment?

If your total bill is 110 percent or less of the non-binding estimate, the mover can require payment in full upon delivery. If the bill exceeds 110 percent of the non-binding estimate, your mover must relinquish possession of the shipment at the time of delivery upon payment of 110 percent of the estimated amount. Your mover should have specified its acceptable form of payment on the estimate, order for service, and bill of lading. Your mover's failure to relinquish possession of a shipment after you offer to pay 110 percent of the estimated charges constitutes its failure to transport the shipment with "reasonable dispatch" and subjects your mover to your cargo delay claims under 49 CFR Part 370.

Your mover must bill for the payment of the balance of any remaining charges after 30 days from delivery.

Subpart E - Pickup of My Shipment of Household Goods

Must My Mover Write Up an Order for Service?

We require your mover to prepare an order for service on every shipment transported for you. You are entitled to a copy of the order for service when your mover prepares it.

The order for service is not a contract. Should you cancel or delay your move or if you decide not to use the mover, you should promptly cancel the order.

If you or your mover change any agreed-upon dates for pickup or delivery of your shipment, or agree to any change in the non-binding estimate, your mover may prepare a written change to the order for service. The written change must be attached to the order for service.

The order for service must contain the following 15 elements:

(1) *Your mover's name and address* and the USDOT number assigned to your mover.

(2) *Your name, address and, if available, telephone number(s).*

(3) *The name, address, and telephone number* of the delivering mover's office or agent at or nearest to the destination of your shipment.

(4) *A telephone number* where you may contact your mover or its designated agent.

(5) *One of the following three dates and times:*
  (i) *The agreed-upon pickup date* and agreed delivery date of your move.
  (ii) *The agreed-upon period(s) of the entire move.*
  (iii) *If your mover is transporting the shipment* on a guaranteed service basis, the guaranteed dates or periods of time for pickup, transportation, and delivery. Your mover must enter any penalty or per diem requirements upon the agreement under this item.

(6) *The names and addresses* of any other motor carriers, when known, that will participate in interline transportation of the shipment.

(7) *The form of payment* your mover will honor at delivery. The payment information must be the same as was entered on the estimate.
(8) *The terms and conditions* for payment of the total charges, including notice of any minimum charges.
(9) *The maximum amount your mover will demand* at the time of delivery to obtain possession of the shipment, when transported on a collect-on-delivery basis.
(10) *If not provided in the bill of lading,* the Surface Transportation Board's required released rates valuation statement, and the charges, if any, for optional valuation coverage. The STB's required released rates may be increased annually by your mover based on the U.S. Department of Commerce's Cost of Living Adjustment.
(11) *A complete description* of any special or accessorial services ordered and minimum weight or volume charges applicable to the shipment.
(12) *Any identification or registration number* your mover assigns to the shipment.
(13) *For non-binding estimated charges,* your mover's reasonably accurate estimate of the amount of the charges, the method of payment of total charges, and the maximum amount (110 percent of the non-binding estimate) your mover will demand at the time of delivery for you to obtain possession of the shipment.
(14) *For binding estimated charges,* the amount of charges your mover will demand based upon the binding estimate and the terms of payment under the estimate.
(15) *An indication* of whether you request notification of the charges before delivery. You must provide your mover with the telephone number(s) or address(es) where your mover will transmit such communications.

You and your mover must sign the order for service. Your mover must provide a dated copy of the order for service to you at the time your mover signs the order. Your mover must provide you the opportunity to rescind the order for service without any penalty for a three-day period after you sign the order for service, if you scheduled the shipment to be loaded more than three days after you sign the order.

Your mover should provide you with documents that are as complete as possible, and with all charges clearly identified. However, as a practical matter, your mover usually cannot give you a complete bill of lading before transporting your goods. This is both because the shipment cannot be weighed until it is in transit and because other charges for service, such as unpacking, storage-in-transit, and various destination charges, cannot be determined until the shipment reaches its destination.

Therefore, your mover can require you to sign a partially complete bill of lading if it contains all relevant information except the actual shipment weight and any other information necessary to determine the final charges for all services provided. Signing the bill of lading allows you to choose the valuation option, request special services, and/or acknowledge the terms and conditions of released valuation.

Your mover also may provide you, strictly for informational purposes, with blank or incomplete documents pertaining to the move.

Before loading your shipment, and upon mutual agreement of both you and your mover, your mover may amend an order for service. Your mover must retain records of an order for service it transported for at least one year from the date your mover wrote the order.

Your mover must inform you, before or at the time of loading, if the mover reasonably expects a special or accessorial service is necessary to transport a shipment safely. Your mover must refuse to accept the shipment when your mover reasonably expects a special or accessorial service is necessary to transport a shipment safely, but you refuse to purchase the special or accessorial service. Your mover must make a written note if you refuse any special or accessorial services that your mover reasonably expects to be necessary.

Must My Mover Write Up an Inventory of the Shipment?

Yes. Your mover must prepare an inventory of your shipment before or at the time of loading. If your mover's driver fails to prepare an inventory, you should write a detailed inventory of your shipment listing any damage or unusual wear to any items. The purpose is to make a record of the existence and condition of each item.

After completing the inventory, you should sign each page and ask the mover's driver to sign each page. Before you sign it, it is important you make sure that the inventory lists every item in the shipment and that the entries regarding the condition of each item are correct. You have the right to note any disagreement. If an item is missing or damaged when your mover delivers the shipment, your subsequent ability to dispute the items lost or damaged may depend upon your notations.

You should retain a copy of the inventory. Your mover may keep the original if the driver prepared it. If your mover's driver completed an inventory, the mover must attach the complete inventory to the bill of lading as an integral part of the bill of lading.

Must My Mover Write Up a Bill of Lading?

The bill of lading is the contract between you and the mover. The mover is required by law to prepare a bill of lading for every shipment it transports. The information on a bill of lading is required to be the same information shown on the order for service. The driver who loads your shipment must give you a copy of the bill of lading before or at the time of loading your furniture and other household goods.

It is your responsibility to read the bill of lading before you accept it. It is your responsibility to understand the bill of lading before you sign it. If you do not agree with something on the bill of lading, do not sign it until you are satisfied it is correct.

The bill of lading requires the mover to provide the service you have requested. You must pay the charges set forth in the bill of lading.

The bill of lading is an important document. Do not lose or misplace your copy. Have it available until your shipment is delivered, all charges are paid, and all claims, if any, are settled.

A bill of lading must include the following 14 elements:

(1) *Your mover's name and address,* or the name and address of the motor carrier issuing the bill of lading.
(2) *The names and addresses* of any other motor carriers, when known, who will participate in the transportation of the shipment.
(3) *The name, address, and telephone number* of the office of the motor carrier you must contact in relation to the transportation of the shipment.
(4) *The form of payment* your mover will honor at delivery. The payment information must be the same that was entered on the estimate and order for service.
(5) *When your mover transports your shipment* under a collect-on-delivery basis, your name, address, and telephone number where the mover will notify you about the charges.
(6) *For non-guaranteed service,* the agreed-upon date or period of time for pickup of the shipment and the agreed-upon date or period of time for the delivery of the shipment. The agreed-upon dates or periods for pickup and delivery entered upon the bill of lading must conform to the agreed-upon dates or periods of time for pickup and delivery entered upon the order for service or a proper amendment to the order for service.
(7) *For guaranteed service,* the dates for pickup and delivery and any penalty or per diem entitlements due you under the agreement.
(8) *The actual date of pickup.*
(9) *The identification number(s) of the vehicle(s)* in which your mover loads your shipment.
(10) *The terms and conditions* for payment of the total charges including notice of any minimum charges.
(11) *The maximum amount* your mover will demand from you at the time of delivery for you to obtain possession of your shipment, when your mover transports under a collect-on-delivery basis.
(12) *If not provided in the order for service,* the Surface Transportation Board's required released rates valuation statement, and the charges, if any, for optional valuation coverage. The Board's required released rates may be increased annually by your mover based on the U.S. Department of Commerce's Cost of Living Adjustment.
(13) *Evidence of any insurance coverage* sold to or procured for you from an independent insurer, including the amount of the premium for such insurance.

Part 375 - Transportation of Household Goods in Interstate Commerce   Appendix A

(14) *Each attachment to the bill of lading.* Each attachment is an integral part of the bill of lading contract. If not provided to you elsewhere by the mover, the following three items must be added as attachments:
  (i) *The binding or non-binding estimate.*
  (ii) *The order for service.*
  (iii) *The inventory.*

A copy of the bill of lading must accompany your shipment at all times while in the possession of your mover or its agent(s). When your mover loads the shipment on a vehicle for transportation, the bill of lading must be in the possession of the driver responsible for the shipment. Your mover must retain bills of lading for shipments it transported for at least one year from the date your mover created the bill of lading.

Should I Reach an Agreement With My Mover About Pickup and Delivery Times?

You and your mover should reach an agreement for pickup and delivery times. It is your responsibility to determine on what date, or between what dates, you need to have the shipment picked up and on what date, or between what dates, you require delivery. It is your mover's responsibility to tell you if it can provide service on or between those dates, or, if not, on what other dates it can provide the service.

In the process of reaching an agreement with your mover, you may find it necessary to alter your moving and travel plans if no mover can provide service on the specific dates you desire.

Do not agree to have your shipment picked up or delivered "as soon as possible." The dates or periods you and your mover agree upon should be definite.

Once an agreement is reached, your mover must enter those dates upon the order for service and the bill of lading.

Once your goods are loaded, your mover is contractually bound to provide the service described in the bill of lading. Your mover's only defense for not providing the service on the dates called for is the defense of force majeure. This is a legal term. It means that when circumstances change, were not foreseen, and are beyond the control of your mover, preventing your mover from performing the service agreed to in the bill of lading, your mover is not responsible for damages resulting from its nonperformance.

This may occur when you do not inform your mover of the exact delivery requirements. For example, because of restrictions trucks must follow at your new location, the mover may not be able to take its truck down the street of your residence and may need to shuttle the shipment using another type of vehicle.

Must My Mover Determine the Weight of My Shipment?

Generally, yes. If your mover transports your household goods on a non-binding estimate under the mover's tariffs based upon weight, your mover must determine the weight of the shipment. If your mover provided a binding estimate and has loaded your shipment without claiming you have added additional items or services, the weight of the shipment will not affect the charges you will pay. If your mover is transporting your shipment based upon the volume of the shipment — that is, a set number of cubic feet (or yards or meters) — the weight of the shipment likewise will not affect the charges you will pay.

Your mover must determine the weight of your shipment before requesting you to pay for any charges dependent upon your shipment's weight.

Most movers have a minimum weight or volume charge for transporting a shipment. Generally, the minimum is the charge for transporting a shipment of at least 3,000 pounds (1,362 kilograms).

If your shipment appears to weigh less than the mover's minimum weight, your mover must advise you on the order for service of the minimum cost before transporting your shipment. Should your mover fail to advise you of the minimum charges and your shipment is less than the minimum weight, your mover must base your final charges upon the actual weight, not upon the minimum weight.

How Must My Mover Determine the Weight of My Shipment?

Your mover must weigh your shipment upon a certified scale.

The weight of your shipment must be obtained by using one of two methods.

Origin Weighing — Your mover may weigh your shipment in the city or area where it loads your shipment. If it elects this option, the driver must weigh the truck before coming to your residence. This is called the tare weight. At the time of this first weighing, the truck may already be partially loaded with another shipment(s). This will not affect the weight of your shipment. The truck should also contain the pads, dollies, hand trucks, ramps, and other equipment normally used in the transportation of household goods shipments.

After loading, the driver will weigh the truck again to obtain the loaded weight, called the gross weight. The net weight of your shipment is then obtained by subtracting the tare weight before loading from the gross weight.

Gross Weight - Tare Weight Before Loading = Net Weight.

Destination Weighing (Also called Back Weighing) — The mover is also permitted to determine the weight of your shipment at the destination after it delivers your load. Weighing your shipment at destination instead of at origin will not affect the accuracy of the shipment weight. The most important difference is that your mover will not determine the exact charges on your shipment before it is unloaded.

Destination weighing is done in reverse of origin weighing. After arriving in the city or area where you are moving, the driver will weigh the truck. Your shipment will still be on the truck. Your mover will determine the gross weight before coming to your new residence to unload. After unloading your shipment, the driver will again weigh the truck to obtain the tare weight. The net weight of your shipment will then be obtained by subtracting the tare weight after delivery from the gross weight.

Gross Weight - Tare Weight After Delivery = Net Weight.

At the time of both weighings, your mover's truck must have installed or loaded all pads, dollies, hand trucks, ramps, and other equipment required in the transportation of your shipment. The driver and other persons must be off the vehicle at the time of both weighings. The fuel tanks on the vehicle must be full at the time of each weighing. In lieu of this requirement, your mover must not add fuel between the two weighings when the tare weighing is the first weighing performed.

Your mover may detach the trailer of a tractor-trailer vehicle combination from the tractor and have the trailer weighed separately at each weighing provided the length of the scale platform is adequate to accommodate and support the entire trailer.

Your mover may use an alternative method to weigh your shipment if it weighs 3,000 pounds (1,362 kilograms) or less. The only alternative method allowed is weighing the shipment upon a platform or warehouse certified scale before loading your shipment for transportation or after unloading.

Your mover must use the net weight of shipments transported in large containers, such as ocean or railroad containers. Your mover will calculate the difference between the tare weight of the container (including all pads, blocking and bracing used in the transportation of your shipment) and the gross weight of the container with your shipment loaded in the container.

You have the right, and your mover must inform you of your right, to observe all weighings of your shipment. Your mover must tell you where and when each weighing will occur. Your mover must give you a reasonable opportunity to be present to observe the weighings.

You may waive your right to observe any weighing or reweighing. This does not affect any of your other rights under Federal law.

Your mover may request you waive your right to have a shipment weighed upon a certified scale. Your mover may want to weigh the shipment upon a trailer's on-board, noncertified scale. You should demand your right to have a certified scale used. The use of a non-certified scale may cause you to pay a higher final bill for your move, if the noncertified scale does not accurately weigh your shipment. Remember that certified scales are inspected and approved for accuracy by a government inspection or licensing agency. Noncertified scales are not inspected and approved for accuracy by a government inspection or licensing agency.

Your mover must obtain a separate weight ticket for each weighing. The weigh master must sign each weight ticket. Each weight ticket must contain the following six items:

(1) *The complete name and location of the scale.*
(2) *The date of each weighing.*
(3) *Identification of the weight entries* as being the tare, gross, or net weights.
(4) *The company or mover identification of the vehicle.*
(5) *Your last name as it appears on the Bill of Lading.*
(6) *Your mover's shipment registration or Bill of Lading number.*

Your mover must retain the original weight ticket or tickets relating to the determination of the weight of your shipment as part of its file on your shipment.

When both weighings are performed on the same scale, one weight ticket may be used to record both weighings.

Your mover must present all freight bills with true copies of all weight tickets. If your mover does not present its freight bill with all weight tickets, your mover is in violation of Federal law.

Before the driver actually begins unloading your shipment weighed at origin and after your mover informs you of the billing weight and total charges, you have the right to demand a reweigh of your shipment. If you believe the weight is not accurate, you have the right to request your mover reweigh your shipment before unloading.

You have the right, and your mover must inform you of your right, to observe all reweighings of your shipment. Your mover must tell you where and when each reweighing will occur. Your mover must give you a reasonable opportunity to be present to observe the reweighings.

You may waive your right to observe any reweighing; however, you must waive that right in writing. You may send the written waiver via fax or e-mail, as well as by overnight courier or certified mail, return receipt requested. This does not affect any of your other rights under Federal law.

Your mover is prohibited from charging you for the reweighing. If the weight of your shipment at the time of the reweigh is different from the weight determined at origin, your mover must recompute the charges based upon the reweigh weight.

Before requesting a reweigh, you may find it to your advantage to estimate the weight of your shipment using the following three-step method:

1. *Count the number of items in your shipment.* Usually there will be either 30 or 40 items listed on each page of the inventory. For example, if there are 30 items per page and your inventory consists of four complete pages and a fifth page with 15 items listed, the total number of items will be 135. If an automobile is listed on the inventory, do not include this item in the count of the total items.
2. *Subtract the weight of any automobile* included in your shipment from the total weight of the shipment. If the automobile was not weighed separately, its weight can be found on its title or license receipt.
3. *Divide the number of items in your shipment into the weight.* If the average weight resulting from this exercise ranges between 35 and 45 pounds (16 and 20 kilograms) per article, it is unlikely a reweigh will prove beneficial to you. In fact, it could result in your paying higher charges.

Experience has shown that the average shipment of household goods will weigh about 40 pounds (18 kilograms) per item. If a shipment contains a large number of heavy items, such as cartons of books, boxes of tools or heavier than average furniture, the average weight per item may be 45 pounds or more (20 kilograms or more).

What Must My Mover Do if I Want To Know the Actual Weight or Charges for My Shipment Before Delivery?

If you request notification of the actual weight or volume and charges upon your shipment, your mover must comply with your request if it is moving your goods on a collect-on-delivery basis. This requirement is conditioned upon your supplying your mover with an address or telephone number where you will receive the communication. Your mover must make its notification by telephone; fax transmissions; e-mail; overnight courier; certified mail, return receipt requested; or in person.

You must receive the mover's notification at least one full 24-hour day before its scheduled delivery, excluding Saturdays, Sundays, and Federal holidays.

Your mover may disregard this 24-hour notification requirement on shipments subject to one of the following three things:

(1) *Back weigh* (when your mover weighs your shipment at its destination).

(2) *Pickup and delivery* encompassing two consecutive weekdays, if you agree.

(3) *Maximum payment amounts at time of delivery* of 110 percent of the estimated charges, if you agree.

Subpart F - Transportation of My Shipment

Must My Mover Transport the Shipment in a Timely Manner?

Yes, your mover must transport your household goods in a timely manner. This is also known as "reasonable dispatch service." Your mover must provide reasonable dispatch service to you, except for transportation on the basis of guaranteed delivery dates.

When your mover is unable to perform either the pickup or delivery of your shipment on the dates or during the periods of time specified in the order for service, your mover must notify you of the delay, at the mover's expense. As soon as the delay becomes apparent to your mover, it must give you notification it will be unable to provide the service specified in the terms of the order for service. Your mover may notify you of the delay in any of the following ways: by telephone; fax transmissions; e-mail; overnight courier; certified mail, return receipt requested; or in person.

When your mover notifies you of a delay, it also must advise you of the dates or periods of time it may be able to pick up and/or deliver the shipment. Your mover must consider your needs in its advisement.

Your mover must prepare a written record of the date, time, and manner of its notification. Your mover must prepare a written record of its amended date or period for delivery. Your mover must retain these records as a part of its file on your shipment. The retention period is one year from the date of notification. Your mover must furnish a copy of the notification to you either by first class mail or in person, if you request a copy of the notice.

Your mover must tender your shipment for delivery on the agreed-upon delivery date or within the period specified on the bill of lading. Upon your request or concurrence, your mover may deliver your shipment on another day.

The establishment of a delayed pickup or delivery date does not relieve your mover from liability for damages resulting from your mover's failure to provide service as agreed. However, when your mover notifies you of alternate delivery dates, it is your responsibility to be available to accept delivery on the dates specified. If you are not available and are not willing to accept delivery, your mover has the right to place your shipment in storage at your expense or hold the shipment on its truck and assess additional charges.

If after the pickup of your shipment, you request your mover to change the delivery date, most movers will agree to do so provided your request will not result in unreasonable delay to its equipment or interfere with another customer's move. However, your mover is under no obligation to consent to amended delivery dates. Your mover has the right to place your shipment in storage at your expense if you are unwilling or unable to accept delivery on the date agreed to in the bill of lading.

If your mover fails to pick up and deliver your shipment on the date entered on the bill of lading and you have expenses you otherwise would not have had, you may be able to recover those expenses from your mover. This is what is called an inconvenience or delay claim. Should your mover refuse to honor such a claim and you continue to believe you are entitled to be paid damages, you may take your mover to court under 49 U.S.C. 14706. The Federal Motor Carrier Safety Administration (FMCSA) has no authority to order your mover to pay such claims.

While we hope your mover delivers your shipment in a timely manner, you should consider the possibility your shipment may be delayed, and find out what payment you can expect if a mover delays service through its own fault, before you agree with the mover to transport your shipment.

What Must My Mover Do if It Is Able To Deliver My Shipment More Than 24 Hours Before I Am Able to Accept Delivery?

At your mover's discretion, it may place your shipment in storage. This will be under its own account and at its own expense in a warehouse located in proximity to the destination of your shipment. Your mover may do this if you fail to request or concur with an early delivery date, and your mover is able to deliver your shipment more than 24 hours before your specified date or the first day of your specified period.

If your mover exercises this option, your mover must immediately notify you of the name and address of the warehouse where your mover places your shipment. Your mover must make and keep a record of its notification as a part of its shipment records. Your mover has full responsibility for the shipment under the terms and conditions of the bill of lading. Your mover is responsible for the charges for redelivery, handling, and storage until it makes final delivery. Your mover may limit its responsibility to the agreed-upon delivery date or the first day of the period of delivery as specified in the bill of lading.

What Must My Mover Do for Me When I Store Household Goods in Transit?

If you request your mover to hold your household goods in storage-in-transit and the storage period is about to expire, your mover must notify you, in writing, about the four following items:

(1) *The date when storage-in-transit* will convert to permanent storage.
(2) *The existence of a nine-month period* after the date of conversion to permanent storage, during which you may file claims against your mover for loss or damage occurring to your goods while in transit or during the storage-in-transit period.
(3) *Your mover's liability will end.*
(4) *Your property will be subject* to the rules, regulations, and charges of the warehouseman.

Your mover must make this notification at least 10 days before the expiration date of one of the following two periods of time:

(1) *The specified period of time* when your mover is to hold your goods in storage.
(2) *The maximum period of time* provided in its tariff for storage-in-transit.

Your mover must notify you by facsimile transmission; overnight courier; e-mail; or certified mail, return receipt requested.

If your mover holds your household goods in storage-in-transit for less than 10 days, your mover must notify you, one day before the storage-in-transit period expires, of the same information specified above.

Your mover must maintain a record of all notifications to you as part of the records of your shipment. Under the applicable tariff provisions regarding storage-in-transit, your mover's failure or refusal to notify you will automatically extend your mover's liability until the end of the day following the date when your mover actually gives you notice.

Subpart G - Delivery of My Shipment

May My Mover Ask Me To Sign a Delivery Receipt Purporting To Release It From Liability?

At the time of delivery, your mover will expect you to sign a receipt for your shipment. Normally, you will sign each page of your mover's copy of the inventory.

Your mover's delivery receipt or shipping document must not contain any language purporting to release or discharge it or its agents from liability.

Your mover may include a statement about your receipt of your property in apparent good condition, except as noted on the shipping documents.

Do not sign the delivery receipt if it contains any language purporting to release or discharge your mover or its agents from liability. Strike out such language before signing, or refuse delivery if the driver or mover refuses to provide a proper delivery receipt.

What Is the Maximum Collect-on-Delivery Amount My Mover May Demand I Pay at the Time of Delivery?

On a binding estimate, the maximum amount is the exact estimate of the charges. Your mover must specify on the estimate, order for service, and bill of lading the form of payment acceptable to it (for example, a certified check).

On a non-binding estimate, the maximum amount is 110 percent of the approximate costs. Your mover must specify on the estimate, order for service, and bill of lading the form of payment acceptable to it (for example, cash).

If My Shipment Is Transported on More Than One Vehicle, What Charges May My Mover Collect at Delivery?

Although all movers try to move each shipment on one truck, it becomes necessary at times to divide a shipment among two or more trucks. This frequently occurs when an automobile is included in the shipment and it is transported on a vehicle specially designed to transport automobiles. When this occurs, your transportation charges are the same as if the entire shipment moved on one truck.

If your shipment is divided for transportation on two or more trucks, the mover may require payment for each portion as it is delivered.

Your mover may delay the collection of all the charges until the entire shipment is delivered, at its discretion, not yours. When you order your move, you should ask the mover about its policies in this regard.

If My Shipment Is Partially Lost or Destroyed, What Charges May My Mover Collect at Delivery?

Movers customarily make every effort to avoid losing, damaging, or destroying any of your items while your shipment is in their possession for transportation. However, despite the precautions taken, articles are sometimes lost or destroyed during the move.

In addition to any money you may recover from your mover to compensate for lost or destroyed articles, you may also recover the transportation charges represented by the portion of the shipment lost or destroyed. Your mover may only apply this paragraph to the transportation of household goods. Your mover may disregard this paragraph if loss or destruction was due to an act or omission by you. Your mover must require you to pay any specific valuation charge due.

For example, if you pack a hazardous material (i.e., gasoline, aerosol cans, motor oil, etc.) and your shipment is partially lost or destroyed by fire in storage or in the mover's trailer, your mover may require you to pay for the full cost of transportation.

Your mover may first collect its freight charges for the entire shipment, if your mover chooses. At the time your mover disposes of claims for loss, damage, or injury to the articles in your shipment, it must refund the portion of its freight charges corresponding to the portion of the lost or destroyed shipment (including any charges for accessorial or terminal services).

Your mover is forbidden from collecting, or requiring you to pay, any freight charges (including any charges for accessorial or terminal services) when your household goods shipment is totally lost or destroyed in transit, unless the loss or destruction was due to an act or omission by you.

How Must My Mover Calculate the Charges Applicable to the Shipment as Delivered?

Your mover must multiply the percentage corresponding to the delivered shipment times the total charges applicable to the shipment tendered by you to obtain the total charges it must collect from you.

If your mover's computed charges exceed the charges otherwise applicable to the shipment as delivered, the lesser of those charges must apply. This will apply only to the transportation of your household goods.

Your mover must require you to pay any specific valuation charge due.

Your mover may not refund the freight charges if the loss or destruction was due to an act or omission by you. For example, you fail to disclose to your mover that your shipment contains perishable live plants. Your mover may disregard its loss or destruction of your plants, because you failed to inform your mover you were transporting live plants.

Your mover must determine, at its own expense, the proportion of the shipment, based on actual or constructive weight, not lost or destroyed in transit.

Your rights are in addition to, and not in lieu of, any other rights you may have with respect to your shipment of household goods your mover lost or destroyed, or partially lost or destroyed, in transit. This applies whether or not you have exercised your rights provided above.

Subpart H - Collection of Charges

Does This Subpart Apply to Most Shipments?

It applies to all shipments of household goods that involve a balance due freight or expense bill or are shipped on credit.

How Must My Mover Present Its Freight or Expense Bill to Me?

At the time of payment of transportation charges, your mover must give you a freight bill identifying the service provided and the charge for each service. It is customary for most movers to use a copy of the bill of lading as a freight bill; however, some movers use an entirely separate document for this purpose.

Except in those instances where a shipment is moving on a binding estimate, the freight bill must specifically identify each service performed, the rate or charge per service performed, and the total charges for each service. If this information is not on the freight bill, do not accept or pay the freight bill.

Movers' tariffs customarily specify that freight charges must be paid in cash, by certified check, or by cashier's check. When this requirement exists, the mover will not accept personal checks. At the time you order your move, you should ask your mover about the form of payment your mover requires.

Some movers permit payment of freight charges by use of a charge or credit card. However, do not assume your nationally recognized charge, credit, or debit card will be acceptable for payment. Ask your mover at the time you request an estimate. Your mover must specify the form of payment it will accept at delivery.

If you do not pay the transportation charges at the time of delivery, your mover has the right, under the bill of lading, to refuse to deliver your goods. The mover may place them in storage, at your expense, until the charges are paid. However, the mover must deliver your goods upon payment of 100 percent of a binding estimate.

If, before payment of the transportation charges, you discover an error in the charges, you should attempt to correct the error with the driver, the mover's local agent, or by contacting the mover's main office. If an error is discovered after payment, you should write the mover (the address will be on the freight bill) explaining the error, and request a refund.

Movers customarily check all shipment files and freight bills after a move has been completed to make sure the charges were accurate. If an overcharge is found, you should be notified and a refund made. If an undercharge occurred, you may be billed for the additional charges due.

On "to be prepaid" shipments, your mover must present its freight bill for all transportation charges within 15 days of the date your mover received the shipment. This period excludes Saturdays, Sundays, and Federal holidays.

On "collect" shipments, your mover must present its freight bill for transportation charges on the date of delivery, or, at its discretion, within 15 days, calculated from the date the shipment was delivered at your destination. This period excludes Saturdays, Sundays, and Federal holidays. (Bills for charges exceeding 110 percent of a non-binding estimate, and for additional services requested or found necessary after the shipment is in transit, will be presented no sooner than 30 days from the date of delivery.)

Your mover's freight bills and accompanying written notices must state the following five items:

(1) *Penalties for late payment.*
(2) *Credit time limits.*
(3) *Service or finance charges.*
(4) *Collection expense charges.*
(5) *Discount terms.*

If your mover extends credit to you, freight bills or a separate written notice accompanying a freight bill or a group of freight bills presented at one time must state, "You may be subject to tariff penalties for failure to timely pay freight charges," or a similar statement. Your mover must state on its freight bills or other notices when it expects payment, and any applicable service charges, collection expense charges, and discount terms.

When your mover lacks sufficient information to compute its tariff charges at the time of billing, your mover must present its freight bill for payment within 15 days following the day when sufficient information becomes available. This period excludes Saturdays, Sundays, and Federal holidays.

Your mover must not extend additional credit to you if you fail to furnish sufficient information to your mover. Your mover must have sufficient information to render a freight bill within a reasonable time after shipment.

When your mover presents freight bills by mail, it must deem the time of mailing to be the time of presentation of the bills. The term "freight bills," as used in this paragraph, includes both paper documents and billing by use of electronic media such as computer tapes, disks, or the Internet (e-mail).

When you mail acceptable checks or drafts in payment of freight charges, your mover must deem the act of mailing the payment within the credit period to be the proper collection of the tariff charges within the credit period for the purposes of Federal law. In case of a dispute as to the date of mailing, your mover must accept the postmark as the date of mailing.

If I Forced My Mover To Relinquish a Collect-on-Delivery Shipment Before the Payment of ALL Charges, How Must My Mover Collect the Balance?

On "collect-on-delivery" shipments, your mover must present its freight bill for transportation charges within 15 days, calculated from the date the shipment was delivered at your destination. This period excludes Saturdays, Sundays, and Federal holidays. (Bills for charges exceeding 110 percent of a non-binding estimate, and charges for additional services requested or found necessary after the shipment is in transit, will be presented no sooner than 30 days after the date of delivery.)

What Actions May My Mover Take To Collect From Me the Charges Upon Its Freight Bill?

Your mover must present a freight bill within 15 days (excluding Saturdays, Sundays, and Federal holidays) of the date of delivery of a shipment at your destination. (Bills for charges exceeding 110 percent of a non-binding estimate, and for additional services requested or found necessary after the shipment is in transit, will be presented no sooner than 30 days after the date of delivery.)

The credit period must be 7 days (excluding Saturdays, Sundays, and Federal holidays).

Your mover must provide in its tariffs the following three things:

(1) *A provision automatically extending the credit period* to a total of 30 calendar days for you if you have not paid its freight bill within the 7-day period.
(2) *A provision indicating* you will be assessed a service charge by your mover equal to one percent of the amount of the freight bill, subject to a $20 minimum charge, for the extension of the credit period. The mover will assess the service charge for each 30-day extension that the charges go unpaid.
(3) *A provision that your mover* must deny credit to you if you fail to pay a duly presented freight bill within the 30-day period. Your mover may grant credit to you, at its discretion, when you satisfy your mover's condition that you will pay all future freight bills duly presented. Your mover must ensure all your payments of freight bills are strictly in accordance with Federal rules and regulations for the settlement of its rates and charges.

Do I Have a Right To File a Claim To Recover Money for Property My Mover Lost or Damaged?

Should your move result in the loss of or damage to any of your property, you have the right to file a claim with your mover to recover money for such loss or damage.

You should file a claim as soon as possible. If you fail to file a claim within 9 months, your mover may not be required to accept your claim. If you institute a court action and win, you may be entitled to attorney's fees, but only in either of two circumstances. You may be entitled to attorney's fees if you submitted your claim to the carrier within 120 days after delivery, and a decision was not rendered through arbitration within the time required by law. You also may be entitled to attorney's fees if you submitted your claim to the carrier within 120 days after delivery, the court enforced an arbitration decision in your favor, and the time for the carrier to comply with the decision has passed.

While the Federal Government maintains regulations governing the processing of loss and damage claims (49 CFR Part 370), it cannot resolve those claims. If you cannot settle a claim with the mover, you may file a civil action to recover your claim in court under 49 U.S.C. 14706. You may obtain the name and address of the mover's agent for service of legal process in your state by contacting the Federal Motor Carrier Safety Administration. You may also obtain the name of a process agent via the Internet by going to http://www.fmcsa.dot.gov and then clicking on Licensing and Insurance (L&I) section.

In addition, your mover must participate in an arbitration program. As described earlier in this pamphlet, an arbitration program gives you the opportunity to settle certain types of unresolved loss or damage claims through a neutral arbitrator. You may find submitting your claim to arbitration under such a program to be a less expensive and more convenient way to seek recovery of your claim. Your mover is required to provide you with information about its arbitration program before you move. If your mover fails to do so, ask the mover for details of its program.

Part 375 - Transportation of Household Goods in Interstate Commerce — Appendix A

Subpart I - Resolving Disputes With My Mover

What May I Do To Resolve Disputes With My Mover?

The Federal Motor Carrier Safety Administration does not help you settle your dispute with your mover.

Generally, you must resolve your own loss and damage disputes with your mover. You enter a contractual arrangement with your mover. You are bound by each of the following three things:

(1) *The terms and conditions you negotiated before your move.*

(2) *The terms and conditions you accepted* when you signed the bill of lading.

(3) *The terms and conditions you accepted* when you signed for delivery of your goods.

You have the right to take your mover to court. We require your mover to offer you arbitration to settle your disputes with it.

If your mover holds your goods "hostage" — refuses delivery unless you pay an amount you believe the mover is not entitled to charge — the Federal Motor Carrier Safety Administration does not have the resources to seek a court injunction on your behalf.

NOTES

Part 376 - Lease and Interchange of Vehicles

Subpart A - General Applicability and Definitions

§376.1 Applicability.
The regulations in this part apply to the following actions by motor carriers registered with the Secretary to transport property:
- (a) **The leasing of equipment** with which to perform transportation regulated by the Secretary.
- (b) **The leasing of equipment to motor private carrier or shippers.**
- (c) **The interchange of equipment** between motor common carriers in the performance of transportation regulated by the Secretary.

§376.2 Definitions.
- (a) **Authorized carrier.** A person or persons authorized to engage in the transportation of property as a motor carrier under the provisions of 49 U.S.C. 13901 and 13902.
- (b) **Equipment.** A motor vehicle, straight truck, tractor, semitrailer, full trailer, any combination of these and any other type of equipment used by authorized carriers in the transportation of property for hire.
- (c) **Interchange.** The receipt of equipment by one motor common carrier of property from another such carrier, at a point which both carriers are authorized to serve, with which to continue a through movement.
- (d) **Owner.** A person (1) to whom title to equipment has been issued, or (2) who, without title, has the right to exclusive use of equipment, or (3) who has lawful possession of equipment registered and licensed in any State in the name of that person.
- (e) **Lease.** A contract or arrangement in which the owner grants the use of equipment, with or without driver, for a specified period to an authorized carrier for use in the regulated transportation of property, in exchange for compensation.
- (f) **Lessor.** In a lease, the party granting the use of equipment, with or without driver, to another.
- (g) **Lessee.** In a lease, the party acquiring the use of equipment with or without driver, from another.
- (h) **Sublease.** A written contract in which the lessee grants the use of leased equipment, with or without driver, to another.
- (i) **Addendum.** A supplement to an existing lease which is not effective until signed by the lessor and lessee.
- (j) **Private carrier.** A person, other than a motor carrier, transporting property by motor vehicle in interstate or foreign commerce when (1) the person is the owner, lessee, or bailee of the property being transported; and (2) the property is being transported for sale, lease, rent, or bailment, or to further a commercial enterprise.
- (k) **Shipper.** A person who sends or receives property which is transported in interstate or foreign commerce.
- (l) **Escrow fund.** Money deposited by the lessor with either a third party or the lessee to guarantee performance, to repay advances, to cover repair expenses, to handle claims, to handle license and State permit costs, and for any other purposes mutually agreed upon by the lessor and lessee.
- (m) **Detention.** The holding by a consignor or consignee of a trailer, with or without power unit and driver, beyond the free time allocated for the shipment, under circumstances not attributable to the performance of the carrier.

Subpart B - Leasing Regulations

§376.11 General leasing requirements.
Other than through the interchange of equipment as set forth in §376.31, and under the exemptions set forth in Subpart C of these regulations, the authorized carrier may perform authorized transportation in equipment it does not own only under the following conditions:
- (a) **Lease.** There shall be a written lease granting the use of the equipment and meeting the requirements contained in §376.12.
- (b) **Receipts for equipment.** Receipts, specifically identifying the equipment to be leased and stating the date and time of day possession is transferred, shall be given as follows:
  - (1) *When possession of the equipment* is taken by the authorized carrier, it shall give the owner of the equipment a receipt. The receipt identified in this section may be transmitted by mail, telegraph, or other similar means of communication.
  - (2) *When possession of the equipment* by the authorized carrier ends, a receipt shall be given in accordance with the terms of the lease agreement if the lease agreement requires a receipt.
  - (3) *Authorized representatives* of the carrier and the owner may take possession of leased equipment and give and receive the receipts required under this subsection.
- (c) **Identification of equipment.** The authorized carrier acquiring the use of equipment under this section shall identify the equipment as being in its service as follows:
  - (1) *During the period of the lease,* the carrier shall identify the equipment in accordance with the FMCSA's requirements in 49 CFR Part 390 of this chapter (Identification of Vehicles).
  - (2) *Unless a copy of the lease* is carried on the equipment, the authorized carrier shall keep a statement with the equipment during the period of the lease certifying that the equipment is being operated by it. The statement shall also specify the name of the owner, the date and length of the lease, any restrictions in the lease relative to the commodities to be transported, and the address at which the original lease is kept by the authorized carrier. This statement shall be prepared by the authorized carrier or its authorized representative.
- (d) **Records of equipment.** The authorized carrier using equipment leased under this section shall keep records of the equipment as follows:
  - (1) *The authorized carrier* shall prepare and keep documents covering each trip for which the equipment is used in its service. These documents shall contain the name and address of the owner of the equipment, the point of origin, the time and date of departure, and the point of final destination. Also, the authorized carrier shall carry papers with the leased equipment during its operation containing this information and identifying the lading and clearly indicating that the transportation is under its responsibility. These papers shall be preserved by the authorized carrier as part of its transportation records. Leases which contain the information required by the provisions in this paragraph may be used and retained instead of such documents or papers. As to lease agreements negotiated under a master lease, this provision is complied with by having a copy of a master lease in the unit of equipment in question and where the balance of documentation called for by this paragraph is included in the freight documents prepared for the specific movement.
  - (2) [Reserved]

§376.12 Written lease requirements.
Except as provided in the exemptions set forth in Subpart C of this part, the written lease required under §376.11(a) shall contain the following provisions. The required lease provisions shall be adhered to and performed by the authorized carrier.
- (a) **Parties.** The lease shall be made between the authorized carrier and the owner of the equipment. The lease shall be signed by these parties or by their authorized representatives.
- (b) **Duration to be specific.** The lease shall specify the time and date or the circumstances on which the lease begins and ends. These times or circumstances shall coincide with the times for the giving of receipts required by §376.11(b).
- (c) **Exclusive possession and responsibilities.**
  - (1) *The lease shall provide* that the authorized carrier lessee shall have exclusive possession, control, and use of the equipment for the duration of the lease. The lease shall further provide that the authorized carrier lessee shall assume complete responsibility for the operation of the equipment for the duration of the lease.
  - (2) *Provision may be made in the lease* for considering the authorized carrier lessee as the owner of the equipment for the purpose of subleasing it under these regulations to other authorized carriers during the lease.
  - (3) *When an authorized carrier of household goods* leases equipment for the transportation of household goods, as defined by the Secretary, the parties may provide in the lease that the provisions required by paragraph (c)(1) of this section apply only during the time the equipment is operated by or for the authorized carrier lessee.
  - (4) *Nothing in the provisions* required by paragraph (c)(1) of this section is intended to affect whether the lessor or driver provided by the lessor is an independent contractor or an employee of the authorized carrier lessee. An independent contractor relationship may exist when a carrier lessee complies with 49 U.S.C. 14102 and attendant administrative requirements.

(d) Compensation to be specified. The amount to be paid by the authorized carrier for equipment and driver's services shall be clearly stated on the face of the lease or in an addendum which is attached to the lease. Such lease or addendum shall be delivered to the lessor prior to the commencement of any trip in the service of the authorized carrier. An authorized representative of the lessor may accept these documents. The amount to be paid may be expressed as a percentage of gross revenue, a flat rate per mile, a variable rate depending on the direction traveled or the type of commodity transported, or by any other method of compensation mutually agreed upon by the parties to the lease. The compensation stated on the lease or in the attached addendum may apply to equipment and driver's services either separately or as a combined amount.

(e) Items specified in lease. The lease shall clearly specify which party is responsible for removing identification devices from the equipment upon the termination of the lease and when and how these devices, other than those painted directly on the equipment, will be returned to the carrier. The lease shall clearly specify the manner in which a receipt will be given to the authorized carrier by the equipment owner when the latter retakes possession of the equipment upon termination of the lease agreement, if a receipt is required at all by the lease. The lease shall clearly specify the responsibility of each party with respect to the cost of fuel, fuel taxes, empty mileage, permits of all types, tolls, ferries, detention and accessorial services, base plates and licenses, and any unused portions of such items. The lease shall clearly specify who is responsible for loading and unloading the property onto and from the motor vehicle, and the compensation, if any, to be paid for this service. Except when the violation results from the acts or omissions of the lessor, the authorized carrier lessee shall assume the risks and costs of fines for overweight and oversize trailers when the trailers are pre-loaded, sealed, or the load is containerized, or when the trailer or lading is otherwise outside of the lessor's control, and for improperly permitted overdimension and overweight loads and shall reimburse the lessor for any fines paid by the lessor. If the authorized carrier is authorized to receive a refund or a credit for base plates purchased by the lessor from, and issued in the name of, the authorized carrier, or if the base plates are authorized to be sold by the authorized carrier to another lessor the authorized carrier shall refund to the initial lessor on whose behalf the base plate was first obtained a prorated share of the amount received.

(f) Payment period. The lease shall specify that payment to the lessor shall be made within 15 days after submission of the necessary delivery documents and other paperwork concerning a trip in the service of the authorized carrier. The paperwork required before the lessor can receive payment is limited to log books required by the Department of Transportation and those documents necessary for the authorized carrier to secure payment from the shipper. In addition, the lease may provide that, upon termination of the lease agreement, as a condition precedent to payment, the lessor shall remove all identification devices of the authorized carrier and, except in the case of identification painted directly on equipment, return them to the carrier. If the identification device has been lost or stolen, a letter certifying its removal will satisfy this requirement. Until this requirement is complied with, the carrier may withhold final payment. The authorized carrier may require the submission of additional documents by the lessor but not as a prerequisite to payment. Payment to the lessor shall not be made contingent upon submission of a bill of lading to which no exceptions have been taken. The authorized carrier shall not set time limits for the submission by the lessor of required delivery documents and other paperwork.

(g) Copies of freight bill or other form of freight documentation. When a lessor's revenue is based on a percentage of the gross revenue for a shipment, the lease must specify that the authorized carrier will give the lessor, before or at the time of settlement, a copy of the rated freight bill or a computer-generated document containing the same information, or, in the case of contract carriers, any other form of documentation actually used for a shipment containing the same information that would appear on a rated freight bill. When a computer-generated document is provided, the lease will permit lessor to view, during normal business hours, a copy of any actual document underlying the computer-generated document. Regardless of the method of compensation, the lease must permit lessor to examine copies of the carrier's tariff or, in the case of contract carriers, other documents from which rates and charges are computed, provided that where rates and charges are computed from a contract of a contract carrier, only those portions of the contract containing the same information that would appear on a rated freight bill need be disclosed. The authorized carrier may delete the names of shippers and consignees shown on the freight bill or other form of documentation.

(h) Charge-back items. The lease shall clearly specify all items that may be initially paid for by the authorized carrier, but ultimately deducted from the lessor's compensation at the time of payment or settlement, together with a recitation as to how the amount of each item is to be computed. The lessor shall be afforded copies of those documents which are necessary to determine the validity of the charge.

(i) Products, equipment, or services from authorized carrier. The lease shall specify that the lessor is not required to purchase or rent any products, equipment, or services from the authorized carrier as a condition of entering into the lease arrangement. The lease shall specify the terms of any agreement in which the lessor is a party to an equipment purchase or rental contract which gives the authorized carrier the right to make deductions from the lessor's compensation for purchase or rental payments.

(j) Insurance.
  (1) *The lease shall clearly specify* the legal obligation of the authorized carrier to maintain insurance coverage for the protection of the public pursuant to FMCSA regulations under 49 U.S.C. 13906. The lease shall further specify who is responsible for providing any other insurance coverage for the operation of the leased equipment, such as bobtail insurance. If the authorized carrier will make a charge back to the lessor for any of this insurance, the lease shall specify the amount which will be charged-back to the lessor.
  (2) *If the lessor purchases any insurance coverage* for the operation of the leased equipment from or through the authorized carrier, the lease shall specify that the authorized carrier will provide the lessor with a copy of each policy upon the request of the lessor. Also, where the lessor purchases such insurance in this manner, the lease shall specify that the authorized carrier will provide the lessor with a certificate of insurance for each such policy. Each certificate of insurance shall include the name of the insurer, the policy number, the effective dates of the policy, the amounts and types of coverage, the cost to the lessor for each type of coverage, and the deductible amount for each type of coverage for which the lessor may be liable.
  (3) *The lease shall clearly specify the conditions* under which deductions for cargo or property damage may be made from the lessor's settlements. The lease shall further specify that the authorized carrier must provide the lessor with a written explanation and itemization of any deductions for cargo or property damage made from any compensation of money owed to the lessor. The written explanation and itemization must be delivered to the lessor before any deductions are made.

(k) Escrow funds. If escrow funds are required, the lease shall specify:
  (1) *The amount* of any escrow fund or performance bond required to be paid by the lessor to the authorized carrier or to a third party.
  (2) *The specific items* to which the escrow fund can be applied.
  (3) *That while the escrow fund* is under the control of the authorized carrier, the authorized carrier shall provide an accounting to the lessor of any transactions involving such fund. The carrier shall perform this accounting in one of the following ways:
    (i) *By clearly indicating* in individual settlement sheets the amount and description of any deduction or addition made to the escrow fund; or
    (ii) *By providing a separate accounting* to the lessor of any transactions involving the escrow fund. This separate accounting shall be done on a monthly basis.
  (4) *The right of the lessor* to demand to have an accounting for transactions involving the escrow fund at any time.
  (5) *That while the escrow fund* is under the control of the carrier, the carrier shall pay interest on the escrow fund on at least a quarterly basis. For purposes of calculating the balance of the escrow fund on which interest must be paid, the carrier may deduct a sum equal to the average advance made to the individual lessor during the period of time for which interest is paid. The interest rate shall be established on the date the interest period begins and shall be at least equal to the average yield or equivalent coupon issue yield on 91-day, 13-week Treasury bills as established in the weekly auction by the Department of Treasury.
  (6) *The conditions the lessor must fulfill* in order to have the escrow fund returned. At the time of the return of the escrow fund, the authorized carrier may deduct monies for those obligations

incurred by the lessor which have been previously specified in the lease, and shall provide a final accounting to the lessor of all such final deductions made to the escrow fund. The lease shall further specify that in no event shall the escrow fund be returned later than 45 days from the date of termination.

(l) **Copies of the lease.** An original and two copies of each lease shall be signed by the parties. The authorized carrier shall keep the original and shall place a copy of the lease on the equipment during the period of the lease unless a statement as provided for in §376.11(c)(2) is carried on the equipment instead. The owner of the equipment shall keep the other copy of the lease.

(m) **This paragraph applies to owners who are not agents** but whose equipment is used by an agent of an authorized carrier in providing transportation on behalf of that authorized carrier. In this situation, the authorized carrier is obligated to ensure that these owners receive all the rights and benefits due an owner under the leasing regulations, especially those set forth in paragraphs (d)-(k) of this section. This is true regardless of whether the lease for the equipment is directly between the authorized carrier and its agent rather than directly between the authorized carrier and each of these owners. The lease between an authorized carrier and its agent shall specify this obligation.

Subpart C - Exemptions for the Leasing Regulations

§376.21 General exemptions.

Except for §376.11(c) which requires the identification of equipment, the leasing regulations in this part shall not apply to:

(a) **Equipment used** in substituted motor-for-rail transportation of railroad freight moving between points that are railroad stations and on railroad billing.

(b) **Equipment used** in transportation performed exclusively within any commercial zone as defined by the Secretary.

(c) **Equipment leased without drivers** from a person who is principally engaged in such a business.

(d) **Any type of trailer** not drawn by a power unit leased from the same lessor.

§376.22 Exemption for private carrier leasing and leasing between authorized carriers.

Regardless of the leasing regulations set forth in this part, an authorized carrier may lease equipment to or from another authorized carrier, or a private carrier may lease equipment to an authorized carrier under the following conditions:

(a) **The identification of equipment requirements** in §376.11(c) must be complied with;

(b) **The lessor must own the equipment or hold it under a lease;**

(c) **There must be a written agreement** between the authorized carriers or between the private carrier and authorized carrier, as the case may be, concerning the equipment as follows:

(1) *It must be signed by the parties or their authorized representatives.*

(2) *It must provide that control and responsibility* for the operation of the equipment shall be that of the lessee from the time possession is taken by the lessee and the receipt required under §376.11(b) is given to the lessor until:

(i) *Possession of the equipment* is returned to the lessor and the receipt required under §376.11(b) is received by the authorized carrier; or

(ii) *in the event* that the agreement is between authorized carriers, possession of the equipment is returned to the lessor or given to another authorized carrier in an interchange of equipment.

(3) *A copy of the agreement* must be carried in the equipment while it is in the possession of the lessee.

(4) *Nothing in this section shall prohibit the use,* by authorized carriers, private carriers, and all other entities conducting lease operations pursuant to this section, of a master lease if a copy of that master lease is carried in the equipment while it is in the possession of the lessee, and if the master lease complies with the provisions of this section and receipts are exchanged in accordance with §376.11(b), and if records of the equipment are prepared and maintained in accordance with §376.11(d).

(d) **Authorized and private carriers** under common ownership and control may lease equipment to each other under this section without complying with the requirements of paragraph (a) of this section pertaining to identification of equipment, and the requirements of paragraphs (c)(2) and (c)(4) of this section pertaining to equipment receipts. The leasing of equipment between such carriers will be subject to all other requirements of this section.

§376.26 Exemption for leases between authorized carriers and their agents.

The leasing regulations set forth in §376.12(e) through (l) do not apply to leases between authorized carriers and their agents.

Subpart D - Interchange Regulations

§376.31 Interchange of equipment.

Authorized common carriers may interchange equipment under the following conditions:

(a) **Interchange agreement.** There shall be a written contract, lease, or other arrangement providing for the interchange and specifically describing the equipment to be interchanged. This written agreement shall set forth the specific points of interchange, how the equipment is to be used, and the compensation for such use. The interchange agreement shall be signed by the parties or by their authorized representatives.

(b) **Operating authority.** The carriers participating in the interchange shall be registered with the Secretary to provide the transportation of the commodities at the point where the physical exchange occurs.

(c) **Through bills of lading.** The traffic transported in interchange service must move on through bills of lading issued by the originating carrier. The rates charged and the revenues collected must be accounted for in the same manner as if there had been no interchange. Charges for the use of the interchanged equipment shall be kept separate from divisions of the joint rates or the proportions of such rates accruing to the carriers by the application of local or proportional rates.

(d) **Identification of equipment.** The authorized common carrier receiving the equipment shall identify equipment operated by it in interchange service as follows:

(1) *The authorized common carrier* shall identify power units in accordance with the FMCSA's requirements in 49 CFR Part 390 of this chapter (Identification of Vehicles). Before giving up possession of the equipment, the carrier shall remove all identification showing it as the operating carrier.

(2) *Unless a copy of the interchange agreement* is carried on the equipment, the authorized common carrier shall carry a statement with each vehicle during interchange service certifying that it is operating the equipment. The statement shall also identify the equipment by company or State registration number and shall show the specific point of interchange, the date and time it assumes responsibility for the equipment, and the use to be made of the equipment. This statement shall be signed by the parties to the interchange agreement or their authorized representatives. The requirements of this paragraph shall not apply where the equipment to be operated in interchange service consists only of trailers or semitrailers.

(3) *Authorized carriers under common ownership* and control may interchange equipment with each other without complying with the requirements of paragraph (d)(1) of this section pertaining to removal of identification from equipment.

(e) **Connecting carriers considered as owner** — An authorized carrier receiving equipment in connection with a through movement shall be considered to the owner of the equipment for the purpose of leasing the equipment to other authorized carriers in furtherance of the movement to destination or the return of the equipment after the movement is completed.

Subpart E - Private Carriers and Shippers

§376.42 Lease of equipment by regulated carriers.

Authorized carriers may lease equipment and drivers from private carriers, for periods of less than 30 days, in the manner set forth in §376.22.

Part 376 - Lease and Interchange of Vehicles

Notes

Part 377 - Payment of Transportation Charges

Subpart A - Handling of C.O.D. Shipments

§377.101 Applicability.
The rules and regulations in this part apply to the transportation by motor vehicle of c.o.d. shipments by all common carriers of property subject to 49 U.S.C. 13702, except such transportation which is auxiliary to or supplemental of transportation by railroad and performed on railroad bills of lading, and except such transportation which is performed for freight forwarders and on freight forwarder bills of lading.

§377.103 Tariff requirements.
No common carrier of property subject to the provisions of 49 U.S.C. 13702, except as otherwise provided in §377.101, shall render any c.o.d. service unless such carrier has published, posted and filed tariffs which contain the rates, charges and rules governing such service, which rules shall conform to the regulations in this part.

§377.105 Collection and remittance.
Every common carrier of property subject to 49 U.S.C. 13702, except as otherwise provided in §377.101, which chooses to provide c.o.d. service may publish and maintain, or cause to be published and maintained for its account, a tariff or tariffs which set forth nondiscriminatory rules governing c.o.d. service and the collection and remittance of c.o.d. funds. Alternatively, any carrier that provides c.o.d. service, but does not wish to publish and maintain, or cause to be published and maintained, its own nondiscriminatory tariff, may adopt a rule requiring remittance of each c.o.d. collection directly to the consignor or other person designated by the consignor as payee within fifteen (15) days after delivery of the c.o.d. shipment to the consignee.

Subpart B - Extension of Credit to Shippers by Motor Common Carriers, Water Common Carriers, and Household Goods Freight Forwarders

§377.201 Scope.
(a) General. These regulations apply to the extension of credit in the transportation of property under Federal Motor Carrier Safety Administration regulation by motor carriers and household goods freight forwarders, except as otherwise provided.

(b) Exceptions. These regulations do not apply to —
  (1) *Contract carriage operations.*
  (2) *Transportation for —*
   (i) *The United States* or any department, bureau, or agency thereof,
   (ii) *Any State,* or political subdivision thereof,
   (iii) *The District of Columbia.*
  (3) *Property transportation incidental to passenger operations.*

§377.203 Extension of credit to shippers.
(a) Authorization to extend credit.
  (1) *A carrier* that meets the requirements in paragraph (a)(2) of this section may —
   (i) *Relinquish possession of freight* in advance of the payment of the tariff charges, and
   (ii) *Extend credit* in the amount of such charges to those who undertake to pay them (such persons are called shippers in this part).
  (2) *For such authorization,* the carrier shall take reasonable actions to assure payment of the tariff charges within the credit periods specified —
   (i) *In this part,* or
   (ii) *In tariff provisions* published pursuant to the regulations in paragraph (d) of this section.

(b) When the credit period begins. The credit period shall begin on the day following presentation of the freight bill.

(c) Length of credit period. Unless a different credit period has been established by tariff publication pursuant to paragraph (d) of this section, the credit period is 15 days. It includes Saturdays, Sundays, and legal holidays.

(d) Carriers may establish different credit periods in tariff rules. Carriers may publish tariff rules establishing credit periods different from those in paragraph (c) of this section. Such credit periods shall not be longer than 30 calendar days.

(e) Service charges.
  (1) *Service charges shall not apply* when credit is extended and payments are made within the standard credit period. The term standard credit period, as used in the preceding sentence, means —
   (i) *The credit period prescribed in paragraph (c) of this section,* or
   (ii) *A substitute credit period* published in a tariff rule pursuant to the authorization in paragraph (d) of this section.
  (2) *Carriers may,* by tariff rule, extend credit for an additional time period, subject if they wish to a service charge for that additional time. The combined length of the carrier's standard credit period (as defined in paragraph (e)(1) of this section) and its additional credit period shall not exceed the 30-day maximum credit period prescribed in paragraph (d) of this section. When such a tariff rule is in effect, shippers may elect to postpone payment until the end of the extended credit period if, in consideration therefor, they include any published service charges when making their payment.
  (3) *Carriers may,* by tariff rule, establish service charges for payments made after the expiration of an authorized credit period. Such a rule shall —
   (i) *Institute such charges* on the day following the last day of an authorized credit period, and
   (ii) *Notify shippers* —
    [A] *That its only purpose* is to prevent a shipper who does not pay on time from having free use of funds due to the carrier,
    [B] *That it does not sanction payment delays,* and
    [C] *That failure to pay* within the authorized credit period will, despite this provision for such charges, continue to require the carrier, before again extending credit, to determine in good faith whether the shipper will comply with the credit regulations in the future.
  (4) *Tariff rules* that establish charges pursuant to paragraph (e)(2) or (3) of this section may establish minimum charges.

(f) Discounts. Carriers may, by tariff rule, authorize discounts for early freight bill payments when credit is extended.

(g) (1) *Collection expense charges.* Carriers may, by tariff rule, assess reasonable and certain liquidated damages for all costs incurred in the collection of overdue freight charges. Carriers may use one of two methods in their tariffs:
  (i) *The first method* is to assess liquidated damages as a separate additional charge to the unpaid freight bill. In doing so, the tariff rule shall disclose the exact amount of the charges by stating either a dollar or specified percentage amount (or a combination of both) of the unpaid freight bill. The tariff shall further specify the time period (which shall at least allow for the authorized credit period) within which the shipper must pay to avoid such liquidated damages.
  (ii) *The second method* is to require payment of the full, non-discounted rate instead of the discounted rate otherwise applicable. The difference between the discount and the full rate constitutes a carrier's liquidated damages for its collection effort. Under this method the tariff shall identify the discount rates that are subject to the condition precedent and which require the shipper to make payment by a date certain. The date certain may not be set to occur by the carrier until at least after the expiration of the carrier's authorized credit period.
  (2) *The damages,* the timing of their applicability, and the conditions, if any, as provided by the tariff-rule methods allowed under paragraphs (g)(1)(i) and (ii) of this section also:
   (i) *Shall be clearly described in the tariff rule;*
   (ii) *Shall be applied* without unlawful prejudice and/or unjust discrimination between similarly situated shippers and/or consignees;
   (iii) *Shall be applied* only to the nonpayment of original, separate and independent freight bills and shall not apply to aggregate balance-due claims sought for collection on past shipments by a bankruptcy trustee, or any other person or agent;
   (iv) *Shall not apply* to instances of clear clerical or ministerial error such as non-receipt of a carrier's freight bill, or shipper's payment check lost in the mail, or carrier mailing of the freight bill to the wrong address;

(v) *Shall not apply in any way* to a charge for a transportation service if the carrier's bill of lading independently provides that the shipper is liable for fees incurred by the carrier in the collection of freight charges on that same transportation service;

(vi) *Shall be applied* only after the authorized credit period, and when the carrier has issued a revised freight bill or notice of imposition of collection expense charges for late payment within 90 days after expiration of the authorized credit period.

(3) *As an alternative to the tariff-rule methods* allowed under paragraphs (g)(1)(i) and (ii) of this section, a carrier may, wholly outside of its tariff, assess collection charges though contract terms in a bill of lading. By using the carrier and its bill of lading, the shipper accepts the bill of lading terms.

(h) **Discrimination prohibited.** Tariff rules published pursuant to paragraphs (d), (e), and (f) of this section shall not result in unreasonable discrimination among shippers.

§377.205 Presentation of freight bills.

(a) **"To be prepaid" shipments.**

(1) *On "to be prepaid" shipments,* the carrier shall present its freight bill for all transportation charges within the time period prescribed in paragraph (a)(2) of this section, except —

(i) As noted in paragraph (d) of this section, or

(ii) As otherwise excepted in this part.

(2) *The time period* for a carrier to present its freight bill for all transportation charges shall be 7 days, measured from the date the carrier received the shipment. This time period does not include Saturdays, Sundays, or legal holidays.

(b) **"Collect" shipments.**

(1) *On "collect" shipments,* the carrier shall present its freight bill for all transportation charges within the time period prescribed in paragraph (b)(2) of this section, except —

(i) As noted in paragraph (d) of this section, or

(ii) As otherwise excepted in this part.

(2) *The time period* for a carrier to present its freight bill for all transportation charges shall be 7 days, measured from the date the shipment was delivered at its destination. This time period does not include Saturdays, Sundays, or legal holidays.

(c) **Bills or accompanying written notices** shall state penalties for late payment, credit time limits and service charge and/or collection expense charge and discount terms. When credit is extended, freight bills or a separate written notice accompanying a freight bill or a group of freight bills presented at one time shall state that "failure timely to pay freight charges may be subject to tariff penalties" (or a statement of similar import). The bills or other notice shall also state the time by which payment must be made and any applicable service charge and/or collection expense charge and discount terms.

(d) **When the carrier lacks sufficient information** to compute tariff charges.

(1) *When information* sufficient to enable the carrier to compute the tariff charges is not then available to the carrier at its billing point, the carrier shall present its freight bill for payment within 7 days following the day upon which sufficient information becomes available at the billing point. This time period does not include Saturdays, Sundays, or legal holidays.

(2) *A carrier shall not extend further credit* to any shipper which fails to furnish sufficient information to allow the carrier to render a freight bill within a reasonable time after the shipment is tendered to the origin carrier.

(3) *As used in this paragraph,* the term "shipper" includes, but is not limited to, freight forwarders, and shippers' associations and shippers' agents.

§377.207 Effect of mailing freight bills or payments.

(a) **Presentation of freight bills by mail.** When carriers present freight bills by mail, the time of mailing shall be deemed to be the time of presentation of the bills. The term freight bills, as used in this paragraph, includes both paper documents and billing by use of electronic media such as computer tapes or disks, when the mails are used to transmit them.

(b) **Payment by mail.** When shippers mail acceptable checks, drafts, or money orders in payment of freight charges, the act of mailing them within the credit period shall be deemed to be the collection of the tariff charges within the credit period for the purposes of the regulations in this part.

(c) **Disputes as to date of mailing.** In case of dispute as to the date of mailing, the postmark shall be accepted as such date.

§377.209 Additional charges.

When a carrier —

(a) **Has collected the amount of tariff charges** represented in a freight bill presented by it as the total amount of such charges, and

(b) **Thereafter presents to the shipper another freight bill** for additional charges — the carrier may extend credit in the amount of such additional charges for a period of 30 calendar days from the date of the presentation of the freight bill for the additional charges.

§377.211 Computation of time.

Time periods involving calendar days shall be calculated pursuant to 49 CFR 386.32(a).

§§377.213-377.215 [Reserved]

§377.217 Interline settlement of revenues.

Nothing in this part shall be interpreted as affecting the interline settlement of revenues from traffic which is transported over through routes composed of lines of common carriers subject to the Secretary's jurisdiction under 49 U.S.C. Subtitle IV, Part B.

Part 378 - Procedures Governing the Processing, Investigation, and Disposition of Overcharge, Duplicate Payment, or Overcollection Claims

§378.1 Applicability.
The regulations set forth in this part govern the processing of claims for overcharge, duplicate payment, or overcollection for the transportation of property in interstate or foreign commerce by motor common carriers and household goods freight forwarders subject to 49 U.S.C. Subtitle IV, Part B.

§378.2 Definitions.
(a) **Carrier** means a motor common carrier or household goods freight forwarder subject to 49 U.S.C. Subtitle IV, Part B.

(b) **Overcharge** means an overcharge as defined in 49 U.S.C. 14704(b). It also includes duplicate payments as defined in paragraph (c) of this section and overcollections as defined in paragraph (d) of this section when a dispute exists between the parties concerning such charges.

(c) **Duplicate payment** means two or more payments for transporting the same shipment. Where one or more payment is not in the exact amount of the applicable tariff rates and charges, refunds shall be made on the basis of the excess amount over the applicable tariff rates and charges.

(d) **Overcollection** means the receipt by a household goods carrier of a payment in excess of the transportation and/or accessorial charges applicable to a particular shipment of household goods, as defined in Part 375 of this chapter, under tariffs lawfully on file with the United States Department of Transportation's Surface Transportation Board.

(e) **Unidentified payment** means a payment which a carrier has received but which the carrier is unable to match with its open accounts receivable or otherwise identify as being due for the performance of transportation services.

(f) **Claimant** means any shipper or receiver, or its authorized agent, filing a request with a carrier for the refund of an overcharge, duplicate payment, or overcollection.

§378.3 Filing and processing claims.
(a) A **claim for overcharge,** duplicate payment, or overcollection shall not be paid unless filed in writing or electronically communicated (when agreed to by the carrier and shipper or receiver involved) with the carrier that collected the transportation charges. The collecting carrier shall be the carrier to process all such claims. When a claim is filed with another carrier that participated in the transportation, that carrier shall transmit the claim to the collecting carrier within 15 days after receipt of the claim. If the collecting carrier is unable to dispose of the claim for any reason, the claim may be filed with or transferred to any participating carrier for final disposition.

(b) A **single claim may include** more than one shipment provided the claim on each shipment involves:
  (1) The same tariff issue or authority or circumstances,
  (2) Single line service by the same carrier, or
  (3) Service by the same interline carriers.

§378.4 Documentation of claims.
(a) **Claims for overcharge,** duplicate payment, or overcollection shall be accompanied by sufficient information to allow the carriers to conduct an investigation and pay or decline the claim within the time limitations set forth in §378.8. Claims shall include the name of the claimant, its file number, if any, and the amount of the refund sought to be recovered, if known.

(b) **Except when the original freight bill** is not a paper document but is electronically transmitted, claims for overcharge shall be accompanied by the original freight bill. Additional information may include, but is not limited to, the following:
  (1) The rate, classification, or commodity description or weight claimed to have been applicable.
  (2) Complete tariff authority for the rate, classification, or commodity description claimed.
  (3) Freight bill payment information.
  (4) Other documents or data which is believed by claimant to substantiate the basis for its claim.

(c) **Claims for duplicate payment and overcollection** shall be accompanied by the original freight bill(s) for which charges were paid (except when the original freight bill is not a paper document but is electronically transmitted) and by freight bill payment information.

(d) **Regardless of the provisions** of paragraphs (a), (b), and (c) of this section, the failure to provide sufficient information and documentation to allow a carrier to conduct an investigation and pay or decline the claim within the allowable time limitation shall not constitute grounds for disallowance of the claim. Rather, the carrier shall comply with §378.5(c) to obtain the additional information required.

(e) **A carrier shall accept copies** instead of the original documents required to be submitted in this section where the carrier is furnished with an agreement entered into by the claimant which indemnifies the carrier for subsequent duplicate claims which might be filed and supported by the original documents.

§378.5 Investigation of claims.
(a) **Upon receipt of a claim, whether written or otherwise,** the processing carrier shall promptly initiate an investigation and establish a file, as required by §378.6.

(b) **If a carrier discovers an overcharge,** duplicate payment, or overcollection which has not been the subject of a claim, it shall promptly initiate an investigation and comply with the provisions in §378.9.

(c) **In the event the carrier processing the claim** requires information or documents in addition to that submitted with the claim, the carrier shall promptly notify the claimant and request the information required. This includes notifying the claimant that a written or electronically transmitted claim must be filed before the carrier becomes subject to the time limits for settling such a claim under §378.8.

§378.6 Claim records.
At the time a claim is received the carrier shall create a separate file and assign it a successive claim file number and note that number on all documents filed in support of the claim and all records and correspondence with respect to the claim, including the written or electronic acknowledgment of receipt required under §378.7. If pertinent to the disposition of the claim, the carrier shall also note that number on the shipping order and delivery receipt, if any, covering the shipment involved.

§378.7 Acknowledgment of claims.
Upon receipt of a written or electronically transmitted claim, the carrier shall acknowledge its receipt in writing or electronically to the claimant within 30 days after the date of receipt except when the carrier shall have paid or declined in writing or electronically within that period. The carrier shall include the date of receipt in its written or electronic claim which shall be placed in the file for that claim.

§378.8 Disposition of claims.
The processing carrier shall pay, decline to pay, or settle each written or electronically communicated claim within 60 days after its receipt by that carrier, except where the claimant and the carrier agree in writing or electronically to a specific extension based upon extenuating circumstances. If the carrier declines to pay a claim or makes settlement in an amount different from that sought, the carrier shall notify the claimant in writing or electronically, of the reason(s) for its action, citing tariff authority or other pertinent information developed as a result of its investigation.

§378.9 Disposition of unidentified payments, overcharges, duplicate payments, and overcollections not supported by claims.
(a) (1) *Carriers shall establish procedures* for identifying and properly applying all unidentified payments. If a carrier does not have sufficient information with which properly to apply such a payment, the carrier shall notify the payor of the unidentified payment within 60 days of receipt of the payment and request information which will enable it to identify the payment. If the carrier does not receive the information requested within 90 days from the date of the notice, the carrier may treat the unidentified payment as a payment in fact of freight charges owing to it. Following the 90-day period, the regular claims procedure under this part shall be applicable.

(2) *Notice shall be in writing* and clearly indicate that it is a final notice and not a bill. Notice shall include: The check number, amount, and date; the payor's name; and any additional basic information the carrier is able to provide. The final notice also must inform payor that:
  (i) *Applicable regulations* allow the carrier to conditionally retain the payment as revenue in the absence of a timely response by the payor; and

(ii) *following the 90-day period* the regular claims procedure shall be applicable.

(3) *Upon a carrier's receipt of information from the payor,* the carrier shall, within 14 days:

(i) *Make a complete refund of such funds to the payor; or*

(ii) *notify the payor* that the information supplied is not sufficient to identify the unapplied payment and request additional information; or

(iii) *notify the payor* of the carrier's determination that such payment was applicable to particular freight charges lawfully due the carrier.

Where no refund is made by the carrier, the carrier shall advise the payor of its right to file a formal claim for refund with the carrier in accordance with the regular claims procedure under this part.

(b) **When a carrier which participates** in a transportation movement, but did not collect the transportation charges, finds that an overpayment has been made, that carrier shall immediately notify the collecting carrier. When the collecting carrier (when single or joint line haul) discovers or is notified by such a participating carrier that an overcharge, duplicate payment, or overcollection exists for any transportation charge which has not been the subject of a claim, the carrier shall create a file as if a claim had been submitted and shall record in the file the date it discovered or was notified of the overpayment. The carrier that collected the charges shall then refund the amount of the overpayment to the person who paid the transportation charges or to the person that made duplicate payment within 30 days from the date of such discovery or notification.

Part 379 - Preservation of Records

§379.1 Applicability.
(a) **The preservation of record rules** contained in this part shall apply to the following:
   (1) *Motor carriers and brokers;*
   (2) *Water carriers; and*
   (3) *Household goods freight forwarders.*
(b) **This part applies also to the preservation** of accounts, records and memoranda of traffic associations, weighing and inspection bureaus, and other joint activities maintained by or on behalf of companies listed in paragraph (a) of this section.

§379.3 Records required to be retained.
Companies subject to this part shall retain records for the minimum retention periods provided in Appendix A to this part. After the required retention periods, the records may be destroyed at the discretion of each company's management. It shall be the obligation of the subject company to maintain records that adequately support financial and operational data required by the Secretary. The company may request a ruling from the Secretary on the retention of any record. The provisions of this part shall not be construed as excusing compliance with the lawful requirements of any other governmental body prescribing longer retention periods for any category of records.

§379.5 Protection and storage of records.
(a) **The company shall protect records** subject to this part from fires, floods, and other hazards, and safeguard the records from unnecessary exposure to deterioration from excessive humidity, dryness, or lack of ventilation.
(b) **The company shall notify the Secretary** if prescribed records are substantially destroyed or damaged before the term of the prescribed retention periods.

§379.7 Preservation of records.
(a) **All records may be preserved by any technology** that is immune to alteration, modification, or erasure of the underlying data and will enable production of an accurate and unaltered paper copy.
(b) **Records not originally preserved on hard copy** shall be accompanied by a statement executed by a person having personal knowledge of the facts indicating the type of data included within the records. One comprehensive statement may be executed in lieu of individual statements for multiple records if the type of data included in the multiple records is common to all such records. The records shall be indexed and retained in such a manner as will render them readily accessible. The company shall have facilities available to locate, identify and produce legible paper copies of the records.
(c) **Any significant characteristic, feature or other attribute** that a particular medium will not preserve shall be clearly indicated at the beginning of the applicable records as appropriate.
(d) **The printed side of forms, such as instructions,** need not be preserved for each record as long as the printed matter is common to all such forms and an identified specimen of the form is maintained on the medium for reference.

§379.9 Companies going out of business.
The records referred to in the regulations in this part may be destroyed after business is discontinued and the company is completely liquidated. The records may not be destroyed until dissolution is final and all pending transactions and claims are completed. When a company is merged with another company under jurisdiction of the Secretary, the successor company shall preserve records of the merged company in accordance with the regulations in this part.

§379.11 Waiver of requirements of the regulations in this part.
A waiver from any provision of the regulations in this part may be made by the Secretary upon his/her own initiative or upon submission of a written request by the company. Each request for waiver shall demonstrate that unusual circumstances warrant a departure from prescribed retention periods, procedures, or techniques, or that compliance with such prescribed requirements would impose an unreasonable burden on the company.

§379.13 Disposition and retention of records.
The schedule in Appendix A to this part shows periods that designated records shall be preserved. The descriptions specified under the various general headings are for convenient reference and identification, and are intended to apply to the items named regardless of what the records are called in individual companies and regardless of the record media. The retention periods represent the prescribed number of years from the date of the document and not calendar years. Records not listed in Appendix A to this part shall be retained as determined by the management of each company.

Appendix A to Part 379 — Schedule of Records and Periods of Retention.

Item and category of records	Retention period
A. Corporate and General	
1. Incorporation and reorganization:	
(a) Charter or certificate of incorporation and amendments.	Note A.
(b) Legal documents related to mergers, consolidations, reorganization, receiverships and similar actions which affect the identity or organization of the company.	Note A.
2. Minutes of Directors, Executive Committees, Stockholders and other corporate meetings.	Note A.
3. Titles, franchises and authorities:	
(a) Certificates of public convenience and necessity issued by regulating bodies.	Until expiration or cancellation.
(b) Operating authorizations and exemptions to operate.	Until expiration or cancellation.
(c) Copies of formal orders of regulatory bodies served upon the company.	Note A.
(d) Deeds, charters, and other title papers.	Until disposition of property.
(e) Patents and patent records.	Note A.
4. Annual reports or statements to stockholders.	3 years.
5. Contracts and agreements:	
(a) Service contracts, such as for operational management, accounting, financial or legal services, and agreements with agents.	Until expiration or termination plus 3 years.
(b) Contracts and other agreements relating to the construction, acquisition or sale of real property and equipment except as otherwise provided in (a) above.	Until expiration or termination plus 3 years.
(c) Contracts for the purchase or sale of material and supplies except as provided in (a) above.	Until expiration.
(d) Shipping contracts for transportation or caretakers of freight.	Until expiration.
(e) Contracts with employees and employee bargaining groups.	Until expiration.
(f) Contracts, leases and agreements, not specifically provided for in this section.	Until expiration or termination plus 1 year.
6. Accountant's auditor's, and inspector's reports:	
(a) Certifications and reports of examinations and audits conducted by public accountants.	3 years.

Appendix A

Part 379 - Preservation of Records

Item and category of records	Retention period
(b) Reports of examinations and audits conducted by internal auditors, time inspectors, and others.	3 years.
7. Other.	Note A.
B. Treasury	
1. Capital stock records:	
(a) Capital stock ledger.	Note A.
(b) Capital stock certificates, records of or stubs of.	Note A.
(c) Stock transfer register.	Note A.
2. Long-term debt records:	
(a) Bond indentures, underwritings, mortgages, and other long-term credit agreements.	Until redemption plus 3 years.
(b) Registered bonds and debenture ledgers.	Until redemption plus 3 years.
(c) Stubs or similar records of bonds or other long-term debt issued.	Note A.
3. Authorizations from regulatory bodies for issuance of securities including applications, reports, and supporting papers.	Note A.
4. Records of securities owned, in treasury, or held by custodians, detailed ledgers and journals, or their equivalent.	Until the securities are sold, redeemed or otherwise disposed of.
5. Other.	Note A.
C. Financial and Accounting	
1. Ledgers:	
(a) General and subsidiary ledgers with indexes.	Until discontinuance of use plus 3 years.
(b) Balance sheets and trial balance sheets of general and subsidiary ledgers.	3 years.
2. Journals:	
(a) General journals.	Until discontinuance of use plus 3 years.
(b) Subsidiary journals and any supporting data, except as otherwise provided for, necessary to explain journal entries.	3 years.
3. Cash books:	
(a) General cash books.	Until discontinuance of use plus 3 years.
(b) Subsidiary cash books.	3 years.
4. Vouchers:	
(a) Voucher registers, indexes, or equivalent.	3 years.
(b) Paid and canceled vouchers, expenditure authorizations, detailed distribution sheets and other supporting data including original bills and invoices, if not provided for elsewhere.	3 years.
(c) Paid drafts, paid checks, and receipts for cash paid out.	3 years.
5. Accounts receivable:	
(a) Record or register of accounts receivable, indexes thereto, and summaries of distribution.	3 years after settlement.
(b) Bills issued for collection and supporting data.	3 years after settlement.

Item and category of records	Retention period
(c) Authorization for writing off receivables.	1 year.
(d) Reports and statements showing age and status of receivables.	1 year.
6. Records of accounting codes and instructions.	3 years after discontinuance.
7. Other.	Note A.
D. Property and Equipment	
NOTE: All accounts, records, and memoranda necessary for making a complete analysis of the cost or value of property shall be retained for the periods shown. If any of the records elsewhere provided for in this schedule are of this character, they shall be retained for the periods shown below, regardless of any lesser retention period assigned.	
1. Property records:	
(a) Records which maintain complete information on cost or other value of all real and personal property or equipment.	3 years after disposition of property.
(b) Records of additions and betterments made to property and equipment.	3 years after disposition of property.
(c) Records pertaining to retirements and replacements of property and equipment.	3 years after disposition of property.
(d) Records pertaining to depreciation.	3 years after disposition of property.
(e) Records of equipment number changes.	3 years after disposition of property.
(f) Records of motor and engine changes.	3 years after disposition of property.
(g) Records of equipment lightweighed and stenciled.	Only current or latest records.
2. Engineering records of property changes actually made.	3 years after disposition of property.
3. Other.	Note A.
E. Personnel and Payroll	
1. Personnel and payroll records.	1 year.
F. Insurance and Claims	
1. Insurance records:	
(a) Schedules of insurance against fire, storms, and other hazards and records of premium payments.	Until expiration plus 1 year.
(b) Records of losses and recoveries from insurance companies and supporting papers.	1 year after settlement.
(c) Insurance policies.	Until expiration of coverage plus 1 year.
2. Claims records:	
(a) Claim registers, card or book indexes, and other records which record personal injury, fire and other claims against the company, together with all supporting data.	1 year after settlement.
(b) Claims registers, card or book indexes, and other records which record overcharges, damages, and other claims filed by the company against others, together with all supporting data.	1 year after settlement.
(c) Records giving the details of authorities issued to agents, carriers, and others for participation in freight claims.	3 years.

Part 379 - Preservation of Records — Appendix A (continued)

Item and category of records	Retention period
(d) Reports, statements and other data pertaining to personal injuries or damage to property when not necessary to support claims or vouchers.	3 years.
(e) Reports, statements, tracers, and other data pertaining to unclaimed, over, short, damaged, and refused freight, when not necessary to support claims or vouchers.	1 year.
(f) Authorities for disposal of unclaimed, damaged, and refused freight.	3 years.
3. Other.	Note A.
G. Taxes	
1. Taxes.	Note A.
H. Purchases and Stores	
1. Purchases and stores.	Note A.
I. Shipping and Agency Documents	
1. Bills of lading and releases:	
(a) Consignors' shipping orders, consignors' shipping tickets, and copies of bills of lading, freight bills from other carriers and other similar documents furnished the carrier for movement of freight.	1 year.
(b) Shippers' order-to-notify bills of lading taken up and canceled.	1 year.
2. Freight waybills:	
(a) Local waybills.	1 year.
(b) Interline waybills received from and made to other carriers.	1 year.
(c) Company freight waybills.	1 year.
(d) Express waybills.	1 year.
3. Freight bills and settlements:	
(a) Paid copy of freight bill retained to support receipt of freight charges:	
(1) Bus express freight bills provided no claim has been filed.	1 year.
(2) All other freight bills.	1 year.
(b) Paid copy of freight bill retained to support payment of freight charges to other carriers:	
(1) Bus express freight bills provided no claim has been filed.	1 year.
(2) All other freight bills.	1 year.
(c) Records of unsettled freight bills and supporting papers.	1 year after disposition.
(d) Records and reports of correction notices.	1 year.
4. Other freight records:	
(a) Records of freight received, forwarded, and delivered.	1 year.
(b) Notice to consignees of arrival of freight; tender of delivery.	1 year.
5. Agency records (to include conductors, pursers, stewards, and others):	
(a) Cash books.	1 year.
(b) Remittance records, bank deposit slips and supporting papers.	1 year.
(c) Balance sheets and supporting papers.	1 year.
(d) Statements of corrections in agents' accounts.	1 year.
(e) Other records and reports pertaining to ticket sales, baggage handled, miscellaneous collections, refunds, adjustments, etc.	1 year.
J. Transportation	
1. Records pertaining to transportation of household goods:	
(a) Estimate of charges.	1 year.
(b) Order for service.	1 year.
(c) Vehicle-load manifest.	1 year.
(d) Descriptive inventory.	1 year.
2. Records and reports pertaining to operation of marine and floating equipment:	
(a) Ship log.	3 years.
(b) Ship articles.	3 years.
(c) Passenger and room list.	3 years.
(d) Floatmen's barge, lighter, and escrow captain's reports, demurrage records, towing reports and checks sheets.	2 years.
3. Dispatchers' sheets, registers, and other records pertaining to movement of transportation equipment.	3 years.
4. Import and export records including bonded freight and steamship engagements.	2 years.
5. Records, reports, orders and tickets pertaining to weighting of freight.	3 years.
6. Records of loading and unloading of transportation equipment.	2 years.
7. Records pertaining to the diversion or reconsignment of freight, including requests, tracers, and correspondence.	2 years.
8. Other.	Note A.
K. Supporting Data for Reports and Statistics	
1. Supporting data for reports filed with the Federal Motor Carrier Administration, the Surface Transportation Board, the Department of Transportation's Bureau of Transportation Statistics and regulatory bodies:	
(a) Supporting data for annual financial, operating and statistical reports.	3 years.
(b) Supporting data for periodical reports of operating revenues, expenses, and income.	3 years.
(c) Supporting data for reports detailing use of proceeds from issuance or sale of company securities.	3 years.

Part 379 - Preservation of Records
(continued)

Item and category of records	Retention period
(d) Supporting data for valuation inventory reports and records. This includes related notes, maps and sketches, underlying engineering, land, and accounting reports, pricing schedules, summary or collection sheets, yearly reports of changes and other miscellaneous data, all relating to the valuation of the company's property by the Federal Highway Administration, the Surface Transportation Board, the Department of Transportation's Bureau of Transportation Statistics or other regulatory body.	3 years after disposition of the property.
2. Supporting data for periodical reports of accidents, inspections, tests, hours of service, repairs, etc.	3 years.
3. Supporting data for periodical statistical of operating results or performance by tonnage, mileage, passengers carried, piggyback traffic, commodities, costs, analyses of increases and decreases, or otherwise.	3 years.
M. Miscellaneous	
1. Index of records.	Until revised as record structure changes.
2. Statement listing records prematurely destroyed or lost.	For the remainder of the period as prescribed for records destroyed.

Note A: Records referenced to this note shall be maintained as determined by the designated records supervisory official. Companies should be mindful of the record retention requirements of the Internal Revenue Service, Securities and Exchange Commission, State and local jurisdictions, and other regulatory agencies. Companies shall exercise reasonable care in choosing retention periods, and the choice of retention periods shall reflect past experiences, company needs, pending litigation, and regulatory requirements.

Part 380 - Special Training Requirements
(Page 43 in the Driver Edition)

Subpart A - Longer Combination Vehicle (LCV) Driver-Training and Driver-Instructor Requirements — General

§380.101 Purpose and scope.
(a) **Purpose.** The purpose of this part is to establish minimum requirements for operators of longer combination vehicles (LCVs) and LCV driver-instructors.
(b) **Scope.** This part establishes:
  (1) *Minimum training requirements for operators of LCVs;*
  (2) *Minimum qualification requirements for LCV driver-instructors; and*
  (3) *Procedures for determining compliance* with this part by operators, instructors, training institutions, and employers.

§380.103 Applicability.
The rules in this part apply to all operators of LCVs in interstate commerce, employers of such persons, and LCV driver-instructors.

§380.105 Definitions.
(a) **The definitions in Part 383 of this subchapter** apply to this part, except where otherwise specifically noted.
(b) **As used in this part:**
Classroom instructor means a qualified LCV driver-instructor who provides knowledge instruction that does not involve the actual operation of a longer combination vehicle or its components. Instruction may take place in a parking lot, garage, or any other facility suitable for instruction.
Longer combination vehicle (LCV) means any combination of a truck-tractor and two or more trailers or semi-trailers, which operate on the National System of Interstate and Defense Highways with a gross vehicle weight (GVW) greater than 36,288 kilograms (80,000 pounds).
LCV Double means an LCV consisting of a truck-tractor in combination with two trailers and/or semi-trailers.
LCV Triple means an LCV consisting of a truck-tractor in combination with three trailers and/or semi-trailers.
Qualified LCV driver-instructor means an instructor meeting the requirements contained in Subpart C of this part. There are two types of qualified LCV driver-instructors:
  (1) *classroom instructor* and
  (2) *skills instructor.*
Skills instructor means a qualified LCV driver-instructor who provides behind-the-wheel instruction involving the actual operation of a longer combination vehicle or its components outside a classroom.
Training institution means any technical or vocational school accredited by an accrediting institution recognized by the U.S. Department of Education. A motor carrier's training program for its drivers or an entity that exclusively offers services to a single motor carrier is not a training institution.

§380.107 General requirements.
(a) **Except as provided in §380.111,** a driver who wishes to operate an LCV shall first take and successfully complete an LCV driver-training program that provides the knowledge and skills necessary to operate an LCV. The specific types of knowledge and skills that a training program shall include are outlined in the appendix to this part.
(b) **Before a person receives training:**
  (1) *That person shall present evidence* to the LCV driver-instructor showing that he/she meets the general requirements set forth in Subpart B of this part for the specific type of LCV training to be taken.
  (2) *The LCV driver-instructor shall verify* that each trainee applicant meets the general requirements for the specific type of LCV training to be taken.
(c) **Upon successful completion** of the training requirement, the driver-student shall be issued an LCV Driver Training Certificate by a certifying official of the training entity in accordance with the requirements specified in Subpart D of this part.

§380.109 Driver testing.
(a) **Testing methods.** The driver-student must pass knowledge and skills tests in accordance with the following requirements, to determine whether a driver-student has successfully completed an LCV driver-training program as specified in Subpart B of this part. The written knowledge test may be administered by any qualified driver-instructor. The skills tests, based on actual operation of an LCV, must be administered by a qualified LCV skills instructor.
  (1) *All tests shall be constructed to determine* if the driver-student possesses the required knowledge and skills set forth in the appendix to this part for the specific type of LCV training program being taught.
  (2) *Instructors shall develop their own tests* for the specific type of LCV-training program being taught, but those tests must be at least as stringent as the requirements set forth in paragraph (b) of this section.
  (3) *LCV driver-instructors* shall establish specific methods for scoring the knowledge and skills tests.
  (4) *Passing scores must meet the requirements* of paragraph (b) of this section.
  (5) *Knowledge and skills tests shall be based* upon the information taught in the LCV training programs as set forth in the appendix to this part.
  (6) *Each knowledge test* shall address the training provided during both theoretical and behind-the-wheel instruction, and include at least one question from each of the units listed in the table to the appendix to this part, for the specific type of LCV training program being taught.
  (7) *Each skills test shall include* all the maneuvers and operations practiced during the Proficiency Development unit of instruction (behind-the-wheel instruction), as described in the appendix to this part, for the specific type of LCV training program being taught.
(b) **Proficiency determinations.** The driver-student must meet the following conditions to be certified as an LCV driver:
  (1) *Answer correctly* at least 80 percent of the questions on each knowledge test; and
  (2) *Demonstrate that he/she can successfully perform* all of the skills addressed in paragraph (a)(7) of this section.
(c) **Automatic test failure.** Failure to obey traffic laws or involvement in a preventable crash during the skills portion of the test will result in automatic failure. Automatic test failure determinations are made at the sole discretion of the qualified LCV driver-instructor.
(d) **Guidance for testing methods** and proficiency determinations. Motor carriers should refer to the Examiner's Manual for Commercial Driver's License Tests for help in developing testing methods and making proficiency determinations. You may obtain a copy of this document by contacting the American Association of Motor Vehicle Administrators (AAMVA), 4300 Wilson Boulevard, Suite 400, Arlington, Virginia 22203.

§380.111 Substitute for driver training.
(a) **Grandfather clause.** The LCV driver-training requirements specified in Subpart B of this part do not apply to an individual who meets the conditions set forth in paragraphs (b), (c), and (d) of this section. A motor carrier must ensure that an individual claiming eligibility to operate an LCV on the basis of this section meets these conditions before allowing him/her to operate an LCV.
(b) **An individual must certify that,** during the 2-year period immediately preceding the date of application for a Certificate of Grandfathering, he/she had:
  (1) *A valid Class A CDL with a "double/triple trailers" endorsement;*
  (2) *No more than one driver's license;*
  (3) *No suspension, revocation, or cancellation of his/her CDL;*
  (4) *No convictions for a major offense* while operating a CMV as defined in §383.51(b) of this subchapter;
  (5) *No convictions* for a railroad-highway grade crossing offense while operating a CMV as defined in §383.51(d) of this subchapter;
  (6) *No convictions for violating* an out-of-service order as defined in §383.51(e) of this subchapter;
  (7) *No more than one conviction* for a serious traffic violation, as defined in §383.5 of this subchapter, while operating a CMV; and

(8) *No convictions* for a violation of State or local law relating to motor vehicle traffic control arising in connection with any traffic crash while operating a CMV.

(c) **An individual must certify and provide evidence that he/she:**
  (1) *Is regularly employed in a job* requiring the operation of a CMV that requires a CDL with a double/triple trailers endorsement; and
  (2) *Has operated,* during the 2 years immediately preceding the date of the application for a Certificate of Grandfathering, vehicles representative of the type of LCV that he/she seeks to continue operating.

(d) **A motor carrier must issue** a Certificate of Grandfathering to a person who meets the requirements of this section and must maintain a copy of the certificate in the individual's Driver Qualification file.

[Form: Longer Combination Vehicle (LCV) Driver-Training Certificate of Grandfathering]

* Full-size forms available free of charge at www.dotcfr.com.

(e) **An applicant may be grandfathered** under this section only during the year following June 1, 2004.

§380.113 Employer responsibilities.

(a) **No motor carrier shall:**
  (1) *Allow, require, permit or authorize an individual* to operate an LCV unless he/she meets the requirements in §380.203 or §380.205 and has been issued the LCV driver-training certificate described in §380.401. This provision does not apply to individuals who are eligible for the substitute for driver training provision in §380.111.
  (2) *Allow, require, permit, or authorize an individual* to operate an LCV which the LCV driver-training certificate, CDL, and CDL endorsement(s) do not authorize the driver to operate. This provision applies to individuals employed by or under contract to the motor carrier.

(b) **A motor carrier that employs** or has under contract LCV drivers shall provide evidence of the certifications required by §380.401 or §380.111 of this part when requested by an authorized FMCSA, State, or local official in the course of a compliance review.

Subpart B - LCV Driver-Training Program

§380.201 General requirements.

(a) **The LCV Driver-Training Program** that is described in the appendix to this part requires training using an LCV Double or LCV Triple and must include the following general categories of instruction:
  (1) Orientation;
  (2) Basic operation;
  (3) Safe operating practices;
  (4) Advanced operations; and
  (5) Nondriving activities.

(b) **The LCV Driver-Training Program** must include the minimum topics of training set forth in the appendix to this part and behind-the-wheel instruction that is designed to provide an opportunity to develop the skills outlined under the Proficiency Development unit of the training program.

§380.203 LCV Doubles.

(a) **To qualify for the training necessary** to operate an LCV Double, a driver-student shall, during the 6 months immediately preceding application for training, have:
  (1) *A valid Class A CDL with a double/triple trailer endorsement;*
  (2) *Driving experience in a Group A vehicle* as described in §383.91 of this subchapter. Evidence of driving experience shall be an employer's written statement that the driver has, for at least 6 months immediately preceding application, operated a Group A vehicle while under his/her employ;
  (3) *No more than one driver's license;*
  (4) *No suspension, revocation, or cancellation of his/her CDL;*
  (5) *No convictions for a major offense,* as defined in §383.51(b) of this subchapter, while operating a CMV;
  (6) *No convictions* for a railroad-highway grade crossing offense, as defined in §383.51(d) of this subchapter, while operating a CMV;
  (7) *No convictions* for violating an out-of-service order as defined in §383.51(e) of this subchapter;
  (8) *No more than one conviction* for a serious traffic violation, as defined in §383.5 of this subchapter, while operating a CMV; and
  (9) *No convictions* for a violation of State or local law relating to motor vehicle traffic control arising in connection with any traffic crash while operating a CMV.

(b) **Driver-students meeting the preliminary requirements** in paragraph (a) of this section shall successfully complete a training program that meets the minimum unit requirements for LCV Doubles as set forth in the appendix to this part.

(c) **Driver-students who successfully complete** the Driver Training Program for LCV Doubles shall be issued a certificate, in accordance with Subpart D of this part, indicating the driver is qualified to operate an LCV Double.

§380.205 LCV Triples.

(a) **To qualify for the training necessary** to operate an LCV Triple, a driver-student shall, during the 6 months immediately preceding application for training, have:
  (1) *A valid Class A CDL with a double/triple trailer endorsement;*
  (2) *Experience operating the vehicle* listed under paragraph (a)(2)(i) or (a)(2)(ii) of this section. Evidence of driving experience shall be an employer's written statement that the driver has, during the 6 months immediately preceding application, operated the applicable vehicle(s):
    (i) Group A truck-tractor/semi-trailer combination as described in §383.91 of this subchapter; or
    (ii) Group A truck-tractor/semi-trailer/trailer combination that operates at a gross vehicle weight of 80,000 pounds or less;
  (3) *No more than one driver's license;*
  (4) *No suspension, revocation, or cancellation of his/her CDL;*
  (5) *No convictions for a major offense,* as defined in §383.51(b) of this subchapter, while operating a CMV;
  (6) *No convictions* for a railroad-highway grade crossing offense, as defined in §383.51(d) of this subchapter, while operating a CMV;
  (7) *No convictions* for violating an out-of-service order, as defined in §383.51(e) of this subchapter;
  (8) *No more than one conviction* for a serious traffic violation, as defined in §383.5 of this subchapter, while operating a CMV; and
  (9) *No convictions* for a violation of State or local law relating to motor vehicle traffic control arising in connection with any traffic crash, while operating a CMV.

(b) **Driver-students meeting the preliminary requirements** in paragraph (a) of this section shall successfully complete a training program that meets the minimum unit requirements for LCV Triples as set forth in the appendix to this part.

(c) **Driver-students who successfully complete** the Driver Training Program for LCV Triples shall be issued a certificate, in accordance with Subpart D of this part, indicating the driver is qualified to operate an LCV Triple.

Subpart C - LCV Driver-Instructor Requirements

§380.301 General requirements.
There are two types of LCV driver-instructors: Classroom instructors and Skills instructors. Except as provided in §380.303, you must meet the conditions under paragraph (a) or paragraph (b) of this section to qualify as an LCV driver-instructor.

(a) Classroom instructor. To qualify as an LCV Classroom instructor, a person shall:
   (1) *Have audited the driver-training course* that he/she intends to instruct.
   (2) *If employed by a training institution,* meet all State requirements for a vocational instructor.

(b) Skills instructor. To qualify as an LCV skills instructor, a person shall:
   (1) *Provide evidence of successful completion* of the Driver-Training Program requirements, as set forth in Subpart B of this part, when requested by employers and/or an authorized FMCSA, State, or local official in the course of a compliance review. The Driver-Training Program must be for the operation of CMVs representative of the subject matter that he/she will teach.
   (2) *If employed by a training institution,* meet all State requirements for a vocational instructor;
   (3) *Possess a valid Class A CDL* with all endorsements necessary to operate the CMVs applicable to the subject matter being taught (LCV Doubles and/or LCV Triples, including any specialized variation thereof, such as a tank vehicle, that requires an additional endorsement); and
   (4) *Have at least 2 years' CMV driving experience* in a vehicle representative of the type of driver training to be provided (LCV Doubles or LCV Triples).

§380.303 Substitute for instructor requirements.
(a) Classroom instructor. The requirements specified under §380.301(a) of this part for a qualified LCV driver-instructor are waived for a classroom instructor-candidate who has 2 years of recent satisfactory experience teaching the classroom portion of a program similar in content to that set forth in the appendix to this part.

(b) Skills instructor. The requirements specified under §380.301(b) of this part for a qualified LCV driver-instructor are waived for a skills instructor-candidate who:
   (1) *Meets the conditions of §380.111(b);*
   (2) *Has CMV driving experience* during the previous 2 years in a vehicle representative of the type of LCV that is the subject of the training course to be provided;
   (3) *Has experience during the previous 2 years* in teaching the operation of the type of LCV that is the subject of the training course to be provided; and
   (4) *If employed by a training institution,* meets all State requirements for a vocational instructor.

§380.305 Employer responsibilities.
(a) No motor carrier shall:
   (1) *Knowingly allow, require, permit or authorize* a driver-instructor in its employ, or under contract to the motor carrier, to provide LCV driver training unless such person is a qualified LCV driver-instructor under the requirements of this subpart; or
   (2) *Contract with a training institution* to provide LCV driver training unless the institution:
      (i) *Uses instructors* who are qualified LCV driver-instructors under the requirements of this subpart;
      (ii) *Is accredited by an accrediting institution* recognized by the U.S. Department of Education;
      (iii) *Is in compliance with all applicable* State training school requirements; and
      (iv) *Identifies drivers* certified under §380.401 of this part, when requested by employers and/or an authorized FMCSA, State, or local official in the course of a compliance review.

(b) A motor carrier that employs or has under contract qualified LCV driver-instructors shall provide evidence of the certifications required by §380.301 or §380.303 of this part, when requested by an authorized FMCSA, State, or local official in the course of a compliance review.

Subpart D - Driver-Training Certification

§380.401 Certification document.
(a) A student who successfully completes LCV driver training shall be issued a Driver-Training Certificate that is substantially in accordance with the following form.

Longer Combination Vehicle (LCV) Driver-Training Certificate

I certify that _____ has presented evidence of meeting the training prerequisites set forth in the Federal Motor Carrier Safety Regulations (49 CFR 380.203(a) and 380.205(a)) for LCV training, and has successfully completed the LCV Driver-Training Course(s) indicated below:

YES	NO		
☐	☐	LCV Doubles	Date Training Completed
☐	☐	LCV Triples	Date Training Completed

I certify that the indicated LCV Driver-Training Course(s) was/were provided by a qualified LCV driver-instructor as defined under 49 CFR 380.105 and meet(s) the minimum requirements set forth in 49 CFR Part 380, Subparts A and B.

DRIVER NAME (First name, MI, Last name)

Commercial Driver's License Number | STATE

ADDRESS OF DRIVER (Street Address, City, State, and Zip Code)

FULL NAME OF TRAINING ENTITY | Telephone Number

BUSINESS ADDRESS (Street Address, City, State, and Zip Code)

SIGNATURE OF TRAINING CERTIFYING OFFICIAL | DATE ISSUED

©MMV Mangan Communications, Inc.

* Full-size forms available free of charge at www.dotcfr.com.

(b) An LCV driver must provide a copy of the Driver-Training Certificate to his/her employer to be filed in the Driver Qualification File.

Subpart E - Entry-Level Driver Training Requirements

§380.501 Applicability.
All entry-level drivers who drive in interstate commerce and are subject to the CDL requirements of Part 383 of this chapter must comply with the rules of this subpart, except drivers who are subject to the jurisdiction of the Federal Transit Administration or who are otherwise exempt under §390.3(f) of this subchapter.

§380.502 Definitions.
(a) The definitions in Part 383 of this chapter apply to this part, except where otherwise specifically noted.
(b) As used in this subpart:
Entry-level driver is a driver with less than one year of experience operating a CMV with a CDL in interstate commerce.
Entry-level driver training is training the CDL driver receives in driver qualification requirements, hours of service of drivers, driver wellness, and whistle blower protection as appropriate to the entry-level driver's current position in addition to passing the CDL test.

§380.503 Entry-level driver training requirements.
Entry-level driver training must include instruction addressing the following four areas:

(a) Driver qualification requirements. The Federal rules on medical certification, medical examination procedures, general qualifications, responsibilities, and disqualifications based on various offenses, orders, and loss of driving privileges (Part 391, Subparts B and E of this subchapter).

(b) Hours of service of drivers. The limitations on driving hours, the requirement to be off-duty for certain periods of time, record of duty status preparation, and exceptions (Part 395 of this subchapter). Fatigue countermeasures as a means to avoid crashes.

(c) Driver wellness. Basic health maintenance including diet and exercise. The importance of avoiding excessive use of alcohol.

(d) Whistleblower protection. The right of an employee to question the safety practices of an employer without the employee's risk of losing a job or being subject to reprisals simply for stating a safety concern (29 CFR Part 1978).

§380.505 Proof of training.

An employer who uses an entry-level driver must ensure the driver has received a training certificate containing all the information contained in §380.513 from the training provider.

§380.507 Driver responsibilities.

Each entry-level driver must receive training required by §380.503.

§380.509 Employer responsibilities.

(a) **Each employer must ensure** each entry-level driver who first began operating a CMV requiring a CDL in interstate commerce after July 20, 2003, receives training required by §380.503.

(b) **Each employer must place a copy** of the driver's training certificate in the driver's personnel or qualification file.

(c) **All records required by this subpart** shall be maintained as required by §390.31 of this subchapter and shall be made available for inspection at the employer's principal place of business within two business days after a request has been made by an authorized representative of the Federal Motor Carrier Safety Administration.

§380.511 Employer recordkeeping responsibilities.

The employer must keep the records specified in §380.505 for as long as the employer employs the driver and for one year thereafter.

§380.513 Required information on the training certificate.

The training provider must provide a training certificate or diploma to the entry-level driver. If an employer is the training provider, the employer must provide a training certificate or diploma to the entry-level driver. The certificate or diploma must contain the following seven items of information:

(a) **Date of certificate issuance.**
(b) **Name of training provider.**
(c) **Mailing address of training provider.**
(d) **Name of driver.**
(e) **A statement that the driver** has completed training in driver qualification requirements, hours of service of drivers, driver wellness, and whistle blower protection requirements substantially in accordance with the following sentence: I certify _____ has completed training requirements set forth in the Federal Motor Carrier Safety Regulations for entry-level driver training in accordance with 49 CFR 380.503.
(f) **The printed name of the person attesting** that the driver has received the required training.
(g) **The signature of the person attesting** that the driver has received the required training.

Appendix to Part 380 LCV Driver-Training Programs, Required Knowledge and Skills

The following table lists topics of instruction required for drivers of longer combination vehicles pursuant to 49 CFR Part 380, Subpart B. The training courses for operators of LCV Doubles and LCV Triples must be distinct and tailored to address their unique operating and handling characteristics. Each course must include the minimum topics of instruction, including behind-the-wheel training designed to provide an opportunity to develop the skills outlined under the Proficiency Development unit of the training program. Only a skills instructor may administer behind-the-wheel training involving the operation of an LCV or one of its components. A classroom instructor may administer only instruction that does not involve the operation of an LCV or one of its components.

Table to the Appendix — Course Topics for LCV Drivers

Section 1: Orientation	
1.1	LCVs in Trucking
1.2	Regulatory Factors
1.3	Driver Qualifications
1.4	Vehicle Configuration Factors
Section 2: Basic Operation	
2.1	Coupling and Uncoupling
2.2	Basic Control and Handling
2.3	Basic Maneuvers
2.4	Turning, Steering and Tracking
2.5	Proficiency Development
Section 3: Safe Operating Practices	
3.1	Interacting with Traffic
3.2	Speed and Space Management
3.3	Night Operations
3.4	Extreme Driving Conditions
3.5	Security Issues
3.6	Proficiency Development
Section 4: Advanced Operations	
4.1	Hazard Perception
4.2	Hazardous Situations
4.3	Maintenance and Troubleshooting
Section 5: Non-Driving Activities	
5.1	Routes and Trip Planning
5.2	Cargo and Weight Considerations

Section 1 — Orientation

The units in this section must provide an orientation to the training curriculum and must cover the role LCVs play within the motor carrier industry, the factors that affect their operations, and the role that drivers play in the safe operation of LCVs.

Unit 1.1 — LCVs in Trucking. This unit must provide an introduction to the emergence of LCVs in trucking and must serve as an orientation to the course content. Emphasis must be placed upon the role the driver plays in transportation.

Unit 1.2 — Regulatory factors. This unit must provide instruction addressing the Federal, State, and local governmental bodies that propose, enact, and implement the laws, rules, and regulations that affect the trucking industry. Emphasis must be placed on those regulatory factors that affect LCVs, including 23 CFR 658.23 and Appendix C to Part 658.

Unit 1.3 — Driver qualifications. This unit must provide classroom instruction addressing the Federal and State laws, rules, and regulations that define LCV driver qualifications. It also must include a discussion on medical examinations, drug and alcohol tests, certification, and basic health and wellness issues. Emphasis must be placed upon topics essential to physical and mental health maintenance, including (1) diet, (2) exercise, (3) avoidance of alcohol and drug abuse, and caution in the use of prescription and nonprescription drugs, (4) the adverse effects of driver fatigue, and (5) effective fatigue countermeasures. Driver-trainees who have successfully completed the Entry-level training segments at §380.503(a) and (c) are considered to have satisfied the requirements of Unit 1.3.

Unit 1.4 — Vehicle configuration factors. This unit must provide classroom instruction addressing the key vehicle components used in the configuration of longer combination vehicles. It also must familiarize the driver-trainee with various vehicle combinations, as well as provide instruction about unique characteristics and factors associated with LCV configurations.

Section 2 — Basic Operation

The units in this section must cover the interaction between the driver and the vehicle. They must teach driver-trainees how to couple and uncouple LCVs, ensure the vehicles are in proper operating condition, and control the motion of LCVs under various road and traffic conditions.

During the driving exercises at off-highway locations required by this section, the driver-trainee must first familiarize himself/herself with basic operating characteristics of an LCV. Utilizing an LCV, students must be able to perform the skills learned in each unit to a level of proficiency required to permit safe transition to on-street driving.

Unit 2.1 — Coupling and uncoupling. This unit must provide instruction addressing the procedures for coupling and uncoupling LCVs. While vehicle coupling and uncoupling procedures are common to all truck-tractor/semi-trailer operations, some factors are peculiar to LCVs. Emphasis must be placed upon preplanning and safe operating procedures.

Unit 2.2 — Basic control and handling. This unit must provide an introduction to basic vehicular control and handling as it applies to LCVs. This must include instruction addressing brake performance, handling characteristics and factors affecting LCV stability while braking, turning, and cornering. Emphasis must be placed upon safe operating procedures.

Unit 2.3 — Basic maneuvers. This unit must provide instruction addressing the basic vehicular maneuvers that will be encountered by LCV drivers. This must include instruction relative to backing, lane positioning and path selection, merging situations, and parking LCVs. Emphasis must be placed upon safe operating procedures as they apply to brake performance and directional stability while accelerating, braking, merging, cornering, turning, and parking.

Unit 2.4 — Turning, steering, and tracking. This unit must provide instruction addressing turning situations, steering maneuvers, and the tracking of LCV trailers. This must include instruction related to trailer sway and off-tracking. Emphasis must be placed on maintaining directional stability.

Unit 2.5 — Proficiency development: basic operations. The purpose of this unit is to enable driver-students to gain the proficiency in basic operation needed to safely undertake on-street instruction in the Safe Operations Practices section of the curriculum.

The activities of this unit must consist of driving exercises that provide practice for the development of basic control skills and mastery of basic maneuvers. Driver-students practice skills and maneuvers learned in the Basic Control and Handling; Basic Maneuvers; and Turning, Steering and Tracking units. A series of basic exercises is practiced at off-highway locations until students develop sufficient proficiency for transition to on-street driving.

Once the driver-student's skills have been measured and found adequate, the driver-student must be allowed to move to on-the-street driving.

Nearly all activity in this unit will take place on the driving range or on streets or roads that have low-density traffic conditions.

Section 3 — Safe Operating Practices

The units in this section must cover the interaction between student drivers, the vehicle, and the traffic environment. They must teach driver-students how to apply their basic operating skills in a way that ensures their safety and that of other road users under various road, weather, and traffic conditions.

Unit 3.1 — Interacting with traffic. This unit must provide instruction addressing the principles of visual search, communication, and sharing the road with other traffic. Emphasis must be placed upon visual search, mirror usage, signaling and/or positioning the vehicle to communicate, and understanding the special situations encountered by LCV drivers in various traffic situations.

Unit 3.2 — Speed and space management. This unit must provide instruction addressing the principles of speed and space management. Emphasis must be placed upon maintaining safe vehicular speed and appropriate space surrounding the vehicle under various traffic and road conditions. Particular attention must be placed upon understanding the special situations encountered by LCVs in various traffic situations.

Unit 3.3 — Night operations. This unit must provide instruction addressing the principles of Night Operations. Emphasis must be placed upon the factors affecting operation of LCVs at night. Night driving presents specific factors that require special attention on the part of the driver. Changes in vehicle safety inspection, vision, communications, speed management, and space management are needed to deal with the special problems night driving presents.

Unit 3.4 — Extreme driving conditions. This unit must provide instruction addressing the driving of LCVs under extreme driving conditions. Emphasis must be placed upon the factors affecting the operation of LCVs in cold, hot, and inclement weather and in the mountains and desert. Changes in basic driving habits are needed to deal with the specific problems presented by these extreme driving conditions.

Unit 3.5 — Security issues. This unit must include a discussion of security requirements imposed by the Department of Homeland Security, Transportation Security Administration; the U.S. Department of Transportation, Research and Special Programs Administration; and any other State or Federal agency with responsibility for highway or motor carrier security.

Unit 3.6 — Proficiency development. This unit must provide driver-students an opportunity to refine, within the on-street traffic environment, their vehicle handling skills learned in the first three sections.

Driver-student performance progress must be closely monitored to determine when the level of proficiency required for carrying out the basic traffic maneuvers of stopping, turning, merging, straight driving, curves, lane changing, passing, driving on hills, driving through traffic restrictions, and parking has been attained. The driver-student must also be assessed for regulatory compliance with all traffic laws.

Nearly all activity in this unit will take place on public roadways in a full range of traffic environments applicable to this vehicle configuration. This must include urban and rural uncontrolled roadways, expressways or freeways, under light, moderate, and heavy traffic conditions. There must be a brief classroom session to familiarize driver-students with the type of on-street maneuvers they will perform and how their performance will be rated.

The instructor must assess the level of skill development of the driver-student and must increase in difficulty, based upon the level of skill attained, the types of maneuvers, roadways and traffic conditions to which the driver-student is exposed.

Section 4 — Advanced Operations

The units in this section must introduce higher level skills that can be acquired only after the more fundamental skills and knowledge taught in sections two and three have been mastered. They must teach the perceptual skills necessary to recognize potential hazards, and must demonstrate the procedures needed to handle an LCV when faced with a hazard.

The Maintenance and Trouble-shooting Unit must provide instruction that addresses how to keep the vehicle in safe and efficient operating condition. The purpose of this unit is to teach the correct way to perform simple maintenance tasks, and how to troubleshoot and report those vehicle discrepancies or deficiencies that must be repaired by a qualified mechanic.

Unit 4.1 — Hazard perception. This unit must provide instruction addressing the principles of recognizing hazards in sufficient time to reduce the severity of the hazard and neutralize a possible emergency situation. While hazards are present in all motor vehicle traffic operations, some are peculiar to LCV operations. Emphasis must be placed upon hazard recognition, visual search, and response to possible emergency-producing situations encountered by LCV drivers in various traffic situations.

Unit 4.2 — Hazardous situations. This unit must address dealing with specific procedures appropriate for LCV emergencies. These must include evasive steering, emergency braking, off-road recovery, brake failures, tire blowouts, rearward amplification, hydroplaning, skidding, jackknifing and the rollover phenomenon. The discussion must include a review of unsafe acts and the role they play in producing hazardous situations.

Unit 4.3 — Maintenance and trouble-shooting. This unit must introduce driver-students to the basic servicing and checking procedures for the various vehicle components and provide knowledge of conducting preventive maintenance functions, making simple emergency repairs, and diagnosing and reporting vehicle malfunctions.

Section 5 — Non-Driving Activities

The units in this section must cover activities that are not directly related to the vehicle itself but must be performed by an LCV driver. The units in this section must ensure these activities are performed in a manner that ensures the safety of the driver, vehicle, cargo, and other road users.

Unit 5.1 — Routes and trip planning. This unit must address the importance of and requirements for planning routes and trips. This must include classroom discussion of Federal and State requirements for a number of topics including permits, vehicle size and weight limitations, designated highways, local access, the reasonable access rule, staging areas, and access zones.

Unit 5.2 — Cargo and weight considerations. This unit must address the importance of proper cargo documentation, loading, securing and unloading cargo, weight distribution, load sequencing and trailer placement. Emphasis must be placed on the importance of axle weight distribution, as well as on trailer placement and its effect on vehicle handling.

Notes

Part 381 - Waivers, Exemptions, and Pilot Programs

Subpart A - General

§381.100 What is the purpose of this part?
This part prescribes the rules and procedures for requesting waivers and applying for exemptions from those provisions of the Federal Motor Carrier Safety Regulations (FMCSRs) which were issued on the authority of 49 U.S.C. 31136 or Chapter 313, and the initiation and administration of pilot programs.

§381.105 Who is required to comply with the rules in this part?
(a) You must comply with the rules in this part if you are going to request a waiver or apply for an exemption.

(b) You should follow the instructions in Subpart D of this part if you would like to recommend the agency initiate a pilot program.

§381.110 What definitions are applicable to this part?
Commercial motor vehicle means any motor vehicle that meets the definition of "commercial motor vehicle" found at 49 CFR 382.107 concerning controlled substances and alcohol use and testing, 49 CFR 383.5 concerning commercial driver's license standards, or 49 CFR 390.5 concerning Parts 390 through 399 of the FMCSRs.

Federal Motor Carrier Safety Administrator (the Administrator) means the chief executive of the Federal Motor Carrier Safety Administration, an agency within the Department of Transportation.

FMCSRs means Federal Motor Carrier Safety Regulations (49 CFR Parts 382 and 383, §§385.21 and 390.21, Parts 391 through 393, 395, 396, and 399).

You means an individual or motor carrier or other entity that is, or will be, responsible for the operation of a CMV(s). The term includes a motor carrier's agents, officers and representatives as well as employees responsible for hiring, supervising, training, assigning, or dispatching of drivers and employees concerned with the installation, inspection, and maintenance of motor vehicle equipment and/or accessories. You also includes any interested party who would like to suggest or recommend that the FMCSA initiate a pilot program.

Subpart B - Procedures for Requesting Waivers

§381.200 What is a waiver?
(a) A waiver is temporary regulatory relief from one or more FMCSR given to a person subject to the regulations, or a person who intends to engage in an activity that would be subject to the regulations.

(b) A waiver provides the person with relief from the regulations for up to three months.

(c) A waiver is intended for unique, non-emergency events and is subject to conditions imposed by the Administrator.

(d) Waivers may only be granted from one or more of the requirements contained in the following parts and sections of the FMCSRs:
  (1) *Part 382 — Controlled Substances and Alcohol Use and Testing;*
  (2) *Part 383 — Commercial Driver's License Standards; Requirements and Penalties;*
  (3) *§390.19 — Motor Carrier Identification Report;*
  (4) *§390.21 — Marking of Commercial Motor Vehicles;*
  (5) *Part 391 — Qualifications of Drivers;*
  (6) *Part 392 — Driving of Commercial Motor Vehicles;*
  (7) *Part 393 — Parts and Accessories Necessary for Safe Operation;*
  (8) *Part 395 — Hours of Service of Drivers;*
  (9) *Part 396 — Inspection, Repair, and Maintenance((except §396.25); and*
  (10) *Part 399 — Step, Handhold and Deck Requirements.*

§381.205 How do I determine when I may request a waiver?
(a) You may request a waiver if one or more FMCSR would prevent you from using or operating CMVs, or make it unreasonably difficult to do so, during a unique, non-emergency event that will take no more than three months to complete.

(b) Before you decide to request a waiver, you should carefully review the regulation to determine whether there are any practical alternatives already available that would allow your use or operation of CMVs during the event. You should also determine whether you need a waiver from all of the requirements in one or more parts of the regulations, or whether a more limited waiver of certain sections within one or more of the parts of the regulations would provide an acceptable level of regulatory relief. For example, if you need relief from one of the recordkeeping requirements concerning driver qualifications, you should not request relief from all of the requirements of Part 391.

§381.210 How do I request a waiver?
(a) You must send a written request (for example, a typed or handwritten (printed) letter), which includes all of the information required by this section, to the Federal Motor Carrier Safety Administrator, U.S. Department of Transportation, 400 Seventh Street, SW., Washington, DC 20590.

(b) You must identify the person who would be covered by the waiver. The application for a waiver must include:
  (1) *Your name, job title,* mailing address, and daytime telephone number;
  (2) *The name of the individual,* motor carrier, or other entity that would be responsible for the use or operation of CMVs during the unique, non-emergency event;
  (3) *Principal place of business* for the motor carrier or other entity (street address, city, State, and zip code); and
  (4) *The USDOT identification number* for the motor carrier, if applicable.

(c) You must provide a written statement that:
  (1) *Describes the unique, non-emergency event* for which the waiver would be used, including the time period during which the waiver is needed;
  (2) *Identifies the regulation that you believe needs to be waived;*
  (3) *Provides an estimate* of the total number of drivers and CMVs that would be operated under the terms and conditions of the waiver; and
  (4) *Explains how you would ensure* that you could achieve a level of safety that is equivalent to, or greater than, the level of safety that would be obtained by complying with the regulation.

§381.215 What will the FMCSA do after the agency receives my request for a waiver?
(a) The Federal Motor Carrier Safety Administration will review your request and make a recommendation to the Administrator. The final decision whether to grant or deny the application for a waiver will be made by the Administrator.

(b) After a decision is signed by the Administrator, you will be sent a copy of the document, which will include the terms and conditions for the waiver or the reason for denying the application for a waiver.

§381.220 How long will it take the agency to respond to my request for a waiver?
You should receive a response from the agency within 60 calendar days from the date the Administrator receives your request. However, depending on the complexity of the issues discussed in your application, and the availability of staff to review the material, a final decision may take up to 120 days.

§381.225 Who should I contact if I have questions about the information I am required to submit to the FMCSA or about the status of my request for a waiver?
You should contact the Office of Bus and Truck Standards and Operations, Federal Motor Carrier Safety Administration, 400 Seventh Street, SW., Washington, DC 20590. The telephone number is (202) 366-1790.

Subpart C - Procedures for Applying for Exemptions

§381.300 What is an exemption?
(a) An exemption is temporary regulatory relief from one or more FMCSR given to a person or class of persons subject to the regulations, or who intend to engage in an activity that would make them subject to the regulations.

(b) An exemption provides the person or class of persons with relief from the regulations for up to two years, and may be renewed.

(c) Exemptions may only be granted from one or more of the requirements contained in the following parts and sections of the FMCSRs:
  (1) *Part 382 — Controlled Substances and Alcohol Use and Testing;*
  (2) *Part 383 — Commerical Driver's License Standards; Requirements and Penalties;*
  (3) *Part 391 — Qualifications of Drivers;*
  (4) *Part 392 — Driving of Commercial Motor Vehicles;*

(5) *Part 393* — *Parts and Accessories Necessary for Safe Operation;*
(6) *Part 395* — *Hours of Service of Drivers;*
(7) *Part 396* — *Inspection, Repair, and Maintenance* (except for §396.25); and
(8) *Part 399* — *Step, Handhold and Deck Requirements.*

§381.305 How do I determine when I may apply for an exemption?

(a) **You may apply for an exemption** if one or more FMCSR prevents you from implementing more efficient or effective operations that would maintain a level of safety equivalent to, or greater than, the level achieved without the exemption.

(b) **Before you decide to apply for an exemption** you should carefully review the regulation to determine whether there are any practical alternatives already available that would allow you to conduct your motor carrier operations. You should also determine whether you need an exemption from all of the requirements in one or more parts of the regulations, or whether a more limited exemption from certain sections within one or more parts of the regulations would provide an acceptable level of regulatory relief. For example, if you need regulatory relief from one of the recordkeeping requirements concerning driver qualifications, you should not request regulatory relief from all of the requirements of Part 391.

§381.310 How do I apply for an exemption?

(a) **You must send a written request** (for example, a typed or handwritten (printed) letter), which includes all of the information required by this section, to the Federal Motor Carrier Safety Administrator, U.S. Department of Transportation, Federal Motor Carrier Safety Administration, 400 Seventh Street, SW., Washington, DC 20590.

(b) **You must identify the person or class of persons** who would be covered by the exemption. The application for an exemption must include:
   (1) *Your name, job title,* mailing address, and daytime telephone number;
   (2) *The name of the individual or motor carrier* that would be responsible for the use or operation of CMVs;
   (3) *Principal place of business* for the motor carrier (street address, city, State, and zip code); and
   (4) *The USDOT identification number* for the motor carrier.

(c) **You must provide a written statement that:**
   (1) *Describes the reason the exemption is needed,* including the time period during which it is needed;
   (2) *Identifies the regulation* from which you would like to be exempted;
   (3) *Provides an estimate* of the total number of drivers and CMVs that would be operated under the terms and conditions of the exemption;
   (4) *Assesses the safety impacts* the exemption may have;
   (5) *Explains how you would ensure* that you could achieve a level a safety that is equivalent to, or greater than, the level of safety that would be obtained by complying with the regulation; and
   (6) *Describes the impacts* (e.g., inability to test innovative safety management control systems, etc.) you could experience if the exemption is not granted by the FMCSA.

(d) **Your application must include a copy** of all research reports, technical papers, and other publications and documents you reference.

§381.315 What will the FMCSA do after the agency receives my application for an exemption?

(a) **The Federal Motor Carrier Safety Administration** will review your application and prepare, for the Administrator's signature, a Federal Register notice requesting public comment on your application for an exemption. The notice will give the public an opportunity to review your request and your safety assessment or analysis (required by §381.310) and any other relevant information known to the agency.

(b) **After a review of the comments received** in response to the Federal Register notice described in paragraph (a) of this section, the Federal Motor Carrier Safety Administration will make a recommendation(s) to the Administrator to either to grant or deny the exemption. Notice of the Administrator's decision will be published in the Federal Register.

(c) (1) *If the exemption is granted,* the notice will identify the provisions of the FMCSRs from which you will be exempt, the effective period, and all terms and conditions of the exemption.
   (2) *If the exemption is denied,* the notice will explain the reason for the denial.

(d) **A copy of your application for an exemption** and all comments received in response to the Federal Register notice will be included in a public docket and be available for review by interested parties.

(1) *Interested parties may view* the information contained in the docket by visiting the Department of Transportation, U.S. DOT Dockets, Room PL-401, 400 Seventh Street, SW., Washington DC. All information in the exemption docket will be available for examination at this address from 10 a.m. to 5 p.m., e.t., Monday through Friday, except Federal holidays.

(2) *Internet users can access all information received* by the U.S. DOT Dockets, Room PL-401, by using the universal resources locator (URL): http://dms.dot.gov. It is available 24 hours each day, 365 days each year. Please follow the instructions online for more information and help.

§381.320 How long will it take the agency to respond to my application for an exemption?

The agency will attempt to issue a final decision within 180 days of the date it receives your application. However, if you leave out important details or other information necessary for the FMCSA to prepare a meaningful request for public comments, the agency will attempt to issue a final decision within 180 days of the date it receives the additional information.

§381.325 Who should I contact if I have questions about the information I am required to submit to the FMCSA or about the status of my application for an exemption?

You should contact the Office of Bus and Truck Standards and Operations, Federal Motor Carrier Safety Administration, 400 Seventh Street, SW., Washington, DC 20590. The telephone number is (202) 366-1790.

§381.330 What am I required to do if the FMCSA grants my application for an exemption?

(a) **You must comply** with all the terms and conditions of the exemption.

(b) **The FMCSA will immediately revoke your exemption if:**
   (1) *You fail to comply* with the terms and conditions of the exemption;
   (2) *The exemption has resulted in a lower level of safety* than was maintained before the exemption was granted; or
   (3) *Continuation of the exemption* is determined by the FMCSA to be inconsistent with the goals and objectives of the FMCSRs.

Subpart D - Initiation of Pilot Programs

§381.400 What is a pilot program?

(a) **A pilot program is a study** in which temporary regulatory relief from one or more FMCSR is given to a person or class of persons subject to the regulations, or a person or class of persons who intend to engage in an activity that would be subject to the regulations.

(b) **During a pilot program,** the participants would be given an exemption from one or more sections or parts of the regulations for a period of up to three years.

(c) **A pilot program is intended for use** in collecting specific data for evaluating alternatives to the regulations or innovative approaches to safety while ensuring that the safety performance goals of the regulations are satisfied.

(d) **The number of participants in the pilot program** must be large enough to ensure statistically valid findings.

(e) **Pilot programs must include an oversight plan** to ensure that participants comply with the terms and conditions of participation, and procedures to protect the health and safety of study participants and the general public.

(f) **Exemptions for pilot programs may be granted** only from one or more of the requirements contained in the following parts and sections of the FMCSRs:
   (1) *Part 382* — Controlled Substances and Alcohol Use and Testing;
   (2) *Part 383* — Commercial Driver's License Standards; Requirements and Penalties;
   (3) *Part 391* — Qualifications of Drivers;
   (4) *Part 392* — Driving of Commercial Motor Vehicles;
   (5) *Part 393* — Parts and Accessories Necessary for Safe Operation;
   (6) *Part 395* — Hours of Service of Drivers;
   (7) *Part 396* — Inspection, Repair, and Maintenance (except for §396.25); and
   (8) *Part 399* — Step, Handhold and Deck Requirements.

§381.405 Who determines whether a pilot program should be initiated?

(a) **Generally, pilot programs are initiated by the FMCSA** when the agency determines that there may be an effective alternative to one or more of the requirements in the FMCSRs, but does not have sufficient research data to support the development of a notice of proposed rulemaking to change the regulation.

(b) **You may request the FMCSA to initiate a pilot program.** However, the decision of whether to propose a pilot program will be made at the discretion of the FMCSA. The FMCSA is not required to publish a notice in the Federal Register requesting public comment on your ideas or suggestions for pilot programs.

§381.410 What may I do if I have an idea or suggestion for a pilot program?

(a) **You may send a written statement** (for example, a typed or handwritten (printed) letter) to the Federal Motor Carrier Safety Administrator, U.S. Department of Transportation, 400 Seventh Street, SW., Washington, DC 20590.

(b) **You should identify the persons or class of persons** who would be covered by the pilot program exemptions. Your letter should include:
(1) *Your name, job title,* mailing address, and daytime telephone number;
(2) *The name of the individuals or motor carrier* that would be responsible for the use or operation of CMVs covered by the pilot program, if there are motor carriers that have expressed an interest in participating in the program;
(3) *Principal place of business* for the motor carrier (street address, city, State, and zip code); and
(4) *The USDOT identification number* for the motor carrier.

(c) **You should provide a written statement that:**
(1) *Presents your estimate* of the potential benefits to the motor carrier industry, the FMCSA, and the general public if the pilot program is conducted, and describes how you developed your estimate;
(2) *Estimates of the amount of time* that would be needed to conduct the pilot program (e.g., the time needed to complete the collection and analysis of data);
(3) *Identifies the regulation* from which the participants would need to be exempted;
(4) *Recommends a reasonable number* of participants necessary to yield statistically valid findings;
(5) *Provides ideas or suggestions* for a monitoring plan to ensure that participants comply with the terms and conditions of participation;
(6) *Provides ideas or suggestions* for a plan to protect the health and safety of study participants and the general public.
(7) *Assesses the safety impacts* the pilot program exemption may have; and
(8) *Provides recommendations* on how the safety measures in the pilot project would be designed to achieve a level a safety that is equivalent to, or greater than, the level of safety that would be obtained by complying with the regulation.

(d) **Your recommendation should include a copy** of all research reports, technical papers, publications and other documents you reference.

§381.415 Who should I contact if I have questions about the information to be included in my suggestion?

You should contact the Office of Bus and Truck Standards and Operations, Federal Motor Carrier Safety Administration, 400 Seventh Street, SW., Washington, DC 20590. The telephone number is (202) 366-1790.

§381.420 What will the FMCSA do after the agency receives my suggestion for a pilot program?

(a) **The Federal Motor Carrier Safety Administration** will review your suggestion for a pilot program and make a recommendation to the Administrator. The final decision whether to propose the development of a pilot program based upon your recommendation will be made by the Administrator.

(b) **You will be sent a copy of the Administrator's decision.** If the pilot program is approved, the agency will follow the administrative procedures contained in Subpart E of this part.

Subpart E - Administrative Procedures for Pilot Programs

§381.500 What are the general requirements the agency must satisfy in conducting a pilot program?

(a) **The FMCSA may conduct pilot programs** to evaluate alternatives to regulations, or innovative approaches, concerning motor carrier, CMV, and driver safety.

(b) **Pilot programs may include exemptions** from the regulations listed in §381.400(f) of this part.
(c) **Pilot programs must, at a minimum,** include all of the program elements listed in §381.505.
(d) **The FMCSA will publish in the Federal Register** a detailed description of each pilot program, including the exemptions to be considered, and provide notice and an opportunity for public comment before the effective date of the pilot program.

§381.505 What are the minimum elements required for a pilot program?

(a) **Safety measures.** Before granting exemptions for a pilot program, the FMCSA will ensure that the safety measures in a pilot program are designed to achieve a level of safety that is equivalent to, or greater than, the level of safety that would be achieved by complying with the regulations.

(b) **Pilot program plan.** Before initiating a pilot program, the FMCSA will ensure that there is a pilot program plan which includes the following elements:
(1) *A scheduled duration* of three years or less;
(2) *A specific data collection and safety analysis plan* that identifies a method of comparing the safety performance for motor carriers, CMVs, and drivers operating under the terms and conditions of the pilot program, with the safety performance of motor carriers, CMVs, and drivers that comply with the regulation;
(3) *A reasonable number of participants* necessary to yield statistically valid findings;
(4) *A monitoring plan* to ensure that participants comply with the terms and conditions of participation in the pilot program;
(5) *Adequate safeguards* to protect the health and safety of study participants and the general public; and
(6) *A plan to inform the States and the public* about the pilot program and to identify approved participants to enforcement personnel and the general public.

§381.510 May the FMCSA end a pilot program before its scheduled completion date?

The FMCSA will immediately terminate a pilot program if there is reason to believe the program is not achieving a level of safety that is at least equivalent to the level of safety that would be achieved by complying with the regulations.

§381.515 May the FMCSA remove approved participants from a pilot program?

The Administrator will immediately revoke participation in a pilot program of a motor carrier, CMV, or driver for failure to comply with the terms and conditions of the pilot program, or if continued participation is inconsistent with the goals and objectives of the safety regulations.

§381.520 What will the FMCSA do with the results from a pilot program?

At the conclusion of each pilot program, the FMCSA will report to Congress the findings and conclusions of the program and any recommendations it considers appropriate, including suggested amendments to laws and regulations that would enhance motor carrier, CMV, and driver safety and improve compliance with the FMCSRs.

Subpart F - Preemption of State Rules

§381.600 Do waivers, exemptions, and pilot programs preempt State laws and regulations?

Yes. During the time period that a waiver, exemption, or pilot program authorized by this part is in effect, no State shall enforce any law or regulation that conflicts with or is inconsistent with the waiver, exemption, or pilot program with respect to a person operating under the waiver or exemption or participating in the pilot program.

Part 381 - Waivers, Exemptions, and Pilot Programs

Notes

Part 382 - Controlled Substances and Alcohol Use and Testing (Page 47 in the Driver Edition)

Subpart A - General

§382.101 Purpose.
The purpose of this part is to establish programs designed to help prevent accidents and injuries resulting from the misuse of alcohol or use of controlled substances by drivers of commercial motor vehicles.

§382.103 Applicability.
(a) **This part applies to every person and to all employers** of such persons who operate a commercial motor vehicle in commerce in any State, and is subject to:
  (1) *The commercial driver's license requirements* of Part 383 of this subchapter;
  (2) *The Licencia Federal de Conductor (Mexico) requirements;* or
  (3) *The commercial driver's license requirements* of the Canadian National Safety Code.
(b) **An employer who employs himself/herself as a driver** must comply with both the requirements in this part that apply to employers and the requirements in this part that apply to drivers. An employer who employs only himself/herself as a driver shall implement a random alcohol and controlled substances testing program of two or more covered employees in the random testing selection pool.
(c) **The exceptions contained in §390.3(f) of this subchapter** do not apply to this part. The employers and drivers identified in §390.3(f) of this subchapter must comply with the requirements of this part, unless otherwise specifically provided in paragraph (d) of this section.
(d) **Exceptions.** This part shall not apply to employers and their drivers:
  (1) *Required to comply* with the alcohol and/or controlled substances testing requirements of Part 655 of this title (Federal Transit Administration alcohol and controlled substances testing regulations); or
  (2) *Who a State must waive* from the requirements of Part 383 of this subchapter. These individuals include active duty military personnel; members of the reserves; and members of the national guard on active duty, including personnel on full-time national guard duty, personnel on part-time national guard training and national guard military technicians (civilians who are required to wear military uniforms), and active duty U.S. Coast Guard personnel; or
  (3) *Who a State has,* at its discretion, exempted from the requirements of Part 383 of this subchapter. These individuals may be:
   (i) *Operators of a farm vehicle which is:*
     [A] *Controlled and operated by a farmer;*
     [B] *Used to transport* either agricultural products, farm machinery, farm supplies, or both to or from a farm;
     [C] *Not used in the operations* of a common or contract motor carrier; and
     [D] *Used within 241 kilometers (150 miles)* of the farmer's farm.
   (ii) *Firefighters or other persons* who operate commercial motor vehicles which are necessary for the preservation of life or property or the execution of emergency governmental functions, are equipped with audible and visual signals, and are not subject to normal traffic regulation.

§382.103 DOT Interpretations
Question 1: Are intrastate drivers of CMVs, who are required to obtain CDLs, required to be alcohol and drug tested by their employer?
Guidance: Yes. The definition of commerce in §382.107 is taken from 49 U.S.C. §31301 which encompasses interstate, intrastate and foreign commerce.
Question 2: Are students who will be trained to be motor vehicle operators subject to alcohol and drug testing? Are they required to obtain a CDL in order to operate training vehicles provided by the school?
Guidance: Yes. §382.107 includes the following definitions:
"Employer" means any person (including the United States, a State, District of Columbia, or a political subdivision of a State) who owns or leases a CMV or assigns persons to operate such a vehicle. The term employer includes an employer's agents, officers and representatives.
"Driver" means any person who operates a CMV.
Truck and bus driver training schools meet the definition of an employer because they own or lease CMVs and assign students to operate them at appropriate points in their training. Similarly, students who actually operate CMVs to complete their course work qualify as drivers.
The CDL regulations provide that "no person shall operate" a CMV before passing the written and driving tests required for that vehicle (49 CFR 383.23(a)(1)). Virtually all of the vehicles used for training purposes meet the definition of a CMV, and student drivers must therefore obtain a CDL.
Question 3: Are Part 382 alcohol and drug testing requirements applicable to firefighters in a State which gives them the option of obtaining a CDL or a non-commercial Class A or B license restricted to operating fire equipment only?
Guidance: No. The applicability of Part 382 is coextensive with Part 383 — the general CDL requirements. Only those persons required to obtain a CDL under Federal law and who actually perform safety-sensitive duties, are required to be tested for drugs and alcohol.
The FMCSA, exercising its waiver authority, granted the States the option of waiving firefighters from CDL requirements. A State which gives firefighters the choice of obtaining either a CDL or a non-commercial license has exercised the option not to require CDLs. Therefore, because a CDL is not required, by extension Part 382 is not applicable.
A firefighter in the State would not be required under Federal law to be tested for drugs and alcohol regardless of the type of license which the employer required as a condition of employment or the driver actually obtained. It is the Federal requirement to obtain a CDL, nonexistent in the State, that entails drug and alcohol testing, not the fact of actually holding a CDL.
Question 4: An employer or State government agency requires CDLs for drivers of motor vehicles: (1) with a GVWR of 26,000 pounds or less; (2) with a GCWR of 26,000 pounds or less inclusive of a towed unit with a GVWR of 10,000 pounds or less; (3) designed to transport 15 or less passengers, including the driver; or (4) which transport HM, but are not required to be placarded under 49 CFR Part 172, Subpart F. Are such drivers required by Part 382 to be tested for the use of alcohol or controlled substances?
Guidance: No. Part 382 requires or authorizes drug and alcohol testing only of those drivers required by Part 383 to obtain a CDL. Since the vehicles described above do not meet the definition of a CMV in Part 383, their drivers are not required by Federal regulations to have a CDL.
Question 5: Are Alaskan drivers with a CDL who operate CMVs and have been waived from certain CDL requirements subject to controlled substances and alcohol testing?
Guidance: Yes. Alaskan drivers with a CDL who operate CMVs are subject to controlled substances and alcohol testing because they have licenses marked either "commercial driver's license" or "CDL". The waived drivers are only exempted from the knowledge and skills tests, and the photograph on license requirements.
Question 6: Do the FMCSA's alcohol and controlled substances testing regulations apply to employers and drivers in U.S. territories or possessions such as Puerto Rico and Guam?
Guidance: No. The rule by definition applies only to employers and drivers domiciled in the 50 states and the District of Columbia.
Question 7: Which drivers are to be included in a alcohol and controlled substances testing program under the FMCSA's rule?
Guidance: Any person who operates a CMV, as defined in §382.107, in intrastate or interstate commerce and is subject to the CDL requirement of 49 CFR Part 383.
Question 8: Is a foreign resident driver operating between the U.S. and a foreign country from a U.S. terminal for a U.S.-based employer subject to the FMCSA alcohol and controlled substances testing regulations?
Guidance: Yes. A driver operating for a U.S.-based employer is subject to Part 382.
Question 9: What alcohol and drug testing provisions apply to foreign drivers employed by foreign motor carriers?
Guidance: Foreign employers are subject to the alcohol and drug testing requirements in Part 382 (see §382.103). All provisions of the rules will be applicable while drivers are operating in the U.S. Foreign drivers may also be subject to State laws, such as probable cause testing by law enforcement officers.

§382.105 Testing procedures.

Each employer shall ensure that all alcohol or controlled substances testing conducted under this part complies with the procedures set forth in Part 40 of this title. The provisions of Part 40 of this title that address alcohol or controlled substances testing are made applicable to employers by this part.

§382.105 DOT Interpretations

Question 1: What does a BAT do when a test involves an independent, self-employed owner-operator with a confirmed alcohol concentration of 0.02 or greater, to notify a company representative as required by §40.65(i)?

Guidance: The independent, self-employed owner-operator will be notified by the BAT immediately and the owner-operator's certification in Step 4 notes that the self-employed owner-operator has been notified. No further notification is necessary. The BAT will provide copies 1 and 2 to the self-employed owner-operator directly.

Question 2: A driver does not have a photo identification card. Must an employer representative identify the driver in the presence of the BAT/urine specimen collector or may the employer representative identify the driver via a telephone conversation?

Guidance: Those subject to Part 382 are subject first, generally, to Part 383. Part 383 requires all States, with an exception in Alaska for a very small group of individuals, to provide a CDL document to the individual that includes, among other things: the full name, signature, and mailing address of the person to whom such license is issued; physical and other information to identify and describe the person including date of birth (month, day, and year), sex, and height; and, a color photograph of the person. Except in these rare Alaskan instances, the FMCSA fully expects most employers to require the driver to present the CDL document to the BAT or urine collector.

A driver subject to alcohol and drug testing should be able to provide the CDL document. In those rare instances that the CDL or other form of photo identification is not produced for verification, an employer representative must be contacted and must provide identification. The FMCSA will allow employer representatives to identify drivers in any way that the employer believes will positively identify the driver.

Question 3: Will foreign drug testing laboratories need to be certified by the National Institute on Drug Abuse (NIDA)? Will they need to be certified by the Department of Health and Human Services (DHHS)?

Guidance: The NIDA, an agency of the DHHS, no longer administers the workplace drug testing laboratory certification program. This program is now administered by the DHHS' Substance Abuse and Mental Health Services Administration. All motor carriers are required to use DHHS-certified laboratories for analysis of alcohol and controlled substances tests as neither Mexico nor Canada has an equivalent laboratory certification program.

Question 4: Particularly in light of the coverage of Canadian and Mexican employees, how should MROs deal, in the verification process, with claims of the use of foreign prescriptions or over-the-counter medication?

Guidance: Possession or use of controlled substances are prohibited when operating a CMV under the FMCSA regulations regardless of the source of the substance. A limited exception exists for a substance's use in accordance with instructions provided by a licensed medical practitioner who knows that the individual is a CMV driver who operates CMVs in a safety-sensitive job and has provided instructions to the CMV driver that the use of the substance will not affect the CMV driver's ability to safely operate a CMV (see §§382.213, 391.41(b)(12), and 392.4(c)). Individuals entering the United States must properly declare controlled substances with the U.S. Customs Service. 21 CFR 1311.27.

The FMCSA expects MROs to properly investigate the facts concerning a CMV driver's claim that a positive controlled substance test result was caused by a prescription written by a knowledgeable, licensed medical practitioner or the use of an over-the-counter substance that was obtained in a foreign country without a prescription. This investigation should be documented in the MRO's files.

If the CMV driver lawfully obtained a substance in a foreign country without a prescription which is a controlled substance in the United States, the MRO must also investigate whether a knowledgeable, licensed medical practitioner provided instructions to the CMV driver that the use of the "over-the-counter" substance would not affect the driver's ability to safely operate a CMV.

Potential violations of §392.4 must be investigated by the law enforcement officer at the time possession or use is discovered to determine whether the exception applies.

§382.107 Definitions.

Words or phrases used in this part are defined in §§386.2 and 390.5 of this subchapter, and §40.3 of this title, except as provided in this section —

Actual knowledge for the purpose of Subpart B of this part, means actual knowledge by an employer that a driver has used alcohol or controlled substances based on the employer's direct observation of the employee, information provided by the driver's previous employer(s), a traffic citation for driving a CMV while under the influence of alcohol or controlled substances or an employee's admission of alcohol or controlled substance use, except as provided in §382.121. Direct observation as used in this definition means observation of alcohol or controlled substances use and does not include observation of employee behavior or physical characteristics sufficient to warrant reasonable suspicion testing under §382.307.

Alcohol means the intoxicating agent in beverage alcohol, ethyl alcohol, or other low molecular weight alcohols including methyl and isopropyl alcohol.

Alcohol concentration (or content) means the alcohol in a volume of breath expressed in terms of grams of alcohol per 210 liters of breath as indicated by an evidential breath test under this part.

Alcohol use means the drinking or swallowing of any beverage, liquid mixture or preparation (including any medication), containing alcohol.

Commerce means:

(1) *Any trade, traffic or transportation* within the jurisdiction of the United States between a place in a State and a place outside of such State, including a place outside of the United States; and

(2) *Trade, traffic, and transportation* in the United States which affects any trade, traffic, and transportation described in paragraph (1) of this definition.

Commercial motor vehicle means a motor vehicle or combination of motor vehicles used in commerce to transport passengers or property if the vehicle —

(1) *Has a gross combination weight rating* of 11,794 or more kilograms (26,001 or more pounds) inclusive of a towed unit with a gross vehicle weight rating of more than 4,536 kilograms (10,000 pounds); or

(2) *Has a gross vehicle weight rating* of 11,794 or more kilograms (26,001 or more pounds); or

(3) *Is designed to transport 16 or more passengers,* including the driver; or

(4) *Is of any size* and is used in the transportation of materials found to be hazardous for the purposes of the Hazardous Materials Transportation Act (49 U.S.C. 5103(b)) and which require the motor vehicle to be placarded under the Hazardous Materials Regulations (49 CFR Part 172, Subpart F).

Confirmation (or confirmatory) drug test means a second analytical procedure performed on a urine specimen to identify and quantify the presence of a specific drug or drug metabolite.

Confirmation (or confirmatory) validity test means a second test performed on a urine specimen to further support a validity test result.

Confirmed drug test means a confirmation test result received by an MRO from a laboratory.

Consortium/Third party administrator (C/TPA) means a service agent that provides or coordinates one or more drug and/or alcohol testing services to DOT-regulated employers. C/TPAs typically provide or coordinate the provision of a number of such services and perform administrative tasks concerning the operation of the employers' drug and alcohol testing programs. This term includes, but is not limited to, groups of employers who join together to administer, as a single entity, the DOT drug and alcohol testing programs of its members (e.g., having a combined random testing pool). C/TPAs are not "employers" for purposes of this part.

Controlled substances mean those substances identified in §40.85 of this title.

Designated employer representative (DER) is an individual identified by the employer as able to receive communications and test results from service agents and who is authorized to take immediate actions to remove employees from safety-sensitive duties and to make required decisions in the testing and evaluation processes. The individual must be an employee of the company. Service agents cannot serve as DERs.

Disabling damage means damage which precludes departure of a motor vehicle from the scene of the accident in its usual manner in daylight after simple repairs.

Subpart A - General §382.109 (b)

(1) *Inclusions.* Damage to motor vehicles that could have been driven, but would have been further damaged if so driven.
(2) *Exclusions.*
  (i) *Damage which can be remedied temporarily* at the scene of the accident without special tools or parts.
  (ii) *Tire disablement without other damage* even if no spare tire is available.
  (iii) *Headlight or taillight damage.*
  (iv) *Damage to turn signals,* horn, or windshield wipers which make them inoperative.

DOT Agency means an agency (or "operating administration") of the United States Department of Transportation administering regulations requiring alcohol and/or drug testing (14 CFR Parts 61, 63, 65, 121, and 135; 49 CFR Parts 199, 219, 382, and 655), in accordance with Part 40 of this title.

Driver means any person who operates a commercial motor vehicle. This includes, but is not limited to: Full time, regularly employed drivers; casual, intermittent or occasional drivers; leased drivers and independent owner-operator contractors.

Employer means a person or entity employing one or more employees (including an individual who is self-employed) that is subject to DOT agency regulations requiring compliance with this part. The term, as used in this part, means the entity responsible for overall implementation of DOT drug and alcohol program requirements, including individuals employed by the entity who take personnel actions resulting from violations of this part and any applicable DOT agency regulations. Service agents are not employers for the purposes of this part.

Licensed medical practitioner means a person who is licensed, certified, and/or registered, in accordance with applicable Federal, State, local, or foreign laws and regulations, to prescribe controlled substances and other drugs.

Performing (a safety-sensitive function) means a driver is considered to be performing a safety-sensitive function during any period in which he or she is actually performing, ready to perform, or immediately available to perform any safety-sensitive functions.

Positive rate for random drug testing means the number of verified positive results for random drug tests conducted under this part plus the number of refusals of random drug tests required by this part, divided by the total number of random drug tests results (i.e., positives, negatives, and refusals) under this part.

Refuse to submit (to an alcohol or controlled substances test) means that a driver:
(1) *Fails to appear for any test* (except a pre-employment test) within a reasonable time, as determined by the employer, consistent with applicable DOT agency regulations, after being directed to do so by the employer. This includes the failure of an employee (including an owner-operator) to appear for a test when called by a C/TPA (see §40.61(a) of this title);
(2) *Fails to remain at the testing site* until the testing process is complete. Provided, that an employee who leaves the testing site before the testing process commences (see §40.63(c) of this title) a pre-employment test is not deemed to have refused to test;
(3) *Fails to provide a urine specimen* for any drug test required by this part or DOT agency regulations. Provided, that an employee who does not provide a urine specimen because he or she has left the testing site before the testing process commences (see §40.63(c) of this title) for a pre-employment test is not deemed to have refused to test;
(4) *In the case* of a directly observed or monitored collection in a drug test, fails to permit the observation or monitoring of the driver's provision of a specimen (see §§40.67(l) and 40.69(g) of this title);
(5) *Fails to provide* a sufficient amount of urine when directed, and it has been determined, through a required medical evaluation, that there was no adequate medical explanation for the failure (see §40.193(d)(2) of this title);
(6) *Fails or declines to take a second test* the employer or collector has directed the driver to take;
(7) *Fails to undergo* a medical examination or evaluation, as directed by the MRO as part of the verification process, or as directed by the DER under §40.193(d) of this title. In the case of a pre-employment drug test, the employee is deemed to have refused to test on this basis only if the pre-employment test is conducted following a contingent offer of employment;
(8) *Fails to cooperate* with any part of the testing process (e.g., refuses to empty pockets when so directed by the collector, behaves in a confrontational way that disrupts the collection process); or
(9) *Is reported by the MRO* as having a verified adulterated or substituted test result.

Safety-sensitive function means all time from the time a driver begins to work or is required to be in readiness to work until the time he/she is relieved from work and all responsibility for performing work. Safety-sensitive functions shall include:
(1) *All time* at an employer or shipper plant, terminal, facility, or other property, or on any public property, waiting to be dispatched, unless the driver has been relieved from duty by the employer;
(2) *All time inspecting equipment* as required by §§392.7 and 392.8 of this subchapter or otherwise inspecting, servicing, or conditioning any commercial motor vehicle at any time;
(3) *All time spent at the driving controls* of a commercial motor vehicle in operation;
(4) *All time,* other than driving time, in or upon any commercial motor vehicle except time spent resting in a sleeper berth (a berth conforming to the requirements of §393.76 of this subchapter);
(5) *All time loading or unloading a vehicle,* supervising, or assisting in the loading or unloading, attending a vehicle being loaded or unloaded, remaining in readiness to operate the vehicle, or in giving or receiving receipts for shipments loaded or unloaded; and
(6) *All time* repairing, obtaining assistance, or remaining in attendance upon a disabled vehicle.

Screening test (or initial test) means:
(1) *In drug testing,* a test to eliminate "negative" urine specimens from further analysis or to identify a specimen that requires additional testing for the presence of drugs.
(2) *In alcohol testing,* an analytical procedure to determine whether an employee may have a prohibited concentration of alcohol in a breath or saliva specimen.

Stand-down means the practice of temporarily removing an employee from the performance of safety-sensitive functions based only on a report from a laboratory to the MRO of a confirmed positive test for a drug or drug metabolite, an adulterated test, or a substituted test, before the MRO has completed verification of the test results.

Violation rate for random alcohol testing means the number of 0.04 and above random alcohol confirmation test results conducted under this part plus the number of refusals of random alcohol tests required by this part, divided by the total number of random alcohol screening tests (including refusals) conducted under this part.

§382.107 DOT Interpretations
Question 1: What is an owner-operator?
Guidance: The FMCSA neither defines the term "owner-operator" nor uses it in regulation. The FMCSA regulates "employers" and "drivers." An owner-operator may act as both an employer and a driver at certain times, or as a driver for another employer at other times depending on contractual arrangements and operational structure.

§382.109 Preemption of State and local laws.
(a) **Except as provided in paragraph (b) of this section,** this part preempts any State or local law, rule, regulation, or order to the extent that:
  (1) *Compliance with both the State or local requirement* in this part is not possible; or
  (2) *Compliance with the State or local requirement* is an obstacle to the accomplishment and execution of any requirement in this part.
(b) **This part shall not be construed to preempt provisions** of State criminal law that impose sanctions for reckless conduct leading to actual loss of life, injury, or damage to property, whether the provisions apply specifically to transportation employees, employers, or the general public.

§382.109 DOT Interpretations
Question 1: An employer is required by State or local law, regulation, or order to bargain with unionized employees over discretionary elements of the DOT alcohol and drug testing regulations (e.g., selection of DHHS-approved laboratories or MROs). May the employer defer the 1995 or 1996 implementation dates for testing employees until the collective bargaining process has produced agreement on these discretionary elements, or must the employer implement testing as required by Part 382?
Guidance: The FMCSA provided large employers 45 weeks and small employers 97 weeks collectively to bargain the discretionary elements of the Part 382 testing program. An employer must implement alcohol and controlled substances testing in accordance with the schedule in §382.115. If observance of the collective bargaining process would make it impossible for the employer to comply with these deadlines, §382.109(a)(1) preempts the State or local bargaining requirement to the extent needed to meet the implementation date.

§382.111 Other requirements imposed by employers.
Except as expressly provided in this part, nothing in this part shall be construed to affect the authority of employers, or the rights of drivers, with respect to the use of alcohol, or the use of controlled substances, including authority and rights with respect to testing and rehabilitation.

§382.113 Requirement for notice.
Before performing each alcohol or controlled substances test under this part, each employer shall notify a driver that the alcohol or controlled substances test is required by this part. No employer shall falsely represent that a test is administered under this part.

§382.113 DOT Interpretations
Question 1: Must a notice be given before each test or will a general notice given to drivers suffice?
Guidance: A driver must be notified before submitting to each test that it is required by Part 382. This notification can be provided to the driver either verbally or in writing. In addition, the FMCSA believes that the use of the DOT Breath Alcohol Testing Form, OMB No. 2105-0529, and the Drug Testing Custody and Control Form, 49 CFR Part 40, Appendix A, will support the verbal or written notice that the test is being conducted in accordance with Part 382.

§382.115 Starting date for testing programs.
(a) **All domestic-domiciled employers** must implement the requirements of this part on the date the employer begins commercial motor vehicle operations.
(b) **All foreign-domiciled employers** must implement the requirements of this part on the date the employer begins commercial motor vehicle operations in the United States.

§382.115 DOT Interpretations
Question 1: In a governmental entity structured into various subunits such as departments, divisions, and offices, how is the number of an employer's drivers determined for purposes of the implementation date of controlled substances and alcohol testing?
Guidance: Part 382 testing applies to governmental entities, including those of the Federal government, the States, and political subdivisions of the States. An employer is defined as any person that owns or leases CMVs, or assigns drivers to operate them. Therefore, any governmental entity, or a subunit of it that controls CMVs and the day-to-day operations of its drivers, may be considered the employer for purposes of Part 382. For example, a city government divided into various departments, such as parks and public works, could consider the departments as separate employers if the CMV operations are separately controlled. The city also has the option of deeming the city as the employer of all of the drivers of the various departments.

§382.117 Public interest exclusion.
No employer shall use the services of a service agent who is subject to public interest exclusion in accordance with 49 CFR Part 40, Subpart R.

§382.119 Stand-down waiver provision.
(a) **Employers are prohibited** from standing employees down, except consistent with a waiver from the Federal Motor Carrier Safety Administration as required under this section.

(b) **An employer subject to this part who seeks a waiver** from the prohibition against standing down an employee before the MRO has completed the verification process shall follow the procedures in 49 CFR 40.21. The employer must send a written request, which includes all of the information required by that section to the Federal Motor Carrier Safety Administrator (or the Administrator's designee), U.S. Department of Transportation, 400 Seventh Street, SW., Washington, DC 20590.
(c) **The final decision** whether to grant or deny the application for a waiver will be made by the Administrator or the Administrator's designee.
(d) **After a decision is signed** by the Administrator or the Administrator's designee, the employer will be sent a copy of the decision, which will include the terms and conditions for the waiver or the reason for denying the application for a waiver.
(e) **Questions regarding waiver applications** should be directed to the Office of Enforcement and Compliance, Federal Motor Carrier Safety Administration, 400 Seventh Street, SW., Washington, DC 20590. The telephone number is (202) 366-5720.

§382.121 Employee admission of alcohol and controlled substances use.
(a) **Employees who admit to alcohol misuse** or controlled substances use are not subject to the referral, evaluation and treatment requirements of this part and Part 40 of this title, provided that:
(1) *The admission is in accordance* with a written employer-established voluntary self-identification program or policy that meets the requirements of paragraph (b) of this section;
(2) *The driver does not self-identify* in order to avoid testing under the requirements of this part;
(3) *The driver makes the admission* of alcohol misuse or controlled substances use prior to performing a safety-sensitive function (i.e., prior to reporting for duty); and
(4) *The driver does not* perform a safety-sensitive function until the employer is satisfied that the employee has been evaluated and has successfully completed education or treatment requirements in accordance with the self-identification program guidelines.
(b) **A qualified voluntary self-identification program** or policy must contain the following elements:
(1) *It must prohibit the employer* from taking adverse action against an employee making a voluntary admission of alcohol misuse or controlled substances use within the parameters of the program or policy and paragraph (a) of this section;
(2) *It must allow the employee* sufficient opportunity to seek evaluation, education or treatment to establish control over the employee's drug or alcohol problem;
(3) *It must permit the employee* to return to safety-sensitive duties only upon successful completion of an educational or treatment program, as determined by a drug and alcohol abuse evaluation expert, i.e., employee assistance professional, substance abuse professional, or qualified drug and alcohol counselor;
(4) *It must ensure that:*
  (i) *Prior to the employee* participating in a safety-sensitive function, the employee shall undergo a return to duty test with a result indicating an alcohol concentration of less than 0.02; and/or
  (ii) *Prior to the employee* participating in a safety-sensitive function, the employee shall undergo a return to duty controlled substance test with a verified negative test result for controlled substances use; and
(5) *It may incorporate employee monitoring* and include non-DOT follow-up testing.

Subpart B - Prohibitions

§382.201 Alcohol concentration.
No driver shall report for duty or remain on duty requiring the performance of safety-sensitive functions while having an alcohol concentration of 0.04 or greater. No employer having actual knowledge that a driver has an alcohol concentration of 0.04 or greater shall permit the driver to perform or continue to perform safety-sensitive functions.

§382.205 On-duty use.
No driver shall use alcohol while performing safety-sensitive functions. No employer having actual knowledge that a driver is using alcohol while performing safety-sensitive functions shall permit the driver to perform or continue to perform safety-sensitive functions.

§382.205 DOT Interpretations
Question 1: What is meant by the terms "use alcohol" or "alcohol use"? Is observation of use sufficient or is an alcohol test result required?
Guidance: The term "alcohol use" is defined in §382.107. The employer is prohibited in §382.205 from permitting a driver to drive when the employer has actual knowledge of the driver's use of alcohol, regardless of the level of alcohol in the driver's body. The form of knowledge is not specified. It may be obtained through observation or other method.

§382.207 Pre-duty use.
No driver shall perform safety-sensitive functions within four hours after using alcohol. No employer having actual knowledge that a driver has used alcohol within four hours shall permit a driver to perform or continue to perform safety-sensitive functions.

§382.209 Use following an accident.
No driver required to take a post-accident alcohol test under §382.303 shall use alcohol for eight hours following the accident, or until he/she undergoes a post-accident alcohol test, whichever occurs first.

§382.211 Refusal to submit to a required alcohol or controlled substances test.
No driver shall refuse to submit to a post-accident alcohol or controlled substances test required under §382.303, a random alcohol or controlled substances test required under §382.305, a reasonable suspicion alcohol or controlled substances test required under §382.307, or a follow-up alcohol or controlled substances test required under §382.311. No employer shall permit a driver who refuses to submit to such tests to perform or continue to perform safety-sensitive functions.

§382.213 Controlled substances use.
(a) No driver shall report for duty or remain on duty requiring the performance of safety-sensitive functions when the driver uses any controlled substance, except when the use is pursuant to the instructions of a licensed medical practitioner, as defined in §382.107, who has advised the driver that the substance will not adversely affect the driver's ability to safely operate a commercial motor vehicle.

(b) No employer having actual knowledge that a driver has used a controlled substance shall permit the driver to perform or continue to perform a safety-sensitive function.

(c) An employer may require a driver to inform the employer of any therapeutic drug use.

§382.213 DOT Interpretations
Question 1: Must a physician specifically advise that substances in a prescription will not adversely affect the driver's ability to safely operate a CMV or may a pharmacist's advice or precautions printed on a container suffice for the advice?
Guidance: A physician must specifically advise the driver that the substances in a prescription will not adversely affect the driver's ability to safely operate a CMV.

§382.215 Controlled substances testing.
No driver shall report for duty, remain on duty or perform a safety-sensitive function, if the driver tests positive or has adulterated or substituted a test specimen for controlled substances. No employer having actual knowledge that a driver has tested positive or has adulterated or substituted a test specimen for controlled substances shall permit the driver to perform or continue to perform safety-sensitive functions.

Subpart B — General
Question 1: If a urine specimen is collected during a given calendar year (e.g., December 30) and the medical review officer (MRO) makes the final determination the following calendar year (e.g., January 3), for which year is the test result considered to be complete?
Guidance: The Federal Motor Carrier Safety Administration considers test results to be complete for the calendar year in which the MRO makes a final determination of the test results, regardless of the date the specimen was collected.

Subpart B — Prohibitions
Question 1: Does the term, "actual knowledge," used in the various prohibitions in Subpart B of Part 382, require direct observation by a supervisor or is it more general?
Guidance: The form of actual knowledge is not specified, but may result from the employer's direct observation of the employee, the driver's previous employer(s), the employee's admission of alcohol use, or other occurrence.

Subpart C - Tests Required

§382.301 Pre-employment testing.
(a) Prior to the first time a driver performs safety-sensitive functions for an employer, the driver shall undergo testing for controlled substances as a condition prior to being used, unless the employer uses the exception in paragraph (b) of this section. No employer shall allow a driver, who the employer intends to hire or use, to perform safety-sensitive functions unless the employer has received a controlled substances test result from the MRO or C/TPA indicating a verified negative test result for that driver.

(b) An employer is not required to administer a controlled substances test required by paragraph (a) of this section if:

  (1) *The driver has participated* in a controlled substances testing program that meets the requirements of this part within the previous 30 days; and

  (2) *While participating in that program, either:*
   - **(i)** *Was tested for controlled substances* within the past 6 months (from the date of application with the employer), or
   - **(ii)** *Participated in the random* controlled substances testing program for the previous 12 months (from the date of application with the employer); and

  (3) *The employer ensures* that no prior employer of the driver of whom the employer has knowledge has records of a violation of this part or the controlled substances use rule of another DOT agency within the previous six months.

(c) (1) *An employer* who exercises the exception in paragraph (b) of this section shall contact the controlled substances testing program(s) in which the driver participates or participated and shall obtain and retain from the testing program(s) the following information:
   - **(i)** *Name(s) and address(es) of the program(s).*
   - **(ii)** *Verification that the driver* participates or participated in the program(s).
   - **(iii)** *Verification that the program(s) conforms to Part 40 of this title.*
   - **(iv)** *Verification that the driver is qualified* under the rules of this part, including that the driver has not refused to be tested for controlled substances.
   - **(v)** *The date the driver was last tested for controlled substances.*
   - **(vi)** *The results of any tests taken* within the previous six months and any other violations of Subpart B of this part.

  (2) *An employer who uses,* but does not employ a driver more than once a year to operate commercial motor vehicles must obtain the information in paragraph (c)(1) of this section at least once every six months. The records prepared under this paragraph shall be maintained in accordance with §382.401. If the employer cannot verify that the driver is participating in a controlled substances testing program in accordance with this part and Part 40 of this title, the employer shall conduct a pre-employment controlled substances test.

(d) An employer may, but is not required to, conduct pre-employment alcohol testing under this part. If an employer chooses to conduct pre-employment alcohol testing, it must comply with the following requirements:

  (1) *It must conduct a pre-employment alcohol test* before the first performance of safety-sensitive functions by every covered employee (whether a new employee or someone who has transferred to a position involving the performance of safety-sensitive functions).

  (2) *It must treat all safety-sensitive employees* performing safety-sensitive functions the same for the purpose of pre-employment alcohol testing (i.e., it must not test some covered employees and not others).

  (3) *It must conduct the pre-employment tests* after making a contingent offer of employment or transfer, subject to the employee passing the pre-employment alcohol test.

  (4) *It must conduct all pre-employment alcohol tests* using the alcohol testing procedures of 49 CFR Part 40 of this title.

(5) *It must not allow a covered employee* to begin performing safety-sensitive functions unless the result of the employee's test indicates an alcohol concentration of less than 0.04.

§382.301 DOT Interpretations

Question 1: What is meant by the phrase, "an employer who uses, but does not employ, a driver * * * " ? Describe a situation to which the phrase would apply.

Guidance: This exception was contained in the original drug testing rules and was generally applied to "trip-lease" drivers involved in interstate commerce. A trip-lease driver is generally a driver employed by one motor carrier, but who is temporarily leased to another motor carrier for one or more trips generally for a time period less than 30 days. The phrase would also apply to volunteer organizations that use loaned drivers.

Question 2: Must school bus drivers be pre-employment tested after they return to work after summer vacation in each year in which they do not drive for 30 consecutive days?

Guidance: A school bus driver whom the employer expects to return to duty the next school year does not have to be pre-employment tested so long as the driver has remained in the random selection pool over the summer. There is deemed to be no break in employment if the driver is expected to return in the fall.

On the other hand, if the driver is taken out of all DOT random pools for more than 30 days, the exception to pre-employment drug testing in §382.301 would be unavailable and a drug test would have to be administered after the summer vacation.

Question 3: Is a pre-employment controlled substances test required if a driver returns to a previous employer after his/her employment had been terminated?

Guidance: Yes. A controlled substances test must be administered any time employment has been terminated for more than 30 days and the exceptions under §382.301(c) were not met.

Question 4: Must all drivers who do not work for an extended period of time (such as layoffs over the winter or summer months) be pre-employment drug tested each season when they return to work?

Guidance: If the driver is considered to be an employee of the company during the extended (layoff) period, a pre-employment test would not be required so long as the driver has been included in the company's random testing program during the layoff period. However, if the driver was not considered to be an employee of the company at any point during the layoff period, or was not covered by a program, or was not covered for more than 30 days, then a pre-employment test would be required.

Question 5: What must an employer do to avail itself of the exceptions to pre-employment testing listed under §382.301(c)?

Guidance: An employer must meet all requirements in §382.301(c) and (d), including maintaining all required documents. An employer must produce the required documents at the time of the Compliance Review for the exception to apply.

Question 6: May a CDL driving skills test examiner conduct a driving skills test administered in accordance with 49 CFR Part 383 before a person subject to Part 382 is tested for alcohol and controlled substances?

Guidance: Yes. A CDL driving skills test examiner, including a third party CDL driving skills test examiner, may administer a driving skills test to a person subject to Part 382 without first testing him/her for alcohol and controlled substances. The intent of the CDL driving skills test is to assess a person's ability to operate a commercial motor vehicle during an official government test of their driving skills. However, this guidance does not allow an employer (including a truck or bus driver training school) to use a person as a current company, lease, or student driver prior to obtaining a verified negative test result. An employer must obtain a verified negative controlled substance test result prior to dispatching a driver on his/her first trip.

§382.303 Post-accident testing.

(a) **As soon as practicable following an occurrence** involving a commercial motor vehicle operating on a public road in commerce, each employer shall test for alcohol for each of its surviving drivers:

(1) *Who was performing safety-sensitive functions* with respect to the vehicle, if the accident involved the loss of human life; or

(2) *Who receives a citation* within 8 hours of the occurrence under State or local law for a moving traffic violation arising from the accident, if the accident involved:

(i) *Bodily injury to any person* who, as a result of the injury, immediately receives medical treatment away from the scene of the accident; or

(ii) *One or more motor vehicles* incurring disabling damage as a result of the accident, requiring the motor vehicle to be transported away from the scene by a tow truck or other motor vehicle.

(b) **As soon as practicable following an occurrence** involving a commercial motor vehicle operating on a public road in commerce, each employer shall test for controlled substances for each of its surviving drivers:

(1) *Who was performing safety-sensitive functions* with respect to the vehicle, if the accident involved the loss of human life; or

(2) *Who receives a citation* within thirty-two hours of the occurrence under State or local law for a moving traffic violation arising from the accident, if the accident involved:

(i) *Bodily injury to any person* who, as a result of the injury, immediately receives medical treatment away from the scene of the accident; or

(ii) *One or more motor vehicles* incurring disabling damage as a result of the accident, requiring the motor vehicle to be transported away from the scene by a tow truck or other motor vehicle.

(c) **The following table notes when a post-accident test** is required to be conducted by paragraphs (a)(1), (a)(2), (b)(1), and (b)(2) of this section:

Table for §382.303(a) and (b)

Type of accident involved	Citation issued to the CMV driver	Test must be performed by employer
i. Human fatality	YES	YES
	NO	YES
ii. Bodily injury with immediate medical treatment away from the scene	YES	YES
	NO	NO
iii. Disabling damage to any motor vehicle requiring tow away	YES	YES
	NO	NO

(d) (1) *Alcohol tests.* If a test required by this section is not administered within two hours following the accident, the employer shall prepare and maintain on file a record stating the reasons the test was not promptly administered. If a test required by this section is not administered within eight hours following the accident, the employer shall cease attempts to administer an alcohol test and shall prepare and maintain the same record. Records shall be submitted to the FMCSA upon request.

(2) *Controlled substance tests.* If a test required by this section is not administered within 32 hours following the accident, the employer shall cease attempts to administer a controlled substances test, and prepare and maintain on file a record stating the reasons the test was not promptly administered. Records shall be submitted to the FMCSA upon request.

(e) **A driver who is subject to post-accident testing** shall remain readily available for such testing or may be deemed by the employer to have refused to submit to testing. Nothing in this section shall be construed to require the delay of necessary medical attention for injured people following an accident or to prohibit a driver from leaving the scene of an accident for the period necessary to obtain assistance in responding to the accident, or to obtain necessary emergency medical care.

(f) **An employer shall provide drivers** with necessary post-accident information, procedures and instructions, prior to the driver operating a commercial motor vehicle, so that drivers will be able to comply with the requirements of this section.

(g) (1) *The results of a breath or blood test* for the use of alcohol, conducted by Federal, State, or local officials having independent authority for the test, shall be considered to meet the requirements of this section, provided such tests conform to the applicable Federal, State or local alcohol testing requirements, and that the results of the tests are obtained by the employer.

(2) *The results of a urine test* for the use of controlled substances, conducted by Federal, State, or local officials having independent authority for the test, shall be considered to meet the requirements of this section, provided such tests conform to the applicable Federal, State or local controlled substances testing requirements, and that the results of the tests are obtained by the employer.

(h) **Exception.** This section does not apply to:

(1) *An occurrence* involving only boarding or alighting from a stationary motor vehicle; or

(2) *An occurrence* involving only the loading or unloading of cargo; or

Subpart C - Tests Required §382.305 (e)

(3) *An occurrence* in the course of the operation of a passenger car or a multipurpose passenger vehicle (as defined in §571.3 of this title) by an employer unless the motor vehicle is transporting passengers for hire or hazardous materials of a type and quantity that require the motor vehicle to be marked or placarded in accordance with §177.823 of this title.

§382.303 DOT Interpretations

Question 1: Why does the FMCSA allow post-accident tests done by Federal, State, or local law enforcement agencies to substitute for a §382.303 test even though the FMCSA does not allow a Federal, State or local law enforcement agency test to substitute for a pre-employment, random, reasonable suspicion, return-to-duty, or follow-up test? Will such substitutions be allowed in the future?

Guidance: A highway accident is generally investigated by a Federal, State, or local law enforcement agency that may determine that probable cause exists to conduct alcohol or controlled substances testing of a surviving driver. The FMCSA believes that testing done by such agencies will be done to document an investigation for a charge of driving under the influence of a substance and should be allowed to substitute for a FMCSA-required test. The FMCSA expects this provision to be used rarely.

The FMCSA is required by statute to provide certain protection for drivers who are tested for alcohol and controlled substances. The FMCSA believes that law enforcement agencies investigating accidents will provide similar protection based on the local court's prior action in such types of testing.

The FMCSA will not allow a similar approach for law enforcement agencies to conduct testing for the other types of testing. A law enforcement agency, however, may act as a consortium to provide any testing in accordance with Parts 40 and 382.

Question 2: May an employer allow a driver, subject to post-accident controlled substances testing, to continue to drive pending receipt of the results of the controlled substances test?

Guidance: Yes. A driver may continue to drive, so long as no other restrictions are imposed by §382.307 or by law enforcement officials.

Question 3: A commercial motor vehicle operator is involved in an accident in which an individual is injured but does not die from the injuries until a later date. The commercial motor vehicle driver does not receive a citation under State or local law for a moving traffic violation arising from the accident. How long after the accident is the employer required to attempt to have the driver subjected to post-accident testing?

Guidance: Each employer is required to test each surviving driver for alcohol and controlled substances as soon as practicable following an accident as required by §382.303. However, if an alcohol test is not administered within 8 hours following the accident, or if a controlled substance test is not administered within 32 hours following the accident, the employer must cease attempts to administer that test. In both cases the employer must prepare and maintain a record stating the reason(s) the test(s) were not promptly administered.

If the fatality occurs following the accident and within the time limits for the required tests, the employer shall attempt to conduct the tests until the respective time limits are reached. The employer is not required to conduct any tests for cases in which the fatality occurs outside of the 8 and 32 hour time limits.

Question 4: What post-accident alcohol and drug testing requirements are there for U.S. employer's drivers involved in an accident occurring outside the U.S.?

Guidance: U.S. employers are responsible for ensuring that drivers who have an accident (as defined in §390.5) in a foreign country are post-accident alcohol and drug tested in conformance with the requirements of 49 CFR Parts 40 and 382. If the test(s) cannot be administered within the required 8 or 32 hours, the employer shall prepare and maintain a record stating the reasons the test(s) was not administered (see §382.303(b)(1) and (b)(4)).

Question 5: What post-accident alcohol and drug testing requirements are there for foreign drivers involved in accidents occurring outside the United States?

Guidance: Post-accident alcohol and drug testing is required for CMV accidents occurring within the U.S. and on segments of interstate movements into Canada between the U.S.-Canadian border and the first physical delivery location of a Canadian consignee. The FMCSA further believes its regulations require testing for segments of interstate movements out of Canada between the last physical pick-up location of a Canadian consignor and the U.S.-Canadian border. The same would be true for movements between the U.S.-Mexican border and a point in Mexico.

For example, a motor carrier has two shipments on a CMV from a shipper in Chicago, Illinois. The first shipment will be delivered to Winnipeg, Manitoba and the second to Lloydminster, Saskatchewan. A driver is required to be post-accident tested for any CMV accident that meets the requirements to conduct 49 CFR 382.303 Post-accident testing, that occurs between Chicago, Illinois and Winnipeg, Manitoba (the first delivery point). The FMCSA would not require a foreign motor carrier to conduct testing of foreign drivers for any accidents between Winnipeg and Lloydminster.

The FMCSA does not believe it has authority over Canadian and Mexican motor carriers that operate within their own countries where the movement does not involve movements into or out of the United States. For example, the FMCSA does not believe it has authority to require testing for transportation of freight from Prince George, British Colombia to Red Deer, Alberta that does not traverse the United States.

If the driver is not tested for alcohol and drugs as required by §382.303 and the motor carrier operates in the U.S. during a four-month period of time after the event that triggered the requirement for such a test, the motor carrier will be in violation of Part 382 and may be subject to penalties under §382.507.

§382.305 Random testing.

(a) Every employer shall comply with the requirements of this section. Every driver shall submit to random alcohol and controlled substance testing as required in this section.

(b) (1) *Except as provided* in paragraphs (c) through (e) of this section, the minimum annual percentage rate for random alcohol testing shall be 10 percent of the average number of driver positions.

(2) *Except as provided* in paragraphs (f) through (h) of this section, the minimum annual percentage rate for random controlled substances testing shall be 50 percent of the average number of driver positions.

(c) The FMCSA Administrator's decision to increase or decrease the minimum annual percentage rate for alcohol testing is based on the reported violation rate for the entire industry. All information used for this determination is drawn from the alcohol management information system reports required by §382.403. In order to ensure reliability of the data, the FMCSA Administrator considers the quality and completeness of the reported data, may obtain additional information or reports from employers, and may make appropriate modifications in calculating the industry violation rate. In the event of a change in the annual percentage rate, the FMSCA Administrator will publish in the Federal Register the new minimum annual percentage rate for random alcohol testing of drivers. The new minimum annual percentage rate for random alcohol testing will be applicable starting January 1 of the calendar year following publication in the Federal Register.

(d) (1) *When the minimum annual percentage rate* for random alcohol testing is 25 percent or more, the FMCSA Administrator may lower this rate to 10 percent of all driver positions if the FMCSA Administrator determines that the data received under the reporting requirements of §382.403 for two consecutive calendar years indicate that the violation rate is less than 0.5 percent.

(2) *When the minimum annual percentage rate* for random alcohol testing is 50 percent, the FMCSA Administrator may lower this rate to 25 percent of all driver positions if the FMCSA Administrator determines that the data received under the reporting requirements of §382.403 for two consecutive calendar years indicate that the violation rate is less than 1.0 percent but equal to or greater than 0.5 percent.

(e) (1) *When the minimum annual percentage rate* for random alcohol testing is 10 percent, and the data received under the reporting requirements of §382.403 for that calendar year indicate that the violation rate is equal to or greater than 0.5 percent, but less than 1.0 percent, the FMCSA Administrator will increase the minimum annual percentage rate for random alcohol testing to 25 percent for all driver positions.

(2) *When the minimum annual percentage rate* for random alcohol testing is 25 percent or less, and the data received under the reporting requirements of §382.403 for that calendar year indicate that the violation rate is equal to or greater than 1.0 percent, the FMCSA Administrator will increase the minimum annual percentage rate for random alcohol testing to 50 percent for all driver positions.

(f) **The FMCSA Administrator's decision** to increase or decrease the minimum annual percentage rate for controlled substances testing is based on the reported positive rate for the entire industry. All information used for this determination is drawn from the controlled substances management information system reports required by §382.403. In order to ensure reliability of the data, the FMCSA Administrator considers the quality and completeness of the reported data, may obtain additional information or reports from employers, and may make appropriate modifications in calculating the industry positive rate. In the event of a change in the annual percentage rate, the FMCSA Administrator will publish in the Federal Register the new minimum annual percentage rate for controlled substances testing of drivers. The new minimum annual percentage rate for random controlled substances testing will be applicable starting January 1 of the calendar year following publication in the Federal Register.

(g) **When the minimum annual percentage rate** for random controlled substances testing is 50 percent, the FMCSA Administrator may lower this rate to 25 percent of all driver positions if the FMCSA Administrator determines that the data received under the reporting requirements of §382.403 for two consecutive calendar years indicate that the positive rate is less than 1.0 percent.

(h) **When the minimum annual percentage rate** for random controlled substances testing is 25 percent, and the data received under the reporting requirements of §382.403 for any calendar year indicate that the reported positive rate is equal to or greater than 1.0 percent, the FMCSA Administrator will increase the minimum annual percentage rate for random controlled substances testing to 50 percent of all driver positions.

(i) (1) *The selection of drivers* for random alcohol and controlled substances testing shall be made by a scientifically valid method, such as a random number table or a computer-based random number generator that is matched with drivers' Social Security numbers, payroll identification numbers, or other comparable identifying numbers.

(2) *Each driver selected* for random alcohol and controlled substances testing under the selection process used, shall have an equal chance of being tested each time selections are made.

(3) *Each driver selected for testing* shall be tested during the selection period.

(j) (1) *To calculate the total number* of covered drivers eligible for random testing throughout the year, as an employer, you must add the total number of covered drivers eligible for testing during each random testing period for the year and divide that total by the number of random testing periods. Covered employees, and only covered employees, are to be in an employer's random driver testing pool, and all covered drivers must be in the random pool. If you are an employer conducting random testing more often than once per month (e.g., daily, weekly, bi-weekly) you do not need to compute this total number of covered drivers rate more than on a once per month basis.

(2) *As an employer,* you may use a service agent (e.g., a C/TPA) to perform random selections for you, and your covered drivers may be part of a larger random testing pool of covered employees. However, you must ensure that the service agent you use is testing at the appropriate percentage established for your industry and that only covered employees are in the random testing pool.

(k) (1) *Each employer shall ensure* that random alcohol and controlled substances tests conducted under this part are unannounced.

(2) *Each employer shall ensure* that the dates for administering random alcohol and controlled substances tests conducted under this part are spread reasonably throughout the calendar year.

(l) **Each employer shall require that each driver** who is notified of selection for random alcohol and/or controlled substances testing proceeds to the test site immediately; provided, however, that if the driver is performing a safety-sensitive function, other than driving a commercial motor vehicle, at the time of notification, the employer shall instead ensure that the driver ceases to perform the safety-sensitive function and proceeds to the testing site as soon as possible.

(m) **A driver shall only be tested for alcohol** while the driver is performing safety-sensitive functions, just before the driver is to perform safety-sensitive functions, or just after the driver has ceased performing such functions.

(n) **If a given driver is subject to random** alcohol or controlled substances testing under the random alcohol or controlled substances testing rules of more than one DOT agency for the same employer, the driver shall be subject to random alcohol and/or controlled substances testing at the annual percentage rate established for the calendar year by the DOT agency regulating more than 50 percent of the driver's function.

(o) **If an employer is required to conduct** random alcohol or controlled substances testing under the alcohol or controlled substances testing rules of more than one DOT agency, the employer may —

(1) *Establish separate pools for random selection,* with each pool containing the DOT-covered employees who are subject to testing at the same required minimum annual percentage rate; or

(2) *Randomly select such employees* for testing at the highest minimum annual percentage rate established for the calendar year by any DOT agency to which the employer is subject.

§382.305 DOT Interpretations

Question 1: Is a driver who is on-duty, but has not been assigned a driving task, considered to be ready to perform a safety-sensitive function as defined in §382.107 subjecting the driver to random alcohol testing?

Guidance: A driver must be about to perform, or immediately available to perform, a safety-sensitive function to be considered subject to random alcohol testing. A supervisor, mechanic, or clerk, etc., who is on call to perform safety-sensitive functions may be tested at any time they are on call, ready to be dispatched while on-duty.

Question 2: What are the employer's obligations, in terms of random testing, with regard to an employee who does not drive as part of the employee's usual job functions, but who holds a CDL and may be called upon at any time, on an occasional or emergency basis, to drive?

Guidance: Such an employee must be in a random testing pool at all times, like a full-time driver. A drug test must be administered each time the employee's name is selected from the pool.

Alcohol testing, however, may only be conducted just before, during, or just after the performance of safety-sensitive functions. A safety-sensitive function as defined in §382.107 means any of those on-duty functions set forth in §395.2 On-Duty time, paragraphs (1) through (7), (generally, driving and related activities). If the employee's name is selected, the employer must wait until the next time the employee is performing safety-sensitive functions, just before the employee is to perform a safety-sensitive function, or just after the employee has ceased performing such functions to administer the alcohol test. If a random selection period expires before the employee performs a safety-sensitive function, no alcohol test should be given, the employee's name should be returned to the pool, and the number of employees subsequently selected should be adjusted accordingly to achieve the required rate.

Question 3: How should a random testing program be structured to account for the schedules of school bus or other drivers employed on a seasonal basis?

Guidance: If no school bus drivers from an employer's random testing pool are used to perform safety sensitive functions during the summer, the employer could choose to make random selections only during the school year. If the employer nevertheless chooses to make selections in the summer, tests may only be administered when the drivers return to duty.

If some drivers continue to perform safety-sensitive functions during the summer, such as driving buses for summer school, an employer could not choose to forego all random selections each summer. Such a practice would compromise the random, unannounced nature of the random testing program. The employer would test all selected drivers actually driving in the summer. With regard to testing drivers not driving during the summer, the employer has two options. One, names of drivers selected who are on summer vacation may be returned to the pool and another selection made. Two, the selected names could be held by the employer and, if the drivers return to perform safety-sensitive functions before the next random selection, the test administered upon the drivers' return.

Finally, it should be noted that reductions in the number of drivers during summer vacations reduces the average number of driving positions over the course of the year, and thus the number of tests which must be administered to meet the minimum random testing rate.

Question 4: Are driver positions that are vacant for a testing cycle to be included in the determination of how many random tests must be conducted?

Guidance: No. The FMCSA random testing program tests employed or utilized drivers, not positions that are vacant.

Question 5: May an employer use the results of another program in which a driver participates to satisfy random testing requirements if the driver is used by the employer only occasionally?
Guidance: The rules establish an employer-based testing program. Employers remain responsible at all times for ensuring compliance with all of the rules, including random testing, for all drivers which they use, regardless of any utilization of third parties to administer parts of the program. Therefore, to use another's program, an employer must make the other program, by contract, consortium agreement, or other arrangement, the employer's own program. This would entail, among other things, being held responsible for the other program's compliance, having records forwarded to the employer's principal place of business on 2 days notice, and being notified of and acting upon positive test results.

Question 6: Once an employee is randomly tested during a calendar year, is his/her name removed from the pool of names for the calendar year?
Guidance: No, the names of those tested earlier in the year must be returned to the pool for each new selection. Each driver must be subject to an equal chance of being tested during each selection process.

Question 7: Is it permissible to make random selections by terminals?
Guidance: Yes. If random selection is done based on locations or terminals, a two-stage selection process must be utilized. The first selection would be made by the locations and the second selection would be of those employees at the location(s) selected. The selections must ensure that each employee in the pool has an equal chance of being selected and tested, no matter where the employee is located.

Question 8: When a driver works for two or more employers, in whose random pool must the driver be included?
Guidance: The driver must be in the pool of each employer for which the driver works.

Question 9: After what period of time may an employer remove a casual driver from a random pool?
Guidance: An employer may remove a casual driver, who is not used by the employer, from its random pool when it no longer expects the driver to be used.

Question 10: If an employee is off work due to temporary lay-off, illness, injury, or vacation, should that individual's name be removed from the random pool?
Guidance: No. The individual's name should not be removed from the random pool so long as there is a reasonable expectation of the employee's return.

Question 11: Is it necessary for an owner-operator, who is not leased to a motor carrier, to belong to a consortium for random testing purposes?
Guidance: Yes.

Question 12: If an employer joins a consortium, and the consortium is randomly testing at the appropriate rates, will these rates meet the requirements of the alcohol and controlled substances testing for the employer even though the required percent of the employer's drivers were not randomly tested?
Guidance: Yes.

Question 13: Is it permissible to combine the drivers from the subsidiaries of a parent employer into one pool, with the parent employer acting as a consortium?
Guidance: Yes.

Question 14: How should an employer compute the number of random tests to be given to ensure that the appropriate testing rate is achieved given the fluctuations in driver populations and the high turnover rate of drivers?
Guidance: An employer should take into account fluctuations by estimating the number of random tests needed to be performed over the course of the year. If the carrier's driver workforce is expected to be relatively constant (i.e., the total number of driver positions is approximately the same) then the number of tests to be performed in any given year could be determined by multiplying the average number of driver positions by the testing rate.

If there are large fluctuations in the number of driver positions throughout the year without any clear indication of the average number of driver positions, the employer should make a reasonable estimate of the number of positions. After making the estimate, the employer should then be able to determine the number of tests necessary.

Question 15: May an employer or consortium include non-DOT-covered employees in a random pool with DOT-covered employees?
Guidance: No.

Question 16: Canadians believe that their laws require employer actions be tied to the nature of the job and the associated safety risk. Canadian employers believe they will have to issue alcohol and drug testing policies that deal with all drivers in an identical manner, not just drivers that cross the border into the United States. If a motor carrier wanted to add cross border work to an intra-Canadian driver's duties, and the driver was otherwise qualified under the FMCSA rules, may the pre-employment test be waived?
Guidance: The FMCSA has long required, since the beginning of the drug testing program in 1988, that transferring from intrastate work into interstate work requires a "pre-employment" test regardless of what type of testing a State might have required under intrastate laws. This policy also applied to motor carriers that had a pre-employment testing program similar to the FMCSA requirement. The FMCSA believes it is reasonable to apply this same interpretation to the first time a Canadian or Mexican driver enters the United States. This policy was delineated in the Federal Register of February 15, 1994 (59 FR 7302, at 7322). The FMCSA believes motor carriers should separate drivers into intra-Canadian and inter-state groups for their policies and the random selection pools. If a driver in the intra-Canadian group (including the random selection pool) were to take on driving duties into the United States, the driver would be subject to a pre-employment test to take on this driving task. Although the circumstance is not actually a first employment with the motor carrier, such a test would be required because it would be the first time the driver would be subject to Part 382.

Question 17: May an employer notify a driver of his/her selection for a random controlled substances test while the driver is in an off-duty status?
Guidance: Yes. Part 382 does not prohibit an employer from notifying a driver of his/her selection for a random controlled substances test while the driver is in an off-duty status.

If an employer selects a driver for a random controlled substances test while the driver is in an off-duty status, and then chooses to notify the driver that he/she has been selected while the driver is still off-duty, the employer must ensure that the driver proceeds immediately to a collection site. Immediately, in this context, means that all the driver's actions, after notification, lead to an immediate specimen collection. If the employer's policy or practice is to notify drivers while they are in an off-duty status, the employer should make that policy clear to all drivers so that they are fully informed of their obligation to proceed immediately to a collection site.

If an employer does not want to notify the driver that he/she has been selected for a random controlled substances test while the driver is in an off-duty status, the employer could set aside the driver's name for notification until the driver returns to work, as long as the driver returns to work before the next selection for random testing is made.

Employers should note that regardless of when a driver is notified, the time the driver spends traveling to and from the collection site, and all time associated with providing the specimen, must be recorded as on-duty time for purposes of compliance with the hours-of-service rules.

Question 18: Is it permissible to select alternates for the purpose of complying with the Random Testing regulations?
Guidance: Yes, it is permissible to select alternates. However, it is only permissible if the primary driver selected will not be available for testing during the selection period because of long-term absence due to layoff, illness, injury, vacation or other circumstances. In the event the initial driver selected is not available for testing, the employer and/or C/TPA must document the reason why an alternate driver was tested. The documentation must be maintained and readily available when requested by the Secretary of Transportation, any DOT agency, or any State or local officials with regulatory authority over the employer or any of its drivers.

Question 19: A motor carrier uses a consortium/third party administrator (C/TPA) to conduct its random selection of driver names. The C/TPA has many motor carriers in its random selection pool. The C/TPA has set up its random selection program to pick driver names and notifies the motor carrier whose driver the C/TPA has selected. The motor carrier notifies the C/TPA the driver is presently on long-term absence due to layoff, illness, injury, or vacation. The motor carrier also notifies the C/TPA it does not expect the driver to return to duty before the C/TPA's next selection of driver names. The C/TPA then randomly orders and selects a driver's name from the motor carrier that employs the driver who is unavailable rather than selecting the next name on the random selection list. Is this a scientifically valid and impartial method for selecting drivers for random testing in a motor carrier's program?

Question 19: A motor carrier uses a consortium/third party administrator (C/TPA) to conduct its random selection of driver names. The C/TPA has many motor carriers in its random selection pool. The C/TPA has set up its random selection program to pick driver names and notifies the motor carrier whose driver the C/TPA has selected. The motor carrier notifies the C/TPA the driver is presently on long-term absence due to layoff, illness, injury, or vacation. The motor carrier also notifies the C/TPA it does not expect the driver to return to duty before the C/TPA's next selection of driver names. The C/TPA then randomly orders and selects a driver's name from the motor carrier that employs the driver who is unavailable rather than selecting the next name on the random selection list. Is this a scientifically valid and impartial method for selecting drivers for random testing in a motor carrier's program?

Guidance: This procedure is a scientifically valid method for selecting driver names. This method is similar to methods used by organizations, including the Department of Labor's Bureau of Labor Statistics, to randomly order, select, and substitute names for sampling with replacement of groups of individual and companies. This procedure has a small degree of theoretical bias for a simple random sampling selection procedure. The theoretical bias, though, is so minimal the FMCSA does not believe the agency should prohibit its use.

This method is useful for operational settings, such as FMCSA's motor carrier random testing program. The method is less impartial toward drivers than other theoretical methods, but maintains a deterrent effect for both motor carriers and drivers. This method should deter motor carriers from claiming drivers are unavailable each time the C/TPA selects one of its drivers, thereby never having its drivers subject to actual random tests.

In addition, employers and C/TPA's should establish operational procedures that will ensure, to the greatest extent possible, that the primary selections for random testing are tested. The operational procedures should include procedures that will ensure the random selection lists are updated in a timely manner. The updates will ensure that drivers who are no longer available to an employer will not be counted in the random selection lists. The operational procedures should also outline the measures for selecting alternates, including documenting the reasons for using an alternate.

Question 20: If an employer is subject to random testing for only a partial calendar year, how should the employer determine the number of random tests required during the year to achieve the appropriate testing rate? (Examples: new employers that begin operating midway through the calendar year; employers which merge or split midway through the calendar year; Canadian or Mexican carriers that begin U.S. operations midway through the calendar year.)

Guidance: The number of random tests required can be computed in the same manner as for any employer that has large fluctuations in the number of driver positions during the year. Use the formulas T = 50% x D/P for controlled substance testing and T = 10% x D/P for alcohol testing, where T is the number of tests required, D is the total number of drivers subject to testing, and P is the number of selection periods in a full calendar year. For any selection period during which the carrier was not subject to §382.305, simply enter a zero in the driver calculations. Example: A carrier starts operating in August and decides to test quarterly (P = 4). It has 16 drivers subject to testing in the third quarter and only 12 drivers subject to testing in the fourth quarter. D = 0 + 0 + 16 + 12 = 28. D/P = 28/4 = 7. T = 50% of 7, or 3.5, which must be rounded up to 4. The carrier must test 4 drivers for controlled substances between its first day of operation in August and the end of the year. Following the requirement to spread testing reasonably throughout the year, two drivers should be tested during the third quarter and two during the fourth quarter.

§382.307 Reasonable suspicion testing.

(a) **An employer shall require a driver** to submit to an alcohol test when the employer has reasonable suspicion to believe that the driver has violated the prohibitions of Subpart B of this part concerning alcohol. The employer's determination that reasonable suspicion exists to require the driver to undergo an alcohol test must be based on specific, contemporaneous, articulable observations concerning the appearance, behavior, speech or body odors of the driver.

(b) **An employer shall require a driver** to submit to a controlled substances test when the employer has reasonable suspicion to believe that the driver has violated the prohibitions of Subpart B of this part concerning controlled substances. The employer's determination that reasonable suspicion exists to require the driver to undergo a controlled substances test must be based on specific, contemporaneous, articulable observations concerning the appearance, behavior, speech or body odors of the driver. The observations may include indications of the chronic and withdrawal effects of controlled substances.

(c) **The required observations for alcohol** and/or controlled substances reasonable suspicion testing shall be made by a supervisor or company official who is trained in accordance with §382.603. The person who makes the determination that reasonable suspicion exists to conduct an alcohol test shall not conduct the alcohol test of the driver.

(d) **Alcohol testing is authorized by this section** only if the observations required by paragraph (a) of this section are made during, just preceding, or just after the period of the work day that the driver is required to be in compliance with this part. A driver may be directed by the employer to only undergo reasonable suspicion testing while the driver is performing safety-sensitive functions, just before the driver is to perform safety-sensitive functions, or just after the driver has ceased performing such functions.

(e) (1) *If an alcohol test required by this section* is not administered within two hours following the determination under paragraph (a) of this section, the employer shall prepare and maintain on file a record stating the reasons the alcohol test was not promptly administered. If an alcohol test required by this section is not administered within eight hours following the determination under paragraph (a) of this section, the employer shall cease attempts to administer an alcohol test and shall state in the record the reasons for not administering the test.

(2) *Notwithstanding the absence* of a reasonable suspicion alcohol test under this section, no driver shall report for duty or remain on duty requiring the performance of safety-sensitive functions while the driver is under the influence of or impaired by alcohol, as shown by the behavioral, speech, and performance indicators of alcohol misuse, nor shall an employer permit the driver to perform or continue to perform safety-sensitive functions, until:

(i) *An alcohol test is administered* and the driver's alcohol concentration measures less than 0.02; or

(ii) *Twenty four hours have elapsed* following the determination under paragraph (a) of this section that there is reasonable suspicion to believe that the driver has violated the prohibitions in this part concerning the use of alcohol.

(3) *Except as provided* in paragraph (e)(2) of this section, no employer shall take any action under this part against a driver based solely on the driver's behavior and appearance, with respect to alcohol use, in the absence of an alcohol test. This does not prohibit an employer with independent authority of this part from taking any action otherwise consistent with law.

(f) **A written record shall be made of the observations** leading to an alcohol or controlled substances reasonable suspicion test, and signed by the supervisor or company official who made the observations, within 24 hours of the observed behavior or before the results of the alcohol or controlled substances tests are released, whichever is earlier.

§382.307 DOT Interpretations

Question 1: May a reasonable suspicion alcohol test be based upon any information or observations of alcohol use or possession, other than a supervisor's actual knowledge?

Guidance: No. Information conveyed by third parties of a driver's alcohol use may not be the only determining factor used to conduct a reasonable suspicion test. A reasonable suspicion test may only be conducted when a trained supervisor has observed specific, contemporaneous, articulable appearance, speech, body odor, or behavior indicators of alcohol use.

Question 2: Why does §382.307(b) allow an employer to use indicators of chronic and withdrawal effects of controlled substances in the observations to conduct a controlled substances reasonable suspicion test, but does not allow similar effects of alcohol use to be used for an alcohol reasonable suspicion test?

Guidance: The use of controlled substances by drivers is strictly prohibited. Because controlled substances remain present in the body for a relatively long period, withdrawal effects may indicate that the driver has used drugs in violation of the regulations, and therefore must be given a reasonable suspicion drug test.

Alcohol is generally a legal substance. Only its use or presence in sufficient concentrations while operating a CMV is a violation of FMCSA regulation. Alcohol withdrawal effects, standing alone, do not, therefore, indicate that a driver has used alcohol in violation of the regulations, and would not constitute reasonable suspicion to believe so.

Question 3: A consignee, consignor, or other party is a motor carrier employer for purposes of 49 CFR Parts 382 through 399. They have trained their supervisors in accordance with 49 CFR 382.603 to conduct reasonable suspicion training on their own drivers. A driver for another motor carrier employer delivers, picks up, or has some contact with the consignee's, consignor's, or other party's trained supervisor. This supervisor believes there is reasonable suspicion, based on their training, that the driver may have used a controlled substance or alcohol in violation of the regulations. May this trained consignee, consignor, or other party's supervisor order a reasonable suspicion test of a driver the supervisor does not supervise for the employing/using motor carrier employer?

Guidance: No, the trained supervisor may not order a reasonable suspicion test of a driver the supervisor does not supervise for the employing/using motor carrier employer. Motor carrier employers may not conduct reasonable suspicion testing based "on reports of a third person who has made the observations, because of that person's possible credibility problems or lack of appropriate training."

The trained supervisor for the consignee, consignor, or other party may, however, choose to do things not required by regulation, but encouraged by the FMCSA. They may inform the driver that they believe the driver may have violated Federal, State, or local regulations and advise them not to perform additional safety-sensitive work. They may contact the employing/using motor carrier employer to alert them of their reasonable suspicion and request the employing/using motor carrier employer take appropriate action. In addition, they may contact the police to request appropriate action.

Question 4: Are the reasonable suspicion testing and training requirements of §§382.307 and 382.603 applicable to an owner-operator who is both an employer and the only employee?

Guidance: No. The requirements of §§382.307 and 382.603 are not applicable to owner-operators in non-supervisory positions. §382.307 requires employers to have a driver submit to an alcohol and/or controlled substances test when the employer has reasonable suspicion to believe that the driver has violated the prohibitions of Subpart B of Part 382. Applying §382.307, Reasonable Suspicion Testing, to an owner-operator who is an employer and the only employee contradicts both "reason" and "suspicion" implicit in the title and the purpose of §382.307. A driver who has self-knowledge that he/she has violated the prohibitions of Subpart B of Part 382 is beyond mere suspicion. Furthermore, §382.603 requires "all persons designated to supervise drivers" to receive training that will enable him/her to determine whether reasonable suspicion exists to require a driver to undergo testing under §382.307. An owner-operator who does not hire or supervise other drivers is not in a supervisory position, nor are they subject to the testing requirements of §382.307. Therefore, such an owner-operator would not be subject to the training requirements of §382.603.

§382.309 Return-to-duty testing.

The requirements for return-to-duty testing must be performed in accordance with 49 CFR Part 40, Subpart O.

§382.311 Follow-up testing.

The requirements for follow-up testing must be performed in accordance with 49 CFR Part 40, Subpart O.

Subpart D - Handling of Test Results, Records Retention, and Confidentiality

§382.401 Retention of records.

(a) **General requirement.** Each employer shall maintain records of its alcohol misuse and controlled substances use prevention programs as provided in this section. The records shall be maintained in a secure location with controlled access.

(b) **Period of retention.** Each employer shall maintain the records in accordance with the following schedule:
  (1) *Five years.* The following records shall be maintained for a minimum of five years:
      (i) *Records of driver alcohol test results* indicating an alcohol concentration of 0.02 or greater,
      (ii) *Records of driver verified* positive controlled substances test results,
      (iii) *Documentation of refusals* to take required alcohol and/or controlled substances tests,
      (iv) *Driver evaluation and referrals,*
      (v) *Calibration documentation,*
      (vi) *Records related to the administration* of the alcohol and controlled substances testing programs, and
      (vii) *A copy of each annual calendar year summary* required by §382.403.
  (2) *Two years.* Records related to the alcohol and controlled substances collection process (except calibration of evidential breath testing devices).
  (3) *One year.* Records of negative and canceled controlled substances test results (as defined in Part 40 of this title) and alcohol test results with a concentration of less than 0.02 shall be maintained for a minimum of one year.
  (4) *Indefinite period.* Records related to the education and training of breath alcohol technicians, screening test technicians, supervisors, and drivers shall be maintained by the employer while the individual performs the functions which require the training and for two years after ceasing to perform those functions.

(c) **Types of records.** The following specific types of records shall be maintained. "Documents generated" are documents that may have to be prepared under a requirement of this part. If the record is required to be prepared, it must be maintained.
  (1) *Records related to the collection process:*
      (i) *Collection logbooks, if used;*
      (ii) *Documents relating to the random selection process;*
      (iii) *Calibration documentation for evidential breath testing devices;*
      (iv) *Documentation of breath alcohol technician training;*
      (v) *Documents generated* in connection with decisions to administer reasonable suspicion alcohol or controlled substances tests;
      (vi) *Documents generated* in connection with decisions on post-accident tests;
      (vii) *Documents verifying existence* of a medical explanation of the inability of a driver to provide adequate breath or to provide a urine specimen for testing; and
      (viii) *A copy of each annual calendar year summary* as required by §382.403.
  (2) *Records related to a driver's test results:*
      (i) *The employer's copy* of the alcohol test form, including the results of the test;
      (ii) *The employer's copy* of the controlled substances test chain of custody and control form;
      (iii) *Documents sent by the MRO to the employer,* including those required by Part 40, Subpart G, of this title;
      (iv) *Documents related to the refusal of any driver* to submit to an alcohol or controlled substances test required by this part;
      (v) *Documents presented by a driver* to dispute the result of an alcohol or controlled substances test administered under this part; and
      (vi) *Documents generated* in connection with verifications of prior employers' alcohol or controlled substances test results that the employer:
          [A] Must obtain in connection with the exception contained in §382.301, and
          [B] Must obtain as required by §382.413.
  (3) *Records related to other violations of this part.*
  (4) *Records related to evaluations:*
      (i) *Records pertaining to a determination* by a substance abuse professional concerning a driver's need for assistance; and
      (ii) *Records concerning a driver's compliance* with recommendations of the substance abuse professional.
  (5) *Records related to education and training:*
      (i) *Materials on alcohol misuse* and controlled substance use awareness, including a copy of the employer's policy on alcohol misuse and controlled substance use;
      (ii) *Documentation of compliance* with the requirements of §382.601, including the driver's signed receipt of education materials;
      (iii) *Documentation of training* provided to supervisors for the purpose of qualifying the supervisors to make a determination concerning the need for alcohol and/or controlled substances testing based on reasonable suspicion;
      (iv) *Documentation of training* for breath alcohol technicians as required by §40.213(a) of this title; and
      (v) *Certification that any training* conducted under this part complies with the requirements for such training.

(6) *Administrative records* related to alcohol and controlled substances testing:
  (i) *Agreements with* collection site facilities, laboratories, breath alcohol technicians, screening test technicians, medical review officers, consortia, and third party service providers;
  (ii) *Names and positions of officials* and their role in the employer's alcohol and controlled substances testing program(s);
  (iii) *Semi-annual laboratory statistical summaries* of urinalysis required by §40.111(a) of this title; and
  (iv) *The employer's* alcohol and controlled substances testing policy and procedures.

(d) **Location of records.** All records required by this part shall be maintained as required by §390.31 of this subchapter and shall be made available for inspection at the employer's principal place of business within two business days after a request has been made by an authorized representative of the Federal Motor Carrier Safety Administration.

(e) **OMB control number.**
  (1) *The information collection requirements of this part* have been reviewed by the Office of Management and Budget pursuant to the Paperwork Reduction Act of 1995 (44 U.S.C. 3501 et seq.) and have been assigned OMB control number 2126-0012.
  (2) *The information collection requirements of this part* are found in the following sections: §§382.105, 382.113, 382.301, 382.303, 382.305, 382.307, 382.401, 382.403, 382.405, 382.409, 382.411, 382.601, 382.603.

§382.401 DOT Interpretations

Question 1: Many small school districts are affiliated through service units which are, in essence, a coalition of individual districts. Can these school districts have one common confidant for purposes of receiving results and keeping records?

Guidance: Yes. Employers may use agents to maintain the records, as long as they are in a secure location with controlled access. The employer must also make all records available for inspection at the employer's principal place of business within two business days after a request has been made by an FMCSA representative.

§382.403 Reporting of results in a management information system.

(a) **An employer shall prepare and maintain** a summary of the results of its alcohol and controlled substances testing programs performed under this part during the previous calendar year, when requested by the Secretary of Transportation, any DOT agency, or any State or local officials with regulatory authority over the employer or any of its drivers.

(b) **If an employer is notified, during the month of January,** of a request by the Federal Motor Carrier Safety Administration to report the employer's annual calendar year summary information, the employer shall prepare and submit the report to the FMCSA by March 15 of that year. The employer shall ensure that the annual summary report is accurate and received by March 15 at the location that the FMCSA specifies in its request. The employer must use the Management Information System (MIS) form and instructions as required by 49 CFR Part 40 (at §40.26 and Appendix H to Part 40). The employer may also use the electronic version of the MIS form provided by the DOT. The Administrator may designate means (e.g., electronic program transmitted via the Internet), other than hard-copy, for MIS form submission. For information on the electronic version of the form, see: http://www.fmcsa.dot.gov/safetyprogs/drugs/engtesting.htm.

(c) **When the report is submitted to the FMCSA** by mail or electronic transmission, the information requested shall be typed, except for the signature of the certifying official. Each employer shall ensure the accuracy and timeliness of each report submitted by the employer or a consortium.

(d) **If you have a covered employee** who performs multi-DOT agency functions (e.g., an employee drives a commercial motor vehicle and performs pipeline maintenance duties for the same employer), count the employee only on the MIS report for the DOT agency under which he or she is randomly tested. Normally, this will be the DOT agency under which the employee performs more than 50% of his or her duties. Employers may have to explain the testing data for these employees in the event of a DOT agency inspection or audit.

(e) **A service agent** (e.g., Consortia/Third party administrator as defined in 49 CFR 382.107) may prepare the MIS report on behalf of an employer. However, a company official (e.g., Designated employer representative) must certify the accuracy and completeness of the MIS report, no matter who prepares it.

§382.403 DOT Interpretations

Question 1: The FMCSA regulations are written on an annual calendar year basis. Will foreign motor carriers, using this system, work from July 1 to June 30, or is everything to be managed on a six-month basis for the first year and then fall into annual calendar years subsequently?

Guidance: All motor carriers must manage their programs and report results under §382.403, if requested by FMCSA, on a January 1 to December 31 basis. This means that foreign motor carriers will report July 1 to December 31 results the first applicable year.

§382.405 Access to facilities and records.

(a) **Except as required by law or expressly authorized** or required in this section, no employer shall release driver information that is contained in records required to be maintained under §382.401.

(b) **A driver is entitled, upon written request,** to obtain copies of any records pertaining to the driver's use of alcohol or controlled substances, including any records pertaining to his or her alcohol or controlled substances tests. The employer shall promptly provide the records requested by the driver. Access to a driver's records shall not be contingent upon payment for records other than those specifically requested.

(c) **Each employer shall permit access to all facilities** utilized in complying with the requirements of this part to the Secretary of Transportation, any DOT agency, or any State or local officials with regulatory authority over the employer or any of its drivers.

(d) **Each employer shall make available copies** of all results for employer alcohol and/or controlled substances testing conducted under this part and any other information pertaining to the employer's alcohol misuse and/or controlled substances use prevention program, when requested by the Secretary of Transportation, any DOT agency, or any State or local officials with regulatory authority over the employer or any of its drivers.

(e) **When requested by the National Transportation Safety Board** as part of an accident investigation, employers shall disclose information related to the employer's administration of a post-accident alcohol and/or controlled substance test administered following the accident under investigation.

(f) **Records shall be made available** to a subsequent employer upon receipt of a written request from a driver. Disclosure by the subsequent employer is permitted only as expressly authorized by the terms of the driver's request.

(g) **An employer may disclose information** required to be maintained under this part pertaining to a driver to the decision maker in a lawsuit, grievance, or administrative proceeding initiated by or on behalf of the individual, and arising from a positive DOT drug or alcohol test or a refusal to test (including, but not limited to, adulterated or substituted test results) of this part (including, but not limited to, a worker's compensation, unemployment compensation, or other proceeding relating to a benefit sought by the driver). Additionally, an employer may disclose information in criminal or civil actions in accordance with §40.323(a)(2) of this title.

(h) **An employer shall release information** regarding a driver's records as directed by the specific written consent of the driver authorizing release of the information to an identified person. Release of such information by the person receiving the information is permitted only in accordance with the terms of the employee's specific written consent as outlined in §40.321(b) of this title.

§382.405 DOT Interpretations

Question 1: May employers who are subject to other Federal agencies' regulations, such as the Nuclear Regulatory Commission, Department of Energy, Department of Defense, etc., allow those agencies to view or have access to test records required to be prepared and maintained by Parts 40 and/or 382?

Guidance: Federal agencies, other than those specifically provided for in §382.405, may have access to an employer's driver test records maintained in accordance with Parts 40 or 382 only when a specific, contemporaneous authorization for release of the test records is allowed by the driver.

Question 2: Must a motor carrier respond to a third-party administrator's request (as directed by the specific, written consent of the driver authorizing release of the information on behalf of an entity such as a motor carrier) to release driver information that is contained in records required to be maintained under §382.401?

Subpart D - Handling of Test Results, Records Retention, and Confidentiality §382.413

Guidance: Yes. However, the third-party administrator must comply with the conditions established concerning confidentiality, test results, and record keeping as stipulated in the "Notice: Guidance on the Role of Consortia and Third-Party Administrators (C/TPA) in DOT Drug and Alcohol Testing Programs" published on July 25, 1995, in Volume 60, No. 142, in the Federal Register. Motor carriers must comply completely with 49 CFR 382.413 and 382.405 as well as any applicable regulatory guidance. Please note that written consent must be obtained from the employee each time Part 382 information is provided to a C/TPA, the consent must be specific to the individual or entity to whom information is being provided, and that blanket or non-specific consents to release information are not allowed.

Question 3: May employers allow unions or the National Labor Relations Board to view or have access to test records required to be prepared and maintained by Parts 40 and/or 382, such as the list(s) of all employees actually tested?

Guidance: Unions and the National Labor Relations Board may have access to the list(s) of all employees in the random pool or the list(s) of all employees actually tested. The dates of births and SSNs must be removed from these lists prior to release. However, access to the employee's negative or positive test records maintained in accordance with Parts 40 or 382 can be granted only when a specific, contemporaneous authorization for release of the test records is allowed by the driver.

Question 4: May an employer (motor carrier) disclose information required to be maintained under 49 CFR Part 382 (pertaining to a driver) to the driver or the decision maker in a lawsuit, grievance, or other proceeding (including, but not limited to, worker's compensation, unemployment compensation) initiated by or on behalf of the driver, without the driver's written consent?

Guidance: Yes, a motor carrier has discretion without the driver's consent as provided by §382.405(g), to disclose information to the driver or the decision maker in a lawsuit, grievance, or other proceeding (including, but not limited to, worker's compensation, unemployment compensation) initiated by or on behalf of the driver concerning prohibited conduct under 49 CFR Part 382.

Also, an employer (motor carrier) may be required to provide the test result information pursuant to other Federal statutes or an order of a competent Federal jurisdiction, such as an administrative subpoena, as allowed by §382.405(a) without the driver's written consent.

Question 5: What is meant by the term "as required by law" in relation to State or local laws for disclosure of public records relating to a driver's testing information and test results?

Guidance: The term "as required by law" in §382.405(a) means Federal statutes or an order of a competent Federal jurisdiction, such as an administrative subpoena. The Omnibus Transportation Employee Testing Act of 1991, and the implementing regulations in Part 382, require that test results and medical information be confidential to the maximum extent possible. (Pub. L. 102-143, Title V, sec. 5(a)(1), 105 Stat. 959, codified at 49 U.S.C. 31306). In addition, the Act preempts inconsistent State or local government laws, rules, regulations, ordinances, standards, or orders that are inconsistent with the regulations issued under the Act.

The FMCSA believes the only State and local officials that may have access to the driver's records under §382.405(d) and 49 U.S.C. 31306, without the driver's written consent, are State or local government officials that have regulatory authority over an employer's (motor carrier's) alcohol and drug testing programs for purposes of enforcement of Part 382. Such State and local agencies conduct employer (motor carrier) compliance reviews under the FMCSA's Motor Carrier Safety Assistance Program (MCSAP) on the FMCSA's behalf in accordance with 49 CFR Part 350.

§382.407 Medical review officer notifications to the employer.

Medical review officers shall report the results of controlled substances tests to employers in accordance with the requirements of Part 40, Subpart G, of this title.

§382.409 Medical review officer record retention for controlled substances.

(a) A medical review officer or third party administrator shall maintain all dated records and notifications, identified by individual, for a minimum of five years for verified positive controlled substances test results.

(b) A medical review officer or third party administrator shall maintain all dated records and notifications, identified by individual, for a minimum of one year for negative and canceled controlled substances test results.

(c) No person may obtain the individual controlled substances test results retained by a medical review officer or third party administrator, and no medical review officer or third party administrator shall release the individual controlled substances test results of any driver to any person, without first obtaining a specific, written authorization from the tested driver. Nothing in this paragraph (c) shall prohibit a medical review officer or third party administrator from releasing, to the employer or to officials of the Secretary of Transportation, any DOT agency, or any State or local officials with regulatory authority over the controlled substances testing program under this part, the information delineated in Part 40, Subpart G, of this title.

§382.411 Employer notifications.

(a) An employer shall notify a driver of the results of a pre-employment controlled substances test conducted under this part, if the driver requests such results within 60 calendar days of being notified of the disposition of the employment application. An employer shall notify a driver of the results of random, reasonable suspicion and post-accident tests for controlled substances conducted under this part if the test results are verified positive. The employer shall also inform the driver which controlled substance or substances were verified as positive.

(b) The designated employer representative shall make reasonable efforts to contact and request each driver who submitted a specimen under the employer's program, regardless of the driver's employment status, to contact and discuss the results of the controlled substances test with a medical review officer who has been unable to contact the driver.

(c) The designated employer representative shall immediately notify the medical review officer that the driver has been notified to contact the medical review officer within 72 hours.

§382.413 Inquiries for alcohol and controlled substances information from previous employers.

Employers shall request alcohol and controlled substances information from previous employers in accordance with the requirements of §40.25 of this title.

§382.413 DOT Interpretations

Question 1: What is to be done if a previous employer does not make the records available in spite of the employer's request along with the driver's written consent?

Guidance: Employers must make a reasonable, good faith effort to obtain the information. If a previous employer refuses, in violation of §382.405, to release the information pursuant to the new employer's and driver's request, the new employer should note the attempt to obtain the information and place the note with the driver's other testing information (59 FR 7501, February 14, 1994).

Question 2: Within 14 days of first using a driver to perform safety-sensitive functions, an employer discovers that a driver had a positive controlled substances and/or 0.04 alcohol concentration test result within the previous two years. No records are discovered that the driver was evaluated by an SAP and has been released by an SAP for return to work. The employer removes the driver immediately from the performance of safety-sensitive duties. Is there a violation of the regulations?

Guidance: Based on the scenario as presented, only the driver is in violation of the rules.

Question 3: Must an employer investigate a driver's alcohol and drug testing background prior to January 1, 1995?

Guidance: No. The first implementation date of the Part 382 testing programs was January 1, 1995. §382.413 requires subsequent employers to obtain information retained by previous employers that the previous employers generated under a Part 382 testing program. Since no employer was allowed to conduct any type of alcohol or drug test under the authority of Part 382 prior to January 1, 1995, no tests conducted prior to 1995 are required to be obtained under §382.413. An employer may, however, under its own authority, request that a driver who was subject to Part 391 drug testing provide prior testing information.

Question 4: Must a motor carrier respond to a third-party administrator's request (as directed by the specific, written consent of the driver authorizing release of the information on behalf of an entity such as a motor carrier) to release driver information that is contained in records required to be maintained under §382.401?

Guidance: Yes. However, the third-party administrator must comply with the conditions established concerning confidentiality, test results, and record keeping as stipulated in the "Notice: Guidance on the Role of Consortia and Third-Party Administrators (C/TPA) in DOT Drug and Alcohol Testing Programs" published on July 25, 1995, in Volume 60, No. 142, in the Federal Register. Motor carriers must comply completely with §§382.413 and 382.405 as well as any applicable regulatory guidance. Please note that written consent must be obtained from the employee each time Part 382 information is provided to a C/TPA, that the consent must be specific to the individual or entity to whom information is being provided, and that blanket or non-specific consents to release information are not allowed.

Subpart E - Consequences for Drivers Engaging in Substance Use-Related Conduct

§382.501 Removal from safety-sensitive function.

(a) **Except as provided in Subpart F of this part,** no driver shall perform safety-sensitive functions, including driving a commercial motor vehicle, if the driver has engaged in conduct prohibited by Subpart B of this part or an alcohol or controlled substances rule of another DOT agency.

(b) **No employer shall permit any driver** to perform safety-sensitive functions; including driving a commercial motor vehicle, if the employer has determined that the driver has violated this section.

(c) **For purposes of this subpart,** commercial motor vehicle means a commercial motor vehicle in commerce as defined in §382.107, and a commercial motor vehicle in interstate commerce as defined in Part 390 of this subchapter.

§382.501 DOT Interpretations

Question 1: What work may the driver perform for an employer, if a driver violates the prohibitions in Subpart B?

Guidance: A driver who has violated the prohibitions of Subpart B may perform any duties for an employer that are not considered "safety-sensitive functions." This may include handling of materials exclusively in a warehouse, regardless of whether the materials are considered hazardous as long as safety-sensitive functions are not performed. Safety-sensitive functions may not be performed until the individual has been evaluated by an SAP, complied with any recommended treatment, has been re-evaluated by an SAP, has been allowed by the SAP to return to work and has passed a return to duty test.

§382.503 Required evaluation and testing.

No driver who has engaged in conduct prohibited by Subpart B of this part shall perform safety-sensitive functions, including driving a commercial motor vehicle, unless the driver has met the requirements of Part 40, Subpart O, of this title. No employer shall permit a driver who has engaged in conduct prohibited by Subpart B of this part to perform safety-sensitive functions, including driving a commercial motor vehicle, unless the driver has met the requirements of Part 40, Subpart O, of this title.

§382.503 DOT Interpretations

Question 1: If (1) a driver has a verified positive test result for controlled substances or an alcohol concentration of 0.04 or greater and (2) the driver subsequently obtains a verified negative result for controlled substances or a test result of less than 0.04 alcohol concentration without having been evaluated by a substance abuse professional (SAP), may the motor carrier accept the subsequent test results and ignore the requirement to refer the driver to an SAP for evaluation and possible treatment?

Guidance: No. A motor carrier must have a report from an SAP showing that the driver has been evaluated and may return to work because he or she:

(1) Does not need treatment,

(2) Needs part-time outpatient treatment, but may continue to drive while being treated on his or her off duty time; or

(3) Needed full-time outpatient or inpatient treatment, has received such treatment, and is ready to return to driving.

The driver must also pass a return-to-duty controlled substances or alcohol test that complies with all of the requirements of Parts 40 and 382.

§382.505 Other alcohol-related conduct.

(a) **No driver tested under the provisions of Subpart C** of this part who is found to have an alcohol concentration of 0.02 or greater but less than 0.04 shall perform or continue to perform safety-sensitive functions for an employer, including driving a commercial motor vehicle, nor shall an employer permit the driver to perform or continue to perform safety-sensitive functions, until the start of the driver's next regularly scheduled duty period, but not less than 24 hours following administration of the test.

(b) **Except as provided in paragraph (a) of this section,** no employer shall take any action under this part against a driver based solely on test results showing an alcohol concentration less than 0.04. This does not prohibit an employer with authority independent of this part from taking any action otherwise consistent with law.

§382.507 Penalties.

Any employer or driver who violates the requirements of this part shall be subject to the civil and/or criminal penalty provisions of 49 U.S.C. 521(b). In addition, any employer or driver who violates the requirements of 49 CFR Part 40 shall be subject to the civil and/or criminal penalty provisions of 49 U.S.C. 521(b).

§382.507 DOT Interpretations

Question 1: What is the fine or penalty for employers who refuse or fail to provide Part 382 testing information to a subsequent employer?

Guidance: Title 49 U.S.C. 521(b)(2)(A) provides for civil penalties not to exceed $500 for each instance of refusing or failing to provide the information required by §382.405. Criminal penalties may also be imposed under 49 U.S.C. 521(b)(6).

Subpart F - Alcohol Misuse and Controlled Substances Use Information, Training, and Referral

§382.601 Employer obligation to promulgate a policy on the misuse of alcohol and use of controlled substances.

(a) **General requirements.** Each employer shall provide educational materials that explain the requirements of this part and the employer's policies and procedures with respect to meeting these requirements.

   (1) *The employer shall ensure* that a copy of these materials is distributed to each driver prior to the start of alcohol and controlled substances testing under this part and to each driver subsequently hired or transferred into a position requiring driving a commercial motor vehicle.

   (2) *Each employer shall provide written notice* to representatives of employee organizations of the availability of this information.

(b) **Required content.** The materials to be made available to drivers shall include detailed discussion of at least the following:

   (1) *The identity of the person* designated by the employer to answer driver questions about the materials;

   (2) *The categories of drivers* who are subject to the provisions of this part;

   (3) *Sufficient information* about the safety-sensitive functions performed by those drivers to make clear what period of the work day the driver is required to be in compliance with this part;

   (4) *Specific information* concerning driver conduct that is prohibited by this part;

   (5) *The circumstances* under which a driver will be tested for alcohol and/or controlled substances under this part, including post-accident testing under §382.303(d);

   (6) *The procedures that will be used* to test for the presence of alcohol and controlled substances, protect the driver and the integrity of the testing processes, safeguard the validity of the test results, and ensure that those results are attributed to the correct driver, including post-accident information, procedures and instructions required by §382.303(d);

   (7) *The requirement that a driver submit* to alcohol and controlled substances tests administered in accordance with this part;

   (8) *An explanation of what constitutes* a refusal to submit to an alcohol or controlled substances test and the attendant consequences;

   (9) *The consequences for drivers* found to have violated Subpart B of this part, including the requirement that the driver be removed immediately from safety-sensitive functions, and the procedures under Part 40, Subpart O, of this title;

Subpart F - Alcohol Misuse & Controlled Substances Use Information, Training, & Referral §382.605

(10) *The consequences for drivers* found to have an alcohol concentration of 0.02 or greater but less than 0.04;

(11) *Information concerning the effects* of alcohol and controlled substances use on an individual's health, work, and personal life; signs and symptoms of an alcohol or a controlled substances problem (the driver's or a co-worker's); and available methods of intervening when an alcohol or a controlled substances problem is suspected, including confrontation, referral to any employee assistance program and/or referral to management.

(c) Optional provision. The materials supplied to drivers may also include information on additional employer policies with respect to the use of alcohol or controlled substances, including any consequences for a driver found to have a specified alcohol or controlled substances level, that are based on the employer's authority independent of this part. Any such additional policies or consequences must be clearly and obviously described as being based on independent authority.

(d) Certificate of receipt. Each employer shall ensure that each driver is required to sign a statement certifying that he or she has received a copy of these materials described in this section. Each employer shall maintain the original of the signed certificate and may provide a copy of the certificate to the driver.

§382.601 DOT Interpretations

Question 1: If a driver refuses to sign a statement certifying that he or she has received a copy of the educational materials required in §382.601 from their employer, will the employee be in violation of §382.601? May the driver's supervisor sign the certificate of receipt indicating that the employee refused to sign?

Guidance: The employer is responsible for ensuring that each driver signs a statement certifying that he or she has received a copy of the materials required in §382.601. The employer is required to maintain the original of the signed certificate and may provide a copy to the driver. The employer would be in violation if it uses a driver, who refuses to comply with §382.601, to perform any safety sensitive function, because §382.601 is a requirement placed on the employer. The employee would not be in violation if he or she drove without signing for the receipt of the policy. It is not permissible for the driver's supervisor to sign the certificate of receipt; however, it is advisable for the employer to note the attempt, the refusal, and the consequences of such action. Also, please note that the signing of the policy by the employee is in no way an acknowledgment that the policy itself complies with the regulations.

Question 2: Does §382.601 require employers to provide educational materials and policies and procedures to drivers after the initial distribution of required educational materials?

Guidance: No.

§382.603 Training for supervisors.

Each employer shall ensure that all persons designated to supervise drivers receive at least 60 minutes of training on alcohol misuse and receive at least an additional 60 minutes of training on controlled substances use. The training will be used by the supervisors to determine whether reasonable suspicion exists to require a driver to undergo testing under §382.307. The training shall include the physical, behavioral, speech, and performance indicators of probable alcohol misuse and use of controlled substances. Recurrent training for supervisory personnel is not required.

§382.603 DOT Interpretations

Question 1: Does §382.603 require employers to provide recurrent training to supervisory personnel?

Guidance: No.

Question 2: May an employer accept proof of supervisory training for a supervisor from another employer?

Guidance: Yes.

§382.605 Referral, evaluation, and treatment.

The requirements for referral, evaluation, and treatment must be performed in accordance with 49 CFR Part 40, Subpart O.

§382.605 DOT Interpretations

Question 1: Must an SAP evaluation be conducted in person or may it be conducted telephonically?

Guidance: Both the initial and follow-up SAP evaluations are clinical processes that must be conducted face-to-face. Body language and appearance offer important physical cues vital to the evaluation process. Tremors, needle marks, dilated pupils, exaggerated movements, yellow eyes, glazed or bloodshot eyes, lack of eye contact, a physical slowdown or hyperactivity, appearance, posture, carriage, and ability to communicate in person are vital components that cannot be determined telephonically. In-person sessions carry with them the added advantage of the SAP's being able to provide immediate attention to individuals who may be a danger to themselves or others.

Question 2: Are employers required to provide intervention and treatment for drivers who have a substance abuse problem or only refer drivers to be evaluated by an SAP?

Guidance: An employer who wants to continue to use or hire a driver who has violated the prohibitions in Subpart B in the past must ensure that a driver has complied with any SAP's recommended treatment prior to the driver returning to safety-sensitive functions. However, employers must only refer to an SAP drivers who have tested positive for controlled substances, tested 0.04 or greater alcohol concentration, or have violated other prohibitions in Subpart B.

Question 3: Under the DOT rules, must an SAP be certified by the DOT in order to perform SAP functions?

Guidance: The DOT does not certify, license, or approve individual SAPs. The SAP must be able to demonstrate to the employer qualifications necessary to meet the DOT rule requirements. The DOT rules define the SAP to be a licensed physician (medical doctor or doctor of osteopathy), a licensed or certified psychologist, a licensed or certified social worker, or a licensed or certified employee assistance professional. All must have knowledge of and clinical experience in the diagnosis and treatment of substance abuse-related disorders (the degrees and certificates alone do not confer this knowledge). In addition, alcohol and drug abuse counselors certified by the National Association of Alcoholism and Drug Abuse Counselors Certification Commission, a national organization that imposes qualification standards for treatment of alcohol-related disorders, are included in the SAP definition.

Question 4: Are employers required to refer a discharged employee to an SAP?

Guidance: The rules require an employer to advise the employee, who engages in conduct prohibited under the DOT rules, of the available resources for evaluation and treatment including the names, addresses, and telephone numbers of SAPs and counseling and treatment programs. In the scenario where the employer discharges the employee, that employer would be considered to be in compliance with the rules if it provided the list to the employee and ensured that SAPs on the list were qualified. This employer has no further obligation (e.g., to facilitate referral to the SAP; ensure that the employee receives an SAP evaluation; pay for the evaluation; or seek to obtain, or maintain the SAP evaluation synopsis).

Question 5: How will the SAP evaluation process differ if the employee is discharged by the employer rather than retained following a rule violation?

Guidance: After engaging in prohibited conduct and prior to performing safety-sensitive duties in any DOT regulated industry, the employee must receive an SAP evaluation. And, when assistance with a problem is clinically indicated, the employee must receive that assistance and demonstrate successful compliance with the recommendation as evaluated through an SAP follow-up evaluation.

The SAP process has the potential to be more complicated when the employee is not retained by the employer. In such circumstances, the SAP will likely not have a connection with the employer for whom the employee worked nor have immediate access to the exact nature of the rule violation. In addition, the SAP may have to hold the synopsis of evaluation and recommendation for assistance report until asked by the employee to forward that information to a new employer who wishes to return the individual to safety-sensitive duties. In some cases, the SAP may provide the evaluation, referral to a treatment professional, and the follow-up evaluation before the employee has received an offer of employment. This circumstance may require the SAP to hold all reports until asked by the individual to forward them to the new employer. If the new employer has a designated SAP, that SAP may conduct the follow-up evaluation despite the fact that the employee's SAP has already done so. In other words, a new employer may determine to its own satisfaction (e.g., by having the prospective employee receive a follow-up SAP evaluation utilizing the employer's designated SAP) that the prospective employee has demonstrated successful compliance with recommended treatment.

Question 6: Do community lectures and self-help groups qualify as education and/or treatment?

Guidance: Self-help groups and community lectures qualify as education but do not qualify as treatment. While self-help groups such as Alcoholics Anonymous (AA) and Narcotics Anonymous (NA) are crucial to many employees' recovery process, these efforts are not considered to be treatment programs in and of themselves. However, they can serve as vital adjuncts in support of treatment program efforts. AA and NA programs require a level of anonymity which makes reporting client progress and prognosis for recovery impossible. If the client provides permission, AA and NA sponsors can provide attendance status reports to the SAP. Therefore, if a client is referred to one of these groups or to community lectures as a result of the SAP evaluation, the employee's attendance, when it can be independently validated, can satisfy an SAP recommendation for education as well as a gauge for determining successful compliance with a treatment program when both education and treatment are recommended by the SAP's evaluation.

Question 7: Can an employee who has violated the rules return to safety-sensitive functions prior to receiving an SAP evaluation?

Guidance: The employee is prohibited from performing any DOT regulated safety-sensitive function until being evaluated by the SAP. An employer is prohibited from permitting the employee to engage in safety-sensitive duties until evaluated. If the evaluation reveals that assistance is needed, the employee must receive the assistance, be re-evaluated by the SAP (and determined to have demonstrated successful compliance with the recommendation), and pass a return-to-duty alcohol and/or drug test prior to performing safety-sensitive duties.

Question 8: Can an employer overrule an SAP treatment recommendation?

Guidance: No. If found to need assistance, the employee cannot return to safety-sensitive functions until an SAP's follow-up evaluation determines that the employee has demonstrated successful compliance with the recommended treatment. An employer who returns a worker to safety-sensitive duties when the employee has not complied with the SAP's recommendation is in violation of the DOT rule and is, therefore, subject to a penalty.

Question 9: Is an employer obligated to return an employee to safety-sensitive duty following the SAP's finding during the follow-up evaluation that the employee has demonstrated successful compliance with the treatment recommendation?

Guidance: Demonstrating successful compliance with prescribed treatment and testing negative on the return-to-duty alcohol test and/or drug test, are not guarantees of employment or of return to work in a safety-sensitive position; they are preconditions the employee must meet in order to be considered for hiring or reinstatement to safety-sensitive duties by an employer.

Question 10: Can an employee receive the follow-up from an SAP who did not conduct the initial SAP evaluation?

Guidance: Although it is preferable for the same SAP to conduct both evaluations, this will not be realistic in some situations. For instance, the initial SAP may no longer be in the area, still under contract to the employer, or still hired by the employer to conduct the service. Additionally, the employee may have moved from the area to a new location. In all cases, the employer responsibility is to ensure that both the initial SAP and the follow-up SAP are qualified according to the DOT rules.

Question 11: Who is responsible for reimbursing the SAP for services rendered? Who is responsible for paying for follow-up testing recommended by the SAP?

Guidance: The DOT rules do not affix responsibility for payment for SAP services upon any single party. The DOT has left discussions regarding payment to employer policies and to labor-management agreements. Therefore, in some instances, this issue has become part of labor-management negotiations.

Some employers have hired or contracted staff for the purpose of providing SAP services. For some employees, especially those who have been released following a violation, payment for SAP services will become their responsibility. In any case, the SAP should be suitable to the employer who chooses to return the employee to safety-sensitive functions. Employer policies should address this payment issue.

Regarding follow-up testing recommended by the SAP, when an employer decides to return the employee to safety-sensitive duty, the employer is essentially determining that the costs associated with hiring and training a new employee exceeds the costs associated with conducting follow-up testing of the returning employee. In any case, whether the employer pays or the employee pays, if the employee returns to performance of safety-sensitive functions, the employer must ensure that follow-up testing occurs as required. The employer will be held accountable if the follow-up testing plan is not followed.

Question 12: Can the SAP direct that an employee be tested for both alcohol and drugs for the return-to-duty test and during the follow-up testing program?

Guidance: If the SAP determines that an employee referred for alcohol misuse also uses drugs, or that an employee referred for drugs use also misuses alcohol, the SAP can require that the individual be tested for both substances. The SAP's decision to test for both can be based upon information gathered during the initial evaluation, the SAP's consultation contacts with the treatment program, and/or the information presented during the follow-up evaluation.

Question 13: Can random testing be substituted for required follow-up testing?

Guidance: Follow-up testing is directly related to a rule violation and subsequent return to safety-sensitive duty. Random tests are independent of rule violations. Therefore, the two test types are to be separated — one cannot be substituted for the other or be conducted in lieu of the other. Follow-up testing should be unpredictable, unannounced, and conducted not less than six times throughout the first 12 months after the employee returns to safety-sensitive functions. Follow-up testing can last up to 60 months. An employee subject to follow-up testing will continue to be subject to an employer's random testing program.

Question 14: If a company has several employees in follow-up testing, can those employees be placed into a follow-up random testing pool and selected for follow-up testing on a random basis?

Guidance: Follow-up testing is not to be conducted in a random way. An employee's follow-up testing program is to be individualized and designed to ensure that the employee is tested the appropriate number of times as directed by the SAP. Random testing is neither individualized nor can it ensure that the employee receives the requisite number of tests.

Question 15: What actions are to occur if an employee tests positive while in the follow-up testing program?

Guidance: Employees testing positive while in follow-up testing are subject to the same specific DOT operating administration rules as if they tested positive on the initial test. In addition, the employees are subject to employer policies related to second violations of DOT rules.

Subpart F - Alcohol Misuse & Controlled Substances Use Information, Training, & Referral §382.605

Question 16: Can an SAP recommend that six follow-up tests be conducted in less than six months and then be suspended after all six are conducted?

Guidance: Follow-up testing must be conducted a minimum of six times during the first twelve months following the employee's return to safety-sensitive functions. The intent of this requirement is that testing be spread throughout the 12 month period and not be grouped into a shorter interval. When the SAP believes that the employee needs to be tested more frequently during the first months after returning to duty, the SAP may recommend more than the minimum six tests or can direct the employer to conduct more of the six tests during the first months rather than toward the latter months of the year.

Question 17: Can you clarify the DOT's intent with respect to an SAP's determination that an individual needs education?

Guidance: An SAP's decision that an individual needs an education program constitutes a clinically based determination that the individual requires assistance in resolving problems with alcohol misuse and controlled substances use. Therefore, the SAP is prohibited from referring the individual to her or his own practice for this recommended education unless exempted by DOT rules.

Question 18: In rare circumstances, it is necessary to refer an individual immediately for inpatient substance abuse services. May the SAP provide direct treatment services or refer the individual to services provided by a treatment facility with which he or she is affiliated, or must the inpatient provider refer the individual to another provider?

Guidance: SAPs are prohibited from referring an employee to themselves or to any program with which they are financially connected. SAP referrals to treatment programs must not give the impression of a conflict of interest. However, an SAP is not prohibited from referring an employee for assistance through a public agency; the employer or person under contract to provide treatment on behalf of the employer; the sole source of therapeutically appropriate treatment under the employee's health insurance program; or the sole source of therapeutically appropriate reasonably accessible to the employee.

Question 19: What arrangement for SAP services would be acceptable in geographical areas where no qualified SAP is readily available?

Guidance: The driver must be given the names, addresses, and phone numbers of the nearest SAPs. Because evaluation by a qualified SAP rarely takes more than one diagnostic session, the requirement for an in-person evaluation is not unreasonable, even if it must be conducted some distance from the employee's home.

Question 20: May an employee who tests positive be retained in a non-driving capacity?

Guidance: Yes. Before an employee returns to performing safety-sensitive functions, the requirements of §382.605 must be met.

Question 21: Are foreign motor carriers required to have an employee assistance program?

Guidance: No. The employee assistance program was an element of the original FMCSA drug testing program under 49 CFR Part 391, which has been superseded by 49 CFR Part 382. All motor carriers under Part 382 alcohol and drug testing regulations must refer drivers, who operate in the U.S. and violate the FMCSA's alcohol and drug testing regulations, to a substance abuse professional.

Special Topics — Responsibility for Payment for Testing

Question 1: Who is responsible for paying for any testing under the alcohol and drug testing program, the employer or the driver?

Guidance: Part 382 is silent as to the responsibility for paying for testing required under the rule. The employer remains responsible at all times for ensuring compliance with the rule, regardless of who pays for testing.

Special Topics — Multiple Service Providers

Question 1: May an employer use more than one MRO, BAT, or SAP?

Guidance: Yes.

Special Topics — Biennial (Periodic) Testing Requirements

Question 1: May an employer perform testing beyond that required by the DOT?

Guidance: An employer may perform any testing provided it is consistent with applicable law and agreements, and is not represented as a DOT test.

Question 2: Does Part 382 require a CMV driver to carry proof of compliance with Part 382 and Part 40?

Guidance: No. The drug and alcohol testing is employer-based and proof of compliance must be maintained by the employer. The only certificate that is required to be in the driver's possession while operating a CMV is the medical examiner's certificate required in §391.41(a) and, if applicable, a waiver of certain physical defects issued under §391.49.

Part 382 - Controlled Substances and Alcohol Use and Testing

Notes

Part 383 - Commercial Driver's License Standards; Requirements and Penalties

(Page 59 in the Driver Edition)

Subpart A - General

§383.1 Purpose and scope.

(a) The purpose of this part is to help reduce or prevent truck and bus accidents, fatalities, and injuries by requiring drivers to have a single commercial motor vehicle driver's license and by disqualifying drivers who operate commercial motor vehicles in an unsafe manner.

(b) This part:
- **(1)** *Prohibits a commercial motor vehicle driver* from having more than one commercial motor vehicle driver's license;
- **(2)** *Requires a driver* to notify the driver's current employer and the driver's State of domicile of certain convictions;
- **(3)** *Requires that a driver* provide previous employment information when applying for employment as an operator of a commercial motor vehicle;
- **(4)** *Prohibits an employer* from allowing a person with a suspended license to operate a commercial motor vehicle;
- **(5)** *Establishes periods of disqualification and penalties* for those persons convicted of certain criminal and other offenses and serious traffic violations, or subject to any suspensions, revocations, or cancellations of certain driving privileges;
- **(6)** *Establishes testing and licensing requirements* for commercial motor vehicle operators;
- **(7)** *Requires States to give knowledge and skills tests* to all qualified applicants for commercial drivers' licenses which meet the Federal standard;
- **(8)** *Sets forth commercial motor vehicle groups and endorsements;*
- **(9)** *Sets forth the knowledge and skills test requirements* for the motor vehicle groups and endorsements;
- **(10)** *Sets forth the Federal standards* for procedures, methods, and minimum passing scores for States and others to use in testing and licensing commercial motor vehicle operators; and
- **(11)** *Establishes requirements* for the State issued commercial license documentation.

§383.3 Applicability.

(a) The rules in this part apply to every person who operates a commercial motor vehicle (CMV) in interstate, foreign, or intrastate commerce, to all employers of such persons, and to all States.

(b) The exceptions contained in §390.3(f) of this subchapter do not apply to this part. The employers and drivers identified in §390.3(f) must comply with the requirements of this part, unless otherwise provided in this section.

(c) Exception for certain military drivers. Each State must exempt from the requirements of this part individuals who operate CMVs for military purposes. This exception is applicable to active duty military personnel; members of the military reserves; member of the national guard on active duty, including personnel on full-time national guard duty, personnel on part-time national guard training, and national guard military technicians (civilians who are required to wear military uniforms); and active duty U.S. Coast Guard personnel. This exception is not applicable to U.S. Reserve technicians.

(d) Exception for farmers, firefighters, emergency response vehicle drivers, and drivers removing snow and ice. A State may, at its discretion, exempt individuals identified in paragraphs (d)(1), (d)(2), and (d)(3) of this section from the requirements of this part. The use of this waiver is limited to the driver's home State unless there is a reciprocity agreement with adjoining States.

- **(1)** *Operators of a farm vehicle which is:*
  - **(i)** *Controlled and operated by a farmer,* including operation by employees or family members;
  - **(ii)** *Used to transport* either agricultural products, farm machinery, farm supplies, or both to or from a farm;
  - **(iii)** *Not used in the operations* of a common or contract motor carrier; and
  - **(iv)** *Used within 241 kilometers (150 miles) of the farmer's farm.*
- **(2)** *Firefighters and other persons who operate CMVs* which are necessary to the preservation of life or property or the execution of emergency governmental functions, are equipped with audible and visual signals and are not subject to normal traffic regulation. These vehicles include fire trucks, hook and ladder trucks, foam or water transport trucks, police SWAT team vehicles, ambulances, or other vehicles that are used in response to emergencies.
- **(3) (i)** *A driver,* employed by an eligible unit of local government, operating a commercial motor vehicle within the boundaries of that unit for the purpose of removing snow or ice from a roadway by plowing, sanding, or salting, if
  - **[A]** *The properly licensed employee* who ordinarily operates a commercial motor vehicle for these purposes is unable to operate the vehicle; or
  - **[B]** *The employing governmental entity* determines that a snow or ice emergency exists that requires additional assistance.
  - **(ii)** *This exemption* shall not preempt State laws and regulations concerning the safe operation of commercial motor vehicles.

(e) Restricted commercial drivers license (CDL) for certain drivers in the State of Alaska.
- **(1)** *The State of Alaska* may, at its discretion, waive only the following requirements of this part and issue a CDL to each driver that meets the conditions set forth in paragraphs (e)(2) and (3) of this section:
  - **(i)** *The knowledge tests standards* for testing procedures and methods of Subpart H, but must continue to administer knowledge tests that fulfill the content requirements of Subpart G for all applicants;
  - **(ii)** *All the skills test requirements;* and
  - **(iii)** *The requirement under §383.153(a)(4)* to have a photograph on the license document.
- **(2)** *Drivers of CMVs in the State of Alaska* must operate exclusively over roads that meet both of the following criteria to be eligible for the exception in paragraph (e)(1) of this section:
  - **(i)** *Such roads are not connected* by land highway or vehicular way to the land-connected State highway system; and
  - **(ii)** *Such roads are not connected* to any highway or vehicular way with an average daily traffic volume greater than 499.
- **(3)** *Any CDL issued* under the terms of this paragraph must carry two restrictions:
  - **(i)** *Holders may not operate CMVs over roads* other than those specified in paragraph (e)(2) of this section; and
  - **(ii)** *The license is not valid for CMV operation* outside the State of Alaska.

(f) Restricted CDL for certain drivers in farm-related service industries.
- **(1)** *A State may, at its discretion,* waive the required knowledge and skills tests of Subpart H of this part and issue restricted CDLs to employees of these designated farm-related service industries:
  - **(i)** *Agri-chemical businesses;*
  - **(ii)** *Custom harvesters;*
  - **(iii)** *Farm retail outlets and suppliers;*
  - **(iv)** *Livestock feeders.*
- **(2)** *A restricted CDL issued pursuant to this paragraph* shall meet all the requirements of this part, except Subpart H of this part. A restricted CDL issued pursuant to this paragraph shall be accorded the same reciprocity as a CDL meeting all of the requirements of this part. The restrictions imposed upon the issuance of this restricted CDL shall not limit a person's use of the CDL in a non-CMV during either validated or non-validated periods, nor shall the CDL affect a State's power to administer its driver licensing program for operators of vehicles other than CMVs.
- **(3)** *A State issuing a CDL* under the terms of this paragraph must restrict issuance as follows:
  - **(i)** *Applicants must have a good driving record* as defined in this paragraph. Drivers who have not held any motor vehicle operator's license for at least one year shall not be eligible for this CDL. Drivers who have between one and two years of driving experience must demonstrate a good driving record for their entire driving history. Drivers with more than two years of driving experience must have a good driving record for the two most recent years. For the purposes of this paragraph, the term *good driving record* means that an applicant:
    - **[A]** *Has not had more than one license* (except in the instances specified in §383.21);
    - **[B]** *Has not had any license suspended, revoked, or canceled;*
    - **[C]** *Has not had any conviction* for any type of motor vehicle for the disqualifying offenses contained in §383.51(b);

[D] Has not had any conviction for any type of motor vehicle for serious traffic violations; and

[E] Has not had any conviction for a violation of State or local law relating to motor vehicle traffic control (other than a parking violation) arising in connection with any traffic accident, and has no record of an accident in which he/she was at fault.

(ii) *Restricted CDLs* shall have the same renewal cycle as unrestricted CDLs, but shall be limited to the seasonal period or periods as defined by the State of licensure, provided that the total number of calendar days in any 12-month period for which the restricted CDL is valid does not exceed 180. If a State elects to provide for more than one seasonal period, the restricted CDL is valid for commercial motor vehicle operation only during the currently approved season, and must be revalidated for each successive season. Only one seasonal period of validity may appear on the license document at a time. The good driving record must be confirmed prior to any renewal or revalidation.

(iii) *Restricted CDL holders* are limited to operating Group B and C vehicles, as described in Subpart F of this part.

(iv) *Restricted CDLs* shall not be issued with *any* endorsements on the license document. Only the limited tank vehicle and hazardous materials endorsement privileges that the restricted CDL automatically confers and are described in paragraph (f)(3)(v) of this section are permitted.

(v) *Restricted CDL holders* may not drive vehicles carrying any placardable quantities of hazardous materials, except for diesel fuel in quantities of 3,785 liters (1,000 gallons) or less; liquid fertilizers (i.e., plant nutrients) in vehicles or implements of husbandry in total quantities of 11,355 liters (3,000 gallons) or less; and solid fertilizers (i.e., solid plant nutrients) that are not transported with any organic substance.

(vi) *Restricted CDL holders* may not hold an unrestricted CDL at the same time.

(vii) *Restricted CDL holders* may not operate a commercial motor vehicle beyond 241 kilometers (150 miles) from the place of business or the farm currently being served.

(g) Restricted CDL for certain drivers in the pyrotechnic industry.

(1) *A State may,* at its discretion, waive the required hazardous materials knowledge tests of Subpart H of this part and issue restricted CDLs to part-time drivers operating commercial motor vehicles transporting less than 227 kilograms (500 pounds) of fireworks classified as DOT Class 1.3G explosives.

(2) *A State issuing a CDL* under the terms of this paragraph must restrict issuance as follows:

(i) *The GVWR of the vehicle to be operated* must be less than 4,537 kilograms (10,001 pounds);

(ii) *If a State believes, at its discretion,* that the training required by §172.704 of this title adequately prepares part-time drivers meeting the other requirements of this paragraph to deal with fireworks and the other potential dangers posed by fireworks transportation and use, the State may waive the hazardous materials knowledge tests of Subpart H of this part. The State may impose any requirements it believes is necessary to ensure itself that a driver is properly trained pursuant to §172.704 of this title.

(iii) *A restricted CDL document* issued pursuant to this paragraph shall have a statement clearly imprinted on the face of the document that is substantially similar as follows: For use as a CDL only during the period from June 30 through July 6 for purposes of transporting less than 227 kilograms (500 pounds) of fireworks classified as DOT Class 1.3G explosives in a vehicle with a GVWR of less than 4,537 kilograms (10,001 pounds).

(3) *A restricted CDL* issued pursuant to this paragraph shall meet all the requirements of this part, except those specifically identified. A restricted CDL issued pursuant to this paragraph shall be accorded the same reciprocity as a CDL meeting all of the requirements of this part. The restrictions imposed upon the issuance of this restricted CDL shall not limit a person's use of the CDL in a non-CMV during either validated or non-validated periods, nor shall the CDL affect a State's power to administer its driver licensing program for operators of vehicles other than CMVs.

(4) *Restricted CDLs* shall have the same renewal cycle as unrestricted CDLs, but shall be limited to the seasonal period of June 30 through July 6 of each year or a lesser period as defined by the State of licensure.

(5) *Persons who operate* commercial motor vehicles during the period from July 7 through June 29 for purposes of transporting less than 227 kilograms (500 pounds) of fireworks classified as DOT Class 1.3G explosives in a vehicle with a GVWR of less than 4,537 kilograms (10,001 pounds) and who also operate such vehicles for the same purposes during the period June 30 through July 6 shall not be issued a restricted CDL pursuant to this paragraph.

§383.3 DOT Interpretations

Question 1: Are school and church bus drivers required to obtain a CDL?
Guidance: Yes, if they drive vehicles designed to transport 16 or more people.

Question 2: Do mechanics, shop help, and other occasional drivers need a CDL if they are operating a CMV or if they only test drive a vehicle?
Guidance: Yes, if the vehicle is operated or test-driven on a public highway.

Question 3: Does Part 383 apply to drivers of recreational vehicles?
Guidance: No, if the vehicle is used strictly for non-business purposes.

Question 4: Does Part 383 apply to drivers of vehicles used in "van pools"?
Guidance: Yes, if the vehicle is designed to transport 16 or more people.

Question 5: May a person operate a CMV wholly on private property, not open to public travel, without a CDL?
Guidance: Yes.

Question 6: Does off-road motorized construction equipment meet the definitions of "motor vehicle" and "commercial motor vehicle" as used in sections 383.5 and 390.5?
Guidance: No. Off-road motorized construction equipment is outside the scope of these definitions.

Question 7: What types of equipment are included in the category of off-road motorized construction equipment?
Guidance: The definition of off-road motorized construction equipment is to be narrowly construed and limited to equipment which, by its design and function is obviously not intended for use on a public road. Examples of such equipment include motor scrapers, backhoes, motor graders, compactors, tractors, trenchers, bulldozers and railroad track maintenance cranes.

Question 8: Do operators of motorized cranes and vehicles used to pump cement at construction sites have to meet the testing and licensing requirements of the CDL program?
Guidance: Yes, because such vehicles are designed to be operated on the public highways and therefore do not qualify as off-road construction equipment. The fact that these vehicles are only driven for limited distances, at less than normal highway speeds and/or incidental to their primary function, does not exempt the operators from the CDL requirements.

Question 9: May a State require persons operating recreational vehicles or other CMVs used by family members for non-business purposes to have a CDL?
Guidance: Yes. States may extend the CDL requirements to recreational vehicles.

Question 10: Do drivers of either a tractor trailer or straight truck that is converted into a mobile office need a CDL?
Guidance: Yes, if the vehicle meets the definition of a CMV.

Question 11: Do State motor vehicle inspectors who drive trucks and motorcoaches on an infrequent basis and for short distances as part of their job have to obtain a CDL?
Guidance: Yes.

Question 12: Are State, county, and municipal workers operating CMVs required to obtain CDLs?
Guidance: Yes, unless they are waived by the State under the firefighting and emergency equipment exemption in §383.3(d).

Question 13: This question, originally published in the 4/4/97 Federal Register, has been superceded. See Section §383.3, Question 32 (below) for new guidance.

Question 14: Are employees of any governmental agency who drive emergency response vehicles that transport HM in quantities requiring placarding subject to the CDL regulations?

Guidance: No, as long as the vehicle does not meet the weight/configuration thresholds for Groups A or B (in §383.91). However, under the HMTUSA of 1990, when a Federal, State, or local government agency "offers HM for transportation in commerce or transports HM in furtherance of a commercial enterprise," its vehicles are subject to the placarding requirements of Part 172, Subpart F. Vehicles that are controlled and operated by government agencies in the conduct of governmental functions normally are not subject to placarding, since governmental activities usually are not commercial enterprises. Based on the above, local police emergency responders driving a vehicle having a gross vehicle or combination weight rating under 26,001 pounds do not need a CDL, according to the Federal minimum standards, when transporting HM as a function of their agency. The drivers should check with their State licensing agency to determine what class of license the State may require to operate the vehicles.

Question 15: Are public transit employees known as "hostlers," who maintain and park transit buses on transit system property, subject to CDL requirements?

Guidance: No, unless operating on public roads.

Question 16: Are non-military amphibious landing craft that are usually used in water but occasionally used on a public highway CMVs?

Guidance: Yes, if they are designed to transport 16 or more people.

Question 17: Are students who will be trained to be motor vehicle operators subject to alcohol and drug testing? Are they required to obtain a CDL in order to operate training vehicles provided by the school?

Guidance: Yes. §382.107 includes the following definitions:

"Employer" means any person (including the United States, a State, District of Columbia or a political subdivision of a State) who owns or leases a CMV or assigns persons to operate such a vehicle. The term employer includes an employer's agents, officers and representatives.

"Driver" means any person who operates a CMV. * * *

Truck and bus driver training schools meet the definition of an employer because they own or lease CMVs and assign students to operate them at appropriate points in their training. Similarly, students who actually operate CMVs to complete their course work qualify as drivers.

The CDL regulations provide that "no person shall operate" a CMV before passing the written and driving tests required for that vehicle (§383.23(a)(1)). Virtually all of the vehicles used for training purposes meet the definition of a CMV, and student drivers must therefore obtain a CDL.

Question 18: May States exempt motor carriers which operate wholly in intrastate commerce from the Federal HMRs, thus exempting from the CDL requirement the driver of an unplacarded vehicle with a GVWR of less than 26,001 pounds?

Guidance: The HMRs apply to motor carriers in intrastate commerce only if they transport hazardous wastes, hazardous substances, flammable cryogenic liquids in portable tanks and cargo tanks, and marine pollutants (as those terms are defined in the HMRs) (see 49 CFR 171.1(a)(3)). Such carriers transporting any other cargo are not required to use HM placards, even if the cargo qualifies as hazardous under the Federal HMRs. Unless the vehicles used by these carriers had GVWRs of 26,001 pounds or more, they would not meet either the placarding or the GVWR test in the jurisdictional definition of a CMV (§383.5), and the driver would be exempt from the CDL requirements.

However, if the State has adopted the HMRs, or the placarding requirements of 49 CFR Part 172, as regulations applicable to intrastate commerce, then the drivers of all vehicles required to use placards must also have CDLs.

If the State promulgates its own rules for the regulation of HM in intrastate commerce, instead of adopting the HMRs, and those rules are approved by the FMCSA under 49 CFR 355.21(c)(3) and paragraph 3(d) of the Tolerance Guidelines (49 CFR Part 350, Appendix C), the drivers of vehicles with GVWRs of less than 26,001 pounds transporting such materials in intrastate commerce are required to obtain CDLs only if State law requires the use of placards.

Question 19: Must a civilian operator of a CMV, as defined in §383.5, who operates wholly within a military facility open to public travel, have a CDL?

Guidance: Yes. The CDL requirement applies to every person who operates a CMV in interstate, foreign, or intrastate commerce. Driving a CMV on a road, street, or way which is open to public travel, even though privately-owned or subject to military control, is *prima facie* evidence of operation in commerce.

Question 20: Does the FMCSA include the Space Cargo Transportation System (SCTS) off-road motorized military equipment under the definitions of "motor vehicle" and "commercial motor vehicle" as used in §383.5?

Guidance: No. Although the SCTS has vehicular aspects (it is mechanically propelled on wheels), the SCTS is obviously incompatible with highway traffic and is found only at locations adjacent to military bases in California and Florida, and is operated by skilled technicians. The SCTS is moved to and from its point of manufacture to its launch site by "driving" the "vehicles" short distances on public roads at speeds of five MPH or less. This is only incidental to their primary functions; the SCTS is not designed to operate in traffic; and its mechanical manipulation often requires a different set of knowledge and skills. In most instances, the SCTS has to be specially marked, escorted, and attended by numerous observers.

Question 21: Are police officers who operate buses and vans which are designed to carry 16 or more persons and are used to transport police officers during demonstrations and other crowd control activities required to obtain a CDL?

Guidance: Yes. The CMVSA applies to anyone who operates a CMV, including employees of Federal, State, and local governments. Crowd control activities do not meet the conditions for a waiver of operators of firefighting and other emergency vehicles in §383.3(d).

Question 22: May fuel be considered "farm supplies" as used in §383.3(d)(1)?

Guidance: Yes. The decision to grant the waiver is left to each individual State.

Question 23: Is the transportation of seed-cotton modules from the cotton field to the gin by a module transport vehicle considered a form of custom harvesting activity that may be included under the FRSI waiver (§383.3(f))?

Guidance: Yes. The transportation of seed-cotton modules from field to gin may, at the State's discretion, be considered as custom harvesting and therefore eligible for the FRSI waiver. However, cotton ginning operations as an industry and, specifically the transport of cotton from the gin, are not eligible activities under the FRSI waiver because these activities are not considered appropriate elements of custom harvesting.

Question 24: Does the amendment of the CMVSA by the Motor Carrier Act of 1991 exempt all custom harvesting operations from the CDL requirements or only the operation of combines?

Guidance: Section 4010 of the Motor Carrier Act of 1991 (Title IV of Pub. L. 102-240, 105 Stat 1914, 2156, December 18, 1991) modifies the definition of a "motor vehicle" in 49 U.S.C. 31301(11) by excluding "custom harvesting farm machinery" from the definition. The conference report clarifies the intent of the exclusion by stating: "The substitute [provision] removes custom harvesting farm machinery from the Act. Operators of such machinery are not covered by the Commercial Motor Vehicle Safety Act of 1986. A State, however, may still impose a requirement for a commercial driver's license if it so desires. The change does not apply to vehicles used to transport this type of machinery." (H.R. Conf. Rep. No. 404, 102d Cong., 1st Sess. 449 (1991)).

Therefore, the intent of Congress was only to exempt operators of combines and other equipment used to cut the grain and not the operators of trucks, tractors, trailers, semitrailers or any other CMV.

Question 25: May a State (1) require an applicant for a CDL farmer waiver (§383.3(d)) to take HM training as a condition for being granted a waiver and (2) reduce the 150-mile provision in the waiver to 50 miles if the driver is transporting HM?

Guidance: Yes. The Federal farm waiver is permissive, not mandatory.

Question 26: Do active duty military personnel, not wearing military uniforms, qualify for a waiver from the CDL requirements if the CMVs are rental trucks or leased buses from the General Services Administration?

Guidance: Yes. The drivers in question do not need to be in military uniforms to qualify for the waivers as long as they are on active duty. In regard to the vehicles, they may be owned or operated by the Department of Defense.

Question 27: Are custom harvesters who harvest trees for tree farmers eligible to be considered "custom harvesters" for purposes of the FRSI waiver from selected CDL requirements?

Guidance: If the State considers a firm that harvests trees for tree farmers to be a custom harvesting operation, then its employees could qualify for the FRSI-restricted CDLs, subject to the stringent conditions and limitations of the waiver provisions in §383.3(f).

Question 28: May a farmer who meets all of the conditions for a farm waiver be waived from the CDL requirements when transporting another farmer's products absent any written contract?
Guidance: If a farmer is transporting another farmer's products and being paid for doing so, he or she is acting as a contract carrier and does not meet the conditions for a farm waiver. The existence of a contract, written or verbal, is not relevant to the CDL waiver provisions.

Question 29: May a State exempt commercial motor vehicle drivers employed by a partnership, corporation, or an association engaged in farming from the CDL requirements under the farmer waiver (49 CFR 383.3(d)) or is the waiver only available to drivers employed by a family-owned farm?
Guidance: The purpose of the farmer exemption was to give relief to family farms (53 FR 37313, September 26, 1988). The conditions for the waiver were established to ensure that the waiver focused on this type of farm operation. However, "farmer" is defined in §390.5 as "any person who operates a farm or is directly involved in the cultivation of land, crops, or livestock which (a) [a]re owned by that person; or (b) [a]re under the direct control of that person." Since farming partnerships, corporations, and associations are legal "persons," States may exempt drivers working for these organizations from the CDL requirements, provided they can meet the strict limits imposed by the waiver conditions.

Question 30: May a State exempt commercial motor vehicle drivers employed by farm cooperatives from the commercial driver's license (CDL) requirements under the farmer waiver (§383(d))?
Guidance: No. The waiver covers only operators of farm vehicles which are controlled and operated by "farmers" as defined in §390.5. The waiver does not extend to ancillary businesses, like cooperatives, that provide farm-related services to members. As stated in the waiver notice (53 FR 37313, September 26, 1988), "[t]he waiver would not be available to operators of farm vehicles who operate over long distances, operate to further a commercial enterprise, or operate under contract or for-hire for farm cooperatives or other farm groups. Such operators drive for a living and do not drive only incidentally to farming."

Question 31: Is a person who grows sod as a business considered a farmer and eligible for the farmer waiver?
Guidance: Yes, a sod farmer is eligible for the farmer waiver provided the State of licensure recognizes the growing of sod to be a farming activity.

Question 32: Do the regulations require that a person driving an empty school bus from the manufacturer to the local distributor obtain a CDL?
Guidance: Yes. Any driver of a bus that is designed to transport 16 or more passengers, or that has a GVWR of 11,794 kilograms (26,001 pounds) is required to obtain a CDL in the applicable class. However, a passenger endorsement is not required.

Question 33: Must the driver of an empty tank vehicle that is being transported from the manufacturer to a local distributor or purchaser have a tank endorsement on his or her commercial drivers license (CDL)?
Guidance: Yes. One of the primary objectives of the CDL program is to ensure that drivers are qualified to safely operate the type of vehicle they will be driving. To achieve this objective, the Federal Motor Carrier Safety Regulations (FMCSRs) require a driver to pass a knowledge and skills test for the CMV group they intend to drive. In addition to this requirement, if the driver will be operating double/triple trailers, a tank vehicle, or a CMV used to transport passengers, they must also obtain an appropriate endorsement on their CDL. The specific requirements for the knowledge and skills tests an applicant must meet to obtain a CDL and the various endorsements can be found in Subpart G of Part 383 of the FMCSRs.

§383.5 Definitions.

As used in this part:

Administrator means the Federal Motor Carrier Safety Administrator, the chief executive of the Federal Motor Carrier Safety Administration, an agency within the Department of Transportation.

Alcohol or **alcoholic beverage** means:
(a) *Beer as defined in 26 U.S.C. 5052(a),* of the Internal Revenue Code of 1954,
(b) *Wine of not less than one-half* of one per centum of alcohol by volume, or
(c) *Distilled spirits as defined in section 5002(a)(8),* of such Code.

Alcohol concentration (AC) means the concentration of alcohol in a person's blood or breath. When expressed as a percentage it means grams of alcohol per 100 milliliters of blood or grams of alcohol per 210 liters of breath.

Alien means any person not a citizen or national of the United States.

Commerce means:
(a) *Any trade, traffic, or transportation* within the jurisdiction of the United States between a place in a State and a place outside of such State, including a place outside of the United States and
(b) *Trade, traffic, and transportation* in the United States which affects any trade, traffic, and transportation described in paragraph (a) of this definition.

Commercial driver's license (CDL) means a license issued by a State or other jurisdiction, in accordance with the standards contained in 49 CFR Part 383, to an individual which authorizes the individual to operate a class of a commercial motor vehicle.

Commercial driver's license information system (CDLIS) means the CDLIS established by FMCSA pursuant to section 12007 of the Commercial Motor Vehicle Safety Act of 1986.

Commercial motor vehicle (CMV) means a motor vehicle or combination of motor vehicles used in commerce to transport passengers or property if the motor vehicle —
(a) *Has a gross combination weight rating* of 11,794 kilograms or more (26,001 pounds or more) inclusive of a towed unit(s) with a gross vehicle weight rating of more than 4,536 kilograms (10,000 pounds); or
(b) *Has a gross vehicle weight rating* of 11,794 or more kilograms (26,001 pounds or more); or
(c) *Is designed to transport 16 or more passengers,* including the driver; or
(d) *Is of any size* and is used in the transportation of hazardous materials as defined in this section.

Controlled substance has the meaning such term has under 21 U.S.C. 802(6) and includes all substances listed on schedules I through V of 21 CFR 1308 (§§1308.11 through 1308.15), as they may be amended by the United States Department of Justice.

Conviction means an unvacated adjudication of guilt, or a determination that a person has violated or failed to comply with the law in a court of original jurisdiction or by an authorized administrative tribunal, an unvacated forfeiture of bail or collateral deposited to secure the person's appearance in court, a plea of guilty or nolo contendere accepted by the court, the payment of a fine or court cost, or violation of a condition of release without bail, regardless of whether or not the penalty is rebated, suspended, or probated.

Disqualification means any of the following three actions:
(a) *The suspension, revocation, or cancellation* of a CDL by the State or jurisdiction of issuance.
(b) *Any withdrawal of a person's privileges* to drive a CMV by a State or other jurisdiction as the result of a violation of State or local law relating to motor vehicle traffic control (other than parking, vehicle weight or vehicle defect violations).
(c) *A determination by the FMCSA* that a person is not qualified to operate a commercial motor vehicle under Part 391 of this chapter.

Driver applicant means an individual who applies to a State to obtain, transfer, upgrade, or renew a CDL.

Driver's license means a license issued by a State or other jurisdiction, to an individual which authorizes the individual to operate a motor vehicle on the highways.

Driving a commercial motor vehicle while under the influence of alcohol means committing any one or more of the following acts in a CMV —
(a) *Driving a CMV* while the person's alcohol concentration is 0.04 or more;
(b) *Driving under the influence of alcohol,* as prescribed by State law; or
(c) *Refusal to undergo such testing* as is required by any State or jurisdiction in the enforcement of §383.51(b) or §392.5(a)(2) of this subchapter.

Eligible unit of local government means a city, town, borough, county, parish, district, or other public body created by or pursuant to State law which has a total population of 3,000 individuals or less.

Employee means any operator of a commercial motor vehicle, including full time, regularly employed drivers; casual, intermittent or occasional drivers; leased drivers and independent, owner-operator contractors (while in the course of operating a commer-

Subpart A - General   §383.5

cial motor vehicle) who are either directly employed by or under lease to an employer.

Employer means any person (including the United States, a State, District of Columbia or a political subdivision of a State) who owns or leases a commercial motor vehicle or assigns employees to operate such a vehicle.

Endorsement means an authorization to an individual's CDL required to permit the individual to operate certain types of commercial motor vehicles.

Fatality means the death of a person as a result of a motor vehicle accident.

Felony means an offense under State or Federal law that is punishable by death or imprisonment for a term exceeding 1 year.

Foreign means outside the fifty United States and the District of Columbia.

Gross combination weight rating (GCWR) means the value specified by the manufacturer as the loaded weight of a combination (articulated) vehicle. In the absence of a value specified by the manufacturer, GCWR will be determined by adding the GVWR of the power unit and the total weight of the towed unit and any load thereon.

Gross vehicle weight rating (GVWR) means the value specified by the manufacturer as the loaded weight of a single vehicle.

Hazardous materials means any material that has been designated as hazardous under 49 U.S.C. 5103 and is required to be placarded under Subpart F of 49 CFR Part 172 or any quantity of a material listed as a select agent or toxin in 42 CFR Part 73.

Imminent hazard means the existence of a condition that presents a substantial likelihood that death, serious illness, severe personal injury, or a substantial endangerment to health, property, or the environment may occur before the reasonably foreseeable completion date of a formal proceeding begun to lessen the risk of that death, illness, injury or endangerment.

Motor vehicle means a vehicle, machine, tractor, trailer, or semitrailer propelled or drawn by mechanical power used on highways, except that such term does not include a vehicle, machine, tractor, trailer, semitrailer operated exclusively on a rail.

Nonresident CDL means a CDL issued by a State under either of the following two conditions:
(a) *To an individual domiciled in a foreign country* meeting the requirements of §383.23(b)(1).
(b) *To an individual domiciled in another State* meeting the requirements of §383.23(b)(2).

Non-CMV means a motor vehicle or combination of motor vehicles not defined by the term "commercial motor vehicle (CMV)" in this section.

Out-of-service order means a declaration by an authorized enforcement officer of a Federal, State, Canadian, Mexican, or local jurisdiction that a driver, a commercial motor vehicle, or a motor carrier operation, is out-of-service pursuant to §§386.72, 392.5, 395.13, 396.9, or compatible laws, or the North American Uniform Out-of-Service Criteria.

Representative vehicle means a motor vehicle which represents the type of motor vehicle that a driver applicant operates or expects to operate.

School bus means a CMV used to transport pre-primary, primary, or secondary school students from home to school, from school to home, or to and from school-sponsored events. School bus does not include a bus used as a common carrier.

Serious traffic violation means conviction of any of the following offenses when operating a CMV, except weight, defect and parking violations:
(a) *Excessive speeding,* involving any single offense for any speed of 15 miles per hour or more above the posted speed limit;
(b) *Reckless driving,* as defined by State or local law or regulation, including but not limited to offenses of driving a CMV in willful or wanton disregard for the safety of persons or property;
(c) *Improper or erratic traffic lane changes;*
(d) *Following the vehicle ahead too closely;*
(e) *A violation,* arising in connection with a fatal accident, of State or local law relating to motor vehicle traffic control;
(f) *Driving a CMV without obtaining a CDL;*
(g) *Driving a CMV without a CDL* in the driver's possession. Any individual who provides proof to the enforcement authority that issued the citation, by the date the individual must appear in court or pay any fine for such a violation, that the individual held a valid CDL on the date the citation was issued, shall not be guilty of this offense; or
(h) *Driving a CMV without the proper class of CDL* and/or endorsements for the specific vehicle group being operated or for the passengers or type of cargo being transported.

State means a State of the United States and the District of Columbia.

State of domicile means that State where a person has his/her true, fixed, and permanent home and principal residence and to which he/she has the intention of returning whenever he/she is absent.

Tank vehicle means any commercial motor vehicle that is designed to transport any liquid or gaseous materials within a tank that is either permanently or temporarily attached to the vehicle or the chassis. Such vehicles include, but are not limited to, cargo tanks and portable tanks, as defined in Part 171 of this title. However, this definition does not include portable tanks having a rated capacity under 1,000 gallons.

United States the term United States means the 50 States and the District of Columbia.

Vehicle means a motor vehicle unless otherwise specified.

Vehicle group means a class or type of vehicle with certain operating characteristics.

§383.5 DOT Interpretations

Question 1:
a. Does "designed to transport" as used in the definition of a CMV in §383.5 mean original design or current design when a number of seats are removed?
b. If all of the seats except the driver's seat are removed from a vehicle originally designed to transport only passengers to convert it to a cargo-carrying vehicle, does this vehicle meet the definition of a CMV in §383.5?

Guidance:
a. "Designed to transport" means the original design. Removal of seats does not change the design capacity of the CMV.
b. No, unless this modified vehicle has a GVWR over 26,000 pounds or is used to transport placarded HM.

Question 2: Are rubberized collapsible containers or "bladder bags" attached to a trailer considered a tank vehicle, thus requiring operators to obtain a CDL with a tank vehicle endorsement?
Guidance: Yes.

Question 3: If a vehicle's GVWR plate and/or VIN number are missing but its actual gross weight is 26,001 pounds or more, may an enforcement officer use the latter instead of GVWR to determine the applicability of the Part 383?
Guidance: Yes. The only apparent reason to remove the manufacturer's GVWR plate or VIN number is to make it impossible for roadside enforcement officers to determine the applicability of Part 383, which has a GVWR threshold of 26,001 pounds. In order to frustrate willful evasion of safety regulations, an officer may therefore presume that a vehicle which does not have a manufacturer's GVWR plate and/or does not have a VIN number has a GVWR of 26,001 pounds or more if: (1) It has a size and configuration normally associated with vehicles that have a GVWR of 26,001 pounds or more; and (2) It has an actual gross weight of 26,001 pounds or more.

A motor carrier or driver may rebut the presumption by providing the enforcement officer the GVWR plate, the VIN number or other information of comparable reliability which demonstrates, or allows the officer to determine, that the GVWR of the vehicle is below the jurisdictional weight threshold.

Question 4: If a vehicle with a manufacturer's GVWR of less than 26,001 pounds has been structurally modified to carry a heavier load, may an enforcement officer use the higher actual gross weight of the vehicle, instead of the GVWR, to determine the applicability of Part 383?
Guidance: Yes. The motor carrier's intent to increase the weight rating is shown by the structural modifications. When the vehicle is used to perform functions normally performed by a vehicle with a higher GVWR, §390.33 allows an enforcement officer to treat the actual gross weight as the GVWR of the modified vehicle.

Question 5: When a State agency contracts with private parties for services involving the operation of CMVs, is the State agency or contractor considered the employer?
Guidance: If the contractor employs individuals and assigns and monitors their driving tasks, the contractor is considered the employer. If the State agency assigns and monitors driving tasks, then the State agency is the employer for purposes of Part 383.

Question 6: A driver operates a tractor of exactly 26,000 pounds GVWR, towing a trailer of exactly 10,000 pounds GVWR, for a GCWR of 36,000 pounds. HM and passengers are not involved. Is it a CMV and does the driver need a CDL?

Guidance: No to both questions. Although the vehicle has a GCWR of 36,000 pounds, it is not a CMV under any part of the definition of that term in §383.5, and a CDL is not federally required.

Question 7: Does the definition of a "commercial motor vehicle" in §383.5 of the CDL requirements include parking lot and/or street sweeping vehicles?

Guidance: If the GVWR of a parking lot or street sweeping vehicle is 26,001 or more pounds, it is a CMV under the CDL regulations.

Question 8: Is an employee of a Federal, State, or local government who operates a CMV, as defined in §383.5, including an emergency medical vehicle, required to obtain a CDL? If so, why are such drivers considered as operating "in commerce"?

Guidance: Government employees who drive CMVs are generally required to obtain a CDL. However, operators of firefighting and related emergency equipment may be exempt from the CDL requirement [53 FR 37313, September 26, 1988], at a State's discretion. Drivers of large advanced life support vehicles operated by municipalities would therefore, at a State's discretion, qualify for the exemption.

Government employees who drive CMVs are operating in "commerce," as defined in §383.5, because they perform functions that affect interstate trade, traffic, or transportation. Nearly all government CMVs are used, directly or indirectly, to facilitate or promote such trade, traffic, and transportation.

Question 9: The definition of a passenger CMV is a vehicle "designed to transport" more than 15 passengers, including the driver. Does that include standing passengers if the vehicle was specifically designed to accommodate standees?

Guidance: No. "Designed to transport" refers only to the number of designated seats; it does not include areas suitable, or even designed, for standing passengers.

Question 10: What is considered a "public road"?

Guidance: A public road is any road under the jurisdiction of a public agency and open to public travel or any road on private property that is open to public travel.

Question 11: Must operators of motor graders or motor scrapers obtain a commercial driver's license (CDL) and be subject to controlled substances and alcohol testing if they operate the equipment on public roads to perform such functions as snow and leaf removal? If so, is a State that exempts such operations from the CDL requirements of its laws subject to sanctions under 49 CFR Part 384?

Guidance: No.

§383.7 Validity of CDL issued by decertified State.

A CDL issued by a State prior to the date the State is notified by the Administrator, in accordance with the provisions of §384.405 of this subchapter, that the State is prohibited from issuing CDLs, will remain valid until its stated expiration date.

Subpart B - Single License Requirement

§383.21 Number of drivers' licenses.

No person who operates a commercial motor vehicle shall at any time have more than one driver's license.

§383.21 DOT Interpretations

Question 1: Are there any circumstances under which the driver of a CMV as defined in §383.5 is allowed to hold more than one driver's license?

Guidance: Yes. A recipient of a new driver's license may hold more than one license during the 10 days beginning on the date the person is issued a driver's license.

Guidance: Since Puerto Rico and the U.S. Territories are not included in the definition of a State in Section 12016 of the CMVSA (49 U.S.C. §31301(13)), they must be considered foreign countries for purposes of the CDL requirements. Under Part 383, a person domiciled in a foreign country is not required to surrender his or her foreign license in order to obtain a nonresident CDL. There are two reasons for permitting this dual licensing to a person domiciled in Puerto Rico: (a) There is no reciprocal agreement with Puerto Rico recognizing its CMV testing and licensing standards as equivalent to the standards in Part 383 and, (b) the nonresident CDL may not be recognized as a valid license to drive in Puerto Rico.

§383.23 Commercial driver's license.

(a) General rule.

(1) Effective April 1, 1992, no person shall operate a commercial motor vehicle unless such person has taken and passed written and driving tests which meet the Federal standards contained in Subparts F, G, and H of this part for the commercial motor vehicle that person operates or expects to operate.

(2) Except as provided in paragraph (b) of this section, no person may legally operate a CMV unless such person possesses a CDL which meets the standards contained in Subpart J of this part, issued by his/her State or jurisdiction of domicile.

(b) Exception.

(1) If a CMV operator is not domiciled in a foreign jurisdiction which the Administrator has determined tests drivers and issues CDLs in accordance with, or under standards similar to, the standards contained in Subparts F, G, and H of this part, the person may obtain a Nonresident CDL from a State which does comply with the testing and licensing standards contained in such Subparts F, G, and H of this part.[1]

(2) If an individual is domiciled in a State while that State is prohibited from issuing CDLs in accordance with §384.405 of this subchapter, that individual is eligible to obtain a Nonresident CDL from any State that elects to issue a Nonresident CDL and which complies with the testing and licensing standards contained in Subparts F, G, and H of this part.

(c) Learner's permit. State learners' permits, issued for limited time periods according to State requirements, shall be considered valid commercial drivers' licenses for purposes of behind-the-wheel training on public roads or highways, if the following minimum conditions are met:

(1) The learner's permit holder is at all times accompanied by the holder of a valid CDL;

(2) He/she either holds a valid automobile driver's license, or has passed such vision, sign/symbol, and knowledge tests as the State issuing the learner's permit ordinarily administers to applicants for automotive drivers' licenses; and

(3) He/she does not operate a commercial motor vehicle transporting hazardous materials as defined in §383.5.

§383.23 DOT Interpretations

Question 1: May a holder of a CMV learner's permit continue to hold his/her basic driver's license from any State without violating the single-license rule?

Guidance: Yes, since the learner's permit is not a license.

Question 2: The requirements for States regarding CMV learner's permits in §383.23 appear to be ambiguous. For example, if the CMV learner's permit is "considered a valid CDL" for instructional purposes, is the State to enter the learner's permit issuance as a CDLIS transaction?

Guidance: No such requirement currently exists.

Question 3: Is a CDL required for CMV operations that occur exclusively in places where the general public is never allowed to operate, such as airport taxiways or other areas restricted from the public?

Guidance: No. FMCSA regulations would not require a CMV driver to obtain a CDL under those circumstances. The Federal rules are minimum standards, however, and State law may require a CDL for operations not covered by Part 383.

Question 4: The holder of a commercial learner's permit (CLP) must be "accompanied by the holder of a valid commercial driver's license (CDL)." What is meant by "accompanied"?

Guidance: The holder of a valid CDL must be physically present in the front seat of the vehicle next to the CLP holder and have the CLP holder under observation and direct supervision. The CDL holder must have the proper CDL class and endorsement(s) necessary to operate the CMV.

---

1. Effective December 29, 1988, the Administrator determined that commercial drivers' licenses issued by Canadian Provinces and Territories in conformity with the Canadian National Safety Code are in accordance with the standards of this part. Effective November 21, 1991, the Administrator determined that the new Licencias Federales de Conductor issued by the United Mexican States are in accordance with the standards of this part. Therefore, under the single license provision of §383.21, a driver holding a commercial driver's license issued under the Canadian National Safety Code or a new Licencia Federal de Conductor issued by Mexico is prohibited from obtaining nonresident CDL, or any other type of driver's license, from a State or other jurisdiction in the United States.

Subpart C - Notification Requirements and Employer Responsibilities §383.37 (d)

Question 5: May a foreign driver with a temporary work visa obtain a commercial driver's license (CDL) to operate a commercial motor vehicle in the United States?

Guidance: A foreign driver holding a temporary work visa may obtain a nonresident CDL if he or she is domiciled in a foreign jurisdiction that does not test drivers and issue commercial licenses under standards equivalent to those in Subparts F, G, and H of Part 383 (see §383.23(b)). However, drivers from Canada and Mexico with temporary work visas are not eligible for nonresident CDLs because FMCSA has determined that commercial licenses issued by Canadian provinces and territories, and the United Mexican States, are in accordance with the standards established by our rules. Therefore, all Mexican and Canadian drivers must have an appropriate license from their home country. Finally, a foreign driver who is in this country on a temporary work visa may not obtain a resident CDL since he or she is not "domiciled" in a U.S. State, as defined in §383.5 ("state of domicile").

Subpart C - Notification Requirements and Employer Responsibilities

§383.31 Notification of convictions for driver violations.

(a) Each person who operates a commercial motor vehicle, who has a commercial driver's license issued by a State or jurisdiction, and who is convicted of violating, in any type of motor vehicle, a State or local law relating to motor vehicle traffic control (other than a parking violation) in a State or jurisdiction other than the one which issued his/her license, shall notify an official designated by the State or jurisdiction which issued such license, of such conviction. The notification must be made within 30 days after the date that the person has been convicted.

(b) Each person who operates a commercial motor vehicle, who has a commercial driver's license issued by a State or jurisdiction, and who is convicted of violating, in any type of motor vehicle, a State or local law relating to motor vehicle traffic control (other than a parking violation), shall notify his/her current employer of such conviction. The notification must be made within 30 days after the date that the person has been convicted. If the driver is not currently employed, he/she must notify the State or jurisdiction which issued the license according to §383.31(a).

(c) Notification. The notification to the State official and employer must be made in writing and contain the following information:

(1) Driver's full name;
(2) Driver's license number;
(3) Date of conviction;
(4) The specific criminal or other offense(s), serious traffic violation(s), and other violation(s) of State or local law relating to motor vehicle traffic control, for which the person was convicted and any suspension, revocation, or cancellation of certain driving privileges which resulted from such conviction(s);
(5) Indication whether the violation was in a commercial motor vehicle;
(6) Location of offense; and
(7) Driver's signature.

§383.31 DOT Interpretations

Question 1: Must an operator of a CMV (as defined in §383.5), who holds a CDL, notify his/her current employer of a conviction for violating a State or local (non-parking) traffic law in any type of vehicle, as required by §383.31(b), even though the conviction is under appeal?

Guidance: Yes. The taking of an appeal does not vacate or annul the conviction, nor does it stay the notification requirements of §383.31. The driver must notify his/her employer within 30 days of the date of conviction.

§383.33 Notification of driver's license suspensions.

Each employee who has a driver's license suspended, revoked, or canceled by a State or jurisdiction, who loses the right to operate a commercial motor vehicle in a State or jurisdiction for any period, or who is disqualified from operating a commercial motor vehicle for any period, shall notify his/her current employer of such suspension, revocation, cancellation, lost privilege, or disqualification. The notification must be made before the end of the business day following the day the employee received notice of the suspension, revocation, cancellation, lost privilege, or disqualification.

§383.33 DOT Interpretations

Question 1: When a driver (a) receives an Administrative Order of Suspension due to a blood alcohol reading in excess of the legal limit with notice that the suspension is not to be effective until 45 days after the notice or after an administrative hearing, and (b) a hearing is subsequently held, in effect suspending the license, what is the effective date of suspension for purposes of notifying the employer under §383.33?

Guidance: The effective date of the suspension for notification purposes is the day the employee received notice of the suspension.

§383.35 Notification of previous employment.

(a) Any person applying for employment as an operator of a commercial motor vehicle shall provide at the time of application for employment, the information specified in paragraph (c) of this section.

(b) All employers shall request the information specified in paragraph (c) of this section from all persons applying for employment as a commercial motor vehicle operator. The request shall be made at the time of application for employment.

(c) The following employment history information for the 10 years preceding the date the application is submitted shall be presented to the prospective employer by the applicant:

(1) A list of the names and addresses of the applicant's previous employers for which the applicant was an operator of a commercial motor vehicle;
(2) The dates the applicant was employed by these employers; and
(3) The reason for leaving such employment.

(d) The applicant shall certify that all information furnished is true and complete.

(e) An employer may require an applicant to provide additional information.

(f) Before an application is submitted, the employer shall inform the applicant that the information he/she provides in accordance with paragraph (c) of this section may be used, and the applicant's previous employers may be contacted for the purpose of investigating the applicant's work history.

§383.37 Employer responsibilities.

No employer may knowingly allow, require, permit, or authorize a driver to operate a CMV in the United States:

(a) During any period in which the driver has a CMV driver's license suspended, revoked, or canceled by a State, has lost the right to operate a CMV in a State, or has been disqualified from operating a CMV;

(b) During any period in which the driver has more than one CMV driver's license;

(c) During any period in which the driver, or the CMV he or she is driving, or the motor carrier operation, is subject to an out-of-service order; or

(d) In violation of a Federal, State, or local law or regulation pertaining to railroad-highway grade crossings.

§383.37 DOT Interpretations

Question 1: §383.37(a) does not allow employers to knowingly use a driver whose license has been suspended, revoked, or canceled. Do motor carriers have latitude in their resulting actions: firing, suspension, layoff, authorized use of unused vacation time during suspension duration, transfer to nondriving position for duration of the suspension?

Guidance: Yes. The employer's minimum responsibility is to prohibit operation of a CMV by such an employee.

Question 2:
a. A motor carrier recently found a driver who had a detectable presence of alcohol, placed him off-duty in accordance with §392.5, and ordered a blood test which disclosed a blood alcohol concentration of 0.05 percent. Is the carrier obligated to place the driver out of service for 24 hours as prescribed by §392.5(c)?
b. Is the carrier obligated to disqualify the driver for a period of one year as prescribed by §383.51(b) and 391.15(c)(3)(i) of the FMCSRs?

Guidance:
a. Only a State or Federal official can place a driver out of service. Instead, the carrier is obligated to place the driver off-duty and prevent him/her from operating or being in control of a CMV until he/she is no longer in violation of §392.5.
b. No. A motor carrier has no authority to disqualify a driver. Disqualification for such an offense only occurs upon a conviction.

Question 3: If an individual driver had two convictions for serious traffic violations while driving a CMV, and neither FMCSA nor his/her State licensing agency took any disqualification action, does the motor carrier have any obligation under FMCSA regulations to refrain from using this driver for 60 days? If so, when does that time period begin?

Guidance: No. Only the State or the FMCSA has the authority to take a disqualification action against a driver. The motor carrier's responsibility under §383.37(a) to refrain from using the driver begins when it learns of the disqualification action and continues until the disqualification period set by the State or the FMCSA is completed.

Question 4: Is a driver who has a CDL, and has been convicted of a felony, disqualified from operating a CMV under the FMCSRs?

Guidance: Not necessarily. The FMCSRs do not prohibit a driver who has been convicted of a felony, such as drug dealing, from operating a CMV unless the offense involved the use of a CMV. If the offense involved a non-CMV, or was unrelated to motor vehicles, there is no FMCSR prohibition to employment of the person as a driver.

Subpart D - Driver Disqualifications and Penalties

§383.51 Disqualification of drivers.

(a) *General.*

(1) *A driver or holder of a CDL who is disqualified must not drive a CMV.*

(2) *An employer* must not knowingly allow, require, permit, or authorize a driver who is disqualified to drive a CMV.

(3) *A driver is subject to disqualification sanctions* designated in paragraphs (b) and (c) of this section, if the holder of a CDL drives a CMV or non-CMV and is convicted of the violations.

(4) *Determining first and subsequent violations.* For purposes of determining first and subsequent violations of the offenses specified in this subpart, each conviction for any offense listed in Tables 1 through 4 to this section resulting from a separate incident, whether committed in a CMV or non-CMV, must be counted.

(5) *Reinstatement after lifetime disqualification.* A State may reinstate any driver disqualified for life for offenses described in paragraphs (b)(1) through (b)(8) of this section (Table 1 to §383.51) after 10 years if that person has voluntarily entered and successfully completed an appropriate rehabilitation program approved by the State. Any person who has been reinstated in accordance with this provision and who is subsequently convicted of a disqualifying offense described in paragraphs (b)(1) through (b)(8) of this section (Table 1 to §383.51) must not be reinstated.

(b) *Disqualification for major offenses.* Table 1 to §383.51 contains a list of the offenses and periods for which a driver must be disqualified, depending upon the type of vehicle the driver is operating at the time of the violation, as follows:

Table 1 to §383.51

If a driver operates a motor vehicle and is convicted of:	For a first conviction or refusal to be tested while operating a CMV, a person required to have a CDL and a CDL holder must be disqualified from operating a CMV for . . .	For a first conviction or refusal to be tested while operating a non-CMV, a CDL holder must be disqualified from operating a CMV for . . .	For a first conviction or refusal to be tested while operating a CMV transporting hazardous materials required to be placarded under the Hazardous Materials Regulations (49 CFR Part 172, Subpart F), a person required to have a CDL and CDL holder must be disqualified from operating a CMV for . . .	For a second conviction or refusal to be tested in a separate incident of any combination of offenses in this Table while operating a CMV, a person required to have a CDL and a CDL holder must be disqualified from operating a CMV for . . .	For a second conviction or refusal to be tested in a separate incident of any combination of offenses in this Table while operating a non-CMV, a CDL holder must be disqualified from operating a CMV for . . .
(1) Being under the influence of alcohol as prescribed by State law ***.	1 year	1 year	3 years	Life	Life
(2) Being under the influence of a controlled substance ***.	1 year	1 year	3 years	Life	Life
(3) Having an alcohol concentration of 0.04 or greater while operating a CMV ***.	1 year	Not applicable	3 years	Life	Not applicable
(4) Refusing to take an alcohol test as required by a State or jurisdiction under its implied consent laws or regulations as defined in §383.72 of this part ***.	1 year	1 year	3 years	Life	Life
(5) Leaving the scene of an accident ***.	1 year	1 year	3 years	Life	Life

Subpart D - Driver Disqualifications and Penalties §383.51 (b)

Table 1 to §383.51 (continued)

If a driver operates a motor vehicle and is convicted of:	For a first conviction or refusal to be tested while operating a CMV, a person required to have a CDL and a CDL holder must be disqualified from operating a CMV for . . .	For a first conviction or refusal to be tested while operating a non-CMV, a CDL holder must be disqualified from operating a CMV for . . .	For a first conviction or refusal to be tested while operating a CMV transporting hazardous materials required to be placarded under the Hazardous Materials Regulations (49 CFR Part 172, Subpart F), a person required to have a CDL and CDL holder must be disqualified from operating a CMV for . . .	For a second conviction or refusal to be tested in a separate incident of any combination of offenses in this Table while operating a CMV, a person required to have a CDL and a CDL holder must be disqualified from operating a CMV for . . .	For a second conviction or refusal to be tested in a separate incident of any combination of offenses in this Table while operating a non-CMV, a CDL holder must be disqualified from operating a CMV for . . .
(6) Using the vehicle to commit a felony, other than a felony described in paragraph (b)(9) of this table * * *.	1 year	1 year	3 years	Life	Life
(7) Driving a CMV when, as a result of prior violations committed operating a CMV, the driver's CDL is revoked, suspended, or canceled, or the driver is disqualified from operating a CMV.	1 year	Not applicable	3 years	Life	Not applicable
(8) Causing a fatality through the negligent operation of a CMV, including but not limited to the crimes of motor vehicle manslaughter, homicide by motor vehicle and negligent homicide.	1 year	Not applicable	3 years	Life	Not applicable
(9) Using the vehicle in the commission of a felony involving manufacturing, distributing, or dispensing a controlled substance * * *.	Life — not eligible for 10-year reinstatement	Life — not eligible for 10-year reinstatement	Life — not eligible for 10-year reinstatement	Life — not eligible for 10-year reinstatement	Life — not eligible for 10-year reinstatement

(c) Disqualification for serious traffic violations. Table 2 to §383.51 contains a list of the offenses and the periods for which a driver must be disqualified, depending upon the type of vehicle the driver is operating at the time of the violation, as follows:

Table 2 to §383.51

If the driver operates a motor vehicle and is convicted of:	For a second conviction of any combination of offenses in this Table in a separate incident within a 3-year period while operating a CMV, a person required to have a CDL and a CDL holder must be disqualified from operating a CMV for . . .	For a second conviction of any combination of offenses in this Table in a separate incident within a 3-year period while operating a non-CMV, a CDL holder must be disqualified from operating a CMV, if the conviction results in the revocation, cancellation, or suspension of the CDL holder's license or non-CMV driving privileges, for . . .	For a third or subsequent conviction of any combination of offenses in this Table in a separate incident within a 3-year period while operating a CMV, a person required to have a CDL and a CDL holder must be disqualified from operating a CMV for . . .	For a third or subsequent conviction of any combination of offenses in this Table in a separate incident within a 3-year period while operating a non-CMV, a CDL holder must be disqualified from operating a CMV, if the conviction results in the revocation, cancellation, or suspension of the CDL holder's license or non-CMV driving privileges, for . . .
(1) Speeding excessively, involving any speed of 24.1 kmph (15 mph) or more above the posted speed limit.	60 days	60 days	120 days	120 days
(2) Driving recklessly, as defined by State or local law or regulation, including but, not limited to, offenses of driving a motor vehicle in willful or wanton disregard for the safety of persons or property.	60 days	60 days	120 days	120 days
(3) Making improper or erratic traffic lane changes.	60 days	60 days	120 days	120 days
(4) Following the vehicle ahead too closely.	60 days	60 days	120 days	120 days
(5) Violating State or local law relating to motor vehicle traffic control (other than a parking violation) arising in connection with a fatal accident.	60 days	60 days	120 days	120 days
(6) Driving a CMV without obtaining a CDL.	60 days	Not applicable	120 days	Not applicable
(7) Driving a CMV without a CDL in the driver's possession[1].	60 days	Not applicable	120 days	Not applicable
(8) Driving a CMV without the proper class of CDL and/or endorsements for the specific vehicle group being operated or for the passengers or type of cargo being transported.	60 days	Not applicable	120 days	Not applicable

1. Any individual who provides proof to the enforcement authority that issued the citation, by the date the individual must appear in court or pay any fine for such a violation, that the individual held a valid CDL on the date the citation was issued, shall not be guilty of this offense.

Subpart D - Driver Disqualifications and Penalties §383.51 (e)

(d) **Disqualification for railroad-highway grade crossing offenses.** Table 3 to §383.51 contains a list of the offenses and the periods for which a driver must be disqualified, when the driver is operating a CMV at the time of the violation, as follows:

Table 3 to §383.51

If the driver is convicted of operating a CMV in violation of a Federal, State or local law because . . .	For a first conviction a person required to have a CDL and a CDL holder must be disqualified from operating a CMV for . . .	For a second conviction of any combination of offenses in this Table in a separate incident within a 3-year period, a person required to have a CDL and a CDL holder must be disqualified from operating a CMV for . . .	For a third or subsequent conviction of any combination of offenses in this Table in a separate incident within a 3-year period, a person required to have a CDL and a CDL holder must be disqualified from operating a CMV for . . .
(1) The driver is not required to always stop, but fails to slow down and check that tracks are clear of an approaching train * * *.	No less than 60 days	No less than 120 days	No less than 1 year
(2) The driver is not required to always stop, but fails to stop before reaching the crossing, if the tracks are not clear * * *.	No less than 60 days	No less than 120 days	No less than 1 year
(3) The driver is always required to stop, but fails to stop before driving onto the crossing * * *.	No less than 60 days	No less than 120 days	No less than 1 year
(4) The driver fails to have sufficient space to drive completely through the crossing without stopping * * *.	No less than 60 days	No less than 120 days	No less than 1 year
(5) The driver fails to obey a traffic control device or the directions of an enforcement official at the crossing * * *.	No less than 60 days	No less than 120 days	No less than 1 year
(6) The driver fails to negotiate a crossing because of insufficient undercarriage clearance * * *.	No less than 60 days	No less than 120 days	No less than 1 year

(e) **Disqualification for violating out-of-service orders.** Table 4 to §383.51 contains a list of the offenses and periods for which a driver must be disqualified when the driver is operating a CMV at the time of the violation, as follows:

Table 4 to §383.51

If the driver operates a CMV and is convicted of . . .	For a first conviction while operating a CMV, a person required to have a CDL and a CDL holder must be disqualified from operating a CMV for . . .	For a second conviction in a separate incident within a 10-year period while operating a CMV, a person required to have a CDL and a CDL holder must be disqualified from operating a CMV for . . .	For a third or subsequent conviction in a separate incident within a 10-year period while operating a CMV, a person required to have a CDL and a CDL holder must be disqualified from operating a CMV for . . .
(1) Violating a driver or vehicle out-of-service order while transporting nonhazardous materials	No less than 90 days or more than 1 year	No less than 1 year or more than 5 years	No less than 3 years or more than 5 years
(2) Violating a driver or vehicle out-of-service order while transporting hazardous materials required to be placarded under Part 172, Subpart F of this title, or while operating a vehicle designed to transport 16 or more passengers, including the driver	No less than 180 days or more than 2 years	No less than 3 years or more than 5 years	No less than 3 years or more than 5 years

§383.51 DOT Interpretations

— General Questions —

Question 1:
a. If a driver received one "excessive speeding" violation in a CMV and the same violation in his/her personal passenger vehicle, would the driver be disqualified? or,
b. If a driver received two "excessive speeding" violations in his/her personal passenger vehicle, would the driver be disqualified?

Guidance: No, in both cases. Convictions for serious traffic violations, such as excessive speeding, only result in disqualification if the offenses were committed in a CMV — unless the State has stricter regulations.

Question 2: §383.51 of the FMCSRs disqualifies drivers if certain offenses were committed while operating a CMV. Will the States be required to identify on the motor vehicle driver's record the class of vehicle being operated when a violation occurs?

Guidance: No, only whether or not the violation occurred in a CMV. The only other indication that may be required is if the vehicle was carrying placardable amounts of HM.

Question 3: If a CDL holder commits an offense that would normally be disqualifying, but the CDL holder is driving under the farm waiver, must conviction result in disqualification and action against the CDL holder?

Guidance: Yes. Possession of the CDL means the driver is not operating under the waiver. In addition, the waiver does not absolve the driver from disqualification under Part 391.

Question 4: What is meant by leaving the scene of an accident involving a CMV?

Guidance: As used in Part 383, the disqualifying offense of "leaving the scene of an accident involving a CMV" is all-inclusive and covers the entire range of situations where the driver of the CMV is required by State law to stop after an accident and either give information to the other party, render aid, or attempt to locate and notify the operator or owner of other vehicles involved in the accident.

Question 5: If a State disqualifies a driver for two serious traffic violations under §383.51(c)(2)(i), and that driver, after being reinstated, commits a third serious violation, what additional period of disqualification must be imposed on that driver?

Guidance: If three years have not elapsed since the original violation, then the driver is now subject to a full 120-day disqualification period.

Question 6: May a State issue a "conditional," "occupational" or "hardship" license that includes CDL driving privileges when a CDL holder loses driving privileges to operate a private passenger vehicle (non-CMV)?

Guidance: Yes, provided the CDL holder loses his/her driving privileges for operating a non-CMV as the result of a conviction for a disqualifying offense that occurred in a non-CMV. A State is prohibited, however, from issuing any type of license which would give the driver even limited privileges to operate a CMV when the conviction is for a disqualifying offense that occurred in a CMV.

Question 7: What information needs to be contained on a "conditional," "occupational" or "hardship" license document that includes CDL driving privileges?

Guidance: The same information that is required under §383.153, including an explanation of restrictions of driving privileges.

Question 8: Is a State obligated to grant reciprocity to another State's "conditional," "occupational" or "hardship" license that includes CDL driving privileges?

Guidance: Yes, in regard to operating a CMV as stated in §383.73(h).

§383.51 DOT Interpretations

— Alcohol Questions —

Question 1: Are States expected to make major changes to their enforcement procedures in order to apply the alcohol disqualifications in the Federal regulations?

Guidance: No. §§383.51 and 392.5 do not require any change in a State's existing procedures for initially stopping vehicles and drivers. Roadblocks, random testing programs, or other enforcement procedures which have been held unconstitutional in the State or which the State does not wish to implement are not required.

Question 2: Is a driver disqualified for driving a CMV while off-duty with a blood alcohol concentration over 0.04 percent?

Guidance: Yes. §383.51 applies to any person who is driving a CMV, as defined in §383.5, regardless of the person's duty status under other regulations. Therefore, the driver, if convicted, would be disqualified under §383.51.

Question 3: Does a temporary license issued pursuant to the administrative license revocation (ALR) procedure authorize the continued operation of CMVs when the license surrendered is a CDL? Does the acceptance of a temporary driver's license place the CDL holder in violation of the one driver's license requirement?

Guidance: The ALR procedure of taking possession of the driver's CDL and issuing a "temporary license" for individuals who either fail a chemical alcohol test or refuse to take the test is valid under the requirements of Part 383. Since the CDL that is being held by the State is still valid until the administrative revocation action is taken, the FMCSA would interpret the document given to the driver as a "receipt" for the CDL, not a new "temporary" license. The driver violates no CDL requirements for accepting the receipt which may be used to the extent authorized.

Question 4: Is a driver disqualified under §383.51 if convicted of driving under the influence of alcohol while operating a personal vehicle?

Guidance: The convictions triggering mandatory disqualification under §383.51 all pertain to offenses that occur while the person is driving a CMV. However, a driver could be disqualified under §383.51(b)(2)(i) if the State has stricter standards which apply to offenses committed in a personal vehicle. (The same principle applies to all other disqualifying offenses listed in §383.51.)

Question 5: Would a driver convicted under a State's "open container" law be disqualified under the CDL regulations if the violation occurred while he/she was operating a CMV?

Guidance: If a conviction under a particular State's "open container law" is a conviction for "driving under the influence" or "driving while intoxicated," and if the person committed the violation while driving a CMV, then the driver is disqualified for one year under §383.51, assuming it is a first offense.

Question 6: Is a driver who possesses a valid commercial driver's license (CDL) issued by their State of residence, but who is suspended by another State for reasons unrelated to the violation of a motor vehicle traffic control law, disqualified from operating a commercial motor vehicle (CMV) in accordance with provisions of the Federal Motor Carrier Safety Regulations?

Guidance: Yes. Currently, both §383.5, which defines the term disqualification as it applies to drivers required to have a CDL, and §391.15, which applies to other CMV drivers subject to Federal Motor Carrier Safety Regulations, include the suspension of a person's license or privilege to drive as an action requiring that person to be disqualified from operating a CMV. Neither of these regulatory provisions limit such suspensions to those imposed by the State where the driver is licensed, nor do these regulations specify the grounds upon which a suspension must be based.

Be advised, however, that the Federal Motor Carrier Safety Administration has proposed in 66 FR 22499, Docket No. FMCSA-00-7382, published May 4, 2001, to limit the basis of the suspension to those resulting from a driving violation. If the rule is finalized, the answer would be no.

Question 7: Must the State use the date of conviction, rather than the offense date, to calculate the starting and ending dates for the driver disqualification period specified in 49 CFR 383.51?

Guidance: Yes, the State must use the date of conviction or a later date, rather than the offense date, as the basis for calculating the starting and ending dates for the driver disqualification period. The State may allow the driver additional time after the conviction date to appeal the conviction before the disqualification period begins. The use of the conviction date (or the date when all appeals are exhausted) ensures that the driver receives due process of law but (if the conviction is upheld) still serves the full disqualification period 49 CFR 383.51 requires. For example, a driver is cited for a disqualifying offense on May 1 and is convicted of the offense on July 1. If the offense date were used for the starting date of the disqualification, it would shorten the actual disqualification by 2 months. Using the conviction date or a later date when all appeals are exhausted ensures that the driver serves the full disqualification period.

Question 8: Must the State use the offense date or the conviction date to determine if two or more serious traffic convictions occurred within a 3-year period?

Subpart E - Testing and Licensing Procedures

Guidance: The State must use the offense date to determine if two or more serious traffic convictions fall within the 3-year period specified in 49 CFR 383.51 Table 2. If the conviction date were used, delays in bringing a case to trial could push the second conviction outside the 3-year period, thus defeating the purpose of the rule. For example, a driver is cited for a first serious traffic violation on February 1, 2001 and is convicted on March 1, 2001. The driver is cited for a second serious traffic violation on January 15, 2004. The trial is set for February 27, 2004, but the driver asks to have the trial delayed because he has something important to do that day. The new trial date is set for March 15, 2004 and he is convicted of the second violation on this date. If the conviction dates are used, the two offenses are not within three years of each other and no disqualification action is taken on the driver. If the offense dates are used, the driver is disqualified regardless of the conviction date because the offenses for which he was convicted are within three years of each other.

§383.52 Disqualification of drivers determined to constitute an imminent hazard.

(a) **The Assistant Administrator or his/her designee** must disqualify from operating a CMV any driver whose driving is determined to constitute an imminent hazard, as defined in §383.5.

(b) **The period of the disqualification** may not exceed 30 days unless the FMCSA complies with the provisions of paragraph (c) of this section.

(c) **The Assistant Administrator or his/her delegate** may provide the driver an opportunity for a hearing after issuing a disqualification for a period of 30 days or less. The Assistant Administrator or his/her delegate must provide the driver notice of a proposed disqualification period of more than 30 days and an opportunity for a hearing to present a defense to the proposed disqualification. A disqualification imposed under this paragraph may not exceed one year in duration. The driver, or a representative on his/her behalf, may file an appeal of the disqualification issued by the Assistant Administrator's delegate with the Assistant Administrator, Adjudications Counsel, Federal Motor Carrier Safety Administration (Room 8217), 400 Seventh Street, SW., Washington, DC 20590.

(d) **Any disqualification imposed in accordance** with the provisions of this section must be transmitted by the FMCSA to the jurisdiction where the driver is licensed and must become a part of the driver's record maintained by that jurisdiction.

(e) **A driver who is simultaneously disqualified** under this section and under other provisions of this subpart, or under State law or regulation, shall serve those disqualification periods concurrently.

§383.53 Penalties.

(a) **General rule.** Any person who violates the rules set forth in Subparts B and C of this part may be subject to civil or criminal penalties as provided for in 49 U.S.C. 521(b).

(b) **Special penalties pertaining to violation of out-of-service orders —**
  (1) *Driver violations.* A driver who is convicted of violating an out-of-service order shall be subject to a civil penalty of not less than $1,100 nor more than $2,750, in addition to disqualification under §383.51(e).
  (2) *Employer violations.* An employer who is convicted of a violation of §383.37(c) shall be subject to a civil penalty of not less than $2,750 nor more than $11,000.

(c) **Special penalties** pertaining to railroad-highway grade crossing violations. An employer who is convicted of a violation of §383.37(d) must be subject to a civil penalty of not more than $10,000.

Subpart E - Testing and Licensing Procedures

§383.71 Driver application procedures.

(a) **Initial Commercial Driver's License.** Prior to obtaining a CDL, a person must meet the following requirements:
  (1) *A person who operates or expects to operate* in interstate or foreign commerce, or is otherwise subject to Part 391 of this title, shall certify that he/she meets the qualification requirements contained in Part 391 of this title. A person who operates or expects to operate entirely in intrastate commerce and is not subject to Part 391, is subject to State driver qualification requirements and must certify that he/she is not subject to Part 391;
  (2) *Pass a knowledge test* in accordance with the standards contained in Subparts G and H of this part for the type of motor vehicle the person operates or expects to operate;
  (3) *Pass a driving or skills test* in accordance with the standards contained in Subparts G and H of this part taken in a motor vehicle which is representative of the type of motor vehicle the person operates or expects to operate; or provide evidence that he/she has successfully passed a driving test administered by an authorized third party;
  (4) *Certify that the motor vehicle* in which the person takes the driving skills test is representative of the type of motor vehicle that person operates or expects to operate;
  (5) *Provide to the State of issuance* the information required to be included on the CDL as specified in Subpart J of this part;
  (6) *Certify that he/she* is not subject to any disqualification under §383.51, or any license suspension, revocation, or cancellation under State law, and that he/she does not have a driver's license from more than one State or jurisdiction;
  (7) *Surrender the applicant's non-CDL driver's licenses* to the State; and
  (8) *Provide the names of all States* where the applicant has previously been licensed to drive any type of motor vehicle during the previous 10 years.
  (9) *If applying for a hazardous materials endorsement,* comply with Transportation Security Administration requirements codified in 49 CFR Part 1572, and provide proof of citizenship or immigration status as specified in Table 1 to this section. A lawful permanent resident of the United States requesting a hazardous materials endorsement must additionally provide his or her Bureau of Citizenship and Immigration Services (BCIS) Alien registration number.

Table 1 to §383.71 - List of Acceptable Proofs of Citizenship or Immigration

Status	Proof of status
U.S. Citizen	• U.S. Passport • Certificate of birth that bears an official seal and was issued by a State, county, municipal authority, or outlying possession of the United States • Certification of Birth Abroad issued by the U.S. Department of State (Form FS-545 or DS 1350) • Certificate of Naturalization (Form N-550 or N-570) • Certificate of U.S. Citizenship (Form N-560 or N-561)
Lawful Permanent Resident	• Permanent Resident Card, Alien Registration Receipt Card (Form I-551) • Temporary I-551 stamp in foreign passport • Temporary I-551 stamp on Form I-94, Arrival/Departure Record, with photograph of the bearer • Reentry Permit (Form I-327)

(b) **License transfer.** When applying to transfer a CDL from one State of domicile to a new State domicile, an applicant shall apply for a CDL from the new State of domicile within no more than 30 days after establishing his/her new domicile. The applicant shall:
  (1) *Provide to the new State of domicile* the certifications contained in §383.71(a)(1) and (6);
  (2) *Provide to the new State of domicile* updated information as specified in Subpart J of this part;
  (3) *If the applicant wishes to retain* a hazardous materials endorsement, he/she must comply with the requirements for such endorsement specified in §383.71(a)(9) and State requirements as specified in §383.73(b)(4);
  (4) *Surrender the CDL* from the old State of domicile to the new State of domicile; and
  (5) *Provide the names of all States* where the applicant has previously been licensed to drive any type of motor vehicle during the previous 10 years.

(c) **License renewal.** When applying for a renewal of a CDL, all applicants shall:
  (1) *Provide certification contained in §383.71(a)(1);*

(2) *Provide update information* as specified in Subpart J of this part; and

(3) *If a person wishes to retain* a hazardous materials endorsement, he/she must comply with the requirements specified in §383.71(a)(9) and pass the test specified in §383.121 for such endorsement.

(4) *Provide the names of all States* where the applicant has previously been licensed to drive any type of motor vehicle during the previous 10 years.

(d) **License upgrades.** When applying to operate a commercial motor vehicle in a different group or endorsement from the group or endorsement in which the applicant already has a CDL, all persons shall:

(1) *Provide the necessary certifications* as specified in §383.71(a)(1) and (a)(4);

(2) *Pass all tests specified in §383.71(a)(2) and (a)(3)* for the new vehicle group and/or different endorsements; and

(3) *To obtain a hazardous materials endorsement,* comply with the requirements for such endorsement specified in §383.71(a)(9).

(e) **Nonresident CDL.** When an applicant is domiciled in a foreign jurisdiction, as defined in §383.5, where the commercial motor vehicle operator testing and licensing standards do not meet the standards contained in Subparts G and H of this part, as determined by the Administrator, such applicant shall obtain a Nonresident CDL from a State which meets such standards. Such applicant shall:

(1) *Complete the requirements* to obtain a CDL contained in §383.71(a); and

(2) *After receipt of the CDL,* and for as long as it is valid, notify the State which issued the CDL of any adverse action taken by any jurisdiction or governmental agency, foreign or domestic, against his/her driving privileges. Such adverse actions would include but not be limited to license suspension or revocation, or disqualification from operating a commercial motor vehicle for the convictions described in §383.51. Notifications shall be made within the time periods specified in §383.33.

(f) *If a State uses the alternative method* described in §383.73(i) to achieve the objectives of the certifications in §383.71(a), then the driver applicant shall satisfy such alternative methods as are applicable to him/her with respect to initial licensing, license transfer, license renewal, and license upgrades.

§383.71 DOT Interpretations

Question 1: What must a driver certify if he/she is in interstate commerce but is excepted or exempted from Part 391 under the provisions of Parts 390 or 391?

Guidance: The State should instruct the driver to certify that he/she is not subject to Part 391.

Question 2: Since an applicant is required to turn in his/her current license when issued an FRSI-restricted CDL, should the applicant return to the State exam office and be re-issued the old license when the seasonal validation period expires?

Guidance: No. This approach violates the requirements of Part 383 and the FRSI waiver regarding the single-license concept. It violates the waiver requirement that the FRSI-restricted CDL is to have the same renewal cycle as an unrestricted CDL and shall serve as an operator's license for vehicles other than CMVs. The license issued under the waiver is a CDL and must be treated the same as an unrestricted CDL in regard to the driver record being maintained through the CDLIS and subject to all disqualifying conditions for the full renewal cycle. The restriction determining when the driver may use the CDL to operate a CMV should be clearly printed on the license.

Question 3: Do the regulations require that a driver be recertified for the hazardous materials "H" endorsement every two years?

Guidance: No. If the driver wishes to retain an HM endorsement, he/she is required at the time of license renewal to pass the test for such endorsement. The only times a driver may be required to pass the test for such endorsement in a condensed time frame is within the 2 years preceding a license transfer if he/she is transferring a CDL from one State of domicile to a new State of domicile (see §383.73(b)(4)), or if the State has exercised its prerogative to establish more stringent requirements.

Question 4: May a CDL driving skills test examiner conduct a driving skills test administered in accordance with 49 CFR Part 383 before a person subject to Part 382 is tested for alcohol and controlled substances?

Guidance: Yes. A CDL driving skills test examiner, including a third party examiner, may administer a driving skills test to a person subject to Part 382 without first testing him/her for alcohol and controlled substances. The intent of the CDL driving skills test is to assess a person's ability to operate a commercial motor vehicle during an official government test of their driving skills. However, this guidance does not allow an employer (including a truck or bus driver training school) to use a person as a current company, lease, or student driver prior to obtaining a verified negative test result. An employer must obtain a verified negative controlled substance test result prior to dispatching a driver on his/her first trip.

§383.72 Implied consent to alcohol testing.

Any person who holds a CDL is considered to have consented to such testing as is required by any State or jurisdiction in the enforcement of §§383.51(b)(2)(i) and 392.5(a)(2) of this chapter. Consent is implied by driving a commercial motor vehicle.

§383.73 State procedures.

(a) **Initial licensure.** Prior to issuing a CDL to a person, a State shall:

(1) *Require the driver applicant* to certify, pass tests, and provide information as described in §§383.71(a)(1) through (6);

(2) *Check that the vehicle* in which the applicant takes his/her test is representative of the vehicle group the applicant has certified that he/she operates or expects to operate;

(3) *Initiate and complete* a check of the applicant's driving record to ensure that the person is not subject to any disqualification under §383.51, or any license suspension, revocation, or cancellation under State law, and that the person does not have a driver's license from more than one State or jurisdiction. The record check must include, but is not limited to, the following:

(i) *A check of the applicant's driving record* as maintained by his/her current State of licensure, if any;

(ii) *A check with the CDLIS* to determine whether the driver applicant already has been issued a CDL, whether the applicant's license has been suspended, revoked, or canceled, or if the applicant has been disqualified from operating a commercial motor vehicle;

(iii) *A check with the National Driver Register (NDR)* to determine whether the driver applicant has:

[A] *Been disqualified* from operating a motor vehicle (other than a commercial motor vehicle);

[B] *Had a license* (other than CDL) suspended, revoked, or canceled for cause in the 3-year period ending on the date of application; or

[C] *Been convicted* of any offenses contained in section 205(a)(3) of the National Driver Register Act of 1982 (23 U.S.C. 401 note); and

(iv) *A request* for the applicant's complete driving record from all States where the applicant was previously licensed over the last 10 years to drive any type of motor vehicle.

EXCEPTION: A State is only required to make the driving record check specified in this paragraph (a)(3) for drivers renewing a CDL for the first time after September 30, 2002, provided a notation is made on the driver's record confirming that the driver record check required by this paragraph (a)(3) has been made and noting the date it was done; and

(4) *Require the driver applicant* to surrender his/her driver's license issued by another State, if he/she has moved from another State.

(5) *For persons* applying for a hazardous materials endorsement, require compliance with the standards for such endorsement specified in §383.71(a)(9).

(b) **License transfers.** Prior to issuing a CDL to a person who has a CDL from another State, a State shall:

(1) *Require the driver applicant* to make the certifications contained in §383.71(a);

(2) *Complete a check* of the driver applicant's record as contained in §383.73(a)(3);

(3) *Request and receive updates* of information specified in Subpart J of this part;

(4) *If such applicant* wishes to retain a hazardous materials endorsement, require compliance with standards for such endorsement specified in §383.71(a)(9) and ensure that the driver has, within the 2 years preceding the transfer, either:

(i) *Passed the test for such endorsement specified in §383.121;* or

(ii) *Successfully completed* a hazardous materials test or training that is given by a third party and that is deemed by the State to substantially cover the same knowledge base as that described in §383.121; and

Subpart E - Testing and Licensing Procedures §383.75 (a)

(5) *Obtain the CDL* issued by the applicant's previous State of domicile.

(c) **License Renewals.** Prior to renewing any CDL a State shall:
   (1) *Require the driver applicant* to make the certifications contained in §383.71(a);
   (2) *Complete a check* of the driver applicant's record as contained in §383.73(a)(3);
   (3) *Request and receive updates of information* specified in Subpart J of this part; and
   (4) *If such applicant wishes to retain* a hazardous materials endorsement, require the driver to pass the test specified in §383.121 and comply with the standards specified in §383.71(a)(9) for such endorsement.

(d) **License upgrades.** Prior to issuing an upgrade of a CDL, a State shall:
   (1) *Require such driver applicant* to provide certifications, pass tests, and meet applicable hazardous materials standards specified in §383.71(d); and
   (2) *Complete a check* of the driver applicant's record as described in §383.73(a)(3).

(e) **Nonresident CDL.** A State may issue a Nonresident CDL to a person domiciled in a foreign country if the Administrator has determined that the commercial motor vehicle testing and licensing standards in the foreign jurisdiction of domicile do not meet the standards contained in this part. State procedures for the issuance of a nonresident CDL, for any modifications thereto, and for notifications to the CDLIS shall at a minimum be identical to those pertaining to any other CDL, with the following exceptions:
   (1) *If the applicant is requesting a transfer* of his/her Nonresident CDL, the State shall obtain the Nonresident CDL currently held by the applicant and issued by another State;
   (2) *The State shall add the word "Nonresident"* to the face of the CDL, in accordance with §383.153(b); and
   (3) *The State shall have established,* prior to issuing any Nonresident CDL, the practical capability of disqualifying the holder of any Nonresident CDL, by withdrawing, suspending, canceling, and revoking his/her Nonresident CDL as if the Nonresident CDL were a CDL issued to a resident of the State.

(f) **License issuance.** After the State has completed the procedures described in §383.73 (a), (b), (c), (d) or (e), it may issue a CDL to the driver applicant. The State shall notify the operator of the CDLIS of such issuance, transfer, renewal, or upgrade within the 10-day period beginning on the date of license issuance.

(g) **Penalties for false information.** If a State determines, in its check of an applicant's license status and record prior to issuing a CDL, or at any time after the CDL is issued, that the applicant has falsified information contained in Subpart J of this part or any of the certifications required in §383.71(a), the State shall at a minimum suspend, cancel, or revoke the person's CDL or his/her pending application, or disqualify the person from operating a commercial motor vehicle for a period of at least 60 consecutive days.

(h) **Reciprocity.** A State shall allow any person who has a valid CDL which is not suspended, revoked, or canceled, and who is not disqualified from operating a commercial motor vehicle, to operate a commercial motor vehicle in the State.

(i) **Alternative procedures.** A State may implement alternative procedures to the certification requirements of §383.71(a)(1), (4), and (6), provided those procedures ensure that the driver meets the requirements of those paragraphs.

§383.73 DOT Interpretations

Question 1: Does the State have any role in certifying compliance with §391.11(b)(2) of the FMCSRs, which requires driver competence in the English language?
Guidance: No. The driver must certify that he or she meets the qualifications of Part 391. The State is under no duty to verify the certification by giving exams or tests.

Question 2: Are States required to change their current medical standards for drivers who need CDLs?
Guidance: No, but interstate drivers must continue to meet the Federal standards, while intrastate drivers are subject to the requirements adopted by the State.

Question 3: To what does the phrase "... as contained in §383.51" refer to in §383.73(a)(3)?

Guidance: The phrase refers only to the word "disqualification." Thus the State must check the applicant's record to ensure that he/she is not subject to any suspensions, revocations, or cancellations for any reason, and is not subject to any disqualifications under §383.51.

Question 4: Is a State required to refuse a CDL to an applicant if the NDR check shows that he/she had a license suspended, revoked, or canceled within 3 years of the date of the application?
Guidance: Yes, if the person's driving license is currently suspended, revoked, or canceled.

Question 5: Must a new State of record accept the out-of-state driving record on CDL transfer applications and include this record as a permanent part of the new State's file?
Guidance: Yes.

Question 6: What does the term "initial licensure" mean as used in §383.73?
Guidance: The term "initial licensure" as used in the context of §383.73 is meant to refer to the procedures a State must follow when a person applies for his/her first CDL.

Question 7: May a State allow an applicant to keep his/her current valid State license when issued an FRSI-restricted CDL?
Guidance: No. That would violate the single-license concept.

Question 8: Does the word "issuing" as used in §383.73(a) include temporary 60-day CDLs as well as permanent CDLs?
Guidance: Yes, the word "issuing" applies to all CDLs whether they are temporary or permanent.

Question 9: When a State chooses to meet the certification requirements of §383.73(a)(1), (b)(1), (c)(1), and (d)(1) by demanding, as part of its licensing process, that a commercial driver maintain with the Department of Motor Vehicles (DMV) currently valid evidence of compliance with the physical qualification standards of Part 391, Subpart E, may the State suspend, cancel, or revoke the driver's CDL if he/she does not maintain such evidence with the DMV?
Guidance: Yes. §383.73 requires a State to obtain from a driver applicant a certification that he/she meets the qualification standards of Part 391, including Subpart E (Physical Qualifications and Examinations). A requirement that a driver maintain currently valid evidence of compliance with Subpart E does not conflict with Part 383, since the CMVSA made it clear that the DOT was to issue "regulations to establish minimum Federal standards * * *" (49 U.S.C. 31305(a)). A State may therefore demand more information or tests than the Federal CDL regulations require. If a driver fails to comply with State requirements which are not inconsistent with Part 383, the State may suspend, cancel or revoke the driver's CDL. This action is not a disqualification for purposes of §383.51, but a withdrawal of the commercial driving privilege.

Question 10: What action should enforcement officers take when a commercial driver's CDL has been declared invalid by the issuing State because of a lapse in the driver's medical certificate?
Guidance: Whatever the reason for the State's decision, a driver with an invalid CDL may not lawfully drive a CMV.

Question 11: May licensing jurisdictions meet their stewardship requirements for surrendered licenses by physically marking the license in some way as not valid and returning it to a driver as part of the driver's application for a new or renewal of an existing CDL?
Guidance: Yes. Provided the licensing jurisdiction meets the test of guaranteeing that the returned license document cannot possibly be mistaken for a valid document by a casual observer. A document perforated with the word "VOID" conspicuously and unmistakably displayed with holes large enough to be easily distinguished by a casual observer in limited light, which cannot be obscured by the holder of the document, would meet the test of being invalidated.

§383.75 Third party testing.

(a) **Third party tests.** A State may authorize a person (including another State, an employer, a private driver training facility or other private institution, or a department, agency or instrumentality of a local government) to administer the skills tests as specified in Subparts G and H of this part, if the following conditions are met:
   (1) *The tests given by the third party* are the same as those which would otherwise be given by the State; and
   (2) *The third party* as an agreement with the State containing, at a minimum, provisions that:
      (i) *Allow the FMCSA,* or its representative, and the State to conduct random examinations, inspections and audits without prior notice;

(ii) *Require the State* to conduct on-site inspections at least annually;

(iii) *Require that all third party examiners* meet the same qualification and training standards as State examiners, to the extent necessary to conduct skills tests in compliance with Subparts G and H;

(iv) *Require that,* at least on an annual basis, State employees take the tests actually administered by the third party as if the State employee were a test applicant, or that States test a sample of drivers who were examined by the third party to compare pass/fail results; and

(v) *Reserve unto the State* the right to take prompt and appropriate remedial action against the third-party testers in the event that the third-party fails to comply with State or Federal standards for the CDL testing program, or with any other terms of the third-party contract.

(b) **Proof of testing by a third party.** A driver applicant who takes and passes driving tests administered by an authorized third party shall provide evidence to the State licensing agency that he/she has successfully passed the driving tests administered by the third party.

§383.75 DOT Interpretations

Question 1: May the CDL knowledge test be administered by a third party?
Guidance: No. The third party testing provision found in §383.75 applies only to the skills portion of the testing procedure. However, if an employee of the State who is authorized to supervise knowledge testing is present during the testing, then the FMCSA regards it as being administered by the State and not by the third party.

Question 2: Do third party skills test examiners have to meet all the requirements of State-employed examiners — i.e. all the State's qualification and training standards?
Guidance: No. §383.75(a)(2)(iii) requires third party examiners to meet the same standards as State examiners only "to the extent necessary to conduct skills tests."

Question 3: Do third-party skills test examiners have to be qualified to administer skills tests in all types of CMVs?
Guidance: No.

§383.77 Substitute for driving skills tests.

At the discretion of a State, the driving skill test as specified in §383.113 may be waived for a CMV operator who is currently licensed at the time of his/her application for a CDL, and substituted with either an applicant's driving record and previous passage of an acceptable skills test, or an applicant's driving record in combination with certain driving experience. The State shall impose conditions and limitations to restrict the applicants from whom a State may accept alternative requirements for the skills test described in §383.113. Such conditions must require at least the following:

(a) **An applicant must certify that,** during the two-year period immediately prior to applying for a CDL, he/she:

(1) *Has not had more than one license* (except in the instances specified in §383.21(b));

(2) *Has not had any license suspended, revoked, or canceled;*

(3) *Has not had any convictions* for any type of motor vehicle for the disqualifying offenses contained in §383.51(b);

(4) *Has not had more than one conviction* for any type of motor vehicle for serious traffic violations; and

(5) *Has not had any conviction* for a violation of State or local law relating to motor vehicle traffic control (other than a parking violation) arising in connection with any traffic accident, and has no record of an accident in which he/she was at fault; and

(b) **An applicant must provide evidence and certify that:**

(1) *He/she is regularly employed* in a job requiring operation of a CMV, and that either:

(2) *He/she has previously taken and passed* a skills test given by a State with a classified licensing and testing system, and that the test was behind-the-wheel in a representative vehicle for that applicant's driver's license classification; or

(3) *He/she has operated,* for at least 2 years immediately preceding application for a CDL, a vehicle representative of the commercial motor vehicle the driver applicant operates or expects to operate.

§383.77 DOT Interpretations

Question 1: May a State grandfather drivers from skills testing under §383.77?
Guidance: Yes, provided the applicant meets all the eligibility conditions under §383.77, including current operation of a CMV (§383.77(b)(1)). Therefore, the pool of applicants eligible for grandfathering is limited to drivers with current CMV operating experience under a CDL waiver (e.g., farm, FRSI, firefighting, emergency and military vehicles).

Question 2: May a driver applicant be "grandfathered" from any CDL knowledge test?
Guidance: No. "Grandfathering" of CDL basic or endorsement knowledge testing is not permitted by Part 383.

Subpart F - Vehicle Groups and Endorsements

§383.91 Commercial motor vehicle groups.

(a) **Vehicle group descriptions.** Each driver applicant must possess and be tested on his/her knowledge and skills, described in Subpart G of this part, for the commercial motor vehicle group(s) for which he/she desires a CDL. The commercial motor vehicle groups are as follows:

(1) *Combination vehicle (Group A)* — Any combination of vehicles with a gross combination weight rating (GCWR) of 11,794 kilograms or more (26,001 pounds or more) provided the GVWR of the vehicle(s) being towed is in excess of 4,536 kilograms (10,000 pounds).

(2) *Heavy Straight Vehicle (Group B)* — Any single vehicle with a GVWR of 11,794 kilograms or more (26,001 pounds or more), or any such vehicle towing a vehicle not in excess of 4,536 kilograms (10,000 pounds) GVWR.

(3) *Small Vehicle (Group C)* — Any single vehicle, or combination of vehicles, that meets neither the definition of Group A nor that of Group B as contained in this section, but that either is designed to transport 16 or more passengers including the driver, or is used in the transportation of materials found to be hazardous for the purposes of the Hazardous Materials Transportation Act and which require the motor vehicle to be placarded under the Hazardous Materials Regulations (49 CFR Part 172, Subpart F).

(b) **Representative vehicle.** For purposes of taking the driving test in accordance with §383.113, a representative vehicle for a given vehicle group contained in §383.91(a), is any commercial motor vehicle which meets the definition of that vehicle group.

(c) **Relation between vehicle groups.** Each driver applicant who desires to operate in a different commercial motor vehicle group from the one which his/her CDL authorizes shall be required to retake and pass all related tests, except the following:

(1) *A driver who has passed* the knowledge and skills tests for a combination vehicle (Group A) may operate a heavy straight vehicle (Group B) or a small vehicle (Group C), provided that he/she possesses the requisite endorsement(s); and

(2) *A driver who has passed* the knowledge and skills tests for a heavy straight vehicle (Group B) may operate any small vehicle (Group C), provided that he/she possesses the requisite endorsement(s).

(d) **Vehicle group illustration.** Figure 1 illustrates typical vehicles within each of the vehicle groups defined in this section.

Figure 1 Vehicle Groups as Established by FMCSA (§383.91)
[Note: Certain types of vehicles, such as passenger and doubles/triples, will require an endorsement. Please consult text for particulars.]

Group: *Description:

A   Any combination of vehicles with a GCWR of 26,001 or more pounds provided the GVWR of the vehicle(s) being towed is in excess of 10,000 pounds. (Holders of a Group A license may, with any appropriate endorsements, operate all vehicles within Groups B and C.)

Examples include, but are not limited to:

Subpart F - Vehicle Groups and Endorsements §383.93 (c)

Group:	*Description:
B	Any single vehicle with a GVWR of 26,001 or more pounds, or any such vehicle towing a vehicle not in excess of 10,000 pounds GVWR. (Holders of a Group B license may, with any appropriate endorsements, operate all vehicles within Group C.)

Examples include, but are not limited to:

C	Any single vehicle, or combination of vehicles, that does not meet the definition of Group A or Group B as contained herein, but that either is designed to transport 16 or more passengers including the driver, or is placarded for hazardous materials.

Examples include, but are not limited to:

* The representative vehicle for the skills test must meet the written description for that group. The silhouettes typify, but do not fully cover, the types of vehicles falling within each group.

§383.91 DOT Interpretations

Question 1: May a State expand a vehicle group to include vehicles that do not meet the Federal definition of the group?
Guidance: Yes, if:
 a. A person who tests in a vehicle that does not meet the Federal standard for the group(s) for which the issued CDL would otherwise be valid, is restricted to vehicles not meeting the Federal definition of such group(s); and
 b. The restriction is fully explained on the license.

Question 2: Is a driver of a combination vehicle with a GCWR of less than 26,001 pounds required to obtain a CDL even if the trailer GVWR is more than 10,000 pounds?
Guidance: No, because the GCWR is less than 26,001 pounds. The driver would need a CDL if the vehicle is transporting HM requiring the vehicle to be placarded or if it is designed to transport 16 or more persons.

Question 3: Can a State which expands the vehicle group descriptions in §383.91 enforce those expansions on out-of-state CMV drivers by requiring them to have a CDL?
Guidance: No. They must recognize out-of-state licenses that have been validly issued in accordance with the Federal standards and operative licensing compacts.

Question 4: What CMV group are drivers of articulated motorcoaches (buses) required to possess?
Guidance: Drivers of articulated motorcoaches are required to possess a Class B CDL.

Question 5: Do tow truck operators need CDLs? If so, in what vehicle group(s)?
Guidance: For CDL purposes, the tow truck and its towed vehicle are treated the same as any other powered unit towing a nonpowered unit:
— If the GCWR of the tow truck and its towed vehicle is 26,001 pounds or more, and the towed vehicle alone exceeds 10,000 pounds GVWR, then the driver needs a Group A CDL.
— If the GVWR of the tow truck alone is 26,001 pounds or more, and the driver either (a) drives the tow truck without a vehicle in tow, or (b) drives the tow truck with a towed vehicle of 10,000 pounds or less GVWR, then the driver needs a Group B CDL.
— A driver of a tow truck or towing configuration that does not fit either configuration description above, requires a Group C CDL only if he or she tows a vehicle required to be placarded for hazardous materials on a "subsequent move," i.e. after the initial movement of the disabled vehicle to the nearest storage or repair facility.

§383.93 Endorsements.
(a) **General.** In addition to taking and passing the knowledge and skills tests described in Subpart G of this part, all persons who operate or expect to operate the type(s) of motor vehicles described in paragraph (b) of this section shall take and pass specialized tests to obtain each endorsement. The State shall issue CDL endorsements only to drivers who successfully complete the tests.
(b) **Endorsement descriptions.** An operator must obtain State-issued endorsements to his/her CDL to operate commercial motor vehicles which are:
 (1) *Double/triple trailers;*
 (2) *Passenger vehicles;*
 (3) *Tank vehicles;*
 (4) *Used to transport hazardous materials as defined in §383.5; or*
 (5) *School buses.*
(c) **Endorsement testing requirements.** The following tests are required for the endorsements contained in paragraph (b) of this section:
 (1) *Double/Triple Trailers — a knowledge test;*
 (2) *Passenger — a knowledge and a skills test;*
 (3) *Tank vehicle — a knowledge test;*
 (4) *Hazardous Materials — a knowledge test; and*
 (5) *School bus — a knowledge and a skills test.*

§383.93 DOT Interpretations

Question 1: Is the HM endorsement needed for operation of State and local government vehicles carrying HM?
Guidance: No.

Question 2: Are drivers of double and triple saddle-mount combinations required to have the double/triple trailers endorsement on their CDLs?
Guidance: Yes, if the following conditions apply:
— There is more than one point of articulation in the combination;
— The GCWR is 26,001 or more pounds; and
— The combined GVWR of the vehicle(s) being towed is in excess of 10,000 pounds.

Question 3: Are drivers delivering empty buses in driveaway-towaway operations required to have the passenger endorsement on their CDLs?
Guidance: No.

Question 4: Would the driver in the following scenarios be required to have a CDL with a HM endorsement?
 a. A driver transports 1,000 or more pounds of Division 1.4 (Class C explosive) materials in a vehicle with a GVWR of less than 26,001 pounds?
 b. A driver transports less than 1,000 pounds of Division 1.4 (Class C explosive) materials in a vehicle with a GVWR of less than 26,001 pounds?
 c. The driver transports any quantity of Division 1.1, 1.2 or 1.3 (Class A or B explosive) materials in any vehicle.
Guidance:
 a. Yes.
 b. No.
 c. Yes.

Question 5: Do drivers of ready-mix concrete mixers need a tank vehicle endorsement ("N") on their CDL?
Guidance: No.

Question 6: Does an unattached tote or portable tank with a cargo capacity of 1,000 gallons or more meet the definition of "portable tank" requiring a tank vehicle endorsement on the driver's CDL?
Guidance: Yes.

Question 7: Must all drivers of vehicles required to be placarded have CDLs containing the HM endorsement?
Guidance: Yes, unless waived.

Question 8: Is a driver who operates a truck tractor pulling a heavy-haul trailer attached to the tractor by means of a "jeep" that meets the definition of a CMV under Part 383 required to have a CDL with a double/triple trailer endorsement?
Guidance: Yes. The "jeep," also referred to as a load divider, is a short frame-type trailer complete with upper coupler, fifth wheel and undercarriage assembly and designed in such a manner that when coupled to a semitrailer and tractor it carries a portion of the trailer kingpin load while transferring the remainder to the tractor's fifth wheel.

Question 9: Do persons transporting battery-powered forklifts need to obtain an HM endorsement?
Guidance: No.

Question 10: Do tow truck operators who hold a CDL require endorsements to tow "endorsable" vehicles?
Guidance: For CDL endorsement purposes, the nature of the tow truck operations determines the need for endorsements:
— If the driver's towing operations are restricted to emergency "first moves" from the site of a breakdown or accident to the nearest appropriate repair facility, then no CDL endorsement of any kind is required.
— If the driver's towing operations include any "subsequent moves" from one repair or disposal facility to another, then endorsements requisite to the vehicles being towed are required. *Exception*: Tow truck operators need not obtain a passenger endorsement.

Question 11: Must a driver have a tank vehicle endorsement to deliver an empty storage container tank, not designed for transportation, with a rated capacity of 1,000 gallons or more that is temporarily attached to a flatbed trailer?
Guidance: No. Part of the definition of a "tank vehicle" in §383.5 is "any commercial motor vehicle that is designed to transport any liquid or gaseous materials within a tank that is either permanently or temporarily attached to the vehicle or the chassis." A flatbed is not "designed to transport any liquid or gaseous materials" simply because it carries an empty storage tank — readily distinguishable from a transportation tank — secured as cargo in compliance with Part 393, Subpart I.

Question 12: Is a person who drives an empty school bus from the manufacturer to the local distributor required to obtain a CDL?
Guidance: Yes. Any driver of a bus that is designed to transport 16 or more passengers or that has a GVWR of 11,794 kilograms (26,001 pounds) or greater is required to obtain a CDL in the applicable class. A passenger endorsement is also required if the bus is designed to transport 16 or more passengers, including the driver.

Question 13: Does a driver who operates a straight truck equipped with a pintle hook towing a full trailer (a semitrailer equipped with a converter dolly) need a doubles/triples endorsement on his or her (CDL)?
Guidance: No. This combination is a truck-tractor towing a single trailer. This configuration does not require a driver to have a doubles/triples endorsement on a CDL.

§383.95 Air brake restrictions.

(a) If an applicant either fails the air brake component of the knowledge test, or performs the skills test in a vehicle not equipped with air brakes, the State shall indicate on the CDL, if issued, that the person is restricted from operating a CMV equipped with air brakes.

(b) For the purposes of the skills test and the restriction, air brakes shall include any braking system operating fully or partially on the air brake principle.

§383.95 DOT Interpretations

Question 1: A driver has a Group B or C CDL valid for airbrake-equipped vehicles. He or she later upgrades to a Group A license by testing in a vehicle that is not equipped with airbrakes. Must the State restrict the upgraded license to nonairbrake-equipped vehicles?
Guidance: No, because the airbrake systems on combination versus single vehicles do not differ significantly.

Question 2: May a driver who has an air brake restriction as defined in §383.95 operate a CMV equipped with an air-over-hydraulic brake system?
Guidance: No. Under §383.95(b), the term "air brakes" includes any braking system operating fully or partially on the air brake principle. Air-over-hydraulic brake systems operate partially on the air brake principle and are therefore air brakes for purposes of the CDL regulations. The NHTSA also considers "air over hydraulic" brakes to be air brakes under FMVSS 121.

Question 3: May a State issue a restriction to a driver who passes the air brake knowledge test and the skills test in a vehicle equipped with an air-over-hydraulic brake system that limits the driver to operate only vehicles equipped with an air-over-hydraulic air brake system?

Guidance: Yes. A State may issue the additional restriction, provided it is fully explained on the CDL. This would give a State the option to allow a driver who tests in a vehicle equipped with an air-over-hydraulic brake system (rather than a full air brake system) to operate a vehicle equipped with either a hydraulic or air-over-hydraulic brake system, while restricting them from operating vehicles equipped with a full air brake system.

Question 4: May a driver with an air brake restriction on his or her CDL operate a CMV equipped with a hydraulic braking system that has an air-assisted parking brake release?
Guidance: Yes. The air brake restriction applies only to the principal braking system used to stop the vehicle. §383.95(b) is not applicable to an air-assisted mechanism to release the parking brake.

Subpart G - Required Knowledge and Skills

§383.110 General requirement.

All drivers of commercial motor vehicles shall have knowledge and skills necessary to operate a commercial moztor vehicle safely as contained in this subpart. A sample of the specific types of items which a State may wish to include in the knowledge and skills tests that it administers to CDL applicants is included in the appendix to this Subpart G.

§383.111 Required knowledge.

All commercial motor vehicle operators must have knowledge of the following general areas:

(a) **Safe operations regulations.** Driver-related elements of the regulations contained in 49 CFR Parts 382, 391, 392, 393, 395, 396, and 397, such as: Motor vehicle inspection, repair, and maintenance requirements; procedures for safe vehicle operations; the effects of fatigue, poor vision, hearing, and general health upon safe commercial motor vehicle operation; the types of motor vehicles and cargoes subject to the requirements; and the effects of alcohol and drug use upon safe commercial motor vehicle operations.

(b) **Commercial motor vehicle safety control systems.** Proper use of the motor vehicle's safety system, including lights, horns, side and rear-view mirrors, proper mirror adjustments, fire extinguishers, symptoms of improper operation revealed through instruments, motor vehicle operation characteristics, and diagnosing malfunctions. Commercial motor vehicle drivers shall have knowledge on the correct procedures needed to use these safety systems in an emergency situation, e.g., skids and loss of brakes.

(c) **Safe vehicle control.**
  (1) *Control systems.* The purpose and function of the controls and instruments commonly found on commercial motor vehicles.
  (2) *Basic control.* The proper procedures for performing various basic maneuvers.
  (3) *Shifting.* The basic shifting rules and terms, as well as shift patterns and procedures for common transmissions.
  (4) *Backing.* The procedures and rules for various backing maneuvers.
  (5) *Visual search.* The importance of proper visual search, and proper visual search methods.
  (6) *Communication.* The principles and procedures for proper communications and the hazards of failure to signal properly.
  (7) *Speed management.* The importance of understanding the effects of speed.
  (8) *Space management.* The procedures and techniques for controlling the space around the vehicle.
  (9) *Night operation.* Preparations and procedures for night driving.
  (10) *Extreme driving conditions.* The basic information on operating in extreme driving conditions and the hazards that are encountered in extreme conditions.
  (11) *Hazard perceptions.* The basic information on hazard perception and clues for recognition of hazards.
  (12) *Emergency maneuvers.* The basic information concerning when and how to make emergency maneuvers.
  (13) *Skid control and recovery.* The information on the causes and major types of skids, as well as the procedures for recovering from skids.

(d) **Relationship of cargo to vehicle control.** The principles and procedures for the proper handling of cargo.

(e) **Vehicle inspections:** The objectives and proper procedures for performing vehicle safety inspections, as follows:
  (1) *The importance of periodic inspection and repair to vehicle safety.*

Subpart G - Required Knowledge and Skills §383.121 (a)

(2) *The effect of undiscovered malfunctions upon safety.*
(3) *What safety-related parts to look for when inspecting vehicles.*
(4) *Pre-trip/enroute/post-trip inspection procedures.*
(5) *Reporting findings.*

(f) **Hazardous materials knowledge, such as:** What constitutes hazardous material requiring an endorsement to transport; classes of hazardous materials; labeling/placarding requirements; and the need for specialized training as a prerequisite to receiving the endorsement and transporting hazardous cargoes.

(g) **Air brake knowledge as follows:**
  (1) *Air brake system nomenclature;*
  (2) *The dangers of contaminated air supply;*
  (3) *Implications of severed or disconnected air lines* between the power unit and the trailer(s);
  (4) *Implications of low air pressure readings;*
  (5) *Procedures to conduct safe and accurate pre-trip inspections.*
  (6) *Procedures for conducting* enroute and post-trip inspections of air actuated brake systems, including ability to detect defects which may cause the system to fail.

(h) **Operators for the combination vehicle group** shall also have knowledge of:
  (1) *Coupling and uncoupling* — The procedures for proper coupling and uncoupling a tractor to semi-trailer.
  (2) *Vehicle inspection* — The objectives and proper procedures that are unique for performing vehicle safety inspections on combination vehicles.

§383.113 Required skills.

(a) **Basic vehicle control skills.** All applicants for a CDL must possess and demonstrate basic motor vehicle control skills for each vehicle group which the driver operates or expects to operate. These skills should include the ability to start, to stop, and to move the vehicle forward and backward in a safe manner.

(b) **Safe driving skills.** All applicants for a CDL must possess and demonstrate the safe driving skills for their vehicle group. These skills should include proper visual search methods, appropriate use of signals, speed control for weather and traffic conditions, and ability to position the motor vehicle correctly when changing lanes or turning.

(c) **Air brake skills.** Except as provided in §393.95, all applicants shall demonstrate the following skills with respect to inspection and operation of air brakes:
  (1) *Pre-trip inspection skills.* Applicants shall demonstrate the skills necessary to conduct a pre-trip inspection which includes the ability to:
    (i) *Locate and verbally identify* air brake operating controls and monitoring devices;
    (ii) *Determine the motor vehicle's* brake system condition for proper adjustments and that air system connections between motor vehicles have been properly made and secured;
    (iii) *Inspect the low pressure warning device(s)* to ensure that they will activate in emergency situations;
    (iv) *Ascertain, with the engine running,* that the system maintains an adequate supply of compressed air;
    (v) *Determine that required* minimum air pressure build up time is within acceptable limits and that required alarms and emergency devices automatically deactivate at the proper pressure level; and
    (vi) *Operationally check the brake system for proper performance.*
  (2) *Driving skills.* Applicants shall successfully complete the skills tests contained in §383.113 in a representative vehicle equipped with air brakes.

(d) **Test area.** Skills tests shall be conducted in on-street conditions or under a combination of on-street and off-street conditions.

(e) **Simulation technology.** A State may utilize simulators to perform skills testing, but under no circumstances as a substitute for the required testing in on-street conditions.

§383.113 DOT Interpretations

Question 1: A driver holding a CDL with an "air brake restriction" wants to operate a commercial motor vehicle of the same vehicle group which is equipped with air brakes. Must the driver retake the complete CDL test, or may the State conduct a partial test to determine the driver's air brake skills?

Guidance: Since the applicant has already demonstrated the ability to drive a vehicle in a specific vehicle group, the State may conduct a test that includes only the Air brake knowledge requirements of §383.111(g) and the Air brake skills, pre-trip inspection skills and driving skills required by §383.113(c). The driving skills test need only demonstrate that the driver can safely and effectively operate the vehicle's air brakes.

Question 2: May a driver use a truck tractor (as defined in 49 CFR 390.5) as a representative vehicle for purposes of completing the skills tests for a Class B commercial driver's license (CDL)?

Guidance: No. A driver must be tested in a truck or bus (as those terms are defined in 49 CFR 390.5), or other single unit vehicle with a gross vehicle weight rating (GVWR) of 11,794 kilograms (26,001 pounds) or more to satisfy the skills testing requirements for a Class B CDL. A truck tractor is designed to operate with a towed unit(s), typically a semi-trailer (as defined in 49 CFR 390.5) and therefore could only be used as a representative vehicle when connected to a semi-trailer, for a Class A CDL.

§383.115 Requirements for double/triple trailers endorsement.

In order to obtain a Double/Triple Trailers endorsement each applicant must have knowledge covering:

(a) **Procedures for assembly and hookup of the units;**
(b) **Proper placement of heaviest trailer;**
(c) **Handling and stability characteristics** including off-tracking, response to steering, sensory feedback, braking, oscillatory sway, rollover in steady turns, yaw stability in steady turns; and
(d) **Potential problems in traffic operations,** including problems the motor vehicle creates for other motorists due to slower speeds on steep grades, longer passing times, possibility for blocking entry of other motor vehicles on freeways, splash and spray impacts, aerodynamic buffeting, view blockages, and lateral placement.

§383.117 Requirements for passenger endorsement.

An applicant for the passenger endorsement must satisfy both of the following additional knowledge and skills test requirements.

(a) **Knowledge test.** All applicants for the passenger endorsement must have knowledge covering at least the following topics:
  (1) *Proper procedures for loading/unloading passengers;*
  (2) *Proper use of emergency exits, including push-out windows;*
  (3) *Proper responses to such emergency situations* as fires and unruly passengers;
  (4) *Proper procedures at railroad crossings and drawbridges;* and
  (5) *Proper braking procedures.*
(b) **Skills test.** To obtain a passenger endorsement applicable to a specific vehicle group, an applicant must take his/her skills test in a passenger vehicle satisfying the requirements of that group as defined in §383.91.

§383.119 Requirements for tank vehicle endorsement.

In order to obtain a Tank Vehicle Endorsement, each applicant must have knowledge covering the following:

(a) **Causes, prevention, and effects** of cargo surge on motor vehicle handling;
(b) **Proper braking procedures for the motor vehicle** when it is empty, full and partially full;
(c) **Differences in handling** of baffled/compartmental tank interiors versus non-baffled motor vehicles;
(d) **Differences in tank vehicle type and construction;**
(e) **Differences in cargo surge** for liquids of varying product densities;
(f) **Effects of road grade and curvature** on motor vehicle handling with filled, half-filled and empty tanks;
(g) **Proper use of emergency systems; and**
(h) **For drivers of DOT specification tank vehicles,** retest and marking requirements.

§383.121 Requirements for hazardous materials endorsement.

In order to obtain a Hazardous Material Endorsement each applicant must have such knowledge as is required of a driver of a hazardous materials laden vehicle, from information contained in 49 CFR Parts 171, 172, 173, 177, 178, and 397 on the following:

(a) **Hazardous materials regulations including:**
  (1) *Hazardous materials table;*

(2) *Shipping paper requirements;*
(3) *Marking;*
(4) *Labeling;*
(5) *Placarding requirements;*
(6) *Hazardous materials packaging;*
(7) *Hazardous materials definitions and preparation;*
(8) *Other regulated material (e.g., ORM-D);*
(9) *Reporting hazardous materials accidents; and*
(10) *Tunnels and railroad crossings.*

(b) **Hazardous materials handling including:**
(1) *Forbidden Materials and Packages;*
(2) *Loading and Unloading Materials;*
(3) *Cargo Segregation;*
(4) *Passenger Carrying Buses and Hazardous Materials;*
(5) *Attendance of Motor Vehicles;*
(6) *Parking;*
(7) *Routes;*
(8) *Cargo Tanks; and*
(9) *"Safe Havens."*

(c) **Operation of emergency equipment including:**
(1) *Use of equipment to protect the public;*
(2) *Special precautions for equipment to be used in fires;*
(3) *Special precautions* for use of emergency equipment when loading or unloading a hazardous materials laden motor vehicle; and
(4) *Use of emergency equipment for tank vehicles.*

(d) **Emergency response procedures including:**
(1) *Special care and precautions for different types of accidents;*
(2) *Special precautions for driving near a fire* and carrying hazardous materials, and smoking and carrying hazardous materials;
(3) *Emergency procedures; and*
(4) *Existence of special requirements* for transporting Class A and B explosives.

§383.123 Requirements for a school bus endorsement.

(a) **An applicant for a school bus endorsement** must satisfy the following three requirements:
(1) *Qualify for passenger vehicle endorsement.* Pass the knowledge and skills test for obtaining a passenger vehicle endorsement.
(2) *Knowledge test.* Must have knowledge covering at least the following three topics:
  (i) *Loading and unloading children,* including the safe operation of stop signal devices, external mirror systems, flashing lights and other warning and passenger safety devices required for school buses by State or Federal law or regulation.
  (ii) *Emergency exits and procedures* for safely evacuating passengers in an emergency.
  (iii) *State and Federal laws and regulations* related to safely traversing highway rail grade crossings.
(3) *Skills test.* Must take a driving skills test in a school bus of the same vehicle group (see §383.91(a)) as the school bus applicant will drive.
(4) *Exception.* Knowledge and skills tests administered before September 30, 2002 and approved by FMCSA as meeting the requirements of this section, meet the requirements of paragraphs (a)(2) and (a)(3) of this section.

(b) **Substitute for driving skills test.**
(1) At the discretion of a State, the driving skills test required in paragraph (a)(3) of this section may be waived for an applicant who is currently licensed, has experience driving a school bus, has a good driving record, and meets the conditions set forth in paragraph (b)(2) of this section.
(2) *An applicant must certify* and the State must verify that, during the two-year period immediately prior to applying for the school bus endorsement, the applicant:
  (i) *Held a valid CDL* with a passenger vehicle endorsement to operate a school bus representative of the group he or she will be driving;
  (ii) *Has not had* his or her driver's license or CDL suspended, revoked or canceled or been disqualified from operating a CMV;
  (iii) *Has not been convicted* of any of the disqualifying offenses in §383.51(b) while operating a CMV or of any offense in a non-CMV that would be disqualifying under §383.51(b) if committed in a CMV;
  (iv) *Has not had more than one conviction* of any of the serious traffic violations defined in §383.5, while operating any type motor vehicle;
  (v) *Has not had any conviction* for a violation of State or local law relating to motor vehicle traffic control (other than a parking violation) arising in connection with any traffic accident;
  (vi) *Has not been convicted* of any motor vehicle traffic violation that resulted in an accident; and
  (vii) *Has been regularly employed* as a school bus driver, has operated a school bus representative of the group the applicant seeks to drive, and provides evidence of such employment.
(3) *After September 30, 2006,* the provisions in paragraph (b) of this section do not apply.

Appendix to Subpart G Required Knowledge and Skills — Sample Guidelines

The following is a sample of the specific types of items which a State may wish to include in the knowledge and skills tests that it administers to CDL applicants. This appendix closely follows the framework of §§383.111 and 383.113. It is intended to provide more specific guidance and suggestion to States. Additional detail in this appendix is not binding and States may depart from it at their discretion provided their CDL program tests for the general areas of knowledge and skill specified in §§383.111 and 383.113.

Examples of specific knowledge elements

(a) **Safe operations regulations.** Driver-related elements of the following regulations:
(1) *Motor vehicle inspection,* repair, and maintenance requirements as contained in Parts 393 and 396 of this title;
(2) *Procedures for safe vehicle operations* as contained in Part 392 of this title;
(3) *The effects of fatigue,* poor vision, hearing, and general health upon safe commercial motor vehicle operation as contained in Parts 391, 392, and 395 of this title;
(4) *The types of motor vehicles and cargoes* subject to the requirements contained in Part 397 of this title; and
(5) *The effects of alcohol and drug use* upon safe commercial motor vehicle operations as contained in Parts 391 and 395 of this title.

(b) **Commercial motor vehicle safety control systems.** Proper use of the motor vehicle's safety system, including lights, horns, side and rear-view mirrors, proper mirror adjustments, fire extinguishers, symptoms of improper operation revealed through instruments, motor vehicle operation characteristics, and diagnosing malfunctions. Commercial motor vehicle drivers shall have knowledge on the correct procedures needed to use these safety systems in an emergency situation, e.g., skids and loss of brakes.

(c) **Safe vehicle control.**
(1) *Control systems.* The purpose and function of the controls and instruments commonly found on commercial motor vehicles.
(2) *Basic control.* The proper procedures for performing various basic maneuvers, including:
  (i) *Starting, warming up, and shutting down the engine;*
  (ii) *Putting the vehicle in motion and stopping;*
  (iii) *Backing in a straight line; and*
  (iv) *Turning the vehicle,* e.g., basic rules, off-tracking, right/left turns and right curves.
(3) *Shifting.* The basic shifting rules and terms, as well as shift patterns and procedures for common transmissions, including:
  (i) *Key elements of shifting,* e.g., controls, when to shift and double clutching;
  (ii) *Shift patterns and procedures; and*
  (iii) *Consequences of improper shifting.*
(4) *Backing.* The procedures and rules for various backing maneuvers, including:
  (i) *Backing principles and rules; and*
  (ii) *Basic backing maneuvers,* e.g., straight-line backing, and backing on a curved path.
(5) *Visual search.* The importance of proper visual search, and proper visual search methods, including:
  (i) *Seeing ahead and to the sides;*
  (ii) *Use of mirrors; and*
  (iii) *Seeing to the rear.*

(6) *Communication.* The principles and procedures for proper communications and the hazards of failure to signal properly, including:
  (i) *Signaling intent,* e.g., signaling when changing speed or direction in traffic;
  (ii) *Communicating presence,* e.g., using horn or lights to signal presence; and
  (iii) *Misuse of communications.*
(7) *Speed management.* The importance of understanding the effects of speed, including:
  (i) *Speed and stopping distance;*
  (ii) *Speed and surface conditions;*
  (iii) *Speed and the shape of the road;*
  (iv) *Speed and visibility;* and
  (v) *Speed and traffic flow.*
(8) *Space management.* The procedures and techniques for controlling the space around the vehicle, including:
  (i) *The importance of space management;*
  (ii) *Space cushions,* e.g., *controlling space ahead/to the rear;*
  (iii) *Space to the sides;* and
  (iv) *Space for traffic gaps.*
(9) *Night operation.* Preparations and procedures for night driving, including:
  (i) *Night driving factors,* e.g., driver factors, (vision, glare, fatigue, inexperience), roadway factors, (low illumination, variation in illumination, familiarity with roads, other road users, especially drivers exhibiting erratic or improper driving), vehicle factors (headlights, auxiliary lights, turn signals, windshields and mirrors); and
  (ii) *Night driving procedures,* e.g., preparing to drive at night and driving at night.
(10) *Extreme driving conditions.* The basic information on operating in extreme driving conditions and the hazards that are encountered in extreme conditions, including:
  (i) *Adverse weather;*
  (ii) *Hot weather;* and
  (iii) *Mountain driving.*
(11) *Hazard perceptions.* The basic information on hazard perception and clues for recognition of hazards, including:
  (i) *Importance of hazards recognition;*
  (ii) *Road characteristics;* and
  (iii) *Road user activities.*
(12) *Emergency maneuvers.* The basic information concerning when and how to make emergency maneuvers, including:
  (i) *Evasive steering;*
  (ii) *Emergency stop;*
  (iii) *Off-road recovery;*
  (iv) *Brake failure;* and
  (v) *Blowouts.*
(13) *Skid control and recovery.* The information on the causes and major types of skids, as well as the procedures for recovering from skids.
(d) **Relationship of cargo to vehicle control.** The principles and procedures for the proper handling of cargo, including:
  (1) *The importance of proper cargo handling,* e.g., consequences of improperly secured cargo, drivers' responsibilities, Federal/State and local regulations.
  (2) *Principles of weight distribution.*
  (3) *Principles and methods of cargo securement.*
(e) **Vehicle inspections:** The objectives and proper procedures for performing vehicle safety inspections, as follows:
  (1) *The importance of periodic inspection and repair* to vehicle safety and to prevention of enroute breakdowns.
  (2) *The effect of undiscovered malfunctions upon safety.*
  (3) *What safety-related parts* to look for when inspecting vehicles, e.g., fluid leaks, interference with visibility, bad tires, wheel and rim defects, braking system defects, steering system defects, suspension system defects, exhaust system defects, coupling system defects, and cargo problems.
  (4) *Pre-trip/enroute/post-trip inspection procedures.*
  (5) *Reporting findings.*
(f) **Hazardous materials knowledge, as follows:**
  (1) *What constitutes hazardous material* requiring an endorsement to transport; and
  (2) *Classes of hazardous materials,* labeling/placarding requirements, and the need for specialized training as a prerequisite to receiving the endorsement and transporting hazardous cargoes.
(g) **Air brake knowledge as follows:**
  (1) *General air brake system nomenclature;*
  (2) *The dangers of contaminated air* (dirt, moisture and oil) supply;
  (3) *Implications of severed or disconnected air lines* between the power unit and the trailer(s);
  (4) *Implications of low air pressure readings;*
  (5) *Procedures to conduct* safe and accurate pre-trip inspections, including knowledge about:
    (i) *Automatic fail-safe devices;*
    (ii) *System monitoring devices;* and
    (iii) *Low pressure warning alarms.*
  (6) *Procedures for conducting* enroute and post-trip inspections of air actuated brake systems, including ability to detect defects which may cause the system to fail, including:
    (i) *Tests which indicate the amount of air loss* from the braking system within a specified period, with and without the engine running; and
    (ii) *Tests which indicate the pressure levels* at which the low air pressure warning devices and the tractor protection valve should activate.
(h) **Operators for the combination vehicle group** shall also have knowledge of:
  (1) *Coupling and uncoupling.* The procedures for proper coupling and uncoupling a tractor to semi-trailer.
  (2) *Vehicle inspection.* The objectives and proper procedures that are unique for performing vehicle safety inspections on combination vehicles.

Examples of Specific Skills Elements

These examples relate to paragraphs (a) and (b) of §383.113 only.
(a) **Basic vehicle control skills.** All applicants for a CDL must possess and demonstrate the following basic motor vehicle control skills for each vehicle group which the driver operates or expects to operate. These skills shall include:
  (1) *Ability to start, warm-up, and shut down the engine;*
  (2) *Ability to put the motor vehicle in motion* and accelerate smoothly, forward and backward;
  (3) *Ability to bring the motor vehicle to a smooth stop;*
  (4) *Ability to back the motor vehicle in a straight line,* and check path and clearance while backing;
  (5) *Ability to position the motor vehicle* to negotiate and then make left and right turns;
  (6) *Ability to shift as required* and select appropriate gear for speed and highway conditions;
  (7) *Ability to back along a curved path;* and
  (8) *Ability to observe the road and the behavior* of other motor vehicles, particularly before changing speed and direction.
(b) **Safe driving skills.** All applicants for a CDL must possess and demonstrate the following safe driving skills for any vehicle group. These skills shall include:
  (1) *Ability to use proper visual search methods.*
  (2) *Ability to signal appropriately* when changing speed or direction in traffic.
  (3) *Ability to adjust speed* to the configuration and condition of the roadway, weather and visibility conditions, traffic conditions, and motor vehicle, cargo and driver conditions;
  (4) *Ability to choose a safe gap* for changing lanes, passing other vehicles, as well as for crossing or entering traffic;
  (5) *Ability to position the motor vehicle correctly* before and during a turn to prevent other vehicles from passing on the wrong side as well as to prevent problems caused by off-tracking;
  (6) *Ability to maintain a safe following distance* depending on the condition of the road, on visibility, and on vehicle weight; and
  (7) *Ability to adjust operation of the motor vehicle* to prevailing weather conditions including speed selection, braking, direction changes and following distance to maintain control.

Subpart H - Tests

§383.131 Test procedures.

(a) **Driver information manuals.** Information on how to obtain a CDL and endorsements shall be included in manuals and made available by States to CDL applicants. All information provided to the applicant shall include the following:
  (1) *Information on the requirements* described in §383.71, the implied consent to alcohol testing described in §383.72, the pro-

§383.133 Part 383 - Commercial Driver's License Standards; Requirements and Penalties

cedures and penalties, contained in §383.51(b) to which a CDL holder is exposed for refusal to comply with such alcohol testing, State procedures described in §383.73, and other appropriate driver information contained in Subpart E of this part;

(2) *Information on vehicle groups and endorsements* as specified in Subpart F of this part;

(3) *The substance of the knowledge and skills* which drivers shall have as outlined in Subpart G of this part for the different vehicle groups and endorsements;

(4) *Details of testing procedures,* including the purpose of the tests, how to respond, any time limits for taking the test, and any other special procedures determined by the State of issuance; and

(5) *Directions for taking the tests.*

(b) **Examiner procedures.** A State shall provide to test examiners details on testing and any other State-imposed requirements in the examiner's manual, and shall ensure that examiners are qualified to administer tests on the basis of training and/or other experience. States shall provide standardized scoring sheets for the skills tests, as well as standardized driving instructions for the applicants. Such examiners' manuals shall contain the following:

(1) *Information on driver application procedures* contained in §383.71, State procedures described in §383.73, and other appropriate driver information contained in Subpart E of this part;

(2) *Details on information which must be given to the applicant;*

(3) *Details on how to conduct the tests;*

(4) *Scoring procedures and minimum passing scores;*

(5) *Information for selecting driving test routes;*

(6) *List of the skills to be tested;*

(7) *Instructions on where and how the skills will be tested;*

(8) *How performance of the skills will be scored; and*

(9) *Causes for automatic failure of skills tests.*

§383.131 DOT Interpretations

Question 1: Are there any Federal regulations which require the States to retain for a specified period of time the CDL knowledge tests (or the test results) used to test CMV drivers?
Guidance: No, there are no Federal regulations regarding such record retention.

§383.133 Testing methods.

(a) **All tests shall be constructed in such a way** as to determine if the applicant possesses the required knowledge and skills contained in Subpart G of this part for the type of motor vehicle or endorsement the applicant wishes to obtain.

(b) **States shall develop their own specifications** for the tests for each vehicle group and endorsement which must be at least as stringent as the Federal standards.

(c) **States shall determine specific methods** for scoring the knowledge and skills tests.

(d) **Passing scores must meet those standards contained in §383.135.**

(e) **Knowledge and skills tests shall be based** solely on the information contained in the driver manuals referred to in §383.131(a).

(f) **Each knowledge test shall be valid and reliable** so as to assure that driver applicants possess the knowledge required under §383.111.

(g) **Each basic knowledge test,** i.e., the test covering the areas referred to in §383.111 for the applicable vehicle group, shall contain at least 30 items, exclusive of the number of items testing air brake knowledge. Each endorsement knowledge test, and the air brake component of the basic knowledge test as described in §383.111(g), shall contain a number of questions that is sufficient to test the driver applicant's knowledge of the required subject matter with validity and reliability.

(h) **The skills tests shall have** administrative procedures, designed to achieve interexaminer reliability, that are sufficient to ensure fairness of pass/fail rates.

§383.133 DOT Interpretations

Question 1: May States administer the CDL knowledge and endorsement test in foreign languages or in other than a written format?
Guidance: Yes.

Question 2: Do the Federal standards limit the number of times a driver may take a test if he or she fails?
Guidance: The rule does not limit the number of times a driver may take a test.

Question 3: Is a State allowed to provide for an alternative test (e.g., oral) or administer an alternate exam format providing the test meets FMCSA requirements?
Guidance: Yes. The knowledge portion of the test may be administered in written form, verbally, in automated formats, or otherwise at the discretion of the State.

§383.135 Minimum passing scores.

(a) **The driver applicant must correctly answer** at least 80 percent of the questions on each knowledge test in order to achieve a passing score on such knowledge test.

(b) **To achieve a passing score on the skills test,** the driver applicant must demonstrate that he/she can successfully perform all of the skills listed in §383.113.

(c) **If the driver applicant does not obey traffic laws,** or causes an accident during the test, he/she shall automatically fail the test.

(d) **The scoring of the basic knowledge and skills tests** shall be adjusted as follows to allow for the air brake restriction (§383.95):

(1) *If the applicant scores less than 80 percent* on the air brake component of the basic knowledge test as described in §383.111(g), the driver will have failed the air brake component and, if the driver is issued a CDL, an air brake restriction shall be indicated on the license; and

(2) *If the applicant performs the skills test* in a vehicle not equipped with air brakes, the driver will have omitted the air brake component as described in §383.113(c) and, if the driver is issued a CDL, the air brake restriction shall be indicated on the license.

Subpart I - Requirement for Transportation Security Administration Approval of Hazardous Materials Endorsement Issuances

§383.141 General.

(a) **Applicability date.** Beginning on the date(s) listed in 49 CFR 1572.13(b), this section applies to State agencies responsible for issuing hazardous materials endorsements for a CDL, and applicants for such endorsements.

(b) **Prohibition.** A State may not issue, renew, upgrade, or transfer a hazardous materials endorsement for a CDL to any individual authorizing that individual to operate a commercial motor vehicle transporting a hazardous material in commerce unless the Transportation Security Administration has determined that the individual does not pose a security risk warranting denial of the endorsement.

(c) **Individual notification.** At least 60 days prior to the expiration date of the CDL or hazardous materials endorsement, a State must notify the holder of a hazardous materials endorsement that the individual must pass a Transportation Security Administration security threat assessment process as part of any application for renewal of the hazardous materials endorsement. The notice must advise a driver that, in order to expedite the security screening process, he or she should file a renewal application as soon as possible, but not later than 30 days before the date of expiration of the endorsement. An individual who does not successfully complete the Transportation Security Administration security threat assessment process referenced in paragraph (b) of this section may not be issued a hazardous materials endorsement.

(d) **Hazardous materials endorsement renewal cycle.** Each State must require that hazardous materials endorsements be renewed every 5 years or less so that individuals are subject to a Transportation Security Administration security screening requirement referenced in paragraph (b) of this section at least every 5 years.

Subpart J - Commercial Driver's License Document

§383.151 General.

The CDL shall be a document that is easy to recognize as a CDL. At a minimum, the document shall contain information specified in §383.153.

§383.153 Information on the document and application.

(a) **All CDLs shall contain the following information:**

(1) *The prominent statement* that the license is a "Commercial Driver's License" or "CDL," except as specified in §383.153(b).

(2) *The full name, signature, and mailing address* of the person to whom such license is issued;

(3) *Physical and other information* to identify and describe such person including date of birth (month, day, and year), sex, and height;
(4) *Color photograph of the driver;*
(5) *The driver's State license number;*
(6) *The name of the State which issued the license;*
(7) *The date of issuance and the date of expiration of the license;*
(8) *The group or groups* of commercial motor vehicle(s) that the driver is authorized to operate, indicated as follows:
  (i) *A for Combination Vehicle;*
  (ii) *B for Heavy Straight Vehicle; and*
  (iii) *C for Small Vehicle.*
(9) *The endorsement(s)* for which the driver has qualified, if any, indicated as follows:
  (i) *T for double/triple trailers;*
  (ii) *P for passenger;*
  (iii) *N for tank vehicle;*
  (iv) *H for hazardous materials;*
  (v) *X for a combination* of tank vehicle and hazardous materials endorsements;
  (vi) *S for school bus; and*
  (vii) *At the discretion of the State,* additional codes for additional groupings of endorsements, as long as each such discretionary code is fully explained on the front or back of the CDL document.
(b) If the CDL is a Nonresident CDL, it shall contain the prominent statement that the license is a "Nonresident Commercial Driver's License" or "Nonresident CDL." The word "Nonresident" must be conspicuously and unmistakably displayed, but may be noncontiguous with the words "Commercial Driver's License" or "CDL."
(c) If the State has issued the applicant an air brake restriction as specified in §383.95, that restriction must be indicated on the license.
(d) Except in the case of a Nonresident CDL:
  (1) *A driver applicant* must provide his/her Social Security Number on the application of a CDL; and
  (2) *The State must provide the Social Security Number to the CDLIS.*

§383.153 DOT Interpretations

Question 1: May a State use the residence address as opposed to the mailing address on the CDL?
Guidance: Yes.

Question 2: May a State issue temporary nonphoto CDLs?
Guidance: Yes, as long as:
 a. The State does not liberalize any existing procedures for issuing nonphoto licenses; and
 b. The State does not allow drivers to operate CMVs indefinitely without a CDL which meets all the standards of §383.153.

Question 3: May a State choose to implement a driver license system involving multiple part license documents?
Guidance: Yes. A two or more part document, as currently used in some States, is acceptable, provided:
 a. All of the documents must be present to constitute a "license;"
 b. Each document is explicitly "tied" to the other document(s), and to a single driver's record. Each document must indicate that the driver is licensed as a CMV driver, if that is the case; and
 c. The multipart license document includes all of the data elements specified in Part 383, Subpart J.

Question 4: If the State restricts the CDL driving privilege, must that restriction be shown on the license?
Guidance: Yes. **Question 5:** Is a State required to show the driver's SSN on the CDL?
Guidance: No. §383.153 does not specify the SSN as a required element of the CDL document although the regulation does require a driver applicant who is domiciled in the U.S. to provide his or her SSN on the CDL application.

Question 6: Is a State prohibited from issuing a CDL to an applicant who, for religious reasons, does not possess an SSN?
Guidance: No. The determination of whether a person needs an SSN is left up to the Social Security Administration.

Question 7: Is a color-digitized image of a driver acceptable for purposes of a CDL?
Guidance: Yes. The FMCSA will accept a color-digitized image of a driver on a CDL in lieu of a color photograph.

Question 8: May a State issue a commercial driver's license (CDL) without a color photograph?
Guidance: Yes, if requiring a photograph (whether in color or black and white) would violate a driver's religious beliefs. The issuing State must determine whether a driver's objection to a photograph has a genuine religious basis. In addition, §383.3(e)(1)(iii) and authorizes Alaska to dispense with a photograph on its CDL.

§383.155 Tamperproofing requirements.

States shall make the CDL tamperproof to the maximum extent practicable. At a minimum, a State shall use the same tamperproof method used for noncommercial drivers' licenses.

Special Topics — Motor Coaches and CDL

Question 1: May a State develop a knowledge test exclusively for motorcoach operators which excludes cargo handling and hazardous materials?
Guidance: Yes. A State could develop a basic knowledge test for bus drivers only, by deleting the cargo handling and HM questions from its normal basic knowledge test. In that case, the driver applicant would still need to pass the specialized knowledge and skills tests for the passenger endorsement, and the State would need to restrict the CDL to passenger operations only.

Question 2: What skills test is required for a CDL holder seeking to add a passenger endorsement?
Guidance: If a person already holds a CDL without a passenger endorsement, and subsequently applies for such endorsement, three situations may arise:
 a. The passenger test vehicle is in the same vehicle group as that shown on the CDL. This situation poses no problem since there is no discrepancy.
 b. The passenger test vehicle is in a greater vehicle group than that shown on the preexisting CDL. This is an upgrade situation. The driver and the State must meet the requirements of §§383.71(d) and 383.73(d), and the upgraded CDL must show the vehicle group of the passenger test vehicle.
 c. The passenger test vehicle is in a lesser vehicle group than that shown on the preexisting CDL. In this situation, the CDL retains the vehicle group of the preexisting CDL, but also restricts the driver, when engaged in CMV passenger operations, to vehicles in the group in which the passenger skills test was taken, or to a lesser group.

Special Topics — State Reciprocity

Question 1: May a State place an "intrastate only" or similar restriction on the CDL of a driver who certifies that he or she is not subject to Part 391?
Guidance: Yes; however, this restriction would not apply to drivers in interstate commerce who are excepted or exempted from Part 391 under the provisions of Parts 390 or 391.

Question 2: May a State allow a driver possessing an out-of-state CDL containing an intrastate restriction to operate a CMV in their jurisdiction?
Guidance: Yes, provided the driver operates exclusively intrastate.

Question 3: May States choose to interpret "intrastate" in ways that differ from established transportation practice?
Guidance: No. States do not have the discretion to change the Federal definition of either "interstate" or "intrastate" commerce.

Special Topics — International

Question 1: The driver's medical exam is part of the Mexican Licencia Federal. If a roadside inspection reveals that a Mexico-based driver has not had the medical portion of the Licencia Federal re-validated, is the driver considered to be without a valid medical certificate or without a valid license?
Guidance: The Mexican Licencia Federal is issued for a period of 10 years but must be re-validated every 2 years. A condition of re-validation is that the driver must pass a new physical examination. The dates for each re-validation are on the Licencia Federal and must be stamped at the completion of each physical. This constitutes documentation that the driver is medically qualified. Therefore, if the Licencia Federal is not re-validated every 2 years as specified by Mexican law, the driver's license is considered invalid.

Part 383 - Commercial Driver's License Standards; Requirements and Penalties

Notes

Part 384 - State Compliance with Commercial Driver's License Program

Subpart A - General

§384.101 Purpose and scope.
(a) Purpose. The purpose of this part is to ensure that the States comply with the provisions of section 12009(a) of the Commercial Motor Vehicle Safety Act of 1986 (49 U.S.C. 31311(a)).

(b) Scope. This part:

(1) *Includes the minimum standards* for the actions States must take to be in substantial compliance with each of the 22 requirements of 49 U.S.C. 31311(a);

(2) *Establishes procedures for determinations to be made* of such compliance by States; and

(3) *Specifies the consequences of State noncompliance.*

§384.103 Applicability.
The rules in this part apply to all States.

§384.105 Definitions.
(a) The definitions in Part 383 of this title apply to this part, except where otherwise specifically noted.

(b) As used in this part:

Issue and **issuance** mean initial licensure, license transfers, license renewals, license upgrades, and nonresident commercial driver's licenses (CDLs), as described in §383.73 of this title.

Licensing entity means the agency of State government that is authorized to issue drivers' licenses.

Year of noncompliance means any Federal fiscal year during which —

(1) *A State fails to submit timely certification* as prescribed in Subpart C of this part; or

(2) *The State does not meet one or more of the standards* of Subpart B of this part, based on a final determination by the FMCSA under §384.307(c) of this part.

§384.107 Matter incorporated by reference.
(a) Incorporation by reference. This part includes references to certain matter or materials. The text of the materials is not included in the regulations contained in this part. The materials are hereby made a part of the regulations in this part. The Director of the Office of the Federal Register has approved the materials incorporated by reference in accordance with 5 U.S.C. 552(a) and 1 CFR part 51. For materials subject to change, only the specific version approved by the Director of the Office of the Federal Register and specified in the regulation are incorporated. Material is incorporated as it exists on the date of the approval and a notice of any change in these materials will be published in the Federal Register.

(b) Materials incorporated. The AAMVAnet, Inc.'s "Commercial Driver License Information System (CDLIS) State Procedures," Version 2.0, October 1998, IBR approved for §384.231(d).

(c) Addresses.

(1) *All of the materials incorporated by reference* are available for inspection at:

(i) *The Department of Transportation Library,* 400 Seventh Street, SW, Washington, DC 20590 in Room 2200. These documents are also available for inspection and copying as provided in 49 CFR Part 7.

(ii) *The National Archives* and Records Administration (NARA). For information on the availability of this material at NARA, call 202-741-6030, or go to: http://www.archives.gov/federal_register/code_of_federal_regulations/ibr_locations.html.

(2) *Information and copies* of all of the materials incorporated by reference may be obtained by writing to: American Association of Motor Vehicle Administrators, Inc., 4301 Wilson Blvd, Suite 400, Arlington, VA 22203.

Subpart B - Minimum Standards for Substantial Compliance by States

§384.201 Testing program.
The State shall adopt and administer a program for testing and ensuring the fitness of persons to operate commercial motor vehicles (CMVs) in accordance with the minimum Federal standards contained in Part 383 of this title.

§384.202 Test standards.
No State shall authorize a person to operate a CMV unless such person passes a knowledge and driving skills test for the operation of a CMV in accordance with Part 383 of this title.

§384.203 Driving while under the influence.
(a) The State must have in effect and enforce through licensing sanctions the disqualifications prescribed in §383.51(b) of this subchapter for driving a CMV with a 0.04 alcohol concentration.

(b) Nothing in this section shall be construed to require a State to apply its criminal or other sanctions for driving under the influence to a person found to have operated a CMV with an alcohol concentration of 0.04, except licensing sanctions including suspension, revocation, or cancellation.

(c) A State that enacts and enforces through licensing sanctions the disqualifications prescribed in §383.51(b) of this subchapter for driving a CMV with a 0.04 alcohol concentration and gives full faith and credit to the disqualification of CMV drivers by other States shall be deemed in substantial compliance with section 12009(a)(3) of the Commercial Motor Vehicle Safety Act of 1986 (49 U.S.C. 31311(a)(3)).

§384.204 CDL issuance and information.
(a) General rule. The State shall authorize a person to operate a CMV only by issuance of a CDL, unless a waiver under the provisions of §383.7 applies, which contains, at a minimum, the information specified in Part 383, Subpart J, of this title.

(b) Exceptions —

(1) *Training.* The State may authorize a person, who does not hold a CDL valid in the type of vehicle in which training occurs, to undergo behind-the-wheel training in a CMV only by means of a learner's permit issued and used in accordance with §383.23(c) of this title.

(2) *Confiscation of CDL pending enforcement.* A State may allow a CDL holder whose CDL is held in trust by that State or any other State in the course of enforcement of the motor vehicle traffic code, but who has not been convicted of a disqualifying offense under §383.51 based on such enforcement, to drive a CMV while holding a dated receipt for such CDL.

§384.205 CDLIS information.
Before issuing a CDL to any person, the State shall, within the period of time specified in §384.232, perform the check of the Commercial Driver's License Information System (CDLIS) in accordance with §383.73(a)(3)(ii) of this title, and, based on that information, shall issue the license, or, in the case of adverse information, promptly implement the disqualifications, licensing limitations, denials, and/or penalties that are called for in any applicable section(s) of this subpart.

§384.206 State record checks.
(a) Required checks —

(1) *Issuing State's records.* Before issuing a CDL to any person, the State shall, within the period of time specified in §384.232, check its own driving record for such person in accordance with §383.73(a)(3) of this title.

(2) *Other States' records.* Before the initial or transfer issuance of a CDL to a person, and before renewing a CDL held by any person, the issuing State must:

(i) *Require the applicant* to provide the names of all States where the applicant has previously been licensed to operate any type of motor vehicle.

(ii) *Within the time period specified in §384.232,* request the complete driving record from all States where the applicant was licensed within the previous 10 years to operate any type of motor vehicle.

(iii) *States receiving a request* for the driving record of a person currently or previously licensed by the State must provide the information within 30 days.

(b) Required action. Based on the findings of the State record checks prescribed in this section, the State shall issue the license, or, in the case of adverse information, promptly implement the disqualifications, licensing limitations, denials, and/or penalties that are called for in any applicable section(s) of this subpart.

§384.207 Notification of licensing.

Within the period defined in §383.73(f) of this title, the State shall:

(a) Notify the operator of the CDLIS of each CDL issuance;

(b) Notify the operator of the CDLIS of any changes in driver identification information; and

(c) In the case of transfer issuances, implement the Change State of Record transaction, as specified by the operator of the CDLIS, in conjunction with the previous State of record and the operator of the CDLIS.

§384.208 Notification of disqualification.

(a) No later than 10 days after disqualifying a CDL holder licensed by another State, or revoking, suspending, or canceling an out-of-State CDL holder's privilege to operate a commercial motor vehicle for at least 60 days, the State must notify the State that issued the license of the disqualification, revocation, suspension, or cancellation.

(b) The notification must include both the disqualification and the violation that resulted in the disqualification, revocation, suspension, or cancellation. The notification and the information it provides must be recorded on the driver's record.

§384.209 Notification of traffic violations.

(a) Required notification with respect to CDL holders. Whenever a person who holds a CDL from another State is convicted of a violation of any State or local law relating to motor vehicle traffic control (other than a parking violation), in any type of vehicle, the licensing entity of the State in which the conviction occurs must notify the licensing entity in the State where the driver is licensed of this conviction within the time period established in paragraph (c) of this section.

(b) Required notification with respect to non-CDL holders. Whenever a person who does not hold a CDL, but who is licensed to drive by another State, is convicted of a violation in a CMV of any State or local law relating to motor vehicle traffic control (other than a parking violation), the licensing entity of the State in which the conviction occurs must notify the licensing entity in the State where the driver is licensed of this conviction within the time period established in paragraph (c) of this section.

(c) Time period for notification of traffic violations.

 (1) *Beginning on September 30, 2005,* the notification must be made within 30 days of the conviction.

 (2) *Beginning on September 30, 2008,* the notification must be made within 10 days of the conviction.

§384.209 DOT Interpretations

Question 1: Must a CDL holder's out-of-State conviction for a traffic violation be included in the driving record of the State of licensure (and thus CDLIS), if there are no traffic violation points assigned to the conviction?

Guidance: All out-of-State convictions of a CDL holder for traffic violations committed in any vehicle must be sent to the State of licensure, but only the convictions for offenses specified in 49 CFR 383.51 must be included in that State's driving record (and thus CDLIS). Assigning points to a conviction is strictly a State decision and has no bearing on the inclusion of the conviction.

The FHWA recommends the inclusion by the State of licensure of all convictions of a CDL holder for traffic violations committed in any vehicle, so that the State will have the full driver record available as an aid in making licensing decisions.

Question 2: Must the licensing agency establish a commercial driver record, including a CDLIS pointer record, for a person holding a non-commercial license issued by that jurisdiction upon receiving notification of a conviction of any offense committed while (illegally) operating a CMV?

Guidance: Yes.

§384.210 Limitation on licensing.

A State must not knowingly issue a CDL or a commercial special license or permit (including a provisional or temporary license) permitting a person to drive a CMV during a period in which:

(a) A person is disqualified from operating a CMV, as disqualification is defined by §383.5 of this subchapter, or under the provisions of §383.73(g) or §384.231(b)(2) of this subchapter;

(b) The CDL holder's noncommercial driving privilege has been revoked, suspended, or canceled; or

(c) Any type of driver's license held by such person is suspended, revoked, or canceled by the State where the driver is licensed for any State or local law related to motor vehicle traffic control (other than parking violations).

§384.211 Return of old licenses.

The State shall not issue a CDL to a person who possesses a driver's license issued by another State or jurisdiction unless such person first surrenders the driver's license issued by such other State or jurisdiction in accordance with §§383.71(a)(7) and (b)(4) of this title.

§384.211 DOT Interpretations

Question 1: May licensing jurisdictions meet their stewardship requirements for surrendered licenses by physically marking the license in some way as not valid and returning it to a driver as part of the driver's application for a new or renewal of an existing CDL?

Guidance: Yes. Provided the licensing jurisdiction meets the test of guaranteeing that the returned license document cannot possibly be mistaken for a valid document by a casual observer. A document perforated with the word "VOID" conspicuously and unmistakably displayed with holes large enough to be easily distinguished by a casual observer in limited light, which cannot be obscured by the holder of the document would meet the test of being invalidated.

§384.212 Domicile requirement.

(a) The State shall issue CDLs only to those persons for whom such State is the State of domicile as defined in §383.5 of this title; except that the State may issue a nonresident CDL under the conditions specified in §§383.23(b), 383.71(e), and 383.73(e) of this title.

(b) The State shall require any person holding a CDL issued by another State to apply for a transfer CDL from the State within 30 days after establishing domicile in the State, as specified in §383.71(b) of this title.

§384.213 State penalties for drivers of CMVs.

The State must impose on drivers of CMVs appropriate civil and criminal penalties that are consistent with the penalties prescribed under Part 383, Subpart D, of this subchapter.

§384.214 Reciprocity.

The State shall allow any person to operate a CMV in the State who is not disqualified from operating a CMV and who holds a CDL which is —

(a) Issued to him or her by any other State or jurisdiction in accordance with Part 383 of this title;

(b) Not suspended, revoked, or canceled; and

(c) Valid, under the terms of Part 383, Subpart F, of this title, for the type of vehicle being driven.

§384.215 First offenses.

(a) General rule. The State must disqualify from operating a CMV each person who is convicted, as defined in §383.5 of this subchapter, in any State or jurisdiction, of a disqualifying offense specified in items (1) through (8) of Table 1 to §383.51 of this subchapter, for no less than one year.

(b) Special rule for hazardous materials offenses. If the offense under paragraph (a) of this section occurred while the driver was operating a vehicle transporting hazardous materials required to be placarded under the Hazardous Materials Transportation Act (implementing regulations at 49 CFR 177.823), the State shall disqualify the person for no less than three years.

§384.216 Second offenses.

(a) General rule. The State must disqualify for life from operating a CMV each person who is convicted, as defined in §383.5 of this subchapter, in any State or jurisdiction, of a subsequent offense as described in Table 1 to §383.51 of this subchapter.

(b) Special rule for certain lifetime disqualifications. A driver disqualified for life under Table 1 to §383.51 may be reinstated after 10 years by the driver's State of residence if the requirements of §383.51(a)(5) have been met.

§384.217 Drug offenses.

The State must disqualify from operating a CMV for life each person who is convicted, as defined in §383.5 of this subchapter, in any State or jurisdiction of a first offense, of using a CMV in the commission of a felony described in item (9) of Table 1 to §383.51 of this subchapter. The State shall not apply the special rule in §384.216(b) to lifetime disqualifications imposed for controlled substance felonies as detailed in item (9) of Table 1 to §383.51 of this subchapter.

Subpart C - Procedures for Determining State Compliance

§384.218 Second serious traffic violation.
The State must disqualify from operating a CMV for a period of not less than 60 days each person who, in a three-year period, is convicted, as defined in §383.5 of this subchapter, in any State(s) or jurisdiction(s), of two serious traffic violations as specified in Table 2 to §383.51.

§384.219 Third serious traffic violation.
The State must disqualify from operating a CMV for a period of not less than 120 days each person who, in a three-year period, is convicted, as defined in §383.5 of this subchapter, in any State(s) or jurisdiction(s), of three serious traffic violations as specified in Table 2 to §383.51. This disqualification period must be in addition to any other previous period of disqualification.

§384.220 National Driver Register information.
Before issuing a CDL to any person, the State shall, within the period of time specified in §384.232, perform the check of the National Driver Register in accordance with §383.73(a)(3)(iii) of this title, and, based on that information, promptly implement the disqualifications, licensing limitations, and/or penalties that are called for in any applicable section(s) of this subpart.

§384.221 Out-of-service regulations (intoxicating beverage).
The State shall adopt, and enforce on operators of CMVs as defined in §§383.5 and 390.5 of this title, the provisions of §392.5 (a) and (c) of this title in accordance with the Motor Carrier Safety Assistance Program as contained in 49 CFR Part 350 and applicable policy and guidelines.

§384.222 Violation of out-of-service orders.
The State must have and enforce laws and/or regulations applicable to drivers of CMVs and their employers, as defined in §383.5 of this subchapter, which meet the minimum requirements of §§383.37(c), Table 4 to 383.51, and 383.53(b) of this subchapter.

§384.223 Railroad-highway grade crossing violation.
The State must have and enforce laws and/or regulations applicable to CMV drivers and their employers, as defined in §383.5 of this subchapter, which meet the minimum requirements of §§383.37(d), Table 3 to 383.51, and 383.53(c) of this subchapter.

§384.224 Noncommercial motor vehicle violations.
The State must have and enforce laws and/or regulations applicable to drivers of non-CMVs, as defined in §383.5 of this subchapter, which meet the minimum requirements of Tables 1 and 2 to §383.51 of this subchapter.

§384.225 Record of violations.
The State must:
(a) **CDL holders.** Record and maintain as part of the driver history all convictions, disqualifications and other licensing actions for violations of any State or local law relating to motor vehicle traffic control (other than a parking violation) committed in any type of vehicle.
(b) **A person required to have a CDL.** Record and maintain as part of the driver history all convictions, disqualifications and other licensing actions for violations of any State or local law relating to motor vehicle traffic control (other than a parking violation) committed while the driver was operating a CMV.
(c) **Make driver history information** required by this section available to the users designated in paragraph (e) of this section, or to their authorized agent, within 10 days of:
  (1) *Receiving the conviction* or disqualification information from another State; or
  (2) *The date of the conviction*, if it occurred in the same State.
(d) **Retain on the driver history record** all convictions, disqualifications and other licensing actions for violations for at least 3 years or longer as required under §384.231(d).
(e) **Only the following users or their authorized agents** may receive the designated information:
  (1) *States* —All information on all driver records.
  (2) *Secretary of Transportation* — All information on all driver records.
  (3) *Driver* — Only information related to that driver's record.
  (4) *Motor Carrier or Prospective Motor Carrier* — After notification to a driver, all information related to that driver's, or prospective driver's, record.

§384.226 Prohibition on masking convictions.
The State must not mask, defer imposition of judgment, or allow an individual to enter into a diversion program that would prevent a CDL driver's conviction for any violation, in any type of motor vehicle, of a State or local traffic control law (except a parking violation) from appearing on the driver's record, whether the driver was convicted for an offense committed in the State where the driver is licensed or another State.

§§384.227-384.230 [Reserved]

§384.231 Satisfaction of State disqualification requirement.
(a) **Applicability.** The provisions of §§384.203, 384.206(b), 384.210, 384.213, 384.215 through 384.219, 384.221 through 384.224, and 384.231 of this part apply to the State of licensure of the person affected by the provision. The provisions of §384.210 of this part also apply to any State to which a person makes application for a transfer CDL.
(b) **Required action —**
  (1) *CDL holders.* A State must satisfy the requirement of this part that the State disqualify a person who holds a CDL by, at a minimum, suspending, revoking, or canceling the person's CDL for the applicable period of disqualification.
  (2) *A person required to have a CDL.* A State must satisfy the requirement of this subpart that the State disqualify a person required to have a CDL who is convicted of an offense or offenses necessitating disqualification under §383.51 of this subchapter. At a minimum, the State must implement the limitation on licensing provisions of §384.210 and the timing and recordkeeping requirements of paragraphs (c) and (d) of this section so as to prevent such a person from legally obtaining a CDL from any State during the applicable disqualification period(s) specified in this subpart.
(c) **Required timing.** The State must disqualify a driver as expeditiously as possible.
(d) **Recordkeeping requirements.** The State must conform to the requirements of the October 1998 edition of the AAMVAnet, Inc.'s "Commercial Driver License Information System (CDLIS) State Procedures," Version 2.0. (Incorporated by reference, see §384.107.) These requirements include the maintenance of such driver records and driver identification data on the CDLIS as the FMCSA finds are necessary to the implementation and enforcement of the disqualifications called for in §§384.215 through 384.219, and 384.221 through 384.224 of this part.

§384.232 Required timing of record checks.
The State shall perform the record checks prescribed in §§384.205, 384.206, and 384.220, no earlier than 10 days prior to issuance for licenses issued before October 1, 1995. For licenses issued after September 30, 1995, the State shall perform the record checks no earlier than 24 hours prior to issuance if the license is issued to a driver who does not currently possess a valid CDL from the same State and no earlier than 10 days prior to issuance for all other drivers.

§384.233 Background records checks.
(a) **The State shall comply with** Transportation Security Administration requirements concerning background records checks for drivers seeking to obtain, renew, transfer or upgrade a hazardous materials endorsement in 49 CFR Part 1572, to the extent those provisions impose requirements on the State.
(b) **The State shall comply with each requirement of 49 CFR 383.141.**

Subpart C - Procedures for Determining State Compliance

§384.301 Substantial compliance — general requirements.
(a) **To be in substantial compliance** with 49 U.S.C. 31311(a), a State must meet each and every standard of Subpart B of this part by means of the demonstrable combined effect of its statutes, regulations, administrative procedures and practices, organizational structures, internal control mechanisms, resource assignments (facilities, equipment, and personnel), and enforcement practices.
(b) (1) *A State* must come into substantial compliance with the requirements of Subpart B of this part in effect as of September 30, 2002 as soon as practical, but, unless otherwise specifically provided in this part, not later than September 30, 2005.
  (2) *Exception.* A State must come into substantial compliance with 49 CFR 383.123 not later than September 30, 2006.

§384.303 [Reserved]

§384.305 State certifications for Federal fiscal years after FY 1994.

(a) *Certification requirement.* Prior to January 1 of each Federal fiscal year after FY 1994, each State shall review its compliance with this part and certify to the Federal Motor Carrier Safety Administrator as prescribed in paragraph (b) of this section. The certification shall be submitted as a signed original and four copies to the State Director or Officer-in-Charge, Federal Motor Carrier Safety Administration, located in that State.

(b) *Certification content.* The certification shall consist of a statement signed by the Governor of the State, or by an official designated by the Governor, and reading as follows: "I (name of certifying official), (position title), of the State (Commonwealth) of _____, do hereby certify that the State (Commonwealth) has continuously been in substantial compliance with all requirements of 49 U.S.C. 31311(a), as defined in 49 CFR 384.301, since [the first day of the current Federal fiscal year], and contemplates no changes in statutes, regulations, or administrative procedures, or in the enforcement thereof, which would affect such substantial compliance through [the last date of the current Federal fiscal year]."

(Approved by the Office of Management and Budget under control number 2125-0542)

§384.307 FMCSA program reviews of State compliance.

(a) *FMCSA Program Reviews.* Each State's CDL program will be subject to review to determine whether or not the State meets the general requirement for substantial compliance in §384.301. The State must cooperate with the review and provide any information requested by the FMCSA.

(b) *Preliminary FMCSA determination and State response.* If, after review, a preliminary determination is made either that the State has not submitted the required annual self-certification or that the State does not meet one or more of the minimum standards for substantial compliance under Subpart B of this part, the State will be informed accordingly.

(c) *Reply.* The State will have up to 30 calendar days to respond to the preliminary determination. The State's reply must explain what corrective action it either has implemented or intends to implement to correct the deficiencies cited in the notice or, alternatively, why the FMCSA preliminary determination is incorrect. The State must provide documentation of corrective action as required by the agency. Corrective action must be adequate to correct the deficiencies noted in the program review and be implemented on a schedule mutually agreed upon by the agency and the State. Upon request by the State, an informal conference will be provided during this time.

(d) *Final FMCSA determination.* If, after reviewing a timely response by the State to the preliminary determination, a final determination is made that the State is not in compliance with the affected standard, the State will be notified of the final determination. In making its final determination, the FMCSA will take into consideration the corrective action either implemented or planned to be implemented in accordance with the mutually agreed upon schedule.

(e) *State's right to judicial review.* Any State aggrieved by an adverse decision under this section may seek judicial review under 5 U.S.C. Chapter 7.

§384.309 Results of compliance determination.

(a) *A State shall be determined* not substantially in compliance with 49 U.S.C. 31311(a) for any fiscal year in which it:
   (1) *Fails to submit the certification as prescribed in this subpart;* or
   (2) *Does not meet one or more of the standards* of Subpart B of this part, as established in a final determination by the FMCSA under 384.307(c).

(b) *A State shall be in substantial compliance* with 49 U.S.C. 31311(a) for any fiscal year in which neither of the eventualities in paragraph (a) of this section occurs.

Subpart D - Consequences of State Noncompliance

§384.401 Withholding of funds based on noncompliance.

(a) *Following the first year of noncompliance.* A State is subject to both of the following sanctions:
   (1) *An amount equal to five percent* of the Federal-aid highway funds required to be apportioned to any State under each of sections 104(b)(1), (b)(3), and (b)(4) of Title 23, U.S.C., shall be withheld on the first day of the fiscal year following such State's first year of noncompliance under this part.
   (2) *The Motor Carrier* Safety Assistance Program (MCSAP) grant funds authorized under section 103(b)(1) of the Motor Carrier Safety Improvement Act of 1999 (Public Law 106-159, 113 Stat. 1754) shall be withheld from a State on the first day of the fiscal year following the fiscal year in which the FMCSA determined that the State was not in substantial compliance with Subpart B of this part.

(b) *Following second and subsequent year(s)* of noncompliance. A State is subject to both of the following sanctions:
   (1) *An amount equal to ten percent* of the Federal-aid funds required to be apportioned to any State under each of sections 104(b)(1), (b)(3), and (b)(4) of Title 23, U.S.C., shall be withheld on the first day of the fiscal year following such State's second or subsequent year of noncompliance under this part.
   (2) *The Motor Carrier* Safety Assistance Program (MCSAP) grant funds authorized under section 103(b)(1) of the Motor Carrier Safety Improvement Act of 1999 (Public Law 106-159, 113 Stat. 1753) shall be withheld from a State on the first day of the fiscal year following the fiscal year in which the FMCSA determined that the State had not returned to substantial compliance with Subpart B of this part.

§384.403 Availability of funds withheld for noncompliance.

(a) *Federal-aid highway funds* withheld from a State under §384.401(a)(1) or (b)(1) shall not thereafter be available for apportionment to the State.

(b) *MCSAP funds withheld from a State* under §384.401(a)(2) or (b)(2) remain available until June 30 of the fiscal year in which they were withheld. If before June 30 the State submits a document signed by the Governor or his or her delegate certifying, and the FMCSA determines, that the State is now in substantial compliance with the standards of Subpart B of this part, the withheld funds shall be restored to the State. After June 30, unrestored funds shall lapse and be allocated in accordance with §350.313 of this subchapter to all States currently in substantial compliance with Subpart B of this part.

§384.405 Decertification of State CDL program.

(a) *Prohibition on CDL licensing activities.* The Administrator may prohibit a State found to be in substantial noncompliance from performing any of the following four licensing transactions:
   (1) *Issuance of initial CDLs.*
   (2) *Renewal of CDLs.*
   (3) *Transfer of out-of-State CDLs to the State.*
   (4) *Upgrade of CDLs.*

(b) *Conditions considered in making* decertification determination. The Administrator will consider, but is not limited to, the following five conditions in determining whether the CDL program of a State in substantial noncompliance should be decertified:
   (1) *The State computer system* does not check the Commercial Driver's License Information System (CDLIS) and/or National Driver Register (NDR) as required by §383.73 of this subchapter when processing CDL applicants, drivers transferring a CDL issued by another State, CDL renewals and/or upgrades.
   (2) *The State does not disqualify drivers* convicted of disqualifying offenses in commercial motor vehicles.
   (3) *The State does not transmit convictions* for out of State drivers to the State where the driver is licensed.
   (4) *The State does not properly administer* knowledge and/or skills tests to CDL applicants or drivers.
   (5) *The State fails to submit a corrective action plan* for a substantial compliance deficiency or fails to implement a corrective action plan within the agreed upon time frame.

(c) *Standard for considering deficiencies.* The deficiencies described in paragraph (b) of this section must affect a substantial number of either CDL applicants or drivers.

(d) *Decertification: preliminary determination.* If the Administrator finds that a State is in substantial noncompliance with Subpart B of this part, as indicated by the factors specified in §384.405(b), among other things, the FMCSA will inform the State that it has made a preliminary determination of noncompliance and that the State's CDL program may therefore be decertified. Any response from the State, including factual or legal arguments or a plan to correct the noncompliance, must be submitted within 30 calendar days after receipt of the preliminary determination.

(e) *Decertification: final determination.* If, after considering all material submitted by the State in response to the FMCSA preliminary determination, the Administrator decides that substantial noncompliance exists which warrants decertification of the CDL program, he or she will issue a decertification order prohibiting the

Subpart D - Consequences of State Noncompliance

State from issuing CDLs until such time as the Administrator determines that the condition(s) causing the decertification has (have) been corrected.

(f) Recertification of a State. The Governor of the decertified State or his or her designated representative must submit a certification and documentation that the condition causing the decertification has been corrected. If the FMCSA determines that the condition causing the decertification has been satisfactorily corrected, the Administrator will issue a recertification order, including any conditions that must be met in order to begin issuing CDLs in the State.

(g) State's right to judicial review. Any State aggrieved by an adverse decision under this section may seek judicial review under 5 U.S.C. Chapter 7.

(h) Validity of previously issued CDLs. A CDL issued by a State prior to the date the State is prohibited from issuing CDLs in accordance with provisions of paragraph (a) of this section, will remain valid until its stated expiration date.

§384.407 Emergency CDL grants.

The FMCSA may provide grants of up to $1,000,000 per State from funds made available under 49 U.S.C. 31107(a), to assist States whose CDL programs may fail to meet the compliance requirements of Subpart B of this part, but which are determined by the FMCSA to be making a good faith effort to comply with these requirements.

Notes

Part 385 - Safety Fitness Procedures

Subpart A - General

§385.1 Purpose and scope.

(a) This part establishes the FMCSA's procedures to determine the safety fitness of motor carriers, to assign safety ratings, to direct motor carriers to take remedial action when required, and to prohibit motor carriers receiving a safety rating of "unsatisfactory" from operating a CMV.

(b) This part establishes the safety assurance program for a new entrant motor carrier initially seeking to register with FMCSA to conduct interstate operations. It also describes the consequences that will occur if the new entrant fails to maintain adequate basic safety management controls.

(c) This part establishes the safety permit program for a motor carrier to transport the types and quantities of hazardous materials listed in §385.403.

(d) The provisions of this part apply to all motor carriers subject to the requirements of this subchapter, except non-business private motor carriers of passengers.

§385.3 Definitions and acronyms.

Applicable safety regulations or requirements means 49 CFR Chapter III, Subchapter B — Federal Motor Carrier Safety Regulations or, if the carrier is an intrastate motor carrier subject to the hazardous materials safety permit requirements in Subpart E of this part, the equivalent State standards; and 49 CFR Chapter I, Subchapter C — Hazardous Materials Regulations.

CMV means a commercial motor vehicle as defined in §390.5 of this subchapter.

Commercial motor vehicle shall have the same meaning as described in §390.5 of this subchapter, except that this definition will also apply to intrastate motor vehicles subject to the hazardous materials safety permit requirements of Subpart E of this part.

FMCSA means the Federal Motor Carrier Safety Administration.

FMCSRs mean Federal Motor Carrier Safety Regulations (49 CFR Parts 350-399).

HMRs means the Hazardous Materials Regulations (49 CFR Parts 100-178).

New entrant is a motor carrier not domiciled in Mexico that applies for a United States Department of Transportation (DOT) identification number in order to initiate operations in interstate commerce.

New entrant registration is the registration (US DOT number) granted a new entrant before it can begin interstate operations in an 18-month monitoring period. A safety audit must be performed on a new entrant's operations within 18 months after receipt of its US DOT number and it must be found to have adequate basic safety management controls to continue operating in interstate commerce at the end of the 18-month period.

Preventable accident on the part of a motor carrier means an accident (1) that involved a commercial motor vehicle, and (2) that could have been averted but for an act, or failure to act, by the motor carrier or the driver.

Reviews. For the purposes of this part:

(1) **Compliance review** means an on-site examination of motor carrier operations, such as drivers' hours of service, maintenance and inspection, driver qualification, commercial drivers license requirements, financial responsibility, accidents, hazardous materials, and other safety and transportation records to determine whether a motor carrier meets the safety fitness standard. A compliance review may be conducted in response to a request to change a safety rating, to investigate potential violations of safety regulations by motor carriers, or to investigate complaints or other evidence of safety violations. The compliance review may result in the initiation of an enforcement action.

(2) **Safety Audit** means an examination of a motor carrier's operations to provide educational and technical assistance on safety and the operational requirements of the FMCSRs and applicable HMRs and to gather critical safety data needed to make an assessment of the carrier's safety performance and basic safety management controls. Safety audits do not result in safety ratings.

(3) **Safety management controls** means the systems, policies, programs, practices, and procedures used by a motor carrier to ensure compliance with applicable safety and hazardous materials regulations which ensure the safe movement of products and passengers through the transportation system, and to reduce the risk of highway accidents and hazardous materials incidents resulting in fatalities, injuries, and property damage.

RSPA means the Research and Special Programs Administration.

Safety ratings:

(1) **Satisfactory safety rating** means that a motor carrier has in place and functioning adequate safety management controls to meet the safety fitness standard prescribed in §385.5. Safety management controls are adequate if they are appropriate for the size and type of operation of the particular motor carrier.

(2) **Conditional safety rating** means a motor carrier does not have adequate safety management controls in place to ensure compliance with the safety fitness standard that could result in occurrences listed in §385.5 (a) through (k).

(3) **Unsatisfactory safety rating** means a motor carrier does not have adequate safety management controls in place to ensure compliance with the safety fitness standard which has resulted in occurrences listed in §385.5 (a) through (k).

(4) **Unrated carrier** means that a safety rating has not been assigned to the motor carrier by the FMCSA.

§385.4 Matter incorporated by reference.

(a) Incorporation by reference. Part 385 includes references to certain matter or materials, as listed in paragraph (b) of this section. The text of the materials is not included in the regulations contained in Part 385. The materials are hereby made a part of the regulations in Part 385. The Director of the Federal Register has approved the materials incorporated by reference in accordance with 5 U.S.C. 552(a) and 1 CFR Part 51. For materials subject to change, only the specific version in the regulation is incorporated. Material is incorporated as it exists on the date of the approval and a notice of any changes in these materials will be published in the Federal Register.

(b) Matter or materials referenced in Part 385. The matter or materials in this paragraph are incorporated by reference in the corresponding sections noted.

(1) "North American Standard Out-of-Service Criteria and Level VI Inspection Procedures and Out-of-Service Criteria for Commercial Highway Vehicles Transporting Transuranics and Highway Route Controlled Quantities of Radioactive Materials as defined in 49 CFR Part 173.403," January 1, 2004. Information and copies may be obtained from the Commercial Vehicle Safety Alliance, 1101 17th Street, NW, Suite 803, Washington, DC 20036. Phone number (202) 775-1623.

(2) *All of the materials incorporated by reference* are available for inspection at: The Federal Motor Carrier Safety Administration, Office of Enforcement and Compliance, 400 Seventh Street, SW, Washington, DC 20590; and the National Archives and Records Administration (NARA). For information on the availability of this material at NARA, call (202) 741-6030, or go to: http://www.archives.gov/federal_register/code_of_federal_regulations/ibr_locations.html.

§385.5 Safety fitness standard.

The Satisfactory safety rating is based on the degree of compliance with the safety fitness standard for motor carriers. For intrastate motor carriers subject to the hazardous materials safety permit requirements of Subpart E of this part, the motor carrier must meet the equivalent State requirements. To meet the safety fitness standard, the motor carrier must demonstrate it has adequate safety management controls in place, which function effectively to ensure acceptable compliance with applicable safety requirements to reduce the risk associated with:

(a) Commercial driver's license standard violations (Part 383),

(b) Inadequate levels of financial responsibility (Part 387),

(c) The use of unqualified drivers (Part 391),

(d) Improper use and driving of motor vehicles (Part 392),

(e) Unsafe vehicles operating on the highways (Part 393),

(f) Failure to maintain accident registers and copies of accident reports (Part 390),

(g) The use of fatigued drivers (Part 395),

(h) Inadequate inspection, repair, and maintenance of vehicles (Part 396),

(i) Transportation of hazardous materials, driving and parking rule violations (Part 397),

(j) Violation of hazardous materials regulations (Parts 170 through 177), and

(k) Motor vehicle accidents and hazardous materials incidents.

§385.7 Factors to be considered in determining a safety rating.

The factors to be considered in determining the safety fitness and assigning a safety rating include information from safety reviews, compliance reviews and any other data. The factors may include all or some of the following:

(a) Adequacy of safety management controls. The adequacy of controls may be questioned if their degree of formalization, automation, etc., is found to be substantially below the norm for similar carriers. Violations, accidents or incidents substantially above the norm for similar carriers will be strong evidence that management controls are either inadequate or not functioning properly.

(b) Frequency and severity of regulatory violations.

(c) Frequency and severity of driver/vehicle regulatory violations identified in roadside inspections.

(d) Number and frequency of out-of-service driver/vehicle violations.

(e) Increase or decrease in similar types of regulatory violations discovered during safety or compliance reviews.

(f) Frequency of accidents; hazardous materials incidents; accident rate per million miles; preventable accident rate per million miles; and other accident indicators; and whether these accident and incident indicators have improved or deteriorated over time.

(g) The number and severity of violations of state safety rules, regulations, standards, and orders applicable to commercial motor vehicles and motor carrier safety that are compatible with Federal rules, regulations, standards, and orders.

§385.9 Determination of a safety rating.

(a) Following a compliance review of a motor carrier operation, the FMCSA, using the factors prescribed in §385.7 as computed under the Safety Fitness Rating Methodology set forth in Appendix B of this part, shall determine whether the present operations of the motor carrier are consistent with the safety fitness standard set forth in §385.5, and assign a safety rating accordingly.

(b) Unless otherwise specifically provided in this part, a safety rating will be issued to a motor carrier within 30 days following the completion of a compliance review.

§385.11 Notification of safety fitness determination.

(a) The FMCSA will provide a motor carrier written notice of any safety rating resulting from a compliance review as soon as practicable, but not later than 30 days after the review. The notice will take the form of a letter issued from the FMCSA's headquarters office and will include a list of FMCSR and HMR compliance deficiencies which the motor carrier must correct.

(b) If the safety rating is "satisfactory" or improves a previous "unsatisfactory" safety rating, it is final and becomes effective on the date of the notice.

(c) In all other cases, a notice of a proposed safety rating will be issued. It becomes the final safety rating after the following time periods:

(1) *For motor carriers* transporting hazardous materials in quantities requiring placarding or transporting passengers by CMV — 45 days after the date of the notice.

(2) *For all other motor carriers operating CMVs* — 60 days after the date of the notice.

(d) A proposed safety rating of "unsatisfactory" is a notice to the motor carrier that the FMCSA has made a preliminary determination that the motor carrier is "unfit" to continue operating in interstate commerce, and that the prohibitions in §385.13 will be imposed after 45 or 60 days if necessary safety improvements are not made.

(e) A motor carrier may request the FMCSA to perform an administrative review of a proposed or final safety rating. The process and the time limits are described in §385.15.

(f) A motor carrier may request a change to a proposed or final safety rating based upon its corrective actions. The process and the time limits are described in §385.17.

§385.13 Unsatisfactory rated motor carriers; prohibition on transportation; ineligibility for Federal contracts.

(a) Generally, a motor carrier rated "unsatisfactory" is prohibited from operating a CMV. Information on motor carriers, including their most current safety rating, is available from the FMCSA on the Internet at http://www.safersys.org, or by telephone at (800) 832-5660.

(1) *Motor carriers transporting hazardous materials* in quantities requiring placarding, and motor carriers transporting passengers in a CMV, are prohibited from operating a CMV beginning on the 46th day after the date of the FMCSA's notice of proposed "unsatisfactory" rating.

(2) *All other motor carriers* rated from reviews completed on or after November 20, 2000 are prohibited from operating a CMV beginning on the 61st day after the date of the FMCSA's notice of proposed "unsatisfactory" rating. If the FMCSA determines the motor carrier is making a good-faith effort to improve its safety fitness, the FMCSA may allow the motor carrier to operate for up to 60 additional days.

(b) A Federal agency must not use a motor carrier that holds an "unsatisfactory" rating to transport passengers in a CMV or to transport hazardous materials in quantities requiring placarding.

(c) A Federal agency must not use a motor carrier for other CMV transportation if that carrier holds an "unsatisfactory" rating which became effective on or after January 22, 2001.

(d) Penalties. If a proposed "unsatisfactory" safety rating becomes final, the FMCSA will issue an order placing its interstate operations out of service. Any motor carrier that operates CMVs in violation of this section will be subject to the penalty provisions listed in 49 U.S.C. 521(b).

§385.14 Motor carriers, brokers, and freight forwarders delinquent in paying civil penalties: prohibition on transportation.

(a) A CMV owner or operator that has failed to pay civil penalties imposed by the FMCSA, or has failed to abide by a payment plan, may be prohibited from operating CMVs in interstate commerce under 49 CFR 386.83.

(b) A broker, freight forwarder, or for-hire motor carrier that has failed to pay civil penalties imposed by the FMCSA, or has failed to abide by a payment plan, may be prohibited from operating in interstate commerce, and its registration may be suspended under the provisions of 49 CFR 386.84.

§385.15 Administrative review.

(a) A motor carrier may request the FMCSA to conduct an administrative review if it believes the FMCSA has committed an error in assigning its proposed safety rating in accordance with §385.15(c) or its final safety rating in accordance with §385.11(b).

(b) The motor carrier's request must explain the error it believes the FMCSA committed in issuing the safety rating. The motor carrier must include a list of all factual and procedural issues in dispute, and any information or documents that support its argument.

(c) The motor carrier must submit its request in writing to the Chief Safety Officer, Federal Motor Carrier Safety Administration, 400 Seventh Street, SW., Washington DC 20590.

(1) *If a motor carrier has received a notice* of a proposed "unsatisfactory" safety rating, it should submit its request within 15 days from the date of the notice. This time frame will allow the FMCSA to issue a written decision before the prohibitions outlined in §385.13 (a)(1) and (2) take effect. Failure to petition within this 15-day period may prevent the FMCSA from issuing a final decision before such prohibitions take effect.

(2) *A motor carrier must make a request* for an administrative review within 90 days of the date of the proposed safety rating issued under §385.11 (c) or a final safety rating issued under §385.11 (b), or within 90 days after denial of a request for a change in rating under §385.17(i).

(d) The FMCSA may ask the motor carrier to submit additional data and attend a conference to discuss the safety rating. If the motor carrier does not provide the information requested, or does not attend the conference, the FMCSA may dismiss its request for review.

(e) The FMCSA will notify the motor carrier in writing of its decision following the administrative review. The FMCSA will complete its review:

(1) *Within 30 days after receiving a request* from a hazardous materials or passenger motor carrier that has received a proposed or final "unsatisfactory" safety rating.

(2) *Within 45 days after receiving a request* from any other motor carrier that has received a proposed or final "unsatisfactory" safety rating.

(f) The decision constitutes final agency action.

(g) Any motor carrier may request a rating change under the provisions of §385.17.

§385.17 Change to safety rating based upon corrective actions.

(a) A motor carrier that has taken action to correct the deficiencies that resulted in a proposed or final rating of "conditional" or "unsatisfactory" may request a rating change at any time.

(b) A motor carrier must make this request in writing to the FMCSA Service Center for the geographic area where the carrier maintains its principal place of business. The addresses and geographical boundaries of the Service Centers are listed in §390.27 of this chapter.

(c) The motor carrier must base its request upon evidence that it has taken corrective actions and that its operations currently meet the safety standard and factors specified in §§385.5 and 385.7. The request must include a written description of corrective actions taken, and other documentation the carrier wishes the FMCSA to consider.

(d) The FMCSA will make a final determination on the request for change based upon the documentation the motor carrier submits, and any additional relevant information.

(e) The FMCSA will perform reviews of requests made by motor carriers with a proposed or final "unsatisfactory" safety rating in the following time periods after the motor carrier's request:

(1) Within 30 days for motor carriers transporting passengers in CMVs or placardable quantities of hazardous materials.

(2) Within 45 days for all other motor carriers.

(f) The filing of a request for change to a proposed or final safety rating under this section does not stay the 45-day period specified in §385.13(a)(1) for motor carriers transporting passengers or hazardous materials. If the motor carrier has submitted evidence that corrective actions have been taken pursuant to this section and the FMCSA cannot make a final determination within the 45-day period, the period before the proposed safety rating becomes final may be extended for up to 10 days at the discretion of the FMCSA.

(g) The FMCSA may allow a motor carrier with a proposed rating of "unsatisfactory" (except those transporting passengers in CMVs or placardable quantities of hazardous materials) to continue to operate in interstate commerce for up to 60 days beyond the 60 days specified in the proposed rating, if the FMCSA determines that the motor carrier is making a good faith effort to improve its safety status. This additional period would begin on the 61st day after the date of the notice of the proposed "unsatisfactory" rating.

(h) If the FMCSA determines that the motor carrier has taken the corrective actions required and that its operations currently meet the safety standard and factors specified in §§385.5 and 385.7, the agency will notify the motor carrier in writing of its upgraded safety rating.

(i) If the FMCSA determines that the motor carrier has not taken all the corrective actions required, or that its operations still fail to meet the safety standard and factors specified in §§385.5 and 385.7, the agency will notify the motor carrier in writing.

(j) Any motor carrier whose request for change is denied in accordance with paragraph (i) of this section may request administrative review under the procedures of §385.15. The motor carrier must make the request within 90 days of the denial of the request for a rating change. If the proposed rating has become final, it shall remain in effect during the period of any administrative review.

§385.19 Safety fitness information.

(a) Final ratings will be made available to other Federal and State agencies in writing, telephonically or by remote computer access.

(b) The final safety rating assigned to a motor carrier will be made available to the public upon request. Any person requesting the assigned rating of a motor carrier shall provide the FMCSA with the motor carrier's name, principal office address, and, if known, the USDOT number or the ICCMC docket number, if any.

(c) Requests should be addressed to the Office of Data Analysis and Information Systems (MC RIS), Federal Motor Carrier Safety Administration, 400 Seventh Street, SW., Washington, DC 20590. The information can also be found at the SAFER website: http://www.safersys.org.

(d) Oral requests by telephone to (800) 832-5660 will be given an oral response.

Subpart B - Safety Monitoring System for Mexico-Domiciled Carriers

§385.101 Definitions

Compliance Review means a compliance review as defined in §385.3 of this part.

Provisional certificate of registration means the registration under §368.6 of this subchapter that the FMCSA grants to a Mexico-domiciled motor carrier to provide interstate transportation of property within the United States solely within the municipalities along the United States-Mexico border and the commercial zones of such municipalities. It is provisional because it will be revoked if the registrant does not demonstrate that it is exercising basic safety management controls during the safety monitoring period established in this subpart.

Provisional operating authority means the registration under §365.507 of this subchapter that the FMCSA grants to a Mexico-domiciled motor carrier to provide interstate transportation within the United States beyond the municipalities along the United States-Mexico border and the commercial zones of such municipalities. It is provisional because it will be revoked if the registrant is not assigned a Satisfactory safety rating following a compliance review conducted during the safety monitoring period established in this subpart.

Safety audit means an examination of a motor carrier's operations to provide educational and technical assistance on safety and the operational requirements of the FMCSRs and applicable HMRs and to gather critical safety data needed to make an assessment of the carrier's safety performance and basic safety management controls. Safety audits do not result in safety ratings.

§385.103 Safety monitoring system.

(a) **General.** Each Mexico-domiciled carrier operating in the United States will be subject to an oversight program to monitor its compliance with applicable Federal Motor Carrier Safety Regulations (FMCSRs), Federal Motor Vehicle Safety Standards (FMVSSs), and Hazardous Materials Regulations (HMRs).

(b) **Roadside monitoring.** Each Mexico-domiciled carrier that receives provisional operating authority or a provisional Certificate of Registration will be subject to intensified monitoring through frequent roadside inspections.

(c) **CVSA decal.** Each Mexico-domiciled carrier granted provisional operating authority under Part 365 of this subchapter must have on every commercial motor vehicle it operates in the United States a current decal attesting to a satisfactory inspection by a Commercial Vehicle Safety Alliance (CVSA) inspector.

(d) **Safety audit.** The FMCSA will conduct a safety audit on a Mexico-domiciled carrier within 18 months after the FMCSA issues the carrier a provisional Certificate of Registration under Part 368 of this subchapter.

(e) **Compliance review.** The FMCSA will conduct a compliance review on a Mexico-domiciled carrier within 18 months after the FMCSA issues the carrier provisional operating authority under Part 365 of this subchapter.

§385.105 Expedited action.

(a) A Mexico-domiciled motor carrier committing any of the following violations identified through roadside inspections, or by any other means, may be subjected to an expedited safety audit or compliance review, or may be required to submit a written response demonstrating corrective action:

(1) *Using drivers* not possessing, or operating without, a valid Licencia Federal de Conductor. An invalid Licencia Federal de Conductor includes one that is falsified, revoked, expired, or missing a required endorsement.

(2) *Operating vehicles* that have been placed out of service for violations of the Commercial Vehicle Safety Alliance (CVSA) North American Standard Out-of-Service Criteria, without making the required repairs.

(3) *Involvement in,* due to carrier act or omission, a hazardous materials incident within the United States involving:

(i) *A highway route controlled quantity* of a Class 7 (radioactive) material as defined in §173.403 of this title;

(ii) *Any quantity* of a Class 1, Division 1.1, 1.2, or 1.3 explosive as defined in §173.50 of this title; or

(iii) *Any quantity* of a poison inhalation hazard Zone A or B material as defined in §§173.115, 173.132, or 173.133 of this title.

(4) *Involvement in,* due to carrier act or omission, two or more hazardous material incidents occurring within the United States and involving any hazardous material not listed in paragraph (a)(3) of this section and defined in Chapter I of this title.

(5) *Using a driver* who tests positive for controlled substances or alcohol or who refuses to submit to required controlled substances or alcohol tests.

(6) *Operating within the United States* a motor vehicle that is not insured as required by Part 387 of this chapter.

(7) *Having a driver or vehicle out-of-service rate* of 50 percent or more based upon at least three inspections occurring within a consecutive 90-day period.

(b) **Failure to respond to an agency demand** for a written response demonstrating corrective action within 30 days will result in the suspension of the carrier's provisional operating authority or provisional Certificate of Registration until the required showing of corrective action is submitted to the FMCSA.

(c) **A satisfactory response to a written demand** for corrective action does not excuse a carrier from the requirement that it undergo a safety audit or compliance review, as appropriate, during the provisional registration period.

§385.107   The safety audit.

(a) **The criteria used in a safety audit to determine** whether a Mexico-domiciled carrier exercises the necessary basic safety management controls are specified in Appendix A to this part.

(b) **If the FMCSA determines, based on the safety audit,** that the Mexico-domiciled carrier has adequate basic safety management controls, the FMCSA will provide the carrier written notice of this finding as soon as practicable, but not later than 45 days after the completion of the safety audit. The carrier's Certificate of Registration will remain provisional and the carrier's on-highway performance will continue to be closely monitored for the remainder of the 18-month provisional registration period.

(c) **If the FMCSA determines, based on the safety audit,** that the Mexico-domiciled carrier's basic safety management controls are inadequate, it will initiate a suspension and revocation proceeding in accordance with §385.111 of this subpart.

(d) **The safety audit is also used to assess** the basic safety management controls of Mexico-domiciled applicants for provisional operating authority to operate beyond United States municipalities and commercial zones on the United States-Mexico border under §365.507 of this subchapter.

§385.109   The compliance review.

(a) **The criteria used in a compliance review** to determine whether a Mexico-domiciled carrier granted provisional operating authority under §365.507 of this subchapter exercises the necessary basic safety management controls are specified in Appendix B to this part.

(b) **Satisfactory Rating.** If the FMCSA assigns a Mexico-domiciled carrier a Satisfactory rating following a compliance review conducted under this subpart, the FMCSA will provide the carrier written notice as soon as practicable, but not later than 45 days after the completion of the compliance review. The carrier's operating authority will remain in provisional status and its on-highway performance will continue to be closely monitored for the remainder of the 18-month provisional registration period.

(c) **Conditional Rating.** If the FMCSA assigns a Mexico-domiciled carrier a Conditional rating following a compliance review conducted under this subpart, it will initiate a revocation proceeding in accordance with §385.111 of this subpart. The carrier's provisional operating authority will not be suspended prior to the conclusion of the revocation proceeding.

(d) **Unsatisfactory Rating.** If the FMCSA assigns a Mexico-domiciled carrier an Unsatisfactory rating following a compliance review conducted under this subpart, it will initiate a suspension and revocation proceeding in accordance with §385.111 of this subpart.

§385.111   Suspension and revocation of Mexico-domiciled carrier registration.

(a) **If a carrier is assigned** an "Unsatisfactory" safety rating following a compliance review conducted under this subpart, or a safety audit conducted under this subpart determines that a carrier does not exercise the basic safety management controls necessary to ensure safe operations, the FMCSA will provide the carrier written notice, as soon as practicable, that its registration will be suspended effective 15 days from the service date of the notice unless the carrier demonstrates, within 10 days of the service date of the notice, that the compliance review or safety audit contains material error.

(b) **For purposes of this section,** material error is a mistake or series of mistakes that resulted in an erroneous safety rating or an erroneous determination that the carrier does not exercise the necessary basic safety management controls.

(c) **If the carrier demonstrates** that the compliance review or safety audit contained material error, its registration will not be suspended. If the carrier fails to show a material error in the safety audit, the FMCSA will issue an Order:

(1) *Suspending the carrier's* provisional operating authority or provisional Certificate of Registration and requiring it to immediately cease all further operations in the United States; and

(2) *Notifying the carrier* that its provisional operating authority or provisional Certificate of Registration will be revoked unless it presents evidence of necessary corrective action within 30 days from the service date of the Order.

(d) **If a carrier is assigned a "Conditional" rating** following a compliance review conducted under this subpart, the provisions of subparagraphs (a) through (c) of this section will apply, except that its provisional registration will not be suspended under paragraph (c)(1) of this section.

(e) **If a carrier subject to this subpart fails to provide** the necessary documents for a safety audit or compliance review upon reasonable request, or fails to submit evidence of the necessary corrective action as required by §385.105 of this subpart, the FMCSA will provide the carrier with written notice, as soon as practicable, that its registration will be suspended 15 days from the service date of the notice unless it provides all necessary documents or information. This suspension will remain in effect until the necessary documents or information are produced and:

(1) *A safety audit* determines that the carrier exercises basic safety management controls necessary for safe operations;

(2) *The carrier is rated Satisfactory or Conditional* after a compliance review; or

(3) *The FMCSA determines,* following review of the carrier's response to a demand for corrective action under §385.105, that the carrier has taken the necessary corrective action.

(f) **If a carrier commits any of the violations** specified in §385.105(a) of this subpart after the removal of a suspension issued under this section, the suspension will be automatically reinstated. The FMCSA will issue an Order requiring the carrier to cease further operations in the United States and demonstrate, within 15 days from the service date of the Order, that it did not commit the alleged violation(s). If the carrier fails to demonstrate that it did not commit the violation(s), the FMCSA will issue an Order revoking its provisional operating authority or provisional Certificate of Registration.

(g) **If the FMCSA receives credible evidence** that a carrier has operated in violation of a suspension order issued under this section, it will issue an Order requiring the carrier to show cause, within 10 days of the service date of the Order, why its provisional operating authority or provisional Certificate of Registration should not be revoked. If the carrier fails to make the necessary showing, the FMCSA will revoke its registration.

(h) **If a Mexico-domiciled** motor carrier operates a commercial motor vehicle in violation of a suspension or out-of-service order, it is subject to the penalty provisions in 49 U.S.C. 521(b)(2)(A), not to exceed $10,000 for each offense.

(i) **Notwithstanding any provision of this subpart,** a carrier subject to this subpart is also subject to the suspension and revocation provisions of 49 U.S.C. 13905 for repeated violations of DOT regulations governing its motor carrier operations.

§385.113   Administrative review.

(a) **A Mexico-domiciled motor carrier** may request the FMCSA to conduct an administrative review if it believes the FMCSA has committed an error in assigning a safety rating or suspending or revoking the carrier's provisional operating authority or provisional Certificate of Registration under this subpart.

(b) **The carrier must submit its request in writing,** in English, to the Associate Administrator for Enforcement, Federal Motor Carrier Safety Administration, 400 Seventh Street, SW., Washington DC 20590.

(c) **The carrier's request must explain the error** it believes the FMCSA committed in assigning the safety rating or suspending or revoking the carrier's provisional operating authority or provisional Certificate of Registration and include any information or documents that support its argument.

(d) **The FMCSA will complete its administrative review** no later than 10 days after the carrier submits its request for review. The Associate Administrator's decision will constitute the final agency action.

§385.115 Reapplying for provisional registration.
(a) **A Mexico-domiciled motor carrier** whose provisional operating authority or provisional Certificate of Registration has been revoked may reapply under Part 365 or 368 of this subchapter, as appropriate, no sooner than 30 days after the date of revocation.
(b) **The Mexico-domiciled motor carrier** will be required to initiate the application process from the beginning. The carrier will be required to demonstrate how it has corrected the deficiencies that resulted in revocation of its registration and how it will ensure that it will have adequate basic safety management controls. It will also have to undergo a pre-authorization safety audit if it applies for provisional operating authority under Part 365 of this subchapter.

§385.117 Duration of safety monitoring system.
(a) **Each Mexico-domiciled carrier subject to this subpart** will remain in the safety monitoring system for at least 18 months from the date FMCSA issues its provisional Certificate of Registration or provisional operating authority, except as provided in paragraphs (c) and (d) of this section.
(b) **If, at the end of this 18-month period,** the carrier's most recent safety audit or safety rating was Satisfactory and no additional enforcement or safety improvement actions are pending under this subpart, the Mexico-domiciled carrier's provisional operating authority or provisional Certificate of Registration will become permanent.
(c) **If, at the end of this 18-month period,** the FMCSA has not been able to conduct a safety audit or compliance review, the carrier will remain in the safety monitoring system until a safety audit or compliance review is conducted. If the results of the safety audit or compliance review are satisfactory, the carrier's provisional operating authority or provisional Certificate of Registration will become permanent.
(d) **If, at the end of this 18-month period,** the carrier's provisional operating authority or provisional Certificate of Registration is suspended under §385.111(a) of this subpart, the carrier will remain in the safety monitoring system until the FMCSA either:
  (1) *Determines that the carrier has taken corrective action;* or
  (2) *Completes measures* to revoke the carrier's provisional operating authority or provisional Certificate of Registration under §385.111(c) of this subpart.

§385.119 Applicability of safety fitness and enforcement procedures.
At all times during which a Mexico-domiciled motor carrier is subject to the safety monitoring system in this subpart, it is also subject to the general safety fitness procedures established in Subpart A of this part and to compliance and enforcement procedures applicable to all carriers regulated by the FMCSA.

Subpart C - Certification of Safety Auditors, Safety Investigators, and Safety Inspectors

§385.201 Who is qualified to perform a review of a motor carrier?
(a) **An FMCSA employee,** or a State or local government employee funded through MCSAP, who was qualified to perform a compliance review before June 17, 2002, may perform a compliance review, safety audit or roadside inspection if he or she complies with §385.203(b).
(b) **A person who was not qualified to perform** a compliance review before June 17, 2002, may perform a compliance review, safety audit or roadside inspection after complying with the requirements of §385.203(a).

§385.203 What are the requirements to obtain and maintain certification?
(a) **After June 17, 2002,** a person who is not qualified under §385.201(a) may not perform a compliance review, safety audit, or roadside inspection unless he or she has been certified by FMCSA or a State or local agency applying the FMCSA standards after successfully completing classroom training and examinations on the FMCSRs and HMRs as described in detail on the FMCSA website (*www.fmcsa.dot.gov*). These employees must also comply with the maintenance of certification/ qualification requirements of paragraph (b) of this section.

(b) **Maintenance of certification/qualification.** A person may not perform a compliance review, safety audit, or roadside inspection unless he or she meets the quality-control and periodic re-training requirements adopted by the FMCSA to ensure the maintenance of high standards and familiarity with amendments to the FMCSRs and HMRs. These maintenance of certification/qualification requirements are described in detail on the FMCSA website (*www.fmcsa.dot.gov*).
(c) **The requirements of paragraphs (a) and (b)** of this section for training, performance and maintenance of certification/qualification, which are described on the FMCSA website (*www.fmcsa.dot.gov*), are also available in hard copy from the Office of Professional Development and Training, FMCSA, 400 7th Street, SW., Washington, DC 20590.

§385.205 How can a person who has lost his or her certification be re-certified?
He or she must successfully complete the requirements of §385.203(a) and (b).

Subpart D - New Entrant Safety Assurance Program

§385.301 What is a motor carrier required to do before beginning interstate operations?
(a) **Before a motor carrier of property or passengers** begins interstate operations, it must register with the FMCSA and receive a USDOT number. In addition, for-hire motor carriers must obtain operating authority from FMCSA following the registration procedures described in 49 CFR Part 365, unless providing transportation exempt from 49 CFR Part 365 registration requirements.
(b) **This subpart applies to motor carriers** domiciled in the United States and Canada.
(c) **A Mexico-domiciled motor carrier** of property or passengers must register with the FMCSA by following the registration procedures described in 49 CFR Part 365 or 368, as appropriate. The regulations in this subpart do not apply to Mexico-domiciled carriers.

§385.303 How does a motor carrier register with the FMCSA?
A motor carrier may contact the FMCSA by internet (*www.fmcsa.dot.gov*); or Washington, DC headquarters by mail at, FMCSA, 400 7th Street SW., Washington, DC 20590; fax (703) 280-4003; or telephone 1-800-832-5660, and request the application materials for a new entrant motor carrier.

§385.305 What happens after the FMCSA receives a request for new entrant registration?
(a) **The requester for new entrant registration** will be directed to the FMCSA Internet website (*www.fmcsa.dot.gov*) to secure and/or complete the application package online.
(b) **The application package will contain the following:**
  (1) *Educational and technical assistance material* regarding the requirements of the FMCSRs and HMRs, if applicable.
  (2) *The Form MCS-150, The Motor Carrier Identification Report.*
  (3) *The Form MCS-150A,* The Safety Certification for Applications for U.S. DOT Number.
  (4) *Application forms* to obtain operating authority under 49 CFR 365, as appropriate.
(c) **Upon completion of the application forms,** the new entrant will be issued a USDOT number.
(d) **For-hire motor carriers,** unless providing transportation exempt from 49 CFR Part 365 registration requirements, must also comply with the procedures established in 49 CFR Part 365 to obtain operating authority before operating in interstate commerce.

§385.307 What happens after a motor carrier begins operations as a new entrant?
After a new entrant satisfies all applicable pre-operational requirements, it will be subject to the new entrant safety monitoring procedures for a period of 18 months. During this 18-month period:
(a) **The new entrant's roadside safety performance** will be closely monitored to ensure the new entrant has basic safety management controls that are operating effectively. An accident rate or driver or vehicle violation rate that is higher than the industry average for similar motor carrier operations may cause the FMCSA to conduct an expedited safety audit or compliance review at any time.

(b) **A safety audit will be conducted on the new entrant,** once it has been in operation for enough time to have sufficient records to allow the agency to evaluate the adequacy of its basic safety management controls. This period will generally be at least 3 months.

(c) **All records and documents required** for the safety audit shall be made available for inspection upon request by an individual certified under FMCSA regulations to perform safety audits.

§385.309 What is the purpose of the safety audit?

The purpose of a safety audit is to:

(a) **Provide educational and technical assistance** to the new entrant; and

(b) **Gather safety data needed to make an assessment** of the new entrant's safety performance and adequacy of its basic safety management controls.

§385.311 What will the safety audit consist of?

The safety audit will consist of a review of the new entrant's safety management systems and a sample of required records to assess compliance with the FMCSRs, applicable HMRs and related recordkeeping requirements as specified in Appendix A of this part. The areas for review include, but are not limited to, the following:

(a) Driver qualification;
(b) Driver duty status;
(c) Vehicle maintenance;
(d) Accident register; and
(e) Controlled substances and alcohol use and testing requirements.

§385.313 Who will conduct the safety audit?

An individual certified under the FMCSA regulations to perform safety audits will conduct the safety audit.

§385.315 Where will the safety audit be conducted?

The safety audit will generally be conducted at the new entrant's business premises.

§385.317 Will a safety audit result in a safety fitness determination by the FMCSA?

A safety audit will not result in a safety fitness determination. Safety fitness determinations follow completion of a compliance review.

§385.319 What happens after the completion of the safety audit?

(a) **Upon the completion of the safety audit,** the auditor will review the findings with the new entrant.

(b) **If the FMCSA determines that the safety audit** discloses that the new entrant has adequate basic safety management controls, the FMCSA will provide the new entrant written notice as soon as practicable, but not later than 45 days after the completion of the safety audit, that it has adequate basic safety management controls. The new entrant's safety performance will continue to be closely monitored for the remainder of the 18-month period of new entrant registration.

(c) **If the FMCSA determines that the findings** of the safety audit disclose that the new entrant's basic safety management controls are inadequate, it will provide the new entrant written notice, as soon as practicable, but not later than 45 days after the completion of the safety audit, that its USDOT new entrant registration will be revoked and its operations placed out-of-service unless it takes the actions specified in the notice to remedy its safety management practices within:

(1) *45 days of the date of the notice* if the new entrant transports passengers in a CMV designed or used to transport 16 or more passengers, including the driver, or transports hazardous materials requiring placarding; or

(2) *60 days of the date of the notice for all other new entrants.*

§385.321 What failures of safety management practices disclosed by the safety audit will result in a notice to a new entrant that its DOT new entrant registration will be revoked?

The failures of safety management practices consist of a lack of basic safety management controls as described in Appendix A of this part and will result in a notice to a new entrant that its DOT new entrant registration will be revoked.

§385.323 May the FMCSA extend the period under §385.319(c) for a new entrant to take corrective action to remedy its safety management practices?

(a) **If a new entrant that transports passengers** in a CMV designed or used to transport 16 or more passengers, including the driver, or transports hazardous materials in quantities requiring placarding, has submitted evidence that corrective actions have been taken pursuant to §385.319(c) and the FMCSA cannot make a determination regarding the adequacy of the corrective actions within the 45 day period, the period may be extended for up to 10 days at the discretion of the FMCSA.

(b) **The FMCSA may extend the 60-day period** in §385.319(c)(2), for up to an additional 60 days provided FMCSA determines that the new entrant is making a good faith effort to remedy its safety management practices.

§385.325 What happens after a new entrant has been notified under §385.319(c) to take corrective action to remedy its safety management practices?

(a) **If the new entrant provides evidence** of corrective action acceptable to the FMCSA within the time period provided in §385.319(c), including any extension of that period authorized under §385.323, the FMCSA will provide written notification to the new entrant that its DOT new entrant registration will not be revoked and it may continue operations.

(b) **If a new entrant, after being notified** that it is required to take corrective action to improve its safety management practices, fails to submit a written response demonstrating corrective action acceptable to FMCSA within the time specified in §385.319(c), including any extension of that period authorized under §385.323, the FMCSA will revoke its new entrant registration and issue an out-of-service order effective on:

(1) *Day 46 from the date of notification* if the new entrant transports passengers in a CMV designed to transport 16 or more passengers, including the driver, or transports hazardous materials in quantities requiring placarding; or

(2) *Day 61 from the date of notification for all other new entrants;* or

(3) *If an extension has been granted* under §385.323, the day following the expiration of the extension date.

(c) **The new entrant may not operate** in interstate commerce on or after the effective date of the out-of-service order.

§385.327 What happens when a new entrant receives a notice under §385.319(c) that its new entrant registration will be revoked and it believes the FMCSA made an error in its determination?

(a) **If a new entrant receives a revocation notice,** it may request the FMCSA to conduct an administrative review if it believes the FMCSA has committed an error in determining that its basic safety management controls were inadequate.

(1) *The request must be made* to the Field Administrator of the appropriate FMCSA Service Center.

(2) *The request must explain the error* the new entrant believes the FMCSA committed in its determination.

(3) *The request must include* a list of all factual and procedural issues in dispute, and any information or documents that support the new entrant's argument.

(b) **The new entrant should submit its request** no later than 15 days from the date of the notice of the inadequacy of its basic safety management controls. Submitting the request within 15 days will allow the FMCSA to issue a written decision before the prohibitions outlined in §385.319(c) take effect. Failure to petition within this 15-day period may prevent the FMCSA from issuing a final decision before the prohibitions take effect.

(c) **The FMCSA may request that the new entrant** submit additional data and attend a conference to discuss the issue(s) in dispute. If the new entrant does not attend the conference, or does not submit the requested data, the FMCSA may dismiss the new entrant's request for review.

(d) **The FMCSA will complete its review** and notify the new entrant in writing of its decision within 30 days after receiving a request for review from a hazardous materials or passenger new entrant and within 45 days from any other new entrant.

Subpart E - Hazardous Materials Safety Permits §385.403

(e) **A new entrant must make a request** for an administrative review within:
(1) *90 days of the date* when it was initially notified under §385.319(c) that its basic safety management controls were inadequate; or
(2) *90 days after it was notified* that its corrective action under §385.319(c) was insufficient and its basic safety management controls remain inadequate.

(f) **The Field Administrator's decision** constitutes the final agency action.

(g) **Notwithstanding this subpart,** a new entrant is subject to the suspension and revocation provisions of 49 U.S.C. 13905 for violations of DOT regulations governing motor carrier operations.

§385.329 May a new entrant that has had its U.S. DOT registration revoked and its operations placed out of service (OOS) reapply?

(a) **A new entrant whose U.S. DOT registration** has been revoked and whose operations have been placed OOS by the FMCSA may reapply under §385.301 no sooner than 30 days after the date of revocation.

(b) **The motor carrier will be required** to initiate the process from the beginning, and will be required to demonstrate that it has corrected the deficiencies that resulted in revocation of its registration and otherwise will ensure that it will have adequate basic safety management controls.

§385.331 What happens if a new entrant operates a CMV after having been issued an order placing its interstate operations out of service (OOS)?

If a new entrant operates a CMV in violation of an out-of-service (OOS) order and §385.325(b), it is subject to the penalty provisions in 49 U.S.C. 521(b)(2)(A), not to exceed $10,000 for each offense.

§385.333 What happens at the end of the 18-month safety monitoring period?

(a) **If a safety audit has been performed** within the 18-month period, and the new entrant is not currently subject to an order placing its operations out-of-service under §385.325(b) or under a notice ordering it to take specified actions to remedy its safety management controls under §385.319(c), the FMCSA will remove the new entrant designation and notify the new entrant in writing that its registration has become permanent. Thereafter, the FMCSA will evaluate the motor carrier on the same basis as any other carrier.

(b) **If a new entrant is determined to be "unfit"** after a compliance review its new entrant registration will be revoked. (See §385.13)

(c) **A new entrant that has reached the conclusion** of the 18-month period but is under an order to correct its safety management practices under §385.319(c) will have its new entrant registration removed following FMCSA's determination that the specified actions have been taken to remedy its safety management practices. The motor carrier will be notified in writing that its new entrant designation is removed and that its registration has become permanent. Thereafter, the FMCSA will evaluate the motor carrier on the same basis as any other carrier.

(d) **If a safety audit or compliance review** has not been performed by the end of the 18-month monitoring period through no fault of the motor carrier, the carrier will be permitted to continue operating as a new entrant until a safety audit or compliance review is performed and a final determination is made regarding the adequacy of its safety management controls. Based on the results of the safety audit or compliance review, the FMCSA will either:
(1) *Remove the new entrant designation* and notify the new entrant in writing that its registration has become permanent; or
(2) *Revoke the new entrant registration* in accordance with §385.319(c).

§385.335 If the FMCSA conducts a compliance review on a new entrant, will the new entrant also be subject to a safety audit?

If the FMCSA conducts a compliance review on a new entrant that has not previously been subject to a safety audit and issues a safety fitness determination, the new entrant will not have to undergo a safety audit under this subpart. However, the new entrant will continue to be subject to the 18-month safety-monitoring period prior to removal of the new entrant designation.

§385.337 What happens if a new entrant refuses to permit a safety audit to be performed on its operations?

(a) **If a new entrant refuses to permit a safety audit** to be performed on its operations, the FMCSA will provide the carrier with written notice that its registration will be revoked and its operations placed out of service unless the new entrant agrees in writing, within 10 days from the service date of the notice, to permit the safety audit to be performed. The initial refusal to permit a safety audit to be performed may subject the new entrant to the penalty provisions in 49 U.S.C. 521(b)(2)(A).

(b) **If the new entrant does not agree** to undergo a safety audit as specified in paragraph (a) of this section, its registration will be revoked and its interstate operations placed out of service effective on the 11th day from the service date of the notice issued under paragraph (a) of this section.

Subpart E - Hazardous Materials Safety Permits

§385.401 What is the purpose and scope of this subpart?

(a) **This subpart contains the requirements** for obtaining and maintaining a safety permit to transport certain hazardous materials. No one may transport the materials listed in §385.403 without a safety permit required by this subpart.

(b) **This subpart includes:**
(1) *Definitions of terms used in this subpart;*
(2) *The list of hazardous materials* that require a safety permit if transported in commerce;
(3) *The requirements and procedures* a carrier must follow in order to be issued a safety permit and maintain a safety permit;
(4) *The procedures for a motor carrier to follow* to initiate an administrative review of a denial, suspension, or revocation of a safety permit.

§385.402 What definitions are used in this subpart?

(a) **The definitions in Parts 390 and 385 of this chapter** apply to this subpart, except where otherwise specifically noted.

(b) **As used in this part,**

Hazardous material has the same meaning as under §171.8 of this title: A substance or material that the Secretary of Transportation has determined is capable of posing an unreasonable risk to health, safety, and property when transported in commerce, and has designated as hazardous under §5103 of Federal hazardous materials transportation law (49 U.S.C. 5103). The term includes hazardous substances, hazardous wastes, marine pollutants, elevated temperature materials, materials designated as hazardous in the Hazardous Materials Table (see §172.101 of this title), and materials that meet the defining criteria for hazard classes and divisions in Part 173 of this title.

Hazmat employee has the same meaning as under §171.8 of this title: A person who is employed by a hazmat employer as defined under §171.8 of this title, and who in the course of employment directly affects hazardous materials transportation safety. This term includes an owner-operator of a motor vehicle that transports hazardous materials in commerce. This term includes an individual who, during the course of employment:
(1) *Loads, unloads, or handles hazardous materials;*
(2) *Manufactures, tests, reconditions,* repairs, modifies, marks, or otherwise represents containers, drums, or packaging as qualified for use in the transportation of hazardous materials;
(3) *Prepares hazardous materials for transportation;*
(4) *Is responsible for the safe transportation* of hazardous materials; or
(5) *Operates a vehicle used to transport hazardous materials.*

Liquefied natural gas (LNG) means a Division 2.1 liquefied natural gas material that is transported in a liquid state with a methane content of 85 percent or more.

Safety permit means a document issued by FMCSA that contains a permit number and confers authority to transport in commerce the hazardous materials listed in §385.403.

Shipment means the offering or loading of hazardous materials at one loading facility using one transport vehicle, or the transport of that transport vehicle.

§385.403 Who must hold a safety permit?

After the date following January 1, 2005, that a motor carrier is required to file a Motor Carrier Identification Report Form (MCS-150) according to the schedule set forth in §390.19(a) of this chapter, the motor carrier may not transport in interstate or intrastate commerce

any of the following hazardous materials, in the quantity indicated for each, unless the motor carrier holds a safety permit:
- (a) **A highway route-controlled quantity** of a Class 7 (radioactive) material, as defined in §173.403 of this title;
- (b) **More than 25 kg (55 pounds)** of a Division 1.1, 1.2, or 1.3 (explosive) material or an amount of a Division 1.5 (explosive) material requiring placarding under Part 172 of this title;
- (c) **More than one liter (1.08 quarts) per package** of a "material poisonous by inhalation," as defined in §171.8 of this title, that meets the criteria for "hazard zone A," as specified in §173.116(a) or §173.133(a) of this title;
- (d) **A "material poisonous by inhalation,"** as defined in §171.8 of this title, that meets the criteria for "hazard zone B," as specified in §173.116(a) or §173.133(a) of this title in a bulk packaging (capacity greater than 450 L [119 gallons]);
- (e) **A "material poisonous by inhalation,"** as defined in §171.8 of this title, that meets the criteria for "hazard zone C," or "hazard zone D," as specified in §173.116(a) of this title, in a packaging having a capacity equal to or greater than 13,248 L (3,500) gallons; or
- (f) **A shipment of compressed or refrigerated** liquefied methane or liquefied natural gas, or other liquefied gas with a methane content of at least 85 percent, in a bulk packaging having a capacity equal to or greater than 13,248 L (3,500 gallons).

§385.405 How does a motor carrier apply for a safety permit?

- (a) **Application form(s).** To apply for a new safety permit or renewal of the safety permit, a motor carrier must complete and submit Form MCS-150B, Combined Motor Carrier Identification Report and HM Permit Application.
  - (1) *The Form MCS-150B* will also satisfy the requirements for obtaining and renewing a DOT identification number; there is no need to complete Form MCS-150, Motor Carrier Identification Report.
  - (2) *A new entrant,* as defined in §385.3, must also submit Form MCS-150A, Safety Certification for Application (Safety Certification for Application for USDOT Number) (see Subpart D of this part).
- (b) **Where to get forms and instructions.** The forms listed in paragraph (a) of this section, and instructions for completing the forms, may be obtained on the Internet at http://www.fmcsa.dot.gov, or by contacting FMCSA at Federal Motor Carrier Safety Administration, MC-PSDRIS, Room 8214, 400 7th Street, SW, Washington, DC 20590, Telephone: 1-800-832-5660.
- (c) **Signature and certification.** An official of the motor carrier must sign and certify that the information is correct on each form the motor carrier submits.
- (d) **Updating information on Form MCS-150B.** A motor carrier holding a safety permit must report to FMCSA any change in the information on its Form MCS-150B within 30 days of the change. The motor carrier must use Form MCS-150B to report the new information (contact information in paragraph (b) of this section).

§385.407 What conditions must a motor carrier satisfy for FMCSA to issue a safety permit?

- (a) **Motor carrier safety performance.**
  - (1) *The motor carrier* must have a "Satisfactory" safety rating assigned by either FMCSA, pursuant to the Safety Fitness Procedures of this part, or the State in which the motor carrier has its principal place of business, if the State has adopted and implemented safety fitness procedures that are equivalent to the procedures in Subpart A of this part; and,
  - (2) *FMCSA will not issue a safety permit to a motor carrier that:*
    - (i) *Does not certify* that it has a satisfactory security program as required in §385.407(b);
    - (ii) *Has a crash rate in the top 30 percent* of the national average as indicated in the FMCSA Motor Carrier Management Information System (MCMIS); or
    - (iii) *Has a driver, vehicle, hazardous materials,* or total out-of-service rate in the top 30 percent of the national average as indicated in the MCMIS.
- (b) **Satisfactory security program.** The motor carrier must certify that it has a satisfactory security program, including:
  - (1) *A security plan* meeting the requirements of Part 172, Subpart I of this title, and addressing how the carrier will ensure the security of the written route plan required by this part;
  - (2) *A communications plan* that allows for contact between the commercial motor vehicle operator and the motor carrier to meet the periodic contact requirements in §385.415(c)(1); and
  - (3) *Successful completion by all hazmat employees* of the security training required in §172.704(a)(4) and (a)(5) of this title.
- (c) **Registration with** the Research and Special Programs Administration (RSPA). The motor carrier must be registered with RSPA in accordance with Part 107, Subpart G of this title.

§385.409 When may a temporary safety permit be issued to a motor carrier?

- (a) **Temporary safety permit.** If a motor carrier does not meet the criteria in §385.407(a), FMCSA may issue it a temporary safety permit. To obtain a temporary safety permit a motor carrier must certify on Form MCS-150B that it is operating in full compliance with the HMRs; with the FMCSRs, and/or comparable State regulations, whichever is applicable; and with the minimum financial responsibility requirements in Part 387 of this chapter or in State regulations, whichever is applicable.
- (b) **FMCSA will not issue** a temporary safety permit to a motor carrier that:
  - (1) *Does not certify* that it has a satisfactory security program as required in §385.407(b);
  - (2) *Has a crash rate in the top 30 percent* of the national average as indicated in the FMCSA's MCMIS; or
  - (3) *Has a driver, vehicle, hazardous materials,* or total out-of-service rate in the top 30 percent of the national average as indicated in the MCMIS.
- (c) **A temporary safety permit** shall be valid for 180 days after the date of issuance or until the motor carrier is assigned a new safety rating, whichever occurs first.
  - (1) *A motor carrier that receives* a Satisfactory safety rating will be issued a safety permit (see §385.421).
  - (2) *A motor carrier that receives* a less than Satisfactory safety rating is ineligible for a safety permit and will be subject to revocation of its temporary safety permit.
- (d) **If a motor carrier has not received a safety rating** within the 180-day time period, FMCSA will extend the effective date of the temporary safety permit for an additional 60 days, provided the motor carrier demonstrates that it is continuing to operate in full compliance with the FMCSRs and HMRs.

§385.411 Must a motor carrier obtain a safety permit if it has a State permit?

Yes. However, if FMCSA is able to verify that a motor carrier has a safety permit issued by a State under a program that FMCSA has determined to be equivalent to the provisions of this subpart, FMCSA will immediately issue a safety permit to the motor carrier upon receipt of an application in accordance with §385.405, without further inspection or investigation.

§385.413 What happens if a motor carrier receives a proposed safety rating that is less than Satisfactory?

- (a) **If a motor carrier does not already have a safety permit,** it will not be issued a safety permit (including a temporary safety permit) unless and until a Satisfactory safety rating is issued to the motor carrier.
- (b) **If a motor carrier holds a safety permit** (including a temporary safety permit), the safety permit will be subject to revocation or suspension (see §385.421).

§385.415 What operational requirements apply to the transportation of a hazardous material for which a permit is required?

- (a) **Information that must be carried in the vehicle.** During transportation, the following must be maintained in each commercial motor vehicle that transports a hazardous material listed in §385.403 and must be made available to an authorized official of a Federal, State, or local government agency upon request.
  - (1) *A copy of the safety permit* or another document showing the permit number, provided that document clearly indicates the number is the FMCSA Safety Permit number;
  - (2) *A written route plan* that meets the requirements of §397.101 of this chapter for highway route-controlled Class 7 (radioactive) materials or §397.67 of this chapter for Division 1.1, 1.2, and 1.3 (explosive) materials; and
  - (3) *The telephone number,* including area code or country code, of an employee of the motor carrier or representative of the motor carrier who is familiar with the routing of the permitted material. The motor carrier employee or representative must be able to verify that the shipment is within the general area for the expected route for the permitted material. The telephone number, when called, must be answered directly by the motor car-

Subpart E - Hazardous Materials Safety Permits §385.423 (b)

rier or its representative at all times while the permitted material is in transportation including storage incidental to transportation. Answering machines are not sufficient to meet this requirement.

(b) (1) *Inspection of vehicle* transporting Class 7 (radioactive) materials. Before a motor carrier may transport a highway route controlled quantity of a Class 7 (radioactive) material, the motor carrier must have a pre-trip inspection performed on each motor vehicle to be used to transport a highway route controlled quantity of a Class 7 (radioactive) material, in accordance with the requirements of the "North American Standard Out-of-Service Criteria and Level VI Inspection Procedures and Out-of-Service Criteria for Commercial Highway Vehicles Transporting Transuranics and Highway Route Controlled Quantities of Radioactive Materials as defined in 49 CFR Part 173.403," January 1, 2004, which is incorporated by reference. The Director of the Federal Register has approved the materials incorporated by reference in accordance with 5 U.S.C. 552(a) and 1 CFR Part 51. Information and copies may be obtained from the Commercial Vehicle Safety Alliance, 1101 17th Street, NW, Suite 803, Washington, DC 20036. Phone number (202) 775-1623.

(2) *All materials incorporated by reference* are available for inspection at the Federal Motor Carrier Safety Administration, Office of Enforcement and Compliance, 400 Seventh Street, SW., Washington, DC 20590; and the National Archives and Records Administration (NARA). For information on the availability of this material at NARA, call (202) 741-6030, or go to: *http://www.archives.gov/federal_registercode_of_federal_regulations/ibr_locations.html.*

(c) Additional requirements. A motor carrier transporting hazardous materials requiring a permit under this part must also meet the following requirements:

(1) *The operator of a motor vehicle* used to transport a hazardous material listed in §385.403 must follow the communications plan required in §385.407(b)(2) to make contact with the carrier at the beginning and end of each duty tour, and at the pickup and delivery of each permitted load. Contact may be by telephone, radio or via an electronic tracking or monitoring system. The motor carrier or driver must maintain a record of communications for 6 months after the initial acceptance of a shipment of hazardous material for which a safety permit is required. The record of communications must contain the name of the driver, identification of the vehicle, permitted material(s) being transported, and the date, location, and time of each contact required under this section.

(2) *The motor carrier* should contact the Transportation Security Administration's Transportation Security Coordination Center (703-563-3236 or 703-563-3237) at any time the motor carrier suspects its shipment of a hazardous material listed in §385.403 is lost, stolen or otherwise unaccounted for.

§385.417 Is a motor carrier's safety permit number available to others?

Upon request, a motor carrier must provide the number of its safety permit to a person who offers a hazardous material listed in §385.403 for transportation in commerce. A motor carrier's safety permit number will also be available to the public on the FMCSA Safety and Fitness Electronic Records System at *http://www.safersys.org*.

§385.419 How long is a safety permit effective?

Unless suspended or revoked, a safety permit (other than a temporary safety permit) is effective for two years, except that:

(a) A safety permit will be subject to revocation if a motor carrier fails to submit a renewal application (Form MCS-150B) in accordance with the schedule set forth for filing Form MCS-150 in §390.19(a) of this chapter; and

(b) An existing safety permit will remain in effect pending FMCSA's processing of an application for renewal if a motor carrier submits the required application (Form MS-150B) in accordance with the schedule set forth in §390.19(a)(2) and (a)(3) of this chapter.

§385.421 Under what circumstances will a safety permit be subject to revocation or suspension by FMCSA?

(a) Grounds. A safety permit will be subject to revocation or suspension by FMCSA for the following reasons:

(1) *A motor carrier fails to submit* a renewal application (Form MCS-150B) in accordance with the schedule set forth in §390.19(a)(2) and (a)(3) of this chapter;

(2) *A motor carrier provides* any false or misleading information on its application (Form MCS-150B), on Form MCS-150A (when required), or as part of updated information it is providing on Form MCS-150B (see §385.405(d));

(3) *A motor carrier is issued a final safety rating* that is less than Satisfactory;

(4) *A motor carrier fails to maintain* a satisfactory security plan as set forth in §385.407(b);

(5) *A motor carrier fails to comply* with applicable requirements in the FMCSRs, the HMRs, or compatible State requirements governing the transportation of hazardous materials, in a manner showing that the motor carrier is not fit to transport the hazardous materials listed in §385.403;

(6) *A motor carrier fails to comply with an out-of-service order;*

(7) *A motor carrier fails to comply* with any other order issued under the FMCSRs, the HMRs, or compatible State requirements governing the transportation of hazardous materials, in a manner showing that the motor carrier is not fit to transport the hazardous materials listed in §385.403;

(8) *A motor carrier fails to maintain* the minimum financial responsibility required by §387.9 of this chapter or an applicable State requirement;

(9) *A motor carrier fails to maintain* current hazardous materials registration with the Research and Special Programs Administration; or

(10) *A motor carrier loses its operating rights* or has its registration suspended in accordance with §386.83 or §386.84 of this chapter for failure to pay a civil penalty or abide by a payment plan.

(b) Determining whether a safety permit is revoked or suspended. A motor carrier's safety permit will be suspended the first time any of the conditions specified in paragraph (a) of this section are found to apply to the motor carrier. A motor carrier's safety permit will be revoked if any of the conditions specified in paragraph (a) of this section are found to apply to the motor carrier and the carrier's safety permit has been suspended in the past for any of the reasons specified in paragraph (a) of this section.

(c) Effective date of suspension or revocation. A suspension or revocation of a safety permit is effective:

(1) *Immediately after FMCSA determines* that an imminent hazard exists, after FMCSA issues a final safety rating that is less than Satisfactory, or after a motor carrier loses its operating rights or has its registration suspended for failure to pay a civil penalty or abide by a payment plan;

(2) *Thirty (30) days after service* of a written notification that FMCSA proposes to suspend or revoke a safety permit, if the motor carrier does not submit a written request for administrative review within that time period; or

(3) *As specified in §385.423(c),* when the motor carrier submits a written request for administrative review of FMCSA's proposal to suspend or revoke a safety permit.

(4) *A motor carrier whose safety permit has been revoked* will not be issued a replacement safety permit or temporary safety permit for 365 days from the time of revocation.

§385.423 Does a motor carrier have a right to an administrative review of a denial, suspension, or revocation of a safety permit?

A motor carrier has a right to an administrative review pursuant to the following procedures and conditions:

(a) Less than Satisfactory safety rating. If a motor carrier is issued a proposed safety rating that is less than Satisfactory, it has the right to request (1) an administrative review of a proposed safety rating, as set forth in §385.15, and (2) a change to a proposed safety rating based on corrective action, as set forth in §385.17. After a motor carrier has had an opportunity for administrative review of, or change to, a proposed safety rating, FMCSA's issuance of a final safety rating constitutes final agency action, and a motor carrier has no right to further administrative review of FMCSA's denial, suspension, or revocation of a safety permit when the motor carrier has been issued a final safety rating that is less than Satisfactory.

(b) Failure to pay civil penalty or abide by payment plan. If a motor carrier is notified that failure to pay a civil penalty will result in suspension or termination of its operating rights, it has the right to an administrative review of that proposed action in a show cause proceeding, as set forth in §386.83(b) or §386.84(b) of this chapter. The decision by FMCSA's Chief Safety Officer in the show cause proceeding constitutes final agency action, and a motor carrier has no right to further administrative review of FMCSA's denial, suspension, or revocation of a safety permit when the motor carrier has lost its operating rights or had its registration suspended for failure to pay a civil penalty or abide by a payment plan.

(c) Other grounds. Under circumstances other than those set forth in paragraphs (a) and (b) of this section, a motor carrier may submit a written request for administrative review within 30 days after service of a written notification that FMCSA has denied a safety permit, that FMCSA has immediately suspended or revoked a safety permit, or that FMCSA has proposed to suspend or revoke a safety permit. The rules for computing time limits for service and requests for extension of time in §§386.31 and 386.33 of this chapter apply to the proceedings on a request for administrative review under this section.

(1) *The motor carrier must send or deliver* its written request for administrative review to FMCSA Chief Safety Officer, with a copy to FMCSA Chief Counsel, at the following addresses:

(i) *FMCSA Chief Safety Officer,* Federal Motor Carrier Safety Administration, c/o Adjudications Counsel (MC-PSDCC), 400 Seventh Street, SW., Washington, DC 20590.

(ii) *FMCSA Chief Counsel,* Federal Motor Carrier Safety Administration, Office of the Chief Counsel, Room 8125, 400 Seventh Street, SW., Washington, DC 20590.

(2) *A request for administrative review* must state the specific grounds for review and include all information, evidence, and arguments upon which the motor carrier relies to support its request for administrative review.

(3) *Within 30 days after service* of a written request for administrative review, the Office of the Chief Counsel shall submit to the Chief Safety Officer a written response to the request for administrative review. The Office of the Chief Counsel must serve a copy of its written response on the motor carrier requesting administrative review.

(4) *The Chief Safety Officer* may decide a motor carrier's request for administrative review on the written submissions, hold a hearing personally, or refer the request to an administrative law judge for a hearing and recommended decision. The Chief Safety Officer or administrative law judge is authorized to specify, and must notify the parties of, specific procedural rules to be followed in the proceeding (which may include the procedural rules in Part 386 of this chapter that are considered appropriate).

(5) *If a request for administrative review* is referred to an administrative law judge, the recommended decision of the administrative law judge becomes the final decision of the Chief Safety Officer 45 days after service of the recommended decision is served, unless either the motor carrier or the Office of the Chief Counsel submits a petition for review to the Chief Safety Officer (and serves a copy of its petition on the other party) within 15 days after service of the recommended decision. In response to a petition for review of a recommended decision of an administrative law judge:

(i) *The other party may submit a written reply* within 15 days of service of the petition for review.

(ii) *The Chief Safety Officer* may adopt, modify, or set aside the recommended decision of an administrative law judge, and may also remand the petition for review to the administrative law judge for further proceedings.

(6) *The Chief Safety Officer* will issue a final decision on any request for administrative review when:

(i) *The request for administrative review* has not been referred to an administrative law judge;

(ii) *A petition for review* of a recommended decision by an administrative law judge has not been remanded to the administrative law judge for further proceedings; or

(iii) *An administrative law judge* has held further proceedings on a petition for review and issued a supplementary recommended decision.

(7) *The decision of the Chief Safety Officer* (including a recommended decision of an administrative law judge that becomes the decision of the Chief Safety Officer under paragraph (c)(5) of this section) constitutes final agency action, and there is no right to further administrative reconsideration or review.

(8) *Any appeal of a final agency action* under this section must be taken to an appropriate United States Court of Appeals. Unless the Court of Appeals issues a stay pending appeal, the final agency action shall not be suspended while the appeal is pending.

Appendix A to Part 385 **Explanation of Safety Audit Evaluation Criteria.**

I. General

(a) Section 210 of the Motor Carrier Safety Improvement Act (49 U.S.C. 31144) directed the Secretary to establish a procedure whereby each owner and each operator granted new authority must undergo a safety review within 18 months after the owner or operator begins operations. The Secretary was also required to establish the elements of this safety review, including basic safety management controls. The Secretary, in turn, delegated this to the FMCSA.

(b) To meet the safety standard, a motor carrier must demonstrate to the FMCSA that it has basic safety management controls in place which function adequately to ensure minimum acceptable compliance with the applicable safety requirements. A "safety audit evaluation criteria" was developed by the FMCSA, which uses data from the safety audit and roadside inspections to determine that each owner and each operator applicant for new entrant registration, provisional operating authority, or provisional Certificate of Registration has basic safety management controls in place. The term "safety audit" is the equivalent to the "safety review" required by §210. Using "safety audit" avoids any possible confusion with the safety reviews previously conducted by the agency that were discontinued on September 30, 1994.

(c) The safety audit evaluation process developed by the FMCSA is used to:

1. *Evaluate basic safety management controls* and determine if each owner and each operator is able to operate safely in interstate commerce; and

2. *Identify owners and operators* who are having safety problems and need improvement in their compliance with the FMCSRs and the HMRs, before they are granted permanent registration.

II. Source of the Data for the Safety Audit Evaluation Criteria

(a) The FMCSA's evaluation criteria are built upon the operational tool known as the safety audit. This tool was developed to assist auditors and investigators in assessing the adequacy of a new entrant's basic safety management controls.

(b) The safety audit is a review of a Mexico-domiciled or new entrant motor carrier's operation and is used to:

1. *Determine if a carrier* has the basic safety management controls required by 49 U.S.C. 31144;

2. *Meet the requirements of Section 350* of the DOT Appropriations Act; and

3. *In the event that a carrier* is found not to be in compliance with applicable FMCSRs and HMRs, the safety audit can be used to educate the carrier on how to comply with U.S. safety rules.

(c) Documents such as those contained in the driver qualification files, records of duty status, vehicle maintenance records, and other records are reviewed for compliance with the FMCSRs and HMRs. Violations are cited on the safety audit. Performance-based information, when available, is utilized to evaluate the carrier's compliance with the vehicle regulations. Recordable accident information is also collected.

III. Determining if the Carrier Has Basic Safety Management Controls

(a) During the safety audit, the FMCSA gathers information by reviewing a motor carrier's compliance with "acute" and "critical" regulations of the FMCSRs and HMRs.

(b) Acute regulations are those where noncompliance is so severe as to require immediate corrective actions by a motor carrier regardless of the overall basic safety management controls of the motor carrier.

(c) Critical regulations are those where noncompliance relates to management and/or operational controls. These are indicative of breakdowns in a carrier's management controls.

(d) The list of the acute and critical regulations, which are used in determining if a carrier has basic safety management controls in place, is included in Appendix B, VII. List of Acute and Critical Regulations.

(e) Noncompliance with acute and critical regulations are indicators of inadequate safety management controls and usually higher than average accident rates.

(f) Parts of the FMCSRs and the HMRs having similar characteristics are combined together into six regulatory areas called "factors." The regulatory factors, evaluated on the basis of the adequacy of the carrier's safety management controls, are:

1. *Factor 1 — General:* Parts 387 and 390;

2. *Factor 2 — Driver:* Parts 382, 383 and 391;

3. *Factor 3 — Operational:* Parts 392 and 395;

Part 385 - Safety Fitness Procedures — Appendix B

4. *Factor 4 — Vehicle: Part 393, 393 and inspection data for the last 12 months;*
5. *Factor 5 — Hazardous Materials: Parts 171, 177, 180 and 397; and*
6. *Factor 6 — Accident: Recordable Accident Rate per Million Miles.*

(g) For each instance of noncompliance with an acute regulation, 1.5 points will be assessed.

(h) For each instance of noncompliance with a critical regulation, 1 point will be assessed.

A. Vehicle Factor

(a) *When at least three vehicle inspections* are recorded in the Motor Carrier Management Information System (MCMIS) during the twelve months before the safety audit or performed at the time of the review, the Vehicle Factor (Part 396) will be evaluated on the basis of the Out-of-Service (OOS) rates and noncompliance with acute and critical regulations. The results of the review of the OOS rate will affect the Vehicle Factor as follows:

1. *If the motor carrier* has had at least three roadside inspections in the twelve months before the safety audit, and the vehicle OOS rate is 34 percent or higher, one point will be assessed against the carrier. That point will be added to any other points assessed for discovered noncompliance with acute and critical regulations of Part 396 to determine the carrier's level of safety management control for that factor; and

2. *If the motor carrier's vehicle OOS rate* is less than 34 percent, or if there are less than three inspections, the determination of the carrier's level of safety management controls will only be based on discovered noncompliance with the acute and critical regulations of Part 396.

(b) *Over two million inspections* occur on the roadside each year. This vehicle inspection information is retained in the MCMIS and is integral to evaluating motor carriers' ability to successfully maintain their vehicles, thus preventing them from being placed OOS during roadside inspections. Each safety audit will continue to have the requirements of Part 396, Inspection, Repair, and Maintenance, reviewed as indicated by the above explanation.

B. The Accident Factor

(a) *In addition to the five regulatory factors,* a sixth factor is included in the process to address the accident history of the motor carrier. This factor is the recordable accident rate, which the carrier has experienced during the past 12 months. Recordable accident, as defined in 49 CFR 390.5, means an accident involving a commercial motor vehicle operating on a public road in interstate or intrastate commerce which results in a fatality; a bodily injury to a person who, as a result of the injury, immediately receives medical treatment away from the scene of the accident; or one or more motor vehicles incurring disabling damage as a result of the accident requiring the motor vehicle to be transported away from the scene by a tow truck or other motor vehicle.

(b) *Experience has shown that urban carriers,* those motor carriers operating entirely within a radius of less than 100 air miles (normally urban areas), have a higher exposure to accident situations because of their environment and normally have higher accident rates.

(c) *The recordable accident rate will be used* in determining the carrier's basic safety management controls in Factor 6, Accident. It will be used only when a carrier incurs two or more recordable accidents within the 12 months before the safety audit. An urban carrier (a carrier operating entirely within a radius of 100 air miles) with a recordable rate per million miles greater than 1.7 will be deemed to have inadequate basic safety management controls for the accident factor. All other carriers with a recordable accident rate per million miles greater than 1.5 will be deemed to have inadequate basic safety management controls for the accident factor. The rates are the result of roughly doubling the national average accident rate in Fiscal Years 1994, 1995, and 1996.

(d) *The FMCSA will continue to consider preventability* when a new entrant contests the evaluation of the accident factor by presenting compelling evidence that the recordable rate is not a fair means of evaluating its accident factor. Preventability will be determined according to the following standard: "If a driver, who exercises normal judgment and foresight, could have foreseen the possibility of the accident that in fact occurred, and avoided it by taking steps within his/her control which would not have risked causing another kind of mishap, the accident was preventable."

C. Factor Ratings

For Factors 1 through 5, if the combined violations of acute and or critical regulations for each factor is equal to three or more points, the carrier is determined not to have basic safety management controls for that individual factor.

If the recordable accident rate is greater than 1.7 recordable accidents per million miles for an urban carrier (1.5 for all other carriers), the carrier is determined to have inadequate basic safety management controls.

IV. Overall Determination of the Carrier's Basic Safety Management Controls

(a) If the carrier is evaluated as having inadequate basic safety management controls in at least three separate factors, the carrier will be considered to have inadequate safety management controls in place and corrective action will be necessary in order to avoid having its new entrant registration, provisional operating authority, or provisional Certificate of Registration revoked.

(b) For example, FMCSA evaluates a carrier finding:

(1) *One instance of noncompliance* with a critical regulation in Part 387 scoring one point for Factor 1;

(2) *Two instances of noncompliance* with acute regulations in Part 382 scoring three points for Factor 2;

(3) *Three instances of noncompliance* with critical regulations in Part 396 scoring three points for Factor 4; and

(4) *Three instances of noncompliance* with acute regulations in Parts 171 and 397 scoring four and one-half (4.5) points for Factor 5.

(c) In this example, the carrier scored three or more points for Factors 2, 4 and 5 and FMCSA determined the carrier had inadequate basic safety management controls in at least three separate factors. FMCSA will require corrective action in order to avoid having the carrier's new entrant registration revoked, or having the provisional operating authority or provisional Certificate of Registration suspended and possibly revoked.

Appendix B to Part 385 Explanation of Safety Rating Process.

(a) Section 215 of the Motor Carrier Safety Act of 1984 (49 U.S.C. 31144) directed the Secretary of Transportation to establish a procedure to determine the safety fitness of owners and operators of commercial motor vehicles operating in interstate or foreign commerce. The Secretary, in turn, delegated this responsibility to the Federal Motor Carrier Safety Administration (FMCSA).

(b) As directed, FMCSA promulgated a safety fitness regulation, entitled "Safety Fitness Procedures," which established a procedure to determine the safety fitness of motor carriers through the assignment of safety ratings and established a "safety fitness standard" which a motor carrier must meet to obtain a satisfactory safety rating.

(c) Critical regulations are those identified as such where noncompliance relates to management and/or operational controls. These are indicative of breakdowns in a carrier's management controls. An example of a critical regulation is §395.3(a)(1), requiring or permitting a property-carrying commercial motor vehicle driver to drive more than 11 hours.

(d) The safety rating process developed by FMCSA is used to:

1. *Evaluate safety fitness* and assign one of three safety ratings (satisfactory, conditional or unsatisfactory) to motor carriers operating in interstate commerce. This process conforms to 49 CFR 385.5, Safety fitness standard, and §385.7, Factors to be considered in determining a safety rating.

2. *Identify motor carriers needing improvement* in their compliance with the Federal Motor Carrier Safety Regulations (FMCSRs) and applicable Hazardous Material Regulations (HMRs). These are carriers rated unsatisfactory or conditional.

(e) The hazardous materials safety permit requirements of Part 385, Subpart E apply to intrastate motor carriers. Intrastate motor carriers that are subject to the hazardous materials safety permit requirements in Subpart E will be rated using equivalent State requirements whenever the FMCSRs are referenced in this appendix.

I. Source of Data for Rating Methodology

(a) The FMCSA's rating process is built upon the operational tool known as the CR. This tool was developed to assist Federal and State safety specialists in gathering pertinent motor carrier compliance and accident information.

(b) The CR is an in-depth examination of a motor carrier's operations and is used (1) to rate unrated motor carriers, (2) to conduct a follow-up investigation on motor carriers rated unsatisfactory or conditional as a result of a previous review, (3) to investigate complaints, or (4) in response to a request by a motor carrier to reevaluate its safety rating. Documents such as those contained in driver qualification files, records of duty status, vehicle maintenance records, and other records are thoroughly examined for compliance with the FMCSRs and HMRs. Violations are cited on the CR document. Performance-based information, when available, is utilized to evaluate the carrier's compliance with the vehicle regulations. Recordable accident information is also collected.

II. Converting CR Information Into a Safety Rating

(a) The FMCSA gathers information through an in-depth examination of the motor carrier's compliance with identified "acute" or "critical" regulations of the FMCSRs and HMRs.

(b) Acute regulations are those identified as such where noncompliance is so severe as to require immediate corrective actions by a motor carrier regardless of the overall safety posture of the motor carrier. An example of an acute regulation is §383.37(b), allowing, requiring, permitting, or authorizing an employee with more than one Commercial Driver's License (CDL) to operate a commercial motor vehicle. Noncompliance with §383.37(b) is usually discovered when the motor carrier's driver qualification file reflects that the motor carrier had knowledge of a driver with more than one CDL, and still permitted the driver to operate a commercial motor vehicle. If the motor carrier did not have such knowledge or could not reasonably be expected to have such knowledge, then a violation would not be cited.

(c) Critical regulations are those identified as such where noncompliance relates to management and/or operational controls. These are indicative of breakdowns in a carrier's management controls. An example of a critical regulation is §395.3(a)(1), requiring or permitting a property-carrying commercial motor vehicle driver to drive more than 11 hours.

(d) The list of the acute and critical regulations which are used in determining safety ratings is included at the end of this document.

(e) Noncompliance with acute regulations and patterns of noncompliance with critical regulations are quantitatively linked to inadequate safety management controls and usually higher than average accident rates. The FMCSA has used noncompliance with acute regulations and patterns of noncompliance with critical regulations since 1989 to determine motor carriers' adherence to the Safety fitness standard in §385.5.

(f) The regulatory factors, evaluated on the basis of the adequacy of the carrier's safety management controls, are
  (1) *Parts 387 and 390;*
  (2) *Parts 382, 383 and 391;*
  (3) *Parts 392 and 395;*
  (4) *Parts 393 and 396* when there are less than three vehicle inspections in the last 12 months to evaluate; and
  (5) *Parts 397, 171, 177 and 180.*

(g) For each instance of noncompliance with an acute regulation or each pattern of noncompliance with a critical regulation during the CR, one point will be assessed. A pattern is more than one violation. When a number of documents are reviewed, the number of violations required to meet a pattern is equal to at least 10 percent of those examined.

(h) However, each pattern of noncompliance with a critical regulation relative to Part 395, Hours of Service of Drivers, will be assessed two points.

A. Vehicle Factor

(a) *When a total of three or more inspections* are recorded in the Motor Carrier Management Information System (MCMIS) during the twelve months prior to the CR or performed at the time of the review, the Vehicle Factor (Parts 393 and 396) will be evaluated on the basis of the Out-of-Service (OOS) rates and noncompliance with acute regulations and/ or a pattern of noncompliance with critical regulations. The results of the review of the OOS rate will affect the Vehicle Factor rating as follows:

  1. If a motor carrier has three or more roadside vehicle inspections in the twelve months prior to the carrier review, or three vehicles inspected at the time of the review, or a combination of the two totaling three or more, and the vehicle OOS rate is 34 percent or greater, the initial factor rating will be conditional. The requirements of Part 396, Inspection, Repair, and Maintenance, will be examined during each review. The results of the examination could lower the factor rating to unsatisfactory if noncompliance with an acute regulation or a pattern of noncompliance with a critical regulation is discovered. If the examination of the Part 396 requirements reveals no such problems with the systems the motor carrier is required to maintain for compliance, the Vehicle Factor remains conditional.

  2. *If a carrier's vehicle OOS rate* is less than 34 percent, the initial factor rating will be satisfactory. If noncompliance with an acute regulation or a pattern of noncompliance with a critical regulation is discovered during the examination of Part 396 requirements, the factor rating will be lowered to conditional. If the examination of Part 396 requirements discovers no such problems with the systems the motor carrier is required to maintain for compliance, the Vehicle Factor remains satisfactory.

(b) *Nearly two million vehicle inspections* occur on the roadside each year. This vehicle inspection information is retained in the MCMIS and is integral to evaluating motor carriers' ability to successfully maintain their vehicles, thus preventing them from being placed OOS during roadside inspections. Since many of the roadside inspections are targeted to visibly defective vehicles and since there are a limited number of inspections for many motor carriers, the use of that data is limited. Each CR will continue to have the requirements of Part 396, Inspection, Repair, and Maintenance, reviewed as indicated by the above explanation.

B. Accident Factor

(a) *In addition to the five regulatory rating factors*, a sixth factor is included in the process to address the accident history of the motor carrier. This factor is the recordable accident rate which the carrier has experienced during the past 12 months. Recordable accident, as defined in 49 CFR 390.5, means an accident involving a commercial motor vehicle operating on a public road in interstate or intrastate commerce which results in a fatality; bodily injury to a person who, as a result of the injury, immediately receives medical treatment away from the scene of the accident; one or more motor vehicles incurring disabling damage as a result of the accident requiring the motor vehicle to be transported away from the scene by a tow truck or other motor vehicle.

(b) *Recordable accidents per million miles* were computed for each CR performed in Fiscal Years 1994, 1995 and 1996. The national average for all carriers rated was 0.747, and .839 for carriers operating entirely within the 100 air mile radius.

(c) *Experience has shown that urban carriers*, those motor carriers operating primarily within a radius of less than 100 air miles (normally in urban areas) have a higher exposure to accident situations because of their environment and normally have higher accident rates.

(d) *The recordable accident rate* will be used to rate Factor 6, Accident. It will be used only when a motor carrier incurs two or more recordable accidents occurred within the 12 months prior to the CR. An urban carrier (a carrier operating entirely within a radius of 100 air miles) with a recordable accident rate greater than 1.7 will receive an unsatisfactory rating for the accident factor. All other carriers with a recordable accident rate greater than 1.5 will receive an unsatisfactory factor rating. The rates are a result of roughly doubling the national average accident rate for each type of carrier rated in Fiscal Years 1994, 1995 and 1996.

(e) *The FMCSA will continue to consider preventability* when a motor carrier contests a rating by presenting compelling evidence that the recordable rate is not a fair means of evaluating its accident factor. Preventability will be determined according to the following standard: "If a driver, who exercises normal judgment and foresight could have foreseen the possibility of the accident that in fact occurred, and avoided it by taking steps within his/her control which would not have risked causing another kind of mishap, the accident was preventable."

C. Factor Ratings

(a) *Parts of the FMCSRs and the HMRs* having similar characteristics are combined together into five regulatory areas called "factors."

(b) *The following table* shows the five regulatory factors, parts of the FMCSRs and HMRs associated with each factor, and the accident factor. Factor Ratings are determined as follows:
Factors

Factor 1 General = Parts 387 and 390

Factor 2 Driver = Parts 382, 383 and 391

Factor 3 Operational = Parts 392 and 395

Part 385 - Safety Fitness Procedures

Appendix B

Factor 4 Vehicle = Parts 393 and 396
Factor 5 Haz. Mat. = Parts 397, 171, 177 and 180
Factor 6 Accident Factor = Recordable Rate
"Satisfactory" — if the acute and/or critical = 0 points
"Conditional" — if the acute and/or critical = 1 point
"Unsatisfactory" — if the acute and/or critical = 2 or more points

III. Safety Rating

A. Rating Table
(a) *The ratings for the six factors* are then entered into a rating table which establishes the motor carrier's safety rating.
(b) *The FMCSA has developed* a computerized rating formula for assessing the information obtained from the CR document and is using that formula in assigning a safety rating.

Motor Carrier Safety Rating Table

Factor ratings		Overall Safety rating
Unsatisfactory	Conditional	
0	2 or fewer	Satisfactory
0	more than 2	Conditional
1	2 or fewer	Conditional
1	more than 2	Unsatisfactory
2 or more	0 or more	Unsatisfactory

B. Proposed Safety Rating
(a) *The proposed safety rating will appear on the CR.* The following appropriate information will appear after the last entry on the CR, MCS-151, Part B.
"Your proposed safety rating is SATISFACTORY."
OR
"Your proposed safety rating is CONDITIONAL." The proposed safety rating will become the final safety rating 45 days after you receive this notice.
OR
"Your proposed safety rating is UNSATISFACTORY." The proposed safety rating will become the final safety rating 45 days after you receive this notice.
(b) *Proposed safety ratings* of conditional or unsatisfactory will list the deficiencies discovered during the CR for which corrective actions must be taken.
(c) *Proposed unsatisfactory safety ratings* will indicate that, if the unsatisfactory rating becomes final, the motor carrier will be subject to the provision of §385.13, which prohibits motor carriers rated unsatisfactory from transporting hazardous materials requiring placarding or more than 15 passengers, including the driver.

IV. Assignment of Final Rating/Motor Carrier Notification
When the official rating is determined in Washington, D.C., the FMCSA notifies the motor carrier in writing of its safety rating as prescribed in §385.11. A proposed conditional safety rating (which is an improvement of an existing unsatisfactory rating) becomes effective as soon as the official safety rating from Washington, D.C. is issued, and the carrier may also avail itself of relief under the §385.15, Administrative Review and §385.17, Change to safety rating based on corrective actions.

V. Motor Carrier Rights to a Change in the Safety Rating
Under §§385.15 and 385.17, motor carriers have the right to petition for a review of their ratings if there are factual or procedural disputes, and to request another review after corrective actions have been taken. They are the procedural avenues a motor carrier which believes its safety rating to be in error may exercise, and the means to request another review after corrective action has been taken.

VI. Conclusion
(a) **The FMCSA believes** this "safety fitness rating methodology" is a reasonable approach for assigning a safety rating which best describes the current safety fitness posture of a motor carrier as required by the safety fitness regulations (§385.9). This methodology has the capability to incorporate regulatory changes as they occur.
(b) **Improved compliance with the regulations** leads to an improved rating, which in turn increases safety. This increased safety is our regulatory goal.

VII. List of Acute and Critical Regulations

§382.115(a) Failing to implement an alcohol and/or controlled substances testing program (domestic motor carrier) (acute).

§382.201 Using a driver known to have an alcohol concentration of 0.04 or greater (acute).

§382.211 Using a driver who has refused to submit to an alcohol or controlled substances test required under Part 382 (acute).

§382.213(b) Using a driver known to have used a controlled substance (acute).

§382.215 Using a driver known to have tested positive for a controlled substance (acute).

§382.301(a) Using a driver before the motor carrier has received a negative pre-employment controlled substance test result (critical).

§382.303(a) Failing to conduct post accident testing on driver for alcohol and/or controlled substances (critical).

§382.305 Failing to implement a random controlled substances and/or an alcohol testing program (acute).

§382.305(b)(1) Failing to conduct random alcohol testing at an annual rate of not less than the applicable annual rate of the average number of driver positions (critical).

§382.305(b)(2) Failing to conduct random controlled substances testing at an annual rate of not less than the applicable annual rate of the average number of driver positions (critical).

§382.309(a) Using a driver who has not undergone a return-to-duty alcohol test with a result indicating an alcohol concentration of less than 0.02 (acute).

§382.309(b) Using a driver who has not undergone a return-to-duty controlled substances test with a result indicating a verified negative result for controlled substances (acute).

§382.503 Allowing a driver to perform safety sensitive function, after engaging in conduct prohibited by Subpart B, without being evaluated by substance abuse professional, as required by §382.605 (critical).

§382.505(a) Using a driver within 24 hours after being found to have an alcohol concentration of 0.02 or greater but less than 0.04 (acute).

§382.605(c)(1) Using a driver who has not undergone a return-to-duty alcohol test with a result indicating an alcohol concentration of less than .02 or with verified negative test result, after engaging in conduct prohibited by Part 382 Subpart B (acute).

§382.605(c)(2)(ii) Failing to subject a driver who has been identified as needing assistance to at least six unannounced follow-up alcohol and/or controlled substance tests in the first 12 months following the driver's return to duty (critical).

§383.23(a) Operating a commercial motor vehicle without a valid commercial driver's license (critical).

§383.37(a) Knowingly allowing, requiring, permitting, or authorizing an employee with a commercial driver's license which is suspended, revoked, or canceled by a state or who is disqualified to operate a commercial motor vehicle (acute).

§383.37(b) Knowingly allowing, requiring, permitting, or authorizing an employee with more than one commercial driver's license to operate a commercial motor vehicle (acute).

§383.51(a) Knowingly allowing, requiring, permitting, or authorizing a driver to drive who is disqualified to drive a commercial motor vehicle (acute).

§387.7(a) Operating a motor vehicle without having in effect the required minimum levels of financial responsibility coverage (acute).

§387.7(d) Failing to maintain at principal place of business required proof of financial responsibility (critical).

§387.31(a) Operating a passenger carrying vehicle without having in effect the required minimum levels of financial responsibility (acute).

Appendix B — Part 385 - Safety Fitness Procedures

§387.31(d)	Failing to maintain at principal place of business required proof of financial responsibility for passenger carrying vehicles (critical).
§390.15(b)(2)	Failing to maintain copies of all accident reports required by State or other governmental entities or insurers (critical).
§390.35	Making, or causing to make fraudulent or intentionally false statements or records and/or reproducing fraudulent records (acute).
§391.11(b)(4)	Using a physically unqualified driver (acute).
§391.15(a)	Using a disqualified driver (acute).
§391.45(a)	Using a driver not medically examined and certified (critical).
§391.45(b)(1)	Using a driver not medically examined and certified during the preceding 24 months (critical).
§391.51(a)	Failing to maintain driver qualification file on each driver employed (critical).
§391.51(b)(2)	Failing to maintain inquiries into driver's driving record in driver's qualification file (critical).
§391.51(b)(7)	Failing to maintain medical examiner's certificate in driver's qualification file (critical).
§392.2	Operating a motor vehicle not in accordance with the laws, ordinances, and regulations of the jurisdiction in which it is being operated (critical).
§392.4(b)	Requiring or permitting a driver to drive while under the influence of, or in possession of, a narcotic drug, amphetamine, or any other substance capable of rendering the driver incapable of safely operating a motor vehicle (acute).
§392.5(b)(1)	Requiring or permitting a driver to drive a motor vehicle while under the influence of, or in possession of, an intoxicating beverage (acute).
§392.5(b)(2)	Requiring or permitting a driver who shows evidence of having consumed an intoxicating beverage within 4 hours to operate a motor vehicle (acute).
§392.6	Scheduling a run which would necessitate the vehicle being operated at speeds in excess of those prescribed (critical).
§392.9(a)(1)	Requiring or permitting a driver to drive without the vehicle's cargo being properly distributed and adequately secured (critical).
§395.1(h)(1)(i)	Requiring or permitting a property-carrying commercial motor vehicle driver to drive more than 15 hours (Driving in Alaska) (critical).
§395.1(h)(1)(ii)	Requiring or permitting a property-carrying commercial motor vehicle driver to drive after having been on duty 20 hours (Driving in Alaska) (critical).
§395.1(h)(1)(iii)	Requiring or permitting a property-carrying commercial motor vehicle driver to drive after having been on duty more than 70 hours in 7 consecutive days (Driving in Alaska) (critical).
§395.1(h)(1)(iv)	Requiring or permitting a property-carrying commercial motor vehicle driver to drive after having been on duty more than 80 hours in 8 consecutive days (Driving in Alaska) (critical).
§395.1(h)(2)(i)	Requiring or permitting a passenger-carrying commercial motor vehicle driver to drive more than 15 hours (Driving in Alaska) (critical).
§395.1(h)(2)(ii)	Requiring or permitting a passenger-carrying commercial motor vehicle driver to drive after having been on duty 20 hours (Driving in Alaska) (critical).
§395.1(h)(2)(iii)	Requiring or permitting a passenger-carrying commercial motor vehicle driver to drive after having been on duty more than 70 hours in 7 consecutive days (Driving in Alaska) (critical).
§395.1(h)(2)(iv)	Requiring or permitting a passenger-carrying commercial motor vehicle driver to drive after having been on duty more than 80 hours in 8 consecutive days (Driving in Alaska) (critical).
§395.1(o)	Requiring or permitting a property-carrying commercial motor vehicle driver to drive after having been on duty 16 consecutive hours (critical).
§395.3(a)(1)	Requiring or permitting a property-carrying commercial motor vehicle driver to drive more than 11 hours (critical).
§395.3(a)(2)	Requiring or permitting a property-carrying commercial motor vehicle driver to drive after the end of the 14th hour after coming on duty (critical).
§395.3(b)(1)	Requiring or permitting a property-carrying commercial motor vehicle driver to drive after having been on duty more than 60 hours in 7 consecutive days (critical).
§395.3(b)(2)	Requiring or permitting a property-carrying commercial motor vehicle driver to drive after having been on duty more than 70 hours in 8 consecutive days (critical).
§395.3(c)(1)	Requiring or permitting a property-carrying commercial motor vehicle driver to restart a period of 7 consecutive days without taking an off-duty period of 34 or more consecutive hours (critical).
§395.3(c)(2)	Requiring or permitting a property-carrying commercial motor vehicle driver to restart a period of 8 consecutive days without taking an off-duty period of 34 or more consecutive hours (critical).
§395.5(a)(1)	Requiring or permitting a passenger-carrying commercial motor vehicle driver to drive more than 10 hours (critical).
§395.5(a)(2)	Requiring or permitting a passenger-carrying commercial motor vehicle driver to drive after having been on duty 15 hours (critical).
§395.5(b)(1)	Requiring or permitting a passenger-carrying commercial motor vehicle driver to drive after having been on duty more than 60 hours in 7 consecutive days (critical).
§395.5(b)(2)	Requiring or permitting a passenger-carrying commercial motor vehicle driver to drive after having been on duty more than 70 hours in 8 consecutive days (critical).
§395.8(a)	Failing to require driver to make a record of duty status (critical).
§395.8(e)	False reports of records of duty status (critical).
§395.8(i)	Failing to require driver to forward within 13 days of completion, the original of the record of duty status (critical).
§395.8(k)(1)	Failing to preserve driver's record of duty status for 6 months (critical).
§395.8(k)(1)	Failing to preserve driver's records of duty status supporting documents for 6 months (critical).
§396.3(b)	Failing to keep minimum records of inspection and vehicle maintenance (critical).
§396.9(c)(2)	Requiring or permitting the operation of a motor vehicle declared "out-of-service" before repairs were made (acute).
§396.11(a)	Failing to require driver to prepare driver vehicle inspection report (critical).
§396.11(c)	Failing to correct Out-of-Service defects listed by driver in a driver vehicle inspection report before the vehicle is operated again (acute).
§396.17(a)	Using a commercial motor vehicle not periodically inspected (critical).
§396.17(g)	Failing to promptly repair parts and accessories not meeting minimum periodic inspection standards (acute).
§397.5(a)	Failing to ensure a motor vehicle containing Division 1.1, 1.2, or 1.3 (explosive) material is attended at all times by its driver or a qualified representative (acute).
§397.7(a)(1)	Parking a motor vehicle containing Division 1.1, 1.2, or 1.3 materials within 5 feet of traveled portion of highway or street (critical).
§397.7(b)	Parking a motor vehicle containing hazardous material(s) other than Division 1.1, 1.2, or 1.3 materials within 5 feet of traveled portion of highway or street (critical).
§397.13(a)	Permitting a person to smoke or carry a lighted cigarette, cigar or pipe within 25 feet of a motor vehicle containing Class 1 materials, Class 5 materials, or flammable materials classified as Division 2.1, Class 3, Divisions 4.1 and 4.2 (critical).

Part 385 - Safety Fitness Procedures — Appendix B

§397.19(a)	Failing to furnish driver of motor vehicle transporting Division 1.1, 1.2, or 1.3 (explosive) materials with a copy of the rules of Part 397 and/or emergency response instructions (critical).
§397.67(d)	Requiring or permitting the operation of a motor vehicle containing explosives in Class 1, Divisions 1.1, 1.2, or 1.3 that is not accompanied by a written route plan (critical).
§397.101(d)	Requiring or permitting the operation of a motor vehicle containing highway route-controlled quantity, as defined in §173.403, of radioactive materials that is not accompanied by a written route plan.
§171.15	Carrier failing to give immediate telephone notice of an incident involving hazardous materials (critical).
§171.16	Carrier failing to make a written report of an incident involving hazardous materials (critical).
§172.313(a)	Accepting for transportation or transporting a package containing a poisonous-by-inhalation material that is not marked with the words "Inhalation Hazard" (acute).
§172.704(a)(4)	Failing to provide security awareness training (critical).
§172.704(a)(5)	Failing to provide in-depth security awareness training (critical).
§172.800(b)	Transporting HM without a security plan (acute).
§172.800(b)	Transporting HM without a security plan that conforms to Subpart I requirements (acute).
§172.800(b)	Failure to adhere to a required security plan (acute).
§172.802(b)	Failure to make copies of security plan available to hazmat employees (critical).
§173.24(b)(1)	Accepting for transportation or transporting a package that has an identifiable release of a hazardous material to the environment (acute).
§173.421(a)	Accepting for transportation or transporting a Class 7 (radioactive) material described, marked, and packaged as a limited quantity when the radiation level on the surface of the package exceeds 0.005 mSv/hour (0.5 mrem/hour) (acute).
§173.431(a)	Accepting for transportation or transporting in a Type A packaging a greater quantity of Class 7 (radioactive) material than authorized (acute).
§173.431(b)	Accepting for transportation or transporting in a Type B packaging a greater quantity of Class 7 (radioactive) material than authorized (acute).
§173.441(a)	Accepting for transportation or transporting a package containing Class 7 (radioactive) material with external radiation exceeding allowable limits (acute).
§173.442(b)	Accepting for transportation or transporting a package containing Class 7 (radioactive) material when the temperature of the accessible external surface of the loaded package exceeds 50 °C (122 °F) in other than an exclusive use shipment, or 85 °C (185 °F) in an exclusive use shipment (acute).
§173.443(a)	Accepting for transportation or transporting a package containing Class 7 (radioactive) material with removable contamination on the external surfaces of the package in excess of permissible limits (acute).
§177.800(c)	Failing to instruct a category of employees in hazardous materials regulations (critical).
§177.801	Accepting for transportation or transporting a forbidden material (acute).
§177.817(a)	Transporting a shipment of hazardous materials not accompanied by a properly prepared shipping paper (critical).
§177.817(e)	Failing to maintain proper accessibility of shipping papers (critical).
§177.823(a)	Moving a transport vehicle containing hazardous material that is not properly marked or placarded (critical).
§177.835(a)	Loading or unloading a Class 1 (explosive) material with the engine running (acute).
§177.835(c)	Accepting for transportation or transporting Division 1.1, 1.2, or 1.3 (explosive) materials in a motor vehicle or combination of vehicles that is not permitted (acute).
§177.835(j)	Transferring Division 1.1, 1.2, or 1.3 (explosive) materials between containers or motor vehicles when not permitted (acute).
§177.841(e)	Transporting a package bearing a poison label in the same transport vehicle with material marked or known to be foodstuff, feed, or any edible material intended for consumption by humans or animals unless an exception in §177.841(e)(i) or (ii) is met (acute).
§180.407(a)	Transporting a shipment of hazardous material in cargo tank that has not been inspected or retested in accordance with §180.407 (critical).
§180.407(c)	Failing to periodically test and inspect a cargo tank (critical).
§180.415	Failing to mark a cargo tank which passed an inspection or test required by §180.407 (critical).
§180.417(a)(1)	Failing to retain cargo tank manufacturer's data report certificate and related papers, as required (critical).
§180.417(a)(2)	Failing to retain copies of cargo tank manufacturer's certificate and related papers (or alternative report) as required (critical).

Notes

Part 386 - Rules of Practice for Motor Carrier, Broker, Freight Forwarder, and Hazardous Materials Proceedings

Subpart A - Scope of Rules; Definitions and General Provisions

§386.1 Scope of rules in this part.

The rules in this part govern proceedings before the Assistant Administrator, who also acts as the Chief Safety Officer of the Federal Motor Carrier Safety Administration (FMCSA), under applicable provisions of the Federal Motor Carrier Safety Regulations (49 CFR Parts 350-399), including the commercial regulations (49 CFR Parts 360-379) and the Hazardous Materials Regulations (49 CFR Parts 171-180). The purpose of the proceedings is to enable the Assistant Administrator to determine whether a motor carrier, property broker, freight forwarder, or its agents, employees, or any other person subject to the jurisdiction of the FMCSA, has failed to comply with the provisions or requirements of applicable statutes and the corresponding regulations and, if such violations are found, to issue an appropriate order to compel compliance with the statute or regulation, assess a civil penalty, or both.

---

§386.1 DOT Interpretations

Question 1: What is the authority of the RDMC to issue provisions as a part of the terms in a Notice of Abatement, Notice of Assessment, Compliance Order and Consent Order?

Guidance: The MCSA of 1984 provided the authority to penalize violators of Notices and Orders issued by the FHWA. Regulations were issued under Part 386 which specify these penalties. Notices to Abate and Notices of Assessment/Claim generally deal with specific regulatory requirements. Consent Orders and Compliance Orders often require remedial measures not specifically mentioned in the FMCSRs since the motor carrier's compliance record often indicates that additional measures are needed to improve safety and compliance with the regulations.

---

§386.2 Definitions.

Abate or **abatement** means to discontinue regulatory violations by refraining from or taking actions identified in a notice to correct noncompliance.

Administration means the Federal Motor Carrier Safety Administration.

Administrative adjudication means a process or proceeding to resolve contested claims in conformity with the Administrative Procedure Act, 5 U.S.C. 554-558.

Administrative law judge means an administrative law judge appointed pursuant to the provisions of 5 U.S.C. 3105.

Agency means the Federal Motor Carrier Safety Administration.

Agency Counsel means the attorney who prosecutes a civil penalty matter on behalf of the Field Administrator.

Assistant Administrator means the Assistant Administrator of the Federal Motor Carrier Safety Administration. The Assistant Administrator is the Chief Safety Officer of the agency pursuant to 49 U.S.C. 113(d). Decisions of the Assistant Administrator in motor carrier, broker, freight forwarder, and hazardous materials proceedings under this part are administratively final.

Broker means a person who, for compensation, arranges or offers to arrange the transportation of property by an authorized motor carrier. A motor carrier, or person who is an employee or bona fide agent of a carrier, is not a broker within the meaning of this section when it arranges or offers to arrange the transportation of shipments which it is authorized to transport and which it has accepted and legally bound itself to transport.

Civil forfeiture proceedings means proceedings to collect civil penalties for violations under the Commercial Motor Vehicle Safety Act of 1986 (49 U.S.C. Chapter 313); the Hazardous Materials Transportation Act of 1975, as amended (49 U.S.C. Chapter 51); the Motor Carrier Safety Act of 1984 (49 U.S.C. Chapter 311, Subchapter III); section 18 of the Bus Regulatory Reform Act of 1982 (49 U.S.C. 31138); section 30 of the Motor Carrier Act of 1980 (49 U.S.C. 31139); and the ICC Termination Act of 1995 (49 U.S.C. Chapters 131-149).

Civil penalty proceedings means proceedings to collect civil penalties for violations of regulations and statutes within the jurisdiction of FMCSA.

Claimant means the representative of the Federal Motor Carrier Safety Administration authorized to make claims.

Commercial regulations means statutes and regulations that apply to persons providing or arranging transportation for compensation subject to the Secretary's jurisdiction under 49 U.S.C. Chapter 135. The statutes are codified in Part B of Subtitle IV, Title 49, U.S.C. (49 U.S.C. 13101 through 14913). The regulations include those issued by the Federal Motor Carrier Safety Administration or its predecessors under authority provided in 49 U.S.C. 13301 or a predecessor statute.

Decisionmaker means the Assistant Administrator of FMCSA, acting in the capacity of the decisionmaker or any person to whom the Assistant Administrator has delegated his/her authority in a civil penalty proceeding. As used in this subpart, the Agency decisionmaker is the official authorized to issue a final decision and order of the Agency in a civil penalty proceeding.

Default means an omission or failure to perform a legal duty within the time specified for action, failure to reply to a Notice of Claim within the time required, or failure to submit a reply in accordance with the requirements of this part. A default may result in issuance of a Final Agency Order or additional penalties against the defaulting party.

Department means the U.S. Department of Transportation.

Dockets means the U.S. Department of Transportation's docket management system, which is the central repository for original copies of all documents filed before the agency decisionmaker.

Driver qualification proceeding means a proceeding commenced under 49 CFR 391.47 or by issuance of a letter of disqualification.

Federal Motor Carrier Commercial Regulations (FMCCRs) means statutes and regulations applying to persons providing or arranging transportation for compensation subject to the Secretary's jurisdiction under 49 U.S.C. Chapter 135. The statutes are codified in Part B of Subtitle IV, Title 49 U.S.C. (49 U.S.C. 13101 through 14913). The regulations include those issued by FMCSA or its predecessors under authority provided in 49 U.S.C. 13301 or a predecessor stature.

Field Administrator means the head of an FMCSA Service Center who has been delegated authority to initiate compliance and enforcement actions on behalf of FMCSA.

Final Agency Order means the final action by FMCSA issued pursuant to this part by the appropriate Field Administrator (for default judgments under §386.14) or the Assistant Administrator, or settlement agreements which become the Final Agency Order pursuant to 386.22, or decisions of the Administrative Law Judge, which become the Final Agency Order pursuant to 386.61 or binding arbitration awards. A person who fails to perform the actions directed in the Final Agency Order commits a violation of that order and is subject to an additional penalty as prescribed in Subpart G of this part.

FMCSRs means the Federal Motor Carrier Safety Regulations.

Formal hearing means an evidentiary hearing on the record in which parties have the opportunity to conduct discovery, present relevant evidence, and cross-examine witnesses.

Freight forwarder means a person holding itself out to the general public (other than as an express, pipeline, rail, sleeping car, motor, or water carrier) to provide transportation of property for compensation in interstate commerce, and in the ordinary course of its business:

(1) *Performs or provides* for assembling, consolidating, break-bulk, and distribution of shipments;

(2) *Assumes responsibility* for transportation from place of receipt to destination; and

(3) *Uses for any part of the transportation* a carrier subject to FMCSA jurisdiction.

Hearing Officer means a neutral Agency employee designated by the Assistant Administrator to preside over an informal hearing.

HMRs means Hazardous Materials Regulations.

Informal hearing means a hearing in which the parties have the opportunity to present relevant evidence to a neutral Hearing Officer, who will prepare findings of fact and recommendations for the Agency decisionmaker. The informal hearing will not be on the transcribed record and discovery will not be allowed. Parties will have the opportunity to discuss their case and present testimony and evidence before the Hearing Officer without the formality of a formal hearing.

Mail means U.S. first class mail, U.S. registered or certified mail, or use of a commercial delivery service.

Motor carrier means a motor carrier, motor private carrier, or motor carrier of migrant workers as defined in 49 U.S.C. 13102 and 31501.

Notice of Claim (NOC) means the initial document issued by FMCSA to assert a civil penalty for alleged violations of the FMCSRs, HMRs, or FMCCRs.

Notice of Violation (NOV) means a document alleging a violation of the FMCSRs, HMRs, or FMCCRs, for which corrective action, other than payment of a civil penalty, is recommended.

Person means any individual, partnership, association, corporation, business trust, or any other organized group of individuals.

Petitioner means a party petitioning to overturn a determination in a driver qualification proceeding.

Reply means a written response to a Notice of Claim, admitting or denying the allegations contained within the Notice of Claim. In addition, the reply provides the mechanism for determining whether the respondent seeks to pay, settle, contest, or seek binding arbitration of the claim. See §386.14. If contesting the allegations, the reply must also set forth all known affirmative defenses and factors in mitigation of the claim.

Respondent means a party against whom relief is sought or claim is made.

Secretary means the Secretary of Transportation.

Submission of written evidence without hearing means the submission of written evidence and legal argument to the Agency decisionmaker, or his/her representative, in lieu of a formal or informal hearing.

§386.3 Separation of functions.

(a) **Civil penalty proceedings will be prosecuted** by Agency Counsel who represent the Field Administrator. In Notices of Violation, the Field Administrator will be represented by Agency Counsel.

(b) **An Agency employee,** including those listed in paragraph (c) of this section, engaged in the performance of investigative or prosecutorial functions in a civil penalty proceeding may not, in that case or a factually related case, discuss or communicate the facts or issues involved with the Agency decisionmaker, Administrative Law Judge, Hearing Officer or others listed in paragraph (d) of this section, except as counsel or a witness in the public proceedings. This prohibition also includes the staff of those covered by this section.

(c) **The Deputy Chief Counsel,** Assistant Chief Counsel for Enforcement and Litigation, and attorneys in the Enforcement and Litigation Division serve as enforcement counsel in the prosecution of all cases brought under this part.

(d) **The Chief Counsel,** the Special Counsel to the Chief Counsel, and attorneys serving as Adjudications Counsel advise the Agency decisionmaker regarding all cases brought under this part.

(e) **Nothing in this part shall preclude** agency decisionmakers or anyone advising an agency decisionmaker from taking part in a determination to launch an investigation or issue a complaint, or similar preliminary decision.

§386.4 Appearances and rights of parties.

(a) **A party may appear in person,** by counsel, or by other representative, as the party elects, in a proceeding under this subpart.

(b) **A person representing a party must file** a notice of appearance in the proceeding, in the manner provided in §386.7 of this subpart. The notice of appearance must list the name, address, telephone number, and facsimile number of the person designated to represent the party. A copy of the notice of appearance must be served on each party, in the manner provided in §386.6 of this subpart. The notice of appearance must be filed and served before the representative can participate in the proceeding. Any changes in an attorney or representative's contact information must be served and filed according to §§386.6 and 386.7 in a timely manner.

(c) **A separate notice of appearance must be filed** by a representative in each case. Blanket appearances on behalf of a party will not be accepted.

§386.5 Form of filings and extensions of time.

(a) **Form.** Each document must be typewritten or legibly handwritten.

(b) **Contents.** Unless otherwise specified in this part, each document must contain a short, plain statement of the facts on which the person's case rests and a brief statement of the action requested in the document. Except by prior order, all contents will be made publicly available.

(c) **Length.** Except for the Notice of Claim and reply, motions, briefs, and other filings may not exceed 20 pages except as permitted by Order following a motion to exceed the page limitation based upon good cause shown. Exhibits or attachments in support of the relevant filing are not included in the page limit.

(d) **Paper and margins.** Filed documents must be printed on 8 1/2" by 11" paper with a one-inch margin on all four sides of text, to include pagination and footnotes.

(e) **Spacing, and font size for typewritten documents.** Typewritten documents will use the following line format: single-spacing for the caption and footnotes, and double-spacing for the main text. All printed matter must appear in at least 12-point font, including footnotes.

(f) **Extensions of time.** Only those requests showing good cause will be granted. No motion for continuance or postponement of a hearing date filed within 15 days of the date set for a hearing will be granted unless accompanied by an affidavit showing extraordinary circumstances warrant a continuance. Unless directed otherwise by the Agency decisionmaker before whom a matter is pending, the parties may stipulate to reasonable extensions of time by filing the stipulation in the official docket and serving copies on all parties on the certificate of service. Motions for extensions of time must be filed in accordance with §386.6 and served in accordance with §386.7. A copy must also be served upon the person presiding over the proceeding at the time of the filing.

§386.6 Service.

(a) **General.** All documents must be served upon the party or the party's designated agent for service of process. If a notice of appearance has been filed in the specific case in question in accordance with §386.4, service is to be made on the party's attorney of record or its designated representative.

(b) **Type of service.** A person may serve documents by personal delivery utilizing governmental or commercial entities, U.S. mail, commercial mail delivery, and upon prior written consent of the parties, facsimile. Written consent for facsimile service must specify the facsimile number where service will be accepted. When service is made by facsimile, a copy will also be served by any other method permitted by this section. Facsimile service occurs when transmission is complete.

(c) **Certificate of service.** A certificate of service will accompany all documents served in a proceeding under this part. The certificate must show the date and manner of service, be signed by the person making service, and list the persons served in accordance with §386.7.

(d) **Date of service.** A document will be considered served on the date of personal delivery; or if mailed, the mailing date shown on the certificate of service, the date shown on the postmark if there is no certificate of service, or other mailing date shown by other evidence if there is no certificate of service or postmark.

(e) **Valid service.** A properly addressed document, sent in accordance with this subpart, which was returned, unclaimed, or refused, is deemed to have been served in accordance with this subpart. The service will be considered valid as of the date and the time the document was mailed, or the date personal delivery of the document was refused. Service by delivery after 5 p.m. in the time zone in which the recipient will receive delivery is deemed to have been made on the next day that is not a Saturday, Sunday, or legal holiday.

(f) **Presumption of service.** There shall be a presumption of service if the document is served where a party or a person customarily receives mail or at the address designated in the entry of appearance. If an entry of appearance has been filed on behalf of the party, service is effective upon service of a document to its representative.

§386.7 Filing of documents.

(a) **Address and method of filing.** A person serving or tendering a document for filing must personally deliver or mail one copy of each document to all parties and counsel or their designated representative of record if represented. A signed original and one copy of each document submitted for the consideration of the Assistant Administrator, an Administrative Law Judge, or Hearing Officer must be personally delivered or mailed to: U.S. DOT Dockets 400 7th Street, SW., Room PL-401, Washington, DC 20590. A person will serve a copy of each document on each party in accordance with §386.6 of this subpart.

§386.8 Computation of time.

(a) **Generally.** In computing any time period set out in these rules or in an order issued hereunder, the time computation begins with the day following the act, event, or default. The last day of the period is included unless it is a Saturday, Sunday, or legal Federal holiday in which case the time period will run to the end of the next day that is not a Saturday, Sunday, or legal Federal holiday. All Saturdays, Sundays, and legal Federal holidays except those falling on the last day of the period will be computed.

(b) Date of entry of orders. In computing any period of time involving the date of the entry of an order, the date of entry is the date the order is served.

(c) Computation of time for delivery by mail.
  (1) *Service of all documents is deemed effected at the time of mailing.*
  (2) *Documents are not deemed filed until received by Dockets.*
  (3) *Whenever a party* has a right or a duty to act or to make any response within a prescribed period after service by mail, or on a date certain after service by mail, 5 days will be added to the prescribed period.

Subpart B - Commencement of Proceedings, Pleadings

§386.11 Commencement of proceedings.

(a) Driver qualification proceedings. These proceedings are commenced by the issuance of a determination by the Director, Office of Truck and Bus Standards and Operations, in a case arising under §391.47 of this chapter or by the issuance of a letter of disqualification.
  (1) *Such determination and letters* must be accompanied by the following:
   (i) *A citation of the regulation under which the action is being taken;*
   (ii) *A copy of all documentary evidence* relied on or considered in taking such action, or in the case of voluminous evidence a summary of such evidence;
   (iii) *Notice to the driver and motor carrier* involved in the case that they may petition for review of the action;
   (iv) *Notice that a hearing will be granted* if the Assistant Administrator determines there are material factual issues in dispute;
   (v) *Notice that failure to petition for review* will constitute a waiver of the right to contest the action; and
   (vi) *Notice that the burden or proof* will be on the petitioner in cases arising under §391.47 of this chapter.
  (2) *At any time before the close of hearing,* upon application of a party, the letter or determination may be amended at the discretion of the administrative law judge upon such terms as he/she approves.

(b) Notice of Violation. The Agency may issue a Notice of Violation as a means of notifying any person subject to the rules in this part that it has received information (i.e., from an investigation, audit, or any other source) wherein it has been alleged the person has violated provisions of the FMCSRs, HMRs, or FMCCRs. The notice of violation serves as an informal mechanism to address compliance deficiencies. If the alleged deficiency is not addressed to the satisfaction of the Agency, formal enforcement action may be taken in accordance with paragraph (c) of this section. A notice of violation is not a prerequisite to the issuance of a Notice of Claim. The notice of violation will address the following issues, as appropriate:
  (1) *The specific alleged violations.*
  (2) *Any specific actions* the Agency determines are appropriate to remedy the identified problems.
  (3) *The means by which the notified person* can inform the Agency that it has received the notice of violation and either has addressed the alleged violation or does not agree with the Agency's assertions in the notice of violation.
  (4) *Any other relevant information.*

(c) Civil penalty proceedings. These proceedings are commenced by the issuance of a Notice of Claim.
  (1) *Each Notice of Claim must contain the following:*
   (i) *A statement setting forth the facts alleged.*
   (ii) *A statement of the provisions of law* allegedly violated by the respondent.
   (iii) *The proposed civil penalty* and notice of the maximum amount authorized to be claimed under statute.
   (iv) *The time, form, and manner* whereby the respondent may pay, contest, or otherwise seek resolution of the claim.
  (2) *In addition to the information* required by paragraph (c)(1) of this section, the Notice of Claim may contain such other matters as the Agency deems appropriate.
  (3) *In proceedings* for collection of civil penalties for violations of the motor carrier safety regulations under the Motor Carrier Safety Act of 1984, the Agency may require the respondent to post a copy of the Notice of Claim in such place or places and for such duration as the Agency may determine appropriate to aid in the enforcement of the law and regulations.

§386.12 Complaint.

(a) Complaint of substantial violation. Any person may file a written complaint with the Assistant Administrator alleging that a substantial violation of any regulation issued under the Motor Carrier Safety Act of 1984 is occurring or has occurred within the preceding 60 days. A substantial violation is one which could reasonably lead to, or has resulted in, serious personal injury or death. Each complaint must be signed by the complainant and must contain:
  (1) *The name, address, and telephone number* of the person who files it;
  (2) *The name and address* of the alleged violator and, with respect to each alleged violator, the specific provisions of the regulations that the complainant believes were violated; and
  (3) *A concise but complete statement* of the facts relied upon to substantiate each allegation, including the date of each alleged violation.

(b) Action on complaint of substantial violation. Upon the filing of a complaint of a substantial violation under paragraph (a) of this section, the Assistant Administrator shall determine whether it is nonfrivolous and meets the requirements of paragraph (a) of this section. If the Assistant Administrator determines the complaint is nonfrivolous and meets the requirements of paragraph (a), he/she shall investigate the complaint. The complainant shall be timely notified of findings resulting from such investigation. The Assistant Administrator shall not be required to conduct separate investigations of duplicative complaints. If the Assistant Administrator determines the complaint is frivolous or does not meet the requirements of the paragraph (a), he/ she shall dismiss the complaint and notify the complainant in writing of the reasons for such dismissal.

(c) Notwithstanding the provisions of Section 552 of Title 5, United States Code, the Assistant Administrator shall not disclose the identity of complainants unless it is determined that such disclosure is necessary to prosecute a violation. If disclosure becomes necessary, the Assistant Administrator shall take every practical means within the Assistant Administrator's authority to assure that the complainant is not subject to harassment, intimidation, disciplinary action, discrimination, or financial loss as a result of such disclosure.

§386.13 Petitions to review and request for hearing: Driver qualification proceedings.

(a) Within 60 days after service of the determination under §391.47 of this chapter or the letter of disqualification, the driver or carrier may petition to review such action. Such petitions must be submitted to the Assistant Administrator and must contain the following:
  (1) *Identification of what action the petitioner wants overturned;*
  (2) *Copies of all evidence* upon which petitioner relies in the form set out in §386.49;
  (3) *All legal and other arguments* which the petitioner wishes to make in support of his/her position;
  (4) *A request for oral hearing,* if one is desired, which must set forth material factual issues believed to be in dispute;
  (5) *Certification that the reply has been filed* in accordance with §386.31; and
  (6) *Any other pertinent material.*

(b) Failure to submit a petition as specified in paragraph (a) of this section shall constitute a waiver of the right to petition for review of the determination or letter of disqualification. In these cases, the determination or disqualification issued automatically becomes the final decision of the Assistant Administrator 30 days after the time to submit the reply or petition to review has expired, unless the Assistant Administrator orders otherwise.

(c) If the petition does not request a hearing, the Assistant Administrator may issue a final decision and order based on the evidence and arguments submitted.

§386.14 Reply.

(a) Time for reply to the Notice of Claim. Respondent must serve a reply to the Notice of Claim in writing within 30 days following service of the Notice of Claim. The reply is to be served in accordance with §386.6 upon the Service Center indicated in the Notice of Claim.

(b) Options for reply. The respondent must reply to the Notice of Claim within the time allotted by choosing one of the following:

- (1) *Paying the full amount* asserted in the Notice of Claim in accordance with §386.18 of this part;
- (2) *Contesting the claim* by requesting administrative adjudication pursuant to paragraph (d) of this section; or
- (3) *Seeking binding arbitration* in accordance with the Agency's program. Although the amount of the proposed penalty may be disputed, referral to binding arbitration is contingent upon an admission of liability that the violations occurred.

(c) Failure to answer the Notice of Claim.
- (1) *Respondent's failure to answer* the Notice of Claim in accordance with paragraph (a) may result in the issuance of a Notice of Default and Final Agency Order by the Field Administrator. The Notice of Default and Final Agency Order will declare respondent to be in default and further declare the Notice of Claim, including the civil penalty proposed in the Notice of Claim, to be the Final Agency Order in the proceeding. The Final Agency Order will be effective five days following service of the Notice of Default and Final Agency Order.
- (2) *The default* constitutes an admission of all facts alleged in the Notice of Claim and a waiver of respondent's opportunity to contest the claim. The default will be reviewed by the Assistant Administrator in accordance with §386.64(b), and the Final Agency Order may be vacated where a respondent demonstrates excusable neglect, a meritorious defense, or due diligence in seeking relief.
- (3) *Failure to pay the civil penalty* as directed in a Final Agency Order constitutes a violation of that order, subjecting the respondent to an additional penalty as prescribed in Subpart G of this part.

(d) Request for administrative adjudication. The respondent may contest the claim and request administrative adjudication pursuant to paragraph (b)(2) of this section. An administrative adjudication is a process to resolve contested claims before the Assistant Administrator, Administrative Law Judge, or Hearing Officer. Once an administrative adjudication option is elected, it is binding on the respondent.
- (1) *Contents.* In addition to the general requirements of this section, the reply must be in writing and state the grounds for contesting the claim and must raise any affirmative defenses the respondent intends to assert. Specifically, the reply:
  - (i) *Must admit or deny* each separately stated and numbered allegation of violation in the claim. A statement that the person is without sufficient knowledge or information to admit or deny will have the effect of a denial. Any allegation in the claim not specifically denied in the reply is deemed admitted. A mere general denial of the claim is insufficient and may result in a default being entered by the Agency decisionmaker upon motion by the Field Administrator.
  - (ii) *Must include all known affirmative defenses,* including those relating to jurisdiction, limitations, and procedure.
  - (iii) *Must state* which one of the following options respondent seeks:
    - [A] *To submit written evidence without hearing;* or
    - [B] *An informal hearing;* or
    - [C] *A formal hearing.*
- (2) [Reserved].

§386.15 [Reserved]

§386.16 Action on replies to the Notice of Claim.

(a) Requests to submit written evidence without a hearing. Where respondent has elected to submit written evidence in accordance with §386.14(d)(1)(iii)(A):
- (1) *Agency Counsel must serve* all written evidence and argument in support of the Notice of Claim no later than 60 days following service of respondent's reply. The written evidence and argument must be served on the Assistant Administrator in accordance with §§386.6 and 386.7. The submission must include all pleadings, notices, and other filings in the case to date.
- (2) *Respondent will,* not later than 45 days following service of Agency Counsel's written evidence and argument, serve its written evidence and argument on the Assistant Administrator in accordance with §§386.6 and 386.7.
- (3) *Agency Counsel may file* a written response to respondent's submission. Any such submission must be filed within 20 days of service of respondent's submission.
- (4) *All written evidence* submitted by the parties must conform to the requirements of §386.49.
- (5) *Following submission* of evidence and argument as outlined in this section, the Assistant Administrator may issue a Final Agency Order and order based on the evidence and arguments submitted, or may issue any other order as may be necessary to adjudicate the matter.

(b) Requests for hearing.
- (1) *If a request* for a formal or informal hearing has been filed, the Assistant Administrator will determine whether there exists a dispute of a material fact at issue in the matter. If so, the matter will be set for hearing in accordance with respondent's reply. If it is determined that there does not exist a dispute of a material fact at issue in the matter, the Assistant Administrator may issue a decision based on the written record, or may request the submission of further evidence or argument.
- (2) *If a respondent* requests a formal or informal hearing in its reply, the Field Administrator must serve upon the Assistant Administrator and respondent a notice of consent or objection with a basis to the request within 60 days of service of respondent's reply. Failure to serve an objection within the time allotted may result in referral of the matter to hearing.
- (3) *Requests for formal hearing.* Following the filing of an objection with basis, the Field Administrator must serve a motion for Final Agency Order pursuant to §386.36 unless otherwise ordered by the Assistant Administrator. The motion must set forth the reasons why the Field Administrator is entitled to judgment as a matter of law. Respondent must, within 45 days of service of the motion for Final Agency Order, submit and serve a response to the Field Administrator's motion. After reviewing the record, the Assistant Administrator will either set the matter for hearing by referral to the Office of Hearings or issue a Final Agency Order based upon the submissions.
- (4) *Requests for informal hearing.*
  - (i) *If the Field Administrator* objects with basis to a request for an informal hearing, he/she must serve the objection, a copy of the Notice of Claim, and a copy of respondent's reply, on the respondent and Assistant Administrator, pursuant to paragraph (b)(2) of this section. Based upon the Notice of Claim, the reply, and the objection with basis, the Assistant Administrator will issue an order granting or denying the request for informal hearing.
    - [A] *Informal hearing granted.* If the request for informal hearing is granted by the Assistant Administrator, a Hearing Officer will be assigned to hear the matter and will set forth the date, time and location for hearing. No further motions will be entertained, and no discovery will be allowed. At hearing, all parties may present evidence, written and oral, to the Hearing Officer, following which the Hearing Officer will issue a report to the Assistant Administrator containing findings of fact and recommending a disposition of the matter. The report will serve as the sole record of the proceedings. The Assistant Administrator may issue a Final Agency Order adopting the report, or issue other such orders as he/she may deem appropriate. By participating in an informal hearing, respondent waives its right to a formal hearing.
    - [B] *Informal hearing denied.* If the request for informal hearing is denied, the Field Administrator must serve a motion for Final Agency Order pursuant to §386.36, unless otherwise directed by the Assistant Administrator. The motion must set forth the reasons why the Field Administrator is entitled to judgment as a matter of law. Respondent must, within 45 days of service of the motion for Final Agency Order, submit and serve a response to the Field Administrator's motion. After reviewing the record, the Assistant Administrator will set the matter for formal hearing by referral to the Office of Hearings, or will issue a Final Agency Order based upon the submissions.
    - [C] *Nothing in this section* shall limit the Assistant Administrator's authority to refer any matter for formal hearing, even in instances where respondent seeks only an informal hearing.

§386.17 Intervention.

After the matter is called for hearing and before the date set for the hearing to begin, any person may petition for leave to intervene. The petition is to be served on the administrative law judge. The petition must set forth the reasons why the petitioner alleges he/she is entitled to intervene. The petition must be served on all parties in accordance with §386.31. Any party may file a response within 10 days of service of the petition. The administrative law judge shall then determine whether to permit or deny the petition. The petition will be allowed if the administrative law judge determines that the final decision could directly and adversely affect the petitioner or the class he/she represents, and if the petitioner may contribute materially to the disposition of the proceedings and his/her interest is not adequately represented by existing parties. Once admitted, a petitioner is a party for the purpose of all subsequent proceedings.

§386.18 Payment of the claim.

(a) **Payment of the full amount claimed** may be made at any time before issuance of a Final Agency Order. After the issuance of a Final Agency Order, claims are subject to interest, penalties, and administrative charges in accordance with 31 U.S.C. 3717; 49 CFR Part 89; and 31 CFR 901.9.

(b) **If respondent elects to pay the full amount** as its response to the Notice of Claim, payment must be served upon the Field Administrator at the Service Center designated in the Notice of Claim within 30 days following service of the Notice of Claim. No written reply is necessary if respondent elects the payment option during the 30-day reply period. Failure to serve full payment within 30 days of service of the Notice of Claim when this option has been chosen may constitute a default and may result in the Notice of Claim, including the civil penalty assessed by the Notice of Claim, becoming the Final Agency Order in the proceeding pursuant to §386.14(c).

(c) **Unless objected to in writing,** submitted at the time of payment, payment of the full amount in response to the Notice of Claim constitutes an admission by the respondent of all facts alleged in the Notice of Claim. Payment waives respondent's opportunity to further contest the claim, and will result in the Notice of Claim becoming the Final Agency Order.

Subpart C - Settlement Agreements

§386.22 Settlement agreements and their contents.

(a) **Settlement agreements.**

(1) When negotiations produce an agreement as to the amount or terms of payment of a civil penalty or the terms and conditions of an order, a settlement agreement shall be drawn and signed by the respondent and the Field Administrator or his/her designee. Such settlement agreement must contain the following:

(i) The statutory basis of the claim;

(ii) A brief statement of the violations;

(iii) The amount claimed and the amount paid;

(iv) The date, time, and place and form of payment;

(v) A statement that the agreement is not binding on the Agency until executed by the Field Administrator or his/her designee;

(vi) A statement that failure to pay in accordance with the terms of the agreement or to comply with the terms of the agreement may result in the reinstatement of any penalties held in abeyance and may also result in the loss of any reductions in civil penalties asserted in the Notice of Claim, in which case the original amount asserted will be due immediately; and

(vii) A statement that the agreement is the Final Agency Order.

(2) A settlement agreement may contain any conditions, actions, or provisions agreed by the parties to redress the violations cited in the Notice of Claim or notice of violation.

(3) A settlement agreement accepted and approved by the Assistant Administrator or Administrative Law Judge is a Final Agency Order which is binding on all parties according to its terms. Consent to a settlement agreement which has not yet been approved by the Assistant Administrator or Administrative Law Judge may not be withdrawn for a period of 30 days.

(b) **Civil Penalty Proceedings** not before Agency Decisionmaker. When the parties have agreed to a settlement at any time prior to the case coming before the Agency decisionmaker, the parties may execute an appropriate agreement for disposing of the case. The agreement does not require approval by the Agency decisionmaker. The agreement becomes the Final Agency Order upon execution by the Field Administrator or his/her designee.

(c) **Civil Penalty Proceedings before Agency Decisionmaker.** When a respondent has agreed to a settlement of a civil penalty before a Final Agency Order has been issued, the parties may execute an appropriate agreement for disposal of the case by consent for the consideration of the Assistant Administrator. The agreement is filed with the Assistant Administrator, who may accept it, reject it and direct that proceedings in the case continue, or take such other action as he/she deems appropriate. If the Assistant Administrator accepts the agreement, he/she shall enter an order in accordance with its terms. The settlement agreement becomes the Final Agency Order as of the date the Assistant Administrator enters an order accepting the settlement agreement.

(d) **Civil Penalty Proceedings** before Administrative Law Judge (ALJ). When a respondent has agreed to a settlement of a civil penalty before the hearing is concluded, the parties may execute an appropriate agreement for disposing of the case by consent for the consideration of the ALJ. The agreement is filed with the ALJ who may accept it, reject it, and direct that proceedings in the case continue, or take such other action as he/she deems appropriate. If the ALJ accepts the agreement, he/she shall enter an order in accordance with its terms. The settlement agreement becomes the Final Agency Order as per §386.61.

(e) **Civil Penalty Proceedings before Hearing Officer.** When a respondent has agreed to a settlement of a civil penalty before the hearing is concluded, the parties may execute an appropriate agreement for disposal of the case for the consideration of the Hearing Officer. The agreement is filed with the Hearing Officer, who, within 20 days of receipt, will make a report and recommendation to the Assistant Administrator who may accept it, reject it, and direct that proceedings in the case continue, or take such other action as he/she deems appropriate. If the Assistant Administrator accepts the agreement, he/she will enter an order in accordance with its terms. The settlement agreement becomes the Final Agency Order as of the date the Assistant Administrator enters an order accepting the settlement agreement.

Subpart D - General Rules and Hearings

§386.31 Official notice.

Upon notification to all parties, the Assistant Administrator or Administrative Law Judge may take official notice of any fact or document not appearing in evidence in the record. Any party objecting to the official notice must file an objection within 10 days after service of the notice. If a Final Agency Order has been issued, and the decision rests on a material and disputable fact of which the Agency decisionmaker has taken official notice, a party may challenge the action of official notice in accordance with §386.64 of this part.

§386.34 Motions.

(a) **General.** An application for an order or ruling not otherwise covered by these rules shall be by motion. All motions filed prior to the calling of the matter for a hearing shall be to the Assistant Administrator. All motions filed after the matter is called for hearing shall be to the administrative law judge.

(b) **Form.** Unless made during hearing, motions shall be made in writing, shall state with particularity the grounds for relief sought, and shall be accompanied by affidavits or other evidence relied upon.

(c) **Answers.** Except when a motion is filed during a hearing, any party may file an answer in support or opposition to a motion, accompanied by affidavits or other evidence relied upon. Such answers shall be served within 20 days after the motion is served or within such other time as the Assistant Administrator or administrative law judge may set.

(d) **Argument.** Oral argument or briefs on a motion may be ordered by the Assistant Administrator or the administrative law judge.

(e) **Disposition.** Motions may be ruled on immediately or at any other time specified by the administrative law judge or the Assistant Administrator.

(f) **Suspension of time.** The pendency of a motion shall not affect any time limits set in these rules unless expressly ordered by the Assistant Administrator or administrative law judge.

§386.35 Motions to dismiss and motions for a more definite statement.

(a) **Motions to dismiss must be made** within the time set for reply or petition to review, except motions to dismiss for lack of jurisdiction, which may be made at any time.

(b) **Motions for a more definite statement** may be made in lieu of a reply. The motion must point out the defects complained of and the details desired. If the motion is granted, the pleading complained of must be remedied within 15 days of the granting of the motion or it will be stricken. If the motion is denied, the party who requested the more definite statement must file his/her pleading within 10 days after the denial.

§386.36 Motions for final agency order.

(a) *Generally.* Unless otherwise provided in this section, the motion and answer will be governed by §386.34. Either party may file a motion for final order. The motion must be served in accordance with §§386.6 and 386.7. If the matter is still pending before the service center, upon filing, the matter is officially transferred from the service center to the Agency decisionmaker, who will then preside over the matter.

(b) *Form and content.*
  (1) *Movant's filing* must contain a motion and memorandum of law, which may be separate or combined and must include all responsive pleadings, notices, and other filings in the case to date.
  (2) *The motion for final order* must be accompanied by written evidence in accordance with §386.49.
  (3) *The motion* will state with particularity the grounds upon which it is based and the substantial matters of law to be argued. A Final Agency Order may be issued if, after reviewing the record in a light most favorable to the non-moving party, the Agency decisionmaker determines no genuine issue exists as to any material fact.

(c) *Answer to Motion.* The non-moving party will, within 45 days of service of the motion for final order, submit and serve a response to rebut movant's motion.

§386.37 Discovery.

(a) *Parties may obtain discovery* by one or more of the following methods: Depositions upon oral examination or written questions; written interrogatories; request for production of documents or other evidence for inspection and other purposes; physical and mental examinations; and requests for admission.

(b) *Discovery may not commence* until the matter is pending before the Assistant Administrator or referred to the Office of Hearings.

(c) *Except as otherwise provided in these rules,* in the Administrative Procedure Act, 5 U.S.C. 551 et seq., or by the Assistant Administrator or administrative law judge, in the absence of specific Agency provisions or regulations, the Federal Rules of Civil Procedure may serve as guidance in administrative adjudications.

§386.38 Scope of discovery.

(a) *Unless otherwise limited by order* of the Assistant Administrator or, in cases that have been called for a hearing, the administrative law judge, in accordance with these rules, the parties may obtain discovery regarding any matter, not privileged, which is relevant to the subject matter involved in the proceeding, including the existence, description, nature, custody, condition, and location of any books, documents, or other tangible things and the identity and location of persons having knowledge of any discoverable matter.

(b) *It is not ground for objection that information sought* will not be admissible at the hearing if the information sought appears reasonably calculated to lead to the discovery of admissible evidence.

(c) *A party may obtain discovery of documents* and tangible things otherwise discoverable under paragraph (a) of this section and prepared in anticipation of or for the hearing by or for another party's representative (including his or her attorney, consultant, surety, indemnitor, insurer, or agent) only upon a showing that the party seeking discovery has substantial need of the materials in the preparation of his or her case and that he or she is unable without undue hardship to obtain the substantial equivalent of the materials by other means. In ordering discovery of such materials when the required showing has been made, the Assistant Administrator or the Administrative Law Judge shall protect against disclosure of the mental impressions, conclusions, opinions, or legal theories of an attorney or other representative of a party concerning the proceeding.

§386.39 Protective orders.

Upon motion by a party or other person from whom discovery is sought, and for good cause shown, the Assistant Administrator or the administrative law judge, if one has been appointed, may make any order which justice requires to protect a party or person from annoyance, embarrassment, oppression, or undue burden or expense, including one or more of the following:

(a) *The discovery not be had;*
(b) *The discovery may be had* only on specified terms and conditions, including a designation of the time or place;
(c) *The discovery may be had* only by a method of discovery other than that selected by the party seeking discovery;
(d) *Certain matters not relevant may not be inquired into,* or that the scope of discovery be limited to certain matters;
(e) *Discovery be conducted with no one present* except persons designated by the Assistant Administrator or the Administrative Law Judge; or
(f) *A trade secret or other confidential research,* development, or commercial information may not be disclosed or be disclosed only in a designated way.

§386.40 Supplementation of responses.

A party who has responded to a request for discovery with a response that was complete when made is under no duty to supplement his/her response to include information thereafter acquired, except as follows:

(a) *A party is under a duty to supplement timely* his/her response with respect to any question directly addressed to:
  (1) *The identity and location* of persons having knowledge of discoverable matters; and
  (2) *The identity of each person* expected to be called as an expert witness at the hearing, the subject matter on which he or she is expected to testify and the substance of his or her testimony.

(b) *A party is under a duty to amend timely* a prior response if he or she later obtains information upon the basis of which:
  (1) *he or she knows the response was incorrect when made; or*
  (2) *he or she knows that the response* though correct when made is no longer true and the circumstances are such that a failure to amend the response is in substance a knowing concealment.

(c) *A duty to supplement responses may be imposed* by order of the Assistant Administrator or the administrative law judge or agreement of the parties.

§386.41 Stipulations regarding discovery.

Unless otherwise ordered, a written stipulation entered into by all the parties and filed with the Assistant Administrator or the administrative law judge, if one has been appointed, may:

(a) *Provide that depositions be taken before any person,* at any time or place, upon sufficient notice, and in any manner, and when so taken may be used like other depositions, and
(b) *Modify the procedures provided by these rules* for other methods of discovery.

§386.42 Written interrogatories to parties.

(a) *Without leave, any party may serve upon any other party* written interrogatories to be answered by the party to whom the interrogatories are directed; or, if that party is a public or private corporation or partnership or association or governmental agency, by any officer or agent, who will furnish the information available to that party.

(b) *The maximum number of interrogatories served* will not exceed 30, including all subparts, unless the Assistant Administrator or Administrative Law Judge permits a larger number on motion and for good cause shown. Other interrogatories may be added without leave, so long as the total number of approved and additional interrogatories does not exceed 30.

(c) *Each interrogatory shall be answered* separately and fully in writing under oath unless it is objected to, in which event the grounds for objection shall be stated and signed by the party, or counsel for the party, if represented, making the response. The party to whom the interrogatories are directed shall serve the answers and any objections within 30 days after the service of the interrogatories, or within such shortened or longer period as the Assistant Administrator or the Administrative Law Judge may allow.

(d) *Motions to compel may be made in accordance with §386.45.*

(e) *A notice of discovery must be served* on the Assistant Administrator or, in cases that have been referred to the Office of Hearings, on the Administrative Law Judge. A copy of the interrogatories, answers, and all related pleadings must be served on all parties to the proceeding.

(f) *An interrogatory otherwise proper* is not necessarily objectionable merely because an answer to the interrogatory involves an opinion or contention that relates to fact or the application of law to fact, but the Assistant Administrator or Administrative Law Judge may order that such an interrogatory need not be answered until after designated discovery has been completed or until a prehearing conference or other later time.

§386.43 Production of documents and other evidence; entry upon land for inspection and other purposes; and physical and mental examination.

(a) Any party may serve on any other party a request to:
  (1) *Produce and permit the party making the request,* or a person acting on his or her behalf, to inspect and copy any designated documents, or to inspect and copy, test, or sample any tangible things which are in the possession, custody, or control of the party upon whom the request is served; or
  (2) *Permit entry upon designated land* or other property in the possession or control of the party upon whom the request is served for the purpose of inspection and measuring, photographing, testing, or for other purposes as stated in paragraph (a)(1) of this section.
  (3) *Submit to a physical or mental examination* by a physician.
(b) The request may be served on any party without leave of the Assistant Administrator or administrative law judge.
(c) The request shall:
  (1) *Set forth the items to be inspected* either by individual item or category;
  (2) *Describe each item or category* with reasonable particularity;
  (3) *Specify a reasonable time, place, and manner* of making the inspection and performing the related acts;
  (4) *Specify the time, place, manner, conditions, and scope* of the physical or mental examination and the person or persons by whom it is to be made. A report of examining physician shall be made in accordance with Rule 35(b) of the Federal Rules of Civil Procedure, Title 28, U.S. Code, as amended.
(d) The party upon whom the request is served shall serve on the party submitting the request a written response within 30 days after service of the request.
(e) The response shall state, with respect to each item or category:
  (1) *That inspection and related activities* will be permitted as requested; or
  (2) *That objection is made in whole or in part,* in which case the reasons for objection shall be stated.
(f) A copy of each request for production and each written response shall be served on all parties and filed with the Assistant Administrator or the administrative law judge, if one has been appointed.

§386.44 Request for admissions.

(a) Request for admission.
  (1) *Any party may serve upon any other party* a request for admission of any relevant matter or the authenticity of any relevant document. Copies of any document about which an admission is requested must accompany the request.
  (2) *Each matter for which an admission is requested* shall be separately set forth and numbered. The matter is admitted unless within 15 days after service of the request, the party to whom the request is directed serves upon the party requesting the admission a written answer signed by the party or his/her attorney.
  (3) *Each answer must specify* whether the party admits or denies the matter. If the matter cannot be admitted or denied, the party shall set out in detail the reasons.
  (4) *A party may not issue a denial* or fail to answer on the ground that he/she lacks knowledge unless he/she has made reasonable inquiry to ascertain information sufficient to allow him/her to admit or deny.
  (5) *A party may file an objection* to a request for admission within 10 days after service. Such motion shall be filed with the administrative law judge if one has been appointed, otherwise it shall be filed with the Assistant Administrator. An objection must explain in detail the reasons the party should not answer. A reply to the objection may be served by the party requesting the admission within 10 days after service of the objection. It is not sufficient ground for objection to claim that the matter about which an admission is requested presents an issue of fact for hearing.
(b) Effect of admission. Any matter admitted is conclusively established unless the Assistant Administrator or administrative law judge permits withdrawal or amendment. Any admission under this rule is for the purpose of the pending action only and may not be used in any other proceeding.
(c) If a party refuses to admit a matter or the authenticity of a document which is later proved, the party requesting the admission may move for an award of expenses incurred in making the proof. Such a motion shall be granted unless there was a good reason for failure to admit.

§386.45 Motion to compel discovery.

(a) If a deponent fails to answer a question propounded or a party upon whom a request is made pursuant to §§386.42 through 386.44, or a party upon whom interrogatories are served fails to respond adequately or objects to the request, or any part thereof, or fails to permit inspection as requested, the discovering party may move the Assistant Administrator or the administrative law judge, if one has been appointed, for an order compelling a response or inspection in accordance with the request.
(b) The motion shall set forth:
  (1) *The nature of the questions or request;*
  (2) *The response or objections of the party* upon whom the request was served; and
  (3) *Arguments in support of the motion.*
(c) For purposes of this section, an evasive answer or incomplete answer or response shall be treated as a failure to answer or respond.
(d) In ruling on a motion made pursuant to this section, the Assistant Administrator or the administrative law judge, if one has been appointed, may make and enter a protective order such as he or she is authorized to enter on a motion made pursuant to §386.39(a).

§386.46 Depositions.

(a) When, how, and by whom taken.
  (1) *The deposition of any witness* may be taken at reasonable times subsequent to the appointment of an Administrative Law Judge. Prior to referral to the Office of Hearings, a party may petition the Assistant Administrator, in accordance with §386.37, for leave to conduct a deposition based on good cause shown.
  (2) *Depositions may be taken* by oral examination or upon written interrogatories before any person having power to administer oaths.
  (3) *The parties may stipulate in writing* or the Administrative Law Judge may upon motion order that a deposition be taken by telephone or other remote electronic means.
  (4) *If a subpoena duces tecum* is to be served on the person to be examined, the designation of the materials to be produced as set forth in the subpoena shall be attached to, or included in, the notice.
  (5) *If the deposition* is to be recorded by videotape or audiotape, the notice shall specify the method of recording.
(b) Application. Any party desiring to take the deposition of a witness must indicate to the witness and all other parties the time when, the place where, and the name and post office address of the person before whom the deposition is to be taken; the name and address of each witness; and the subject matter concerning which each such witness is expected to testify.
(c) Notice. A party desiring to take a deposition must give notice to the witness and all other parties. Notice must be in writing. Notice of the deposition must be given not less than 20 days from when the deposition is to be taken if the deposition is to be held within the continental United States and not less than 30 days from when the deposition is to be taken if the deposition is to be held elsewhere, unless a shorter time is agreed to by the parties or by leave of the Assistant Administrator or Administrative Law Judge by motion for good cause shown.
(d) Depositions upon written questions. Within 14 days after the notice and written questions are served, a party may serve cross-questions upon all other parties. Within 7 days after being served with cross-questions, a party may serve redirect questions upon all other parties. Within 7 days after being served with redirect questions, a party may serve recross questions upon all other parties. The Assistant Administrator or Administrative Law Judge may enlarge or shorten the time for cause shown.
(e) Taking and receiving in evidence. Each witness testifying upon deposition must be sworn, and any other party must be given the right to cross-examine. The questions propounded and the answers to them, together with all objections made, must be reduced to writing; read by or to, and subscribed by the witness; and certified by the person administering the oath. The person who took the deposition must seal the deposition transcript in an envelope and file it in accordance with §386.7. Subject to objections to the questions and answers as were noted at the time of taking the deposition and which would have been valid if the witness were personally present and testifying, the deposition may

be read and offered in evidence by the party taking it as against any party who was present or represented at the taking of the deposition or who had due notice of it.

(f) Witness Limit. No party may seek deposition testimony of more than five witnesses without leave of the Agency decisionmaker for good cause shown. Individual depositions are not to exceed 8 hours for any one witness.

(g) Motion to terminate or limit examination. During the taking of a deposition, a party or deponent may request suspension of the deposition on grounds of bad faith in the conduct of the examination, oppression of a deponent or party or improper questions propounded. The deposition will then be adjourned. The objecting party or deponent must, however, immediately move for a ruling on his or her objections to the deposition conduct or proceedings before the Assistant Administrator or Administrative Law Judge, who then may limit the scope or manner of the taking of the deposition.

§386.47 Use of deposition at hearings.

(a) Generally. At the hearing, any part or all of a deposition, so far as admissible under the rules of evidence, may be used against any party who was present or represented at the taking of the deposition or who had due notice thereof in accordance with any one of the following provisions:

(1) *Any deposition may be used by any party* for the purpose of contradicting or impeaching the testimony of the deponent as a witness.

(2) *The deposition of expert witnesses,* particularly the deposition of physicians, may be used by any party for any purpose, unless the Assistant Administrator or administrative law judge rules that such use would be unfair or a violation of due process.

(3) *The deposition of a party* or of anyone who at the time of taking the deposition was an officer, director, or duly authorized agent of a public or private organization, partnership, or association which is a party, may be used by any other party for any purpose.

(4) *The deposition of a witness,* whether or not a party, may be used by any party for any purpose if the presiding officer finds:

  (i) *That the witness is dead;* or
  (ii) *That the witness is out of the United States* or more than 100 miles from the place of hearing unless it appears that the absence of the witness was procured by the party offering the deposition; or
  (iii) *That the witness is unable to attend to testify* because of age, sickness, infirmity, or imprisonment; or
  (iv) *That the party offering the deposition* has been unable to procure the attendance of the witness by subpoena; or
  (v) *Upon application and notice,* that such exceptional circumstances exist as to make it desirable, in the interest of justice and with due regard to the importance of presenting the testimony of witnesses orally in open hearing, to allow the deposition to be used.

(5) *If only part of a deposition* is offered in evidence by a party, any other party may require him or her to introduce all of it which is relevant to the part introduced, and any party may introduce any other parts.

(b) Objections to admissibility. Except as provided in this paragraph, objection may be made at the hearing to receiving in evidence any deposition or part thereof for any reason which would require the exclusion of the evidence if the witness were then present and testifying.

(1) *Objections to the competency of a witness* or to the competency, relevancy or materiality of testimony are not waived by failure to make them before or during the taking of the deposition, unless the ground of the objection is one which might have been obviated or removed if presented at that time.

(2) *Errors and irregularities* occurring at the oral examination in the manner of taking the deposition, in the form of the questions or answers, in the oath or affirmation, or in the conduct of parties and errors of any kind which might be obviated, removed, or cured if promptly presented, are waived unless reasonable objection thereto is made at the taking of the deposition.

(3) *Objections to the form or written interrogatories* are waived unless served in writing upon the party propounding them.

(c) Effect of taking using depositions. A party shall not be deemed to make a person his or her own witness for any purpose by taking his or her deposition. The introduction in evidence of the deposition or any part thereof for any purpose other than that of contradicting or impeaching the deponent makes the deponent the witness of the party introducing the deposition, but this shall not apply to the use by any other party of a deposition as described in paragraph (a)(2) of this section. At the hearing, any party may rebut any relevant evidence contained in a deposition whether introduced by him or her or by any other party.

§386.48 Medical records and physicians' reports.

In cases involving the physical qualifications of drivers, copies of all physicians' reports, test results, and other medical records that a party intends to rely upon shall be served on all other parties at least 30 days prior to the date set for a hearing. Except as waived by the Director, Office of Truck and Bus Standards and Operations, reports, test results and medical records not served under this rule shall be excluded from evidence at any hearing.

§386.49 Form of written evidence.

All written evidence should be submitted in the following forms:

(a) A written statement of a person having personal knowledge of the facts alleged, or

(b) Documentary evidence in the form of exhibits attached to a written statement identifying the exhibit and giving its source.

§386.51 Amendment and withdrawal of pleadings.

(a) Except in instances covered by other rules, anytime more than 15 days prior to the hearing, a party may amend his/her pleadings by serving the amended pleading on the Assistant Administrator or the Administrative Law Judge, if one has been appointed, and on all parties. Within 15 days prior to the hearing, an amendment shall be allowed only at the discretion of the Administrative Law Judge. When an amended pleading is filed, other parties may file a response and objection within 10 days.

(b) A party may withdraw his/her pleading any time more than 15 days prior to the hearing by serving a notice of withdrawal on the Assistant Administrator or the Administrative Law Judge. Within 15 days prior to the hearing a withdrawal may be made only at the discretion of the Assistant Administrator or the Administrative Law Judge. The withdrawal will be granted absent a finding that the withdrawal will result in injustice, prejudice, or irreparable harm to the non-moving party, or is otherwise contrary to the public interest.

§386.52 Appeals from interlocutory rulings.

(a) General. Unless otherwise provided in this subpart, a party may not appeal a ruling or decision of the Administrative Law Judge to the Assistant Administrator until the Administrative Law Judge's decision has been entered on the record. A decision or order of the Assistant Administrator on the interlocutory appeal does not constitute a Final Agency Order for the purposes of judicial review under §386.67.

(b) Interlocutory appeal for cause. If a party files a written request for an interlocutory appeal for cause with the Administrative Law Judge, or orally requests an interlocutory appeal for cause, the proceedings are stayed until the Administrative Law Judge issues a decision on the request. If the Administrative Law Judge grants the request, the proceedings are stayed until the Assistant Administrator issues a decision on the interlocutory appeal. The Administrative Law Judge must grant an interlocutory appeal for cause if a party shows that delay of the appeal would be detrimental to the public interest or would result in undue prejudice to any party.

(d) Procedure. A party must file a notice of interlocutory appeal, with any supporting documents, with the Assistant Administrator, and serve copies on each party and the Administrative Law Judge, not later than 10 days after the Administrative Law Judge's oral decision has been issued, or a written decision has been served. A party must file a reply brief, if any, with the Assistant Administrator and serve a copy of the reply brief on each party, not later than 10 days after service of the appeal brief. The Assistant Administrator will render a decision on the interlocutory appeal, within a reasonable time after receipt of the interlocutory appeal.

(e) The Assistant Administrator may reject frivolous, repetitive, or dilatory appeals, and may issue an order precluding one or more parties from making further interlocutory appeals, and may order such further relief as required.

§386.53 Subpoenas, witness fees.

(a) Applications for the issuance of subpoenas must be submitted to the Assistant Administrator, or in cases that have been called for a hearing, to the administrative law judge. The application must show the general relevance and reasonable scope of the evidence sought. Any person served with a subpoena may, within 7 days after service, file a motion to quash or modify. The motion must be filed with the official who approved the subpoena. The filing of a motion shall stay the effect of the subpoena until a decision is reached.

(b) **Witnesses shall be entitled to the same fees and mileage** as are paid witnesses in the courts of the United States. The fees shall be paid by the party at whose instance the witness is subpoenaed or appears.

(c) **Paragraph (a) of this section shall not apply** to the Administrator or employees of the FMCSA or to the production of documents in their custody. Applications for the attendance of such persons or the production of such documents at a hearing shall be made to the Assistant Administrator or administrative law judge, if one is appointed, and shall set forth the need for such evidence and its relevancy.

§386.54 Administrative Law Judge.

(a) **Powers of an Administrative Law Judge.** The Administrative Law Judge may take any action and may prescribe all necessary rules and regulations to govern the conduct of the proceedings to ensure a fair and impartial hearing, and to avoid delay in the disposition of the proceedings. In accordance with the rules in this subchapter, an Administrative Law Judge may do the following:

(1) *Give notice of and hold prehearing conferences and hearings.*

(2) *Administer oaths and affirmations.*

(3) *Issue subpoenas authorized by law.*

(4) *Rule on offers of proof.*

(5) *Receive relevant and material evidence.*

(6) *Regulate the course* of the administrative adjudication in accordance with the rules of this subchapter and the Administrative Procedure Act.

(7) *Hold conferences* to settle or simplify the issues by consent of the parties.

(8) *Dispose of procedural motions and requests,* except motions that under this part are made directly to the Assistant Administrator.

(9) *Issue orders* permitting inspection and examination of lands, buildings, equipment, and any other physical thing and the copying of any document.

(10) *Make findings of fact and conclusions of law, and issue decisions.*

(11) *To take any other action* authorized by these rules and permitted by law.

(b) **Limitations on the power of the Administrative Law Judge.** The Administrative Law Judge is bound by the procedural requirements of this part and the precedent opinions of the Agency. This section does not preclude an Administrative Law Judge from barring a person from a specific proceeding based on a finding of obstreperous or disruptive behavior in that proceeding.

(c) **Disqualification.** The Administrative Law Judge may disqualify himself or herself at any time, either at the request of any party or upon his or her own initiative. Assignments of Administrative Law Judges are made by the Chief Administrative Law Judge upon the request of the Assistant Administrator. Any request for a change in such assignment, including disqualification, will be considered only for good cause which would unduly prejudice the proceeding.

§386.55 Prehearing conferences.

(a) **Convening.** At any time before the hearing begins, the administrative law judge, on his/her own motion or on motion by a party, may direct the parties or their counsel to participate with him/her in a prehearing conference to consider the following:

(1) *Simplification and clarification of the issues;*

(2) *Necessity or desirability of amending pleadings;*

(3) *Stipulations as to the facts* and the contents and authenticity of documents;

(4) *Issuance of and responses to subpoenas;*

(5) *Taking of depositions* and the use of depositions in the proceedings;

(6) *Orders for discovery, inspection and examination* of premises, production of documents and other physical objects, and responses to such orders;

(7) *Disclosure of the names and addresses* of witnesses and the exchange of documents intended to be offered in evidence; and

(8) *Any other matter* that will tend to simplify the issues or expedite the proceedings.

(b) **Order.** The administrative law judge shall issue an order which recites the matters discussed, the agreements reached, and the rulings made at the prehearing conference. The order shall be served on the parties and filed in the record of the proceedings.

§386.56 Hearings.

(a) **As soon as practicable after his/her appointment,** the administrative law judge shall issue an order setting the date, time, and place for the hearing. The order shall be served on the parties and become a part of the record of the proceedings. The order may be amended for good cause shown.

(b) **Conduct of hearing.** The administrative law judge presides over the hearing. Hearings are open to the public unless the administrative law judge orders otherwise.

(c) **Evidence.** Except as otherwise provided in these rules and the Administrative Procedure Act, 5 U.S.C. 551 et seq., the Federal Rules of Evidence shall be followed.

(d) **Information obtained by investigation.** Any document, physical exhibit, or other material obtained by the Administration in an investigation under its statutory authority may be disclosed by the Administration during the proceeding and may be offered in evidence by counsel for the Administration.

(e) **Record.** The hearing shall be stenographically transcribed and reported. The transcript, exhibits, and other documents filed in the proceedings shall constitute the official record of the proceedings. A copy of the transcript and exhibits will be made available to any person upon payment of prescribed costs.

§386.57 Proposed findings of fact, conclusions of law.

The administrative law judge shall afford the parties reasonable opportunity to submit proposed findings of fact, conclusions of law, and supporting reasons therefor. If the administrative law judge orders written proposals and arguments, each proposed finding must include a citation to the specific portion of the record relied on to support it. Written submissions, if any, must be served within the time period set by the administrative law judge.

§386.58 Burden of proof.

(a) **Enforcement cases.** The burden of proof shall be on the Administration in enforcement cases.

(b) **Conflict of medical opinion.** The burden of proof in cases arising under §391.47 of this chapter shall be on the party petitioning for review under §386.13(a).

Subpart E - Decision

§386.61 Decision.

(a) **Administrative Law Judge.** After receiving the proposed findings of fact, conclusions of law, and arguments of the parties, the Administrative Law Judge shall issue a decision. If the proposed findings of fact, conclusions of law, and arguments were oral, he/she may issue an oral decision. The decision of the Administrative Law Judge becomes the final decision of the Assistant Administrator 45 days after it is served unless a petition or motion for review is filed under §386.62. The decision shall be served on all parties and on the Assistant Administrator.

(b) **Hearing Officer.** The Hearing Officer will prepare a report to the Assistant Administrator containing findings of fact and recommended disposition of the matter within 45 days after the conclusion of the hearing. The Assistant Administrator will issue a Final Agency Order adopting the report, or may make other such determinations as appropriate. The Assistant Administrator's decision to adopt a Hearing Officer's report may be reviewed in accordance with §386.64.

§386.62 Review of administrative law judge's decision.

(a) **All petitions to review must be accompanied** by exceptions and briefs. Each petition must set out in detail objections to the initial decision and shall state whether such objections are related to alleged errors of law or fact. It shall also state the relief requested. Failure to object to any error in the initial decision shall waive the right to allege such error in subsequent proceedings.

(b) **Reply briefs may be filed** within 30 days after service of the appeal brief.

(c) **No other briefs shall be permitted** except upon request of the Assistant Administrator.

(d) **Copies of all briefs must be served on all parties.**

(e) **No oral argument will be permitted** except on order of the Assistant Administrator.

§386.63 Decision on review.

Upon review of a decision, the Assistant Administrator may adopt, modify, or set aside the administrative law judge's findings of fact and conclusions of law. He/she may also remand proceedings to the administrative law judge with instructions for such further proceedings

§386.64 Reconsideration.

(a) **Within 20 days following service** of the Final Agency Order, any party may petition the Assistant Administrator for reconsideration of the order. If a civil penalty was imposed, the filing of a petition for reconsideration stays the entire action, unless the Assistant Administrator orders otherwise.

(b) **In the event a Notice of Default** and Final Agency Order is issued by the Field Administrator as a result of the respondent's failure to reply in accordance with §386.14(a), the only issue that will be considered upon reconsideration is whether a default has occurred under §386.14(c). The Final Agency Order may be vacated where a respondent can demonstrate excusable neglect, a meritorious defense, or due diligence in seeking relief.

(c) **Either party may serve an answer** to a petition for reconsideration within 30 days of the service date of the petition.

(d) **Following the close of the 30-day period,** the Assistant Administrator will rule on the petition.

(e) **The ruling on the petition** will be the Final Agency Order. A petition for reconsideration of the Assistant Administrator's ruling will not be permitted.

§386.65 Failure to comply with final order.

If, within 30 days of receipt of a final agency order issued under this part, the respondent does not submit in writing his/her acceptance of the terms of an order directing compliance, or, where appropriate, pay a civil penalty, or file an appeal under §386.67, the case may be referred to the Attorney General with a request that an action be brought in the appropriate United States District Court to enforce the terms of a compliance order or collect the civil penalty.

§386.66 Motions for rehearing or for modification.

(a) **No motion for rehearing or for modification** of an order shall be entertained for 1 year following the date the Assistant Administrator's order goes into effect. After 1 year, any party may file a motion with the Assistant Administrator requesting a rehearing or modification of the order. The motion must contain the following:

(1) *A copy of the order about which the change is requested;*

(2) *A statement of the changed circumstances* justifying the request; and

(3) *Copies of all evidence intended to be relied on* by the party submitting the motion.

(b) **Upon receipt of the motion,** the Assistant Administrator may make a decision denying the motion or modifying the order in whole or in part. He/she may also, prior to making his/her decision, order such other proceedings under these rules as he/she deems necessary and may request additional information from the party making the motion.

§386.67 Judicial review.

(a) **Any party to the underlying proceeding,** who, after an administrative adjudication, is adversely affected by a Final Agency Order issued under 49 U.S.C. 521 may, within 30 days of service of the Final Agency Order, petition for review of the order in the United States Court of Appeals in the circuit where the violation is alleged to have occurred, or where the violator has its principal place of business or residence, or in the United States Court of Appeals for the District of Columbia Circuit.

(b) **Judicial review will be based on a determination** of whether the findings and conclusions in the Final Agency Order were supported by substantial evidence or were otherwise not in accordance with law. No objection that has not been raised before the Agency will be considered by the court, unless reasonable grounds existed for failure or neglect to do so. The commencement of proceedings under this section will not, unless ordered by the court, operate as a stay of the Final Agency Order of the Agency.

Subpart F - Injunctions and Imminent Hazards

§386.71 Injunctions.

Whenever it is determined that a person has engaged, or is about to engage, in any act or practice constituting a violation of Section 31502 of Title 49, United States Code; of the Motor Carrier Safety Act of 1984; the Hazardous Materials Transportation Act; or any regulation or order issued under that section or those Acts for which the Federal Motor Carrier Safety Administrator exercises enforcement responsibility, the Chief Counsel may request the United States Attorney General to bring an action in the appropriate United States District Court for such relief as is necessary or appropriate, including mandatory or prohibitive injunctive relief, interim equitable relief, and punitive damages, as provided by Section 213(c) of the Motor Carrier Safety Act of 1984 and Section 111(a) of the Hazardous Materials Transportation Act (49 U.S.C. 507(c) 5122).

§386.72 Imminent hazard.

(a) **Whenever it is determined that an imminent hazard exists** as a result of the transportation by motor vehicle of a particular hazardous material, the Chief Counsel or Deputy Chief Counsel of the FMCSA may bring, or request the United States Attorney General to bring, an action in the appropriate United States District Court for an order suspending or restricting the transportation by motor vehicle of the hazardous material or for such other order as is necessary to eliminate or ameliorate the imminent hazard, as provided by 49 U.S.C. 5122. In this paragraph, "imminent hazard" means the existence of a condition that presents a substantial likelihood that death, serious illness, severe personal injury, or a substantial endangerment to health, property, or the environment may occur before a notice of investigation proceeding, or other administrative hearing or formal proceeding, to abate the risk of harm can be completed.

(b) (1) *Whenever it is determined* that a violation of 49 U.S.C. 31502 or the Motor Carrier Safety Act of 1984, as amended, or the Commercial Motor Vehicle Safety Act of 1986, as amended, or a regulation issued under such section or Acts, or a combination of such violations, poses an imminent hazard to safety, the Director of the Office of Enforcement and Compliance or a State Director, or his or her delegate, shall order a vehicle or employee operating such vehicle out of service, or order an employer to cease all or part of the employer's commercial motor vehicle operations, as provided by 49 U.S.C. 521(b)(5). In making any such order, no restrictions shall be imposed on any employee or employer beyond that required to abate the hazard. In this paragraph, "imminent hazard" means any condition of vehicle, employee, or commercial motor vehicle operations which substantially increases the likelihood of serious injury or death if not discontinued immediately.

(2) *Upon the issuance* of an order under paragraph (b)(1) of this section, the motor carrier employer or driver employee shall comply immediately with such order. Opportunity for review shall be provided in accordance with 5 U.S.C. 554, except that such review shall occur not later than 10 days after issuance of such order, as provided by section 213(b) of the Motor Carrier Safety Act of 1984 (49 U.S.C. 521(b)(5)). An order to an employer to cease all or part of its operations shall not prevent vehicles in transit at the time the order is served from proceeding to their immediate destinations, unless any such vehicle or its driver is specifically ordered out of service forthwith. However, vehicles and drivers proceeding to their immediate destination shall be subject to compliance upon arrival.

(3) *For purposes of this section* the term "immediate destination" is the next scheduled stop of the vehicle already in motion where the cargo on board can be safely secured.

(4) *Failure to comply immediately* with an order issued under this section shall subject the motor carrier employer or driver to penalties prescribed in Subpart G of this part.

Subpart G - Penalties

§386.81 General.

(a) **The amounts of civil penalties that can be assessed** for regulatory violations subject to the proceedings in this subchapter are established in the statutes granting enforcement powers. The determination of the actual civil penalties assessed in each proceeding is based on those defined limits or minimums and consideration of information available at the time the claim is made concerning the nature, gravity of the violation and, with respect to the violator, the degree of culpability, history of prior offenses, ability to pay, effect on ability to continue to do business, and such other matters as justice and public safety may require. In addition to these factors, a civil penalty assessed under 49 U.S.C. 14901(a) and (d) concerning household goods is also based on the degree of harm caused to a shipper and whether the shipper has been adequately compensated before institution of the civil penalty proceeding. In adjudicating the claims and orders under the administrative procedures herein, additional information may

Part 386 - Rules of Practice for Motor Carrier, Broker, Freight Forwarder, & Haz. Mat. Proceedings §386.84 (d)

be developed regarding these factors that may affect the final amount of the claim.
(b) When assessing penalties for violations of notices and orders or settling claims based on these assessments, consideration will be given to good faith efforts to achieve compliance with the terms of the notices and orders.

§386.82 Civil penalties for violations of notices and orders.

(a) Additional civil penalties are chargeable for violations of notices and orders which are issued under civil forfeiture proceedings pursuant to 49 U.S.C. 521(b). These notices and orders are as follows:
  (1) *Notice to abate* — §386.11 (b)(2) and (c)(1)(iv);
  (2) *Notice to post* — §386.11(b)(3);
  (3) *Final order* — §§386.14, 386.17, 386.22, and 386.61; and
  (4) *Out-of-service order* — §386.72(b)(1).
(b) A schedule of these additional penalties is provided in the Appendix A to this part. All the penalties are maximums, and discretion will be retained to meet special circumstances by setting penalties for violations of notices and orders, in some cases, at less than the maximum.
(c) Claims for penalties provided in this section and in the Appendix A to this part shall be made through the civil forfeiture proceedings contained in this part. The issues to be decided in such proceedings will be limited to whether violations of notices and orders occurred as claimed and the appropriate penalty for such violations. Nothing contained herein shall be construed to authorize the reopening of a matter already finally adjudicated under this part.

§386.83 Sanction for failure to pay civil penalties or abide by payment plan; operation in interstate commerce prohibited.

(a) (1) *General rule.* A CMV owner or operator that fails to pay a civil penalty in full within 90 days after the date specified for payment by the FMCSA's final agency order is prohibited from operating in interstate commerce starting on the next (i.e., the 91st) day. The prohibition continues until the FMCSA has received full payment of the penalty.
  (2) *Civil penalties paid in installments.* The FMCSA Service Center may allow a CMV owner or operator to pay a civil penalty in installments. If the CMV owner or operator fails to make an installment payment on schedule, the payment plan is void and the entire debt is payable immediately. A CMV owner or operator that fails to pay the full outstanding balance of its civil penalty within 90 days after the date of the missed installment payment, is prohibited from operating in interstate commerce on the next (i.e., the 91st) day. The prohibition continues until the FMCSA has received full payment of the entire penalty.
  (3) *Appeals to Federal Court.* If the CMV owner or operator appeals the final agency order to a Federal Circuit Court of Appeals, the terms and payment due date of the final agency order are not stayed unless the Court so directs.
(b) Show Cause Proceeding.
  (1) *The FMCSA will notify a CMV owner or operator in writing* if it has not received payment within 45 days after the date specified for payment by the final agency order or the date of a missed installment payment. The notice will include a warning that failure to pay the entire penalty within 90 days after payment was due, will result in the CMV owner or operator being prohibited from operating in interstate commerce.
  (2) *The notice will order the CMV owner or operator* to show cause why it should not be prohibited from operating in interstate commerce on the 91st day after the date specified for payment. The prohibition may be avoided only by submitting to the Chief Safety Officer:
    (i) *Evidence that the respondent* has paid the entire amount due; or
    (ii) *Evidence that the respondent* has filed for bankruptcy under Chapter 11, Title 11, United States Code. Respondents in bankruptcy must also submit the information required by paragraph (d) of this section.
  (3) *The notice will be delivered* by certified mail or commercial express service. If a CMV owner's or operator's principal place of business is in a foreign country, the notice will be delivered to the CMV owner's or operator's designated agent.
(c) A CMV owner or operator that continues to operate in interstate commerce in violation of this section may be subject to additional sanctions under paragraph IV (h) of Appendix A to Part 386.

(d) This section does not apply to any person who is unable to pay a civil penalty because the person is a debtor in a case under Chapter 11, Title 11, United States Code. CMV owners or operators in bankruptcy proceedings under Chapter 11 must provide the following information in their response to the FMCSA:
  (1) *The chapter of the Bankruptcy Code* under which the bankruptcy proceeding is filed (i.e., Chapter 7 or 11);
  (2) *The bankruptcy case number;*
  (3) *The court in which the bankruptcy proceeding was filed;* and
  (4) *Any other information requested by the agency* to determine a debtor's bankruptcy status.

§386.84 Sanction for failure to pay civil penalties or abide by payment plan; suspension or revocation of registration.

(a) (1) *General rule.* The registration of a broker, freight forwarder, or for-hire motor carrier that fails to pay a civil penalty in full within 90 days after the date specified for payment by the FMCSA's final agency order, will be suspended starting on the next (i.e., the 91st) day. The suspension continues until the FMCSA has received full payment of the penalty.
  (2) *Civil penalties paid in installments.* The FMCSA Service Center may allow a respondent broker, freight forwarder, or for-hire motor carrier to pay a civil penalty in installments. If the respondent fails to make an installment payment on schedule, the payment plan is void and the entire debt is payable immediately. The registration of a respondent that fails to pay the remainder of its civil penalty in full within 90 days after the date of the missed installment payment, is suspended on the next (i.e., the 91st) day. The suspension continues until the FMCSA has received full payment of entire penalty.
  (3) *Appeals to Federal Court.* If the respondent broker, freight forwarder, or for-hire motor carrier appeals the final agency order to a Federal Circuit Court of Appeals, the terms and payment due date of the final agency order are not stayed unless the Court so directs.
(b) Show Cause Proceeding.
  (1) *The FMCSA will notify* a respondent broker, freight forwarder, or for-hire motor carrier in writing if it has not received payment within 45 days after the date specified for payment by the final agency order or the date of a missed installment payment. The notice will include a warning that failure to pay the entire penalty within 90 days after payment was due, will result in the suspension of the respondent's registration.
  (2) *The notice will order the respondent* to show cause why its registration should not be suspended on the 91st day after the date specified for payment. The prohibition may be avoided only by submitting to the Chief Safety Officer:
    (i) *Evidence that the respondent has paid* the entire amount due; or
    (ii) *Evidence that the respondent has filed* for bankruptcy under Chapter 11, Title 11, United States Code. Respondents in bankruptcy must also submit the information required by paragraph (d) of this section.
  (3) *The notice will be delivered* by certified mail or commercial express service. If a respondent's principal place of business is in a foreign country, it will be delivered to the respondent's designated agent.
(c) The registration of a broker, freight forwarder or for-hire motor carrier that continues to operate in interstate commerce in violation of this section after its registration has been suspended may be revoked after an additional notice and opportunity for a proceeding in accordance with 49 U.S.C. 13905(c). Additional sanctions may be imposed under paragraph IV (h) of Appendix A to Part 386.
(d) This section does not apply to any person who is unable to pay a civil penalty because the person is a debtor in a case under Chapter 11, Title 11, United States Code. Brokers, freight forwarders, or for-hire motor carriers in bankruptcy proceedings under Chapter 11 must provide the following information in their response to the FMCSA:
  (1) *The chapter of the Bankruptcy Code* under which the bankruptcy proceeding is filed (i.e., Chapter 7 or 11);
  (2) *The bankruptcy case number;*
  (3) *The court in which the bankruptcy proceeding was filed;* and
  (4) *Any other information requested by the agency* to determine a debtor's bankruptcy status.

Appendix A   Part 386 - Rules of Practice for Motor Carrier, Broker, Freight Forwarder, & Haz. Mat. Proceedings

Appendix A to Part 386   Penalty Schedule; Violations of Notices and Orders.

I. Notice To Abate
Violation — Failure to cease violations of the regulations in the time prescribed in the notice. (The time within to comply with a notice to abate shall not begin to run with respect to contested violations, i.e., where there are material issues in dispute under §386.14, until such time as the violation has been established.)

Penalty — Reinstatement of any deferred assessment or payment of a penalty or portion thereof.

II. [Reserved]

III. Final Order
Violation — Failure to comply with Final Agency Order.

Penalty — Automatic reinstatement of any penalty previously reduced or held in abeyance and restoration of the full amount assessed in the Notice of Claim less any payments previously made.

IV. Out-of-Service Order[1]

a. *Violation* — Operation of a commercial vehicle by a driver during the period the driver was placed out of service.

Penalty — Up to $2,100 per violation.

(For purposes of this violation, the term "driver" means an operator of a commercial motor vehicle, including an independent contractor who, while in the course of operating a commercial motor vehicle, is employed or used by another person.)

b. *Violation* — Requiring or permitting a driver to operate a commercial vehicle during the period the driver was placed out of service.

Penalty — Up to $16,000 per violation.

(This violation applies to motor carriers, including an independent contractor who is not a "driver," as defined under paragraph IVa above.)

c. *Violation* — Operation of a commercial motor vehicle by a driver after the vehicle was placed out of service and before the required repairs are made.

Penalty — $2,100 each time the vehicle is so operated.

(This violation applies to drivers as defined in IVa above.)

d. *Violation* — Requiring or permitting the operation of a commercial motor vehicle placed out of service before the required repairs are made.

Penalty — Up to $16,000 each time the vehicle is so operated after notice of the defect is received.

(This violation applies to motor carriers, including an independent owner-operator who is not a "driver," as defined in IVa above.)

e. *Violation* — Failure to return written certification of correction as required by the out-of-service order.

Penalty — Up to $650 per violation.

f. *Violation* — Knowingly falsifies written certification of correction required by the out-of-service order.

Penalty — Considered the same as the violations described in paragraphs IVc and IVd above, and subject to the same penalties.

NOTE: Falsification of certification may also result in criminal prosecution under 18 U.S.C. 1001.

g. *Violation* — Operating in violation of an order issued under §386.72(b) to cease all or part of the employer's commercial motor vehicle operations, i.e., failure to cease operations as ordered.

Penalty — Up to $16,000 per day the operation continues after the effective date and time of the order to cease.

h. *Violation* — Conducting operations during a period of suspension under §§386.83 or 386.84 for failure to pay penalties.

Penalty — Up to $11,000 for each day that operations are conducted during the suspension period.

Appendix B to Part 386   Penalty schedule; violations and maximum civil penalties.

The Debt Collection Improvement Act of 1996 [Public Law 104-134, Title III, Chapter 10, §31001, par. (s), 110 Stat. 1321-373] amended the Federal Civil Penalties Inflation Adjustment Act of 1990 to require agencies to adjust for inflation "each civil monetary penalty provided by law within the jurisdiction of the Federal agency * * *"

and to publish that regulation in the Federal Register. Pursuant to that authority, the inflation-adjusted civil penalties listed in paragraphs (a) through (g) of this appendix supersede the corresponding civil penalty amounts listed in Title 49, United States Code.

What are the types of violations and maximum monetary penalties?

(a) **Violations of the Federal Motor Carrier Safety Regulations (FMCSRs).**

(1) *Recordkeeping.* A person or entity that fails to prepare or maintain a record required by Parts 40, 382, 385, and 390-99 of this subchapter, or prepares or maintains a required record that is incomplete, inaccurate, or false, is subject to a maximum civil penalty of $550 for each day the violation continues, up to $5,500.

(2) *Knowing falsification of records.* A person or entity that knowingly falsifies, destroys, mutilates, or changes a report or record required by Parts 382, 385, and 390-99 of this subchapter, knowingly makes or causes to be made a false or incomplete record about an operation or business fact or transaction, or knowingly makes, prepares, or preserves a record in violation of a regulation or order of the Secretary is subject to a maximum civil penalty of $5,500 if such action misrepresents a fact that constitutes a violation other than a reporting or recordkeeping violation.

(3) *Non-recordkeeping violations.* A person or entity that violates Parts 382, 385, or 390-99 of this subchapter, except a recordkeeping requirement, is subject to a civil penalty not to exceed $11,000 for each violation.

(4) *Non-recordkeeping violations by drivers.* A driver who violates Parts 382, 385, and 390-99 of this subchapter, except a recordkeeping violation, is subject to a civil penalty not to exceed $2,750.

(5) *Violation of 49 CFR 392.5.* A driver placed out of service for 24 hours for violating the alcohol prohibitions of 49 CFR 392.5(a) or (b) who drives during that period is subject to a civil penalty not to exceed $3,750 for each violation.

(b) **Commercial driver's license (CDL) violations.** Any person who violates 49 CFR Part 383, Subparts B, C, E, F, G, or H is subject to a civil penalty of $3,750.

(c) **Special penalties pertaining to violations** of out-of-service orders by CDL-holders. A CDL-holder who is convicted of violating an out-of-service order shall be subject to a civil penalty of not less than $2,100 nor more than $3,750. An employer of a CDL-holder who knowingly allows, requires, permits, or authorizes that employee to operate a CMV during any period in which the CDL-holder is subject to an out-of-service order, is subject to a civil penalty of not less than $3,750 or more than $16,000.

(d) **Financial responsibility violations.** A motor carrier that fails to maintain the levels of financial responsibility prescribed by Part 387 of this subchapter is subject to a maximum penalty of $16,000 for each violation. Each day of a continuing violation constitutes a separate offense.

(e) **Violations of the Hazardous Materials Regulations (HMRs)** and Safety Permitting Regulations found in Subpart E of Part 385. This paragraph applies to violations by motor carriers, drivers, shippers and other persons who transport hazardous materials on the highway in commercial motor vehicles or cause hazardous materials to be so transported.

(1) *All knowing violations* of 49 U.S.C. Chapter 51 or orders or regulations issued under the authority of that chapter applicable to the transportation or shipment of hazardous materials by commercial motor vehicle on highways are subject to a civil penalty of not less than $275 and not more than $32,500 for each violation. Each day of a continuing violation constitutes a separate offense.

(2) *All knowing violations* of 49 U.S.C. Chapter 51 or orders, regulations, or exemptions issued under the authority of that chapter applicable to the manufacture, fabrication, marking, maintenance, reconditioning, repair or testing of a packaging or container which is represented, marked, certified or sold as being qualified for use in the transportation or shipment of hazardous materials by commercial motor vehicle on highways, are subject to a civil penalty of not less than $275 and not more than $32,500 for each violation.

(3) *Whenever regulations* issued under the authority of 49 U.S.C. Chapter 51 require compliance with the FMCSRs while transporting hazardous materials, any violations of the FMCSRs will be considered a violation of the HMRs and subject to a civil penalty of not less than $275 and not more than $32,500.

---

1. Editor's Note: Section IV appears to have been deleted from the CFR in error following an amendment appearing in the May 18, 2005, Federal Register.

Part 386 - Rules of Practice for Motor Carrier, Broker, Freight Forwarder, & Haz. Mat. Proceedings   Appendix B

(f) Operating after being declared unfit by assignment of a final unsatisfactory safety rating. A motor carrier operating a commercial motor vehicle in interstate commerce after receiving a final unsatisfactory safety rating is subject to a civil penalty of not more than $11,000 (49 CFR 385.13). Each day the transportation continues constitutes a separate offense.

(g) Violations of the commercial regulations (CRs). Penalties for violations of the CRs are specified in 49 U.S.C. Chapter 149. These penalties relate to transportation subject to the Secretary's jurisdiction under 49 U.S.C. Chapter 135. Unless otherwise noted, a separate violation occurs for each day the violation continues.

(1) *A person who fails to make a report,* to specifically, completely, and truthfully answer a question, or to make, prepare, or preserve a record in the form and manner prescribed is liable for a minimum penalty of $550 per violation.

(2) *A person who operates as a carrier or broker* for the transportation of property in violation of the registration requirements of 49 U.S.C. 13901 is liable for a minimum penalty of $550 per violation.

(3) *A person who operates as a motor carrier of passengers* in violation of the registration requirements of 49 U.S.C. 13901 is liable for a minimum penalty of $2,200 per violation.

(4) *A person who operates as a foreign motor carrier* or foreign motor private carrier in violation of the provisions of 49 U.S.C. 13902 (c) is liable for a minimum penalty of $550 per violation.

(5) *A person who operates as a foreign motor carrier* or foreign motor private carrier without authority, before the implementation of the land transportation provisions of the North American Free Trade Agreement, outside the boundaries of a commercial zone along the United States-Mexico border is liable for a maximum penalty of $11,000 for an intentional violation and a maximum penalty of $27,500 for a pattern of intentional violations.

(6) *A person who operates as a motor carrier or broker* for the transportation of hazardous wastes in violation of the registration provisions of 49 U.S.C. 13901 is liable for a maximum penalty of $22,000 per violation.

(7) *A motor carrier or freight forwarder of household goods,* or their receiver or trustee, that does not comply with any regulation relating to the protection of individual shippers is liable for a minimum penalty of $1,100 per violation.

(8) *A person —*
 (i) *Who falsifies,* or authorizes an agent or other person to falsify, documents used in the transportation of household goods by motor carrier or freight forwarder to evidence the weight of a shipment or
 (ii) *Who charges for services* which are not performed or are not reasonably necessary in the safe and adequate movement of the shipment is liable for a minimum penalty of $2,200 for the first violation and $5,500 for each subsequent violation.

(9) *A person who knowingly accepts or receives* from a carrier a rebate or offset against the rate specified in a tariff required under 49 U.S.C. 13702 for the transportation of property delivered to the carrier commits a violation for which the penalty is equal to three times the amount accepted as a rebate or offset and three times the value of other consideration accepted or received as a rebate or offset for the six-year period before the action is begun.

(10) *A person who offers, gives, solicits, or receives* transportation of property by a carrier at a different rate than the rate in effect under 49 U.S.C. 13702 is liable for a maximum penalty of $110,000 per violation. When acting in the scope of his/her employment, the acts or omissions of a person acting for or employed by a carrier or shipper are considered to be the acts and omissions of that carrier or shipper, as well as that person.

(11) *Any person who offers, gives, solicits, or receives* a rebate or concession related to motor carrier transportation subject to jurisdiction under subchapter I of 49 U.S.C. Chapter 135, or who assists or permits another person to get that transportation at less than the rate in effect under 49 U.S.C. 13702, commits a violation for which the penalty is $200 for the first violation and $275 for each subsequent violation.

(12) *A freight forwarder, its officer, agent, or employee,* that assists or willingly permits a person to get service under 49 U.S.C. 13531 at less than the rate in effect under 49 U.S.C. 13702 commits a violation for which the penalty is up to $550 for the first violation and up to $2,200 for each subsequent violation.

(13) *A person who gets or attempts to get service* from a freight forwarder under 49 U.S.C. 13531 at less than the rate in effect under 49 U.S.C. 13702 commits a violation for which the penalty is up to $550 for the first violation and up to $2,200 for each subsequent violation.

(14) *A person* who knowingly authorizes, consents to, or permits a violation of 49 U.S.C. 14103 relating to loading and unloading motor vehicles or who knowingly violates subsection (a) of 49 U.S.C. 14103 is liable for a penalty of not more than $11,000 per violation.

(15) *A person, or an officer, employee,* or agent of that person, who tries to evade regulation under Part B of Subtitle IV, Title 49, U.S.C., for carriers or brokers is liable for a penalty of $220 for the first violation and at least $275 for a subsequent violation.

(16) *A person required to make a report* to the Secretary, answer a question, or make, prepare, or preserve a record under Part B of Subtitle IV, Title 49, U.S.C., or an officer, agent, or employee of that person, is liable for a maximum penalty of $5,500 per violation if it does not make the report, does not completely and truthfully answer the question within 30 days from the date the Secretary requires the answer, does not make or preserve the record in the form and manner prescribed, falsifies, destroys, or changes the report or record, files a false report or record, makes a false or incomplete entry in the record about a business related fact, or prepares or preserves a record in violation of a regulation or order of the Secretary.

(17) *A motor carrier,* water carrier, freight forwarder, or broker, or their officer, receiver, trustee, lessee, employee, or other person authorized to receive information from them, who discloses information identified in 49 U.S.C. 14908 without the permission of the shipper or consignee is liable for a maximum penalty of $2,200.

(18) *A person who violates* a provision of Part B, Subtitle IV, Title 49, U.S.C., or a regulation or order under Part B, or who violates a condition of registration related to transportation that is subject to jurisdiction under Subchapter I or III or Chapter 135, or who violates a condition of registration of a foreign motor carrier or foreign motor private carrier under section 13902, is liable for a penalty of $550 for each violation if another penalty is not provided in 49 U.S.C. Chapter 149.

(19) *A violation* of Part B, Subtitle IV, Title 49, U.S.C., committed by a director, officer, receiver, trustee, lessee, agent, or employee of a carrier that is a corporation is also a violation by the corporation to which the penalties of Chapter 149 apply. Acts and omissions of individuals acting in the scope of their employment with a carrier are considered to be the actions and omissions of the carrier as well as the individual.

(20) *In a proceeding* begun under 49 U.S.C. 14902 or 14903, the rate that a carrier publishes, files, or participates in under section 13702 is conclusive proof against the carrier, its officers, and agents that it is the legal rate for the transportation or service. Departing, or offering to depart, from that published or filed rate is a violation of 49 U.S.C. 14902 and 14903.

Notes

Part 387 - Minimum Levels of Financial Responsibility for Motor Carriers
(Page 75 in the Driver Edition)

Subpart A - Motor Carriers of Property

§387.1 Purpose and scope.
This subpart prescribes the minimum levels of financial responsibility required to be maintained by motor carriers of property operating motor vehicles in interstate, foreign, or intrastate commerce. The purpose of these regulations is to create additional incentives to motor carriers to maintain and operate their vehicles in a safe manner and to assure that motor carriers maintain an appropriate level of financial responsibility for motor vehicles operated on public highways.

§387.1 DOT Interpretations
Question 1: May a State require a higher level of financial responsibility coverage than is required by Part 387?
Guidance: Yes.

§387.3 Applicability.
(a) **This subpart applies to for-hire motor carriers** operating motor vehicles transporting property in interstate or foreign commerce.
(b) **This subpart applies to motor carriers** operating motor vehicles transporting hazardous materials, hazardous substances, or hazardous wastes in interstate, foreign, or intrastate commerce.
(c) **Exception.**
  (1) *The rules in this part* do not apply to a motor vehicle that has a gross vehicle weight rating (GVWR) of less than 10,000 pounds. This exception does not apply if the vehicle is used to transport any quantity of a Division 1.1, 1.2, or 1.3 material, any quantity of a Division 2.3, Hazard Zone A, or Division 6.1, Packing Group I, Hazard Zone A, or to a highway route controlled quantity of a Class 7 material as it is defined in 49 CFR 173.403, in interstate or foreign commerce.
  (2) *The rules in this part* do not apply to the transportation of non-bulk oil, non-bulk hazardous materials, substances, or wastes in intrastate commerce, except that the rules in this part do apply to the transportation of a highway route controlled quantity of a Class 7 material as defined in 49 CFR 173.403, in intrastate commerce.

§387.3 DOT Interpretations
Question 1: At what GVWR, as assigned by a manufacturer, does the requirement to comply with the financial responsibility regulations begin?
Guidance: Generally, Part 387, Subpart A applies if the vehicle has a GVWR of 10,000 pounds or more. Part 387, Subpart A, does not apply to the intrastate transportation of nonbulk oil, nonbulk HM, substances or wastes. Motor vehicles used to transport any quantity of Divisions 1.1, 1.2 or 1.3 (explosive) materials, poison gas, or highway route controlled quantity of radioactive materials in interstate or foreign commerce are subject to Federal regulation regardless of the GVWR.

Question 2: Does the GVWR apply to the power unit only?
Guidance: No.

Question 3: When are tow trucks subject to financial responsibility coverage?
Guidance: For-hire tow trucks with a GVWR or GCWR of 10,000 pounds or more performing emergency moves in interstate or foreign commerce are required to maintain minimum levels of financial responsibility in the amount of $750,000. For-hire tow trucks performing secondary moves are required to maintain levels of coverage applicable to the commodity being transported by the vehicle being towed.

Question 4: Are Federal, State or local political subdivisions subject to the financial responsibility regulations?
Guidance: No.

Question 5: Is a motor vehicle owned by an owner-operator, and being dead-headed (returning empty), or a tractor that is being bob-tailed (operating without a trailer), subject to the financial responsibility regulations?
Guidance: A motor vehicle deadheading or bobtailing while in the service of a motor carrier would be subject to the financial responsibility regulations.

Question 6: Is a motor carrier transporting mail under contract for the U.S. Postal Service wholly within the boundaries of a single State subject to the minimum levels of financial responsibility requirements of Part 387?
Guidance: Yes. The transportation of U.S. mail is considered to be interstate commerce because of the intermingling of inter- and intrastate mail on every vehicle.

Question 7: Are motor carriers transporting HM that are covered under exceptions to the HMRs subject to financial responsibility regulations?
Guidance: Yes. Even though an HM may be covered under a packaging, placarding, transportation, or other exception to the HMRs, if the item meets the definition of a hazardous material per 49 CFR 171.8, it is still considered HM for the purposes of Part 387. The motor carrier must still provide for financial responsibility at the appropriate level for the commodity being transported.

Question 8: Are motor vehicles being transported considered to be HM for purposes of the financial responsibility requirements, thus requiring the higher limits set forth in the regulations?
Guidance: Yes. Even though vehicles being transported by motor vehicle are subject only to 49 CFR 173.220 of the HMRs, they meet the definition of "Hazardous material" in 49 CFR 171.8 because "Vehicle, flammable gas powered" and "Vehicle, flammable liquid powered" are designated as hazardous in 49 CFR 172.101 [UN 3166]. For that reason, vehicles transporting other vehicles would have to carry $1,000,000 of public liability insurance.

Question 9: Is a travel trailer or motor home that has propane cylinders attached subject to Part 387 of the FMCSRs?
Guidance: No. The FHWA considers such propane cylinders to be an integral part of the recreational vehicle and not subject to the financial responsibility regulations.

§387.5 Definitions.
As used in this subpart —

Accident — includes continuous or repeated exposure to the same conditions resulting in public liability which the insured neither expected nor intended.

Bodily injury — means injury to the body, sickness, or disease including death resulting from any of these.

Cancellation of insurance — the withdrawal of insurance coverage by either the insurer or the insured.

Endorsement — an amendment to an insurance policy.

Environmental restoration — restitution for the loss, damage, or destruction of natural resources arising out of the accidental discharge, dispersal, release or escape into or upon the land, atmosphere, watercourse, or body of water of any commodity transported by a motor carrier. This shall include the cost of removal and the cost of necessary measure taken to minimize or mitigate damage to human health, the natural environment, fish, shellfish, and wildlife.

Evidence of security — a surety bond or a policy of insurance with the appropriate endorsement attached.

Financial responsibility — the financial reserves (e.g., insurance policies or surety bonds) sufficient to satisfy liability amounts set forth in this part covering public liability.

For-hire carriage means the business of transporting, for compensation, the goods or property of another.

In bulk — the transportation, as cargo, of property, except Division 1.1, 1.2, or 1.3 materials, and Division 2.3, Hazard Zone A gases, in containment systems with capacities in excess of 3500 water gallons.

In bulk (Division 1.1, 1.2, and 1.3 explosives) — the transportation, as cargo, of any Division 1.1, 1.2, or 1.3 materials in any quantity.

In bulk (Division 2.3, Hazard Zone A or Division 6.1, Packing Group I, Hazard Zone A materials) — the transportation, as cargo, of any Division 2.3, Hazard Zone A, or Division 6.1, Packing Group I, Hazard Zone A material, in any quantity.

Insured and principal — the motor carrier named in the policy of insurance, surety bond, endorsement, or notice of cancellation, and also the fiduciary of such motor carrier.

Insurance premium — the monetary sum an insured pays an insurer for acceptance of liability for public liability claims made against the insured.

Motor carrier means a for-hire motor carrier or a private motor carrier. The term includes, but is not limited to, a motor carrier's agent, officer, or representative; an employee responsible for hiring, supervising, training, assigning, or dispatching a driver; or an employee concerned with the installation, inspection, and maintenance of motor vehicle equipment and/or accessories.

Property damage — means damage to or loss of use of tangible property.

Public liability — liability for bodily injury or property damage and includes liability for environmental restoration.

State means a State of the United States, the District of Columbia, Puerto Rico, the Virgin Islands, American Samoa, Guam, and the Northern Mariana Islands.

§387.5 DOT Interpretations

Question 1: Does the definition of the term "in bulk" include solids as well as liquids even though the definition refers to containment systems with capacities in excess of 3,500 water gallons?

Guidance: Yes, the term "3,500 water gallons" is used as a volumetric value and includes solids as well as liquids.

§387.7 Financial responsibility required.

(a) No motor carrier shall operate a motor vehicle until the motor carrier has obtained and has in effect the minimum levels of financial responsibility as set forth in §387.9 of this subpart.

(b) (1) *Policies of insurance,* surety bonds, and endorsements required under this section shall remain in effect continuously until terminated. Cancellation may be effected by the insurer or the insured motor carrier giving 35 days notice in writing to the other. The 35 days notice shall commence to run from the date the notice is mailed. Proof of mailing shall be sufficient proof of notice.

(2) *Exception.* Policies of insurance and surety bonds may be obtained for a finite period of time to cover any lapse in continuous compliance.

(3) *Exception.* A Mexico-domiciled motor carrier operating solely in municipalities in the United States on the U.S.-Mexico international border or within the commercial zones of such municipalities with a Certificate of Registration issued under Part 368 may meet the minimum financial responsibility requirements of this subpart by obtaining insurance coverage, in the required amounts, for periods of 24 hours or longer, from insurers that meet the requirements of §387.11 of this subpart. A Mexican motor carrier so insured must have available for inspection in each of its vehicles copies of the following documents:

(i) The Certificate of Registration;

(ii) The required insurance endorsement (Form MCS-90); and

(iii) An insurance identification card, binder, or other document issued by an authorized insurer which specifies both the effective date and the expiration date of the temporary insurance coverage authorized by this exception.

Mexican motor carriers insured under this exception are also exempt from the notice of cancellation requirements stated on Form MCS-90.

(c) Policies of insurance and surety bonds required under this section may be replaced by other policies of insurance or surety bonds. The liability of the retiring insurer or surety, as to events after the termination date, shall be considered as having terminated on the effective date of the replacement policy of insurance or surety bond or at the end of the 35 day cancellation period required in paragraph (b) of this section, whichever is sooner.

(d) Proof of the required financial responsibility shall be maintained at the motor carrier's principal place of business. The proof shall consist of:

(1) "*Endorsement(s) for Motor Carrier Policies* of Insurance for Public Liability Under Sections 29 and 30 of the Motor Carrier Act of 1980" (Form MCS- 90) issued by an insurer(s);

(2) A "*Motor Carrier Surety Bond for Public Liability* Under Section 30 of the Motor Carrier Act of 1980" (Form MCS-82) issued by a surety; or

(3) *A written decision, order, or authorization* of the Federal Motor Carrier Safety Administration authorizing a motor carrier to self-insure under §387.309, provided the motor carrier maintains a satisfactory safety rating as determined by the Federal Motor Carrier Safety Administration under Part 385 of this chapter.

(e) The proof of minimum levels of financial responsibility required by this section shall be considered public information and be produced for review upon reasonable request by a member of the public.

(f) All vehicles operated within the United States by motor carriers domiciled in a contiguous foreign country, shall have on board the vehicle a legible copy, in English, of the proof of the required financial responsibility (Forms MCS-90 or MCS-82) used by the motor carrier to comply with paragraph (d) of this section.

(g) Any motor vehicle in which there is no evidence of financial responsibility required by paragraph (f) of this section shall be denied entry into the United States.

§387.7 DOT Interpretations

Question 1: May a large corporation which has many wholly owned subsidiaries have one policy for the parent corporation and maintain the policy and the Form MCS-90 at the corporate headquarters?

Guidance: Generally, the required financial responsibility must be in the exact name of the motor carrier and the proof of that coverage must be maintained at the motor carrier's principal place of business. A parent corporation may, however, have a single policy of insurance or surety bond covering the parent and its subsidiaries, provided the name of the parent and the name of each subsidiary are listed on the policy or bond. Further, the required proof must have listed thereon the name of the parent and its subsidiaries. A copy of that proof of financial responsibility coverage must be maintained at each motor carrier subsidiary's principal place of business.

Question 2: What is the definition of "Certificate of Registration" in §387.7(b)(3)?

Guidance: "Certificate of Registration" means a document issued by the FHWA to all Mexican motor carriers, for-hire as well as private, that allows them to enter the U.S., but restricts them to the commercial zone for a particular border municipality, as previously adopted by the ICC. The border municipality is the Port of Entry wherever the motor carrier's vehicle enters the U.S.

Question 3: How does a Mexican motor carrier prove that it is complying with §387.7?

Guidance: Mexican motor carriers are permitted to obtain trip insurance and are required to carry, on the vehicle, a Form MCS-90 along with an insurance verification document listing the date and time the insurance coverage began and expires.

Question 4: Is the financial responsibility requirement met when an owner-operator (lessor) provides the motor carrier (lessee) a copy of the policy and Form MCS-90 where the carrier is named as an additional insured to the policy (Form MCS-90)?

Guidance: No. The motor carrier has the responsibility to obtain the proper financial responsibility levels.

§387.9 Financial responsibility, minimum levels.

The minimum levels of financial responsibility referred to in §387.7 of this subpart are hereby prescribed as follows:

Schedule of Limits — Public liability

Type of carriage	Commodity transported	Jan. 1, 1985
(1) For-hire (In interstate or foreign commerce, with a gross vehicle weight rating of 10,001 or more pounds).	Property (nonhazardous)	$750,000
(2) For-hire and Private (In interstate, foreign, or intrastate commerce, with a gross vehicle weight rating of 10,001 or more pounds).	Hazardous substances, as defined in 49 CFR 171.8, transported in cargo tanks, portable tanks, or hopper-type vehicles with capacities in excess of 3,500 water gallons; or in bulk Division 1.1, 1.2, and 1.3 materials, Division 2.3, Hazard Zone A, or Division 6.1, Packing Group I, Hazard Zone A material; in bulk Division 2.1 or 2.2; or highway route controlled quantities of a Class 7 material, as defined in 49 CFR §173.403	$5,000,000
(3) For-hire and Private (In interstate or foreign commerce, in any quantity; or in intrastate commerce, in bulk only; with a gross vehicle weight rating of 10,001 or more pounds).	Oil listed in 49 CFR 172.101; hazardous waste, hazardous materials, and hazardous substances defined in 49 CFR 171.8 and listed in 49 CFR 172.101, but not mentioned in (2) above or (4) below	$1,000,000

Schedule of Limits — Public liability (continued)

Type of carriage	Commodity transported	Jan. 1, 1985
(4) For-hire and Private (In interstate or foreign commerce, with a gross vehicle weight rating of less than 10,000 pounds).	Any quantity of Division 1.1, 1.2, or 1.3 material; any quantity of Division 2.3, Hazard Zone A, or Division 6.1, Packing Group I, Hazard Zone A material; or highway route controlled quantities of a Class 7 material as defined in 49 CFR 173.403	$5,000,000

§387.9 DOT Interpretations

Question 1: Is gasoline listed as a hazardous material, and, if so, what is the minimum level of financial responsibility currently required?

Guidance: Gasoline is a listed hazardous material in the table found at 49 CFR 172.101. §387.9 requires for-hire and private motor carriers transporting any quantity of oil in interstate or foreign commerce to have a minimum $1,000,000 of financial responsibility coverage. The Clean Water Act of 1973, as amended, declares that gasoline is an "oil," not a "hazardous substance." The $1,000,000 coverage also applies to for-hire and private motor carriers transporting gasoline "in-bulk" in intrastate commerce.

Question 2: Is a motor carrier transporting liquefied petroleum gas (LPG) in any quantity required to have $1,000,000 or $5,000,000 of financial responsibility coverage?

Guidance: Liquefied petroleum gas (LPG) is a flammable compressed gas. All transportation of LPG in containment systems with capacities in excess of 3,500 water gallons requires $5 million financial responsibility coverage. Interstate and foreign commerce movements of LPG in containment systems *not* in excess of 3,500 water gallons requires $1 million coverage. Intrastate movements of LPG in those smaller containment systems are subject *only* to state financial responsibility requirements.

Question 3: What is the definition of a "hopper type" vehicle as indicated in §387.9?

Guidance: A "hopper type" vehicle is one which is capable of discharging its load through a bottom opening without tilting. This vehicle type would also include belly dump trailers. Rear dump trailers and roll-off containers do not meet the definition of a bottom discharging vehicle.

Question 4: What level of insurance is required for a carrier operating a multi-compartment cargo tank that is transporting a hazardous substance, where each compartment is less than 3,500 water gallon capacity, and the total capacity is greater than 3,500 water gallons capacity?

Guidance: $5,000,000 of insurance is required. The table in §387.9 requires that amount of coverage for hazardous substances transported in "cargo tanks, portable tanks, or hopper-type vehicles with capacities in excess of 3,500 water gallons." The transporting vehicle must have "a gross vehicle weight rating of 10,000 or more pounds." Section 171.8 of Title 49 CFR defines a "cargo tank motor vehicle" as a motor vehicle with one or more cargo tanks permanently attached to or forming an integral part of the motor vehicle. Additionally, the use of the plural to describe the tanks and the singular to describe the truck implies that the standard is met if several tanks with a combined capacity of 3,500 water gallons are transported on the same vehicle. This is consistent with the purpose of the financial responsibility requirement — in this case, to protect the public from financial loss following an accidental release of hazardous material — because all of the compartments in a single tank trailer could be damaged in one crash. Here, the compartments on the vehicle have a total capacity of greater than 3,500 water gallons therefore, $5,000,000 of insurance is required.

Question 5: What level of insurance is required for a motor carrier operating a tube trailer where the cylinders are manifolded together. Each separate cylinder has a capacity less than 3,500 water gallons, but the total capacity of all the cylinders on the vehicle is in excess of 3,500 water gallons.

Guidance: $5,000,000 of insurance is required, for the reasons given above. The table in §387.9 refers to "in bulk Division 2.1 or 2.2 materials." The definition of in bulk in §387.5 includes "the transportation, as cargo, of property ... in containment systems with capacities in excess of 3,500 water gallons." In this case, a group of cylinders manifolded together qualify as "containment systems." As in Guidance A, the table describes the vehicle in the singular. As long as the containment systems transported on a single vehicle have a total capacity of at least 3,500 water gallons, $5,000,000 of insurance is required.

§387.11 State authority and designation of agent.

A policy of insurance or surety bond does not satisfy the financial responsibility requirements of this subpart unless the insurer or surety furnishing the policy or bond is —

(a) **Legally authorized to issue such policies or bonds** in each State in which the motor carrier operates; or

(b) **Legally authorized to issue such policies or bonds** in the State in which the motor carrier has its principal place of business or domicile, and is willing to designate a person upon whom process, issued by or under the authority of any court having jurisdiction of the subject matter, may be served in any proceeding at law or equity brought in any State in which the motor carrier operates; or

(c) **Legally authorized to issue such policies or bonds** in any State of the United States and eligible as an excess or surplus lines insurer in any State in which business is written, and is willing to designate a person upon whom process, issued by or under the authority of any court having jurisdiction of the subject matter, may be served in any proceeding at law or equity brought in any State in which the motor carrier operates.

§387.11 DOT Interpretations

Question 1: How does a Mexican motor carrier demonstrate that its insurance company complies with §387.11?

Guidance: With a properly executed Form MCS-90 from an insurance company licensed in the U.S.

§387.13 Fiduciaries.

The coverage of fiduciaries shall attach at the moment of succession of such fiduciaries.

§387.15 Forms.

Endorsements for policies of insurance (Illustration I) and surety bonds (Illustration II) must be in the form prescribed by the FMCSA and approved by the OMB. Endorsements to policies of insurance and surety bonds shall specify that coverage thereunder will remain in effect continuously until terminated, as required in §387.7 of this subpart. The continuous coverage requirement does not apply to Mexican motor carriers insured under 387.7(b)(3) of this subpart. The endorsement and surety bond shall be issued in the exact name of the motor carrier.

§387.15 ILLUSTRATION I

[Form MCS-90 (3/82) — Endorsement for Motor Carrier Policies of Insurance for Public Liability Under Sections 29 and 30 of the Motor Carrier Act of 1980]

* Full-size forms available free of charge at www.dotcfr.com.

§387.15 ILLUSTRATION II

[Form MCS-82 (4/83) — Motor Carrier Public Liability Surety Bond Under Sections 29 and 30 of the Motor Carrier Act of 1980]

* Full-size forms available free of charge at www.dotcfr.com.

§387.15 DOT Interpretations

Question 1: May the motor carrier meet the financial responsibility requirements by aggregating insurance in layers?

Guidance: Yes. A motor carrier may aggregate coverage, by purchasing insurance in layers with each layer consisting of a separate policy and endorsement. The first layer of coverage is referred to as primary insurance and each additional layer is referred to as excess insurance. Example: ABC Motor Carrier transports Division 1.1 explosive material and is required to maintain $5 million coverage. ABC Motor Carrier decides to meet this requirement by purchasing a primary insurance policy of $1 million from insurance company A, an excess policy of $1 million from insurance company B, and a $3 million excess policy from insurance company C. Each policy would have a separate endorsement (Form MCS-90). The endorsement provided by insurer A would state "This insurance is primary and the company shall not be liable for amounts in excess of $1,000,000 for each accident." The endorsement provided by insurer B would state "This insurance is excess and the company shall not be liable for amounts in excess of $1 million for each accident in excess of the underlying limit of $1 million for each accident." The endorsement provided by insurer C would state "This insurance is excess and the company shall not be liable for amounts in excess of $3 million for each accident in excess of the underlying limit of $2 million for each accident."

Question 2: May the Form MCS-90 required by Part 387 for proof of minimum financial responsibility be modified?

Guidance: The prescribed text of the document may not be changed. However, the format (i.e., number of pages, layout of the text, etc.) may be altered.

Question 3: Is the use of a printed or stamped signature on the Form MCS-90 endorsement acceptable?

Guidance: Yes.

Question 4: Must a motor carrier obtain a new Form MCS-90 each year if it retains the same insurance company?

Guidance: If the insurance policy, as identified by the policy number on the Form MCS-90, is still valid upon the renewal of insurance, no new Form MCS-90 is required. If the policy number has changed or the insurance policy has been canceled in accordance with the terms shown on Form MCS-90, then a new Form MCS-90 must be completed and attached to the valid insurance policy.

Question 5: Does the term "insured," as used on Form MCS–90, Endorsement for Motor Carrier Policies of Insurance for Public Liability, or "Principal", as used on Form MCS–82, Motor Carrier Liability Surety Bond, mean the motor carrier named in the endorsement or surety bond?

Guidance: Yes. Under 49 CFR 387.5, "insured and principal" is defined as "the motor carrier named in the policy of insurance, surety bond, endorsement, or notice of cancellation, and also the fiduciary of such motor carrier." Form MCS–90 and Form MCS–82 are not intended, and do not purport, to require a motor carrier's insurer or surety to satisfy a judgment against any party other than the carrier named in the endorsement or surety bond or its fiduciary.

§387.17 Violation and penalty.

Any person (except an employee who acts without knowledge) who knowingly violates the rules of this subpart shall be liable to the United States for civil penalty of no more than $11,000 for each violation, and if any such violation is a continuing one, each day of violation will constitute a separate offense. The amount of any such penalty shall be assessed by the FMCSA's Administrator, by written notice. In determining the amount of such penalty, the Administrator, or his/her authorized delegate shall take into account the nature, circumstances, extent, the gravity of the violation committed and, with respect to the person found to have committed such violation, the degree of culpability, any history of prior offenses, ability to pay, effect on ability to continue to do business, and such other matters as justice may require.

Subpart B - Motor Carriers of Passengers

§387.25 Purpose and scope.

This subpart prescribes the minimum levels of financial responsibility required to be maintained by for-hire motor carriers of passengers operating motor vehicles in interstate or foreign commerce. The purpose of these regulations is to create additional incentives to carriers to operate their vehicles in a safe manner and to assure that they maintain adequate levels of financial responsibility.

Subpart B - Motor Carriers of Passengers §387.31 (e)

§387.25 DOT Interpretations
Question 1: May a State require a higher level of financial responsibility coverage than is required by Part 387?
Guidance: Yes.

§387.27 Applicability.
(a) **This subpart applies** to for-hire motor carriers transporting passengers in interstate or foreign commerce.
(b) **Exception.** The rules in this subpart do not apply to —
 (1) *A motor vehicle transporting only school children and teachers* to or from school;
 (2) *A motor vehicle providing taxicab service* and having a seating capacity of less than 7 passengers and not operated on a regular route or between specified points;
 (3) *A motor vehicle carrying less than 16 individuals* in a single daily round trip to commute to and from work; and
 (4) *A motor vehicle operated by a motor carrier* under contract providing transportation of preprimary, primary, and secondary students for extracurricular trips organized, sponsored, and paid by a school district.

§387.27 DOT Interpretations
Question 1: Is a nonprofit corporation, providing for-hire interstate transportation of passengers, subject to the minimum levels of financial responsibility for motor carriers of passengers?
Guidance: Yes.
Question 2: What determines the level of coverage required for a passenger carrier: the number of passengers or the number of seats in the vehicle?
Guidance: The level of financial responsibility required is predicated upon the manufacturer's designed seating capacity, not on the number of passengers riding in the vehicle at a particular time. The minimum levels of financial responsibility required for various seating capacities are found in §387.33.
Question 3: Are luxury limousines with a seating capacity of fewer than seven passengers and not operated on a regular route or between specified points exempted under §387.27(b)(2)?
Guidance: No. Taxi cab service is highly regulated by local governments, usually conducted in marked vehicles, which makes them readily identifiable to enforcement officials. Limousines are not taxi cabs and are therefore not exempted from the financial responsibility requirements.
Question 4: When must a contract school bus operator comply with Part 387?
Guidance: When the contractor is not engaged in transportation to or from school and the transportation is not organized, sponsored, and paid for by the school district.
Question 5: Does the exemption for the transportation of school children end at the high school level or does it extend to educational institutions beyond high school, for example junior college or college?
Guidance: The exemption does not extend beyond the high school level.
Question 6: Do the financial responsibility requirements of Subpart B of Part 387 apply to school buses used by the federal government of Mexico to transport students on field trips to the United States?
Guidance: No. The financial responsibility requirements of Subpart B are only applicable to for-hire motor carriers transporting passengers in interstate or foreign commerce.

§387.29 Definitions.
As used in this subpart —

Accident includes continuous or repeated exposure to the same conditions resulting in public liability which the insured neither expected nor intended.

Bodily injury means injury to the body, sickness, or disease including death resulting from any of these.

Endorsement — an amendment to an insurance policy.

Financial responsibility — the financial reserves (e.g., insurance policies or surety bonds) sufficient to satisfy liability amounts set forth in this subpart covering public liability.

For-hire carriage means the business of transporting, for compensation, passengers and their property, including any compensated transportation of the goods or property or another.

Insured and principal — the motor carrier named in the policy of insurance, surety bond, endorsement, or notice of cancellation, and also the fiduciary of such motor carrier.

Insurance premium — the monetary sum an insured pays an insurer for acceptance of liability for public liability claims made against the insured.

Motor carrier means a for-hire motor carrier. The term includes, but is not limited to, a motor carrier's agent, officer, or representative; an employee responsible for hiring, supervising, training, assigning, or dispatching a driver; or an employee concerned with the installation, inspection, and maintenance of motor vehicle equipment and/or accessories.

Property damage means damage to or loss of use of tangible property.

Public liability — liability for bodily injury or property damage.

Seating capacity — any plan view location capable of accommodating a person at least as large as a 5th percentile adult female, if the overall seat configuration and design and vehicle design is such that the position is likely to be used as a seating position while the vehicle is in motion, except for auxiliary seating accommodations such as temporary or folding jump seats. Any bench or split bench seat in a passenger car, truck or multi-purpose passenger vehicle with a gross vehicle weight rating less than 10,000 pounds, having greater than 50 inches of hip room (measured in accordance with SEA Standards J1100(a)) shall have not less than three designated seating positions, unless the seat design or vehicle design is such that the center position cannot be used for seating.

§387.31 Financial responsibility required.
(a) **No motor carrier shall operate a motor vehicle** transporting passengers until the motor carrier has obtained and has in effect the minimum levels of financial responsibility as set forth in §387.33 of this subpart.
(b) **Policies of insurance, surety bonds, and endorsements** required under this section shall remain in effect continuously until terminated.
 (1) *Cancellation may be effected* by the insurer or the insured motor carrier giving 35 days notice in writing to the other. The 35 days notice shall commence to run from the date the notice is mailed. Proof of mailing shall be sufficient proof of notice.
 (2) *Exception.* Policies of insurance and surety bonds may be obtained for a finite period of time to cover any lapse in continuous compliance.
 (3) *Exception.* Mexican motor carriers may meet the minimum financial responsibility requirements of this subpart by obtaining insurance coverage, in the required amounts, for periods of 24 hours or longer, from insurers that meet the requirements of §387.35 of this subpart. A Mexican motor carrier so insured must have available for inspection in each of its vehicles copies of the following documents:
  (i) *The required insurance endorsement (Form MCS-90B);* and
  (ii) *An insurance identification card,* binder, or other document issued by an authorized insurer which specifies both the effective date and the expiration date of the temporary insurance coverage authorized by this exception.
 Mexican motor carriers insured under this exception are also exempt from the notice of cancellation requirements stated on Form MCS-90B.
(c) **Policies of insurance and surety bonds** required under this section may be replaced by other policies of insurance or surety bonds. The liability of retiring insurer or surety, as to events after the termination date, shall be considered as having terminated on the effective date of the replacement policy of insurance or surety bond or at the end or the 35 day cancellation period required in paragraph (b) of this section, whichever is sooner.
(d) **Proof of the required financial responsibility** shall be maintained at the motor carrier's principal place of business. The proof shall consist of —
 (1) *"Endorsement(s) for Motor Carriers* of Passengers Policies of Insurance for Public Liability Under Section 18 of the Bus Regulatory Reform Act of 1982" (Form MCS-90B) issued by an insurer(s); or
 (2) *A "Motor Carrier of Passengers Surety Bond* for Public Liability Under Section 18 of the Bus Regulatory Reform Act of 1982" (Form MCS-82B) issued by a surety.
(e) **The proof of minimum levels of financial responsibility** required by this section shall be considered public information and be produced for review upon reasonable request by a member of the public.

235

(f) All passenger carrying vehicles operated within the United States by motor carriers domiciled in a contiguous foreign country, shall have on board the vehicle a legible copy, in English, of the proof of the required financial responsibility (Forms MCS-90B or MCS-82B) used by the motor carrier to comply with paragraph (d) of this section.

(g) Any motor vehicle in which there is no evidence of financial responsibility required by paragraph (f) of this section shall be denied entry into the United States.

§387.31 DOT Interpretations

Question 1: May a large corporation which has many wholly-owned subsidiaries have one policy of insurance for the parent corporation and maintain the policy and Form MCS-90B at the corporate headquarters?

Guidance: Generally, the required financial responsibility must be in the exact name of the motor carrier and the proof of that coverage must be maintained at the motor carrier's principal place of business. A parent corporation may, however, have a single policy of insurance or surety bond covering the parent and its subsidiaries, provided the name of the parent and the name of each subsidiary are listed on the policy or bond. Further, the required proof must have listed thereon the name of the parent and its subsidiaries. A copy of that proof of financial responsibility coverage must be maintained at each motor carrier subsidiary's principal place of business.

§387.33 Financial responsibility, minimum levels.

The minimum levels of financial responsibility referred to in §387.31 of this subpart are hereby prescribed as follows:

Schedule of Limits
Public Liability

For-hire motor carriers of passengers operating in interstate or foreign commerce.

Vehicle Seating Capacity	Effective Dates	
	Nov. 19, 1983	Nov. 19, 1985
(1) Any vehicle with a seating capacity of 16 passengers or more	$2,500,000	$5,000,000
(2) Any vehicle with a seating capacity of 15 passengers or less[1]	$750,000	$1,500,000

1. Except as provided in §387.27(b)

§387.35 State authority and designation of agent.

A policy of insurance or surety bond does not satisfy the financial responsibility requirements of this subpart unless the insurer or surety furnishing the policy or bond is —

(a) Legally authorized to issue such policies or bonds in each State in which the motor carrier operates, or

(b) Legally authorized to issue such policies or bonds in the State in which the motor carrier has its principal place of business or domicile, and is willing to designate a person upon whom process, issued by or under the authority of any court having jurisdiction of the subject matter, may be served in any proceeding at law or equity brought in any State in which the motor carrier operates; or

(c) Legally authorized to issue such policies or bonds in any State of the United States and eligible as an excess or surplus lines insurer in any State in which business is written, and is willing to designate a person upon whom process, issued by or under the authority of any court having jurisdiction of the subject matter, may be served in any proceeding at law or equity brought in any State in which the motor carrier operates.

§387.37 Fiduciaries.

The coverage of fiduciaries shall attach at the moment of succession of such fiduciaries.

§387.39 Forms.

Endorsements for policies of insurance (Illustration I) and surety bonds (Illustration II) must be in the form prescribed by the FMCSA and approved by the OMB. Endorsements to policies of insurance and surety bonds shall specify that coverage thereunder will remain in effect continuously until terminated, as required in §387.31 of this subpart. The continuous coverage requirement does not apply to Mexican motor carriers insured under §387.31(b)(3) of this subpart. The endorsement and surety bond shall be issued in the exact name of the motor carrier.

(Approved by the Office of Management and Budget under control number 2125-0518).

* Full-size forms available free of charge at www.dotcfr.com.

* Full-size forms available free of charge at www.dotcfr.com.

Subpart C - Surety Bonds and Policies of Insurance for Motor Carriers and Property Brokers §387.301 (b)

Full-size forms available free of charge at www.dotcfr.com.

§387.39 DOT Interpretations

Question 1: May a motor carrier of passengers meet the financial responsibility requirements by aggregating insurance in layers?

Guidance: Yes. A motor carrier of passengers may aggregate coverage, by purchasing insurance in layers with each layer consisting of a separate policy and endorsement. The first layer of coverage is referred to as primary insurance and each additional layer is referred to as excess insurance. Each policy would have a separate endorsement (Form MCS-90B). The endorsement provided by insurer A would state "This insurance is primary and the company shall not be liable for amounts in excess of $1,500,000 or $5,000,000 for each accident." The endorsement provided by insurer B would state "This insurance is excess and the company shall not be liable for amounts in excess of $1 million for each accident in excess of the underlying limit of $1,500,000 or $5,000,000 million for each accident." The endorsement provided by insurer C would state "This insurance is excess and the company shall not be liable for amounts in excess of $3 million for each accident in excess of the underlying limit of $2 million for each accident."

Question 2: May the Form MCS-90B required by Part 387 for proof of minimum financial responsibility be modified?

Guidance: The prescribed text of the document may not be changed. However, the format (i.e., number of pages, layout of the text, etc.) may be altered.

Question 3: Is the use of a facsimile signature (e.g., printed, stamped, autopenned, etc.) on the Form MCS-90B endorsement acceptable?

Guidance: Yes.

Question 4: Does the term "insured," as used on Form MCS-90B, Endorsement for Motor Carrier Policies of Insurance for Public Liability, or "Principal", as used on Form MCS-82B, Motor Carrier Liability Surety Bond, mean the motor carrier named in the endorsement or surety bond?

Question 4: Does the term "insured," as used on Form MCS-90B, Endorsement for Motor Carrier Policies of Insurance for Public Liability, or "Principal", as used on Form MCS-82B, Motor Carrier Liability Surety Bond, mean the motor carrier named in the endorsement or surety bond?

Guidance: Yes. Under 49 CFR 387.29, "insured and principal" is defined as "the motor carrier named in the policy of insurance, surety bond, endorsement, or notice of cancellation, and also the fiduciary of such motor carrier." Form MCS-90B and Form MCS-82B are not intended, and do not purport, to require a motor carrier's insurer or surety to satisfy a judgment against any party other than the carrier named in the endorsement or surety bond or its fiduciary.

§387.41 Violation and penalty.

Any person (except an employee who acts without knowledge) who knowingly violates the rules of this subpart shall be liable to the United States for civil penalty of no more than $11,000 for each violation, and if any such violation is a continuing one, each day of violation will constitute a separate offense. The amount of any such penalty shall be assessed by the Administrator or his/her designee, by written notice. In determining the amount of such penalty, the Administrator or his/her designee shall take into account the nature, circumstances, extent, the gravity of the violation committed and, with respect to the person found to have committed such violation, the degree of culpability, any history of prior offenses, ability to pay, effect on ability to continue to do business, and such other matters as justice may require.

Subpart C - Surety Bonds and Policies of Insurance for Motor Carriers and Property Brokers

§387.301 Surety bond, certificate of insurance, or other securities.

(a) Public liability.

(1) *No common or contract carrier* or foreign (Mexican) motor private carrier or foreign motor carrier transporting exempt commodities subject to Subtitle IV, Part B, Chapter 135 of Title 49 of the United States Code shall engage in interstate or foreign commerce, and no certificate or permit shall be issued to such a carrier or remain in force unless and until there shall have been filed with and accepted by the FMCSA surety bonds, and certificates of insurance, proof of qualifications as self-insurer, or other securities or agreements, in the amounts prescribed in §387.303, conditioned to pay any final judgment recovered against such motor carrier for bodily injuries to or the death of any person resulting from the negligent operation, maintenance or use of motor vehicles in transportation subject to Subtitle IV, Part B, Chapter 135 of Title 49 of the U.S. Code, or for loss of or damage to property of others, or, in the case of motor carriers of property operating freight vehicles described in §387.303(b)(2) of this part, for environmental restoration.

(2) *Motor Carriers of property* which are subject to the conditions set forth in paragraph (a)(1) of this section and transport the commodities described in §387.303(b)(2), are required to obtain security in the minimum limits prescribed in §387.303(b)(2).

(b) Common carriers — cargo insurance; exempt commodities. No common carrier by motor vehicle subject to Subtitle IV, Part B, Chapter 135 of Title 49 of the U.S. Code, nor any foreign (Mexican) common carrier of exempt commodities shall engage in interstate or foreign commerce, nor shall any certificate be issued to such a carrier or remain in force unless and until there shall have been filed with and accepted by the FMCSA, a surety bond, certificate of insurance, proof of qualifications as a self-insurer, or other securities or agreements in the amounts prescribed in §387.303, conditioned upon such carrier making compensation to shippers or consignees for all property belonging to shippers or consignees and coming into the possession of such carrier in connection with its transportation service: Provided, That the requirements of this paragraph shall not apply in connection with the transportation of the following commodities:

Agricultural ammonium nitrate.

Agricultural nitrate of soda.

Anhydrous ammonia — used as a fertilizer only.
Ashes, wood or coal.
Bituminous concrete (also known as blacktop or amosite), including mixtures of asphalt paving.
Cement, dry, in containers or in bulk.
Cement, building blocks.
Charcoal.
Chemical fertilizer.
Cinder blocks.
Cinders, coal.
Coal.
Coke.
Commercial fertilizer.
Concrete materials and added mixtures.
Corn cobs.
Cottonseed hulls.
Crushed stone.
Drilling salt.
Dry fertilizer.
Fish scrap.
Fly ash.
Forest products; viz: Logs, billets, or bolts, native woods, Canadian wood or Mexican pine; pulpwood, fuel wood, wood kindling; and wood sawdust or shavings (shingle tow) other than jewelers' or paraffined.
Foundry and factory sweepings.
Garbage.
Gravel, other than bird gravel.
Hardwood and parquet flooring.
Haydite.
Highway construction materials, when transported in dump trucks and unloaded at destination by dumping.
Ice.
Iron ore.
Lime and limestone.
Liquid fertilizer solutions, in bulk, in tank vehicles.
Lumber.
Manure.
Meat scraps.
Mud drilling salt.
Ores, in bulk, including ore concentrates.
Paving materials, unless contain oil hauled in tank vehicles.
Peat moss.
Peeler cores.
Plywood.
Poles and piling, other than totem poles.
Potash, used as commercial fertilizer.
Pumice stone, in bulk in dump vehicles.
Salt, in bulk or in bags.
Sand, other than asbestos, bird, iron, monazite, processed, or tobacco sand.
Sawdust.
Scoria stone.
Scrap iron.
Scrap steel.
Shells, clam, mussel, or oyster.
Slag, other than slag with commercial value for the further extraction of metals.
Slag, derived aggregates — cinders.
Slate, crushed or scrap.
Slurry, as waste material.
Soil, earth or marl, other than infusorial, diatomaceous, tripoli, or inoculated soil or earth.
Stone, unglazed and unmanufactured, including ground agricultural limestone.
Sugar beet pulp.
Sulphate of ammonia, bulk, used as fertilizer.
Surfactants.
Trap rock.
Treated poles.
Veneer.
Volcanic scoria.
Waste, hazardous and nonhazardous, transported solely for purposes of disposal.
Water, other than mineral or prepared water.
Wood chips, not processed.
Wooden pallets, unassembled.
Wrecked or disabled motor vehicles.
Other materials or commodities of low value, upon specific application to and approval by the FMCSA.

(c) **Continuing compliance required.** Such security as is accepted by the FMCSA in accordance with the requirements of Section 13906 of Title 49 of the U.S. Code shall remain in effect at all times.

§387.303 **Security for the protection of the public: Minimum limits.**

(a) **Definitions:**
  (1) **Primary security** means public liability coverage provided by the insurance or surety company responsible for the first dollar of coverage.
  (2) **Excess security** means public liability coverage above the primary security, or above any additional underlying security, up to and including the required minimum limits set forth in paragraph (b)(2) of this section.

(b) (1) *Motor carriers subject to §387.301(a)(1) are required to have security for the required minimum limits as follows:*
  (i) *Small Freight Vehicles:*

Kind of equipment	Transportation provided	Minimum limits
Fleet including only vehicles under 10,000 pounds GVWR.	Commodities not subject to §387.303(b)(2).	$300,000

  (ii) *Passenger Carriers:*

Kind of Equipment		
Vehicle Seating Capacity	Effective Dates	
	Nov. 19, 1983	Nov. 19, 1985
(1) Any vehicle with a seating capacity of 16 passengers or more.	$2,500,000	$5,000,000
(2) Any vehicle with a seating capacity of 15 passengers or less.	$750,000	$1,500,000

(2) *Motor carriers subject to §387.301(a)(2) are required to have security for the required minimum limits as follows:*

Kind of equipment	Commodity transported	July 1, 1983[1]	July 1, 1984[1]
(a) Freight Vehicles of 10,001 Pounds or More GVWR.	Property (non-hazardous).	$500,000	$750,000
(b) Freight Vehicles of 10,001 Pounds or More GVWR.	Hazardous substances, as defined in §171.8, transported in cargo tanks, portable tanks, or hopper-type vehicles with capacities in excess of 3,500 water gallons, or in bulk Class A or B explosives, poison gas (Poison A) liquefied compressed gas or compressed gas, or highway route controlled quantity radioactive materials as defined in §173.455.	$1,000,000	$5,000,000

Subpart C - Surety Bonds and Policies of Insurance for Motor Carriers and Property Brokers §387.309 (a)

Kind of equipment	Commodity transported	July 1, 1983[1]	July 1, 1984[1]
(c) Freight Vehicles of 10,001 Pounds or More GVWR.	Oil listed in §172.101; hazardous waste, hazardous materials and hazardous substances defined in §171.8 and listed in §172.101, but not mentioned in (b) above or (d) below.	$500,000	$1,000,000
(d) Freight Vehicles Under 10,001 Pounds GVWR.	Any quantity of Class A or B explosives; any quantity of poison gas (Poison A); or highway route controlled quantity radioactive materials as defined in §173.455.	$1,000,000	$5,000,000

1. The effective date of the current required minimum limit in §387.303(b)(2) was January 6, 1983, in accordance with the requirements of Pub. L 97-424, 96 Stat. 2097.

(3) *Motor carriers subject to the minimum limits* governed by this section, which are also subject to Department of Transportation limits requirements, are at no time required to have security for more than the required minimum limits established by the Secretary of Transportation in the applicable provisions of 49 CFR Part 387 — Minimum Levels of Financial Responsibility for Motor Carriers.

(4) *Foreign motor carriers* and foreign motor private carriers. Foreign motor carriers and foreign motor private carriers (Mexican), subject to the requirements of 49 U.S.C. 13902(c) and 49 CFR Part 368 regarding obtaining certificates of registration from the FMCSA, must meet our minimum financial responsibility requirements by obtaining insurance coverage, in the required amounts, for periods of 24 hours or longer, from insurance or surety companies, that meet the requirements of 49 CFR 387.315. These carriers must have available for inspection, in each vehicle operating in the United States, copies of the following documents:
  (i) *The certificate of registration;*
  (ii) *The required insurance endorsement (Form MCS-90); and*
  (iii) *An insurance identification card,* binder, or other document issued by an authorized insurer which specifies both the effective date and the expiration date of the insurance coverage.

Notwithstanding the provisions of §387.301(a)(1), the filing of evidence of insurance is not required as a condition to the issuance of a certificate of registration. Further, the reference to continuous coverage at §387.313(a)(6) and the reference to cancellation notice at §387.313(d) are not applicable to these carriers.

(c) **Motor common carriers: Cargo liability.** Security required to compensate shippers or consignees for loss damage to property belonging to shippers or consignees and coming into the possession of motor carriers in connection with their transportation service:
  (1) *for loss of or damage to property carried* on any one motor vehicle — $5,000,
  (2) *for loss of or damage to* or aggregate of losses or damages of or to property occurring at any one time and place — $10,000.

§387.305 Combination vehicles.
The following combinations will be regarded as one motor vehicle for purposes of this part, (a) a tractor and trailer or semitrailer when the tractor is engaged solely in drawing the trailer or semitrailer, and (b) a truck and trailer when both together bear a single load.

§387.307 Property broker surety bond or trust fund.
(a) **Security.** A property broker must have a surety bond or trust fund in effect for $10,000. The FMCSA will not issue a property broker license until a surety bond or trust fund for the full limits of liability prescribed herein is in effect. The broker license shall remain valid or effective only as long as a surety bond or trust fund remains in effect and shall ensure the financial responsibility of the broker.
(b) **Evidence of Security.** Evidence of a surety bond must be filed using the FMCSA's prescribed Form BMC 84. Evidence of a trust fund with a financial institution must be filed using the FMCSA's prescribed Form BMC 85. The surety bond or the trust fund shall ensure the financial responsibility of the broker by providing for payments to shippers or motor carriers if the broker fails to carry out its contracts, agreements, or arrangements for the supplying of transportation by authorized motor carriers.
(c) **Financial Institution** — when used in this section and in forms prescribed under this section, where not otherwise distinctly expressed or manifestly incompatible with the intent thereof, shall mean — Each agent, agency, branch or office within the United States of any person, as defined by the ICC Termination Act, doing business in one or more of the capacities listed below:
  (1) *An insured bank* (as defined in section 3(h) of the Federal Deposit Insurance Act (12 U.S.C. 1813(h));
  (2) *A commercial bank or trust company;*
  (3) *An agency or branch of a foreign bank in the United States;*
  (4) *An insured institution* (as defined in section 401(a) of the National Housing Act (12 U.S.C. 1724(a));
  (5) *A thrift institution* (savings bank, building and loan association, credit union, industrial bank or other);
  (6) *An insurance company;*
  (7) *A loan or finance company;* or
  (8) *A person subject to supervision* by any state or federal bank supervisory authority.
(d) **Forms and Procedures.**
  (1) *Forms for broker surety bonds* and trust agreements. Form BMC-84 broker surety bond will be filed with the FMCSA for the full security limits under subsection (a); or Form BMC-85 broker trust fund agreement will be filed with the FMCSA for the full security limits under paragraph (a) of this section.
  (2) *Broker surety bonds and trust fund agreements* in effect continuously. Surety bonds and trust fund agreements shall specify that coverage thereunder will remain in effect continuously until terminated as herein provided.
    (i) *Cancellation notice.* The surety bond and the trust fund agreement may be cancelled as only upon 30 days written notice to the FMCSA, on prescribed Form BMC 36, by the principal or surety for the surety bond, and on prescribed Form BMC 85, by the trustor/broker or trustee for the trust fund agreement. The notice period commences upon the actual receipt of the notice at the FMCSA's Washington, DC office.
    (ii) *Termination by replacement.* Broker surety bonds or trust fund agreements which have been accepted by the FMCSA under these rules may be replaced by other surety bonds or trust fund agreements, and the liability of the retiring surety or trustee under such surety bond or trust fund agreements shall be considered as having terminated as of the effective date of the replacement surety bond or trust fund agreement. However, such termination shall not affect the liability of the surety or the trustee hereunder for the payment of any damages arising as the result of contracts, agreements or arrangements made by the broker for the supplying of transportation prior to the date such termination becomes effective.
  (3) *Filing and copies.* Broker surety bonds and trust fund agreements must be filed with the FMCSA in duplicate.

§387.309 Qualifications as a self-insurer and other securities or agreements.
(a) **As a self-insurer.** The FMCSA will consider and will approve, subject to appropriate and reasonable conditions, the application of a motor carrier to qualify as a self-insurer, if the carrier furnishes a true and accurate statement of its financial condition and other evidence that establishes to the satisfaction of the FMCSA the ability of the motor carrier to satisfy its obligation for bodily injury liability, property damage liability, or cargo liability. Application Guidelines: In addition to filing Form BMC 40, applicants for authority to self-insure against bodily injury and property damage claims should submit evidence that will allow the FMCSA to determine:
  (1) *The adequacy of the tangible net worth* of the motor carrier in relation to the size of operations and the extent of its request for self-insurance authority. Applicant should demonstrate that it will maintain a net worth that will ensure that it will be able to meet its statutory obligations to the public to indemnify all claimants in the event of loss.
  (2) *The existence* of a sound self-insurance program. Applicant should demonstrate that it has established, and will maintain, an insurance program that will protect the public against all claims to the same extent as the minimum security limits applicable to applicant under §387.303 of this part. Such a program may include, but not be limited to, one or more of the following: irrevocable letters of credit; irrevocable trust funds; reserves; sinking funds; third party financial guarantees, parent company

or affiliate sureties; excess insurance coverage; or other similar arrangements.

(3) *The existence of an adequate safety program.* Applicant must submit evidence of a current "satisfactory" safety rating by the United States Department of Transportation. Non-rated carriers need only certify that they have not been rated. Applications by carriers with a less than satisfactory rating will be summarily denied. Any self-insurance authority granted by the FMCSA will automatically expire 30 days after a carrier receives a less than satisfactory rating from DOT.

(4) *Additional information.* Applicant must submit such additional information to support its application as the FMCSA may require.

(b) **Other securities or agreements.** The FMCSA also will consider applications for approval of other securities or agreements and will approve any such application if satisfied that the security or agreement offered will afford the security for protection of the public contemplated by 49 U.S.C. 13906.

§387.311 Bonds and certificates of insurance.

(a) **Public liability.** Each Form BMC 82 surety bond filed with the FMCSA must be for the full limits of liability required under §387.303(b)(1). Form MCS-82 surety bonds and other forms of similar import prescribed by the Department of Transportation, may be aggregated to comply with the minimum security limits required under §387.303(b)(1) or §387.303(b)(2). Each Form BMC 91 certificate of insurance filed with the FMCSA will always represent the full security minimum limits required for the particular carrier, while it remains in force, under §387.303(b)(1) or §387.303(b)(2), whichever is applicable. Any previously executed Form BMC 91 filed before the current revision which is left on file with the FMCSA after the effective date of this regulation, and not canceled within 30 days of that date will be deemed to certify the same coverage limits as would the filing of a revised Form BMC 91. Each Form BMC 91X certificate of insurance filed with the FMCSA will represent the full security limits under §387.303(b)(1) or §387.303(b)(2) or the specific security limits of coverage as indicated on the face of the form. If the filing reflects aggregation, the certificate must show clearly whether the insurance is primary or, if excess coverage, the amount of underlying coverage as well as amount of the maximum limits of coverage.[1] Each Form BMC 91MX certificate of insurance filed with the FMCSA will represent the security limits of coverage as indicated on the face of the form. The Form BMC 91MX must show clearly whether the insurance is primary or, if excess coverage, the amount of underlying coverage as well as amount of the maximum limits of coverage.

(b) **Cargo liability.** Each Form BMC 83 surety bond filed with the FMCSA must be for the full limits of liability required under §387.303(c). Each Form BMC 34 certificate of insurance filed with the FMCSA will represent the full security limits under §387.303(c) or the specific security limits of coverage as indicated on the face of the form. If the filing reflects aggregation, the certificate must show clearly whether the insurance is primary or, if excess coverage, the amount of underlying coverage as well as amount of the maximum limits of coverage.

(c) **Each policy of insurance** in connection with the certificate of insurance which is filed with the FMCSA, shall be amended by attachment of the appropriate endorsement prescribed by the FMCSA and the certificate of insurance filed must accurately reflect that endorsement.

§387.313 Forms and procedures.

(a) **Forms for endorsements, certificates of insurance and others.**

(1) *In form prescribed.* Endorsements for policies of insurance and surety bonds, certificates of insurance, applications to qualify as a self-insurer, or for approval of other securities or agreements, and notices of cancellation must be in the form prescribed and approved by the FMCSA.

(2) *Aggregation of Insurance.*[2] When insurance is provided by more than one insurer in order to aggregate security limits for carriers operating only freight vehicles under 10,000 pounds Gross Vehicle Weight Rating, as defined in §387.303(b)(1), a separate Form BMC 90, with the specific amounts of underlying and limits of coverage shown thereon or appended thereto, and Form BMC 91X certificate is required of each insurer.

For aggregation of insurance for all other carriers to cover security limits under §387.303(b)(1) or (b)(2), a separate Department of Transportation prescribed form endorsement and Form BMC 91X certificate is required of each insurer. When insurance is provided by more than one insurer to aggregate coverage for security limits under §387.303(c) a separate Form BMC 32 endorsement and Form BMC 34 certificate of insurance is required for each insurer.

For aggregation of insurance for foreign motor private carriers of nonhazardous commodities to cover security limits under §387.303(b)(4), a separate Form BMC 90 with the specific amounts of underlying and limits of coverage shown thereon or appended thereto, or Department of Transportation prescribed form endorsement, and Form BMC 91MX certificate is required for each insurer.

(3) *Use of Certificates and Endorsements in BMC Series.* — Form BMC 91 certificates of insurance will be filed with the FMCSA for the full security limits under §387.303(b)(1) or (b)(2).

Form BMC 91X certificate of insurance will be filed to represent full coverage or any level of aggregation for the security limits under §387.303(b)(1) or (b)(2).

Form BMC 90 endorsement will be used with each filing of Form BMC 91 or Form BMC 91X certificate with the FMCSA which certifies to coverage not governed by the requirements of the Department of Transportation.

Form BMC 32 endorsement and Form BMC 34 certificate of insurance and Form BMC 83 surety bonds are used for the limits of cargo liability under §387.303(c).

Form BMC 91MX certificate of insurance will be filed to represent any level of aggregation for the security limits under §387.303(b)(4).

(4) *Use of Endorsements in MCS Series.* When Security limits certified under §387.303(b)(1) or (b)(2) involves coverage also required by the Department of Transportation a Form MCS endorsement prescribed by the Department of Transportation such as, and including, the Form MCS 90 endorsement is required.

(5) *Surety bonds.* When surety bonds are used rather than certificates of insurance, Form BMC 82 is required for the security limits under §387.303(b)(1) not subject to regulation by the Department of Transportation, and Form MCS 82, or any form of similar import prescribed by the Department of Transportation, is used for the security limits subject also to minimum coverage requirements of the Department of Transportation.

(6) *Surety bonds and certificates in effect continuously.* Surety bonds and certificates of insurance shall specify that coverage thereunder will remain in effect: continuously until terminated as herein provided, except (1) when filed expressly to fill prior gaps or lapses in coverage or to cover grants of emergency temporary authority of unusually short duration and the filing clearly so indicates, or (2) in special or unusual circumstances, when special permission is obtained for filing certificates of insurance or surety bonds on terms meeting other particular needs of the situation.

(b) **Filing and copies.** Certificates of insurance, surety bonds, and notices of cancellation must be filed with the FMCSA in triplicate.

(c) **Name of insured.** Certificates of insurance and surety bonds shall be issued in the full and correct name of the individual, partnership, corporation or other person to whom the certificate, permit, or license is, or is to be, issued. In the case of a partnership, all partners shall be named.

(d) **Cancellation notice.** Except as provided in paragraph (e) of this section, surety bonds, certificates of insurance and other securities or agreements shall not be cancelled or withdrawn until 30 days after written notice has been submitted to the FMCSA at its offices in Washington, DC, on the prescribed form (Form BMC-35, Notice of Cancellation Motor Carrier Policies of Insurance under 49 U.S.C. 13906, and BMC-36, Notice of Cancellation Motor Carrier and Broker Surety Bonds, as appropriate) by the insurance company, surety or sureties, motor carrier, broker or other party thereto, as the case may be, which period of thirty (30) days shall commence to run from the date such notice on the prescribed form is actually received by the FMCSA.

(e) **Termination by replacement.** Certificates of insurance or surety bonds which have been accepted by the FMCSA under these rules may be replaced by other certificates of insurance, surety bonds or

---

1. Aggregation to meet the requirements of §387.303(b)(1) will not be allowed until the completion of our rulemaking in Ex Parte No. MC-5 (Sub-No. 2), *Motor Carrier and Freight Forwarder Insurance Procedures and Minimum Amounts of Liability.*
2. See footnote for Rule 387.311. Also, it should be noted that DOT is considering prescribing adaptions of the Form MCS 90 endorsement and the Form MCS 82 surety bond for use by passenger carriers and Rules §§387.311 and 387.313 have been written sufficiently broad to provide for this contingency when new forms are prescribed by that Agency.

Subpart C - Surety Bonds and Policies of Insurance for Motor Carriers and Property Brokers §387.323 (c)

other security, and the liability of the retiring insurer or surety under such certificates of insurance or surety bonds shall be considered as having terminated as of the effective date of the replacement certificate of insurance, surety bond or other security, provided the said replacement certificate, bond or other security is acceptable to the FMCSA under the rules and regulations in this part.

§387.315 Insurance and surety companies.

A certificate of insurance or surety bond will not be accepted by the FMCSA unless issued by an insurance or surety company that is authorized (licensed or admitted) to issue bonds or underlying insurance policies:

(a) **In each state in which the motor carrier** is authorized by the FMCSA to operate, or

(b) **In the state in which the motor carrier** has its principal place of business or domicile, and will designate in writing upon request by the FMCSA, a person upon whom process, issued by or under the authority of a court of competent jurisdiction, may be served in any proceeding at law or equity brought in any state in which the carrier operates, or

(c) **In any state,** and is eligible as an excess or surplus lines insurer in any state in which business is written, and will make the designation of process agent described in paragraph (b) of this section.

§387.317 Refusal to accept, or revocation by the FMCSA of surety bonds, etc.

The FMCSA may, at any time, refuse to accept or may revoke its acceptance of any surety bond, certificate of insurance, qualifications as a self-insurer, surety or other securities or agreements if, in its judgment such security does not comply with these sections or for any reason fails to provide satisfactory or adequate protection for the public. Revocation of acceptance of any certificate of insurance, surety bond or other security shall not relieve the motor carrier from compliance with §387.301(d).

§387.319 Fiduciaries.

(a) **Definitions.** The terms "insured" and "principal" as used in a certificate of insurance, surety bond, and notice of cancellation, filed by or for a motor carrier, include the motor carrier and its fiduciary as of the moment of succession. The term "fiduciary" means any person authorized by law to collect and preserve property of incapacitated, financially disabled, bankrupt, or deceased holders of operating rights, and assignees of such holders.

(b) **Insurance coverage in behalf of fiduciaries** to apply concurrently. The coverage furnished under the provisions of this section on behalf of fiduciaries shall not apply subsequent to the effective date of other insurance, or other security, filed with and approved by the FMCSA in behalf of such fiduciaries. After the coverage provided in this section shall have been in effect thirty (30) days, it may be cancelled or withdrawn within the succeeding period of thirty (30) days by the insurer, the insured, the surety, or the principal upon ten (10) days notice in writing to the FMCSA at its office in Washington, DC, which period of ten (10) days shall commence to run from the date such notice is actually received by the FMCSA. After such coverage has been in effect for a total of sixty (60) days, it may be cancelled or withdrawn only in accordance with §1043.7.

§387.321 Operations in foreign commerce.

No motor carrier may operate in the United States in the course of transportation between places in a foreign country or between a place in one foreign country and a place in another foreign country unless and until there shall have been filed with and accepted by the FMCSA a certificate of insurance, surety bond, proof of qualifications as a self-insurer, or other securities or agreements in the amount prescribed in §387.303(b), conditioned to pay any final judgment recovered against such motor carrier for bodily injuries to or the death of any person resulting from the negligent operation, maintenance, or use of motor vehicles in transportation between places in a foreign country or between a place in one foreign country and a place in another foreign country, insofar as such transportation takes place in the United States, or for loss of or damage to property of others. The security for the protection of the public required by this section shall be maintained in effect at all times and shall be subject to the provisions of §§387.309 through 387.319. The requirements of §387.315(a) shall be satisfied if the insurance or surety company, in addition to having been approved by the FMCSA, is legally authorized to issue policies or surety bonds in at least one of the States in the United States, or one of the Provinces in Canada, and has filed with the FMCSA the name and address of a person upon whom legal process may be served in each State in or through which the motor carrier operates. Such designation may from time to time be changed by like designation similarly filed, but shall be maintained during the effectiveness of any certificate of insurance or surety bond issued by the company, and thereafter with respect to any claims arising during the effectiveness of such certificate or bond. The term "motor carrier" as used in this section shall not include private carriers or carriers operating under the partial exemption from regulation in 49 U.S.C. 13503 and 13506.

§387.323 Electronic filing of surety bonds, trust fund agreements, certificates of insurance and cancellations.

(a) **Insurers may, at their option and in accordance** with the requirements and procedures set forth in paragraphs (a) through (d) of this section, file forms BMC 34, BMC 35, BMC 36, BMC 82, BMC 83, BMC 84, BMC 85, BMC 91, and BMC 91X electronically, in lieu of using the prescribed printed forms.

(b) **Each insurer must obtain authorization** to file electronically by registering with the FMCSA. An individual account number and password for computer access will be issued to each registered insurer.

(c) **Filings may be transmitted online via the Internet** at: http://fhwa-li.volpe.dot.gov or via American Standard Code Information Interchange (ASCII). All ASCII transmission must be in fixed format, i.e., all records must have the same number of fields and same length. The record layouts for ASCII electronic transactions are described in the following table:

Electronic Insurance Filing Transactions

Field name	Number of positions	Description	Required F=filing C=cancel B=both	Start field	End field
Record type	1 Numeric	1 = Filing 2 = Cancellation	B	1	1
Insurer number	8 Text	FMCSA Assigned Insurer Number (Home Office) With Suffix (Issuing Office), If Different, e.g. 12345-01	B	2	9
Filing type	1 Numeric	1 = BI & PD 2 = Cargo 3 = Bond 4 = Trust Fund	B	10	10
FMCSA docket number	8 Text	FMCSA Assigned MC or FF Number, e.g., MC000045	B	11	18
Insured legal name	120 Text	Legal Name	B	19	138
Insured d/b/a name	60 Text	Doing Business As Name If Different From Legal Name	B	139	198
Insured address	35 Text	Either Street or Mailing Address	B	199	233
Insured city	30 Text		B	234	263
Insured state	2 Text		B	264	265
Insured zip code	9 Numeric	(Do Not Include Dash If Using 9 Digit Code)	B	266	274
Insured country	2 Text	(Will Default to US)	B	275	276
Form code	10 Text	BMC-91, BMC-91X, BMC-34, BMC-35, etc.	B	277	286
Full, primary or excess coverage	1 Text	If BMC-91X, P or E = Indicator of Primary or Excess Policy; 1 = Full under §387.303(b)(1); 2 = Full under §387.303(b)(2).	F	287	287

241

Electronic Insurance Filing Transactions (continued)

Field name	Number of positions	Description	Required F=filing C=cancel B=both	Start field	End field
Limit of liability	5 Numeric	$ in Thousands	F	288	292
Underlying limit of liability	5 Numeric	$ in Thousands (Will Default to $000 If Primary)	F	293	297
Effective date	8 Text	MM/DD/YY Format for Both Filing or Cancellation	B	298	305
Policy number	25 Text	Surety Companies May Enter Bond Number	B	306	330

(d) **All registered insurers agree to furnish** upon request to the FMCSA a duplicate original of any policy (or policies) and all endorsements, surety bond, trust fund agreement, or other filing.

Subpart D - Surety Bonds and Policies of Insurance for Freight Forwarders

§387.401 Definitions.

(a) **Freight forwarder** means a person holding itself out to the general public (other than as an express, pipeline, rail, sleeping car, motor, or water carrier) to provide transportation of property for compensation in interstate commerce, and in the ordinary course of its business:

(1) *Performs or provides* for assembling, consolidating, break-bulk, and distribution of shipments; and

(2) *Assumes responsibility for transportation* from place of receipt to destination; and

(3) *Uses for any part of the transportation* a carrier subject to FMCSA jurisdiction.

(b) **Household goods freight forwarder (HHGFF)** means a freight forwarder of household goods, unaccompanied baggage, or used automobiles.

(c) **Motor vehicle** means any vehicle, machine, tractor, trailer, or semi-trailer propelled or drawn by mechanical power and used to transport property, but does not include any vehicle, locomotive, or car operated exclusively on a rail or rails. The following combinations will be regarded as one motor vehicle:

(1) *A tractor that draws a trailer or semitrailer; and*

(2) *A truck and trailer bearing a single load.*

§387.403 General requirements.

(a) **Cargo.** A freight forwarder (including a HHGFF) may not operate until it has filed with the FMCSA an appropriate surety bond, certificate of insurance, qualifications as a self-insurer, or other securities or agreements, in the amounts prescribed at §387.405, for loss of or damage to property.

(b) **Public liability.** A HHGFF may not perform transfer, collection, and delivery service until it has filed with the FMCSA and appropriate surety bond, certificate of insurance, qualifications as a self-insurer, or other securities or agreements, in the amounts prescribed at §387.405, conditioned to pay any final judgment recovered against such HHGFF for bodily injury to or the death of any person, or loss of or damage to property (except cargo) of others, or, in the case of freight vehicles described at 49 CFR 387.303(b)(2), for environmental restoration, resulting from the negligent operation, maintenance, or use of motor vehicles operated by or under its control in performing such service.

§387.405 Limits of liability.

The minimum amounts for cargo and public liability security are identical to those prescribed for motor carriers at 49 CFR 387.303.

§387.407 Surety bonds and certificates of insurance.

(a) **The limits of liability under §387.405** may be provided by aggregation under the procedures at 49 CFR Part 387, Subpart C.

(b) **Each policy of insurance** used in connection with a certificate of insurance filed with the FMCSA shall be amended by attachment of the appropriate endorsement prescribed by the FMCSA (or the Department of Transportation, where applicable).

§387.409 Insurance and surety companies.

A certificate of insurance or surety bond will not be accepted by the FMCSA unless issued by an insurance or surety company that is authorized (licensed or admitted) to issue bonds or underlying insurance policies:

(a) **In each state in which the freight forwarder** is authorized by the FMCSA to perform service, or

(b) **In the state in which the freight forwarder** has its principal place of business or domicile, and will designate in writing upon request by the FMCSA, a person upon whom process, issued by or under the authority of a court of competent jurisdiction, may be served in any proceeding at law or equity brought in any state in which the freight forwarder performs service; or

(c) **In any state,** and is eligible as an excess or surplus lines insurer in any state in which business is written, and will make the designation of process agent prescribed in paragraph (b) of this section.

§387.411 Qualifications as a self-insurer and other securities or agreements.

(a) **Self-insurer.** The FMCSA will approve the application of a freight forwarder to qualify as a self-insurer if it is able to meet its obligations for bodily-injury, property-damage, and cargo liability without adversely affecting its business.

(b) **Other securities and agreements.** The FMCSA will grant applications for approval of other securities and agreements if the public will be protected as contemplated by 49 U.S.C. 13906(c).

§387.413 Forms and procedure.

(a) **Forms.** Endorsements for policies of insurance, surety bonds, certificates of insurance, applications to qualify as a self-insurer or for approval of other securities or agreements, and notices of cancellation must be in the form prescribed at 49 CFR Part 387, Subpart C.

Cross Reference: For list of forms prescribed, see §1003.3 of this chapter.

(b) **Procedure.** Certificates of insurance, surety bonds, and notices of cancellation must be filed with the FMCSA in triplicate.

(c) **Names.** Certificates of insurance and surety bonds shall be issued in the full name (including any trade name) of the individual, partnership (all partners named), corporation, or other person holding or to be issued the permit.

(d) **Cancellation.** Except as provided in paragraph (e) of this section, certificates of insurance, surety bonds and other securities and agreements shall not be cancelled or withdrawn until 30 days after the FMCSA receives written notice from the insurance company, surety, freight forwarder, or other party, as the case may be.

(e) **Termination by replacement.** Certificates of insurance or surety bonds may be replaced by other certificates of insurance, surety bonds, or other security, and the liability of the retiring insurer or surety shall be considered as having terminated as of the replacement's effective date, if acceptable to the FMCSA.

§387.415 Acceptance and revocation by the FMCSA.

The FMCSA may at any time refuse to accept or may revoke its acceptance of any surety bond, certificate of insurance, qualifications as a self-insurer, or other security or agreement that does not comply with these rules or fails to provide adequate public protection.

§387.417 Fiduciaries.

(a) **Interpretations.** The terms "insured" and "principal" as used in a certificate of insurance, surety bond, and notice of cancellation, filed by or for a freight forwarder, include the freight forwarder and its fiduciary (as defined at 49 CFR 387.319(a)) as of the moment of succession.

(b) **Span of security coverage.** The coverage furnished for a fiduciary shall not apply after the effective date of other insurance or security, filed with and accepted by the FMCSA for such fiduciary. After the coverage shall have been in effect 30 days, it may be cancelled or withdrawn within the succeeding 30 days by the insurer, the insured, the surety, or the principal 10 days after the FMCSA receives written notice. After such coverage has been in effect 60 days, it may be cancelled or withdrawn only in accordance with §387.413(d).

§387.419 Electronic filing of surety bonds, certificates of insurance and cancellations.

Insurers may, at their option and in accordance with the requirements and procedures set forth at 49 CFR 387.323, file certificates of insurance, surety bonds, and other securities and agreements electronically.

Part 388 - Cooperative Agreements with States

§388.1 Eligibility.
Any State may agree with the Federal Motor Carrier Safety Administration to enforce the safety laws and regulations of said State and the United States concerning motor carrier transportation by filing with the Administrator at Washington, DC 20590, a written acceptance of the terms herein.

§388.2 Extent of acceptance.
The written acceptance may be in letter form, signed by competent authority of said State charged with regulations of motor carrier safety and hazardous materials transportation and shall specify the terms herein pertaining to the obligations of a State in which said State will participate. To the extent that a State agrees to participate in the terms herein, officials of the Federal Motor Carrier Safety Administration will reciprocate.

§388.3 Cancellation.
Cancellation or withdrawal, in whole or in part, from any agreement made under this chapter may be effected by written notice from either party indicating the effective date of said cancellation or withdrawal.

§388.4 Exchange of information.
(a) Federal Motor Carrier Safety Administration furnishing information to State. Information that comes to the attention of an employee of the Federal Motor Carrier Safety Administration in the course of his/her official duties of investigation, inspection, or examination of the property, equipment, and records of a motor carrier or others, pursuant to 49 U.S.C. 504(c), and that is believed to be a violation of any law or regulation of the State pertaining to unsafe motor carrier operations and practices, shall be communicated to the appropriate State authority by an official of the Federal Motor Carrier Safety Administration.

(b) State furnishing information to Federal Motor Carrier Safety Administration. Information that comes to the attention of a duly authorized agent of the State in the course of his/her official duties of investigation, inspection, or examination of the property, equipment, and records of a motor carrier or others, and that is believed to be a violation of any provision of the safety or hazardous materials laws of the United States concerning highway transportation or the regulations of the Federal Motor Carrier Safety Administration thereunder, shall be communicated to the Field Administrator.

§388.5 Requests for assistance.
(a) State request for Federal Motor Carrier Safety Administration assistance. Upon written request of the appropriate State authority, the officials of the Federal Motor Carrier Safety Administration for that State shall, as time, personnel, and funds permit, obtain evidence for use by said State in the enforcement of its laws and regulations concerning unsafe motor carrier operations. Evidence obtained in this manner shall be transmitted to the appropriate State authority together with the name and address of an agent or employee, if any, having knowledge of the facts, who shall be made available when necessary to testify as a witness in an enforcement proceeding or other action.

(b) Federal Motor Carrier Safety Administration request for State assistance. Upon written request from a Regional Director of Motor Carriers, the appropriate State authority, shall, as time, personnel, and funds permit, obtain evidence in the State for use by the Federal Motor Carrier Safety Administration in its enforcement of the safety and hazardous materials laws and regulations of the United States concerning highway transportation. Evidence obtained in this manner shall be transmitted to the Field Administrator, together with the name and address of an agent or employee, if any, having knowledge of the facts, who shall be made available when necessary to testify as a witness in an enforcement proceeding or other action.

§388.6 Joint investigation, inspection, or examination.
Upon agreement by the Field Administrator and the appropriate State authority, there will be conducted a joint investigation, inspection, or examination of the property, equipment, or records of motor carriers or others, for the enforcement of the safety and hazardous materials laws and regulations of the United States and the State concerning highway transportation. The said Field Administrator and the appropriate State authority shall decide as to the location and time, the objectives sought, and the identity of the person who will supervise the joint effort and make the necessary decisions. Any agent or employee of either agency who has personal knowledge of pertinent facts shall be made available when necessary to testify as a witness in an enforcement proceeding or other action.

§388.7 Joint administrative activities related to enforcement of safety and hazardous materials laws and regulations.
To facilitate the interchange of information and evidence, and the conduct of joint investigation and administrative action, the Field Administrator and the appropriate State authority shall, when warranted, schedule joint conferences of staff members of both agencies. Information shall be exchanged as to the nature and extent of the authority and capabilities of the respective agencies to enforce the safety and hazardous materials laws and regulations of the State or of the United States concerning motor carrier transportation. The Federal Motor Carrier Safety Administration and the State (or appropriate State authority) shall use their best efforts to inform each other of changes in their rules and regulations and cooperate with and assist each other in conducting training schools for Federal and State enforcement officials engaged in such duties.

§388.8 Supplemental agreements.
The terms specified in this part may be supplemented from time to time by specific agreement between the Federal Motor Carrier Safety Administration and the appropriate State authority in order to further implement the provisions of 49 U.S.C. 502.

Part 388 - Cooperative Agreements with States

Notes

Part 389 - Rulemaking Procedures — Federal Motor Carrier Safety Regulations

Subpart A - General

§389.1 Applicability.
This part prescribes rulemaking procedures that apply to the issuance, amendment and revocation of rules under an Act.

§389.3 Definitions.
Act means statutes granting the Secretary authority to regulate motor carrier safety.
Administrator means the Federal Motor Carrier Safety Administrator.

§389.5 Regulatory docket.
(a) Information and data deemed relevant by the Administrator relating to rule making actions, including notices of proposed rule making; comments received in response to notices; petitions for rule making and reconsideration; denials of petitions for rule making and reconsideration; records of additional rule making proceedings under 389.25; and final rules are maintained at Headquarters, Federal Motor Carrier Safety Administration, Nassif Building, 400 Seventh Street, SW., Washington, DC 20590.

(b) Any person may examine docketed material, at any time during regular business hours after the docket is established, except material ordered withheld from the public under §552(b) of Title 5 of the United States Code, and may obtain a copy of it upon payment of a fee.

§389.7 Records.
Records of the Administrator relating to rule making proceedings are available for inspection as provided in §552(b) of Title 5 of the United States Code and Part 7 of the regulations of the Secretary of Transportation (Part 7 of this Title; 32 FR 9284 et seq.).

Subpart B - Procedures for Adoption of Rules

§389.11 General.
Unless the Administrator, for good cause, finds a notice is impractical, unnecessary, or contrary to the public interest, and incorporates such a finding and a brief statement of the reasons for it in the rule, a notice of proposed rulemaking must be issued, and interested persons are invited to participate in the rulemaking proceedings involving rules under an Act.

§389.13 Initiation of rule making.
The Administrator initiates rule making on his/her own motion. However, in so doing, he/she may, in his/her discretion, consider the recommendations of his/her staff or other agencies of the United States or of other interested persons.

§389.15 Contents of notices of proposed rule making.
(a) Each notice of proposed rule making is published in the Federal Register, unless all persons subject to it are named and are personally served with a copy of it.

(b) Each notice, whether published in the Federal Register or personally served, includes:
  (1) *A statement of the time, place, and nature* of the proposed rule making proceeding;
  (2) *A reference to the authority under which it is issued;*
  (3) *A description of the subjects* and issues involved or the substance and terms of the proposed rule;
  (4) *A statement of the time* within which written comments must be submitted; and
  (5) *A statement of how and to what extent* interested persons may participate in the proceeding.

§389.17 Participation by interested persons.
(a) Any interested person may participate in rule making proceedings by submitting comments in writing containing information, views, or arguments.

(b) In his/her discretion, the Administrator may invite any interested person to participate in the rule making procedures described in §389.25.

§389.19 Petitions for extension of time to comment.
A petition for extension of the time to submit comments must be received in duplicate not later than three (3) days before expiration of the time stated in the notice. The filing of the petition does not automatically extend the time for petitioner's comments. Such a petition is granted only if the petitioner shows good cause for the extension, and if the extension is consistent with the public interest. If an extension is granted, it is granted to all persons, and it is published in the Federal Register.

§389.21 Contents of written comments.
All written comments must be in English and submitted in five (5) legible copies, unless the number of copies is specified in the notice. Any interested person must submit as part of his/her written comments all material that he/she considers relevant to any statement of fact made by him/her. Incorporation of material by reference is to be avoided. However, if such incorporation is necessary, the incorporated material shall be identified with respect to document and page.

§389.23 Consideration of comments received.
All timely comments are considered before final action is taken on a rule making proposal. Late filed comments may be considered as far as practicable.

§389.25 Additional rule making proceedings.
The Administrator may initiate any further rule making proceedings that he/she finds necessary or desirable. For example, interested persons may be invited to make oral arguments, to participate in conferences between the Administrator or his/her representative at which minutes of the conference are kept, to appear at informal hearings presided over by officials designated by the Administrator at which a transcript or minutes are kept, or participate in any other proceeding to assure informed administrative action and to protect the public interest.

§389.27 Hearings.
(a) Sections 556 and 557 of Title 5, United States Code, do not apply to hearings held under this part. Unless otherwise specified, hearings held under this part are informal, nonadversary, fact-finding procedures at which there are no formal pleadings or adverse parties. Any rule issued in a case in which an informal hearing is held is not necessarily based exclusively on the record of the hearing.

(b) The Administrator designates a representative to conduct any hearing held under this part. The Chief Counsel of the Federal Motor Carrier Safety Administration designates a member of his/her staff to serve as legal officer at the hearing.

§389.29 Adoption of final rules.
Final rules are prepared by representatives of the office concerned and the Office of the Chief Counsel. The rule is then submitted to the Administrator for his/her consideration. If the Administrator adopts the rule, it is published in the Federal Register, unless all persons subject to it are named and are personally served with a copy of it.

§389.31 Petitions for rule making.
(a) Any interested person may petition the Administrator to establish, amend, or repeal a rule.

(b) Each petition filed under this section must:
  (1) *Be submitted in duplicate* to the Administrator, Federal Motor Carrier Safety Administration, 400 Seventh Street, SW., Washington, DC 20590;
  (2) *Set forth the text or substance* of the rule or amendment proposed, or specify the rule that the petitioner seeks to have repealed, as the case may be;
  (3) *Explain the interest of the petitioner in the action requested;*
  (4) *Contain any information and arguments available* to the petitioner to support the action sought.

§389.33 Processing of petition.
(a) Unless the Administrator otherwise specifies, no public hearing, argument, or other proceeding is held directly on a petition before its disposition under this section.

(b) Grants. If the Administrator determines that the petition contains adequate justification, he/she initiates rule making action under this Subpart B.

(c) Denials. If the Administrator determines that the petition does not justify rule making, he/she denies the petition.

(d) Notification. Whenever the Administrator determines that a petition should be granted or denied, the Office of the Chief Counsel prepares a notice of that grant or denial for issuance to the petitioner, and the Administrator issues it to the petitioner.

§389.35 Petitions for reconsideration.

(a) Any interested person may petition the Administrator for reconsideration of any rule issued under this part. The petition must be in English and submitted in five (5) legible copies to the Administrator, Federal Motor Carrier Safety Administration, 400 Seventh Street, SW., Washington, DC 20590, and received not later than thirty (30) days after publication of the rule in the Federal Register. Petitions filed after that time will be considered as petitions filed under §389.31. The petition must contain a brief statement of the complaint and an explanation as to why compliance with the rule is not practicable, is unreasonable, or is not in the public interest.

(b) If the petitioner requests the consideration of additional facts, he/she must state the reason they were not presented to the Administrator within the prescribed time.

(c) The Administrator does not consider repetitious petitions.

(d) Unless the Administrator otherwise provides, the filing of a petition under this section does not stay the effectiveness of the rule.

§389.37 Proceedings on petitions for reconsideration.

The Administrator may grant or deny, in whole or in part, any petition for reconsideration without further proceedings. In the event he/she determines to reconsider any rule, he/she may issue a final decision on reconsideration without further proceedings, or he/she may provide such opportunity to submit comment or information and data as he/she deems appropriate. Whenever the Administrator determines that a petition should be granted or denied, he/she prepares a notice of the grant or denial of a petition for reconsideration, for issuance to the petitioner, and issues it to the petitioner. The Administrator may consolidate petitions relating to the same rule.

Part 390 - Federal Motor Carrier Safety Regulations; General (Page 85 in the Driver Edition)

Subpart A - General Applicability and Definitions

§390.1 Purpose.
This part establishes general applicability, definitions, general requirements and information as they pertain to persons subject to this chapter.

§390.3 General applicability.
(a) The rules in Subchapter B of this chapter are applicable to all employers, employees, and commercial motor vehicles, which transport property or passengers in interstate commerce.

(b) The rules in Part 383, Commercial Driver's License Standards; Requirements and Penalties, are applicable to every person who operates a commercial motor vehicle, as defined in §383.5 of this Subchapter, in interstate or intrastate commerce and to all employers of such persons.

(c) The rules in Part 387, Minimum Levels of Financial Responsibility for Motor Carriers, are applicable to motor carriers as provided in §387.3 or 387.27 of this subchapter.

(d) Additional requirements. Nothing in Subchapter B of this chapter shall be construed to prohibit an employer from requiring and enforcing more stringent requirements relating to safety of operation and employee safety and health.

(e) Knowledge of and compliance with the regulations.
  (1) *Every employer* shall be knowledgeable of and comply with all regulations contained in this subchapter which are applicable to that motor carrier's operations.
  (2) *Every driver and employee* shall be instructed regarding, and shall comply with, all applicable regulations contained in this subchapter.
  (3) *All motor vehicle equipment and accessories* required by this subchapter shall be maintained in compliance with all applicable performance and design criteria set forth in this subchapter.

(f) Exceptions. Unless otherwise specifically provided, the rules in this subchapter do not apply to —
  (1) *All school bus operations* as defined in §390.5;
  (2) *Transportation performed* by the Federal government, a State, or any political subdivision of a State, or an agency established under a compact between States that has been approved by the Congress of the United States;
  (3) *The occasional transportation* of personal property by individuals not for compensation nor in the furtherance of a commercial enterprise;
  (4) *The transportation of human corpses or sick and injured persons;*
  (5) *The operation of fire trucks and rescue vehicles* while involved in emergency and related operations;
  (6) (i) *The operation* of commercial motor vehicles designed or used to transport between 9 and 15 passengers (including the driver), not for direct compensation, provided the vehicle does not otherwise meet the definition of a commercial motor vehicle, except that motor carriers operating such vehicles are required to comply with §§390.15, 390.19, and 390.21(a) and (b)(2).
  (ii) *The operation* of commercial motor vehicles designed or used to transport between 9 and 15 passengers (including the driver) for direct compensation, provided the vehicle is not being operated beyond a 75 air-mile radius (86.3 statute miles or 138.9 kilometers) from the driver's normal work-reporting location, and provided the vehicle does not otherwise meet the definition of a commercial motor vehicle, except that motor carriers operating such vehicles are required to comply with §§390.15, 390.19, and 390.21(a) and (b)(2).

(g) Motor carriers that transport hazardous materials in intrastate commerce. The rules in the following provisions of subchapter B of this chapter apply to motor carriers that transport hazardous materials in intrastate commerce and to the motor vehicles that transport hazardous materials in intrastate commerce:
  (1) *Part 385, Subparts A and E,* for carriers subject to the requirements of §385.403 of this chapter.
  (2) *Part 386,* Rules of practice for motor carrier, broker, freight forwarder, and hazardous materials proceedings, of this chapter.
  (3) *Part 387,* Minimum Levels of Financial Responsibility for Motor Carriers, to the extent provided in §387.3 of this chapter.
  (4) *§390.19,* Motor carrier identification report, and §390.21, Marking of CMVs, for carriers subject to the requirements of §385.403 of this chapter. Intrastate motor carriers operating prior to January 1, 2005, are excepted from §390.19(a)(1).

§390.3 DOT Interpretations

Question 1: Does the government exception in §390.3(f)(2) apply to motor carriers doing business with the government?
Guidance: No. The exception applies only when the government is the motor carrier.

Question 2: Are the FMCSRs applicable to drivers and CMVs which transport tools, equipment, and supplies across State lines in a CMV?
Guidance: Yes, the FMCSRs are applicable to drivers and CMVs in interstate commerce which transport property. The property in this situation is the tools, equipment and supplies.

Question 3: Are the operations of a church which provides bus tours to the general public for compensation subject to the FMCSRs as a for-hire motor carrier?
Guidance: Yes, the church is a for-hire motor carrier of passengers subject to the FMCSRs.

Question 4: Are the FMCSRs applicable to the rail movement of trailers and intermodal container chassis that previously or subsequently were moved by highway by a motor carrier in interstate commerce?
Guidance: No. They are only subject when being moved as a motor vehicle by highway by a motor carrier.

Question 5: Are personnel involved in road testing CMVs across a State line subject to the FMCSRs?
Guidance: Yes, any driver (including mechanics, technicians, driver trainees and other personnel) operating a CMV in interstate commerce must be in compliance with the FMCSRs.

Question 6: How does one distinguish between intra- and interstate commerce for the purposes of applicability of the FMCSRs?
Guidance: Interstate commerce is determined by the essential character of the movement, manifested by the shipper's fixed and persistent intent at the time of shipment, and is ascertained from all of the facts and circumstances surrounding the transportation. When the intent of the transportation being performed is interstate in nature, even when the route is within the boundaries of a single State, the driver and CMV are subject to the FMCSRs.

Question 7: Are Red Cross vehicles/drivers subject to the FMCSRs?
Guidance: Red Cross vehicles/drivers used to provide emergency relief under the provisions of §390.23 are not subject to the FMCSRs while providing the relief. However, these vehicles/drivers would be subject when operating at other times, provided they are used in interstate commerce and the vehicles meet the definition of a CMV.

Question 8: May a motor carrier require fingerprinting as a pre-employment condition?
Guidance: The FMCSRs do not require or prohibit fingerprinting as a condition of employment. §390.3(d) allows employers to enforce more stringent requirements.

Question 9: Are the FMCSRs applicable to drivers/vehicles operated by a State or local educational institution which is a political subdivision of the State?
Guidance: §390.3(f)(2) specifically exempts transportation performed by a State or a political subdivision including any agency of a State or locality from the FMCSRs. The drivers, however, may be subject to the CDL requirements and/or State laws that are similar to the FMCSRs.

Question 10: Are the FMCSRs applicable to drivers/vehicles operated by a transit authority owned and operated by a State or a political subdivision of the State?
Guidance: §390.3(f)(2) specifically exempts transportation performed by the Federal Government, a State, or any political subdivision of a State from the FMCSRs. However, this exemption does not apply to the CDL requirements in Part 383. Also, if governmental entities engage in interstate charter transportation of passengers, they must comply with accident report retention requirements of Part 390.

Question 11: Is the interstate transportation of students, teachers and parents to school events such as athletic contests and field trips performed by municipalities subject to the FMCSRs? If a fee is charged to defer the municipality's expenses, does this affect the applicability of the regulations?

Guidance: §390.3(f)(2) specifically exempts transportation performed by the Federal Government, a State, or any political subdivision of a State from the FMCSRs. Charging a fee to defer governmental costs does not affect this exemption.

However, this exemption does not apply to the CDL requirements in Part 383. Also, if governmental entities engage in interstate charter transportation of passengers, they must comply with accident report retention requirements of Part 390.

Question 12: What is the applicability of the FMCSRs to school bus operations performed by Indian Tribal Governments?

Guidance: Transportation performed by the Federal Government, States, or political subdivisions of a State is generally excepted from the FMCSRs. This general exception includes Indian Tribal Governments, which for purposes of §390.3(f) are equivalent to a State governmental entity. When a driver is employed and a bus is operated by the governmental entity, the operation would not be subject to the FMCSRs, with the following exceptions: The requirements of Part 383 as they pertain to commercial driver licensing standards are applicable to every driver operating a CMV, and the accident report retention requirements of Part 390 are applicable when the governmental entity is performing interstate charter transportation of passengers.

Question 13: A motor carrier dispatches an empty CMV from State A into adjoining State B in order to transport cargo or passengers between two points in State B, and then to return empty to State A. Does the transportation of cargo or passengers within State B constitute interstate commerce?

Guidance: Yes. The courts and the ICC developed a test that clarifies the legal status of intrastate portions of interstate trips. The character of the intrastate leg depends on the shipper's fixed and persistent intent when the transportation began. The fixed and persistent intent in this case was to move property — the vehicle itself — across State lines and between two points in State B where it was used to haul cargo or passengers. The transportation within State B, therefore, constitutes interstate commerce. In some cases the motor carrier may be the shipper.

Question 14: What is the applicability of the FMCSRs to motor carriers owning and operating school buses that contract with a municipality to provide pupil transportation services?

Guidance: For the purposes of the FMCSRs, Parts 390-399, "school bus operation" means the use of a school bus to transport school children and/or school personnel from home to school and from school to home. A "school bus" is a passenger motor vehicle designed to carry more than 10 passengers in addition to the driver, and used primarily for school bus operations (see §390.5). School bus operations and transportation performed by government entities are specifically exempted from the FMCSRs under §390.3(f).

However, anyone operating school buses under contract with a school is a for-hire motor carrier. When a nongovernment, for-hire motor carrier transports children to school-related functions other than "school bus operation" such as sporting events, class trips, etc., and operates across State lines, its operation must be conducted in accordance with the FMCSRs. This applies to motor carriers that operate CMVs as defined under Part 390, which includes vehicles which have a GVWR of 10,001 pounds or more or are designed or used to carry passengers for compensation, except 6-passenger taxicabs not operating on fixed routes.

In certain instances, carriers providing school bus transportation are not subject to the Bus Regulatory Reform Act of 1982 and the minimum financial responsibility requirements (Part 387) issued under this Act. Transportation of school children and teachers that is organized, sponsored, and paid for by the school district is not subject to Part 387. Therefore, school bus contractors must comply with the FMCSRs for interstate trips such as sporting events and class trips but are not required by Federal regulations to carry a specific level of insurance coverage.

For those operations provided by school bus contractors that are subject to the FMCSRs, the motor carriers must keep driver and vehicle records as required by the regulations. This would include driver qualifications records (Part 391), driver records of duty status (Part 395), accident report retention (Part 390), and inspection, repair, and maintenance records (Part 396) for the drivers and vehicles that are used on the trips that are subject to the FMCSRs. These records are not required under the FMCSRs for the other vehicles in the motor carrier's fleet that are not subject to the regulations.

Question 15: May drivers be coerced into employing loading or unloading assistance (lumpers)?

Guidance: No. The Motor Carrier Act of 1980 made it illegal to coerce someone into unwanted loading or unloading and require payment for it (49 U.S.C. 14103, previously 49 U.S.C. 11109). The FHWA is responsible for the enforcement of regulations forbidding coercion in the use of lumpers.

Question 16:
a. Are vehicles which, in the course of interstate transportation over the highway, are off the highway, loading, unloading or waiting, subject to the FMCSRs during these times?
b. Are vehicles and drivers used wholly within terminals and on premises or plant sites subject to the FMCSRs?

Guidance:
a. Yes.
b. No.

Question 17: What protection is afforded a driver for refusing to violate the FMCSRs?

Guidance: Section 405 of the STAA — Surface Transportation Assistance Act of 1982 (49 U.S.C. 31105) states, in part, that no person shall discharge, discipline, or in any manner discriminate against an employee with respect to the employee's compensation, terms, conditions, or privileges of employment for refusing to operate a vehicle when such operation constitutes a violation of any Federal rule, regulation, standard, or order applicable to CMV safety. In such a case, a driver may submit a signed complaint to the Occupational Safety and Health Administration.

Question 18: Are persons who operate CMVs for the personal conveyance of their friends or family members "private motor carriers of passengers (nonbusiness)" as defined in §390.5?

Guidance: No. Nonbusiness private motor carriers of passengers (PMCPs) do not include individuals providing personal conveyance of passengers for recreational purposes. A nonbusiness PMCP must be engaged in some group activity. For example, organizations that are exempt under the Internal Revenue Code (26 U.S.C. 501) and provide transportation for their members would generally be considered nonbusiness PMCPs: Religious, charitable, scientific, and educational organizations, scouting groups, sports clubs, fraternal societies or lodges, etc.

Question 19: "Unless otherwise specifically provided," §390.3(f)(2) exempts certain government entities and their drivers from compliance with 49 CFR Chapter III, Subchapter B, i.e., Parts 350-399. Which parts are covered by this exemption and which are "otherwise specifically" excluded?

Guidance: Government employers and drivers are exempt from compliance with Parts 325, 385, 387, and 390-399. However, they must comply with the drug and alcohol testing requirements in Part 382 and the CDL requirements in Part 383. Parts 350, 355, 384, 386, 388, and 389 do not directly regulate CMV operators, public or private, and the question of an exemption therefore does not arise.

Question 20: Do the FMCSRs apply to Indian Tribal Governments?

Guidance: Under §390.3(f)(2), transportation performed by the Federal Government, States, or political subdivisions of a State is generally exempt from the FMCSRs. Indian Tribal Governments are considered equivalent to a State governmental entity for purposes of this exemption. Thus, when a driver is employed by and is operating a CMV owned by a governmental entity, neither the driver, the vehicle, nor the entity is subject to the FMCSRs, with the following exceptions:

(1) The requirements of Part 383 relating to CMV driver licensing standards;

(2) The drug testing requirements in Part 382;

(3) Alcohol testing when an employee is performing, about to perform, or just performed safety-sensitive functions. For the purposes of alcohol testing, safety-sensitive functions are defined in §382.107 as any of those on-duty functions set forth in §395.2 On-Duty time, paragraphs (1) through (6), (generally, driving and related activities) and;

(4) The accident report retention requirements of §390.15 are applicable when the governmental entity is performing interstate charter transportation of passengers.

Subpart A - General Applicability and Definitions §390.3 (g)

Guidance: The exemption would apply to this kind of transportation, provided: (1) The underlying activities are not undertaken for profit, i.e., (a) prize money is declared as ordinary income for tax purposes, and (b) the cost of the underlying activities is not deducted as a business expense for tax purposes; and, where relevant; (2) corporate sponsorship is not involved. Drivers must confer with their State of licensure to determine the licensing provisions to which they are subject.

Question 22: If, after December 18, 1995, a Mexico-based driver is found operating beyond the boundaries of the four border States allowed by the North American Free Trade Agreement (NAFTA), is that driver in violation of the FMCSRs? If so, which one?

Guidance: No. Driving beyond the four border States is not, in and of itself, a violation of the FMCSRs.

Question 23: Is transportation within the boundaries of a State between a place in an Indian Reservation and a place outside such reservation interstate commerce?

Guidance: No, such transportation is considered to be intrastate commerce. An Indian reservation is geographically located within the area of a State. Enforcement on Indian reservations is inherently Federal, unless such authority has been granted to the States by Congressional enactment, accepted by the States where appropriate, and consented to by the Indian tribes.

Question 24: To what extent does the FHWA have jurisdiction to regulate the qualifications and hours of service of CMV drivers engaged in interstate or foreign commerce if the drivers only occasionally operate in interstate or foreign commerce?

Guidance: The FHWA published an interpretation in the Federal Register on July 23, 1981 (46 FR 37902) on this subject. The FHWA must show that the driver or motor carrier has engaged in interstate or foreign commerce within a reasonable period of time prior to its assertion of jurisdiction under 49 U.S.C. 31136 and 31502.

The FHWA must show that the driver or motor carrier has actually operated in interstate commerce within a reasonable period of time prior to its assertion of jurisdiction. Mere solicitation of business that would involve operations in interstate commerce is not sufficient to establish jurisdiction. If jurisdiction is claimed over a driver who has not driven in interstate commerce, evidence must be presented that the carrier has operated in interstate commerce and that the driver could reasonably be expected to make one of the carrier's interstate runs. Satisfactory evidence would include, but not be limited to, statements from drivers and carriers and any employment agreements.

Evidence of driving or being available for use in interstate commerce makes the driver subject to the FMCSRs for a 4-month period from the date of the proof. For that period, the motor carrier is also required to comply with those portions of the FMCSRs that deal with drivers, driving, and records related to or generated by drivers, primarily those in 49 CFR Parts 387, 391, 392, 395 and 396. The FHWA believes that the 4-month period is reasonable because it avoids both a week-by-week determination of jurisdiction, which is excessively narrow, and the assertion that a driver who is used or available for use once remains subject to the FMCSRs for an unlimited time, which is overly inclusive.

Editor's Note:
The following memorandum was issued February 8, 2000:

Purpose
On July 6, 1999, a memorandum was issued to all field offices concerning the authority of the Office of Motor Carrier and Highway Safety (OMCHS) to regulate the qualifications and maximum hours of service of commercial motor vehicle (CMV) drivers who operate both in interstate and intrastate commerce. Concerns about that memo have been expressed by (1) State agencies uncertain about its implications for the Motor Carrier Safety Assistance Program (MCSAP) (specifically, the tolerance guidelines for States' intrastate hours-of-service regulations); (2) motor carriers trying to determine whether Federal or State safety regulations would apply to intrastate trips made by drivers who also handled interstate runs; and (3) FHWA field office personnel.

After considering the issues raised by the July memo, I have decided to change the policy of the FHWA. This memorandum explains when the agency will exercise jurisdiction over intrastate operations of motor carriers and drivers that sometimes operate interstate.

Background
The statutes on which most of the Federal Motor Carrier Safety Regulations (FMCSRs) are based apply only to "interstate commerce." The extent of the jurisdiction conferred by that term has been decided by the Federal courts in a long series of cases. Most of the motor carrier cases analyzing "interstate commerce" involve disputes about overtime pay under the Fair Labor Standards Act (FLSA). The FLSA exempts employers from the requirement to pay overtime to any employee "with respect to whom the Secretary of Transportation has power to establish qualifications and maximum hours of service" under the Motor Carrier Act of 1935 (i.e., 49 U.S.C. 31502). Since the 1935 Act applies only to "interstate commerce," the courts have had to determine whether drivers not currently operating across State lines may nonetheless be subject to the "power" of the Secretary, and thus not entitled to overtime pay.

In 1981 the Federal Highway Administration (FHWA), on behalf of its Bureau of Motor Carrier Safety, published a notice in the Federal Register (46 FR 37902, July 23, 1981) discussing the more important FLSA cases and interpreting its "jurisdiction to regulate the qualifications and maximum hours of service of commercial motor vehicle drivers engaged in interstate or foreign commerce." The notice summarized the conclusions of these cases as follows:

If in the regular course of employment a driver is, or could be, called upon to transport a shipment in interstate commerce the driver would be subject to the FHWA's jurisdiction under 49 U.S.C. 304 [i.e., the Motor Carrier Act of 1935, now codified at 49 U.S.C. 31502]. 49 U.S.C. 304 provides the authority to regulate the qualifications and maximum hours of service of employees and safety of operation and equipment of common carriers, contract carriers, private carriers of property, and carriers of migrant workers. These cases establish the basic tests for determining whether a driver is subject to Federal jurisdiction under 49 U.S.C. 304. They hold that even a minor involvement in interstate commerce as a regular part of an employee's duties will subject that employee to the jurisdiction of the FHWA. In two of the cases mentioned, "Morris v. McComb" [332 U.S. 422, Supreme Court, 1947] and "Starrett v. Bruce" [391 F.2d 320 (10th Cir. 1968)], the courts found jurisdiction over drivers even though those drivers had not driven at all in interstate commerce. The findings of jurisdiction were based on the probability of those drivers being assigned to interstate runs in the regular course of their employment.

The 1981 notice reached the following conclusion:

The FHWA view is that in order to establish jurisdiction under 49 U.S.C. 304 [now 49 U.S.C. 31502] the carrier must be shown to have engaged in interstate commerce within a reasonable period of time prior to the time at which jurisdiction is in question. The carrier's involvement in interstate commerce must be established by some concrete evidence such as an actual trip in interstate commerce or proof, in the case of a "for hire" carrier, that interstate business had been solicited. If jurisdiction is claimed over a driver who has not driven in interstate commerce, evidence must be presented that the carrier has engaged in interstate commerce and that the driver could reasonably have been expected to make one of the carrier's interstate runs. Satisfactory evidence would be statements from drivers and carriers, and any employment agreements.

Evidence of driving in interstate commerce or being subject to being used in interstate commerce should be accepted as proof that the driver is subject to 49 U.S.C. 304 for a 4-month period from the date of the proof. The FHWA believes that the 4-month period is reasonable because it avoids both the too strict week-by-week approach and the situation where a driver could be used or be subject to being used once and remain subject to jurisdiction under 49 U.S.C. 304 for an unlimited time.

Although the notice of interpretation was never included in the Code of Federal Regulations, the FHWA summarized it in the Regulatory Guidance for the FMCSRs published on April 4, 1997 (Q. 24 under Part 390, 63 FR 16370, at 16406).

Despite the 1981 and 1997 publications, the Office of Motor Carriers (OMC) and the OMCHS never applied the so-called 4-month rule, or at least not universally. The July 6 memorandum was designed to create a new, consistent policy for OMC. As mentioned above, however, it has created more problems than it resolved. Therefore, this document is being issued to establish a new national policy for the FHWA.

National Policy

Safety is the highest priority of the FHWA. Enforcement of the hours of service regulations is a critical part of that mandate. Drivers who operate in interstate commerce must be in compliance with 49 CFR Part 395 before, during and after interstate trips. Although the case law discussed in the 1981 notice of interpretation clearly supports an assertion of jurisdiction over a driver for four months after a single interstate trip, a 4-month rule is not necessary to prevent fatigue. The rules in Part 395 control hours of service in periods of either 7 consecutive days (if the carrier does not operate every day of the week) or 8 consecutive days (if the carrier operates every day of the week). Because compliance with Part 395 during the 7- or 8-day period before and after an interstate trip will keep driver fatigue within manageable bounds, the FMCSA will replace the 4-month rule with a 14/15-day rule.

1. Any driver who begins a trip in interstate commerce must continue to meet the requirements of 49 CFR 395.3(a) and (b) through the end of the next 7 to 8 consecutive days, depending on which rule the motor carrier operates under.

   The driver must continue to comply with the requirements of 49 CFR Part 395, even if he/she operates exclusively in intrastate commerce for the remainder of the 60/70 hour period (i.e. 7-8 day schedule) at the end of the interstate trip. The driver must also continue to comply with the 10- and 15-hour rules as well as the 60- or 70-hour rules for the remainder of that day, and the following 7 days (if the 60-hour rule was applicable) or 8 days (if the 70-hour rule was applicable).

   A driver who begins a trip in interstate commerce in a CMV must have in his/her possession a copy of records of duty status for the previous 7 consecutive days, as required by 49 CFR 395.8(k)(2) unless they meet 49 CFR 395.1(e), even if the driver operated only in intrastate commerce during that 7-day period. During the 7-day period prior to the interstate trip the driver may follow the State regulations applicable to intrastate commerce with regard to the states' CMV driving and on-duty requirements.

2. FHWA investigators should cite drivers for violations of the 10- or 15-hour rules or the 60- or 70-hour rules that are committed while on the interstate trip or during the 7 or 8 days after completing the interstate trip (depending on which rule the motor carrier operates under).

   The driver remains subject to Part 395 for 7 or 8 days after a trip in interstate commerce even if he/she drives only in intrastate commerce for that period. Violations of the policies stated here which are discovered during compliance reviews should be treated like any other violations of the FMCSRs in determining the motor carrier's safety rating and enforcement action may be taken.

3. The MCSAP Tolerance Guidelines in Appendix C to 49 CFR Part 350 are unchanged. This policy statement simply clarifies the difference between Paragraphs 2 and 3 of the Guidelines, i.e., between the type of trips subject to Federal jurisdiction, as opposed to those subject only to State jurisdiction.

The FMCSA does not disagree with the legal conclusions the FHWA reached in the 1981 notice of interpretation. However, in the interest of simplicity and workability, the so-called 4-month rule is being replaced with a 14/15-day rule.

Question 25: Do the Federal Motor Carrier Safety Regulations apply to transportation performed by the Federal government of a foreign country, or by a state, provincial, or territorial government of a foreign country?

Guidance: Yes. Although §390.3(f)(2) includes an exception for transportation performed by the Federal government, a State, or any political subdivision of a State, the exceptions are only applicable to government entities in the United States.

Question 26: Is the operation of fire trucks and rescue vehicles in interstate commerce by a private firefighting company subject to the FMCSRs when the company provides its services under contract to Federal or State agencies?

Guidance: Generally, 49 CFR Parts 390-399 (FMCSRs) are not applicable to the operation of fire trucks and rescue vehicles by private contract fire companies while such vehicles are being used in emergency and related operations, i.e., while their personnel are engaged in firefighting or participating in rescue operations, and when their vehicles are returning from the emergency or rescue scene [see 49 CFR 390.3(f)(5)]. In such cases, private contract fire companies' drivers and vehicles are not subject to most of the safety regulations.

In addition to 49 CFR 390.3(f)(5), private contract firefighting companies are also exempted by 49 CFR 390.23 when providing direct assistance during national, regional or local emergencies. The term "emergency," as used in §390.23, means an occurrence, natural or manmade, that interrupts the delivery of services (such as electricity, medical care, sewer, water, telecommunications, and telecommunications transmissions) or supplies (such as food and fuel), or that otherwise immediately threatens human life or public welfare. The occurrence must result in a declaration of an emergency by the President of the United States, the Governor of a State, or their authorized representatives having authority to declare emergencies; such as the FMCSA Field Administrator for the geographical area in which the occurrence happens; or by other Federal, State or local government officials having authority to declare emergencies. Direct assistance means transportation or other relief services provided by a motor carrier (including a private contract fire company) or its driver(s) incident to the immediate restoration of essential services or essential supplies. Direct assistance does not include transportation related to long-term rehabilitation of damaged physical infrastructure or routine commercial deliveries after the initial threat to human life and property has passed.

With regard to non-emergency and rescue activities, such as training exercises, emergency preparedness drills, or pre-positioning of personnel and equipment prior to an actual emergency, private contract fire companies must comply with the FMCSR while operating commercial motor vehicles in interstate commerce.

Question 27: Section 390.3(f)(5) provides an exemption from the FMCSRs for the operation of fire trucks and rescue vehicles while such vehicles are being used in emergency and related operations. What is meant by the phrase "emergency and related operations"?

Guidance: The term "emergency," as used in §390.3(f)(5), includes any occurrence, natural or manmade, that immediately threatens human life or public welfare, and requires the work of firefighters or rescue personnel to respond to the threat. Such occurrences include, but are not limited to, fires, floods, motor vehicle crashes, and medical emergencies. An emergency, however, need not have been formally declared by a governmental authority in order to utilize this exemption.

The term "related operations" includes driving fire trucks or rescue vehicles to the scene of an emergency, and driving such vehicles while returning from the emergency or rescue scene. "Related operations" does not include the pre-positioning of fire trucks or rescue vehicles in anticipation of emergencies, or the use of such vehicles in training or emergency preparedness exercises.

Question 28: Is the operation of motor vehicles designed or used to transport between 9 and 15 passengers (including the driver), in interstate commerce, by private firefighting companies transporting their employees subject to the FMCSRs?

Guidance: No. Although the 9- to 15-passenger vehicles are being operated in interstate commerce, firefighting companies transporting their own employees would be considered private motor carriers of passengers with regard to the operation of these vehicles because the passengers are not being transported for compensation. Vehicles designed or used to transport 9- to 15-passengers, in interstate commerce, but not for compensation, are excluded from the definition of "commercial motor vehicle" found at 49 CFR 390.5. Therefore, the FMCSRs are not applicable to the operation of such vehicles, even if the firefighting company operates other vehicles that are subject to the safety regulations.

Question 29: §390.3(f)(5) provides an exemption from the FMCSRs for the operation of fire trucks and rescue vehicles while such vehicles are being used in emergency and related operations. §390.23 provides an exception to most of the FMCSRs for motor carriers providing direct assistance during an emergency. What are the differences between these provisions when they are applied to contract wildfire suppression services?

Guidance: §390.3(f)(5) provides an exception to all of the requirements in Subchapter B of Chapter III, Title 49 of the Code of Federal Regulations (49 CFR Parts 350 through 399) for certain operations of fire trucks and rescue vehicles. By contrast the exception provided by §390.23 is limited to all of the requirements in 49 CFR Parts 390 through 399 and may be used by any motor carrier, including contract wildfire suppression services, providing direct assistance during an emergency, as defined in 49 CFR 390.5.

The exception provided by §390.3(f)(5) may be used by operators of fire trucks and rescue vehicles while such vehicles are used in emergency and related operations, regardless of whether there is an emergency declaration. The exception provided in §390.23 always requires a declaration of an emergency by the President of the United States, the Governor of a State, or their authorized representatives having authority to declare emergencies, such as the FMCSA Field Administrator for the geographical area in which the occurrence happens; or by other Federal, State, or local government officials having authority to declare emergencies.

Question 30: §390.3(f)(5) provides an exemption from the FMCSRs for the operation of fire trucks and rescue vehicles while such vehicles are being used in emergency and related operations. Is this exemption applicable to all fire trucks and rescue vehicles, or is it limited to such vehicles when they are used for emergency and related operations associated with occurrences in or around residential or commercial buildings or structures?

Guidance: §390.3(f)(5) is applicable to all fire trucks and rescue vehicles while such vehicles are being used in emergency and related operations, regardless of whether the emergency or related operation involves occurrences in or around residential or commercial buildings or structures. For example, §390.3(f)(5) is applicable to fire trucks and rescue vehicles used by wildfire suppression services when these vehicles are used in emergency and related operations, regardless of whether there are buildings or structures in the immediate vicinity of the fire suppression activities.

Question 31: §390.3(f)(5) provides an exemption from the FMCSRs for the operation of fire trucks and rescue vehicles while such vehicles are being used in emergency and related operations. What is meant by the phrase "fire trucks and rescue vehicles?"

Guidance: For the purposes of §390.3(f)(5), the term "fire trucks and rescue vehicles" should be considered to include a wide range of fire and rescue apparatus used by fire fighters, such as, but not limited to, pumper trucks (which may or may not be equipped with water tanks) and rescue trucks (used to transport a crew and various emergency equipment; they may or may not be equipped with water pumping equipment) used primarily or exclusively for fire and rescue operations.

The term "fire trucks and rescue vehicles" should not be considered to include certain wildfire suppression services support vehicles such as: trucks operated by caterers or other food vendors; cargo tank vehicles and trailers operated by water supply companies; cargo tank vehicles and trailers used to transport fuel for helicopters and auxiliary equipment such as generators; vehicles used to transport tents (or other temporary shelters), portable showers, or portable/mobile restrooms; or, buses designed or used to transport 16 or more passengers, including the driver. Although cargo tank vehicles and trailers operated by water supply companies should not be considered fire trucks or rescue vehicles, wildfire suppression efforts that require significant use of water supply companies are likely to result in the declaration of an emergency, as defined in 49 CFR 390.5. If an emergency is declared, all motor carriers, including water supply companies, providing direct assistance (as defined in 49 CFR 390.5) in responding to the emergency would be covered by §390.23, an exception to all of the requirements of 49 CFR Parts 390 through 399.

§390.5 Definitions.

Unless specifically defined elsewhere, in this subchapter:

Accident means —
  (1) *Except as provided* in paragraph (2) of this definition, an occurrence involving a commercial motor vehicle operating on a highway in interstate or intrastate commerce which results in:
    (i) *A fatality;*
    (ii) *Bodily injury to a person* who, as a result of the injury, immediately receives medical treatment away from the scene of the accident; or
    (iii) *One or more motor vehicles* incurring disabling damage as a result of the accident, requiring the motor vehicle(s) to be transported away from the scene by a tow truck or other motor vehicle.
  (2) *The term accident does not include:*
    (i) *An occurrence* involving only boarding and alighting from a stationary motor vehicle; or
    (ii) *An occurrence* involving only the loading or unloading of cargo.

Alcohol concentration (AC) means the concentration of alcohol in a person's blood or breath. When expressed as a percentage it means grams of alcohol per 100 milliliters of blood or grams of alcohol per 210 liters of breath.

Bus means any motor vehicle designed, constructed, and/or used for the transportation of passengers, including taxicabs.

Business district means the territory contiguous to and including a highway when within any 600 feet along such highway there are buildings in use for business or industrial purposes, including but not limited to, hotels, banks, or office buildings which occupy at least 300 feet of frontage on one side or 300 feet collectively on both sides of the highway.

Charter transportation of passengers means transportation, using a bus, of a group of persons who pursuant to a common purpose, under a single contract, at a fixed charge for the motor vehicle, have acquired the exclusive use of the motor vehicle to travel together under an itinerary either specified in advance or modified after having left the place of origin.

Commercial motor vehicle means any self-propelled or towed motor vehicle used on a highway in interstate commerce to transport passengers or property when the vehicle —
  (1) *Has a gross vehicle weight rating* or gross combination weight rating, or gross vehicle weight or gross combination weight, of 4,536 kg (10,001 pounds) or more, whichever is greater; or
  (2) *Is designed or used to transport* more than 8 passengers (including the driver) for compensation; or
  (3) *Is designed or used to transport* more than 15 passengers, including the driver, and is not used to transport passengers for compensation; or
  (4) *Is used in transporting material* found by the Secretary of Transportation to be hazardous under 49 U.S.C. 5103 and transported in a quantity requiring placarding under regulations prescribed by the Secretary under 49 CFR, Subtitle B, Chapter I, Subchapter C.

Conviction means an unvacated adjudication of guilt, or a determination that a person has violated or failed to comply with the law in a court of original jurisdiction or by an authorized administrative tribunal, an unvacated forfeiture of bail or collateral deposited to secure the person's appearance in court, a plea of guilty or nolo contendere accepted by the court, the payment of a fine or court cost, or violation of a condition of release without bail, regardless of whether or not the penalty is rebated, suspended, or probated.

Direct assistance means transportation and other relief services provided by a motor carrier or its driver(s) incident to the immediate restoration of essential services (such as, electricity, medial care, sewer, water, telecommunications, and telecommunication transmissions) or essential supplies (such as, food and fuel). It does not include transportation related to long-term rehabilitation of damaged physical infrastructure or routine commercial deliveries after the initial threat to life and property has passed.

Direct compensation means payment made to the motor carrier by the passengers or a person acting on behalf of the passengers for the transportation services provided, and not included in a total package charge or other assessment for highway transportation services.

Disabling damage means damage which precludes departure of a motor vehicle from the scene of the accident in its usual manner in daylight after simple repairs.
  (1) *Inclusions.* Damage to motor vehicles that could have been driven, but would have been further damaged if so driven.
  (2) *Exclusions.*
    (i) *Damage which can be remedied temporarily* at the scene of the accident without special tools or parts.
    (ii) *Tire disablement without other damage* even if no spare tire is available.
    (iii) *Headlamp or taillight damage.*
    (iv) *Damage to turn signals,* horn, or windshield wipers which makes them inoperative.

Driveaway-towaway operation means an operation in which an empty or unladen motor vehicle with one or more sets of wheels on the surface of the roadway is being transported:
  (1) *Between vehicle manufacturer's facilities;*
  (2) *Between a vehicle manufacturer* and a dealership or purchaser;
  (3) *Between a dealership,* or other entity selling or leasing the vehicle, and a purchaser or lessee;
  (4) *To a motor carrier's terminal* or repair facility for the repair of disabling damage (as defined in §390.5) following a crash; or
  (5) *To a motor carrier's terminal* or repair facility for repairs associated with the failure of a vehicle component or system; or
  (6) *By means of a saddle-mount or tow-bar.*

Driver means any person who operates any commercial motor vehicle.

Driving a commercial motor vehicle while under the influence of alcohol means committing any one or more of the following acts in a CMV: Driving a CMV while the person's alcohol concentration is 0.04 or more; driving under the influence of alcohol, as prescribed by State law; or refusal to undergo such testing as is required by any State or jurisdiction in the enforcement of Table 1 to §§383.51 or 392.5(a)(2) of this subchapter.

Emergency means any hurricane, tornado, storm (e.g. thunderstorm, snowstorm, icestorm, blizzard, sandstorm, etc.), high water, wind-driven water, tidal wave, tsunami, earthquake, volcanic eruption, mud slide, drought, forest fire, explosion, blackout or other occurrence, natural or man-made, which interrupts the delivery of essential services (such as, electricity, medical care, sewer, water, telecommunications, and telecommunication transmissions) or essential supplies (such as, food and fuel) or otherwise immediately threatens human life or public welfare, provided such hurricane, tornado, or other event results in:

(1) *A declaration of an emergency* by the President of the United States, the Governor of a State, or their authorized representatives having authority to declare emergencies; by the FMCSA Field Administrator for the geographical area in which the occurrence happens; or by other Federal, state, or local government officials having authority to declare emergencies, or

(2) *A request by a police officer* for tow trucks to move wrecked or disabled motor vehicles.

Emergency relief means an operation in which a motor carrier or driver of a commercial motor vehicle is providing direct assistance to supplement State and local efforts and capabilities to save lives or property or to protect public health and safety as a result of an emergency as defined in this section.

Employee means any individual, other than an employer, who is employed by an employer and who in the course of his or her employment directly affects commercial motor vehicle safety. Such term includes a driver of a commercial motor vehicle (including an independent contractor while in the course of operating a commercial motor vehicle), a mechanic, and a freight handler. Such term does not include an employee of the United States, any State, any political subdivision of a State, or any agency established under a compact between States and approved by the Congress of the United States who is acting within the course of such employment.

Employer means any person engaged in a business affecting interstate commerce who owns or leases a commercial motor vehicle in connection with that business, or assigns employees to operate it, but such term does not include the United States, any State, any political subdivision of a State, or an agency established under a compact between States approved by the Congress of the United States.

Exempt intracity zone means the geographic area of a municipality or the commercial zone of that municipality described in Appendix F to Subchapter B of this chapter. The term "exempt intracity zone" does not include any municipality or commercial zone in the State of Hawaii. For purposes of §391.62, a driver may be considered to operate a commercial motor vehicle wholly within an exempt intracity zone notwithstanding any common control, management, or arrangement for a continuous carriage or shipment to or from a point without such zone.

Exempt motor carrier means a person engaged in transportation exempt from economic regulation by the Federal Motor Carrier Safety Administration (FMCSA) under 49 U.S.C. 13506. "Exempt motor carriers" are subject to the safety regulations set forth in this subchapter.

Farm vehicle driver means a person who drives only a commercial motor vehicle that is —

(1) *Controlled and operated* by a farmer as a private motor carrier of property;

(2) *Being used to transport either —*
  (i) *Agricultural products,* or
  (ii) *Farm machinery, farm supplies,* or both, to or from a farm;

(3) *Not being used in the operation of a for-hire motor carrier;*

(4) *Not carrying hazardous materials* of a type or quantity that requires the commercial motor vehicle to be placarded in accordance with §177.823 of this subtitle; and

(5) *Being used within 150 air-miles of the farmer's farm.*

Farmer means any person who operates a farm or is directly involved in the cultivation of land, crops, or livestock which —

(1) *Are owned by that person;* or

(2) *Are under the direct control of that person.*

Fatality means any injury which results in the death of a person at the time of the motor vehicle accident or within 30 days of the accident.

Federal Motor Carrier Safety Administrator means the chief executive of the Federal Motor Carrier Safety Administration, an agency within the Department of Transportation.

For-hire motor carrier means a person engaged in the transportation of goods or passengers for compensation.

Gross combination weight rating (GCWR) means the value specified by the manufacturer as the loaded weight of a combination (articulated) motor vehicle. In the absence of a value specified by the manufacturer, GCWR will be determined by adding the GVWR of the power unit and the total weight of the towed unit and any load thereon.

Gross vehicle weight rating (GVWR) means the value specified by the manufacturer as the loaded weight of a single motor vehicle.

Hazardous material means a substance or material which has been determined by the Secretary of Transportation to be capable of posing an unreasonable risk to health, safety, and property when transported in commerce, and which has been so designated.

Hazardous substance means a material, and its mixtures or solutions, that is identified in the appendix to §172.101, List of Hazardous Substances and Reportable Quantities, of this title when offered for transportation in one package, or in one transport motor vehicle if not packaged, and when the quantity of the material therein equals or exceeds the reportable quantity (RQ). This definition does not apply to petroleum products that are lubricants or fuels, or to mixtures or solutions of hazardous substances if in a concentration less than that shown in the table in §171.8 of this title, based on the reportable quantity (RQ) specified for the materials listed in the appendix to §172.101.

Hazardous waste means any material that is subject to the hazardous waste manifest requirements of the EPA specified in 40 CFR Part 262 or would be subject to these requirements absent an interim authorization to a State under 40 CFR Part 123, Subpart F.

Highway means any road, street, or way, whether on public or private property, open to public travel. "Open to public travel" means that the road section is available, except during scheduled periods, extreme weather or emergency conditions, passable by four-wheel standard passenger cars, and open to the general public for use without restrictive gates, prohibitive signs, or regulation other than restrictions based on size, weight, or class of registration. Toll plazas of public toll roads are not considered restrictive gates.

Interstate commerce means trade, traffic, or transportation in the United States —

(1) *Between a place in a State* and a place outside of such State (including a place outside of the United States);

(2) *Between two places in a State* through another State or a place outside of the United States; or

(3) *Between two places in a State* as part of trade, traffic, or transportation originating or terminating outside the State or the United States.

Intrastate commerce means any trade, traffic, or transportation in any State which is not described in the term "interstate commerce."

Medical examiner means a person who is licensed, certified, and/or registered, in accordance with applicable State laws and regulations, to perform physical examinations. The term includes but is not limited to, doctors of medicine, doctors of osteopathy, physician assistants, advanced practice nurses, and doctors of chiropractic.

Motor carrier means a for-hire motor carrier or a private motor carrier. The term includes a motor carrier's agents, officers and representatives as well as employees responsible for hiring, supervising, training, assigning, or dispatching of drivers and employees concerned with the installation, inspection, and maintenance of motor vehicle equipment and/or accessories. For purposes of Subchapter B, this definition includes the terms *employer,* and *exempt motor carrier.*

Motor vehicle means any vehicle, machine, tractor, trailer, or semitrailer propelled or drawn by mechanical power and used upon the highways in the transportation of passengers or property, or any combination thereof determined by the Federal Motor Carrier Safety Administration, but does not include any vehicle, locomotive, or car operated exclusively on a rail or rails, or a trolley bus operated by electric power derived from a fixed overhead wire, furnishing local passenger transportation similar to street-railway service.

Multiple-employer driver means a driver, who in any period of 7 consecutive days, is employed or used as a driver by more than one motor carrier.

Subpart A - General Applicability and Definitions §390.5

Operator — See driver.

Other terms — Any other term used in this subchapter is used in its commonly accepted meaning, except where such other term has been defined elsewhere in this subchapter. In that event, the definition therein given shall apply.

Out-of-service order means a declaration by an authorized enforcement officer of a Federal, State, Canadian, Mexican, or local jurisdiction that a driver, a commercial motor vehicle, or a motor carrier operation is out of service pursuant to 49 CFR 386.72, 392.5, 392.9a, 395.13, or 396.9, or compatible laws, or the North American Standard Out-of-Service Criteria.

Person means any individual, partnership, association, corporation, business trust, or any other organized group of individuals.

Previous employer means any DOT regulated person who employed the driver in the preceding 3 years, including any possible current employer.

Principal place of business means the single location designated by the motor carrier, normally its headquarters, for purposes of identification under this subchapter. The motor carrier must make records required by Parts 382, 387, 390, 391, 395, 396, and 397 of this subchapter available for inspection at this location within 48 hours (Saturdays, Sundays, and Federal holidays excluded) after a request has been made by a special agent or authorized representative of the Federal Motor Carrier Safety Administration.

Private motor carrier means a person who provides transportation of property or passengers, by commercial motor vehicle, and is not a for-hire motor carrier.

Private motor carrier of passengers (business) means a private motor carrier engaged in the interstate transportation of passengers which is provided in the furtherance of a commercial enterprise and is not available to the public at large.

Private motor carrier of passengers (nonbusiness) means private motor carrier involved in the interstate transportation of passengers that does not otherwise meet the definition of a private motor carrier of passengers (business).

Radar detector means any device or mechanism to detect the emission of radio microwaves, laser beams or any other future speed measurement technology employed by enforcement personnel to measure the speed of commercial motor vehicles upon public roads and highways for enforcement purposes. Excluded from this definition are radar detection devices that meet both of the following requirements:

(1) *Transported outside the driver's compartment* of the commercial motor vehicle. For this purpose, the driver's compartment of a passenger-carrying CMV shall include all space designed to accommodate both the driver and the passengers; and

(2) *Completely inaccessible to,* inoperable by, and imperceptible to the driver while operating the commercial motor vehicle.

Regional Director of Motor Carriers means the Field Administrator, Federal Motor Carrier Safety Administration, for a given geographical area of the United States.

Residential district means the territory adjacent to and including a highway which is not a business district and for a distance of 300 feet or more along the highway is primarily improved with residences.

School bus means a passenger motor vehicle which is designed or used to carry more than 10 passengers in addition to the driver, and which the Secretary determines is likely to be significantly used for the purpose of transporting preprimary, primary, or secondary school students to such schools from home or from such schools to home.

School bus operation means the use of a school bus to transport only school children and/or school personnel from home to school and from school to home.

Secretary means the Secretary of Transportation.

Single-employer driver means a driver who, in any period of 7 consecutive days, is employed or used as a driver solely by a single motor carrier. This term includes a driver who operates a commercial motor vehicle on an intermittent, casual, or occasional basis.

Special agent — See Appendix B to Subchapter B — Special agents.

State means a State of the United States and the District of Columbia and includes a political subdivision of a State.

Trailer includes:

(1) **Full trailer** means any motor vehicle other than a pole trailer which is designed to be drawn by another motor vehicle and so constructed that no part of its weight, except for the towing device, rests upon the self-propelled towing motor vehicle. A semitrailer equipped with an auxiliary front axle (converter dolly) shall be considered a full trailer.

(2) **Pole trailer** means any motor vehicle which is designed to be drawn by another motor vehicle and attached to the towing motor vehicle by means of a "reach" or "pole," or by being "boomed" or otherwise secured to the towing motor vehicle, for transporting long or irregularly shaped loads such as poles, pipes, or structural members, which generally are capable of sustaining themselves as beams between the supporting connections.

(3) **Semitrailer** means any motor vehicle, other than a pole trailer, which is designed to be drawn by another motor vehicle and is constructed so that some part of its weight rests upon the self-propelled towing motor vehicle.

Truck means any self-propelled commercial motor vehicle except a truck tractor, designed and/or used for the transportation of property.

Truck tractor means a self-propelled commercial motor vehicle designed and/or used primarily for drawing other vehicles.

United States means the 50 States and the District of Columbia.

§390.5 DOT Interpretations

Question 1: Do the definitions of "farm," "farmer" and "agricultural crops" apply to greenhouse operations?
Guidance: Yes.

Question 2: Is a vehicle used to transport or tow anhydrous ammonia nurse tanks considered a CMV and subject to FMCSRs?
Guidance: Yes, provided the vehicle's GVWR or GCWR meets or exceeds that of a CMV as defined in §390.5 and/or the vehicle transports HM in a quantity that requires placarding.

Question 3: If a vehicle's GVWR plate and/or VIN number are missing but its actual gross weight is 10,001 pounds or more, may an enforcement officer use the latter instead of GVWR to determine the applicability of the FMCSRs?
Guidance: Yes. The only apparent reason to remove the manufacturer's GVWR plate or VIN number is to make it impossible for roadside enforcement officers to determine the applicability of the FMCSRs, which have a GVWR threshold of 10,001 pounds. In order to frustrate willful evasion of safety regulations, an officer may therefore presume that a vehicle which does not have a manufacturer's GVWR plate and/or does not have a VIN number has a GVWR of 10,001 pounds or more if: (1) It has a size and configuration normally associated with vehicles that have a GVWR of 10,001 pounds or more; and (2) It has an actual gross weight of 10,001 pounds or more.

A motor carrier or driver may rebut the presumption by providing the enforcement officer the GVWR plate, the VIN number or other information of comparable reliability which demonstrates, or allows the officer to determine, that the GVWR of the vehicle is below the jurisdictional weight threshold.

Question 4: If a vehicle with a manufacturer's GVWR of less than 10,001 pounds has been structurally modified to carry a heavier load, may an enforcement officer use the higher actual gross weight of the vehicle, instead of the GVWR, to determine the applicability of the FMCSRs?
Guidance: Yes. The motor carrier's intent to increase the weight rating is shown by the structural modifications. When the vehicle is used to perform functions normally performed by a vehicle with a higher GVWR, §390.33 allows an enforcement officer to treat the actual gross weight as the GVWR of the modified vehicle.

Question 5: A driver used by a motor carrier operates a CMV to and from his/her residence out of State. Is this considered interstate commerce?
Guidance: If the driver is operating a CMV at the direction of the motor carrier, it is considered interstate commerce and is subject to the FMCSRs. If the motor carrier is allowing the driver to use the vehicle for private personal transportation, such transportation is not subject to the FMCSRs.

Question 6: Is transporting an empty CMV across State lines for purposes of repair and maintenance considered interstate commerce?
Guidance: Yes. The FMCSRs are applicable to drivers and CMVs in interstate commerce which transport property. The property in this situation is the empty CMV.

Question 7: Does off-road motorized construction equipment meet the definitions of "motor vehicle" and "commercial motor vehicle" as used in §§383.5 and 390.5?
Guidance: No. Off-road motorized construction equipment is outside the scope of these definitions: (1) When operated at construction sites: and (2) when operated on a public road open to unrestricted public travel, provided the equipment is not used in furtherance of a transportation purpose. Occasionally driving such equipment on a public road to reach or leave a construction site does not amount to furtherance of a transportation purpose. Since construction equipment is not designed to operate in traffic, it should be accompanied by escort vehicles or in some other way separated from the public traffic. This equipment may also be subject to State or local permit requirements with regard to escort vehicles, special markings, time of day, day of the week, and/or the specific route.

Question 8: What types of equipment are included in the category of off-road motorized construction equipment?
Guidance: The definition of off-road motorized construction equipment is to be narrowly construed and limited to equipment which, by its design and function is obviously not intended for use on a public road. Examples of such equipment include motor scrapers, backhoes, motor graders, compactors, tractors, trenchers, bulldozers and railroad track maintenance cranes.

Question 9: Are mobile cranes operating in interstate commerce subject to the FMCSRs?
Guidance: Yes, the definition of CMV encompasses mobile cranes.

Question 10: Does the FHWA define for-hire transportation of passengers the same as the former ICC did?
Guidance: To the extent FHWA's authority stems from 49 U.S.C. 31502 or other sections of Title 49 which are rooted in the Interstate Commerce Act, the FHWA is bound by judicial precedent and legislative history in interpreting that Act, much of which relates to the operations of the former ICC. However, since the MCSA of 1984 re-established the FHWA's jurisdictional authority and resulted in a re-promulgation of the FMCSRs, the FHWA has been establishing its own precedents based on "safety" rather than "economics" as the overriding consideration. This has resulted in some deviation in the definition of terms by the two agencies, e.g., commercial zones, for-hire transportation, etc.

The term "for-hire motor carrier" as defined in Part 390 means a person engaged in the transportation of goods or passengers for compensation. The FMCSA has determined that any business entity that assesses a fee, monetary or otherwise, directly or indirectly for the transportation of passengers is operating as a for-hire carrier. Thus, the transportation for compensation in interstate commerce of passengers by motor vehicles (except in six-passenger taxicabs operating on fixed routes) in the following operations would typically be subject to all parts of the FMCSRs, including Part 387: whitewater river rafters, hotel/motel shuttle transporters, rental car shuttle services, etc. These are examples of for-hire carriage because some fee is charged, usually indirectly in a total package charge or other assessment for transportation performed.

Question 11: A company has a truck with a GVWR under 10,001 pounds towing a trailer with a GVWR under 10,001 pounds. However, the GVWR of the truck added to the GVWR of the trailer is greater than 10,001 pounds. Would the company operating this vehicle in interstate commerce have to comply with the FMCSRs?
Guidance: §390.5 of the FMCSRs includes in the definition of CMV a vehicle with a GVWR or GCWR of 10,001 or more pounds. The section further defines GCWR as the value specified by the manufacturer as the loaded weight of a combination (articulated) vehicle. Therefore, if the GVWR of the truck added to the GVWR of the trailer exceeds 10,001 pounds, the driver and vehicle are subject to the FMCSRs.

Question 12: A CMV becomes stuck in a median or on a shoulder, and has had no contact with another vehicle, a pedestrian, or a fixed object prior to becoming stuck. If a tow truck is used to pull the CMV back onto the traveled portion of the road, would this be considered an accident?
Guidance: No.

Question 13: To what extent would the windshield and/or mirrors of a vehicle have to be damaged in order for it to be considered "disabling damage" as used in the definition of an accident in §390.5?
Guidance: The decision as to whether damage to a windshield and/or mirrors is disabling is left to the discretion of the investigating officer.

Question 14: Is the tillerman who controls the steerable rear axle of a vehicle so equipped a driver subject to the FMCSRs while operating in interstate commerce?
Guidance: Yes. Although the tillerman does not control the vehicle's speed or braking, the rear-axle steering he/she performs is essential to prevent the trailer from offtracking into other lanes or vehicles or off the highway entirely. Because this function is critical to the safe operation of vehicles with steerable rear axles, the tillerman is a driver.

Question 15: Does the definition of a "commercial motor vehicle" in §390.5 of the FMCSRs include parking lot and/or street sweeping vehicles?
Guidance: If the GVWR of a parking lot or street sweeping vehicle is 10,001 or more pounds, and it operates in interstate commerce, it is a CMV.

Question 16: Does a driver leasing company that hires, assigns, trains, and/or supervises drivers for a private or for-hire motor carrier become a motor carrier as defined by 49 CFR 390.5?
Guidance: No.

Question 17: May a motor carrier that employs owner-operators who have their own operating authority issued by the FHWA or the Surface Transportation Board transfer the responsibility for compliance with the FMCSRs to the owner-operators?
Guidance: No. The term "employee," as defined in §390.5, specifically includes an independent contractor employed by a motor carrier. The existence of operating authority has no bearing upon the issue. The motor carrier is, therefore, responsible for compliance with the FMCSRs by its driver employees, including those who are owner-operators.

Question 18: Must a person who is injured in an accident and immediately receives treatment away from the scene of the accident be transported in an ambulance?
Guidance: No. Any type of vehicle may be used to transport an injured person from the accident scene to the treatment site.

Question 19: What is the meaning of "immediate" as used in the definition of "accident"?
Guidance: The term "immediate" means without an unreasonable delay. A person immediately receives medical treatment if he or she is transported directly from the scene of an accident to a hospital or other medical facility as soon as it is considered safe and feasible to move the injured person away from the scene of the accident.

Question 20: A person involved in an incident discovers that he or she is injured after leaving the scene of the incident and receives medical attention at that time. Does the incident meet the definition of accident in 49 CFR 390.5?
Guidance: No. The incident does not meet the definition of accident in 49 CFR 390.5 because the person did not receive treatment immediately after the incident.

Question 21: Do electronic devices which are advertised as radar jammers meet the definition of a radar detector in 49 CFR 390.5?
Guidance: Devices that are said to reflect incoming energy passively or to transmit steadily on the same frequency as police radar units are not radar detectors because they do not detect radio microwaves. Devices that are said to detect and isolate the incoming signal and then to transmit on the same frequency to interfere with the police unit would qualify as radar detectors.

Question 22: Is a motor vehicle drawing a non-self-propelled mobile home that has one or more set of wheels on the roadway, a driveaway-towaway operation?
Guidance: Yes, if the mobile home is a commodity. For example, the mobile home is transported from the manufacturer to the dealer or from the dealer or other seller to the buyer.

Question 23: Can a truck tractor drawing a trailer be a driveaway-towaway operation?
Guidance: Yes, if the trailer is a commodity. For example, the trailer is transported from the manufacturer to the dealer or from the dealer or other seller to the buyer.

Question 24: Are trailers which are stacked upon each other and drawn by a motor vehicle by attachment to the bottom trailer, a driveaway-towaway operation.
Guidance: No. Only the bottom trailer has one or more sets of wheels on the roadway. The other trailers are cargo.

Question 25: The definition of a passenger CMV is a vehicle "designed to transport" more than 15 passengers, including the driver. Does that include standing passengers if the vehicle was specifically designed to accommodate standees?

Guidance: No. "Designed to transport" refers only to the number of designated seats; it does not include areas suitable, or even designed, for standing passengers.

Question 26: What is considered a "public road"?

Guidance: A public road is any road under the jurisdiction of a public agency and open to public travel or any road on private property that is open to public travel.

Question 27: An individual is transported to a hospital for observation or "check up" after an occurrence involving a CMV. Is this observation or check up considered "medical treatment," making the occurrence an "accident" for purposes of the FMCSRs?

Guidance: No. An individual who does not receive active medical intervention for injuries directly related to the occurrence, has not received "medical treatment" as that term is used in §390.5. The observation or check up alone would not make the occurrence an "accident" for purposes of the FMCSRs.

Question 28: Is the §390.5 definition of an accident met when a driver of a commercial motor vehicle (CMV) is changing lanes and a passenger car driver behind the CMV loses control, leaves the roadway, and hits a building sustaining damage requiring the vehicle to be towed?

Guidance: No. An occurrence in which a motor carrier's vehicle does not leave the roadway, or strike another vehicle, person or object does not meet the definition of an accident. No contact between the vehicles is not a recordable accident.

Question 29: A corporation (the parent corporation) owns subsidiary corporations that are for-hire motor carriers, each having their own separate operating authorities. The parent corporation does not operate commercial motor vehicles. However, the parent corporation exercises or retains management supervision, including supervision for safety compliance, and provides policy/procedural manuals and driver safety manuals for the subsidiary corporations (for-hire motor carriers). Is the parent corporation considered a motor carrier as defined by 49 CFR 390.5?

Guidance: No. A motor carrier is defined in 49 CFR 390.5 as a for-hire motor carrier or a private motor carrier. The term includes a motor carrier's agents, officers and representatives as well as employees responsible for hiring, supervising, training, assigning, or dispatching of drivers and employees concerned with the installation, inspection, and maintenance of motor vehicle equipment and/or accessories. As long as the parent corporation does not engage in the transportation of goods or passengers for compensation (i.e., exercising daily control over drivers and equipment; and, in the case of a for-hire motor carrier, soliciting customers, and billing and collecting freight charges), it would not be considered a motor carrier. The exercise of managerial control by the parent corporation by establishing operational policies and procedures, or through other forms of general oversight, does not, in and of itself, make it a motor carrier under FMCSA regulations.

§390.7 Rules of construction.

(a) *In Part 325 of Subchapter A and in this subchapter,* unless the context requires otherwise:
  (1) *Words imparting the singular include the plural;*
  (2) *Words imparting the plural include the singular;*
  (3) *Words imparting the present tense include the future tense.*

(b) *In this subchapter the word —*
  (1) **Officer** includes any person authorized by law to perform the duties of the office;
  (2) **Writing** includes printing and typewriting;
  (3) **Shall** is used in an imperative sense;
  (4) **Must** is used in an imperative sense;
  (5) **Should** is used in a recommendatory sense;
  (6) **May** is used in a permissive sense; and
  (7) **Includes** is used as a word of inclusion, not limitation.

Subpart B - General Requirements and Information

§390.9 State and local laws, effect on.

Except as otherwise specifically indicated, Subchapter B of this chapter is not intended to preclude States or subdivisions thereof from establishing or enforcing State or local laws relating to safety, the compliance with which would not prevent full compliance with these regulations by the person subject thereto.

§390.9 DOT Interpretations

Question 1: If an interstate driver gets stopped by a State enforcement officer for an inspection, would the inspecting officer be enforcing the Federal regulations or State regulations?

Guidance: A State enforcement officer can only enforce State laws. However, under the Motor Carrier Safety Assistance Program, quite often State laws are the same as or similar to the FMCSRs.

§390.11 Motor carrier to require observance of driver regulations.

Whenever in Part 325 of Subchapter A or in this subchapter a duty is prescribed for a driver or a prohibition is imposed upon the driver, it shall be the duty of the motor carrier to require observance of such duty or prohibition. If the motor carrier is a driver, the driver shall likewise be bound.

§390.13 Aiding or abetting violations.

No person shall aid, abet, encourage, or require a motor carrier or its employees to violate the rules of this chapter.

§390.15 Assistance in investigations and special studies.

(a) *A motor carrier must make* all records and information pertaining to an accident available to an authorized representative or special agent of the Federal Motor Carrier Safety Administration, an authorized State or local enforcement agency representative or authorized third party representative, upon request or as part of any investigation within such time as the request or investigation may specify. A motor carrier shall give an authorized representative all reasonable assistance in the investigation of any accident including providing a full, true and correct response to any question of the inquiry.

(b) *For accidents that occur after April 29, 2003,* motor carriers must maintain an accident register for three years after the date of each accident. For accidents that occurred on or prior to April 29, 2003, motor carriers must maintain an accident register for a period of one year after the date of each accident. Information placed in the accident register must contain at least the following:

  (1) *A list of accidents* as defined at §390.5 of this chapter containing for each accident:
    (i) *Date of accident.*
    (ii) *City or town, or most near,* where the accident occurred and the State where the accident occurred.
    (iii) *Driver Name.*
    (iv) *Number of injuries.*
    (v) *Number of fatalities.*
    (vi) *Whether hazardous materials,* other than fuel spilled from the fuel tanks of motor vehicle involved in the accident, were released.

  (2) *Copies of all accident reports* required by State or other governmental entities or insurers.

(Approved by the Office of Management and Budget under control number 2126-0009)

§390.15 DOT Interpretations

Question 1: May a motor carrier create an accident register of its own, or is there a specified form that must be used?

Guidance: There is no specified form. A motor carrier may create or use any accident register as long as it includes the elements required by §390.15.

Question 2: Would the accident report retention requirement in §390.15(b)(2) include an "Adjuster's Report" that is normally considered to be an internal document of an insurance company?

Guidance: No. The intent of §390.15(b)(2) is that motor carriers maintain copies of all documents which the motor carrier is required by the insurance company to complete and/or maintain. §390.15(b)(2) does not require motor carriers to maintain documents, such as "Adjuster's Reports," that are typically internal documents of the insurance company.

§390.16

Question 3: What types of documents must a motor carrier retain to support its accident register and be in compliance with §390.15(b)?
Guidance: The documents required by §390.15(b)(2) include all information about a particular accident generated by a motor carrier or driver to fulfill its accident reporting obligations to State or other governmental entities or that motor carrier's insurer. The language of paragraph (b)(2) does not require a motor carrier to seek out, obtain, and retain copies of accident reports prepared by State investigators or insurers.

Question 4: Does a foreign-based motor carrier's accident register have to include accidents that occur in Canada or Mexico?
Guidance: Motor carriers must record accidents occurring within the U.S. and on segments of interstate movements into Canada between the U.S.-Canadian border and the first physical delivery location of a Canadian consignee. The FHWA further believes its regulations require the documentation of accidents for segments of interstate movements out of Canada between the last physical pick-up location in Canada and the U.S.-Canadian border. The same would be true for movements between the U.S.-Mexican border and a point in Mexico. However, the FHWA does not have authority over Canadian and Mexican motor carriers that operate within their own countries where the transportation does not involve movements into or out of the United States.

§390.16 [Reserved]

§390.17 Additional equipment and accessories.

Nothing in this subchapter shall be construed to prohibit the use of additional equipment and accessories, not inconsistent with or prohibited by this subchapter, provided such equipment and accessories do not decrease the safety of operation of the commercial motor vehicles on which they are used.

§390.19 Motor carrier identification report.

(a) **Each motor carrier that conducts operations** in interstate commerce (or intrastate commerce if the carrier requires a Safety Permit as per §385.400 of this chapter) must file a Motor Carrier Identification Report, Form MCS-150, or the Combined Motor Carrier Identification Report and HM Permit Application, Form MCS-150B for permitted carriers, at the following times:

(1) *Before it begins operations; and*
(2) *Every 24 months, according to the following schedule:*

USDOT Number ending in:	Must file by last day of:
1	January
2	February
3	March
4	April
5	May
6	June
7	July
8	August
9	September
0	October

(3) *If the next-to-last digit of its USDOT number is odd,* the motor carrier shall file its update in every odd-numbered calendar year. If the next-to-last digit of the USDOT number is even, the motor carrier shall file its update in every even-numbered calendar year.

(b) **The Motor Carrier Identification Report,** Form MCS-150, and the Combined Motor Carrier Identification Report and HM Permit Application, Form MCS-150B, with complete instructions, are available from the FMCSA Web site at: http://www.fmcsa.dot.gov (Keyword "MCS-150" or "MCS-150B"); from all FMCSA Service Centers and Division offices nationwide; or by calling 1-800-832-5660.

(c) **The completed Motor Carrier Identification Report,** Form MCS-150, or Combined Motor Carrier Identification Report and HM Permit Application, Form MCS-150B, must be filed with FMCSA Office of Information Management.

(1) *The form may be filed electronically* according to the instructions at the agency's web site, or it may be sent to Federal Motor Carrier Safety Administration, Data Analysis and Information Systems, MC-PSDRIS, 400 Seventh Street, SW, Washington, DC 20590.

(2) *A for-hire motor carrier should submit* the Form MCS-150, or Form MCS-150B, along with its application for operating authority (Form OP-1 or OP-2), to the appropriate address referenced on that form, or may submit it electronically or by mail separately to the address mentioned in this section.

(d) **Only the legal name or a single trade name** of the motor carrier may be used on the motor carrier identification report (Form MCS-150 or MCS-150B).

(e) **A motor carrier that fails to file** a Motor Carrier Identification Report, Form MCS-150, or the Combined Motor Carrier Identification Report and HM Permit Application, Form MCS-150B, or furnishes misleading information or makes false statements upon Form MCS-150 or Form MCS-150B, is subject to the penalties prescribed in 49 U.S.C. 521(b)(2)(B).

(f) **Upon receipt and processing** of the Motor Carrier Identification Report, Form MCS-150, or the Combined Motor Carrier Identification Report and HM Permit Application, Form MCS-150B, the FMCSA will issue the motor carrier an identification number (USDOT Number). The motor carrier must display the number on each self-propelled CMV, as defined in §390.5, along with the additional information required by §390.21.

(g) **A motor carrier that registers its vehicles** in a State that participates in the Performance and Registration Information Systems Management (PRISM) program (authorized under section 4004 of the Transportation Equity Act for the 21st Century [(Public Law 105-178, 112 Stat. 107)] is exempt from the requirements of this section, provided it files all the required information with the appropriate State office.

(Approved by the Office of Management and Budget under control number 2126-0013)

§390.21 Marking of CMVs.

(a) **General.** Every self-propelled CMV, as defined in §390.5, subject to Subchapter B of this chapter must be marked as specified in paragraphs (b), (c), and (d) of this section.

(b) **Nature of marking.** The marking must display the following information:

(1) *The legal name or a single trade name* of the motor carrier operating the self-propelled CMV, as listed on the motor carrier identification report (Form MCS-150) and submitted in accordance with §390.19.
(2) *The motor carrier identification number* issued by the FMCSA, preceded by the letters "USDOT".
(3) *If the name of any person* other than the operating carrier appears on the CMV, the name of the operating carrier must be followed by the information required by paragraphs (b)(1), and (2) of this section, and be preceded by the words "operated by."
(4) *Other identifying information* may be displayed on the vehicle if it is not inconsistent with the information required by this paragraph.
(5) *Each motor carrier* shall meet the following requirements pertaining to its operation:
  (i) *All CMVs* that are part of a motor carrier's existing fleet on July 3, 2000, and which are marked with an ICCMC number must come into compliance with paragraph (b)(2) of this section by July 3, 2002.
  (ii) *All CMVs* that are part of a motor carrier's existing fleet on July 3, 2000, and which are not marked with the legal name or a single trade name on both sides of their CMVs, as shown on the Motor Carrier Identification Report, Form MCS-150, must come into compliance with paragraph (b)(1) of this section by July 5, 2005.
  (iii) *All CMVs added to a motor carrier's fleet* on or after July 3, 2000, must meet the requirements of this section before being put into service and operating on public ways.

(c) **Size, shape, location, and color of marking.** The marking must—
(1) *Appear on both sides of the self-propelled CMV;*
(2) *Be in letters that contrast sharply in color* with the background on which the letters are placed;
(3) *Be readily legible,* during daylight hours, from a distance of 50 feet (15.24 meters) while the CMV is stationary; and
(4) *Be kept and maintained in a manner* that retains the legibility required by paragraph (c)(3) of this section.

(d) **Construction and durability.** The marking may be painted on the CMV or may consist of a removable device, if that device meets the identification and legibility requirements of paragraph (c) of this section, and such marking must be maintained as required by paragraph (c)(4) of this section.

Subpart B - General Requirements and Information §390.23 (c)

(e) Rented CMVs. A motor carrier operating a self-propelled CMV under a rental agreement having a term not in excess of 30 calendar days meets the requirements of this section if:
  (1) *The CMV is marked* in accordance with the provisions of paragraphs (b) through (d) of this section; or
  (2) *The CMV is marked* as set forth in paragraph (e)(2)(i) through (iv) of this section:
   (i) *The legal name or a single trade name* of the lessor is displayed in accordance with paragraphs (c) and (d) of this section.
   (ii) *The lessor's identification number* preceded by the letters "USDOT" is displayed in accordance with paragraphs (c) and (d) of this section; and
   (iii) *The rental agreement* entered into by the lessor and the renting motor carrier conspicuously contains the following information:
    [A] *The name and complete physical address* of the principal place of business of the renting motor carrier;
    [B] *The identification number* issued the renting motor carrier by the FMCSA, preceded by the letters "USDOT," if the motor carrier has been issued such a number. In lieu of the identification number required in this paragraph, the following may be shown in the rental agreement:
     [1] *Information which indicates* whether the motor carrier is engaged in "interstate" or "intrastate" commerce; and
     [2] *Information which indicates* whether the renting motor carrier is transporting hazardous materials in the rented CMV;
    [C] *The sentence:* "This lessor cooperates with all Federal, State, and local law enforcement officials nationwide to provide the identity of customers who operate this rental CMV"; and
   (iv) *The rental agreement* entered into by the lessor and the renting motor carrier is carried on the rental CMV during the full term of the rental agreement. See the leasing regulations at 49 CFR 376 for information that should be included in all leasing documents.
(f) Driveaway services. In driveaway services, a removable device may be affixed on both sides or at the rear of a single driven vehicle. In a combination driveaway operation, the device may be affixed on both sides of any one unit or at the rear of the last unit. The removable device must display the legal name or a single trade name of the motor carrier and the motor carrier's USDOT number.

§390.21 DOT Interpretations
Question 1: What markings must be displayed on a CMV when used by two or more motor carriers?
Guidance: The markings of the motor carrier responsible for the operation of the CMV must be displayed at the time of transportation. If 2 or more names are on the vehicle, the name of the operating motor carrier must be preceded by the words "operated by."

§390.23 Relief from regulations.
(a) Parts 390 through 399 of this chapter shall not apply to any motor carrier or driver operating a commercial motor vehicle to provide emergency relief during an emergency, subject to the following time limits:
  (1) *Regional emergencies.*
   (i) *The exemption provided* by paragraph (a)(1) of this section is effective only when:
    [A] *An emergency has been declared* by the President of the United States, the Governor of a State, or their authorized representatives having authority to declare emergencies; or
    [B] *The FMCSA Field Administrator* has declared that a regional emergency exists which justifies an exemption from Parts 390 through 399 of this chapter.
   (ii) *Except as provided in §390.25,* this exemption shall not exceed the duration of the motor carrier's or driver's direct assistance in providing emergency relief, or 30 days from the date of the initial declaration of the emergency or the exemption from the regulations by the FMCSA Field Administrator, whichever is less.
  (2) *Local emergencies.*
   (i) *The exemption provided* by paragraph (a)(2) of this section is effective only when:
    [A] *An emergency has been declared* by a Federal, State or local government official having authority to declare an emergency; or
    [B] *The FMCSA Field Administrator* has declared that a local emergency exists which justifies an exemption from Parts 390 through 399 of this chapter.
   (ii) *This exemption shall not exceed* the duration of the motor carrier's or driver's direct assistance in providing emergency relief, or 5 days from the date of the initial declaration of the emergency or the exemption from the regulations by the FMCSA Field Administrator, whichever is less.
  (3) *Tow trucks responding to emergencies.*
   (i) *The exemption provided* by paragraph (a)(3) of this section is effective only when a request has been made by a Federal, State or local police officer for tow trucks to move wrecked or disabled motor vehicles.
   (ii) *This exemption shall not exceed* the length of the motor carrier's or driver's direct assistance in providing emergency relief, or 24 hours from the time of the initial request for assistance by the Federal, State or local police officer, whichever is less.
(b) Upon termination of direct assistance to the regional or local emergency relief effort, the motor carrier or driver is subject to the requirements of Parts 390 through 399 of this chapter, with the following exception: A driver may return empty to the motor carrier's terminal or the driver's normal work reporting location without complying with Parts 390 through 399 of this chapter. However, a driver who informs the motor carrier that he or she needs immediate rest must be permitted at least 10 consecutive hours off duty before the driver is required to return to such terminal or location. Having returned to the terminal or other location, the driver must be relieved of all duty and responsibilities. Direct assistance terminates when a driver or commercial motor vehicle is used in interstate commerce to transport cargo not destined for the emergency relief effort, or when the motor carrier dispatches such driver or commercial motor vehicle to another location to begin operations in commerce.
(c) When the driver has been relieved of all duty and responsibilities upon termination of direct assistance to a regional or local emergency relief effort, no motor carrier shall permit or require any driver used by it to drive nor shall any such driver drive in commerce until:
  (1) *The driver has met the requirements* of §§395.3(a) and 395.5(a) of this chapter; and
  (2) *The driver has had at least 34 consecutive hours off-duty when:*
   (i) *The driver has been on duty* for more than 60 hours in any 7 consecutive days at the time the driver is relieved of all duty if the employing motor carrier does not operate every day in the week, or
   (ii) *The driver has been on duty* for more than 70 hours in any 8 consecutive days at the time the driver is relieved of all duty if the employing motor carrier operates every day in the week.

§390.23 DOT Interpretations
Question 1: Does §390.23 create an exemption from the FMCSRs each and every time the delivery of electricity is interrupted, no matter how isolated or minor the occurrence?
Guidance: The rule creates an exemption from the FMCSRs when interruptions of electricity are severe enough to trigger a declaration of an emergency by a public official authorized to do so.

An interruption of electricity that does not produce a declaration by a public official is not an emergency for purposes of the regulation and does not exempt a motor carrier or driver from the FMCSRs. A call reporting a downed power line, whether directed to the State police or a public utility company, does not create a declared emergency.

The authority to declare emergencies has been delegated to different officials in the various States. The FHWA has not attempted to list these officials. In order to utilize the exemption provided by §390.23, drivers and motor carriers must therefore ascertain that a declaration of an emergency was made by a State or local official authorized to do so.

Question 2: §390.23(a) provides that Parts 390 through 399 do not apply to any motor carrier or driver operating a CMV to provide direct assistance in an emergency. Is a motor carrier or driver required to keep a record of the driver's on-duty or driving time while providing relief?
Guidance: No.

Question 3: After providing emergency relief under §390.23, what on-duty hours must a driver use to determine how much off-duty time he/she must have before returning to the service of the employing motor carrier?
Guidance: The driver must total the number of hours worked while the driver actually provided direct assistance to the emergency relief effort.

Question 4: Upon termination of direct assistance to a regional or local emergency relief effort, as specified in §390.23(a), may utility company line crews return directly to the motor carrier's terminal or the driver's normal work reporting location without complying with Parts 390-399?
Guidance: Yes, provided drivers who ask for immediate rest are given 8 consecutive hours off-duty before returning to the terminal or other work reporting location. Because the returning vehicles are transporting only crew members, tools, equipment, or materials not used in the emergency relief effort, they are considered to be "return[ing] empty" for purposes of §390.23(b).

Question 5: When an interstate tow truck operator responds to a request for assistance from a Federal, State or local police officer to move wrecked or disabled motor vehicles, what should the Record of Duty Status (RODS) required by §395.8 reflect for the time spent in the exempt status?
Guidance: The time spent responding to the police call is exempt under §390.23(a)(3). The entry on the RODS for the time spent in this activity should be entered as "exempt," or "exempt under §390.23(a)(3)." Any time logged by the driver while engaged in activities that are NOT exempt must be accounted for on the RODS, but exempt time is not included in the computation of maximum driving time under §395.3. Please note that this exemption is only operative during the time that the tow truck operator is providing direct assistance to the emergency, or twenty-four hours from the time of the request, whichever is less. The driver and the motor carrier are also at all times subject to the prohibitions of §392.3 pertaining to ill or fatigued drivers. Section 390.23(c) applies to local and regional emergencies, not tow truck emergency operations.

§390.25 Extension of relief from regulations — emergencies.

The FMCSA Field Administrator may extend the 30-day time period of the exemption contained in §390.23(a)(1), but not the 5-day time period contained in §390.23(a)(2) or the 24-hour period contained in §390.23(a)(3). Any motor carrier or driver seeking to extend the 30-day limit shall obtain approval from the FMCSA Field Administrator in the region in which the motor carrier's principal place of business is located before the expiration of the 30-day period. The motor carrier or driver shall give full details of the additional relief requested. The FMCSA Field Administrator shall determine if such relief is necessary taking into account both the severity of the ongoing emergency and the nature of the relief services to be provided by the carrier or driver. If the FMCSA Field Administrator approves an extension of the exemption, he or she shall establish a new time limit and place on the motor carrier or driver any other restrictions deemed necessary.

§390.27 Locations of motor carrier safety service centers.

Service center	Territory included	Location of office
Eastern	CT, DC, DE, MA, MD, ME, NJ, NH, NY, PA, PR, RI, VA, VT, Virgin Islands, WV	City Crescent Building, #10 South Howard Street, Suite 4000, Baltimore, MD 21201-2819
Midwestern	IA, IL, IN, KS, MI, MO, MN, NE, OH, WI	19900 Governors Drive, Suite 210, Olympia Fields, IL 60461-1021
Southern	AL, AR, FL, GA, KY, LA, MS, NC, NM, OK, SC, TN, TX	61 Forsyth Street, SW, Suite 17T75, Atlanta, GA 30303-3104
Western	American Samoa, AK, AZ, CA, CO, Guam, HI, ID, Mariana Islands, MT, ND, NV, OR, SD, UT, WA, WY	201 Mission Street, Suite 2100, San Francisco, CA 94105-1838

Note 1: Canadian carriers, for information regarding proper service center, contact a FMCSA division (State) office in AK, ME, MI, MT, NY, ND, VT, or WA.

Note 2: Mexican carriers, for information regarding proper service center, contact a FMCSA division (State) office in AZ, CA, NM, or TX.

§390.29 Location of records or documents.

(a) **A motor carrier with multiple offices or terminals** may maintain the records and documents required by this subchapter at its principal place of business, a regional office, or driver work-reporting location unless otherwise specified in this subchapter.

(b) **All records and documents** required by this subchapter which are maintained at a regional office or driver work-reporting location shall be made available for inspection upon request by a special agent or authorized representative of the Federal Motor Carrier Safety Administration at the motor carrier's principal place of business or other location specified by the agent or representative within 48 hours after a request is made. Saturdays, Sundays, and Federal holidays are excluded from the computation of the 48-hour period of time.

§390.31 Copies of records or documents.

(a) **All records and documents required to be maintained** under this subchapter must be preserved in their original form for the periods specified, unless the records and documents are suitably photographed and the microfilm is retained in lieu of the original record for the required retention period.

(b) **To be acceptable in lieu of original records,** photographic copies of records must meet the following minimum requirements:

  (1) *Photographic copies* shall be no less readily accessible than the original record or document as normally filed or preserved would be and suitable means or facilities shall be available to locate, identify, read, and reproduce such photographic copies.

  (2) *Any significant characteristic, feature or other attribute* of the original record or document, which photography in black and white will not preserve, shall be clearly indicated before the photograph is made.

  (3) *The reverse side of printed forms* need not be copied if nothing has been added to the printed matter common to all such forms, but an identified specimen of each form shall be on the film for reference.

  (4) *Film used for photographing copies* shall be of permanent record-type meeting in all respects the minimum specifications of the National Bureau of Standards, and all processes recommended by the manufacturer shall be observed to protect it from deterioration or accidental destruction.

  (5) *Each roll of film shall include a microfilm* of a certificate or certificates stating that the photographs are direct or facsimile reproductions of the original records. Such certificate(s) shall be executed by a person or persons having personal knowledge of the material covered thereby.

(c) **All records and documents required to be maintained** under this subchapter may be destroyed after they have been suitably photographed for preservation.

(d) **Exception.** All records except those requiring a signature may be maintained through the use of computer technology provided the motor carrier can produce, upon demand, a computer printout of the required data.

§390.31 DOT Interpretations

Question 1: May records required by the FMCSRs be maintained in an electronic format?
Guidance: Yes, provided the motor carrier can produce the information required by the regulations. Documents requiring a signature must be capable of replication (i.e., photocopy, facsimile, etc.) in such form that will provide an opportunity for signature verification upon demand. If computer records are used, all of the relevant data on the original documents must be included in order for the record to be valid.

Question 2: How long does a motor carrier have to produce records if a motor carrier maintains all records in an electronic format?
Guidance: A motor carrier must produce all records maintained in an electronic format within 2 working days after the request. Documents requiring a signature must be capable of replication (e.g., photocopy, facsimile, etc.) in such form that will provide an opportunity for signature verification upon demand.

Question 3: Using record scanning technology, these requirements can be fulfilled. Is my understanding of §390.31 paragraph (c) correct that once qualifying documents have been suitably scanned, original paper documents may be destroyed?
Guidance: Yes, scanned records, which include a verifiable signature, would fulfill the requirements of §390.31 and the original paper documents may be destroyed as stated in §390.31(c).

Question 4: If my understanding of §390.31 and its associated interpretations is correct, will this negate the necessity to maintain the original road test document as required by §391.31(g)(1)?
Guidance: Yes, as long as the road test document has been properly scanned.

§390.33 Commercial motor vehicles used for purposes other than defined.

Whenever a commercial motor vehicle of one type is used to perform the functions normally performed by a commercial motor vehicle of another type, the requirements of this subchapter and Part 325 of Subchapter A shall apply to the commercial motor vehicle and to its operation in the same manner as though the commercial motor vehicle were actually a commercial motor vehicle of the latter type.

Example: If a commercial motor vehicle other than a bus is used to perform the functions normally performed by a bus, the regulations pertaining to buses and to the transportation of passengers shall apply to that commercial motor vehicle.

§390.35 Certificates, reports, and records: Falsification, reproduction, or alteration.

No motor carrier, its agents, officers, representatives, or employees shall make or cause to make —

(a) A fraudulent or intentionally false statement on any application, certificate, report, or record required by Part 325 of Subchapter A or this subchapter;

(b) A fraudulent or intentionally false entry on any application, certificate, report, or record required to be used, completed, or retained, to comply with any requirement of this subchapter or Part 325 of Subchapter A; or

(c) A reproduction, for fraudulent purposes, of any application, certificate, report, or record required by this subchapter or Part 325 of Subchapter A.

§390.37 Violation and penalty.

Any person who violates the rules set forth in this subchapter or Part 325 of Subchapter A may be subject to civil or criminal penalties.

Subpart C [Reserved]

Special Topics — Serious Pattern of Violations
Question 1: What constitutes a "serious pattern" of violations?
Guidance: A serious pattern constitutes violations that are both widespread and continuing over a period of time. A serious pattern is more than isolated violations. A serious pattern does not require a specific number of violations.

Notes

Part 391 - Qualifications of Drivers and Longer Combination Vehicle (LCV) Driver Instructors (Page 95 in the Driver Edition)

Subpart A - General

§391.1 Scope of the rules in this part; additional qualifications; duties of carrier-drivers.
(a) **The rules in this part** establish minimum qualifications for persons who drive commercial motor vehicles as, for, or on behalf of motor carriers. The rules in this part also establish minimum duties of motor carriers with respect to the qualifications of their drivers.

(b) **A motor carrier who employs himself/herself as a driver** must comply with both the rules in this part that apply to motor carriers and the rules in this part that apply to drivers.

§391.2 General exemptions.
(a) **Farm custom operation.** The rules in this part do not apply to a driver who drives a commercial motor vehicle controlled and operated by a person engaged in custom-harvesting operations, if the commercial motor vehicle is used to —
  (1) *Transport farm machinery, supplies, or both,* to or from a farm for custom-harvesting operations on a farm; or
  (2) *Transport custom-harvested crops to storage or market.*

(b) **Apiarian industries.** The rules in this part do not apply to a driver who is operating a commercial motor vehicle controlled and operated by a beekeeper engaged in the seasonal transportation of bees.

(c) **Certain farm vehicle drivers.** The rules in this part do not apply to a farm vehicle driver except a farm vehicle driver who drives an articulated (combination) commercial motor vehicle, as defined in §390.5. (For limited exemptions for farm vehicle drivers of articulated commercial motor vehicles, see §391.67.)

§391.2 DOT Interpretations
Question 1: Must exempt intracity zone (see §390.5) drivers comply with the medical requirements of this subpart?
Guidance: No, provided:
  a. the driver was otherwise qualified and operating in a municipality or exempt intracity zone thereof throughout the 1-year period ending November 18, 1988; and,
  b. the driver's medical condition has not substantially worsened since August 23, 1988.

Question 2: What driver qualification requirements must a farm vehicle driver (as defined in §390.5) comply with in Part 391?
Guidance: Drivers meeting the definition of "farm vehicle driver" who operate straight trucks are exempted from all driver qualification requirements of Part 391. All drivers of articulated motor vehicles with a GCWR of 10,001 pounds or more are required to possess a current medical certificate as required in §§391.41 and 391.45.

Subpart B - Qualification and Disqualification of Drivers

§391.11 General qualifications of drivers.
(a) **A person shall not drive a commercial motor vehicle** unless he/she is qualified to drive a commercial motor vehicle. Except as provided in §391.63, a motor carrier shall not require or permit a person to drive a commercial motor vehicle unless that person is qualified to drive a commercial motor vehicle.

(b) **Except as provided in Subpart G of this part,** a person is qualified to drive a motor vehicle if he/she —
  (1) *Is at least 21 years old;*
  (2) *Can read and speak the English language sufficiently* to converse with the general public, to understand highway traffic signs and signals in the English language, to respond to official inquiries, and to make entries on reports and records;
  (3) *Can, by reason of experience, training, or both,* safely operate the type of commercial motor vehicle he/she drives;
  (4) *Is physically qualified* to drive a commercial motor vehicle in accordance with Subpart E - Physical Qualifications and Examinations of this part;
  (5) *Has a currently valid* commercial motor vehicle operator's license issued only by one State or jurisdiction;
  (6) *Has prepared and furnished* the motor carrier that employs him/her with the list of violations or the certificate as required by §391.27;
  (7) *Is not disqualified* to drive a commercial motor vehicle under the rules in §391.15; and
  (8) *Has successfully completed a driver's road test* and has been issued a certificate of driver's road test in accordance with §391.31, or has presented an operator's license or a certificate of road test which the motor carrier that employs him/her has accepted as equivalent to a road test in accordance with §391.33.

§391.11 DOT Interpretations
Question 1: Is there a maximum age limit for driving in interstate commerce?
Guidance: The FMCSRs do not specify any maximum age limit for drivers.

Question 2: Does the age requirement in §391.11(b)(1) apply to CMV drivers involved entirely in intrastate commerce?
Guidance: No. Neither the CDL requirements in Part 383 nor the FMCSRs in Parts 390-399 require drivers engaged purely in intrastate commerce to be 21 years old. The States may set lower age thresholds for intrastate drivers.

Question 3: What effect does the Age Discrimination in Employment Act have on the minimum age requirement for an interstate driver?
Guidance: None. The Age Discrimination in Employment Act, 29 U.S.C. 621-634, recognizes an exception when age is a bona fide occupational qualification. 29 U.S.C. 623(f)(1).

Question 4: May a motor carrier be exempt from driver qualification requirements by hiring a driver leasing company or temporary help service?
Guidance: No. The FMCSRs apply to, and impose responsibilities on, motor carriers and their drivers. The FHWA does not regulate driver leasing companies or temporary help service companies.

Question 5: May a motor carrier lawfully permit a person not yet qualified as a driver in accordance with §391.11 to operate a vehicle in interstate commerce for the purpose of attending a training and indoctrination course in the operation of that specific vehicle?
Guidance: No. If the trip is in interstate commerce, the driver must be fully qualified to operate a CMV.

Question 6: Does the Military Selective Service Act of 1967 require a motor carrier to place a returning veteran in his/her previous position (driving interstate) even though he/she fails to meet minimum physical standards?
Guidance: No. The Act does not require a motor carrier to place a returning veteran who does not meet the minimum physical standards into his/her previous driving position. The returning veteran must meet the physical requirements and obtain a medical examiner's certificate before driving in interstate operations.

§391.13 Responsibilities of drivers.
In order to comply with the requirements of §392.9(a) and §393.9 of this subchapter, a motor carrier shall not require or permit a person to drive a commercial motor vehicle unless the person —

(a) **Can, by reason** of experience, training, or both, determine whether the cargo he/she transports (including baggage in a passenger-carrying commercial motor vehicle) has been properly located, distributed, and secured in or on the commercial motor vehicle he/she drives;

(b) **Is familiar with methods and procedures** for securing cargo in or on the commercial motor vehicle he/she drives.

§391.15 Disqualification of drivers.
(a) **General.** A driver who is disqualified shall not drive a commercial motor vehicle. A motor carrier shall not require or permit a driver who is disqualified to drive a commercial motor vehicle.

(b) **Disqualification for loss of driving privileges.**
  (1) *A driver is disqualified* for the duration of the driver's loss of his/her privilege to operate a commercial motor vehicle on public highways, either temporarily or permanently, by reason of the revocation, suspension, withdrawal, or denial of an operator's license, permit, or privilege, until that operator's license, permit, or privilege is restored by the authority that revoked, suspended, withdrew, or denied it.
  (2) *A driver who receives a notice* that his/her license, permit, or privilege to operate a commercial motor vehicle has been revoked, suspended, or withdrawn shall notify the motor carrier that employs him/her of the contents of the notice before the end of the business day following the day the driver received it.

(c) **Disqualification for criminal and other offenses.**
  (1) *General rule.* A driver who is convicted of (or forfeits bond or collateral upon a charge of) a disqualifying offense specified in

paragraph (c)(2) of this section is disqualified for the period of time specified in paragraph (c)(3) of this section, if —
  (i) *The offense was committed* during on-duty time as defined in §395.2(a) of this subchapter or as otherwise specified; and
  (ii) *The driver is employed by a motor carrier* or is engaged in activities that are in furtherance of a commercial enterprise in interstate, intrastate, or foreign commerce;
 (2) *Disqualifying offenses.* The following offenses are disqualifying offenses:
  (i) *Driving a commercial motor vehicle* while under the influence of alcohol. This shall include:
   [A] *Driving a commercial motor vehicle* while the person's alcohol concentration is 0.04 percent or more;
   [B] *Driving under the influence of alcohol,* as prescribed by State law; or
   [C] *Refusal to undergo such testing* as is required by any State or jurisdiction in the enforcement of §391.15 (c)(2)(i)[A] or [B], or §392.5(a)(2).
  (ii) *Driving a commercial motor vehicle* under the influence of a 21 CFR 1308.11 Schedule I identified controlled substance, an amphetamine, a narcotic drug, a formulation of an amphetamine, or a derivative of a narcotic drug;
  (iii) *Transportation, possession, or unlawful use* of a 21 CFR 1308.11 Schedule I identified controlled substance, amphetamines, narcotic drugs, formulations of an amphetamine, or derivatives of narcotic drugs while the driver is on duty, as the term on-duty time is defined in §395.2 of this subchapter;
  (iv) *Leaving the scene of an accident* while operating a commercial motor vehicle; or
  (v) *A felony involving the use of a commercial motor vehicle.*
 (3) *Duration of disqualification.*
  (i) *First offenders.* A driver is disqualified for 1 year after the date of conviction or forfeiture of bond or collateral, if, during the 3 years preceding that date, the driver was not convicted of, or did not forfeit bond or collateral upon a charge of an offense that would disqualify the driver under the rules of this section. Exemption. The period of disqualification is 6 months if the conviction or forfeiture of bond or collateral solely concerned the transportation or possession of substances named in paragraph (c)(2)(iii) of this section.
  (ii) *Subsequent offenders.* A driver is disqualified for 3 years after the date of his/her conviction or forfeiture of bond or collateral if, during the 3 years preceding that date, he/she was convicted of, or forfeited bond or collateral upon a charge of, an offense that would disqualify him/her under the rules in this section.

(d) Disqualification for violation of out-of-service orders.
 (1) *General rule.* A driver who is convicted of violating an out-of-service order is disqualified for the period of time specified in paragraph (d)(2) of this section.
 (2) *Duration of disqualification for violation of out-of-service orders.*
  (i) *First violation.* A driver is disqualified for not less than 90 days nor more than one year if the driver is convicted of a first violation of an out-of-service order.
  (ii) *Second violation.* A driver is disqualified for not less than one year nor more than five years if, during any 10-year period, the driver is convicted of two violations of out-of-service orders in separate incidents.
  (iii) *Third or subsequent violation.* A driver is disqualified for not less than three years nor more than five years if, during any 10-year period, the driver is convicted of three or more violations of out-of-service orders in separate incidents.
  (iv) *Special rule* for hazardous materials and passenger offenses. A driver is disqualified for a period of not less than 180 days nor more than two years if the driver is convicted of a first violation of an out-of-service order while transporting hazardous materials required to be placarded under the Hazardous Materials Transportation Act (49 U.S.C. 5101 et seq.), or while operating commercial motor vehicles designed to transport more than 15 passengers, including the driver. A driver is disqualified for a period of not less than three years nor more than five years if, during any 10-year period, the driver is convicted of any subsequent violations of out-of-service orders, in separate incidents, while transporting hazardous materials required to be placarded under the Hazardous Materials Transportation Act, or while operating commercial motor vehicles designed to transport more than 15 passengers, including the driver.

§391.15 DOT Interpretations

Question 1: May a driver convicted of a disqualifying offense be "disqualified" by a motor carrier?
Guidance: No. Motor carriers have no authority to disqualify drivers. However, a conviction for a disqualifying offense automatically disqualifies a driver from driving for the period specified in the regulations. Thus, so long as a motor carrier knows, or should have known, of a driver's conviction for a disqualifying offense, it is prohibited from using the driver during the disqualification period.

Question 2: Is a decision of probation before judgment sufficient for disqualification?
Guidance: Yes, provided the State process includes a finding of guilt.

Question 3: Is a driver holding a valid driver's license from his or her home State but whose privilege to drive in another State has been suspended or revoked, disqualified from driving by §391.15(b)?
Guidance: Yes, the driver would be disqualified from interstate operations until his privileges are restored by the authority that suspended or revoked them, provided the suspension resulted from a driving violation. It is immaterial that he holds a valid license from another State. All licensing actions should be accomplished through the CDLIS or the controlling interstate compact.

Question 4: What are the differences between the disqualification provisions listed in §§383.51 and 383.5 and those listed in §391.15?
Guidance: Part 383 disqualifications are applicable generally to drivers who drive CMVs above 26,000 pounds GVWR, regardless of where the CMV is driven in the U.S. Part 391 disqualifications are applicable generally to drivers who drive CMVs above 10,000 pounds GVWR, only when the vehicle is used in interstate commerce in a State, including the District of Columbia.

Question 5: Do the disqualification provisions of §391.15 apply to offenses committed by a driver who is using a company vehicle for personal reasons while off-duty?
Guidance: No. For example, an owner-operator using his own vehicle in an off-duty status, or a driver using a company truck, or tractor for transportation to a motel, restaurant or home, would be outside the scope of this section if he returns to the same terminal from which he went off-duty (see §383.51 for additional information).

Question 6: If a driver has his/her privileges to drive a pleasure vehicle revoked or suspended by State authorities, but his/her privileges to operate a CMV are left intact, would the driver be disqualified under the terms set forth in §391.15?
Guidance: No. The driver would not be disqualified from operating a CMV.

Question 7: If a driver is convicted of one of the specified offenses in §391.15(c), but is allowed to retain his driver's license, is he/she still disqualified?
Guidance: Yes. A driver who is convicted of one of the specified offenses in §391.15(c), or has forfeited bond in collateral on account of one of these offenses, and who is allowed to retain his/her driver's license, is still disqualified. The loss of a driver's license and convictions of certain offenses in §391.15(c) are entirely separate grounds for disqualification.

Question 8: If a driver has his/her license suspended for driving while under the influence of alcohol, and 2 months later, as a result of this same incident, the driver is convicted of a DWI, must the periods of disqualification be combined since these are both disqualifying offenses?
Guidance: No. Disqualification during the suspension of an operating license continues until the license is restored by the jurisdiction that suspended it. Disqualification for conviction of DWI is for a fixed term. The fact that the driver was already disqualified for driving under the influence of alcohol because of the suspension action may mean that the total time under disqualification for the DWI conviction may exceed the stated term.

Question 9: If a driver commits a felony while operating a CMV but not in the employ of a motor carrier, is the offense disqualifying?
Guidance: No. There are 2 conditions required to be present for a felony conviction to be a disqualifying offense under §391.15:
 (1) The offense was committed during on-duty time; and
 (2) the driver was employed by a motor carrier or was engaged in activities that were in furtherance of a commercial enterprise.
However, neither of these conditions is a prerequisite for a disqualifying offense under §383.51.

Subpart C - Background and Character §391.23 (b)

Question 10: Is a driver who possesses a valid commercial driver's license (CDL) issued by their State of residence, but who is suspended by another State for reasons unrelated to the violation of a motor vehicle traffic control law, disqualified from operating a commercial motor vehicle (CMV) in accordance with provisions of the Federal Motor Carrier Safety Regulations?

Guidance: Yes. Currently, both §383.5, which defines the term disqualification as it applies to drivers required to have a CDL, and §391.15, which applies to other CMV drivers subject to Federal Motor Carrier Safety Regulations, include the suspension of a person's license or privilege to drive as an action requiring that person to be disqualified from operating a CMV. Neither of these regulatory provisions limit such suspensions to those imposed by the State where the driver is licensed, nor do these regulations specify the grounds upon which a suspension must be based.

Be advised, however, that the Federal Motor Carrier Safety Administration has proposed in 66 FR 22499, Docket No. FHWA-00-7382, published May 4, 2001, to limit the basis of the suspension to those resulting from a driving violation. If the rule is finalized, the answer would be no.

Subpart C - Background and Character

§391.21 Application for employment.

(a) Except as provided in Subpart G of this part, a person shall not drive a commercial motor vehicle unless he/she has completed and furnished the motor carrier that employs him/her with an application for employment that meets the requirements of paragraph (b) of this section.

(b) The application for employment shall be made on a form furnished by the motor carrier. Each application form must be completed by the applicant, must be signed by him/her, and must contain the following information:

(1) *The name and address of the employing motor carrier;*

(2) *The applicant's name,* address, date of birth, and social security number;

(3) *The addresses* at which the applicant has resided during the 3 years preceding the date on which the application is submitted;

(4) *The date on which the application is submitted;*

(5) *The issuing State, number, and expiration date* of each unexpired commercial motor vehicle operator's license or permit that has been issued to the applicant;

(6) *The nature and extent of the applicant's experience* in the operation of motor vehicles, including the type of equipment (such as buses, trucks, truck tractors, semitrailers, full trailers, and pole trailers) which he/she has operated;

(7) *A list of all motor vehicle accidents* in which the applicant was involved during the 3 years preceding the date the application is submitted, specifying the date and nature of each accident and any fatalities or personal injuries it caused;

(8) *A list of all violations* of motor vehicle laws or ordinances (other than violations involving only parking) of which the applicant was convicted or forfeited bond or collateral during the 3 years preceding the date the application is submitted;

(9) *A statement setting forth in detail* the facts and circumstances of any denial, revocation, or suspension of any license, permit, or privilege to operate a motor vehicle that has been issued to the applicant, or a statement that no such denial, revocation, or suspension has occurred;

(10)(i) *A list of the names and addresses* of the applicant's employers during the 3 years preceding the date the application is submitted,

(ii) *The dates he or she was employed by that employer,*

(iii) *The reason for leaving the employ of that employer,*

(iv) *After October 29, 2004, whether the*

[A] Applicant was subject to the FMCSRs while employed by that previous employer,

[B] Job was designated as a safety sensitive function in any DOT regulated mode subject to alcohol and controlled substances testing requirements as required by 49 CFR Part 40;

(11) *For those drivers* applying to operate a commercial motor vehicle as defined by Part 383 of this subchapter, a list of the names and addresses of the applicant's employers during the 7-year period preceding the 3 years contained in paragraph (b)(10) of this section for which the applicant was an operator of a commercial motor vehicle, together with the dates of employment and the reasons for leaving such employment; and

(12) *The following certification and signature line,* which must appear at the end of the application form and be signed by the applicant: This certifies that this application was completed by me, and that all entries on it and information in it are true and complete to the best of my knowledge.

_____   _____
(Date)   (Applicant's signature)

(c) A motor carrier may require an applicant to provide information in addition to the information required by paragraph (b) of this section on the application form.

(d) Before an application is submitted, the motor carrier must inform the applicant that the information he/she provides in accordance with paragraph (b)(10) of this section may be used, and the applicant's previous employers will be contacted, for the purpose of investigating the applicant's safety performance history information as required by paragraphs (d) and (e) of §391.23. The prospective employer must also notify the driver in writing of his/her due process rights as specified in §391.23(i) regarding information received as a result of these investigations.

§391.21 DOT Interpretations

Question 1: If a driver submits an application for employment and has someone else type, write, or print the answers to the questions for him and he signs the application, does this constitute a valid application?

Guidance: Yes. The applicant, by signing the application, certifies that all entries on it and information therein are true and complete to the best of the applicant's knowledge.

Question 2: Is there a prescribed or specified form that must be used when a driver applies for employment, or can a carrier develop its own application?

Guidance: There is no specified form to be used in an application for employment. Carriers may develop their own forms, which may be tailored to their specific needs. The application form must, at the minimum, contain the information specified in §391.21(b).

Question 3: §391.21(b)(11) requires that an application for employment contain 10 years of prior employment information on the driver. If a foreign motor carrier's home country requires that an application for employment contain only five years of data, will a foreign carrier need to change its application to collect 10 years of data? Will the foreign carrier be required to go back and collect 10 years of data on its current drivers? What will a U.S. motor carrier who employs foreign drivers be required to do in this regard?

Guidance: A foreign motor carrier would not be required to collect 10 years of prior employment information as long as a foreign driver has an appropriate foreign commercial driver's license, i.e., (1) the Licencia Federal de Conductor (Mexico), or (2) the Canadian National Safety Code commercial driver's license. A U.S. motor carrier, on the other hand, would be required to collect 10 years of prior employment information when hiring foreign drivers. The carrier should also remember to contact the U.S. Immigration and Naturalization Service for their regulations and policies with respect to hiring foreign drivers.

Question 4: Must a driver's application for employment include a social security number (SSN), as required by §391.21(b)(2), if the applicant has religious objections to the SSN and the Social Security Administration does not require him or her to hold such a number?

Guidance: No.

§391.23 Investigation and inquiries.

(a) Except as provided in Subpart G of this part, each motor carrier shall make the following investigations and inquiries with respect to each driver it employs, other than a person who has been a regularly employed driver of the motor carrier for a continuous period which began before January 1, 1971:

(1) *An inquiry into the driver's driving record* during the preceding 3 years to the appropriate agency of every State in which the driver held a motor vehicle operator's license or permit during those 3 years; and

(2) *An investigation* of the driver's safety performance history with Department of Transportation regulated employers during the preceding three years.

(b) A copy of the driver record(s) obtained in response to the inquiry or inquiries to each State driver record agency required by paragraph (a)(1) of this section must be placed in the driver qualification

263

file within 30 days of the date the driver's employment begins and be retained in compliance with §391.51. If no driving record exists from the State or States, the motor carrier must document a good faith effort to obtain such information, and certify that no record exists for that driver in that State. The inquiry to the State driver record agencies must be made in the form and manner each agency prescribes.

(c) (1) *Replies to the investigations* of the driver's safety performance history required by paragraph (a)(2) of this section, or documentation of good faith efforts to obtain the investigation data, must be placed in the driver investigation history file, after October 29, 2004, within 30 days of the date the driver's employment begins. Any period of time required to exercise the driver's due process rights to review the information received, request a previous employer to correct or include a rebuttal, is separate and apart from this 30-day requirement to document investigation of the driver safety performance history data.

(2) *The investigation may consist* of personal interviews, telephone interviews, letters, or any other method for investigating that the carrier deems appropriate. Each motor carrier must make a written record with respect to each previous employer contacted, or good faith efforts to do so. The record must include the previous employer's name and address, the date the previous employer was contacted, or the attempts made, and the information received about the driver from the previous employer. Failures to contact a previous employer, or of them to provide the required safety performance history information, must be documented. The record must be maintained pursuant to §391.53.

(3) *Prospective employers* should report failures of previous employers to respond to an investigation to the FMCSA following procedures specified at §386.12 of this chapter and keep a copy of such reports in the Driver Investigation file as part of documenting a good faith effort to obtain the required information.

(4) *Exception.* For a driver with no previous employment experience working for a DOT regulated employer during the preceding three years, documentation that no investigation was possible must be placed in the driver history investigation file, after October 29, 2004, within the required 30 days of the date the driver's employment begins.

(d) **The prospective motor carrier must investigate,** at a minimum, the information listed in this paragraph from all previous employers of the applicant that employed the driver to operate a CMV within the previous three years. The investigation request must contain specific contact information on where the previous motor carrier employers should send the information requested.

(1) *General driver identification* and employment verification information.

(2) *The data elements* as specified in §390.15(b)(1) of this chapter for accidents involving the driver that occurred in the three-year period preceding the date of the employment application.
  (i) Any accidents as defined by §390.5 of this chapter.
  (ii) Any accidents the previous employer may wish to provide that are retained pursuant to §390.15(b)(2), or pursuant to the employer's internal policies for retaining more detailed minor accident information.

(e) **In addition to the investigations required** by paragraph (d) of this section, the prospective motor carrier employers must investigate the information listed below in this paragraph from all previous DOT regulated employers that employed the driver within the previous three years from the date of the employment application, in a safety-sensitive function that required alcohol and controlled substance testing specified by 49 CFR Part 40.

(1) *Whether, within the previous three years,* the driver had violated the alcohol and controlled substances prohibitions under Subpart B of Part 382 of this chapter, or 49 CFR Part 40.

(2) *Whether the driver* failed to undertake or complete a rehabilitation program prescribed by a substance abuse professional (SAP) pursuant to §382.605 of this chapter, or 49 CFR Part 40, Subpart O. If the previous employer does not know this information (e.g., an employer that terminated an employee who tested positive on a drug test), the prospective motor carrier must obtain documentation of the driver's successful completion of the SAP's referral directly from the driver.

(3) *For a driver who had successfully completed* a SAP's rehabilitation referral, and remained in the employ of the referring employer, information on whether the driver had the following testing violations subsequent to completion of a §382.605 or 49 CFR Part 40, Subpart O referral:
  (i) *Alcohol tests* with a result of 0.04 or higher alcohol concentration;
  (ii) *Verified positive drug tests;*
  (iii) *Refusals to be tested* (including verified adulterated or substituted drug test results).

(f) **A prospective motor carrier employer** must provide to the previous employer the driver's written consent meeting the requirements of §40.321(b) for the release of the information in paragraph (e) of this section. If the driver refuses to provide this written consent, the prospective motor carrier employer must not permit the driver to operate a commercial motor vehicle for that motor carrier.

(g) **After October 29, 2004, previous employers must:**
(1) *Respond to each request* for the DOT defined information in paragraphs (d) and (e) of this section within 30 days after the request is received. If there is no safety performance history information to report for that driver, previous motor carrier employers are nonetheless required to send a response confirming the non-existence of any such data, including the driver identification information and dates of employment.
(2) *Take all precautions reasonably necessary* to ensure the accuracy of the records.
(3) *Provide specific contact information* in case a driver chooses to contact the previous employer regarding correction or rebuttal of the data.
(4) *Keep a record of each request* and the response for one year, including the date, the party to whom it was released, and a summary identifying what was provided.
(5) *Exception.* Until May 1, 2006, carriers need only provide information for accidents that occurred after April 29, 2003.

(h) **The release of information under this section** may take any form that reasonably ensures confidentiality, including letter, facsimile, or e-mail. The previous employer and its agents and insurers must take all precautions reasonably necessary to protect the driver safety performance history records from disclosure to any person not directly involved in forwarding the records, except the previous employer's insurer, except that the previous employer may not provide any alcohol or controlled substances information to the previous employer's insurer.

(i) (1) *The prospective employer* must expressly notify drivers with Department of Transportation regulated employment during the preceding three years — via the application form or other written document prior to any hiring decision — that he or she has the following rights regarding the investigative information that will be provided to the prospective employer pursuant to paragraphs (d) and (e) of this section:
  (i) *The right to review information provided by previous employers;*
  (ii) *The right to have errors* in the information corrected by the previous employer and for that previous employer to re-send the corrected information to the prospective employer;
  (iii) *The right to have a rebuttal statement* attached to the alleged erroneous information, if the previous employer and the driver cannot agree on the accuracy of the information.

(2) *Drivers who have previous* Department of Transportation regulated employment history in the preceding three years, and wish to review previous employer-provided investigative information must submit a written request to the prospective employer, which may be done at any time, including when applying, or as late as 30 days after being employed or being notified of denial of employment. The prospective employer must provide this information to the applicant within five (5) business days of receiving the written request. If the prospective employer has not yet received the requested information from the previous employer(s), then the five-business days deadline will begin when the prospective employer receives the requested safety performance history information. If the driver has not arranged to pick up or receive the requested records within thirty (30) days of the prospective employer making them available, the prospective motor carrier may consider the driver to have waived his/her request to review the records.

(j) (1) *Drivers wishing* to request correction of erroneous information in records received pursuant to paragraph (i) of this section must send the request for the correction to the previous employer that provided the records to the prospective employer.
(2) *After October 29, 2004,* the previous employer must either correct and forward the information to the prospective motor carrier employer, or notify the driver within 15 days of receiving a

Subpart C - Background and Character §391.25 (c)

driver's request to correct the data that it does not agree to correct the data. If the previous employer corrects and forwards the data as requested, that employer must also retain the corrected information as part of the driver's safety performance history record and provide it to subsequent prospective employers when requests for this information are received. If the previous employer corrects the data and forwards it to the prospective motor carrier employer, there is no need to notify the driver.

(3) *Drivers wishing to rebut information* in records received pursuant to paragraph (i) of this section must send the rebuttal to the previous employer with instructions to include the rebuttal in that driver's safety performance history.

(4) *After October 29, 2004,* within five business days of receiving a rebuttal from a driver, the previous employer must:
  (i) *Forward a copy of the rebuttal* to the prospective motor carrier employer;
  (ii) *Append the rebuttal to the driver's information* in the carrier's appropriate file, to be included as part of the response for any subsequent investigating prospective employers for the duration of the three-year data retention requirement.

(5) *The driver may submit a rebuttal initially* without a request for correction, or subsequent to a request for correction.

(6) *The driver may report failures* of previous employers to correct information or include the driver's rebuttal as part of the safety performance information, to the FMCSA following procedures specified at §386.12.

(k) (1) *The prospective motor carrier employer* must use the information described in paragraphs (d) and (e) of this section only as part of deciding whether to hire the driver.

(2) *The prospective motor carrier employer,* its agents and insurers must take all precautions reasonably necessary to protect the records from disclosure to any person not directly involved in deciding whether to hire the driver. The prospective motor carrier employer may not provide any alcohol or controlled substances information to the prospective motor carrier employer's insurer.

(l) (1) *No action or proceeding* for defamation, invasion of privacy, or interference with a contract that is based on the furnishing or use of information in accordance with this section may be brought against —
  (i) *A motor carrier investigating the information,* described in paragraphs (d) and (e) of this section, of an individual under consideration for employment as a commercial motor vehicle driver,
  (ii) *A person who has provided such information;* or
  (iii) *The agents or insurers* of a person described in paragraph (l)(1)(i) or (ii) of this section, except insurers are not granted a limitation on liability for any alcohol and controlled substance information.

(2) *The protections in paragraph (l)(1) of this section* do not apply to persons who knowingly furnish false information, or who are not in compliance with the procedures specified for these investigations.

(Approved by the Office of Management and Budget under control number 2126-0004)

§391.23 DOT Interpretations

Question 1: When a motor carrier receives a request for driver information from another motor carrier about a former or current driver, is it required to supply the requested information?
Guidance: Generally no. See §382.405, however, for requests pertaining to drug and alcohol records.

Question 2: May motor carriers use third parties to ask State agencies for copies of the driving record of driver-applicants?
Guidance: Yes. Driver information services or companies acting as the motor carrier's agent may be used to contact State agencies. However, the motor carrier is responsible for ensuring the information obtained is accurate.

§391.25 Annual inquiry and review of driving record.

(a) **Except as provided in Subpart G of this part,** each motor carrier shall, at least once every 12 months, make an inquiry into the driving record of each driver it employs, covering at least the preceding 12 months, to the appropriate agency of every State in which the driver held a commercial motor vehicle operator's license or permit during the time period.

(b) **Except as provided in Subpart G of this part,** each motor carrier shall, at least once every 12 months, review the driving record of each driver it employs to determine whether that driver meets minimum requirements for safe driving or is disqualified to drive a commercial motor vehicle pursuant to §391.15.
  (1) *The motor carrier must consider any evidence* that the driver has violated any applicable Federal Motor Carrier Safety Regulations in this subchapter or Hazardous Materials Regulations (49 CFR Chapter I, Subchapter C).
  (2) *The motor carrier must consider* the driver's accident record and any evidence that the driver has violated laws governing the operation of motor vehicles, and must give great weight to violations, such as speeding, reckless driving, and operating while under the influence of alcohol or drugs, that indicate that the driver has exhibited a disregard for the safety of the public.

(c) **Recordkeeping.**
  (1) *A copy of the response from each State agency* to the inquiry required by paragraph (a) of this section shall be maintained in the driver's qualification file.
  (2) *A note,* including the name of the person who performed the review of the driving record required by paragraph (b) of this section and the date of such review, shall be maintained in the driver's qualification file.

§391.25 DOT Interpretations

Question 1: To what extent must a motor carrier review a driver's overall driving record to comply with the requirements of §391.25?
Guidance: The motor carrier must consider as much information about the driver's experience as is reasonably available. This would include all known violations, whether or not they are part of an official record maintained by a State, as well as any other information that would indicate the driver has shown a lack of due regard for the safety of the public. Violations of traffic and criminal laws, as well as the driver's involvement in motor vehicle accidents, are such indications and must be considered. A violation of size and weight laws should also be considered.

Question 2: Is a driver service or leasing company that is not a motor carrier permitted to perform annual reviews of driving records (§391.25) on the drivers it furnishes to motor carriers?
Guidance: The driver service or leasing company may perform annual reviews if designated by a motor carrier to do so.

Question 3: May motor carriers use third parties to ask State agencies for copies of driving records to be examined during the carrier's annual review of each driver's record?
Guidance: Yes. Although an examination of the official driving record maintained by the State is not required during the annual review, motor carriers that choose to do so may use third-party agents, such as driver information services or companies, to obtain the information. However, the motor carrier is responsible for ensuring the information is accurate.

Question 4: Does the use of a third-party computerized system that provides motor carriers with a complete department of motor vehicle report for every State in which the driver held a commercial motor vehicle operator's license or permit when a driver is enrolled in the system, and then automatically provides an update anytime the State licensing agency enters new information on the driving record, satisfy the requirements of §391.25?
Guidance: Yes. Since motor carriers would be provided with complete department of motor vehicle report for every State in which the driver held a commercial motor vehicle operator's license or permit when a driver is enrolled in the system, and the provided with an update anytime the State licensing agency enters new information on the driving record, the requirements of §391.25(a) would be satisfied. When the motor carrier manager reviews the information on the driving record, and the License Monitor system records the identity of the manger who conducted the review, the requirements of §391.25(b) and (c) would be satisfied.

With regard to the requirement that the response from each State agency, and a note identifying the person who performed the review, may be maintained in the driver's qualification files, motor carriers may satisfy the recordkeeping requirement by using computerized records in accordance with 49 CFR 390.31. Section allows all records that do not require signatures to be maintained through the use of computer technology provided the motor carrier can produce, upon demand, a computer printout of the required data. Therefore, motor carriers using an automated computer system would not be required to maintain paper copies of the driving records, or a note identifying the person who performed the review, in each individual driver qualification file provided a computer printout can be produced upon demand of a Federal or State enforcement official.

§391.27 Record of violations.

(a) **Except as provided in Subpart G of this part,** each motor carrier shall, at least once every 12 months, require each driver it employs to prepare and furnish it with a list of all violations of motor vehicle traffic laws and ordinances (other than violations involving only parking) of which the driver has been convicted or on account of which he/she has forfeited bond or collateral during the preceding 12 months.

(b) **Each driver shall furnish the list required** in accordance with paragraph (a) of this section. If the driver has not been convicted of, or forfeited bond or collateral on account of, any violation which must be listed, he/she shall so certify.

(c) **The form of the driver's list or certification** shall be prescribed by the motor carrier. The following form may be used to comply with this section:

```
                    DRIVER'S CERTIFICATION
I certify that the following is a true and complete list of traffic violations (other than parking violations) for which I have been
convicted or forfeited bond or collateral during the past 12 months.

Date of conviction:    Offense:        Location:        Type of motor vehicle operated:
___/___/___           _____      _____       _____
___/___/___           _____      _____       _____
___/___/___           _____      _____       _____
___/___/___           _____      _____       _____
___/___/___           _____      _____       _____

If no violations are listed above, I certify that I have not been convicted or forfeited bond or collateral on account of any
violation required to be listed during the past 12 months.
Date of certification: ___/___/___
Driver's signature: _____
Motor carrier's name: _____
Motor carrier's address: _____
City: _____
State: _____ Zip Code: _____-_____
Reviewed by: _____
                      Signature
Title: _____
                                          ©MMV Mangan Communications, Inc.
```

* Full-size forms available free of charge at www.dotcfr.com.

(d) **The motor carrier shall retain the list or certificate** required by this section, or a copy of it, in its files as part of the driver's qualification file.

(e) **Drivers who have provided information** required by §383.31 of this subchapter need not repeat that information in the annual list of violations required by this section.

§391.27 DOT Interpretations

Question 1: Are notifications to a motor carrier by a driver convicted of a driver violation as required by §383.31 to be maintained in the driver's qualification file as part of the supporting documentation or certifications noted in the requirements listed in §391.27(d)?
Guidance: §391.27(d) does not require documentation in the qualification file. However, §391.51 does require that such notifications be maintained in the qualification file.

Subpart D - Tests

§391.31 Road test.

(a) **Except as provided in Subpart G,** a person shall not drive a commercial motor vehicle unless he/she has first successfully completed a road test and has been issued a certificate of driver's road test in accordance with this section.

(b) **The road test shall be given by the motor carrier** or a person designated by it. However, a driver who is a motor carrier must be given the test by a person other than himself/herself. The test shall be given by a person who is competent to evaluate and determine whether the person who takes the test has demonstrated that he/she is capable of operating the commercial motor vehicle, and associated equipment, that the motor carrier intends to assign him/her.

(c) **The road test must be of sufficient duration** to enable the person who gives it to evaluate the skill of the person who takes it at handling the commercial motor vehicle, and associated equipment, that the motor carrier intends to assign to him/her. As a minimum, the person who takes the test must be tested, while operating the type of commercial motor vehicle the motor carrier intends to assign him/her, on his/her skill at performing each of the following operations:

(1) *The pre-trip inspection required by §392.7 of this subchapter;*

(2) *Coupling and uncoupling of combination units,* if the equipment he/she may drive includes combination units;

(3) *Placing the commercial motor vehicle in operation;*

(4) *Use of the commercial motor vehicle's* controls and emergency equipment;

(5) *Operating the commercial motor vehicle* in traffic and while passing other motor vehicles;

(6) *Turning the commercial motor vehicle;*

(7) *Braking, and slowing* the commercial motor vehicle by means other than braking; and

(8) *Backing and parking the commercial motor vehicle.*

(d) **The motor carrier shall provide a road test form** on which the person who gives the test shall rate the performance of the person who takes it at each operation or activity which is a part of the test. After he/she completes the form, the person who gave the test shall sign it.

(e) **If the road test is successfully completed,** the person who gave it shall complete a certificate of driver's road test in substantially the form prescribed in paragraph (f) of this section.

(f) **The form for the certificate of driver's road** test is substantially as follows:

```
                  CERTIFICATION OF ROAD TEST
Driver's name: _____
Social Security Number: _____-___-_____
Operator's or Chauffeur's License No.: _____ State: _____
Type of power unit: _____
Type of trailer(s): _____
If passenger carrier, type of bus: _____
This is to certify that the above-named driver was given a road test under my supervision on: ___/___/___
consisting of approximately: _____ miles of driving.
It is my considered opinion that this driver possesses sufficient driving skill to operate safely the type of commercial motor
vehicle listed above.
Signature of Examiner: _____
Title: _____
Organization of Examiner: _____
Address of Examiner: _____
City: _____ State: _____ Zip Code: _____-_____
                                          ©MMV Mangan Communications, Inc.
```

* Full-size forms available free of charge at www.dotcfr.com.

(g) **A copy of the certificate** required by paragraph (e) of this section shall be given to the person who was examined. The motor carrier shall retain in the driver qualification file of the person who was examined —

(1) *The original of the signed road test form* required by paragraph (d) of this section; and

(2) *The original, or a copy of, the certificate* required by paragraph (e) of this section.

§391.31 DOT Interpretations

Question 1: Are employers still required to administer road tests since all States have implemented CDL skills testing?
Guidance: The employer may accept a CDL in lieu of a road test if the driver is required to successfully complete a road test to obtain a CDL in the State of issuance. However, if the employer intends to assign to the driver a vehicle necessitating the doubles/triples or tank vehicle endorsement, the employer must administer the road test under §391.31 in a representative vehicle.

Question 2: How does a student enrolled in a driver training school comply with the requirement to pass a road test?
Guidance: The road test is administered only after the student has demonstrated a sufficient degree of proficiency on a range or off-road course. A student who passes the road test and is qualified to operate in interstate commerce could cross a State line in the process of receiving training.

Question 3: May a carrier use a blanket certification of road test for specific vehicles (driver's names, etc., left out)?
Guidance: No.

Question 4: May a motor carrier designate another person or organization to administer the road test?
Guidance: Yes. A motor carrier may designate another person or organization to administer the road test as long as the person who administers the road test is competent to evaluate and determine the results of the tests.

Subpart E - Physical Qualifications and Examinations

§391.33 Equivalent of road test.
(a) In place of, and as equivalent to, the road test required by §391.31, a person who seeks to drive a commercial motor vehicle may present, and a motor carrier may accept —
  (1) A valid Commercial Driver's License as defined in §383.5 of this subchapter, but not including double/triple trailer or tank vehicle endorsements, which has been issued to him/her to operate specific categories of commercial motor vehicles and which, under the laws of that State, licenses him/her after successful completion of a road test in a commercial motor vehicle of the type the motor carrier intends to assign to him/her; or
  (2) A copy of a valid certificate of driver's road test issued to him/her pursuant to §391.31 within the preceding 3 years.
(b) If a driver presents, and a motor carrier accepts, a license or certificate as equivalent to the road test, the motor carrier shall retain a legible copy of the license or certificate in its files as part of the driver's qualification file.
(c) A motor carrier may require any person who presents a license or certificate as equivalent to the road test to take a road test or any other test of his/her driving skill as a condition to his/her employment as a driver.

§391.33 DOT Interpretations
Question 1: If a driver was grandfathered from the skills test when he or she obtained a CDL, may an employer forego the administration of a road test as required by §391.31?
Guidance: Yes. While the grandfathered driver has not actually taken the CDL skills test, he or she has met the conditions described in §383.77, that are used as a substitute means of determining the driver's ability to operate the vehicle. Therefore, a grandfathered CDL holder may be treated the same as any other CDL holder in regards to foregoing employer skills testing.

While it is not a requirement for drivers who hold CDL tank vehicle and double/triple trailers endorsements to undergo skills tests, it remains the prerogative of the motor carrier to require and enforce more stringent requirements than the minimum Federal regulations.

Subpart E - Physical Qualifications and Examinations

§391.41 Physical qualifications for drivers.
(a) A person shall not drive a commercial motor vehicle unless he/she is physically qualified to do so and, except as provided in §391.67, has on his/her person the original, or a photographic copy, of a medical examiner's certificate that he/she is physically qualified to drive a commercial motor vehicle.[1]
(b) A person is physically qualified to drive a commercial motor vehicle if that person —
  (1) *Has no loss of a foot, a leg, a hand, or an arm,* or has been granted a skill performance evaluation certificate pursuant to §391.49;
  (2) *Has no impairment of:*
    (i) *A hand or finger* which interferes with prehension or power grasping; or
    (ii) *An arm, foot, or leg* which interferes with the ability to perform normal tasks associated with operating a commercial motor vehicle; or any other significant limb defect or limitation which interferes with the ability to perform normal tasks associated with operating a commercial motor vehicle; or has been granted a skill performance evaluation certificate pursuant to §391.49.
  (3) *Has no established medical history* or clinical diagnosis of diabetes mellitus currently requiring insulin for control;
  (4) *Has no current clinical diagnosis* of myocardial infarction, angina pectoris, coronary insufficiency, thrombosis, or any other cardiovascular disease of a variety known to be accompanied by syncope, dyspnea, collapse, or congestive cardiac failure;
  (5) *Has no established medical history* or clinical diagnosis of a respiratory dysfunction likely to interfere with his/her ability to control and drive a commercial motor vehicle safely;
  (6) *Has no current clinical diagnosis* of high blood pressure likely to interfere with his/her ability to operate a commercial motor vehicle safely;
  (7) *Has no established medical history* or clinical diagnosis of rheumatic, arthritic, orthopedic, muscular, neuromuscular, or vascular disease which interferes with his/her ability to control and operate a commercial motor vehicle safely;
  (8) *Has no established medical history* or clinical diagnosis of epilepsy or any other condition which is likely to cause loss of consciousness or any loss of ability to control a commercial motor vehicle;
  (9) *Has no mental,* nervous, organic, or functional disease or psychiatric disorder likely to interfere with his/her ability to drive a commercial motor vehicle safely;
  (10) *Has distant visual acuity* of at least 20/40 (Snellen) in each eye without corrective lenses or visual acuity separately corrected to 20/40 (Snellen) or better with corrective lenses, distant binocular acuity of at least 20/40 (Snellen) in both eyes with or without corrective lenses, field of vision of at least 70° in the horizontal Meridian in each eye, and the ability to recognize the colors of traffic signals and devices showing standard red, green, and amber;
  (11) *First perceives a forced whispered voice* in the better ear at not less than 5 feet with or without the use of a hearing aid or, if tested by use of an audiometric device, does not have an average hearing loss in the better ear greater than 40 decibels at 500 Hz, 1,000 Hz, and 2,000 Hz with or without a hearing aid when the audiometric device is calibrated to American National Standard (formerly ASA Standard) Z24.5-1951;
  (12)(i) *Does not use a controlled substance* identified in 21 CFR 1308.11 Schedule I, an amphetamine, a narcotic, or any other habit-forming drug.
    (ii) *Exception.* A driver may use such a substance or drug, if the substance or drug is prescribed by a licensed medical practitioner who:
      [A] *Is familiar with the driver's medical history* and assigned duties; and
      [B] *Has advised the driver* that the prescribed substance or drug will not adversely affect the driver's ability to safely operate a commercial motor vehicle; and
  (13) *Has no current clinical diagnosis of alcoholism.*

§391.41 DOT Interpretations
Question 1: Who is responsible for ensuring that medical certifications meet the requirements?
Guidance: Medical certification determinations are the responsibility of the medical examiner. The motor carrier has the responsibility to ensure that the medical examiner is informed of the minimum medical requirements and the characteristics of the work to be performed. The motor carrier is also responsible for ensuring that only medically qualified drivers are operating CMVs in interstate commerce.

Question 2: Do the physical qualification requirements of the FMCSRs infringe upon a person's religious beliefs if such beliefs prohibit being examined by a licensed doctor of medicine or osteopathy?
Guidance: No. To determine whether a governmental regulation infringes on a person's right to freely practice his religion, the interest served by the regulation must be balanced against the degree to which a person's rights are adversely affected. *Biklen v. Board of Education,* 333 F. Supp. 902 (N.D.N.Y. 1971) aff'd 406 U.S. 951 (1972).

If there is an important objective being promoted by the requirement and the restriction on religious freedom is reasonably adapted to achieving that objective, the requirement should be upheld. *Burgin v. Henderson,* 536 F.2d 501 (2d. Cir. 1976).

Based on the tests developed by the courts and the important objective served, the regulation meets Constitutional standards. It does not deny a driver his First Amendment rights.

Question 3: What are the physical qualification requirements for operating a CMV in interstate commerce?
Guidance: The physical qualification regulations for drivers in interstate commerce are found at §391.41. Instructions to medical examiners performing physical examinations of these drivers are found at §391.43. Interpretive guidelines are distributed upon request.

---

1. The United States and Canada entered into a Reciprocity Agreement, effective March 30, 1999, recognizing that a Canadian commercial driver's license is proof of medical fitness to drive. Therefore, Canadian commercial motor vehicle (CMV) drivers are no longer required to have in their possession a medical examiner's certificate if the driver has been issued, and possesses, a valid commercial driver's license issued by a Canadian Province or Territory. However, Canadian drivers who are insulin-using diabetics, who have epilepsy, or who are hearing impaired as defined in §391.41(b)(11) are not qualified to drive CMVs in the United States. Furthermore, Canadian drivers who do not meet the medical fitness provisions of the Canadian National Safety Code for Motor Carriers but who have been issued a waiver by one of the Canadian Provinces or Territories are not qualified to drive CMVs in the United States.

The qualification standards cover 13 areas which directly relate to the driving function. All but four of the standards require a judgement by the medical examiner. A person's qualification to drive is determined by a medical examiner who is knowledgeable about the driver's functions and whether a particular condition would interfere with the driver's ability to operate a CMV safely. In the case of vision, hearing, insulin-using diabetes, and epilepsy, the current standards are absolute, providing no discretion to the medical examiner.

Question 4: Is a driver who is taking prescription methadone qualified to drive a CMV in interstate commerce?

Guidance: Methadone is a habit-forming narcotic which can produce drug dependence and is not an allowable drug for operators of CMVs.

Question 5: May the medical examiner restrict a driver's duties?

Guidance: No. The only conditions a medical examiner may impose upon a driver otherwise qualified involve the use of corrective lenses or hearing aids, securement of a waiver or limitation of driving to exempt intracity zones (see §391.43(g)). A medical examiner who believes a driver has a condition not specified in §391.41 that would affect his ability to operate a CMV safely should refuse to sign the examiner's certificate.

Question 6: If an interstate driver tests positive for alcohol or controlled substances under Part 382, must the driver be medically re-examined and obtain a new medical examiner's certificate to drive again?

Guidance: The driver is not required to be medically re-examined or to obtain a new medical examiner's certificate provided the driver is seen by an SAP who evaluates the driver, does not make a clinical diagnosis of alcoholism, and provides the driver with documentation allowing the driver to return to work. However, if the SAP determines that alcoholism exists, the driver is not qualified to drive a CMV in interstate commerce. The ultimate responsibility rests with the motor carrier to ensure the driver is medically qualified and to determine whether a new medical examination should be completed.

Question 7: Are drivers prohibited from using CB radios and earphones?

Guidance: No. CB radios and earphones are not prohibited under the regulations, as long as they do not distract the driver and the driver is capable of complying with §391.41(b)(11).

Question 8: Is the use of coumadin, an anticoagulant, an automatic disqualification for drivers operating CMVs in interstate commerce?

Guidance: No. Although the FHWA 1987 "Conference on Cardiac Disorders and Commercial Drivers" recommended that drivers who are taking anticoagulants not be allowed to drive, the agency has not adopted a rule to that effect. The medical examiner and treating specialist may, but are not required to, accept the Conference recommendations. Therefore, the use of coumadin is not an automatic disqualification, but a factor to be considered in determining the driver's physical qualification status.

§391.43 Medical examination; certificate of physical examination.

(a) Except as provided by paragraph (b) of this section, the medical examination shall be performed by a licensed medical examiner as defined in §390.5 of this subchapter.

(b) A licensed optometrist may perform so much of the medical examination as pertains to visual acuity, field of vision, and the ability to recognize colors as specified in paragraph (10) of §391.41(b).

(c) Medical examiners shall:
 (1) *Be knowledgeable* of the specific physical and mental demands associated with operating a commercial motor vehicle and the requirements of this subpart, including the medical advisory criteria prepared by the FMCSA as guidelines to aid the medical examiner in making the qualification determination; and
 (2) *Be proficient in the use of* and use the medical protocols necessary to adequately perform the medical examination required by this section.

(d) Any driver authorized to operate a commercial motor vehicle within an exempt intracity zone pursuant to §391.62 of this part shall furnish the examining medical examiner with a copy of the medical findings that led to the issuance of the first certificate of medical examination which allowed the driver to operate a commercial motor vehicle wholly within an exempt intracity zone.

(e) Any driver operating under a limited exemption authorized by §391.64 shall furnish the medical examiner with a copy of the annual medical findings of the endocrinologist, ophthalmologist or optometrist, as required under that section. If the medical examiner finds the driver qualified under the limited exemption in §391.64, such fact shall be noted on the Medical Examiner's Certificate.

(f) The medical examination shall be performed, and its results shall be recorded, substantially in accordance with the following instructions and examination form. Existing forms may be used until current printed supplies are depleted or until September 30, 2004, whichever occurs first.

Instructions for Performing and Recording Physical Examinations

The medical examiner must be familiar with 49 CFR 391.41, Physical qualifications for drivers, and should review these instructions before performing the physical examination. Answer each question "yes" or "no" and record numerical readings where indicated on the physical examination form.

The medical examiner must be aware of the rigorous physical, mental, and emotional demands placed on the driver of a commercial motor vehicle. In the interest of public safety, the medical examiner is required to certify that the driver does not have any physical, mental, or organic condition that might affect the driver's ability to operate a commercial motor vehicle safely.

General information. The purpose of this history and physical examination is to detect the presence of physical, mental, or organic conditions of such a character and extent as to affect the driver's ability to operate a commercial motor vehicle safely. The examination should be conducted carefully and should at least include all of the information requested in the following form. History of certain conditions may be cause for rejection. Indicate the need for further testing and/or require evaluation by a specialist. Conditions may be recorded which do not, because of their character or degree, indicate that certification of physical fitness should be denied. However, these conditions should be discussed with the driver and he/she should be advised to take the necessary steps to insure correction, particularly of those conditions which, if neglected, might affect the driver's ability to drive safely.

General appearance and development. Note marked overweight. Note any postural defect, perceptible limp, tremor, or other conditions that might be caused by alcoholism, thyroid intoxication or other illnesses.

Head-eyes. When other than the Snellen chart is used, the results of such test must be expressed in values comparable to the standard Snellen test. If the driver wears corrective lenses for driving, these should be worn while driver's visual acuity is being tested. If contact lenses are worn, there should be sufficient evidence of good tolerance of and adaptation to their use. Indicate the driver's need to wear corrective lenses to meet the vision standard on the Medical Examiner's Certificate by checking the box, "Qualified only when wearing corrective lenses." In recording distance vision use 20 feet as normal. Report all vision as a fraction with 20 as the numerator and the smallest type read at 20 feet as the denominator. Monocular drivers are not qualified to operate commercial motor vehicles in interstate commerce.

Ears. Note evidence of any ear disease, symptoms of aural vertigo, or Meniere's Syndrome. When recording hearing, record distance from patient at which a forced whispered voice can first be heard. For the whispered voice test, the individual should be stationed at least 5 feet from the examiner with the ear being tested turned toward the examiner. The other ear is covered. Using the breath which remains after a normal expiration, the examiner whispers words or random numbers such as 66, 18, 23, etc. The examiner should not use only sibilants (s-sounding test materials). The opposite ear should be tested in the same manner. If the individual fails the whispered voice test, the audiometric test should be administered. For the audiometric test, record decibel loss at 500 Hz, 1,000 Hz, and 2,000 Hz. Average the decibel loss at 500 Hz, 1,000 Hz and 2,000 Hz and record as described on the form. If the individual fails the audiometric test and the whispered voice test has not been administered, the whispered voice test should be performed to determine if the standard applicable to that test can be met.

Throat. Note any irremediable deformities likely to interfere with breathing or swallowing.

Heart. Note murmurs and arrhythmias, and any history of an enlarged heart, congestive heart failure, or cardiovascular disease that is accompanied by syncope, dyspnea, or collapse. Indicate onset date, diagnosis, medication, and any current limitation. An electrocardiogram is required when findings so indicate.

Blood pressure (BP). If a driver has hypertension and/or is being medicated for hypertension, he or she should be recertified more frequently. An individual diagnosed with Stage 1 hypertension (BP is 140/90-159/99) may be certified for one year. At recertification, an individual with a BP equal to or less than 140/90 may be certified for

Subpart E - Physical Qualifications and Examinations §391.43 (f)

one year; however, if his or her BP is greater than 140/90 but less than 160/100, a one-time certificate for 3 months can be issued. An individual diagnosed with Stage 2 (BP is 160/100-179/109) should be treated and a one-time certificate for 3-month certification can be issued. Once the driver has reduced his or her BP to equal to or less than 140/90, he or she may be recertified annually thereafter. An individual diagnosed with Stage 3 hypertension (BP equal to or greater than 180/110) should not be certified until his or her BP is reduced to 140/90 or less, and may be recertified every 6 months.

Lungs. Note abnormal chest wall expansion, respiratory rate, breath sounds including wheezes or alveolar rales, impaired respiratory function, dyspnea, or cyanosis. Abnormal finds on physical exam may require further testing such as pulmonary tests and/or x-ray of chest.

Abdomen and Viscera. Note enlarged liver, enlarged spleen, abnormal masses, bruits, hernia, and significant abdominal wall muscle weakness and tenderness. If the diagnosis suggests that the condition might interfere with the control and safe operation of a commercial motor vehicle, further testing and evaluation is required.

Genital-urinary and rectal examination. A urinalysis is required. Protein, blood or sugar in the urine may be an indication of further testing to rule out any underlying medical problems. Note hernias. A condition causing discomfort should be evaluated to determine the extent to which the condition might interfere with the control and safe operation of a commercial motor vehicle.

Neurological. Note impaired equilibrium, coordination, or speech pattern; paresthesia; asymmetric deep tendon reflexes; sensory or positional abnormalities; abnormal patellar and Babinski's reflexes; ataxia. Abnormal neurological responses may be an indication for further testing to rule out an underlying medical condition. Any neurological condition should be evaluated for the nature and severity of the condition, the degree of limitation present, the likelihood of progressive limitation, and the potential for sudden incapacitation. In instances where the medical examiner has determined that more frequent monitoring of a condition is appropriate, a certificate for a shorter period should be issued.

Spine, musculoskeletal. Previous surgery, deformities, limitation of motion, and tenderness should be noted. Findings may indicate additional testing and evaluation should be conducted.

Extremities. Carefully examine upper and lower extremities and note any loss or impairment of leg, foot, toe, arm, hand, or finger. Note any deformities, atrophy, paralysis, partial paralysis, clubbing, edema, or hypotonia. If a hand or finger deformity exists, determine whether prehension and power grasp are sufficient to enable the driver to maintain steering wheel grip and to control other vehicle equipment during routine and emergency driving operations. If a foot or leg deformity exists, determine whether sufficient mobility and strength exist to enable the driver to operate pedals properly. In the case of any loss or impairment to an extremity which may interfere with the driver's ability to operate a commercial motor vehicle safely, the medical examiner should state on the medical certificate "medically unqualified unless accompanied by a Skill Performance Evaluation Certificate." The driver must then apply to the Field Service Center of the FMCSA, for the State in which the driver has legal residence, for a Skill Performance Evaluation Certificate under §391.49.

Laboratory and Other Testing. Other test(s) may be indicated based upon the medical history or findings of the physical examination.

Diabetes. If insulin is necessary to control a diabetic driver's condition, the driver is not qualified to operate a commercial motor vehicle in interstate commerce. If mild diabetes is present and it is controlled by use of an oral hypoglycemic drug and/or diet and exercise, it should not be considered disqualifying. However, the driver must remain under adequate medical supervision.

Upon completion of the examination, the medical examiner must date and sign the form, provide his/her full name, office address and telephone number. The completed medical examination form shall be retained on file at the office of the medical examiner.

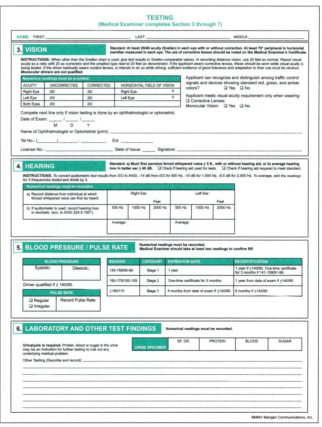

* Full-size forms available free of charge at www.dotcfr.com.

§391.43   Part 391 - Qualifications of Drivers and Longer Combination Vehicle (LCV) Driver Instructors

* Full-size forms available free of charge at www.dotcfr.com.

Subpart E - Physical Qualifications and Examinations §391.43 (h)

being tested turned toward the examiner. The other ear is covered. Using the breath which remains after a normal expiration, the examiner whispers words or random numbers such as 66, 18, 23, etc. The examiner should not use only sibilants (s sounding materials). The opposite ear should be tested in the same manner. If the individual fails the whispered voice test, the audiometric test should be administered.

If an individual meets the criteria by the use of a hearing aid, the following statement must appear on the Medical Examiner's Certificate "Qualified only when wearing a hearing aid".

(See Hearing Disorders and Commercial Motor Vehicle Drivers at: http://www.fmcsa.dot.gov/rulesregs/medreports.htm)

Drug Use:
§391.41(b)(12)
A person is physically qualified to drive a commercial motor vehicle if that person:

Does not use a controlled substance identified in 21 CFR 1308.11, an amphetamine, a narcotic, or any other habit-forming drug. *Exception:* A driver may use such a substance or drug, if the substance or drug is prescribed by a licensed medical practitioner who is familiar with the driver's medical history and assigned duties; and has advised the driver that the prescribed substance or drug will not adversely affect the driver's ability to safely operate a commercial motor vehicle.

This exception does not apply to methadone. The intent of the medical certification process is to medically evaluate a driver to ensure that the driver has no medical condition which interferes with the safe performance of driving tasks on a public road. If a driver uses a Schedule I drug or other substance, an amphetamine, a narcotic, or any other habit-forming drug, it may be cause for the driver to be found medically unqualified. Motor carriers are encouraged to obtain a practitioner's written statement about the effects on transportation safety of the use of a particular drug.

A test for controlled substances is not required as part of this biennial certification process. The FMCSA or the driver's employer should be contacted directly for information on controlled substances and alcohol testing under Part 382 of the FMCSRs.

The term "uses" is designed to encompass instances of prohibited drug use determined by a physician through established medical means. This may or may not involve body fluid testing. If body fluid testing takes place, positive test results should be confirmed by a second test of greater specificity. The term "habit-forming" is intended to include any drug or medication generally recognized as capable of becoming habitual, and which may impair the user's ability to operate a commercial motor vehicle safely.

The driver is medically unqualified for the duration of the prohibited drug(s) use and until a second examination shows the driver is free from the prohibited drug(s) use. Recertification may involve a substance abuse evaluation, the successful completion of a drug rehabilitation program, and a negative drug test result. Additionally, given that the certification period is normally two years, the examiner has the option to certify for a period of less than two years if this examiner determines more frequent monitoring is required.

(See Conference on Neurological Disorders and Commercial Drivers and Conference on Psychiatric Disorders and Commercial Drivers at: http://www.fmcsa.dot.gov/rulesregs/medreports.htm)

Alcoholism:
§391.41(b)(13)
A person is physically qualified to drive a commercial motor vehicle if that person:

Has no current clinical diagnosis of alcoholism.

The term "current clinical diagnosis of" is specifically designed to encompass a current alcoholic illness or those instances where the individual's physical condition has not fully stabilized, regardless of the time element. If an individual shows signs of having an alcohol-use problem, he or she should be referred to a specialist. After counseling and/or treatment, he or she may be considered for certification.

* Full-size forms available free of charge at www.dotcfr.com.

(g) If the medical examiner finds that the person he/she examined is physically qualified to drive a commercial motor vehicle in accordance with §391.41(b), the medical examiner shall complete a certificate in the form prescribed in paragraph (h) of this section and furnish one copy to the person who was examined and one copy to the motor carrier that employs him/her.

(h) The medical examiner's certificate shall be substantially in accordance with the following form. Existing forms may be used until current printed supplies are depleted or until November 6, 2001, whichever occurs first.

[Medical Examiner's Certificate form]

* Full-size forms available free of charge at www.dotcfr.com.

§391.43 DOT Interpretations

Question 1: May a motor carrier, for the purposes of §391.41, or a State driver licensing agency, for the purposes of §383.71, accept the results of a medical examination performed by a foreign medical examiner?

Guidance: Yes. Foreign drivers operating in the U.S. with a driver's license recognized as equivalent to the CDL may be medically certified in accordance with the requirements of Part 391, Subpart E, by a medical examiner in the driver's home country who is licensed, certified, and/or registered to perform physical examinations in that country. However, U.S. drivers operating in interstate commerce within the U.S. must be medically certified in accordance with Part 391, Subpart E, by a medical examiner licensed, certified, and/or registered to perform physical examinations in the U.S.

Question 2: May a urine sample collected for purposes of performing a Subpart H test be used to test for diabetes as part of a driver's FHWA-required physical examination?

Guidance: In general, no. However, the DOT has recognized an exception to this general policy whereby, after 60 milliliters of urine have been set aside for Subpart H testing, any remaining portion of the sample may be used for other nondrug testing, but only if such other nondrug testing is required by the FHWA (under Part 391, Subpart E) such as testing for glucose and protein levels.

Question 3: Is a chest x-ray required under the minimum medical requirements of the FMCSRs?

Guidance: No, but a medical examiner may take an x-ray if appropriate.

Question 4: Does §391.43 of the FMCSRs require that physical examinations of applicants for employment be conducted by medical examiners employed by or designated by the carrier?

Guidance: No.

Question 5: Does a medical certificate displaying a facsimile of a medical examiner's signature meet the "signature of examining health care professional" requirement?

Guidance: Yes.

Question 6: The driver's medical exam is part of the Mexican Licencia Federal. If a roadside inspection reveals that a Mexico-based driver has not had the medical portion of the Licencia Federal re-validated, is the driver considered to be without a valid medical certificate or without a valid license?

Guidance: The Mexican Licencia Federal is issued for a period of 10 years but must be re-validated every 2 years. A condition of re-validation is that the driver must pass a new physical examination. The dates for each re-validation are on the Licencia Federal and must be stamped at the completion of each physical. This constitutes documentation that the driver is medically qualified. Therefore, if the Licencia Federal is not re-validated every 2 years as specified by Mexican law, the driver's license is considered invalid.

Question 7: If a motor carrier sends a potential interstate driver to a medical examiner to have both a pre-employment medical examination and a pre-employment controlled substances test performed, how must the medical examiner conduct the medical examination including the certification the driver meets the physical qualifications of §391.41(b)?

Guidance: The medical examiner must complete the physical examination first without collecting the Part 382 controlled substances urine specimen. If the potential driver meets the requirements of Part 391, Subpart E [especially §391.41(b)] and the medical examiner chooses to certify the potential driver as qualified to operate commercial motor vehicles (CMV) in interstate commerce, the medical examiner may prepare the medical examiner's certificate.

After the medical examiner has completed the medical examiner's certificate and provided a copy to the potential driver and to the motor carrier who will use the potential driver's services, the medical examiner may collect the specimen for the 49 CFR Part 382 pre-employment controlled substances test. The motor carrier is held fully responsible for ensuring the potential driver is not used to operate CMVs until the carrier receives a verified negative controlled substances test result from the medical review officer. A Department of Transportation pre-employment controlled substances test is not a medical examination test.

§391.45 Persons who must be medically examined and certified.

Except as provided in §391.67, the following persons must be medically examined and certified in accordance with §391.43 as physically qualified to operate a commercial motor vehicle:

(a) **Any person who has not been medically examined** and certified as physically qualified to operate a commercial motor vehicle;

(b) (1) *Any driver* who has not been medically examined and certified as qualified to operate a commercial motor vehicle during the preceding 24 months; or

(2) *Any driver* authorized to operate a commercial motor vehicle only with an exempt intracity zone pursuant to §391.62, or only by operation of the exemption in §391.64, if such driver has not been medically examined and certified as qualified to drive in such zone during the preceding 12 months; and

(c) **Any driver whose ability to perform** his/her normal duties has been impaired by a physical or mental injury or disease.

§391.45 DOT Interpretations

Question 1: Is it intended that the words "person" and "driver" be used interchangeably in §391.45?
Guidance: Yes.

Question 2: Do the FMCSRs require applicants, possessing a current medical certificate, to undergo a new physical examination as a condition of employment?
Guidance: No. However, if a motor carrier accepts such a currently valid certificate from a driver subject to Part 382, the driver is subject to additional controlled substance testing requirements unless otherwise excepted in Subpart H.

Question 3: Must a driver who is returning from an illness or injury undergo a medical examination even if his current medical certificate has not expired?
Guidance: The FMCSRs do not require an examination in this case unless the injury or illness has impaired the driver's ability to perform his/her normal duties. However, the motor carrier may require a driver returning from any illness or injury to take a physical examination. But, in either case, the motor carrier has the obligation to determine if an injury or illness renders the driver medically unqualified.

§391.47 Resolution of conflicts of medical evaluation.

(a) **Applications.** Applications for determination of a driver's medical qualifications under standards in this part will only be accepted if they conform to the requirements of this section.

(b) **Content.** Applications will be accepted for consideration only if the following conditions are met.

(1) *The application must contain* the name and address of the driver, motor carrier, and all physicians involved in the proceeding.

(2) *The applicant must submit proof* that there is a disagreement between the physician for the driver and the physician for the motor carrier concerning the driver's qualifications.

(3) *The applicant must submit a copy* of an opinion and report including results of all tests of an impartial medical specialist in the field in which the medical conflict arose. The specialist should be one agreed to by the motor carrier and the driver.

(i) *In cases where the driver* refuses to agree on a specialist and the applicant is the motor carrier, the applicant must submit a statement of his/her agreement to submit the matter to an impartial medical specialist in the field, proof that he/she has requested the driver to submit to the medical specialist, and the response, if any, of the driver to his/her request.

(ii) *In cases where the motor carrier* refuses to agree on a medical specialist, the driver must submit an opinion and test results of an impartial medical specialist, proof that he/she has requested the motor carrier to agree to submit the matter to the medical specialist and the response, if any, of the motor carrier to his/her request.

(4) *The applicant must include a statement* explaining in detail why the decision of the medical specialist identified in paragraph (b)(3) of this section is unacceptable.

(5) *The applicant must submit proof* that the medical specialist mentioned in paragraph (b)(3) of this section was provided, prior to his/her determination, the medical history of the driver and an agreed-upon statement of the work the driver performs.

(6) *The applicant must submit* the medical history and statement of work provided to the medical specialist under paragraph (b)(5) of this section.

(7) *The applicant must submit* all medical records and statements of the physicians who have given opinions on the driver's qualifications.

(8) *The applicant must submit a description* and a copy of all written and documentary evidence upon which the party making application relies in the form set out in 49 CFR 386.37.

(9) *The application must be accompanied* by a statement of the driver that he/she intends to drive in interstate commerce not subject to the commercial zone exemption or a statement of the carrier that he/she has used or intends to use the driver for such work.

(10) *The applicant must submit* three copies of the application and all records.

(c) **Information.** The Director, Office of Bus and Truck Standards and Operations (MC PSDPSD) may request further information from the applicant if he/she determines that a decision cannot be made on the evidence submitted. If the applicant fails to submit the information requested, the Director may refuse to issue a determination.

(d) (1) *Action.* Upon receiving a satisfactory application the Director, Office of Bus and Truck Standards and Operations (MC PSDPSD) shall notify the parties (the driver, motor carrier, or any other interested party) that the application has been accepted and that a determination will be made. A copy of all evidence received shall be attached to the notice.

(2) *Reply.* Any party may submit a reply to the notification within 15 days after service. Such reply must be accompanied by all evidence the party wants the Director, Office of Bus and Truck Standards and Operations (MC PSDPSD) to consider in making his/her determination. Evidence submitted should include all medical records and test results upon which the party relies.

(3) *Parties.* A party for the purposes of this section includes the motor carrier and the driver, or anyone else submitting an application.

(e) **Petitions to review, burden of proof.** The driver or motor carrier may petition to review the Director's determination. Such petition must be submitted in accordance with §386.13(a) of this chapter. The burden of proof in such a proceeding is on the petitioner.

(f) **Status of driver.** Once an application is submitted to the Director, Office of Bus and Truck Standards and Operations (MC PSDPSD), the driver shall be deemed disqualified until such time as the Director, Office of Bus and Truck Standards and Operations (MC PSDPSD) makes a determination, or until the Director, Office of Bus and Truck Standards and Operations (MC PSDPSD) orders otherwise.

§391.47 DOT Interpretations

Question 1: Does the FHWA issue formal medical decisions as to the physical qualifications of drivers on an individual basis?
Guidance: No, except upon request for resolution of a conflict of medical evaluations.

§391.49 Alternative physical qualification standards for the loss or impairment of limbs.

(a) **A person who is not** physically qualified to drive under §391.41 (b)(1) or (b)(2) and who is otherwise qualified to drive a commercial motor vehicle, may drive a commercial motor vehicle, if the Division Administrator, FMCSA, has granted a Skill Performance Evaluation (SPE) Certificate to that person.

(b) **SPE certificate.**

(1) *Application.* A letter of application for an SPE certificate may be submitted jointly by the person (driver applicant) who seeks an SPE certificate and by the motor carrier that will employ the driver applicant, if the application is accepted.

(2) *Application address.* The application must be addressed to the applicable field service center, FMCSA, for the State in which the co-applicant motor carrier's principal place of business is located. The address of each, and the States serviced, are listed in §390.27 of this chapter.

(3) *Exception.* A letter of application for an SPE certificate may be submitted unilaterally by a driver applicant. The application must be addressed to the field service center, FMCSA, for the State in which the driver has legal residence. The driver applicant must comply with all the requirements of paragraph (c) of this section except those in (c)(1)(i) and (iii). The driver applicant shall respond to the requirements of paragraphs (c)(2)(i) to (v) of this section, if the information is known.

Subpart E - Physical Qualifications and Examinations §391.49 (f)

(c) A letter of application for an SPE certificate shall contain:
   (1) *Identification of the applicant(s):*
      (i) *Name and complete address of the motor carrier coapplicant;*
      (ii) *Name and complete address of the driver applicant;*
      (iii) *The U.S. DOT Motor Carrier Identification Number,* if known; and
      (iv) *A description* of the driver applicant's limb impairment for which SPE certificate is requested.
   (2) *Description of the type of operation* the driver will be employed to perform:
      (i) *State(s) in which the driver will operate* for the motor carrier coapplicant (if more than 10 States, designate general geographic area only);
      (ii) *Average period of time* the driver will be driving and/or on duty, per day;
      (iii) *Type of commodities or cargo to be transported;*
      (iv) *Type of driver operation* (i.e., sleeper team, relay, owner operator, etc.); and
      (v) *Number of years experience* operating the type of commercial motor vehicle(s) requested in the letter of application and total years of experience operating all types of commercial motor vehicles.
   (3) *Description of the commercial motor vehicle(s)* the driver applicant intends to drive:
      (i) *Truck, truck tractor, or bus make, model, and year (if known);*
      (ii) *Drive train;*
         [A] *Transmission type* (automatic or manual — if manual, designate number of forward speeds);
         [B] *Auxiliary transmission (if any)* and number of forward speeds; and
         [C] *Rear axle* (designate single speed, 2 speed, or 3 speed).
      (iii) *Type of brake system;*
      (iv) *Steering, manual or power assisted;*
      (v) *Description of type of trailer(s)* (i.e., van, flatbed, cargo tank, drop frame, lowboy, or pole);
      (vi) *Number of semitrailers or full trailers to be towed at one time;*
      (vii) *For commercial motor vehicles* designed to transport passengers, indicate the seating capacity of commercial motor vehicle; and
      (viii) *Description of any modification(s)* made to the commercial motor vehicle for the driver applicant; attach photograph(s) where applicable.
   (4) *Otherwise qualified:*
      (i) *The coapplicant motor carrier* must certify that the driver applicant is otherwise qualified under the regulations of this part;
      (ii) *In the case of a unilateral application,* the driver applicant must certify that he/she is otherwise qualified under the regulations of this part.
   (5) *Signature of applicant(s):*
      (i) *Driver applicant's signature and date signed;*
      (ii) *Motor carrier official's signature* (if application has a coapplicant), title, and date signed. Depending upon the motor carrier's organizational structure (corporation, partnership, or proprietorship), the signer of the application shall be an officer, partner, or the proprietor.

(d) The letter of application for an SPE certificate shall be accompanied by:
   (1) *A copy of the results* of the medical examination performed pursuant to §391.43;
   (2) *A copy of the medical certificate* completed pursuant to §391.43(h);
   (3) *A medical evaluation summary* completed by either a board qualified or board certified physiatrist (doctor of physical medicine) or orthopedic surgeon. The coapplicant motor carrier or the driver applicant shall provide the physiatrist or orthopedic surgeon with a description of the job-related tasks the driver applicant will be required to perform;
      (i) *The medical evaluation summary* for a driver applicant disqualified under §391.41(b)(1) shall include:
         [A] *An assessment of the functional capabilities* of the driver as they relate to the ability of the driver to perform normal tasks associated with operating a commercial motor vehicle; and
         [B] *A statement by the examiner* that the applicant is capable of demonstrating precision prehension (e.g., manipulating knobs and switches) and power grasp prehension (e.g., holding and maneuvering the steering wheel) with each upper limb separately. This requirement does not apply to an individual who was granted a waiver, absent a prosthetic device, prior to the publication of this amendment.
      (ii) *The medical evaluation summary* for a driver applicant disqualified under §391.41(b)(2) shall include:
         [A] *An explanation as to how and why* the impairment interferes with the ability of the applicant to perform normal tasks associated with operating a commercial motor vehicle;
         [B] *An assessment and medical opinion* of whether the condition will likely remain medically stable over the lifetime of the driver applicant; and
         [C] *A statement by the examiner* that the applicant is capable of demonstrating precision prehension (e.g., manipulating knobs and switches) and power grasp prehension (e.g., holding and maneuvering the steering wheel) with each upper limb separately. This requirement does not apply to an individual who was granted an SPE certificate, absent an orthotic device, prior to the publication of this amendment.
   (4) *A description* of the driver applicant's prosthetic or orthotic device worn, if any;
   (5) *Road test:*
      (i) *A copy of the driver applicant's road test* administered by the motor carrier coapplicant and the certificate issued pursuant to §391.31(b) through (g); or
      (ii) *A unilateral applicant* shall be responsible for having a road test administered by a motor carrier or a person who is competent to administer the test and evaluate its results.
   (6) *Application for employment:*
      (i) *A copy* of the driver applicant's application for employment completed pursuant to §391.21; or
      (ii) *A unilateral applicant* shall be responsible for submitting a copy of the last commercial driving position's employment application he/she held. If not previously employed as a commercial driver, so state.
   (7) *A copy of the driver applicant's SPE certificate* of certain physical defects issued by the individual State(s), where applicable; and
   (8) *A copy* of the driver applicant's State Motor Vehicle Driving Record for the past 3 years from each State in which a motor vehicle driver's license or permit has been obtained.

(e) Agreement. A motor carrier that employs a driver with an SPE certificate agrees to:
   (1) *File promptly* (within 30 days of the involved incident) with the Medical Program Specialist, FMCSA service center, such documents and information as may be required about driving activities, accidents, arrests, license suspensions, revocations, or withdrawals, and convictions which involve the driver applicant. This applies whether the driver's SPE certificate is a unilateral one or has a coapplicant motor carrier;
      (i) *A motor carrier who is a coapplicant* must file the required documents with the Medical Program Specialist, FMCSA for the State in which the carrier's principal place of business is located; or
      (ii) *A motor carrier who employs a driver* who has been issued a unilateral SPE certificate must file the required documents with the Medical Program Specialist, FMCSA service center, for the State in which the driver has legal residence.
   (2) *Evaluate the driver* with a road test using the trailer the motor carrier intends the driver to transport or, in lieu of, accept a certificate of a trailer road test from another motor carrier if the trailer type(s) is similar, or accept the trailer road test done during the Skill Performance Evaluation if it is a similar trailer type(s) to that of the prospective motor carrier. Job tasks, as stated in paragraph (e)(3) of this section, are not evaluated in the Skill Performance Evaluation;
   (3) *Evaluate the driver* for those nondriving safety related job tasks associated with whatever type of trailer(s) will be used and any other nondriving safety related or job related tasks unique to the operations of the employing motor carrier; and
   (4) *Use the driver* to operate the type of commercial motor vehicle defined in the SPE certificate only when the driver is in compliance with the conditions and limitations of the SPE certificate.

(f) The driver shall supply each employing motor carrier with a copy of the SPE certificate.

(g) The State Director, FMCSA, may require the driver applicant to demonstrate his or her ability to safely operate the commercial motor vehicle(s) the driver intends to drive to an agent of the State Director, FMCSA. The SPE certificate form will identify the power unit (bus, truck, truck tractor) for which the SPE certificate has been granted. The SPE certificate forms will also identify the trailer type used in the Skill Performance Evaluation; however, the SPE certificate is not limited to that specific trailer type. A driver may use the SPE certificate with other trailer types if a successful trailer road test is completed in accordance with paragraph (e)(2) of this section. Job tasks, as stated in paragraph (e)(3) of this section, are not evaluated during the Skill Performance Evaluation.

(h) The State Director, FMCSA, may deny the application for SPE certificate or may grant it totally or in part and issue the SPE certificate subject to such terms, conditions, and limitations as deemed consistent with the public interest. The SPE certificate is valid for a period not to exceed 2 years from date of issue, and may be renewed 30 days prior to the expiration date.

(i) The SPE certificate renewal application shall be submitted to the Medical Program Specialist, FMCSA service center, for the State in which the driver has legal residence, if the SPE certificate was issued unilaterally. If the SPE certificate has a coapplicant, then the renewal application is submitted to the Medical Program Specialist, FMCSA field service center, for the State in which the coapplicant motor carrier's principal place of business is located. The SPE certificate renewal application shall contain the following:

(1) *Name and complete address* of motor carrier currently employing the applicant;
(2) *Name and complete address of the driver;*
(3) *Effective date of the current SPE certificate;*
(4) *Expiration date of the current SPE certificate;*
(5) *Total miles driven under the current SPE certificate;*
(6) *Number of accidents* incurred while driving under the current SPE certificate, including date of the accident(s), number of fatalities, number of injuries, and the estimated dollar amount of property damage;
(7) *A current medical examination report;*
(8) *A medical evaluation summary* pursuant to paragraph (d)(3) of this section, if an unstable medical condition exists. All handicapped conditions classified under §391.41(b)(1) are considered unstable. Refer to paragraph (d)(3)(ii) of this section for the condition under §391.41(b)(2) which may be considered medically stable.
(9) *A copy of driver's* current State motor vehicle driving record for the period of time the current SPE certificate has been in effect;
(10) *Notification of any change* in the type of tractor the driver will operate;
(11) *Driver's signature and date signed; and*
(12) *Motor carrier coapplicant's signature and date signed.*

(j) (1) *Upon granting an SPE certificate,* the State Director, FMCSA, will notify the driver applicant and co-applicant motor carrier (if applicable) by letter. The terms, conditions, and limitations of the SPE certificate will be set forth. A motor carrier shall maintain a copy of the SPE certificate in its driver qualification file. A copy of the SPE certificate shall be retained in the motor carrier's file for a period of 3 years after the driver's employment is terminated. The driver applicant shall have the SPE certificate (or a legible copy) in his/her possession whenever on duty.

(2) *Upon successful completion* of the skill performance evaluation, the State Director, FMCSA, for the State where the driver applicant has legal residence, must notify the driver by letter and enclose an SPE certificate substantially in the following form:

* Full-size forms available free of charge at www.dotcfr.com.

(k) The State Director, FMCSA, may revoke an SPE certificate after the person to whom it was issued is given notice of the proposed revocation and has been allowed a reasonable opportunity to appeal.

(l) Falsifying information in the letter of application, the renewal application, or falsifying information required by this section by either the applicant or motor carrier is prohibited.

§391.49 DOT Interpretations

Question 1: Since 49 CFR 391.49 does not mandate a Skill Performance Evaluation, does the term "performance standard" mean that the State must give a driving test or other Skill Performance Evaluation to the driver for every waiver issued or does this term mean that, depending upon the medical condition, the State may give some other type of performance test? For example, in the case of a vision waiver, would a vision examination suffice as a performance standard?

Guidance: Under the Tolerance Guidelines, Appendix C, Paragraph 3(j), each State that creates a waiver program for intrastate drivers is responsible for determining what constitutes "sound medical judgment," as well as determining the performance standard. In the example used above, a vision examination would suffice as a performance standard. It is the responsibility of each State establishing a waiver program to determine what constitutes an appropriate performance standard.

Subpart F - Files and Records

§391.51 General requirements for driver qualification files.

(a) **Each motor carrier shall maintain a driver qualification file** for each driver it employs. A driver's qualification file may be combined with his/her personnel file.

(b) **The qualification file for a driver must include:**
  (1) *The driver's application* for employment completed in accordance with §391.21;
  (2) *A copy of the response* by each State agency concerning a driver's driving record pursuant to §391.23(a)(1);
  (3) *The certificate of driver's road test* issued to the driver pursuant to §391.31(e), or a copy of the license or certificate which the motor carrier accepted as equivalent to the driver's road test pursuant to §391.33;
  (4) *The response of each State agency* to the annual driver record inquiry required by §391.25(a);
  (5) *A note relating to the annual review* of the driver's driving record as required by §391.25(c)(2);
  (6) *A list or certificate* relating to violations of motor vehicle laws and ordinances required by §391.27;
  (7) *The medical examiner's certificate* of his/her physical qualification to drive a commercial motor vehicle as required by §391.43(f) or a legible photographic copy of the certificate; and
  (8) *A letter* from the Field Administrator, Division Administrator, or State Director granting a waiver of a physical disqualification, if a waiver was issued under §391.49.

(c) **Except as provided in paragraph (d) of this section,** each driver's qualification file shall be retained for as long as a driver is employed by that motor carrier and for three years thereafter.

(d) **The following records may be removed** from a driver's qualification file three years after the date of execution:
  (1) *The response of each State agency* to the annual driver record inquiry required by §391.25(a);
  (2) *The note relating to the annual review* of the driver's driving record as required by §391.25(c)(2);
  (3) *The list or certificate* relating to violations of motor vehicle laws and ordinances required by §391.27;
  (4) *The medical examiner's certificate* of the driver's physical qualification to drive a commercial motor vehicle or the photographic copy of the certificate as required by §391.43(f); and
  (5) *The letter issued under §391.49* granting a waiver of a physical disqualification.

(Approved by the Office of Management and Budget under control number 2126-004)

§391.51 DOT Interpretations

Question 1: When a motor carrier purchases another motor carrier, must the drivers of the acquired motor carrier be requalified by the purchasing motor carrier?
Guidance: No.

Question 2: Is a driver training school required to keep a driver qualification file on each student?
Guidance: Yes, if operating in interstate commerce.

Question 3: Before December 23, 1994, motor carriers were required to maintain documentary evidence that their drivers had completed the written examination specified by 49 CFR 391.35 (1994). The rule removing §391.35 became effective on that date (59 FR 60319, November 23, 1994). Are motor carriers required to maintain such documentary evidence for drivers employed prior to December 23, 1994?
Guidance: No.

Question 4: If a motor carrier maintains complete driver qualification files but cannot produce them at the time of the review or within two business days, is it in violation of §391.51?
Guidance: Yes. Driver qualification files must be produced on demand. Producing driver qualification files after the completion of the review does not cure a record-keeping violation of §391.51.

Question 5: Must a driver/employee who was employed prior to the deletion of the section of the FMCSRs requiring certain documentary proof of written examination, and who does not have such proof in his driver qualification file, complete the exam?
Guidance: No. The requirement of former 49 CFR 391.35(h) that a driver qualification file contains certain documents substantiating the driver examination may not be the basis of a citation after November 23, 1994, the date on which all requirements pertinent to a driver's written test were rescinded (59 FR 60319).

§391.53 Driver investigation history file.

(a) **After October 29, 2004,** each motor carrier must maintain records relating to the investigation into the safety performance history of a new or prospective driver pursuant to paragraphs (d) and (e) of §391.23. This file must be maintained in a secure location with controlled access.
  (1) *The motor carrier must ensure* that access to this data is limited to those who are involved in the hiring decision or who control access to the data. In addition, the motor carrier's insurer may have access to the data, except the alcohol and controlled substances data.
  (2) *This data must only be used for the hiring decision.*

(b) **The file must include:**
  (1) *A copy of the driver's written authorization* for the motor carrier to seek information about a driver's alcohol and controlled substances history as required under §391.23(d).
  (2) *A copy of the response(s) received* for investigations required by paragraphs (d) and (e) of §391.23 from each previous employer, or documentation of good faith efforts to contact them. The record must include the previous employer's name and address, the date the previous employer was contacted, and the information received about the driver from the previous employer. Failures to contact a previous employer, or of them to provide the required safety performance history information, must be documented.

(c) **The safety performance histories received** from previous employers for a driver who is hired must be retained for as long as the driver is employed by that motor carrier and for three years thereafter.

(d) **A motor carrier must make all records and information** in this file available to an authorized representative or special agent of the Federal Motor Carrier Safety Administration, an authorized State or local enforcement agency representative, or an authorized third party, upon request or as part of any inquiry within the time period specified by the requesting representative.

(Approved by the Office of Management and Budget under control number 2126-004)

§391.55 LCV Driver-Instructor qualification files.

(a) **Each motor carrier must maintain a qualification file** for each LCV driver-instructor it employs or uses. The LCV driver-instructor qualification file may be combined with his/her personnel file.

(b) **The LCV driver-instructor qualification file** must include the information in paragraphs (b)(1) and (b)(2) of this section for a skills instructor or the information in paragraph (b)(1) of this section for a classroom instructor, as follows:
  (1) *Evidence that the instructor* has met the requirements of 49 CFR 380.301 or 380.303;
  (2) *A photographic copy* of the individual's currently valid CDL with the appropriate endorsements.

Subpart G - Limited Exemptions

§391.61 Drivers who were regularly employed before January 1, 1971.

The provisions of §391.21 (relating to applications for employment), §391.23 (relating to investigations and inquiries), and §391.33 (relating to road tests) do not apply to a driver who has been a single-employer driver (as defined in §390.5 of this subchapter) of a motor carrier for a continuous period which began before January 1, 1971, as long as he/she continues to be a single-employer driver of that motor carrier.

§391.62 Limited exemptions for intra-city zone drivers.

The provisions of §§391.11(b)(1) and 391.41(b)(1) through (b)(11) do not apply to a person who:

(a) **Was otherwise qualified to operate** and operated a commercial motor vehicle in a municipality or exempt intracity zone thereof throughout the one-year period ending November 18, 1988;
(b) **Meets all the other requirements of this section;**
(c) **Operates wholly within the exempt intracity zone** (as defined in 49 CFR 390.5);
(d) **Does not operate a vehicle used in the transportation** of hazardous materials in a quantity requiring placarding under regulations issued by the Secretary under 49 U.S.C. Chapter 51.; and

(e) *Has a medical or physical condition which:*
  (1) *Would have prevented such person* from operating a commercial motor vehicle under the Federal Motor Carrier Safety Regulations contained in this subchapter;
  (2) *Existed on July 1, 1988,* or at the time of the first required physical examination after that date; and
  (3) *The examining physician* has determined this condition has not substantially worsened since July 1, 1988, or at the time of the first required physical examination after that date.

§391.63 Multiple-employer drivers.

(a) *If a motor carrier employs a person* as a multiple-employer driver (as defined in §390.5 of this subchapter), the motor carrier shall comply with all requirements of this part, except that the motor carrier need not —
  (1) *Require the person* to furnish an application for employment in accordance with §391.21;
  (2) *Make the investigations and inquiries* specified in §391.23 with respect to that person;
  (3) *Perform the annual driving record inquiry required by §391.25(a);*
  (4) *Perform the annual review* of the person's driving record required by §391.25(b); or
  (5) *Require the person* to furnish a record of violations or a certificate in accordance with §391.27.
(b) *Before a motor carrier* permits a multiple-employer driver to drive a commercial motor vehicle, the motor carrier must obtain his/her name, his/her social security number, and the identification number, type and issuing State of his/her commercial motor vehicle operator's license. The motor carrier must maintain this information for three years after employment of the multiple-employer driver ceases.

(Approved by the Office of Management and Budget under control number 2125-0081)

---

§391.63 DOT Interpretations

Question 1: Is a person employed by a nonmotor carrier in his normal duties considered an intermittent, casual, or occasional driver when employed by a motor carrier as a driver on a part-time basis?
Guidance: No. A person who drives for one motor carrier (even if it is only one day per month) would not meet the definition of an intermittent, casual, or occasional driver in §390.5 since he/she is employed by only one motor carrier. The motor carrier must fully qualify the driver and maintain a qualification file on the employee as a regularly employed driver.

Question 2: How does §391.63 apply when motor carriers obtain, from a driver leasing service, intermittent, casual, or occasional drivers who are on temporary assignments to multiple motor carriers?
Guidance: If an intermittent, casual, or occasional driver has only been fully qualified by a driver leasing service or similar non-motor carrier entity, and has never been fully qualified by a motor carrier, the first motor carrier employing such a driver must ensure that the driver is fully qualified, and must keep a complete driver qualification file for that driver. It was the intention of §§391.63 and 391.65 to require that a driver, before entering the status of an "intermittent, casual, or occasional" driver, be fully qualified by a motor carrier. In a contractual relationship between a motor carrier and a driver leasing service, this may be accomplished by a motor carrier designating a driver leasing service as its agent to perform the qualification procedures in accordance with Parts 383 and 391. However, in such a case, the motor carrier will be held liable for any violations of the FMCSRs committed by its agent.

Question 3: Must a motor carrier that employs an intermittent, casual, or occasional driver to operate a CMV, as defined in §383.5, (1) require the driver to prepare and submit an employment application in accordance with §391.21 and (2) conduct the background investigation of the driver's previous employers required by §391.23?
Guidance: §391.63(a)(1)-(2) exempts from compliance with §§391.21 and 391.23 motor carriers that use intermittent, casual or occasional drivers to operate CMVs with a gross vehicle (or combination) weight rating (GVWR/GCWR) of 10,001 pounds or more. These exemptions also apply to carriers operating the heavier CMVs subject to Parts 382 and 383.

However, the more limited driver information and motor carrier investigation required by Parts 382 and 383 are not covered by §391.63. Therefore, a carrier using intermittent, casual or occasional drivers to operate CMVs with a GVWR/GCWR of 26,001 pounds or more need not require an employment application in accordance with §391.21, but the driver must furnish the information required by §383.35(c). The carrier may conduct a background investigation of the driver's previous employers (§383.35(f)), and it must investigate his/her previous alcohol and controlled substance test results (§382.413).

§391.64 Grandfathering for certain drivers participating in vision and diabetes waiver study programs.

(a) *The provisions of §391.41(b)(3) do not apply* to a driver who was a participant in good standing on March 31, 1996, in a waiver study program concerning the operation of commercial motor vehicles by insulin-controlled diabetic drivers; provided:
  (1) *The driver is physically examined every year,* including an examination by a board-certified/eligible endocrinologist attesting to the fact that the driver is:
    (i) *Otherwise qualified under §391.41;*
    (ii) *Free of insulin reactions* (an individual is free of insulin reactions if that individual does not have severe hypoglycemia or hypoglycemia unawareness, and has less than one documented, symptomatic hypoglycemic reaction per month);
    (iii) *Able to and has demonstrated willingness* to properly monitor and manage his/her diabetes; and
    (iv) *Not likely to suffer* any diminution in driving ability due to his/her diabetic condition.
  (2) *The driver agrees to and complies with the following conditions:*
    (i) *A source of rapidly absorbable glucose* shall be carried at all times while driving;
    (ii) *Blood glucose levels shall be self-monitored* one hour prior to driving and at least once every four hours while driving or on duty prior to driving using a portable glucose monitoring device equipped with a computerized memory;
    (iii) *Submit blood glucose logs* to the endocrinologist or medical examiner at the annual examination or when otherwise directed by an authorized agent of the FMCSA;
    (iv) *Provide a copy* of the endocrinologist's report to the medical examiner at the time of the annual medical examination; and
    (v) *Provide a copy* of the annual medical certification to the employer for retention in the driver's qualification file and retain a copy of the certification on his/her person while driving for presentation to a duly authorized Federal, State or local enforcement official.
(b) *The provisions of §391.41(b)(10) do not apply* to a driver who was a participant in good standing on March 31, 1996, in a waiver study program concerning the operation of commercial motor vehicles by drivers with visual impairment in one eye; provided:
  (1) *The driver is physically examined every year,* including an examination by an ophthalmologist or optometrist attesting to the fact that the driver:
    (i) *Is otherwise qualified under §391.41;* and
    (ii) *Continues to measure at least 20/40* (Snellen) in the better eye.
  (2) *The driver provides a copy* of the ophthalmologist or optometrist report to the medical examiner at the time of the annual medical examination.
  (3) *The driver provides a copy* of the annual medical certification to the employer for retention in the driver's qualification file and retains a copy of the certification on his/her person while driving for presentation to a duly authorized federal, state or local enforcement official.

§391.65 Drivers furnished by other motor carriers.

(a) *A motor carrier may employ a driver* who is not a regularly employed driver of that motor carrier without complying with the generally applicable driver qualification file requirements in this part, if —
  (1) *The driver is regularly employed by another motor carrier;* and
  (2) *The motor carrier* which regularly employs the driver certifies that the driver is fully qualified to drive a commercial motor vehicle in a written statement which —
    (i) *Is signed and dated* by an officer or authorized employee of the regularly employing carrier;

Subpart G - Limited Exemptions §391.71

(ii) *Contains the driver's name and signature;*
(iii) *Certifies that the driver* has been regularly employed as defined in §390.5;
(iv) *Certifies that the driver* is fully qualified to drive a commercial motor vehicle under the rules in Part 391 of the Federal Motor Carrier Safety Regulations;
(v) *States the expiration date* of the driver's medical examiner's certificate;
(vi) *Specifies an expiration date for the certificate,* which shall be not longer than 2 years or, if earlier, the expiration date of the driver's current medical examiner's certificate; and
(vii) *After April 1, 1977,* is substantially in accordance with the following form:

DRIVERS FURNISHED BY OTHER MOTOR CARRIERS

Driver's name: _____
Social Security Number: _____ - _____ - _____
Signature of Driver: _____

I certify that the above named driver, as defined in §390.5 is regularly driving a commercial motor vehicle operated by the below named carrier and is fully qualified under Part 391, Federal Motor Carrier Safety Regulations. His or her current medical examiner's certificate expires on: ____ / ____ / ____

This certificate expires: ____ / ____ / ____
(Date not later than expiration date of medical certificate.)

Issued on: ____ / ____ / ____
Issued by: _____
(Name of carrier.)
Address of Carrier: _____
City: _____ State: _____ Zip Code: _____ - _____
Signature: _____
Title: _____

©MMV Mangan Communications, Inc.

---

* Full-size forms available free of charge at www.dotcfr.com.

(b) A motor carrier that obtains a certificate in accordance with paragraph (a)(2) of this section shall:
(1) *Contact the motor carrier* which certified the driver's qualifications under this section to verify the validity of the certificate. This contact may be made in person, by telephone, or by letter.
(2) *Retain a copy of that certificate in its files for three years.*

(c) A motor carrier which certifies a driver's qualifications under this section shall be responsible for the accuracy of the certificate. The certificate is no longer valid if the driver leaves the employment of the motor carrier which issued the certificate or is no longer qualified under the rules in this part.

§391.65 DOT Interpretations

Question 1: May a nonmotor carrier which owns a CMV prepare the qualification certificate provided for in §391.65?
Guidance: No, only a motor carrier which regularly employs a driver may issue the required certification.

Question 2: May the certificate of qualification as prescribed by §391.65 be incorporated into another carrier's forms such as a lease and/or interchange agreement?
Guidance: Yes. However, the certificate of qualification must be signed and dated by an officer or authorized employee of the regularly employing carrier.

Question 3: Is a motor carrier required to accept a certificate from the driver's regularly employing motor carrier certifying that the driver is qualified per §391.65?
Guidance: No. If the motor carrier chooses not to accept the certificate issued by the regularly employing motor carrier furnishing the driver, the motor carrier must then assume responsibility for assuring itself that the driver is fully qualified in accordance with Part 391.

Question 4: If a driver furnished by another motor carrier is in the second carrier's service for a period of 7 consecutive days or more, may the driver still fall under the exemption in §391.65?
Guidance: No. The driver becomes a regularly employed driver of the second motor carrier and the exemption in §391.65 is inapplicable.

§391.67 Farm vehicle drivers of articulated commercial motor vehicles.

The following rules in this part do not apply to a farm vehicle driver (as defined in §390.5 of this subchapter) who is 18 years of age or older and who drives an articulated commercial motor vehicle:

(a) Section 391.11(b)(1), (b)(6) and (b)(8) (relating to general qualifications of drivers);
(b) Subpart C (relating to disclosure of, investigation into, and inquiries about the background, character, and driving record of drivers);
(c) Subpart D (relating to road tests); and
(d) Subpart F (relating to maintenance of files and records).

§391.68 Private motor carrier of passengers (nonbusiness).

The following rules in this part do not apply to a private motor carrier of passengers (nonbusiness) and its drivers:

(a) Section 391.11(b)(1), (b)(6) and (b)(8) (relating to general qualifications of drivers);
(b) Subpart C (relating to disclosure of, investigation into, and inquiries about the background, character, and driving record of, drivers);
(c) So much of §§391.41 and 391.45 as require a driver to be medically examined and to have a medical examiner's certificate on his/her person; and
(d) Subpart F (relating to maintenance of files and records).

§391.69 Private motor carrier of passengers (business).

The provisions of §391.21 (relating to applications for employment), §391.23 (relating to investigations and inquiries), and §391.31 (relating to road tests) do not apply to a driver who was a single-employer driver (as defined in §390.5 of this subchapter) of a private motor carrier of passengers (business) as of July 1, 1994, so long as the driver continues to be a single-employer driver of that motor carrier.

§391.71 [Reserved]

Part 391 - Qualifications of Drivers and Longer Combination Vehicle (LCV) Driver Instructors

Notes

Part 392 - Driving of Commercial Motor Vehicles (Page 109 in the Driver Edition)

Subpart A - General

§392.1 Scope of the rules in this part.
Every motor carrier, its officers, agents, representatives, and employees responsible for the management, maintenance, operation, or driving of commercial motor vehicles, or the hiring, supervising, training, assigning, or dispatching of drivers, shall be instructed in and comply with the rules in this part.

§392.2 Applicable operating rules.
Every commercial motor vehicle must be operated in accordance with the laws, ordinances, and regulations of the jurisdiction in which it is being operated. However, if a regulation of the Federal Motor Carrier Safety Administration imposes a higher standard of care than that law, ordinance or regulation, the Federal Motor Carrier Safety Administration regulation must be complied with.

§392.3 Ill or fatigued operator.
No driver shall operate a commercial motor vehicle, and a motor carrier shall not require or permit a driver to operate a commercial motor vehicle, while the driver's ability or alertness is so impaired, or so likely to become impaired, through fatigue, illness, or any other cause, as to make it unsafe for him/her to begin or continue to operate the commercial motor vehicle. However, in a case of grave emergency where the hazard to occupants of the commercial motor vehicle or other users of the highway would be increased by compliance with this section, the driver may continue to operate the commercial motor vehicle to the nearest place at which that hazard is removed.

> **§392.3 DOT Interpretations**
>
> *Question 1:* What protection is afforded a driver for refusing to violate the FMCSRs?
>
> *Guidance:* Section 405 of the STAA — Surface Transportation Assistance Act of 1982 (49 U.S.C. 31105) states, in part, that no person shall discharge, discipline, or in any manner discriminate against an employee with respect to the employee's compensation, terms, conditions, or privileges of employment for refusing to operate a vehicle when such operation constitutes a violation of any Federal rule, regulation, standard, or order applicable to CMV safety. In such a case, a driver may submit a signed complaint to the Occupational Safety and Health Administration.

§392.4 Drugs and other substances.
(a) **No driver shall be on duty and possess,** be under the influence of, or use, any of the following drugs or other substances:
  (1) *Any 21 CFR 1308.11 Schedule I substance;*
  (2) *An amphetamine or any formulation thereof* (including, but not limited, to "pep pills," and "bennies");
  (3) *A narcotic drug or any derivative thereof;* or
  (4) *Any other substance,* to a degree which renders the driver incapable of safely operating a motor vehicle.

(b) **No motor carrier shall require or permit a driver** to violate paragraph (a) of this section.

(c) **Paragraphs (a)(2), (3), and (4) do not apply** to the possession or use of a substance administered to a driver by or under the instructions of a licensed medical practitioner, as defined in §382.107 of this subchapter, who has advised the driver that the substance will not affect the driver's ability to safely operate a motor vehicle.

(d) **As used in this section,** "possession" does not include possession of a substance which is manifested and transported as part of a shipment.

§392.5 Alcohol prohibition.
(a) **No driver shall —**
  (1) *Use alcohol,* as defined in §382.107 of this subchapter, or be under the influence of alcohol, within 4 hours before going on duty or operating, or having physical control of, a commercial motor vehicle; or
  (2) *Use alcohol,* be under the influence of alcohol, or have any measured alcohol concentration or detected presence of alcohol, while on duty, or operating, or in physical control of a commercial motor vehicle; or
  (3) *Be on duty* or operate a commercial motor vehicle while the driver possesses wine of not less than one-half of one per centum of alcohol by volume, beer as defined in 26 U.S.C. 5052(a), of the Internal Revenue Code of 1954, and distilled spirits as defined in section 5002(a)(8), of such Code. However, this does not apply to possession of wine, beer, or distilled spirits which are:
      (i) *Manifested and transported as part of a shipment;* or
      (ii) *Possessed or used by bus passengers.*

(b) **No motor carrier shall require or permit a driver to —**
  (1) *Violate any provision of paragraph (a) of this section;* or
  (2) *Be on duty* or operate a commercial motor vehicle if, by the driver's general appearance or conduct or by other substantiating evidence, the driver appears to have used alcohol within the preceding four hours.

(c) **Any driver who is found to be in violation** of the provisions of paragraph (a) or (b) of this section shall be placed out-of-service immediately for a period of 24 hours.
  (1) *The 24-hour out-of-service period* will commence upon issuance of an out-of-service order.
  (2) *No driver shall violate the terms* of an out-of-service order issued under this section.

(d) **Any driver who is issued** an out-of-service order under this section shall:
  (1) *Report such issuance to his/her employer within 24 hours;* and
  (2) *Report such issuance to a State official,* designated by the State which issued his/her driver's license, within 30 days unless the driver chooses to request a review of the order. In this case, the driver shall report the order to the State official within 30 days of an affirmation of the order by either the Division Administrator or State Director for the geographical area or the Administrator.

(e) **Any driver who is subject to an out-of-service order** under this section may petition for review of that order by submitting a petition for review in writing within 10 days of the issuance of the order to the Division Administrator or State Director for the geographical area in which the order was issued. The Division Administrator or State Director may affirm or reverse the order. Any driver adversely affected by such order of the Division Administrator or State Director may petition the Administrator for review in accordance with 49 CFR 386.13.

> **§392.5 DOT Interpretations**
>
> *Question 1:* Do possession and use of alcoholic beverages in the passenger area of a motorcoach constitute "possession" of such beverages under §392.5(a)(3)?
> *Guidance:* No.
>
> *Question 2:* Can a motor carrier, which finds a driver with a detectable presence of alcohol, place him/her out of service in accordance with §392.5?
> *Guidance:* No. The term "out of service" in the context of §392.5 refers to an act by a State or Federal official. However, the motor carrier must prevent the driver from being on-duty or from operating or being in physical control of a CMV for at least as long as is necessary to prevent a violation of §392.5.
>
> *Question 3:* Does the prohibition against carrying alcoholic beverages in §392.5 apply to a driver who uses a company vehicle, for personal reasons, while off-duty?
> *Guidance:* No. For example, an owner-operator using his/her own vehicle in an off-duty status, or a driver using a company truck or tractor for transportation to a motel, restaurant, or home, would normally be outside the scope of this section.
>
> *Question 4:* Would an alcohol test, performed by an employer pursuant to 49 CFR Part 382, with a result greater than 0.00 BAC, but less than 0.02 BAC, establish that a driver was in violation of 49 CFR 392.5(a)(2), having any measured alcohol concentration while on duty?
> *Guidance:* No. The FMCSA believes that a 0.02 BAC is the lowest level at which a scientifically accurate breath/blood alcohol concentration can be measured in an employer-based test under Part 382. The FMCSA further believes that this use of a 0.02 BAC standard is consistent with FMCSA's long established zero tolerance standard for alcohol. This guidance in no way impedes or precludes any action taken by a law enforcement official because of a finding that a BAC level was less than 0.02 BAC.

§392.6 Schedules to conform with speed limits.

No motor carrier shall schedule a run nor permit nor require the operation of any commercial motor vehicle between points in such period of time as would necessitate the commercial motor vehicle being operated at speeds greater than those prescribed by the jurisdictions in or through which the commercial motor vehicle is being operated.

§392.6 DOT Interpretations

Question 1: How many miles may a driver record on his/her daily record of duty status and still be presumed to be in compliance with the speed limits?

Guidance: Drivers are required to conform to the posted speed limits prescribed by the jurisdictions in or through which the vehicle is being operated. Where the total trip is on highways with a speed limit of 65 mph, trips of 550-600 miles completed in 10 hours are considered questionable and the motor carrier may be asked to document that such trips can be made. Trips of 600 miles or more will be assumed to be incapable of being completed without violations of the speed limits and may be required to be documented. In areas where a 55 mph speed limit is in effect, trips of 450-500 miles are open to question, and runs of 500 miles or more are considered incapable of being made in compliance with the speed limit and hours of service limitation.

§392.7 Equipment, inspection and use.

No commercial motor vehicle shall be driven unless the driver is satisfied that the following parts and accessories are in good working order, nor shall any driver fail to use or make use of such parts and accessories when and as needed:

- Service brakes, including trailer brake connections.
- Parking (hand) brake.
- Steering mechanism.
- Lighting devices and reflectors.
- Tires.
- Horn.
- Windshield wiper or wipers.
- Rear-vision mirror or mirrors.
- Coupling devices.

§392.7 DOT Interpretations

Question 1: Must a driver prepare a written report of a pretrip inspection performed under §392.7?

Guidance: No.

Question 2: Must both drivers of a team operation comply with the provisions of §392.7 before driving?

Guidance: Section 392.7 states that a driver must be satisfied that the vehicle is in good working order before operating the vehicle. If a driver is satisfied with a co-driver's inspection, or a safety lane inspection, then the requirement of this section will have been met.

§392.8 Emergency equipment, inspection and use.

No commercial motor vehicle shall be driven unless the driver thereof is satisfied that the emergency equipment required by §393.95 of this subchapter is in place and ready for use; nor shall any driver fail to use or make use of such equipment when and as needed.

§392.9 Inspection of cargo, cargo securement devices and systems.

(a) *General.* A driver may not operate a commercial motor vehicle and a motor carrier may not require or permit a driver to operate a commercial motor vehicle unless —

 (1) *The commercial motor vehicle's cargo* is properly distributed and adequately secured as specified in §§393.100 through 393.142 of this subchapter.

 (2) *The commercial motor vehicle's tailgate,* tailboard, doors, tarpaulins, spare tire and other equipment used in its operation, and the means of fastening the commercial motor vehicle's cargo, are secured; and

 (3) *The commercial motor vehicle's cargo* or any other object does not obscure the driver's view ahead or to the right or left sides (except for drivers of self-steer dollies), interfere with the free movement of his/her arms or legs, prevent his/her free and ready access to accessories required for emergencies, or prevent the free and ready exit of any person from the commercial motor vehicle's cab or driver's compartment.

(b) *Drivers of trucks and truck tractors.* Except as provided in paragraph (b)(4) of this section, the driver of a truck or truck tractor must —

 (1) *Assure himself/herself* that the provisions of paragraph (a) of this section have been complied with before he/she drives that commercial motor vehicle;

 (2) *Inspect the cargo* and the devices used to secure the cargo within the first 50 miles after beginning a trip and cause any adjustments to be made to the cargo or load securement devices as necessary, including adding more securement devices, to ensure that cargo cannot shift on or within, or fall from the commercial motor vehicle; and

 (3) *Reexamine the commercial motor vehicle's cargo* and its load securement devices during the course of transportation and make any necessary adjustment to the cargo or load securement devices, including adding more securement devices, to ensure that cargo cannot shift on or within, or fall from, the commercial motor vehicle. Reexamination and any necessary adjustments must be made whenever —

 (i) *The driver makes a change of his/her duty status; or*
 (ii) *The commercial motor vehicle has been driven for 3 hours; or*
 (iii) *The commercial motor vehicle* has been driven for 150 miles, whichever occurs first.

 (4) *The rules in this paragraph (b)* do not apply to the driver of a sealed commercial motor vehicle who has been ordered not to open it to inspect its cargo or to the driver of a commercial motor vehicle that has been loaded in a manner that makes inspection of its cargo impracticable.

§392.9 DOT Interpretations

Question 1: Is a vehicle's cargo compartment considered sealed according to the terms of §392.9(b)(4) when it is secured with a padlock, to which the driver holds a key?

Guidance: No. The driver has ready access to the cargo compartment by using the padlock key and would be required to perform the examinations of the cargo and load-securing devices described in §392.9(b).

Question 2: Does the FMCSA have authority to enforce the safe loading requirements against a shipper that is not the motor carrier?

Guidance: No, unless HM as defined in §172.101 are involved. It is the responsibility of the motor carrier and the driver to ensure that any cargo aboard a vehicle is properly loaded and secured.

Question 3: How may the motor carrier determine safe loading when a shipper has loaded and sealed the trailer?

Guidance: Under these circumstances, a motor carrier may fulfill its responsibilities for proper loading a number of ways. Examples are:
 a. Arrange for supervision of loading to determine compliance; or
 b. Obtain notation on the connecting line freight bill that the lading was properly loaded; or
 c. Obtain approval to break the seal to permit inspection.

Question 4: Is there a requirement that a driver must personally load, block, brace, and tie down the cargo on the property carrying CMV he/she drives?

Guidance: No. But the driver is required to be familiar with methods and procedures for securing cargo, and may have to adjust the cargo or load securing devices pursuant to §392.9(b).

§392.9a Operating authority.

(a) *Operating authority required.* A motor vehicle providing transportation requiring operating authority must not be operated—
 (1) *Without the required operating authority* or
 (2) *Beyond the scope of the operating authority granted.*

(b) *Penalties.* Every motor vehicle providing transportation requiring operating authority shall be ordered out of service if it is determined that the motor carrier responsible for the operation of such a vehicle is operating in violation of paragraph (a) of this section. In addition, the motor carrier may be subject to penalties in accordance with 49 U.S.C. 14901.

(c) *Administrative Review.* Upon issuance of the out-of-service order under paragraph (b) of this section, the driver shall comply immediately with such order. Opportunity for review shall be provided in accordance with 5 U.S.C. 554 not later than 10 days after issuance of such order.

Subpart B - Driving of Commercial Motor Vehicles

§392.10 Railroad grade crossings; stopping required.
(a) Except as provided in paragraph (b) of this section, the driver of a commercial motor vehicle specified in paragraphs (a)(1) through (6) of this section shall not cross a railroad track or tracks at grade unless he/she first: Stops the commercial motor vehicle within 50 feet of, and not closer than 15 feet to, the tracks; thereafter listens and looks in each direction along the tracks for an approaching train; and ascertains that no train is approaching. When it is safe to do so, the driver may drive the commercial motor vehicle across the tracks in a gear that permits the commercial motor vehicle to complete the crossing without a change of gears. The driver must not shift gears while crossing the tracks.
 (1) *Every bus transporting passengers,*
 (2) *Every commercial motor vehicle* transporting any quantity of a Division 2.3 chlorine.
 (3) *Every commercial motor vehicle* which, in accordance with the regulations of the Department of Transportation, is required to be marked or placarded with one of the following classifications:
   (i) Division 1.1
   (ii) Division 1.2, or Division 1.3
   (iii) Division 2.3 Poison gas
   (iv) Division 4.3
   (v) Class 7
   (vi) Class 3 Flammable
   (vii) Division 5.1
   (viii) Division 2.2
   (ix) Division 2.3 Chlorine
   (x) Division 6.1 Poison
   (xi) Division 2.2 Oxygen
   (xii) Division 2.1
   (xiii) Class 3 Combustible liquid
   (xiv) Division 4.1
   (xv) Division 5.1
   (xvi) Division 5.2
   (xvii) Class 8
   (xviii) Division 1.4
 (4) *Every cargo tank motor vehicle,* whether loaded or empty, used for the transportation of any hazardous material as defined in the Hazardous Materials Regulations of the Department of Transportation, Parts 107 through 180 of this title.
 (5) *Every cargo tank motor vehicle* transporting a commodity which at the time of loading has a temperature above its flashpoint as determined by §173.120 of this title.
 (6) *Every cargo tank motor vehicle,* whether loaded or empty, transporting any commodity under exemption in accordance with the provisions of Subpart B of Part 107 of this title.
(b) A stop need not be made at:
 (1) *A streetcar crossing,* or railroad tracks used exclusively for industrial switching purposes, within a business district, as defined in §390.5 of this chapter.
 (2) *A railroad grade crossing* when a police officer or crossing flagman directs traffic to proceed.
 (3) *A railroad grade crossing* controlled by a functioning highway traffic signal transmitting a green indication which, under local law, permits the commercial motor vehicle to proceed across the railroad tracks without slowing or stopping.
 (4) *An abandoned railroad grade crossing* which is marked with a sign indicating that the rail line is abandoned.
 (5) *An industrial or spur line railroad grade crossing* marked with a sign reading "Exempt." Such "Exempt" signs shall be erected only by or with the consent of the appropriate State or local authority.

§392.10 DOT Interpretations
Question 1: Is §392.10(a)(4) applicable to drivers operating cargo tank vehicles that were used to transport hazardous materials for which placarding or marking was required, but are no longer required because the cargo tank has been emptied, or the quantity of the material has been reduced, or the temperature or characteristics of the material have changed?
Guidance: No, provided the cargo tank vehicle no longer displays placards or markings indicating that the vehicle is transporting hazardous materials for which placarding or marking is required, and either:
 (1) the vehicle has been sufficiently cleaned of residue and purged of vapors; or
 (2) the vehicle is refilled with a material which is not a hazardous material; or
 (3) the original material no longer is an elevated temperature material or otherwise is no longer considered hazardous according to the regulations.
Although §392.10(a)(4) does not distinguish between loaded and empty cargo tank vehicles, or cargo tank vehicles transporting materials or substances that are not, at the time the vehicle is being driven across the railroad grade crossing, required to be placarded or marked, the Federal Motor Carrier Safety Administration intends that the scope of the regulation be limited to those cases in which the vehicle is placarded or marked.

§392.11 Railroad grade crossings; slowing down required.
Every commercial motor vehicle other than those listed in §392.10 shall, upon approaching a railroad grade crossing, be driven at a rate of speed which will permit said commercial motor vehicle to be stopped before reaching the nearest rail of such crossing and shall not be driven upon or over such crossing until due caution has been taken to ascertain that the course is clear.

§§392.12-392.13 [Reserved]

§392.14 Hazardous conditions; extreme caution.
Extreme caution in the operation of a commercial motor vehicle shall be exercised when hazardous conditions, such as those caused by snow, ice, sleet, fog, mist, rain, dust, or smoke, adversely affect visibility or traction. Speed shall be reduced when such conditions exist. If conditions become sufficiently dangerous, the operation of the commercial motor vehicle shall be discontinued and shall not be resumed until the commercial motor vehicle can be safely operated. Whenever compliance with the foregoing provisions of this rule increases hazard to passengers, the commercial motor vehicle may be operated to the nearest point at which the safety of passengers is assured.

§392.14 DOT Interpretations
Question 1: Who makes the determination, the driver or carrier, that conditions are sufficiently dangerous to warrant discontinuing the operation of a CMV?
Guidance: Under this section, the driver is clearly responsible for the safe operation of the vehicle and the decision to cease operation because of hazardous conditions.

§392.15 [Reserved]

§392.16 Use of seat belts.
A commercial motor vehicle which has a seat belt assembly installed at the driver's seat shall not be driven unless the driver has properly restrained himself/herself with the seat belt assembly.

§392.16 DOT Interpretations
Question 1: May a driver be exempted from wearing seat belts because of a medical condition such as claustrophobia?
Guidance: No.
Question 2: Are motorcoach passengers required to wear seat belts?
Guidance: No.

§392.18 [Reserved]

Subpart C - Stopped Commercial Motor Vehicles

§§392.20-392.21 [Reserved]

§392.22 Emergency signals; stopped commercial motor vehicles.

(a) Hazard warning signal flashers. Whenever a commercial motor vehicle is stopped upon the traveled portion of a highway or the shoulder of a highway for any cause other than necessary traffic stops, the driver of the stopped commercial motor vehicle shall immediately activate the vehicular hazard warning signal flashers and continue the flashing until the driver places the warning devices required by paragraph (b) of this section. The flashing signals shall be used during the time the warning devices are picked up for storage before movement of the commercial motor vehicle. The flashing lights may be used at other times while a commercial motor vehicle is stopped in addition to, but not in lieu of, the warning devices required by paragraph (b) of this section.

(b) Placement of warning devices.

(1) *General rule.* Except as provided in paragraph (b)(2) of this section, whenever a commercial motor vehicle is stopped upon the traveled portion or the shoulder of a highway for any cause other than necessary traffic stops, the driver shall, as soon as possible, but in any event within 10 minutes, place the warning devices required by §393.95 of this subchapter, in the following manner:

(i) *One on the traffic side of and 4 paces* (approximately 3 meters or 10 feet) from the stopped commercial motor vehicle in the direction of approaching traffic;

(ii) *One at 40 paces* (approximately 30 meters or 100 feet) from the stopped commercial motor vehicle in the center of the traffic lane or shoulder occupied by the commercial motor vehicle and in the direction of approaching traffic; and

(iii) *One at 40 paces* (approximately 30 meters or 100 feet) from the stopped commercial motor vehicle in the center of the traffic lane or shoulder occupied by the commercial motor vehicle and in the direction away from approaching traffic.

(2) *Special rules.*

(i) *Fusees and liquid-burning flares.* The driver of a commercial motor vehicle equipped with only fusees or liquid-burning flares shall place a lighted fusee or liquid-burning flare at each of the locations specified in paragraph (b)(1) of this section. There shall be at least one lighted fusee or liquid-burning flare at each of the prescribed locations, as long as the commercial motor vehicle is stopped. Before the stopped commercial motor vehicle is moved, the driver shall extinguish and remove each fusee or liquid-burning flare.

(ii) *Daylight hours.* Except as provided in paragraph (b)(2)(iii) of this section, during the period lighted lamps are not required, three bidirectional reflective triangles, or three lighted fusees or liquid-burning flares shall be placed as specified in paragraph (b)(1) of this section within a time of 10 minutes. In the event the driver elects to use only fusees or liquid-burning flares in lieu of bidirectional reflective triangles or red flags, the driver must ensure that at least one fusee or liquid-burning flare remains lighted at each of the prescribed locations as long as the commercial motor vehicle is stopped or parked.

(iii) *Business or residential districts.* The placement of warning devices is not required within the business or residential district of a municipality, except during the time lighted lamps are required and when street or highway lighting is insufficient to make a commercial motor vehicle clearly discernible at a distance of 500 feet to persons on the highway.

(iv) *Hills, curves, and obstructions.* If a commercial motor vehicle is stopped within 500 feet of a curve, crest of a hill, or other obstruction to view, the driver shall place the warning signal required by paragraph (b)(1) of this section in the direction of the obstruction to view a distance of 100 feet to 500 feet from the stopped commercial motor vehicle so as to afford ample warning to other users of the highway.

(v) *Divided or one-way roads.* If a commercial motor vehicle is stopped upon the traveled portion or the shoulder of a divided or one-way highway, the driver shall place the warning devices required by paragraph (b)(1) of this section, one warning device at a distance of 200 feet and one warning device at a distance of 100 feet in a direction toward approaching traffic in the center of the lane or shoulder occupied by the commercial motor vehicle. He/she shall place one warning device at the traffic side of the commercial motor vehicle within 10 feet of the rear of the commercial motor vehicle.

(vi) *Leaking, flammable material.* If gasoline or any other flammable liquid, or combustible liquid or gas seeps or leaks from a fuel container or a commercial motor vehicle stopped upon a highway, no emergency warning signal producing a flame shall be lighted or placed except at such a distance from any such liquid or gas as will assure the prevention of a fire or explosion.

§392.24 Emergency signals; flame-producing.

No driver shall attach or permit any person to attach a lighted fusee or other flame-producing emergency signal to any part of a commercial motor vehicle.

§392.25 Flame producing devices.

No driver shall use or permit the use of any flame-producing emergency signal for protecting any commercial motor vehicle transporting Division 1.1, Division 1.2, or Division 1.3 explosives; any cargo tank motor vehicle used for the transportation of any Class 3 or Division 2.1, whether loaded or empty; or any commercial motor vehicle using compressed gas as a motor fuel. In lieu thereof, emergency reflective triangles, red electric lanterns, or red emergency reflectors shall be used, the placement of which shall be in the same manner as prescribed in §392.22(b).

Subpart D - Use of Lighted Lamps and Reflectors

§§392.30-392.32 [Reserved]

§392.33 Obscured lamps or reflective devices/material.

(a) No commercial motor vehicle shall be driven when any of the lamps or reflective devices/material required by subpart B of part 393 of this title are obscured by the tailboard, or by any part of the load or its covering, by dirt, or other added vehicle or work equipment or otherwise.

(b) Exception. The conspicuity treatments on the front end protection devices of the trailer may be obscured by part of the load being transported.

Subpart E - License Revocation; Duties of Driver

§§392.40-392.41 [Reserved]

§392.42 [Removed]

> **§392.42 DOT Interpretations**
> *Editor's Note:* This section was removed from the regulations. Regulatory information related to this interpretation is now contained in §391.15(b)(2).
> **Question 1:** If a driver's driving privilege is suspended as a result of a violation committed off-duty, in a personal vehicle, is the driver required to notify the employing motor carrier under the provisions of §392.42?
> *Guidance:* Yes.

Subpart F - Fueling Precautions

§392.50 Ignition of fuel; prevention.

No driver or any employee of a motor carrier shall:

(a) Fuel a commercial motor vehicle with the engine running, except when it is necessary to run the engine to fuel the commercial motor vehicle;

(b) Smoke or expose any open flame in the vicinity of a commercial motor vehicle being fueled;

(c) Fuel a commercial motor vehicle unless the nozzle of the fuel hose is continuously in contact with the intake pipe of the fuel tank;

(d) Permit, insofar as practicable, any other person to engage in such activities as would be likely to result in fire or explosion.

§392.51 Reserve fuel; materials of trade.

Small amounts of fuel for the operation or maintenance of a commercial motor vehicle (including its auxiliary equipment) may be designated as materials of trade (see 49 CFR 171.8).

(a) The aggregate gross weight of all materials of trade on a motor vehicle may not exceed 200 kg (440 pounds).

(b) Packaging for gasoline must be made of metal or plastic and conform to requirements of 49 CFR Parts 171, 172, 173, and 178

or requirements of the Occupational Safety and Health Administration contained in 29 CFR 1910.106.
- (c) **For Packing Group II (including gasoline),** Packing Group III (including aviation fuel and fuel oil), or ORM-D, the material is limited to 30 kg (66 pounds) or 30 L (8 gallons).
- (d) **For diesel fuel,** the capacity of the package is limited to 450 L (119 gallons).
- (e) **A Division 2.1 material in a cylinder is limited** to a gross weight of 100 kg (220 pounds). (A Division 2.1 material is a flammable gas, including liquefied petroleum gas, butane, propane, liquefied natural gas, and methane).

§392.52 [Reserved]

Subpart G - Prohibited Practices

§392.60 Unauthorized persons not to be transported.
- (a) **Unless specifically authorized in writing to do so** by the motor carrier under whose authority the commercial motor vehicle is being operated, no driver shall transport any person or permit any person to be transported on any commercial motor vehicle other than a bus. When such authorization is issued, it shall state the name of the person to be transported, the points where the transportation is to begin and end, and the date upon which such authority expires. No written authorization, however, shall be necessary for the transportation of:
  - (1) *Employees or other persons* assigned to a commercial motor vehicle by a motor carrier;
  - (2) *Any person transported when aid is being rendered* in case of an accident or other emergency;
  - (3) *An attendant delegated to care for livestock.*
- (b) **This section shall not apply to the operation** of commercial motor vehicles controlled and operated by any farmer and used in the transportation of agricultural commodities or products thereof from his/her farm or in the transportation of supplies to his/her farm.

§392.60 DOT Interpretations
Question 1: Does §392.60 require a driver to carry a copy of the written authorization (required to transport passengers) on board a CMV?
Guidance: No, the authorization must be maintained at the carrier's principal place of business. At the discretion of the motor carrier, a driver may also carry a copy of the authorization.

§392.61 [Reserved]

§392.62 Safe operation, buses.
No person shall drive a bus and a motor carrier shall not require or permit a person to drive a bus unless —
- (a) **All standees on the bus** are rearward of the standee line or other means prescribed in §393.90 of this subchapter;
- (b) **All aisle seats in the bus** conform to the requirements of §393.91 of this subchapter; and
- (c) **Baggage or freight on the bus is stowed and secured** in a manner which assures —
  - (1) *Unrestricted freedom of movement* to the driver and his proper operation of the bus;
  - (2) *Unobstructed access to all exits by any occupant of the bus;* and
  - (3) *Protection of occupants of the bus* against injury resulting from the falling or displacement of articles transported in the bus.

§392.63 Towing or pushing loaded buses.
No disabled bus with passengers aboard shall be towed or pushed; nor shall any person use or permit to be used a bus with passengers aboard for the purpose of towing or pushing any disabled motor vehicle, except in such circumstances where the hazard to passengers would be increased by observance of the foregoing provisions of this section, and then only in traveling to the nearest point where the safety of the passengers is assured.

§392.64 Riding within closed commercial motor vehicles without proper exits.
No person shall ride within the closed body of any commercial motor vehicle unless there are means on the inside thereof of obtaining exit. Said means shall be in such condition as to permit ready operation by the occupant.

§392.65 [Reserved]

§392.66 Carbon monoxide; use of commercial motor vehicle when detected.
- (a) **No person shall dispatch or drive** any commercial motor vehicle or permit any passengers thereon, when the following conditions are known to exist, until such conditions have been remedied or repaired:
  - (1) *Where an occupant has been affected by carbon monoxide;*
  - (2) *Where carbon monoxide has been detected* in the interior of the commercial motor vehicle;
  - (3) *When a mechanical condition* of the commercial motor vehicle is discovered which would be likely to produce a hazard to the occupants by reason of carbon monoxide.
- (b) [Reserved]

§392.67 Heater, flame-producing; on commercial motor vehicle in motion.
No open flame heater used in the loading or unloading of the commodity transported shall be in operation while the commercial motor vehicle is in motion.

§§392.68-392.69 [Reserved]

§392.71 Radar detectors; use and/or possession.
- (a) **No driver shall use a radar detector** in a commercial motor vehicle, or operate a commercial motor vehicle that is equipped with or contains any radar detector.
- (b) **No motor carrier shall require or permit a driver** to violate paragraph (a) of this section.

Part 392 - Driving of Commercial Motor Vehicles

Notes

Part 393 - Parts and Accessories Necessary for Safe Operation

(Page 113 in the Driver Edition)

Subpart A - General

§393.1 Scope of the rules in this part.

(a) **The rules in this part** establish minimum standards for commercial motor vehicles as defined in §390.5 of this title. Only motor vehicles (as defined in §390.5) and combinations of motor vehicles which meet the definition of a commercial motor vehicle are subject to the requirements of this part. All requirements that refer to motor vehicles with a GVWR below 4,536 kg (10,001 pounds) are applicable only when the motor vehicle or combination of motor vehicles meets the definition of a commercial motor vehicle.

(b) **Every employer and employee** shall comply and be conversant with the requirements and specifications of this part. No employer shall operate a commercial motor vehicle, or cause or permit it to be operated, unless it is equipped in accordance with the requirements and specifications of this part.

§393.3 Additional equipment and accessories.

Nothing contained in this subchapter shall be construed to prohibit the use of additional equipment and accessories, not inconsistent with or prohibited by this subchapter, provided such equipment and accessories do not decrease the safety of operation of the motor vehicles on which they are used.

§393.5 Definitions.

As used in this part, the following words and terms are construed to mean:

Aggregate working load limit. The summation of the working load limits or restraining capacity of all devices used to secure an article of cargo on a vehicle.

Agricultural commodity trailer. A trailer that is designed to transport bulk agricultural commodities in off-road harvesting sites and to a processing plant or storage location, as evidenced by skeletal construction that accommodates harvest containers, a maximum length of 28 feet, and an arrangement of air control lines and reservoirs that minimizes damage in field operations.

Air brake system. A system, including an air-over-hydraulic brake subsystem, that uses air as a medium for transmitting pressure or force from the driver control to the service brake, but does not include a system that uses compressed air or vacuum only to assist the driver in applying muscular force to hydraulic or mechanical components.

Air-over-hydraulic brake subsystem. A subsystem of the air brake system that uses compressed air to transmit a force from the driver control to a hydraulic brake system to actuate the service brakes.

Anchor point. Part of the structure, fitting or attachment on a vehicle or article of cargo to which a tiedown is attached.

Antilock Brake System or **ABS** means a portion of a service brake system that automatically controls the degree of rotational wheel slip during braking by:

(1) *Sensing the rate of angular rotation of the wheels;*

(2) *Transmitting signals* regarding the rate of wheel angular rotation to one or more controlling devices which interpret those signals and generate responsive controlling output signals; and

(3) *Transmitting those controlling signals* to one or more modulators which adjust brake actuating forces in response to those signals.

Article of cargo. A unit of cargo, other than a liquid, gas, or aggregate that lacks physical structure (e.g., grain, gravel, etc.) including articles grouped together so that they can be handled as a single unit or unitized by wrapping, strapping, banding or edge protection device(s).

Auxiliary driving lamp. A lighting device mounted to provide illumination forward of the vehicle which supplements the upper beam of a standard headlighting system. It is not intended for use alone or with the lower beam of a standard headlamp system.

Bell pipe concrete. Pipe whose flanged end is of larger diameter than its barrel.

Blocking. A structure, device or another substantial article placed against or around an article of cargo to prevent horizontal movement of the article of cargo.

Boat trailer. A trailer designed with cradle-type mountings to transport a boat and configured to permit launching of the boat from the rear of the trailer.

Bracing. A structure, device, or another substantial article placed against an article of cargo to prevent it from tipping, that may also prevent it from shifting.

Brake. An energy conversion mechanism used to stop, or hold a vehicle stationary.

Brake power assist unit. A device installed in a hydraulic brake system that reduces the operator effort required to actuate the system, but which if inoperative does not prevent the operator from braking the vehicle by a continued application of muscular force on the service brake control.

Brake power unit. A device installed in a brake system that provides the energy required to actuate the brakes, either directly or indirectly through an auxiliary device, with the operator action consisting only of modulating the energy application level.

Brake tubing/hose. Metallic brake tubing, nonmetallic brake tubing and brake hose are conduits or lines used in a brake system to transmit or contain the medium (fluid or vacuum) used to apply the motor vehicle's brakes.

Chassis. The load-supporting frame of a commercial motor vehicle, exclusive of any appurtenances which might be added to accommodate cargo.

Clearance Lamps. Lamps that provide light to the front or rear, mounted on the permanent structure of the vehicle, such that they indicate the overall width of the vehicle.

Container chassis trailer. A semitrailer of skeleton construction limited to a bottom frame, one or more axles, specially built and fitted with locking devices for the transport of intermodal cargo containers, so that when the chassis and container are assembled, the units serve the same function as an over the road trailer.

Converter dolly. A motor vehicle consisting of a chassis equipped with one or more axles, a fifth wheel and/or equivalent mechanism, and drawbar, the attachment of which converts a semitrailer to a full trailer.

Crib-type log trailer means a trailer equipped with stakes, bunks, a front-end structure, and a rear structure to restrain logs. The stakes prevent movement of the logs from side to side on the vehicle while the front-end and rear structures prevent movement of the logs from front to back on the vehicle.

Curb weight. The weight of a motor vehicle with standard equipment, maximum capacity of fuel, oil, and coolant; and, if so equipped, air conditioning and additional weight of optional engine. Curb weight does not include the driver.

Dunnage. All loose materials used to support and protect cargo.

Dunnage bag. An inflatable bag intended to fill otherwise empty space between articles of cargo, or between articles of cargo and the wall of the vehicle.

Edge protector. A device placed on the exposed edge of an article to distribute tiedown forces over a larger area of cargo than the tiedown itself, to protect the tie-down and/or cargo from damage, and to allow the tiedown to slide freely when being tensioned.

Electric brake system. A system that uses electric current to actuate the service brake.

Emergency brake. A mechanism designed to stop a motor vehicle after a failure of the service brake system.

Emergency brake system. A mechanism designed to stop a vehicle after a single failure occurs in the service brake system of a part designed to contain compressed air or brake fluid or vacuum (except failure of a common valve, manifold brake fluid housing or brake chamber housing).

Fifth wheel. A device mounted on a truck tractor or similar towing vehicle (e.g., converter dolly) which interfaces with and couples to the upper coupler assembly of a semitrailer.

Frame vehicle. A vehicle with skeletal structure fitted with one or more bunk units for transporting logs. A bunk unit consists of U-shaped front and rear bunks that together cradle logs. The bunks are welded, gusseted or otherwise firmly fastened to the vehicle's main beams, and are an integral part of the vehicle.

Friction mat. A device placed between the deck of a vehicle and article of cargo, or between articles of cargo, intended to provide greater friction than exists naturally between these surfaces.

Front fog lamp. A lighting device whose beam provides downward illumination forward of the vehicle and close to the ground, and is to be used only under conditions of rain, snow, dust, smoke or fog. A pair of fog lamps may be used alone, with parking, tail, side, marker, clearance and identification lamps, or with a lower beam headlamp at the driver's discretion in accordance with state and local use law.

Fuel tank fitting. Any removable device affixed to an opening in the fuel tank with the exception of the filler cap.

g. The acceleration due to gravity, 32.2 ft/sec^2 (9.81 m/sec^2).

Grommet. A device that serves as a support and protection to that which passes through it.

Hazard warning signal. Lamps that flash simultaneously to the front and rear, on both the right and left sides of a commercial motor vehicle, to indicate to an approaching driver the presence of a vehicular hazard.

Head lamps. Lamps used to provide general illumination ahead of a motor vehicle.

Heater. Any device or assembly of devices or appliances used to heat the interior of any motor vehicle. This includes a catalytic heater which must meet the requirements of §177.834(l)(2) of this title when Class 3 (flammable liquid) or Division 2.1 (flammable gas) is transported.

Heavy hauler trailer. A trailer which has one or more of the following characteristics, but which is not a container chassis trailer:

(1) *Its brake lines are designed* to adapt to separation or extension of the vehicle frame; or

(2) *Its body consists only of a platform* whose primary cargo-carrying surface is not more than 1,016 mm (40 inches) above the ground in an unloaded condition, except that it may include sides that are designed to be easily removable and a permanent "front-end structure" as that term is used in §393.106 of this title.

Hook-lift container. A specialized container, primarily used to contain and transport materials in the waste, recycling, construction/demolition and scrap industries, which is used in conjunction with specialized vehicles, in which the container is loaded and unloaded onto a tilt frame body by an articulating hook-arm.

Hydraulic brake system. A system that uses hydraulic fluid as a medium for transmitting force from a service brake control to the service brake, and that may incorporate a brake power assist unit, or a brake power unit.

Identification lamps. Lamps used to identify certain types of commercial motor vehicles.

Integral securement system. A system on certain roll-on/roll-off containers and hook-lift containers and their related transport vehicles in which compatible front and rear hold down devices are mated to provide securement of the complete vehicle and its articles of cargo.

Lamp. A device used to produce artificial light.

Length of a manufactured home. The largest exterior length in the traveling mode, including any projections which contain interior space. Length does not include bay windows, roof projections, overhangs, or eaves under which there is no interior space, nor does it include drawbars, couplings or hitches.

License plate lamp. A lamp used to illuminate the license plate on the rear of a motor vehicle.

Longwood means all logs, that are not shortwood, i.e., are over 4.9 m (16 feet) long. Such logs are usually described as long logs or tree-length.

Low chassis vehicle.

(1) *A trailer or semitrailer* manufactured on or after January 26, 1998, having a chassis which extends behind the rearmost point of the rearmost tires and which has a lower rear surface that meets the guard width, height, and rear surface requirements of §571.224 in effect on the date of manufacture, or a subsequent edition.

(2) *A motor vehicle,* not described by paragraph (1) of this definition, having a chassis which extends behind the rearmost point of the rearmost tires and which has a lower rear surface that meets the guard configuration requirements of §393.86(b)(1).

Manufactured home means a structure, transportable in one or more sections, which in the traveling mode, is eight body feet or more in width or forty body feet or more in length, or, when erected on site, is three hundred twenty or more square feet, and which is built on a permanent chassis and designed to be used as a dwelling with or without a permanent foundation when connected to the required utilities, and includes the plumbing, heating, air-conditioning, and electrical systems contained therein. Calculations used to determine the number of square feet in a structure will be based on the structure's exterior dimensions measured at the largest horizontal projections when erected on site. These dimensions will include all expandable rooms, cabinets, and other projections containing interior space, but do not include bay windows. This term includes all structures which meet the above requirements except the size requirements and with respect to which the manufacturer voluntarily files a certification pursuant to 24 CFR 3282.13 and complies with the standards set forth in 24 CFR Part 3280.

Metal coil means an article of cargo comprised of elements, mixtures, compounds, or alloys commonly known as metal, metal foil, metal leaf, forged metal, stamped metal, metal wire, metal rod, or metal chain that are packaged as a roll, coil, spool, wind, or wrap, including plastic or rubber coated electrical wire and communications cable.

Multi-piece windshield. A windshield consisting of two or more windshield glazing surface areas.

Parking brake system. A mechanism designed to prevent the movement of a stationary motor vehicle.

Play. Any free movement of components.

Pulpwood trailer. A trailer or semitrailer that is designed exclusively for harvesting logs or pulpwood and constructed with a skeletal frame with no means for attachment of a solid bed, body, or container.

Rail vehicle. A vehicle whose skeletal structure is fitted with stakes at the front and rear to contain logs loaded crosswise.

Rear extremity. The rearmost point on a motor vehicle that falls above a horizontal plane located 560 mm (22 inches) above the ground and below a horizontal plane located 1,900 mm (75 inches) above the ground when the motor vehicle is stopped on level ground; unloaded; its fuel tanks are full; the tires (and air suspension, if so equipped) are inflated in accordance with the manufacturer's recommendations; and the motor vehicle's cargo doors, tailgate, or other permanent structures are positioned as they normally are when the vehicle is in motion. Nonstructural protrusions such as taillamps, rubber bumpers, hinges, and latches are excluded from the determination of the rearmost point.

Reflective material. A material conforming to Federal Specification L-S-300, "Sheeting and Tape, Reflective; Non-exposed Lens, Adhesive Backing," (September 7, 1965) meeting the performance standard in either Table 1 or Table 1A of SAE Standard J594f, "Reflex Reflectors" (January, 1977).

Reflex reflector. A device which is used on a vehicle to give an indication to an approaching driver by reflected lighted from the lamps on the approaching vehicle.

Saddle-mount. A device, designed and constructed as to be readily demountable, used in driveaway-towaway operations to perform the functions of a conventional fifth wheel:

(1) **Upper-half.** "Upper-half" of a "saddle-mount" means that part of the device which is securely attached to the towed vehicle and maintains a fixed position relative thereto, but does not include the "king-pin;"

(2) **Lower-half.** "Lower-half" of a "saddle-mount" means that part of the device which is securely attached to the towing vehicle and maintains a fixed position relative thereto but does not include the "king-pin;" and

(3) **King-pin.** "King-pin" means that device which is used to connect the "upper-half" to the "lower-half" in such manner as to permit relative movement in a horizontal plane between the towed and towing vehicles.

Service brake system. A primary brake system used for slowing and stopping a vehicle.

Shoring bar. A device placed transversely between the walls of a vehicle and cargo to prevent cargo from tipping or shifting.

Shortwood. All logs typically up to 4.9 m (16 feet) long. Such logs are often described as cut-up logs, cut-to-length logs, bolts or pulpwood. Shortwood may be loaded lengthwise or crosswise, though that loaded crosswise is usually no more than 2.6 m (102 inches) long.

Side extremity. The outermost point on a side of the motor vehicle that is above a horizontal plane located 560 mm (22 inches) above the ground, below a horizontal plane located 1,900 mm (75 inches) above the ground, and between a transverse vertical plane tangent to the rear extremity of the vehicle and a transverse vertical plane located 305 mm (12 inches) forward of that plane when the vehicle is unloaded; its fuel tanks are full; and the tires (and air suspension, if so equipped) are inflated in accordance with the manufacturer's recommendations. Non-structural protrusions such as taillights, hinges, and latches are excluded from the determination of the outermost point.

Side marker lamp (Intermediate). A lamp mounted on the side, on the permanent structure of the motor vehicle that provides light to the side to indicate the approximate middle of the vehicle, when the motor vehicle is 9.14 meters (30 feet) or more in length.

Side Marker Lamps. Lamps mounted on the side, on the permanent structure of the motor vehicle as near as practicable to the front

Subpart A - General — §393.7 (b)

and rear of the vehicle, that provide light to the side to indicate the overall length of the motor vehicle.

Sided vehicle. A vehicle whose cargo compartment is enclosed on all four sides by walls of sufficient strength to contain articles of cargo, where the walls may include latched openings for loading and unloading, and includes vans, dump bodies, and a sided intermodal container carried by a vehicle.

Special purpose vehicle.
(1) *A trailer or semitrailer* manufactured on or after January 26, 1998, having work-performing equipment that, while the motor vehicle is in transit, resides in or moves through the area that could be occupied by the horizontal member of the rear impact guard, as defined by the guard width, height, and rear surface requirements of §571.224 (paragraphs S5.1.1 through S5.1.3), in effect on the date of manufacture, or a subsequent edition.
(2) *A motor vehicle,* not described by paragraph (1) of this definition, having work-performing equipment that, while the motor vehicle is in transit, resides in or moves through the area that could be occupied by the horizontal member of the rear impact guard, as defined by the guard width, height and rear surface requirements of §393.86(b)(1).

Split service brake system. A brake system consisting of two or more subsystems actuated by a single control designed so that a leakage-type failure of a pressure component in a single subsystem (except structural failure of a housing that is common to two or more subsystems) shall not impair the operation of any other subsystem.

Steering wheel lash. The condition in which the steering wheel may be turned through some part of a revolution without associated movement of the front wheels.

Stop lamps. Lamps shown to the rear of a motor vehicle to indicate that the service brake system is engaged.

Tail lamps. Lamps used to designate the rear of a motor vehicle.

Tiedown. A combination of securing devices which forms an assembly that attaches articles of cargo to, or restrains articles of cargo on, a vehicle or trailer, and is attached to anchor point(s).

Tow bar. A strut or column-like device temporarily attached between the rear of a towing vehicle and the front of the vehicle being towed.

Tractor-pole trailer. A combination vehicle that carries logs lengthwise so that they form the body of the vehicle. The logs are supported by a bunk located on the rear of the tractor, and another bunk on the skeletal trailer. The tractor bunk may rotate about a vertical axis, and the trailer may have a fixed, scoping, or cabled reach, or other mechanical freedom, to allow it to turn.

Trailer kingpin. A pin (with a flange on its lower end) which extends vertically from the front of the underside of a semitrailer and which locks into a fifth wheel.

Turn signals. Lamps used to indicate a change in direction by emitting a flashing light on the side of a motor vehicle towards which a turn will be made.

Upper coupler assembly. A structure consisting of an upper coupler plate, king-pin and supporting framework which interfaces with and couples to a fifth wheel.

Upper coupler plate. A plate structure through which the king-pin neck and collar extend. The bottom surface of the plate contacts the fifth wheel when coupled.

Vacuum brake system. A system that uses a vacuum and atmospheric pressure for transmitting a force from the driver control to the service brake, not including a system that uses vacuum only to assist the driver in applying muscular force to hydraulic or mechanical components.

Void filler. Material used to fill a space between articles of cargo and the structure of the vehicle that has sufficient strength to prevent movement of the articles of cargo.

Well. The depression formed between two cylindrical articles of cargo when they are laid with their eyes horizontal and parallel against each other.

Wheels back vehicle.
(1) *A trailer or semitrailer* manufactured on or after January 26, 1998, whose rearmost axle is permanently fixed and is located such that the rearmost surface of the tires (of the size recommended by the vehicle manufacturer for the rear axle) is not more than 305 mm (12 inches) forward of the transverse vertical plane tangent to the rear extremity of the vehicle.
(2) *A motor vehicle,* not described by paragraph (1) of this definition, whose rearmost axle is permanently fixed and is located such that the rearmost surface of the tires (of the size recommended by the vehicle manufacturer for the rear axle) is not more than 610 mm (24 inches) forward of the transverse vertical plane tangent to the rear extremity of the vehicle.

Width of a manufactured home. The largest exterior width in the traveling mode, including any projections which contain interior space. Width does not include bay windows, roof projections, overhangs, or eaves under which there is no interior space.

Windshield. The principal forward facing glazed surface provided for forward vision in operating a motor vehicle.

Working load limit (WLL). The maximum load that may be applied to a component of a cargo securement system during normal service, usually assigned by the manufacturer of the component.

§393.7 Matter incorporated by reference.

(a) Incorporation by reference. Part 393 includes references to certain matter or materials, as listed in paragraph (b) of this section. The text of the materials is not included in the regulations contained in Part 393. The materials are hereby made a part of the regulations in Part 393. The Director of the Federal Register has approved the materials incorporated by reference in accordance with 5 U.S.C. 552(a) and 1 CFR Part 51. For materials subject to change, only the specific version approved by the Director of the Federal Register and specified in the regulation are incorporated. Material is incorporated as it exists on the date of the approval and a notice of any change in these materials will be published in the Federal Register.

(b) Matter or materials referenced in Part 393. The matter or materials listed in this paragraph are incorporated by reference in the corresponding sections noted.

(1) *Auxiliary Upper Beam Lamps,* Society of Automotive Engineers (SAE) J581, July 2004, incorporation by reference approved for §393.24(b).
(2) *Front Fog Lamp,* SAE J583, August 2004, incorporation by reference approved for §393.24(b).
(3) *Stop Lamps* for Use on Motor Vehicles Less Than 2032 mm in Overall Width, SAE J586, March 2000, incorporation by reference approved for §393.25(c).
(4) *Stop Lamps and Front- and Rear-Turn Signal Lamps* for Use on Motor Vehicles 2032 mm or more in Overall Width, SAE J2261, January 2002, incorporated by reference approved for §393.25(c).
(5) *Tail Lamps (Rear Position Lamps)* for Use on Motor Vehicles Less Than 2032 mm in Overall Width, SAE J585, March 2000, incorporation by reference approved for §393.25(c).
(6) *Tail Lamps (Rear Position Lamps)* for Use on Vehicles 2032 mm or More in Overall Width, SAE J2040, March 2002, incorporation by reference approved for §393.25(c).
(7) *Turn Signal Lamps* for Use on Motor Vehicles Less Than 2032 mm in Overall Width, SAE J588, March 2000, incorporation by reference approved for §393.25(c).
(8) *Sidemarker Lamps* for Use on Road Vehicles Less Than 2032 mm in Overall Width, SAE J592, August 2000, incorporation by reference approved for §393.25(c).
(9) *Directional Flashing Optical Warning Devices* for Authorized Emergency, Maintenance, and Service Vehicles, SAE J595, January 2005, incorporation by reference approved for §393.25(e).
(10) *Optical Warning Devices* for Authorized Emergency, Maintenance, and Service Vehicles, SAE J845, May 1997, incorporation by reference approved for §393.25(e).
(11) *Gaseous Discharge Warning Lamp* for Authorized Emergency, Maintenance, and Service Vehicles, SAE J1318, May 1998, incorporation by reference approved for §393.25(e).
(12) *Reflex Reflectors,* SAE J594, December 2003, incorporation by reference approved for §393.26(c).
(13) *Standard Specification* for Retroreflective Sheeting for Traffic Control, American Society of Testing and Materials, ASTM D 4956–04, 2004, incorporation by reference approved for §393.26(c).
(14) *Automobile,* Truck, Truck-Tractor, Trailer, and Motor Coach Wiring, SAE J1292, October 1981, incorporated by reference approved for §393.28.
(15) *Long Stroke Air Brake Actuator Marking,* SAE J1817, July 2001, incorporation by reference approved for §393.47(e).
(16) *American National Standard for Safety Glazing Materials* for Glazing Motor Vehicles and Motor Vehicle Equipment Operating on Land Highways-Safety Standard, SAE Z26.1– 1996, August 1997, incorporation by reference approved for §393.62(d).
(17) *Specification for Sound Level Meters,* American National Standards Institute, S1.4–1983, incorporation by reference approved for §393.94(c).
(18) *Standard Specification* for Strapping, Flat Steel and Seals, American Society for Testing and Materials (ASTM), D3953–

97, February 1998, incorporation by reference approved for §393.104(e).
(19) *Welded Steel Chain Specifications,* National Association of Chain Manufacturers, September 28, 2005, incorporation by reference approved for § 393.104(e).
(20) *Recommended Standard Specification* for Synthetic Web Tiedowns, Web Sling and Tiedown Association, WSTDA-T1, 1998, incorporation by reference approved for §393.104(e).
(21) *Wire Rope Users Manual,* 2nd Edition, Wire Rope Technical Board November 1985, incorporation by reference approved for §393.104(e).
(22) *Cordage Institute rope standards* approved for incorporation into §393.104(e):
   (i) *PETRS-2,* Polyester Fiber Rope, 3-Strand and 8-Strand Constructions, January 1993;
   (ii) *PPRS-2,* Polypropylene Fiber Rope, 3-Strand and 8-Strand Constructions, August 1992;
   (iii) *CRS-1,* Polyester/Polypropylene Composite Rope Specifications, Three-Strand and Eight-Strand Standard Construction, May 1979;
   (iv) *NRS-1,* Nylon Rope Specifications, Three-Strand and Eight-Strand Standard Construction, May 1979; and
   (v) *C-1,* Double Braided Nylon Rope Specifications DBN, January 1984.
(c) **Availability.** The materials incorporated by reference are available as follows:
   (1) *Standards of the Underwriters Laboratories, Inc.* Information and copies may be obtained by writing to: Underwriters Laboratories, Inc., 333 Pfingsten Road, Northbrook, Illinois 60062.
   (2) *Specifications of* the American Society for Testing and Materials. Information and copies may be obtained by writing to: American Society for Testing and Materials, 100 Barr Harbor Drive, West Conshohocken, Pennsylvania 19428-2959.
   (3) *Specifications of* the National Association of Chain Manufacturers. Information and copies may be obtained by writing to: National Association of Chain Manufacturers, P.O. Box 22681, Lehigh Valley, Pennsylvania 18002-2681.
   (4) *Specifications of* the Web Sling and Tiedown Association. Information and copies may be obtained by writing to: Web Sling and Tiedown Association, Inc., 5024-R Campbell Boulevard, Baltimore, Maryland 21236-5974.
   (5) *Manuals of the Wire Rope Technical Board.* Information and copies may be obtained by writing to: Wire Rope Technical Committee, P.O. Box 849, Stevensville, Maryland 21666.
   (6) *Standards of the Cordage Institute.* Information and copies may be obtained by writing to: Cordage Institute, 350 Lincoln Street, 115, Hingham, Massachusetts 02043.
   (7) *Standards of the Society of Automotive Engineers (SAE).* Information and copies may be obtained by writing to: Society of Automotive Engineers, Inc., 400 Commonwealth Drive, Warrendale, Pennsylvania 15096.
   (8) *Standards of the American National Standards Institute (ANSI).* Information and copies may be obtained by writing to: American National Standards Institute, 25 West 43rd Street, New York, New York 10036.
   (9) *[Reserved].*
   (10) *All of the materials incorporated by reference* are available for inspection at:
      (i) *The Federal Motor Carrier Safety Administration,* Office of Bus and Truck Standards and Operations, 400 Seventh Street, SW., Washington, DC 20590; and
      (ii) *The National Archives* and Records Administration (NARA). For information on the availability of this material at NARA, call 202-741-6030, or go to: http://www.archives.gov/federal_register/code_of_federal_regulations/ibr_locations.html.

Subpart B - Lamps, Reflective Devices, and Electrical Wiring

§393.9 Lamps operable, prohibition of obstructions of lamps and reflectors.

(a) **All lamps required by this subpart** shall be capable of being operated at all times. This paragraph shall not be construed to require that any auxiliary or additional lamp be capable of operating at all times.

(b) **Lamps and reflective devices/material** required by this subpart must not be obscured by the tailboard, or by any part of the load, or its covering by dirt, or other added vehicle or work equipment, or otherwise. Exception: The conspicuity treatments on the front end protection devices may be obscured by part of the load being transported.

§393.11 Lamps and reflective devices.

(a) (1) *Lamps and reflex reflectors.* Table 1 specifies the requirements for lamps, reflective devices and associated equipment by the type of commercial motor vehicle. The diagrams in this section illustrate the position of the lamps, reflective devices and associated equipment specified in Table 1. All commercial motor vehicles manufactured on or after December 25, 1968, must, at a minimum, meet the applicable requirements of 49 CFR 571.108 (FMVSS No. 108) in effect at the time of manufacture of the vehicle. Commercial motor vehicles manufactured before December 25, 1968, must, at a minimum, meet the requirements of Subpart B of Part 393 in effect at the time of manufacture.

(2) *Exceptions:* Pole trailers and trailer converter dollies must meet the Part 393 requirements for lamps, reflective devices and electrical equipment in effect at the time of manufacture. Trailers which are equipped with conspicuity material which meets the requirements of §393.11(b) are not required to be equipped with the reflex reflectors listed in Table 1 if—
   (i) *The conspicuity material is placed* at the locations where reflex reflectors are required by Table 1; and
   (ii) *The conspicuity material when installed* on the motor vehicle meets the visibility requirements for the reflex reflectors.

(b) **Conspicuity Systems.** Each trailer of 2,032 mm (80 inches) or more overall width, and with a GVWR over 4,536 kg (10,000 pounds), manufactured on or after December 1, 1993, except pole trailers and trailers designed exclusively for living or office use, shall be equipped with either retroreflective sheeting that meets the requirements of FMVSS No. 108 (S5.7.1), reflex reflectors that meet the requirements FMVSS No. 108 (S5.7.2), or a combination of retroreflective sheeting and reflex reflectors that meet the requirements of FMVSS No. 108 (S5.7.3). The conspicuity system shall be installed and located as specified in FMVSS No. 108 [S5.7.1.4 (for retroreflective sheeting), S5.7.2.2 (for reflex reflectors), S5.7.3 (for a combination of sheeting and reflectors)] and have certification and markings as required by S5.7.1.5 (for retroreflective tape) and S5.7.2.3 (for reflex reflectors).

(c) **Prohibition on the use of amber stop lamps and tail lamps.** No commercial motor vehicle may be equipped with an amber stop lamp, a tail lamp, or other lamp which is optically combined with an amber stop lamp or tail lamp.

(d) **Prohibition on the use** of auxiliary lamps that supplement the identification lamps. No commercial motor vehicle may be equipped with lamps that are in a horizontal line with the required identification lamps unless those lamps are required by this regulation.

Subpart B - Lamps, Reflective Devices, and Electrical Wiring §393.11 (d)

Table 1 - Required Lamps and Reflectors on Commercial Motor Vehicles

Item on the vehicle	Quantity	Color	Location	Position	Height above the road surface in millimeters (mm) (with English units in parenthesis) measured from the center of the lamp at curb weight	Vehicles for which the devices are required
Headlamps	2	White	Front	On the front at the same height, with an equal number at each side of the vertical center line as far apart as practicable.	Not less than 559 mm (22 inches) nor more than 1,372 mm (54 inches).	A, B, C
Turn Signal (Front) [2, 12]	2	Amber	At or near the front	One on each side of the vertical centerline at the same height and as far apart as practicable.	Not less than 381 mm (15 inches) nor more than 2,108 mm (83 inches).	A, B, C
Identification Lamps (Front) [1]	3	Amber	Front	As close as practicable to the top of the vehicle, at the same height, and as close as practicable to the vertical centerline of the vehicle (or the vertical centerline of the cab where different from the centerline of the vehicle) with lamp centers spaced not less than 152 mm (6 inches) or more than 305 mm (12 inches) apart. Alternatively, the front lamps may be located as close as practicable to the top of the cab.	All three on same level as close as practicable to the top of the motor vehicle.	B, C
Tail Lamps [5, 11]	2	Red	Rear	One lamp on each side of the vertical centerline at the same height and as far apart as practicable	Both on the same level between 381 mm (15 inches) and 1,829 mm (72 inches).	A, B, C, D, E, F, G, H
Stop Lamps [5, 13]	2	Red	Rear	One lamp on each side of the vertical centerline at the same height and as far apart as practicable	Both on the same level between 381 mm (15 inches) and 1,829 mm (72 inches).	A, B, C, D, E, F, G
Clearance Lamps [8, 9, 10, 15, 17]	2	Amber	One on each side of the front of the vehicle	One on each side of the vertical centerline to indicate overall width.	Both on the same level as high as practicable.	B, C, D, G, H
	2	Red	One on each side of the rear of the vehicle	One on each side of the vertical centerline to indicate overall width.	Both on the same level as high as practicable.	B, D, G, H
Reflex Reflector, Intermediate (Side)	2	Amber	One on each side	At or near the midpoint between the front and rear side marker lamps, if the length of the vehicle is more than 9,144 mm (30 feet).	Between 381 mm (15 inches) and 1,524 (60 inches).	A, B, D, F, G
Reflex Reflector (Rear) [5, 6, 8]	2	Red	Rear	One on each side of the vertical centerline, as far apart as practicable and at the same height.	Both on the same level, between 381 mm (15 inches) and 1,524 mm (60 inches).	A, B, C, D, E, F, G
Reflex Reflector (Rear Side)	2	Red	One on each side (rear)	As far to the rear as practicable.	Both on the same level, between 381 mm (15 inches) and 1,524 mm (60 inches).	A, B, D, F, G
Reflex Reflector (Front Side) [16]	2	Amber	One on each side (front)	As far to the front as practicable.	Between 381 mm (15 inches) and 1,524 mm (60 inches).	A, B, C, D, F, G
License Plate Lamp (Rear) [11]	1	White	At rear license plate to illuminate the plate from the top or sides		No requirements.	A, B, C, D, F, G
Side Marker Lamp (Front) [16]	2	Amber	One on each side	As far to the front as practicable.	Not less than 381 mm (15 inches).	A, B, C, D, F
Side Marker Lamp Intermediate	2	Amber	One on each side	At or near the midpoint between the front and rear side marker lamps, if the length of the vehicle is more than 9,144 mm (30 feet).	Not less than 381 mm (15 inches).	A, B, D, F, G
Side Marker Lamp (Rear) [4, 8]	2	Red	One on each side	As far to the rear as practicable.	Not less than 381 mm (15 inches), and on the rear of trailers not more than 1,524 mm (60 inches).	A, B, D, F, G

Table 1 - Required Lamps and Reflectors on Commercial Motor Vehicles (continued)

Item on the vehicle	Quantity	Color	Location	Position	Height above the road surface in millimeters (mm) (with English units in parenthesis) measured from the center of the lamp at curb weight	Vehicles for which the devices are required
Turn Signal (Rear) [5, 12]	2	Amber or Red	Rear	One lamp on each side of the vertical centerline as far apart as practicable.	Both on the same level, between 381 mm (15 inches) and 2,108 mm (83 inches).	A, B, C, D, E, F, G
Identification Lamp (Rear) [3, 7, 15]	3	Red	Rear	One as close as practicable to the vertical centerline. One on each side with lamp centers spaced not less than 152 mm (6 inches) or more than 305 mm (12 inches) apart.	All three on the same level as close as practicable to the top of the vehicle.	B, D, G
Vehicular Hazard Warning Signal Flasher Lamps [5, 12]	2	Amber	Front	One lamp on each side of the vertical centerline, as far apart as practicable.	Both on the same level, between 381 mm (15 inches) and 2,108 mm (83 inches).	A, B, C
	2	Amber or Red	Rear	One lamp on each side of the vertical centerline, as far apart as practicable.	Both on the same level, between 381 mm (15 inches) and 2,108 mm (83 inches).	A, B, C, D, E, F, G
Backup Lamp [14]	1 or 2	White	Rear	Rear.	No requirement.	A, B, C
Parking Lamp	2	Amber or white	Front	One lamp on each side of the vertical centerline, as far apart as practicable.	Both on the same level, between 381 mm (15 inches) and 2,108 mm (83 inches).	A

Legend: Types of commercial motor vehicles shown in the last column of Table 1
A. Buses and trucks less than 2,032 mm (80 inches) in overall width.
B. Buses and trucks 2,032 mm (80 inches) or more in overall width.
C. Truck tractors.
D. Semitrailers and full trailers 2,032 mm (80 inches) or more in overall width except converter dollies.
E. Converter dolly.
F. Semitrailers and full trailers less than 2,032 mm (80 inches) in overall width.
G. Pole trailers.
H. Projecting loads.
Note: Lamps and reflectors may be combined as permitted by §393.22 and S5.4 of 49 CFR 571.108, Equipment combinations.

1. Identification lamps may be mounted on the vertical centerline of the cab where different from the centerline of the vehicle, except where the cab is not more than 42 inches wide at the front roofline, then a single lamp at the center of the cab shall be deemed to comply with the requirements for identification lamps. No part of the identification lamps or their mountings may extend below the top of the vehicle windshield.
2. Unless the turn signals on the front are so constructed (double-faced) and located as to be visible to passing drivers, two turn signals are required on the rear of the truck tractor, one at each side as far apart as practicable.
3. The identification lamps need not be visible or lighted if obscured by a vehicle in the same combination.
4. Any semitrailer or full trailer manufactured on or after March 1, 1979, shall be equipped with rear side-marker lamps at a height of not less than 381 mm (15 inches), and on the rear of trailers not more than 1,524 mm (60 inches) above the road surface, as measured from the center of the lamp on the vehicle at curb weight.
5. Each converter dolly, when towed singly by another vehicle and not as part of a full trailer, shall be equipped with one stop lamp, one tail lamp, and two reflectors (one on each side of the vertical centerline, as far apart as practicable) on the rear. Each converter dolly shall be equipped with rear turn signals and vehicular hazard warning signal flasher lamps when towed singly by another vehicle and not as part of a full trailer, if the converter dolly obscures the turn signals at the rear of the towing vehicle.
6. Pole trailers shall be equipped with two reflex reflectors on the rear, one on each side of the vertical centerline as far apart as practicable, to indicate the extreme width of the trailer.
7. Pole trailers, when towed by motor vehicles with rear identification lamps meeting the requirements of §393.11 and mounted at a height greater than the load being transported on the pole trailer, are not required to have rear identification lamps.
8. Pole trailers shall have on the rearmost support for the load:
    (1) two front clearance lamps, one on each side of the vehicle, both on the same level and as high as practicable to indicate the overall width of the pole trailer;
    (2) two rear clearance lamps, one on each side of the vehicle, both on the same level and as high as practicable to indicate the overall width of the pole trailer;
    (3) two rear side marker lamps, one on each side of the vehicle, both on the same level, not less than 375 mm (15 inches) above the road surface;
    (4) two rear reflex reflectors, one on each side, both on the same level, not less than 375 mm (15 inches) above the road surface to indicate maximum width of pole trailer; and
    (5) one red reflector on each side of the rearmost support for the load. Lamps and reflectors may be combined as allowed in §393.22.
9. Any motor vehicle transporting a load which extends more than 102 mm (4 inches) beyond the overall width of the motor vehicle shall be equipped with the following lamps in addition to other required lamps when operated during the hours when headlamps are required to be used:
    (1) The foremost edge of that portion of the load which projects beyond the side of the vehicle shall be marked (at its outermost extremity) with an amber lamp visible from the front and side.
    (2) The rearmost edge of that portion of the load which projects beyond the side of the vehicle shall be marked (at its outermost extremity) with a red lamp visible from the rear and side.
    (3) If the projecting load does not measure more than 914 mm (3 feet) from front to rear, it shall be marked with an amber lamp visible from the front, both sides, and rear, except that if the projection is located at or near the rear it shall be marked by a red lamp visible from front, side, and rear.
10. Projections beyond rear of motor vehicles. Motor vehicles transporting loads which extend more than 1,219 mm (4 feet) beyond the rear of the motor vehicle, or which have tailboards or tailgates extending more than 1,219 mm (4 feet) beyond the body, shall have these projections marked as follows when the vehicle is operated during the hours when headlamps are required to be used:
    (1) On each side of the projecting load, one red side marker lamp, visible from the side, located so as to indicate maximum overhang.
    (2) On the rear of the projecting load, two red lamps, visible from the rear, one at each side; and two red reflectors visible from the rear, one at each side, located so as to indicate maximum width.
11. To be illuminated when tractor headlamps are illuminated.
12. Every bus, truck, and truck tractor shall be equipped with a signaling system that, in addition to signaling turning movements, shall have a switch or combination of switches that will cause the two front turn signals and the two rear signals to flash simultaneously as a vehicular traffic signal warning, required by §392–22(a). The system shall be capable of flashing simultaneously with the ignition of the vehicle on or off.
13. To be actuated upon application of service brakes.
14. Backup lamp required to operate when bus, truck, or truck tractor is in reverse.
15. (1) For the purposes of Section 393.11, the term "overall width" refers to the nominal design dimension of the widest part of the vehicle, exclusive of the signal lamps, marker lamps, outside rearview mirrors, flexible fender extensions, and mud flaps.
    (2) Clearance lamps may be mounted at a location other than on the front and rear if necessary to indicate the overall width of a vehicle, or for protection from damage during normal operation of the vehicle.
    (3) On a trailer, the front clearance lamps may be mounted at a height below the extreme height if mounting at the extreme height results in the lamps failing to mark the overall width of the trailer.
    (4) On a truck tractor, clearance lamps mounted on the cab may be located to indicate the width of the cab, rather than the width of the vehicle.
    (5) When the rear identification lamps are mounted at the extreme height of a vehicle, rear clearance lamps are not required to be located as close as practicable to the top of the vehicle.
16. A trailer subject to this part that is less than 1829 mm (6 feet) in overall length, including the trailer tongue, need not be equipped with front side marker lamps and front side reflex reflectors.
17. A boat trailer subject to this part whose overall width is 2032 mm (80 inches) or more need not be equipped with both front and rear clearance lamps provided an amber (front) and red (rear) clearance lamp is located at or near the midpoint on each side so as to indicate its extreme width.

Subpart B - Lamps, Reflective Devices, and Electrical Wiring §393.11 (d)

Figure 1 - Truck Tractor Illustration for §393.11

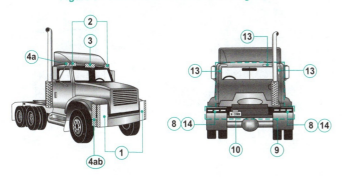

Figure 2 - Straight Truck Illustration for §393.11

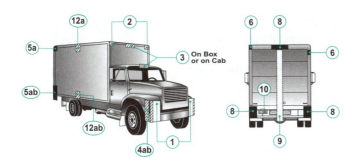

Figure 4 - Straight Truck Illustration for §393.11

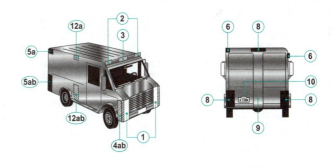

Figure 3 - Straight Truck Illustration for §393.11

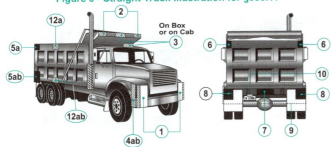

Figure 5 - Straight Truck Illustration for §393.11

Figure 6 - Straight Truck Illustration for §393.11

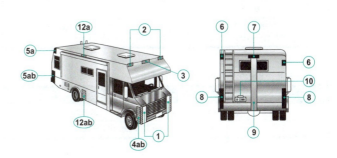

Figure 7 - Bus Illustration for §393.11

§393.11 — Part 393 - Parts and Accessories Necessary for Safe Operation

Legend for Figures 1 Through 7 — 49 CFR 393.11 Truck and Bus Vehicle Illustrations (Does not apply to Figures 8 through 18 for trailers)

Area	Equipment
1	Headlamps — Lower Beam
	Headlamps — Upper Beam
	Parking Lamps — Attention: *Required only on vehicles less than 2032 mm wide*
	Front Turn Signal/Hazard Warning Lamps
2	Front Clearance Lamps — Attention: *Required for vehicles 2032 mm wide or wider*
3	Front Identification Lamps (ID)
4a	Front Side Marker Lamps
4b	Front Side Reflex Reflectors
5a	Rear Side Marker Lamps — *Not required on Truck Tractors*
5b	Rear Side Reflex Reflectors — *Not required on Truck Tractors*
6	Rear Clearance Lamps — Attention: *Required for vehicles 2032 mm wide or wider, but not required on Truck Tractors*
7	Rear Identification Lamps (ID) — Attention: *Required for vehicles 2032 mm wide or wider, but not required on Truck Tractors*
8	Tail Lamps
	Stop Lamps
	Rear Turn Signal/Hazard Warning Lamps
	Rear Reflex Reflectors
9	Backup Lamp
10	License Plate Lamp
11	Center High Mounted Stop Lamp — Attention: *Required for vehicles less than 2032 mm wide and 4536 kg*

Additional Equipment for Specific Trucks and Bus Vehicles

Area	Equipment
12a	Intermediate Side Marker Lamps
12b	Intermediate Side Reflex Reflectors

Truck Tractors

Area	Description / Conspicuity Treatment
13	Rear Upper Body Marking
14	Rear Marking

Figure 8 - Semi Trailer Illustration for §393.11

Figure 9 - Semi Trailer Illustration for §393.11

Figure 10 - Semi Trailer Illustration for §393.11

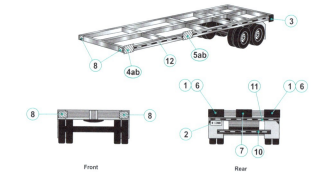

Figure 11 - Container Chassis Illustration for §393.11

Subpart B - Lamps, Reflective Devices, and Electrical Wiring §393.11 (d)

Figure 12 - Pole Trailer Illustration for §393.11 - All Vehicle Widths

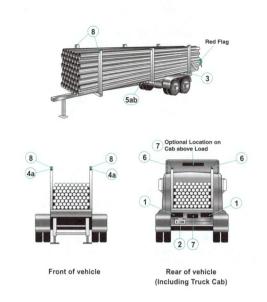

Figure 13 - Converter Dolly Illustration for §393.11

Figure 14 - Semi-Trailer Illustration for §393.11

Figure 15 - Semi-Trailer Illustration for §393.11

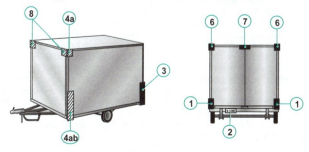

Figure 16 - Semi-Trailer Illustration for §393.11

Figure 17 - Semi-Trailer Illustration for §393.11

Figure 18 - Semi-Trailer Illustration for §393.11

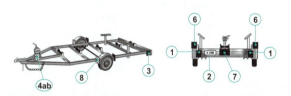

Legend for Figures 8 Through 18 — 49 CFR 393.11 Trailer Illustrations (Does not apply to Figures 1 through 7 for trucks and buses)

Area	Equipment
1	Tail Lamps
	Stop Lamps
	Rear Turn Signal Lamps
	Rear Reflex Reflectors
2	License Plate Lamp(s)
3	Rear Side Marker Lamps
	Rear Side Reflex Reflectors
4a	Front Side Marker Lamps
4b	Front Side Reflex Reflectors

Additional Equipment for Trailers Exceeding the Following Parameters

Length 9.1 m (30 ft.) or Longer

Area	Equipment
5a	Intermediate Side Marker Lamps
5b	Intermediate Side Reflex Reflectors

Width 2.032 m (80 in.) or Wider

Area	Equipment
6	Rear Clearance Lamps
7	Rear Identification Lamps
8	Front Clearance Lamps

Width 2.032 m (80 in.) or Wider and GVWR 4,536 kg (10,000 lb.) or more

Area	Description / Conspicuity Treatment
9	Rear Upper Body Marking
10	Bumper Bar Marking
11	Rear Lower Body Marking
12	Side Marking

§393.11 DOT Interpretations

Question 1: What is the definition of "body" with respect to trucks and trailers?
Guidance: The FMCSRs do not include a definition of "body." However, a truck or trailer body generally means the structure or fixture designed to contain, or support, the material or property to be transported on the vehicle.

Question 2: May retroreflective tape be used in place of side reflex reflectors?
Guidance: §393.26(b) cross references FMVSS 108 (49 CFR 571.108, S5.1.1.4) which allows reflective material to be used for side reflex reflectors under the conditions described below. Retroreflective tape conforming to Federal specification L-S-300, "Sheeting and Tape, Reflective; Non-exposed Lens, Adhesive Backing," September 7, 1965, may be used in place of side reflex reflectors if this material as used on the vehicle, meets the performance standards in either Table I or Table IA of Society of Automotive Engineers J594f, Reflex Reflectors, January 1977.

Question 3: §393.11, Footnote 5, requires that each converter dolly be equipped with turn signals at the rear if the converter dolly obscures the turn signals at the rear of the towing vehicle when towed singly by another vehicle. Are turn signals required on the rear of the converter dolly when the towing of the unladen dolly prevents other motorists from seeing only a portion of the lenses of the turn signals on the towing vehicle?
Guidance: Yes. Although a portion of the rear turn signal lenses on the towing vehicle may be visible to other drivers, the turn signal generally would not satisfy the visibility requirements of FMVSS No. 108 (49 CFR 571.108) if the converter dolly prevents other motorists from seeing the entire lens. The visibility requirements of FMVSS No. 108 help to ensure that other drivers can see the turn signal from a range of positions to the rear of the vehicle. Therefore, turn signals on the towing vehicle are considered to be obscured by the converter dolly if other motorists' view of the lens is even partially blocked.

Question 4: Does a CMV equipped with amber tail lamps in addition to the red tail lamps required to designate the rear of a CMV meet the lighting requirements of §393.11?
Guidance: No. §393.11 requires that lighting devices on CMVs placed in operation after March 7, 1989, meet the requirements of FMVSS No. 108 in effect at the time of manufacture. The NHTSA has issued interpretations which indicate that the use of amber tail lamps impairs the effectiveness of the required lighting equipment and as such is prohibited by FMVSS No. 108 (S5.1.3). Since NHTSA does not allow vehicle manufacturers to install amber tail lamps, the FHWA has concluded that the use of amber tail lamps on vehicles placed in operation after March 7, 1989, is prohibited by §393.11.
In the case of vehicles placed in operation on or before March 7, 1989, §393.11 requires that vehicles meet either the lighting requirements of Part 393 or FMVSS No. 108 in effect at the time of manufacture. Prior to the December 7, 1988, final rule on Part 393 (53 FR 49397), amber tail lamps were prohibited by §393.25. §393.25(e)(3) (in the October 1, 1988 edition of the Code of Federal Regulations) required all rear lamps, with certain exceptions, to be red. Since tail lamps were not included in the exceptions, the use of amber tail lamps was implicitly prohibited. Therefore, a vehicle placed in operation on or before March 7, 1989, must not be equipped with amber tail lamps because the use of such lamps meets neither the lighting requirements of Part 393 nor FMVSS No. 108 in effect at the time of manufacture.

§393.13 Retroreflective sheeting and reflex reflectors, requirements for semitrailers and trailers manufactured before December 1, 1993.

(a) Applicability. All trailers and semitrailers manufactured prior to December 1, 1993, which have an overall width of 2,032 mm (80 inches) or more and a gross vehicle weight rating of 4,536 kg (10,001 pounds) or more, except trailers that are manufactured exclusively for use as offices or dwellings, pole trailers (as defined in §390.5 of this subchapter), and trailers transported in a drive-away-towaway operation, must be equipped with retroreflective sheeting or an array of reflex reflectors that meet the requirements of this section. Motor carriers operating trailers, other than container chassis (as defined in §393.5), have until June 1, 2001, to comply with the requirements of this section. Motor carriers operating container chassis have until December 1, 2001, to comply with the requirements of this section.

(b) Retroreflective sheeting and reflex reflectors. Motor carriers are encouraged to retrofit their trailers with a conspicuity system that meets all of the requirements applicable to trailers manufactured on or after December 1, 1993, including the use of retroreflective sheeting or reflex reflectors in a red and white pattern (see Federal Motor Vehicle Safety Standard No. 108 (49 CFR 571.108), S5.7, Conspicuity systems). Motor carriers which do not retrofit their trailers to meet the requirements of FMVSS No. 108, for example by using an alternative color pattern, must comply with the remainder of this paragraph and with paragraph (c) or (d) of this section. Retroreflective sheeting or reflex reflectors in colors or color combinations other than red and white may be used on the sides or lower rear area of the semitrailer or trailer until June 1, 2009. The alternate color or color combination must be uniform along the sides and lower rear area of the trailer. The retroreflective sheeting or reflex reflectors on the upper rear area of the trailer must be white and conform to the requirements of FMVSS No. 108 (S5.7). Red retroreflective sheeting or reflex reflectors shall not be used along the sides of the trailer unless it is used as part of a red and white pattern. Retroreflective sheeting shall have a width of at least 50 mm (2 inches).

(c) Locations for retroreflective sheeting.

(1) *Sides.* Retroreflective sheeting shall be applied to each side of the trailer or semitrailer. Each strip of retroreflective sheeting shall be positioned as horizontally as practicable, beginning and ending as close to the front and rear as practicable. The strip need not be continuous but the sum of the length of all of the segments shall be at least half of the length of the trailer and the spaces between the segments of the strip shall be distributed as evenly as practicable. The centerline for each strip of retroreflective sheeting shall be between 375 mm (15 inches) and 1,525 mm (60 inches) above the road surface when measured with the trailer empty or unladen, or as close as practicable to this area. If necessary to clear rivet heads or other similar obstructions, 50 mm (2 inches) wide retroreflective sheeting may be separated into two 25 mm (1 inch) wide strips of the same length and color, separated by a space of not more than 25 mm (1 inch).

(2) *Lower rear area.* The rear of each trailer and semitrailer must be equipped with retroreflective sheeting. Each strip of retroreflective sheeting shall be positioned as horizontally as practicable, extending across the full width of the trailer, beginning and ending as close to the extreme edges as practicable. The centerline for each of the strips of retroreflective sheeting shall be between 375 mm (15 inches) and 1,525 mm (60 inches) above the road surface when measured with the trailer empty or unladen, or as close as practicable to this area.

(3) *Upper rear area.* Two pairs of white strips of retroreflective sheeting, each pair consisting of strips 300 mm (12 inches) long, must be positioned horizontally and vertically on the right and left upper corners of the rear of the body of each trailer and semitrailer, as close as practicable to the top of the trailer and as far apart as practicable. If the perimeter of the body, as viewed from the rear, is not square or rectangular, the strips may be applied along the perimeter, as close as practicable to the uppermost and outermost areas of the rear of the body on the left and right sides.

(d) Locations for reflex reflectors.

(1) *Sides.* Reflex reflectors shall be applied to each side of the trailer or semitrailer. Each array of reflex reflectors shall be positioned as horizontally as practicable, beginning and ending as close to the front and rear as practicable. The array need not be continuous but the sum of the length of all of the array segments shall be at least half of the length of the trailer and the spaces between the segments of the strip shall be distributed as evenly as practicable. The centerline for each array of reflex reflectors shall be between 375 mm (15 inches) and 1,525 mm (60 inches) above the road surface when measured with the trailer empty or unladen, or as close as practicable to this area. The center of each reflector shall not be more than 100 mm (4 inches) from the center of each adjacent reflector in the segment of the array. If reflex reflectors are arranged in an alternating color pattern, the length of reflectors of the first color shall be as close as practicable to the length of the reflectors of the second color.

(2) *Lower rear area.* The rear of each trailer and semitrailer must be equipped with reflex reflectors. Each array of reflex reflectors shall be positioned as horizontally as practicable, extending across the full width of the trailer, beginning and ending as close to the extreme edges as practicable. The centerline for

each array of reflex reflectors shall be between 375 mm (15 inches) and 1,525 mm (60 inches) above the road surface when measured with the trailer empty or unladen, or as close as practicable to this area. The center of each reflector shall not be more than 100 mm (4 inches) from the center of each adjacent reflector in the segment of the array.

(3) *Upper rear area.* Two pairs of white reflex reflector arrays, each pair at least 300 mm (12 inches) long, must be positioned horizontally and vertically on the right and left upper corners of the rear of the body of each trailer and semitrailer, as close as practicable to the top of the trailer and as far apart as practicable. If the perimeter of the body, as viewed from the rear, is not square or rectangular, the arrays may be applied along the perimeter, as close as practicable to the uppermost and outermost areas of the rear of the body on the left and right sides. The center of each reflector shall not be more than 100 mm (4 inches) from the center of each adjacent reflector in the segment of the array.

§393.17 Lamps and reflectors — combinations in driveaway-towaway operation.

A combination of motor vehicles engaged in driveaway-towaway operation must be equipped with operative lamps and reflectors conforming to the rules in this section.

(a) **The towing vehicle must be equipped as follows:**
  (1) *On the front,* there must be at least two headlamps, an equal number at each side, two turn signals, one at each side, and two clearance lamps, one at each side.
  (2) *On each side,* there must be at least one side-marker lamp, located near the front of the vehicle.
  (3) *On the rear,* there must be at least two tail lamps, one at each side, and two stop lamps, one at each side.

(b) **Except as provided in paragraph (c) of this section,** the rearmost towed vehicle of the combination (including the towed vehicle or a tow-bar combination, the towed vehicle of a single saddle-mount combination, and the rearmost towed vehicle of a double or triple saddle-mount combination) or, in the case of a vehicle full-mounted on a saddle-mount vehicle, either the full-mounted vehicle or the rearmost saddle-mounted vehicle must be equipped as follows:
  (1) *On each side,* there must be at least one side-marker lamp, located near the rear of the vehicle.
  (2) *On the rear,* there must be at least two tail lamps, two stop lamps, two turn signals, two clearance lamps, and two reflectors, one of each type at each side. In addition, if any vehicle in the combination is 80 inches or more in overall width, there must be three identification lamps on the rear.

(c) **If the towed vehicle in a combination** is a mobile structure trailer, it must be equipped in accordance with the following lighting devices. For the purposes of this part, **mobile structure trailer** means a trailer that has a roof and walls, is at least 10 feet wide, and can be used off road for dwelling or commercial purposes.
  (1) *When the vehicle is operated* in accordance with the terms of a special permit prohibiting operation during the times when lighted lamps are required under §392.30, it must have on the rear —
    (i) *Two stop lamps,* one on each side of the vertical centerline, at the same height, and as far apart as practicable;
    (ii) *Two tail lamps,* one on each side of the vertical centerline, at the same height, and as far apart as practicable;
    (iii) *Two red reflex reflectors,* one on each side of the vertical centerline, at the same height, and as far apart as practicable; and
    (iv) *Two turn signal lamps,* one on each side of the vertical centerline, at the same height, and as far apart as practicable.
  (2) *At all other times,* the vehicle must be equipped as specified in paragraph (b) of this section.

(d) **An intermediate towed vehicle in a combination** consisting of more than two vehicles (including the first saddle-mounted vehicle of a double saddle-mount combination and the first and second saddle-mount vehicles of a triple saddle-mount combination) must have one side-marker lamp on each side, located near the rear of the vehicle.

Figure 19 - Single-Saddle-Mount Diagram to Illustrate §393.17

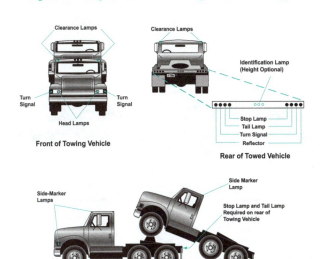

Figure 20 - Double-Saddle-Mount Diagram to Illustrate §393.17

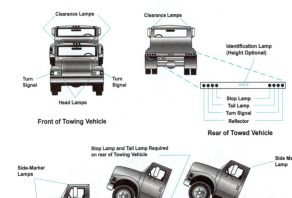

Figure 21 - Tow-bar Diagram to Illustrate §393.17

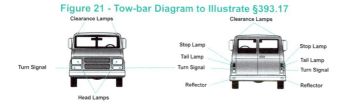

Lamps may be combined as permitted by §393.22. The color of exterior lighting devices and reflectors shall conform to requirements of §393.11.

§393.17 DOT Interpretations

Question 1: What are the lighting requirements when a tow truck is pulling a wrecked or disabled vehicle?
Guidance: A wrecker pulling a vehicle would be considered a driveaway-towaway operation and would have to be equipped with the lighting devices specified in §393.17 when operating in interstate commerce.

§393.19 Hazard warning signals.

The hazard warning signal operating unit on each commercial motor vehicle shall operate independently of the ignition or equivalent switch, and when activated, cause all turn signals required by §393.11 to flash simultaneously.

§393.20 [Reserved]

§393.22 Combination of lighting devices and reflectors.

(a) **Permitted combinations.** Except as provided in paragraph (b) of this section, two or more lighting devices and reflectors (whether or not required by the rules in this part) may be combined optically if —
  (1) *Each required lighting device and reflector* conforms to the applicable rules in this part; and
  (2) *Neither the mounting* nor the use of a nonrequired lighting device or reflector impairs the effectiveness of a required lighting device or reflector or causes that device or reflector to be inconsistent with the applicable rules in this part.
(b) **Prohibited combinations.**
  (1) A *turn signal lamp* must not be combined optically with either a head lamp or other lighting device or combination of lighting devices that produces a greater intensity of light than the turn signal lamp.
  (2) A *turn signal lamp* must not be combined optically with a stop lamp unless the stop lamp function is always deactivated when the turn signal function is activated.
  (3) A *clearance lamp* must not be combined optically with a tail lamp or identification lamp.

§393.23 Power supply for lamps.

All required lamps must be powered by the electrical system of the motor vehicle with the exception of battery powered lamps used on projecting loads.

§393.24 Requirements for head lamps, auxiliary driving lamps and front fog lamps.

(a) **Headlamps.** Every bus, truck and truck tractor shall be equipped with headlamps as required by §393.11(a). The headlamps shall provide an upper and lower beam distribution of light, selectable at the driver's will and be steady-burning. The headlamps shall be marked in accordance with FMVSS No. 108. Auxiliary driving lamps and/or front fog lamps may not be used to satisfy the requirements of this paragraph.
(b) **Auxiliary driving lamps and front fog lamps.** Commercial motor vehicles may be equipped with auxiliary driving lamps and/or front fog lamps for use in conjunction with, but not in lieu of the required headlamps. Auxiliary driving lamps shall meet SAE Standard J581 Auxiliary Upper Beam Lamps, July 2004, and front fog lamps shall meet SAE Standard J583 Front Fog Lamp, August 2004. (See §393.7 for information on the incorporation by reference and availability of these documents.)
(c) **Mounting.** Headlamps shall be mounted and aimable in accordance with FMVSS No. 108. Auxiliary driving lamps and front fog lamps shall be mounted so that the beams are aimable and the mounting shall prevent the aim of the lighting device from being disturbed while the vehicle is operating on public roads.
(d) **Aiming.** Headlamps, auxiliary driving lamps and front fog lamps shall be aimed to meet the aiming specifications in FMVSS No. 108 (49 CFR 571.108), SAE J581, and SAE J583, respectively.

§393.24 DOT Interpretations

Question 1: Must additional lamps that are not required be operative if all required lamps are operative?
Guidance: No.

§393.25 Requirements for lamps other than head lamps.

(a) **Mounting.** All lamps shall be securely mounted on a rigid part of the vehicle. Temporary lamps must be securely mounted to the load and are not required to be mounted to a permanent part of the vehicle.
(b) **Visibility.** Each lamp shall be located so that it meets the visibility requirements specified by FMVSS No. 108 in effect at the time of manufacture of the vehicle. Vehicles which were not subject to FMVSS No. 108 at the time of manufacture shall have each lamp located so that it meets the visibility requirements specified in the SAE standards listed in paragraph (c) of this section. If motor vehicle equipment (e.g., mirrors, snow plows, wrecker booms, backhoes, and winches) prevents compliance with this paragraph by any required lamp, an auxiliary lamp or device meeting the requirements of this paragraph shall be provided. This shall not be construed to apply to lamps on one unit which are obscured by another unit of a combination of vehicles.
(c) **Specifications.** All required lamps (except marker lamps on projecting loads, lamps which are temporarily attached to vehicles transported in driveaway-towaway operations, and lamps on converter dollies and pole trailers) on vehicles manufactured on or after December 25, 1968, shall, at a minimum, meet the applicable requirements of FMVSS No. 108 in effect on the date of manufacture of the vehicle. Marker lamps on projecting loads, all lamps which are temporarily attached to vehicles transported in driveaway-towaway operations, and all lamps on converter dollies and pole trailers must meet the following applicable SAE standards: J586—Stop Lamps for Use on Motor Vehicles Less Than 2032 mm in Overall Width, March 2000; J2261—Stop Lamps and Front- and Rear-Turn Signal Lamps for Use on Motor Vehicles 2032 mm or More in Overall Width, January 2002; J585—Tail Lamps (Rear Position Lamps) for Use on Motor Vehicles Less Than 2032 mm in Overall Width, March 2000; J588—Turn Signal Lamps for Use on Motor Vehicles Less Than 2032 mm in Overall Width, March 2000; J2040—Tail Lamps (Rear Position Lamps) for Use on Vehicles 2032 mm or More in Overall Width, March 2002; J592—Sidemarker Lamps for Use on Road Vehicles Less Than 2032 mm in Overall Width, August 2000. (See §393.7 for information on the incorporation by reference and availability of these documents.)
(d) **[Reserved]**
(e) **Lamps to be steady-burning.** All exterior lamps (both required lamps and any additional lamps) shall be steady-burning with the exception of turn signal lamps; hazard warning signal lamps; school bus warning lamps; amber warning lamps or flashing warning lamps on tow trucks and commercial motor vehicles transporting oversized loads; and warning lamps on emergency and service vehicles authorized by State or local authorities. Lamps combined into the same shell or housing with a turn signal are not required to be steady burning while the turn signal is in use. Amber warning lamps must meet SAE J845—Optical Warning Devices for Authorized Emergency, Maintenance and Service Vehicles, May 1997. Amber flashing warning lamps must meet SAE J595—Directional Flashing Optical Warning Devices for Authorized Emergency, Maintenance and Service Vehicles, January 2005. Amber gaseous discharge warning lamps must meet SAE—J1318 Gaseous Discharge Warning Lamp for Authorized Emergency, Maintenance, and Service Vehicles, May 1998. (See

Subpart C - Brakes

§393.7(b) for information on the incorporation by reference and availability of these documents.)

(f) Stop lamp operation. The stop lamps on each vehicle shall be activated upon application of the service brakes. The stop lamps are not required to be activated when the emergency feature of the trailer brakes is used or when the stop lamp is optically combined with the turn signal and the turn signal is in use.

§393.25 DOT Interpretations

Question 1: Are lighting devices on mobile homes/house trailers required to be permanently mounted?

Guidance: No. The movement of mobile homes/house trailers is considered to be a driveaway-towaway operation.

Question 2: Are there any special lighting requirements for large containers?

Guidance: No.

Question 3: What are the lighting requirements when a container assumes the structural requirements of a trailer?

Guidance: All relevant requirements of the regulations must be met by this container/trailer.

§393.26 Requirements for reflectors.

(a) Mounting. Reflex reflectors shall be mounted at the locations required by §393.11. In the case of motor vehicles so constructed that requirement for a 381 mm (15-inch) minimum height above the road surface is not practical, the reflectors shall be mounted as close as practicable to the required mounting height range. All permanent reflex reflectors shall be securely mounted on a rigid part of the vehicle. Temporary reflectors on projecting loads must be securely mounted to the load and are not required to be permanently mounted to a part of the vehicle. Temporary reflex reflectors on vehicles transported in driveaway-towaway operations must be firmly attached.

(b) Specifications. All required reflex reflectors (except reflex reflectors on projecting loads, vehicles transported in a driveaway-towaway operation, converter dollies and pole trailers) on vehicles manufactured on or after December 25, 1968, shall meet the applicable requirements of FMVSS No. 108 in effect on the date of manufacture of the vehicle. Reflex reflectors on projecting loads, vehicles transported in a driveaway-towaway operation, and all reflex reflectors on converter dollies and pole trailers must conform to SAE J594—Reflex Reflectors, December 2003.

(c) Substitute material for side reflex reflectors. Reflective material conforming to ASTM D 4956–04, Standard Specification for Retroreflective Sheeting for Traffic Control, may be used in lieu of reflex reflectors if the material as used on the vehicle, meets the performance standards in either Table I of SAE J594 or Table IA of SAE J594—Reflex Reflectors, December 2003. (See §393.7(b) for information on the incorporation by reference and availability of these documents.)

(d) Use of additional retroreflective surfaces. Additional retroreflective surfaces may be used in conjunction with, but not in lieu of the reflex reflectors required in Subpart B of Part 393, and the substitute material for side reflex reflectors allowed by paragraph (c) of this section, provided:

(1) *Designs do not resemble* traffic control signs, lights, or devices, except that straight edge striping resembling a barricade pattern may be used.

(2) *Designs do not tend* to distort the length and/or width of the motor vehicle.

(3) *Such surfaces shall be at least 3 inches* from any required lamp or reflector unless of the same color as such lamp or reflector.

(4) *No red color shall be used* on the front of any motor vehicle, except for display of markings or placards required by §177.823 of this title.

(5) *Retroreflective license plates* required by State or local authorities may be used.

§393.27 [Reserved]

§393.28 Wiring systems.

Electrical wiring shall be installed and maintained to conform to SAE J1292—Automobile, Truck, Truck-Tractor, Trailer, and Motor Coach Wiring, October 1981, except the jumper cable plug and receptacle need not conform to SAE J560. The reference to SAE J1292 shall not be construed to require circuit protection on trailers. (See §393.7(b) for information on the incorporation by reference and availability of this document.)

§393.28 DOT Interpretations

Question 1: Does a frame channel of a CMV constitute a protective "sheath or tube" as specified in §393.28?

Guidance: No. To be acceptable, a sheath or tube must enclose the wires throughout their circumference. In the absence of a sheath or tube, the group of wires must be protected by nonconductive tape, braid, or other covering capable of withstanding severe abrasion.

§393.29 [Removed and Reserved]

§393.30 Battery installation.

Every storage battery on every vehicle, unless located in the engine compartment, shall be covered by a fixed part of the motor vehicle or protected by a removable cover or enclosure. Removable covers or enclosures shall be substantial and shall be securely latched or fastened. The storage battery compartment and adjacent metal parts which might corrode by reason of battery leakage shall be painted or coated with an acid-resisting paint or coating and shall have openings to provide ample battery ventilation and drainage. Wherever the cable to the starting motor passes through a metal compartment, the cable shall be protected against grounding by an acid and waterproof insulating bushing. Wherever a battery and a fuel tank are both placed under the driver's seat, they shall be partitioned from each other, and each compartment shall be provided with an independent cover, ventilation, and drainage.

§§393.31 - 393.33 [Reserved]

Subpart C - Brakes

§393.40 Required brake systems.

(a) Each commercial motor vehicle must have brakes adequate to stop and hold the vehicle or combination of motor vehicles. Each commercial motor vehicle must meet the applicable service, parking, and emergency brake system requirements provided in this section.

(b) Service brakes.

(1) *Hydraulic brake systems.* Motor vehicles equipped with hydraulic brake systems and manufactured on or after September 2, 1983, must, at a minimum, have a service brake system that meets the requirements of FMVSS No. 105 in effect on the date of manufacture. Motor vehicles which were not subject to FMVSS No. 105 on the date of manufacture must have a service brake system that meets the applicable requirements of §§393.42, 393.48, 393.49, 393.51, and 393.52 of this subpart.

(2) *Air brake systems.* Buses, trucks and truck-tractors equipped with air brake systems and manufactured on or after March 1, 1975, and trailers manufactured on or after January 1, 1975, must, at a minimum, have a service brake system that meets the requirements of FMVSS No. 121 in effect on the date of manufacture. Motor vehicles which were not subject to FMVSS No. 121 on the date of manufacture must have a service brake system that meets the applicable requirements of §§393.42, 393.48, 393.49, 393.51, and 393.52 of this subpart.

(3) *Vacuum brake systems.* Motor vehicles equipped with vacuum brake systems must have a service brake system that meets the applicable requirements of §§393.42, 393.48, 393.49, 393.51, and 393.52 of this subpart.

(4) *Electric brake systems.* Motor vehicles equipped with electric brake systems must have a service brake system that meets the applicable requirements of §§393.42, 393.48, 393.49 and 393.52 of this subpart.

(c) Parking brakes. Each commercial motor vehicle must be equipped with a parking brake system that meets the applicable requirements of §393.41.

(d) Emergency brakes — partial failure of service brakes.

(1) *Hydraulic brake systems.* Motor vehicles manufactured on or after September 2, 1983, and equipped with a split service brake system must, at a minimum, meet the partial failure requirements of FMVSS No. 105 in effect on the date of manufacture.

(2) *Air brake systems.* Buses, trucks and truck tractors manufactured on or after March 1, 1975, and trailers manufactured on or after January 1, 1975, must be equipped with an emergency brake system which, at a minumum, meets the requirements of FMVSS No. 121 in effect on the date of manufacture.

(3) *Vehicles not subject to* FMVSS Nos. 105 and 121 on the date of manufacture. Buses, trucks and truck tractors not subject to FMVSS Nos. 105 or 121 on the date of manufacture must

meet the requirements of §393.40(e). Trailers not subject to FMVSS No. 121 at the time of manufacture must meet the requirements of §393.43.

(e) Emergency brakes, vehicles manufactured on or after July 1, 1973.

(1) *A bus, truck, truck tractor, or a combination* of motor vehicles manufactured on or after July 1, 1973, and not covered under paragraphs (d)(1) or (d)(2) of this section, must have an emergency brake system which consists of emergency features of the service brake system or an emergency system separate from the service brake system. The emergency brake system must meet the applicable requirements of §§393.43 and 393.52.

(2) *A control by which the driver* applies the emergency brake system must be located so that the driver can operate it from the normal seating position while restrained by any seat belts with which the vehicle is equipped. The emergency brake control may be combined with either the service brake control or the parking brake control. However, all three controls may not be combined.

(f) Interconnected systems.

(1) *If the brake systems required* by §393.40(a) are interconnected in any way, they must be designed, constructed, and maintained so that in the event of a failure of any part of the operating mechanism of one or more of the systems (except the service brake actuation pedal or valve), the motor vehicle will have operative brakes and, for vehicles manufactured on or after July 1, 1973, be capable of meeting the requirements of §393.52(b).

(2) *A motor vehicle* to which the requirements of FMVSS No. 105 (S5.1.2), dealing with partial failure of the service brake, applied at the time of manufacture meets the requirements of §393.40(f)(1) if the motor vehicle is maintained in conformity with FMVSS No. 105 and the motor vehicle is capable of meeting the requirements of §393.52(b), except in the case of a structural failure of the brake master cylinder body.

(3) *A bus is considered* to meet the requirements of §393.40(f)(1) if it meets the requirements of §393.44 and §393.52(b).

§393.40 DOT Interpretations
Question 1: May a system such as "driveline brakes" be used as an emergency brake provided it complies with the requirements of §393.52?
Guidance: Yes. CMVs which were not subject to the emergency brake requirements of FMVSS Nos. 105 or 121 may use "driveline brakes" provided those vehicles meet the requirements of §393.52.

§393.41 Parking brake system.

(a) Hydraulic-braked vehicles manufactured on or after September 2, 1983. Each truck and bus (other than a school bus) with a GVWR of 4,536 kg (10,000 pounds) or less which is subject to this part and school buses with a GVWR greater than 4,536 kg (10,000 pounds) shall be equipped with a parking brake system as required by FMVSS No. 571.105 (S5.2) in effect at the time of manufacture. The parking brake shall be capable of holding the vehicle or combination of vehicles stationary under any condition of loading in which it is found on a public road (free of ice and snow). Hydraulic-braked vehicles which were not subject to the parking brake requirements of FMVSS No. 571.105 (S5.2) must be equipped with a parking brake system that meets the requirements of paragraph (c) of this section.

(b) Air-braked power units manufactured on or after March 1, 1975, and air-braked trailers manufactured on or after January 1, 1975. Each air-braked bus, truck and truck tractor manufactured on and after March 1, 1975, and each air-braked trailer except an agricultural commodity trailer, converter dolly, heavy hauler trailer or pulpwood trailer, shall be equipped with a parking brake system as required by FMVSS No. 121 (S5.6) in effect at the time of manufacture. The parking brake shall be capable of holding the vehicle or combination of vehicles stationary under any condition of loading in which it is found on a public road (free of ice and snow). An agricultural commodity trailer, heavy hauler or pulpwood trailer shall carry sufficient chocking blocks to prevent movement when parked.

(c) Vehicles not subject to FMVSS Nos. 105 and 121 on the date of manufacture.

(1) *Each singly driven motor vehicle* not subject to parking brake requirements of FMVSS Nos. 105 or 121 at the time of manufacturer, and every combination of motor vehicles must be equipped with a parking brake system adequate to hold the vehicle or combination on any grade on which it is operated, under any condition of loading in which it is found on a public road (free of ice and snow).

(2) *The parking brake system shall,* at all times, be capable of being applied by either the driver's muscular effort or by spring action. If other energy is used to apply the parking brake, there must be an accumulation of that energy isolated from any common source and used exclusively for the operation of the parking brake.
Exception: This paragraph shall not be applicable to air-applied, mechanically-held parking brake systems which meet the parking brake requirements of FMVSS No. 121 (S5.6).

(3) *The parking brake system* shall be held in the applied position by energy other than fluid pressure, air pressure, or electric energy. The parking brake system shall not be capable of being released unless adequate energy is available to immediately reapply the parking brake with the required effectiveness.

§393.41 DOT Interpretations
Question 1: May the "park" position of a CMV's transmission be used as a parking brake to comply with the §393.41?
Guidance: No. The "park" position of the transmission is only a locking device used to lock the transmission.

Question 2: Does §393.41 prohibit air brake systems from being equipped with a means to release the spring brakes for purposes of towing disabled vehicles in emergency situations?
Guidance: No, provided the brakes are designed and maintained so they cannot be released unless adequate energy is available to make immediate reapplication of the brakes when the brake system is operable.

Question 3: Are parking brakes required on every CMV manufactured before March 7, 1990?
Guidance: No.

§393.42 Brakes required on all wheels.

(a) Every commercial motor vehicle shall be equipped with brakes acting on all wheels.

(b) Exception.

(1) *Trucks or truck tractors* having three or more axles and manufactured before July 25, 1980, are not required to have brakes on the front wheels. However, these vehicles must meet the requirements of §393.52.

(2) *Motor vehicles being towed* in a driveaway-towaway operation are not required to have operative brakes provided the combination of vehicles meets the requirements of §393.52. This exception is not applicable to:
  (i) Any motor vehicle towed by means of a tow-bar when another motor vehicle is full-mounted on the towed vehicle; and
  (ii) *Any combination of motor vehicles* utilizing three or more saddle-mounts.

(3) *Any semitrailer or pole trailer* (laden or unladen) with a gross weight of 1,361 kg (3,000 pounds) or less which is subject to this part is not required to be equipped with brakes if the axle weight of the towed vehicle does not exceed 40 percent of the sum of the axle weights of the towing vehicle.

(4) *Any full trailer or four-wheel pole trailer* (laden or unladen) with a gross weight of 1,361 kg (3,000 pounds) or less which is subject to this part is not required to be equipped with brakes if the sum of the axle weights of the towed vehicle does not exceed 40 percent of the sum of the axle weights of the towing vehicle.

(5) *Brakes are not required* on the steering axle of a three-axle dolly which is steered by a co-driver.

(6) *Loaded housemoving dollies,* specialized trailers and dollies used to transport industrial furnaces, reactors, and similar motor vehicles are not required to be equipped with brakes, provided the speed at which the combination of vehicles will be operated does not exceed 32 km/hour (20 mph) and brakes on the combination of vehicles are capable of stopping the combination within 12.2 meters (40 feet) from the speed at which the vehicle is being operated or 32 km/hour (20 mph), whichever is less.

Figure 22 - Illustrations of Brake Requirements for Light-Duty Trailers in §393.42

(Semi-trailer or 2-wheel pole trailer of 1,360 kilograms (3,000 pounds) gross weight or less must be equipped with brakes if W-3 is greater than 40 percent of the sum of W-1 and W-2.)

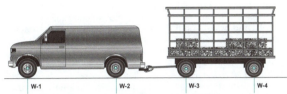

(Full trailer or 4-wheel pole trailer of 1,360 kilograms (3,000 pounds) gross weight or less must be equipped with brakes if the sum of W-3 and W-4 is greater than 40 percent of the sum of W-1 and W-2.)

§393.42 DOT Interpretations

Question 1: Do retractable or lift axles have to be equipped with brakes?
Guidance: Yes, when the wheels are in contact with the roadway.

Question 2: Are unladen converter dollies covered by the exemption in §393.42(b)(3)?
Guidance: Yes. However, if the converter dolly is laden, the brakes must be operable.

Question 3: §393.42(b)(3) of the FMCSRs states that any full trailer, any semitrailer, or any pole trailer having a GVWR of 3,000 pounds or less must be equipped with brakes if the weight of the towed vehicle resting on the towing vehicle exceeds 40 percent of the GVWR of the towing vehicle. Is the manufacturer of the trailer responsible for ensuring that the trailer is equipped with brakes when required?
Guidance: No. The motor carrier pulling the trailer is responsible for ensuring that the trailer is in compliance with all applicable FMCSRs.

§393.43 Breakaway and emergency braking.

(a) Towing vehicle protection system. Every motor vehicle, if used to tow a trailer equipped with brakes, shall be equipped with a means for providing that in the case of a breakaway of the trailer, the service brakes on the towing vehicle will be capable of stopping the towing vehicle. For air braked towing units, the tractor protection valve or similar device shall operate automatically when the air pressure on the towing vehicle is between 138 kPa and 310 kPa (20 psi and 45 psi).

(b) Emergency brake requirements, air brakes. Every truck or truck tractor equipped with air brakes, when used for towing other vehicles equipped with air brakes, shall be equipped with two means of activating the emergency features of the trailer brakes. One of these means shall operate automatically in the event of reduction of the towing vehicle air supply to a fixed pressure which shall not be lower than 20 pounds per square inch nor higher than 45 pounds per square inch. The other means shall be a manually controlled device readily operable by a person seated in the driving seat. Its emergency position or method of operation shall be clearly indicated. In no instance may the manual means be so arranged as to permit its use to prevent operation of the automatic means. The automatic and manual means required by this section may be, but are not required to be, separate.

(c) Emergency brake requirements, vacuum brakes. Every truck tractor and truck when used for towing other vehicles equipped with vacuum brakes, shall have, in addition to the single control required by §393.49 to operate all brakes of the combination, a second manual control device which can be used to operate the brakes on the towed vehicles in emergencies. Such second control shall be independent of brake air, hydraulic, and other pressure, and independent of other controls, unless the braking system be so arranged that failure of the pressure on which the second control depends will cause the towed vehicle brakes to be applied automatically. The second control is not required by this rule to provide modulated or graduated braking.

(d) Breakaway braking requirements for trailers. Every trailer required to be equipped with brakes shall have brakes which apply automatically and immediately upon breakaway from the towing vehicle. With the exception of trailers having three or more axles, all brakes with which the trailer is required to be equipped must be applied upon breakaway from the towing vehicle. The brakes must remain in the applied position for at least 15 minutes.

(e) Emergency valves. Air brake systems installed on towed vehicles shall be so designed, by the use of "no-bleed-back" relay emergency valves or equivalent devices, that the supply reservoir used to provide air for brakes shall be safeguarded against backflow of air to the towing vehicle upon reduction of the towing vehicle air pressure.

(f) Exception. The requirements of paragraphs (b), (c) and (d) of this section shall not be applicable to commercial motor vehicles being transported in driveaway-towaway operations.

§393.43 DOT Interpretations

Question 1: Are tractor protection valves required by §393.43(b), or may similar devices be used?
Guidance: No. Similar devices may be used provided the devices meet the performance requirements of §393.43(b).

Question 2: Are all brakes on a trailer required to be applied automatically upon breakaway?
Guidance: Yes.

§393.44 Front brake lines, protection.

On every bus, if equipped with air brakes, the braking system shall be so constructed that in the event any brake line to any of the front wheels is broken, the driver can apply the brakes on the rear wheels despite such breakage. The means used to apply the brakes may be located forward of the driver's seat as long as it can be operated manually by the driver when the driver is properly restrained by any seat belt assembly provided for use. Every bus shall meet this requirement or comply with the regulations in effect at the time of its manufacture.

§393.44 DOT Interpretations

Question 1: Does the term "rear wheels" include the tag axle on a bus/motorcoach?
Guidance: Yes. The braking system on a bus/motorcoach must be constructed so that if any brake line to either front wheel is broken, the driver can apply the brakes to all of the wheels on each rear axle.

§393.45 Brake tubing and hoses; hose assemblies and end fittings.

(a) General construction requirements for tubing and hoses, assemblies, and end fittings. All brake tubing and hoses, brake hose assemblies, and brake hose end fittings must meet the applicable requirements of FMVSS No. 106 (49 CFR 571.106).

(b) Brake tubing and hose installation. Brake tubing and hose must—
(1) *Be long and flexible enough* to accommodate without damage all normal motions of the parts to which it is attached;
(2) *Be secured against chaffing,* kinking, or other mechanical damage; and
(3) *Be installed in a manner* that prevents it from contacting the vehicle's exhaust system or any other source of high temperatures.

(c) Nonmetallic brake tubing. Coiled nonmetallic brake tubing may be used for connections between towed and towing motor vehicles or between the frame of a towed vehicle and the unsprung subframe of an adjustable axle of the motor vehicle if—
(1) *The coiled tubing* has a straight segment (pigtail) at each end that is at least 51 mm (2 inches) in length and is encased in a spring guard or similar device which prevents the tubing from kinking at the fitting at which it is attached to the vehicle; and
(2) *The spring guard or similar device* has at least 51 mm (2 inches) of closed coils or similar surface at its interface with the fitting and extends at least 38 mm (1 1/2 inches) into the coiled segment of the tubing from its straight segment.

(d) Brake tubing and hose connections. All connections for air, vacuum, or hydraulic braking systems shall be installed so as to ensure an attachment free of leaks, constrictions or other conditions which would adversely affect the performance of the brake system.

§393.46 [Reserved]

§393.47 Brake actuators, slack adjusters, linings/pads and drums/rotors.

(a) **General requirements.** Brake components must be constructed, installed and maintained to prevent excessive fading and grabbing. The means of attachment and physical characteristics must provide for safe and reliable stopping of the commercial motor vehicle.

(b) **Brake chambers.** The service brake chambers and spring brake chambers on each end of an axle must be the same size.

(c) **Slack adjusters.** The effective length of the slack adjuster on each end of an axle must be the same.

(d) **Linings and pads.** The thickness of the brake linings or pads shall meet the applicable requirements of this paragraph—

(1) *Steering axle brakes.* The brake lining/pad thickness on the steering axle of a truck, truck-tractor or bus shall not be less than 4.8 mm (3/16 inch) at the shoe center for a shoe with a continuous strip of lining; less than 6.4 mm (1/4 inch) at the shoe center for a shoe with two pads; or worn to the wear indicator if the lining is so marked, for air drum brakes. The steering axle brake lining/pad thickness shall not be less than 3.2 mm (1/8 inch) for air disc brakes, or 1.6 mm (1/16 inch) or less for hydraulic disc, drum and electric brakes.

(2) *Non-steering axle brakes.* An air braked commercial motor vehicle shall not be operated with brake lining/pad thickness less than 6.4 mm (1/4 inch) or to the wear indicator if the lining is so marked (measured at the shoe center for drum brakes); or less than 3.2 mm (1/8 inch) for disc brakes. Hydraulic or electric braked commercial motor vehicles shall not be operated with a lining/pad thickness less than 1.6 mm (1/16 inch) (measured at the shoe center) for disc or drum brakes.

(e) **Clamp and Roto-Chamber** Brake Actuator Readjustment limits. The pushrod travel for clamp and roto-chamber type actuators must be less than 80 percent of the rated strokes listed in SAE J1817—Long Stroke Air Brake Actuator Marking, July 2001 (See §393.7(b) for information on incorporation by reference and availability of this document), or 80 percent of the rated stroke marked on the brake chamber by the chamber manufacturer, or the readjustment limit marked on the brake chamber by the chamber manufacturer. The pushrod travel for Type 16 and 20 long stroke clamp type brake actuators must be less than 51 mm (2 inches) or 80 percent of the rated stroke marked on the brake chamber by the chamber manufacturer, or the readjustment limit marked on the brake chamber by the chamber manufacturer.

(f) **Wedge Brake Adjustment.** The movement of the scribe mark on the lining shall not exceed 1.6 mm (1/16 inch).

(g) **Drums and rotors.** The thickness of the drums or rotors shall not be less than the limits established by the brake drum or rotor manufacturer.

§393.48 Brakes to be operative.

(a) **General rule.** Except as provided in paragraphs (b) and (c) of this section, all brakes with which a commercial motor vehicle is equipped must be operable at all times.

(b) **Devices to reduce or remove front-wheel braking effort.** A commercial motor vehicle may be equipped with a device to reduce the front wheel braking effort (or in the case of a three-axle truck or truck tractor manufactured before March 1, 1975, a device to remove the front-wheel braking effort) if that device meets the applicable requirements of paragraphs (b)(1) and (2) of this section.

(1) *Manually operated devices.* Manually operated devices to reduce or remove front-wheel braking effort may only be used on buses, trucks, and truck tractors manufactured before March 1, 1975. Such devices must not be used unless the vehicle is being operated under adverse conditions such as wet, snowy, or icy roads.

(2) *Automatic devices.* Automatic devices must not reduce the front-wheel braking force by more than 50 percent of the braking force available when the automatic device is disconnected (regardless of whether or not an antilock system failure has occurred on any axle). The device must not be operable by the driver except upon application of the control that activates the braking system. The device must not be operable when the brake control application pressure exceeds 85 psig (for vehicles equipped with air brakes) or 85 percent of the maximum system pressure (for vehicles which are not equipped with air brakes).

(c) **Exception.** Paragraph (a) of this section does not apply to—

(1) *A towed vehicle with disabling damage* as defined in §390.5;

(2) *A vehicle which is towed* in a driveaway-towaway operation and is included in the exemption to the requirement for brakes on all wheels, §393.42(b);

(3) *Unladen converter dollies* with a gross weight of 1,361 kg (3,000 lbs) or less, and manufactured prior to March 1, 1998;

(4) *The steering axle* of a three-axle dolly which is steered by a co-driver;

(5) *Loaded house moving dollies,* specialized trailers and dollies used to transport industrial furnaces, reactors, and similar motor vehicles provided the speed at which the combination of vehicles will be operated does not exceed 32 km/hour (20 mph) and brakes on the combination of vehicles are capable of stopping the combination within 12.2 meters (40 feet) from the speed at which the vehicle is being operated or 32 km/hour (20 mph), whichever is less.

(6) *Raised lift axles.* Brakes on lift axles need not be capable of being operated while the lift axle is raised. However, brakes on lift axles must be capable of being applied whenever the lift axle is lowered and the tires contact the roadway.

§393.48 DOT Interpretations

Question 1: Do surge brakes comply with §393.48?

Guidance: No. §393.48 requires that brakes be operable at all times. Generally, surge brakes are only operative when the vehicle is moving in the forward direction and as such do not comply with §393.48 (see Question 1 in §393.49).

Question 2: If a CMV manufactured on or after July 25, 1980 (see §393.42) has brake components on the front axle, and the brakes are not operable, does the vehicle comply with §393.48?

Guidance: No.

Question 3: If a truck or truck tractor manufactured prior to July 25, 1980, and having 3 or more axles, has inoperable brakes on the front axle or some of the brake components are missing, would the vehicle be in violation of §393.48?

Guidance: Yes. §393.48(a) requires that all brakes with which the vehicle is equipped must be operable at all times. Although §393.42(b)(1) provides an exception to the requirement for brakes on all wheels for trucks and truck tractors with 3 or more axles and manufactured prior to July 25, 1980, the exception does not affect the applicability of §393.48 for those cases in which the vehicle is equipped with inoperable front wheel brakes or only has certain portions of the front wheel brake system (e.g., shoes, linings, chambers, hoses) in place.

Question 4: Are the brakes on a vehicle towed in a driveaway-towaway operation or towed disabled vehicle required to be operable at all times?

Guidance: §393.48(c) provides an exception to the requirement that brakes be operable at all times. This exception covers disabled vehicles being towed and vehicles towed in a driveaway-towaway operation.

The driveaway-towaway exception in §393.48(c) is contingent upon the conditions outlined in §393.42(b)(2). Towed vehicles must have brakes as may be necessary to ensure compliance with the performance requirements of §393.52. A motor vehicle towed by means of a tow-bar when any other vehicle is full-mounted on the towed vehicle, or any combination of motor vehicles utilizing 3 or more saddle-mounts, would not be covered under the exception found at §393.48(c).

With regard to the disabled-vehicle provision of §393.48(c)(1), the combination vehicle would have to meet the applicable performance requirements of §393.52.

§393.49 Single valve to operate all brakes.

Every motor vehicle, the date of manufacture of which is subsequent to June 30, 1953, which is equipped with power brakes, shall have the braking system so arranged that one application valve shall when applied operate all the service brakes on the motor vehicle or combination of motor vehicles. This requirement shall not be construed to prohibit motor vehicles from being equipped with an additional valve to be used to operate the brakes on a trailer or trailers or as provided in §393.44. This section shall not be applicable to driveaway-towaway operations unless the brakes on such operations are designed to be operated by a single valve.

§393.49 DOT Interpretations

Question 1: Does a combination of vehicles using a surge brake to activate the towed vehicle's brakes comply with §393.49?

Guidance: No. The surge brake cannot keep the trailer brakes in an applied position. Therefore, the brakes on the combination of vehicles are not under the control of a single valve as required by §393.49 (see Question 1 in §393.48)

§393.50 Reservoirs required.

(a) **Reservoir capacity for air-braked power units** manufactured on or after March 1, 1975, and air-braked trailers manufactured on or after January 1, 1975. Buses, trucks, and truck-tractors manufactured on or after March 1, 1975, and air-braked trailers manufactured on or after January 1, 1975, must meet the reservoir requirements of FMVSS No. 121, S5.1.2, in effect on the date of manufacture.

(b) **Reservoir capacity for air-braked vehicles** not subject to FMVSS No. 121 on the date of manufacture and all vacuum braked vehicles. Each motor vehicle using air or vacuum braking must have either reserve capacity, or a reservoir, that would enable the driver to make a full service brake application with the engine stopped without depleting the air pressure or vacuum below 70 percent of that indicated by the air or vacuum gauge immediately before the brake application is made. For the purposes of this paragraph, a full service brake application means depressing the brake pedal or treadle valve to the limit of its travel.

(c) **Safeguarding of air and vacuum.** Each service reservoir system on a motor vehicle shall be protected against a loss of air pressure or vacuum due to a failure or leakage in the system between the service reservoir and the source of air pressure or vacuum, by check valves or equivalent devices whose proper functioning can be checked without disconnecting any air or vacuum line, or fitting.

(d) **Drain valves for air braked vehicles.** Each reservoir must have a condensate drain valve that can be manually operated. Automatic condensate drain valves may be used provided

  (1) they may be operated manually, or
  (2) a manual means of draining the reservoirs is retained.

§393.51 Warning signals, air pressure and vacuum gauges.

(a) **General Rule.** Every bus, truck and truck tractor, except as provided in paragraph (f), must be equipped with a signal that provides a warning to the driver when a failure occurs in the vehicle's service brake system. The warning signal must meet the applicable requirements of paragraphs (b), (c), (d) or (e) of this section.

(b) **Hydraulic brakes.** Vehicles manufactured on or after September 1, 1975, must meet the brake system indicator lamp requirements of FMVSS No. 571.105 (S5.3) applicable to the vehicle on the date of manufacture. Vehicles manufactured on or after July 1, 1973 but before September 1, 1975, or to which FMVSS No. 571.105 was not applicable on the date of manufacture, must have a warning signal which operates before or upon application of the brakes in the event of a hydraulic-type complete failure of a partial system. The signal must be either visible within the driver's forward field of view or audible. The signal must be continuous. (NOTE: FMVSS No. 105 was applicable to trucks and buses from September 1, 1975 to October 12, 1976, and from September 1, 1983, to the present. FMVSS No. 105 was not applicable to trucks and buses manufactured between October 12, 1976, and September 1, 1983. Motor carriers have the option of equipping those vehicles to meet either the indicator lamp requirements of FMVSS No. 105, or the indicator lamp requirements specified in this paragraph for vehicles which were not subject to FMVSS No. 105 on the date of manufacture.)

(c) **Air brakes.** A commercial motor vehicle (regardless of the date of manufacture) equipped with service brakes activated by compressed air (air brakes) or a commercial motor vehicle towing a vehicle with service brakes activated by compressed air (air brakes) must be equipped with a pressure gauge and a warning signal. Trucks, truck tractors, and buses manufactured on or after March 1, 1975, must, at a minimum, have a pressure gauge and a warning signal which meets the requirements of FMVSS No. 121 (S5.1.4 for the pressure gauge and S5.1.5 for the warning signal) applicable to the vehicle on the date of manufacture of the vehicle. Power units to which FMVSS No. 571.121 was not applicable on the date of manufacture of the vehicle must be equipped with —

  (1) *A pressure gauge,* visible to a person seated in the normal driving position, which indicates the air pressure (in kilopascals (kPa) or pounds per square inch (psi)) available for braking; and

  (2) *A warning signal* that is audible or visible to a person in the normal driving position and provides a continuous warning to the driver whenever the air pressure in the service reservoir system is at 379 kPa (55 psi) and below, or one-half of the compressor governor cutout pressure, whichever is less.

(d) **Vacuum brakes.** A commercial motor vehicle (regardless of the date it was manufactured) having service brakes activated by vacuum or a vehicle towing a vehicle having service brakes activated by vacuum must be equipped with —

  (1) *A vacuum gauge,* visible to a person seated in the normal driving position, which indicates the vacuum (in millimeters or inches of mercury) available for braking; and

  (2) *A warning signal that is audible or visible* to a person in the normal driving position and provides a continuous warning to the driver whenever the vacuum in the vehicle's supply reservoir is less than 203 mm (8 inches) of mercury.

(e) **Hydraulic brakes applied or assisted** by air or vacuum. Each vehicle equipped with hydraulically activated service brakes which are applied or assisted by compressed air or vacuum, and to which FMVSS No. 105 was not applicable on the date of manufacture, must be equipped with a warning signal that conforms to paragraph (b) of this section for the hydraulic portion of the system; paragraph (c) of this section for the air assist/air applied portion; or paragraph (d) of this section for the vacuum assist/vacuum applied portion. This paragraph shall not be construed as requiring air pressure gauges or vacuum gauges, only warning signals.

(f) **Exceptions.** The rules in paragraphs (c), (d) and (e) of this section do not apply to property carrying commercial motor vehicles which have less than three axles and

  (1) *were manufactured before July 1, 1973,* and

  (2) *have a manufacturer's gross vehicle weight rating* less than 4,536 kg (10,001 pounds).

§393.51 DOT Interpretations

Question 1: Is the low pressure warning device required to activate before the tractor protection valve?

Guidance: No. §393.51 does not explicitly require the warning device to operate before the protection valve. It is implied that if the operating pressure of the warning device is at least 1/2 of the governor cut-out pressure, and that pressure is not less than the pressure at which the protection valve (or similar device) activates, the requirements of §393.51 are satisfied.

Question 2: Is the vacuum portion of vacuum-assisted hydraulic brake systems required to have a warning device?

Guidance: No. Only the hydraulic portion of vacuum-assisted hydraulic brake systems is required to have a warning device. FMVSS No. 105 does not require a warning device for the vacuum portion of the vacuum-assisted hydraulic brake systems. It is the intention of the FHWA that §393.51 be consistent with FMVSS No. 105.

Question 3: Are vacuum gauges required on the vacuum portion of vacuum-assisted hydraulic brakes?

Guidance: No. §393.51(d)(2) requires only that CMVs with vacuum brakes (not hydraulic brakes applied or assisted by vacuum) be equipped with a vacuum gauge.

Question 4: Is a warning device required in a CMV with a single hydraulic brake system which uses the driveline parking brake as the emergency brake system?

Guidance: No. Warning devices are not required on such CMVs because the driver will be given ample warning of system failure by the movement and feel of the brake pedal.

Question 5: What difference, if any, is there between a warning device and a warning signal?

Guidance: For purposes of §393.51, the terms may be used interchangeably.

§393.52 Brake performance.

(a) **Upon application of its service brakes,** a motor vehicle or combination of motor vehicles must under any condition of loading in which it is found on a public highway, be capable of —

  (1) *Developing a braking force* at least equal to the percentage of its gross weight specified in the table in paragraph (d) of this section;

  (2) *Decelerating to a stop from 20 miles per hour* at not less than the rate specified in the table in paragraph (d) of this section; and

§393.52

Part 393 - Parts and Accessories Necessary for Safe Operation

(3) *Stopping from 20 miles per hour in a distance,* measured from the point at which movement of the service brake pedal or control begins, that is not greater than the distance specified in the table in paragraph (d) of this section; or, for motor vehicles or motor vehicle combinations that have a GVWR or GVW greater than 4,536 kg (10,000 pounds),

(4) *Developing only the braking force* specified in paragraph (a)(1) of this section and the stopping distance specified in paragraph (a)(3) of this section, if braking force is measured by a performance-based brake tester which meets the requirements of functional specifications for performance-based brake testers for commercial motor vehicles, where braking force is the sum of the braking force at each wheel of the vehicle or vehicle combination as a percentage of gross vehicle or combination weight.

(b) **Upon application of its emergency brake system** and with no other brake system applied, a motor vehicle or combination of motor vehicles must, under any condition of loading in which it is found on a public highway, be capable of stopping from 20 miles per hour in a distance, measured from the point at which movement of the emergency brake control begins, that is not greater than the distance specified in the table in paragraph (d) of this section.

(c) **Conformity to the stopping-distance requirements** of paragraphs (a) and (b) of this section shall be determined under the following conditions:

(1) *Any test must be made* with the vehicle on a hard surface that is substantially level, dry, smooth, and free of loose material.

(2) *The vehicle must be in the center* of a 12-foot-wide lane when the test begins and must not deviate from that lane during the test.

(d) **Vehicle brake performance table:**

Type of motor vehicle	Service brake systems			Emergency brake systems
	Braking force as a percentage of gross vehicle or combination weight	Deceleration in feet per second per second	Application and braking distance in feet from initial speed of 20 mph	Application and braking distance in feet from initial speed of 20 mph
A. Passenger-carrying vehicles.				
(1) Vehicles with a seating capacity of 10 persons or less, including driver, and built on a passenger car chassis.	65.2	21	20	54
(2) Vehicles with a seating capacity of more than 10 persons, including driver, and built on a passenger car chassis; vehicles built on a truck or bus chassis and having a manufacturer's GVWR of 10,000 pounds or less.	52.8	17	25	66
(3) All other passenger-carrying vehicles.	43.5	14	35	85
B. Property-carrying vehicles.				
(1) Single unit vehicles having a manufacturer's GVWR of 10,000 pounds or less.	52.8	17	25	66
(2) Single unit vehicles having a manufacturer's GVWR of more than 10,000 pounds, except truck tractors. Combinations of a 2-axle towing vehicle and trailer having a GVWR of 3,000 pounds or less. All combinations of 2 or less vehicles in drive-away or tow-away operation.	43.5	14	35	85
(3) All other property-carrying vehicles and combinations of property-carrying vehicles.	43.5	14	40	90

Notes:

(a) There is a definite mathematical relationship between the figures in columns 2 and 3. If the decelerations set forth in column 3 are divided by 32.2 feet per-second per-second, the figures in column 2 will be obtained. (For example, 21 divided by 32.2 equals 65.2 percent.) Column 2 is included in the tabulation because certain brake-testing devices utilize this factor.

(b) The decelerations specified in column 3 are an indication of the effectiveness of the basic brakes, and as measured in practical brake testing are the maximum decelerations attained at some time during the stop. These decelerations as measured in brake tests cannot be used to compute the values in column 4 because the deceleration is not sustained at the same rate over the entire period of the stop. The deceleration increases from zero to a maximum during a period of brake system application and brake-force buildup. Also, other factors may cause the deceleration to decrease after reaching a maximum. The added distance that results because maximum deceleration is not sustained is included in the figures in column 4 but is not indicated by the usual brake-testing devices for checking deceleration.

(c) The distances in column 4 and the decelerations in column 3 are not directly related. "Brake-system application and braking distance in feet" (column 4) is a definite measure of the overall effectiveness of the braking system, being the distance traveled between the point at which the driver starts to move the braking controls and the point at which the vehicle comes to rest. It includes distance traveled while the brakes are being applied and distance traveled while the brakes are retarding the vehicle.

(d) The distance traveled during the period of brake-system application and brake-force buildup varies with vehicle type, being negligible for many passenger cars and greatest for combinations of commercial vehicles. This fact accounts for the variation from 20 to 40 feet in the values in column 4 for the various classes of vehicles.

(e) The terms "GVWR" and "GVW" refer to the manufacturer's gross vehicle weight rating and the actual gross vehicle weight, respectively.

§393.52 DOT Interpretations

Question 1: May the information in the stopping distance table be used to determine the stopping distances at speeds greater than 20 mph?

Guidance: No, the table is not intended to be used to predict or determine stopping distances at speeds greater than 20 mph.

§393.53 Automatic brake adjusters and brake adjustment indicators.

(a) Automatic brake adjusters (hydraulic brake systems). Each commercial motor vehicle manufactured on or after October 20, 1993, and equipped with a hydraulic brake system, shall meet the automatic brake adjustment system requirements of Federal Motor Vehicle Safety Standard No. 105 (49 CFR 571.105, S5.1) applicable to the vehicle at the time it was manufactured.

(b) Automatic brake adjusters (air brake systems). Each commercial motor vehicle manufactured on or after October 20, 1994, and equipped with an air brake system shall meet the automatic brake adjustment system requirements of Federal Motor Vehicle Safety Standard No. 121 (49 CFR 571.121, S5.1.8) applicable to the vehicle at the time it was manufactured.

(c) Brake adjustment indicator (air brake systems). On each commercial motor vehicle manufactured on or after October 20, 1994, and equipped with an air brake system which contains an external automatic adjustment mechanism and an exposed pushrod, the condition of service brake under-adjustment shall be displayed by a brake adjustment indicator conforming to the requirements of Federal Motor Vehicle Safety Standard No. 121 (49 CFR 571.121, S5.1.8) applicable to the vehicle at the time it was manufactured.

§393.55 Antilock brake systems.

(a) Hydraulic brake systems. Each truck and bus manufactured on or after March 1, 1999 (except trucks and buses engaged in driveaway-towaway operations), and equipped with a hydraulic brake system, shall be equipped with an antilock brake system that meets the requirements of Federal Motor Vehicle Safety Standard (FMVSS) No. 105 (49 CFR 571.105, S5.5).

(b) ABS malfunction indicators for hydraulic braked vehicles. Each hydraulic braked vehicle subject to the requirements of paragraph (a) of this section shall be equipped with an ABS malfunction indicator system that meets the requirements of FMVSS No. 105 (49 CFR 571.105, S5.3).

(c) Air brake systems.

(1) *Each truck tractor manufactured* on or after March 1, 1997 (except truck tractors engaged in driveaway-towaway operations), shall be equipped with an antilock brake system that meets the requirements of FMVSS No. 121 (49 CFR 571.121, S5.1.6.1(b)).

(2) *Each air braked commercial motor vehicle* other than a truck tractor, manufactured on or after March 1, 1998 (except commercial motor vehicles engaged in driveaway-towaway operations), shall be equipped with an antilock brake system that meets the requirements of FMVSS No. 121 (49 CFR 571.121, S5.1.6.1(a) for trucks and buses, S5.2.3 for semitrailers, converter dollies and full trailers).

(d) ABS malfunction circuits and signals for air braked vehicles.

(1) *Each truck tractor manufactured* on or after March 1, 1997, and each single-unit air braked vehicle manufactured on or after March 1, 1998, subject to the requirements of paragraph (c) of this section, shall be equipped with an electrical circuit that is capable of signaling a malfunction that affects the generation or transmission of response or control signals to the vehicle's antilock brake system (49 CFR 571.121, S5.1.6.2(a)).

(2) *Each truck tractor manufactured* on or after March 1, 2001, and each single-unit vehicle that is equipped to tow another air-braked vehicle, subject to the requirements of paragraph (c) of this section, shall be equipped with an electrical circuit that is capable of transmitting a malfunction signal from the antilock brake system(s) on the towed vehicle(s) to the trailer ABS malfunction lamp in the cab of the towing vehicle, and shall have the means for connection of the electrical circuit to the towed vehicle. The ABS malfunction circuit and signal shall meet the requirements of FMVSS No. 121 (49 CFR 571.121, S5.1.6.2(b)).

(3) *Each semitrailer,* trailer converter dolly, and full trailer manufactured on or after March 1, 2001, and subject to the requirements of paragraph (c)(2) of this section, shall be equipped with an electrical circuit that is capable of signaling a malfunction in the trailer's antilock brake system, and shall have the means for connection of this ABS malfunction circuit to the towing vehicle. In addition, each trailer manufactured on or after March 1, 2001, subject to the requirements of paragraph (c)(2) of this section, that is designed to tow another air-brake equipped trailer shall be capable of transmitting a malfunction signal from the antilock brake system(s) of the trailer(s) it tows to the vehicle in front of the trailer. The ABS malfunction circuit and signal shall meet the requirements of FMVSS No. 121 (49 CFR 571.121, S5.2.3.2).

(e) Exterior ABS malfunction indicator lamps for trailers. Each trailer (including a trailer converter dolly) manufactured on or after March 1, 1998 and before March 1, 2009, and subject to the requirements of paragraph (c)(2) of this section, shall be equipped with an ABS malfunction indicator lamp which meets the requirements of FMVSS No. 121 (49 CFR 571.121, S5.2.3.3).

Subpart D - Glazing and Window Construction

§393.60 Glazing in specified openings.

(a) Glazing material. Glazing material used in windshields, windows, and doors on a motor vehicle manufactured on or after December 25, 1968, shall at a minimum meet the requirements of Federal Motor Vehicle Safety Standard (FMVSS) No. 205 in effect on the date of manufacture of the motor vehicle. The glazing material shall be marked in accordance with FMVSS No. 205 (49 CFR 571.205, S6).

(b) Windshields required. Each bus, truck and truck-tractor shall be equipped with a windshield. Each windshield or portion of a multi-piece windshield shall be mounted using the full periphery of the glazing material.

(c) Windshield condition. With the exception of the conditions listed in paragraphs (c)(1), (c)(2), and (c)(3) of this section, each windshield shall be free of discoloration or damage in the area extending upward from the height of the top of the steering wheel (excluding a 51 mm (2 inch) border at the top of the windshield) and extending from a 25 mm (1 inch) border at each side of the windshield or windshield panel.

EXCEPTIONS:
(1) Coloring or tinting which meets the requirements of paragraph (d) of this section;
(2) Any crack that is not intersected by any other cracks;
(3) Any damaged area which can be covered by a disc 19 mm (3/4 inch) in diameter if not closer than 76 mm (3 inches) to any other similarly damaged area.

(d) Coloring or tinting of windshields and windows. Coloring or tinting of windshields and the windows to the immediate right and left of the driver is allowed, provided the parallel luminous transmittance through the colored or tinted glazing is not less than 70 percent of the light at normal incidence in those portions of the windshield or windows which are marked as having a parallel luminous transmittance of not less than 70 percent. The transmittance restriction does not apply to other windows on the commercial motor vehicle.

(e) Prohibition on obstructions to the driver's field of view.

(1) *Devices mounted at the top of the windshield.* Antennas, transponders, and similar devices must not be mounted more than 152 mm (6 inches) below the upper edge of the windshield. These devices must be located outside the area swept by the windshield wipers, and outside the driver's sight lines to the road and highway signs and signals.

(2) *Decals and stickers mounted* on the windshield. Commercial Vehicle Safety Alliance (CVSA) inspection decals, and stickers and/or decals required under Federal or State laws may be placed at the bottom or sides of the windshield provided such decals or stickers do not extend more than 115 mm (4 1/2 inches) from the bottom of the windshield and are located outside the area swept by the windshield wipers, and outside the driver's sight lines to the road and highway signs or signals.

§393.60 DOT Interpretations

Question 1: May windshields and side windows be tinted?
Guidance: Yes, as long as the light transmission is not restricted to less than 70 percent of normal (refer to the American Standards Association publication Z26.1-1966 and Z26.1a-1969).

Question 2: May a decal designed to comply with the periodic inspection documentation requirements of §396.17 be displayed on the windshields or side windows of a CMV?
Guidance: Yes, provided the decal is being used in lieu of an inspection report and is in compliance with §393.60(c).

Question 3: If a crack extended into the thickness of the glass at such an angle as to measure 1/4" or more, measuring from the top edge of the crack on the outside surface of the windshield to vertical line drawn through the windshield to the far edge of this angled crack on the inside of the windshield, would this constitute a crack of 1/4" or more in width as defined in §393.60(b)(2)?
Guidance: No. The crack, in order to fall outside the exception, would have to be a gap of 1/4" or more on the same surface of the windshield.

§393.61 Truck and truck tractor window construction.

Each truck and truck tractor (except trucks engaged in armored car service) shall have at least one window on each side of the driver's compartment. Each window must have a minimum area of 1,290 cm^2 (200 in^2) formed by a rectangle 33 cm by 45 cm (13 inches by 17 3/4 inches). The maximum radius of the corner arcs shall not exceed 152 mm (6 inches). The long axis of the rectangle shall not make an angle of more than 45 degrees with the surface on which the unladen vehicle stands. If the cab is designed with a folding door or doors or with clear openings where doors or windows are customarily located, no windows shall be required in those locations.

§393.61 DOT Interpretations

Question 1: Do school buses used for purposes other than school bus operations (as defined in §390.5), have to meet additional emergency exits requirements under §393.61?
Guidance: Yes. §393.61(b)(2) says that "a bus, including a school bus, manufactured on and after September 1, 1973," must conform with NHTSA's §571.217 (FMVSS 217). At the time this provision was adopted, FMVSS 217 applied only to other buses and it was optional for school buses. The FHWA inserted the language, "including school buses," in §393.61(b)(2) to make clear that school buses used in interstate commerce and, therefore, subject to the FMCSRs, were required to comply with the bus exit standards in Standard FMVSS 217.

§393.61(b)(3) regarding push-out windows provides that older buses must conform with the requirements of §§393.61(b) or 571.217. Buses which are subject to §571.217 would follow NHTSA's interpretation on push-out windows. Buses which are subject to §393.61(b)(1) of the FMCSRs are required to have emergency windows that are either push-out windows or that have laminated safety glass that can be pushed out in a manner similar to a push-out window.

Question 2: For emergency exits which consist of laminated safety glass, is the window frame or sash required to move outward from the bus as is the case with push-out windows?
Guidance: No. Laminated safety glass is an alternative to the use of push-out windows for buses manufactured before September 1, 1973. §393.61(c) requires that every glazed opening used to satisfy the emergency exit space requirements, "if not glazed with laminated safety glass, shall have a frame or sash so designed, constructed, and maintained that it will yield outwardly to provide the required free opening. * * * " Laminated safety glass meeting Test No. 25, Egress, American National Standard "Safety Code for Safety Glazing Materials for Glazing Motor Vehicles Operating on Land Highways," Z26.1-1966 as supplemented by Z26.1a-1969 (referenced in §§393.61(c) and 393.60(a)) is intended to provide an adequate means of emergency exit on older buses without resorting to push-out windows.

However, buses with a seating capacity of more than 10 people manufactured after September 1, 1973, must have push-out windows that conform to 49 CFR 571.217.

Question 3: When calculating the minimum emergency exit space required on school buses used in non-school bus operations, should two or three passengers per bench seat be used in determining the adult seating capacity?
Guidance: The NHTSA has indicated that "School buses can transport 3 to a seat if the passengers are in grades 1 through 5, and 2 per seat in grades 9 through 12." (May 9, 1995, 60 FR 24562, 24567) Therefore, for vehicles originally manufactured as school buses, the total pupil seating capacity provided by the bus manufacturer should be multiplied by 2/3 to determine the adult seating capacity for the purposes of §393.61. This generally yields the same result as using two adults per bench seat.

Question 4: Do school buses which meet the school bus emergency exit requirements established by the NHTSA's November 2, 1992, final rule on FMVSS No. 217 have to be retrofitted with additional emergency exits when used in interstate commerce for non-school bus operations?
Guidance: No. On May 9, 1995, the NHTSA amended FMVSS No. 217 to permit non-school buses to meet either the current non-school bus emergency exit requirements or the upgraded school bus exit requirements established by the November 2, 1992 (57 FR 49413), final rule which became effective on September 1, 1994. Therefore, school buses which meet the upgraded emergency exit standards meet the requirements of §393.61 without the retrofitting of additional exits.

Question 5: Which edition of FMVSS No. 217 is required to be used in determining the emergency exit space requirements when retrofitting buses?
Guidance: The cross reference to FMVSS No. 217 applies to the requirements in effect at the time of manufacture of the bus. Motor carriers are not, however, prohibited from retrofitting their buses to the most up-to-date requirements in FMVSS No. 217. Therefore, at a minimum, motor carriers must meet the non-school bus emergency exit requirements in effect at the time of manufacture, and have the option of retrofitting their buses to meet the emergency exit requirements established by the November 2, 1992 (57 FR 49413), final rule which became effective on September 1, 1994.

§393.62 Emergency exits for buses.

(a) Buses manufactured on or after September 1, 1994. Each bus with a GVWR of 4,536 kg (10,000 pounds) or less must meet the emergency exit requirements of FMVSS No. 217 (S5.2.2.3) in effect on the date of manufacture. Each bus with a GVWR of more than 4,536 kg (10,000 pounds) must have emergency exits which meet the applicable emergency exit requirements of FMVSS No. 217 (S5.2.2 or S5.2.3) in effect on the date of manufacture.

(b) Buses manufactured on or after September 1, 1973, but before September 1, 1994.
  (1) *Each bus* (including a school bus used in interstate commerce for non-school bus operations) with a GVWR of more than 4,536 kg (10,000 lbs) must meet the requirements of FMVSS No. 217, S5.2.2 in effect on the date of manufacture.
  (2) *Each bus* (including a school bus used in interstate commerce for non-school bus operations) with a GVWR of 4,536 kg (10,000 lbs) or less must meet the requirements of FMVSS No. 217, S5.2.2.3 in effect on the date of manufacture.

(c) Buses manufactured before September 1, 1973. For each seated passenger space provided, inclusive of the driver there shall be at least 432 cm^2 (67 square inches) of glazing if such glazing is not contained in a push-out window; or, at least 432 cm^2 (67 square inches) of free opening resulting from opening of a push-out type window. No area shall be included in this minimum prescribed area unless it will provide an unobstructed opening of at least 1,290 cm^2 (200 in^2) formed by a rectangle 33 cm by 45 cm (13 inches by 17 3/4 inches). The maximum radius of the corner arcs shall not exceed 152 mm (6 inches). The long axis of the rectangle shall not make an angle of more than 45 degrees with the surface on which the unladen vehicle stands. The area shall be measured either by removal of the glazing if not of the push-out type, or of the movable sash if of the push-out type. The exit must comply with paragraph (d) of this section. Each side of the bus must have at least 40 percent of emergency exit space required by this paragraph.

(d) Laminated safety glass/push-out window requirements for buses manufactured before September 1, 1973. Emergency exit space used to satisfy the requirements of paragraph (c) of this section must have laminated safety glass or push-out windows designed and maintained to yield outward to provide a free opening.

(1) *Safety glass.* Laminated safety glass must meet Test No. 25, Egress, of American National Standard for Safety Glazing Materials for Glazing Motor Vehicles and Motor Vehicle Equipment Operating on Land Highways—Safety Standards ANSI/SAE Z26.1/96, August 1997. (See §393.7 (b) for information on incorporation by reference and availability of this document.)

(2) *Push-out windows.* Each push-out window shall be releasable by operating no more than two mechanisms and allow manual release of the exit by a single occupant. For mechanisms which require rotary or straight (parallel to the undisturbed exit surface) motions to operate the exit, no more than 89 Newtons (20 pounds) of force shall be required to release the exit. For exits which require a straight motion perpendicular to the undisturbed exit surface, no more than 267 Newtons (60 pounds) shall be required to release the exit.

(e) Emergency exit identification. Each bus and each school bus used in interstate commerce for non-school bus operations, manufactured on or after September 1, 1973, shall meet the applicable emergency exit identification or marking requirements of FMVSS No. 217, S5.5, in effect on the date of manufacture. The emergency exits and doors on all buses (including school buses used in interstate commerce for non-school bus operations) must be marked "Emergency Exit" or "Emergency Door" followed by concise operating instructions describing each motion necessary to unlatch or open the exit located within 152 mm (6 inches) of the release mechanism.

(f) Exception for the transportation of prisoners. The requirements of this section do not apply to buses used exclusively for the transportation of prisoners.

§393.62 DOT Interpretations

Question 1: May a bus being operated by a for-hire motor carrier of passengers, under contract with a governmental agency to provide transportation of prisoners in interstate commerce, be allowed to operate with security bars covering the emergency push-out windows and with locked emergency door exits?

Guidance: Yes. Even when the transportation is performed by a contract carrier, the welfare, safety, and security of the prisoners is under the authority of the governmental corrections agency and, thus, the agency may require additional security measures. For these types of operations, a carrier may meet the special security requirements of the governmental corrections agency regarding emergency exits. However, CMVs that have been modified to meet the security requirements of the corrections agency may not be used for other purposes that are subject to the FMCSRs unless they meet the emergency exit requirements.

§393.63 [Reserved]

Subpart E - Fuel Systems

§393.65 All fuel systems.

(a) Application of the rules in this section. The rules in this section apply to systems for containing and supplying fuel for the operation of motor vehicles or for the operation of auxiliary equipment installed on, or used in connection with, motor vehicles.

(b) Location. Each fuel system must be located on the motor vehicle so that —

(1) *No part of the system* extends beyond the widest part of the vehicle;

(2) *No part of a fuel tank* is forward of the front axle of a power unit;

(3) *Fuel spilled vertically from a fuel tank* while it is being filled will not contact any part of the exhaust or electrical systems of the vehicle, except the fuel level indicator assembly;

(4) *Fill pipe openings are located* outside the vehicle's passenger compartment and its cargo compartment;

(5) *A fuel line does not extend* between a towed vehicle and the vehicle that is towing it while the combination of vehicles is in motion; and

(6) *No part of the fuel system* of a bus manufactured on or after January 1, 1973, is located within or above the passenger compartment.

(c) Fuel tank installation. Each fuel tank must be securely attached to the motor vehicle in a workmanlike manner.

(d) Gravity or syphon feed prohibited. A fuel system must not supply fuel by gravity or syphon feed directly to the carburetor or injector.

(e) Selection control valve location. If a fuel system includes a selection control valve which is operable by the driver to regulate the flow of fuel from two or more fuel tanks, the valve must be installed so that either —

(1) *The driver may operate it* while watching the roadway and without leaving his/her driving position; or

(2) *The driver must stop the vehicle* and leave his/her seat in order to operate the valve.

(f) Fuel lines. A fuel line which is not completely enclosed in a protective housing must not extend more than 2 inches below the fuel tank or its sump. Diesel fuel crossover, return, and withdrawal lines which extend below the bottom of the tank or sump must be protected against damage from impact. Every fuel line must be —

(1) *Long enough and flexible enough* to accommodate normal movements of the parts to which it is attached without incurring damage; and

(2) *Secured against* chafing, kinking, or other causes of mechanical damage.

(g) Excess flow valve. When pressure devices are used to force fuel from a fuel tank, a device which prevents the flow of fuel from the fuel tank if the fuel feed line is broken must be installed in the fuel system.

§393.65 DOT Interpretations

Question 1: May a fuel fill pipe opening be placed above the passenger floor level if it is not physically within the passenger compartment?

Guidance: Yes. In addition, the fill pipe may intrude into the passenger compartment as long as the fill pipe opening complies with §393.65(b)(4), and the fill pipe is protected by a housing or covering to prevent leakage of fuel or fumes into the passenger compartment.

Question 2: Must a motor vehicle that meets the definition of a "commercial motor vehicle" in §390.5 because it transports hazardous materials in a quantity requiring placarding under the Hazardous Materials Regulations (49 CFR Parts 171-180) comply with the fuel system requirements of Subpart E of Part 393, even though it has a gross vehicle weight rating (GVWR) of 10,000 pounds or less?

Guidance: No. FMVSS No. 301 contains fuel system integrity requirements for passenger cars and multipurpose passenger vehicles, trucks, and buses that have a GVWR of 10,000 pounds or less and use fuel with a boiling point above 0 °Celsius (32 °Fahrenheit). Subpart E of Part 393 was issued to provide fuel system requirements to cover motor vehicles with a GVWR of 10,001 or more pounds. The fuel systems of placarded motor vehicles with a GVWR of less than 10,001 pounds are adequately addressed by FMVSS No. 301 and compliance with Subpart E of Part 393 would be redundant. However, commercial motor vehicles that are not covered by FMVSS No. 301 must continue to comply with Subpart E of Part 393.

§393.67 Liquid fuel tanks.

(a) Application of the rules in this section. The rules in this section apply to tanks containing or supplying fuel for the operation of commercial motor vehicles or for the operation of auxiliary equipment installed on, or used in connection with commercial motor vehicles.

(1) *A liquid fuel tank manufactured on or after* January 1, 1973, and a side-mounted gasoline tank must conform to all rules in this section.

§393.67 — **Part 393 - Parts and Accessories Necessary for Safe Operation**

(2) *A diesel fuel tank manufactured before* January 1, 1973, and mounted on a bus must conform to the rules in paragraphs (c)(7)(iii) and (d)(2) of this section.

(3) *A diesel fuel tank manufactured before* January 1, 1973, and mounted on a vehicle other than a bus must conform to the rules in paragraph (c)(7)(iii) of this section.

(4) *A gasoline tank,* other than a side-mounted gasoline tank, manufactured before January 1, 1973, and mounted on a bus must conform to the rules in paragraphs (c) (1) through (10) and (d)(2) of this section.

(5) *A gasoline tank,* other than a side-mounted gasoline tank, manufactured before January 1, 1973, and mounted on a vehicle other than a bus must conform to the rules in paragraphs (c) (1) through (10), inclusive, of this section.

(6) *Private motor carrier of passengers.* Motor carriers engaged in the private transportation of passengers may continue to operate a commercial motor vehicle which was not subject to this section or 49 CFR 571.301 at the time of its manufacture, provided the fuel tank of such vehicle is maintained to the original manufacturer's standards.

(7) *Motor vehicles that meet* the fuel system integrity requirements of 49 CFR 571.301 are exempt from the requirements of this subpart, as they apply to the vehicle's fueling system.

(b) **Definitions.** As used in this section —
  (1) The term **liquid fuel tank** means a fuel tank designed to contain a fuel that is liquid at normal atmospheric pressures and temperatures.
  (2) A **side-mounted fuel tank** is a liquid fuel tank which —
    (i) *If mounted on a truck tractor,* extends outboard of the vehicle frame and outside of the plan view outline of the cab; or
    (ii) *If mounted on a truck,* extends outboard of a line parallel to the longitudinal centerline of the truck and tangent to the outboard side of a front tire in a straight ahead position. In determining whether a fuel tank on a truck or truck tractor is side-mounted, the fill pipe is not considered a part of the tank.

(c) **Construction of liquid fuel tanks.**
  (1) *Joints.* Joints of a fuel tank body must be closed by arc-, gas-, seam-, or spot-welding, by brazing, by silver soldering, or by techniques which provide heat resistance and mechanical securement at least equal to those specifically named. Joints must not be closed solely by crimping or by soldering with a lead-based or other soft solder.
  (2) *Fittings.* The fuel tank body must have flanges or spuds suitable for the installation of all fittings.
  (3) *Threads.* The threads of all fittings must be Dryseal American Standard Taper Pipe Thread or Dryseal SAE Short Taper Pipe Thread, specified in Society of Automotive Engineers Standard J476, as contained in the 1971 edition of the "SAE Handbook," except that straight (nontapered) threads may be used on fittings having integral flanges and using gaskets for sealing. At least four full threads must be in engagement in each fitting.
  (4) *Drains and bottom fittings.*
    (i) *Drains or other bottom fittings* must not extend more than three-fourths of an inch below the lowest part of the fuel tank or sump.
    (ii) *Drains or other bottom fittings* must be protected against damage from impact.
    (iii) *If a fuel tank has drains* the drain fittings must permit substantially complete drainage of the tank.
    (iv) *Drains or other bottom fittings* must be installed in a flange or spud designed to accommodate it.
  (5) *Fuel withdrawal fittings.* Except for diesel fuel tanks, the fittings through which fuel is withdrawn from a fuel tank must be located above the normal level of fuel in the tank when the tank is full.
  (6) [Reserved]
  (7) *Fill pipe.*
    (i) *Each fill pipe* must be designed and constructed to minimize the risk of fuel spillage during fueling operations and when the vehicle is involved in a crash.
    (ii) *For diesel-fueled vehicles,* the fill pipe and vents of a fuel tank having a capacity of more than 94.75 L (25 gallons) of fuel must permit filling the tank with fuel at a rate of at least 75.8 L/m (20 gallons per minute) without fuel spillage.
    (iii) *For gasoline- and methanol-fueled vehicles* with a GVWR of 3,744 kg (8,500 pounds) or less, the vehicle must permit filling the tank with fuel dispensed at the applicable fill rate required by the regulations of the Environmental Protection Agency under 40 CFR 80.22.
    (iv) *For gasoline- and methanol-fueled vehicles* with a GVWR of 14,000 pounds (6,400 kg) or less, the vehicle must comply with the applicable fuel-spitback prevention and onboard refueling vapor recovery regulations of the Environmental Protection Agency under 40 CFR Part 86.
    (v) *Each fill pipe must be fitted with a cap* that can be fastened securely over the opening in the fill pipe. Screw threads or a bayonet type point are methods of conforming to the requirements of paragraph (c) of this section.
  (8) *Safety venting system.* A liquid fuel tank with a capacity of more than 25 gallons of fuel must have a venting system which, in the event the tank is subjected to fire, will prevent internal tank pressure from rupturing the tank's body, seams, or bottom opening (if any).
  (9) *Pressure resistance.* The body and fittings of a liquid fuel tank with a capacity of more than 25 gallons of fuel must be capable of withstanding an internal hydrostatic pressure equal to 150 percent of the maximum internal pressure reached in the tank during the safety venting systems test specified in paragraph (d)(1) of this section.
  (10) *Air vent.* Each fuel tank must be equipped with a nonspill air vent (such as a ball check). The air vent may be combined with the fill-pipe cap or safety vent, or it may be a separate unit installed on the fuel tank.
  (11) *Markings.* If the body of a fuel tank is readily visible when the tank is installed on the vehicle, the tank must be plainly marked with its liquid capacity. The tank must also be plainly marked with a warning against filling it to more than 95 percent of its liquid capacity.
  (12) *Overfill restriction.* A liquid fuel tank manufactured on or after January 1, 1973, must be designed and constructed so that —
    (i) *The tank cannot be filled,* in a normal filling operation, with a quantity of fuel that exceeds 95 percent of the tank's liquid capacity; and
    (ii) *When the tank is filled,* normal expansion of the fuel will not cause fuel spillage.

(d) **Liquid fuel tank tests.** Each liquid fuel tank must be capable of passing the tests specified in paragraphs (d)(1) and (2) of this section. The specified tests are a measure of performance only. Alternative procedures which assure that equipment meets the required performance standards may be used.
  (1) *Safety venting system test —*
    (i) *Procedure.* Fill the tank three-fourths full with fuel, seal the fuel feed outlet, and invert the tank. When the fuel temperature is between 50 °F. and 80 °F., apply an enveloping flame to the tank so that the temperature of the fuel rises at a rate of not less than 6 °F. and not more than 8 °F. per minute.
    (ii) *Required performance.* The safety venting system required by paragraph (c)(8) of this section must activate before the internal pressure in the tank exceeds 50 pounds per square inch, gauge, and the internal pressure must not thereafter exceed the pressure at which the system activated by more than five pounds per square inch despite any further increase in the temperature of the fuel.
  (2) *Leakage test —*
    (i) *Procedure.* Fill the tank to capacity with fuel having a temperature between 50 °F. and 80 °F. With the fill-pipe cap installed, turn the tank through an angle of 150° in any direction about any axis from its normal position.
    (ii) *Required performance.* Neither the tank nor any fitting may leak more than a total of one ounce by weight of fuel per minute in any position the tank assumes during the test.

Subpart F - Coupling Devices and Towing Methods

(e) Side-mounted liquid fuel tank tests. Each side-mounted liquid fuel tank must be capable of passing the tests specified in paragraphs (e)(1) and (2) of this section and the test specified in paragraphs (d)(1) and (2) of this section. The specified tests are a measure of performance only. Alternative procedures which assure that equipment meets the required performance criteria may be used.

(1) *Drop test.*
  (i) *Procedure.* Fill the tank with a quantity of water having a weight equal to the weight of the maximum fuel load of the tank and drop the tank 30 feet onto an unyielding surface so that it lands squarely on one corner.
  (ii) *Required performance.* Neither the tank nor any fitting may leak more than a total of 1 ounce by weight of water per minute.

(2) *Fill-pipe test.*
  (i) *Procedure.* Fill the tank with a quantity of water having a weight equal to the weight of the maximum fuel load of the tank and drop the tank 10 feet onto an unyielding surface so that it lands squarely on its fill-pipe.
  (ii) *Required performance.* Neither the tank nor any fitting may leak more than a total of 1 ounce by weight of water per minute.

(f) Certification and markings. Each liquid fuel tank shall be legibly and permanently marked by the manufacturer with the following minimum information:

(1) *The month and year of manufacture,*
(2) *The manufacturer's name* on tanks manufactured on and after July 1, 1989, and means of identifying the facility at which the tank was manufactured, and
(3) *A certificate that it conforms* to the rules in this section applicable to the tank. The certificate must be in the form set forth in either of the following:
  (i) *If a tank conforms* to all rules in this section pertaining to side-mounted fuel tanks: "Meets all FMCSA side-mounted tank requirements."
  (ii) *If a tank conforms to all rules in this section* pertaining to tanks which are not side-mounted fuel tanks: "Meets all FMCSA requirements for non-side-mounted fuel tanks."
  (iii) *The form of certificate* specified in paragraph (f)(3)(i) or (ii) of this section may be used on a liquid fuel tank manufactured before July 11, 1973, but it is not mandatory for liquid fuel tanks manufactured before March 7, 1989. The form of certification manufactured on or before March 7, 1989, must meet the requirements in effect at the time of manufacture.

(4) *Exception.* The following previously exempted vehicles are not required to carry the certification and marking specified in paragraphs (f)(1) through (3) of this section:
  (i) *Ford vehicles with GVWR over 10,000 pounds* identified as follows: The vehicle identification numbers (VINs) contain A, K, L, M, N, W, or X in the fourth position.
  (ii) *GM G-Vans* (Chevrolet Express and GMC Savanna) and full-sized C/K trucks (Chevrolet Silverado and GMC Sierra) with GVWR over 10,000 pounds identified as follows: The VINs contain either a "J" or a "K" in the fourth position. In addition, the seventh position of the VINs on the G-Van will contain a "1."

§393.67 DOT Interpretations

Question 1: May a properly vented fuel cap be used on a fuel tank equipped with another fuel venting system?
Guidance: Yes (see §393.3).

Question 2: Do the FMCSRs specify a particular pressure relief system?
Guidance: No, but the performance standards of §393.67(d) must be met.

Question 3: What standards under the FMCSRs must be met when a liquid fuel tank is repaired or replaced?
Guidance: A replacement/repaired tank must meet the applicable standards in §393.67.

§393.68 Compressed natural gas fuel containers.

(a) Applicability. The rules in this section apply to compressed natural gas (CNG) fuel containers used for supplying fuel for the operation of commercial motor vehicles or for the operation of auxiliary equipment installed on, or used in connection with commercial motor vehicles.

(b) CNG containers manufactured on or after March 26, 1995. Any motor vehicle manufactured on or after March 26, 1995, and equipped with a CNG fuel tank must meet the CNG container requirements of FMVSS No. 304 (49 CFR 571.304) in effect at the time of manufacture of the vehicle.

(c) Labeling. Each CNG fuel container shall be permanently labeled in accordance with the requirements of FMVSS No. 304, S7.4.

§393.69 Liquefied petroleum gas systems.

(a) A fuel system that uses liquefied petroleum gas as a fuel for the operation of a motor vehicle or for the operation of auxiliary equipment installed on, or used in connection with, a motor vehicle must conform to the "Standards for the Storage and Handling of Liquefied Petroleum Gases" of the National Fire Protection Association, Battery March Park, Quincy, MA 02269, as follows:

(1) *A fuel system installed before* December 31, 1962, must conform to the 1951 edition of the Standards.
(2) *A fuel system installed on or after* December 31, 1962, and before January 1, 1973, must conform to Division IV of the June 1959 edition of the Standards.
(3) *A fuel system installed on or after* January 1, 1973, and providing fuel for propulsion of the motor vehicle must conform to Division IV of the 1969 edition of the Standards.
(4) *A fuel system installed on or after* January 1, 1973, and providing fuel for the operation of auxiliary equipment must conform to Division VII of the 1969 edition of the Standards.

(b) When the rules in this section require a fuel system to conform to a specific edition of the Standards, the fuel system may conform to the applicable provisions in a later edition of the Standards specified in this section.

(c) The tank of a fuel system must be marked to indicate that the system conforms to the Standards.

Subpart F - Coupling Devices and Towing Methods

§393.70 Coupling devices and towing methods, except for driveaway-towaway operations.

(a) Tracking. When two or more vehicles are operated in combination, the coupling devices connecting the vehicles shall be designed, constructed, and installed, and the vehicles shall be designed and constructed, so that when the combination is operated in a straight line on a level, smooth, paved surface, the path of the towed vehicle will not deviate more than 3 inches to either side of the path of the vehicle that tows it.

(b) **Fifth wheel assemblies.**
  (1) *Mounting.*
    (i) *Lower half.* The lower half of a fifth wheel mounted on a truck tractor or converter dolly must be secured to the frame of that vehicle with properly designed brackets, mounting plates or angles and properly tightened bolts of adequate size and grade, or devices that provide equivalent security. The installation shall not cause cracking, warping, or deformation of the frame. The installation must include a device for positively preventing the lower half of the fifth wheel from shifting on the frame to which it is attached.
    (ii) *Upper half.* The upper half of a fifth wheel must be fastened to the motor vehicle with at least the same security required for the installation of the lower half on a truck tractor or converter dolly.
  (2) *Locking.* Every fifth wheel assembly must have a locking mechanism. The locking mechanism, and any adapter used in conjunction with it, must prevent separation of the upper and lower halves of the fifth wheel assembly unless a positive manual release is activated. The release may be located so that the driver can operate it from the cab. If a motor vehicle has a fifth wheel designed and constructed to be readily separable, the fifth wheel locking devices shall apply automatically on coupling.
  (3) *Location.* The lower half of a fifth wheel shall be located so that, regardless of the condition of loading, the relationship between the kingpin and the rear axle or axles of the towing motor vehicle will properly distribute the gross weight of both the towed and towing vehicles on the axles of those vehicles, will not unduly interfere with the steering, braking, and other maneuvering of the towing vehicle, and will not otherwise contribute to unsafe operation of the vehicles comprising the combination. The upper half of a fifth wheel shall be located so that the weight of the vehicles is properly distributed on their axles and the combination of vehicles will operate safely during normal operation.

(c) **Towing of full trailers.** A full trailer must be equipped with a tow-bar and a means of attaching the tow-bar to the towing and towed vehicles. The tow-bar and the means of attaching it must —
  (1) *Be structurally adequate* for the weight being drawn;
  (2) *Be properly and securely mounted;*
  (3) *Provide for adequate articulation* at the connection without excessive slack at that location; and
  (4) *Be provided with a locking device* that prevents accidental separation of the towed and towing vehicles. The mounting of the trailer hitch (pintle hook or equivalent mechanism) on the towing vehicle must include reinforcement or bracing of the frame sufficient to produce strength and rigidity of the frame to prevent its undue distortion.

(d) **Safety devices in case** of tow-bar failure or disconnection. Every full trailer and every converter dolly used to convert a semitrailer to a full trailer must be coupled to the frame, or an extension of the frame, of the motor vehicle which tows it with one or more safety devices to prevent the towed vehicle from breaking loose in the event the tow-bar fails or becomes disconnected. The safety device must meet the following requirements:
  (1) *The safety device must not be attached* to the pintle hook or any other device on the towing vehicle to which the tow-bar is attached. However, if the pintle hook or other device was manufactured prior to July 1, 1973, the safety device may be attached to the towing vehicle at a place on a pintle hook forging or casting if that place is independent of the pintle hook.
  (2) *The safety device must have* no more slack than is necessary to permit the vehicles to be turned properly.
  (3) *The safety device,* and the means of attaching it to the vehicles, must have an ultimate strength of not less than the gross weight of the vehicle or vehicles being towed.
  (4) *The safety device must be connected* to the towed and towing vehicles and to the tow-bar in a manner which prevents the tow-bar from dropping to the ground in the event it fails or becomes disconnected.
  (5) *Except as provided* in paragraph (d)(6) of this section, if the safety device consists of safety chains or cables, the towed vehicle must be equipped with either two safety chains or cables or with a bridle arrangement of a single chain or cable attached to its frame or axle at two points as far apart as the configuration of the frame or axle permits. The safety chains or cables shall be either two separate pieces, each equipped with a hook or other means for attachment to the towing vehicle, or a single piece leading along each side of the tow-bar from the two points of attachment on the towed vehicle and arranged into a bridle with a single means of attachment to be connected to the towing vehicle. When a single length of cable is used, a thimble and twin-base cable clamps shall be used to form the forward bridle eye. The hook or other means of attachment to the towing vehicle shall be secured to the chains or cables in a fixed position.
  (6) *If the towed vehicle is a converter dolly* with a solid tongue and without a hinged tow-bar or other swivel between the fifth wheel mounting and the attachment point of the tongue eye or other hitch device —
    (i) *Safety chains or cables,* when used as the safety device for that vehicle, may consist of either two chains or cables or a single chain or cable used alone;
    (ii) *A single safety device,* including a single chain or cable used alone as the safety device, must be in line with the centerline of the trailer tongue; and
    (iii) *The device may be attached* to the converter dolly at any point to the rear of the attachment point of the tongue eye or other hitch device.
  (7) *Safety devices* other than safety chains or cables must provide strength, security of attachment, and directional stability equal to, or greater than, safety chains or cables installed in accordance with paragraphs (d)(5) and (6) of this section.
  (8)(i) *When two safety devices,* including two safety chains or cables, are used and are attached to the towing vehicle at separate points, the points of attachment on the towing vehicle shall be located equally distant from, and on opposite sides of, the longitudinal centerline of the towing vehicle.
    (ii) *Where two chains or cables* are attached to the same point on the towing vehicle, and where a bridle or a single chain or cable is used, the point of attachment must be on the longitudinal centerline or within 152 mm (6 inches) to the right of the longitudinal centerline of the towing vehicle.
    (iii) *A single safety device,* other than a chain or cable, must also be attached to the towing vehicle at a point on the longitudinal centerline or within 152 mm (6 inches) to the right of the longitudinal centerline of the towing vehicle.

§393.70 DOT Interpretations

Question 1: Is there a minimum number of fasteners required to fasten the upper fifth wheel plate to the frame of a trailer?

Guidance: The FMCSRs do not specify a minimum number of fasteners. However, the industry recommends that a minimum of ten 5/8 inch bolts be used. If 1/2 inch bolts are used, the industry recommends at least 14 bolts. The CVSA has adopted these industry standards as a part of its vehicle out-of-service criteria.

Question 2: When two safety chains are used, must the ultimate combined breaking strength of each chain be equal to the gross weight of the towed vehicle(s) or would the requirements be met if the combined breaking strength of the two chains is equal to the gross weight of the towed vehicle(s)?

Guidance: If the ultimate combined breaking strength of the two chains is equal to the gross weight of the towed vehicle(s), the requirements of §393.70(d) are satisfied. It should be noted that some States may have more stringent requirements for safety chains.

Question 3: §393.70(d) requires that every full trailer must be coupled to the frame, or an extension of the frame, of the motor vehicle which tows it with one or more safety devices to prevent the towed vehicle from breaking loose in the event the tow-bar fails or becomes disconnected. The safety device must be connected to the towed and towing vehicles and to the tow-bar in a manner which prevents the tow-bar from dropping to the ground in the event it fails or becomes disconnected. Would the use of a pair of safety chains/cables between the towing vehicle and the front of a fixed-length draw bar, or an extendible draw bar, with a separate pair of safety chains/cables between the end of the draw bar and the front of the towed vehicle meet the requirements of §393.70(d)?

Guidance: Generally, separate safety devices at the front and rear of the draw bar could be used to satisfy the requirements of §393.70(d) provided the safety devices are attached to the drawbar and the vehicles in a manner that prevents the drawbar from dropping to the ground in the event that it fails or becomes disconnected. Also, the arrangement of the safety device(s) must be such that the vehicles will not separate if the draw bar fails or becomes disconnected.

Subpart F - Coupling Devices and Towing Methods §393.71 (h)

If the drawbar design is such that bolts, connecting pins, etc., are used to connect structural members of the drawbar, and are located at or near the midpoint of the drawbar (beyond the attachment points for the safety chain at the ends of the draw bar) the safety devices would have to extend from either the frame of the towed or towing vehicle to a point beyond the bolts, connecting pins or similar devices.

In the case of an extendible draw bar or reach, if a separate safety device(s) is used for the front and rear of the drawbar, a means must be provided to ensure that the drawbar will not separate at the movable portion of the drawbar. The use of welded tube stops would satisfy the intent of §393.70(d) if the ultimate strength of the welds exceeds the impact forces associated with the drawbar extending suddenly with a fully loaded trailer attached.

§393.71 Coupling devices and towing methods, driveaway-towaway operations.

(a) Number in combination.
  (1) *No more than three saddle-mounts* may be used in any combination.
  (2) *No more than one tow-bar or ball-and-socket type* coupling device may be used in any combination.
  (3) *When motor vehicles are towed* by means of triple saddle-mounts, the towed vehicles shall have brakes acting on all wheels which are in contact with the roadway.

(b) Carrying vehicles on towing vehicles.
  (1) *When adequately and securely attached* by means equivalent in security to that provided in paragraph (j)(2) of this section, a motor vehicle or motor vehicles may be full-mounted on the structure of a towing vehicle engaged in any driveaway-towaway operation.
  (2) *No motor vehicle or motor vehicles* may be full-mounted on a towing vehicle unless the relationship of such full-mounted vehicles to the rear axle or axles results in proper distribution of the total gross weight of the vehicles and does not unduly interfere with the steering, braking, or maneuvering of the towing vehicle, or otherwise contribute to the unsafe operation of the vehicles comprising the combination.
  (3) *Saddle-mounted vehicles* must be arranged such that the gross weight of the vehicles is properly distributed to prevent undue interference with the steering, braking, or maneuvering of the combination of vehicles.

(c) Carrying vehicles on towed vehicles.
  (1) *When adequately and securely attached* by means equivalent in security to that provided in paragraph (j)(2) of this section, a motor vehicle or motor vehicles may be full-mounted on the structure of towed vehicles engaged in any driveaway-towaway operation.
  (2) *No motor vehicle shall be full-mounted* on a motor vehicle towed by means of a tow-bar unless the towed vehicle is equipped with brakes and is provided with means for effective application of brakes acting on all wheels and is towed on its own wheels.
  (3) *No motor vehicle or motor vehicles* shall be full-mounted on a motor vehicle towed by means of a saddle-mount unless the center line of the kingpin or equivalent means of attachment of such towed vehicle shall be so located on the towing vehicle that the relationship to the rear axle or axles results in proper distribution of the total gross weight of the vehicles and does not unduly interfere with the steering, braking, or maneuvering of the towing vehicle or otherwise contribute to the unsafe operation of vehicles comprising the combination; and unless a perpendicular to the ground from the center of gravity of the full-mounted vehicles lies forward of the center line of the rear axle of the saddle-mounted vehicle.
  (4) *If a motor vehicle towed* by means of a double saddle-mount has any vehicle full-mounted on it, such saddle-mounted vehicle shall at all times while so loaded have effective brakes acting on those wheels which are in contact with the roadway.

(d) Bumper tow-bars on heavy vehicles prohibited. Tow-bars of the type which depend upon the bumpers as a means of transmitting forces between the vehicles shall not be used to tow a motor vehicle weighing more than 5,000 pounds.

(e) Front wheels of saddle-mounted vehicles restrained. A motor vehicle towed by means of a saddle-mount shall have the motion of the front wheels restrained if under any condition of turning of such wheels they will project beyond the widest part of either the towed or towing vehicle.

(f) Vehicles to be towed in forward position. Unless the steering mechanism is adequately locked in a straight-forward position, all motor vehicles towed by means of a saddle-mount shall be towed with the front end mounted on the towing vehicle.

(g) Means required for towing. No motor vehicles or combination of motor vehicles shall be towed in driveaway-towaway operations by means other than a tow-bar, ball-and-socket type coupling device, saddle-mount connections which meet the requirements of this section, or in the case of a semi-trailer equipped with an upper coupler assembly, a fifth-wheel meeting the requirements of §393.70.

(h) Requirements for tow-bars. Tow-bars shall comply with the following requirements:
  (1) *Tow-bars, structural adequacy and mounting.* Every tow-bar shall be structurally adequate and properly installed and maintained. To insure that it is structurally adequate, it must, at least, meet the requirements of the following table:

Gross weight of towed vehicle (pounds)[1]	Longitudinal strength in tension and compression[2]		Strength as a beam (in any direction concentrated load at center)[2,3]
	All towbars	New towbars acquired and used by a motor carrier after Sept. 30, 1948	
	Pounds		
Less than 5,000	3,000	6,500	3,000
5,000 and over			
Less than 10,000	6,000	([1])	([1])
10,000 and over			
Less than 15,000	9,000	([1])	([1])

1. The required strength of tow-bars for towed vehicles of 15,000 pounds and over gross weight and of new tow-bars acquired and used after Sept. 30, 1948, for towed vehicles of 5,000 pounds and over gross weight shall be computed by means of the following formulae: Longitudinal strength=gross weight of towed vehicle x 1.3. Strength as a beam=gross weight of towed vehicle x 0.6.
2. In testing, the whole unit shall be tested with all clamps, joints, and pins so mounted and fastened as to approximate conditions of actual operation.
3. This test shall be applicable only to tow-bars which are, in normal operation, subjected to a bending movement such as tow-bars for house trailers.

  (2) *Tow-bars, jointed.* The tow-bar shall be so constructed as to freely permit motion in both horizontal and vertical planes between the towed and towing vehicles. The means used to provide the motion shall be such as to prohibit the transmission of stresses under normal operation between the towed and towing vehicles, except along the longitudinal axis of the tongue or tongues.
  (3) *Tow-bar fastenings.* The means used to transmit the stresses to the chassis or frames of the towed and towing vehicles may be either temporary structures or bumpers or other integral parts of the vehicles: Provided, however, That the means used shall be so constructed, installed, and maintained that when tested as an assembly, failure in such members shall not occur when the weakest new tow-bar which is permissible under paragraph (h)(1) of this section is subjected to the tests given therein.
  (4) *Means of adjusting length.* On tow-bars, adjustable as to length, the means used to make such adjustment shall fit tightly and not result in any slackness or permit the tow-bar to bend. With the tow-bar supported rigidly at both ends and with a load of 50 pounds at the center, the sag, measured at the center, in any direction shall not exceed 0.25 inch under any condition of adjustment as to length.
  (5) *Method of clamping.* Adequate means shall be provided for securely fastening the tow-bar to the towed and towing vehicles.
  (6) *Tow-bar connection to steering mechanism.* The tow-bar shall be provided with suitable means of attachment to and actuation of the steering mechanism, if any, of the towed vehicle. The attachment shall provide for sufficient angularity of movement of the front wheels of the towed vehicle so that it may follow substantially in the path of the towing vehicle without cramping the tow-bar. The tow-bar shall be provided with suitable joints to permit such movement.

(7) *Tracking.* The tow-bar shall be so designed, constructed, maintained, and mounted as to cause the towed vehicle to follow substantially in the path of the towing vehicle. Tow-bars of such design or in such condition[1] as to permit the towed vehicle to deviate more than 3 inches to either side of the path of a towing vehicle moving in a straight line as measured from the center of the towing vehicle are prohibited.

(8) *Passenger car-trailer type couplings.* Trailer couplings used for driveaway-towaway operations of passenger car trailers shall conform to Society of Automotive Engineers Standard No. J684c, "Trailer Couplings and Hitches — Automotive Type," July 1970.[2]

(9) *Marking tow-bars.* Every tow-bar acquired and used in driveaway-towaway operations by a motor carrier shall be plainly marked with the following certification of the manufacturer thereof (or words of equivalent meaning):

This tow-bar complies with the requirements of the Federal Motor Carrier Safety Administration for (maximum gross weight for which tow-bar is manufactured) vehicles.

Allowable Maximum Gross Weight _____

Manufactured _____
(month and year)

by _____
(name of manufacturer)

Tow bar certification manufactured before March 7, 1989 must meet requirements in effect at the time of manufacture.

(10) *Safety devices in case of tow-bar failure or disconnection.*

(i) *The towed vehicle* shall be connected to the towing vehicle by a safety device to prevent the towed vehicle from breaking loose in the event the tow-bar fails or becomes disconnected. When safety chains or cables are used as the safety device for that vehicle, at least two safety chains or cables meeting the requirements of paragraph (h)(10)(ii) of this section shall be used. The tensile strength of the safety device and the means of attachment to the vehicles shall be at least equivalent to the corresponding longitudinal strength for tow-bars required in the table of paragraph (h)(1) of this section. If safety chains or cables are used as the safety device, the required strength shall be the combined strength of the combination of chains and cables.

(ii) *If chains or cables are used as the safety device,* they shall be crossed and attached to the vehicles near the points of bumper attachments to the chassis of the vehicles. The length of chain used shall be no more than necessary to permit free turning of the vehicles. The chains shall be attached to the tow-bar at the point of crossing or as close to that point as is practicable.

(iii) *A safety device* other than safety chains or cables must provide strength, security of attachment, and directional stability equal to, or greater than, that provided by safety chains or cables installed in accordance with paragraph (h)(10)(ii) of this section. A safety device other than safety chains or cables must be designed, constructed, and installed so that, if the tow-bar fails or becomes disconnected, the tow-bar will not drop to the ground.

(i) [Reserved]

(j) Requirements for upper-half of saddle-mounts. The upper-half of any saddle-mount shall comply with the following requirements:

(1) *Upper-half connection to towed vehicle.* The upper-half shall be securely attached to the frame or axle of the towed vehicle by means of U-bolts or other means providing at least equivalent security.

(2) *U-bolts or other attachments.* U-bolts used to attach the upper half to the towed vehicle shall be made of steel rod, free of defects, so shaped as to avoid at any point a radius of less than 1 inch: Provided, however, That a lesser radius may be utilized if the U-bolt is so fabricated as not to cause more than 5 percent reduction in cross-sectional area at points of curvature, in which latter event the minimum radius shall be one-sixteenth inch. U-bolts shall have a diameter not less than required by the following table:

Diameter of U-Bolts in Inches

Weight in pounds of heaviest towed vehicle	Double or triple saddle-mount			Single saddle-mount[1]
	Front mount	Middle or front mount	Rear mount	
Up to 5,000	0.625	0.5625	0.500	0.500
5,000 and over	0.6875	0.625	0.5625	0.5625

1. The total weight of all the vehicles being towed shall govern. If other devices are used to accomplish the same purposes as U-bolts they shall have at least equivalent strength of U-bolts made of mild steel. Cast iron shall not be used for clamps or any other holding devices.

(3) *U-bolts and points of support, location.* The distance between the most widely separated U-bolts shall not be less than 9 inches. The distance between the widely separated points where the upper-half supports the towed vehicle shall not be less than 9 inches, except that saddle-mounts employing ball and socket joints shall employ a device which clamps the axle of the towed vehicle throughout a length of not less than 5 inches.

(4) *Cradle-type upper-halves, specifications.* Upper-halves of the cradle-type using vertical members to restrain the towed vehicle from relative movement in the direction of motion of the vehicles shall be substantially constructed and adequate for the purpose. Such cradle-mounts shall be equipped with at least one bolt or equivalent means to provide against relative vertical movement between the upper-half and the towed vehicle. Bolts, if used, shall be at least one-half inch in diameter. Devices using equivalent means shall have at least equivalent strength. The means used to provide against relative vertical motion between the upper-half and the towed vehicle shall be such as not to permit a relative motion of over one-half inch. The distance between the most widely separated points of support between the upper-half and the towed vehicle shall be at least 9 inches.

(5) *Lateral movement of towed vehicle.*

(i) *Towed vehicles having a straight axle* or an axle having a drop of less than 3 inches, unless the saddle-mount is constructed in accordance with paragraph (m)(2) of this section, shall be securely fastened by means of chains or cables to the upper-half so as to insure against relative lateral motion between the towed vehicle and the upper-half. The chains or cables shall be at least 3/16-inch diameter and secured by bolts of at least equal diameter.

(ii) *Towed vehicles* with an axle with a drop of 3 inches or more, or connected by a saddle-mount constructed in accordance with paragraph (m)(2) of this section, need not be restrained by chains or cables provided that the upper-half is so designed as to provide against such relative motion.

(iii) *Chains or cables shall not be required* if the upper-half is so designed as positively to provide against lateral movement of the axle.

(k) Requirements for lower half of saddle-mounts. The lower half of any saddle-mount shall comply with the following requirements:

(1) *U-bolts or other attachments.* U-bolts used to attach the lower half to the towing vehicle shall be made of steel rod, free of defects, so shaped as to avoid at any point a radius of less than 1 inch: Provided, however, That a lesser radius may be utilized if the U-bolt is so fabricated as not to cause more than 5 percent reduction in cross-sectional area at points of curvature, in which latter event the minimum radius shall be one-sixteenth inch. U-bolts shall have a total cross-sectional area not less than as required by the following table:

Total Cross-Sectional Area of U-Bolts in Square Inches

Weight in pounds of heaviest towed vehicle	Double or triple saddle-mount			Single saddle-mount[1]
	Front mount	Middle or front mount	Rear mount	
Up to 5,000	1.2	1.0	0.8	0.8
5,000 and over	1.4	1.2	1.0	1.0

1. The total weight of all the vehicles being towed shall govern. If other devices are used to accomplish the same purposes as U-bolts they shall have at least equivalent strength of U-bolts made of mild steel. Cast iron shall not be used for clamps or any other holding devices.

---

1. Editor's Note: The phrase 'or in such condition' in the text above replaces the phrase 'on in our condition' in the CFR.
2. Editor's Note: The CFR contains the following footnote at this location: 'See footnote to §393.24(c).' However, the footnote to §393.24(c) was removed following an amendment that appeared in the August 15, 2005, Federal Register.

Subpart F - Coupling Devices and Towing Methods §393.71 (m)

(2) *Shifting.* Adequate provision shall be made by design and installation to provide against relative movement between the lower-half and the towing vehicle especially during periods of rapid acceleration and deceleration. To insure against shifting, designs of the tripod type shall be equipped with adequate and securely fastened hold-back chains or similar devices.

(3) *Swaying.*
  (i) *Adequate provision* shall be made by design and installation to provide against swaying or lateral movement of the towed vehicle relative to the towing vehicle. To insure against swaying, lower-halves designed with cross-members attached to but separable from vertical members shall have such cross-members fastened to the vertical members by at least two bolts on each side. Such bolts shall be of at least equivalent cross-sectional area as those required for U-bolts for the corresponding saddle-mount as given in the table in paragraph (k)(1) of this section. The minimum distance between the most widely separated points of support of the cross-member by the vertical member shall be three inches as measured in a direction parallel to the longitudinal axis of the towing vehicle.
  (ii) *The lower-half* shall have a bearing surface on the frame of the towing vehicle of such dimensions that the pressure exerted by the lower-half upon the frame of the towing vehicle shall not exceed 200 pounds per square inch under any conditions of static loading. Hardwood blocks or blocks of other suitable material, such as hard rubber, aluminum or brakelining, if used between the lower half and the frame of the towing vehicle shall be at least 1/2 inch thick, 3 inches wide, and a combined length of 6 inches.
  (iii) *Under no condition* shall the highest point of support of the towed vehicle by the upper-half be more than 24 inches, measured vertically, above the top of the frame of the towing vehicle, measured at the point where the lower-half rests on the towing vehicle.

(4) *Wood blocks.*
  (i) *Hardwood blocks of good quality* may be used to build up the height of the front end of the towed vehicle, provided that the total height of such wood blocks shall not exceed 8 inches and not over two separate pieces are placed upon each other to obtain such height; however, hardwood blocks, not over 4 in number, to a total height not to exceed 14 inches, may be used if the total cross-sectional area of the U-bolts used to attach the lower-half of the towing vehicle is at least 50 percent greater than that required by the table contained in paragraph (k)(1) of this section, or, if other devices are used in lieu of U-bolts, they shall provide for as great a resistance to bending as is provided by the larger U-bolts above prescribed.
  (ii) *Hardwood blocks* must be at least 4 inches in width and the surfaces between blocks or block and lower-half or block and upper-half shall be planed and so installed and maintained as to minimize any tendency of the towed vehicle to sway or rock.

(5) *Cross-member, general requirements.* The cross-member, which is that part of the lower-half used to distribute the weight of the towed vehicle equally to each member of the frame of the towing vehicle, if used, shall be structurally adequate and properly installed and maintained adequately to perform this function.

(6) *Cross-member, use of wood.* No materials, other than suitable metals, shall be used as the cross-member, and wood may not be used structurally in any manner that will result in its being subject to tensile stresses. Wood may be used in cross-members if supported throughout its length by suitable metal cross-members.

(7) *Lower half strength.* The lower half shall be capable of supporting the loads given in the following table. For the purpose of test, the saddle-mount shall be mounted as normally operated and the load applied through the upper half:

Minimum Test Load in Pounds

Weight in pounds of heaviest towed vehicle	Double or triple saddle-mount			Single saddle-mount[1]
	Front mount	Middle or front mount	Rear mount	
Up to 5,000	15,000	10,000	5,000	5,000
5,000 and over	30,000	20,000	10,000	10,000

1. The total weight of all the vehicles being towed shall govern.

(l) **Requirements for kingpins of saddle-mounts.** The kingpin of any saddle-mount shall comply with the following requirements:
  (1) *Kingpin size.*
    (i) *Kingpins shall be constructed of steel* suitable for the purpose, free of defects, and having a diameter not less than required by the following table:

Diameter of Solid Kingpin in Inches

Weight in pounds of heaviest towed vehicle	Double or triple saddle-mount						Single saddle-mount[1]	
	Front mount		Middle or front mount		Rear mount			
	Mild steel	H.T.S.[2]	Mild steel	H.T.S.[2]	Mild steel	H.T.S.[2]	Mild steel	H.T.S.[2]
Up to 5,000	1.125	1.000	1.000	0.875	0.875	0.750	0.875	0.750
5,000 and over	1.500	1.125	1.250	1.000	1.000	0.875	1.000	0.875

1. The total weight of all the vehicles being towed shall govern.
2. High-tensile steel is steel having a minimum ultimate strength of 65,000 pounds per square inch.

  (ii) *If a ball and socket joint* is used in place of a kingpin, the diameter of the neck of the ball shall be at least equal to the diameter of the corresponding solid kingpin given in the above table. If hollow kingpins are used, the metallic cross-sectional area shall be at least equal to the cross-sectional area of the corresponding solid kingpin.

  (2) *Kingpin fit.* If a kingpin bushing is not used, the king-pin shall fit snugly into the upper and lower-halves but shall not bind. Those portions of the upper or lower-halves in moving contact with the kingpin shall be smoothly machined with no rough or sharp edges. The bearing surface thus provided shall not be less in depth than the radius of the kingpin.

  (3) *Kingpin bushing on saddle-mounts.* The kingpin of all new saddle-mounts acquired and used shall be snugly enclosed in a bushing at least along such length of the kingpin as may be in moving contact with either the upper or lower-halves. The bearing surface thus provided shall not be less in depth than the radius of the kingpin.

  (4) *Kingpin to restrain vertical motion.* The kingpin shall be so designed and installed as to restrain the upper-half from moving in a vertical direction relative to the lower-half.

(m) **Additional requirements for saddle-mounts.** Saddle-mounts shall comply with the following requirements:
  (1) *Bearing surface between upper and lower-halves.* The upper and lower-halves shall be so constructed and connected that the bearing surface between the two halves shall not be less than 16 square inches under any conditions of angularity between the towing and towed vehicles: Provided, however, That saddle-mounts using a ball and socket joint shall have a ball of such dimension that the static bearing load shall not exceed 800 pounds per square inch, based on the projected cross-sectional area of the ball: And further provided, That saddle-mounts having the upper-half supported by ball, taper, or roller-bearings shall not have such bearings loaded beyond the limits prescribed for such bearings by the manufacturer thereof. The upper-half shall rest evenly and smoothly upon the lower-half and the contact surfaces shall be lubricated and maintained so that there shall be a minimum of frictional resistance between the parts.
  (2) *Saddle-mounts, angularity.* All saddle-mounts acquired and used shall provide for angularity between the towing and towed vehicles due to vertical curvatures of the highway. Such means shall not depend upon either the looseness or deformation of the parts of either the saddle-mount or the vehicles to provide for such angularity.
  (3) *Tracking.* The saddle-mount shall be so designed, constructed, maintained, and installed that the towed vehicle or vehicles will follow substantially in the path of the towing vehicle without swerving. Towed vehicles shall not deviate more than 3 inches to either side of the path of the towing vehicle when moving in a straight line.
  (4) *Prevention of frame bending.* Where necessary, provision shall be made to prevent the bending of the frame of the towing vehicle by insertion of suitable blocks inside the frame channel to prevent kinking. The saddle-mount shall not be so located as to cause deformation of the frame by reason of cantilever action.

(5) *Extension of frame.* No saddle-mount shall be located at a point to the rear of the frame of a towing vehicle.

(6) *Nuts, secured.* All nuts used on bolts, U-bolts, king-pins, or in any other part of the saddle-mount shall be secured against accidental disconnection by means of cotter-keys, lock-washers, double nuts, safety nuts, or equivalent means. Parts shall be so designed and installed that nuts shall be fully engaged.

(7) *Inspection of all parts.* The saddle-mount shall be so designed that it may be disassembled and each separate part inspected for worn, bent, cracked, broken, or missing parts.

(8) *Saddle-mounts, marking.* Every new saddle-mount acquired and used in driveaway-towaway operations by a motor carrier shall have the upper-half and the lower-half separately marked with the following certification of the manufacturer thereof (or words of equivalent meaning).

This saddle-mount complies with the requirements of the Federal Motor Carrier Safety Administration for vehicles up to 5,000 pounds (or over 5,000 pounds):

Manufactured _____
(month and year)

by _____
(name of manufacturer)

(n) **Requirements for devices** used to connect motor vehicles or parts of motor vehicles together to form one vehicle.

(1) *Front axle attachment.* The front axle of one motor vehicle intended to be coupled with another vehicle as defined in paragraph (g)(2)(ii) of this section shall be attached with U-bolts meeting the requirements of paragraph (j)(2) of this section.

(2) *Rear axle attachment.* The rear axle of one vehicle shall be coupled to the frame of the other vehicle by means of a connecting device which when in place forms a rectangle. The device shall be composed of two pieces, top and bottom. The device shall be made of 4-inch by 1/2-inch steel bar bent to shape and shall have the corners reinforced with a plate at least 3 inches by 1/2 inch by 8 inches long. The device shall be bolted together with 3/4-inch bolts and at least three shall be used on each side. Wood may be used as spacers to keep the frames apart and it shall be at least 4 inches square.

§393.71 DOT Interpretations

Question 1: May a fifth wheel be considered as a coupling device when towing a semi-trailer in a driveaway-towaway operation?

Guidance: Yes. §393.71(g) requires the use of a tow-bar or a saddle-mount. Since a saddle-mount performs the function of a conventional fifth wheel, the use of a fifth wheel is consistent with the requirements of this section.

Subpart G - Miscellaneous Parts and Accessories

§393.75 Tires.

(a) **No motor vehicle shall be operated on any tire that —**
(1) *has body ply or belt material* exposed through the tread or sidewall,
(2) *has any tread or sidewall separation,*
(3) *is flat or has an audible leak,* or
(4) *has a cut to the extent that the ply or belt material is exposed.*

(b) **Any tire on the front wheels** of a bus, truck, or truck tractor shall have a tread groove pattern depth of at least 4/32 of an inch when measured at any point on a major tread groove. The measurements shall not be made where tie bars, humps, or fillets are located.

(c) **Except as provided in paragraph (b) of this section,** tires shall have a tread groove pattern depth of at least 2/32 of an inch when measured in a major tread groove. The measurement shall not be made where tie bars, humps or fillets are located.

(d) **No bus shall be operated** with regrooved, recapped or retreaded tires on the front wheels.

(e) **A regrooved tire with a load-carrying capacity** equal to or greater than 2,232 kg (4,920 pounds) shall not be used on the front wheels of any truck or truck tractor.

(f) **Tire loading restrictions** (except on manufactured homes). No motor vehicle (except manufactured homes, which are governed by paragraph (g) of this section) shall be operated with tires that carry a weight greater than that marked on the sidewall of the tire or, in the absence of such a marking, a weight greater than that specified for the tires in any of the publications of any of the organizations listed in Federal Motor Vehicle Safety Standard No. 119 (49 CFR 571.119, S5.1(b)) unless:

(1) *The vehicle is being operated* under the terms of a special permit issued by the State; and
(2) *The vehicle is being operated* at a reduced speed to compensate for the tire loading in excess of the manufacturer's rated capacity for the tire. In no case shall the speed exceed 80 km/hr (50 mph).

(g) (1) *Tire loading restrictions for manufactured homes* built before January 1, 2002. Manufactured homes that are labeled pursuant to 24 CFR 3282.362 (c)(2)(i) before January 1, 2002, must not be transported on tires that are loaded more than 18 percent over the load rating marked on the sidewall of the tire or, in the absence of such a marking, more than 18 percent over the load rating specified in any of the publications of any of the organizations listed in FMVSS No. 119 (49 CFR 571.119, S5.1(b)). Manufactured homes labeled before January 1, 2002, transported on tires overloaded by 9 percent or more must not be operated at speeds exceeding 80 km/hr (50 mph).

(2) *Tire loading restrictions for manufactured homes* built on or after January 1, 2002. Manufactured homes that are labeled pursuant to 24 CFR 3282.362 (c)(2)(i) on or after January 1, 2002, must not be transported on tires loaded beyond the load rating marked on the sidewall of the tire or, in the absence of such a marking, the load rating specified in any of the publications of any of the organizations listed in FMVSS No. 119 (49 CFR 571.119, S5.1(b)).

(h) *Tire inflation pressure.*
(1) *No motor vehicle shall be operated on a tire* which has a cold inflation pressure less than that specified for the load being carried.
(2) *If the inflation pressure of the tire* has been increased by heat because of the recent operation of the vehicle, the cold inflation pressure shall be estimated by subtracting the inflation buildup factor shown in Table 1 from the measured inflation pressure.

Table 1 - Inflation Pressure Measurement Correction for Heat

Average speed of vehicle in the previous hour	Minimum inflation pressure buildup	
	Tires with 1,814 kg (4,000 lbs.) maximum load rating or less	Tires with over 1,814 kg (4,000 lbs.) load rating
66-88.5 km/hr (41-55 mph)	34.5 kPa (5 psi)	103.4 kPa (15 psi)

§393.75 DOT Interpretations

Question 1: If a CMV has a defective tire, may the driver remove the defective tire from the axle and drive with three tires on an axle instead of four?

Guidance: Yes, provided the weight on all of the remaining tires does not exceed the maximum allowed under §393.75(f).

Question 2: May a CMV be operated with tires that carry a greater weight than the weight marked on the sidewall of the tires?

Guidance: Yes, but only if the CMV is being operated under the terms of a State-issued special permit, and at a reduced speed that is appropriate to compensate for tire loading in excess of the rated capacity.

Question 3: May a vehicle transport HM when equipped with retreaded tires?

Guidance: Yes. The only CMV that may not utilize retreaded tires is a bus, and then only on its front wheels.

Question 4: May tires be filled with materials other than air (e.g., silicone, polyurethane)?

Guidance: §393.75 does not prohibit the use of tires filled with material other than air. However, §393.3 may prohibit the use of such tires under certain circumstances. Some substances used in place of air in tires may not maintain a constant physical state at different temperatures. While these substances are solid at lower temperatures, the increase in temperature from highway use may result in the substance changing from a solid to a liquid. The use of a substance which could undergo such a change in its physical characteristics is not safe, and is not in compliance with §393.3.

Subpart G - Miscellaneous Parts and Accessories

§393.76 Sleeper berths.
(a) Dimensions.
(1) *Size.* A sleeper berth must be at least the following size:

Date of installation on motor vehicle	Length measured on centerline of longitudinal axis (inches)	Width measured on centerline of transverse axis (inches)	Height measured from highest point of top of mattress (inches)[1]
Before Jan. 1, 1953	72	18	18
After Dec. 31, 1952, and before Oct. 1, 1975	75	21	21
After Sept. 30, 1975	75	24	24

1. In the case of a sleeper berth which utilizes an adjustable mechanical suspension system, the required clearance can be measured when the suspension system is adjusted to the height to which it would settle when occupied by a driver.

(2) *Shape.* A sleeper berth installed on a motor vehicle on or after January 1, 1953 must be of generally rectangular shape, except that the horizontal corners and the roof corners may be rounded to radii not exceeding 10 1/2 inches.

(3) *Access.* A sleeper berth must be constructed so that an occupant's ready entrance to, and exit from, the sleeper berth is not unduly hindered.

(b) Location.
(1) *A sleeper berth must not be installed* in or on a semitrailer or a full trailer other than a house trailer.

(2) *A sleeper berth located* within the cargo space of a motor vehicle must be securely compartmentalized from the remainder of the cargo space. A sleeper berth installed on or after January 1, 1953 must be located in the cab or immediately adjacent to the cab and must be securely fixed with relation to the cab.

(c) Exit from the berth.
(1) *Except as provided* in paragraph (c)(2) of this section, there must be a direct and ready means of exit from a sleeper berth into the driver's seat or compartment. If the sleeper berth was installed on or after January 1, 1963, the exit must be a doorway or opening at least 18 inches high and 36 inches wide. If the sleeper berth was installed before January 1, 1963, the exit must have sufficient area to contain an ellipse having a major axis of 24 inches and a minor axis of 16 inches.

(2) *A sleeper berth installed before January 1, 1953 must either:*
  (i) *Conform to the requirements* of paragraph (c)(1) of this section; or
  (ii) *Have at least two exits,* each of which is at least 18 inches high and 21 inches wide, located at opposite ends of the vehicle and useable by the occupant without the assistance of any other person.

(d) Communication with the driver. A sleeper berth which is not located within the driver's compartment and has no direct entrance into the driver's compartment must be equipped with a means of communication between the occupant and the driver. The means of communication may consist of a telephone, speaker tube, buzzer, pull cord, or other mechanical or electrical device.

(e) Equipment. A sleeper berth must be properly equipped for sleeping. Its equipment must include:
(1) Adequate bedclothing and blankets; and
(2) Either:
  (i) Springs and a mattress; or
  (ii) An innerspring mattress; or
  (iii) A cellular rubber or flexible foam mattress at least four inches thick; or
  (iv) A mattress filled with a fluid and of sufficient thickness when filled to prevent "bottoming-out" when occupied while the vehicle is in motion.

(f) Ventilation. A sleeper berth must have louvers or other means of providing adequate ventilation. A sleeper berth must be reasonably tight against dust and rain.

(g) Protection against exhaust and fuel leaks and exhaust heat. A sleeper berth must be located so that leaks in the vehicle's exhaust system or fuel system do not permit fuel, fuel system gases, or exhaust gases to enter the sleeper berth. A sleeper berth must be located so that it will not be overheated or damaged by reason of its proximity to the vehicle's exhaust system.

(h) Occupant restraint. A motor vehicle manufactured on or after July 1, 1971, and equipped with a sleeper berth must be equipped with a means of preventing ejection of the occupant of the sleeper berth during deceleration of the vehicle. The restraint system must be designed, installed, and maintained to withstand a minimum total force of 6,000 pounds applied toward the front of the vehicle and parallel to the longitudinal axis of the vehicle.

§393.76 DOT Interpretations
Question 1: If a compartment in a CMV is no longer used as a sleeper berth, must it be maintained and equipped as a sleeper berth as required in §393.76?
Guidance: No.

§393.77 Heaters.
On every motor vehicle, every heater shall comply with the following requirements:

(a) Prohibited types of heaters. The installation or use of the following types of heaters is prohibited:
(1) *Exhaust heaters.* Any type of exhaust heater in which the engine exhaust gases are conducted into or through any space occupied by persons or any heater which conducts engine compartment air into any such space.
(2) *Unenclosed flame heaters.* Any type of heater employing a flame which is not fully enclosed, except that such heaters are not prohibited when used for heating the cargo of tank motor vehicles.
(3) *Heaters permitting fuel leakage.* Any type of heater from the burner of which there could be spillage or leakage of fuel upon the tilting or overturning of the vehicle in which it is mounted.
(4) *Heaters permitting air contamination.* Any heater taking air, heated or to be heated, from the engine compartment or from direct contact with any portion of the exhaust system; or any heater taking air in ducts from the outside atmosphere to be conveyed through the engine compartment, unless said ducts are so constructed and installed as to prevent contamination of the air so conveyed by exhaust or engine compartment gases.
(5) *Solid fuel heaters except wood charcoal.* Any stove or other heater employing solid fuel except wood charcoal.
(6) *Portable heaters.* Portable heaters shall not be used in any space occupied by persons except the cargo space of motor vehicles which are being loaded or unloaded.

(b) Heater specifications. All heaters shall comply with the following specifications:
(1) *Heating elements, protection.* Every heater shall be so located or protected as to prevent contact therewith by occupants, unless the surface temperature of the protecting grilles or of any exposed portions of the heaters, inclusive of exhaust stacks, pipes, or conduits shall be lower than would cause contact burns. Adequate protection shall be afforded against igniting parts of the vehicle or burning occupants by direct radiation. Wood charcoal heaters shall be enclosed within a metal barrel, drum, or similar protective enclosure which enclosure shall be provided with a securely fastened cover.
(2) *Moving parts, guards.* Effective guards shall be provided for the protection of passengers or occupants against injury by fans, belts, or any other moving parts.
(3) *Heaters, secured.* Every heater and every heater enclosure shall be securely fastened to the vehicle in a substantial manner so as to provide against relative motion within the vehicle during normal usage or in the event the vehicle overturns. Every heater shall be so designed, constructed, and mounted as to minimize the likelihood of disassembly of any of its parts, including exhaust stacks, pipes, or conduits, upon overturn of the vehicle in or on which it is mounted. Wood charcoal heaters shall be secured against relative motion within the enclosure required by paragraph (c)(1) of this section, and the enclosure shall be securely fastened to the motor vehicle.
(4) *Relative motion between fuel tank and heater.* When either in normal operation or in the event of overturn, there is or is likely to be relative motion between the fuel tank for a heater and the heater, or between either of such units and the fuel lines between them, a suitable means shall be provided at the point of greatest relative motion so as to allow this motion without causing failure of the fuel lines.
(5) *Operating controls to be protected.* On every bus designed to transport more than 15 passengers, including the driver, means shall be provided to prevent unauthorized persons from tampering with the operating controls. Such means may include remote control by the driver; installation of controls at inaccessible places; control of adjustments by key or keys;

§393.78

enclosure of controls in a locked space, locking of controls, or other means of accomplishing this purpose.

(6) *Heater hoses.* Hoses for all hot water and steam heater systems shall be specifically designed and constructed for that purpose.

(7) *Electrical apparatus.* Every heater employing any electrical apparatus shall be equipped with electrical conductors, switches, connectors, and other electrical parts of ample current-carrying capacity to provide against overheating; any electric motor employed in any heater shall be of adequate size and so located that it will not be overheated; electrical circuits shall be provided with fuses and/or circuit breakers to provide against electrical overloading; and all electrical conductors employed in or leading to any heater shall be secured against dangling, chafing, and rubbing and shall have suitable protection against any other condition likely to produce short or open circuits.

NOTE: Electrical parts certified as proper for use by Underwriters' Laboratories, Inc., shall be deemed to comply with the foregoing requirements.

(8) *Storage battery caps.* If a separate storage battery is located within the personnel or cargo space, such battery shall be securely mounted and equipped with nonspill filler caps.

(9) *Combustion heater exhaust construction.* Every heater employing the combustion of oil, gas, liquefied petroleum gas, or any other combustible material shall be provided with substantial means of conducting the products of combustion to the outside of the vehicle: Provided, however, That this requirement shall not apply to heaters used solely to heat the cargo space of motor vehicles where such motor vehicles or heaters are equipped with means specifically designed and maintained so that the carbon monoxide concentration will never exceed 0.2 percent in the cargo space. The exhaust pipe, stack, or conduit if required shall be sufficiently substantial and so secured as to provide reasonable assurance against leakage or discharge of products of combustion within the vehicle and, if necessary, shall be so insulated as to make unlikely the burning or charring of parts of the vehicle by radiation or by direct contact. The place of discharge of the products of combustion to the atmosphere and the means of discharge of such products shall be such as to minimize the likelihood of their reentry into the vehicle under all operating conditions.

(10) *Combustion chamber construction.* The design and construction of any combustion-type heater except cargo space heaters permitted by the proviso of paragraph (c)(9) of this section and unenclosed flame heaters used for heating cargo of tank motor vehicles shall be such as to provide against the leakage of products of combustion into air to be heated and circulated. The material employed in combustion chambers shall be such as to provide against leakage because of corrosion, oxidation, or other deterioration. Joints between combustion chambers and the air chambers with which they are in thermal and mechanical contact shall be so designed and constructed as to prevent leakage between the chambers and the materials employed in such joints shall have melting points substantially higher than the maximum temperatures likely to be attained at the points of jointure.

(11) *Heater fuel tank location.* Every bus designed to transport more than 15 passengers, including the driver, with heaters of the combustion type shall have fuel tanks therefor located outside of and lower than the passenger space. When necessary, suitable protection shall be afforded by shielding or other means against the puncturing of any such tank or its connections by flying stones or other objects.

(12) *Heater, automatic fuel control.* Gravity or siphon feed shall not be permitted for heaters using liquid fuels. Heaters using liquid fuels shall be equipped with automatic means for shutting off the fuel or for reducing such flow of fuel to the smallest practicable magnitude, in the event of overturn of the vehicle. Heaters using liquefied petroleum gas as fuel shall have the fuel line equipped with automatic means at the source of supply for shutting off the fuel in the event of separation, breakage, or disconnection of any of the fuel lines between the supply source and the heater.

(13) *"Tell-tale" indicators.* Heaters subject to paragraph (c)(14) of this section and not provided with automatic controls shall be provided with "tell-tale" means to indicate to the driver that the heater is properly functioning. This requirement shall not apply to heaters used solely for the cargo space in semitrailers or full trailers.

(14) *Shut-off control.* Automatic means, or manual means if the control is readily accessible to the driver without moving from the driver's seat, shall be provided to shut off the fuel and electrical supply in case of failure of the heater to function for any reason, or in case the heater should function improperly or overheat. This requirement shall not apply to wood charcoal heaters or to heaters used solely to heat the contents of cargo tank motor vehicles, but wood charcoal heaters must be provided with a controlled method of regulating the flow of combustion air.

(15) *Certification required.* Every combustion-type heater, except wood charcoal heaters, the date of manufacture of which is subsequent to December 31, 1952, and every wood charcoal heater, the date of manufacture of which is subsequent to September 1, 1953, shall be marked plainly to indicate the type of service for which such heater is designed and with a certification by the manufacturer that the heater meets the applicable requirements for such use. For example, "Meets I.C.C. Bus Heater Requirements," "Meets I.C.C. Flue-Vented Cargo Space Heater Requirements," and after December 31, 1967, such certification shall read "Meets FMCSA Bus Heater Requirements," "Meets FMCSA Flue-Vented Cargo Space Heater Requirements," etc.

(i) *Exception.* The certification for a catalytic heater which is used in transporting flammable liquid or gas shall be as prescribed under §177.834(l) of this title.

§393.78 Windshield wiping and washing systems.

(a) **Vehicles manufactured on or after December 25, 1968.** Each bus, truck, and truck-tractor manufactured on or after December 25, 1968, must have a windshield wiping system that meets the requirements of FMVSS No. 104 (S4.1) in effect on the date of manufacture. Each of these vehicles must have a windshield washing system that meets the requirements of FMVSS No. 104 (S4.2.2) in effect on the date of manufacture.

(b) **Vehicles manufactured between June 30, 1953,** and December 24, 1968. Each truck, truck-tractor, and bus manufactured between June 30, 1953, and December 24, 1968, shall be equipped with a power-driven windshield wiping system with at least two wiper blades, one on each side of the centerline of the windshield. Motor vehicles which depend upon vacuum to operate the windshield wipers, shall have the wiper system constructed and maintained such that the performance of the wipers will not be adversely affected by a change in the intake manifold pressure.

(c) **Driveaway-towaway operations.** Windshield wiping and washing systems need not be in working condition while a commercial motor vehicle is being towed in a driveaway-towaway operation.

§393.78 DOT Interpretations
Question 1: Are windshield washer systems required?
Guidance: No, only windshield wipers are required.

§393.79 Windshield defrosting and defogging systems.

(a) **Vehicles manufactured on or after December 25, 1968.** Each bus, truck, and truck-tractor manufactured on or after December 25, 1968, must have a windshield defrosting and defogging system that meets the requirements of FMVSS No. 103 in effect on the date of manufacture.

(b) **Vehicles manufactured before December 25, 1968.** Each bus, truck, and truck-tractor shall be equipped with a means for preventing the accumulation of ice, snow, frost, or condensation that could obstruct the driver's view through the windshield while the vehicle is being driven.

§393.80 Rear-vision mirrors.

(a) **Every bus, truck, and truck tractor shall be equipped** with two rear-vision mirrors, one at each side, firmly attached to the outside of the motor vehicle, and so located as to reflect to the driver a view of the highway to the rear, along both sides of the vehicle. All such regulated rear-vision mirrors and their replacements shall meet, as a minimum, the requirements of FMVSS No. 111 (49 CFR 571.111) in force at the time the vehicle was manufactured.

(b) **Exceptions.**

(1) *Mirrors installed on a vehicle manufactured* prior to January 1, 1981, may be continued in service, provided that if the mirrors are replaced they shall be replaced with mirrors meeting, as a minimum, the requirements of FMVSS No. 111 (49 CFR 571.111) in force at the time the vehicle was manufactured.

(2) *Only one outside mirror shall be required,* which shall be on the driver's side, on trucks which are so constructed that the driver has a view to the rear by means of an interior mirror.

Subpart G - Miscellaneous Parts and Accessories §393.86 (b)

(3) *In driveway-towaway operations,* the driven vehicle shall have at least one mirror furnishing a clear view to the rear.

§393.81 Horn.

Every bus, truck, truck-tractor, and every driven motor vehicle in driveaway-towaway operations shall be equipped with a horn and actuating elements which shall be in such condition as to give an adequate and reliable warning signal.

§393.81 DOT Interpretations
Question 1: Do the FMCSRs specify what type of horn is to be used on a CMV?
Guidance: No.
Question 2: Are there established criteria in the FMCSRs to determine the minimum sound level of horns on CMVs?
Guidance: No.

§393.82 Speedometer.

Each bus, truck, and truck-tractor must be equipped with a speedometer indicating vehicle speed in miles per hour and/or kilometers per hour. The speedometer must be accurate to within plus or minus 8 km/hr (5 mph) at a speed of 80 km/hr (50 mph).

§393.82 DOT Interpretations
Question 1: What does the phrase "reasonable accuracy" mean?
Guidance: "Reasonable accuracy" is interpreted to mean accuracy to within plus or minus 5 mph at a speed of 50 mph.

§393.83 Exhaust systems.

(a) **Every motor vehicle having a device** (other than as part of its cargo) capable of expelling harmful combustion fumes shall have a system to direct the discharge of such fumes. No part shall be located where its location would likely result in burning, charring, or damaging the electrical wiring, the fuel supply, or any combustible part of the motor vehicle.

(b) **No exhaust system shall discharge to the atmosphere** at a location immediately below the fuel tank or the fuel tank filler pipe.

(c) **The exhaust system of a bus** powered by a gasoline engine shall discharge to the atmosphere at or within 6 inches forward of the rearmost part of the bus.

(d) **The exhaust system of a bus** using fuels other than gasoline shall discharge to the atmosphere either:
  (1) *At or within 15 inches forward* of the rearmost part of the vehicle; or
  (2) *To the rear of all doors or windows* designed to be open, except windows designed to be opened solely as emergency exits.

(e) **The exhaust system of every truck and truck tractor** shall discharge to the atmosphere at a location to the rear of the cab or, if the exhaust projects above the cab, at a location near the rear of the cab.

(f) **No part of the exhaust system** shall be temporarily repaired with wrap or patches.

(g) **No part of the exhaust system** shall leak or discharge at a point forward of or directly below the driver/sleeper compartment. The exhaust outlet may discharge above the cab/sleeper roofline.

(h) **The exhaust system must be securely fastened to the vehicle.**

(i) **Exhaust systems may use hangers** which permit required movement due to expansion and contraction caused by heat of the exhaust and relative motion between engine and chassis of a vehicle.

§393.83 DOT Interpretations
Question 1: Is a heat shield mandatory on a vertical exhaust stack?
Guidance: No. However, §393.83 requires the placement of the exhaust system in such a manner as to prevent the burning, charring, or damaging of the electrical wiring, the fuel supply, or any combustible part of the CMV.
Question 2: Does §393.83 specify the type of exhaust system, vertical or horizontal, to be used on trucks or truck tractors?
Guidance: No.

§393.84 Floors.

The flooring in all motor vehicles shall be substantially constructed, free of unnecessary holes and openings, and shall be maintained so as to minimize the entrance of fumes, exhaust gases, or fire. Floors shall not be permeated with oil or other substances likely to cause injury to persons using the floor as a traction surface.

§393.85 [Reserved]

§393.86 Rear impact guards and rear end protection.

(a) (1) *General requirements* for trailers and semitrailers manufactured on or after January 26, 1998. Each trailer and semitrailer with a gross vehicle weight rating of 4,536 kg (10,000 pounds) or more, and manufactured on or after January 26, 1998, must be equipped with a rear impact guard that meets the requirements of Federal Motor Vehicle Safety Standard No. 223 (49 CFR 571.223) in effect at the time the vehicle was manufactured. When the rear impact guard is installed on the trailer or semitrailer, the vehicle must, at a minimum, meet the requirements of FMVSS No. 224 (49 CFR 571.224) in effect at the time the vehicle was manufactured. The requirements of paragraph (a) of this section do not apply to pole trailers (as defined in §390.5 of this chapter); pulpwood trailers, low chassis vehicles, special purpose vehicles, wheels back vehicles (as defined in §393.5); and trailers towed in driveaway-towaway operations (as defined in §390.5).

(2) *Impact guard width.* The outermost surfaces of the horizontal member of the guard must extend to within 100 mm (4 inches) of the side extremities of the vehicle. The outermost surface of the horizontal member shall not extend beyond the side extremity of the vehicle.

(3) *Guard height.* The vertical distance between the bottom edge of the horizontal member of the guard and the ground shall not exceed 560 mm (22 inches) at any point across the full width of the member. Guards with rounded corners may curve upward within 255 mm (10 inches) of the longitudinal vertical planes that are tangent to the side extremities of the vehicle.

(4) *Guard rear surface.* At any height 560 mm (22 inches) or more above the ground, the rearmost surface of the horizontal member of the guard must be within 305 mm (12 inches) of the rear extremity of the vehicle. This paragraph shall not be construed to prohibit the rear surface of the guard from extending beyond the rear extremity of the vehicle. Guards with rounded corners may curve forward within 255 mm (10 inches) of the side extremity.

(5) *Cross-sectional vertical height.* The horizontal member of each guard must have a cross sectional vertical height of at least 100 mm (3.94 inches) at any point across the guard width.

(6) *Certification and labeling requirements* for rear impact protection guards. Each rear impact guard used to satisfy the requirements of paragraph (a)(1) of this section must be permanently marked or labeled as required by FMVSS No. 223 (49 CFR 571.223, S5.3). The label must be on the forward-facing surface of the horizontal member of the guard, 305 mm (12 inches) inboard of the right end of the guard. The certification label must contain the following information:
  (i) *The impact guard manufacturer's name and address;*
  (ii) *The statement* "Manufactured in _____" (inserting the month and year that the guard was manufactured); and
  (iii) *The letters "DOT,"* constituting a certification by the guard manufacturer that the guard conforms to all requirements of FMVSS No. 223.

(b) (1) *Requirements for motor vehicles* manufactured after December 31, 1952 (except trailers or semitrailers manufactured on or after January 26, 1998). Each motor vehicle manufactured after December 31, 1952, (except truck tractors, pole trailers, pulpwood trailers, or vehicles in driveaway-towaway operations) in which the vertical distance between the rear bottom edge of the body (or the chassis assembly if the chassis is the rearmost part of the vehicle) and the ground is greater than 76.2 cm (30 inches) when the motor vehicle is empty, shall be equipped with a rear impact guard(s). The rear impact guard(s) must be installed and maintained in such a manner that:
  (i) *The vertical distance* between the bottom of the guard(s) and the ground does not exceed 76.2 cm (30 inches) when the motor vehicle is empty;
  (ii) *The maximum lateral distance* between the closest points between guards, if more than one is used, does not exceed 61 cm (24 inches);
  (iii) *The outermost surfaces* of the horizontal member of the guard are no more than 45.7 cm (18 inches) from each side extremity of the motor vehicle;
  (iv) *The impact guard(s)* are no more than 61 cm (24 inches) forward of the rear extremity of the motor vehicle.

(2) *Construction and attachment.* The rear impact guard(s) must be substantially constructed and attached by means of bolts, welding, or other comparable means.

(3) *Vehicle components and structures* that may be used to satisfy the requirements of paragraph (b) of this section. Low chassis

vehicles, special purpose vehicles, or wheels back vehicles constructed and maintained so that the body, chassis, or other parts of the vehicle provide the rear end protection comparable to impact guard(s) conforming to the requirements of paragraph (b)(1) of this section shall be considered to be in compliance with those requirements.

§393.87 Warning flags on projecting loads.

(a) *Any commercial motor vehicle* transporting a load which extends beyond the sides by more than 102 mm (4 inches) or more than 1,219 mm (4 feet) beyond the rear must have the extremities of the load marked with red or orange fluorescent warning flags. Each warning flag must be at least 457 mm (18 inches) square.

(b) *Position of flags.* There must be a single flag at the extreme rear if the projecting load is two feet wide or less. Two warning flags are required if the projecting load is wider than two feet. Flags must be located to indicate maximum width of loads which extend beyond the sides and/or rear of the vehicle.

§393.87 DOT Interpretations

Question 1: May a triangular-shaped flag or device be used by itself to mark an oversized load?

Guidance: No. However, nothing prohibits using a triangular-shaped flag in conjunction with the prescribed flag.

§393.88 Television receivers.

Any motor vehicle equipped with a television viewer, screen or other means of visually receiving a television broadcast shall have the viewer or screen located in the motor vehicle at a point to the rear of the back of the driver's seat if such viewer or screen is in the same compartment as the driver and the viewer or screen shall be so located as not to be visible to the driver, while he/she is driving the motor vehicle. The operating controls for the television receiver shall be so located that the driver cannot operate them without leaving the driver's seat.

§393.88 DOT Interpretations

Question 1: Does §393.88 restrict the use of closed circuit monitor devices being used as a safety viewing system that would eliminate blind-side motor carrier accidents?

Guidance: No. The restriction of this section would not apply because the device cannot receive television broadcasts or be used for the viewing of video tapes.

§393.89 Buses, driveshaft protection.

Any driveshaft extending lengthways under the floor of the passenger compartment of a bus shall be protected by means of at least one guard or bracket at that end of the shaft which is provided with a sliding connection (spline or other such device) to prevent the whipping of the shaft in the event of failure thereof or of any of its component parts. A shaft contained within a torque tube shall not require any such device.

§393.89 DOT Interpretations

Question 1: For the purposes of §393.89, would a spline and yoke that is secured by a nut be considered a sliding connection?

Guidance: No. To be considered a sliding connection, the spline must be able to move within the sleeve. When the end of the spline is secured by a nut, it no longer has that freedom.

Question 2: On multiple drive shaft buses, does §393.89 require that all segments of the drive shaft be protected no matter the segments' length?

Guidance: Yes. Each drive shaft must have one guard or bracket for each end of a shaft which is provided with a sliding connection (spline or other such device).

Question 3: How does an existing pillow bearing (shaft support) on a multiple driveshaft system affect the requirement?

Guidance: It does not affect the requirement. It is part of the requirement.

§393.90 Buses, standee line or bar.

Except as provided below, every bus, which is designed and constructed so as to allow standees, shall be plainly marked with a line of contrasting color at least 2 inches wide or equipped with some other means so as to indicate to any person that he/she is prohibited from occupying a space forward of a perpendicular plane drawn through the rear of the driver's seat and perpendicular to the longitudinal axis of the bus. Every bus shall have clearly posted at or near the front, a sign with letters at least one-half inch high stating that it is a violation of the Federal Motor Carrier Safety Administration's regulations for a bus to be operated with persons occupying the prohibited area. The requirements of this section shall not apply to any bus being transported in driveaway-towaway operation or to any level of the bus other that the level in which the driver is located nor shall they be construed to prohibit any seated person from occupying permanent seats located in the prohibited area provided such seats are so located that persons sitting therein will not interfere with the driver's safe operation of the bus.

§393.91 Buses, aisle seats prohibited.

No bus shall be equipped with aisle seats unless such seats are so designed and installed as to automatically fold and leave a clear aisle when they are unoccupied. No bus shall be operated if any seat therein is not securely fastened to the vehicle.

§393.92 [Reserved]

§393.93 Seats, seat belt assemblies, and seat belt assembly anchorages.

(a) *Buses.*

(1) *Buses manufactured on or after January 1, 1965,* and before July 1, 1971. After June 30, 1972, every bus manufactured on or after January 1, 1965, and before July 1, 1971, must be equipped with a Type 1 or Type 2 seat belt assembly that conforms to Federal Motor Vehicle Safety Standard No. 209[1] (§571.209) installed at the driver's seat and seat belt assembly anchorages that conform to the location and geometric requirements of Federal Motor Vehicle Safety Standard No. 210[1] (§571.210) for that seat belt assembly.

(2) *Buses manufactured on or after July 1, 1971.* Every bus manufactured on or after July 1, 1971, must conform to the requirements of Federal Motor Vehicle Safety Standard No. 208[1] (§571.208) (relating to installation of seat belt assemblies) and Federal Motor Vehicle Safety Standard No. 210[1] (§571.210) (relating to installation of seat belt assembly anchorages).

(3) *Buses manufactured on or after January 1, 1972.* Every bus manufactured on or after January 1, 1972, must conform to the requirements of Federal Motor Vehicle Safety Standard No. 207[1] (§571.207) (relating to seating systems).

(b) *Trucks and truck tractors.*

(1) *Trucks and truck tractors* manufactured on and after January 1, 1965, and before July 1, 1971. Except as provided in paragraph (d) of this section, after June 30, 1972, every truck and truck tractor manufactured on or after January 1, 1965, and before July 1, 1971, must be equipped with a Type 1 or Type 2 seat belt assembly that conforms to Federal Motor Vehicle Safety Standard No. 209 (§571.209) installed at the driver's seat and at the right front outboard seat, if the vehicle has one, and seat belt assembly anchorages that conform to the location and geometric requirements of Federal Motor Vehicle Safety Standard No. 210 (§571.210) for each seat belt assembly that is required by this subparagraph.

(2) *Trucks and truck tractors* manufactured on or after July 1, 1971. Every truck and truck tractor manufactured on or after July 1, 1971, except a truck or truck tractor being transported in driveaway-towaway operation and having an incomplete vehicle seating and cab configuration, must conform to the requirements of Federal Motor Vehicle Safety Standard No. 208[2] (§571.208) (relating to installation of seat belt assemblies) and Federal Motor Vehicle Safety Standard No. 210[2] (§571.210) (relating to installation of seat belt assembly anchorages).

(3) *Trucks and truck tractors* manufactured on or after January 1, 1972. Every truck and truck tractor manufactured on or after January 1, 1972, except a truck or truck tractor being transported in driveaway-towaway operation and having an incomplete vehicle seating and cab configuration, must conform to the requirements of Federal Motor Vehicle Safety Standard No. 207[2] (§571.207) (relating to seating systems).

(c) **Effective date of standards.** Whenever paragraph (a) or (b) of this section requires conformity to a Federal Motor Vehicle Safety Standard, the vehicle or equipment must conform to the version of the Standard that is in effect on the date the vehicle is manufactured or on the date the vehicle is modified to conform to

---

1. Individual copies of Federal Motor Vehicle Safety Standards may be obtained from the National Highway Traffic Safety Administration, Nassif Building, 400 Seventh Street SW., Washington, D.C. 20590.
2. See footnote to § 393.93(a).

Subpart H - Emergency Equipment §393.95 (k)

the requirements of paragraph (a) or (b) of this section, whichever is later.

(d) **Trucks and truck tractors manufactured** on or after January 1, 1965, and before July 1, 1971, and operated in the State of Hawaii, must comply with the provisions of paragraph (b) of this section on and after January 1, 1976.

§393.93 DOT Interpretations
Question 1: If a CMV, other than a motorcoach, is equipped with a passenger seat, is a seat belt required for the passenger seat?
Guidance: Yes.

§393.94 Interior noise levels in power units.
(a) **Applicability of this section.** The interior noise level requirements apply to all trucks, truck-tractors, and buses.
(b) **General rule.** The interior sound level at the driver's seating position of a motor vehicle must not exceed 90 dB(A) when measured in accordance with paragraph (c) of this section.
(c) **Test procedure.**
  (1) *Park the vehicle at a location* so that no large reflecting surfaces, such as other vehicles, signboards, buildings, or hills, are within 50 feet of the driver's seating position.
  (2) *Close all vehicle doors, windows, and vents.* Turn off all power-operated accessories.
  (3) *Place the driver in his/her normal seated position* at the vehicle's controls. Evacuate all occupants except the driver and the person conducting the test.
  (4) *The sound level meters* used to determine compliance with the requirements of this section must meet the American National Standards Institute "Specification for Sound Level Meters," ANSI S1.4—1983. (See §393.7(b) for information on the incorporation by reference and availability of this document.)
  (5) *Locate the microphone,* oriented vertically upward, 6 inches to the right of, in the same plane as, and directly in line with, the driver's right ear.
  (6) *With the vehicle's transmission in neutral gear,* accelerate its engine to either its maximum governed engine speed, if it is equipped with an engine governor, or its speed at its maximum rated horsepower, if it is not equipped with an engine governor. Stabilize the engine at that speed.
  (7) *Observe the A-weighted sound level reading* on the meter for the stabilized engine speed condition. Record that reading, if the reading has not been influenced by extraneous noise sources such as motor vehicles operating on adjacent roadways.
  (8) *Return the vehicle's engine speed to idle* and repeat the procedures specified in paragraphs (c)(6) and (7) of this section until two maximum sound levels within 2 dB of each other are recorded. Numerically average those two maximum sound level readings.
  (9) *The average obtained* in accordance with paragraph (c)(8) of this section is the vehicle's interior sound level at the driver's seating position for the purpose of determining whether the vehicle conforms to the rule in paragraph (b) of this section. However, a 2 dB tolerance over the sound level limitation specified in that paragraph is permitted to allow for variations in test conditions and variations in the capabilities of meters.
  (10) *If the motor vehicle's engine radiator fan drive* is equipped with a clutch or similar device that automatically either reduces the rotational speed of the fan or completely disengages the fan from its power source in response to reduced engine cooling loads the vehicle may be parked before testing with its engine running at high idle or any other speed the operator may choose, for sufficient time but not more than 10 minutes, to permit the engine radiator fan to automatically disengage.

Subpart H - Emergency Equipment

§393.95 Emergency equipment on all power units.
Each truck, truck tractor, and bus (except those towed in driveaway-towaway operations) must be equipped as follows:
(a) **Fire Extinguishers.**
  (1) *Minimum ratings:*
    (i) *A power unit* that is used to transport hazardous materials in a quantity that requires placarding (See §177.823 of this title) must be equipped with a fire extinguisher having an Underwriters' Laboratories rating of 10 B:C or more.
    (ii) *A power unit* that is not used to transport hazardous materials must be equipped with either:
      [A] *A fire extinguisher* having an Underwriters' Laboratories rating of 5 B:C or more; or
      [B] *Two fire extinguishers,* each of which has an Underwriters' Laboratories rating of 4 B:C or more.
  (2) *Labeling and marking.* Each fire extinguisher required by this section must be labeled or marked by the manufacturer with its Underwriters' Laboratories rating.
  (3) *Visual Indicators.* The fire extinguisher must be designed, constructed, and maintained to permit visual determination of whether it is fully charged.
  (4) *Condition, location, and mounting.* The fire extinguisher(s) must be filled and located so that it is readily accessible for use. The extinguisher(s) must be securely mounted to prevent sliding, rolling, or vertical movement relative to the motor vehicle.
  (5) *Extinguishing agents.* The fire extinguisher must use an extinguishing agent that does not need protection from freezing. Extinguishing agents must comply with the toxicity provisions of the Environmental Protection Agency's Significant New Alternatives Policy (SNAP) regulations under 40 CFR Part 82, Subpart G.
(b) **Spare fuses.** Power units for which fuses are needed to operate any required parts and accessories must have at least one spare fuse for each type/size of fuse needed for those parts and accessories.
(c) [Reserved]
(d) [Reserved]
(e) [Reserved]
(f) **Warning devices for stopped vehicles.** Except as provided in paragraph (g) of this section, one of the following options must be used:
  (1) *Three bidirectional emergency reflective triangles* that conform to the requirements of Federal Motor Vehicle Safety Standard No. 125, §571.125 of this title; or
  (2) *At least 6 fusees or 3 liquid-burning flares.* The vehicle must have as many additional fusees or liquid-burning flares as are necessary to satisfy the requirements of §392.22.
  (3) *Other warning devices* may be used in addition to, but not in lieu of, the required warning devices, provided those warning devices do not decrease the effectiveness of the required warning devices.
(g) **Restrictions on the use of flame-producing devices.** Liquid-burning flares, fusees, oil lanterns, or any signal produced by a flame shall not be carried on any commercial motor vehicle transporting Division 1.1, 1.2, 1.3 (explosives) hazardous materials; any cargo tank motor vehicle used for the transportation of Division 2.1 (flammable gas) or Class 3 (flammable liquid) hazardous materials whether loaded or empty; or any commercial motor vehicle using compressed gas as a motor fuel.
(h) [Reserved]
(i) [Reserved]
(j) **Requirements for fusees and liquid-burning flares.** Each fusee shall be capable of burning for 30 minutes, and each liquid-burning flare shall contain enough fuel to burn continuously for at least 60 minutes. Fusees and liquid-burning flares shall conform to the requirements of Underwriters Laboratories, Inc., UL No. 912, Highway Emergency Signals, Fourth Edition, July 30, 1979, (with an amendment dated November 9, 1981). (See §393.7(c) for information on the incorporation by reference and availability of this document.) Each fusee and liquid-burning flare shall be marked with the UL symbol in accordance with the requirements of UL 912.
(k) **Requirements for red flags.** Red flags shall be not less than 12 inches square, with standards adequate to maintain the flags in an upright position.

§393.95 DOT Interpretations
Question 1: Are pressure gauges the only acceptable means for a visual determination that a fire extinguisher is fully charged?
Guidance: No, as long as there is some means to permit a visual determination that a fire extinguisher is fully charged.

Subpart I - Protection Against Shifting and Falling Cargo

§393.100 Which types of commercial motor vehicles are subject to the cargo securement standards of this subpart, and what general requirements apply?

(a) **Applicability.** The rules in this subpart are applicable to trucks, truck tractors, semitrailers, full trailers, and pole trailers.

(b) **Prevention against loss of load.** Each commercial motor vehicle must, when transporting cargo on public roads, be loaded and equipped, and the cargo secured, in accordance with this subpart to prevent the cargo from leaking, spilling, blowing or falling from the motor vehicle.

(c) **Prevention against shifting of load.** Cargo must be contained, immobilized or secured in accordance with this subpart to prevent shifting upon or within the vehicle to such an extent that the vehicle's stability or maneuverability is adversely affected.

§393.100 DOT Interpretations

Question 1: When securing cargo, is the use of a tiedown every 10 linear feet, or fraction thereof, adequate?
Guidance: Yes, as long as the aggregate strength of the tiedowns is equal to the requirements of §393.102, and each article is secured.

Question 2: Are CMVs transporting metal objects required to use option C?
Guidance: Only those CMVs which cannot comply with options A, B, or D, are required to conform to option C (see §393.100(c)).

Question 3: Are the requirements of §393.100 the only cargo securement requirements motor carriers must comply with?
Guidance: No. A motor carrier, when transporting cargo, must comply with all the applicable cargo securement requirements of Subpart I and §392.9.

Question 4: Do the rules for protection against shifting or falling cargo apply to CMVs with enclosed cargo areas?
Guidance: Yes. All CMVs transporting cargo must comply with the applicable provisions of §§393.100-393.106 (Subpart I) to prevent the shifting or falling of cargo aboard the vehicle.

Question 5: How many tiedowns are required for the transportation of logs on pole trailers with trip-bolsters or other stanchions?
Guidance: The regulations do not specify a minimum number of tiedowns. §393.100(b) provides motor carriers with several options for complying with §393.100. Although option B specifically addresses the use of tiedowns for each 10 linear feet of lading or fraction thereof (with certain exceptions), option D indicates the motor carrier may use "other means * * * which are similar to, and at least as effective * * *" as options A, B, and C. Therefore, the trip-bolsters or other stanchions in conjunction with securement devices meeting the requirements of §393.102 may (depending on the amount by which the logs exceed the length of the trailer) be used to satisfy option D.

Question 6: Are logs which are bundled together with tiedowns and transported on pole trailers with trip-bolsters or stanchions required to be fastened to the vehicle?
Guidance: Yes. Generally, cargo is not considered to be secured in accordance with Subpart I of Part 393 unless tiedowns or other securement devices prevent the cargo from moving relative to the vehicle. Two rules in §393.100 are directly applicable to the transportation of logs on a pole trailer.
§393.100(b)(2), Option B, requires one tiedown assembly for each 10 linear feet of lading or fraction thereof. However, "a pole trailer * * * is required only to have two * * * of those tiedown assemblies at each end of the trailer," i.e., at the stanchions, because the cargo cannot effectively be secured at mid-trailer where its structure is limited to the pole or boom.
§393.100(b)(4), Option D, allows the motor carrier to use a securement system that is similar to, and at least as effective as Option B.
§393.100(d) states that the rules in §393.100 do not apply to the transportation of "one or more articles which, because of their size, shape, or weight, must be carried on special purpose vehicles or must be fastened by special methods." However, since pole trailers are explicitly included in §393.100(b)(2), they are not special purpose vehicles and logs must be secured in accordance with §393.100(b).

§393.102 What are the minimum performance criteria for cargo securement devices and systems?

(a) **Performance criteria—**
  (1) *Breaking Strength.* Tiedown assemblies (including chains, wire rope, steel strapping, synthetic webbing, and cordage) and other attachment or fastening devices used to secure articles of cargo to, or in, commercial motor vehicles must be designed, installed, and maintained to ensure that the maximum forces acting on the devices or systems do not exceed the manufacturer's breaking strength rating under the following conditions, applied separately:
  (i) 0.8 g deceleration in the forward direction;
  (ii) 0.5 g acceleration in the rearward direction; and
  (iii) 0.5 g acceleration in a lateral direction.
  (2) *Working Load Limit.* Tiedown assemblies (including chains, wire rope, steel strapping, synthetic webbing, and cordage) and other attachment or fastening devices used to secure articles of cargo to, or in, commercial motor vehicles must be designed, installed, and maintained to ensure that the forces acting on the devices or systems do not exceed the working load limit for the devices under the following conditions, applied separately:
  (i) 0.435 g deceleration in the forward direction;
  (ii) 0.5 g acceleration in the rearward direction; and
  (iii) 0.25 g acceleration in a lateral direction.

(b) **Performance criteria for devices to prevent vertical movement of loads that are not contained within the structure of the vehicle.** Securement systems must provide a downward force equivalent to at least 20 percent of the weight of the article of cargo if the article is not fully contained within the structure of the vehicle. If the article is fully contained within the structure of the vehicle, it may be secured in accordance with Sec. 393.106(b).

(c) **Equivalent means of securement.** The means of securing articles of cargo are considered to meet the performance requirements of this section if the cargo is
  (1) *Immobilized,* such so that it cannot shift or tip to the extent that the vehicle's stability or maneuverability is adversely affected; or
  (2) Transported in a sided vehicle that has walls of adequate strength, such that each article of cargo within the vehicle is in contact with, or sufficiently close to a wall or other articles, so that it cannot shift or tip to the extent that the vehicle's stability or maneuverability is adversely affected; or
  (3) Secured in accordance with the applicable requirements of §§ 393.104 through 393.136.

§393.102 DOT Interpretations

Question 1: Does §393.102(b) prohibit the use of securement devices for which manufacturing standards have not been incorporated by reference?
Guidance: Section 393.102(b) requires that chain, wire rope, synthetic webbing, cordage, and steel strapping meet minimum manufacturing standards. It does not, however, prohibit the use of other types of securement devices or establish manufacturing standards for those devices. Therefore, if the securement device(s) has an aggregate working load limit of at least 1/2 the weight of the article, and the load is secured to prevent it from shifting or falling from the vehicle, §§393.100 and 393.102(b) would be satisfied.

If the cargo is not firmly braced against a front-end structure that conforms to the requirements of §393.106, the securement system would have to provide protection against longitudinal movement [§393.104(a)]. If the load may shift sideways in transit then §393.104(b) would also be applicable.

Question 2: Does §393.102(b) require that securement devices be marked or labeled with their working load limit or any other information?
Guidance: No. Although §393.102(b) requires chain, wire rope, synthetic webbing, cordage, and steel strapping tiedowns to meet applicable manufacturing standards, it explicitly excludes marking identification provisions of those manufacturing standards. Since §393.102(b) does not establish manufacturing standards or marking requirements for other types of securement devices, such devices are not required to be marked with their working load limit.

Subpart I - Protection Against Shifting and Falling Cargo — §393.108 (e)

§393.104 What standards must cargo securement devices and systems meet in order to satisfy the requirements of this subpart?

(a) *General.* All devices and systems used to secure cargo to or within a vehicle must be capable of meeting the requirements of §393.102.

(b) *Prohibition on the use of damaged securement devices.* All tiedowns, cargo securement systems, parts and components used to secure cargo must be in proper working order when used to perform that function with no damaged or weakened components, such as, but not limited to, cracks or cuts that will adversely affect their performance for cargo securement purposes, including reducing the working load limit.

(c) *Vehicle structures and anchor points.* Vehicle structures, floors, walls, decks, tiedown anchor points, headerboards, bulkheads, stakes, posts, and associated mounting pockets used to contain or secure articles of cargo must be strong enough to meet the performance criteria of § 393.102, with no damaged or weakened components, such as, but not limited to, cracks or cuts that will adversely affect their performance for cargo securement purposes, including reducing the working load limit.

(d) *Material for dunnage, chocks, cradles, shoring bars,* blocking and bracing. Material used as dunnage or dunnage bags, chocks, cradles, shoring bars, or used for blocking and bracing, must not have damage or defects which would compromise the effectiveness of the securement system.

(e) *Manufacturing standards for tiedown assemblies.* Tiedown assemblies (including chains, wire rope, steel strapping, synthetic webbing, and cordage) and other attachment or fastening devices used to secure articles of cargo to, or in, commercial motor vehicles must conform to the following applicable standards:

An assembly component of . . .	Must conform to . . .
(1) Steel strapping[1,2]	Standard Specification for Strapping, Flat Steel and Seals, American Society for Testing and Materials (ASTM) D3953-97, dated February 1998.[4]
(2) Chain	National Association of Chain Manufacturers' Welded Steel Chain Specifications, dated September 28, 2005.[4]
(3) Webbing	Web Sling and Tiedown Association's Recommended Standard Specification for Synthetic Web Tiedowns, WSTDA-T1, 1998.[4]
(4) Wire rope[3]	Wire Rope Technical Board's Wire Rope Users Manual, 2nd Edition, November 1985.[4]
(5) Cordage	Cordage Institute rope standard: (i) PETRS-2, Polyester Fiber Rope, three-Strand and eight-Strand Constructions, January 1993;[4] (ii) PPRS-2, Polypropylene Fiber Rope, three-Strand and eight-Strand Constructions, August 1992;[4] (iii) CRS-1, Polyester/Polypropylene Composite Rope Specifications, three-Strand and eight-Strand Standard Construction, May 1979;[4] (iv) NRS-1, Nylon Rope Specifications, three-Strand and eight-Strand Standard Construction, May 1979;[4] and (v) C-1, Double Braided Nylon Rope Specifications DBN, January 1984.[4]

1. Steel strapping not marked by the manufacturer with a working load limit will be considered to have a working load limit equal to one-fourth of the breaking strength listed in ASTM D3953-97.
2. Steel strapping 25.4 mm (1 inch) or wider must have at least two pairs of crimps in each seal and, when an end-over-end lap joint is formed, must be sealed with at least two seals.
3. Wire rope which is not marked by the manufacturer with a working load limit shall be considered to have a working load limit equal to one-fourth of the nominal strength listed in the manual.
4. See §393.7 for information on the incorporation by reference and availability of this document.

(f) *Use of tiedowns.*
   (1) Tiedowns and securing devices must not contain knots.
   (2) If a tiedown is repaired, it must be repaired in accordance with the applicable standards in paragraph (e) of this section, or the manufacturer's instructions.
   (3) Each tiedown must be attached and secured in a manner that prevents it from becoming loose, unfastening, opening or releasing while the vehicle is in transit.

(4) *Edge protection must be used* whenever a tiedown would be subject to abrasion or cutting at the point where it touches an article of cargo. The edge protection must resist abrasion, cutting and crushing.

§393.106 What are the general requirements for securing articles of cargo?

(a) *Applicability.* The rules in this section are applicable to the transportation of all types of articles of cargo, except commodities in bulk that lack structure or fixed shape (*e.g.,* liquids, gases, grain, liquid concrete, sand, gravel, aggregates) and are transported in a tank, hopper, box, or similar device that forms part of the structure of a commercial motor vehicle. The rules in this section apply to the cargo types covered by the commodity specific rules of § 393.116 through § 393.136. The commodity-specific rules take precedence over the general requirements of this section when additional requirements are given for a commodity listed in those sections.

(b) *General.* Cargo must be firmly immobilized or secured on or within a vehicle by structures of adequate strength, dunnage or dunnage bags, shoring bars, tiedowns or a combination of these.

(c) *Cargo placement and restraint.*
   (1) *Articles of cargo that are likely to roll* must be restrained by chocks, wedges, a cradle or other equivalent means to prevent rolling. The means of preventing rolling must not be capable of becoming unintentionally unfastened or loose while the vehicle is in transit.
   (2) *Articles or cargo placed beside each other* and secured by transverse tiedowns must either:
      (i) *Be placed in direct contact with each other, or*
      (ii) *Be prevented from shifting towards each other while in transit.*

(d) *Aggregate working load limit for tiedowns.* The aggregate working load limit of tiedowns used to secure an article or group of articles against movement must be at least one-half times the weight of the article or group of articles. The aggregate working load limit is the sum of:
   (1) One-half the working load limit of each tiedown that goes from an anchor point on the vehicle to an anchor point on an article of cargo;
   (2) One-half the working load limit of each tiedown that is attached to an anchor point on the vehicle, passes through, over, or around the article of cargo, and is then attached to an anchor point on the same side of the vehicle.
   (3) The working load limit for each tiedown that goes from an anchor point on the vehicle, through, over, or around the article of cargo, and then attaches to another anchor point on the other side of the vehicle.

§393.106 DOT Interpretations

Question 1: When describing a headerboard or cab protection device, the regulations state that similar devices may be used. What is meant by the term "similar devices"?

Guidance: The term "similar devices" has reference to devices equivalent in strength and function, though not necessarily in appearance and construction, to headerboards.

§393.108 How is the working load limit of a tiedown, or the load restraining value of a friction mat, determined?

(a) *The working load limit (WLL) of a tiedown,* associated connector or attachment mechanism is the lowest working load limit of any of its components (including tensioner), or the working load limit of the anchor points to which it is attached, whichever is less.

(b) *The working load limits of tiedowns* may be determined by using either the tiedown manufacturer's markings or by using the tables in this section. The working load limits listed in the tables are to be used when the tiedown material is not marked by the manufacturer with the working load limit. Tiedown materials which are marked by the manufacturer with working load limits that differ from the tables, shall be considered to have a working load limit equal to the value for which they are marked.

(c) *Synthetic cordage* (e.g., nylon, polypropylene, polyester) which is not marked or labeled to enable identification of its composition or working load limit shall be considered to have a working load limit equal to that for polypropylene fiber rope.

(d) *Welded steel chain which is not marked or labeled* to enable identification of its grade or working load limit shall be considered to have a working load limit equal to that for grade 30 proof coil chain.

(e) (1) *Wire rope which is not marked by the manufacturer* with a working load limit shall be considered to have a working load limit

§393.110

equal to one-fourth of the nominal strength listed in the Wire Rope Users Manual.

(2) *Wire which is not marked or labeled* to enable identification of its construction type shall be considered to have a working load limit equal to that for 6 x 37, fiber core wire rope.

(f) *Manila rope which is not marked by the manufacturer* with a working load limit shall be considered to have a working load limit based on its diameter as provided in the tables of working load limits.

(g) *Friction mats which are not marked or rated* by the manufacturer shall be considered to provide resistance to horizontal movement equal to 50 percent of the weight placed on the mat.

Tables to §393.108
[Working Load Limits (WLL), Chain]

Size mm (inches)	WLL in kg (pounds)				
	Grade 30 proof coil	Grade 43 high test	Grade 70 transport	Grade 80 alloy	Grade 100 alloy
1. 7 (1/4)	580 (1,300)	1,180 (2,600)	1,430 (3,150)	1,570 (3,500)	1,950 (4,300)
2. 8 (5/16)	860 (1,900)	1,770 (3,900)	2,130 (4,700)	2,000 (4,500)	2,600 (5,700)
3. 10 (3/8)	1,200 (2,650)	2,450 (5,400)	2,990 (6,600)	3,200 (7,100)	4,000 (8,800)
4. 11 (7/16)	1,680 (3,700)	3,270 (7,200)	3,970 (8,750)		
5. 13 (1/2)	2,030 (4,500)	4,170 (9,200)	5,130 (11,300)	5,400 (12,000)	6,800 (15,000)
6. 16 (5/8)	3,130 (6,900)	5,910 (13,000)	7,170 (15,800)	8,200 (18,100)	10,300 (22,600)
Chain Mark Examples: Example 1 Example 2 Example 3	3 30 300	4 43 430	7 70 700	8 80 800	10 100 1000

Wire Rope (6 x 37, Fiber Core)

Diameter mm (inches)	WLL kg (pounds)
7 (1/4)	640 (1,400)
8 (5/16)	950 (2,100)
10 (3/8)	1,360 (3,000)
11 (7/16)	1,860 (4,100)
13 (1/2)	2,400 (5,300)
16 (5/8)	3,770 (8,300)
20 (3/4)	4,940 (10,900)
22 (7/8)	7,300 (16,100)
25 (1)	9,480 (20,900)

Manila Rope

Diameter mm (inches)	WLL kg (pounds)
10 (3/8)	90 (205)
11 (7/16)	120 (265)
13 (1/2)	150 (315)
16 (5/8)	210 (465)
20 (3/4)	290 (640)
25 (1)	480 (1,050)

Polypropylene Fiber Rope WLL
(3-Strand and 8-Strand Constructions)

Diameter mm (inches)	WLL kg (pounds)
10 (3/8)	180 (400)
11 (7/16)	240 (525)
13 (1/2)	280 (625)
16 (5/8)	420 (925)
20 (3/4)	580 (1,275)
25 (1)	950 (2,100)

Polyester Fiber Rope WLL (3-Strand and 8-Strand Constructions)

Diameter mm (inches)	WLL kg (pounds)
10 (3/8)	250 (555)
11 (7/16)	340 (750)
13 (1/2)	440 (960)
16 (5/8)	680 (1,500)
20 (3/4)	850 (1,880)
25 (1)	1,500 (3,300)

Nylon Rope

Diameter mm (inches)	WLL kg (pounds)
10 (3/8)	130 (278)
11 (7/16)	190 (410)
13 (1/2)	240 (525)
16 (5/8)	420 (935)
20 (3/4)	640 (1,420)
25 (1)	1,140 (2,520)

Double Braided Nylon Rope

Diameter mm (inches)	WLL kg (pounds)
10 (3/8)	150 (336)
11 (7/16)	230 (502)
13 (1/2)	300 (655)
16 (5/8)	510 (1,130)
20 (3/4)	830 (1,840)
25 (1)	1,470 (3,250)

Steel Strapping

Width x thickness mm (inches)	WLL kg (pounds)
31.7 x .74 (1 1/4 x 0.029)	540 (1,190)
31.7 x .79 (1 1/4 x 0.031)	540 (1,190)
31.7 x .89 (1 1/4 x 0.035)	540 (1,190)
31.7 x 1.12 (1 1/4 x 0.044)	770 (1,690)
31.7 x 1.27 (1 1/4 x 0.05)	770 (1,690)
31.7 x 1.5 (1 1/4 x 0.057)	870 (1,925)
50.8 x 1.12 (2 x 0.044)	1,200 (2,650)
50.8 x 1.27 (2 x 0.05)	1,200 (2,650)

Synthetic Webbing

Width mm (inches)	WLL kg (pounds)
45 (1 3/4)	790 (1,750)
50 (2)	910 (2,000)
75 (3)	1,360 (3,000)
100 (4)	1,810 (4,000)

§393.110 **What else do I have to do to determine the minimum number of tiedowns?**

(a) When tiedowns are used as part of a cargo securement system, the minimum number of tiedowns required to secure an article or group of articles against movement depends on the length of the article(s) being secured, and the requirements of paragraphs (b) and (c) of this section. These requirements are in addition to the rules under § 393.106.

(b) *When an article is not blocked or positioned* to prevent movement in the forward direction by a headerboard, bulkhead, other cargo that is positioned to prevent movement, or other appropriate blocking devices, it must be secured by at least:
(1) *One tiedown for articles 5 feet* (1.52 meters) or less in length, and 1,100 pounds (500 kg) or less in weight;
(2) *Two tiedowns if the article is:*
(i) *5 feet* (1.52 meters) or less in length and more than 1,100 pounds (500 kg) in weight; or
(ii) *Longer than 5 feet* (1.52 meters) but less than or equal to 10 feet (3.04 meters) in length, irrespective of the weight.

Subpart I - Protection Against Shifting and Falling Cargo §393.116 (d)

(3) *Two tiedowns if the article is longer than 10 feet* (3.04 meters), and one additional tiedown for every 10 feet (3.04 meters) of article length, or fraction thereof, beyond the first 10 feet (3.04 meters) of length.

(c) **If an individual article is blocked, braced, or immobilized** to prevent movement in the forward direction by a headerboard, bulkhead, other articles which are adequately secured or by an appropriate blocking or immobilization method, it must be secured by at least one tiedown for every 3.04 meters (10 feet) of article length, or fraction thereof.

(d) **Special rule for special purpose vehicles.** The rules in this section do not apply to a vehicle transporting one or more articles of cargo such as, but not limited to, machinery or fabricated structural items (e.g., steel or concrete beams, crane booms, girders, and trusses, etc.) which, because of their design, size, shape, or weight, must be fastened by special methods. However, any article of cargo carried on that vehicle must be securely and adequately fastened to the vehicle.

§393.112 Must a tiedown be adjustable?

Each tiedown, or its associated connectors, or its attachment mechanisms must be designed, constructed, and maintained so the driver of an in-transit commercial motor vehicle can tighten them. However, this requirement does not apply to the use of steel strapping.

§393.114 What are the requirements for front end structures used as part of a cargo securement system?

(a) **Applicability.** The rules in this section are applicable to commercial motor vehicles transporting articles of cargo that are in contact with the front end structure of the vehicle. The front end structure on these cargo-carrying vehicles must meet the performance requirements of this section.

(b) **Height and width.**
  (1) *The front end structure must extend* either to a height of 4 feet above the floor of the vehicle or to a height at which it blocks forward movement of any item or article of cargo being carried on the vehicle, whichever is lower.
  (2) *The front end structure must have a width* which is at least equal to the width of the vehicle or which blocks forward movement of any article of cargo being transported on the vehicle, whichever is narrower.

(c) **Strength.** The front end structure must be capable of withstanding the following horizontal forward static load:
  (1) *For a front end structure* less than 6 feet in height, a horizontal forward static load equal to one-half (0.5) of the weight of the articles of cargo being transported on the vehicle uniformly distributed over the entire portion of the front end structure that is within 4 feet above the vehicle's floor or that is at or below a height above the vehicle's floor at which it blocks forward movement of any article of the vehicle's cargo, whichever is less; or
  (2) *For a front end structure* 6 feet in height or higher, a horizontal forward static load equal to four-tenths (0.4) of the weight of the articles of cargo being transported on the vehicle uniformly distributed over the entire front end structure.

(d) **Penetration resistance.** The front end structure must be designed, constructed, and maintained so that it is capable of resisting penetration by any article of cargo that contacts it when the vehicle decelerates at a rate of 20 feet per second, per second. The front end structure must have no aperture large enough to permit any article of cargo in contact with the structure to pass through it.

(e) **Substitute devices.** The requirements of this section may be met by the use of devices performing the same functions as a front end structure, if the devices are at least as strong as, and provide protection against shifting articles of cargo at least equal to, a front end structure which conforms to those requirements.

Specific Securement Requirements by Commodity Type

§393.116 What are the rules for securing logs?

(a) **Applicability.** The rules in this section are applicable to the transportation of logs with the following exceptions:
  (1) *Logs that are unitized* by banding or other comparable means may be transported in accordance with the general cargo securement rules of §§393.100 through 393.114.
  (2) *Loads that consist* of no more than four processed logs may be transported in accordance with the general cargo securement rules of §§393.100 through 393.114.
  (3) *Firewood, stumps, log debris* and other such short logs must be transported in a vehicle or container enclosed on both sides, front, and rear and of adequate strength to contain them. Longer logs may also be so loaded.

(b) **Components of a securement system.**
  (1) *Logs must be transported on a vehicle* designed and built, or adapted, for the transportation of logs. Any such vehicle must be fitted with bunks, bolsters, stakes or standards, or other equivalent means, that cradle the logs and prevent them from rolling.
  (2) *All vehicle components* involved in securement of logs must be designed and built to withstand all anticipated operational forces without failure, accidental release or permanent deformation. Stakes or standards that are not permanently attached to the vehicle must be secured in a manner that prevents unintentional separation from the vehicle in transit.
  (3) *Tiedowns must be used* in combination with the stabilization provided by bunks, stakes, and bolsters to secure the load unless the logs:
    (i) *are transported in a crib-type log trailer* (as defined in 49 CFR 393.5), and
    (ii) *are loaded in compliance* with paragraphs (b)(2) and (c) of this section.
  (4) *The aggregate working load limit* for tiedowns used to secure a stack of logs on a frame vehicle, or a flatbed vehicle equipped with bunks, bolsters,or stakes must be at least one-sixth the weight of the stack of logs.

(c) **Use of securement system.**
  (1) *Logs must be solidly packed,* and the outer bottom logs must be in contact with and resting solidly against the bunks, bolsters, stakes or standards.
  (2) *Each outside log on the side of a stack of logs* must touch at least two stakes, bunks, bolsters, or standards. If one end does not actually touch a stake, it must rest on other logs in a stable manner and must extend beyond the stake, bunk, bolster or standard.
  (3) *The center of the highest outside log* on each side or end must be below the top of each stake, bunk or standard.
  (4) *Each log that is not held in place* by contact with other logs or the stakes, bunks, or standards must be held in place by a tiedown. Additional tiedowns or securement devices must be used when the condition of the wood results in such low friction between logs that they are likely to slip upon each other.

(d) **Securement of shortwood logs loaded crosswise** on frame, rail and flatbed vehicles. In addition to the requirements of paragraphs (b) and (c) of this section, each stack of logs loaded crosswise must meet the following rules:
  (1) *In no case* may the end of a log in the lower tier extend more than one-third of the log's total length beyond the nearest supporting structure on the vehicle.
  (2) *When only one stack of shortwood* is loaded crosswise, it must be secured with at least two tiedowns. The tiedowns must attach to the vehicle frame at the front and rear of the load, and must cross the load in this direction.
  (3) *When two tiedowns are used,* they must be positioned at approximately one-third and two-thirds of the length of the logs.
  (4) *A vehicle* that is more than 10 meters (33 feet) long must be equipped with center stakes, or comparable devices, to divide it into sections approximately equal in length. Where a vehicle is so divided, each tiedown must secure the highest log on each side of the center stake, and must be fastened below these logs. It may be fixed at each end and tensioned from the middle, or fixed in the middle and tensioned from each end, or it may pass through a pulley or equivalent device in the middle and be tensioned from one end.
  (5) *Any structure or stake* that is subjected to an upward force when the tiedowns are tensioned must be anchored to resist that force.
  (6) *If two stacks of shortwood* are loaded side-by-side, in addition to meeting the requirements of paragraphs (d)(1) through (d)(5) of this section, they must be loaded so that:
    (i) *There is no space between the two stacks of logs;*
    (ii) *The outside of each stack* is raised at least 2.5 cm (1 in) within 10 cm (4 in) of the end of the logs or the side of the vehicle;
    (iii) *The highest log* is no more than 2.44 m (8 ft) above the deck; and
    (iv) *At least one tiedown* is used lengthwise across each stack of logs.

(e) Securement of logs loaded lengthwise on flatbed and frame vehicles —
  (1) *Shortwood.* In addition to meeting the requirements of paragraphs (b) and (c) of this section, each stack of shortwood loaded lengthwise on a frame vehicle or on a flatbed must be cradled in a bunk unit or contained by stakes and
   (i) *Secured to the vehicle* by at least two tiedowns, or
   (ii) *If all the logs in any stack* are blocked in the front by a front-end structure strong enough to restrain the load, or by another stack of logs, and blocked in the rear by another stack of logs or vehicle end structure, the stack may be secured with one tiedown. If one tiedown is used, it must be positioned about midway between the stakes, or
   (iii) *Be bound by at least two tiedown type devices* such as wire rope, used as wrappers that encircle the entire load at locations along the load that provide effective securement. If wrappers are being used to bundle the logs together, the wrappers are not required to be attached to the vehicle.
  (2) *Longwood.* Longwood must be cradled in two or more bunks and must either:
   (i) *Be secured to the vehicle* by at least two tiedowns at locations that provide effective securement, or
   (ii) *Be bound by at least two tiedown type devices,* such as wire rope, used as wrappers that encircle the entire load at locations along the load that provide effective securement. If a wrapper(s) is being used to bundle the logs together, the wrapper is not required to be attached to the vehicle.

(f) Securement of logs transported on pole trailers.
  (1) *The load must be secured by at least one tiedown* at each bunk, or alternatively, by at least two tiedowns used as wrappers that encircle the entire load at locations along the load that provide effective securement.
  (2) *The front and rear wrappers* must be at least 3.04 meters (10 feet) apart.
  (3) *Large diameter single and double log loads* must be immobilized with chock blocks or other equivalent means to prevent shifting.
  (4) *Large diameter logs that rise above bunks* must be secured to the underlying load with at least two additional wrappers.

§393.118 What are the rules for securing dressed lumber or similar building products?

(a) Applicability. The rules in this section apply to the transportation of bundles of dressed lumber, packaged lumber, building products such as plywood, gypsum board or other materials of similar shape. Lumber or building products which are not bundled or packaged must be treated as loose items and transported in accordance with §§393.100 through 393.114 of this subpart. For the purpose of this section, "bundle" refers to packages of lumber, building materials or similar products which are unitized for securement as a single article of cargo.

(b) Positioning of bundles. Bundles must be placed side by side in direct contact with each other, or a means must be provided to prevent bundles from shifting towards each other.

(c) Securement of bundles transported using no more than one tier. Bundles carried on one tier must be secured in accordance with the general provisions of §§393.100 through 393.114.

(d) Securement of bundles transported using more than one tier. Bundles carried in more than one tier must be either:
  (1) *Blocked against lateral movement* by stakes on the sides of the vehicle and secured by tiedowns laid out over the top tier, as outlined in the general provisions of §§393.100 through 393.114; or
  (2) *Restrained from lateral movement* by blocking or high friction devices between tiers and secured by tiedowns laid out over the top tier, as outlined in the general provisions of §§393.100 through 393.114; or
  (3) *Placed directly on top of other bundles* or on spaces and secured in accordance with the following:
   (i) *The length of spacers between bundles* must provide support to all pieces in the bottom row of the bundle.
   (ii) *The width of individual spacers* must be equal to or greater than the height.
   (iii) *If spacers are comprised of layers of material,* the layers must be unitized or fastened together in a manner which ensures that the spacer performs as a single piece of material.
   (iv) *The arrangement of the tiedowns for the bundles must be:*
    [A] *Secured by tiedowns* over the top tier of bundles, in accordance with the general provisions of §§393.100 through 393.114 with a minimum of two tiedowns for bundles longer than 1.52 meters (5 ft); and
    [B] Secured by tiedowns as follows:
     (1) *If there are 3 tiers,* the middle and top bundles must be secured by tiedowns in accordance with the general provisions of §§ 393.100 through 393.114; or
     (2) (i) *If there are more than 3 tiers,* then one of the middle bundles and the top bundle must be secured by tiedown devices in accordance with the general provision of §§ 393.100 through 393.114, and the maximum height for the middle tier that must be secured may not exceed 6 feet about the deck of the trailer; or
       (ii) *Otherwise, the second tier from the bottom* must be secured in accordance with the general provisions of §§ 393.100 through 393.114; or
  (4) *Secured by tiedowns* over each tier of bundles, in accordance with §§393.100 through 393.114 using a minimum of two tiedowns over each of the top bundles longer than 1.52 meters (5 ft), in all circumstances; or
  (5) *When loaded in a sided vehicle* or container of adequate strength, dressed lumber or similar building products may be secured in accordance with the general provisions of §§ 393.100 through 393.114.

§393.120 What are the rules for securing metal coils?

(a) Applicability. The rules in this section apply to the transportation of one or more metal coils which, individually or grouped together, weigh 2268 kg (5000 pounds) or more. Shipments of metal coils that weigh less than 2268 kg (5000 pounds) may be secured in accordance with the provisions of §§393.100 through 393.114.

(b) Securement of coils transported with eyes vertical on a flatbed vehicle, in a sided vehicle or intermodal container with anchor points.
  (1) *An individual coil.* Each coil must be secured by tiedowns arranged in a manner to prevent the coils from tipping in the forward, rearward, and lateral directions. The restraint system must include the following:
   (i) *At least one tiedown attached diagonally* from the left side of the vehicle or intermodal container (near the forward-most part of the coil), across the eye of the coil, to the right side of the vehicle or intermodal container (near the rear-most part of the coil);
   (ii) *At least one tiedown attached diagonally* from the right side of the vehicle or intermodal container (near the forward-most part of the coil), across the eye of the coil, to the left side of the vehicle or intermodal container (near the rear-most part of the coil);
   (iii) *At least one tiedown* attached transversely over the eye of the coil; and
   (iv) *Either blocking and bracing,* friction mats or tiedowns must be used to prevent longitudinal movement in the forward direction.
  (2) *Coils grouped in rows.* When coils are grouped and loaded side by side in a transverse or longitudinal row, the each row of coils must be secured by the following:
   (i) *At least one tiedown attached to the front* of the row of coils, restraining against forward motion, and whenever practicable, making an angle no more than 45 degrees with the floor of the vehicle or intermodal container when viewed from the side of the vehicle or container;
   (ii) *At least one tiedown attached to the rear* of the row of coils, restraining against rearward motion, and whenever practicable, making an angle no more than 45 degrees with the floor of the vehicle or intermodal container when viewed from the side of the vehicle or container;
   (iii) *At least one tiedown* over the top of each coil or transverse row of coils, restraining against vertical motion. Tiedowns going over the top of a coil(s) must be as close as practicable to the eye of the coil and positioned to prevent the tiedown from slipping or becoming unintentionally unfastened while the vehicle is in transit; and
   (iv) *Tiedowns must be arranged* to prevent shifting or tipping in the forward, rearward and lateral directions.

(c) Securement of coils transported with eyes crosswise on a flatbed vehicle, in a sided vehicle or intermodal container with anchor points.

Subpart I - Protection Against Shifting and Falling Cargo §393.122 (b)

(1) *An individual coil.* Each coil must be secured by the following:
  (i) *A means* (e.g., timbers, chocks or wedges, a cradle, etc.) to prevent the coil from rolling. The means of preventing rolling must support the coil off the deck, and must not be capable of becoming unintentionally unfastened or loose while the vehicle is in transit. If timbers, chocks or wedges are used, they must be held in place by coil bunks or similar devices to prevent them from coming loose. The use of nailed blocking or cleats as the sole means to secure timbers, chocks or wedges, or a nailed wood cradle, is prohibited;
  (ii) *At least one tiedown through its eye,* restricting against forward motion, and whenever practicable, making an angle no more than 45 degrees with the floor of the vehicle or intermodal container when viewed from the side of the vehicle or container; and
  (iii) *At least one tiedown through its eye,* restricting against rearward motion, and whenever practicable, making an angle no more than 45 degrees with the floor of the vehicle or intermodal container when viewed from the side of the vehicle or container.
(2) *Prohibition on crossing of tiedowns* when coils are transported with eyes crosswise. Attaching tiedowns diagonally through the eye of a coil to form an X-pattern when viewed from above the vehicle is prohibited.

(d) **Securement of coils transported** with eyes lengthwise on a flatbed vehicle, in a sided vehicle or intermodal container with anchor points.
  (1) *An individual coil — option 1.* Each coil must be secured by:
    (i) *A means* (e.g., timbers, chocks or wedges, a cradle, etc.) to prevent the coil from rolling. The means of preventing rolling must support the coil off the deck, and must not be capable of becoming unintentionally unfastened or loose while the vehicle is in transit. If timbers, chocks or wedges are used, they must be held in place by coil bunks or similar devices to prevent them from coming loose. The use of nailed blocking or cleats as the sole means to secure timbers, chocks or wedges, or a nailed wood cradle, is prohibited;
    (ii) *At least one tiedown* attached diagonally through its eye from the left side of the vehicle or intermodal container (near the forwardmost part of the coil), to the right side of the vehicle or intermodal container (near the rearmost part of the coil), making an angle no more than 45 degrees, whenever practicable, with the floor of the vehicle or intermodal container when viewed from the side of the vehicle or container;
    (iii) *At least one tiedown* attached diagonally through its eye, from the right side of the vehicle or intermodal container (near the forward-most part of the coil), to the left side of the vehicle or intermodal container (near the rearmost part of the coil), making an angle no more than 45 degrees, whenever practicable, with the floor of the vehicle or intermodal container when viewed from the side of the vehicle or container;
    (iv) *At least one tiedown* attached transversely over the top of the coil; and
    (v) *Either blocking,* or friction mats to prevent longitudinal movement.
  (2) *An individual coil — option 2.* Each coil must be secured by:
    (i) *A means* (e.g., timbers, chocks or wedges, a cradle, etc.) to prevent the coil from rolling. The means of preventing rolling must support the coil off the deck, and must not be capable of becoming unintentionally unfastened or loose while the vehicle is in transit. If timbers, chocks or wedges are used, they must be held in place by coil bunks or similar devices to prevent them from coming loose. The use of nailed blocking or cleats as the sole means to secure timbers, chocks or wedges, or a nailed wood cradle, is prohibited;
    (ii) *At least one tiedown* attached straight through its eye from the left side of the vehicle or intermodal container (near the forwardmost part of the coil), to the left side of the vehicle or intermodal container (near the rearmost part of the coil), and, whenever practicable, making an angle no more than 45 degrees with the floor of the vehicle or intermodal container when viewed from the side of the vehicle or container;
    (iii) *At least one tiedown* attached straight through its eye, from the right side of the vehicle or intermodal container (near the forward-most part of the coil), to the right side of the vehicle or intermodal container (near the rearmost part of the coil), and whenever practicable, making an angle no more than 45 degrees with the floor of the vehicle or intermodal container when viewed from the side of the vehicle or container;
    (iv) *At least one tiedown* attached transversely over the top of the coil; and
    (v) *Either blocking or friction mats* to prevent longitudinal movement.
  (3) *An individual coil — option 3.* Each coil must be secured by:
    (i) *A means* (e.g., timbers, chocks or wedges, a cradle, etc.) to prevent the coil from rolling. The means of preventing rolling must support the coil off the deck, and must not be capable of becoming unintentionally unfastened or loose while the vehicle is in transit. If timbers, chocks or wedges are used, they must be held in place by coil bunks or similar devices to prevent them from coming loose. The use of nailed blocking or cleats as the sole means to secure timbers, chocks or wedges, or a nailed wood cradle, is prohibited;
    (ii) *At least one tiedown over the top of the coil,* located near the forward-most part of the coil;
    (iii) *At least one tiedown over the top of the coil* located near the rearmost part of the coil; and
    (iv) *Either blocking or friction mats* to prevent longitudinal movement.he forward direction.
  (4) *Rows of coils.* Each transverse row of coils having approximately equal outside diameters must be secured with:
    (i) *A means* (e.g., timbers, chocks or wedges, a cradle, etc.) to prevent each coil in the row of coils from rolling. The means of preventing rolling must support each coil off the deck, and must not be capable of becoming unintentionally unfastened or loose while the vehicle is in transit. If timbers, chocks or wedges are used, they must be held in place by coil bunks or similar devices to prevent them from coming loose. The use of nailed blocking or cleats as the sole means to secure timbers, chocks or wedges, or a nailed wood cradle, is prohibited;
    (ii) *At least one tiedown* over the top of each coil or transverse row, located near the forward-most part of the coil;
    (iii) *At least one tiedown* over the top of each coil or transverse row, located near the rearmost part of the coil; and
    (iv) *Either blocking, bracing or friction mats* to prevent longitudinal movement.

(e) **Securement of coils transported in a sided vehicle** without anchor points or an intermodal container without anchor points. Metal coils transported in a vehicle with sides without anchor points or an intermodal container without anchor points must be loaded in a manner to prevent shifting and tipping. The coils may also be secured using a system of blocking and bracing, friction mats, tiedowns, or a combination of these to prevent any horizontal movement and tipping.

§393.122 What are the rules for securing paper rolls?

(a) **Applicability.** The rules in this section apply to shipments of paper rolls which, individually or together, weigh 2268 kg (5000 lb) or more. Shipments of paper rolls that weigh less than 2268 kg (5000 lb), and paper rolls that are unitized on a pallet, may either be secured in accordance with the rules in this section or the requirements of §§393.100 through 393.114.

(b) **Securement of paper rolls** transported with eyes vertical in a sided vehicle.
  (1) *Paper rolls must be placed* tightly against the walls of the vehicle, other paper rolls, or other cargo, to prevent movement during transit.
  (2) *If there are not enough paper rolls in the shipment* to reach the walls of the vehicle, lateral movement must be prevented by filling the void, blocking, bracing, tiedowns or friction mats. The paper rolls may also be banded together.
  (3) *When any void behind a group of paper rolls,* including that at the rear of the vehicle, exceeds the diameter of the paper rolls, rearward movement must be prevented by friction mats, blocking, bracing, tiedowns, or banding to other rolls.
  (4)(i) *If a paper roll is not prevented* from tipping or falling sideways or rearwards by vehicle structure or other cargo, and its width is more than 2 times its diameter, it must be prevented from tipping or falling by banding it to other rolls, bracing, or tiedowns.
    (ii) *If the forwardmost roll(s) in a* group of paper rolls has a width greater than 1.75 times its diameter and it is not prevented from tipping or falling forwards by vehicle structure or other cargo, then it must be prevented from tipping or

falling forwards by banding it to other rolls, bracing, or tiedowns.
  - (iii) *If the forwardmost roll(s) in a* group of paper rolls has a width equal to or less than 1.75 times its diameter, and it is restrained against forward movement by friction mat(s) alone, then banding, bracing, or tiedowns are not required to prevent tipping or falling forwards.
  - (iv) *If a paper roll or the forwardmost* roll in a group of paper rolls has a width greater than 1.25 times its diameter, and it is not prevented from tipping or falling forwards by vehicle structure or other cargo, and it is not restrained against forward movement by friction mat(s) alone, then it must be prevented from tipping or falling by banding it to other rolls, bracing or tiedowns.
  - (5) *If paper rolls are banded together,* the rolls must be placed tightly against each other to form a stable group. The bands must be applied tightly, and must be secured so that they cannot fall off the rolls or to the deck.
  - (6) *A friction mat* used to provide the principal securement for a paper roll must protrude from beneath the roll in the direction in which it is providing that securement.
- (c) **Securement of split loads of paper rolls** transported with eyes vertical in a sided vehicle.
  - (1) *If a paper roll in a split load* is not prevented from forward movement by vehicle structure or other cargo, it must be prevented from forward movement by filling the open space, or by blocking, bracing, tiedowns, friction mats, or some combination of these.
  - (2) *A friction mat* used to provide the principal securement for a paper roll must protrude from beneath the roll in the direction in which it is providing that securement.
- (d) **Securement of stacked loads of paper rolls** transported with eyes vertical in a sided vehicle.
  - (1) *Paper rolls must not be loaded* on a layer of paper rolls beneath unless the lower layer extends to the front of the vehicle.
  - (2) *Paper rolls in the second and subsequent layers* must be prevented from forward, rearward or lateral movement by means as allowed for the bottom layer, or by use of a blocking roll from a lower layer.
  - (3) *The blocking roll must be at least 38 mm* (1.5 in) taller than other rolls, or must be raised at least 38 mm (1.5 in) using dunnage.
  - (4) *A roll in the rearmost row* of any layer raised using dunnage may not be secured by friction mats alone.
- (e) **Securement of paper rolls transported** with eyes crosswise in a sided vehicle.
  - (1) *The paper rolls must be prevented* from rolling or shifting longitudinally by contact with vehicle structure or other cargo, by chocks, wedges or blocking and bracing of adequate size, or by tiedowns.
  - (2) *Chocks, wedges or blocking* must be held securely in place by some means in addition to friction, so they cannot become unintentionally unfastened or loose while the vehicle is in transit.
  - (3) *The rearmost roll* must not be secured using the rear doors of the vehicle or intermodal container, or by blocking held in place by those doors.
  - (4) *If there is more than a total of 203 mm* (8 in) of space between the ends of a paper roll, or a row of rolls, and the walls of the vehicle, void fillers, blocking, bracing, friction mats, or tiedowns must be used to prevent the roll from shifting towards either wall.
- (f) **Securement of stacked loads of paper rolls** transported with eyes crosswise in a sided vehicle.
  - (1) *Rolls must not be loaded in a second layer* unless the bottom layer extends to the front of the vehicle.
  - (2) *Rolls must not be loaded in a third or higher layer* unless all wells in the layer beneath are filled.
  - (3) *The foremost roll in each upper layer,* or any roll with an empty well in front of it, must be secured against forward movement by:
    - (i) *Banding it to other rolls,* or
    - (ii) *Blocking against* an adequately secured eye-vertical blocking roll resting on the floor of the vehicle which is at least 1.5 times taller than the diameter of the roll being blocked, or
    - (iii) *Placing it in a well* formed by two rolls on the lower row whose diameter is equal to or greater than that of the roll on the upper row.
  - (4) *The rearmost roll* in each upper layer must be secured by banding it to other rolls if it is located in either of the last two wells formed by the rearmost rolls in the layer below.
  - (5) *Rolls must be secured* against lateral movement by the same means allowed for the bottom layer when there is more than a total of 203 mm (8 in) of space between the ends of a paper roll, or a row of rolls, and the walls of the vehicle.
- (g) **Securement of paper rolls transported** with the eyes lengthwise in a sided vehicle.
  - (1) *Each roll must be prevented* from forward movement by contact with vehicle structure, other cargo, blocking or tiedowns.
  - (2) *Each roll must be prevented* from rearward movement by contact with other cargo, blocking, friction mats or tiedowns.
  - (3) *The paper rolls must be prevented* from rolling or shifting laterally by contact with the wall of the vehicle or other cargo, or by chocks, wedges or blocking of adequate size.
  - (4) *Chocks, wedges or blocking* must be held securely in place by some means in addition to friction, so they cannot become unintentionally unfastened or loose while the vehicle is in transit.
- (h) **Securement of stacked loads of paper rolls** transported with the eyes lengthwise in a sided vehicle.
  - (1) *Rolls must not be loaded in a higher layer* if another roll will fit in the layer beneath.
  - (2) *An upper layer must be formed* by placing paper rolls in the wells formed by the rolls beneath.
  - (3) *A roll in an upper layer must be secured* against forward and rearward movement by any of the means allowed for the bottom layer, by use of a blocking roll, or by banding to other rolls.
- (i) **Securement of paper rolls transported** on a flatbed vehicle or in a curtain-sided vehicle.
  - (1) *Paper rolls with eyes vertical or with eyes lengthwise.*
    - (i) *The paper rolls must be loaded and secured* as described for a sided vehicle, and the entire load must be secured by tiedowns in accordance with the requirements of §§393.100 through 393.114.
    - (ii) *Stacked loads of paper rolls with eyes vertical are prohibited.*
  - (2) *Paper rolls with eyes crosswise.*
    - (i) *The paper rolls must be prevented* from rolling or shifting longitudinally by contact with vehicle structure or other cargo, by chocks, wedges or blocking and bracing of adequate size, or by tiedowns.
    - (ii) *Chocks, wedges or blocking* must be held securely in place by some means in addition to friction so that they cannot become unintentionally unfastened or loose while the vehicle is in transit.
    - (iii) *Tiedowns must be used* in accordance with the requirements of §§393.100 through 393.114 to prevent lateral movement.

§393.124 What are the rules for securing concrete pipe?

- (a) **Applicability.**
  - (1) *The rules in this section* apply to the transportation of concrete pipe on flatbed trailers and vehicles, and lowboy trailers.
  - (2) *Concrete pipe bundled tightly together* into a single rigid article that has no tendency to roll, and concrete pipe loaded in a sided vehicle or container must be secured in accordance with the provisions of §§393.100 through 393.114.
- (b) **General specifications for tiedowns.**
  - (1) *The aggregate working load limit of all tiedowns* on any group of pipes must not be less than half the total weight of all the pipes in the group.
  - (2) *A transverse tiedown through a pipe* on an upper tier or over longitudinal tiedowns is considered to secure all those pipes beneath on which that tiedown causes pressure.
- (c) **Blocking.**
  - (1) *Blocking may be one or more pieces* placed symmetrically about the center of a pipe.
  - (2) *One piece must extend at least half the distance* from the center to each end of the pipe, and two pieces must be placed on the opposite side, one at each end of the pipe.
  - (3) *Blocking must be placed firmly against the pipe,* and must be secured to prevent it moving out from under the pipe.
  - (4) *Timber blocking must have minimum dimensions* of at least 10 x 15 cm (4 x 6 in).
- (d) **Arranging the load.**
  - (1) *Pipe of different diameter.* If pipe of more than one diameter are loaded on a vehicle, groups must be formed that consist of pipe of only one size, and each group must be separately secured.
  - (2) *Arranging a bottom tier.* The bottom tier must be arranged to cover the full length of the vehicle, or as a partial tier in one group or two groups.
  - (3) *Arranging an upper tier.* Pipe must be placed only in the wells formed by adjacent pipes in the tier beneath. A third or higher tier must not be started unless all wells in the tier beneath are filled.

Subpart I - Protection Against Shifting and Falling Cargo §393.128 (b)

(4) *Arranging the top tier.* The top tier must be arranged as a complete tier, a partial tier in one group, or a partial tier in two groups.

(5) *Arranging bell pipe.*
  (i) *Bell pipe must be loaded* on at least two longitudinal spacers of sufficient height to ensure that the bell is clear of the deck.
  (ii) *Bell pipe loaded in one tier* must have the bells alternating on opposite sides of the vehicle.
  (iii) *The ends of consecutive pipe* must be staggered, if possible, within the allowable width, otherwise they must be aligned.
  (iv) *Bell pipe loaded in more than one tier* must have the bells of the bottom tier all on the same side of the vehicle.
  (v) *Pipe in every upper tier* must be loaded with bells on the opposite side of the vehicle to the bells of the tier below.
  (vi) *If the second tier is not complete,* pipe in the bottom tier which do not support a pipe above must have their bells alternating on opposite sides of the vehicle.

(e) **Securing pipe with an inside diameter** up to 1,143 mm (45 in). In addition to the requirements of paragraphs (b), (c) and (d) of this section, the following rules must be satisfied:[1]
  (1) *Stabilizing the bottom tier.*
    (i) *The bottom tier must be immobilized longitudinally* at each end by blocking, vehicle end structure, stakes, a locked pipe unloader, or other equivalent means.
    (ii) *Other pipe in the bottom tier* may also be held in place by blocks and/or wedges; and
    (iii) *Every pipe in the bottom tier* must also be held firmly in contact with the adjacent pipe by tiedowns though the front and rear pipes:
      [A] *At least one tiedown* through the front pipe of the bottom tier must run aft at an angle not more than 45 degrees with the horizontal, whenever practicable.
      [B] *At least one tiedown* through the rear pipe of the bottom tier must run forward at an angle not more than 45 degrees with the horizontal, whenever practicable.
  (2) *Use of tiedowns.*
    (i) *Each pipe may be secured individually* with tiedowns through the pipe.
    (ii) *If each pipe is not secured individually with a tiedown, then:*
      [A] *Either one 1/2-inch diameter chain or wire rope,* or two 3/8-inch diameter chain or wire rope, must be placed longitudinally over the group of pipes;
      [B] *One transverse tiedown* must be used for every 3.04 m (10 ft) of load length. The transverse tiedowns may be placed through a pipe, or over both longitudinal tiedowns between two pipes on the top tier.
      [C] *If the first pipe of a group in the top tier* is not placed in the first well formed by pipes at the front of the tier beneath, it must be secured by an additional tiedown that runs rearward at an angle not more than 45 degrees to the horizontal, whenever practicable. This tiedown must pass either through the front pipe of the upper tier, or outside it and over both longitudinal tiedowns; and
      [D] *If the last pipe of a group in the top tier* is not placed in the last well formed by pipes at the rear of the tier beneath, it must be secured by an additional tiedown that runs forward at an angle not more than 45 degrees to the horizontal, whenever practicable. This tiedown must pass either through the rear pipe of the upper tier or outside it and over both longitudinal tiedowns.

(f) **Securing large pipe,** with an inside diameter over 1143 mm (45 in). In addition to the requirements of paragraphs (b), (c) and (d) of this section, the following rules must be satisfied:
  (1) *The front pipe and the rear pipe* must be immobilized by blocking, wedges, vehicle end structure, stakes, locked pipe unloader, or other equivalent means.
  (2) *Each pipe must be secured by tiedowns through the pipe:*
    (i) *At least one tiedown through each pipe* in the front half of the load, which includes the middle one if there is an odd number, and must run rearward at an angle not more than 45 degrees with the horizontal, whenever practicable.
    (ii) *At least one tiedown through each pipe* in the rear half of the load, and must run forward at an angle not more than 45 degrees with the horizontal, whenever practicable, to hold each pipe firmly in contact with adjacent pipe; and
    (iii) *If the front or rear pipe* is not also in contact with vehicle end structure, stakes, a locked pipe unloader, or other equivalent means, at least two tiedowns positioned as described in paragraphs (f)(2)(i) and (ii) of this section, must be used through that pipe.
  (3) *If only one pipe is transported,* or if several pipes are transported without contact between other pipes, the requirements in this paragraph apply to each pipe as a single front and rear article.

§393.126 What are the rules for securing intermodal containers?

(a) **Applicability.** The rules in this section apply to the transportation of intermodal containers. Cargo contained within an intermodal container must be secured in accordance with the provisions of §§393.100 through 393.114 or, if applicable, the commodity specific rules of this part.

(b) **Securement of intermodal containers** transported on container chassis vehicle(s).
  (1) *All lower corners* of the intermodal container must be secured to the container chassis with securement devices or integral locking devices that cannot unintentionally become unfastened while the vehicle is in transit.
  (2) *The securement devices* must restrain the container from moving more than 1.27 cm (1/2 in) forward, more than 1.27 cm (1/2 in) aft, more than 1.27 cm (1/2 in) to the right, more than 1.27 cm (1/2 in) to the left, or more than 2.54 cm (1 in) vertically.
  (3) *The front and rear of the container must be secured independently.*

(c) **Securement of loaded intermodal containers** transported on vehicles other than container chassis vehicle(s).
  (1) *All lower corners of the intermodal container* must rest upon the vehicle, or the corners must be supported by a structure capable of bearing the weight of the container and that support structure must be independently secured to the motor vehicle.
  (2) *Each container must be secured to the vehicle by:*
    (i) *Chains, wire ropes or integral devices* which are fixed to all lower corners; or
    (ii) *Crossed chains* which are fixed to all upper corners; and,
  (3) *The front and rear of the container* must be secured independently. Each chain, wire rope, or integral locking device must be attached to the container in a manner that prevents it from being unintentionally unfastened while the vehicle is in transit.

(d) **Securement of empty intermodal containers** transported on vehicles other than container chassis vehicle(s). Empty intermodal containers transported on vehicles other than container chassis vehicles do not have to have all lower corners of the intermodal container resting upon the vehicle, or have all lower corners supported by a structure capable of bearing the weight of the empty container, provided:
  (1) *The empty intermodal container* is balanced and positioned on the vehicle in a manner such that the container is stable before the addition of tiedowns or other securement equipment; and,
  (2) *The amount of overhang* for the empty container on the trailer does not exceed five feet on either the front or rear of the trailer;
  (3) *The empty intermodal container* must not interfere with the vehicle's maneuverability; and,
  (4) *The empty intermodal container* is secured to prevent lateral, longitudinal, or vertical shifting.

§393.128 What are the rules for securing automobiles, light trucks and vans?

(a) **Applicability.** The rules in this section apply to the transportation of automobiles, light trucks, and vans which individually weigh 4,536 kg. (10,000 lb) or less. Vehicles which individually are heavier than 4,536 kg (10,000 lb) must be secured in accordance with the provisions of §393.130 of this part.

(b) **Securement of automobiles, light trucks, and vans.**
  (1) *Automobiles, light trucks, and vans* must be restrained at both the front and rear to prevent lateral, forward, rearward, and vertical movement using a minimum of two tiedowns.
  (2) *Tiedowns that are designed* to be affixed to the structure of the automobile, light truck, or van must use the mounting points on those vehicles that have been specifically designed for that purpose.
  (3) *Tiedowns that are designed* to fit over or around the wheels of an automobile, light truck, or van must provide restraint in the lateral, longitudinal and vertical directions.

---

1. Editor's Note: The paragraph lettering in the text above corrects a typographical error in the CFR in which paragraph (e) text was preceeded by the letter (a).

(4) *Edge protectors are not required* for synthetic webbing at points where the webbing comes in contact with the tires.

§393.130 What are the rules for securing heavy vehicles, equipment and machinery?

(a) **Applicability.** The rules in this section apply to the transportation of heavy vehicles, equipment and machinery which operate on wheels or tracks, such as front end loaders, bulldozers, tractors, and power shovels and which individually weigh 4,536 kg (10,000 lb.) or more. Vehicles, equipment and machinery which is lighter than 4,536 kg (10,000 lb.) may also be secured in accordance with the provisions of this section, with §393.128, or in accordance with the provisions of §§393.100 through 393.114.

(b) **Preparation of equipment being transported.**
 (1) *Accessory equipment,* such as hydraulic shovels, must be completely lowered and secured to the vehicle.
 (2) *Articulated vehicles shall be restrained* in a manner that prevents articulation while in transit.

(c) **Securement of heavy vehicles, equipment or machinery** with crawler tracks or wheels.
 (1) *In addition to the requirements* of paragraph (b) of this section, heavy equipment or machinery with crawler tracks or wheels must be restrained against movement in the lateral, forward, rearward, and vertical direction using a minimum of four tiedowns.
 (2) *Each of the tiedowns* must be affixed as close as practicable to the front and rear of the vehicle, or mounting points on the vehicle that have been specifically designed for that purpose.

§393.132 What are the rules for securing flattened or crushed vehicles?

(a) **Applicability.** The rules in this section apply to the transportation of vehicles such as automobiles, light trucks, and vans that have been flattened or crushed.

(b) **Prohibition on the use of synthetic webbing.** The use of synthetic webbing to secure flattened or crushed vehicles is prohibited except that such webbing may be used to connect wire rope or chain to anchor points on the commercial motor vehicle. However, the webbing (regardless of whether edge protection is used) must not come into contact with the flattened or crushed cars.

(c) **Securement of flattened or crushed vehicles.** Flattened or crushed vehicles must be transported on vehicles which have—
 (1) *Containment walls or comparable means* on four sides which extend to the full height of the load and which block against movement of the cargo in the forward, rearward and lateral directions; or
 (2) (i) *Containment walls or comparable means* on three sides which extend to the full height of the load and which block against movement of the cargo in the direction for which there is a containment wall or comparable means, and
  (ii) *A minimum of two tiedowns are required per vehicle stack;* or
 (3) (i) *Containment walls on two sides* which extend to the full height of the load and which block against movement of the cargo in the forward and rearward directions, and
  (ii) *A minimum of three tiedowns are required per vehicle stack;* or
 (4) *A minimum of four tiedowns per vehicle stack.*
 (5) *In addition to the requirements* of paragraphs (c)(2), (3), and (4), the following rules must be satisfied:
  (i) *Vehicles used to transport* flattened or crushed vehicles must be equipped with a means to prevent liquids from leaking from the bottom of the vehicle, and loose parts from falling from the bottom and all four sides of the vehicle extending to the full height of the cargo.
  (ii) *The means used to contain loose parts* may consist of structural walls, sides or sideboards, or suitable covering material, alone or in combinations.
  (iii) *The use of synthetic material* for containment of loose parts is permitted.

§393.134 What are the rules for securing roll-on/roll-off or hook lift containers?

(a) **Applicability.** The rules in this section apply to the transportation of roll-on/roll-off or hook lift containers.

(b) **Securement of a roll-on/roll-off and hook lift container.** Each roll-on/roll-off and hook lift container carried on a vehicle which is not equipped with an integral securement system must be:
 (1) *Blocked against forward movement* by the lifting device, stops, a combination of both or other suitable restraint mechanism;
 (2) *Secured to the front of the vehicle* by the lifting device or other suitable restraint against lateral and vertical movement;
 (3) *Secured to the rear of the vehicle* with at least one of the following mechanisms:
  (i) *One tiedown* attached to both the vehicle chassis and the container chassis;
  (ii) *Two tiedowns installed lengthwise,* each securing one side of the container to one of the vehicle's side rails; or
  (iii) *Two hooks, or an equivalent mechanism,* securing both sides of the container to the vehicle chassis at least as effectively as the tiedowns in the two previous items.
 (4) *The mechanisms used to secure the rear end* of a roll-on/roll off or hook lift container must be installed no more than two meters (6 ft 7 in) from the rear of the container.
 (5) *In the event that one or more of the front stops* or lifting devices are missing, damaged or not compatible, additional manually installed tiedowns must be used to secure the container to the vehicle, providing the same level of securement as the missing, damaged or incompatible components.

§393.136 What are the rules for securing large boulders?

(a) **Applicability.**
 (1) *The rules in this section* are applicable to the transportation of any large piece of natural, irregularly shaped rock weighing in excess of 5,000 kg (11,000 lb.) or with a volume in excess of 2 cubic-meters on an open vehicle, or in a vehicle whose sides are not designed and rated to contain such cargo.
 (2) *Pieces of rock weighing more than 100 kg (220 lb.),* but less than 5,000 kg (11,000 lb.) must be secured, either in accordance with this section, or in accordance with the provisions of §§393.100 through 393.114, including:
  (i) *Rock contained* within a vehicle which is designed to carry such cargo; or
  (ii) *Secured individually by tiedowns,* provided each piece can be stabilized and adequately secured.
 (3) *Rock which has been formed or cut to a shape* and which provides a stable base for securement must also be secured, either in accordance with the provisions of this section, or in accordance with the provisions of §§393.100 through 393.114.

(b) **General requirements for the positioning of boulders on the vehicle.**
 (1) *Each boulder must be placed* with its flattest and/or largest side down.
 (2) *Each boulder must be supported* on at least two pieces of hard wood blocking at least 10 cm x 10 cm (4 inches x 4 inches) side dimensions extending the full width of the boulder.
 (3) *Hardwood blocking pieces* must be placed as symmetrically as possible under the boulder and should support at least three-fourths of the length of the boulder.
 (4) *If the flattest side of a boulder* is rounded or partially rounded, so that the boulder may roll, it must be placed in a crib made of hardwood timber fixed to the deck of the vehicle so that the boulder rests on both the deck and the timber, with at least three well-separated points of contact that prevent its tendency to roll in any direction.
 (5) *If a boulder is tapered,* the narrowest end must point towards the front of the vehicle.

(c) **General tiedown requirements.**
 (1) *Only chain may be used as tiedowns to secure large boulders.*
 (2) *Tiedowns which are in direct contact* with the boulder should, where possible, be located in valleys or notches across the top of the boulder, and must be arranged to prevent sliding across the rock surface.

(d) **Securement of a cubic shaped boulder.** In addition to the requirements of paragraphs (b) and (c) of this section, the following rules must be satisfied:
 (1) *Each boulder must be secured individually* with at least two chain tiedowns placed transversely across the vehicle.
 (2) *The aggregate working load limit of the tiedowns* must be at least half the weight of the boulder.
 (3) *The tiedowns must be placed as closely as possible* to the wood blocking used to support the boulder.

(e) **Securement of a non-cubic shaped boulder** — with a stable base. In addition to the requirements of paragraphs (b) and (c) of this section, the following rules must be satisfied:
 (1) *The boulder must be secured individually* with at least two chain tiedowns forming an "X" pattern over the boulder.
 (2) *The aggregate working load limit of the tiedowns* must be at least half the weight of the boulder.

Subpart J - Frames, Cab and Body Components, Wheels, Steering, and Suspension Systems §393.209 (e)

(3) *The tiedowns must pass* over the center of the boulder and must be attached to each other at the intersection by a shackle or other connecting device.

(f) **Securement of a non-cubic shaped boulder** — with an unstable base. In addition to the requirements of paragraphs (b) and (c) of this section, each boulder must be secured by a combination of chain tiedowns as follows:

(1) *One chain must surround the top of the boulder* (at a point between one-half and two-thirds of its height). The working load limit of the chain must be at least half the weight of the boulder.

(2) *Four chains must be attached* to the surrounding chain and the vehicle to form a blocking mechanism which prevents any horizontal movement. Each chain must have a working load limit of at least one-fourth the weight of the boulder. Whenever practicable, the angle of the chains must not exceed 45 degrees from the horizontal.

Subpart J - Frames, Cab and Body Components, Wheels, Steering, and Suspension Systems

§393.201 Frames.

(a) **The frame or chassis** of each commercial motor vehicle shall not be cracked, loose, sagging or broken.

(b) **Bolts or brackets securing** the cab or the body of the vehicle to the frame must not be loose, broken, or missing.

(c) **The frame rail flanges between the axles** shall not be bent, cut or notched, except as specified by the manufacturer.

(d) **Parts and accessories shall not be welded** to the frame or chassis of a commercial motor vehicle except in accordance with the vehicle manufacturer's recommendations. Any welded repair of the frame must also be in accordance with the vehicle manufacturer's recommendations.

(e) **No holes shall be drilled** in the top or bottom rail flanges, except as specified by the manufacturer.

§393.201 DOT Interpretations

Question 1: Are crossmembers of CMVs considered part of the frame?
Guidance: Yes.
Question 2: Does §393.201 of the FMCSRs apply to trailers?
Guidance: No. Section 393.201 is specific to buses, trucks, and truck tractors.
Question 3: Are welded repairs or modifications to the frame of a CMV violations of the FMCSRs?
Guidance: Welding would not be a violation of the FMCSRs unless the process used for the metals being welded or the location of the weld reduced the safety of operation of the vehicle. The safety of a repaired and/or modified vehicle would depend on the structural design of the frame, as well as the modifications performed. The manufacturer of the vehicle should be contacted for assistance.

§393.203 Cab and body components.

(a) **The cab compartment doors or door parts** used as an entrance or exist shall not be missing or broken. Doors shall not sag so that they cannot be properly opened or closed. No door shall be wired shut or otherwise secured in the closed position so that it cannot be readily opened.
EXCEPTION: When the vehicle is loaded with pipe or bar stock that blocks the door and the cab has a roof exit.

(b) **Bolts or brackets securing the cab** or the body of the vehicle to the frame shall not be loose, broken, or missing.

(c) **The hood must be securely fastened.**

(d) **All seats must be securely mounted.**

(e) **The front bumper must not be missing,** loosely attached, or protruding beyond the confines of the vehicle so as to create a hazard.

§393.205 Wheels.

(a) **Wheels and rims shall not be cracked or broken.**

(b) **Stud or bolt holes on the wheels** shall not be elongated (out of round).

(c) **Nuts or bolts shall not be missing or loose.**

§393.207 Suspension systems.

(a) **Axles.** No axle positioning part shall be cracked, broken, loose or missing. All axles must be in proper alignment.

(b) **Adjustable axles.** Adjustable axle assemblies shall not have locking pins missing or disengaged.

(c) **Leaf springs.** No leaf spring shall be cracked, broken, or missing nor shifted out of position.

(d) **Coil springs.** No coil spring shall be cracked or broken.

(e) **Torsion bar.** No torsion bar or torsion bar suspension shall be cracked or broken.

(f) **Air suspensions.** The air pressure regulator valve shall not allow air into the suspension system until at least 55 psi is in the braking system. The vehicle shall be level (not tilting to the left or right). Air leakage shall not be greater than 3 psi in a 5-minute time period when the vehicle's air pressure gauge shows normal operating pressure.

(g) **Air suspension exhaust controls.** The air suspension exhaust controls must not have the capability to exhaust air from the suspension system of one axle of a two-axle air suspension trailer unless the controls are either located on the trailer, or the power unit and trailer combination are not capable of traveling at a speed greater than 10 miles per hour while the air is exhausted from the suspension system. This paragraph shall not be construed to prohibit —

(1) *Devices that could exhaust air* from both axle systems simultaneously; or

(2) *Lift axles* on multi-axle units.

§393.209 Steering wheel systems.

(a) **The steering wheel shall be secured** and must not have any spokes cracked through or missing.

(b) **Steering wheel lash.**

(1) *The steering wheel lash shall not exceed the following parameters:*

Steering wheel diameter	Manual steering system	Power steering system
406 mm or less (16 inches or less)	51 mm (2 inches)	108 mm (4 1/4 inches)
457 mm (18 inches)	57 mm (2 1/4 inches)	121 mm (4 3/4 inches)
483 mm (19 inches)	60 mm (2 3/8 inches)	127 mm (5 inches)
508 mm (20 inches)	64 mm (2 1/2 inches)	133 mm (5 1/4 inches)
533 mm (21 inches)	67 mm (2 5/8 inches)	140 mm (5 1/2 inches)
559 mm (22 inches)	70 mm (2 3/4 inches)	146 mm (5 3/4 inches)

(2) *For steering wheel diameters* not listed in paragraph (b)(1) of this section the steering wheel lash shall not exceed 14 degrees angular rotation for manual steering systems, and 30 degrees angular rotation for power steering systems.

(c) **Steering column.** The steering column must be securely fastened.

(d) **Steering system.** Universal joints and ball-and-socket joints shall not be worn, faulty or repaired by welding. The steering gear box shall not have loose or missing mounting bolts or cracks in the gear box or mounting brackets. The pitman arm on the steering gear output shaft shall not be loose. Steering wheels shall turn freely through the limit of travel in both directions.

(e) **Power steering systems.** All components of the power system must be in operating condition. No parts shall be loose or broken. Belts shall not be frayed, cracked or slipping. The system shall not leak. The power steering system shall have sufficient fluid in the reservoir.

Special Topics — CMV Parts and Accessories

Question 1: Do tires marked "NHS" (not for highway service) mean that highway use is prohibited by §393.75?
Guidance: No, provided the use of such tires does not decrease the safety of operations (see Periodic Inspection Requirements, Appendix G to Subpart B).

Part 394 [Reserved]

Part 393 - Parts and Accessories Necessary for Safe Operation

Notes

Part 395 - Hours of Service of Drivers[1]

(Page 145 in the Driver Edition)

§395.0 Rescission.
Any regulations on hours of service of drivers in effect before April 28, 2003, which were amended or replaced by the final rule adopted on April 28, 2003 [69 FR 22456] are rescinded and not in effect.

§395.1 Scope of rules in this part.
(a) *General.*
  (1) *The rules in this part* apply to all motor carriers and drivers, except as provided in paragraphs (b) through (o) of this section.
  (2) *The exceptions from Federal requirements* contained in paragraphs (l) through (n) do not preempt State laws and regulations governing the safe operation of commercial motor vehicles.

(b) *Adverse driving conditions.*
  (1) *Except as provided* in paragraph (h)(2) of this section, a driver who encounters adverse driving conditions, as defined in §395.2, and cannot, because of those conditions, safely complete the run within the maximum driving time permitted by §§395.3(a) or 395.5(a) may drive and be permitted or required to drive a commercial motor vehicle for not more than 2 additional hours in order to complete that run or to reach a place offering safety for the occupants of the commercial motor vehicle and security for the commercial motor vehicle and its cargo. However, that driver may not drive or be permitted to drive —
    (i) *For more than 13 hours in the aggregate* following 10 consecutive hours off duty for drivers of property-carrying commercial motor vehicles;
    (ii) *After the end* of the 14th hour since coming on duty following 10 consecutive hours off duty for drivers of property-carrying commercial motor vehicles;
    (iii) *For more than 12 hours in the aggregate* following 8 consecutive hours off duty for drivers of passenger-carrying commercial motor vehicles; or
    (iv) *After he/she has been on duty* 15 hours following 8 consecutive hours off duty for drivers of passenger-carrying commercial motor vehicles.
  (2) *Emergency conditions.* In case of any emergency, a driver may complete his/her run without being in violation of the provisions of the regulations in this part, if such run reasonably could have been completed absent the emergency.

(c) *Driver-salesperson.* The provisions of §395.3(b) shall not apply to any driver-salesperson whose total driving time does not exceed 40 hours in any period of 7 consecutive days.

(d) *Oilfield operations.*
  (1) *In the instance* of drivers of commercial motor vehicles used exclusively in the transportation of oilfield equipment, including the stringing and picking up of pipe used in pipelines, and servicing of the field operations of the natural gas and oil industry, any period of 8 consecutive days may end with the beginning of any off-duty period of 24 or more successive hours.
  (2) *In the case of specially trained drivers* of commercial motor vehicles which are specially constructed to service oil wells, on-duty time shall not include waiting time at a natural gas or oil well site; provided, that all such time shall be fully and accurately accounted for in records to be maintained by the motor carrier. Such records shall be made available upon request of the Federal Motor Carrier Safety Administration.

(e) *Short-haul operations—*
  (1) *100 air-mile radius driver.* A driver is exempt from the requirements of §395.8 if:
    (i) *The driver operates* within a 100 air-mile radius of the normal work reporting location;
    (ii) *The driver*, except a driver-salesperson, returns to the work reporting location and is released from work within 12 consecutive hours;
    (iii)[A] *A property-carrying* commercial motor vehicle driver has at least 10 consecutive hours off duty separating each 12 hours on duty;
      [B] *A passenger-carrying* commercial motor vehicle driver has at least 8 consecutive hours off duty separating each 12 hours on duty;
    (iv)[A] *A property-carrying* commercial motor vehicle driver does not exceed 11 hours maximum driving time following 10 consecutive hours off duty; or
      [B] *A passenger-carrying* commercial motor vehicle driver does not exceed 10 hours maximum driving time following 8 consecutive hours off duty; and
    (v) *The motor carrier that employs the driver* maintains and retains for a period of 6 months accurate and true time records showing:
      [A] The time the driver reports for duty each day;
      [B] The total number of hours the driver is on duty each day;
      [C] The time the driver is released from duty each day; and
      [D] The total time for the preceding 7 days in accordance with §395.8(j)(2) for drivers used for the first time or intermittently.
  (2) *Operators of property-carrying* commercial motor vehicles not requiring a commercial driver's license. Except as provided in this paragraph, a driver is exempt from the requirements of §395.3 and §395.8 and ineligible to use the provisions of §395.1(e)(1), (g) and (o) if:
    (i) *The driver operates* a property-carrying commercial motor vehicle for which a commercial driver's license is not required under Part 383 of this subchapter;
    (ii) *The driver operates* within a 150 air-mile radius of the location where the driver reports to and is released from work, i.e., the normal work reporting location;
    (iii) *The driver returns* to the normal work reporting location at the end of each duty tour;
    (iv) *The driver* has at least 10 consecutive hours off duty separating each on-duty period;
    (v) *The driver* does not drive more than 11 hours following at least 10 consecutive hours off duty;
    (vi) *The driver does not drive:*
      [A] After the 14th hour after coming on duty on 5 days of any period of 7 consecutive days; and
      [B] After the 16th hour after coming on duty on 2 days of any period of 7 consecutive days;
    (vii) *The driver does not drive:*
      [A] After having been on duty for 60 hours in 7 consecutive days if the employing motor carrier does not operate commercial motor vehicles every day of the week;
      [B] After having been on duty for 70 hours in 8 consecutive days if the employing motor carrier operates commercial motor vehicles every day of the week;
    (viii) *Any period* of 7 or 8 consecutive days may end with the beginning of any off-duty period of 34 or more consecutive hours.
    (ix) *The motor carrier that employs the driver* maintains and retains for a period of 6 months accurate and true time records showing:
      [A] The time the driver reports for duty each day;
      [B] The total number of hours the driver is on duty each day;
      [C] The time the driver is released from duty each day;
      [D] The total time for the preceding 7 days in accordance with §395.8(j)(2) for drivers used for the first time or intermittently.

(f) *Retail store deliveries.* The provisions of §395.3 (a) and (b) shall not apply with respect to drivers of commercial motor vehicles engaged solely in making local deliveries from retail stores and/or retail catalog businesses to the ultimate consumer, when driving solely within a 100-air mile radius of the driver's work-reporting location, during the period from December 10 to December 25, both inclusive, of each year.

(g) *Sleeper berths —*
  (1) *Property-carrying commercial motor vehicle —*
    (i) *In General.* A driver who operates a property-carrying commercial motor vehicle equipped with a sleeper berth, as defined in §§395.2 and 393.76 of this subchapter,

---

1. *Editor's Note:* The Federal Motor Carrier Safety Administration (FMCSA) has posted the following note at the beginning of each interpretation for sections appearing in Part 395: 'The FMCSA is currently updating and revising its regulatory guidance to Part 395 of the Federal Motor Carrier Safety Regulations (FMCSRs) to conform to the provisions of the new hours-of-service regulations, and to provide additional guidance concerning the application of the new regulations. All prior interpretations and regulatory guidance relating to Part 395 of the FMCSRs, as well as FMCSA and FHWA memoranda and letters concerning Part 395, may no longer be relied upon as authoritative to the extent they are inconsistent with the final rule published April 28, 2003 and the Technical Amendments published September 30, 2003. All interpretations and guidance for Parts other than Part 395 remain valid.

[A] *Must, before driving, accumulate*
  [1] *At least 10 consecutive hours off duty;*
  [2] *At least 10 consecutive hours of sleeper-berth time;*
  [3] *A combination* of consecutive sleeper-berth and off-duty time amounting to at least 10 hours; or
  [4] *The equivalent* of at least 10 consecutive hours off duty if the driver does not comply with paragraph (g)(1)(i)[A][1], [2], or [3] of this section;
[B] *May not drive* more than 11 hours following one of the 10-hour off-duty periods specified in paragraph (g)(1)(i)[A][1] through [4] of this section; and
[C] *May not drive* after the 14th hour after coming on duty following one of the 10-hour off-duty periods specified in paragraph (g)(1)(i)[A][1] through [4] of this section; and
[D] *Must exclude* from the calculation of the 14-hour limit any sleeper berth period of at least 8 but less than 10 consecutive hours.

(ii) *Specific requirements.* — The following rules apply in determining compliance with paragraph (g)(1)(i) of this section:
[A] *The term* "equivalent of at least 10 consecutive hours off duty" means a period of
  [1] *At least 8* but less than 10 consecutive hours in a sleeper berth, and
  [2] *A separate period* of at least 2 but less than 10 consecutive hours either in the sleeper berth or off duty, or any combination thereof.
[B] *Calculation* of the 11-hour driving limit includes all driving time; compliance must be re-calculated from the end of the first of the two periods used to comply with paragraph (g)(1)(ii)[A] of this section.
[C] *Calculation* of the 14-hour limit includes all time except any sleeper-berth period of at least 8 but less than 10 consecutive hours; compliance must be re-calculated from the end of the first of the two periods used to comply with the requirements of paragraph (g)(1)(ii)[A] of this section.

(2) *Specially trained driver* of a specially constructed oil well servicing commercial motor vehicle at a natural gas or oil well location. A specially trained driver who operates a commercial motor vehicle specially constructed to service natural gas or oil wells that is equipped with a sleeper berth, as defined in §§395.2 and 393.76 of this subchapter, or who is off duty at a natural gas or oil well location, may accumulate the equivalent of 10 consecutive hours off duty time by taking a combination of at least 10 consecutive hours of off-duty time, sleeper-berth time, or time in other sleeping accommodations at a natural gas or oil well location; or by taking two periods of rest in a sleeper berth, or other sleeping accommodation at a natural gas or oil well location, providing:

(i) *Neither rest period is shorter than 2 hours;*
(ii) *The driving time* in the period immediately before and after each rest period, when added together, does not exceed 11 hours;
(iii) *The driver does not drive* after the 14th hour after coming on duty following 10 hours off duty, where the 14th hour is calculated:
  [A] *By excluding any sleeper berth* or other sleeping accommodation period of at least 2 hours which, when added to a subsequent sleeper berth or other sleeping accommodation period, totals at least 10 hours, and
  [B] *By including all on-duty time,* all off-duty time not spent in the sleeper berth or other sleeping accommodations, all such periods of less than 2 hours, and any period not described in paragraph (g)(2)(iii)[A] of this section; and
(iv) *The driver may not return to driving* subject to the normal limits under §395.3 without taking at least 10 consecutive hours off duty, at least 10 consecutive hours in the sleeper berth or other sleeping accommodations, or a combination of at least 10 consecutive hours off duty, sleeper berth time, or time in other sleeping accommodations.

(3) *Passenger-carrying commercial motor vehicles.* A driver who is driving a passenger-carrying commercial motor vehicle that is equipped with a sleeper berth, as defined in §§395.2 and 393.76 of this subchapter, may accumulate the equivalent of 8 consecutive hours of off-duty time by taking a combination of at least 8 consecutive hours off-duty and sleeper berth time; or by taking two periods of rest in the sleeper berth, providing:[1]

(i) *Neither rest period is shorter than two hours;*
(ii) *The driving time in the period* immediately before and after each rest period, when added together, does not exceed 10 hours;
(iii) *The on-duty time in the period* immediately before and after each rest period, when added together, does not include any driving time after the 15th hour; and
(iv) *The driver may not return to driving* subject to the normal limits under §395.5 without taking at least 8 consecutive hours off duty, at least 8 consecutive hours in the sleeper berth, or a combination of at least 8 consecutive hours off duty and sleeper berth time.

(h) **State of Alaska —**
(1) *Property-carrying commercial motor vehicle.* The provisions of §395.3(a) and (b) do not apply to any driver who is driving a commercial motor vehicle in the State of Alaska. A driver who is driving a property-carrying commercial motor vehicle in the State of Alaska must not drive or be required or permitted to drive —
  (i) *More than 15 hours following 10 consecutive hours off duty;* or
  (ii) *After being on duty for 20 hours or more* following 10 consecutive hours off duty.
  (iii) *After having been on duty for 70 hours* in any period of 7 consecutive days, if the motor carrier for which the driver drives does not operate every day in the week; or
  (iv) *After having been on duty for 80 hours* in any period of 8 consecutive days, if the motor carrier for which the driver drives operates every day in the week.

(2) *Passenger-carrying commercial motor vehicle.* The provisions of §395.5 do not apply to any driver who is driving a passenger-carrying commercial motor vehicle in the State of Alaska. A driver who is driving a passenger-carrying commercial motor vehicle in the State of Alaska must not drive or be required or permitted to drive —
  (i) *More than 15 hours following 8 consecutive hours off duty;*
  (ii) *After being on duty for 20 hours or more* following 8 consecutive hours off duty;
  (iii) *After having been on duty for 70 hours* in any period of 7 consecutive days, if the motor carrier for which the driver drives does not operate every day in the week; or
  (iv) *After having been on duty for 80 hours* in any period of 8 consecutive days, if the motor carrier for which the driver drives operates every day in the week.

(3) *A driver who is driving a commercial motor vehicle* in the State of Alaska and who encounters adverse driving conditions (as defined in §395.2) may drive and be permitted or required to drive a commercial motor vehicle for the period of time needed to complete the run.
  (i) *After a property-carrying* commercial motor vehicle driver completes the run, that driver must be off duty for at least 10 consecutive hours before he/she drives again; and
  (ii) *After a passenger-carrying* commercial motor vehicle driver completes the run, that driver must be off duty for at least 8 consecutive hours before he/she drives again.

(i) **State of Hawaii.** The rules in §395.8 do not apply to a driver who drives a commercial motor vehicle in the State of Hawaii, if the motor carrier who employs the driver maintains and retains for a period of 6 months accurate and true records showing —
(1) *The total number of hours the driver is on duty each day;* and
(2) *The time at which the driver* reports for, and is released from, duty each day.

(j) **Travel time —**
(1) *When a property-carrying* commercial motor vehicle driver at the direction of the motor carrier is traveling, but not driving or assuming any other responsibility to the carrier, such time must be counted as on-duty time unless the driver is afforded at least 10 consecutive hours off duty when arriving at destination, in which case he/she must be considered off duty for the entire period.
(2) *When a passenger-carrying* commercial motor vehicle driver at the direction of the motor carrier is traveling, but not driving or assuming any other responsibility to the carrier, such time must be counted as on-duty time unless the driver is afforded at least 8 consecutive hours off duty when arriving at destina-

---

1. Subparagraphs (g)(3)(i)-(iv) were deleted from the CFR following the incorporation of an amendment appearing in the August 25, 2005, Federal Register due to inaccurate amendatory instructions.

Part 395 - Hours of Service of Drivers §395.1 (o)

tion, in which case he/she must be considered off duty for the entire period.

(k) Agricultural operations. The provisions of this part shall not apply to drivers transporting agricultural commodities or farm supplies for agricultural purposes in a State if such transportation:
  (1) *Is limited* to an area within a 100 air-mile radius from the source of the commodities or the distribution point for the farm supplies, and
  (2) *Is conducted* during the planting and harvesting seasons within such State, as determined by the State.

(l) Ground water well drilling operations. In the instance of a driver of a commercial motor vehicle who is used primarily in the transportation and operations of a ground water well drilling rig, any period of 7 or 8 consecutive days may end with the beginning of any off-duty period of 24 or more successive hours.

(m) Construction materials and equipment. In the instance of a driver of a commercial motor vehicle who is used primarily in the transportation of construction materials and equipment, any period of 7 or 8 consecutive days may end with the beginning of any off-duty period of 24 or more successive hours.

(n) Utility service vehicles. In the instance of a driver of a utility service vehicle, any period of 7 or 8 consecutive days may end with the beginning of any off-duty period of 24 or more successive hours.

(o) Property-carrying driver. A property-carrying driver is exempt from the requirements of §395.3(a)(2) if:
  (1) *The driver has returned* to the driver's normal work reporting location and the carrier released the driver from duty at that location for the previous five duty tours the driver has worked;
  (2) *The driver has returned* to the normal work reporting location and the carrier releases the driver from duty within 16 hours after coming on duty following 10 consecutive hours off duty; and
  (3) *The driver has not taken this exemption* within the previous 6 consecutive days, except when the driver has begun a new 7- or 8-consecutive day period with the beginning of any off-duty period of 34 or more consecutive hours as allowed by §395.3(c).

§395.1 DOT Interpretations

Question 1: What hours-of-service regulations apply to drivers operating between the United States and Mexico or between the United States and Canada?
Guidance: When operating CMVs, as defined in §390.5, in the United States, all hours-of-service provisions apply to all drivers of CMVs, regardless of nationality, point of origin, or where the driving time or on-duty time was accrued.

Question 2: If a driver invokes the exception for adverse driving conditions, does a supervisor need to sign the driver's record of duty status when he/she arrives at the destination?
Guidance: No.

Question 3: May a driver use the adverse driving conditions exception if he/she has accumulated driving time and on-duty (not driving) time, that would put the driver over 15 hours or over 70 hours in 8 consecutive days?
Guidance: No. The adverse driving conditions exception applies only to the 10-hour rule.

Question 4: Are there allowances made in the FMCSRs for delays caused by loading and unloading?
Guidance: No. Although the regulations do make some allowances for unforeseen contingencies such as in §395.1(b), adverse driving conditions, and §395.1(b)(2), emergency conditions, loading and unloading delays are not covered by these sections.

Question 5: How may a driver utilize the adverse driving conditions exception or the emergency conditions exception as found in §395.1(b), to preclude an hours of service violation?
Guidance: An absolute prerequisite for any such claim must be that the trip involved is one which could normally and reasonably have been completed without a violation and that the unforeseen event occurred after the driver began the trip.

Drivers who are dispatched after the motor carrier has been notified or should have known of adverse driving conditions are not eligible for the two hours additional driving time provided for under §395.1(b), adverse driving conditions. The term "in any emergency" shall not be construed as encompassing such situations as a driver's desire to get home, shippers' demands, market declines, shortage of drivers, or mechanical failures.

Question 6: What does "servicing" of the field operations of the natural gas and oil industry cover?
Guidance: Servicing of field operations, as described by the ICC report issued with this exemption, covers those services generally performed by specialized companies supporting the petroleum drilling and producing industry, "including testing, mudfilling, cementing, hydraulic fracturing, voltage, logging, and resistivity measurements, and cleaning of industrial equipment, as the particular requirement might arise in the normal course of well digging or maintenance operations * * * " (89 M.C.C. 19, at 28, March 29, 1962). Water servicing companies, whose operations are exclusive to servicing the natural gas and oil industry, are also covered by the provisions of §395.1(d).

§395.1(d) applies only to situations involving drilling or the operation of wells. It does not apply to exploration activities.

Question 7: What is considered "oilfield equipment" for the purposes of 395.1(d)(1)?
Guidance: Oilfield equipment is not specifically defined in this section. However, its meaning is broader than the "specially constructed" commercial motor vehicles referred to in §395.1(d)(2), and may encompass a spectrum of equipment ranging from an entire vehicle to hand-held devices.

Question 8: What kinds of oilfield equipment may drivers operate while taking advantage of the special rule in §395.1(d)(2)?
Guidance: The special rule in §395.1(d)(2) applies only to drivers transporting the equipment identified by the former Interstate Commerce Commission (now part of the Federal Highway Administration) in a 1962 report to accompany the oilfield rule. The report indicated the specialized equipment normally consists of heavy machinery permanently mounted on commercial motor vehicles, designed to fill a specific need.

Question 9: Are drivers required to be dedicated permanently to the oilfield industry, or must they exclusively transport oilfield equipment or service the field operations of the industry only for each eight-day (or shorter) period ended by an off-duty period of 24 or more consecutive hours?
Guidance: A driver must exclusively transport oilfield equipment or service the field operations of the industry for each eight-day (or shorter) period before his/her off-duty period of 24 or more consecutive hours. However, he/she must be in full compliance with the requirements of 395.3(b) before driving other commercial motor vehicles not used to service the field operations of the natural gas or oil industry.

Question 10: A driver is used exclusively to transport materials (such as sand or water) which are used exclusively to service the field operations of the natural gas or oil industry. Occasionally, the driver has leftover materials that must be transported back to a motor carrier facility or service depot. Would such a return trip be covered by §395.1(d)(1)?
Guidance: Yes. Transporting excess materials back to a facility from the well site is part of the servicing operations. However, such servicing operations are limited to transportation back and forth between the service depot or motor carrier facility and the field site. Transportation of materials from one depot to another, from a railhead to a depot, or from a motor carrier terminal to a depot, is not considered to be in direct support of field operations.

Question 11: May specially trained drivers of specially constructed oil well servicing vehicles cumulate the 8 consecutive hours off duty required by §395.3 by combining off-duty time or sleeper-berth time at a natural gas or oil well site with off-duty time or sleeper-berth time while en route to or from the well?
Guidance: These drivers may cumulate the required 8 consecutive hours off duty by combining two separate periods, each at least 2 hours long, of off-duty time or sleeper-berth time at a natural gas or oil well location with sleeper-berth time in a CMV while en route to or from such a location. They may also cumulate the required 8 consecutive hours off duty by combining an off-duty period of at least 2 hours at a well site with: (1) Another off-duty period at the well site that, when added to the first such period, equals at least 8 hours, or (2) a period in a sleeper-berth, either at or away from the well site, or in other sleeping accommodations at the well site, that, when added to the first off-duty period, equals at least 8 hours.

However, such drivers may not combine a period of less than 8 hours off duty away from a natural gas or oil well site with another period of less than 8 hours off duty at such well sites. The special provisions for drivers at well sites are strictly limited to those locations.

The following table indicates what types of off-site and on-site time periods may be combined.

	On Site Off Duty Time	On Site Sleeper Berth	On Site Other Sleeping Accommodation
Away from Site Off Duty Time			
Away from Site Sleeper Berth Time	X Combination must be 8 or more hours.	X Combination must be 8 or more hours.	X Combination must be 8 or more hours.
Away from Site Other Sleeping Accomodation			

Question 12: What constitutes the 100-air-mile radius exemption?
Guidance: The term "air mile" is internationally defined as a "nautical mile" which is equivalent to 6,076 feet or 1,852 meters. Thus, the 100 air miles are equivalent to 115.08 statute miles or 185.2 kilometers.

Question 13: What documentation must a driver claiming the 100-air-mile radius exemption [§395.1(e)] have in his/her possession?
Guidance: None.

Question 14: Must a motor carrier retain 100-air-mile driver time records at its principal place of business?
Guidance: No. However, upon request by an authorized representative of the FMCSA or State official, the records must be produced within a reasonable period of time (2 working days) at the location where the review takes place.

Question 15: May an operation that changes its normal work-reporting location on an intermittent basis utilize the 100-air-mile radius exemption?
Guidance: Yes. However, when the motor carrier changes the normal reporting location to a new reporting location, that trip (from the old location to the new location) must be recorded on the record of duty status because the driver has not returned to his/her normal work reporting location.

Question 16: May a driver use a record of duty status form as a time record to meet the requirement contained in the 100-air-mile radius exemption?
Guidance: Yes, provided the form contains the mandatory information.

Question 17: Is the "mandatory information" referred to in the previous guidance that required of a normal RODS under §395.8(d) or that of the 100-air-mile radius exemption under §395.1(e)(5)?
Guidance: The "mandatory information" referred to is the time records specified by §395.1(e)(5) which must show: (1) The time the driver reports for duty each day; (2) the total number of hours the driver is on duty each day; (3) the time the driver is released from duty each day; and (4) the total time for the preceding 7 days in accordance with §395.8(j)(2) for drivers used for the first time or intermittently.
Using the RODS to comply with §395.1(e)(5) is not prohibited as long as the RODS contains driver identification, the date, the time the driver began work, the time the driver ended work, and the total hours on duty.

Question 18: Must the driver's name and each date worked appear on the time record prepared to comply with §395.1(e), 100-air-mile radius driver?
Guidance: Yes. The driver's name or other identification and date worked must be shown on the time record.

Question 19: May drivers who work split shifts take advantage of the 100-air-mile radius exemption found at §395.1(e)?
Guidance: Yes. Drivers who work split shifts may take advantage of the 100-air-mile radius exemption if: 1. The drivers operate within a 100-air-mile radius of their normal work-reporting locations; 2. The drivers return to their work-reporting locations and are released from work at the end of each shift and each shift is less than 12 consecutive hours; 3. The drivers are off-duty for more than 8 consecutive hours before reporting for their first shift of the day and spend less than 12 hours, in the aggregate, on-duty each day; 4. The drivers do not exceed a total of 10 hours driving time and are afforded 8 or more consecutive hours off-duty prior to their first shift of the day; and 5. The employing motor carriers maintain and retain the time records required by 395.1(e)(5).

Question 20: May a driver who is taking advantage of the 100-air-mile radius exemption in §395.1(e) be intermittently off-duty during the period away from the work-reporting location?

Guidance: Yes, a driver may be intermittently off-duty during the period away from the work-reporting location provided the driver meets all requirements for being off-duty. If the driver's period away from the work-reporting location includes periods of off-duty time, the time record must show both total on-duty time and total off-duty time during his/her tour of duty. In any event, the driver must return to the work-reporting location and be released from work within 12 consecutive hours.

Question 21: When a driver fails to meet the provisions of the 100-air-mile radius exemption (§395.1(e)), is the driver required to have copies of his/her records of duty status for the previous seven days? Must the driver prepare daily records of duty status for the next seven days? *Guidance:* The driver must only have in his/her possession a record of duty status for the day he/she does not qualify for the exemption. A driver must begin to prepare the record of duty status for the day immediately after he/she becomes aware that the terms of the exemption cannot be met. The record of duty status must cover the entire day, even if the driver has to record retroactively changes in status that occurred between the time that the driver reported for duty and the time in which he/she no longer qualified for the 100 air-mile radius exemption. This is the only way to ensure that a driver does not claim the right to drive 10 hours after leaving his/her exempt status, in addition to the hours already driven under the 100-air-mile exemption.

Question 22: A driver returns to his/her normal work reporting location from a location beyond the 100-air-mile radius and goes off duty for 7 hours. May the driver return to duty after being off-duty for 7 hours and utilize the 100-air-mile radius exemption?
Guidance: No. The 7-hour off-duty period has not met the requirement of 8 consecutive hours separating each 12-hour on-duty period. The driver must first accumulate 8 consecutive hours off-duty before operating under the 100-air-mile radius exemption.

Question 23: Is the exemption contained in §395.1(f) concerning department store deliveries during the period from December 10 to December 25 limited to only drivers employed by department stores?
Guidance: No. The exemption applies to all drivers engaged solely in making local deliveries from retail stores and/or retail catalog businesses to the ultimate consumer, when driving solely within a 100-air-mile radius of the driver's work-reporting location, during the dates specified.

Question 24: May time spent in sleeping facilities being transported as cargo (e.g., boats, campers, travel trailers) be recorded as sleeper berth time?
Guidance: No, it cannot be recorded as sleeper berth time.

Question 25: May sleeper berth time and off-duty periods be combined to meet the 8-hour off-duty requirement?
Guidance: Yes, as long as the 8-hour period is consecutive and not broken by on-duty or driving activities. This does not apply to drivers at natural gas or oil well locations who may separate the periods.

Question 26: May a driver record sleeper berth time as off-duty time on line one of the record of duty status?
Guidance: No. The driver's record of duty status must accurately reflect the driver's activities.

Question 27: After accumulating 8 consecutive hours of off-duty time, a driver spends 2 hours in the sleeper berth. The driver then drives a CMV for 10 hours, then spends 6 hours in the sleeper berth. May the driver combine the two sleeper berth periods to meet the required 8 consecutive hours of off-duty time per §395.1(h), then drive for up to 10 more hours?
Guidance: No. The 10 hours of driving time between the first and second sleeper berth periods must be considered in determining the amount of time that the driver may drive after the second sleeper berth period. Sleeper berths are intended to be used between periods of on- duty time. When a driver has already been off duty for more than 8 consecutive hours, and has therefore had adequate opportunity to rest, he/she may not "save" additional hours before going on duty and add them to the next sleeper berth period. In short, a driver must be on duty before he/she begins to accumulate sleeper berth time. The driver in your scenario is operating in violation of the hours of service regulations for the entire second 10-hour driving period until that driver is able to secure at least 8 consecutive hours of off-duty time.

Question 28: Does the emergency conditions exception in 49 CFR 395.1(b)(2) apply to a driver who planned on arriving at a specific rest area to complete his 10 hours driving and found the rest area full, forcing the driver to continue past the ten hours driving looking for another safe parking area?

Guidance: No. The emergency conditions exception does not apply to the driver. It is general knowledge that rest areas have become increasingly crowded for commercial motor vehicle parking, thus, it is incumbent on drivers to look for a parking spot before the last few minutes of a 10 hour driving period. The driver should provide the reason for exceeding the 10 hours driving in the Remarks section of the record of duty status.

Question 29: Must a motor carrier that uses a 100-air-mile radius driver write zero (0) hours on the time record for each day the driver is off duty (not working for the motor carrier)?

Guidance: No. Section 395.1(e)(5) requires a motor carrier to maintain "accurate and true time records" for each driver. These records must show the time the driver goes on and off duty, as well as the total number of hours on duty, each day. The lack of a time record for a 100-air-mile radius driver on any given day is therefore a statement by the motor carrier that the driver was not on duty that day. If an investigator discovers that the driver was in fact on duty, despite the absence of a time record, the motor carrier has violated §395.1(e)(5) because it has not maintained "true and accurate time records." Appropriate enforcement action may then be taken.

Question 30: Does the exception in §395.1(k) for "drivers transporting agricultural commodities or farm supplies for agricultural purposes" cover the transportation of poultry or poultry feed?

Guidance: No. The exception was created by Sec. 345(a)(1) of the National Highway System Designation Act of 1995 [Public Law 104-50, 109 Stat. 568, at 613], which provides in part that the hours of service regulations "shall not apply to drivers transporting agricultural commodities or farm supplies for agricultural purposes..." The terms "agricultural commodities or farm supplies for agricultural purposes" were not defined, but the context clarifies their meaning. Because the statute made the exception available only "during the planting and harvesting seasons" in each State, Congress obviously intended to restrict it to agriculture in the traditional (and etymological) sense, i.e., the cultivation of fields. "Agricultural commodities" therefore means products grown on and harvested from the land, and "farm supplies for agricultural purposes" means products directly related to the growing or harvesting of agricultural commodities.

Drivers transporting livestock or slaughtered animals, or the grain, corn, hay, etc., used to feed animals, may not use the "agricultural operations" exception.

Question 31: Does fuel used in the production of agricultural commodities qualify as "farm supplies" under 49 CFR 395.1(k)?

Guidance: Fuel qualifies as a farm supply if (1) it is "for agricultural purposes," e.g. used in tractors or other equipment that cultivate agricultural commodities or trucks that haul them, but not in automobiles, station wagons, SUVs or other vehicles designed primarily to carry passengers, or for residential heating or cooking; (2) it is transported within the planting and harvesting season, as determined by the State, and within a 100 air-mile radius of the distribution point for fuel; (3) the motor carrier is operating in interstate commerce; and (4) the entire fuel load on the vehicle is to be delivered to one or more farms. A carrier may not use the exemption if any portion of the fuel load is to be delivered to a non-farm customer.

Question 32: Can a for-hire motor carrier located in Canada transport farm supplies and/or equipment for agricultural purposes to a location in the U.S. without having to comply with Part 395?

Guidance:
Yes, if a Canadian driver meets all of the requirements of the 49 CFR 395.1(k) definition of "agricultural operations," the provisions of Part 395 do not apply so long as the trip occurs only during the official "planting and harvesting season" as designated by each State.

Question 33: How is "point of origin" defined for the purpose of § 395.1(k)?

Guidance: The term "point of origin" is not used in the NHS Designation Act; the statutory term is "source of the [agricultural] commodities." The exemption created by the Act applies to two types of transportation. The first type is transportation from the source of the agricultural commodity - where the product is grown or raised - to a location within a 100 air-mile radius of the source. The second type is transportation from a retail distribution point of the farm supply to a location (farm or other location where the farm supply product would be used) within a 100 air-mile radius of the retail distribution point.

The legislative history of the agricultural exemption indicates it was intended to only apply to retail store deliveries. Thus, it is clear Congress intended to limit this exemption to retail distributors of farm supplies.

Second-stage movements, such as grain hauled from an elevator (or sugar beets from a cold storage facility) to a processing plant, are more likely to fall outside the exempt radius. Similarly, the exemption does not apply to a wholesaler's transportation of an agricultural chemical to a local cooperative because this is not a retail delivery to an ultimate consumer, even if it is within the 100 air-mile radius.

§395.2 Definitions.

As used in this part, the following words and terms are construed to mean:

Adverse driving conditions means snow, sleet, fog, other adverse weather conditions, a highway covered with snow or ice, or unusual road and traffic conditions, none of which were apparent on the basis of information known to the person dispatching the run at the time it was begun.

Automatic on-board recording device means an electric, electronic, electromechanical, or mechanical device capable of recording driver's duty status information accurately and automatically as required by §395.15. The device must be integrally synchronized with specific operations of the commercial motor vehicle in which it is installed. At a minimum, the device must record engine use, road speed, miles driven, the date, and time of day.

Driver-salesperson means any employee who is employed solely as such by a private carrier of property by commercial motor vehicle, who is engaged both in selling goods, services, or the use of goods, and in delivering by commercial motor vehicle the goods sold or provided or upon which the services are performed, who does so entirely within a radius of 100 miles of the point at which he/she reports for duty, who devotes not more than 50 percent of his/her hours on duty to driving time. The term **selling goods** for purposes of this section shall include in all cases solicitation or obtaining of reorders or new accounts, and may also include other selling or merchandising activities designed to retain the customer or to increase the sale of goods or services, in addition to solicitation or obtaining of reorders or new accounts.

Driving time means all time spent at the driving controls of a commercial motor vehicle in operation.

Eight consecutive days means the period of 8 consecutive days beginning on any day at the time designated by the motor carrier for a 24-hour period.

Ground water well drilling rig means any vehicle, machine, tractor, trailer, semi-trailer, or specialized mobile equipment propelled or drawn by mechanical power and used on highways to transport water well field operating equipment, including water well drilling and pump service rigs equipped to access ground water.

Multiple stops means all stops made in any one village, town, or city may be computed as one.

On duty time means all time from the time a driver begins to work or is required to be in readiness to work until the time the driver is relieved from work and all responsibility for performing work. On duty time shall include:

(1) *All time at a plant, terminal, facility, or other property* of a motor carrier or shipper, or on any public property, waiting to be dispatched, unless the driver has been relieved from duty by the motor carrier;

(2) *All time inspecting, servicing, or conditioning* any commercial motor vehicle at any time;

(3) *All driving time as defined in the term driving time;*

(4) *All time, other than driving time,* in or upon any commercial motor vehicle except time spent resting in a sleeper berth;

(5) *All time loading or unloading* a commercial motor vehicle, supervising, or assisting in the loading or unloading, attending a commercial motor vehicle being loaded or unloaded, remaining in readiness to operate the commercial motor vehicle, or in giving or receiving receipts for shipments loaded or unloaded;

(6) *All time repairing, obtaining assistance,* or remaining in attendance upon a disabled commercial motor vehicle;

(7) *All time spent* providing a breath sample or urine specimen, including travel time to and from the collection site, in order to comply with the random, reasonable suspicion, post-accident, or follow-up testing required by Part 382 of this subchapter when directed by a motor carrier;

(8) *Performing any other work* in the capacity, employ, or service of a motor carrier; and

(9) *Performing any compensated work* for a person who is not a motor carrier.

Seven consecutive days means the period of 7 consecutive days beginning on any day at the time designated by the motor carrier for a 24-hour period.

Sleeper berth means a berth conforming to the requirements of §393.76 of this chapter.

Transportation of construction materials and equipment means the transportation of construction and pavement materials, construction equipment, and construction maintenance vehicles, by a driver to or from an active construction site (a construction site between mobilization of equipment and materials to the site to the final completion of the construction project) within a 50 air mile radius of the normal work reporting location of the driver. This paragraph does not apply to the transportation of material found by the Secretary to be hazardous under 49 U.S.C. 5103 in a quantity requiring placarding under regulations issued to carry out such section.

Twenty-four-hour period means any 24-consecutive-hour period beginning at the time designated by the motor carrier for the terminal from which the driver is normally dispatched.

Utility service vehicle means any commercial motor vehicle:

(1) *Used in the furtherance* of repairing, maintaining, or operating any structures or any other physical facilities necessary for the delivery of public utility services, including the furnishing of electric, gas, water, sanitary sewer, telephone, and television cable or community antenna service;

(2) *While engaged in any activity* necessarily related to the ultimate delivery of such public utility services to consumers, including travel or movement to, from, upon, or between activity sites (including occasional travel or movement outside the service area necessitated by any utility emergency as determined by the utility provider); and

(3) *Except for any occasional emergency use,* operated primarily within the service area of a utility's subscribers or consumers, without regard to whether the vehicle is owned, leased, or rented by the utility.

§395.2 DOT Interpretations

Question 1: A company told all of its drivers that it would no longer pay for driving from the last stop to home and that this time should not be shown on the time cards. Is it a violation of the FMCSRs to operate a CMV from the last stop to home and not show that time on the time cards?

Guidance: The FMCSRs do not address questions of pay. All the time spent operating a CMV for, or at the direction of, a motor carrier must be recorded as driving time.

Question 2: What conditions must be met for a CMV driver to record meal and other routine stops made during a tour of duty as off-duty time?

Guidance:

1. The driver must have been relieved of all duty and responsibility for the care and custody of the vehicle, its accessories, and any cargo or passengers it may be carrying.
2. The duration of the driver's relief from duty must be a finite period of time which is of sufficient duration to ensure that the accumulated fatigue resulting from operating a CMV will be significantly reduced.
3. If the driver has been relieved from duty, as noted in (1) above, the duration of the relief from duty must have been made known to the driver prior to the driver's departure in written instructions from the employer. There are no record retention requirements for these instructions on board a vehicle or at a motor carrier's principal place of business.
4. During the stop, and for the duration of the stop, the driver must be at liberty to pursue activities of his/her own choosing and to leave the premises where the vehicle is situated.

Question 3: A driver has been given written permission by his/her employer to record meal and other routine stops made during a tour of duty as off-duty time. Is the driver required to record such time as off-duty, or is it the driver's decision whether such time is recorded as off-duty?

Guidance: It is the employer's choice whether the driver shall record stops made during a tour of duty as off-duty time. However, employers may permit drivers to make the decision as to how the time will be recorded.

Question 4: A driver has been given written permission by his/her employer to record meal and other routine stops made during a tour of duty as off-duty time. Is the driver allowed to record his stops during a tour of duty as off-duty time when the CMV is laden with HM and the CMV is parked in a truck stop parking lot?

Guidance: Drivers may record meal and other routine stops made during a tour of duty as off-duty time, except when a CMV is laden with explosive HM classified as hazard divisions 1.1, 1.2, or 1.3 (formerly Class A or B explosives). In addition, when HM classified under hazard divisions 1.1, 1.2, or 1.3 are on a CMV, the employer and the driver must comply with §397.5 of the FMCSRs.

Question 5: Do telephone calls to or from the motor carrier that momentarily interrupt a driver's rest period constitute a change of the driver's duty status?

Guidance: Telephone calls of this type do not prevent the driver from obtaining adequate rest. Therefore, the FHWA does not consider these brief telephone calls to be a break in the driver's off-duty status.

Question 6: If a driver is required by a motor carrier to carry a pager/beeper to receive notification to contact the motor carrier for a duty assignment, how should this time be recorded?

Guidance: The time is to be recorded as off-duty.

Question 7: May a sleeper berth be used for a period of less than 2 hours' duration?

Guidance: Yes. The sleeper berth may be used for such periods of inactivity. Periods of time of less than 2 hours spent in a sleeper berth may not be used to accumulate the 8 hours of off-duty time required by §395.3 of the FMCSRs.

Question 8: If a "driver trainer" occasionally drives a CMV, thereby becoming a "driver" (regardless of whether he/she is paid for driving), must the driver record all nondriving (training) time as on-duty (not driving)?

Guidance: Yes.

Question 9: A driver drives on streets and highways during the week and jockeys CMVs in the yard (private property) on weekends. How is the yard time to be recorded?

Guidance: On-duty (driving).

Question 10: How does compensation relate to on-duty time?

Guidance: The fact that a driver is paid for a period of time does not always establish that the driver was on-duty for the purposes of Part 395 during that period of time. A driver may be relieved of duty under certain conditions and still be paid.

Question 11: Must nontransportation-related work for a motor carrier be recorded as on-duty time?

Guidance: Yes. All work for a motor carrier, whether compensated or not, must be recorded as on-duty time. The term "work" as used in the definition of "on-duty time" in §395.2 of the FMCSRs is not limited to driving or other nontransportation-related employment.

Question 12: How should time spent in transit on a ferry boat be recorded?

Guidance: Time spent on a ferry by drivers may be recorded as off-duty time if they are completely relieved from work and all responsibility and obligation to the motor carriers for which they drive. This relief must be consistent with existing regulations of the ferry company and the U.S. Coast Guard.

Question 13: What is the duty status of a co-driver (truck) who is riding seated next to the driver?

Guidance: On-duty (not driving).

Question 14: How must a CMV driver driving a non-CMV at the direction of a motor carrier record this time?

Guidance: If CMV drivers operate motor vehicles with GVWRs of 10,000 pounds or less at the direction of a motor carrier, the FHWA requires those drivers to maintain records of duty status and record such time operating as on-duty (not driving).

Question 15: How must the time spent operating a motor vehicle on the rails (roadrailers) be recorded?

Guidance: On-duty (not driving).

Question 16: Must a driver engaged in union activities affecting the employing motor carrier record such time as on-duty (not driving) time?

Guidance: The union activities of a driver employed by a unionized motor carrier must be recorded as on-duty (not driving) time if the collective bargaining agreement requires the motor carrier to pay the driver for time engaged in such activities. Otherwise these activities may be recorded as off duty time unless they are combined with normal duties performed for the carrier.

Efforts by a driver to organize co-workers employed by a non-unionized motor carrier, either on the carrier's premises or elsewhere, may be recorded as off duty time unless the organizing activities are combined with normal duties performed for the carrier.

Question 17: How is the 50 percent driving time in the definition of "driver-salesperson" in §395.2 determined?

Guidance: The driving time is determined on a weekly basis. The driver must be employed solely as a driver-salesperson. The driver-salesperson may not participate in any other type of work activity.

Question 18: May a driver change to and from a driver-salesman status at any time?

Guidance: Yes, if the change is made on a weekly basis.

Question 19: May the time a driver spends attending safety meetings, ceremonies, celebrations, or other company-sponsored safety events be recorded as off-duty time?

Guidance: Yes, if attendance is voluntary.

Question 20: How must a driver record time spent on-call awaiting dispatch?

Guidance: The time that a driver is free from obligations to the employer and is able to use that time to secure appropriate rest may be recorded as off-duty time. The fact that a driver must also be available to receive a call in the event the driver is needed at work, even under the threat of discipline for non-availability, does not by itself impair the ability of the driver to use this time for rest.

If the employer generally requires its drivers to be available for call after a mandatory rest period which complies with the regulatory requirement, the time spent standing by for a work-related call, following the required off-duty period, may be properly recorded as off-duty time.

Question 21: How does a driver record the hours spent driving in a school bus operation when he/she also drives a CMV for a company subject to the FMCSRs?

Guidance: If the school bus meets the definition of a CMV, it must be recorded as driving time.

Question 22: A motor carrier relieves a driver from duty. What is a suitable facility for resting?

Guidance: The only resting facility which the FHWA regulates is the sleeper berth. The sleeper berth requirements can be found in §393.76.

Question 23: How many times may a motor carrier relieve a driver from duty within a tour of duty?

Guidance: There is no limitation on the number of times a driver can be relieved from duty during a tour of duty.

Question 24: If a driver is transported by automobile from the point of a breakdown to a terminal, and then dispatched on another run, how is the time spent in the automobile entered on the record of duty status? How is the time entered if the driver goes off-duty once he reaches the terminal?

Guidance: The time spent in the automobile would be on-duty (not driving) if dispatched on another run once he/she reaches the terminal, and off-duty if he/she is given 8 consecutive hours off-duty upon reaching the terminal.

Question 25: When a driver experiences a delay on an impassable highway, should the time he/she is delayed be entered on the record of duty status as driving time or on-duty (not driving)?

Guidance: Delays on impassable highways must be recorded as driving time because §395.2 defines "driving time" as all time spent at the driving controls of a CMV in operation.

Question 26: Is time spent operating controls in a CMV to perform an auxiliary, non-driving function (e.g., lifting a loaded container, compacting waste, etc.) considered driving time? Does the location of the controls have a bearing on the answer?

Guidance: The location of the controls does have a bearing on the answer. §395.2 defines "driving time" as all time spent at the driving controls of a CMV in operation. If a driver, seated at the driving controls of the vehicle, is able to simultaneously perform the driving and auxiliary function (for example, one hand on the steering wheel and one hand on a control mechanism), the time spent performing the auxiliary function must be recorded as "driving time." If a driver, seated at the driving controls of the vehicle, is unable to simultaneously perform the driving and auxiliary function, the time spent performing the auxiliary function may be recorded as "on-duty not driving time."

Question 27: A motor carrier has full-time drivers who are also volunteer fire fighters. Some of the drivers carry pagers and leave their normal activities only when notified of a fire. Others consistently work 3 to 4 non-consecutive 24-hour shifts at a fire station each month, resting between calls. The drivers receive no monetary compensation for their work. How should the time spent on these activities be logged on the record of duty status when the drivers return to work?

Guidance: When drivers are free from obligations to their employers, that time may be recorded as off-duty time. Drivers who are allowed by the motor carrier to leave their normal activities to fight fires and those who spend full days in a fire station are clearly off duty. Their time should be recorded as such.

Question 28: How should time spent at National Guard meetings and training sessions be recorded for the hours-of-service requirements?

Guidance: A member of a military reserve component, serving in either an inactive duty status, such as weekend drills, or in an active duty status, such as annual training, may log that time as "off-duty time" regardless of whether such duty time is paid or unpaid. This is consistent with the rights and benefit entitlements provided in the Uniformed Services Employment and Reemployment Rights Act (38 U.S.C. 4301 et seq.)

Question 29: Although firefighters, emergency medical technicians, paramedics and other public safety professionals are often exempt from the hours-of-service (HOS) regulations under the governmental exception [49 CFR 390.3(f)(2)], they sometimes have second jobs with interstate motor carriers for which they are required to comply with the HOS rules. When one of these individuals has a second job with an interstate motor carrier and works a 24-hour shift for the fire/rescue/emergency services department, is all of the time spent during the shift considered on-duty time?

Guidance: No. Firefighters and other public safety professionals working 24-hour shifts may record time during which they are required or permitted to rest as off-duty time. However, all time that the public safety specialist is required to perform work (e.g., administrative work, cleaning/repairing equipment, operating equipment, etc.) would be considered on-duty time.

Question 30: If a driver is required repeatedly to respond to satellite or similar communications received during his or her sleeper berth period, does this activity affect a driver's duty status?

Guidance: Yes. The driver cannot be required to do any work for the motor carrier during sleeper berth time. A driver who is required to access a communications system for the purpose of reading messages from the carrier, responding to certain messages (either verbally or by typing a message), or otherwise acknowledging them, is performing work. For the purpose of this guidance, "repeatedly" means a pattern or series of interruptions that prevent a driver from obtaining restorative sleep during the sleeper berth period.

Question 31: If a driver is required repeatedly to respond to satellite or similar communications received during a 10-hour (8-hour for passenger transportation) off-duty period, does this activity affect a driver's duty status?

Guidance: Yes. The driver cannot be required to do any work for the motor carrier during the 10-hour or the 8-hour off-duty period. A driver who is required to access a communications system for the purpose of reading messages from the carrier, responding to certain messages (either verbally or by typing a message), or otherwise acknowledging them, is performing work. For the purpose of this guidance, "repeatedly" means a pattern or series of interruptions that prevent a driver from obtaining restorative sleep during the off-duty period.

Question 32: If a driver drives in a non-commercial vehicle to take a physical examination, should the duty status be recorded as on-duty not driving, or as off-duty? Would the answer change if the motor carrier directs the driver to go for the examination?

Guidance: So long as the driver schedules and attends the physical examination at a time of his or her own choosing, the time may be recorded as off-duty. If, however, the motor carrier directs the driver to attend at a specific time, the time is to be recorded as on-duty not driving.

§395.3 Maximum driving time for property-carrying vehicles.

Subject to the exceptions and exemptions in §395.1:

(a) No motor carrier shall permit or require any driver used by it to drive a property-carrying commercial motor vehicle, nor shall any such driver drive a property-carrying commercial motor vehicle:

§395.5 Part 395 - Hours of Service of Drivers

(1) *More than 11 cumulative hours* following 10 consecutive hours off duty; or
(2) *For any period* after the end of the 14th hour after coming on duty following 10 consecutive hours off duty, except when a property-carrying driver complies with the provisions of §395.1(o) or §395.1(e)(2).
(b) No motor carrier shall permit or require a driver of a property-carrying commercial motor vehicle to drive, nor shall any driver drive a property-carrying commercial motor vehicle, regardless of the number of motor carriers using the driver's services, for any period after —
(1) *Having been on duty 60 hours* in any period of 7 consecutive days if the employing motor carrier does not operate commercial motor vehicles every day of the week; or
(2) *Having been on duty 70 hours* in any period of 8 consecutive days if the employing motor carrier operates commercial motor vehicles every day of the week.
(c) (1) *Any period of 7 consecutive days* may end with the beginning of any off-duty period of 34 or more consecutive hours; or
(2) *Any period of 8 consecutive days* may end with the beginning of any off-duty period of 34 or more consecutive hours.

§395.3 DOT Interpretations

Question 1: May a motor carrier switch from a 60-hour/7-day limit to a 70-hour/8-day limit or vice versa?
Guidance: Yes. The only restriction regarding the use of the 70-hour/8-day rule is that the motor carrier must have CMVs operating every day of the week. The 70-hour/8-day rule is a permissive provision in that a motor carrier with vehicles operating every day of the week is not required to use the 70-hour/8-day rules for calculating its drivers' hours of service. The motor carrier may, however, assign some or all of its drivers to operate under the 70-hour/8-day rule if it so chooses. The assignment of individual drivers to the 60-hour/7-day or the 70-hour/8-day time rule is left to the discretion of the motor carrier.
Question 2: Does a driver, employed full time by one motor carrier using the 60-hours in 7-days rule, and part-time by another motor carrier using the 70-hours in 8-days rule, have the option of using either rule in computing his hours of service?
Guidance: No. The motor carrier that employs the driver on a full-time basis determines which rule it will use to comply with §395.3(b). The driver does not have the option to select the rule he/she wishes to use.
Question 3: May a carrier which provides occasional, but not regular service on every day of the week, have the option of the 60 hours in 7 days or 70 hours in 8 days with respect to all drivers, during the period in which it operates one or more vehicles on each day of the week?
Guidance: Yes.
Question 4: A Canadian driver is subjected to a log book inspection in the U.S. The driver has logged one or more 13-hour driving periods while in Canada during the previous 7 days, but has complied with all the FMCSRs while operating in the U.S. Has the driver violated the 10- hour driving requirement in the U.S.?
Guidance: No. Canadian drivers are required to comply with the FMCSRs only when operating in the U.S.
Question 5: May a driver domiciled in the United States comply with the Canadian hours of service regulations while driving in Canada? If so, would the driving and on-duty time accumulated in Canada be counted toward compliance with one or more of the limits imposed by part 395 when the driver re-enters the United States?
Guidance: A driver domiciled in the United States may comply with the Canadian hours of service regulations while driving in Canada. Upon re-entering the United States, however, the driver is subject to all of the requirements of part 395, including the 10- and 15-hour rules, and the 60- or 70- hour rules applicable to the previous 7 or 8 consecutive days.

In other words, a driver who takes full advantage of Canadian law may have to stop driving for a time immediately after returning to the U.S. in order to restore compliance with part 395. Despite its possible effect on decisions a U.S. driver must make while in Canada, this interpretation does not involve an exercise of extraterritorial jurisdiction.
Question 6: If a motor carrier operates under the 70-hour/8-day rule, does any aspect of the 60-hour rule apply to its operations? If a motor carrier operates under the 60-hour/7-day rule, does any part of the 70-hour rule apply to its operations?

Guidance: If a motor carrier operates 7 days per week and chooses to require all of its drivers to comply with the 70-hour/8-day rule, the 60-hour/7-day rule would not be applicable to these drivers. If this carrier chooses to assign some or all of its drivers to the 60-hour/7-day rule, the 70-hour rule would not be applicable to these drivers. Conversely, if a motor carrier does not operate 7 days per week, it must operate under the 60-hour/7-day rule and the 70-hour rule would not apply to its operations.
Question 7: What is the liability of a motor carrier for hours of service violations? *Guidance:* The carrier is liable for violations of the hours of service regulations if it had or should have had the means by which to detect the violations. Liability under the FMCSRs does not depend upon actual knowledge of the violations.
Question 8: Are carriers liable for the actions of their employees even though the carrier contends that it did not require or permit the violations to occur?
Guidance: Yes. Carriers are liable for the actions of their employees. Neither intent to commit, nor actual knowledge of, a violation is a necessary element of that liability. Carriers "permit" violations of the hours of service regulations by their employees if they fail to have in place management systems that effectively prevent such violations.
Question 9: May time spent in resting or sleeping in motor homes being delivered be recorded as off-duty time?
Guidance: The Federal Highway Administration believes the time drivers spend resting or sleeping in the motor homes while stopped or parked (e.g., at a rest area or parking lot) could be considered off-duty time. Drivers may take at least eight consecutive hours off-duty for the purpose of obtaining restorative sleep. The driver may also take less than eight hours off-duty and take a nap. This time would not count toward the required eight consecutive hours off-duty. There are certain conditions which must be met in order for this time (less than eight consecutive hours) to qualify as off-duty time.
1. The driver must have been relieved of all duty and responsibility for the care and custody of the vehicle, its accessories, and any cargo or passengers it may be carrying.
2. The duration of the driver's relief from duty must be a finite period of time which is of sufficient duration to ensure that the accumulated fatigue resulting from operating a commercial motor vehicle will be significantly reduced.
3. If the driver has been relieved from duty, as noted in (1) above, the duration of the relief from duty must have been made known to the driver prior to the driver's departure in written instructions from the employer. There are no record retention requirements for these instructions onboard a vehicle or at a motor carrier's principal place of business.
4. During the stop, and for the duration of the stop, the driver must be at liberty to pursue activities of his/her own choosing and to leave the premises where the vehicle is situated.

§395.5 Maximum driving time for passenger-carrying vehicles.

Subject to the exceptions and exemptions in §395.1:
(a) No motor carrier shall permit or require any driver used by it to drive a passenger-carrying commercial motor vehicle, nor shall any such driver drive a passenger-carrying commercial motor vehicle:
(1) *More than 10 hours* following 8 consecutive hours off duty; or
(2) *For any period* after having been on duty 15 hours following 8 consecutive hours off duty.
(b) No motor carrier shall permit or require a driver of a passenger-carrying commercial motor vehicle to drive, nor shall any driver drive a passenger-carrying commercial motor vehicle, regardless of the number of motor carriers using the driver's services, for any period after —
(1) *Having been on duty 60 hours* in any 7 consecutive days if the employing motor carrier does not operate commercial motor vehicles every day of the week; or
(2) *Having been on duty 70 hours* in any period of 8 consecutive days if the employing motor carrier operates commercial motor vehicles every day of the week.

§395.7 [Reserved]

§395.8 Driver's record of duty status.

(a) Except for a private motor carrier of passengers (nonbusiness), every motor carrier shall require every driver used by the motor carrier to record his/her duty status for each 24 hour period using the methods prescribed in either paragraph (a)(1) or (2) of this section.

Part 395 - Hours of Service of Drivers   §395.8 (g)

(1) *Every driver who operates* a commercial motor vehicle shall record his/her duty status, in duplicate, for each 24-hour period. The duty status time shall be recorded on a specified grid, as shown in paragraph (g) of this section. The grid and the requirements of paragraph (d) of this section may be combined with any company forms. The previously approved format of the Daily Log, Form MCS-59 or the Multi-day Log, MCS-139 and 139A, which meets the requirements of this section, may continue to be used.

(2) *Every driver who operates* a commercial motor vehicle shall record his/her duty status by using an automatic on-board recording device that meets the requirements of §395.15 of this part. The requirements of §395.8 shall not apply, except paragraphs (e) and (k)(1) and (2) of this section.

(b) **The duty status shall be recorded as follows:**
  (1) *"Off duty" or "OFF"*
  (2) *"Sleeper berth" or "SB" (only if a sleeper berth is used).*
  (3) *"Driving" or "D."*
  (4) *"On-duty not driving" or "ON."*

(c) **For each change of duty status** (e.g., the place of reporting for work, starting to drive, on-duty not driving and where released from work), the name of the city, town, or village, with State abbreviation, shall be recorded.

NOTE: If a change of duty status occurs at a location other than a city, town, or village, show one of the following: (1) the highway number and nearest milepost followed by the name of the nearest city, town, or village and State abbreviation, (2) the highway number and the name of the service plaza followed by the name of the nearest city, town, or village and State abbreviation, or (3) the highway numbers of the nearest two intersecting roadways followed by the name of the nearest city, town, or village and State abbreviation.

(d) **The following information must be included on the form** in addition to the grid:
  (1) *Date;*
  (2) *Total miles driving today;*
  (3) *Truck or tractor and trailer number;*
  (4) *Name of carrier;*
  (5) *Driver's signature/certification;*
  (6) *24-hour period starting time (e.g. midnight, 9:00 a.m., noon, 3:00 p.m.);*
  (7) *Main office address;*
  (8) *Remarks;*
  (9) *Name of co-driver;*
  (10) *Total hours (far right edge of grid);*
  (11) *Shipping document number(s),* or name of shipper and commodity.

(e) **Failure to complete the record of duty activities** of this section or §395.15, failure to preserve a record of such duty activities, or making of false reports in connection with such duty activities shall make the driver and/or the carrier liable to prosecution.

(f) **The driver's activities shall be recorded** in accordance with the following provisions:
  (1) *Entries to be current.* Drivers shall keep their records of duty status current to the time shown for the last change of duty status.
  (2) *Entries made by driver only.* All entries relating to driver's duty status must be legible and in the driver's own handwriting.
  (3) *Date.* The month, day and year for the beginning of each 24-hour period shall be shown on the form containing the driver's duty status record.

(4) *Total miles driving today.* Total mileage driven during the 24-hour period shall be recorded on the form containing the driver's duty status record.

(5) *Commercial motor vehicle identification.* The driver shall show the number assigned by the motor carrier, or the license number and licensing State of each commercial motor vehicle operated during each 24-hour period on his/her record of duty status. The driver of an articulated (combination) commercial motor vehicle shall show the number assigned by the motor carrier, or the license number and licensing State of each motor vehicle used in each commercial motor vehicle combination operated during that 24-hour period on his/her record of duty status.

(6) *Name of motor carrier.* The name(s) of the motor carrier(s) for which work is performed shall be shown on the form containing the driver's record of duty status. When work is performed for more than one motor carrier during the same 24-hour period, the beginning and finishing time, showing a.m. or p.m., worked for each motor carrier shall be shown after each motor carrier's name. Drivers of leased commercial motor vehicles shall show the name of the motor carrier performing the transportation.

(7) *Signature/certification.* The driver shall certify to the correctness of all entries by signing the form containing the driver's duty status record with his/her legal name or name of record. The driver's signature certifies that all entries required by this section made by the driver are true and correct.

(8) *Time base to be used.*
  (i) *The driver's duty status record* shall be prepared, maintained, and submitted using the time standard in effect at the driver's home terminal, for a 24-hour period beginning with the time specified by the motor carrier for that driver's home terminal.
  (ii) *The term "7 or 8 consecutive days"* means the 7 or 8 consecutive 24-hour periods as designated by the carrier for the driver's home terminal.
  (iii) *The 24-hour period starting time* must be identified on the driver's duty status record. One-hour increments must appear on the graph, be identified, and preprinted. The words "Midnight" and "Noon" must appear above or beside the appropriate one-hour increment.

(9) *Main office address.* The motor carrier's main office address shall be shown on the form containing the driver's duty status record.

(10) *Recording days off duty.* Two or more consecutive 24-hour periods off duty may be recorded on one duty status record.

(11) *Total hours.* The total hours in each duty status: off duty other than in a sleeper berth; off duty in a sleeper berth; driving, and on duty not driving, shall be entered to the right of the grid, the total of such entries shall equal 24 hours.

(12) *Shipping document number(s),* or name of shipper and commodity shall be shown on the driver's record of duty status.

(g) **Graph grid.** The following graph grid must be incorporated into a motor carrier recordkeeping system which must also contain the information required in paragraph (d) of this section.

Graph Grid-Horizontally

1: OFF DUTY
2: SLEEPER BERTH
3: DRIVING
4: ON DUTY (NOT DRIVING)
REMARKS

Graph Grid-Vertically

(h) **Graph grid preparation.** The graph grid may be used horizontally or vertically and shall be completed as follows:
   (1) *Off duty.* Except for time spent resting in a sleeper berth, a continuous line shall be drawn between the appropriate time markers to record the period(s) of time when the driver is not on duty, is not required to be in readiness to work, or is not under any responsibility for performing work.
   (2) *Sleeper berth.* A continuous line shall be drawn between the appropriate time markers to record the period(s) of time off duty resting in a sleeper berth, as defined in §395.2. (If a non-sleeper berth operation, sleeper berth need not be shown on the grid.)
   (3) *Driving.* A continuous line shall be drawn between the appropriate time markers to record the period(s) of driving time, as defined in §395.2.
   (4) *On duty not driving.* A continuous line shall be drawn between the appropriate time markers to record the period(s) of time on duty not driving specified in §395.2.
   (5) *Location — Remarks.* The name of the city, town, or village, with State abbreviation where each change of duty status occurs shall be recorded.
   NOTE: If a change of duty status occurs at a location other than a city, town, or village, show one of the following: (1) the highway number and nearest milepost followed by the name of the nearest city, town, or village and State abbreviation, (2) the highway number and the name of the service plaza followed by the name of the nearest city, town, or village and State abbreviation, or (3) the highway numbers of the nearest two intersecting roadways followed by the name of the nearest city, town, or village and State abbreviation.

(i) **Filing driver's record of duty status.** The driver shall submit or forward by mail the original driver's record of duty status to the regular employing motor carrier within 13 days following the completion of the form.

(j) **Drivers used by more than one motor carrier.**
   (1) *When the services of a driver* are used by more than one motor carrier during any 24-hour period in effect at the driver's home terminal, the driver shall submit a copy of the record of duty status to each motor carrier. The record shall include:
      (i) *All duty time* for the entire 24-hour period;
      (ii) *The name of each motor carrier* served by the driver during that period; and
      (iii) *The beginning and finishing time,* including a.m. or p.m., worked for each carrier.
   (2) *Motor carriers,* when using a driver for the first time or intermittently, shall obtain from the driver a signed statement giving the total time on duty during the immediately preceding 7 days and the time at which the driver was last relieved from duty prior to beginning work for the motor carriers.

(k) **Retention of driver's record of duty status.**
   (1) *Each motor carrier* shall maintain records of duty status and all supporting documents for each driver it employs for a period of six months from the date of receipt.
   (2) *The driver shall retain* a copy of each record of duty status for the previous 7 consecutive days which shall be in his/her possession and available for inspection while on duty.
   NOTE: Driver's record of duty status. The graph grid, when incorporated as part of any form used by a motor carrier, must be of sufficient size to be legible.

Part 395 - Hours of Service of Drivers §395.8 (k)

The following executed specimen grid illustrates how a driver's duty status should be recorded for a trip to Richmond, Virginia, to Newark, New Jersey. The grid reflects the midnight to midnight 24 hour period.

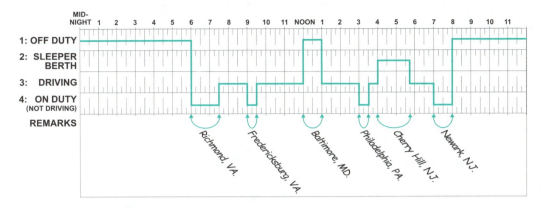

Graph Grid (midnight to midnight operation)
The driver in this instance reported for duty at the motor carrier's terminal. The driver reported for work at 6 a.m., helped load, checked with dispatch, made a pre-trip inspection, and performed other duties until 7:30 a.m., when the driver began driving. At 9 a.m., the driver had a minor accident in Fredericksburg, Virginia, and spent one half hour handling details with the local police. The driver arrived at the company's Baltimore, Maryland, terminal at noon and went to lunch while minor repairs were made to the tractor. At 1 p.m. the driver resumed the trip and made a delivery in Philadelphia, Pennsylvania, between 3 p.m. and 3:30 p.m., at which time the driver started driving again. Upon arrival at Cherry Hill, New Jersey, at 4 p.m., the driver entered the sleeper berth for a rest break until 5:45 p.m., at which time the driver resumed driving again. At 7 p.m. the driver arrived at the company's terminal in Newark, New Jersey. Between 7 p.m. and 8 p.m. the driver prepared the required paperwork, including completing the driver's record of duty status, driver vehicle inspection report, insurance report for the Fredericksburg, Virginia, accident, checked for the next day's dispatch, etc. At 8 p.m., the driver went off duty.
(Approved by the Office of Management and Budget under control number 2125-0016.)

§395.8 DOT Interpretations

Question 1: How should a change of duty status for a short period of time be shown on the driver's record of duty status?
Guidance: Short periods of time (less than 15 minutes) may be identified by drawing a line from the appropriate on-duty (not driving) or driving line to the remarks section and entering the amount of time, such as "6 minutes," and the geographic location of the duty status change.

Question 2: May a rubber stamp signature be used on a driver's record of duty status?
Guidance: No, a driver's record of duty status must bear the signature of the driver whose time is recorded thereon.

Question 3: If a driver's record of duty status is not signed, may enforcement action be taken on the current day's record if it contains false information?
Guidance: Enforcement action can be taken against the driver even though that record may not be signed. The regulations require the driver to keep the record of duty status current to the time of last change of duty status (whether or not the record has been signed). Also, §395.8(e) states that making false reports shall make the driver and/or the carrier liable to prosecution.

Question 4: Must drivers, alternating between interstate and intrastate commerce, record their intrastate driving time on their record of duty status?
Guidance: Yes, to account for all on-duty time for the prior 7 or 8 days preceding an interstate movement.

Question 5: May a driver, being used for the first time, submit records of duty status for the preceding 7 days in lieu of a signed statement?
Guidance: The carrier may accept true and accurate copies of the driver's record of duty status for the preceding 7 days in lieu of the signed statement required by §395.8(j)(2).

Question 6: How should multiple short stops in a town or city be recorded on a record of duty status?
Guidance: All stops made in any one city, town, village or municipality may be computed as one. In such cases the sum of all stops should be shown on a continuous line as on-duty (not driving). The aggregate driving time between such stops should be entered on the record of duty status immediately following the on-duty (not driving) entry. The name of the city, town, village, or municipality, followed by the State abbreviation where all the stops took place, must appear in the "remarks" section of the record of duty status.

Question 7: Is the Canadian bilingual or any other record of duty status form acceptable in the U.S.?
Guidance: Yes, provided the grid format and specific information required are included.

Question 8: May a motor carrier return a driver's completed record of duty status to the driver for correction of inaccurate or incomplete entries?
Guidance: Yes, although the regulations do not require a driver to submit "corrected" records of duty status. A driver may submit corrected records of duty status to the motor carrier at any time. It is suggested the carrier mark the second submission "CORRECTED COPY" and staple it to the original submission for the required retention period.

Question 9: May a duplicate copy of a record of duty status be submitted if an original was seized by an enforcement official?
Guidance: A driver must prepare a second original record of duty status to replace any page taken by an enforcement official. The driver should note that the first original had been taken by an enforcement official and the circumstances under which it was taken.

Question 10: What regulation, interpretation, and/or administrative ruling requires a motor carrier to retain supporting documents and what are those documents?
Guidance: §395.8(k)(1) requires motor carriers to retain all supporting documents at their principal places of business for a period of 6 months from date of receipt.

Supporting documents are the records of the motor carrier which are maintained in the ordinary course of business and used by the motor carrier to verify the information recorded on the driver's record of duty status. Examples are: bills of lading, carrier pros, freight bills, dispatch records, driver call-in records, gate record receipts, weight/scale tickets, fuel receipts, fuel billing statements, toll receipts, international registration plan receipts, international fuel tax agreement receipts, trip permits, port of entry receipts, cash advance receipts, delivery receipts, lumper receipts, interchange and inspection reports, lessor settlement sheets, over/short and damage reports, agricultural inspection reports, CVSA reports, accident reports, telephone billing statements, credit card receipts, driver fax reports, on-board computer reports, border crossing reports, custom declarations, traffic citations, overweight/oversize reports and citations, and/or other documents directly related to the motor carrier's operation, which are retained by the motor carrier in connection with the operation of its transportation business. Supporting documents may include other documents which the motor carrier maintains and can be used to verify information on the driver's records of duty status. If these records are maintained at locations other than the principal place of business but are not used by the motor carrier for verification purposes, they must be forwarded to the principal place of business upon a request by an authorized representative of the FHWA or State official within 2 business days.

Question 11: Is a driver who works for a motor carrier on an occasional basis and who is regularly employed by a non-motor carrier entity required to submit either records of duty status or a signed statement regarding the hours of service for all on-duty time as "on-duty time" as defined by §395.2?

Guidance: Yes.

Question 12: May a driver use "white-out" liquid paper to correct a record of duty status entry?

Guidance: Any method of correction would be acceptable so long as it does not negate the obligation of the driver to certify by his or her signature that all entries were made by the driver and are true and correct.

Question 13: Are drivers required to draw continuous lines between the off-duty, sleeper berth, driving, and on-duty (not driving) lines on a record of duty status when changing their duty status?

Guidance: No. Under §395.8(h) the FMCSRs require that continuous lines be drawn between the appropriate time markers within each duty status line, but they do not require that continuous lines be drawn between the appropriate duty status lines when drivers change their duty status.

Question 14: What documents satisfy the requirement to show a shipping document number on a record of duty status as found in §395.8(d)(11)?

Guidance: The following are some of the documents acceptable to satisfy the requirement: shipping manifests, invoices/freight bills, trip reports, charter orders, special order numbers, bus bills or any other document that identifies a particular movement of passengers or cargo.

In the event of multiple shipments, a single document will satisfy the requirement. If a driver is dispatched on a trip, which is subsequently completed, and then is dispatched on another trip on that calendar day, two shipping document numbers or two shippers and commodities must be shown in the remarks section of the record of duty status.

Question 15: If a driver from a foreign country only operates in the U.S. one day a week, is he required to keep a record of duty status for every day?

Guidance: A foreign driver, when in the U.S., must produce a current record of duty status, and sufficient documentation to account for his duty time for the previous 6 days.

Question 16: Are drivers required to include their total on-duty time for the previous 7 to 8 days (as applicable) on the driver's record of duty status?

Guidance: No.

Question 17: Can military time be used on the grid portion of the driver's record of duty status?

Guidance: Yes. The references to 9 a.m., 3 p.m., etc. in §395.8(d)(6) are examples only. Military time is also acceptable.

Question 18: §395.8(d)(4) requires that the name of the motor carrier be shown on the driver's record of duty status. If a company owns more than one motor carrier subject to the FMCSRs, may the company use logs listing the names of all such motor carrier employers and require the driver to identify the carrier for which he or she drives?

Guidance: Yes, provided three conditions are met. First, the driver must identify his or her motor carrier employer by a method that would be visible on a photocopy of the log. A dark check mark by the carrier's name would be acceptable. However, a colored highlight of the name would not be acceptable, since these colors are often transparent to photocopiers.

Second, the driver may check off the name of the motor carrier employer only if he or she works for a single carrier during the 24 hour period covered by the log.

Third, if the parent company uses Multiday Logs (Form 139 or 139A), the log for each day must list all motor carrier employers and the driver must identify his or her carrier each day.

Question 19: Regulatory guidance issued by the Office of Motor Carriers states that a driver's record-of-duty-status (RODS) may be used as the 100 air-mile radius time record "... provided the form contains the mandatory information." Is this "mandatory information" that required of a normal RODS under §395.8(d) or that of the 100 air-mile radius exemption under §395.1(e)(5)?

Guidance: The "mandatory information" referred to is the time records specified by §395.1(e)(5) which must show:

(1) The time the driver reports for duty each day;
(2) the total number of hours the driver is on duty each day;
(3) the time the driver is released from duty each day; and
(4) the total time for the preceding 7 days in accordance with §395.8(j)(2) for drivers used for the first time or intermittently.

Using the RODS to comply with §395.1(e)(5) is not prohibited as long as the RODS contains driver identification, the date, the time the driver began work, the time the driver ended work, and the total hours on duty.

Question 20: When a driver fails to meet the provisions of the 100 air-mile radius exemption (§395.1(e)), is the driver required to have copies of his/her records of duty status for the previous seven days? Must the driver prepare daily records of duty status for the next seven days?

Guidance: The driver must only have in his/her possession a record of duty status for the day he/she does not qualify for the exemption. The record of duty status must cover the entire day, even if the driver has to record retroactively changes in status that occurred between the time that the driver reported for duty and the time in which he/she no longer qualified for the 100 air-mile radius exemption. This is the only way to ensure that a driver does not claim the right to drive 10 hours after leaving his/her exempt status, in addition to the hours already driven under the 100 air-mile exemption.

Question 21: What is the carrier's liability when its drivers falsify records of duty status?

Guidance: A carrier is liable both for the actions of its drivers in submitting false documents and for its own actions in accepting false documents. Motor carriers have a duty to require drivers to observe the FMCSRs.

Question 22: If a driver logs his/her duty status as "driving" but makes multiple short stops (each less than 15 minutes) for on-duty or off-duty activities, marks a vertical line on the grid for each stop, and records the elapsed time for each in the remarks section of the grid, would the aggregate time spent on those non-driving activities be counted against the 10-hour driving limit?

Guidance: No. On-duty not driving time or off-duty time is not counted against the 10-hour driving limit.

Question 23: When the driver's duty status changes, do §§395.8(c) or 395.8(h)(5) require a description of on-duty not driving activities ("fueling," "pre-trip," "loading," "unloading," etc.) in the remarks section in addition to the name of the nearest city, town or village followed by the State abbreviation?

Guidance: No. Many motor carriers require drivers to identify work performed during a change of duty status. Part 395 neither requires nor prohibits this practice.

Question 24: When must a driver complete the signature/certification of the driver's record of duty status?

Guidance: In general, the driver must sign the record of duty status immediately after all required entries have been made for the 24-hour period. However, if the driver is driving at the end of the 24-hour period, he/she must sign during the next stop. A driver may also sign the record of duty status upon going off duty if he/she expects to remain off duty until the end of the 24-hour period.

Question 25: Is a driver (United States or foreign) required to maintain a record of duty status (log book) in a foreign country before entering the U.S.?

Guidance: No. The FHWA does not require drivers to prepare records of duty status while operating outside the jurisdiction of the United States. However, it may be advantageous for any driver (U.S. or foreign) to prepare records of duty status for short-term foreign trips. Upon entering the U.S., each driver must either: (a) Have in his/her possession a record of duty status current on the day of the examination showing the total hours worked for the prior seven consecutive days, including time spent outside the U.S.; or, (b) Demonstrate that he/she is operating as a "100 air-mile (161 air-kilometer) radius driver" under §395.1(e).

Question 26: If a driver is permitted to use a CMV for personal reasons, how must the driving time be recorded?

Guidance: When a driver is relieved from work and all responsibility for performing work, time spent traveling from a driver's home to his/her terminal (normal work reporting location), or from a driver's terminal to his/her home, may be considered off-duty time. Similarly, time spent traveling short distances from a driver's en route lodgings (such as en route terminals or motels) to restaurants in the vicinity of such lodgings may be considered off-duty time. The type of conveyance used from the terminal to the driver's home, from the driver's home to the terminal, or to restaurants in the vicinity of en route lodgings would not alter the situation unless the vehicle is laden. A driver may not operate a laden CMV as a personal conveyance. The driver who uses a motor carrier's CMV for transportation home, and is subsequently called by the employing carrier and is then dispatched from home, would be on-duty from the time the driver leaves home.

A driver placed out of service for exceeding the requirements of the hours of service regulations may not drive a CMV to any location to obtain rest.

Question 27: Would a driver who prepares his/her log on a computer, "digitally" signs the log, and then transmits it directly to the carrier, be in compliance with 49 CFR §395.8(f)(2)?

Guidance: No. The driver's activities must be recorded in accordance with the provisions of §395.8(f)(2). This section requires that all entries relating to driver's duty status must be legible and in the driver's own handwriting.

Question 28: May a driver use a computer to generate his or her record of duty status (log book) and then manually sign the computer printouts in lieu of handwritten logs?

Guidance: A driver may use a computer to generate the graph grid and entries for the record of duty status or log book, provided the computer-generated output includes the minimum information required by §395.8 and is formatted in accordance with the rules. In addition, the driver must:

1. Be capable of printing the record of duty status for the current 24-hour period at the request of an enforcement officer.
2. Print the record of duty status at the end of each 24-hour period, and sign it in his or her handwriting to certify that all entries required by this section are true and correct.
3. Maintain a copy of printed and signed records of duty status for the previous 7 consecutive days and make it available for inspection at the request of an enforcement officer.

§§395.10-395.12 [Reserved]

§395.13 Drivers declared out of service.

(a) Authority to declare drivers out of service. Every special agent of the Federal Motor Carrier Safety Administration (as defined in Appendix B to this subchapter) is authorized to declare a driver out of service and to notify the motor carrier of that declaration, upon finding at the time and place of examination that the driver has violated the out of service criteria as set forth in paragraph (b) of this section.

(b) Out of service criteria.
   (1) *No driver shall drive* after being on duty in excess of the maximum periods permitted by this part.
   (2) *No driver* required to maintain a record of duty status under §395.8 or §395.15 of this part shall fail to have a record of duty status current on the day of examination and for the prior seven consecutive days.
   (3) *Exception.* A driver failing only to have possession of a record of duty status current on the day of examination and the prior day, but has completed records of duty status up to that time (previous 6 days), will be given the opportunity to make the duty status record current.

(c) Responsibilities of motor carriers.
   (1) *No motor carrier shall:*
      (i) *Require or permit a driver* who has been declared out of service to operate a commercial motor vehicle until that driver may lawfully do so under the rules in this part.
      (ii) *Require a driver* who has been declared out of service for failure to prepare a record of duty status to operate a commercial motor vehicle until that driver has been off duty for the appropriate number of consecutive hours required by this part and is in compliance with this section. The appropriate consecutive hours off-duty may include sleeper berth time.
   (2) *A motor carrier shall complete* the "Motor Carrier Certification of Action Taken" portion of the form MCS-63 (Driver-Vehicle Examination Report) and deliver the copy of the form either personally or by mail to the Division Administrator or State Director, Federal Motor Carrier Safety Administration, at the address specified upon the form within 15 days following the date of examination. If the motor carrier mails the form, delivery is made on the date it is postmarked.

(d) Responsibilities of the driver.
   (1) *No driver who has been declared out of service* shall operate a commercial motor vehicle until that driver may lawfully do so under the rules of this part.
   (2) *No driver who has been declared out of service,* for failing to prepare a record of duty status, shall operate a commercial motor vehicle until the driver has been off duty for the appropriate number of consecutive hours required by this part and is in compliance with this section.
   (3) *A driver to whom a form has been tendered* declaring the driver out of service shall within 24 hours thereafter deliver or mail the copy to a person or place designated by motor carrier to receive it.
   (4) *Section 395.13 does not alter* the hazardous materials requirements prescribed in §397.5 pertaining to attendance and surveillance of commercial motor vehicles.

§395.13 DOT Interpretations

Question 1: May a driver operate any motor vehicle, at the direction of the motor carrier, after being placed out of service for an hours of service violation?

Guidance: An out of service order issued under §395.13 extends only to the operation of CMVs. State procedures may differ.

Question 2: May a driver operating a CMV under a lease arrangement with a motor carrier, after being placed out of service for an hours of service violation, cancel the lease and continue to operate the vehicle as a private personal conveyance?

Guidance: No. Cancellation of a lease does not relieve the driver of the responsibility of complying with the out of service order which prohibits the driver from operating a CMV.

§395.15 Automatic on-board recording devices.

(a) Authority to use automatic on-board recording device.
   (1) *A motor carrier may require a driver* to use an automatic on-board recording device to record the driver's hours of service in lieu of complying with the requirements of §395.8 of this part.
   (2) *Every driver required by a motor carrier* to use an automatic on-board recording device shall use such device to record the driver's hours of service.

(b) Information requirements.
   (1) *Automatic on-board recording devices* shall produce, upon demand, a driver's hours of service chart, electronic display, or printout showing the time and sequence of duty status changes including the drivers' starting time at the beginning of each day.
   (2) *The device shall provide a means* whereby authorized Federal, State, or local officials can immediately check the status of a driver's hours of service. This information may be used in conjunction with handwritten or printed records of duty status, for the previous 7 days.
   (3) *Support systems used in conjunction* with on-board recorders at a driver's home terminal or the motor carrier's principal place of business must be capable of providing authorized Federal,

State, or local officials with summaries of an individual driver's hours of service records, including the information specified in §395.8(d) of this part. The support systems must also provide information concerning on-board system sensor failures and identification of edited data. Such support systems should meet the information interchange requirements of the American National Standard Code for Information Interchange (ANSCII) (EIARS-232/CCITT V.24 port (National Bureau of Standards "Code for Information Interchange," FIPS PUB 1-1)).

(4) *The driver shall have in his/her possession* records of duty status for the previous 7 consecutive days available for inspection while on duty. These records shall consist of information stored in and retrievable from the automatic on-board recording device, handwritten records, computer generated records, or any combination thereof.

(5) *All hard copies of the driver's record of duty status* must be signed by the driver. The driver's signature certifies that the information contained thereon is true and correct.

(c) **The duty status and additional information** shall be recorded as follows:
(1) *"Off duty" or "OFF", or by an identifiable code or character;*
(2) *"Sleeper berth" or "SB"* or by an identifiable code or character (only if the sleeper berth is used);
(3) *"Driving" or "D", or by an identifiable code or character; and*
(4) *"On-duty not driving" or "ON",* or by an identifiable code or character.
(5) *Date;*
(6) *Total miles driving today;*
(7) *Truck or tractor and trailer number;*
(8) *Name of carrier;*
(9) *Main office address;*
(10) *24-hour period starting time* (e.g., midnight, 9:00 a.m., noon, 3:00 p.m.);
(11) *Name of co-driver;*
(12) *Total hours; and*
(13) *Shipping document number(s),* or name of shipper and commodity.

(d) **Location of duty status change.**
(1) *For each change of duty status* (e.g., the place and time of reporting for work, starting to drive, on-duty not driving and where released from work), the name of the city, town, or village, with State abbreviation, shall be recorded.
(2) *Motor carriers are permitted to use location codes* in lieu of the requirements of paragraph (d)(1) of this section. A list of such codes showing all possible location identifiers shall be carried in the cab of the commercial motor vehicle and available at the motor carrier's principal place of business. Such lists shall be made available to an enforcement official on request.

(e) **Entries made by driver only.** If a driver is required to make written entries relating to the driver's duty status, such entries must be legible and in the driver's own handwriting.

(f) **Reconstruction of records of duty status.** Drivers are required to note any failure of automatic on-board recording devices, and to reconstruct the driver's record of duty status for the current day, and the past 7 days, less any days for which the drivers have records, and to continue to prepare a handwritten record of all subsequent duty status until the device is again operational.

(g) **On-board information.** Each commercial motor vehicle must have on-board the commercial motor vehicle an information packet containing the following items:
(1) *An instruction sheet describing in detail* how data may be stored and retrieved from an automatic on-board recording system; and
(2) *A supply of blank driver's records* of duty status graph-grids sufficient to record the driver's duty status and other related information for the duration of the current trip.

(h) **Submission of driver's record of duty status.**
(1) *The driver shall submit,* electronically or by mail, to the employing motor carrier, each record of the driver's duty status within 13 days following the completion of each record;
(2) *The driver shall review and verify* that all entries are accurate prior to submission to the employing motor carrier; and
(3) *The submission of the record of duty status* certifies that all entries made by the driver are true and correct.

(i) **Performance of recorders.** Motor carriers that use automatic on-board recording devices for recording their drivers' records of duty status in lieu of the handwritten record shall ensure that:
(1) *A certificate is obtained from the manufacturer* certifying that the design of the automatic on-board recorder has been sufficiently tested to meet the requirements of this section and under the conditions it will be used;
(2) *The automatic on-board recording device* permits duty status to be updated only when the commercial motor vehicle is at rest, except when registering the time a commercial motor vehicle crosses a State boundary;
(3) *The automatic on-board recording device* and associated support systems are, to the maximum extent practicable, tamper-proof and do not permit altering of the information collected concerning the driver's hours of service;
(4) *The automatic on-board recording device* warns the driver visually and/or audibly that the device has ceased to function. Devices installed and operational as of October 31, 1988, and authorized to be used in lieu of the handwritten record of duty status by the FMCSA are exempted from this requirement.
(5) *Automatic on-board recording devices* with electronic displays shall have the capability of displaying the following:
(i) *Driver's total hours of driving today;*
(ii) *The total hours on duty today;*
(iii) *Total miles driving today;*
(iv) *Total hours on duty* for the 7 consecutive day period, including today;
(v) *Total hours on duty* for the prior 8 consecutive day period, including the present day; and
(vi) *The sequential changes in duty status* and the times the changes occurred for each driver using the device.
(6) *The on-board recorder* is capable of recording separately each driver's duty status when there is a multiple-driver operation;
(7) *The on-board recording device/system* identifies sensor failures and edited data when reproduced in printed form. Devices installed and operational as of October 31, 1988, and authorized to be used in lieu of the handwritten record of duty status by the FMCSA are exempted from this requirement.
(8) *The on-board recording device* is maintained and recalibrated in accordance with the manufacturer's specifications;
(9) *The motor carrier's drivers* are adequately trained regarding the proper operation of the device; and
(10) *The motor carrier must maintain* a second copy (back-up copy) of the electronic hours-of-service files, by month, in a different physical location than where the original data is stored.

(j) **Rescission of authority.**
(1) *The FMCSA may,* after notice and opportunity to reply, order any motor carrier or driver to comply with the requirements of §395.8 of this part.
(2) *The FMCSA may issue such an order* if the FMCSA has determined that —
(i) *The motor carrier has been issued* a conditional or unsatisfactory safety rating by the FMCSA;
(ii) *The motor carrier has required or permitted* a driver to establish, or the driver has established, a pattern of exceeding the hours of service limitations of this part;
(iii) *The motor carrier has required or permitted* a driver to fail, or the driver has failed, to accurately and completely record the driver's hours of service as required in this section; or
(iv) *The motor carrier or driver* has tampered with or otherwise abused the automatic on-board recording device on any commercial motor vehicle.

§395.15 DOT Interpretations

Question 1: Must a motor carrier maintain a second (back-up) copy of the electronic hours-of-service files, by month, in a different physical location than where the original data is stored if the motor carrier retains the original hours-of-service printout signed by the driver and provides the driver with a copy?

Guidance: No. By creating and maintaining the signed original record-of-duty status printed from the electronic hours-of-service file, the motor carrier has converted the electronic document into a paper document subject to §395.8(k). That section requires the motor carrier to retain at its principal place of business the records of duty status and supporting documents for a period of 6 months from date of receipt. If the motor carrier did not generate a paper copy of the electronic document and retain a signed original, it would be required to maintain the electronic file and a second (back-up) copy.

Question 2: May a driver who uses an automatic on-board recording device amend his/her record of duty status during a trip?

Part 395 - Hours of Service of Drivers

Guidance: No. §395.15(i)(3) requires automatic on-board recording devices, to the maximum extent possible, be tamperproof and preclude the alteration of information collected concerning a driver's hours of service. If drivers, who use automatic on-board recording devices, were allowed to amend their record of duty status while in transit, legitimate amendments could not be distinguished from falsifications. Records of duty status maintained and generated by an automatic on-board recording device may only be amended by a supervisory motor carrier official to accurately reflect the driver's activity. Such supervisory motor carrier official must include an explanation of the mistake in the remarks section of either the original or amended record of duty status. Both the original and amended record of duty status must be retained by the motor carrier.

Question 3: May an automatic on-board recording device use an algorithm to identify the location of each change in duty status relative to the nearest city, town, or village?

Guidance: Yes, provided that the accuracy of the algorithm is sufficient to ensure correlation between the driving time and distance data provided through the on-board recorder's integral connection to the vehicle's systems. Furthermore, the description of the location must be of sufficient precision to enable enforcement personnel to quickly determine the geographic location on a standard map or road atlas.

Hours of Service Frequently Asked Questions

A. LATEST REVISIONS

A-1. When are carriers and drivers required to comply with the latest revisions of the HOS rule?

Answer: Carrier and drivers are required to comply with the latest revisions of the HOS rule on October 1, 2005, the effective date of the rule. Carriers and drivers will not be allowed to operate under the HOS rule prior to its effective date.

A-2. How does the 2005 HOS rule differ from the current (April 2003) HOS rule?

Answer: Important changes were made in three areas.

(1) Sleeper Berth: To use any of the HOS provisions regarding sleeper berths, a driver must now have one of the following:

Continuous Sleeper Berth Provision: At least 10 consecutive and uninterrupted hours in the sleeper berth.

Sleeper Berth Provision: The equivalent of at least 10 consecutive hours off-duty (equivalent means at least 8 hours but less than 10 consecutive hours in a sleeper berth and a separate period of at least 2 hours but less than 10 consecutive hours either in the sleeper berth or off duty, or any combination of both).

Continuous Off-Duty and Sleeper Berth Provision: At least 10 consecutive hours sleeper berth and off-duty time combined and uninterrupted. Further details are on the internet at www.fmcsa.dot.gov/documents/rulesregs/hos/logbook-examples.pdf.

(2) Operators of property-carrying commercial motor vehicles not requiring a commercial driver's license: Drivers of non-commercial driver's license (CDL) vehicles (those vehicles not requiring a CDL to operate) who are operating within a 150 air-mile radius of their normal work reporting location and return to their normal work reporting location at the end of their duty tour are now covered by a separate HOS provision. Drivers meeting these conditions are not eligible for the existing 100 air-mile radius provision in §395.1(e) or the current 16-hour exception in §395.1(o), since those conflict with this new "Non-CDL, 150 Air-Mile Radius" provision. These drivers are required to comply with the following:

(a) The 11 hours driving, minimum 10 hours off-duty, 14 consecutive hour duty period, 60/70 hours in 7/8 days, 34-hour restart all apply.

(b) On any 2 days of every 7 consecutive days, the driver may extend the 14-hour duty period to 16 hours.

(c) There is no requirement that the driver be released from duty at the end of the 14- or 16-hour duty periods. The driver may continue to perform non-driving duties, which would be counted against the 60/70 hour weekly limitation.

(d) Time records may be used in lieu of records of duty status (RODS).

(3) 34-Hour Restart: Previously, a driver was required to be in compliance with the "60/70 on-duty hours in 7/8 days" limitation before the driver could start counting a 34-hour restart period. Now the 34-hour restart period may begin at the start of any consecutive 34-hour off-duty period.

A-3. Are previous interpretations and guidance regarding HOS still valid?

Answer: The Federal Motor Carrier Safety Administration (FMCSA) will be updating and revising its regulatory guidance to Part 395 of the Federal Motor Carrier Safety Regulations (FMCSRs) to provide additional guidance concerning the application of HOS regulations. All prior interpretations and regulatory guidance relating to Part §395 of the FMCSRs, as well as FMCSA and Federal Highway Administration memoranda and letters concerning Part 395, may no longer be relied upon as authoritative to the extent they are inconsistent with the current rule. All interpretations and guidance for Parts other than Part 395 remain valid.

A-4. Where can I obtain more details about the 2005 revisions of the HOS rules?

Answer: Extensive information and downloadable HOS documents are available on the Internet at www.fmcsa.dot.gov/rules-regulations/truck/driver/hos/hos-2005.htm. In particular, note the "Frequently Asked Questions" (FAQs) link on that page. You may also contact the FMCSA Office in your State. A directory of those offices is available at www.fmcsa.dot.gov/about/contact/offices/displayfieldroster.htm.

B. GENERAL PROVISIONS

B-1. Do these HOS regulations apply to intrastate commerce?

Answer: No. Intrastate commercial motor vehicle regulations are under the jurisdiction of each State. The HOS regulations apply directly only to interstate commerce. However, most States have adopted intrastate regulations which are identical or very similar to the Federal hours-of-service regulations. A driver involved exclusively in intrastate operations should contact the State agency handling commercial vehicle enforcement in the driver's home State with any questions. Usually this is the state police or highway patrol, although in some States, the function is handled by the department of motor vehicles, department of public safety, or public service commission.

B-2. What are the penalties for violating the HOS rules?

Answer: Drivers or carriers who violate the HOS rules face serious penalties:

- Drivers may be placed out-of-service (shut down) at roadside until the driver has accumulated enough off-duty time to be back in compliance;
- State and local enforcement officials may assess fines;
- FMCSA may levy civil penalties on driver or carrier, ranging from $1,000 to $11,000 per violation depending on severity;
- The carrier's safety rating can be downgraded for a pattern of violations; and

Federal criminal penalties can be brought against carriers who knowingly and willfully allow or require HOS violations, or drivers who knowingly and willfully violate the HOS regulations.

B-3. Are drivers of passenger-carrying commercial motor vehicles (CMV) required to comply with the same HOS rule as property-carrying drivers?

Answer: No. Motorcoach operators and drivers will continue to operate under the HOS rules as specified in §395.5

B-4. What happens if a driver operates both a bus and truck for part of each day or each week?

Answer: A driver will be subject to the limits on driving time applicable to the CMV the driver is driving (11 hours for a property-carrying CMV, 10 hours for a passenger CMV), and will be required to meet the off-duty requirements applicable to the type of CMV the driver will drive immediately after that off-duty period (10 hours if the next assignment is in a property-carrying CMV, 8 hours if it is in a passenger CMV). For example, if a bus driver completes 8 hours off-duty for the motorcoach company, the driver must remain off-duty for another 2 hours before driving for the trucking company. After completing 10 consecutive hours off-duty, the driver may drive for 11 hours for the trucking company. Following 8 consecutive hours off-duty, the driver may then drive for the bus company.

B-5. If a State has an 8-hour off-duty requirement for intrastate operations, may a driver who takes 8 hours off-duty after completing an intrastate trip begin driving on an interstate trip?

Answer: No. The driver of a property carrying vehicle must take an additional 2 consecutive hours off-duty, for a total of 10 consecutive hours, before beginning an interstate trip.

Part 395 - Hours of Service of Drivers

B-6. How would "waiting time" at a terminal, plant, or port be logged?

Answer: "Waiting time" at a terminal, plant, or port may be recorded as off-duty, sleeper berth, or on duty/not driving, depending on specific circumstances. For "waiting time" to be off-duty, the following off-duty conditions must be met:

1. The driver must be relieved of all duty and responsibility for the care and custody of the vehicle, its accessories, and any cargo or passengers it may be carrying.
2. During the stop, and for the duration of the stop, the driver must be at liberty to pursue activities of his/her own choosing and to leave the premises where the vehicle is situated.

If circumstances permit a driver to utilize a valid sleeper berth without being disturbed for a specific period of "waiting time," that time in the sleeper berth may be recorded as "sleeper berth" time. However, a driver must take eight consecutive hours in a sleeper berth, plus another two consecutive hours off duty or in a sleeper berth, in order to meet the requirement for the equivalent of 10 consecutive hours off duty. In most other circumstances, such as when the driver is required to remain with the vehicle to move it when necessary, the "waiting time" should be recorded as "on duty/not driving."

These provisions should not be confused with waiting time of drivers of vehicles that are specially constructed to service oil wells.

B-7. May a driver be called after 8 hours off-duty to report to work 2 hours later?

Answer: Yes. The HOS rule does not control communication between the driver and the motor carrier during the driver's off-duty time, so the call may occur. However, the driver cannot be required to do any work for the motor carrier during the 10 hours of off-duty time.

B-8. How does the HOS rule apply to Mexican and Canadian drivers? Are Canadian and Mexican military or other government employees exempt?

Answer: Mexican and Canadian drivers operating in the United States must comply with FMCSA's HOS regulations. Although compliance with the HOS regulations is checked by looking backward in time, and activity occurring outside the U.S. may be taken into account, State and Federal officials may only impose penalties for violations that occurred in this country.

For example, upon entering this country, Canadian and Mexican drivers must show a current RODS for the previous 7 consecutive days. U.S. officials cannot penalize a driver for actions that occurred abroad, but failure to have the previous 7 days of RODS while in the U.S. is a violation of §395.8(k)(2). Additionally, Mexican and Canadian drivers of property-carrying commercial motor vehicles may not drive in the U.S. unless their last off-duty period (either here or abroad) amounted to 10 consecutive hours (or an authorized sleeper-berth equivalent). If such a driver took only 8 consecutive hours off-duty in Mexico or Canada just before starting a trip into the U.S., he/she would be required to take 10 consecutive hours off-duty immediately after entering this country.

Canadian and Mexican military and other government employees are NOT exempt from the HOS regulations. The general exemption in §390.3(f)(2) applies only to U.S. Federal, State, and local governments.

B-9. How are property-carrying and passenger-carrying drivers determined as the terms are used in the HOS rule?

Answer: It is easiest to determine passenger-carrying, with any other CMV drivers to be considered property-carrying. The definition of a CMV in §390.5 should be used to determine passenger-carrying. If a driver is operating a CMV "designed or used to transport more than 8 passengers (including the driver) for compensation; or designed or used to transport more than 15 passengers, including the driver, and is not used to transport passengers for compensation," the driver would be considered to be passenger-carrying regardless of whether there were actually any passengers on the vehicle. This would include, for example, new buses being delivered (driven) from manufacturer to dealer.

C. SHORT-HAUL OPERATIONS

General Questions

C-1. What is a "short-haul" operation?

Answer: The HOS regulations do not specifically define or use the term "short haul" except as a caption for §395.1(e), which includes requirements for drivers using the 100 air-mile radius exception and those covered by the "non-CDL, as defined in Part 383, 150 air-mile radius" provision.

C-2. What is an "air-mile"?

Answer: The term "air-mile" is internationally defined as a "nautical mile" which is equivalent to 6,076 feet. Thus, the 100 air-miles are equivalent to 115.08 statute miles, and 150 air-miles are equivalent to 172.6 statute miles.

C-3. What are the recordkeeping requirements for a driver who is utilizing either the 100 or non-CDL, as defined in Part 383, 150 air-mile radius provisions?

Answer: Under both provisions, a driver may use time records in lieu of RODS.

C-4. May drivers who work split shifts take advantage of the short-haul operations provisions found in Part §395.1(e)?

Answer: For property-drivers, the concept of "split shifts" is no longer relevant due to the limitations of the 14-hour rule. The provisions in §395.1(e) only provide an exception to the RODS requirements. Generally, they do not exempt the driver from any requirements of the HOS rules.

100 air-mile radius driver - A driver may go on- and off-duty multiple times during a duty tour, after completing at least 10 hours off duty, but the total of all on- and off-duty time accumulates toward their 12 hours. Once a driver is on duty more than 12 hours they no longer meet the 100 air-mile radius exemption.

Operators of property-carrying commercial motor vehicles not requiring a commercial driver's license - A driver may go on- and off-duty multiple times during a duty tour, but the total of all on- and off-duty time accumulates towards the 14- or 16-hour time limit, whichever is applicable at the time, until the driver has a period of 10 or more consecutive hours off-duty.

Prior Regulatory Guidance (§395.1 Question 19) on this subject no longer applies to property-carrying drivers.

C-5. How does a driver comply if during a 7-day period the driver operates some days under the 100 air-mile radius exception, some days under the "non-CDL 150 air-mile radius" provision, and some days under neither?

Answer: The driver complies with the provisions of the 100 air-mile radius exception or the non-CDL, as defined by Part 383, 150 air-mile radius provision if either of those are applicable for the entire duty period (usually one day). For example, if a driver operates within the 100 air-mile radius for part of the day and then travels outside the radius during the same duty period, the exception would not apply. The driver must remain under the conditions of the exception for the entire duty period. Compliance may vary from one duty period to the next, depending on operating circumstances. A driver operating under the 100 air-mile radius exception for one day and then outside the radius for the second day would only be required to make a RODS for the second day.

100 Air-Mile Radius Provision

C-6. How would you summarize the 100 air-mile radius HOS provision in §395.1(e)(1)?

Answer: The 100 air-mile radius exception in Part §395.1(e)(1) is an option to use time records in lieu of RODS on days when the driver meets the conditions of the exception, which are:

- The driver operates within a 100 air-mile (115 statute miles) radius of the normal work reporting location, and
- The driver returns to the work reporting location and be released from duty within 12 consecutive hours, and
- The driver maintains time records as specified in the rule, and
- The driver is not covered by the "non-CDL 150 air-mile radius" provision.

C-7. May a "100 air-mile radius" driver utilize the "16-hour duty period" exception in Part §395.1(o)?

Answer: Yes. A driver normally operating under the 100 air-mile radius exception in §395.1(e) may also meet the requirements in §395.1(o) enabling the driver to have one period of 16 hours on-duty each week (or after a 34-hour restart). However, on the day in which the 16-hour exception is utilized, the driver would not meet the 12-hour duty-period requirement of the 100 air-mile radius exception and would therefore be required to make a RODS for that day.

Non-CDL 150 Air-Mile Radius Provision

C-8. What drivers are covered by the Non-CDL 150 air-mile radius provision?

Part 395 - Hours of Service of Drivers

Answer: Operators of property-carrying commercial motor vehicles not requiring a CDL, as defined in Part 383, may be covered by the Non-CDL 150 air-mile radius provision. Note that the applicability depends on the type of vehicle being driven, not whether the operator possesses a CDL.

C-9. How would you summarize the Non-CDL 150 air-mile radius provision in Part §395.1(e)(2)?

Answer: Drivers of non-CDL vehicles (those vehicles not requiring a CDL, as defined in Part 383 to operate) who are operating within a 150 air-mile radius of their normal work reporting location and return to their normal work reporting location at the end of their duty tour are now covered by separate HOS provisions. Drivers meeting these conditions are not eligible for the existing 100 air-mile radius provision in §395.1(e)(1) or the current 16-hour exception in §395.1(o), since those conflict with this new Non-CDL 150 air-mile radius provision. These drivers are required to comply with the following:

(a) The 11 hours driving, minimum 10 hours off-duty, 14 consecutive hour duty period, 60/70 hours in 7/8 days, 34-hour restart all apply.

(b) On any 2 days of every 7 consecutive days, the driver may extend the 14-hour duty period to 16 hours.

(c) There is no requirement that the driver be released from duty at the end of the 14- or 16-hour duty periods. The driver may continue to perform non-driving duties, which would be counted against the 60/70 hour weekly limitation.

(d) Time records may be used in lieu of records of duty status.

D. 14-HOUR DUTY PERIOD

D-1. May a driver be on duty for more than 14 consecutive hours?

Answer: Yes. A driver may remain on duty for more than 14 hours; however, the driver of a property-carrying CMV cannot drive after the 14th hour after coming on duty. Also, the additional on-duty time will be counted toward the 60/70-hour on-duty limit.

D-2. If a carrier allows a driver to log mealtime or similar activities as off-duty time, does that permit a driver to extend the 14-hour duty period?

Answer: No. Off-duty breaks during the day do not extend the workday to permit a driver to drive after the 14th consecutive hour on duty. However, time logged as off duty is not counted in calculating a driver's 60/70-hour on-duty limit.

E. 16-HOUR EXCEPTION

E-1. What is a "duty tour" as the term is used in Part §395.1(o)?

Answer: The 16-hour exemption in §395.1(o) is designed for one-day "duty tours." The duty tour is the interval between the time a driver comes on-duty and is released from duty on a daily basis. This period begins and ends at the driver's normal work reporting location and may only be used following 10 or more consecutive hours off-duty, 10 or more consecutive hours in the sleeper berth, or a combination of 10 or more consecutive hours off-duty and sleeper berth time.

E-2. If a driver is "on duty, not driving" during the 15th and 16th hour of his duty tour and does not drive after that, has he used the 16-hour exception in §395.1(o)?

Answer: No. Example: If a driver was on duty 16 hours on Wednesday, but didn't drive after being on duty 14 hours, could the driver use the 16 hour extension on Friday and be allowed to drive after the 14th hour as long as all other conditions and regulations (11-, 16-, and 60/70- hour rules) were met?

In this scenario, the driver may choose to use the 16-hour extension on Friday as long as the driver meets all of the requirements for the 16-hour exception outlined in Part §395.1(o) and also remains in compliance with Part §395.3(a)(1) and Part §395.3(b). Although the 16 hours on-duty on Wednesday will count toward the driver's 60/70 calculations, the driver has not utilized the 16-hour exception unless the driver has actually driven after the 14th hour.

E-3. May a driver having more than one work reporting location use the §395.1(o), 16-hour exception?

Answer: As stated in §395.1(o) and current §395.1 Interpretation Question 15, a driver having more than one work reporting location could use the §395.1(o) 16-hour exception; however, its availability would be limited by the requirement of §395.1(o)(1) that the "carrier released the driver from duty at that location for the previous five duty tours the driver has worked…" A driver alternating between two normal work locations on a weekly basis would not be able to utilize the exception unless he worked six days per week, and then the exception could only be used on the sixth day.

E-4. May a driver utilize the adverse driving rule, which extends the driving time by two additional hours, in conjunction with the 16-hour exception?

Answer: No. A driver may not use the exception for adverse driving conditions while also using the 16-hour exception for property-carrying drivers. Section 395.1(b)(1)(ii) of the adverse driving conditions exception specifically states that a property-carrying driver may not drive or be permitted to drive after he/she has been on-duty after the end of the 14th hour after coming on-duty following 10 consecutive hours off-duty.

E-5. When the "16 hour exception" is used, may sleeper berth periods or extended off-duty periods be included in the "duty tour?" How does this affect team drivers?

Answer: The §395.1(o) exception for property-carrying drivers is for drivers who return to the normal work reporting location and are released from duty at the end of each of the previous 5 duty tours. The use of 10 consecutive hours off duty or the equivalent (sleeper berth, off duty, or any allowable combination thereof) before returning to the work reporting location would interrupt the duty tour, and the driver would not be eligible to use the 16-hour exception that day or again until after 5 or more duty tours when the driver did return to the work reporting location.

F. 34-HOUR RESTART

F-1. Does any period of 34 consecutive hours off-duty automatically restart the calculation of the 60/70-hour on-duty period?

Answer: Yes. Any period of 34 consecutive hours off-duty will restart the 60/70 hour calculation.

F-2. If a driver works at another job, unrelated to trucking, during his 34-hour off-duty restart period, and then begins a duty shift for the trucking company, does the 34-hour restart provision apply?

Answer: No. Performing compensated work for a person not a motor carrier is considered on-duty time, which would interrupt the 34-hour period.

F-3. If a driver is on-call, but has not been called for 34 hours, may those 34 hours be counted as a 34-hour restart?

Answer: Yes, provided the carrier has not required the driver to report for work until after the 34-hour period has ended.

F-4. If a driver takes the 34-hour restart in Canada or Mexico just before entering the U.S., will it be recognized as such in the U.S.?

Answer: Yes. Duty status changes and periods occurring in Canada or Mexico before entering the U.S. are included in HOS calculations while in the U.S.

F-5. How should the "recap" section of the RODS page be completed when using a 34-hour restart to begin a new 60/70 hour period?

Answer: The RODS pages printed by most commercial firms include a "recap" on each page for drivers to calculate compliance with the 60/70 hour limits and show "time remaining" within those limits. This "recap," however, is not required or addressed by the FMCSRs. Therefore, the "recap" may be completed in any manner desired.

G. SLEEPER BERTHS

G-1. May a driver spend part of his or her 34-hours of consecutive off-duty time in a sleeper berth?

Answer: Yes, provided the 34-hour period is consecutive and not broken by on-duty or driving activities.

G-2. If a team driver goes directly from 10 consecutive hours off-duty to the sleeper berth at the start of his duty period, can the sleeper-berth period be excluded from calculation of the 14-hour limit?

Answer: Yes. It would be a "…combination of consecutive sleeper-berth and off-duty time amounting to at least 10 hours" per §395.1(g)(1). The driver would not be permitted to perform any duties, such as pre-trip inspections, prior to using the sleeper berth.

G-3. How does a driver who is utilizing the sleeper berth provision calculate his or her compliance with the 14-hour rule?

Answer: A sleeper-berth period of at least 8 consecutive hours is excluded from calculation of the 14-hour limitation. All other sleeper berth periods are included in the 14-hour calculation (unless part of a sleeper-berth/off-duty combination of 10 or more consecutive hours).

H. OILFIELD OPERATIONS

H-1. Are drivers of vehicles that are specially constructed to service oil wells required to log waiting time as on-duty time under the new rule?

Part 395 - Hours of Service of Drivers

Answer: No. The new rule retains the current exception in §395.1(d)(2), which provides that drivers of vehicles that are specially constructed to service oil wells are not required to log time waiting at a natural gas or oil well site as "on-duty not driving" time. This specific group of drivers is allowed to extend, by the amount of their waiting time, the 14-hour period after coming on-duty during which driving is allowed.

H-2. Is off-duty time at a yard for oil-field equipment excluded from the 14-hour calculation?
Answer: No. Off-duty time at a yard for oil-field equipment is counted toward the calculation of the 14-hour rule. Only waiting time at a natural gas or oil well site may be excluded from on-duty time.

H-3. May "oilfield" drivers take advantage of the 16-hour exception provided for property-carrying drivers under §395.1(o)?
Answer: No. The exception in §395.1(o) is only available to drivers who otherwise strictly observe the 14-hour limit. Since §395.1(d)(2) allows drivers of commercial motor vehicles specially constructed to service oil wells to exclude waiting time at a natural gas or oil well site from on-duty time, these drivers do not strictly observe the 14-hour limit on a daily basis. An oilfield driver may choose to use the exception provided in either §395.1(d)(2) or §395.1(o), but not both.

H-4. Mechanics are often dispatched with oilfield service crews. Some of the mechanic's service vehicles meet the definition of a CMV. Can these mechanics use the oilfield operations exceptions found in §395.1(d)?
Answer: Based on the language of §395.1(d)(1), dedicated oilfield mechanics operating CMVs are able to take advantage of the 24-hour restart provision since they are servicing the vehicles/equipment associated with field operations. However, the mechanics may not take advantage of the provisions of §395.1(d)(2) to exclude waiting time at a natural gas or oil well site from on-duty time because the vehicle being operated is not specially constructed to service oil wells.

I. DRIVER-SALESPERSONS

I-1. What HOS exceptions are available to "driver-salespersons"?
Answer:
- Under §395.1(c), a driver meeting the "driver-salesperson" definition in §395.2 (private carrier, solely delivering and selling goods or services, 100 air-mile radius, no more than 50% of on-duty time is driving) does not have to comply with the 60/70-hour limitation if the driver does not exceed 40 hours driving in any 7-consecutive-day period.
- A property-carrying driver-salesperson may use the "no RODS" provision of §395.1(e)(1) if the driver-salesperson meets the requirements of operating within a 100-air-mile radius and has at least 10 consecutive hours off-duty separating each 12 hours on-duty. Although a driver-salesperson is not required to return to the work reporting location to be released from work within 12 hours, the driver may not drive after the 14th hour after coming on duty. Driver-salespersons using the 100-air-mile radius exception must complete a RODS on days in which they exceed 12 hours on duty.
- A driver-salesperson may be eligible to use the 16-hour exception of §395.1(o) if the driver meets all of the requirements of that section.
- A property-carrying driver-salesperson may use the 150-mile exemption, if applicable.

J. OTHER EXEMPTIONS

J-1. Are there other hours-of-service exemptions not included in this regulation?
Answer: Yes. The Motor Carrier Safety Act of 2005 (Part IV of SAFETEA-LU) includes several exemptions to the hours-of-service for specific industries. Although not included in this regulation, these exemptions are in effect.

Sleeper Berth Examples

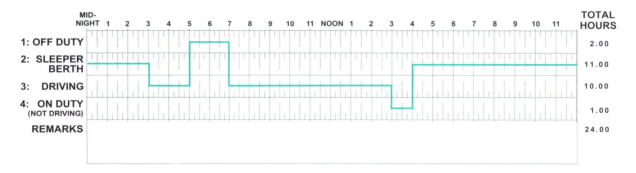

No violation.
Compliance with the 11-hour and 14-hour rules is re-calculated from the end of the first of the two periods used to obtain 10 hours off-duty.

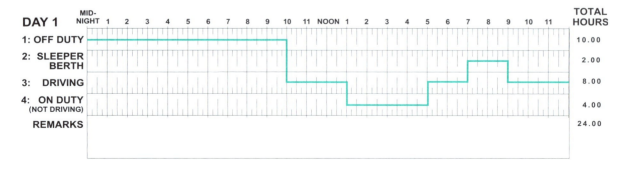

No violation on Day 1.

Part 395 - Hours of Service of Drivers

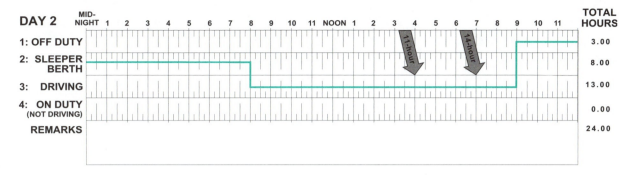

There is an 11-hour violation on Day 2 from 4:00 p.m. until 9:00 p.m. There is also a 14-hour violation on Day 2 from 7:00 p.m. until 9:00 p.m. Compliance with the 11-hour and 14-hour rules is re-calculated from the end of the first of the two periods used to obtain 10 hours off-duty.

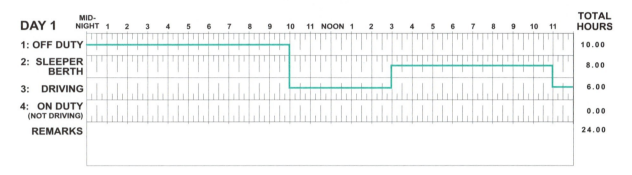

No violation on Day 1.

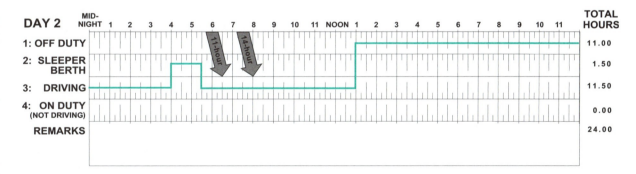

There is an 11-hour violation on Day 2 starting at 6:30 a.m. until 1:00 p.m. There is also a 14-hour violation on Day 2 from 8:00 a.m. until 1:00 p.m. Compliance with the 11-hour and 14-hour rules is re-calculated from the end of the first of the two periods used to obtain 10 hours off-duty.

Part 395 - Hours of Service of Drivers

Notes

Part 396 - Inspection, Repair, and Maintenance (Page 159 in the Driver Edition)

§396.1 Scope.

General — Every motor carrier, its officers, drivers, agents, representatives, and employees directly concerned with the inspection or maintenance of motor vehicles shall comply and be conversant with the rules of this part.

§396.3 Inspection, repair, and maintenance.

(a) *General.* Every motor carrier shall systematically inspect, repair, and maintain, or cause to be systematically inspected, repaired, and maintained, all motor vehicles subject to its control.

  (1) *Parts and accessories* shall be in safe and proper operating condition at all times. These include those specified in Part 393 of this subchapter and any additional parts and accessories which may affect safety of operation, including but not limited to, frame and frame assemblies, suspension systems, axles and attaching parts, wheels and rims, and steering systems.

  (2) *Pushout windows,* emergency doors, and emergency door marking lights in buses shall be inspected at least every 90 days.

(b) *Required records.* For vehicles controlled for 30 consecutive days or more, except for a private motor carrier of passengers (nonbusiness), the motor carriers shall maintain, or cause to be maintained, the following record for each vehicle:

  (1) *An identification of the vehicle* including company number, if so marked, make, serial number, year, and tire size. In addition, if the motor vehicle is not owned by the motor carrier, the record shall identify the name of the person furnishing the vehicle;

  (2) *A means to indicate the nature and due date* of the various inspection and maintenance operations to be performed;

  (3) *A record of inspection, repairs, and maintenance* indicating their date and nature; and

  (4) *A record of tests* conducted on pushout windows, emergency doors, and emergency door marking lights on buses.

(c) *Record retention.* The records required by this section shall be retained where the vehicle is either housed or maintained for a period of 1 year and for 6 months after the motor vehicle leaves the motor carrier's control.

§396.3 DOT Interpretations

Question 1: What is meant by "systematic inspection, repair, and maintenance"?

Guidance: Generally, systematic means a regular or scheduled program to keep vehicles in a safe operating condition. §396.3 does not specify inspection, maintenance, or repair intervals because such intervals are fleet specific and, in some instances, vehicle specific. The inspection, repair, and maintenance intervals are to be determined by the motor carrier. The requirements of §§396.11, 396.13, and 396.17 are in addition to the systematic inspection, repair, and maintenance required by §396.3.

Question 2: Section 396.3(b)(4) refers to a record of tests. What tests are required of push-out windows and emergency door lamps on buses?

Guidance: Generally, inspection of a push-out window would require pushing out the window. However, if the window may be destroyed by pushing out to test its proper functioning, a visual inspection may qualify as a test if the inspector can ascertain the proper functioning of the window without opening it. Checking to ensure that the rubber push-out molding is properly in place and has not deteriorated and that any handles or marking instructions have not been tampered with would meet the test requirement. Inspection of emergency door marking lights would require opening the door to test the lights.

Question 3: Who has the responsibility of inspecting and maintaining leased vehicles and their maintenance records?

Guidance: The motor carrier must either inspect, repair, maintain, and keep suitable records for all vehicles subject to its control for 30 consecutive days or more, or cause another party to perform such activities. The motor carrier is solely responsible for ensuring that the vehicles under its control are in safe operating condition and that defects have been corrected.

Question 4: Is computerized recordkeeping of CMV inspection and maintenance information permissible under §396.3 of the FMCSRs?

Guidance: Yes, if the minimum inspection, repair, and maintenance records required are included in the computer information system and can be reproduced on demand.

Question 5: Where must vehicle inspection and maintenance records be retained if a vehicle is not housed or maintained at a single location?

Guidance: The motor carrier may retain the records at a location of its choice. If the vehicle maintenance records are retained at a location apart from the vehicle, the motor carrier is not relieved of its responsibility for ensuring that the records are current and factual. In all cases, however, upon request of the FHWA the maintenance records must be made available within a reasonable period of time (2 working days).

§396.5 Lubrication.

Every motor carrier shall ensure that each motor vehicle subject to its control is —

(a) Properly lubricated; and

(b) Free of oil and grease leaks.

§396.7 Unsafe operations forbidden.

(a) *General.* A motor vehicle shall not be operated in such a condition as to likely cause an accident or a breakdown of the vehicle.

(b) *Exemption.* Any motor vehicle discovered to be in an unsafe condition while being operated on the highway may be continued in operation only to the nearest place where repairs can safely be effected. Such operation shall be conducted only if it is less hazardous to the public than to permit the vehicle to remain on the highway.

§396.9 Inspection of motor vehicles in operation.

(a) *Personnel authorized to perform inspections.* Every special agent of the FMCSA (as defined in Appendix B to this subchapter) is authorized to enter upon and perform inspections of motor carrier's vehicles in operation.

(b) *Prescribed inspection report.* The Driver Vehicle Examination Report shall be used to record results of motor vehicle inspections conducted by authorized FMCSA personnel.

(c) *Motor vehicles declared "out of service".*

  (1) *Authorized personnel* shall declare and mark "out of service" any motor vehicle which by reason of its mechanical condition or loading would likely cause an accident or a breakdown. An "Out of Service Vehicle" sticker shall be used to mark vehicles "out of service."

  (2) *No motor carrier* shall require or permit any person to operate nor shall any person operate any motor vehicle declared and marked "out of service" until all repairs required by the "out of service notice" have been satisfactorily completed. The term "operate" as used in this section shall include towing the vehicle, except that vehicles marked "out of service" may be towed away by means of a vehicle using a crane or hoist. A vehicle combination consisting of an emergency towing vehicle and an "out of service" vehicle shall not be operated unless such combination meets the performance requirements of this subchapter except for those conditions noted on the Driver Equipment Compliance Check.

  (3) *No person shall remove* the "Out of Service Vehicle" sticker from any motor vehicle prior to completion of all repairs required by the "out of service notice".

(d) *Motor carrier disposition.*

  (1) *The driver of any motor vehicle* receiving an inspection report shall deliver it to the motor carrier operating the vehicle upon his/her arrival at the next terminal or facility. If the driver is not scheduled to arrive at a terminal or facility of the motor carrier operating the vehicle within 24 hours, the driver shall immediately mail the report to the motor carrier.

  (2) *Motor carriers shall examine the report.* Violations or defects noted thereon shall be corrected.

  (3) *Within 15 days* following the date of the inspection, the motor carrier shall —

    (i) *Certify that all violations noted* have been corrected by completing the "Signature of Carrier Official, Title, and Date Signed" portions of the form; and

    (ii) *Return the completed roadside inspection form* to the issuing agency at the address indicated on the form and retain a copy at the motor carrier's principal place of business or where the vehicle is housed for 12 months from the date of the inspection.

§396.9 DOT Interpretations

Question 1: Under what conditions may a vehicle that has been placed "out of service" under §396.3 be moved?
Guidance: The vehicle may be moved by being placed entirely upon another vehicle, towed by a vehicle equipped with a crane or hoist, or driven if the "out of service" condition no longer exists.

Question 2: Is it the intent of §396.9 to allow "out of service" vehicles to be towed?
Guidance: Yes; however, not all out of service vehicles may be towed away from the inspection location. The regulation sets up a flexible situation that will permit the inspecting officer to use his/her best judgment on a case-by-case basis.

§396.11 Driver vehicle inspection report(s).

(a) *Report required.* Every motor carrier shall require its drivers to report, and every driver shall prepare a report in writing at the completion of each day's work on each vehicle operated and the report shall cover at least the following parts and accessories:
— Service brakes including trailer brake connections
— Parking (hand) brake
— Steering mechanism
— Lighting devices and reflectors
— Tires
— Horn
— Windshield wipers
— Rear vision mirrors
— Coupling devices
— Wheels and rims
— Emergency equipment

(b) *Report content.* The report shall identify the vehicle and list any defect or deficiency discovered by or reported to the driver which would affect the safety of operation of the vehicle or result in its mechanical breakdown. If no defect or deficiency is discovered by or reported to the driver, the report shall so indicate. In all instances, the driver shall sign the report. On two-driver operations, only one driver needs to sign the driver vehicle inspection report, provided both drivers agree as to the defects or deficiencies identified. If a driver operates more than one vehicle during the day, a report shall be prepared for each vehicle operated.

(c) *Corrective action.* Prior to requiring or permitting a driver to operate a vehicle, every motor carrier or its agent shall repair any defect or deficiency listed on the driver vehicle inspection report which would be likely to affect the safety of operation of the vehicle.

(1) *Every motor carrier or its agent* shall certify on the original driver vehicle inspection report which lists any defect or deficiency that the defect or deficiency has been repaired or that repair is unnecessary before the vehicle is operated again.

(2) *Every motor carrier* shall maintain the original driver vehicle inspection report, the certification of repairs, and the certification of the driver's review for three months from the date the written report was prepared.

(d) *Exceptions.* The rules in this section shall not apply to a private motor carrier of passengers (nonbusiness), a driveaway-towaway operation, or any motor carrier operating only one commercial motor vehicle.

§396.11 DOT Interpretations

Question 1: Does §396.11 require the DVIR to be turned in each day by a driver dispatched on a trip of more than one day's duration?
Guidance: A driver must prepare a DVIR at the completion of each day's work and shall submit those reports to the motor carrier upon his/her return to the home terminal. This does not relieve the motor carrier from the responsibility of effecting repairs and certification of any items listed on the DVIR, prepared at the end of each day's work, that would be likely to affect the safety of the operation of the motor vehicle.

Question 2: Does §396.11 require that the power unit and the trailer be inspected?
Guidance: Yes. A driver must be satisfied that both the power unit and the trailer are in safe operating condition before operating the combination.

Question 3: May more than one power unit be included on the DVIR if two or more power units were used by a driver during one day's work?
Guidance: No. A separate DVIR must be prepared for each power unit operated during the day's work.

Question 4: Does §396.11 require a motor carrier to use a specific type of DVIR?
Guidance: A motor carrier may use any type of DVIR as long as the report contains the information and signatures required.

Question 5: Does §396.11 require a separate DVIR for each vehicle and a combination of vehicles or is one report adequate to cover the entire combination?
Guidance: One vehicle inspection report may be used for any combination, provided the defects or deficiencies, if any, are identified for each vehicle and the driver signs the report.

Question 6: Does §396.11(c) require a motor carrier to effect repairs of all items listed on a DVIR prepared by a driver before the vehicle is subsequently driven?
Guidance: The motor carrier must effect repairs of defective or missing parts and accessories listed in Appendix G to the FMCSRs before allowing the vehicle to be driven.

Question 7: What constitutes a "certification" as required by §396.11(c)(1) and (2)?
Guidance: A motor carrier or its agent must state, in writing, that certain defects or deficiencies have been corrected or that correction was unnecessary. The declaration must be immediately followed by the signature of the person making it.

Question 8: Who must certify under §396.11(c) that repairs have been made when a motor vehicle is repaired en route by the driver or a commercial repair facility?
Guidance: Either the driver or the commercial repair facility.

Question 9: Must certification for trailer repairs be made?
Guidance: Yes. Certification must be made that all reported defects or deficiencies have been corrected or that correction was unnecessary. The certification need only appear on the carrier's copy of the report if the trailer is separated from the tractor.

Question 10: What responsibility does a vehicle leasing company, engaged in the daily rental of CMVs, have regarding the placement of the DVIR in the power unit?
Guidance: A leasing company has no responsibility to comply with §396.11 unless it is the carrier. It is the responsibility of a motor carrier to comply with Part 396 regardless of whether the vehicles are owned or leased.

Question 11: Which carrier is to be provided the original of the DVIR in a trip lease arrangement?
Guidance: The motor carrier controlling the vehicle during the term of the lease (i.e. the lessee) must be given the original of the DVIR. The controlling motor carrier is also responsible for obtaining and retaining records relating to repairs.

Question 12: Must the motor carrier's certification be shown on all copies of the DVIR?
Guidance: Yes.

Question 13: Must a DVIR carried on a power unit during operation cover both the power unit and trailer being operated at the time?
Guidance: No. The DVIR must cover the power unit being operated at the time. The trailer identified on the report may represent one pulled on the preceding trip.

Question 14: In instances where the DVIR has not been prepared or cannot be located, is it permissible under §396.11 for a driver to prepare a DVIR based on a pre-trip inspection and a short drive of a motor vehicle?
Guidance: Yes. §396.11 of the FMCSRs places the responsibility on the motor carrier to require its drivers to prepare and submit the DVIR. If, in unusual circumstances, the DVIR has not been prepared or cannot be located the motor carrier may cause a road test and inspection to be performed for safety of operation and the DVIR to be prepared.

Question 15: Is it permissible to use the back of a record of duty status (daily log) as a DVIR?
Guidance: Yes, but the retention requirements of §396.11 and §395.8 must be met.

Question 16: Does §396.11 require that specific parts and accessories that are inspected be identified on the DVIR?
Guidance: No.

Question 17: Is the Ontario pre-trip/post-trip inspection report acceptable as a DVIR under §396.11?
Guidance: Yes, provided the report from the preceding trip is carried on board the motor vehicle while in operation and all entries required by §396.11 and 396.13 are contained on the reports.

Part 396 - Inspection, Repair, and Maintenance §396.17 (d)

Question 18: Where must DVIRs be maintained?
Guidance: Since §396.11 is not specific, the DVIRs may be kept at either the motor carrier's principal place of business or the location where the vehicle is housed or maintained.

Question 19: Who is responsible for retaining DVIRs for leased vehicles including those of owner-operators?
Guidance: The motor carrier is responsible for retaining the original copy of each DVIR and the certification of repairs for at least 3 months from the date the report was prepared.

Question 20: Is a multi-day DVIR acceptable under §§396.11 and 396.13?
Guidance: Yes, provided all information and certifications required by §§396.11 and 396.13 are contained on the report.

Question 21: Is a DVIR required by a motor carrier operating only one tractor trailer combination?
Guidance: No. One tractor semitrailer/full trailer combination is considered one motor vehicle. However, a carrier operating a single truck tractor and multiple semitrailers, which are not capable of being operated as one combination unit, would be required to prepare DVIRs.

Question 22: Are motor carriers required to retain the "legible copy" of the last vehicle inspection report (referenced in §396.11(c)(3)) which is carried on the power unit?
Guidance: No. The record retention requirement refers only to the original copy retained by the motor carrier.

Question 23: Does the record retention requirement of §396.11(c)(2) apply to all DVIRs, or only those reports on which defects or deficiencies have been noted?
Guidance: The record retention requirement applies to all DVIRs.

Question 24: How would the DVIR requirements apply to a driver who works two or more shifts in a single calendar day?
Guidance: §396.11(a) requires every driver to prepare a DVIR at the completion of each day's work on each vehicle operated. A driver who operates two or more vehicles in a 24-hour-period must prepare a DVIR at the completion of the tour of duty in each vehicle.

Question 25: §396.11 requires the driver, at the completion of each day's work, to prepare a written report on each vehicle operated that day. Does this section require a "post trip inspection" of the kind described in §396.15?
Guidance: No. However, the written report must include all defects in the parts and accessories listed in §396.11(a) that were discovered by or reported to the driver during that day.

Question 26: Is the motor carrier official or agent who certifies that defects or deficiencies have been corrected or that correction was unnecessary required to be a mechanic or have training concerning commercial motor vehicle maintenance?
Guidance: No. §396.11 does not establish minimum qualifications for motor carrier officials or agents who certify that defects or deficiencies on DVIRs are corrected. With the exception of individuals performing the periodic or annual inspection (§396.19), and motor carrier employees responsible for ensuring that brake-related inspection, repair, or maintenance tasks are performed correctly (§396.25), Part 396 of the FMCSRs does not establish minimum qualifications for maintenance personnel. Motor carriers, therefore, are not prohibited from having DVIRs certified by company officials or agents who do not have experience repairing or maintaining commercial motor vehicles.

§396.13 Driver inspection.

Before driving a motor vehicle, the driver shall:
(a) Be satisfied that the motor vehicle is in safe operating condition;
(b) Review the last driver vehicle inspection report; and
(c) Sign the report, only if defects or deficiencies were noted by the driver who prepared the report, to acknowledge that the driver has reviewed it and that there is a certification that the required repairs have been performed. The signature requirement does not apply to listed defects on a towed unit which is no longer part of the vehicle combination.

§396.13 DOT Interpretations

Question 1: If a DVIR does not indicate that certain defects have been repaired, and the motor carrier has not certified in writing that such repairs were considered unnecessary, may the driver refuse to operate the motor vehicle?
Guidance: The driver is prohibited from operating the motor vehicle if the motor carrier fails to make that certification. Operation of the vehicle by the driver would cause the driver and the motor carrier to be in violation of §396.11(c) and both would be subject to appropriate penalties. However, a driver may sign the certification of repairs as an agent of the motor carrier if he/she is satisfied that the repairs have been performed.

Question 2: At the end of the day's work and upon completion of the required DVIR, what does the driver do with the copy of the previous DVIR carried on the power unit?
Guidance: There is no requirement that the driver submit the copy of that previous DVIR to the motor carrier nor is there a retention requirement for the motor carrier.

§396.15 Driveaway-towaway operations and inspections.

(a) **General.** Effective December 7, 1989, every motor carrier, with respect to motor vehicles engaged in driveaway-towaway operations, shall comply with the requirements of this part.
EXCEPTION: Maintenance records required by §396.3, the vehicle inspection report required by §396.11, and the periodic inspection required by §396.17 of this part shall not be required for any vehicle which is part of the shipment being delivered.

(b) **Pre-trip inspection.** Before the beginning of any driveaway-towaway operation of motor vehicles in combination, the motor carrier shall make a careful inspection and test to ascertain that:
   (1) *The towbar or saddle-mount connections* are properly secured to the towed and towing vehicle;
   (2) *They function adequately* without cramping or binding of any of the parts; and
   (3) *The towed motor vehicle* follows substantially in the path of the towing vehicle without whipping or swerving.

(c) **Post-trip inspection.** Motor carriers shall maintain practices to ensure that following completion of any trip in driveaway-towaway operation of motor vehicles in combination, and before they are used again, the towbars and saddle-mounts are disassembled and inspected for worn, bent, cracked, broken, or missing parts. Before reuse, suitable repair or replacement shall be made of any defective parts and the devices shall be properly reassembled.

§396.17 Periodic inspection.

(a) **Every commercial motor vehicle** shall be inspected as required by this section. The inspection shall include, at a minimum, the parts and accessories set forth in Appendix G of this subchapter.
NOTE: The term commercial motor vehicle includes each vehicle in a combination vehicle. For example, for a tractor semitrailer, fulltrailer combination, the tractor, semitrailer, and the fulltrailer (including the converter dolly if so equipped) shall each be inspected.

(b) **Except as provided in §396.23,** a motor carrier shall inspect or cause to be inspected all motor vehicles subject to its control.

(c) **A motor carrier shall not use** a commercial motor vehicle unless each component identified in Appendix G has passed an inspection in accordance with the terms of this section at least once during the preceding 12 months and documentation of such inspection is on the vehicle. The documentation may be:
   (1) *The inspection report* prepared in accordance with paragraph 396.21(a), or
   (2) *Other forms of documentation,* based on the inspection report (e.g., sticker or decal), which contains the following information:
      (i) *The date of inspection;*
      (ii) *Name and address* of the motor carrier or other entity where the inspection report is maintained;
      (iii) *Information uniquely identifying* the vehicle inspected if not clearly marked on the motor vehicle; and
      (iv) *A certification that the vehicle* has passed an inspection in accordance with §396.17.

(d) **A motor carrier may perform** the required annual inspection for vehicles under the carrier's control which are not subject to an inspection under §396.23(b)(1).

(e) **In lieu of the self inspection provided for** in paragraph (d) of this section, a motor carrier may choose to have a commercial garage, fleet leasing company, truck stop, or other similar commercial business perform the inspection as its agent, provided that business operates and maintains facilities appropriate for commercial vehicle inspections and it employs qualified inspectors, as required by §396.19.

(f) *Vehicles passing* roadside or periodic inspections performed under the auspices of any State government or equivalent jurisdiction or the FMCSA, meeting the minimum standards contained in Appendix G of this subchapter, will be considered to have met the requirements of an annual inspection for a period of 12 months commencing from the last day of the month in which the inspection was performed, except as provided in §396.23(b)(1).

(g) **It shall be the responsibility of the motor carrier** to ensure that all parts and accessories not meeting the minimum standards set forth in Appendix G to this subchapter are repaired promptly.

(h) **Failure to perform properly the annual inspection** set forth in this section shall cause the motor carrier to be subject to the penalty provisions provided by 49 U.S.C. 521(b).

§396.17 DOT Interpretations

Question 1: Some of a motor carrier's vehicles are registered in a State with a mandated inspection program which has been determined to be as effective as the Federal periodic inspection program, but these vehicles are not used in that State. Is the motor carrier required to make sure the vehicles are inspected under that State's program in order to meet the Federal periodic inspection requirements?

Guidance: If the State requires all vehicles registered in the State to be inspected through its mandatory program then the motor carrier must go through the State program to satisfy the Federal requirements. If, however, the State inspection program includes an exception or exemption for vehicles which are registered in the State but domiciled outside of the State, then the motor carrier may meet the Federal requirements through a self-inspection, a third party inspection, a CVSA inspection, or a periodic inspection performed in any State with a program that the FHWA determines is comparable to, or as effective as, the Part 396 requirements.

Question 2: May the due date for the next inspection satisfy the requirements for the inspection date on the sticker or decal?

Guidance: No. The rule requires that the date of the inspection be included on the report and sticker or decal. This date may consist of a month and a year.

Question 3: Must each vehicle in a combination carry separate periodic inspection documentation?

Guidance: Yes, unless a single document clearly identifies all of the vehicles in the CMV combination.

Question 4: Does the sticker have to be located in a specific location on the vehicle?

Guidance: No. The rule does not specify where the sticker, decal or other form of documentation must be located. It is the responsibility of the driver to produce the documentation when requested. Therefore, the driver must know the location of the sticker and ensure that all information on it is legible and current. The driver must also be able to produce the inspection report if that form of documentation is used.

Question 5: Is new equipment required to pass a periodic inspection under §396.17?

Guidance: Yes, but a dealer who meets the inspection requirements may provide the documentation for the initial periodic inspection.

Question 6: Are the Federal periodic inspection requirements applicable to U.S. Government trailers operated by motor carriers engaged in interstate commerce?

Guidance: Yes. The transportation is not performed by a governmental entity but by a for-hire carrier in interstate commerce.

Question 7: Does a CMV equipped with tires marked "Not for Highway Use" meet the periodic inspection requirements?

Guidance: No. Appendix G to Subchapter B - Minimum Periodic Inspection Standards, lists tires so labeled as a defect or deficiency which would prevent a vehicle from passing an inspection.

Question 8: Is a CMV subject to a roadside inspection by State or Federal inspectors if it displays a periodic inspection decal or other evidence of a periodic inspection being conducted in the past 12 months?

Guidance: Yes. Evidence of a valid periodic inspection only precludes a citation for a violation of §396.17.

Question 9: Is a State required to accept the periodic inspection program of another State having a periodic inspection program meeting minimum FHWA standards as contained in Appendix G to the FMCSRs?

Guidance: Yes. Section 210 of the MCSA (49 U.S.C. 31142) establishes the principle that State inspections meeting federally approved criteria must be recognized by every other State.

Question 10: Do vehicles inspected under a periodic Canadian inspection program comply with the FHWA periodic inspection standards?

Guidance: Yes. The FHWA has determined that the inspection programs of all of the Canadian Provinces meet or exceed the Federal requirements for a periodic inspection program.

Question 11: Must a specific form be used to record the periodic inspection mandated by §396.17?

Guidance: No. §396.21 does not designate any particular form, decal, or sticker, but does specify the information which must be shown on these documents.

Question 12: May an inspector certify a CMV as meeting the periodic inspection standards of §396.17 if he/she cannot see all components required to be inspected under Appendix G?

Guidance: No. The affixing of a decal or sticker or preparation of a report as proof of inspection indicates compliance with all requirements of Appendix G to Part 396.

Question 13: If an intermodal container is attached to a chassis at the time of a periodic inspection, must the container also be inspected to comply with §396.17 inspection requirements?

Guidance: Yes. Safe loading is one of the inspection areas covered under Appendix G. If the chassis is loaded at the time of inspection, the method of securement of the container to the chassis must be included in the inspection. Although integral securement devices such as twist locks are not listed in Appendix G, the operation of these devices must be included in the inspection without removal of the container.

Question 14: Is it acceptable for the proof of periodic inspection to be written in Spanish?

Guidance: Yes. There is no requirement under §396.17, or Appendix G to Subchapter B that the proof of periodic inspection be written in English.

§396.19 Inspector qualifications.

(a) **It shall be the motor carrier's responsibility** to ensure that the individual(s) performing an annual inspection under §396.17 (d) or (e) is qualified as follows:

(1) *Understands the inspection criteria* set forth in 49 CFR Part 393 and Appendix G of this subchapter and can identify defective components;

(2) *Is knowledgeable of and has mastered* the methods, procedures, tools and equipment used when performing an inspection; and

(3) *Is capable of performing an inspection* by reason of experience, training, or both as follows:

(i) *Successfully completed* a State or Federal-sponsored training program or has a certificate from a State or Canadian Province which qualifies the person to perform commercial motor vehicle safety inspections, or

(ii) *Have a combination* of training and/or experience totaling at least 1 year. Such training and/or experience may consist of:

[A] *Participation in* a truck manufacturer-sponsored training program or similar commercial training program designed to train students in truck operation and maintenance;

[B] *Experience as a mechanic or inspector* in a motor carrier maintenance program;

[C] *Experience as a mechanic or inspector* in truck maintenance at a commercial garage, fleet leasing company, or similar facility; or

[D] *Experience as a commercial vehicle inspector* for a State, Provincial or Federal Government.

(b) **Evidence of that individual's qualifications** under this section shall be retained by the motor carrier for the period during which that individual is performing annual motor vehicle inspections for the motor carrier, and for one year thereafter. However, motor carriers do not have to maintain documentation of inspector qualifications for those inspections performed either as part of a State periodic inspection program or at the roadside as part of a random roadside inspection program.

§396.19 DOT Interpretations

Question 1: May an entity other than a motor carrier maintain the evidence of inspector qualifications required by §396.19(b)?

Guidance: Yes. In those cases in which the inspection is performed by a commercial garage or similar facility or a leasing company, the motor carrier may allow the commercial garage or leasing company to maintain a copy of the inspector's qualifications on behalf of the motor carrier. The motor carrier, however, is responsible for obtaining copies of evidence of the inspector's qualifications upon the request of Federal, State, or local officials. If, for whatever reason, the motor carrier is unable to obtain this information from the third party, the motor carrier may be cited for noncompliance with §396.19.

Question 2: Is there a specific form or format to be used in ensuring that inspectors are qualified in accordance with §396.19?

Guidance: No. §396.19(b) requires the motor carrier to retain evidence satisfying the standards without specifying any particular form.

§396.21 Periodic inspection recordkeeping requirements.

(a) **The qualified inspector performing the inspection** shall prepare a report which:
   (1) *Identifies the individual performing the inspection;*
   (2) *Identifies the motor carrier operating the vehicle;*
   (3) *Identifies the date of the inspection;*
   (4) *Identifies the vehicle inspected;*
   (5) *Identifies the vehicle components inspected* and describes the results of the inspection, including the identification of those components not meeting the minimum standards set forth in Appendix G to this subchapter; and
   (6) *Certifies the accuracy and completeness* of the inspection as complying with all the requirements of this section.

(b) (1) *The original or a copy of the inspection report* shall be retained by the motor carrier or other entity who is responsible for the inspection for a period of fourteen months from the date of the inspection report. The original or a copy of the inspection report shall be retained where the vehicle is either housed or maintained.
   (2) *The original or a copy of the inspection report* shall be available for inspection upon demand of an authorized Federal, state, or local official.
   (3) *Exception.* Where the motor carrier operating the commercial motor vehicles did not perform the commercial motor vehicle's last annual inspection, the motor carrier shall be responsible for obtaining the original or a copy of the last annual inspection report upon demand of an authorized Federal, State, or local official.

§396.21 DOT Interpretations

Question 1: What recordkeeping requirements under §396.21 is a carrier subject to when it utilizes an FHWA-approved State inspection program?

Guidance: The motor carrier must comply with the recordkeeping requirements of the State. The requirements specified in §396.21(a) and (b) are applicable only in those instances where the motor carrier self-inspects its CMVs or has an agent perform the periodic inspection.

§396.23 Equivalent to periodic inspection.

(a) **The motor carrier** may meet the requirements of §396.17 through a State or other jurisdiction's roadside inspection program. The inspection must have been performed during the preceding 12 months. In using the roadside inspection, the motor carrier would need to retain a copy of an annual inspection report showing that the inspection was performed in accordance with the minimum periodic inspection standards set forth in Appendix G to this subchapter. When accepting such an inspection report, the motor carrier must ensure that the report complies with the requirements of §396.21(a).

(b) (1) *If a commercial motor vehicle* is subject to a mandatory State inspection program which is determined by the Administrator to be as effective as §396.17, the motor carrier shall meet the requirement of §396.17 through that State's inspection program. Commercial motor vehicle inspections may be conducted by State personnel, at State authorized commercial facilities, or by the motor carrier under the auspices of a State authorized self-inspection program.

   (2) *Should the FMCSA determine* that a State inspection program, in whole or in part, is not as effective as §396.17, the motor carrier must ensure that the periodic inspection required by §396.17 is performed on all commercial motor vehicles under its control in a manner specified in §396.17.

§396.23 DOT Interpretations

Question 1: Is a CVSA Level I or Level V inspection a "State * * * roadside inspection program" through which a motor carrier may meet the periodic inspection requirements of §396.17? If so, what evidence of inspection is required?

Guidance: A CVSA Level I or Level V inspection is equivalent to the Federal periodic inspection requirements. A CMV that passes such an inspection has therefore met §396.17, unless the vehicle is subject to a mandatory State inspection program that the FHWA has determined is comparable to, or as effective as, the Federal requirements [see §396.23(b)(1)]. A CVSA decal displayed on the CMV, or a copy of the Level I or Level V inspection report maintained in the vehicle, constitutes sufficient evidence of inspection.

§396.25 Qualifications of brake inspectors.

(a) **The motor carrier shall ensure** that all inspections, maintenance, repairs or service to the brakes of its commercial motor vehicles, are performed in compliance with the requirements of this section.

(b) **For purposes of this section,** brake inspector means any employee of a motor carrier who is responsible for ensuring all brake inspections, maintenance, service, or repairs to any commercial motor vehicle, subject to the motor carrier's control, meet the applicable Federal standards.

(c) **No motor carrier shall require or permit** any employee who does not meet the minimum brake inspector qualifications of §396.25 (d) to be responsible for the inspection, maintenance, service or repairs of any brakes on its commercial motor vehicles.

(d) **The motor carrier shall ensure** that each brake inspector is qualified as follows:
   (1) *Understands the brake service or inspection task* to be accomplished and can perform that task; and
   (2) *Is knowledgeable of and has mastered* the methods, procedures, tools and equipment used when performing an assigned brake service or inspection task; and
   (3) *Is capable of performing* the assigned brake service or inspection by reason of experience, training or both as follows:
      (i) *Has successfully completed* an apprenticeship program sponsored by a State, a Canadian Province, a Federal agency or a labor union, or a training program approved by a State, Provincial or Federal agency, or has a certificate from a State or Canadian Province which qualifies the person to perform the assigned brake service or inspection task (including passage of Commercial Driver's License air brake tests in the case of a brake inspection); or
      (ii) *Has brake-related training or experience* or a combination thereof totaling at least one year. Such training or experience may consist of:
         [A] *Participation in a training program* sponsored by a brake or vehicle manufacturer or similar commercial training program designed to train students in brake maintenance or inspection similar to the assigned brake service or inspection tasks; or
         [B] *Experience performing* brake maintenance or inspection similar to the assigned brake service or inspection task in a motor carrier maintenance program; or
         [C] *Experience performing* brake maintenance or inspection similar to the assigned brake service or inspection task at a commercial garage, fleet leasing company, or similar facility.

(e) **No motor carrier shall employ** any person as a brake inspector unless the evidence of the inspector's qualifications, required under this section is maintained by the motor carrier at its principal place of business, or at the location at which the brake inspector is employed. The evidence must be maintained for the period during which the brake inspector is employed in that capacity and for one year thereafter. However, motor carriers do not have to maintain evidence of qualifications to inspect air brake systems for such inspections performed by persons who have passed the air brake knowledge and skills test for a Commercial Driver's License.

§396.25 DOT Interpretations

Question 1: Does a CDL with an airbrake endorsement qualify a person as a brake inspector under §396.25?

Guidance: No.

Question 2: May a driver who does not have the necessary experience perform the adjustment under directions issued by telephone by a qualified inspector?

Guidance: Yes. A driver is permitted to perform brake adjustments at a roadside inspection providing they are done under the supervision of a qualified brake adjuster and the carrier is willing to assume responsibility for the proper adjustment.

Question 3: May a driver or other motor carrier employee be qualified as a brake inspector under §396.25 by way of experience or training to perform brake adjustments without being qualified to perform other brake-related tasks such as the repair or replacement of brake components?

Guidance: Yes. A driver may be qualified by the motor carrier to perform a limited number of tasks in connection with the brake system, e.g., inspect and/or adjust the vehicle's brakes, but not repair them.

Question 4: Would a mechanic who is employed by a leasing company and only works on CMVs that the leasing company leases to other motor carriers be required to meet the brake inspector certification requirements?

Guidance: No. The mechanic is not required to meet the certification requirements of §396.25(d) since he or she is not employed by a motor carrier.

Part 397 - Transportation of Hazardous Materials; Driving and Parking Rules
(Page 163 in the Driver Edition)

Subpart A - General

§397.1 Application of the rules in this part.
(a) The rules in this part apply to each motor carrier engaged in the transportation of hazardous materials by a motor vehicle which must be marked or placarded in accordance with §177.823 of this title and to —
  (1) Each officer or employee of the motor carrier who performs supervisory duties related to the transportation of hazardous materials; and
  (2) Each person who operates or who is in charge of a motor vehicle containing hazardous materials.
(b) Each person designated in paragraph (a) of this section must know and obey the rules in this part.

§397.1 DOT Interpretations
Question 1: Who is subject to Part 397?
Guidance: Part 397 applies to motor carriers that transport HM in interstate commerce in types and quantities requiring marking or placarding under 49 CFR 177.823. The routing requirements of Part 397 establish guidelines State and Indian tribal routing agencies must employ in designating and/or restricting routes for the transportation of HM. Interstate motor carriers transporting HM, in interstate or intrastate commerce, must comply with the designations and restrictions established by the routing agencies.

Question 2: Is the interstate transportation of anhydrous ammonia, in nurse tanks, subject to Part 397?
Guidance: The requirements of Part 397 do not apply to the direct application of ammonia to fields from nurse tanks. However, Part 397 does apply to the transportation of nurse tanks on public highways, when performed by interstate motor carriers.

§397.2 Compliance with Federal Motor Carrier Safety Regulations.
A motor carrier or other person to whom this part is applicable must comply with the rules in Parts 390 through 397, inclusive, of this subchapter when he/she is transporting hazardous materials by a motor vehicle which must be marked or placarded in accordance with §177.823 of this title.

§397.3 State and local laws, ordinances, and regulations.
Every motor vehicle containing hazardous materials must be driven and parked in compliance with the laws, ordinances, and regulations of the jurisdiction in which it is being operated, unless they are at variance with specific regulations of the Department of Transportation which are applicable to the operation of that vehicle and which impose a more stringent obligation or restraint.

§397.5 Attendance and surveillance of motor vehicles.
(a) Except as provided in paragraph (b) of this section, a motor vehicle which contains a Division 1.1, 1.2, or 1.3 (explosive) material must be attended at all times by its driver or a qualified representative of the motor carrier that operates it.
(b) The rules in paragraph (a) of this section do not apply to a motor vehicle which contains Division 1.1, 1.2, or 1.3 material if all the following conditions exist —
  (1) The vehicle is located on the property of a motor carrier, on the property of a shipper or consignee of the explosives, in a safe haven, or, in the case of a vehicle containing 50 pounds or less of a Division 1.1, 1.2, or 1.3 material, on a construction or survey site; and
  (2) The lawful bailee of the explosives is aware of the nature of the explosives the vehicle contains and has been instructed in the procedures which must be followed in emergencies; and
  (3) The vehicle is within the bailee's unobstructed field of view or is located in a safe haven.
(c) A motor vehicle which contains hazardous materials other than Division 1.1, 1.2, or 1.3, materials, and which is located on a public street or highway, or the shoulder of a public highway, must be attended by its driver. However, the vehicle need not be attended while its driver is performing duties which are incident and necessary to the driver's duties as the operator of the vehicle.
(d) For purposes of this section —
  (1) A motor vehicle is attended when the person in charge of the vehicle is on the vehicle, awake, and not in a sleeper berth, or is within 100 feet of the vehicle and has it within his/her unobstructed field of view.
  (2) A qualified representative of a motor carrier is a person who —
    (i) Has been designated by the carrier to attend the vehicle;
    (ii) Is aware of the nature of the hazardous materials contained in the vehicle he/she attends;
    (iii) Has been instructed in the procedures he/she must follow in emergencies; and
    (iv) Is authorized to move the vehicle and has the means and ability to do so.
  (3) A safe haven in an area specifically approved in writing by local, State, or Federal governmental authorities for the parking of unattended vehicles containing Division 1.1, 1.2, or 1.3 materials.
(e) The rules in this section do not relieve the driver from any obligation imposed by law relating to the placing of warning devices when a motor vehicle is stopped on a public street or highway.

§397.5 DOT Interpretations
Question 1: What defines a "public highway" or "shoulder" of a public highway for the purpose of determining violations under §397.5(c)?
Guidance: The applicable engineering/highway design plans.

Question 2: Must a driver of a motor vehicle transporting HM, other than Division 1.1, 1.2, or 1.3 (Class A or B) explosives, always maintain an unobstructed view and be within 100 feet of that vehicle?
Guidance: No. If the vehicle is not located on a public street or highway or on the shoulder of a public highway, then the vehicle need not be within 100 feet of the driver's unobstructed view, unless it contains Division 1.1, 1.2, or 1.3 (Class A or B) materials.

Question 3: May a motor carrier consider fuel stop operators as "qualified representative(s)" for purposes of the attendance and surveillance requirements of §397.5?
Guidance: Yes. However, the fuel stop operator must be able to perform the required functions.

Question 4: Who determines what is a "safe haven"?
Guidance: The selection of safe havens is a decision of the "competent government authorities" having jurisdiction over the area. The definition found in §397.5(d)(3) is purposely void of any specific guidelines or criteria. A truck stop may be considered a safe haven if it is so designated by local or State governmental authorities.

Question 5: Section 397.5(d)(3) describes a safe haven as " * * * an area specifically approved in writing by local, State, or Federal governmental authorities for the parking of unattended vehicles containing Division 1.1, 1.2, or 1.3 materials." Do guidelines exist for establishing approval criteria for safe havens? Is there a national list of approved safe havens available to the public?
Guidance: The FMCSA believes the safe haven concept is becoming increasingly obsolete due to readily available alternatives for providing "attendance at all times" for vehicles laden with explosives. The FMCSA is aware of two documents that may be used as resources for establishing approval criteria for safe havens. The first document, Construction and Maintenance Procedure Recommendations for Proposed Federal Guidelines of Safe Havens for Vehicles Carrying Class A or Class B Explosives (1985), contains design, construction, and maintenance guidelines. The second document, Recommended National Criteria for the Establishment and Operation of Safe Havens (1990), contains recommended national uniform criteria for approval of safe havens and an inventory of all State-approved safe havens in existence at the time of the report. These two documents may be used both as resources for establishing guidelines for safe haven design and construction, and as source documents for finding other materials that may be used toward the same purpose. These two documents are available to the public through the U.S. Department of Commerce, National Technical Information Service (NTIS), Springfield, Virginia 22161 (phone: (703) 487-4650). The NTIS publications database is also accessible on the internet's world wide web at http://www.fedworld.gov/ntis.

Question 6: May video monitors be used to satisfy the attendance requirements in §397.5?
Guidance: The purpose of the attendance requirement is to ensure that motor vehicles containing hazardous materials are attended at all times and that, in the event of an emergency involving the motor vehicle, the attendant is able to respond immediately. The use of video monitors could satisfy the attendance requirements in §397.5, provided the monitors are operable and continuously manned, the attendant is within 30.48 meters (100 feet) of the parked vehicle with an unobstructed view, and the attendant is able to go to the vehicle immediately from the monitoring location.

§397.7 Parking.

(a) A motor vehicle which contains Division 1.1, 1.2, or 1.3 materials must not be parked under any of the following circumstances —
  (1) *On or within 5 feet* of the traveled portion of a public street or highway;
  (2) *On private property* (including premises of fueling or eating facility) without the knowledge and consent of the person who is in charge of the property and who is aware of the nature of the hazardous materials the vehicle contains; or
  (3) *Within 300 feet* of a bridge, tunnel, dwelling, or place where people work, congregate, or assemble, except for brief periods when the necessities of operation require the vehicle to be parked and make it impracticable to park the vehicle in any other place.
(b) A motor vehicle which contains hazardous materials other than Division 1.1, 1.2, or 1.3 materials must not be parked on or within five feet of the traveled portion of public street or highway except for brief periods when the necessities of operation require the vehicle to be parked and make it impracticable to park the vehicle in any other place.

§397.7 DOT Interpretations

Question 1: When is a vehicle considered "parked"?
Guidance: For the purposes of Part 397, "parked" means the vehicle is stopped for a purpose unrelated to the driving function, (e.g., fueling, eating, loading, unloading).

Question 2: What constitutes "knowledge and consent of the person in charge," as used in §397.7(a)(2)?
Guidance: In order to satisfy the requirement for "knowledge and consent," actual notice of "the nature of the hazardous materials the vehicle contains" must be given to the person in charge, and that person must affirmatively agree to allow the vehicle to be parked on the property under his/her control.

Question 3: Is the motor carrier or driver relieved from the requirements of §397.7(a)(3) if the person in charge of the private property is notified of the explosive HM contained in the vehicle?
Guidance: No. A vehicle transporting Division 1.1, 1.2, or 1.3 (Class A or B) explosives must meet the 300-foot separation requirement, regardless of any notification made to any person.

Question 4: What is meant by the term "brief periods when necessities of operation require * * *" in §397.7(a)(3)?
Guidance: Brief periods of time depend upon the "necessities of operation" in question. Parking a vehicle containing Division 1.1, 1.2, or 1.3 (Class A or B) materials closer than 300 feet to buildings, dwellings, etc. for periods up to 1 hour for a driver to eat would not be permitted under the provisions of §397.7(a)(3). Parking at fueling facilities to obtain fuel, oil, etc., or at a carrier's terminal would be considered necessities of operation.

Question 5: May a safe haven be designated within 300 feet of an area where buildings and other structures are likely to be occupied by large numbers of people?
Guidance: The selection and designation of safe havens are a decision of the "competent government authorities" having jurisdiction over the area.

Question 6: If a motor vehicle is transporting Division 1.1, 1.2, or 1.3 (Class A or B) explosives and is parked in a safe haven, must it be in compliance with the parking requirements of §397.7?
Guidance: Yes. Safe havens, as outlined in §397.5, relate to attendance and surveillance requirements. The parking restrictions of §397.7 still apply.

Question 7: May a driver transporting Division 1.1, 1.2, or 1.3 (Class A or B) materials park within 100 feet of an eating establishment in order to meet the attendance and surveillance requirements?
Guidance: No, because it will result in a violation of §397.7(a)(3).

§397.9 [Reserved]

§397.9 DOT Interpretations

Editor's Note: This section was removed from the regulations. Regulatory information related to this interpretation is now contained in §397.67.

Question 1: May a motor vehicle which contains HM use expressways or major thoroughfares to make deliveries within a populated area?
Guidance: Yes, unless otherwise specifically prohibited by State or local authorities. In many instances a more circuitous route may present greater hazards due to increased exposure. However, in those situations where a vehicle is passing through a populated or congested area, use of a beltway or other bypass would be considered the appropriate route, regardless of the additional economic burden.

§397.11 Fires.

(a) A motor vehicle containing hazardous materials must not be operated near an open fire unless its driver has first taken precautions to ascertain that the vehicle can safely pass the fire without stopping.
(b) A motor vehicle containing hazardous materials must not be parked within 300 feet of an open fire.

§397.13 Smoking.

No person may smoke or carry a lighted cigarette, cigar, or pipe on or within 25 feet of —
(a) A motor vehicle which contains Class 1 materials, Class 5 materials, or flammable materials classified as Division 2.1, Class 3, Divisions 4.1 and 4.2; or
(b) An empty tank motor vehicle which has been used to transport Class 3, flammable materials, or Division 2.1 flammable gases, which when so used, was required to be marked or placarded in accordance with the rules in §177.823 of this title.

§397.13 DOT Interpretations

Question 1: May a driver of a CMV transporting HM, listed in §397.13, smoke while at the controls or in the sleeper berth of the vehicle?
Guidance: No. All persons are prohibited from smoking or carrying lighted smoking materials at any time while on or within 25 feet of such a vehicle. The word "on" includes any time while in the cab, sleeper berth, etc.

§397.15 Fueling.

When a motor vehicle which contains hazardous materials is being fueled —
(a) Its engine must not be operating; and
(b) A person must be in control of the fueling process at the point where the fuel tank is filled.

§397.17 Tires.

(a) A driver must examine each tire on a motor vehicle at the beginning of each trip and each time the vehicle is parked.
(b) If, as the result of an examination pursuant to paragraph (a) of this section, or otherwise, a tire if found to be flat, leaking, or improperly inflated, the driver must cause the tire to be repaired, replaced, or properly inflated before the vehicle is driven. However, the vehicle may be driven to the nearest safe place to perform the required repair, replacement, or inflation.
(c) If, as the result of an examination pursuant to paragraph (a) of this section, or otherwise, a tire is found to be overheated, the driver shall immediately cause the overheated tire to be removed and placed at a safe distance from the vehicle. The driver shall not operate the vehicle until the cause of the overheating is corrected.
(d) Compliance with the rules in this section does not relieve a driver from the duty to comply with the rules in §§397.5 and 397.7.

§397.19 Instructions and documents.

(a) A motor carrier that transports Division 1.1, 1.2, or 1.3 (explosive) materials must furnish the driver of each motor vehicle in which the explosives are transported with the following documents:
  (1) A copy of the rules in this part;
  (2) [Reserved]
  (3) A document containing instructions on procedures to be followed in the event of accident or delay. The documents must include the names and telephone numbers of persons (includ-

ing representatives of carriers or shippers) to be contracted, the nature of the explosives being transported, and the precautions to be taken in emergencies such as fires, accidents, or leakages.

(b) **A driver who receives documents** in accordance with paragraph (a) of this section must sign a receipt for them. The motor carrier shall maintain the receipt for a period of one year from the date of signature.

(c) **A driver of a motor vehicle which contains** Division 1.1, 1.2, or 1.3 materials must be in possession of, be familiar with, and be in compliance with:

(1) The documents specified in paragraph (a) of this section;
(2) The documents specified in §177.817 of this title; and
(3) The written route plan specified in §397.67.

Subpart B [Reserved]

Subpart C - Routing of Non-Radioactive Hazardous Materials

§397.61 Purpose and scope.

This subpart contains routing requirements and procedures that States and Indian tribes are required to follow if they establish, maintain, or enforce routing designations over which a non-radioactive hazardous material (NRHM) in a quantity which requires placarding may or may not be transported by a motor vehicle. It also provides regulations for motor carriers transporting placarded or marked NRHM and procedures for dispute resolutions regarding NRHM routing designations.

§397.63 Applicability.

The provisions of this subpart apply to any State or Indian tribe that establishes, maintains, or enforces any routing designations over which NRHM may or may not be transported by motor vehicle. They also apply to any motor carrier that transports or causes to be transported placarded or marked NRHM in commerce.

§397.65 Definitions.

For purposes of this subpart, the following definitions apply:

Administrator. The Federal Motor Carrier Safety Administrator, who is the chief executive of the Federal Motor Carrier Safety Administration, an agency within the United States Department of Transportation, or his/her designate.

Commerce. Any trade, traffic, or transportation in the United States which:

(1) Is between a place under the jurisdiction of a State or Indian tribe and any place outside of such jurisdiction; or
(2) Is solely within a place under the jurisdiction of a State or Indian tribe but which affects trade, traffic, or transportation described in subparagraph (a).

FMCSA. The Federal Motor Carrier Safety Administration, an agency within the Department of Transportation.

Hazardous material. A substance or material, including a hazardous substance, which has been determined by the Secretary of Transportation to be capable of posing an unreasonable risk to health, safety, or property when transported in commerce, and which has been so designated.

Indian tribe. Has the same meaning as contained in §4 of the Indian Self-Determination and Education Act, 25 U.S.C. 450b.

Motor carrier. A for-hire motor carrier or a private motor carrier of property. The term includes a motor carrier's agents, officers and representatives as well as employees responsible for hiring, supervising, training, assigning, or dispatching of drivers.

Motor vehicle. Any vehicle, machine, tractor, trailer, or semitrailer propelled or drawn by mechanical power and used upon the highways in the transportation of passengers or property, or any combination thereof.

NRHM. A non-radioactive hazardous material transported by motor vehicle in types and quantities which require placarding, pursuant to Table 1 or 2 of 49 CFR 172.504.

Political subdivision. A municipality, public agency or other instrumentality of one or more States, or a public corporation, board, or commission established under the laws of one or more States.

Radioactive material. Any material having a specific activity greater than 0.002 microcuries per gram (uCi/g), as defined in 49 CFR 173.403.

Routing agency. The State highway agency or other State agency designated by the Governor of that State, or an agency designated by an Indian tribe, to supervise, coordinate, and approve the NRHM routing designations for that State or Indian tribe.

Routing designations. Any regulation, limitation, restriction, curfew, time of travel restriction, lane restriction, routing ban, port-of-entry designation, or route weight restriction, applicable to the highway transportation of NRHM over a specific highway route or portion of a route.

Secretary. The Secretary of Transportation.

State. A State of the United States, the District of Columbia, the Commonwealth of Puerto Rico, the Commonwealth of the Northern Mariana Islands, the Virgin Islands, American Samoa or Guam.

§397.67 Motor carrier responsibility for routing.

(a) **A motor carrier transporting NRHM** shall comply with NRHM routing designations of a State or Indian tribe pursuant to this subpart.

(b) **A motor carrier carrying hazardous materials** required to be placarded or marked in accordance with 49 CFR 177.823 and not subject to a NRHM routing designations pursuant to this subpart, shall operate the vehicle over routes which do not go through or near heavily populated areas, places where crowds are assembled, tunnels, narrow streets, or alleys, except where the motor carrier determines that:

(1) There is no practicable alternative;
(2) A reasonable deviation is necessary to reach terminals, points of loading and unloading, facilities for food, fuel, repairs, rest, or a safe haven; or
(3) A reasonable deviation is required by emergency conditions, such as a detour that has been established by a highway authority, or a situation exists where a law enforcement official requires the driver to take an alternative route.

(c) **Operating convenience is not a basis** for determining whether it is practicable to operate a motor vehicle in accordance with paragraph (b) of this section.

(d) **Before a motor carrier requires or permits** a motor vehicle containing explosives in Class 1, Divisions 1.1, 1.2, 1.3, as defined in 49 CFR 173.50 and 173.53 respectively, to be operated, the carrier or its agent shall prepare a written route plan that complies with this section and shall furnish a copy to the driver. However, the driver may prepare the written plan as agent for the motor carrier when the trip begins at a location other than the carrier's terminal.

§397.69 Highway routing designations; preemption.

(a) **Any State or Indian tribe that establishes or modifies** a highway routing designation over which NRHM may or may not be transported on or after November 14, 1994, and maintains or enforces such designation, shall comply with the highway routing standards set forth in §397.71 of this subpart. For purposes of this subpart, any highway routing designation affecting the highway transportation of NRHM, made by a political subdivision of a State is considered as one made by that State, and all requirements of this subpart apply.

(b) **Except as provided in §§397.75 and 397.219,** a NRHM route designation made in violation of paragraph (a) of this section is preempted pursuant to section 105(b)(4) of the Hazardous Materials Transportation Act (49 U.S.C. app. 1804(b)(4)). This provision shall become effective after November 14, 1996.

(c) **A highway routing designation** established by a State, political subdivision, or Indian tribe before November 14, 1994 is subject to preemption in accordance with the preemption standards in paragraphs (a)(1) and (a)(2) of §397.203 of this subpart.

(d) **A State, political subdivision, or Indian tribe** may petition for a waiver of preemption in accordance with §397.213 of this part.

§397.71 Federal standards.

(a) **A State or Indian tribe shall comply** with the Federal standards under paragraph (b) of this section when establishing, maintaining or enforcing specific NRHM routing designations over which NRHM may or may not be transported.

(b) **The Federal standards are as follows:**

(1) Enhancement of public safety. The State or Indian tribe shall make a finding, supported by the record to be developed in accordance with paragraphs (b)(2)(ii) and (b)(3)(iv) of this section, that any NRHM routing designation enhances public safety in the areas subject to its jurisdiction and in other areas which are directly affected by such highway routing designation. In making such a finding, the State or Indian tribe shall consider:

(i) The factors listed in paragraph (b)(9) of this section; and
(ii) The DOT "Guidelines for Applying Criteria to Designate Routes for Transporting Hazardous Materials," DOT/RSPA/

OHMT-89-02, July 1989[1] or its most current version; or an equivalent routing analysis which adequately considers overall risk to the public.

(2) *Public participation.* Prior to the establishment of any NRHM routing designation, the State or Indian tribe shall undertake the following actions to ensure participation by the public in the routing process:

(i) *The State or Indian tribe* shall provide the public with notice of any proposed NRHM routing designation and a 30-day period in which to comment. At any time during this period or following review of the comments received, the State or Indian tribe shall decide whether to hold a public hearing on the proposed NRHM route designation. The public shall be given 30 days prior notice of the public hearing which shall be conducted as described in paragraph (b)(2)(ii) of this section. Notice for both the comment period and the public hearing, if one is held, shall be given by publication in at least two newspapers of general circulation in the affected area or areas and shall contain a complete description of the proposed routing designation, together with the date, time, and location of any public hearings. Notice for both the comment period and any public hearing may also be published in the official register of the State.

(ii) *If it is determined* that a public hearing is necessary, the State or Indian tribe shall hold at least one public hearing on the record during which the public will be afforded the opportunity to present their views and any information or data related to the proposed NRHM routing designation. The State shall make available to the public, upon payment of prescribed costs, copies of the transcript of the hearing, which shall include all exhibits and documents presented during the hearing or submitted for the record.

(3) *Consultation with others.* Prior to the establishment of any NRHM routing designation, the State or Indian tribe shall provide notice to, and consult with, officials of affected political subdivisions, States and Indian tribes, and any other affected parties. Such actions shall include the following:

(i) *At least 60 days* prior to establishing a routing designation, the State or Indian tribe shall provide notice, in writing, of the proposed routing designation to officials responsible for highway routing in all other affected States or Indian tribes. A copy of this notice may also be sent to all affected political subdivisions. This notice shall request approval, in writing, by those States or Indian tribes, of the proposed routing designations. If no response is received within 60 days from the day of receipt of the notification of the proposed routing designation, the routing designation shall be considered approved by the affected State or Indian tribe.

(ii) *The manner in which consultation* under this paragraph is conducted is left to the discretion of the State or Indian tribe.

(iii) *The State or Indian tribe* shall attempt to resolve any concern or disagreement expressed by any consulted official related to the proposed routing designation.

(iv) *The State or Indian tribe* shall keep a record of the names and addresses of the officials notified pursuant to this section and of any consultation or meeting conducted with these officials or their representatives. Such record shall describe any concern or disagreement expressed by the officials and any action undertaken to resolve such disagreement or address any concern.

(4) *Through routing.* In establishing any NRHM routing designation, the State or Indian tribe shall ensure through highway routing for the transportation of NRHM between adjacent areas. The term "through highway routing" as used in this paragraph means that the routing designation must ensure continuity of movement so as to not impede or unnecessarily delay the transportation of NRHM. The State or Indian tribe shall utilize the procedures established in paragraphs (b)(2) and (b)(3) of this section in meeting these requirements. In addition, the State or Indian tribe shall make a finding, supported by a risk analysis conducted in accordance with paragraph (b)(1) of this section, that the routing designation enhances public safety. If the risk analysis shows —

(i) *That the current routing* presents at least 50 percent more risk to the public than the deviation under the proposed routing designation, then the proposed routing designation may go into effect.

(ii) *That the current routing* presents a greater risk but less than 50 percent more risk to the public than the deviation under the proposed routing restriction, then the proposed routing restriction made by a State or Indian tribe shall only go into effect if it does not force a deviation of more than 25 miles or result in an increase of more than 25 percent of that part of a trip affected by the deviation, whichever is shorter, from the most direct route through a jurisdiction as compared to the intended deviation.

(iii) *That the current route* has the same or less risk to the public than the deviation resulting from the proposed routing designation, then the routing designation shall not be allowed.

(5) *Agreement of other States; burden on commerce.* Any NRHM routing designation which affects another State or Indian tribe shall be established, maintained, or enforced only if:

(i) It does not unreasonably burden commerce, and

(ii) It is agreed to by the affected State or Indian tribe within 60 days of receipt of the notice sent pursuant to paragraph (b)(3)(i) of this section, or it is approved by the Administrator pursuant to §397.75.

(6) *Timeliness.* The establishment of a NRHM routing designation by any State or Indian tribe shall be completed within 18 months of the notice given in either paragraph (b)(2) or (b)(3) of this section, whichever occurs first.

(7) *Reasonable routes to terminals and other facilities.* In establishing or providing for reasonable access to and from designated routes, the State or Indian tribe shall use the shortest practicable route considering the factors listed in paragraph (b)(9) of this section. In establishing any NRHM routing designation, the State or Indian tribe shall provide reasonable access for motor vehicles transporting NRHM to reach:

(i) *Terminals,*

(ii) *Points of loading, unloading, pickup and delivery, and*

(iii) *Facilities for food, fuel, repairs, rest, and safe havens.*

(8) *Responsibility for local compliance.* The States shall be responsible for ensuring that all of their political subdivisions comply with the provisions of this subpart. The States shall be responsible for resolving all disputes between such political subdivisions within their jurisdictions. If a State or any political subdivision thereof, or an Indian tribe chooses to establish, maintain, or enforce any NRHM routing designation, the Governor, or Indian tribe, shall designate a routing agency for the State or Indian tribe, respectively. The routing agency shall ensure that all NRHM routing designations within its jurisdiction comply with the Federal standards in this section. The State or Indian tribe shall comply with the public information and reporting requirements contained in §397.73.

(9) *Factors to consider.* In establishing any NRHM routing designation, the State or Indian tribe shall consider the following factors:

(i) *Population density.* The population potentially exposed to a NRHM release shall be estimated from the density of the residents, employees, motorists, and other persons in the area, using United States census tract maps or other reasonable means for determining the population within a potential impact zone along a designated highway route. The impact zone is the potential range of effects in the event of a release. Special populations such as schools, hospitals, prisons, and senior citizen homes shall, among other things, be considered when determining the potential risk to the populations along a highway routing. Consideration shall be given to the amount of time during which an area will experience a heavy population density.

(ii) *Type of highway.* The characteristics of each alternative NRHM highway routing designation shall be compared. Vehicle weight and size limits, underpass and bridge clearances, roadway geometrics, number of lanes, degree of access control, and median and shoulder structures are examples of characteristics which a State or Indian tribe shall consider.

(iii) *Types and quantities of NRHM.* An examination shall be made of the type and quantity of NRHM normally transported along highway routes which are included in a proposed NRHM routing designation, and consideration shall be given to the relative impact zone and risks of each type and quantity.

---

1. This document may be obtained from Office of Enforcement and Compliance (MC-PSDECH), Federal Motor Carrier Safety Administration, U.S. Department of Transportation, 400 7th Street, SW., Washington, D.C. 20590-0001.

Subpart C - Routing of Non-Radioactive Hazardous Materials §397.75 (e)

(iv) *Emergency response capabilities.* In consultation with the proper fire, law enforcement, and highway safety agencies, consideration shall be given to the emergency response capabilities which may be needed as a result of a NRHM routing designation. The analysis of the emergency response capabilities shall be based upon the proximity of the emergency response facilities and their capabilities to contain and suppress NRHM releases within the impact zones.

(v) *Results of consultation* with affected persons. Consideration shall be given to the comments and concerns of all affected persons and entities provided during public hearings and consultations conducted in accordance with this section.

(vi) *Exposure and other risk factors.* States and Indian tribes shall define the exposure and risk factors associated with any NRHM routing designations. The distance to sensitive areas shall be considered. Sensitive areas include, but are not limited to, homes and commercial buildings; special populations in hospitals, schools, handicapped facilities, prisons and stadiums; water sources such as streams and lakes; and natural areas such as parks, wetlands, and wildlife reserves.

(vii) *Terrain considerations.* Topography along and adjacent to the proposed NRHM routing designation that may affect the potential severity of an accident, the dispersion of the NRHM upon release and the control and clean up of NRHM if released shall be considered.

(viii) *Continuity of routes.* Adjacent jurisdictions shall be consulted to ensure routing continuity for NRHM across common borders. Deviations from the most direct route shall be minimized.

(ix) *Alternative routes.* Consideration shall be given to the alternative routes to, or resulting from, any NRHM route designation. Alternative routes shall be examined, reviewed, or evaluated to the extent necessary to demonstrate that the most probable alternative routing resulting from a routing designation is safer than the current routing.

(x) *Effects on commerce.* Any NRHM routing designation made in accordance with this subpart shall not create an unreasonable burden upon interstate or intrastate commerce.

(xi) *Delays in transportation.* No NRHM routing designations may create unnecessary delays in the transportation of NRHM.

(xii) *Climatic conditions.* Weather conditions unique to a highway route such as snow, wind, ice, fog, or other climatic conditions that could affect the safety of a route, the dispersion of the NRHM upon release, or increase the difficulty of controlling it and cleaning it up shall be given appropriate consideration.

(xiii) *Congestion and accident history.* Traffic conditions unique to a highway routing such as: traffic congestion; accident experience with motor vehicles, traffic considerations that could affect the potential for an accident, exposure of the public to any release, ability to perform emergency response operations, or the temporary closing of a highway for cleaning up any release shall be given appropriate consideration.

§397.73 Public information and reporting requirements.

(a) **Public information.** Information on NRHM routing designations must be made available by the States and Indian tribes to the public in the form of maps, lists, road signs or some combination thereof. If road signs are used, those signs and their placements must comply with the provisions of the Manual on Uniform Traffic Control Devices[1], published by the FMCSA, particularly the Hazardous Cargo signs identified as R14-2 and R14-3 shown in Section 2B-43 of that Manual.

(b) **Reporting and publishing requirements.** Each State or Indian tribe, through its routing agency, shall provide information identifying all NRHM routing designations which exist within their jurisdictions on November 14, 1994 to the FMCSA, Office of Enforcement and Compliance (MC-PSDECH), 400 7th St., SW., Washington, D.C. 20590-0001 by March 13, 1995. The State or Indian tribe shall include descriptions of these routing designations, along with the dates they were established. This information may also be published in each State's official register of State regulations. Information on any subsequent changes or new NRHM routing designations shall be furnished within 60 days after establishment to the FMCSA. This information will be available from the FMCSA, consolidated by the FMCSA, and published annually in whole or as updates in the Federal Register. Each State may also publish this information in its official register of State regulations.

(Approved by the Office of Management and Budget under control number 2125-0554)

§397.75 Dispute resolution.

(a) **Petition.** One or more States or Indian tribes may petition the Administrator to resolve a dispute relating to an agreement on a proposed NRHM routing designation. In resolving a dispute under these provisions, the Administrator will provide the greatest level of safety possible without unreasonably burdening commerce, and ensure compliance with the Federal standards established at §397.71 of this subpart.

(b) **Filing.** Each petition for dispute resolution filed under this section must:

(1) *Be submitted to the Administrator,* Federal Motor Carrier Safety Administration, U.S. Department of Transportation, 400 7th Street, SW., Washington, DC 20590-0001. Attention: Office of the Chief Counsel (MC-PSDCC).

(2) *Identify the State or Indian tribe* filing the petition and any other state, political subdivision, or Indian tribe whose NRHM routing designation is the subject of the dispute.

(3) *Contain a certification* that the petitioner has complied with the notification requirements of paragraph (c) of this section, and include a list of the names and addresses of each state, political subdivision, or Indian tribe official who was notified of the filing of the petition.

(4) *Clearly set forth the dispute* for which resolution is sought, including a complete description of any disputed NRHM routing designation and an explanation of how the disputed routing designation affects the petitioner or how it impedes through highway routing. If the routing designation being disputed results in alternative routing, then a comparative risk analysis for the designated route and the resulting alternative routing shall be provided.

(5) *Describe any actions taken* by the State or Indian tribe to resolve the dispute.

(6) *Explain the reasons* why the petitioner believes that the Administrator should intervene in resolving the dispute.

(7) *Describe any proposed actions* that the Administrator should take to resolve the dispute and how these actions would provide the greatest level of highway safety without unreasonably burdening commerce and would ensure compliance with the Federal standards established in this subpart.

(c) **Notice.**

(1) *Any State or Indian tribe* that files a petition for dispute resolution under this subpart shall mail a copy of the petition to any affected State, political subdivision, or Indian tribe, accompanied by a statement that the State, political subdivision, or Indian tribe may submit comments regarding the petition to the Administrator within 45 days.

(2) *By serving notice* on any other State, political subdivision, or Indian tribe determined by the Administrator to be possibly affected by the issues in dispute or the resolution sought, or by publication in the Federal Register, the Administrator may afford those persons an opportunity to file written comments on the petition.

(3) *Any affected State,* political subdivision, or Indian tribe submitting written comments to the Administrator with respect to a petition filed under this section shall send a copy of the comments to the petitioner and certify to the Administrator as to having complied with this requirement. The Administrator may notify other persons participating in the proceeding of the comments and provide an opportunity for those other persons to respond.

(d) **Court actions.** After a petition for dispute resolution is filed in accordance with this section, no court action may be brought with respect to the subject matter of such dispute until a final decision has been issued by the Administrator or until the last day of the one-year period beginning on the day the Administrator receives the petition, whichever occurs first.

(e) **Hearings; alternative dispute resolution.** Upon receipt of a petition filed pursuant to paragraph (a) of this section, the Administrator may schedule a hearing to attempt to resolve the dispute and,

---

1. This publication may be purchased from the Superintendent of Documents, U.S. Government Printing Office (GPO), Washington, D.C. 20402 and has Stock No. 050-001-81001-8. It is available for inspection and copying as prescribed in 49 CFR Part 7, Appendix D. See 23 CFR Part 655, Subpart F.

if a hearing is scheduled, will notify all parties to the dispute of the date, time, and place of the hearing. During the hearing the parties may offer any information pertinent to the resolution of the dispute. If an agreement is reached, it may be stipulated by the parties, in writing, and, if the Administrator agrees, made part of the decision in paragraph (f) of this section. If no agreement is reached, the Administrator may take the matter under consideration and announce his or her decision in accordance with paragraph (f) of this section. Nothing in this section shall be construed as prohibiting the parties from settling the dispute or seeking other methods of alternative dispute resolution prior to the final decision by the Administrator.

(f) *Decision.* The Administrator will issue a decision based on the petition, the written comments submitted by the parties, the record of the hearing, and any other information in the record. The decision will include a written statement setting forth the relevant facts and the legal basis for the decision.

(g) *Record.* The Administrator will serve a copy of the decision upon the petitioner and any other party who participated in the proceedings. A copy of each decision will be placed on file in the public docket. The Administrator may publish the decision or notice of the decision in the Federal Register.

§397.77 Judicial review of dispute decision.

Any State or Indian tribe adversely affected by the Administrator's decision under §397.75 of this subpart may seek review by the appropriate district court of the United States under such proceeding only by filing a petition with such court within 90 days after such decision becomes final.

Subpart D - Routing of Class 7 (Radioactive) Materials

§397.101 Requirements for motor carriers and drivers.

(a) **Except as provided in paragraph (b) of this section** or in circumstances when there is only one practicable highway route available, considering operating necessity and safety, a carrier or any person operating a motor vehicle that contains a Class 7 (radioactive) material, as defined in 49 CFR 172.403, for which placarding is required under 49 CFR Part 172 shall:

(1) *Ensure that the motor vehicle* is operated on routes that minimize radiological risk;

(2) *Consider available information* on accident rates, transit time, population density and activities, and the time of day and the day of week during which transportation will occur to determine the level of radiological risk; and

(3) *Tell the driver which route to take* and that the motor vehicle contains Class 7 (radioactive) materials.

(b) **Except as otherwise permitted in this paragraph** and in paragraph (f) of this section, a carrier or any person operating a motor vehicle containing a highway route controlled quantity of Class 7 (radioactive) materials, as defined in 49 CFR 173.403(l), shall operate the motor vehicle only over preferred routes.

(1) *For purposes of this subpart,* a preferred route is an Interstate System highway for which an alternative route is not designated by a State routing agency; a State-designated route selected by a State routing agency pursuant to §397.103; or both of the above.

(2) *The motor carrier* or the person operating a motor vehicle containing a highway route controlled quantity of Class 7 (radioactive) materials, as defined in 49 CFR 173.403(l) and (y), shall select routes to reduce time in transit over the preferred route segment of the trip. An Interstate System bypass or Interstate System beltway around a city, when available, shall be used in place of a preferred route through a city, unless a State routing agency has designated an alternative route.

(c) **A motor vehicle may be operated over a route,** other than a preferred route, only under the following conditions:

(1) *The deviation from the preferred route* is necessary to pick up or deliver a highway route controlled quantity of Class 7 (radioactive) materials, to make necessary rest, fuel or motor vehicle repair stops, or because emergency conditions make continued use of the preferred route unsafe or impossible;

(2) *For pickup and delivery* not over preferred routes, the route selected must be the shortest-distance route from the pickup location to the nearest preferred route entry location, and the shortest-distance route to the delivery location from the nearest preferred route exit location. Deviation from the shortest-distance pickup or delivery route is authorized if such deviation:

(i) *Is based upon the criteria* in paragraph (a) of this section to minimize the radiological risk; and

(ii) *Does not exceed* the shortest-distance pickup or delivery route by more than 25 miles and does not exceed 5 times the length of the shortest-distance pickup or delivery route.

(iii) *Deviations from preferred routes,* or pickup or delivery routes other than preferred routes, which are necessary for rest, fuel, or motor vehicle repair stops or because of emergency conditions, shall be made in accordance with the criteria in paragraph (a) of this section to minimize radiological risk, unless due to emergency conditions, time does not permit use of those criteria.

(d) **A carrier (or a designated agent)** who operates a motor vehicle which contains a package of highway route controlled quantity of Class 7 (radioactive) materials, as defined in 49 CFR 173.403(l), shall prepare a written route plan and supply a copy before departure to the motor vehicle driver and a copy to the shipper (before departure for exclusive use shipments, as defined in 49 CFR 173.403(i), or within fifteen working days following departure for all other shipments). Any variation between the route plan and routes actually used, and the reason for it, shall be reported in an amendment to the route plan delivered to the shipper as soon as practicable but within 30 days following the deviation. The route plan shall contain:

(1) *A statement of the origin and destination points,* a route selected in compliance with this section, all planned stops, and estimated departure and arrival times; and

(2) *Telephone numbers* which will access emergency assistance in each State to be entered.

(e) **No person may transport a package** of highway route controlled quantity of Class 7 (radioactive) materials on a public highway unless:

(1) *The driver has received* within the two preceding years, written training on:

(i) *Requirements in* 49 CFR Parts 172, 173, and 177 pertaining to the Class 7 (radioactive) materials transported;

(ii) *The properties and hazards* of the Class 7 (radioactive) materials being transported; and

(iii) *Procedures to be followed* in case of an accident or other emergency.

(2) *The driver has in his or her immediate possession* a certificate of training as evidence of training required by this section, and a copy is placed in his or her qualification file (see §391.51 of this subchapter), showing:

(i) *The driver's name and operator's license number;*

(ii) *The dates training was provided;*

(iii) *The name and address of the person providing the training;*

(iv) *That the driver has been trained* in the hazards and characteristics of highway route controlled quantity of Class 7 (radioactive) materials; and

(v) *A statement* by the person providing the training that information on the certificate is accurate.

(3) *The driver has in his or her immediate possession* the route plan required by paragraph (d) of this section and operates the motor vehicle in accordance with the route plan.

(f) **A person may transport irradiated reactor fuel** only in compliance with a plan if required under 49 CFR 173.22(c) that will ensure the physical security of the material. Variation for security purposes from the requirements of this section is permitted so far as necessary to meet the requirements imposed under such a plan, or otherwise imposed by the U.S. Nuclear Regulatory Commission in 10 CFR Part 73.

(g) **Expect for packages shipped in compliance** with the physical security requirements of the U.S. Nuclear Regulatory Commission in 10 CFR Part 73, each carrier who accepts for transportation a highway route controlled quantity of Class 7 (radioactive) material (see 49 CFR 173.401(l)), must, within 90 days following the acceptance of the package, file the following information concerning the transportation of each such package with the Office of Enforcement and Compliance (MC-PSDECH), Federal Motor Carrier Safety Administration, 400 Seventh Street, SW., Washington, DC 20590-0001:

(1) *The route plan* required under paragraph (d) of this section, including all required amendments reflecting the routes actually used;

(2) *A statement identifying* the names and addresses of the shipper, carrier and consignee; and

(3) *A copy of the shipping paper* or the description of the Class 7 (radioactive) material in the shipment required by 49 CFR 172.202 and 172.203.

§397.103 Requirements for State routing designations.

(a) The State routing agency, as defined in §397.201(c), shall select routes to minimize radiological risk using "Guidelines for Selecting Preferred Highway Routes for Highway Route Controlled Quantity Shipments of Radioactive Materials," or an equivalent routing analysis which adequately considers overall risk to the public. Designations must be preceded by substantive consultation with affected local jurisdictions and with any other affected States to ensure consideration of all impacts and continuity of designated routes.

(b) State routing agencies may designate preferred routes as an alternative to, or in addition to, one or more Interstate System highways, including interstate system bypasses, or Interstate System beltways.

(c) A State-designated route is effective when —
 (1) *The State gives written notice* by certified mail, return receipt requested, to the Office of Enforcement and Compliance (MC-PSDECH), Attn: National Hazardous Materials Route Registry, 400 Seventh Street, SW., Washington, DC 20590.
 (2) *Receipt thereof is acknowledged in writing by the FMCSA.*

(d) A list of State-designated preferred routes and a copy of the "Guidelines for Selecting Preferred Highway Routes for Highway Route Controlled Quantity Shipments of Radioactive Materials" are available upon request to the Office of Enforcement and Compliance (MC-PSDECH), 400 Seventh Street, SW., Washington, DC 20590.

Subpart E - Preemption Procedures

§397.201 Purpose and scope of the procedures.

(a) This subpart prescribes procedures by which:
 (1) *Any person,* including a State, political subdivision thereof, or Indian tribe, directly affected by any highway routing designation for hazardous materials may apply to the Administrator for a determination as to whether that highway routing designation is preempted under 49 U.S.C. 5125, or §§397.69 or 397.203 of this part; and
 (2) *A State, political subdivision thereof, or Indian tribe* may apply to the Administrator for a waiver of preemption with respect to any highway routing designation that the State, political subdivision thereof, or Indian tribe acknowledges to be preempted by 49 U.S.C. 5125, or §397.69 or §397.203 of this part, or that has been determined by a court of competent jurisdiction to be so preempted.

(b) Unless otherwise ordered by the Administrator, an application for a preemption determination which includes an application for a waiver of preemption will be treated and processed solely as an application for a preemption determination.

(c) For purposes of this part:

Act means 49 U.S.C. 5101 et seq., formerly known as the Hazardous Materials Transportation Act.

Administrator means the Federal Highway Administrator, who is the chief executive of the Federal Motor Carrier Safety Administration, an agency of the United States Department of Transportation, or his/her designate.

Hazardous material means a substance or material, including a hazardous substance, which has been determined by the Secretary of Transportation to be capable of posing an unreasonable risk to health, safety, or property, when transported in commerce, and which has been so designated.

Indian tribe has the same meaning as contained in Section 4 of the Indian Self-Determination and Education Act, 25 U.S.C. 450b.

Person means an individual, firm, copartnership, corporation, company, association, joint-stock association, including any trustee, receiver, assignee, or similar representative thereof, or government, Indian tribe, or agency or instrumentality of any government or Indian tribe when it offers hazardous materials for transportation in commerce or transports hazardous materials in furtherance of a commercial enterprise, but such term does not include the United States Postal Service.

Political subdivision includes a municipality; a public agency or other instrumentality of one or more States, or a public corporation, board, or commission established under the laws of one or more States.

Routing agency means the State highway agency or other State agency designated by the Governor of a State, or an agency designated by an Indian tribe, to supervise, coordinate, and approve the highway routing designations for that State or Indian tribe. Any highway routing designation made by a political subdivision of a State shall be considered a designation made by that State.

Routing designation includes any regulation, limitation, restriction, curfew, time of travel restriction, lane restriction, routing ban, port-of-entry designation, or route weight restriction applicable to the highway transportation of hazardous materials over a specific highway route or portion of a route.

State means a State of the United States, the District of Columbia, the Commonwealth of Puerto Rico, the Commonwealth of the Northern Mariana Islands, the Virgin Islands, American Samoa, Guam, or any other territory or possession of the United States designated by the Secretary.

§397.203 Standards for determining preemption.

(a) Any highway routing designation established, maintained, or enforced by a State, political subdivision thereof, or Indian tribe is preempted if —
 (1) *Compliance with* both the highway routing designation and any requirement under the Act or of a regulation issued under the Act is not possible;
 (2) *The highway routing designation* as applied or enforced creates an obstacle to the accomplishment and execution of the Act or the regulations issued under the Act; or
 (3) *The highway routing designation* is preempted pursuant to §397.69(b) of this part.

(b) [Reserved]

§397.205 Preemption application.

(a) Any person, including a State, political subdivision thereof, or Indian tribe directly affected by any highway routing designation of another State, political subdivision, or Indian tribe, may apply to the Administrator for a determination of whether that highway routing designation is preempted by the Act or §397.203 of this subpart. The Administrator shall publish notice of the application in the Federal Register.

(b) Each application filed under this section for a determination must:
 (1) *Be submitted to the Administrator,* Federal Motor Carrier Safety Administration, U.S. Department of Transportation, Washington, DC 20590-0001. Attention: Office of the Chief Counsel (MC-CC), Hazardous Materials Preemption;
 (2) *Set forth a detailed description* of the highway routing designation of the State, political subdivision thereof, or Indian tribe for which the determination is sought;
 (3) *If applicable,* specify the provisions of the Act or the regulations issued under the Act under which the applicant seeks preemption of the highway routing designation of the State, political subdivision thereof, or Indian tribe;
 (4) *Explain why the applicant believes* the highway routing designation of the State, political subdivision thereof, or Indian tribe should or should not be preempted under the standards of §397.203; and
 (5) *State how the applicant* is affected by the highway routing designation of the State, political subdivision thereof, or Indian tribe.

(c) The filing of an application for a determination under this section does not constitute grounds for noncompliance with any requirement of the Act or any regulation issued under the Act.

(d) Once the Administrator has published notice in the Federal Register of an application received under paragraph (a) of this section, no applicant for such determination may seek relief with respect to the same or substantially the same issue in any court until final action has been taken on the application or until 180 days after filing of the application, whichever occurs first. Nothing in this section shall be construed as prohibiting any person, including a State, political subdivision thereof, or Indian tribe, directly affected by any highway routing designation from seeking a determination of preemption in any court of competent jurisdiction in lieu of applying to the Administrator under paragraph (a) of this section.

§397.207 Preemption notice.

(a) If the applicant is other than a State, political subdivision thereof, or Indian tribe, the applicant shall mail a copy of the application to the State, political subdivision thereof, or Indian tribe concerned, accompanied by a statement that comments may be submitted regarding the application to the Administrator within 45 days. The application filed with the Administrator must include a certification that the applicant has complied with this paragraph and must include the names and addresses of each official to whom a copy of the application was sent.

(b) **The Administrator may afford interested persons** an opportunity to file written comments on the application by serving notice on any persons readily identifiable by the Administrator as persons who will be affected by the ruling sought or by publication in the Federal Register.

(c) **Each person submitting written comments** to the Administrator with respect to an application filed under this section shall send a copy of the comments to the applicant and certify to the Administrator that he or she has complied with this requirement. The Administrator may notify other persons participating in the proceeding of the comments and provide an opportunity for those other persons to respond.

§397.209 Preemption processing.

(a) **The Administrator may initiate** an investigation of any statement in an application and utilize in his or her evaluation any relevant facts obtained by that investigation. The Administrator may solicit and accept submissions from third persons relevant to an application and will provide the applicant an opportunity to respond to all third person submissions. In evaluating an application, the Administrator may consider any other source of information. The Administrator may convene a hearing or conference, if a hearing or conference will advance the evaluation of the application.

(b) **The Administrator may dismiss the application** without prejudice if:

(1) *He or she determines* that there is insufficient information upon which to base a determination; or

(2) *He or she requests additional information* from the applicant and it is not submitted.

§397.211 Preemption determination.

(a) **Upon consideration of the application** and other relevant information received, the Administrator issues a determination.

(b) **Notwithstanding that an application** for a determination has not been filed under §397.205, the Administrator, on his or her own initiative, may issue a determination as to whether a particular highway routing designation of a State, political subdivision thereof, or Indian tribe is preempted under the Act or the regulations issued under the Act.

(c) **The determination includes a written statement** setting forth the relevant facts and the legal basis for the determination, and provides that any person aggrieved thereby may file a petition for reconsideration within 20 days in accordance with §397.223.

(d) **Unless the determination is issued** pursuant to paragraph (b) of this section, the Administrator serves a copy of the determination upon the applicant. In all preemption determinations, the Administrator serves a copy of the determination upon any other person who participated in the proceeding or who is readily identifiable by the Administrator as affected by the determination. A copy of each determination is placed on file in the public docket. The Administrator may publish the determination or notice of the determination in the Federal Register.

(e) **If no petition for reconsideration is filed** within 20 days in accordance with §397.223, a determination issued under this section constitutes the final agency decision as to whether a particular highway routing designation of a State, political subdivision thereof, or Indian tribe is preempted under the Act or regulations issued thereunder. The fact that a determination has not been issued under this section with respect to a particular highway routing designation of a State, political subdivision thereof, or Indian tribe carries no implication as to whether the requirement is preempted under the Act or regulations issued thereunder.

§397.213 Waiver of preemption application.

(a) **Any State, political subdivision thereof, or Indian tribe** may apply to the Administrator for a waiver of preemption with respect to any highway routing designation that the State, political subdivision thereof, or Indian tribe acknowledges to be preempted by the Act, §397.203 of this subpart, or a court of competent jurisdiction. The Administrator may waive preemption with respect to such requirement upon a determination that such requirement —

(1) *Affords an equal* or greater level of protection to the public than is afforded by the requirements of the Act or regulations issued under the Act, and

(2) *Does not unreasonably burden commerce.*

(b) **Each application filed under this section** for a waiver of preemption determination must:

(1) *Be submitted to the Administrator,* Federal Motor Carrier Safety Administration, U.S. Department of Transportation, Washington, DC 20590-0001. Attention: Office of the Chief Counsel (MC-CC), Hazardous Materials Preemption Docket;

(2) *Set forth a detailed description* of the highway routing designation of the State, political subdivision thereof, or Indian tribe for which the determination is being sought;

(3) *Include a copy* of any relevant court order or determination issued pursuant to §397.211;

(4) *Contain an express acknowledgment* by the applicant that the highway routing designation of the State, political subdivision thereof, or Indian tribe is preempted under the Act or the regulations issued under the Act, unless it has been so determined by a court of competent jurisdiction or in a determination issued under this subpart;

(5) *Specify each provision of the Act* or the regulations issued under the Act that preempts the highway routing designation of the State, political subdivision thereof, or Indian tribe;

(6) *State why the applicant believes* that the highway routing designation of the State, political subdivision thereof, or Indian tribe affords an equal or greater level of protection to the public than is afforded by the requirements of the Act or the regulations issued under the Act;

(7) *State why the applicant believes* that the highway routing designation of the State, political subdivision thereof, or Indian tribe does not unreasonably burden commerce; and

(8) *Specify what steps* the State, political subdivision thereof, or Indian tribe is taking to administer and enforce effectively the preempted requirement.

§397.215 Waiver notice.

(a) **The applicant State, political subdivision thereof,** or Indian tribe shall mail a copy of the application and any subsequent amendments or other documents relating to the application to each person whom the applicant reasonably ascertains will be affected by the determination sought. The copy of the application must be accompanied by a statement that the person may submit comments regarding the application to the Administrator within 45 days. The application filed with the Administrator must include a certification with the application has complied with this paragraph and must include the names and addresses of each person to whom the application was sent.

(b) **Notwithstanding the provisions** of paragraph (a) of this section, if the State, political subdivision thereof, or Indian tribe determines that compliance with paragraph (a) of this section would be impracticable, the applicant shall:

(1) *Comply with the requirements* of paragraph (a) of this section with regard to those persons whom it is reasonable and practicable to notify; and

(2) *Include with the application filed* with the Administrator a description of the persons or class or classes of persons to whom notice was not sent.

(c) **The Administrator may require the applicant** to provide notice in addition to that required by paragraphs (a) and (b) of this section, or may determine that the notice required by paragraph (a) of this section is not impracticable, or that notice should be published in the Federal Register.

(d) **The Administrator may** serve notice on any other persons readily identifiable by the Administrator as persons who will be affected by the determination sought and may afford those persons an opportunity to file written comments on the application.

(e) **Any person submitting written comments** to the Administrator with respect to an application filed under this section shall send a copy of the comments to the applicant. The person shall certify to the Administrator that he or she has complied with the requirements of this paragraph. The Administrator may notify other persons participating in the proceeding of the comments and provide an opportunity for those other persons to respond.

§397.217 Waiver processing.

(a) **The Administrator may initiate an investigation** of any statement in an application and utilize any relevant facts obtained by that investigation. The Administrator may solicit and accept submissions from third persons relevant to an application and will provide the applicant an opportunity to respond to all third person submissions. In evaluating an application, the Administrator may convene a hearing or conference, if a hearing or conference will advance the evaluation of the application.

Subpart E - Preemption Procedures

(b) The Administrator may dismiss the application without prejudice if:
- **(1)** *He or she determines* that there is insufficient information upon which to base a determination;
- **(2)** *Upon his or her request,* additional information is not submitted by the applicant; or
- **(3)** *The applicant fails to provide the notice required by this subpart.*

(c) Except as provided in this subpart, the Administrator will only consider an application for a waiver of preemption determination if:
- **(1)** *The applicant expressly acknowledges* in its application that the highway routing designation of the State, political subdivision thereof, or Indian tribe for which the determination is sought is preempted by the Act or the regulations thereunder; or
- **(2)** *The highway routing designation* of the State, political subdivision thereof, or Indian tribe has been determined by a court of competent jurisdiction or in a determination issued pursuant to §397.211 to be preempted by the Act or the regulations issued thereunder.

(d) When the Administrator has received all substantive information necessary to process an application for a waiver of preemption determination, notice of that fact will be served upon the applicant. Additional notice to all other persons who received notice of the proceeding may be served by publishing a notice in the Federal Register.

§397.219 Waiver determination and order.

(a) Upon consideration of the application and other relevant information received or obtained during the proceeding, the Administrator issues an order setting forth his or her determination.

(b) The Administrator may issue a waiver of preemption order only if he or she finds that the requirement of the State, political subdivision thereof, or Indian tribe affords the public a level of safety at least equal to that afforded by the requirements of the Act and the regulations issued under the Act and does not unreasonably burden commerce. In determining whether the requirement of the State, political subdivision thereof, or Indian tribe unreasonably burdens commerce, the Administrator may consider the following factors:
- **(1)** *The extent* to which increased costs and impairment of efficiency result from the highway routing designation of the State, political subdivision thereof, or Indian tribe;
- **(2)** *Whether the highway routing designation* of the State, political subdivision thereof, or Indian tribe has a rational basis;
- **(3)** *Whether the highway routing designation* of the State, political subdivision thereof, or Indian tribe achieves its stated purpose; and
- **(4)** *Whether there is need for uniformity* with regard to the subject concerned and if so, whether the highway routing designation of the State, political subdivision thereof, or Indian tribe competes or conflicts with those of other States, political subdivisions thereof, or Indian tribes.

(c) The order includes a written statement setting forth the relevant facts and the legal basis for the determination, and provides that any person aggrieved by the order may file a petition for reconsideration in accordance with §397.223.

(d) The Administrator serves a copy of the order upon the applicant, any other person who participated in the proceeding and upon any other person readily identifiable by the Administrator as one who may be affected by the order. A copy of each order is placed on file in the public docket. The Administrator may publish the order or notice of the order in the Federal Register.

(e) If no petition for reconsideration is filed within 20 days in accordance with §397.223, an order issued under this section constitutes the final agency decision regarding whether a particular requirement of a State, political subdivision thereof, or Indian tribe is preempted under the Act or any regulations issued thereunder, or whether preemption is waived.

§397.221 Timeliness.

If the Administrator fails to take action on the application within 90 days of serving the notice required by §397.217(d), the applicant may treat the application as having been denied in all respects.

§397.223 Petition for reconsideration.

(a) Any person aggrieved by an order issued under §397.211 or §397.219 may file a petition for reconsideration with the Administrator. The petition must be filed within 20 days of service of the determination or order issued under the above sections.

(b) The petition must contain a concise statement of the basis for seeking reconsideration, including any specific factual or legal errors, or material information not previously available.

(c) The petitioner shall mail a copy of the petition to each person who participated, either as an applicant or routing, in the waiver of preemption proceeding, accompanied by a statement that the person may submit comments concerning the petition to the Administrator within 20 days. The petition filed with the Administrator must contain a certification that the petitioner has complied with this paragraph and include the names and addresses of all persons to whom a copy of the petition was sent.

(d) The Administrator's decision under this section constitutes the final agency decision. If no petition for reconsideration is filed under this section, then the determination issued under §397.211 or §397.219 becomes the final agency decision at the end of the 20 day period.

§397.225 Judicial review.

A party to a proceeding under §397.205(a), §397.213(a), or §397.223(a) may seek review by the appropriate district court of the United States of the decision of the Administrator under such proceeding only by filing a petition with such court within 60 days after the final agency decision.

Part 397 - Transportation of Hazardous Materials; Driving and Parking Rules

Notes

Part 398 - Transportation of Migrant Workers (Page 171 in the Driver Edition)

§398.1 Definitions.

(a) Migrant worker. "Migrant worker" means any individual proceeding to or returning from employment in agriculture as defined in section 3(f) of the Fair Labor Standards Act of 1938, as amended (29 U.S.C. 203(f)) or section 3121(g) of the Internal Revenue Code of 1954 (26 U.S.C. 3121(g)).

(b) Carrier of migrant workers by motor vehicle. "Carrier of migrant worker by motor vehicle" means any person, including any "contract carrier by motor vehicle", but not including any "common carrier by motor vehicle", who or which transports in interstate or foreign commerce at any one time three or more migrant workers to or from their employment by any motor vehicle other than a passenger automobile or station wagon, except a migrant worker transporting himself/herself or his/her immediate family.

(c) Motor carrier. "Motor carrier" means any carrier of migrant workers by motor vehicle as defined in paragraph (b) of this section.

(d) Motor vehicle. "Motor vehicle" means any vehicle, machine, tractor, trailer, or semitrailer propelled or drawn by mechanical power and used upon the highways in the transportation of passengers or property, or any combination thereof, determined by the Administration, but does not include a passenger automobile or station wagon, any vehicle, locomotive, or car operated exclusively on a rail or rails, or a trolley bus operated by electric power derived from a fixed overhead wire, furnishing local passenger transportation in street railway service.

(e) Bus. "Bus" means any motor vehicle designed, constructed, and used for the transportation of passengers: Except passenger automobiles or station wagons other than taxicabs.

(f) Truck. "Truck" means any self-propelled motor vehicle except a truck tractor, designed and constructed primarily for the transportation of property.

(g) Truck tractor. "Truck tractor" means a self propelled motor vehicle designed and used primarily for drawing other vehicles and not so constructed as to carry a load other than a part of the weight of the vehicle and load so drawn.

(h) Semitrailer. "Semitrailer" means any motor vehicle other than a "pole trailer", with or without motive power designed to be drawn by another motor vehicle and so constructed that some part of its weight rests upon the towing vehicle.

(i) Driver or operator. "Driver or operator" means any person who drives any motor vehicle.

(j) Highway. "Highway" means the entire width between the boundary lines of every way publicly maintained when any part thereof is open to the use of the public for purposes of vehicular traffic.

§398.2 Applicability.

(a) General. The regulations prescribed in this part are applicable to carriers of migrant workers by motor vehicle, as defined in §398.1(b), but only in the case of transportation of any migrant worker for a total distance of more than 75 miles (120.7 kilometers) in interstate commerce, as defined in 49 CFR 390.5.

(b) Exception.
(1) *The regulations prescribed in this part* are not applicable to carriers of migrant workers by motor vehicle, as defined in §398.1(b), when:
  (i) *The motor vehicle* is designed or used to transport between 9 and 15 passengers (including the driver);
  (ii) *The motor carrier* is directly compensated for the transportation service; and
  (iii) *The vehicle used to transport migrant workers* is operated beyond a 75 air-mile radius (86.3 statute miles or 138.9 kilometers) from the driver's normal work-reporting location.
(2) *Carriers of migrant workers* by motor vehicle that operate vehicles, designed or used to transport between 9 and 15 passengers (including the driver) for direct compensation, in interstate commerce, must comply with the applicable requirements of 49 CFR Parts 385, 390, 391, 392, 393, 395, and 396, when the motor vehicle is operated beyond a 75 air-mile radius (86.3 statute miles or 138.9 kilometers) from the driver's normal work-reporting location.

§398.3 Qualifications of drivers or operators.

(a) Compliance required. Every motor carrier, and its officers, agents, representatives and employees who drive motor vehicles or are responsible for the hiring, supervision, training, assignment or dispatching of drivers shall comply and be conversant with the requirements of this part.

(b) Minimum physical requirements. No person shall drive, nor shall any motor carrier require or permit any person to drive, any motor vehicle unless such person possesses the following minimum qualifications:

(1) *No loss of foot, leg, hand or arm.*
(2) *No mental, nervous, organic, or functional disease,* likely to interfere with safe driving.
(3) *No loss of fingers,* impairment of use of foot, leg, fingers, hand or arm, or other structural defect or limitation, likely to interfere with safe driving.
(4) *Eyesight:* Visual acuity of at least 20/40 (Snellen) in each eye either without glasses or by correction with glasses; form field of vision in the horizontal meridian shall not be less than a total of 140°; ability to distinguish colors red, green and yellow; drivers requiring correction by glasses shall wear properly prescribed glasses at all times when driving.
(5) *Hearing:* Hearing shall not be less than 10/20 in the better ear, for conversational tones, without a hearing aid.
(6) *Liquor, narcotics and drugs:* Shall not be addicted to the use of narcotics or habit forming drugs, or the excessive use of alcoholic beverages or liquors.
(7) *Initial and periodic physical examination of drivers:* No person shall drive nor shall any motor carrier require or permit any person to drive any motor vehicle unless within the immediately preceding 36 month period such person shall have been physically examined and shall have been certified in accordance with the provisions of paragraph (b)(8) of this section by a licensed doctor of medicine or osteopathy as meeting the requirements of this subsection.
(8) *Certificate of physical examination:* Every motor carrier shall have in its files at its principal place of business for every driver employed or used by it a legible certificate of a licensed doctor of medicine or osteopathy based on a physical examination as required by paragraph (b)(7) of this section or a legible photographically reproduced copy thereof, and every driver shall have in his/her possession while driving, such a certificate or a photographically reproduced copy thereof covering himself/herself.
(9) *Doctor's certificate:* The doctor's certificate shall certify as follows:

DOCTOR'S CERTIFICATE
(Driver of Migrant Workers)

This is to certify that I have this day examined _____ in accordance with §398.3(b) of the Federal Motor Carrier Safety Regulations of the Federal Motor Carrier Safety Administration and that I find him/her:

Qualified under said rules: [ ]
Qualified only when wearing glasses: [ ]
I have kept on file in my office a completed examination.
Date: ____ / ____ / ____
Place: _____
Signature of examining doctor: _____
Address of doctor: _____
City: _____
State: ____ Zip Code: _____ - _____
Signature of driver: _____
Address of driver: _____
City: _____
State: ____ Zip Code: _____ - _____

©MMV Mangan Communications, Inc.

* Full-size forms available free of charge at www.dotcfr.com.

(c) Minimum age and experience requirements. No person shall drive, nor shall any motor carrier require or permit any person to drive, any motor vehicle unless such person possesses the following minimum qualifications:

(1) *Age.* Minimum age shall be 21 years.
(2) *Driving skill.* Experience in driving some type of motor vehicle (including private automobiles) for not less than one year, including experience throughout the four seasons.

(3) *Knowledge of regulations.* Familiarity with the rules and regulations prescribed in this part pertaining to the driving of motor vehicles.

(4) *Knowledge of English.* Every driver shall be able to read and speak the English language sufficiently to understand highway traffic signs and signals and directions given in English and to respond to official inquiries.

(5) *Driver's permit.* Possession of a valid permit qualifying the driver to operate the type of vehicle driven by him/her in the jurisdiction by which the permit is issued.

§398.4 Driving of motor vehicles.

(a) **Compliance required.** Every motor carrier shall comply with the requirements of this part, shall instruct its officers, agents, representatives and drivers with respect thereto, and shall take such measures as are necessary to insure compliance therewith by such persons. All officers, agents, representatives, drivers, and employees of motor carriers directly concerned with the management, maintenance, operation, or driving of motor vehicles, shall comply with and be conversant with the requirements of this part.

(b) **Driving rules to be obeyed.** Every motor vehicle shall be driven in accordance with the laws, ordinances, and regulations of the jurisdiction in which it is being operated, unless such laws, ordinances and regulations are at variance with specific regulations of this Administration which impose a greater affirmative obligation or restraint.

(c) **Driving while ill or fatigued.** No driver shall drive or be required or permitted to drive a motor vehicle while his/her ability or alertness is so impaired through fatigue, illness, or any other cause as to make it unsafe for him/her to begin or continue to drive, except in case of grave emergency where the hazard to passengers would be increased by observance of this section and then only to the nearest point at which the safety of passengers is assured.

(d) **Alcoholic beverages.** No driver shall drive or be required or permitted to drive a motor vehicle, be in active control of any such vehicle, or go on duty or remain on duty, when under the influence of any alcoholic beverage or liquor, regardless of its alcoholic content, nor shall any driver drink any such beverage or liquor while on duty.

(e) **Schedules to conform with speed limits.** No motor carrier shall permit nor require the operation of any motor vehicle between points in such period of time as would necessitate the vehicle being operated at speeds greater than those prescribed by the jurisdictions in or through which the vehicle is being operated.

(f) **Equipment and emergency devices.** No motor vehicle shall be driven unless the driver thereof shall have satisfied himself/herself that the following parts, accessories, and emergency devices are in good working order; nor shall any driver fail to use or make use of such parts, accessories, and devices when and as needed:

Service brakes, including trailer brake connections.
Parking (hand) brake.
Steering mechanism.
Lighting devices and reflectors.
Tires.
Horn.
Windshield wiper or wipers.
Rear-vision mirror or mirrors.
Coupling devices.
Fire extinguisher, at least one properly mounted.
Road warning devices, at least one red burning fusee and at least three flares (oil burning pot torches), red electric lanterns, or red emergency reflectors.

(g) **Safe loading.**

(1) *Distribution and securing of load.* No motor vehicle shall be driven nor shall any motor carrier permit or require any motor vehicle to be driven if it is so loaded, or if the load thereon is so improperly distributed or so inadequately secured, as to prevent its safe operation.

(2) *Doors, tarpaulins, tailgates and other equipment.* No motor vehicle shall be driven unless the tailgate, tailboard, tarpaulins, doors, all equipment and rigging used in the operation of said vehicle, and all means of fastening the load, are securely in place.

(3) *Interference with driver.* No motor vehicle shall be driven when any object obscures his/her view ahead, or to the right or left sides, or to the rear, or interferes with the free movement of his/her arms or legs, or prevents his/her free and ready access to the accessories required for emergencies, or prevents the free and ready exit of any person from the cab or driver's compartment.

(4) *Property on motor vehicles.* No vehicle transporting persons and property shall be driven unless such property is stowed in a manner which will assure:

(i) *Unrestricted freedom of motion to the driver* for proper operation of the vehicle;

(ii) *Unobstructed passage to all exits by any person;* and

(iii) *Adequate protection to passengers and others* from injury as a result of the displacement or falling of such articles.

(5) *Maximum passengers on motor vehicles.* No motor vehicle shall be driven if the total number of passengers exceeds the seating capacity which will be permitted on seats prescribed in 398.5(f) when that section is effective. All passengers carried on such vehicle shall remain seated while the motor vehicle is in motion.

(h) **Rest and meal stops.** Every carrier shall provide for reasonable rest stops at least once between meal stops. Meal stops shall be made at intervals not to exceed six hours and shall be for a period of not less than 30 minutes duration.

(i) **Kinds of motor vehicles** in which workers may be transported. Workers may be transported in or on only the following types of motor vehicles: A bus, a truck with no trailer attached, or a semi-trailer attached to a truck-tractor provided that no other trailer is attached to the semitrailer. Closed vans without windows or means to assure ventilation shall not be used.

(j) **Limitation on distance of travel in trucks.** Any truck when used for the transportation of migrant workers, if such workers are being transported in excess of 600 miles, shall be stopped for a period of not less than eight consecutive hours either before or upon completion of 600 miles travel, and either before or upon completion of any subsequent 600 miles travel to provide rest for drivers and passengers.

(k) **Lighting devices and reflectors.** No motor vehicle shall be driven when any of the required lamps or reflectors are obscured by the tailboard, by any and all lighting devices required by Subpart B of Part 393 of this subchapter shall be lighted during darkness or at any other time when there is not sufficient light to render vehicles and persons visible upon the highway at a distance of 500 feet.

(l) **Ignition of fuel; prevention.** No driver or any employee of a motor carrier shall:

(1) *Fuel a motor vehicle with the engine running,* except when it is necessary to run the engine to fuel the vehicle;

(2) *Smoke or expose any open flame* in the vicinity of a vehicle being fueled;

(3) *Fuel a motor vehicle* unless the nozzle of the fuel hose is continuously in contact with the intake pipe of the fuel tank;

(4) *Permit any other person to engage in such activities* as would be likely to result in fire or explosion.

(m) **Reserve fuel.** No supply of fuel for the propulsion of any motor vehicle or for the operation of any accessory thereof shall be carried on the motor vehicle except in a properly mounted fuel tank or tanks.

(n) **Driving by unauthorized person.** Except in case of emergency, no driver shall permit a motor vehicle to which he/she is assigned to be driven by any person not authorized to drive such vehicle by the motor carrier in control thereof.

(o) **Protection of passengers from weather.** No motor vehicle shall be driven while transporting passengers unless the passengers therein are protected from inclement weather conditions such as rain, snow, or sleet, by use of the top or protective devices required by §398.5(f).

(p) **Unattended vehicles; precautions.** No motor vehicle shall be left unattended by the driver until the parking brake has been securely set, the wheels chocked, and all reasonable precautions have been taken to prevent the movement of such vehicle.

(q) **Railroad grade crossings; stopping required;** sign on rear of vehicle. Every motor vehicle shall, upon approaching any railroad grade crossing, make a full stop not more than 50 feet, nor less than 15 feet from the nearest rail of such railroad grade crossing, and shall not proceed until due caution has been taken to ascertain that the course is clear; except that a full stop need not be made at:

(1) *A street car crossing* within a business or residence district of a municipality;

(2) *A railroad grade crossing* where a police officer or a traffic-control signal (not a railroad flashing signal) directs traffic to proceed;

(3) *An abandoned or exempted grade crossing* which is clearly marked as such by or with the consent of the proper State authority, when such marking can be read from the driver's position.

All such motor vehicles shall display a sign on the rear reading, "This Vehicle Stops at Railroad Crossings."

§398.5 Parts and accessories necessary for safe operation.

(a) **Compliance.** Every motor carrier and its officers, agents, drivers, representatives, and employees directly concerned with the installation and maintenance of equipment and accessories shall comply and be conversant with the requirements and specifications of this part, and no motor carrier shall operate any motor vehicle, or cause or permit it to be operated, unless it is equipped in accordance with said requirements and specifications.

(b) **Lighting devices.** Every motor vehicle shall be equipped with the lighting devices and reflectors required by Subpart B of Part 393 of this subchapter.

(c) **Brakes.** Every motor vehicle shall be equipped with brakes as required by Subpart C of Part 393 of this subchapter, except 393.44 of this subchapter, and shall satisfy the braking performance requirements contained therein.

(d) **Coupling devices; fifth wheel mounting and locking.** The lower half of every fifth wheel mounted on any truck tractor or dolly shall be securely affixed to the frame thereof by U bolts of adequate size, securely tightened, or by other means providing at least equivalent security. Such U bolts shall not be of welded construction. The installation shall be such as not to cause cracking, warping, or deformation of the frame. Adequate means shall be provided positively to prevent the shifting of the lower half of a fifth wheel on the frame to which it is attached. The upper half of every fifth wheel shall be fastened to the motor vehicle with at least the security required for the securing of the lower half to a truck-tractor or dolly. Locking means shall be provided in every fifth wheel mechanism including adapters when used, so that the upper and lower halves may not be separated without the operation of a positive manual release. A release mechanism operated by the driver from the cab shall be deemed to meet this requirement. On fifth wheels designed and constructed as to be readily separable, the fifth wheel locking devices shall apply automatically on coupling for any motor vehicle the date of manufacture of which is subsequent to December 31, 1952.

(e) **Tires.** Every motor vehicle shall be equipped with tires of adequate capacity to support its gross weight. No motor vehicle shall be operated on tires which have been worn so smooth as to expose any tread fabric or which have any other defect likely to cause failure. No vehicle shall be operated while transporting passengers while using any tire which does not have tread configurations on that part of the tire which is in contact with the road surface. No vehicle transporting passengers shall be operated with re-grooved, re-capped, or re-treaded tires on front wheels.

(f) **Passenger compartment.** Every motor vehicle transporting passengers, other than a bus, shall have a passenger compartment meeting the following requirements:

(1) *Floors.* A substantially smooth floor, without protruding obstructions more than two inches high, except as are necessary for securing seats or other devices to the floor, and without cracks or holes.

(2) *Sides.* Side walls and ends above the floor at least 60 inches high, by attachment of sideboards to the permanent body construction if necessary. Stake body construction shall be construed to comply with this requirement only if all six-inch or larger spaces between stakes are suitably closed to prevent passengers from falling off the vehicle.

(3) *Nails, screws, splinters.* The floor and the interior of the sides and ends of the passenger-carrying space shall be free of inwardly protruding nails, screws, splinters, or other projecting objects likely to be injurious to passengers or their apparel.

(4) *Seats.* On and after November 1, 1957, a seat shall be provided for each worker transported. The seats shall be: Securely attached to the vehicle during the course of transportation; not less than 16 inches nor more than 19 inches above the floor; at least 13 inches deep; equipped with backrests extending to a height of at least 36 inches above the floor, with at least 24 inches of space between the backrests or between the edges of the opposite seats when face to face; designed to provide at least 18 inches of seat for each passenger; without cracks more than two inches wide, and the exposed surfaces, if made of wood, planed or sanded smooth and free of splinters.

(5) *Protection from weather.* Whenever necessary to protect the passengers from inclement weather conditions, be equipped with a top at least 80 inches high above the floor and facilities for closing the sides and ends of the passenger-carrying compartment. Tarpaulins or other such removable devices for protection from the weather shall be secured in place.

(6) *Exit.* Adequate means of ingress and egress to and from the passenger space shall be provided on the rear or at the right side. Such means of ingress and egress shall be at least 18 inches wide. The top and the clear opening shall be at least 60 inches high, or as high as the side wall of the passenger space if less than 60 inches. The bottom shall be at the floor of the passenger space.

(7) *Gates and doors.* Gates or doors shall be provided to close the means of ingress and egress and each such gate or door shall be equipped with at least one latch or other fastening device of such construction as to keep the gate or door securely closed during the course of transportation; and readily operative without the use of tools.

(8) *Ladders or steps.* Ladders or steps for the purpose of ingress or egress shall be used when necessary. The maximum vertical spacing of footholds shall not exceed 12 inches, except that the lowest step may be not more than 18 inches above the ground when the vehicle is empty.

(9) *Hand Holds.* Hand holds or devices for similar purpose shall be provided to permit ingress and egress without hazard to passengers.

(10) *Emergency exit.* Vehicles with permanently affixed roofs shall be equipped with at least one emergency exit having a gate or door, latch and hand hold as prescribed in paragraphs (f)(7) and (9) of this section and located on a side or rear not equipped with the exit prescribed in paragraph (f)(6) of this section.

(11) *Communication with driver.* Means shall be provided to enable the passengers to communicate with the driver. Such means may include telephone, speaker tubes, buzzers, pull cords, or other mechanical or electrical means.

(g) **Protection from cold.** Every motor vehicle shall be provided with a safe means of protecting passengers from cold or undue exposure, but in no event shall heaters of the following types be used:

(1) *Exhaust heaters.* Any type of exhaust heater in which the engine exhaust gases are conducted into or through any space occupied by persons or any heater which conducts engine compartment air into any such space.

(2) *Unenclosed flame heaters.* Any type of heater employing a flame which is not fully enclosed.

(3) *Heaters permitting fuel leakage.* Any type of heater from the burner of which there could be spillage or leakage of fuel upon the tilting or overturning of the vehicle in which it is mounted.

(4) *Heaters permitting air contamination.* Any heater taking air, heated or to be heated, from the engine compartment or from direct contact with any portion of the exhaust system; or any heater taking air in ducts from the outside atmosphere to be conveyed through the engine compartment, unless said ducts are so constructed and installed as to prevent contamination of the air so conveyed by exhaust or engine compartment gases.

(5) *Any heater not securely fastened to the vehicle.*

§398.6 Hours of service of drivers; maximum driving time.

No person shall drive nor shall any motor carrier permit or require a driver employed or used by it to drive or operate for more than 10 hours in the aggregate (excluding rest stops and stops for meals) in any period of 24 consecutive hours, unless such driver be afforded 8 consecutive hours rest immediately following the 10 hours aggregate driving. The term "24 consecutive hours" as used in this part means any such period starting at the time the driver reports for duty.

§398.7 Inspection and maintenance of motor vehicles.

Every motor carrier shall systematically inspect and maintain or cause to be systematically maintained, all motor vehicles and their accessories subject to its control, to insure that such motor vehicles and accessories are in safe and proper operating condition.

§398.8 Administration inspection of motor vehicles in operation.

(a) **Administration personnel authorized** to perform inspections. All persons designated as Special Agents of the Federal Motor Carrier Safety Administration, as detailed in Appendix B of Chapter III of this title, are authorized to enter upon and perform inspections of motor carrier's vehicles in operation.

(b) Prescribed inspection report. Form MCS 63, Driver Equipment Compliance Check, shall be used to record findings from motor vehicles selected for final inspection by authorized Administration employees.

(c) Motor vehicles declared "out of service".

(1) *Authorized Administration employees* shall declare and mark "out of service" any motor vehicle which by reason of its mechanical condition or loading is so imminently hazardous to operate as to be likely to cause an accident or a breakdown. Form MCS 64, "Out of Service Vehicle" sticker shall be used to mark vehicles "out of service".

(2) *No motor carrier* shall require or permit any person to operate nor shall any person operate any motor vehicle declared and marked, "out of service" until all repairs required by the "out of service notice" on Form MCS 63 have been satisfactorily completed. The term operate as used in this section shall include towing the vehicle; provided, however, that vehicles marked "out of service" may be towed away by means of a vehicle using a crane or hoist; and provided further, that the vehicle combination consisting of the emergency towing vehicle and the "out of service" vehicle meets the performance requirements of 393.52.

(3) *No person shall remove* the "Out of Service Vehicle" sticker from any motor vehicle prior to completion of all repairs required by the "out of service notice" on Form MC S63.

(4) *The person or persons completing the repairs* required by the "out of service notice" shall sign the "Certification of Repairman" in accordance with the terms prescribed on Form MCS 63, entering the name of his/her shop or garage and the date and time the required repairs were completed. If the driver completes the required repairs, he/she shall sign and complete the "Certification of Repairman".

(d) Motor carrier's disposition of Form MCS 63.

(1) *Motor carriers shall carefully examine* Forms MCS 63. Any and all violations or mechanical defects noted thereon shall be corrected. To the extent drivers are shown not to be in compliance with the Federal Motor Carrier Safety Regulations, appropriate corrective action shall be taken by the motor carrier.

(2) *Motor carriers shall complete* the "Motor Carrier Certification of Action Taken" on form MCS 63 in accordance with the terms prescribed thereon. Motor carriers shall return Forms MCS 63 to the address indicated upon Form MCS 63 within fifteen (15) days following the date of the vehicle inspection.

Part 399 - Employee Safety and Health Standards (Page 175 in the Driver Edition)

Subparts A-K [Reserved]

Subpart L - Step, Handhold, and Deck Requirements for Commercial Motor Vehicles

§399.201 Purpose and scope.

This subpart prescribes step, handhold, and deck requirements on commercial motor vehicles. These requirements are intended to enhance the safety of motor carrier employees.

§399.203 Applicability.

This subpart applies to all trucks and truck-tractors, having a high profile cab-over-engine (COE) configuration, for entrance, egress and back of cab access, manufactured on and after September 1, 1982.

§399.205 Definitions.

Cab-over-engine (COE). A truck or truck-tractor having all, or the front portion, of the engine under the cab.

COE — High profile. A COE having the door sill step above the height of the front tires.

Deck plate. A horizontal surface designed to provide a person with stable footing for the performance of work such as the connection and disconnection of air and electrical lines, gaining access to permanently-mounted equipment or machinery or for similar needs.

Door sill step. Any step normally protected from the elements by the cab door when closed.

Effective peripheral grip. Any shaped surface, free of sharp edges, in which a full grasp can be made to secure a handhold by a person.

Fingertip grasp. A handhold surface which provides a person contact restricted to finger segments 1 and/or 2 only; or which limits wrap-around closure of finger segment 1 with the palm of the hand to 90 degrees as shown in Illustration I.

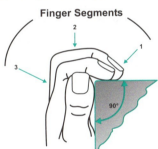

Illustration I • Fingertip Grasp

Full grasp. A handhold surface which provides a person contact with finger segments 2 and 3 and which provides space for finger segment 1 to wrap around toward the palm of the hand beyond the 90-degree surface restriction shown in Illustration I. The handhold need not require contact between fingers and thumb. For example, the hand position shown in Illustration II qualifies as full grasp.

Illustration II • Full Grasp

Ground. The flat horizontal surface on which the tires of a motor vehicle rest.

Handhold. That which qualifies as providing full grasp if a person is able to find a hand position on the handhold which allows more than fingertip grasp.

Handprint. The surface area contacted by the hand when grasping a handhold. The size of this area is the width of the hand across the metacarpal and half the circumference of the handhold. The hand breadth of the typical person is 88.9 millimeters (3.5 inches).

Person. Any individual within the 5th percentile female adult through the 95th percentile male adult of anthropometric measures as described by the 1962 Health Examination Survey, "Weight, Height and Selected Body Dimensions of Adults, United States 1960-1962" which is incorporated by reference. It is Public Health Service publication No. 1000-Series 11-No. 8 and is for sale from the U.S. Department of Commerce, National Technical Information Service, 5285 Port Royal Road, Springfield, Virginia 22161. When ordering use NTIS Accession No. PB 267174. It is also available for inspection at the National Archives and Records Administration (NARA). For information on the availability of this material at NARA, call 202–741–6030, or go to: http://www.archives.gov/federal_register/code_of_federal_regulations/ibr_locations.html. This incorporation by reference was approved by the Director of the Federal Register on July 17, 1979. These materials are incorporated as they exist on the date of the approval and a notice of any change in these materials will be published in the Federal Register.

Slip resistant material. Any material designed to minimize the accumulation of grease, ice, mud or other debris and afford protection from accidental slipping.

§399.207 Truck and truck-tractor access requirements.

(a) General rule. Any person entering or exiting the cab or accessing the rear portion of a high profile COE truck or truck-tractor shall be afforded sufficient steps and handholds, and/or deck plates to allow the user to have at least 3 limbs in contact with the truck or truck-tractor at any time. This rule applies to intermediate positions as well as transition between intermediate positions. To allow for changes in climbing sequence, the step design shall include, as a minimum, one intermediate step of sufficient size to accommodate two feet.

EXCEPTION. If air and electrical connections necessary to couple or uncouple a truck-tractor from a trailer are accessible from the ground, no step, handholds or deck plates are required to permit access to the rear of the cab.

(b) Performance requirements. All high profile COE trucks or truck-tractors shall be equipped on each side of the vehicle where a seat is located, with a sufficient number of steps and handholds to conform with the requirements of paragraph (a) of this section and shall meet the performance requirements:

  (1) *Vertical height.* All measurements of vertical height shall be made from ground level with the vehicle at unladen weight.

  (2) *Distance between steps.* The distance between steps, up to and including the door sill step, shall provide any person a stable resting position which can be sustained without body motion and by exerting no more arm force than 35 percent of the person's body weight per grasp during all stages of entry and exit. This criterion applies to intermediate positions as well as transition between intermediate positions above ground level.

   (i) *When the ground* provides the person foot support during entry or is the final step in the sequence during exit, and the step is 508 millimeters (20 inches) or more above ground, the stable resting position shall be achievable by the person using both hands to grasp the handhold(s) and requiring no more arm force than 35 percent of body weight per grasp.

   (ii) *The vertical height of the first step* shall be no more than 609 millimeters (24 inches) from ground level.

  (3) *Construction.* Each step or deck plate shall be of a slip resistant design which minimizes the accumulation of foreign material. Wherever practicable, a self-cleaning material should be used.

  (4) *Foot accommodation.* Step depth or clearance and step width necessary to accommodate a climbing person are defined by using a minimum 127 millimeter (5 inch) diameter disc as shown in Illustration III.

   (i) *Single foot accommodation.* The disc shall fit on a tread rung, or in a step recess, with no exterior overhang.

(ii) *Two-foot accommodation.* Two discs shall fit on a tread rung, or in a step recess, with no exterior overhang.

Single-foot Accommodation

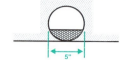

Two-foot Accommodation

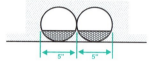

Illustration III • Foot Accommodation

NOTE: The 127 millimeter (5 inch) disc is only intended to test for a minimum depth and width requirement. The step need not retain the disc at rest.

(5) *Step strength.* Each step must withstand a vertical static load of at least 204 kilograms (450 pounds) uniformly distributed over any 127 millimeter (5 inch) increment of step width.

(6) *Handhold location.* A handhold must be located within the reach of any person entering or exiting the vehicle.

(7) *Exterior mounting specifications for handholds.* Each handhold, affixed to the exterior of the vehicle, shall have at least 38 millimeters (1.5 inches) clearance between the handhold and the surface to which it is mounted for the distance between its mounting points.

(8) *Handhold size and shape.* Each handhold shall be free of sharp edges (minimum 1 millimeter [0.04 inch] radius) and have an effective peripheral grip length that permits full grasp by any person.

(9) *Handhold strength.* Each handhold shall withstand a horizontal static load of at least 114 kilograms (250 pounds) uniformly distributed over the area of a hand print and applied away from the mounting surface.

(10) *Deck plates.* Deck plates shall be on the rear of a truck-tractor as necessary to couple or uncouple air and/or electrical connections.

(11) *Deck plate strength.* Each deck plate shall be capable of withstanding the vertical static load of at least 205 kilograms (450 pounds) uniformly distributed over a 127 millimeter (5 inch) diameter disc.

§399.207 DOT Interpretations

Question 1: If a high-profile COE truck or truck-tractor is equipped with a seat on the passenger's side, must steps and handholds be provided for any person entering or exiting on that side of the vehicle?

Guidance: Yes, all high-profile COE trucks and truck tractors shall be equipped on each side of the vehicle where a seat is located, with a sufficient number of steps and handholds to comply with the requirements of §399.207(a).

Question 2: What does the foot accommodation rule mean when it states: "The step need not retain the disc at rest"?

Guidance: The note under §399.207(b)(4) states that the disc referred to is a measuring device. The step or rung does not have to be configured in such a manner as to keep the measuring disc from falling off the step or rung.

Question 3: In §399.207(b)(4), Illustration III, what does the unshaded area within the disc suggest?

Guidance: The unshaded area illustrates the height of the open area required for a driver to insert his or her foot.

Question 4: May the step be a rung? If so, what minimum diameter must the rung be?

Guidance: Yes, the step may be a rung. There is no minimum requirement for the diameter of a step rung. However, it must meet the performance requirements in §399.207(b)(5).

§399.209 Test procedures.

(a) **The force exerted on a handhold will be measured** using a handheld spring scale or force transducer which can be attached to the vehicle and is free to rotate into alignment with a person's hand position.

(b) **Hand grasp will be evaluated by observing** the handgrip of any individual who conforms with the definition of "person" appearing in §399.205 of this subpart.

§399.211 Maintenance.

All steps, handholds, and/or deck plates required by this subpart shall be adequately maintained to serve their intended function.

Appendix A to Subchapter B - [Reserved]

Appendix B to Subchapter B - Special Agents

CAUTIONARY NOTE: This appendix relates only to Federal authority to enforce the regulations in this subchapter. In its present form, it has no application for the States and is not to be included in any adoption of these regulations by State authorities as a condition of eligibility for grants under Part 350 of this chapter.

1. **Authority.** Persons appointed as special agents of the Federal Motor Carrier Safety Administration ("Administration"), are authorized to enter upon, to inspect, and to examine any and all lands, buildings, and equipment of motor carriers and other persons subject to the Interstate Commerce Act, the Department of Transportation Act, and other related Acts, and to inspect and copy any and all accounts, books, records, memoranda, correspondence, and other documents of such carriers and other persons.
2. **Compliance.** Motor carriers and other persons subject to these Acts shall submit their accounts, books, records, memoranda, correspondence, and other documents for inspection and copying, and they shall submit their lands, buildings, and equipment for examination and inspection, to any special agent of the Administration upon demand and display of an Administration credential identifying him/her as a special agent.
3. **Definition of special agent.** Special agents are Federal Motor Carrier Safety Administration (FMCSA) employees who are identified by credentials issued by the FMCSA authorizing them to enforce 42 U.S.C. 4917 and to exercise relevant authority of the Secretary of Transportation under 49 U.S.C. 113, chapters 5, 51, 57, 131-149, 311, 313, and 315 and other statutes, as delegated to FMCSA by 49 CFR 1.73, and under regulations issued on the authority of those statutes. Special agents are authorized to inspect and copy records and to inspect and examine land, buildings, and equipment in the manner and to the extent provided by law.
4. **Facsimile of the Administration Credential:**

UNITED STATES OF AMERICA
DEPARTMENT OF TRANSPORTATION
FEDERAL MOTOR CARRIER SAFETY ADMINISTRATION

This is to certify that _____ whose photograph and signature appear hereon is duly accredited as _____ with authority to enter upon, to inspect, and examine lands, buildings, and equipment, and to inspect and copy records and papers of carriers and other persons, in performance of his/her duties under the Department of Transportation Act, related acts, and regulations of the Department.
By direction of the Secretary

_____   _____
(Certifying Authority)   (Bearer)

Appendix C to Subchapter B - [Reserved]

Appendix D to Subchapter B - [Reserved]

Appendix E to Subchapter B - [Reserved]

Appendix F to Subchapter B - Commercial Zones

NOTE: The text of these definitions is identical to the text of 49 CFR Part 1048, revised as of October 1, 1975, which is no longer in print.

Commercial Zones
Section
1. New York, N.Y.
2. Chicago, Ill.
3. St. Louis, Mo.-East St. Louis, Ill.
4. Washington, D.C.
5. Los Angeles, Calif., and contiguous and adjacent municipalities.
6. Philadelphia, Pa.
7. Cincinnati, Ohio.
8. Kansas City, Mo.-Kansas City, Kans.
9. Boston, Mass.
10. Davenport, Iowa; Rock Island and Moline, Ill.
11. Commercial zones of municipalities in New Jersey within 5 miles of New York, N.Y.
12. Commercial zones of municipalities in Westchester and Nassau Counties, N.Y.
13. Tucson, Ariz.
14. Albuquerque, N. Mex.
18. Ravenswood, W. Va.
19. Lake Charles, La.
20. Syracuse, N.Y.
21. Baltimore, Md.
22. Cleveland, Ohio.
23. Detroit, Mich.
24. Seattle, Wash.
25. Albany, N.Y.
26. Minneapolis-St. Paul, Minn.
27. New Orleans, La.
28. Pittsburgh, Pa.
29. Portland, Oreg.
30. Vancouver, Wash.
31. Charleston, S.C.
32. Charleston, W. Va.
33. Memphis, Tenn.
34. Houston, Tex.
35. Pueblo, Colo.
36. Warren, Ohio.
37. Louisville, Ky.
38. Sioux City, Iowa.
39. Beaumont, Tex.
40. Metropolitan Government of Nashville and Davidson County, Tenn.
41. Consolidated City of Indianapolis, Ind.
42. Lexington-Fayette Urban County, Ky.
43. Definitions.
44. Commercial zones determined generally, with exceptions.
45. Controlling distances and population data.

Section 1   New York, N.Y.

(a) The application of §372.241 Commercial Zones determined generally, with exceptions, is hereby extended to New York, N.Y.

(b) The exemption provided by section 203(b)(8) of the Interstate Commerce Act, of transportation by motor vehicle, in interstate or foreign commerce, performed wholly within the zone the limits of which are defined in paragraph (a) of this section, is hereby removed as to all such transportation except:

(1) *Transportation which is performed* wholly within the following territory: The area within the corporate limits of the cities of New York, Yonkers, Mount Vernon, North Pelham, Pelham, Pelham Manor, Great Neck Estates, Floral Park, and Valley Stream, N.Y., and Englewood, N.J.; the area within the borough limits of Alpine, Tenafly, Englewood Cliffs, Leonia, Fort Lee, Edgewater, Cliffside Park, Fairview, Palisades Park, and Ridgefield, Bergen County, N.J.; and that part of Hudson County, N.J., east of Newark Bay and the Hackensack River;

(2) *Transportation which is performed* in respect of a shipment which has had a prior, or will have a subsequent movement by water carrier, and which is performed wholly between points named in subparagraph (1) of this paragraph, on the one hand, and, on the other, those points in Newark and Elizabeth, N.J., identified as follows: All points in that area within the corporate limits of the cities of Newark and Elizabeth, N.J., west of Newark Bay and bounded on the south by the main line of the Central Railroad of New Jersey, on the west by the Newark & Elizabeth Branch of the Central Railroad Company of New Jersey, and on the north by the property line of the Penn Central Transportation Company.

(3) *Transportation which is performed* in respect of a shipment by rail carrier, and which is performed wholly between points named in subparagraph (1) of this paragraph, on the one hand, and, on the other,

  (a) *Those portions of Kearny, N.J.,* within an area bounded on the north by the main line of the Jersey City Branch of the Penn Central Transportation Co., on the south and east by Fish House Road and Pennsylvania Avenue, and on the west by the property line of the Penn Central Transportation Co. Truck-Train Terminal.

(b) *(i) That portion of Newark, N.J.,* within an area bounded on the north by South Street and Delancey Street, on the east by Doremus Avenue, on the south by the freight right-of-way of the Penn Central Transportation Co. (Waverly Yard, Newark, N.J., to Greenville Piers, Jersey City, N.J., line), and on the west by the Penn Central Transportation Co.'s Hunter Street produce yard, and

(ii) that portion of Newark, N.J., within an area bounded on the north by Poinier Street, on the east by Broad Street, on the south by the passenger right-of-way of the Penn Central Transportation Co.'s main line and on the west by Frelinghuysen Avenue.

(c) *That portion of Port Reading, N.J.,* within an area bounded on the east by the Arthur Kill, on the south by the right-of-way of the Reading Co., on the west by Cliff Road, and on the north by Woodbridge-Carteret Road, and

(d) *That portion of Elizabeth, N.J.,* within an area bounded by a line extending from Newark Bay westward along Trumbull Street to its intersection with Division Street; thence northward along Trumbull Street to its intersection with East North Avenue; thence eastward along East North Avenue to its intersection with the New Jersey Turnpike, thence along the New Jersey Turnpike to the Elizabeth Channel; thence easterly along the Elizabeth Channel to Newark Bay; thence along the western shore of Newark Bay to the point of the beginning.

Section 2 Chicago, Ill.

The zone adjacent to and commercially a part of Chicago, Ill., within which transportation by motor vehicle, in interstate or foreign commerce, not under a common control, management, or arrangement for a continuous carriage or shipment to or from a point beyond the zone is partially exempt from regulation under section 203(b)(8) of the Interstate Commerce Act (49 U.S.C. 303(b)(8)), includes and is comprised of all points as follows:

The area within the corporate limits of Chicago, Evanston, Oak Park, Cicero, Berwyn, River Forest, Willow Springs, Bridgeview, Hickory Hills, Worth, Homewood, and Lansing, Ill.; the area within the township limits of Niles, Maine, Leyden, Norwood Park, Proviso, Lyons, Riverside, Stickney, Worth, Calumet, Bremen, and Thornton Townships, Cook County, Ill.; the area comprised of that part of Lemont Township, Cook County, and that part of Downers Grove Township, Du Page County, Ill., bounded by a line beginning at the intersection of Archer Avenue and the southern corporate limits of Willow Springs, Ill., and extending in a southwesterly direction along Archer Avenue to its junction with Chicago Joliet Road (Sag Lemont Highway), thence in a westerly direction over Chicago Joliet Road to its junction with Walker Road, thence directly north along an imaginary line to the southern shoreline of the Chicago Sanitary and Ship Canal, thence in a northeasterly direction along said shoreline to the corporate limits of Willow Springs, including points on the indicated portions of the highways specified; the area within Burr Ridge, Du Page County, bounded by a line beginning at the intersection of County Line Road and Frontage Road, thence southwesterly along Frontage Road to its intersection with Garfield Street, thence northerly along Garfield Street to its junction with 74th Street, thence westerly along an imaginary line to the junction of 74th Street and Grant Street, thence southerly along Grant Street to its junction with 75th Street, thence westerly along 75th Street to its junction with Brush Hill Road, thence southerly along Brush Hill Road to its junction with Frontage Road, thence northeasterly along Frontage Road to its junction with County Line Road; and the area within the corporate limits of Hammond, Whiting, East Chicago, and Gary, Ind.

Section 3 St. Louis, Mo.-East St. Louis, Ill.

(a) The zone adjacent to and commercially a part of St. Louis, Mo.-East St. Louis, Ill., within which transportation by motor vehicle in interstate or foreign commerce, not under a common control, management or arrangement for a continuous carriage to or from a point beyond the zone is partially exempt from regulation under section 203(b)(8) of the Interstate Commerce Act (49 U.S.C. 303(b)(8)), includes and is comprised of all points as follows:

(1) *All points within the corporate limits of St. Louis, Mo.;*

(2) *All points in St. Louis County, Mo.,* within a line drawn 0.5 mile south, west, and north of the following line: — Beginning at the Jefferson Barracks Bridge across the Mississippi River and extending westerly along Missouri Highway 77 to its junction with U.S. Highway 61 Bypass, thence along U.S. Highway 61 Bypass to its junction with U.S. Highway 66, thence westerly along U.S. Highway 66 to its junction with Bowles Avenue, thence northerly along Bowles Avenue, actual or projected, to the Meramec River, thence easterly along the south bank of the Meramec River to a point directly south of the western boundary of Kirkwood, thence across the Meramec River to and along the western boundary of Kirkwood to Marshall Road, thence westerly along Marshall Road to its junction with Treecourt Avenue, thence northerly along Treecourt Avenue to its junction with Big Bend Road, thence easterly along Big Bend Road to the western boundary of Kirkwood, thence northerly along the western boundary of Kirkwood to its junction with Dougherty Ferry Road, thence westerly along Dougherty Ferry Road to its junction with Interstate Highway 244, thence northerly along Interstate Highway 244 to its junction with Manchester Road, thence easterly along Manchester Road to its junction with the northwest corner of Kirkwood, thence along the western and northern boundaries of Kirkwood to the western boundary of Huntleigh, Mo., thence along the western and northern boundaries of Huntleigh to its junction with Lindbergh Boulevard, thence northerly along Lindbergh Boulevard to its junction with Lackland Avenue, thence in a westerly direction along Lackland Avenue to its junction with the right-of-way of the proposed Circumferential Expressway (Interstate Highway 244), thence in a northerly direction along said right-of-way to its junction with the right-of-way of the Chicago, Rock Island and Pacific Railroad, thence in an easterly direction along said right-of-way to its junction with Dorsett Road, thence in an easterly direction along Dorsett Road to its junction with Lindbergh Boulevard, thence in a northerly direction along Lindbergh Boulevard to its junction with St. Charles Rock Road, thence westerly along St. Charles Rock Road to its function with the Missouri River, thence northerly along the east shore of the Missouri River to its junction with the Norfolk and Western Railway Co. right-of-way, thence easterly along the southern boundary of the Norfolk and Western Railway Co. right-of-way to Lindbergh Boulevard, thence in an easterly direction along Lindbergh Boulevard to the western boundary of St. Ferdinand (Florissant), Mo., thence along the western, northern, and eastern boundaries of St. Ferdinand to junction Interstate Highway 270, and thence along Interstate Highway 270 to the corporate limits of St. Louis (near Chain of Rocks Bridge); and

(3) *All points within the corporate limits* of East St. Louis, Belleville, Granite City, Madison, Venice, Brooklyn, National City, Fairmont City, Washington Park, and Sauget, Ill.; that part of the village of Cahokia, Ill., bounded by Illinois Highway 3 on the east, First Avenue and Red House (Cargill) Road on the south and southwest, the east line of the right-of-way of the Alton and Southern Railroad on the west, and the corporate limits of Sauget, Ill., on the northwest and north; that part of Centerville, Ill., bounded by a line beginning at the junction of 26th Street and the corporate limit of East St. Louis, Ill., and extending northeasterly along 26th Street to its junction with Bond Avenue, thence southeasterly along Bond Avenue to its junction with Owen Street, thence southwesterly along Owen Street to its junction with Church Road, thence southeasterly along Church Road to its junction with Illinois Avenue, thence southwesterly along Illinois Avenue to the southwesterly side of the right-of-way of the Illinois Central Railroad Co., thence along the southwesterly side of the right-of-way of the Illinois Central Railroad Co. to the corporate limits of East St. Louis, Ill, thence along the corporate limits of East St. Louis, Ill., to the point of beginning; and that area bounded by a line commencing at the intersection of the right-of-way of the Alton and Southern Railroad and the Madison, Ill., corporate limits near 19th Street, and extending east and south along said right-of-way to its intersection with the right-of-way of Illinois Terminal Railroad Co., thence southwesterly along the Illinois Terminal Railroad Co. right-of-way to its intersection with Illinois Highway 203, thence northwesterly along said highway to its intersection with the Madison, Ill., corporate boundary near McCambridge Avenue, thence northerly along the Madison, Ill., corporate boundary to the point of beginning.

(b) The exemption provided by section 203(b)(8) of the Interstate Commerce Act in respect of transportation by motor vehicle, in interstate or foreign commerce, between Belleville, Ill., on the one hand, and, on the other, any other point in the commercial zone, the limits of which are defined in paragraph (a) of this section, is hereby removed, and the said transportation is hereby subjected to all applicable provisions of the Interstate Commerce Act.

Section 4 Washington, D.C.

The zone adjacent to and commercially a part of Washington, D.C., within which transportation by motor vehicle, in interstate or foreign commerce, not under a common control, management, or arrangement for a continuous carriage to or from a point beyond the zone is partially exempt from regulation under section 203(b)(8) of the Interstate Commerce Act (49 U.S.A. 303(b)(8)) includes and it is comprised of all as follows:

Beginning at the intersection of MacArthur Boulevard and Falls Road (Maryland Highway 189) and extending northeasterly along Falls Road to its junction with Scott Drive, thence west on Scott Drive to its junction with Viers Drive, thence west on Viers Drive to its junction with Glen Mill Road, thence northeast on Glen Mill Road to its junction with Maryland Highway 28, thence west on Maryland Highway 28 to its junction with Shady Grove Road, thence northeast on Shady Grove Road approximately 2.7 miles to Crabbs Branch, thence southeasterly along the course of Crabbs Branch to Rock Creek, thence southerly along the course of Rock Creek to Viers Mill Road (Maryland Highway 586), thence southeasterly along Viers Mill Road approximately 0.3 mile to its junction with Aspen Hill Road, thence northeasterly along Aspen Hill Road to its junction with Brookeville Road (Maryland Highway 97), thence southeasterly along Brookeville Road to its junction with Maryland Highway 183, thence northeasterly along Maryland Highway 183 to Colesville, Md., thence southeasterly along Beltsville Road to its junction with Powder Mill Road (Maryland Highway 212), thence easterly over Powder Mill Road to its junction with Montgomery Road, thence notheasterly along Montgomery Road, approximately 0.2 mile, to its junction with an unnumbered highway extending northeasterly to the north of Ammendale Normal Institute, thence along such unnumbered highway for a distance of about 2.2 miles to its junction somewhat north of Virginia Manor, Md., with an unnumbered highway extending easterly through Muirkirk, Md., thence along such unnumbered highway through Muirkirk to its junction, approximately 1.8 miles east of the Baltimore and Ohio Railroad, with an unnumbered highway, thence southwesterly along such unnumbered highway for a distance of about 0.5 mile to its junction with an unnumbered highway, thence southeasterly along such unnumbered highway through Springfield and Hillmeade, Md., to its junction with Defense Highway (U.S. Highway 50), thence southwesterly along Defense Highway approximately 0.8 mile to its junction with Enterprise Road (Maryland Highway 556), thence southerly over Enterprise Road to its junction with Central Avenue (Maryland Highway 214), thence westerly over Central Avenue about 0.5 mile to its crossing of Western Branch, thence southerly down the course of Western Branch to Maryland Highway 202, thence westerly approximately 0.3 mile along Maryland Highway 202 to its junction with White House Road, thence southwesterly along White House Road to its junction with Maryland Highway 221, thence southeasterly along Maryland Highway 221 to its junction with Maryland Highway 4, thence westerly along Maryland Highway 4 to the boundary of Andrews Air Force Base, thence south and west along said boundary to Brandywine Road (Maryland Highway 5), thence northwesterly along Maryland Highway 5 to its junction with Maryland Highway 337, thence southwesterly along Maryland Highway 337 to its junction with Maryland Highway 224, thence southerly along Maryland Highway 224 to a point opposite the mouth of Broad Creek, thence due west across the Potomac River to the west bank thereof, thence southerly along the west bank of the Potomac River to Gunston Cove, thence up the course of Gunston Cove to Pohick Creek, thence up the course of Pohick Creek to Virginia Highway 611, thence southwesterly along Virginia Highway 611 to the Fairfax-Prince William County line, thence along said county line to Virginia Highway 123, thence northerly along Virginia Highway 123 to its junction with Virginia Highway 636, thence northeasterly along Virginia Highway 636 to its junction with Virginia Highway 638, thence northwesterly along Virginia Highway 638 to its junction with Virginia Highway 620, thence westerly along Virginia Highway 620 to its junction with Virginia Highway 655, thence northeasterly along Virginia Highway 655 to its junction with U.S. Highway 211, thence westerly along U.S. Highway 211 to its junction with Virginia Highway 608, thence northerly along Virginia Highway 608 to its junction with U.S. Highway 50, thence westerly along U.S. Highway 50 to the Fairfax-Loudoun County line, thence northeasterly along said county line to its intersection with Dulles International Airport, thence along the southern, western, and northern boundaries of said airport to the Fairfax-Loudoun Coundy line (at or near Dulles Airport Access Road), thence northeasterly along said county line to its junction with Virginia Highway 7, thence southeasterly along Virginia Highway 7 to its junction with Virginia Highway 193, thence along Virginia Highway 193 to its junction with Scott Run Creek, thence northerly down the course of Scott Run Creek to the Potomac River, thence due north across the river to MacArthur Boulevard to its junction with Maryland Highway 189, the point of beginning.

Section 5 Los Angeles, Calif., and contiguous and adjacent municipalities.

(a) The exemption provided by section 203(b)(8) of Part II of the Interstate Commerce Act to the extent it affects transportation by motor vehicle, in interstate or foreign commerce, performed wholly within Los Angeles, Calif., or wholly within any municipality contiguous or adjacent to Los Angeles, Calif., or wholly a part of Los Angeles, as defined in paragraph (b) of this section, or wholly within the zone adjacent to and commercially a part of the San Pedro, Wilmington, and Terminal Island Districts of Los Angeles and Long Beach, as defined in paragraph (c) of this section, or wholly within the zone of any independent municipality contiguous or adjacent to Los Angeles, as determined under §372.241, or otherwise, between any point in Los Angeles County, Calif., north of the line described below, on the one hand, and, on the other, any point in Los Angeles County, Calif., south thereof is hereby removed and the said transportation is hereby subjected to all the applicable provisions of the Interstate Commerce Act:

Beginning at the Pacific Ocean, and extending easterly along the northern and eastern corporate limits of Manhattan Beach to the northern corporate limits of Redondo Beach, thence along the northern and eastern corporate limits of Redondo Beach to the intersection of Inglewood Avenue and Redondo Beach Boulevard, thence along Redondo Beach Boulevard to the corporate limits of Torrance, thence along the northwestern and eastern corporate limits of Torrance to 182d Street, thence along 182d Street, Walnut, and Main Streets to Alondra Boulevard, thence along Alondra Boulevard to its intersection with Dwight Avenue, thence southerly along Dwight Avenue and an imaginary straight line extending southward to Greenleaf Boulevard, thence eastward along Greenleaf Boulevard to the northwestern corner of the corporate limits of Long Beach, thence along the northern and eastern corporate limits of Long Beach to Artesia Boulevard, thence east on Artesia Boulevard to the Los Angeles-Orange County line.

(b) For the purpose of administration and enforcement of Part II of the Interstate Commerce Act, the zone adjacent to and commercially a part of Los Angeles and contiguous municipalities (except the San Pedro, Wilmington, and Terminal Island districts of Los Angeles and Long Beach, Calif.), in which transportation by motor vehicle in interstate or foreign commerce, not under a common control, management, or arrangement for a continuous carriage or shipment to or from a point beyond the zone, will be partially exempt from regulation under section 203(b)(8) of the act, is hereby defined to include the area of a line extending in a generally northwesterly and northerly direction from the intersection of Inglewood Avenue and Redondo Beach Boulevard along the eastern and northern corporate limits of Redondo Beach, Calif., to the eastern corporate limits of Manhattan Beach, Calif., thence along the eastern and northern corporate limits of Manhattan Beach to the Pacific Ocean, thence along the shoreline of the Pacific Ocean to the western corporate limits of Los Angeles at a point east of Topanga Canyon, and thence along the western corporate limits of Los Angeles to a point near Santa Susana Pass; south of a line extending in a generally easterly direction from a point near Santa Susana Pass along the northern corporate limits of Los Angeles to the eastern corporate limits of Burbank, Calif., thence along the eastern corporate limits of Burbank to the northern corporate limits of Glendale, Calif., and thence along the northern corporate limits of Glendale and Pasadena, Calif., to the northeastern corner of Pasadena; west of a line extending in a generally southerly and southwesterly direction from the northeastern corner of Pasadena along the eastern and a portion of the southern corporate limits of Pasadena to the eastern corporate limits of San Marino, Calif., thence along the eastern corporate limits of San Marino and the eastern and a portion of the southern corporate limits of Alhambra, Calif., to the western corporate limits of Monterey Park, Calif., and the western corporate limits of Montebello, Calif., thence along the western corporate limits of Montebello, Calif., to the Rio Hondo, and the Los Angeles River to the northern corporate limits of Long Beach; and north of a line extending in a generally westerly direction from the Los Angeles River along the northern corporate limits of Long Beach and thence along Greenleaf Boulevard to its intersection with an imaginary straight line extending southward from Dwight Avenue, thence north on the imaginary straight line extending southward from Dwight Avenue, and thence northerly along Dwight Avenue to Alondra Boulevard, thence west along Alondra Boulevard, Main, Walnut, and 182d Streets to the eastern corporate limits of Torrance, thence along a portion of the eastern and the northwestern corporate limits of Torrance to Redondo Beach Boulevard, and thence along Redondo Beach Boulevard to Inglewood Avenue.

(c) **For the purpose of administration and enforcement** of Part II of the Interstate Commerce Act, the zone adjacent to and commercially a part of the San Pedro, Wilmington, and Terminal Island districts of Los Angeles and Long Beach in which transportation by motor vehicle in interstate or foreign commerce, not under a common control, management, or arrangement for a continuous carriage or shipment to or from a point beyond the zone, will be partially exempt from regulation under section 203(b)(8) of the act, is hereby defined to include the area east of a line extending in a generally northerly and northwesterly direction from the Pacific Ocean along the western corporate limits of Los Angeles to 258th Street, thence along 258th Street to the eastern corporate limits of Torrance, and thence along a portion of the eastern, and along the southern and western, corporate limits of Torrance to the northwestern corner of Torrance, south of a line extending in a generally easterly direction from the northwestern corner of Torrance along the northwestern and a portion of the eastern corporate limits of Torrance to 182d Street, thence along 182d, Walnut, Main, and Alondra Boulevard to its intersection with Dwight Avenue, thence southerly along Dwight Avenue and an imaginary straight line extending southward from Dwight Avenue to Greenleaf Boulevard and thence along Greenleaf Boulevard and the northern corporate limits of Long Beach to the northeastern corner of Long Beach; west of the eastern corporate limits of Long Beach; and north of the southern corporate limits of Long Beach and Los Angeles.

Section 6 Philadelphia, Pa.

The zone adjacent to and commercially a part of Philadelphia, Pa., within which transportation by motor vehicle, in interstate or foreign commerce, not under a common control, management, or arrangement for a continuous carriage or shipment to or from a point beyond such zone, is partially exempt from regulation under section 203(b)(8) of the Interstate Commerce Act (49 U.S.C. 303(b)(8)) includes and is comprised of all points as follows:

(a) **The area within Pennsylvania** included within the corporate limits of Philadelphia and Bensalem and Lower Southampton Townships in Bucks County; Conshohocken and West Conshohocken, Pa., and Lower Moreland, Abington, Cheltenham, Springfield, Whitemarsh, and Lower Merion Townships in Montgomery County; an area in Upper Dublin Township, Montgomery County, bounded by a line beginning at the intersection of Pennsylvania Avenue and Fort Washington Avenue and extending northeast along Fort Washington Avenue to its junction with Susquehanna Road, thence southeast along Susquehanna Road to its junction with the right-of-way of the Pennsylvania Railroad Company, thence southwest along the right-of-way of the Pennsylvania Railroad Company to Pennsylvania Avenue, thence northwest along Pennsylvania Avenue to its junction with Fort Washington Avenue, the point of beginning; Haverford Township in Delaware County; and an area in Delaware County south and east of a line extending southward from the intersection of the western and northern boundaries of Upper Darby Township along Darby Creek to Bishop Avenue, thence along Bishop Avenue to Baltimore Pike, thence west along Baltimore Pike to Pennsylvania Highway 320, thence south along Pennsylvania Highway 320 to the corporate limits of Chester, thence along the northern corporate limit of Chester in a westerly direction to the eastern boundary of Upper Chichester Township, thence south to the southern boundary of said township along the eastern boundary thereof, and thence west along the southern boundary of said township to the Delaware State line, and thence south along the Delaware State line to the Delaware River, and

(b) **The area in New Jersey** included in the corporate limits of Camden, Gloucester City, Woodlynne, Merchantville, and Palmyra Boroughs, and the area included in Pennsauken Township in Camden County.

Section 7 Cincinnati, Ohio.

The zone adjacent to and commercially a part of Cincinnati, Ohio, within which transportation by motor vehicle, in interstate or foreign commerce, not under a common control, management, or arrangement for a continuing carriage to or from a point beyond the zone is partially exempt from regulation under section 203(b)(8) of the Interstate Commerce Act (49 U.S.C. 203(b)(8)), includes and is comprised of all points as follows:

    Addyston, Ohio.
    Cheviot, Ohio.
    Cincinnati, Ohio.
    Cleves, Ohio.
    Elmwood Place, Ohio.
    Fairfax, Ohio.
    Mariemont, Ohio.
    North Bend, Ohio.
    Norwood, Ohio.
    St. Bernard, Ohio.
    Covington, Ky.
    Newport, Ky.
    Cold Spring, Ky.

That part of Ohio bounded by a line commencing at the intersection of the Colerain-Springfield Township line and corporate limits of Cincinnati, Ohio, and extending along said township line in a northerly direction to its intersection with the Butler-Hamilton County line, thence in an easterly direction along said county line to its intersection with Ohio Highway 4, thence in a northerly direction along Ohio Highway 4 to its intersection with Seward Road, thence in a northerly direction along said road to its intersection with Port Union Road, thence east along Port Union Road to the Fairfield Township-Union Township line, thence northward along said township line to its intersection with the right-of-way of the Pennsylvania Railroad Co., thence southeasterly along the right-of-way of the Pennsylvania Railroad Co. to its intersection with Princeton-Glendale Road (Ohio Highway 747), thence southward along said road to its intersection with Mulhauser Road, thence in an easterly direction along said road to the terminus thereof west of the tracks of the Pennsylvania Railroad Co., thence continue in an easterly direction in a straight line to Allen Road, thence along the latter to the junction thereof with Cincinnati-Dayton road, thence in a southerly direction along Cincinnati-Dayton Road, to the Butler, Hamilton county line, thence along said county line to the Warren-Hamilton County line in an easterly direction to the Symmes-Sycamore Township line, thence in a southerly direction along the Symmes-Sycamore Township line to its intersection with the Columbia Township line, thence in a westerly direction along Sycamore-Columbia Township line to Madeira Township, thence in a clockwise direction around the boundary of Madeira Township to the Sycamore-Columbia Township line, thence in a westerly direction along said township line to Silverton Township, thence in a southerly direction along said corporate limits to junction with Redbank Road, thence in a southerly direction over Redbank Road to the Cincinnati Corporate limits.

That part of Kenton County, Ky., lying on and north of a line commencing at the intersection of the Kenton-Boone County line and Dixie Highway (U.S. Highways 25 and 42), and extending over said highway to the corporate limits of Covington, Ky., including communities on the described line.

That part of Campbell County, Ky., lying on and north of a line commencing at the southern corporate limits of Newport, Ky., and extending along Licking Pike (Kentucky Highway 9) to junction with Johns Hill Road, thence along Johns Hill Road to junction with Alexandria Pike (U.S. Highway 27), thence northward along Alexandria Pike to junction with River Road (Kentucky Highway 445), thence over the latter to the Ohio River, including communities on the described line.

That part of Boone County, Ky., bounded by a line beginning at the Boone-Kenton County line west of Erlanger, Ky., and extending in a northwesterly direction along Donaldson Highway to its intersection with Zig-Zag Road, thence along Zig-Zag Road to its intersection with Kentucky Highway 18, thence along Kentucky Highway 18 to its intersection with Kentucky Highway 237, thence along Kentucky Highway 237 to its intersection with Kentucky Highway 20, and thence easterly along Kentucky Highway 20 to the Boone-Kenton County line.

That part of Boone and Kenton Counties, Ky., bounded by a line commencing at the intersection of the Boone-Kenton County line and U.S. Highway 42, and extending in a southwesterly direction along U.S. Highway 42 to its junction with Gunpowder Road, thence southerly along Gunpowder Road to its junction with Sunnybrook Road, thence easterly along Sunnybrook Road to its junction with Interstate Highway 75, thence in a straight line in a northeasterly direction to Richardson Road, thence in an easterly direction over Richardson Road to its junction with Kentucky State Route 1303, thence in a northerly direction over Kentucky State Route 1303 to the southern boundary of Edgewood, Kenton County, Ky.

Section 8 Kansas City, Mo.-Kansas City, Kans.

The zone adjacent to and commercially a part of Kansas City, Mo.-Kansas City, Kans., within which transportation by motor vehicle, in interstate or foreign commerce, not under a common control, management, or arrangement for a continuing carriage to or from a point beyond the zone is partially exempt from regulation under section

203(b)(8) of the Interstate Commerce Act (49 U.S.C. 303(b)(8)), includes and is comprised of all points as follows:

Beginning on the north side of the Missouri River at the western boundary line of Parkville, Mo., thence along the western and northern boundaries of Parkville to the Kansas City, Mo., corporate limits, thence along the western, northern, and eastern corporate limits of Kansas City, Mo., to its junction with U.S. Bypass 71 (near Liberty, Mo.), thence along U.S. Bypass 71 to Liberty, thence along the northern and eastern boundaries of Liberty to its junction with U.S. Bypass 71 south of Liberty, thence south along U.S. Bypass 71 to its junction with the Independence, Mo., corporate limits, thence along the eastern Independence, Mo., corporate limits to its junction with Interstate Highway 70, thence along Interstate Highway 70 to its junction with the Blue Springs, Mo., corporate limits, thence along the western, northern, and eastern corporate limits of Blue Springs, Mo., to its junction with U.S. Highway 40, thence east along U.S. Highway 40 to its junction with Brizen-Dine Road, thence south along the southerly extension of Brizen-Dine Road to its junction with Missouri Highway AA, thence along Missouri Highway AA to its junction with the Blue Springs, Mo., corporate limits, thence along the southern and western corporate limits of Blue Springs, Mo., to its junction with U.S. Highway 40, thence west along U.S. Highway 40 to its junction with the Lee's Summit, Mo., corporate limits.

Thence along the eastern Lee's Summit corporate limits to the Jackson-Cass County line, thence west along Jackson-Cass County line to the eastern corporate limits of Belton, Mo., thence along the eastern, southern, and western corporate limits of Belton to the western boundary of Richards-Gebaur Air Force Base, thence along the western boundary of said Air Force Base to Missouri Highway 150, thence west along Missouri Highway 150 to the Kansas-Missouri State line, thence north along the Kansas-Missouri State line, to 110th Street, thence west along 110th Street to its junction with U.S. Highway 69, thence north along U.S. Highway 69 to its junction with 103d Street, thence west along 103d Street to its junction with Quivera Road (the corporate boundary of Lenexa, Kans.), thence along the eastern and southern boundaries of Lenexa to Black Bob Road, thence south along Black Bob Road to 119th Street, thence east along 119th Street to the corporate limits of Olathe, Kans., thence south and east along the Olathe corporate limits to Schlagel Road, thence south along Schlagel Road to Olathe Morse Road, thence west along Olathe Morse Road to the northeast corner of Johnson County Airport, thence south, west, and north along the boundaries of said airport to Pflumm Road, thence north along Pflumm Road to its junction with Olathe Martin City Road, thence west along Olathe Martin City Road to its junction with Murden Road, thence south along Murden Road to its junction with Olathe Morse Road (the corporate boundary of Olathe, Kans.), thence west and north along said corporate boundary to its intersection with U.S. Highway 56, thence southwest along U.S. Highway 56 to its junction with 159th Street.

Thence west along 159th Street to its junction with the Johnson County Industrial Airport, thence south, west, north and east along the boundaries of said airport to the point of beginning, on 159th Street, thence, east along 159th Street to its junction with U.S. Highway 56, thence northeast along U.S. Highway 56 to its junction with Parker Road, thence north along Parker Road to the northern boundary of Olathe, thence east and north along the northern corporate limits of Olathe to Pickering Road, thence north along Pickering Road to 107th Street (the corporate boundary of Lenexa, Kans.), thence along the western and northern boundaries of Lenexa to Pflumm Road, thence north along Pflumm Road to its junction with Kansas Highway 10, thence along Kansas Highway 10 to its junction with Kansas Highway 7, thence along an imaginary line due west across the Kansas River to the Wyandotte County-Leavenworth County line (142d Street) at Loring, Kans., thence westerly along County Route No. 82, a distance of three-fourths of a mile to the entrance of the facilities at Mid-Continent Underground Storage, Loring, thence from Loring in a northerly direction along Loring Lane and Linwood Avenue to the southern boundary of Bonner Springs, Kans.

Thence along the southern, western, and northern boundaries of Bonner Springs to its intersection with Kansas Highway 7, thence southeast along Kansas Highway 7 to its junction with Kansas Highway 32, thence east on Kansas Highway 32 to the corporate boundary of Kansas City, Kans., thence north, west, and east along the corporate boundaries of Kansas City, Kans., to its junction with Cernech Road and Pomeroy Drive, thence northwesterly along Pomeroy Drive to its junction with 79th Street, thence along 79th Street to its junction with Walcotte Drive at Pomeroy, Kans., thence due west 1.3 miles to its junction with an unnamed road, thence north along such unnamed road to the entrance of Powell Port facility, thence due north to the southern bank of the Missouri River, thence east along the southern bank of Missouri River to a point directly across from the western boundary of Parkville, Mo., thence across the Missouri River to the point of the beginning.

Section 9 Boston, Mass.

For the purpose of administration and enforcement of Part II of the Interstate Commerce Act, the zone adjacent to and commercially a part of Boston, Mass., and contiguous municipalities in which transportation by motor vehicle in interstate or foreign commerce, not under a common control, management, or arrangement for a continuous carriage or shipment to or from a point beyond the zone, will be partially exempt under section 203(b)(8) of the act from regulation, is hereby defined to include the following:

Boston, Mass.; Winthrop, Mass.; Chelsea, Mass.; Revere, Mass.; Everett, Mass.; Malden, Mass.; Medford, Mass.; Somerville, Mass.; Cambridge, Mass.; Watertown, Mass.; Brookline, Mass.; Newton, Mass.; Needham, Mass.; Dedham, Mass.; Milton, Mass.; Quincy, Mass.

Section 10 Davenport, Iowa; Rock Island and Moline, Ill.

For the purpose of administration and enforcement of Part II of the Interstate Commerce Act, the zones adjacent to and commercially a part of Davenport, Iowa, Rock Island and Moline, Ill., in which transportation by motor vehicle, in interstate or foreign commerce, not under a common control, management, or arrangement for a continuous carriage or shipment to or from a point beyond such municipalities or zones, will be partially exempt from regulation under section 203(b)(8) of the act (49 U.S.C. 303(b)(8) are hereby determined to be coextensive and to include and to be comprised of the following:

(a) **All points within the corporate limits** of the city of Davenport and the city of Bettendorf, and in Davenport Township, Iowa.

(b) **All points north of Davenport Township** within that portion of Sheridan Township, Iowa, bounded by a line as follows: Beginning at the points where U.S. Highway 61 crosses the Davenport-Sheridan Township line and extending northward along U.S. Highway 61 to the right-of-way of the Chicago, Milwaukee, St. Paul & Pacific Railroad Co., thence northwesterly along said right-of-way to its junction with the first east-west unnumbered highway, thence westerly approximately 0.25 mile to its junction with a north-south unnumbered highway, thence southerly along such unnumbered highway to the northeast corner of Mount Joy Airport, thence along the northern and western boundaries of said airport to the southwestern corner thereof, and thence south in a straight line to the northern boundary of Davenport Township.

(c) (1) *That part of Iowa lying west* of the municipal limits of Davenport south of Iowa Highway 22, north of the Mississippi River and east of the present western boundary of the Dewey Portland Cement Co., at Linwood, including points on such boundaries, and

(2) *that part of Iowa east* of the municipal limits of Bettendorf, south of U.S. Highway 67, west of a private road running between U.S. Highway 67 and Riverside Power Plant of the Iowa-Illinois Gas & Electric Co., and north of the Mississippi River, including points on such boundaries.

(d) **The municipalities of Carbon Cliff, Silvis,** East Moline, Moline, Rock Island, and Milan, Ill., and that part of Illinois lying south or east of such municipalities, within a line as follows: Beginning at a point where Illinois Highway 84 crosses the southern municipal limits of Carbon Cliff and extending southerly along such highway to its junction with Colona Road, thence westerly along Colona Road to Bowlesburg Road, thence southerly on Bowlesburg Road to the southern boundary of Hampton Township, thence along the southern boundaries of Hampton and South Moline Townships to U.S. Highway 150, thence southerly along U.S. Highway 150 to the southern boundary of the Moline Airport, thence along the southern and western boundaries of the Moline Airport to Illinois Highway 92, and thence along Illinois Highway 92 to the corporate limits of Milan.

(e) **All points in Illinois within one-half mile** on each side of Rock Island County State Aid Route No. 9 extending southwesterly from the corporate limits of Milan for a distance of 1 mile, including points on such highway.

Section 11 Commercial zones of municipalities in New Jersey within 5 miles of New York, N.Y.

(a) **The application of §372.241 is hereby extended** to each municipality in New Jersey, any part of which is within 5 miles of the corporate limits of New York, N.Y.

(b) **The exemption provided by section 203(b)(8)** of the Interstate Commerce Act, of transportation by motor vehicle, in interstate or foreign commerce, performed wholly within any commercial zone, the limits of which are defined in paragraph (a) of this section, is hereby removed as to all such transportation except

(1) *transportation which is performed* wholly between any two points in New Jersey, or

(2) *transportation which is performed* wholly between points in New Jersey named in §372.201, on the one hand, and, on the other, points in New York named in §372.201.

Section 12 Commercial zones of municipalities in Westchester and Nassau Counties, N.Y.

(a) **The application of §372.241 is hereby extended** to each municipality in Westchester or Nassau Counties, N.Y.

(b) **The exemption provided by section 203(b)(8)** of the Interstate Commerce Act, of transportation by motor vehicle, in interstate or foreign commerce, performed wholly within any commercial zone, the limits of which are defined in paragraph (a) of this section, is hereby removed as to all such transportation except

(1) *transportation which is performed* wholly between points in New York neither of which is New York City, N.Y., or

(2) *transportation which is performed* wholly between points in Westchester or Nassau County named in §372.201, on the one hand, and, on the other, New York City, N.Y., or points in New Jersey named in §372.201.

Section 13 Tucson, Ariz.

That zone adjacent to and commercially a part of Tucson, Ariz., within which transportation by motor vehicle, in interstate or foreign commerce, not under a common control, management, or arrangement for a continuous carriage or shipment to or from a point beyond the zone, is partially exempt, under section 203(b)(8) of the Interstate Commerce Act (49 U.S.C. 303(b)(8)) from regulation, includes, and is comprised of, all points as follows:

(a) **The municipality of Tucson, Ariz., itself.**

(b) **All points within a line** drawn 5 miles beyond the corporate limits of Tucson, Ariz.

(c) **All points in that area south of the line** described in paragraph (b) of this section, bounded by a line as follows: Beginning at the point where the line described in paragraph (b) of this section, intersects Wilmot Road, thence south along Wilmot Road to junction Nogales Old Vail Connection, thence west along Nogales Old Vail Connection, actual or extended, to the Santa Cruz River, thence north along the east bank of the Santa Cruz River to its joinder with the line described in paragraph (b) of this section.

(d) **All of any municipality any part of which** is within the limits of the combined areas defined in paragraphs (b) and (c) of this section.

(e) **All of any municipality wholly surrounded,** or so surrounded except for a water boundary, by the city of Tucson or by any municipality included under the terms of paragraph (d) of this section.

Section 14 Albuquerque, N. Mex.

The zone adjacent to and commercially a part of Albuquerque, N. Mex., within which transportation by motor vehicle, in interstate or foreign commerce, not under a common control, management, or arrangement for a continuous carriage or shipment to or from a point beyond the zone, is partially exempt, under section 203(b)(8) of the Interstate Commerce Act (49 U.S.C. 303(b)(8)), from regulation, includes, and is comprised of, all points as follows:

(a) **The municipality of Albuquerque, N. Mex., itself.**

(b) **All points within a line** drawn 5 miles beyond the corporate limits of Albuquerque, N. Mex.

(c) **All points in that area north of the line** described in paragraph (b) of this section, bounded by a line as follows: Beginning at the intersection of the line described in paragraph (b) of this section and New Mexico Highway 528, extending in a notheasterly direction along New Mexico Highway 528 to its intersection with New Mexico Highway 44, thence easterly along New Mexico Highway 44 to its intersection with New Mexico Highway 422, thence southerly along New Mexico Highway 422 to its intersection with the line described in paragraph (b) of this section.

(d) **All of any municipality any part of which** is within the limits of the combined areas defined in paragraphs (b) and (c) of this section;

(e) **All of any municipality wholly surrounded,** or so surrounded except for a water boundary, by the city of Albuquerque, N. Mex., or by any municipality included under the terms of paragraph (b) of this section.

Section 18 Ravenswood, W. Va.

That zone adjacent to and commercially a part of Ravenswood, W. Va., within which transportation by motor vehicle, in interstate or foreign commerce, not under common control, management, or arrangement for a continuous carriage or shipment to or from a point beyond the zone, is partially exempt, under section 203(b)(8) of the Interstate Commerce Act (49 U.S.C. 303(b)(8)), from regulation, includes, and is comprised of, all points as follows:

(a) **The municipality of Ravenswood, W. Va., itself.**

(b) **All points within a line** drawn 3 miles beyond the corporate limits of Ravenswood, W. Va., and

(c) **All points in West Virginia in that area** south and southwest of those described in paragraph (b) of this section, bounded by a line as follows: Beginning at the point where the Ohio River meets the line described in paragraph (b) of this section southwest of Ravenswood, thence southerly along the east bank of the Ohio River to the point where the mouth of the Lick Run River empties into the Ohio River; thence in a northeasterly direction along the northern bank of the Lick Run River to the point where it crosses West Virginia Highway 2 south of Ripley Landing, W. Va.; thence in a northerly direction along West Virginia Highway 2 to its intersection with the line described in paragraph (b) of this section west of Pleasant View, W. Va.

Section 19 Lake Charles, La.

That zone adjacent to and commercially a part of Lake Charles, La., within which transportation by motor vehicle, in interstate of foreign commerce, not under common control, management, or arrangement for a continuous carriage or shipment to or from a point beyond the zone, is partially exempt, under section 203(b)(8) of the Interstate Commerce Act (49 U.S.C. 303(b)(8)), from regulation, includes, and is comprised of, all points as follows:

(a) **The municipality of Lake Charles, La., itself;**

(b) **All points within a line** drawn 4 miles beyond the corporate limits of Lake Charles, La.;

(c) **All points in that area south and west** of the line described in paragraph (b) of this section, bounded by a line, as follows: beginning at the point where the line described in paragraph (b) of this section intersects Louisiana Highway 385; thence south along Louisiana Highway 385 to its intersection with the Calcasieu-Cameron Parish line; thence west along the Calcasieu-Cameron Parish line to its intersection with Louisiana Highway 27; thence northerly along Louisiana Highway 27 to a point thereon 2 miles south of U.S. Highway 90; thence east along a line parallel to U.S. Highway 90 to Louisiana Highway 108; thence north along Louisiana Highway 108 to junction U.S. Highway 90; thence east along U.S. Highway 90 to the intersection thereof with the line described in paragraph (b) of this section;

(d) **All of the municipality any part of which** is within the limits of the combined areas in paragraphs (b) and (c) of this section; and

(e) **All of any municipality wholly surrounded,** or so surrounded except for a water boundary, by the City of Lake Charles or by any municipality included under the terms of paragraph (d) of this section.

Section 20 Syracuse, N.Y.

The zone adjacent to and commercially a part of Syracuse, N.Y., within which transportation by motor vehicle, in interstate or foreign commerce, not under a common control, management, or arrangement for a continuing carriage to or from a point beyond the zone is partially exempt from regulation under section 203(b)(8) of the Interstate Commerce Act (49 U.S.C. 303(b)(8)), includes and is comprised of all points as follows:

(a) **The municipality of Syracuse, NY, itself;**

(b) **All other municipalities and unincorporated areas** within 5 miles of the corporate limits of Syracuse, N.Y., and all of any other municipality any part of which lies within 5 miles of such corporate limits;

(c) **Those points in the town of Geddes,** Onondaga County, N.Y., which are not within 5 miles of the corporate limits of Syracuse, N.Y.;

(d) **Those points in the towns** of Van Buren and Lysander, Onondaga County, N.Y., not within 5 miles of the corporate limits of Syracuse, N.Y., and within an area bounded by a line beginning at the intersection of Van Buren Road with the line described in (b) above, thence northwesterly along Van Buren Road to its intersection with the cleared right-of-way of Niagara Mohawk Power Company, thence northwesterly and north along said right-of-way to its intersection between Church Road and Emerick Road, with the cleared right-of-way of New York State Power Authority, thence easterly along said cleared right-of-way to its intersection with the

Appendix F to Subchapter B - Commercial Zones — Section 24

Seneca River, thence south along the Seneca River to its intersection, near Gaskin Road, with the cleared right-of-way of Niagara Mohawk Power Company, thence southwesterly along said cleared right-of-way to its intersection with the eastern limits of the Village of Baldwinsville, thence south along such Village limits to their intersection with a line of railroad presently operated by the Erie-Lackawanna Railroad Company, thence southeasterly along said line of railroad to its intersection with the Van-Buren Lysander Town line, thence southeasterly along the Van-Buren Lysander Town line to its intersection with the Van-Buren Geddes Town line, thence southeasterly along the Van-Buren Geddes Town line to the line described in (b) above.

Section 21 Baltimore, Md.

The zone adjacent to and commercially a part of Baltimore, Md., within which transportation by motor vehicle, in interstate or foreign commerce, not under a common control, management, or arrangement for a continuous carriage to or from a point beyond the zone is partially exempt from regulation under section 203(b)(8) of the Interstate Commerce Act (49 U.S.C. 303(b)(8)) includes and it is comprised of all as follows:

(a) **The municipality of Baltimore itself;**

(b) **All points within a line** drawn 5 miles beyond the boundaries of Baltimore;

(c) **All points in that area east of the line** described in paragraph (b) of this section bounded by a line as follows: Beginning at the point where the line described in paragraph (b) of this section crosses Dark Head Creek and extending in a southeasterly direction along the center of Dark Head Creek and beyond to a point off Wilson Point, thence in a northeasterly direction to and along the center of Frog Mortar Creek to Stevens Road, thence northerly along Stevens Road to Eastern Avenue, thence easterly along Eastern Avenue to Bengies Road, thence northwesterly along Bengies Road, to the right-of-way of the Penn Central Transportation Co., thence westerly along such right-of-way to the junction thereof with the line described in paragraph (b) of this section;

(d) **All points in that area south of the line** described in paragraph (b) of this section, bounded on the west by the right-of-way of the line of the Penn Central Transportation Co., extending between Stony Run and Severn, Md., and on the south by that part of Maryland Highway 176, extending easterly from the said railroad to its junction with the line described in paragraph (b) of this section;

(e) **All points in that area southwest of the line** described in paragraph (b) of this section, bounded by a line as follows: Beginning at the point where the line described in paragraph (b) of this section crosses the Baltimore-Washington Expressway and extending in a southwesterly direction along the Baltimore-Washington Expressway to its intersection with Maryland Highway 176, thence westerly along Maryland Highway 176 to its intersection with the Howard-Anne Arundel County line, thence southwesterly along said county line to its intersection with Maryland Highway 32, thence northwesterly along Maryland Highway 32 to its intersection with the Little Patuxent River, thence northerly along the Little Patuxent River to the intersection of its north fork and its east fork located approximately 1 mile north of the intersection of Maryland Highway 32 and Berger Road, thence easterly along the east fork of the Little Patuxent River to its intersection with Broken Land Parkway, thence southerly along Broken Land Parkway to its intersection with Snowden River Parkway, thence easterly along Snowden River Parkway, to its intersection with relocated Maryland Highway 175, thence southeasterly along relocated Maryland Highway 175, to its intersection with Lark Brown Road, thence northeasterly along Lark Brown Road to its intersection with Maryland Highway 175, thence southerly along Maryland Highway 175 to its intersection with Interstate Highway 95, thence northeasterly along Interstate Highway 95 to its intersection with the line described in paragraph (b) of this section;

(f) **All points in that area north of the line** described in paragraph (b) of this section bounded by a line as follows: Beginning at the junction of the line described in paragraph (b) of this section and the Baltimore-Harrisburg Expressway (Interstate Highway 83), thence northerly along Interstate Highway 83 to its junction with Shawan Road, thence easterly along Shawan Road to its junction with York Road (Maryland Highway 45) and continuing to a point 1,500 feet east of Maryland Highway 45, thence southerly along a line 1,500 feet east of the parallel to Maryland Highway 45 to its junction with the line described in paragraph (b) of this section;

(g) **All points in that area west of the line** described in paragraph (b) of this section bounded by a line as follows: Beginning at the point where the line described in paragraph (b) of this section intersects U.S. Highway 40 west of Baltimore, Md., and extending in a westerly direction along U.S. Highway 40 to its intersection with St. John's Lane, thence southerly along St. John's Lane to its intersection with Maryland Highway 144, thence easterly along Maryland Highway 144 to its intersection with the line in paragraph (b) of this section;

(h) **All of any municipality any part of which** is within the limits of the combined areas defined in paragraphs (b), (c), (d), (e), (f), and (g) of this section;

(i) **All of any municipality wholly surrounded,** or surrounded except for a water boundary, by the city of Baltimore or by any municipality included under the terms of (h) above.

Section 22 Cleveland, Ohio.

The zone adjacent to and commercially a part of Cleveland, Ohio, within which transportation by motor vehicle, in interstate or foreign commerce, not under a common control, management, or arrangement for a continuous carriage to or from a point beyond the zone is partially exempt from regulation under section 203(b)(8) of the Interstate commerce Act (49 U.S.C. 303(b)(8)) includes and it is comprised of all as follows:

(a) **All points in Cuyahoga County, Ohio, and**

(b) **All points in Wickliffe, Willoughby Hills,** Waite Hill, Willoughby, Willowick, Eastlake, Lakeline, Timberlake, and Mentor, Lake County, Ohio.

Section 23 Detroit, Mich.

For the purpose of administration and enforcement of Part II of the Interstate Commerce Act, the zone adjacent to and commercially a part of Detroit, Mich., in which transportation by motor vehicle in interstate or foreign commerce, not under a common control, management, or arrangement for a continuous carriage or shipment to or from a point beyond the zone, will be partially exempt under section 203(b)(8) of the act (49 U.S.C. 303(b)(8)) from regulation, is hereby determined to include, and to be comprised of, all that area within a line as follows:

Beginning at a point on Lake St. Clair opposite the intersection of Fifteen Mile Road and Michigan Highway 29 and extending south and southwest along the shore of Lake St. Clair, to the Detroit River, thence along such River (east of Belle Isle) and Trenton Channel to a point opposite Sibley Road, thence west to and along Sibley Road to Waltz Road, thence north along Waltz Road to Wick Road, thence west along Wick Road to Cogswell Road, thence north along Cogswell Road to Van Born Road, thence east along Van Born Road to Newburgh Road, thence north along Newburgh Road to its junction with Halsted Road, thence north along Halsted Road to West Maple Road, thence east along West Maple Road to Telegraph Road, thence north along Telegraph Road to Sixteen Mile Road, thence east along Sixteen Mile Road to Utica Road, thence southeasterly along Utica Road to Fifteen Mile Road (also called East Maple Road), thence along Fifteen Mile Road and across Michigan Highway 29 to Lake St. Clair, the point of beginning.

Section 24 Seattle, Wash.

The zone adjacent to and commercially a part of Seattle, Wash., within which transportation by motor vehicle, in interstate or foreign commerce, not under common control, management, or arrangement for continuous carriage or shipments to or from a point beyond such zone, is partially exempt from regulation under section 203(b)(8) of the Interstate Commerce Act (49 U.S.C. 303(b)(8)) includes and is comprised of all points as follows:

(a) **The municipality of Seattle itself.**

(b) **All points within a line** drawn 5 miles beyond the municipal limits of Seattle, except points on Bainbridge Island, Vashon Island, and Blake Island.

(c) **All points more than 5 miles** beyond the municipal limits of Seattle

   (1) *within a line as follows:* Beginning at that point south of Seattle where the eastern shore of Puget Sound intersects the line described in paragraph (b) of this section, thence southerly along the eastern shore of Puget Sound to Southwest 192d Street, thence easterly along Southwest 192d Street to the point where it again intersects the line described in paragraph (b) of this section; and

   (2) *within a line as follows:* Beginning at the junction of the southern corporate limits of Kent, Wash., and Washington Highway 181, and extending south along Washington Highway 181 to the northern corporate limits of Auburn, Wash., thence along the western, southern, and eastern corporate limits of Auburn to the junction of the northern corporate limits of Auburn and

Washington Highway 167, thence northerly along Washington Highway 167 to its junction with the southern corporate limits of Kent, Wash., including all points on the highways named.

(d) **All points more than 5 miles** beyond the municipal limits of Seattle within a line as follows: Beginning at the junction of the northern corporate limits of Lynwood, Wash., and U.S. Highway 99, thence north along U.S. Highway 99 to its junction with Washington Highway 525, thence along Washington Highway 525 to its junction with West Casino Road, thence east along West Casino Road to the western boundary of the Everett facilities of the Boeing Co. at or near 4th Avenue West, thence along the western, northern and eastern boundaries of the facilities of the Boeing Co. to West Casino Road, thence east along West Casino Road to its junction with U.S. Highway 99, thence south along U.S. Highway 99 to 112th Street, thence easterly along 112th Street to its junction with Interstate Highway 5, thence southerly along Interstate Highway 5 to its intersection with the present zone limits, including all points on the named routes.

(e) **All of any municipality any part of which** is within the limits set forth in (b) above.

(f) **All of any municipality wholly surrounded,** or so surrounded except for a water boundary, by the city of Seattle or by any municipality included under the terms of (b) above.

Section 25   Albany, N.Y.

For the purpose of administration and enforcement of Part II of the Interstate Commerce Act, the zone adjacent to and commercially a part of Albany, N.Y., in which transportation by motor vehicle in interstate or foreign commerce, not under a common control, management, or arrangement for a continuos carriage or shipment to or from a point beyond the zone, will be partially exempt under section 203(b)(8) of the act (49 U.S.C. 303(b)(8)) from regulations, is hereby determined to include, and to be comprised of, the following:

(a) **The municipality of Albany itself,**

(b) **All points within a line** drawn 5 miles beyond the municipal limits of Albany,

(c) **All points in that area more than 5 miles** beyond the municipal limits of Albany bounded by a line as follows: Beginning at that point on Swatling Road (in the Town of Colonie) where it crosses the line described in (b) above and extending northerly along such road to the municipal limits of Cohoes, thence along the western and northern boundary of Cohoes to the Mohawk River, thence along such river to the northern boundary of the Town of Waterford, thence along the northern and eastern boundaries of the Town of Waterford to the northern boundary of the City of Troy (all of which city is included under the next following provision),

(d) **All of any municipality any part of which** is within the limits of the combined areas defined in (b) and (c) above, and

(e) **All of any municipality wholly surrounded,** or so surrounded except for a water boundary, by the municipality of Albany or by any other municipality included under the terms of (d) above.

Section 26   Minneapolis-St. Paul, Minn.

The zone adjacent to and commercially a part of Minneapolis-St. Paul, Minn., within which transportation by motor vehicle, in interstate or foreign commerce, not under a common control, management, or arrangement for a continuous carriage to or from a point beyond the zone is partially exempt from regulation under section 203(b)(8) of the Interstate Commerce Act (49 U.S C.303(b)(8)) include and it is comprised of all as follows:

Beginning at the intersection of Minnesota Highway 36 and the Minnesota River and extending along the Minnesota River to the southwest corner of the city of Bloomington, thence north along the western boundaries of the city of Bloomington and the village of Edina to the southern boundary of the city of Hopkins, thence along the southern, western, and northern boundaries of the city of Hopkins to the western boundary of the city of St. Louis Park, thence north along the western boundaries of the city of St. Louis Park and the village of Golden Valley to the southeast corner of the village of Plymouth, thence west along the southern boundary of Plymouth to Interstate Highway 494, thence north along Interstate Highway 494 to Minnesota Highway 55, thence southeast along Minnesota Highway 55 to the western boundary of the village of Golden Valley, thence north along the western boundaries of the villages of Golden Valley and New Hope to the northwestern corner of the village of New Hope, thence east along the northern boundary of the village of New Hope and the city of Crystal to the western boundary of the village of Brooklyn Center, thence north along the western boundary of the village of Brooklyn Center to its northern boundary, thence east along such northern boundary to the Hennepin County-Anoka County line, thence north along such country line to the northwestern corner of the village of Spring Lake Park in Anoka County, thence east along the northern boundary of the village of Spring Lake Park to the northwest corner of Mounds View Township in Ramsey County, thence east and south along the northern and eastern boundaries of Mounds View Township to the northwestern corner of the village of Little Canada, thence east and south along the northern and eastern boundaries of Little Canada to the northwest corner of the village of Maplewood, thence east and south along the northern and eastern boundaries of the village of Maplewood to the northeastern corner of the village of North St. Paul, thence south along the eastern boundary of the village of North St. Paul to the southeast corner of such village, thence south along the eastern boundary of the village of Maplewood to the northeastern corner of the village of Newport, thence south and west along the eastern and southern boundaries of the village of Newport to U.S. Highway 61, thence southeasterly along U.S. Highway 61, to the eastern boundary of the village of St. Paul Park, thence along the eastern, southern, and western boundaries of the village of St. Paul Park to a point on the Mississippi River opposite the southeast corner of the original village of Inver Grove, thence westerly across the river and along the southern and western boundaries of the original village of Inver Grove to the northwest corner of such village, thence due north to the southern boundary of South St. Paul, thence north and west along the western and southern boundaries of South St. Paul to the southeastern corner of West St. Paul, thence west along the southern boundary of West St. Paul to County Highway 63, thence south along County Highway 63 to its junction with County Highway 63A, thence west along County Highway 63A to its junction with Minnesota Highway 49, thence north along Minnesota Highway 49 to its junction with County Highway 28, thence west along County Highway 28 to its junction with Minnesota Highway 13, thence southwest along Minnesota Highway 13 to its junction with Minnesota Highway 36, thence north and northwest along Minnesota Highway 36 to the Minnesota River, the point of beginning.

Section 27   New Orleans, La.

The zone adjacent to and commercially a part of New Orleans, La., within which transportation by motor vehicle, in interstate or foreign commerce, not under common control, management, or arrangement for a continuous carriage or shipment to or from a point beyond the zone is partially exempt from regulation under section 203(b)(8) of the Interstate Commerce Act (49 U.S.C. 303(b)(8)), includes and is comprised of all points in the area bounded as follows:

Commencing at a point on the shore of Lake Pontchartrain where it is crossed by the Jefferson Parish-Orleans Parish line; thence easterly along the shore of Lake Pontchartrain to the Rigolets; thence through the Rigolets in an easterly direction to Lake Borgne; thence southwesterly along the shore of Lake Borgne to the Bayou Bienvenue; thence in a general westerly direction along the Bayou Bienvenue (which also constitutes the Orleans Parish-St. Bernard Parish line) to Paris Road; thence in a southerly direction along Paris Road to the Back Protection Levee; thence in a southeasterly direction along the Back Protection Levee (across Lake Borgne Canal) to a point 1 mile north of Louisiana Highway 46; thence in an easterly direction 1 mile north of Louisiana Highway 46 to longitude 89°50'W.; thence south along longitude line 89°50'W. (crossing Louisiana Highway 46 approximately three-eighths of a mile east of Toca) to Forty Arpent Canal; thence westerly, northwesterly, and southerly along Forty Arpent Canal to Scarsdale Canal; thence northwesterly along Scarsdale Canal and beyond it in the same direction to the middle of the Mississippi River; thence southerly along the middle of the Mississippi River to the Augusta Canal; thence in a westerly direction along the Augusta Canal to the Gulf Intracoastal Waterway; thence in a northerly direction along the middle of the Gulf Intracoastal Waterway (Harvey Canal) to the point where Lapalco Boulevard runs perpendicular to the Gulf Intracoastal Waterway (Harvey Canal); thence in a westerly direction along Lapalco Boulevard to its junction with Barataria Boulevard; thence north on Barataria Boulevard to a point approximately 2 miles south of the Mississippi River where a high tension transmission line crosses Barataria Boulevard; thence in a westerly direction following such transmission line to the intersection thereof with U.S. Highway 90; thence westerly along U.S. Highway 90 to the Jefferson Parish-St. Charles Parish line; thence north along such parish line to the middle of the Mississippi River; thence westerly along the middle of the Mississippi River to a point south of Almedia Road; thence north to Almedia Road; thence in a northerly direction along Almedia Road to its junction with Highway 61; thence north to the shore of Lake Pontchartrain; thence along the shore of Lake Pontchartrain in an easterly direction to the Jefferson Parish-Orleans Parish line, the point of beginning.

Appendix F to Subchapter B - Commercial Zones Section 33

Section 28 Pittsburgh, Pa.

For the purpose of administration and enforcement of Part II of the Interstate Commerce Act, the zone adjacent to and commercially a part of Pittsburgh, Pa., in which transportation by motor vehicle in interstate or foreign commerce, not under a common control, management, or arrangement for a continuous carriage or shipment to or from a point beyond the zone, will be partially exempt under section 203(b)(8) of the act (49 U.S.C. 303(b)(8)) from regulation is hereby determined to include, and to be comprised of, the following:

(a) **All points in Allegheny County, Pa.,** except Forward, Elizabeth, South Versailles, Marshall (including the Borough of Bradford Woods), Pine Richland, West Deer and Fawn Townships and that part of Frazer Township north of a line made by extending easterly in a straight line the southern boundary of West Deer Township.

(b) **Borough of Trafford situated in both** Allegheny and Westmoreland Counties;

(c) **Borough of Ambridge and Harmony Township** located in Beaver County; and

(d) **The City of New Kensington and Borough of Arnold** in Westmoreland County.

Section 29 Portland, Oreg.

For the purpose of administration and enforcement of Part II of the Interstate Commerce Act, the zone adjacent to and commercially a part of Portland, Oreg., in which transportation by motor vehicle in interstate or foreign commerce, not under a common control, management, or arrangement for a continuous carriage or shipment to or from a point beyond the zone, will be partially exempt under section 203(b)(8) of the act (49 U.S.C. 303(b)(8)) from regulation, is hereby determined to include, and to be comprised of, the following:

(a) **The municipality itself.**

(b) **All points in Oregon within a line** drawn 5 miles beyond the corporate limits of Portland.

(c) **All of any municipality any part of which** is within the line described in (b) above.

(d) **All of any municipality wholly surrounded,** or so surrounded except for a water boundary, by the city of Portland or by any municipality included under the terms of (c) above.

Section 30 Vancouver, Wash.

For the purpose of administration and enforcement of Part II of the Interstate Commerce Act, the zone adjacent to and commercially a part of Vancouver, Wash., in which transportation by motor vehicle in interstate or foreign commerce, not under a common control, management, or arrangement for a continuous carriage or shipment to or from a point beyond the zone, will be partially exempt under section 203(b)(8) of the act (49 U.S.C. 303(b)(8)) from regulation, is hereby determined to include, and to be comprised of, the following:

(a) **The municipality itself.**

(b) **All points in Washington within a line** drawn 4 miles beyond the corporate limits of Vancouver.

(c) **All of any municipality any part of which** is within the line described in (b) above.

(d) **All of any municipality wholly surrounded,** or so surrounded except for a water boundary, by the City of Vancouver or by any municipality included under the terms of (c) above.

Section 31 Charleston, S.C.

The zone adjacent to and commercially a part of Charleston, S.C., within which transportation by motor vehicle, in interstate or foreign commerce, not under a common control, management, or arrangement for a continuous carriage or shipment to or from a point beyond the zone is partially exempt, under section 203(b)(8) of the Interstate Commerce Act (49 U.S.C. 303(b)(8)), from regulation, includes and is comprised of, all points and places as follows:

(a) **The municipality of Charleston itself.**

(b) **All points within a line** drawn 4 miles beyond the boundaries of Charleston.

(c) **All points in that area north of the line** described in paragraph (b) of this section, bounded by a line as follows: Beginning at the point where the line described in paragraph (b) of this section crosses Cooper River and extending in a northerly direction along the center of Cooper River to Goose Creek; thence north and west along the center of Goose Creek to the dam of the reservoir of the Charleston waterworks; thence northwesterly along the west bank of the Charleston waterworks reservoir for approximately one mile to an unnamed creek; thence westerly along the center of this unnamed creek for approximately one mile to U.S. Highway 52; thence northerly along U.S. Highway 52 to junction South Carolina Highway S-10-75; thence westerly along South Carolina Highway S-10-75 approximately one and one half miles to a point one quarter mile west of the track of the Southern Railway Company; thence southeasterly along a line one quarter of a mile west of, and parallel to, the track of the Southern Railway Company to the junction thereof with the line described in paragraph (b) of this section.

(d) **All of any municipality any part of which** is within the limits of the combined areas defined in paragraphs (b) and (c) of this section.

(e) **All of any municipality wholly surrounded,** or so surrounded except for a water boundary, by the city of Charleston or by any municipality included under the terms of paragraph (d) of this section.

Section 32 Charleston, W. Va.

That zone adjacent to and commercially a part of Charleston, W. Va., within which transportation by motor vehicle, in interstate or foreign commerce, not under a common control, management, or arrangement for a continuous carriage or shipment to or from a point beyond the zone, is partially exempt, under section 203(b)(8) of the Interstate Commerce Act (49 U.S.C. 303(b)(8)), from regulation, includes, and is comprised of, all points and places as follows:

(a) **The municipality of Charleston, W. Va., itself.**

(b) **All points within a line** drawn 4 miles beyond the corporate limits of Charleston, W. Va.

(c) **All points in that area northwest** of those described in (b) above, bounded by a line as follows: Beginning at a point on the line described in (b) above, one-half mile south of U.S. Highway 60 west of Charleston, thence westerly along a line one-half mile south of and parallel to U.S. Highway 60 to a point one-half mile south of the junction of U.S. Highway 60 with West Virginia Highway 17 near 2 3/4 Mile Creek, thence westerly along a line one-half mile south of and parallel to West Virginia Highway 17 to the Coal River, thence north along the center of the Coal River to West Virginia Highway 17, thence northerly along West Virginia Highway 17 to Scary Creek, near Scary, W. Va., thence east along Scary Creek to the center of the Kanawha River, thence northerly along the center of the Kanawha River to a point opposite the mouth of Blake Creek (between Nitro and Poca, W. Va.), thence easterly along a straight line drawn through the junction of U.S. Highway 35 and West Virginia Highway 25 to a point one-half mile beyond said junction, thence southerly along a line one-half mile northeast of and parallel to West Virginia Highway 25 to the junction of the line described in (b) above.

(d) **All points in that area southeast** of those described in (b) above, bounded by a line as follows: Beginning at a point on the line described in (b) above one-half mile south of the Kanawha River, thence easterly along a line one-half mile south of, and parallel to, the Kanawha River to junction with a straight line intersecting the highway bridge at Chelyan, W. Va., thence northerly along said straight line across the Kanawha River to a point one-half mile north of the Kanawha River, thence westerly along a line one-half mile north of and parallel to the Kanawha River to the junction of the line described in (b) above.

(e) **All of any municipality any part of which** is within the limits of the combined areas defined in (b), (c), and (d) above.

Section 33 Memphis, Tenn.

That zone adjacent to and commercially a part of Memphis, Tenn., within which transportation by motor vehicle, in interstate or foreign commerce, not under a common control management, or arrangement for a continuous carriage or shipment to or from a point beyond the zone, is partially exempt, under section 203(b)(8) of the Interstate Commerce Act (49 U.S.C. 303(b)(8)), from regulation, includes, and is comprised of, all points as follows:

(a) **The municipality of Memphis, Tenn., itself.**

(b) **All points within a line** drawn 5 miles beyond the corporate limits of Memphis, Tenn.

(c) **All points in that part of Shelby County, Tenn.,** north of the line described in paragraph (b) of this section, bounded by a line as follows: Beginning at the intersection of the line described in paragraph (b) of this section and U.S. Highway 51 north of Memphis, thence northeasterly along U.S. Highway 51 for approximately 3 miles to its intersection with Lucy Road, thence easterly along Lucy Road for approximately 1.4 miles to its intersection with Chase Road, thence northerly along Chase Road for approximately 0.6 mile to its intersection with Lucy Road thence easterly along Lucy Road for approximately 0.8 mile to its intersection with Main Road, thence southeasterly along Main Road approximately 0.3 mile to its intersection with Amherst Road, thence southerly and easterly along Amherst Road for approximately 0.8 mile to its intersection with Raleigh-Millington Road, thence southerly along Raleigh-Mill-

ington Road for approximately 2 miles to its intersection with the line described in paragraph (b) of this section north of Memphis;
(d) **All of any municipality any part of which** is within the limits of the combined areas described in paragraphs (b) and (c) of this section.

Section 34 Houston, Tex.

The zone adjacent to, and commercially a part of Houston, Tex., and contiguous municipalities in which transportation by motor vehicle, in interstate or foreign commerce, not under common control, management, or arrangement for a continuous carriage or shipment to or from a point beyond the zone, will be partially exempt under section 203(b)(8) of the act from regulation, is hereby defined to include the area which would result by the application of the general formula promulgated in §372.241, and in addition thereto, the municipalities of Baytown, La Porte and Lomax, Tex.

Section 35 Pueblo, Colo.

The zone adjacent to and commercially a part of Pueblo, Colo., within which transportation by motor vehicle, in interstate or foreign commerce, not under a common control, management, or arrangement for a continuous carriage or shipment to or from a point beyond such zone is partially exempt from regulation under section 203(b)(8) of the Interstate Commerce Act (49 U.S.C. 303(b)(8)), includes and is comprised of all points as follows:
(a) **The municipality of Pueblo, Colo., itself;**
(b) **All points within a line** drawn 4 miles beyond the corporate limits of Pueblo, Colo.;
(c) **All of the area known as the Pueblo Memorial Airport,** consisting of about 3,500 acres, not within 4 miles of the corporate limits of Pueblo, Colo., and within an area located on the East of Pueblo, the nearest point being about 3.80 miles from the city limits of Pueblo, and bounded on the south by the tracks of the Santa Fe Railroad and the Missouri Pacific Railroad, and a public highway known as Baxter Road and designated as U.S. Highway 50 Bypass and Colorado Highway 96, with such property extending north, west, and east of the described southern base line.

Section 36 Warren, Ohio.

The zone adjacent to and commercially a part of Warren, Ohio within which transportation by motor vehicle, in interstate or foreign commerce, not under a common control, management, or arrangement for a continuous carriage or shipment to or from a point beyond the zone, is partially exempt, under section 203(b)(8) of the Interstate Commerce Act (49 U.S.C. 303(b)(8)) from regulation includes, and is comprised of, all points as follows:
(a) **The municipality of Warren, Ohio, itself.**
(b) **All points within a line** drawn 4 miles beyond the corporate limits of Warren, Ohio.
(c) **All points in that area, south of the line** in paragraph (b) of this section, bounded by a line as follows: Beginning at the point where the line described in paragraph (b) of this section intersects Ellsworth-Baily Road, thence south along Ellsworth-Baily Road to the Ohio Turnpike, thence southeast along the Ohio Turnpike to New Hallock-Young Road, thence northeast along New Hallock-Young Road to Hallock-Young Road, thence east along Hallock-Young Road to junction Ohio Highway 45 (Salem-Warren Road), thence north along Ohio Highway 45 (Salem-Warren Road) to its intersection with the line described in paragraph (b) of this section.

Section 37 Louisville, Ky.

The zone adjacent to and commercially a part of Louisville, Ky., within which transportation by motor vehicle, in interstate or foreign commerce, not under a common control, management, or arrangement for a continuous carriage or shipment to or from a point beyond such zone, is partially exempt from regulation under section 203(b)(8) of the Interstate Commerce Act (49 U.S.C. 303(b)(8)) includes and is comprised of all points as follows:
(a) **The municipality of Louisville, Ky., itself;**
(b) **All other municipalities and unincorporated areas** within 5 miles of the corporate limits of Louisville, Ky., and all of any municipality any part of which lies within 5 miles of such corporate limits; and
(c) **Those points not within 5 miles** of the corporate limits of Louisville, Ky., and within an area bounded by a line beginning at the junction of Kentucky Highway 146 (LaGrange Road) and Kentucky Highway 1447 (Westport Road), thence over Kentucky Highway 146 to the junction of Kentucky Highway 146 and Kentucky Highway 841 (Jefferson Freeway), thence over Kentucky Highway 841 to the junction of Kentucky Highway 841 and Kentucky Highway 1447, thence over Kentucky Highway 1447 to junction Kentucky Highway 1447 and Kentucky Highway 146, the point of beginning, all within Jefferson County, Ky.

Section 38 Sioux City, Iowa.

The zone adjacent to and commercially a part of Sioux City, Iowa, within which transportation by motor vehicle, in interstate or foreign commerce, not under a common control, management, or arrangement for a continuous carriage or shipment to or from a point beyond such zone, is partially exempt from regulation under section 203(b)(8) of the Interstate Commerce Act (49 U.S.C. 303(b)(8)) includes and is comprised of all points as follows:
(a) **The area which would result by application** of the general formula promulgated in §372.241; and in addition thereto.
(b) **That area bounded by a line** beginning at the intersection of Interstate Highway 29 and the line described in paragraph (a) of this section, and extending southeasterly along Interstate Highway 29 to its intersection with the Liberty-Lakeport Township, Iowa, line, thence westerly along the Liberty-Lakeport Township, Iowa, line to the Missouri River, thence northerly along the east bank of the Missouri River to its intersection with the line described in paragraph (a) of this section, thence along the line described in paragraph (a) of this section, to the point of beginning.

Section 39 Beaumont, Tex.

The zone adjacent to and commercially a part of Beaumont, Tex., within which transportation by motor vehicle, in interstate or foreign commerce, not under a common control, management, or arrangement for a continuous carriage or shipment to or from a point beyond such zone, is partially exempt from regulation under section 203(b)(8) of the Interstate Commerce Act (49 U.S.C. 303(b)(8)) includes and is comprised of all points as follows:
(a) **The areas which would result by application** of the general formula promulgated in §372.241 for Beaumont, Tex., and in addition thereto.
(b) **That area bounded by a line beginning at that point** where the west bank of Hillebrandt Bayou intersects the line described in paragraph (a) of this section; thence along the west bank of Hillebrandt Bayou to its confluence with Taylors Bayou; thence in a southeasterly direction along the west and south banks of Taylors Bayou to its confluence with the Intracoastal Waterway; thence along the west and north banks of the Intra-coastal Waterway to its confluence with Sabine River and Sabine Lake at a point immediately east of Groves; thence in a northeasterly direction along the north and west banks of Sabine Lake and Sabine River to the Orange-Newton County line; thence westerly along said county line to the west right-of-way line of State Highway 87; thence southerly along the west right-of-way line of State Highway 87 to the north right-of-way line of Interstate Highway 10; thence westerly along the north right-of-way line of Interstate Highway 10 to intersection with the line described in paragraph (a) of this section; thence along the line described in paragraph (a) of this section, to the point of beginning.

Section 40 Metropolitan Government of Nashville and Davidson County, Tenn.

The zone adjacent to and commercially a part of the Metropolitan Government of Nashville and Davidson County, Tenn. within which transportation by motor vehlcle, in interstate or foreign commerce, not under a common control, management, or arrangement for a continuous carriage or shipment to or from a point beyond the zone, is partially exempt from regulation under section 203(b)(8) of the Interstate Commerce Act (49 U.S.C. 303(b)(8)) includes and is comprised of all points as follows:
(a) **The Metropolitan Government** of Nashville and Davidson County itself.
(b) **All of any municipality wholly surrounded,** or so surrounded except for a water boundary, by the Metropolitan Government of Nashville and Davidson County.

Section 41 Consolidated City of Indianapolis, Ind.

The zone adjacent to and commercially a part of the Consolidated City of Indianapolis, Ind., within which transportation by motor vehicle, in interstate or foreign commerce, not under a common control, management, or arrangement for a continuous carriage or shipment to or from a point beyond the zone, is partially exempt from regulation under section 203(b)(8) of the Interstate Commerce Act (49 U.S.C. 303(b)(8)) includes and is comprised of all points as follows:
(a) **The Consolidated City of Indianapolis, Ind., itself.**
(b) **All of any municipality wholly surrounded,** or so surrounded except for a water boundary, by the Consolidated City of Indianapolis.

Appendix G to Subchapter B - Minimum Periodic Inspection Standards

Section 42 Lexington-Fayette Urban County, Ky.

The zone adjacent to and commercially a part of Lexington-Fayette Urban County, Ky., within which transportation by motor vehicle, in interstate or foreign commerce, not under a common control, management, or arrangement for a continuous carriage or shipment to or from a point beyond the zone, is partially exempt from regulation under section 203(b)(8) of the Interstate Commerce Act (49 U.S.C. 303(b)(8)) includes and is comprised of all points as follows:

(a) **Lexington-Fayette Urban County, Ky., itself.**
(b) **All other municipalities and unincorporated areas** within 5 miles of the intersection of U.S. Highway 27 (Nicholasville Road) with the corporate boundary line between Jessamine County, Ky., and Lexington-Fayette Urban County, Ky.

Section 43 Definitions.

For the purposes of this part, the following terms are defined:

(a) **Municipality** means any city, town, village, or borough which has been created by special legislative act or which has been, otherwise, individually incorporated or chartered pursuant to general State laws, or which is recognized as such, under the Constitution or by the laws of the State in which located, and which has a local government. It does not include a town of the township or New England type.
(b) **Contiguous municipalities** means municipalities, as defined in paragraph (a) of this section, which have at some point a common municipal or corporate boundary.
(c) **Unincorporated area** means any area not within the corporate or municipal boundaries of any municipality as defined in paragraph (a) of this section.

Section 44 Commercial zones determined generally, with exceptions.

The commercial zone of each municipality in the United States, with the exceptions indicated in the note at the end of this section, within which the transportation of passengers or property, in interstate or foreign commerce, when not under a common control, management, or arrangement for a continuous carriage or shipment to or from a point without such zone, is exempt from all provisions of Part II, Interstate Commerce Act, except the provisions of section 204 relative to the qualifications and maximum hours of service of employees and safety of operation or standards of equipment shall be deemed to consist of:

(a) **The municipality itself, hereinafter called the base municipality;**
(b) **All municipalities which are contiguous to the base municipality;**
(c) **All other municipalities and all unincorporated areas** within the United States which are adjacent to the base municipality as follows:
  (1) *When the base municipality* has a population less than 2,500 all unincorporated areas within two miles of its corporate limits and all of any other municipality any part of which is within two miles of the corporate limits of the base municipality,
  (2) *When the base municipality* has a population of 2,500 but less than 25,000, all unincorporated areas within 3 miles of its corporate limits and all of any other municipality any part of which is within 3 miles of the corporate limits of the base municipality,
  (3) *When the base municipality* has a population of 25,000 but less than 100,000, all unincorporated areas within 4 miles of its corporate limits and all of any other municipality any part of which is within 4 miles of the corporate limits of the base municipality, and
  (4) *When the base municipality* has a population of 100,000 or more, all unincorporated areas within 5 miles of its corporate limits and all of any other municipality any part of which is within 5 miles of the corporate limits of the base municipality, and
(d) **All municipalities wholly surrounded,** or so surrounded except for a water boundary, by the base municipality, by any municipality contiguous thereto, or by any municipality adjacent thereto which is included in the commercial zone of such base municipality under the provisions of paragraph (c) of this section.

NOTE: Except: Municipalities the commercial zones of which have been or are hereafter individually or specially determined.

Section 45 Controlling distances and population data.

In the application of §372.241:

(a) **Air-line distances or mileages** about corporate limits of municipalities shall be used.
(b) **The population of any municipality** shall be deemed to be the highest figure shown for that municipality in any decennial census since (and including) the 1940 decennial census.

Appendix G to Subchapter B - Minimum Periodic Inspection Standards

(Page 177 in the Driver Edition)

A vehicle does not pass an inspection if it has one of the following defects or deficiencies:

1. **Brake System.**
   a. Service Brakes.
   (1) *Absence of braking action* on any axle required to have brakes upon application of the service brakes (such as missing brakes or brake shoe(s) failing to move upon application of a wedge. S cam, cam, or disc brake).
   (2) *Missing or broken mechanical components* including: shoes, lining pads, springs, anchor pins, spiders, cam rollers, push rods, and air chamber mounting bolts.
   (3) *Loose brake components* including air chambers, spiders, and cam shaft support brackets.
   (4) *Audible air leak at brake chamber* (Example: ruptured diaphragm, loose chamber clamp, etc.).
   (5) *Readjustment limits.* The maximum stroke at which brakes should be readjusted is given below. Any brake 1/4" or more past the readjustment limit or any two brakes less than 1/4" beyond the readjustment limit shall be cause for rejection. Stroke shall be measured with engine off and reservoir pressure of 80 to 90 psi with brakes fully applied.

Bolt Type Brake Chamber Data

Type	Effective area (sq. in.)	Outside dia. (in.)	Maximum stroke at which brakes should be readjusted
A	12	6 15/16	1 3/8
B	24	9 3/16	1 3/4
C	16	8 1/16	1 3/4
D	6	5 1/4	1 1/4
E	9	6 3/16	1 3/8
F	36	11	2 1/4
G	30	9 7/8	2

Rotochamber Data

Type	Effective area (sq. in.)	Outside dia. (in.)	Maximum stroke at which brakes should be readjusted
9	9	4 9/32	1 1/2
12	12	4 13/16	1 1/2
16	16	5 13/32	2
20	20	5 15/16	2
24	24	6 13/32	2
30	30	7 1/16	2 1/4
36	36	7 5/8	2 3/4
50	50	8 7/8	3

Clamp Type Brake Chamber Data

Type	Effective area (sq. in.)	Outside dia. (in.)	Maximum stroke at which brakes should be readjusted
6	6	4 1/2	1 1/4
9	9	5 1/4	1 3/8
12	12	5 11/16	1 3/8
16	16	6 3/8	1 3/4
20	20	6 25/32	1 3/4
24	24	7 7/32	1 3/4[1]
30	30	8 3/32	2
36	36	9	2 1/4

1. (2" for long stroke design).

WEDGE BRAKE DATA. — Movement of the scribe mark on the lining shall not exceed 1/16 inch.

Appendixes

(6) *Brake linings or pads.*
   (a) *Lining or pad is not firmly attached to the shoe;*
   (b) *Saturated with oil, grease, or brake fluid; or*
   (c) *Non-steering axles:* Lining with a thickness less than 1/4 inch at the shoe center for air drum brakes, 1/16 inch or less at the shoe center for hydraulic and electric drum brakes, and less than 1/8 inch for air disc brakes.
   (d) *Steering axles:* Lining with a thickness less than 1/4 inch at the shoe center for drum brakes, less than 1/8 inch for air disc brakes and 1/16 inch or less for hydraulic disc and electric brakes.
(7) *Missing brake on any axle required to have brakes.*
(8) *Mismatch across any power unit steering axle of:*
   (a) *Air chamber sizes.*
   (b) *Slack adjuster length.*

b. *Parking Brake System.* No brakes on the vehicle or combination are applied upon actuation of the parking brake control, including driveline hand controlled parking brakes.

c. *Brake Drum or Rotors.*
(1) *With any external crack or cracks* that open upon brake application (do not confuse short hairline heat check cracks with flexural cracks).
(2) *Any portion of the drum or rotor* missing or in danger of falling away.

d. *Brake Hose.*
(1) *Hose with any damage* extending through the outer reinforcement ply. (Rubber impregnated fabric cover is not a reinforcement ply). (Thermoplastic nylon may have braid reinforcement or color difference between cover and inner tube. Exposure of second color is cause for rejection.
(2) *Bulge or swelling when air pressure is applied.*
(3) *Any audible leaks.*
(4) *Two hoses improperly joined* (such as a splice made by sliding the hose ends over a piece of tubing and clamping the hose to the tube).
(5) *Air hose cracked, broken or crimped.*

e. *Brake Tubing.*
(1) *Any audible leak.*
(2) *Tubing cracked, damaged by heat, broken or crimped.*

f. *Low Pressure Warning Device* missing, inoperative, or does not operate at 55 psi and below, or 1/2 the governor cut-out pressure, whichever is less.

g. *Tractor Protection Valve.* Inoperable or missing tractor protection valve(s) on power unit.

h. *Air Compressor.*
(1) *Compressor drive belts* in condition of impending or probable failure.
(2) *Loose compressor mounting bolts.*
(3) *Cracked, broken or loose pulley.*
(4) *Cracked or broken mounting brackets, braces or adapters.*

i. *Electric Brakes.*
(1) *Absence of braking action* on any wheel required to have brakes.
(2) *Missing or inoperable breakaway braking device.*

j. *Hydraulic Brakes.* (Including Power Assist Over Hydraulic and Engine Drive Hydraulic Booster).
(1) *Master cylinder less than 1/4 full.*
(2) *No pedal reserve with engine running except by pumping pedal.*
(3) *Power assist unit fails to operate.*
(4) *Seeping or swelling brake hose(s) under application of pressure.*
(5) *Missing or inoperative check valve.*
(6) *Has any visually observed* leaking hydraulic fluid in the brake system.
(7) *Has hydraulic hose(s) abraded (chafed)* through outer cover-to-fabric layer.
(8) *Fluid lines or connections* leaking restricted, crimped, cracked or broken.
(9) *Brake failure or low fluid warning light on and/or inoperative.*

k. *Vacuum Systems.* Any vacuum system which:
(1) *Has insufficient vacuum reserve* to permit one full brake application after engine is shut off.
(2) *Has vacuum hose(s) or line(s)* restricted, abraded (chafed) through outer cover to cord ply, crimped, cracked, broken or has collapse of vacuum hose(s) when vacuum is applied.
(3) *Lacks an operative low-vacuum warning device as required.*

2. Coupling Devices.
a. *Fifth Wheels.*
(1) *Mounting to frame.*
   (a) *Any fasteners missing or ineffective.*
   (b) *Any movement between mounting components.*
   (c) *Any mounting angle iron cracked or broken.*
(2) *Mounting plates and pivot brackets.*
   (a) *Any fasteners missing or ineffective.*
   (b) *Any welds or parent metal cracked.*
   (c) *More than 3/8-inch horizontal movement* between pivot bracket pin and bracket.
   (d) *Pivot bracket pin missing or not secured.*
(3) *Sliders.*
   (a) *Any latching fasteners missing or ineffective.*
   (b) *Any fore or aft stop missing or not securely attached.*
   (c) *Movement more than 3/8 inch* between slider bracket and slider base.
   (d) *Any slider component cracked in parent metal or weld.*
(4) *Lower coupler.*
   (a) *Horizontal movement* between the upper and lower fifth wheel halves exceeds 1/2 inch.
   (b) *Operating handle not in closed or locked position.*
   (c) *Kingpin not properly engaged.*
   (d) *Separation between upper and lower coupler* allowing light to show through from side to side.
   (e) *Cracks in the fifth wheel plate.*
   EXCEPTIONS: Cracks in fifth wheel approach ramps and casting shrinkage cracks in the ribs of the body of a cast fifth wheel.
   (f) *Locking mechanism parts* missing, broken, or deformed to the extent the kingpin is not securely held.

b. *Pintle Hooks.*
(1) *Mounting to frame.*
   (a) *Any missing or ineffective fasteners* (a fastener is not considered missing if there is an empty hole in the device but no corresponding hole in the frame or vise versa).
   (b) *Mounting surface cracks* extending from point of attachment (e.g., cracks in the frame at mounting bolt holes).
   (c) *Loose mounting.*
   (d) *Frame cross member* providing pintle hook attachment cracked.
(2) *Integrity.*
   (a) *Cracks anywhere in pintle hook assembly.*
   (b) *Any welded repairs to the pintle hook.*
   (c) *Any part of the horn section reduced by more than 20%.*
   (d) *Latch insecure.*

c. *Drawbar/Towbar Eye.*
(1) *Mounting.*
   (a) *Any cracks in attachment welds.*
   (b) *Any missing or ineffective fasteners.*
(2) *Integrity.*
   (a) *Any cracks.*
   (b) *Any part of the eye reduced by more than 20%.*

d. *Drawbar/Towbar Tongue.*
(1) *Slider (power or manual).*
   (a) *Ineffective latching mechanism.*
   (b) *Missing or ineffective stop.*
   (c) *Movement of more than 1/4 inch between slider and housing.*
   (d) *Any leaking,* air or hydraulic cylinders, hoses, or chambers (other than slight oil weeping normal with hydraulic seals).
(2) *Integrity.*
   (a) *Any cracks.*
   (b) *Movement of 1/4 inch* between subframe and drawbar at point of attachment.

e. *Safety Devices.*
(1) *Safety devices missing.*
(2) *Unattached or incapable of secure attachment.*
(3) *Chains and hooks.*
   (a) *Worn to the extent* of a measurable reduction in link cross section.
   (b) *Improper repairs* including welding, wire, small bolts, rope and tape.
(4) *Cable.*
   (a) *Kinked or broken cable strands.*
   (b) *Improper clamps or clamping.*

Appendix G to Subchapter B - Minimum Periodic Inspection Standards

 f. *Saddle-Mounts.*
  (1) *Method of attachment.*
   (a) *Any missing or ineffective fasteners.*
   (b) *Loose mountings.*
   (c) *Any cracks or breaks in a stress or load bearing member.*
   (d) *Horizontal movement* between upper and lower saddle-mount halves exceeds 1/4 inch.

3. **Exhaust System.**
   a. *Any exhaust system* determined to be leaking at a point forward of or directly below the driver/sleeper compartment.
   b. *A bus exhaust system leaking or discharging to the atmosphere:*
      (1) *Gasoline powered* — excess of 6 inches forward of the rearmost part of the bus.
      (2) *Other than gasoline powered* — in excess of 15 inches forward of the rearmost part of the bus.
      (3) *Other than gasoline powered* — forward of a door or window designed to be opened.
      EXCEPTION: Emergency exits.
   c. *No part of the exhaust system of any motor vehicle* shall be so located as would be likely to result in burning, charring, or damaging the electrical wiring, the fuel supply, or any combustible part of the motor vehicle.

4. **Fuel System.**
   a. *A fuel system with a visible leak at any point.*
   b. *A fuel tank filler cap missing.*
   c. *A fuel tank not securely attached to the motor vehicle* by reason of loose, broken or missing mounting bolts or brackets (some fuel tanks use springs or rubber bushings to permit movement).

5. **Lighting Devices.** All lighting devices and reflectors required by Section 393 shall be operable.

6. **Safe loading.**
   a. *Part(s) of vehicle or condition of loading* such that the spare tire or any part of the load or dunnage can fall onto the roadway.
   b. *Protection Against Shifting Cargo* — Any vehicle without a front end structure or equivalent device as required.

7. **Steering Mechanism.**
   a. *Steering Wheel Free Play* (on vehicles equipped with power steering the engine must be running).

Steering wheel diameter	Manual steering system	Power steering system
16"	2"	4 1/2"
18"	2 1/4"	4 3/4"
20"	2 1/2"	5 1/4"
22"	2 3/4"	5 3/4"

 b. *Steering Column.*
  (1) *Any absence or looseness of U bolt(s) or positioning part(s).*
  (2) *Worn, faulty, or obviously repair welded universal joint(s).*
  (3) *Steering wheel not properly secured.*
 c. *Front Axle Beam and All Steering Components* Other Than Steering Column.
  (1) *Any crack(s).*
  (2) *Any obvious welded repair(s).*
 d. *Steering Gear Box.*
  (1) *Any mounting bolt(s) loose or missing.*
  (2) *Any crack(s) in gear box or mounting brackets.*
 e. *Pitman Arm.* Any looseness of the pitman arm on the steering gear output shaft.
 f. *Power Steering.* Auxiliary power assist cylinder loose.
 g. *Ball and Socket Joints.*
  (1) *Any movement under steering load of a stud nut.*
  (2) *Any motion,* other than rotational, between any linkage member and it's attachment point of more than 1/4 inch.
 h. *Tie Rods and Drag Links.*
  (1) *Loose clamp(s) or clamp bolt(s) on tie rods or drag links.*
  (2) *Any looseness in any threaded joint.*
 i. *Nuts.* Nut(s) loose or missing on tie rods pitman arm, drag link, steering arm, or tie rod arm.
 j. *Steering System.* Any modification or other condition that interferes with free movement of any steering component.

8. **Suspension.**
   a. *Any U bolt(s), spring hanger(s), or other axle positioning part(s)* cracked, broken, loose or missing resulting in shifting of an axle from its normal position. (After a turn, lateral axle displacement is normal with some suspensions. Forward or rearward operation in a straight line will cause the axle to return to alignment).
   b. *Spring Assembly.*
      (1) *Any leaves in a leaf spring assembly broken or missing.*
      (2) *Any broken main leaf* in a leaf spring assembly. (Includes assembly with more than one main spring).
      (3) *Coil spring broken.*
      (4) *Rubber spring missing.*
      (5) *One or more leaves displaced in a manner* that could result in contact with a tire, rim, brake drum or frame.
      (6) *Broken torsion bar spring in a torsion bar suspension.*
      (7) *Deflated air suspension,* i.e., system failure, leak, etc.
   c. *Torque, Radius or Tracking Components.* Any part of a torque, radius or tracking component assembly or any part used for attaching the same to the vehicle frame or axle that is cracked, loose, broken or missing. (Does not apply to loose bushings in torque or track rods.)

9. **Frame.**
   a. *Frame Members.*
      (1) *Any cracked, broken, loose, or sagging frame member.*
      (2) *Any loose or missing fasteners* including fasteners attaching functional component such as engine, transmission, steering gear, suspension, body parts, and fifth wheel.
   b. *Tire and Wheel Clearance.* Any condition, including loading, that causes the body or frame to be in contact with a tire or any part of the wheel assemblies.
   c. (1) *Adjustable Axle Assemblies* (Sliding Subframes). Adjustable axle assembly with locking pins missing or not engaged.

10. **Tires.**
    a. *Any tire on any steering axle of a power unit.*
       (1) *With less than 4/32-inch tread* when measured at any point on a major tread groove.
       (2) *Has body ply or belt material* exposed through the tread or sidewall.
       (3) *Has any tread or sidewall separation.*
       (4) *Has a cut where the ply or belt material is exposed.*
       (5) *Labeled "Not for Highway Use"* or displaying other marking which would exclude use on steering axle.
       (6) *A tube-type radial tire without radial tube stem markings.* These markings include a red band around the tube stem, the word "radial" embossed in metal stems, or the word "radial" molded in rubber stems.
       (7) *Mixing bias and radial tires on the same axle.*
       (8) *Tire flap protrudes through valve slot in rim and touches stem.*
       (9) *Regrooved tire except motor vehicles* used solely in urban or suburban service (see exception in §393.75(e)).
       (10) *Boot, blowout patch or other ply repair.*
       (11) *Weight carried exceeds tire load limit.* This includes overloaded tire resulting from low air pressure.
       (12) *Tire is flat or has noticeable* (e.g., can be heard or felt) *leak.*
       (13) *Any bus equipped with recapped or retreaded tire(s).*
       (14) *So mounted or inflated* that it comes in contact with any part of the vehicle.
    b. *All tires other than those found on the steering axle of a power unit:*
       (1) *Weight carried exceeds tire load limit.* This includes overloaded tire resulting from low air pressure.
       (2) *Tire is flat or has noticeable* (e.g., can be heard or felt) *leak.*
       (3) *Has body ply or belt material* exposed through the tread or sidewall.
       (4) *Has any tread or sidewall separation.*
       (5) *Has a cut where ply or belt material is exposed.*
       (6) *So mounted or inflated* that it comes in contact with any part of the vehicle. (This includes a tire that contacts its mate.)
       (7) *Is marked "Not for highway use"* or otherwise marked and having like meaning.
       (8) *With less than 2/32-inch tread* when measured at any point on a major tread groove.

11. **Wheels and Rims.**
    a. *Lock or Side Ring.* Bent, broken, cracked, improperly seated, sprung or mismatched ring(s).
    b. *Wheels and Rims.* Cracked or broken or has elongated bolt holes.
    c. *Fasteners (both spoke and disc wheels).* Any loose, missing, broken, cracked, stripped or otherwise ineffective fasteners.

Appendixes

d. *Welds.*

(1) *Any cracks in welds* attaching disc wheel disc to rim.

(2) *Any crack in welds* attaching tubeless demountable rim to adapter.

(3) *Any welded repair on aluminum wheel(s) on a steering axle.*

(4) *Any welded repair* other than disc to rim attachment on steel disc wheel(s) mounted on the steering axle.

12. Windshield Glazing.

(Not including a 2-inch border at the top, a 1-inch border at each side and the area below the topmost portion of the steering wheel.) Any crack, discoloration or vision reducing matter except:

(1) *coloring or tinting applied at time of manufacture;*

(2) *any crack not over 1/4-inch wide,* if not intersected by any other crack;

(3) *any damaged area* not more than 3/4 inches in diameter, if not closer than 3 inches to any other such damaged area;

(4) *labels, stickers, decalcomania, etc. (see §393.60 for exceptions).*

13. Windshield Wipers.

Any power unit that has an inoperative wiper, or missing or damaged parts that render it ineffective.

Comparison of Appendix G, and the new North American Uniform Driver-Vehicle Inspection Procedure
(North American Commercial Vehicle Critical Safety Inspection Items and Out-Of-Service Criteria)

The vehicle portion of the FMCSA's North American Uniform Driver Vehicle Inspection Procedure (NAUD VIP) requirements, CVSA's North American Commercial Vehicle Critical Safety Inspection Items and Out-Of-Service Criteria and Appendix G of Subchapter B are similar documents and follow the same inspection procedures. The same items are required to be inspected by each document. FMCSA's and CVSA's out-of-service criteria are intended to be used in random roadside inspections to identify critical vehicle inspection items and provide criteria for placing a vehicle(s) out-of-service. A vehicle(s) is placed out-of-service only when by reason of its mechanical condition or loading it is determined to be so imminently hazardous as to likely cause an accident or breakdown, or when such condition(s) would likely contribute to loss of control of the vehicle(s) by the driver. A certain amount of flexibility is given to the inspecting official whether to place the vehicle out-of-service at the inspection site or if it would be less hazardous to allow the vehicle to proceed to a repair facility for repair. The distance to the repair facility must not exceed 25 miles. The roadside type of inspection, however, does not necessarily mean that a vehicle has to be defect-free in order to continue in service.

In contrast, the Appendix G inspection procedure requires that all items required to be inspected are in proper adjustment, are not defective and function properly prior to the vehicle being placed in service.

Differences Between the Out-Of-Service Criteria & FMCSA's Annual Inspection

1. Brake System.

The Appendix G criteria rejects vehicles with any defective brakes, any air leaks, etc. The out-of-service criteria allows 20% defective brakes on non steering axles and a certain latitude on air leaks before placing a vehicle out-of-service.

2. Coupling Devices.

Appendix G rejects vehicles with any fifth wheel mounting fastener missing or ineffective. The out-of-service criteria allows up to 20% missing or ineffective fasteners on frame mountings and pivot bracket mountings and 25% on slider latching fasteners. The out-of-service criteria also allows some latitude on cracked welds.

3. Exhaust System.

Appendix G follows §393.83 verbatim. The CVSA out-of-service criteria allows vehicles to exhaust forward of the dimensions given in §393.83 as long as the exhaust does not leak or exhaust under the chassis.

4. Fuel System.

Same for Appendix G and the out-of-service criteria.

5. Lighting Devices.

Appendix G requires all lighting devices required by Section 393 to be operative at all times. The out-of-service criteria only requires one stop light and functioning turn signals on the rear most vehicle of a combination vehicle to be operative at all times. In addition one operative headlamp and tail lamp are required during the hours of darkness.

6. Safe Loading.

Same for both Appendix G and the out-of-service criteria.

7. Steering Mechanism.

Steering lash requirements of Appendix G follows the new requirements of §393.209.

8. Suspension.

Appendix G follows the new requirements of §393.207 which does not allow any broken leaves in a leaf spring assembly. The out-of-service criteria allows up to 25% broken or missing leaves before being placed out-of-service.

9. Frame.

The out-of-service criteria allows a certain latitude in frame cracks before placing a vehicle out-of-service. Appendix G follows the new requirements of §393.201 which does not allow any frame cracks.

10. Tires.

Appendix G follows the requirements of §393.75 which requires a tire tread depth of 4/32 inch on power unit steering axles and 2/32 inch on all other axles. The out-of-service criteria only requires 2/32-inch tire tread depth on power unit steering axles and 1/32 inch on all other axles.

11. Wheel and Rims.

The out-of-service criteria allows a certain amount latitude for wheel and rim cracks and missing or defective fasteners. Appendix G meets the requirements of the new §393.205 which does not allow defective wheels and rims non-effective nuts and bolts.

12. Windshield Glazing.

The out-of-service criteria places in a restricted service condition any vehicle that has a crack or discoloration in the windshield area lying within the sweep of the wiper on the drivers side and does not address the remaining area of the windshield. Appendix G addresses requirements for the whole windshield as specified in §393.60.

13. Windshield Wipers.

Appendix G requires windshield wipers to be operative at all times. The out-of-service criteria only requires that the windshield wiper on the driver's side to be inspected during inclement weather.

Medical Advisory Criteria for Evaluation Under 49 CFR Part 391.41

NOTE: Unlike regulations which are codified and have a statutory base, the recommendations in this advisory are simply guidance established to help the medical examiner determine a driver's medical qualifications pursuant to §391.41 of the Federal Motor Carrier Safety Regulations (FMCSRs). The Office of Motor Carrier Research and Standards routinely sends copies of these guidelines to medical examiners to assist them in making an evaluation. The medical examiner may, but is not required to, accept the recommendations. §390.3(d) of the FMCSRs allows employers to have more stringent medical requirements.

§391.41(b)(1) — A person is physically qualified to drive a commercial motor vehicle if that person:

> Has no loss of a foot, leg, hand, or arm, or has been granted a Skill Performance Evaluation (SPE) Certificate pursuant to §391.49. and

§391.41(b)(2) — A person is physically qualified to drive a commercial motor vehicle if that person has no impairment of:

> (i) *A hand or finger which interferes with prehension or power grasping;*
>
> (ii) *An arm, foot, or leg* which interferes with the ability to perform normal tasks associated with operating a commercial motor vehicle;
>
> (iii) *Any other significant limb defect or limitation* which interferes with the ability to perform normal tasks associated with operating a commercial motor vehicle;
>
> (iv) *Has been granted* a Skill Performance Evaluation (SPE) certificate pursuant to §391.49.

A person who suffers loss of a foot, leg, hand or arm or whose limb impairment in any way interferes with the safe performance of normal tasks associated with operating a commercial motor vehicle is subject to the SPE Certification Program pursuant to §391.49, assuming the person is otherwise qualified.

With the advancement of technology, medical aids and equipment, modifications have been developed to compensate for certain disabilities. The SPE Certification Program (formerly the Limb Waiver Program) was designed to allow persons with the loss of a foot or limb or with functional impairment to qualify under the Federal Motor Carrier Safety Regulations (FMCSRs) by use of prosthetic devices or equipment modifications which enable them to safely operate a commercial motor vehicle. Since there are no medical aids equivalent to the original body or limb, certain risks are still present, and thus restrictions may be included on individual SPE certificates when a State Director for the FMCSA determines they are necessary to be consistent with safety and public interest.

If the driver is found otherwise medically qualified (391.41(b)(3) through (13)), the medical examiner must check on the medical certificate that the driver is qualified only if accompanied by a SPE certificate. The driver and the employing motor carrier are subject to appropriate penalty if the driver operates a motor vehicle in interstate or foreign commerce without a current SPE certificate for his/her physical disability.

§391.41(b)(3) — A person is physically qualified to drive a commercial motor vehicle if that person:

> Has no established medical history or clinical diagnosis of diabetes mellitus currently requiring insulin for control.

Diabetes mellitus is a disease which, on occasion, can result in a loss of consciousness or disorientation in time and space. Individuals who require insulin for control have conditions which can get out of control by the use of too much or too little insulin, or food intake not consistent with the insulin dosage. Incapacitation may occur from symptoms of hyperglycemic or hypoglycemic reactions (drowsiness, semiconsciousness, diabetic coma, or insulin shock).

The administration of insulin is within itself, a complicated process requiring insulin, syringe, needle, alcohol sponge and a sterile technique. Factors related to long-haul commercial motor vehicle operations such as fatigue, lack of sleep, poor diet, emotional conditions, stress, and concomitant illness, compound the diabetic problem. Because of these inherent dangers, the FMCSA has consistently held that a diabetic who uses insulin for control does not meet the minimum physical requirements of the FMCSRs.

Hypoglycemic drugs, taken orally, are sometimes prescribed for diabetic individuals to help stimulate natural body production of insulin. If the condition can be controlled by the use of oral medication and diet, then an individual may be qualified under the present rule.

See Conference Report on Diabetic Disorders and Commercial Drivers and Insulin-Using Commercial Motor Vehicle Drivers at: http://www.fmcsa.dot.gov/rulesregs/medreports.htm.

§391.41(b)(4) — A person is physically qualified to drive a commercial motor vehicle if that person:

> Has no current clinical diagnosis of myocardial infarction, angina pectoris, coronary insufficiency, thrombosis, or
>
> Any other cardiovascular disease of a variety known to be accompanied by syncope, dyspnea, collapse, or congestive cardiac failure.

The term "has no current clinical diagnosis of" is specifically designed to encompass (1) a current cardiovascular condition; and/or (2) a cardiovascular condition which has not fully stabilized regardless of the time limit. The term "known to be accompanied by" is designed to include a clinical diagnosis of a cardiovascular disease (1) which is accompanied by symptoms of syncope, dyspnea, collapse, or congestive cardiac failure; and/or (2) which is likely to cause syncope, dyspnea, collapse, or congestive cardiac failure.

It is the intent of the Federal Motor Carrier Safety Regulations to render unqualified, a driver who has a current cardiovascular disease which is accompanied by and/or likely to cause symptoms of syncope, dyspnea, collapse, or congestive cardiac failure. However, the subjective decision of whether the nature and severity of an individual's condition will likely cause symptoms of cardiovascular insufficiency is on an individual basis and qualification rests with the medical examiner and the motor carrier. In those cases where there is an occurrence of cardiovascular insufficiency (myocardial infarction, thrombosis, etc.), it is suggested that, before a driver is certified, he/she have a normal resting and stress EKG, no residual complications, no physical limitations, and is taking no medication likely to interfere with safe driving.

Coronary artery bypass surgery and pacemaker implantation are remedial procedures and thus not unqualifying. Implantable cardioverter defibrillators are disqualifying due to risk of syncope. Coumadin is a medical treatment which can improve the health and safety of the driver and should not, by its use, medically disqualify the commercial driver. The emphasis should be on the underlying medical condition(s) which require treatment and the general health of the driver. FMCSA should be contacted at (202) 366-1790 for additional recommendations regarding the physical qualification of drivers on coumadin.

(See Cardiovascular Advisory Panel Guidelines for the Medical Examination of Commercial Motor Vehicle Drivers at: http://www.fmcsa.dot.gov/rulesregs/medreports.htm).

§391.41(b)(5) — A person is physically qualified to drive a commercial motor vehicle if that person:

> Has no established medical history or clinical diagnosis of a respiratory dysfunction likely to interfere with his/her ability to control and drive a commercial motor vehicle safely.

Since a driver must be alert at all times, any change in his or her mental state is in direct conflict with highway safety. Even the slightest impairment in respiratory function under emergency conditions (when greater oxygen supply is necessary for performance) may be detrimental to safe driving.

There are many conditions that interfere with oxygen exchange and may result in incapacitation, including emphysema, chronic asthma, carcinoma, tuberculosis, chronic bronchitis and sleep apnea. If the medical examiner detects a respiratory dysfunction, that in any way is likely to interfere with the driver's ability to safely control and drive a commercial motor vehicle, the driver must be referred to a specialist for further evaluation and therapy.

Anticoagulation therapy for deep vein thrombosis and/or pulmonary thromboembolism is not unqualifying once optimum dose is achieved, provided lower extremity venous examinations remain normal and the treating physician gives a favorable recommendation.

See Conference on Pulmonary/Respiratory Disorders and Commercial Drivers at: http://www.fmcsa.dot.gov/rulesregs/medreports.htm.

§391.41(b)(6) — A person is physically qualified to drive a commercial motor vehicle if that person:

> Has no current clinical diagnosis of high blood pressure likely to interfere with his/her ability to operate a commercial motor vehicle safely.

Hypertension alone is unlikely to cause sudden collapse; however, the likelihood increases when target organ damage, particularly cerebral vascular disease is present. This advisory criteria is based on FMCSA's Cardiovascular Advisory Guidelines for the Examination of CMV Drivers, which used the Sixth Report of the Joint National Committee on Prevention, Detection, Evaluation, and Treatment of High Blood Pressure (1997).

Stage 1 hypertension corresponds to a systolic BP of 140-159 mmHg and/or a diastolic BP of 90-99 mmHg. The driver with a BP in this range is at low risk for hypertension-related acute incapacitation and may be medically certified to drive for a one-year period. Certification examinations should be done annually thereafter and should be less than 140/90. If less than 160/100, certification may be extended one time for three months.

A blood pressure of 160-179 systolic and/or 100-109 diastolic is considered **Stage 2** hypertension, and the driver is not necessarily unqualified during evaluation and institution of treatment. The driver is given a one time certification of three months to reduce his or her blood pressure to less than 140/90. A blood pressure in this range is an absolute indication for antihypertensive drug therapy. Provided treatment is well tolerated and the driver demonstrates a BP value of less than 140/90, he or she may be certified for one year from the date of the initial exam. The driver is certified annually thereafter.

A blood pressure at or greater than 180 (systolic) and 110 (diastolic) is considered **Stage 3**, high risk for an acute BP-related event. The driver may not be qualified, even temporarily, until reduced to less than 140/90 and treatment is well tolerated. The driver may be certified for 6 months and biannually (every 6 months) thereafter if at recheck BP is less than 140/90.

Annual recertification is recommended if the medical examiner does not know the severity of hypertension prior to treatment.

An elevated blood pressure finding should be confirmed by at least two subsequent measurements on different days.

Treatment includes non-pharmacologic and pharmacologic modalities as well as counseling to reduce other risk factors. Most antihypertensive medications also have side effects, the importance of which must be judged on an individual basis. Individuals must be alerted to the hazards of these medications while driving. Side effects of somnolence or syncope are particularly undesirable in commercial drivers.

Secondary hypertension is based on the above stages.

Evaluation is warranted if patient is persistently hypertensive on maximal or near-maximal doses of 2-3 pharmacologic agents. Some causes of secondary hypertension may be amenable to surgical intervention or specific pharmacologic therapy. (See Cardiovascular Advisory Panel Guidelines for the Medical Examination of Commercial Motor Vehicle Drivers at: http://www.fmcsa.dot.gov/rulesregs/medreports.htm).

Reading	Category	Expiration Date	Recertification
140-159/ 90-99	Stage 1	1 year	1 year if <140/90. One-time certificate for 3 months if 140-159/90-99.
160-179/ 100-109	Stage 2	One-time certificate for 3 months	1 year from date of exam if <140/90.
≥ 180/110	Stage 3	Disqualified	6 months from date of exam if <140/90, then every 6 months if <140/90.

Driver qualified if <140/90.

A person is physically qualified to drive a commercial motor vehicle if that person:

Has no established medical history or clinical diagnosis of a rheumatic, arthritic, orthopedic, muscular, neuromuscular or vascular disease which interferes with the ability to control and operate a commercial motor vehicle.

§391.41(b)(7) — A person is physically qualified to drive a commercial motor vehicle if that person:

Has no established medical history or clinical diagnosis of a rheumatic, arthritic, orthopedic, muscular, neuromuscular or vascular disease which interferes with his/her ability to control and operate a commercial motor vehicle safely.

Certain diseases are known to have acute episodes of transient muscle weakness, poor muscular coordination (ataxia), abnormal sensations (paresthesia), decreased muscle tone (hypotonia), visual disturbances and pain which may be suddenly incapacitating. With each recurring episode, these symptoms may become more pronounced and remain for longer periods of time. Other diseases have more insidious onsets and display symptoms of muscle wasting (atrophy), swelling and paresthesia which may not suddenly incapacitate a person but may restrict his/her movements and eventually interfere with the ability to safely operate a motor vehicle. In many instances these diseases are degenerative in nature or may result in deterioration of the involved area.

Once the individual has been diagnosed as having a rheumatic, arthritic, orthopedic, muscular, neuromuscular or vascular disease, then he/she has an established history of that disease. The physician, when examining an individual, should consider the following:

(1) *The nature and severity* of the individual's condition (such as sensory loss or loss of strength;

(2) *The degree of limitation present (such as range of motion;*

(3) *The likelihood of progressive limitation* (not always present initially but manifest itself over time;

(4) *The likelihood of sudden incapacitation.*

If severe functional impairment exists, the driver does not qualify. In cases where more frequent monitoring is required, a certificate for a shorter period of time may be issued.

See Conference on Neurological Disorders and Commercial Drivers at: http://www.dot.gov/rulesregs/medreports.htm.

§391.41(b)(8) — A person is physically qualified to drive a commercial motor vehicle if that person:

Has no established medical history or clinical diagnosis of epilepsy; or any other condition which is likely to cause the loss of consciousness; or any loss of ability to control a commercial motor vehicle.

Epilepsy is a chronic functional disease characterized by seizures or episodes that occur without warning, resulting in loss of voluntary control which may lead to loss of consciousness and/or seizures. Therefore, the following drivers cannot be qualified:

(1) *a driver who has a medical history of epilepsy: or*

(2) *a driver who has a current clinical diagnosis of epilepsy; or*

(3) *a driver who is taking antiseizure medication.*

If an individual has had a sudden episode of a nonepileptic seizure or loss of consciousness of unknown cause which did not require antiseizure medication, the decision as to whether that person's condition will likely cause the loss of consciousness or loss of ability to control a commercial motor vehicle is made on an individual basis by the medical examiner in consultation with the treating physician. Before certification is considered, it is suggested that a 6-month waiting period elapse from the time of the episode. Following the waiting period, it is suggested that the individual have a complete neurological examination. If the results of the examination are negative and antiseizure medication is not required, then the driver may be qualified.

In those individual cases where a driver had a seizure or an episode of loss of consciousness that resulted from a known medical condition (e.g., drug reaction, high temperature, acute infectious disease, dehydration, or acute metabolic disturbance), certification should be deferred until the driver has fully recovered from that condition, has no existing residual complications, and is not taking antiseizure medication.

Drivers with a history of epilepsy/seizures off antiseizure medication and seizure-free for 10 years may be qualified to operate a CMV in interstate commerce. Interstate drivers with a history of a single unprovoked seizure may be qualified to drive a CMV in interstate commerce if seizure-free and off antiseizure medication for a 5-year period or more.

See Conference on Neurological Disorders and Commercial Drivers at: http://www.fmcsa.dot.gov/rulesregs/medreports.htm.

§391.41(b)(9) — A person is physically qualified to drive a commercial motor vehicle if that person:

Has no mental, nervous, organic, or functional disease or psychiatric disorder likely to interfere with the driver's ability to drive a commercial motor vehicle safely.

Emotional or adjustment problems contribute directly to an individual's level of memory, reasoning, attention, and judgment. These problems often underlie physical disorders. A variety of functional disorders can cause drowsiness, dizziness, confusion, weakness, or paralysis that may lead to incoordination, inattention, loss of functional control and susceptibility to crashes while driving. Physical fatigue, headache, impaired coordination, recurring physical ailments, and chronic "nagging" pain may be present to such a degree that certification for commercial driving is inadvisable. Somatic and psychosomatic complaints should be thoroughly examined when determining an individual's overall fitness to drive. Disorders of a periodically incapacitating nature, even in the early stages of development, may warrant disqualification.

Many bus and truck drivers have documented that "nervous trouble" related to neurotic, personality, emotional or adjustment problems is responsible for a significant fraction of their preventable crashes. The degree to which an individual is able to appreciate, evaluate and adequately respond to environmental strain and emotional stress is critical when assessing an individual's mental alertness and flexibility to cope with the stresses of commercial motor vehicle driving.

When examining the driver, it should be kept in mind that individuals who live under chronic emotional upsets may have deeply ingrained maladaptive or erratic behavior patterns. Excessively antagonistic, instinctive, impulsive, openly aggressive, paranoid or severely depressed behavior greatly interfere with the driver's ability to drive safely. Those individuals who are highly susceptible to frequent states of emotional instability (schizophrenia, affective psychoses, paranoia, anxiety or depressive neurosis) may warrant disqualification.

Careful consideration should be given to the side effects and interactions of medications in the overall qualification determination. See Psychiatric Conference Report for specific recommendations on the use of these medications and potential hazards for driving.

See Conference on Psychiatric Disorders and Commercial Drivers at: http://www.fmcsa.dot/rulesregs/medreports.htm.

§391.41(b)(10) — A person is physically qualified to drive a commercial motor vehicle if that person:

Has a distant visual acuity of at least 20/40 (Snellen) in each eye with or without corrective lenses, or visual acuity separately corrected to 20/40 (Snellen) or better with corrective lenses; and

distant binocular acuity of at least 20/40 (Snellen) in both eyes with or without corrective lenses; and

field of vision of at least 70 degrees in the horizontal meridian in each eye; and

the ability to recognize the colors of traffic signals and devices showing standard red, green, and amber.

The term "ability to recognize the colors of" is interpreted to mean if a person can recognize and distinguish among traffic control signals and devices showing standard red, green, and amber, he/she meets the minimum standard, even though he/she may have some type of color perception deficiency. If certain color perception tests are administered (such as Ishihara, Pseudoisochromatic, Yarn, etc.), and doubtful findings are discovered, a controlled test using signal red, green, and amber may be employed to determine the driver's ability to recognize these colors.

Contact lenses are permissible if there is sufficient evidence to indicate that the driver has good tolerance and is well adapted to their use. Use of a contact lens in one eye for distant visual acuity and another lens in the other eye for near vision is not acceptable, nor are telescopic lenses acceptable for driving commercial motor vehicles.

If an individual meets the criteria by the use of glasses or contact lenses, the following statement shall appear on the Medical Examiner's Certificate:

"Qualified only if wearing corrective lenses." CMV drivers who do not meet the Federal vision standards may call (202) 366-1790.

See Visual Disorders and Commercial Drivers at: http://www.fmcsa.dot.gov/rulesregs/medreports.htm.

§391.41(b)(11) — A person is physically qualified to drive a commercial motor vehicle if that person:

> First perceives a forced whispered voice in the better ear at not less than five feet with or without the use of a hearing aid, or
>
> if tested by use of an audiometric device, does not have an average hearing loss in the better ear greater than 40 decibels at 500 Hz, 1,000 Hz and 2,000 Hz with or without a hearing aid when the audiometric device is calibrated to the American National Standard [formerly American Standard Association (ASA)] Z24.5 — 1951.

Since the prescribed standard under the FMCSRs is the American National Standards Institute (ANSI), it may be necessary to convert the audiometric results from the International Standards Organization (ISO) standard to the ANSI standard. Instructions are included on the Medical Examination Report form.

If an individual meets the criteria by using a hearing aid, the driver must wear that hearing aid and have it in operation at all times while driving. Also, the driver must be in possession of a spare power source for the hearing aid.

For the whispered voice test, the individual should be stationed at least 5 feet from the examiner with the ear being tested turned toward the examiner. The other ear is covered. Using the breath which remains after a normal expiration, the examiner whispers words or random numbers such as 66, 18, 23, etc. The examiner should not use only sibilants (s-sounding test materials). If the individual fails the whispered voice test, the audiometric test should be administered.

If an individual meets the criteria by the use of a hearing aid, the following statement must appear on the Medical Examiner's Certificate "Qualified only when wearing a hearing aid."

See Hearing Disorders and Commercial Motor Vehicle Drivers at: http://www.fmcsa.dot.gov/rulesregs/medreports.htm.

§391.41(b)(12) — A person is physically qualified to drive a commercial motor vehicle if that person:

> Does not use a controlled substance identified in 21 CFR 1308.11 Schedule I, an amphetamine, a narcotic, or any other habit-forming drug.
>
> *EXCEPTION:* A driver may use such a substance or drug, if the substance or drug is prescribed by a licensed medical practitioner who is familiar with the driver's medical history and assigned duties; and has advised the driver that the prescribed substance or drug will not adversely affect the driver's ability to safely operate a commercial motor vehicle.

This exception does not apply to the use of methadone.

The intent of the medical certification process is to medically evaluate a driver to ensure that the driver has no medical condition which interferes with the safe performance of driving tasks on a public road. If a driver uses a Schedule I drug or other substance, an amphetamine, a narcotic, or any other habit-forming drug, it may be cause for the driver to be found medically unqualified. Motor carriers are encouraged to obtain a practitioner's written statement about the effects on transportation safety of the use of a particular drug.

A test for controlled substances is not required as part of this biennial certification process. The FMCSA or the driver's employer should be contacted directly for information on controlled substances and alcohol testing under Part 382 of the FMCSRs.

The term "uses" is designed to encompass instances of prohibited drug use determined by a physician through established medical means. This may or may not involve body fluid testing. If body fluid testing takes place, positive test results should be confirmed by a second test of greater specificity. The term "habit-forming" is intended to include any drug or medication generally recognized as capable of becoming habitual, and which may impair the user's ability to operate a commercial motor vehicle safely.

The driver is medically unqualified for the duration of the prohibited drug(s) use and until a second examination shows the driver is free from the prohibited drug(s) use. Recertification may involve a substance abuse evaluation, the successful completion of a drug rehabilitation program, and a negative drug test result. Additionally, given that the certification period is normally two years, the examiner has the option to certify for a period of less than two years if this examiner determines more frequent monitoring is required.

See Conference on Neurological Disorders and Commercial Drivers and Conference on Psychiatric Disorders and Commercial Drivers at: http://www.fmcsa.dot.gov/rulesregs/medreports.htm.

§391.41(b)(13) — A person is physically qualified to drive a commercial motor vehicle if that person:

> Has no current clinical diagnosis of alcoholism.

The term "current clinical diagnosis" is specifically designed to encompass a current alcoholic illness or those instances where the individual's physical condition has not fully stabilized, regardless of the time element. If an individual shows signs of having an alcohol-use problem, he or she should be referred to a specialist. After counseling and/or treatment, he or she may be considered for certification.

Interstate Motor Operations

OVERVIEW OF FEDERAL AND STATE REGULATIONS CONCERNING INTERSTATE MOTOR OPERATIONS

FEBRUARY 2004

INTRODUCTION:

This booklet is designed to assist persons who are interested in interstate surface transportation businesses. The rules, regulations, and requirements governing interstate surface transportation are administered by two agencies of the federal government and applicable state agencies. The federal agencies are the Federal Motor Carrier Safety Administration and the Surface Transportation Board.

The intent of this booklet is to furnish a brief summary of interstate motor carrier rules, regulations, and requirements to those individuals new to the industry.

FEDERAL MOTOR CARRIER SAFETY ADMINISTRATION TELEPHONE NUMBERS

Automated Response System - (202) 358-7000
USDOT Registration Number - (703) 280-4001
Insurance Filings - (202) 358-2423
Hazardous Materials Registration (RSPA) - (202) 366-4109 or 1-800-467-4922
Status of Applications - (202) 366-9805
Questions on hazardous materials (RSPA) - (202) 366-4488 or 1-800-467-4922
DOT Safety Rating or Form MCS-150 - (800) 832-5660
Commercial Driver's License - (202) 366-5014

STATE REGULATIONS:

Before beginning new or expanded interstate operations, you must contact the appropriate regulatory agencies in all states in and through which you will conduct business to obtain information regarding state rules applicable to interstate motor operations. It is your responsibility to comply with registration, fuel tax, and other state regulations and procedures.

Transportation agencies in 38 states register interstate authorities under the single state registration system (SSRS). Under the SSRS, as an interstate motor carrier you may register your operation by contacting your base state (principal place of business) and, for one fee, register for all states in which operations will be conducted. If your home state does not participate in the SSRS, you may contact a neighboring state and declare that state your "base" for registration purposes. State SSRS contacts are listed on the following pages.

Fuel taxes are levied by the individual states. For more information you must contact the state agency which handles fuel taxes.

Worker compensation is another area regulated by the individual states. Rules regarding workers' compensation vary greatly from state to state. You may find it useful to contact the state insurance board for the state in which your business is located. The respective insurance boards should be able to furnish you with detailed information on workers' compensation rules and regulations. These offices normally are located in the state capital, and their telephone numbers may be obtained from the state government section of telephone directories or through local telephone information operators.

Addendum — Useful Addresses and Telephone Numbers

USEFUL ADDRESSES AND TELEPHONE NUMBERS FOR STATE AGENCIES

Following is a list of state motor carrier regulatory bodies. Additionally, the address and telephone number for SSRS information is included for those 38 states that participate in the program (asterisk denotes participating state). Should you have difficulty reaching a particular state office, consult your local telephone directory or call the state government information operator.

STATE REGULATORY BODY

ALABAMA
Public Service Commission,
Insurance and Registration Section
P.O. Box 304260
Montgomery, AL 36130
100 North Union Street, Room 980
Montgomery, AL 36104
(334) 242-5176
Fax (334) 242-2534

ALASKA
Not Regulated

ARIZONA
Department of Transportation
Motor Vehicle Division
P.O. Box 2100
Mail Drop 555M
Phoenix, AZ 85001
(602) 255-0072

ARKANSAS*
Highway & Transportation Department,
Motor Carrier Authority Unit
P.O. Box 8051
Little Rock, AR 72203-8051
(501) 569-2358
SSRS: Same agency, same address and telephone number

CALIFORNIA*
(Passengers only)
Passenger & Household Goods Carriers: Public Utilities Commission License Section
SSRS Unit, 505 Van Ness Avenue
San Francisco, CA 94102-3298
(415) 703-2177
(All other Motor Carriers)
Department of Motor Vehicles IRP/SSRS Unit, MS-G875
2415 First Ave.
Sacramento, CA 95818-2606
P.O. Box 932370
Sacramento, CA 94232-3700
(916) 657-6636

COLORADO*
Public Utilities Commission
Logan Tower OL2
1580 Logan Street
Denver, CO 80203
(303) 894-2000
SSRS: Same address
(303) 894-2867

CONNECTICUT*
Department of Transportation,
Bureau of Public Transportation
P.O. Box 317546
Newington, CT 06131-7546
(860) 594-2865
SSRS: DMV Interstate Registration Plan
60 State Street
Wethersfield, CT 06161-1010
(860) 263-5281

DELAWARE
Department of Transportation
Property: Not Regulated
Passengers: Transportation Authority
P.O. Box 778
Dover, DE 19903
(302) 744-2701

DISTRICT OF COLUMBIA
Property: Office of Public Space
941 N. Capitol St. NE
Washington, DC 20002
(202) 442-4670
Passengers:
Washington Metropolitan Area
Transit Commission
1828 L Street, N.W., Suite 703
Washington, DC 20036
(202) 331-1671
Fax (202) 653-2179

FLORIDA
Not Regulated

GEORGIA*
Department of Motor Vehicle Safety
2206 East View Parkway
Conyers, GA 30013
(404) 362-6484
SSRS: Same address and telephone number

HAWAII
Public Utilities Commission
465 South King Street, Suite 103
Honolulu, HI 96813
(808) 586-2020

IDAHO*
Department of Transportation
P.O. Box 7129
Boise, ID 83707-1129
(208) 334-8611
Fax (208) 334-2006
SSRS: Same address and telephone number

ILLINOIS*
Commerce Commission
527 East Capitol Avenue
Springfield, IL 62701
(217) 782-4654
SSRS: Same address and telephone number

INDIANA*
Department of Revenue
5252 Decatur Blvd., Suite R
Indianapolis, IN 46241
(317) 615-7200
SSRS: Same address and telephone number

IOWA*
Department of Transportation,
Motor Carrier Services
P.O. Box 10382
Des Moines, IA 50306-0382
(515) 237-3224
SSRS: Same address and telephone number

KANSAS*
State Corporation Commission
1500 S.W. Arrowhead Road
Topeka, KS 66604-4027
(785) 271-3100
SSRS: Same address
(785) 271-3145

KENTUCKY*
Transportation Cabinet, Div. of Motor Carriers
P.O. Box 2007
Frankfort, KY 40602
(502) 564-4540
SSRS: Same address and telephone number

LOUISIANA*
Public Service Commission
P.O. Box 91154
Baton Rouge, LA 70821-9154
(225) 342-4439
SSRS: Same address and telephone number

MAINE*
Department of Motor Vehicles,
Commercial Vehicle Section
29 State House Station
Augusta, ME 04333-0029
(207) 624-9000 ext. 52127
SSRS: Same address and telephone number

MARYLAND
Public Service Commission, Trans. Div.
6 St. Paul St.
Baltimore, MD 21202
(410) 767-8128

MASSACHUSETTS*
Dept. of Telecommunications and Energies
Transportation Division
1 South Station
Boston, MA 02110
(617) 305-3559
SSRS: Same address and telephone number

MICHIGAN*
Public Service Commission
6545 Mercantile Way
Lansing, MI 48911
P.O. Box 30221
Lansing, MI 48909
(517) 241-6030
SSRS: Same agency and address
(517) 241-6043

MINNESOTA*
Department of Transportation,
Freight & Commercial Vehicle Operations
1110 Centre Pointe Curve, MS420
Mendota Heights, MN 55120
(651) 405-6060
SSRS: Same address and telephone number

(continued)

Useful Addresses and Telephone Numbers — Addendum

MISSISSIPPI*
Department of Transportation
412 E. Woodrow Wilson
Jackson, MS 39216
(601) 359-9740
SSRS: Same address and telephone number

MISSOURI*
MoDOT Motor Carrier Services
1320 Creek Trail Drive
Jefferson City, MO 65109
P.O. Box 893
Jefferson City, MO 65102
(866) 831-6277 Option 3
SSRS: Same address and telephone number

MONTANA*
Public Service Commission
1701 Prospect Avenue
P.O. Box 202601
Helena, MT 59620-2601
(406) 444-6199
SSRS: Same address and telephone number

NEBRASKA*
Department of Motor Vehicles,
Motor Carrier Services Division
301 Centennial Mall South
Lincoln, NE 68508-2529
(402) 471-4435 or (888) 622-1222
SSRS: Same address and telephone number

NEVADA
Passenger & Household Goods Carriers:
Transportation Services Authority
75 Bank Street
Sparks, NV 89431
(775) 688-2823
Property: DMV
555 Wright Way
Carson City, NV 89711
(775) 684-4711

NEW HAMPSHIRE*
Department of Safety, Bureau of Common Carriers
33 Hazen Drive
Concord, NH 03305
(603) 271-2447
SSRS: Same address and telephone number

NEW JERSEY
Department of Transportation
Motor Vehicle Services
1035 Parkway Ave.
Trenton, NJ 08625
(609) 292-6500

NEW MEXICO*
Public Regulations Commission, Trans. Div.
P.O. Box 1269
Santa Fe, NM 87504-1269
(505) 827-4519
SSRS: Same address
(505) 476-0122 or
(505) 827-4517

NEW YORK*
Dept. of Trans., Motor Carrier & Freight Safety
Building 7-A Room 501
1220 Washington Ave.
Albany, NY 12232
(518) 457-1016
SSRS: Same address and telephone number

NORTH CAROLINA*
Department of Trans., Div. of Motor Vehicles
1425 Rock Quarry Rd., Suite 100
Raleigh, NC 27610
(919) 861-3720
SSRS: Same address and telephone number

NORTH DAKOTA*
Department of Transportation
608 E. Boulevard Avenue
Bismarck, ND 58505-0780
(701) 328-2500
SSRS: Same address
(701) 328-2725

OHIO*
Public Utilities Commission, Trans. Dept.
180 East Broad Street, 14th Floor
Columbus, OH 43215
(614) 466-3392
SSRS: Same address and telephone number

OKLAHOMA*
Corporation Commission
Jim Thorpe Office Building
2101 North Lincoln Boulevard, Suite 312
Oklahoma City, OK 73105
(405) 521-2251
SSRS: Same address and telephone number

OREGON
Department of Transportation, Motor Carrier Div.
550 Capitol Street N.E.
Salem, OR 97301
(503) 378-6699

PENNSYLVANIA
Public Utility Commission, Bureau of Trans.
Safety Division
3rd Floor Keystone Bldg.
P.O. Box 3265
Harrisburg, PA 17105-3265
(717) 772-2254

RHODE ISLAND*
Public Utilities Commission, Motor Carrier Div.
89 Jefferson Boulevard
Warwick, RI 02888-1046
(401) 941-4500
SSRS: Same address and telephone number

SOUTH CAROLINA*
Department of Public Safety,
Motor Carrier Services Office
10311 Wilson Blvd.
P.O. Box 1498
Blythewood, SC 29016
(803) 896-3870
SSRS: Same address and telephone number

SOUTH DAKOTA*
Public Utilities Commission, Transportation Div.
500 East Capitol Avenue
Pierre, SD 57501
(605) 773-5280
SSRS: Same address and telephone number

TENNESSEE*
Tennessee Department of Safety
1148 Foster Avenue
Cooper Hall
Nashville, TN 37210
(615) 687-2285
SSRS: Same address and telephone number

TEXAS*
Department of Transportation, Motor Carrier Div.
P.O. Box 12984
Austin, TX 78711
(800) 299-1700 Option 2, 1
SSRS: Same address and telephone number

UTAH*
Department of Commerce
Motor Carrier Division
4501 South 2700 West
Salt Lake City, UT 84119
Box 148240
Salt Lake City, UT 84114-8240
(801) 965-4205
SSRS: Same address
(802) 965-4279

VERMONT
Property: Not regulated
Passengers: Transportation Board
120 State Street
Montpelier, VT 05603
(802) 828-4824

VIRGINIA*
Department of Transportation, Motor Carrier Div.
2300 W. Broad St.
Richmond, VA 23220
P.O. Box 27412
Richmond, VA 23269
(866) 368-5463
SSRS: Same address and telephone number

WASHINGTON*
Utilities and Trans. Licensing Services Section
1300 S. Evergreen Park Dr. SW
Olympia, WA 98504
(360) 664-1222
SSRS: Same address and telephone number

WEST VIRGINIA*
Public Service Comm., Motor Carrier Division
201 Brooks St.
P.O. Box 812
Charleston, WV 25323
(304) 340-0346
SSRS: Same address and telephone number

WISCONSIN*
Dept. of Trans., Div. of Motor Vehicles
P.O. Box 7967
Madison, WI 53707-7967
(608) 266-1356
SSRS: Same address and telephone number

WYOMING
Dept. of Trans., Motor Vehicle Services, Reg. Sec.
5300 Bishop Boulevard
Cheyenne, WY 82009-3340
(307) 777-4829

Motor Carrier Safety Progress Report
Federal Motor Carrier Safety Administration
(as of September 30, 2005)

SAFETY OUTCOMES	2002	2003	2004
• Large Truck Fatalities	4,939	4,986	5,190
• Large Truck Fatality Rate (per 100 million truck vehicle miles traveled)	2.3	2.3	*
• Intercity Bus Fatalities	54	36	58
• Large Truck Injuries	130,000	122,000	116,000
• Large Truck Injury Rate (per 100 million truck vehicle miles traveled)	60.5	56.6	*

Sources: NHTSA (fatalities and injuries), FHWA (vehicle miles traveled).
* Data not available.

DATA QUALITY	2003	2004
ACCURACY		
• Percentage of FMCSA reported crashes matched to a carrier	86%	87%
• Percentage of FMCSA reported inspections matched to a carrier	96%	97%
TIMELINESS		
• Average time to upload a crash to FMCSA	136 days	84 days
• Average time to upload an inspection to FMCSA	26 days	15 days
COMPLETENESS		
• Percentage of fatal crashes reported to FMCSA	93%	92%

PROGRAM OUTPUTS	FY 2003	FY 2004	FY 2005
INCREASING ENFORCEMENT			
• Number of Federal Compliance Reviews	9,068	7,637	7,943
• Number of State Compliance Reviews	3,744	3,745	4,560
• Number of enforcement cases initiated	5,753	5,192	4,427
- Unsat/Unfit out-of-service orders	316	415	596
• Roadside inspections, trucks	2,991,788	2,946,630	2,887,837
• Roadside inspections, buses	42,377	42,790	47,467
• States participating in PRISM	25	37	42
INCREASING SAFETY AND SECURITY AWARENESS			
• New Entrant Safety Audits:			
- Total	7,205	25,316	33,720**
- Federal	4,119	10,013	10,065
- State	2,998	15,031	22,091
- Seminar	88	272	567
• ITS-CVO: Number of Federal, State, and industry attendees at briefings	2,703	2,205	1,235
• Web site visits to Analysis and Information (A&I) Online	935,865	1,417,701	1,674,741
• HM Security Sensitivity Visits (SSVs)	1,797	1,476	2,378
• Federal/State personnel training:			
- For Compliance Reviews	93	93	176
- For roadside inspections	2,790	3,586	3,793
- For hazardous materials	1,906	2,611	2,149
- For in-service	199	1,332	1,910
IMPROVING SAFETY INFORMATION AND TECHNOLOGY			
• States participating in CVISN (In Planning, Design, Deployment)	7, 6, 34	8, 3, 31	8, 1, 33
• States that have completed Core CVISN Capability Deployment	4	9	9
RULEMAKINGS (July-September 2005)			

• Transportation of Household Goods; RIN 2126-AA32; FMCSA-1997-2979; Consumer Protection Regulations; Final Rule (July 12, 2005).
• Parts and Accessories Necessary for Safe Operation; RIN 2126-AA61; FMCSA-1997-2364; General Amendments; Final Rule (August 15, 2005).
• Hours of Service of Drivers; RIN 2126-AA90; FMCSA-2004-19608; Final Rule (August 25, 2005).

** Includes safety audits conducted by contractors.

BRIDGE FORMULA WEIGHTS

Three questions are addressed by this section with regard to the Bridge Formula: What is it? Why is it necessary? How is it used?

WHAT IS IT?

$$W = 500 \left(\frac{LN}{N-1} + 12N + 36 \right)$$

W = the maximum weight in pounds that can be carried on a group of two or more axles to the nearest 500 pounds.

L = the distance in feet between the outer axles of any two or more consecutive axles.

N = the number of axles being considered.

This formula limits the weight on groups of axles in order to reduce the risk of damage to highway bridges. Allowable weight depends on the number of axles a vehicle has and the distance between those axles. However, the single- or tandem-axle weight limits supersede the Bridge Formula limits for all axles not more than 96 inches apart.

WHY IS THE FORMULA NECESSARY?

Bridges on Interstate System highways are used by a wide variety of traffic. They are designed to support expected loadings. However, as trucks grew heavier in the 1950's and 1960's, something had to be done to protect bridges. The solution was to tie allowable weights to the number and spacing of axles.

Axle spacing is as important as axle weight in bridge design. A bridge is analogous to thin ice on a pond. Walking on the ice concentrates a person's weight on the small area covered by the individual's feet, and the ice may break. Lying down, however, spreads the same weight over a much larger area, and the ice is less likely to break. Consider trucks crossing a bridge:

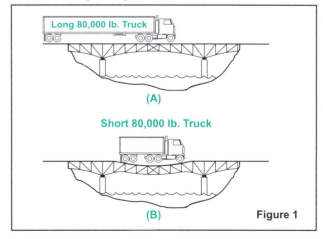

Figure 1

In Figure 1 (A), the stress on bridge members as the longer truck rolls across is much less than that caused by the short vehicle in Figure 1 (B), even though both trucks have the same total weight and individual axle weights. The weight of the longer vehicle is spread out, while the shorter vehicle has all of the weight concentrated on a small area.

The Federal-Aid Highway Amendments of 1974 increased the weights allowed on the Interstate System to 20,000 pounds on a single axle, 34,000 pounds on a tandem axle, and 80,000 pounds gross weight (23 U.S.C. 127). But Congress balanced this concession to productivity by enacting the Bridge Formula. The result is that motor vehicles may be loaded to the maximum weight only if each group of axles on the vehicle and their spacing also satisfy the requirements of the formula. This prevents the vehicle from overstressing bridges in the same way that a person lying down on thin ice would minimize the risk of breaking through.

Until 1982, federal law set only upper limits (or ceilings) on Interstate System weight limits. A few states retained significantly lower weight limits, which eventually became barriers to long-distance truck traffic. In 1982, federal law was amended to make Interstate System weight limits, including the Bridge Formula limits, both the maximum and the minimum weights (i.e., floors and ceilings) that states must allow on the Interstate System.

HOW IS THE FORMULA USED?

Some definitions are needed to use the Bridge Formula correctly.

Gross Weight – The weight of a vehicle or vehicle combination and any load thereon. The federal gross weight limit on the Interstate System is 80,000 pounds.

Single-Axle Weight – The total weight on one or more axles whose centers are not more than 40 inches apart. The federal single-axle weight limit on the Interstate System is 20,000 pounds.

Tandem-Axle Weight – The total weight on two or more consecutive axles more than 40 inches but not more than 96 inches apart. The federal tandem-axle weight limit on the Interstate System is 34,000 pounds.

Interstate System weight limits in some states may be higher than these figures due to "grandfather" rights. When the Interstate System axle and gross weight limits were adopted in 1956, states were allowed to keep or "grandfather" those which were higher. In 1975, states were also allowed to keep "grandfathered" Bridge Formula limits that were higher than those established for the Interstate System.

Bridge Formula calculations yield a series of weights (see the Bridge Formula Table). However, the single-axle weight limit replaces the Bridge Formula weight limit on axles not more than 40 inches apart, and the tandem-axle weight limit replaces the Bridge Formula weight limit for axles over 40 but not more than 96 inches apart. At 97 inches apart, two axles can carry 38,000 pounds and three axles 42,000 pounds, as shown in Figure 2.

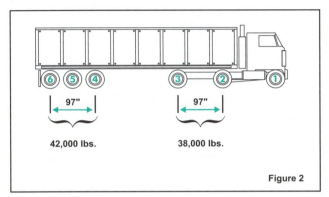

Figure 2

Federal law provides that any two or more consecutive axles may not exceed the weight computed by the formula even though single axles, tandem axles, and gross weight are within legal limits. In other words, the axle group that includes the entire truck – sometimes called the "outer bridge" group – must comply with the Bridge Formula. But interior combinations of axles, such as the "tractor bridge" (axles 1, 2, and 3) and "trailer bridge" (axles 2, 3, 4, and 5), must also be in compliance with weights computed by the formula (Figure 3).

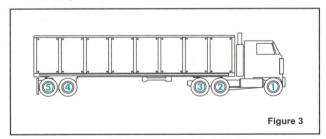

Figure 3

The most common vehicle checked for compliance with weight limit requirements is shown in Figure 3. While the Bridge Formula applies to each combination of two or more axles, experience shows that axle combinations 1 through 3, 1 through 5, and 2 through 5 are critical and must be checked. If these combinations are found to be satisfactory, all of the others on this type of vehicle will normally be satisfactory.

The vehicle with weights and axle dimensions as shown in Figure 4 will be used to illustrate a Bridge Formula check.

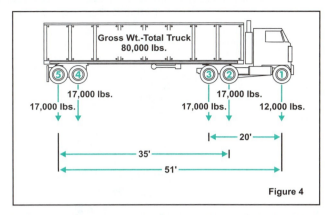

Figure 4

Before checking a vehicle for compliance with the Bridge Formula, its single-axle, tandem-axle, and gross weight should be checked. Here the single axle (number 1) does not exceed 20,000 pounds, tandems 2-3 and 4-5 do not exceed 34,000 pounds each, and the gross weight does not exceed 80,000 pounds. These preliminary requirements are thus satisfied. The first Bridge Formula combination is checked as follows:

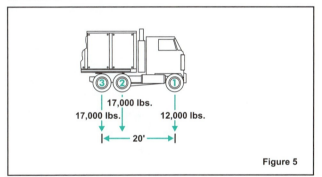

Figure 5

Check of 1 through 3 (Figure 5)
Actual weight = 12,000 + 17,000 + 17,000 = 46,000 pounds.

N = 3 axles.

L = 20 feet.

$$W = 500 \left(\frac{LN}{N-1} + 12N + 36 \right)$$

$$W = 500 \left(\frac{(20 \times 3)}{(3-1)} + (12 \times 3) + 36 \right) = 51,000\#$$

W maximum = 51,000#, which is more than the actual weight of 46,000#, so the Bridge Formula requirement is satisfied.

Example – From the Bridge Table
This same number (51,000#) could have been obtained from the Bridge Table by reading down the left side to L = 20 and across to the right where N = 3.

Bridge Formula Weights — Addendum

BRIDGE FORMULA TABLE

PERMISSIBLE GROSS LOADS FOR VEHICLES IN REGULAR OPERATION[1]

Distance in feet (L) between the extremes of any group of 2 or more consecutive axles

Based on weight formula $W = 500\left(\dfrac{LN}{N-1} + 12N + 36\right)$

Maximum load in pounds carried on any group of 2 or more consecutive axles

N =	2 AXLES	3 AXLES	4 AXLES	5 AXLES	6 AXLES	7 AXLES	8 AXLES	9 AXLES
4	34,000							
5	34,000							
6	34,000							
7	34,000							
8 and less	34,000	34,000						
more than 8	38,000	42,000						
9	39,000	42,500						
10	40,000	43,500						
11		44,000						
12		45,000	50,000					
13		45,500	50,500					
14		46,500	51,500					
15		47,000	52,000					
16		48,000	52,500	58,000				
17		48,500	53,500	58,500				
18		49,500	54,000	59,000				
19		50,000	54,500	60,000				
20		51,000	55,500	60,500	66,000			
21		51,500	56,000	61,000	66,500			
22		52,500	56,500	61,500	67,000			
23		53,000	57,500	62,500	68,000			
24		54,000	58,000	63,000	68,500	74,000		
25		54,500	58,500	63,500	69,000	74,500		
26		55,500	59,500	64,000	69,500	75,000		
27		56,000	60,000	65,000	70,000	75,500		
28		57,000	60,500	65,500	71,000	76,500	82,000	
29		57,500	61,500	66,000	71,500	77,000	82,500	
30		58,500	62,000	66,500	72,000	77,500	83,000	
31		59,000	62,500	67,500	72,500	78,000	83,500	
32		60,000	63,500	68,000	73,000	78,500	84,500	90,000
33			64,000	68,500	74,000	79,000	85,000	90,500
34			64,500	69,000	74,500	80,000	85,500	91,000
35			65,500	70,000	75,000	80,500	86,000	91,500
36			66,000	70,500	75,500	81,000	86,500	92,000
37			66,500	71,000	76,000	81,500	87,000	93,000
38			67,500	71,500	77,000	82,000	87,500	93,500
39			68,000	72,500	77,500	82,500	88,500	94,000
40			68,500	73,000	78,000	83,500	89,000	94,500
41			69,500	73,500	78,500	84,000	89,500	95,000
42			70,000	74,000	79,000	84,500	90,000	95,500
43			70,500	75,000	80,000	85,000	90,500	96,000
44			71,500	75,500	80,500	85,500	91,000	96,500
45			72,000	76,000	81,000	86,000	91,500	97,500
46			72,500	76,500	81,500	87,000	92,500	98,000
47			73,500	77,500	82,000	87,500	93,000	98,500
48			74,000	78,000	83,000	88,000	93,500	99,000
49			74,500	78,500	83,500	88,500	94,000	99,500
50			75,500	79,000	84,000	89,000	94,500	100,000
51			76,000	80,000	84,500	89,500	95,000	100,500
52			76,500	80,500	85,000	90,500	95,500	101,000
53			77,500	81,000	86,000	91,000	96,500	102,000
54			78,000	81,500	86,500	91,500	97,000	102,500
55			78,500	82,500	87,000	92,000	97,500	103,000
56			79,500	83,000	87,500	92,500	98,000	103,500
57			80,000	83,500	88,000	93,000	98,500	104,000
58				84,000	89,000	94,000	99,000	104,500
59				85,000	89,500	94,500	99,500	105,000
60				85,500	90,000	95,000	100,500	105,500

Tandem-Axle Weight (see first page)

Example (see previous page) — 20, 51,000

Exception (see following page) — 36: 66,000; 37: 66,500; 38: 67,500

[1] The permissible loads are computed to the nearest 500 pounds as required by statute.

The following loaded vehicles must not operate over H15-44 bridges: 3-S2 (5-axle) with wheelbase less than 38 feet; 2-S1-2 (5-axle) with wheelbase less than 45 feet; 3-3 (6-axle) with wheelbase less than 45 feet; and 7-, 8-, and 9-axle vehicles regardless of wheelbase.

Weights shown in the white section are over the Federal GVW (gross vehicle weight) on the Interstate System (see first page).

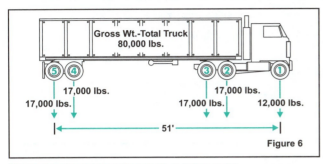

Figure 6

Now check axles 1 through 5 (Figure 6)
Actual weight = 12,000 + 17,000 + 17,000 + 17,000 + 17,000 = 80,000#.

W maximum, from the Bridge Table for "L" of 51 feet and "N" of 5 = 80,000#.

Therefore, this axle spacing is satisfactory.

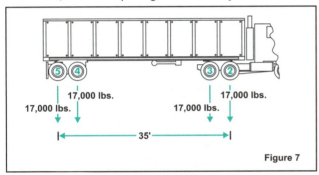

Figure 7

Now check axles 2 through 5 (Figure 7)
Actual weight = 17,000 + 17,000 + 17,000 + 17,000 = 68,000#.

W maximum, from the Bridge Table for "L" of 35 feet and "N" of 4 = 65,500#.

This is a violation because the actual weight exceeds the weight allowed by the Bridge Formula. To correct the situation, some load must be removed from the vehicle or the axle spacing (35 feet) must be increased.

EXCEPTION TO FORMULA AND BRIDGE TABLE
Federal law (23 U.S.C. 127) includes one exception to the Bridge Formula and the Bridge Table – two consecutive sets of tandem axles may carry 34,000 pounds each if the overall distance between the first and last axles of these tandems is 36 feet or more. For example, a five-axle tractor-semitrailer combination may carry 34,000 pounds both on the tractor tandem (axles 2 and 3) and the trailer tandem (axles 4 and 5), provided axles 2 and 5 are spaced at least 36 feet apart. Without this exception, the Bridge Formula would allow an actual weight of only 66,000 to 67,500 pounds on tandems spaced 36 to 38 feet apart.

BRIDGE FORMULA APPLICATION TO SINGLE UNIT TRUCKS
The procedure described above can be used to check any axle combinations, but several closely spaced axles usually produce the most critical situation.

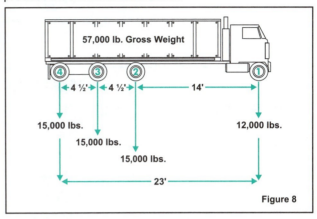

Figure 8

The truck in Figure 8 satisfies the single axle weight limit (12,000# is less than 20,000#), the tandem axle limit (30,000# is less than 34,000#), and gross weight limit (57,000# is less than 80,000#). With these restrictions satisfied, a check will be made for Bridge Formula requirements, axles 1 through 4.

Actual weight = 12,000 + 15,000 + 15,000 + 15,000 = 57,000#.

W maximum for "N" of 4 and "L" of 23 feet = 57,500# (from the Bridge Table).

Since axles 1 through 4 are satisfactory, check axles 2 through 4:

W (actual) = 15,000 + 15,000 + 15,000 = 45,000#.

W maximum for "N" of 3 and "L" of 9 feet = 42,500# (from the Bridge Table).

This is a violation. The load would have to be reduced, axles added, or spacing increased, to comply with the Bridge Formula.

CAUTION:
This section paraphrases the actual provision in 23 U.S.C. 127 and 23 CFR 658 for the sake of clarity. In case of a dispute, the statute and regulations will govern.

Previous editions of this information released under the title "Bridge Gross Weight Formula," dated April 1984, remain valid. Neither the formula nor any resulting maximum gross weight values (table entries) have been changed.

Federal Motor Carrier Safety Administration Field Offices

The field organizations deliver program services to the Federal Motor Carrier Safety Administration's (FMCSA) partners and customers. This organization consists of field operations, service centers, and state-level motor carrier division offices. These offices answer questions and provide guidance concerning the Federal Motor Carrier Safety Regulations. You may write to the service center or call the FMCSA's state office in the State Capital, or in some states, in the nearest satellite office, listed below.

HEADQUARTERS

Federal Motor Carrier Safety Administration
400 7th Street, SW
Washington, D.C. 20590
Phone: (800) 832-5660

REGIONAL OFFICES

Eastern Service Center
Phone (443) 703-2240
Fax (443) 703-2253
802 Cromwell Park Drive
Suite N
Glen Burnie, MD 21061

Midwestern Service Center
Phone (708) 283-3577
Fax (708) 283-3579
19900 Governors Drive
Suite 210
Olympia Fields, IL 60461

Southern Service Center
Phone (404) 327-7400
Fax (404) 327-7349
1800 Century Boulevard NE
Suite 1700
Atlanta, GA 30345

Western Service Center
Phone (303) 407-2350
Fax (303) 407-2339
Golden Hills Office Centre
12600 W. Colfax Avenue
Suite B-300
Lakewood, CO 80215

SATELLITE OFFICES

Alabama Division
Phone (334) 223-7244
Fax (334) 223-7700
500 Eastern Boulevard, Suite 200
Montgomery, AL 36117

Alaska Division
Phone (907) 271-4068
Fax (907) 271-4069
Frontier Building, Suite 260
3601 C Street
Anchorage, AK 99503

Arizona Division
Phone (602) 379-6851
Fax (602) 379-3627
One Arizona Center
400 East Van Buren, Suite 401
Phoenix, AZ 85004-2223

Arkansas Division
Phone (501) 324-5050
Fax (501) 324-6562
2527 Federal Building
700 W. Capitol Avenue
Little Rock, AR 72201

California Division
Phone (916) 930-2760
Fax (916) 930-2778
1325 J Street, Suite 1540
Sacramento, CA 95814

Colorado Division
Phone (720) 963-3130
Fax (720) 963-3131
12300 West Dakota Avenue, Suite 130
Lakewood, CO 80228

Connecticut Division
Phone (860) 659-6700
Fax (860) 659-6725
628-2 Hebron Avenue, Suite 303
Glastonbury, CT 06033

Delaware Division
Phone (302) 734-8173
Fax (302) 734-5380
J. Allen Frear Federal Building
300 South New Street, Suite 1105
Dover, DE 19904-6726

District of Columbia Division
Phone (202) 219-3553
Fax (202) 219-3546
1990 K Street NW, Suite 510
Washington, DC 20006

Florida Division
Phone (850) 942-9338
Fax (850) 942-9680
545 John Knox Road, Room 102
Tallahassee, FL 32303

Georgia Division
Phone (678) 284-5130
Fax (678) 284-5146
Two Crown Center
1745 Phoenix Boulevard, Suite 380
Atlanta, GA 30349

Hawaii Division
Phone (808) 541-2700
Fax (808) 541-2702
300 Ala Moana Boulevard, Room 3-243
Box 50226
Honolulu, HI 96850

Idaho Division
Phone (208) 334-1842
Fax (208) 334-1046
3200 North Lake Harbor Lane, Suite 161
Boise, ID 83703

Illinois Division
Phone (217) 492-4608
Fax (217) 492-4986
3250 Executive Park Drive
Springfield, IL 62703-4514

Indiana Division
Phone (317) 226-7474
Fax (317) 226-5657
575 N. Pennsylvania Street, Room 261
Indianapolis, IN 46204

Iowa Division
Phone (515) 233-7400
Fax (515) 233-7494
105 6th Street
Ames, IA 50010-6337

Kansas Division
Phone (785) 271-1260
Fax (785) 228-9725
1303 SW First American Place, Suite 200
Topeka, KS 66604-4040

Kentucky Division
Phone (502) 223-6779
Fax (502) 223-6767
330 West Broadway
Frankfort, KY 40601

Louisiana Division
Phone (225) 757-7640
Fax (225) 757-7636
5304 Flanders Drive, Suite A
Baton Rouge, LA 70808

Maine Division
Phone (207) 622-8358
Fax (207) 622-8477
Edmund S. Muskie Federal Building
40 Western Avenue, Room 608
Augusta, ME 04330

Maryland Division
Phone (410) 962-2889
Fax (410) 962-3916
City Crescent Building
Baltimore, MD 21201

Massachusetts Division
Phone (617) 494-2770
Fax (617) 494-2783
55 Broadway, Building 3, Room 135
Cambridge, MA 02142

Michigan Division
Phone (517) 377-1866
Fax (517) 377-1868
315 W. Allegan, Room 219
Lansing, MI 48933

Minnesota Division
Phone (651) 291-6150
Fax (651) 291-6001
380 Jackson Street, Galtier Plaza,
Suite 500
St. Paul, MN 55101

Mississippi Division
Phone (601) 965-4219
Fax (601) 965-4674
666 North Street, Suite 103
Jackson, MS 39202-3199

SATELLITE OFFICES CONTINUED

Missouri Division
Phone (573) 636-3246
Fax (573) 636-8901
3219 Emerald Lane, Suite 500
Jefferson City, MO 65109-6863

Montana Division
Phone (406) 449-5304
Fax (406) 449-5318
2880 Skyway Drive
Helena, MT 59602

Nebraska Division
Phone (402) 437-5986
Fax (402) 437-5146
Federal Motor Carrier Safety Admin.
100 Centennial Mall North, Room 220
Lincoln, NE 68508

Nevada Division
Phone (775) 687-5335
Fax (775) 687-8353
705 North Plaza Street, Suite 204
Carson City, NV 89701

New Hampshire Division
Phone (603) 228-3112
Fax (603) 223-0390
70 Commercial St., Suite 102
Concord, NH 03301

New Jersey Division
Phone (609) 637-4222
Fax (609) 538-4913
U.S. Department of Transportation
Federal Motor Carrier Safety Admin.
840 Bear Tavern Road, Suite 310
West Trenton, NJ 08628

New Mexico Division
Phone (505) 346-7858
Fax (505) 346-7859
2400 Louisiana Blvd. NE,
Suite 520 AFC-5
Albuquerque, NM 87110

New York Division
Phone (518) 431-4145
Fax (518) 431-4140
Leo W. O'Brien Federal Building,
Rm. 719
Clinton Avenue & N. Pearl Street
Albany, NY 12207

North Carolina Division
Phone (919) 856-4378
Fax (919) 856-4369
310 New Bern Avenue, Suite 468
Raleigh, NC 27601

North Dakota Division
Phone (701) 250-4346
Fax (701) 250-4389
1471 Interstate Loop
Bismarck, ND 58503

Ohio Division
Phone (614) 280-5657
Fax (614) 280-6875
200 N. High Street, Room 328
Columbus, OH 43215

Oklahoma Division
Phone (405) 605-6047
Fax (405) 605-6176
300 North Meridian, Suite 106 South
Oklahoma City, OK 73107

Oregon Division
Phone (503) 399-5775
Fax (503) 399-5838
The Equitable Center
530 Center Street NE, Suite 100
Salem, OR 97301

Pennsylvania Division
Phone (717) 221-4443
Fax (717) 221-4552
228 Walnut St., Room 560
Harrisburg, PA 17101

Puerto Rico Division
Phone (787) 766-5985
Fax (787) 766-5015
Torre Chardón, 350 Chardón St.
Hato Rey, PR 00918

Rhode Island Division
Phone (401) 431-6010
Fax (401) 431-6019
20 Risho Ave., Suite E
East Providence, RI 02914

South Carolina Division
Phone (803) 765-5414
Fax (803) 765-5413
1835 Assembly St., Suite 1253
Columbia, SC 29201-2451

South Dakota Division
Phone (605) 224-8202
Fax (605) 224-1766
116 East Dakota Avenue, Suite B
Pierre, SD 57501

Tennessee Division
Phone (615) 781-5781
Fax (615) 781-5755
640 Grassmere Park, Suite 111
Nashville, TN 37211

Texas Division
Phone (512) 536-5980
Fax (512) 916-5980
300 East 8th Street, Room 865
Austin, TX 78701

Utah Division
Phone (801) 963-0096
Fax (801) 963-0086
2520 West 4700 South, Suite 9B
Salt Lake City, UT 84118-1847

Vermont Division
Phone (802) 828-4480
Fax (802) 828-4424
87 State Street, Room 222
Montpelier, VT 05602
P.O. Box 568
Montpelier, VT 05601

Virginia Division
Phone (804) 771-8585
Fax (804) 771-8681
400 N. 8th St., Suite 780
P.O. Box 10230
Richmond, VA 23240-0230

Washington Division
Phone (360) 753-9875
Fax (360) 753-9024
Evergreen Plaza Building
711 South Capitol Way,
Suite 502
Olympia, WA 98501

West Virginia Division
Phone (304) 347-5935
Fax (304) 347-5617
U.S. DOT FMCSA
700 Washington Street East
Geary Plaza, Suite 205
Charleston, WV 25301

Wisconsin Division
Phone (608) 829-7530
Fax (608) 829-7540
567 D'Onofrio Drive, Suite 101
Highpoint Office Park
Madison, WI 53719-2814

Wyoming Division
Phone (307) 772-2305
Fax (307) 772-2905
1637 Stillwater Ave., Suite F
Cheyenne, WY 82009

COSTS OF HIGHWAY CRASHES WORKSHEET

Direct Costs	**Cost**
Workers' compensation benefits	$_____
Health care costs for off-duty injuries	$_____
Increases in medical insurance premiums	$_____
Auto insurance and liability claims and settlements	$_____
Physical and vocational rehabilitation costs	$_____
Life insurance and survivor benefits	$_____
Group health insurance dependent coverage	$_____
Property damage (equipment, products, etc.)	$_____
Motor vehicle repair and replacement	$_____
TOTAL	$_____

Indirect Costs	**Cost**
Supervisor's time (rescheduling, making special arrangements)	$_____
Fleet manager's time to coordinate vehicle repair, replacement, etc.	$_____
Reassignment of personnel to cover for missing employees (less efficiency)	$_____
Overtime pay (to cover work of missing employees)	$_____
Employee replacement	$_____
Reentry and retraining of injured employees	$_____
Administrative costs (documentation of injuries, treatment, absences; crash investigation)	$_____
Inspection costs	$_____
Failure to meet customer requirements resulting in loss of business	$_____
TOTAL	$_____

Addendum — Costs of Highway Crashes Worksheet

REVENUE NECESSARY TO PAY FOR ACCIDENT LOSSES

THIS TABLE SHOWS THE DOLLARS OF REVENUE REQUIRED TO PAY FOR DIFFERENT AMOUNTS OF COSTS FOR ACCIDENTS

**It is necessary for a motor carrier to generate an additional $1,250,000 revenue to pay the cost of a $25,000 accident, assuming an average profit of 2%.
The amount of revenue required to pay for losses will vary with the profit margin.**

YEARLY ACCIDENT COSTS	PROFIT MARGIN				
	1%	2%	3%	4%	5%
$1,000	100,000	50,000	33,000	25,000	20,000
5,000	500,000	250,000	167,000	125,000	100,000
10,000	1,000,000	500,000	333,000	250,000	200,000
25,000	2,500,000	1,250,000	833,000	625,000	500,000
50,000	5,000,000	2,500,000	1,667,000	1,250,000	1,000,000
100,000	10,000,000	5,000,000	3,333,000	2,500,000	2,000,000
150,000	15,000,000	7,500,000	5,000,000	3,750,000	3,000,000
200,000	20,000,000	10,000,000	6,666,000	5,000,000	4,000,000

REVENUE REQUIRED TO COVER LOSSES

Accident costs (direct + indirect) consist of any or all of the following:

Direct Costs:
Cargo Damage
Vehicle Damage
Injury(s) Costs
Medical Costs
Loss of Revenue
Administrative Costs
Police Report
Possible Effect on Cost of Insurance
Possible Effect on Cost of Workmen's Compensation Insurance
Towing Costs
Storage of Damage Vehicle

Indirect (Hidden) Costs:
Lost Clients/Customers
Lost Sales
Meetings Missed
Salaries Paid to Employees in Accident
Lost Time at Work
Cost to Hire/Train Replacement Employees
Supervisor's Time
Loss of Personal Property
Replacement Vehicle Rental
Damaged Equipment Downtime
Accelerated Depreciation of Equipment
Accident Reporting
Medical Costs Paid by Company
Poor Public Relations/Publicity
Increased Public Relations Costs
Government Agency Costs

Addendum

NOTES

Index

A

Accidents
    Definition 390.5 **251**
    Investigation 390.15(a) **255**
    Recordkeeping 390.15(b) **255**
Adverse Driving Conditions 395.1(b) 329
Age of Driver 391.11(b)(1) 261
Air Brakes Part 383 App to Sub G 190-191
Alaska
    Hours of Service 395.1(h) **330**
    Restricted CDLs 383.3(e) **171**
Alcohol
    Concentration 382.201 **156**
    Consequences
        Alcohol-Related Conduct 382.505 **166**
        Evaluation and Testing 382.503 **166**
        Penalties 382.507 **166**
        Safety-Sensitive Functions, Removal from 382.501-382.505 **166**
    Disqualification from Driving 383.51(b), 391.15(c) **178**, **261**
    Driving Under the Influence
        Definition 383.5 **174**
        Driver Disqualification 383.51(b), 391.15(c)(2)(i) **178**, **262**
    Evaluation 382.605 **167**
    Following Accident 382.209 **157**
    Misuse 382.601 **166**
    On-Duty Use 382.205 **156**
    Pre-Duty Use 382.207 **157**
    Prohibition 392.5 **279**
    Referral 382.605 **167**
    Supervisor Training 382.603 **167**
    Testing
        Confirmation Test
            First Steps 40.251 **35**
            Post-Test Procedures 40.255 **35**
            Procedures 40.253 **35**
        Devices 40.229, 40.231 **32**
            Proper Use and Care 40.233, 40.235 **33**
        Employer Responsibilities Part 40 Subpart B **3-6**
        Follow-Up 382.311 **163**
        Form 40.225, 40.227, App G to Part 40 **32**, **51-52**
        Management Information System (MIS) Data Collection Form 40.26, App H to Part 40 **6**, **52-55**
        Personnel Part 40 Subpart J **30-32**
        Post-Accident 382.303 **158**
        Pre-Employment 382.301 **157**
        Problems
            Cancellation 40.267-40.275 **37-38**
            Insufficient Breath 40.265 **36**
            Insufficient Saliva 40.263 **36**
            Refusal to Take 40.261 **36**
        Procedures 382.105 **154**
        Random 382.305 **159**
        Reasonable Suspicion 382.307 **162**
        Records
            Access 382.405 **164**
            Confidentiality 40.321, 40.323 **42**
            Employer Notifications 382.411 **165**
            Inquiries for 382.413 **165**
            Releasing 40.329, 40.331 **43**
            Retention 40.333, 382.401 **43**, **163**
        Refusal to Submit 382.211 **157**
        Results, Reporting 382.403 **164**
        Return-to-Duty 382.309 **163**
        Screening Test
            Breath Tube ASD 40.245 **34**
            EBT or Non-Evidential Breath ASD 40.243 **33**
            First Steps 40.241 **33**
            Post-Test Procedures 40.247 **34**
            Saliva ASD 40.245 **34**
        Sites 40.221 **32**
            Security 40.223 **32**
        Starting Date 382.115 **156**
    Treatment 382.605 **167**

Applications
    Certificate of Registration to Operate in U.S. Municipalities on the U.S.-Mexico Border
        Appeals 368.8 **87**
        Applying 368.3 **87**
        Carrying Certificate in Vehicle 368.7 **87**
        Certificates 368.1 **87**
        Change in Applicant Information 368.4 **87**
        Definitions 368.2 **87**
        FMCSA Action on Application 368.6 **87**
        Re-registration 368.5 **87**
    Operating Authority
        Applying 365.101-365.123 **77-78**
        Contacting Another Party 365.303 **78**
        Definitions 365.403 **78**
        FAX Filings 365.309 **78**
        Form OP-1 365.105 **77**
        Mexico-Domiciled Carriers 365.501-App A to Subpart E of Part 365 **79-82**
        Opposing Requests for Authority 365.201-365.207 **78**
        Replies to Motions 365.307 **78**
        Rules 365.301 **78**
        Serving Copies of Pleadings 365.305 **78**
        Transfer of Operating Rights 365.401-365.413 **78-79**
Automatic Brake Adjusters 393.53 303

B

Battery Installation 393.30 297
Bills
    Bills of Lading 373.101 **103**
        Freight Forwarders 373.201 **103**
    Expense Bills 373.103 **103**
    Low Value Packages 373.105 **103**
Boulders, Securing 393.136 326
Brake Adjusters, Automatic 393.53 303
Brakes
    Adjustment Indicator 393.53(c) **303**
    Air Brakes Part 383 App to Sub G **190-191**
    Antilock 393.55 **303**
    Automatic Adjusters
        Air Brake Systems 393.53(b) **303**
        Hydraulic Brake Systems 393.53(a) **303**
    Breakaway 393.43 **299**
    Emergency 393.43 **299**
    Front Brake Lines, Protection 393.44 **299**
    Lining 393.47 **300**
    Operative 393.48 **300**
    Parking Brake Systems 393.41 **298**
    Performance 393.52 **301**
    Required Systems 393.40 **297**
    Reservoirs Required 393.50 **301**
    Single Valve Required 393.49 **300**
    Tubing and Hose
        Connections 393.45(d) **299**
    Tubing and Hose 393.45 **299**
    Warning Signals and Gauges 393.51 **301**
    Wheels, Required on All 393.42 **298**
Bridge Formula Weights Addendum 392
Brokers of Property
    Accounting 371.13 **95**
    Applicability 371.1 **95**
    Definitions 371.2 **95**
    Duties and Obligations 371.10 **95**
    Misrepresentation 371.7 **95**
    Rebating and Compensation 371.9 **95**
    Records Kept 371.3 **95**
Buses
    Aisle Seats Prohibited 393.91 **316**
    Defrosting and Defogging Systems 393.79 **314**
    Driveshaft Protection 393.89 **316**
    Emergency Doors
        Inspection 396.3(a)(2) **349**
        Test Records 396.3(b)(4) **349**

Buses

Buses (continued)
- Emergency Equipment 393.95 **317**
- Emergency Exits 393.62 **304**
  - Marking 393.62(e) **305**
  - Window Requirements 393.62(d) **304**
- Financial Responsibility 387.31 **235**
- Horn 393.81 **315**
- Lighting Devices 393.11 **288**
- Pushing 392.63 **283**
- Rear-Vision Mirrors 393.80 **314**
- Reflectors 393.11 **288**
- Safe Operation 392.62 **283**
- Seats, Seat Belt Assemblies, and Seat Belt Assembly Anchorages 393.93(a) **316**
- Speedometer 393.82 **315**
- Standee Line or Bar 393.90 **316**
- Towing 392.63 **283**
- Windshield Wiping and Washing Systems 393.78 **314**

C

C.O.D. Shipments 377.101-377.105 135
Cab and Body Components 393.203 327
Carbon Monoxide 392.66 283
Cargo, Inspection 392.9 280
Cargo, Securing
- Applicability 393.106(a) **319**
- Boulders 393.136 **326**
- Concrete Pipe 393.124 **324**
- Containers, Roll-on/Roll-off or Hook Lift 393.134 **326**
- Devices
  - Performance Criteria 393.102 **318**
  - Standards 393.104 **319**
- Front End Structures 393.114 **321**
- Intermodal Containers 393.126 **325**
- Load
  - Loss 393.100(b) **318**
  - Shifting 393.100(c) **318**
- Logs 393.116 **321**
- Lumber, Dressed 393.118 **322**
- Metal Coils 393.120 **322**
- Paper Rolls 393.122 **323**
- Placement and Restraint 393.106(c) **319**
- Tiedowns
  - Adjusting 393.112 **321**
  - Manufacturing Standards 393.104(e) **319**
  - Number 393.110 **320**
  - Use 393.104(f) **319**
- Vehicles
  - Automobiles, Light Trucks, and Vans 393.128 **325**
  - Flattened or Crushed 393.132 **326**
  - Heavy Vehicles, Equipment, and Machinery 393.130 **326**
- Types 393.100(a) **318**

Certificates, Falsification 390.35 259
Claims
- Loss and Damage
  - Acknowledgement 370.5 **93**
  - Applicability 370.1 **93**
  - Disposition 370.9 **93**
  - Filing 370.3 **93**
  - Investigation 370.7 **93**
- Overcharge, Duplicate Payment, or Overcollection
  - Acknowledgement 378.7 **137**
  - Applicability 378.1 **137**
  - Definitions 378.2 **137**
  - Disposition 378.8, 378.9 **137**
  - Documentation 378.4 **137**
  - Filing 378.3 **137**
  - Investigation 378.5 **137**
  - Processing 378.3 **137**
  - Records 378.6 **137**

Class 7 Materials 397.101, 397.103 360, 361
Commercial Driver's License
- Application Information 383.153 **192**
- Application Procedures 383.71 **183**
  - State Procedures 383.73 **184**
- Definition 383.5 **174**
- Document Information 383.153 **192**
- Employer Responsibilities 383.37 **177**
- Penalties 383.53 **183**
- Required Skills 383.113 **189**
- Restricted Licenses
  - Drivers in Alaska 383.3(e) **171**
  - Farm-Related Service Industries 383.3(f) **171**
  - Pyrotechnic Industry 383.3(g) **172**
- Single License Requirement 383.21 **176**
- State Compliance
  - CDL Issuance and Information 384.204 **195**
  - CDLIS Information 384.205 **195**
  - Decertification 384.405 **198**
  - Definitions 384.105 **195**
  - Determining Compliance 384.301-384.309 **197-198**
  - Disqualification
    - Notification 384.208 **196**
    - Requirement 384.231 **197**
  - Domicile Requirement 384.212 **196**
  - Driving While Under the Influence 384.203 **195**
  - Drug Offenses 384.217 **196**
  - Emergency Grants 384.407 **199**

Commercial Driver's License (continued)
- State Compliance (continued)
  - Licensing
    - Limitation 384.210 **196**
    - Notification 384.207 **196**
    - Return of Old Licenses 384.211 **196**
  - Masking Convictions 384.226 **197**
  - National Driver Register Information 384.220 **197**
  - Noncommercial Motor Vehicle Violations 384.224 **197**
  - Noncompliance
    - Availability of Funds 384.403 **198**
    - Consequences 384.401 **198**
  - Offenses
    - Drug 384.217 **196**
    - First 384.215 **196**
    - Second 384.216 **196**
  - Out-of-Service
    - Regulations 384.221 **197**
    - Violations 384.222 **197**
  - Penalties for Drivers of CMVs 384.213 **196**
  - Railroad-Highway Grade Crossing Violation 384.223 **197**
  - Reciprocity 384.214 **196**
  - Record Checks 384.206 **195**
    - Background 384.233 **197**
    - Required Timing 384.232 **197**
  - Testing
    - Program 384.201 **195**
    - Standards 384.202 **195**
  - Traffic Violations
    - Notification of 384.209 **196**
    - Record of 384.225 **197**
    - Second 384.218 **197**
    - Third 384.219 **197**
- Tamperproofing 383.155 **193**
- Testing
  - Air Brakes 383.95 **188**
  - Commercial Motor Vehicle Groups 383.91 **186**
  - Driving Skills Test Substitutes 383.77 **186**
  - Endorsements 383.93 **187**
    - Double/Triple Trailers Endorsement 383.115 **189**
    - Hazardous Materials Endorsement 383.121 **189**
    - Passenger Endorsement 383.117 **189**
    - School Bus 383.123 **190**
    - Tank Vehicle Endorsement 383.119 **189**
  - Implied Consent to Alcohol Testing 383.72 **184**
  - Methods 383.133 **192**
  - Passing Score 383.135 **192**
  - Procedures 383.131 **191**
  - Third Party Testing 383.75 **185**
- Validity of CDL Issued by Decertified State 383.7 **176**

Commercial Motor Vehicles (see also Motor Vehicles, Inspection entry) 279-283
- Brakes on Wheels 393.42 **298**
- Carbon Monoxide 392.66 **283**
- Definition 382.107, 383.5, 390.5 **154, 174, 251**
- Driving Time, Maximum 395.3, 395.5 **335, 336**
- Emergency Equipment 392.8 **280**
- Emergency Signals
  - Flame-Producing 392.24, 392.25 **282**
  - Warning Signals 392.22 **282**
- Equipment 392.7 **280**
- Exits 392.64 **283**
- Groups 383.91 **186**
- Hazardous Conditions 392.14 **281**
- Lighting Devices 393.11 **288**
- Marking 390.21 **256**
- Notification Requirements
  - Convictions 383.31 **177**
  - License Suspensions 383.33 **177**
  - Previous Employment 383.35 **177**
- Open Flame Heaters 392.67 **283**
- Operating Authority 392.9a **280**
- Operating Rules 392.2 **279**
- Other Purposes 390.33 **259**
- Parking Brake System 393.41 **298**
- Radar Detectors 392.71 **283**
- Railroad Crossings
  - Slowing Down 392.11 **281**
  - Stopping 392.10 **281**
- Required Knowledge to Operate 383.111 **188**
- Reservoirs 393.50 **301**
- Seat Belts 392.16 **281**
- Speed Limits 392.6 **280**
- Unsafe 396.7 **349**

Commercial Zones 372.201-372.243, App F to Subchapter B 99-102, 371
- Definitions 372.239 **102**

Concrete Pipe, Securing 393.124 324
Controlled Substances
- Disqualification from Driving 383.51, 391.15(c) **178, 261**
- Driving Under the Influence, Driver Disqualification 383.51(b), 391.15(c)(2)(ii)-(iii) **178, 262**
- Misuse 382.601 **166**
- Prohibition 392.4 **279**
- Safety-Sensitive Functions, Removal from 382.501-382.505 **166**
- Testing
  - Cancellation 40.199-209 **29-30**
  - Consent or Release 40.27 **6**
  - Dilute Specimen 40.197 **28**
  - Employer Responsibilities Part 40 Subpart B **3-6**
  - Follow-Up 382.311 **163**
  - Insufficient Urine 40.193 **27**
    - Due to Long-Term Medical Condition 40.195 **28**

Controlled Substances (continued)
   Testing (continued)
      Laboratories 40.81 **13**
         Blind Specimens 40.103, 40.105 **16**
         Cutoff Concentrations 40.87 **14**
         Disclosing Information 40.111 **16**
         Documentation 40.109 **16**
         Drugs Tested for 40.85 **14**
         Inspection 40.107 **16**
         Relationship with MRO 40.101, 40.125 **15**, **18**
         Reporting 40.97 **14**
         Specimen
            Criteria 40.93, 40.95 **14**
            Processing 40.83 **13**
            Retention 40.99 **15**
         Validity Testing 40.89, 40.91 **14**
      Management Information System Data 40.26 **6**
      Positive 382.215 **157**
      Post-Accident 382.303 **158**
      Pre-Employment 382.301 **157**
      Procedures 382.105 **154**
      Random 382.305 **159**
      Reasonable Suspicion 382.307 **162**
      Records
         Access 382.405 **164**
         Confidentiality 40.321, 40.323 **42**
         Inquiries for 382.413 **165**
         Releasing 40.329, 40.331 **43**
         Retention 40.333, 382.401 **43**, **163**
      Refusal to Submit 382.211 **157**
      Refusal to Take 40.191 **26**
      Results, Reporting 382.403 **164**
      Return-to-Duty 382.309 **163**
      Starting Date 382.115 **156**
      Substituting a Test Specimen 382.215 **157**
      Urine Collection
         Collector 40.31 **6**
         Specimen
            Check 40.65 **11**
            Preparation 40.71 **12**
            Process 40.73 **12**
         Training Requirements 40.33 **6**
         Directly Observed 40.67 **11**
         Documentation 40.45, 40.47 **9**, **10**
         Kits App A to Part 40 **49**
         Location 40.41 **8**
         Materials 40.49 **10**
         Monitored 40.69 **12**
         Process 40.61, 40.63 **10**, **11**
         Protecting Security and Integrity 40.43 **8**
         Sending to Lab 40.51 **10**
   Use 382.213 **157**
Cooperative Agreements with States
   Acceptance 388.2 **243**
   Assistance 388.5 **243**
   Cancellation 388.3 **243**
   Eligibility 388.1 **243**
   Information, Exchange of 388.4 **243**
   Joint Administrative Activities 388.7 **243**
   Joint Investigation, Inspection, or Examination 388.6 **243**
   Supplemental Agreements 388.8 **243**
Coupling Devices and Towing Methods
   Driveaway-Towaway Operations 393.71 **309**
   Non-Driveaway-Towaway Operations 393.70 **307**

D

Definitions 390.5 **251**
   Applications
      Certificate of Registration to Operate in U.S. Municipalities on the U.S.-Mexico Border 368.2 **87**
      Operating Authority 365.403 **78**
   Brokers of Property 371.2 **95**
   Claims 378.2 **137**
   Commercial Driver's License Program, State Compliance 384.105(b) **195**
   Commercial Driver's License Standards 383.5 **174**
   Commercial Zones 372.239 **102**
   Drug and Alcohol Testing Programs 40.3, 382.107 **1**, **154**
   Entry-Level Driver Training Requirements 380.502 **145**
   Exemptions 372.107 **97**
   Freight Forwarders 387.401 **242**
   Hazardous Materials
      Non-Radioactive 397.65 **357**
      Safety Permits 385.402 **207**
   Hours of Service 395.2 **333**
   Household Goods, Transportation of 375.103 **109**
   Lease and Interchange of Vehicles 376.2 **131**
   Longer Combination Vehicle (LCV) 380.105 **143**
   Migrant Workers, Transporting 398.1 **365**
   Motor Carriers
      Passengers 387.29 **235**
      Property 387.5 **231**
   Noise Emission Standards 325.5 **57**
   Parts and Accessories Necessary for Safe Operation 393.5 **285**
   Passenger Carrier Regulations 374.113, 374.303 **105**
   Preemption Procedures 397.201(c) **361**
   Registration with States 367.1 **85**
   Rulemaking Procedures 389.3 **245**

Definitions (continued)
   Rules of Practice 386.2 **217**
   Safety Fitness Procedures 385.3 **201**
      Mexico-Domiciled Carriers 385.101 **203**
   State Laws 355.5 **71**
   Step, Handhold, and Deck Requirements 399.205 **369**
   Transportation Workplace Drug and Alcohol Testing Programs 40.3 **1**
Defrosting and Defogging Systems 393.79 **314**
Disqualification of Drivers 383.51, 383.52, 391.15 **178**, **183**, **261**
Doctor's Examination (see also Physical Examination entry) 391.43 **268**
Documents
   Copies 390.31 **258**
   Location 390.29 **258**
Double/Triple Trailers Endorsement 383.115 **189**
Driveaway-Towaway Operations
   Coupling Devices and Towing Methods 393.71 **309**
   Emergency Equipment 393.95 **317**
   Inspections 396.15 **351**
   Lamps and Reflectors 393.17 **295**
Driver's License (see also Commercial Driver's License entry) Part 383 **171–193**
Drivers
   Adverse Driving Conditions 395.1(b) **329**
   Age 391.11(b)(1) **261**
   Alcohol and Controlled Substances Use, Admit to Using (see also Alcohol and Controlled Substances entries) 382.121 **156**
   Disqualification 383.51, 383.52, 391.15 **178**, **183**, **261**
   Driver-Salesperson 395.1(c) **329**
   Driving Record
      Annual Inquiry and Review 391.25 **265**
      Investigation and Inquiries 391.23 **263**
      Violations 391.27 **266**
   Emergency Equipment Inspection 392.8 **280**
   Employment Application 391.21 **263**
   Entry-Level Driver Training Requirements (see also Entry-Level Driver Training Requirements entry) 380.503 **145**
   Exemptions
      Apiarian Industries 391.2(b) **261**
      Employed Prior to January 1, 1971 391.61 **275**
      Farm Vehicles 391.2, 391.67 **261**, **277**
      Furnished by Other Motor Carriers 391.65 **276**
      Intracity Zone 391.62 **275**
      Multiple Employer 391.63 **276**
      Private Motor Carrier of Passengers
         Business 391.69 **277**
         Nonbusiness 391.68 **277**
      Vision and Diabetes Waiver Study Programs 391.64 **276**
   Hazardous Conditions 392.14 **281**
   Hours of Service Part 395 **329–347**
   Ill or Fatigued 392.3 **279**
   Maximum Driving Time 395.3, 395.5 **335**, **336**
   Migrant Workers, Motor Vehicles Transporting (see also Migrant Workers, Transporting entry) Part 398 **365–368**
   Motor Vehicle Inspection 392.7, 396.13 **280**, **351**
   Oilfield Operations 395.1(d) **329**
   Operating Rules 392.2 **279**
   Out of Service 395.13 **341**
      Alcohol Use 392.5(c)-(e) **279**
   Property-Carrying Driver 395.1(o) **331**
   Qualifications
      Certificate of Physical Examination 391.43 **268**
      Files 391.51 **275**
      General 391.11 **261**
      Medical Examination 391.43, 391.45 **268**, **272**
         Conflicts 391.47 **272**
      Physical 391.41 **267**
         Limbs, Loss or Impairment 391.49 **272**
   Record of Duty Status 395.8 **336**
   Responsibilities 391.13 **261**
   Road Test 391.31 **266**
      Certificate 391.31(f) **266**
      Equivalent 391.33 **267**
   Testing
      Follow-Up 382.311 **163**
      Post-Accident 382.303 **158**
      Pre-Employment 382.301 **157**
      Random 382.305 **159**
      Reasonable Suspicion 382.307 **162**
      Return-to-Duty 382.309 **163**
   Vehicle Inspection Records 396.11 **350**
   Violations, Notification of Convictions 383.31 **177**
Driveshaft Protection, Buses 393.89 **316**
Drug Testing (see also Testing under Controlled Substances entry) Part 40 Subpart C **157–163**

E

Emergency Equipment
   Fire Extinguishers 393.95(a) **317**
   Flame-Producing Devices 393.95(g) **317**
   Fusees 393.95(j) **317**
   Inspection 392.8 **280**
   Liquid-Burning Flares 393.95(j) **317**
   Red Flags 393.95(k) **317**
   Spare Fuses 393.95(b) **317**
   Stopped Vehicles 393.95(f) **317**
   Use 392.8 **280**

Emergency Signals

Emergency Signals
    Flame-Producing 392.24, 392.25 **282**
    Warning Signals 392.22 **282**
Employment Application 391.21 263
Endorsement
    Descriptions 383.93(b) **187**
    Double/Triple Trailers 383.115 **189**
    Hazardous Materials 383.121 **189**
    Passenger 383.117 **189**
    School Bus 383.123 **190**
    Tank Vehicle 383.119 **189**
    Testing Requirements 383.93(c) **187**
Entry-Level Driver Training Requirements 380.503 145
    Applicability 380.501 **145**
    Definitions 380.502 **145**
    Driver Responsibilities 380.507 **146**
    Employer Responsibilities 380.509 **146**
        Recordkeeping 380.511 **146**
    Proof of Training 380.505 **146**
    Training Certificate, Required Information 380.513 **146**
Exemptions 372.101-372.117 97-99
    Applying for 381.300-381.330 **149-150**
    Definitions 372.107 **97**
    Preemption of State Rules 381.600 **151**
Exhaust Systems 325.91, 393.83 62, 315
Exits
    Commercial Motor Vehicles 392.64 **283**
    Emergency Exits
        Buses 393.62 **304**
    Motor Vehicles Transporting Migrant Workers 398.5(f)(10) **367**
    Motor Vehicles Transporting Migrant Workers 398.5(f)(6) **367**
    Sleeper Berth 393.76(c) **313**

F

Farm Vehicle Drivers 391.2, 391.67 261, 277
Fees, Insurance and Registration
    Filing 360.3 **75**
    Records Search, Review, Copying, Certification, and Related Services 360.1 **75**
    Updating 360.5 **76**
Fifth Wheel Assemblies 393.70(b), 398.5(d) 308, 367
Financial Responsibility
    Certificates of Insurance 387.301, 387.311 **237, 240**
        Companies 387.315 **241**
        Electronic Filing 387.323 **241**
        Fiduciaries 387.319 **241**
        Foreign Commerce 387.321 **241**
        Forms and Procedures 387.313 **240**
    Freight Forwarders
        Definitions 387.401 **242**
        Electronic Filing 387.419 **242**
        Fiduciaries 387.417 **242**
        Forms and Procedures 387.413 **242**
        Insurance and Surety Companies 387.409 **242**
        Limits of Liability 387.405 **242**
        Self-Insurer Qualifications 387.411 **242**
        Surety Bonds and Certificates of Insurance 387.407 **242**
    Motor Carriers Transporting Passengers
        Agent Designation 387.35 **236**
        Definitions 387.29 **235**
        Fiduciaries 387.37 **236**
        Financial Responsibility Required 387.31 **235**
        Forms 387.39 **236**
        Minimum Levels of Financial Responsibility 387.33 **236**
        State Authority 387.35 **236**
    Motor Carriers Transporting Property
        Agent Designation 387.11 **233**
        Definitions 387.5 **231**
        Fiduciaries 387.13 **233**
        Financial Responsibility Required 387.7 **232**
        Forms 387.15 **233**
        Minimum Levels of Financial Responsibility 387.9 **232**
        State Authority 387.11 **233**
    Securities 387.301 **237**
    Public Protection 387.303 **238**
    Self-Insurer Qualifications 387.309 **239**
    Surety Bonds 387.301 **237**
        Companies 387.315 **241**
        Electronic Filing 387.323 **241**
        Fiduciaries 387.319 **241**
        Foreign Commerce 387.321 **241**
        Property Broker 387.307 **239**
Fire Extinguishers 393.95(a) 317
Flags, Requirements for 393.95(k) 317
Floors 393.84 315
Fuel
    Ignition, Prevention 392.50 **282**
        Motor Vehicles Transporting Migrant Workers 398.4(l) **366**
    Liquefied Petroleum Gas Systems 393.69 **307**
    Liquid Fuel Tanks 393.67 **305**
    Motor Vehicle Containing Hazardous Materials 397.15 **356**
    Reserve 392.51 **282**
    Systems 393.65 **305**

G

Glazing and Window Construction
    Pushout Windows
        Inspection 396.3(a)(2) **349**
        Test Records 396.3(b)(4) **349**
    Specified Openings 393.60 **303**
    Window Obstructions 393.60(e) **303**

H

Hawaii
    Hours of Service 395.1(i) **330**
    Seat Belts 393.93(d) **317**
Hazard Warning Signal Flashers 392.22(a) 282
Hazard Warning Signals 393.19 296
Hazardous Materials
    Attendance and Surveillance of Motor Vehicles 397.5 **355**
    Compliance with Federal Motor Carrier Safety Regulations 397.2 **355**
    Endorsement 383.121 **189**
    Fires 397.11 **356**
    Fueling 397.15 **356**
    Highway Routing Designations, Preemption 397.69 **357**
    Instructions and Documents 397.19 **356**
    Non-Radioactive
        Definitions 397.65 **357**
        Dispute Resolution 397.75 **359**
        Federal Standards 397.71 **357**
        Motor Carrier Responsibility 397.67 **357**
        Public Information 397.73(a) **359**
        Reporting Requirements 397.73(b) **359**
    Parking 397.7 **356**
    Smoking 397.13 **356**
    State and Local Laws, Ordinances, and Regulations 397.3 **355**
    Tires 397.17 **356**
Hazardous Materials Safety Permits
    Applying for 385.405 **208**
    Conditions Necessary for Issue 385.407 **208**
    Definitions 385.402 **207**
    Effective Dates 385.419 **209**
    Motor Carriers Who Hold One 385.403 **207**
    Number Availability 385.417 **209**
    Operational Requirements 385.415 **208**
    Revocation 385.421 **209**
        Administrative Review 385.423 **209**
    Safety Ratings 385.413 **208**
    State Permits 385.411 **208**
    Suspension 385.421 **209**
        Administrative Review 385.423 **209**
    Temporary Safety Permits 385.409 **208**
Head Lamps (see also Head Lamps under Lamps entry) 393.24 296
Hearings (see also Hearings under Rules of Practice entry) 386.31-386.58 221-225
Heaters
    Flame-Producing 392.67 **283**
    Requirements 393.77 **313**
    Types Not Permitted 398.5(g) **367**
Horn 393.81 315
Hours of Service
    100 Air-Mile Radius Driver 395.1(e)(1) **329**
    Adverse Driving Conditions 395.1(b) **329**
    Agricultural Operations 395.1(k) **331**
    Automatic On-Board Recording Devices 395.15 **341**
    Construction Materials and Equipment 395.1(m) **331**
    Definitions 395.2 **333**
    Driver's Record of Duty Status 395.8 **336**
    Drivers Declared Out of Service 395.13 **341**
    Emergency Conditions 395.1(b)(2) **329**
    Maximum Driving Time
        Passenger-Carrying Vehicles 395.5 **336**
        Property-Carrying Vehicles 395.3 **335**
    Oilfield Operations 395.1(d) **329**
    Property-Carrying Driver 395.1(o) **331**
    Sleeper Berths 395.1(g) **329**
    Travel Time 395.1(j) **330**
    Utility Service Vehicles 395.1(n) **331**
Household Goods, Transportation of
    Advertisements 375.207 **110**
    Agents 375.205 **110**
    Arbitration Program 375.211 **110**
    Bill of Lading 375.505 **114**
    Charges
        Collecting 375.215-375.221 **111**
        Estimates (see also Estimates, this heading) 375.401 **111**
    Complaints 375.209 **110**
    Definitions 375.103 **109**
    Delays 375.605 **115**
    Delivery
        Delays 375.605 **115**
        Early 375.607 **115**
        Maximum COD Amount 375.703 **116**
        Release of Liability 375.701 **116**
        Shipment Lost or Destroyed
            Partially 375.707 **116**
            Totally 375.709 **116**
        Timely Manner 375.601 **115**

Household Goods, Transportation of (continued)
   Delivery (continued)
      Transporting on More Than One Vehicle 375.705 **116**
   Estimates 375.401 **111**
      Binding 375.403 **112**
      Household Goods Brokers Providing 375.409 **113**
      Non-Binding 375.405 **112**
         Relinquishing Possession of COD Shipment Transported Under Non-Binding Estimate 375.407 **113**
   Freight or Expense Bill
      Collecting 375.807 **116**
      Presenting 375.803, 375.805 **116**
   Information
      Collection Requirements 375.105 **109**
      Provided to Prospective Individual Shipper 375.213 **110**
   Inquiries 375.209 **110**
   Inventory 375.503 **114**
   Liability
      Considerations 375.201, 375.203 **109**
      Insurance Coverage 375.303 **111**
      Release of Liability on Delivery Receipt 375.701 **116**
   Order for Service 375.501 **113**
   Penalties 375.901 **116**
   Prospective Individual Shipper, Information Provided to 375.213 **110**
   Service Options 375.301 **111**
   Storing Household Goods in Transit 375.609 **115**
   Tendering Shipment for Delivery 375.603 **115**
   Timely Manner 375.601 **115**
   Weight of Shipment
      Determining 375.507, 375.509 **114**
      Knowing Weight or Charges Before Tendering Delivery 375.521 **115**
      Less Than 3,000 Pounds 375.511 **114**
      Observing 375.513, 375.515 **114**, **115**
      Re-Weighing 375.517 **115**
      Weight Tickets 375.519 **115**
   Your Rights and Responsibilities When You Move Pamphlet App A to Part 375 **117**

I

Imminent Hazard 386.72 **226**
Injunctions 386.71 **226**
Inspections
   "Out of Service" Vehicles 396.9(c) **349**
   Cargo, Cargo Securement Devices and Systems 392.9 **280**
   Driveaway-Towaway Operations 396.15 **351**
   Driver Inspections 396.13 **351**
   Driver Vehicle Inspection Report 396.11 **350**
   Emergency Equipment 392.8 **280**
   Equipment 392.7 **280**
   Inspection, Repair, and Maintenance Records 396.3 **349**
   Inspector Qualifications 396.19 **352**
      Brake Inspectors 396.25 **353**
   Laboratories 40.107 **16**
   Minimum Periodic Inspection Standards App G to Subchapter B **381**
   Motor Vehicles in Operation 396.9 **349**
   Motor Vehicles Transporting Migrant Workers 398.7 **367**
      Administration Inspection 398.8 **367**
   Periodic 396.17 **351**
      Equivalent 396.23 **353**
      Recordkeeping Requirements 396.21 **353**
   Truck Drivers 392.9(b) **280**
Insurance Fees 360.1-360.5 **75-76**
Intermodal Containers, Securing 393.126 **325**
Intracity Zone Drivers
   Certificate of Physical Examination 391.43(d) **268**
   Exemptions 391.62 **275**
   Medical Examination 391.45(b)(2) **272**
Investigations 391.23 **263**
   Assistance 390.15 **255**

K

Knowledge
   Motor Vehicle Operators 383.111 **188**
   Regulations 390.3(e) **247**
   Sample Guidelines Part 383 App to Sub G **190-191**

L

Lamps (see also Lighting and Reflectors entry) Part 393 Subpart B **288-297**
   Auxiliary Driving Lamps 393.24
      Aiming 393.24(d) **296**
      Mounting 393.24(c) **296**
   Auxiliary Driving Lamps 393.24(b) **296**
   Driveaway-Towaway Operations 393.17 **295**
   Front Fog Lamps 393.24
      Aiming 393.24(d) **296**
      Mounting 393.24(c) **296**
   Front Fog Lamps 393.24(b) **296**
   Head Lamps 393.24 **296**
      Aiming 393.24(d) **296**
      Requirements 393.24(a) **296**
   Obscured 392.33 **282**
   Operable 393.9 **288**

Lamps (continued)
   Other than Head Lamps 393.25 **296**
      Mounting 393.25(a) **296**
      Specifications 393.25(c) **296**
      Steady-Burning 393.25(e) **296**
      Visibility 393.25(b) **296**
   Stop Lamps 393.25(f) **297**
Laws (see also State Laws entry) Part 355 **71-72**
Lease and Interchange of Vehicles
   Applicability 376.1 **131**
   Definitions 376.2 **131**
   Equipment
      Identification 376.11(c) **131**
      Interchange 376.31 **133**
      Receipts 376.11(b) **131**
      Records 376.11(d) **131**
   Regulated Carriers 376.42 **133**
   Exemptions 376.21-376.26 **133**
   Written Requirements 376.12 **131**
License (see also Commercial Driver's License entry) Part 383 **171-193**
Lighting and Reflectors
   Combination 393.22 **296**
   Driveaway-Towaway Operation 393.17 **295**
   Emergency Reflectors 393.95 **317**
   Equipment Requirements 393.11 **288**
   Motor Vehicles Transporting Migrant Workers 398.4(k), 398.5(b) **366**, **367**
   Obscured 392.33 **282**
   Requirements 393.26
      Additional Retroreflective Surfaces 393.26(d) **297**
      Mounting 393.26(a) **297**
      Specifications 393.26(b) **297**
      Substitute for Side Reflex Reflectors 393.26(c) **297**
      Wiring 393.28 **297**
   Retroreflective Sheeting and Reflex Reflectors 393.13 **294**
Loading
   Buses 392.62 **283**
   Motor Vehicles Transporting Migrant Workers 398.4(g) **366**
Logs 395.8 **336**
Longer Combination Vehicle (LCV)
   Definitions 380.105 **143**
   Driver Testing 380.109 **143**
   Driver-Instructor Requirements 380.301, Part 391 **145**, **261-277**
      Employer Responsibilities 380.305 **145**
      Qualification Files 391.55 **275**
      Substitute for 380.303 **145**
   Driver-Training Program 380.107, 380.201, App to Part 380 **143**, **144**, **146**
      Certification 380.401 **145**
      Doubles 380.203 **144**
      Substitute for 380.111 **143**
      Triples 380.205 **144**
   Employer Responsibilities 380.113 **144**
      Driver-Instructor Requirements 380.305 **145**
   Substitute
      Driver Training 380.111 **143**
      Instructor Requirements 380.303 **145**
Lumber 393.116, 393.118 **321**, **322**

M

Maintenance (see also Inspections entry) 396.3 **349**
   Lubrication 396.5 **349**
   Motor Vehicles Transporting Migrant Workers 398.7 **367**
   Records 396.3(b), (c) **349**
   Unsafe Vehicles 396.7 **349**
Marking
   Buses
      Emergency Exits 393.62(e) **305**
   Commercial Motor Vehicles 390.21 **256**
   Liquid Fuel Tanks 393.67(c)(11), (f) **307**
   Saddle-Mounts 393.71(m)(8) **312**
   Tow-Bars 393.71(h)(9) **310**
Medical Advisory Criteria Addendum **385**
Medical Review Officers
   Employee Notification of Positive, Adulterated, Substituted, or Invalid Test Results 40.131 **19**
   Laboratory, Relationship with 40.101, 40.125 **15**, **18**
   Qualifications 40.121 **17**
   Record Retention 382.409 **165**
   Responsibilities 40.123 **17**
   Split Specimen Test
      Employee Notification 40.153, 40.171 **22**, **24**
      Laboratory Procedure
         First 40.175 **25**
         Report to MRO 40.183, 40.185, 40.187 **25**
         Second 40.177, 40.179, 40.181 **25**
      Payment 40.173 **25**
   Test Results
      Dilute 40.155 **23**
      Invalid 40.159 **23**
      Involving Drugs 40.137 **20**
      Involving Opiates 40.139 **20**
      Negative 40.127 **18**
      Positive or Refusal to Test Without Interviewing Employee 40.133 **19**
      Positive, Adulterated, Substituted, or Invalid 40.129 **18**
         Changing 40.149 **21**
         Employee Notification 40.131 **19**
         Verification 40.145 **21**

Medical Review Officers

Medical Review Officers (continued)
  Test Results (continued)
    Rejected 40.161 23
    Reporting 40.163, 40.165, 40.167 23, 24
    Verification
      Adulteration or Substitution 40.145 21
      Changing 40.149 21
      Decision 40.141 20
      Interview 40.135 20
      Prohibitions 40.151 22
    Reporting Medical Information 40.327 42

Metal Coils, Securing 393.120 322

Mexico-Domiciled Carriers
  Certificate of Registration 368.1-368.8 87
  Operating Authority 365.501-App A to Subpart E of Part 365 79-82
  Safety Monitoring 385.101-385.119 203-205

Migrant Workers, Transporting
  Applicability of Regulations 398.2 365
  Definitions 398.1 365
  Driver Qualifications 398.3 365
  Maximum Driving Time 398.6 367
  Motor Vehicles
    Accessories 398.5 367
    Administration Inspection 398.8 367
    Brakes 398.5(c) 367
    Driving 398.4 366
    Emergency Exits 398.5(f)(10) 367
    Equipment and Emergency Devices 398.4(f) 366
    Exits 398.5(f)(6) 367
    Fuel 398.4(l)-(m) 366
    Heaters 398.5(g) 367
    Inspection and Maintenance 398.7 367
    Lighting Devices and Reflectors 398.4(k), 398.5(b) 366, 367
    Out of Service 398.8(c) 368
    Parts 398.5 367
    Passenger Compartment 398.5(f) 367
    Safe Loading 398.4(g) 366
    Tires 398.5(e) 367

Mirrors, Rear Vision 393.80 314

Motor Carrier Safety Assistance Program 350.101 63
  Basic Program Funds 350.201, 350.209 63, 64
    Certification Format 350.211 64
    Criteria 350.323 67
    Use 350.315 66
  Commercial Vehicle Safety Plan
    Consequences 350.215 65
    Content 350.213 65
    Response Received by State 350.207 64
    Shared Expenses, State and Federal 350.303 66
  Compatibility with FMCSRs and HMRs
    Consequences for Incompatibility 350.335 68
    Ensuring 350.331 67
    Interstate Commerce 350.337 68
    Obtaining a New Exemption 350.343 69
    Review 350.333 67
    Tolerance Guidelines 350.339 68
    Variances
      Allowing 350.341 68
      Applying for 350.345 69
  Definitions 350.105 63
  Funding 350.205 64
    Activities Eligible for Reimbursement 350.309, 350.311 66
    Allocation 350.313 66
    Basic Program Funds (see also Basic Program Funds, this heading) 350.201, 350.209 63, 64
    Border Activity Funds 350.321 67
      States Qualifying 350.329 67
    High Priority Activity Funds 350.319 66
      States Qualifying 350.329 67
    Incentive Funds 350.317 66
      States Qualifying 350.327 67
    Level of Effort 350.301 66
    Term 350.307 66
    U.S. Territories 350.305 66
  Jurisdictions Eligible 350.107 63
  National Program Elements 350.109 63
  Traffic Enforcement 350.111 63

Motor Carrier Safety Progress Report Addendum 391

Motor Carriers
  Aiding or Abetting Violations 390.13 255
  Assistance in Investigations and Special Studies 390.15 255
  Driver Regulations, Observance of 390.11 255
  Identification Report 390.19 256

Motor Vehicles, Inspection (see also Commercial Motor Vehicles entry) 396.9 349

N

Noise Emission Standards
  Correction Factors
    Application 325.79 62
    Ground Surface 325.75 61
    Microphone Distance 325.73 61
    Open Site Requirements, Computation of 325.77 61
  Definitions 325.5 57
  Effective Date 325.3 57

Noise Emission Standards (continued)
  Exhaust Systems 325.91 62
  Highway Operations
    Ambient Conditions 325.35 59
    Location and Operation of Sound Level Measurement System 325.37 59
    Measurement Procedure 325.39 59
    Site Characteristics 325.33 58
  Measurement
    Ambient Conditions
      Highway Operations 325.35 59
      Stationary Test 325.55 60
    Procedure
      Highway Operations 325.39 59
      Stationary Test 325.59 60
    Site Characteristics
      Highway Operations 325.33 58
      Stationary Test 325.53 60
  Systems
    Calibration 325.25 58
    Location and Operation
      Highway Operations 325.37 59
      Stationary Test 325.57 60
    Types 325.23 58
    Tolerances 325.9 58
    Windscreen 325.27 58
  Motor Vehicle Inspection and Examination 325.13 58
  Noise Levels, Allowable 325.7 57
  Stationary Test
    Ambient Conditions 325.55 60
    Location and Operation of Sound Level Measurement Systems 325.57 60
    Measurement Procedure 325.59 60
    Site Characteristics 325.53 60
  Tires 325.93 62
  Windscreen 325.27 58

Noise Levels, Vehicle Interior 393.94 317

O

Oilfield Operations 395.1(d) 329

On-Board Recording Devices 395.15 341

Operating Authority (see also Operating Authority under Applications entry) Part 365 77-82

Out of Service
  Drivers 395.13 341
    Alcohol Use 392.5(c)-(e) 279
  Motor Vehicles 396.9(c), 398.8(c) 349, 368
  Violation 383.51(e), 383.53(b), 391.15(d) 181, 183, 262

P

Paper Rolls, Securing 393.122 323

Parking Brake Systems 393.41 298

Passenger Carrier Regulations
  Baggage
    Declaring Excess Value 374.403, 374.405 107
    Liability 374.401 107
  Definitions 374.113, 374.303 105
  Discrimination 374.101-374.113 105
  Incidental Charter Rights 374.501-374.505 107
  Intercity 374.301-374.319 105-106
  Smoking Prohibited 374.201 105

Passenger-Carrying Vehicles, Maximum Driving Time 395.5 336

Passengers
  Endorsement 383.117 189
  Motor Vehicles Transporting Migrant Workers 398.5(f) 367
  Private Motor Carrier
    Business 391.69 277
    Nonbusiness 391.68 277
  Unauthorized 392.60 283

Payment of Transportation Charges
  C.O.D. Shipments 377.101-377.105 135
  Credit 377.201-377.217 135-136

Penalties (see also Penalties under Rules of Practice entry) 386.81-386.84 226-227

Physical Examination
  Certificate 391.43 268
  Instructions for Performing 391.43(f) 268
  Requirements for 391.45 272

Physical Requirements for Drivers 391.41 267

Pilot Programs 381.400-381.520 150-151
  Preemption of State Rules 381.600 151

Post-Trip Inspection, Driveaway-Towaway Operations 396.15(c) 351

Preemption Procedures (see also Waivers entry) Part 397 Subpart E 361-363
  Application 397.205 361
    Timeliness 397.221 363
    Waiver 397.213 362
  Definitions 397.201(c) 361
  Determination 397.203, 397.211 361, 362
  Judicial Review 397.225 363
  Notice 397.207 361
  Processing 397.209 362
  Reconsideration 397.223 363

Pre-Trip Inspection
  Air Brakes 383.113(c)(1) 189
  Driveaway-Towaway Operations 396.15(b) 351
  Equipment 392.7 280
Proceedings (see also Proceedings under Rules of Practice entry) 386.11-386.17 219-221
Process Agent, Designation of
  Applicability 366.1 83
  Blanket Designations 366.5 83
  Cancellation or Change 366.6 83
  Eligible Persons 366.3 83
  Form 366.2 83
  Required States 366.4 83
Property-Carrying Vehicles, Maximum Driving Time 395.3 335
Public Interest Exclusions Part 40 Subpart R 45-49

R

Radar Detectors 392.71 283
Radioactive Materials 397.101, 397.103 360, 361
Railroad Crossings
  Slowing Down 392.11 281
  Stopping 392.10 281
Rear Impact Guards/Rear End Protection 393.86 315
Rear-Vision Mirrors 393.80 314
Receipts (see also Bills entry) 373.101-373.201 103
Record of Duty Status 395.8 336
  On-Board Recording Devices 395.15 341
  Out of Service Drivers 395.13(b)(2), (c)(1)(ii), (d)(2) 341
  Retention of Records 395.8(k) 338
Records
  Access 382.405 164
  Accident 390.15 255
  Companies Going Out of Business 379.9 139
  Controlled Substances and Alcohol Use Testing 40.333, 382.401 43, 163
  Copies 390.31 258
  Disposition 379.13 139
  Driver Qualification Files 391.51 275
  Driving Record, Annual Review and Inquiry 391.25(c) 265
  Falsification 390.35 259
  Location 390.29 258
  Motor Carrier Inspection, Repair, and Maintenance 396.3(b)-(c) 349
  Periodic Inspections 396.21 353
  Preservation 379.7 139
    Applicability 379.1 139
  Protection 379.5 139
  Record of Duty Status 395.8(k) 338
  Retention 379.13 139
    Periods App A to Part 379 139
    Required 379.3 139
  Schedule of App A to Part 379 139
  Storage 379.5 139
  Violations 391.27 266
  Waiver of Requirements 379.11 139
Reflectors (see also Lighting and Reflectors entry) 393.11 288
Regional Offices, Motor Carrier Safety Service Centers 390.27 258
Registration Fees 360.1-360.5 75-76
Registration with States
  Accounting 367.6 86
  Application App A to Part 367 86
  Definitions 367.1 85
  Receipts 367.5 85
  Requirements 367.4 85
  Selection of State 367.3 85
  State Participation 367.2 85
  Violations of Provisions 367.7 86
Reports
  Alcohol and Controlled Substances Testing 382.403 164
  DOT Drug Testing Semi-Annual Laboratory Report App. B and D to Part 40 49, 50
  Driver Vehicle Inspection 396.11 350
  Drug Test Results 40.163-40.167 23
  Falsification 390.35 259
  Motor Carrier Identification Report 390.19 256
  Routing of Non-Radioactive Hazardous Materials 397.73 359
  Substance Abuse Professional 40.311 41
Reserve Fuel
  Materials of Trade 392.51 282
  Motor Vehicles Transporting Migrant Workers 398.4(m) 366
Retail Store Deliveries 395.1(f) 329
Rights and Responsibilities When You Move Pamphlet App A to Part 375 117
Road Test 391.31 266
  Certificate 391.31(f) 266
  Equivalent 391.33 267
Routing Regulations
  Authority to Serve a Particular Area 356.1 73
  Elimination of Gateways 356.11 73
  Elimination of Restrictions 356.9 73
  Redesignated Highways 356.13 73
  Regular Route Motor Passenger Service 356.3 73
  Tacking 356.7 73
  Traversal Authority 356.5 73

Rulemaking Procedures
  Additional Proceedings 389.25 245
  Adoption of Final Rules 389.29 245
  Applicability 389.1 245
  Definitions 389.3 245
  Extension of Time, Petitions 389.19 245
  Hearings 389.27 245
  Initiation 389.13 245
  Notice Contents 389.15 245
  Participation in 389.17 245
  Petitions 389.31 245
    Extension of Time 389.19 245
    Processing 389.33 245
    Reconsideration 389.35, 389.37 246
  Records 389.7 245
  Regulatory Docket 389.5 245
  Written Comments
    Consideration 389.23 245
    Contents 389.21 245
Rules of Practice
  Admissions, Request for 386.44 223
  Appeal 386.67 226
  Decision 386.61 225
    Appeal 386.67 226
    Failure to Comply with Final Order 386.65 226
    Reconsideration 386.64 226
    Rehearing 386.66 226
    Review of 386.62 225
      After Review 386.63 225
  Definitions 386.2 217
  Depositions 386.46 223
    Hearings 386.47 224
  Discovery
    Methods 386.37 222
    Motion to Compel 386.45 223
    Protective Orders 386.39 222
    Responses, Supplementation of 386.40 222
    Scope 386.38 222
    Stipulations 386.41 222
  Document Production 386.43 223
  Documents
    Filing 386.5 218
    Filing 386.7 218
    Service 386.6 218
  Examinations 386.43 223
  Hearings
    Administrative Law Judge 386.54 225
    Admissions, Request for 386.44 223
    Appeals 386.52 224
    Burden of Proof 386.58 225
    Conclusions of Law 386.57 225
    Conduct 386.56(b) 225
    Deposition 386.47 224
    Evidence 386.56(c) 225
      Written, Form of 386.49 224
    Intervention 386.17 220
    Investigation, Information Obtained by 386.56(d) 225
    Medical Records and Physicians' Reports 386.48 224
    Motions 386.35, 386.36 221
    Pleadings, Amendment and Withdrawal 386.51 224
    Prehearing Conferences 386.55 225
    Proposed Findings of Fact 386.57 225
    Record 386.56(e) 225
    Request for 386.13 219
      Action on Requests 386.16 220
    Subpoenas 386.53 224
  Imminent Hazard 386.72 226
  Injunctions 386.71 226
  Land, Entry Upon 386.43 223
  Motions 386.35 221
    Compel Discovery 386.45 223
    Dismiss 386.36(a) 221
    More Definite Statement 386.36(b) 221
    Rehearing 386.66 226
  Notice of Claim
    Payment 386.18 221
    Reply 386.14 219
  Penalties 386.81 226
    Failure to Pay
      Operation in Interstate Commerce Prohibited 386.83 227
      Suspension or Revocation of Registration 386.84 227
    Penalty Schedule
      Notices and Orders, Violations of App A to Part 386 228
    Violations of Notices and Orders 386.82 227
  Proceedings
    Commencement 386.11 219
    Complaint 386.12 219
    Hearing, Request for 386.13 219
      Action on 386.16 220
    Petitions to Review 386.13 219
      Action on 386.16 220
  Scope 386.1 217
  Service 386.31 221
  Service 386.8 219
  Settlement Agreements 386.22 221
  Written Interrogatories 386.42 222

S

Saddle-Mounts
    Kingpins 393.71(l) **311**
    Lower Half 393.71(k) **310**
    Upper Half 393.71(j) **310**

Safety Fitness Procedures
    Certification of Auditors, Investigators, and Inspectors 385.201-385.205 **205**
    Definitions 385.3 **201**
    Delinquent in Paying Penalties 385.14 **202**
    Information 385.19 **203**
    Monitoring Mexico-Domiciled Carriers 385.101-385.119 **203-205**
    New Entrant Safety Assurance Program 385.301-385.337 **205-207**
    Safety Audit Evaluation Criteria App A to Part 385 **210**
    Safety Rating
        Administrative Review 385.15 **202**
        Changes 385.17 **203**
        Determining 385.7, 385.9 **202**
        Notification 385.11 **202**
        Process, Explanation of App B to Part 385 **211**
        Unsatisfactory Rated Motor Carriers 385.13 **202**
    Standard, Meeting 385.5 **201**

Safety Rating (see also Safety Rating under Safety Fitness Procedures entry) 385.7, 385.9 202

Salvage Processing 370.11 94

School Bus, Endorsement 383.123 190

Seat Belts
    Buses 393.93(a) **316**
    Trucks and Truck Tractors 393.93(b) **316**
    Use 392.16 **281**

Service Agents, Roles and Responsibilities Part 40 Subpart Q 44-45

Sleeper Berths 393.76 313

Special Agents App B to Subchapter B 371

Speed Limits 392.6 280
    Motor Vehicles Transporting Migrant Workers 398.4(e) **366**

Speedometer 393.82 315

Split Specimen Tests (see also Split Specimen Test under Medical Review Officers entry) Part 40 Subpart H 24-26

Standee Line or Bar on Buses 393.90 316

State Laws
    Adopting and Enforcing Compatible Laws and Regulations 355.25 **71**
    Applicability 355.3 **71**
    Definitions 355.5 **71**
    Purpose 355.1 **71**
    Regulatory Review 355.21 **71**
        Guidelines App A to Part 355 **71**
        Submission of Results 355.23 **71**

Steering Wheel Systems 393.209 327

Step, Handhold, and Deck Requirements
    Definitions 399.205 **369**
    Maintenance 399.211 **370**
    Test Procedures 399.209 **370**
    Truck and Truck-Tractor Access Requirements 399.207 **369**

Stopped Vehicles
    Emergency Signals 392.22 **282**
    Warning Devices 393.95(f) **317**

Substance Abuse Professionals
    Certification Organization Recognition for Members 40.283 **38**
    Education and Treatment Referral 40.299, 40.303 **40**
    Equivalency Requirements for Certification Organizations App E to Part 40 **50**
    Evaluation 40.285 **38**
    Evaluation, Referral, and Treatment Process 40.291 **39**
    Follow-Up Evaluation 40.301 **40**
    Follow-Up Tests 40.307 **40**
        Employer's Responsibilities 40.309 **41**
    Initial Evaluation 40.293 **39**
        Changing 40.297 **40**
    Qualifications 40.281 **38**
    Reports 40.311 **41**
    Required Information 40.287 **39**
    Second Opinions 40.295 **40**

Suspension Systems 393.207 327

T

Tank Vehicle Endorsement 383.119 189

Television Receivers 393.88 316

Terminal Areas 372.300-372.303 102

Tiedowns
    Adjusting 393.112 **321**
    Manufacturing Standards 393.104(e) **319**
    Number 393.110 **320**
    Use 393.104(f) **319**

Time
    Computation 386.8 **218**
    Extenstion 386.5 **218**

Tires 325.93, 393.75 62, 312
    Vehicles Containing Hazardous Materials 397.17 **356**

Trucks and Truck Tractors
    Access Requirements 399.207 **369**
    Brakes (see also Brakes entry) Part 393 Subpart C **297-303**
    Defrosting and Defogging Systems 393.79 **314**
    Driver Inspections 392.9(b) **280**
    Emergency Equipment 393.95 **317**
    Exhaust Systems 393.83 **315**
    Frames 393.201 **327**
    Horn 393.81 **315**
    Lighting Devices and Reflectors 393.11 **288**
    Rear-Vision Mirrors 393.80 **314**
    Seat Belts 393.93(b) **316**
    Securing 393.128 **325**
    Speedometer 393.82 **315**
    Window Construction 393.61 **304**
    Windshield Wiping and Washing Systems 393.78 **314**

Turn Signaling Systems 393.19
    Specifications 393.25(c) **296**

U

Urine Collection (see also Testing, Urine Collection under Controlled Substances entry) Part 40 Subpart E 10-13

V

Vehicles, Securing 393.128-393.132 325-326

Violations
    Aiding or Abetting 390.13 **255**
    Notification of Convictions 383.31 **177**
    Out of Service 383.51(e), 383.53(b), 391.15(d) **181, 183, 262**
    Record 391.27 **266**

W

Waivers 149
    Determination and Order 397.219 **363**
    Notice 397.215 **362**
    Preemption Application 397.213 **362**
    Preemption of State Rules 381.600 **151**
    Processing 397.217 **362**
    Stand-Down Waiver Provision 382.119 **156**
    Vision and Diabetes Waiver Study Programs, Grandfathering for Drivers Participating in 391.64 **276**

Warning Devices (see also Emergency Signals entry) 392.22 282
    Placement 392.22(b) **282**
    Stopped Vehicles 393.95(f) **317**
    Warning Signal Flashers 392.22(a) **282**

Wheels 393.205 327
    Brakes Required 393.42 **298**

Windscreen 325.27 58

Windshield Wiping and Washing Systems 393.78 314

Wiring
    Battery Installation 393.30 **297**
    Systems 393.28 **297**